# Contemporary Authors®

## NEW REVISION SERIES

ISSN 0275-7176

# Contemporary Authors®

A Bio-Bibliographical Guide to
Current Writers in Fiction, General Nonfiction,
Poetry, Journalism, Drama, Motion Pictures,
Television, and Other Fields

DANIEL JONES
JOHN D. JORGENSON
Editors

NEW REVISION SERIES
volume 61

GALE
DETROIT • NEW YORK • TORONTO • LONDON

## STAFF

Daniel Jones and John D. Jorgenson, *Editors, New Revision Series*

Thomas Wiloch, *Sketchwriting Coordinator and Online Research Specialist*

Tim Akers, Pamela S. Dear, Jeff Hunter, Jerry Moore, Deborah A. Schmitt, Polly A. Vedder, Tim White and Kathleen Wilson, *Contributing Editors*

Mary Artzner-Wolf, Bruce Boston, Ken Burtle, Jason Dobrowski, Bruce Emery, Joan Goldsworthy, Rena Korb, Jane Kelly Kosek, Howard Meagher, Robert Miltner, John Miranski, James Pollard, Trudy Ring, Bryan Ryan, Susan Salter, Arlene True, Shanna Weagle, Denise Wiloch, and Tim Winter-Damon, *Sketchwriters*

Emily J. McMurray and Pamela L. Shelton, *Copyeditors*

James P. Draper, *Managing Editor*

Victoria B. Cariappa, *Research Manager*

Julia C. Daniel, Tamara C. Nott, Tracie A. Richardson Norma Sawaya, and Cheryl L. Warnock, *Research Associates*

Talitha Dutton, *Research Assistant*



This book is printed on acid-free paper that meets the minimum requirements of American National Standard for Information Sciences-Permanence Paper for Printed Library Materials, ANSI Z39.48-1984.

Library of Congress Catalog Card Number 81-640179
ISBN 0-7876-2004-1
ISSN 0275-7176

Printed in the United States of America

10 9 8 7 6 5 4 3 2 1

# Contents



**Indexing note:** All *Contemporary Authors New Revision Series* entries are indexed in the *Contemporary Authors* cumulative index, which is published separately and distributed with even-numbered *Contemporary Authors* original volumes and odd-numbered *Contemporary Authors New Revision Series* volumes.

**As always, the most recent *Contemporary Authors* cumulative index continues to be the user's guide to the location of an individual author's listing.**

# Preface

The *Contemporary Authors New Revision Series* (*CANR*) provides updated information on authors listed in earlier volumes of *Contemporary Authors* (*CA*). Although entries for individual authors from any volume of *CA* may be included in a volume of the *New Revision Series, CANR* updates only those sketches requiring significant change. However, in response to requests from librarians and library patrons for the most current information possible on high-profile writers of greater public and critical interest, *CANR* revises entries for these authors whenever new and noteworthy information becomes available.

Authors are included on the basis of specific criteria that indicate the need for a revision. These criteria include a combination of bibliographical additions, changes in addresses or career, major awards, and personal information such as name changes or death dates. All listings in this volume have been revised or augmented in various ways and contain up-to-the-minute publication information in the Writings section, most often verified by the author and/or by consulting a variety of online resources. Many sketches have been extensively rewritten, often including informative new Sidelights. As always, a *CANR* listing entails no charge or obligation.

The key to locating an author's most recent entry is the *CA* cumulative index, which is published separately and distributed with even-numbered original volumes and odd-numbered revision volumes. It provides access to all entries in *CA* and *CANR*. Always consult the latest index to find an author's most recent entry.

For the convenience of users, the *CA* cumulative index also includes references to all entries in these Gale literary series: *Authors and Artists for Young Adults, Authors in the News, Bestsellers, Black Literature Criticism, Black Writers, Children's Literature Review, Concise Dictionary of American Literary Biography, Concise Dictionary of British Literary Biography, Contemporary Authors Autobiography Series, Contemporary Authors Bibliographical Series, Contemporary Literary Criticism, Dictionary of Literary Biography, Dictionary of Literary Biography Documentary Series, Dictionary of Literary Biography Yearbook, DISCovering Authors, DISCovering Authors: British, DISCovering Authors: Canadian, DISCovering Authors: Modules* (including modules for Dramatists, Most-Studied Authors, Multicultural Authors, Novelists, Poets, and Popular/Genre Authors), *Drama Criticism, Hispanic Literature Criticism, Hispanic Writers, Junior DISCovering Authors, Major Authors and Illustrators for Children and Young Adults, Major 20th-Century Writers, Native North American Literature, Poetry Criticism, Short Story Criticism, Something about the Author, Something about the Author Autobiography Series, Twentieth-Century Literary Criticism, World Literature Criticism, World Literature Criticism Supplement,* and *Yesterday's Authors of Books for Children.*

**A Sample Index Entry:**

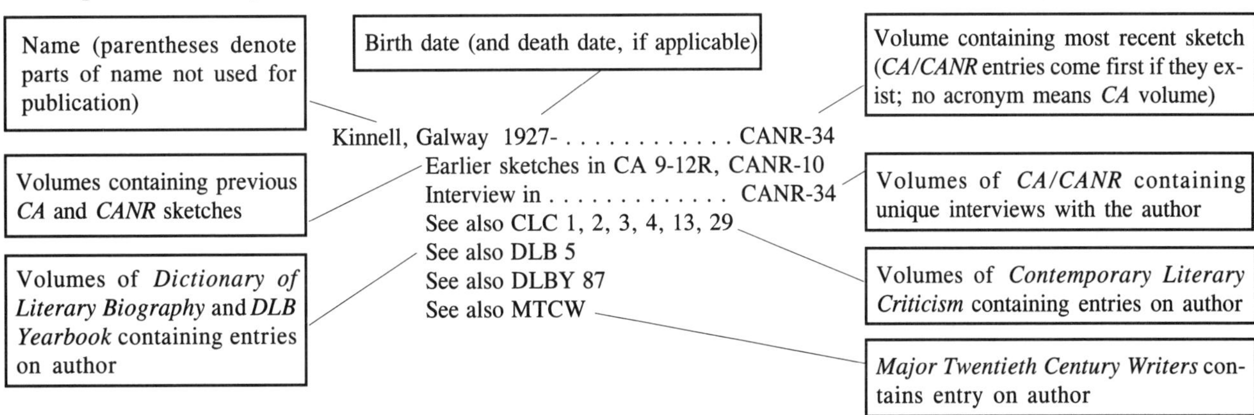


For the most recent *CA* information on Kinnell, users should refer to Volume 34 of the *New Revision Series,* as designated by "CANR-34"; if that volume is unavailable, refer to CANR-10. If CANR-10 is also unavailable, refer to CA 9-12R, published in 1974, for Kinnell's first revision entry.

## How Are Entries Compiled?

The editors make every effort to secure new information directly from the authors. Copies of all sketches in selected *CA* and *CANR* volumes previously published are routinely sent to listees at their last-known addresses, and returns from these authors are then assessed. For deceased writers, or those who fail to reply to requests for data, we consult other reliable biographical sources, such as those indexed in Gale's *Biography and Genealogy Master Index,* and biobliographical sources, such as *Magazine Index, Newspaper Abstracts, LC MARC,* and a variety of online databases. Further details come from published interviews, feature stories, book reviews, online literary magazines and journals, author web sites, and often the authors' publishers supply material.

** Indicates that a listing has been compiled from secondary sources but has not been personally verified for this edition by the author under review.*

## What Kinds of Information Does an Entry Provide?

Sketches in *CANR* contain the following biographical and bibliographical information:

- **Entry heading:** the most complete form of author's name, plus any pseudonyms or name variations used for writing
- **Personal information:** author's date and place of birth, family data, ethnicity, educational background, political and religious affiliations, and hobbies and leisure interests
- **Addresses:** author's home, office, or agent's addresses, plus e-mail and fax numbers, as available
- **Career summary:** name of employer, position, and dates held for each career post; resume of other vocational achievements; military service
- **Membership information:** professional, civic, and other association memberships and any official posts held
- **Awards and honors:** military and civic citations, major prizes and nominations, fellowships, grants, and honorary degrees
- **Writings:** a comprehensive, chronological list of titles, publishers, dates of original publication and revised editions, and production information for plays, television scripts, and screenplays
- **Adaptations:** a list of films, plays, and other media which have been adapted from the author's work
- **Work in progress:** current or planned projects, with dates of completion and/or publication, and expected publisher, when known
- **Sidelights:** a biographical portrait of the author's development; information about the critical reception of the author's works; revealing comments, often by the author, on personal interests, aspirations, motivations, and thoughts on writing
- **Biographical and critical sources:** a list of books and periodicals in which additional information on an author's life and/or writings appears

## Related Titles in the *CA* Series

***Contemporary Authors Autobiography Series*** complements *CA* original and revised volumes with specially commissioned autobiographical essays by important current authors, illustrated with personal photographs they provide. Common topics include their motivations for writing, the people and experiences that shaped their careers, the rewards they derive from their work, and their impressions of the current literary scene.

***Contemporary Authors Bibliographical Series*** surveys writings by and about important American authors since World War II. Each volume concentrates on a specific genre and features approximately ten writers; entries list works written by and about the author and contain a bibliographical essay discussing the merits and deficiencies of major critical and scholarly studies in detail.

## Available in Electronic Formats

**CD-ROM.** Full-text bio-bibliographic entries from the entire *CA* series, covering approximately 101,000 writers, are available on CD-ROM through lease and purchase plans. The disc combines entries from the *CA, CANR,* and *Contemporary Authors Permanent Series* (*CAP*) print series to provide the most recent author listing. It can be searched by name, title, subject/genre, nationality/ethnicity, personal data, and as well as advanced searching using boolean logic. The disc is updated every six months. For more information, call 1-800-877-GALE. *CA* is also available on CD-ROM from SilverPlatter Information, Inc.

**Online.** The *Contemporary Authors* database is made available online to libraries and their patrons through online public access catalog (OPAC) vendors. Currently, *CA* is offered through Ameritech Library Services' Vista Online (formerly Dynix).

**GaleNet.** *CA* is available on a subscription basis through GaleNet, a new online information resource that features an easy-to-use end-user interface, the powerful search capabilities of the BRS/Search retrieval software, and ease of access through the World Wide Web. For more information, call 1-800-877-GALE.

**Magnetic Tape.** *CA* is available for licensing on magnetic tape in a fielded format. The database is available for internal data processing and nonpublishing purposes only. For more information, call 1-800-877-GALE.

## Suggestions Are Welcome

The editors welcome comments and suggestions from users on any aspects of the *CA* series. If readers would like to recommend authors for inclusion in future volumes of the series, they are cordially invited to write: The Editors, *Contemporary Authors New Revision Series,* 835 Penobscot Bldg., 645 Griswold St., Detroit, MI 48226-4094; call toll-free at 1-800-347-GALE; or fax at 1-313-961-6599.

# *CA* Numbering System and Volume Update Chart

Occasionally questions arise about the *CA* numbering system and which volumes, if any, can be discarded. Despite numbers like "29-32R," "97-100" and "157," the entire *CA* print series consists of only 147 physical volumes with the publication of *CA* Volume 159. The following charts note changes in the numbering system and cover design, and indicate which volumes are essential for the most complete, up-to-date coverage.

***CA* First Revision**

- 1-4R through 41-44R (11 books)
  *Cover:* Brown with black and gold trim.
  There will be no further First Revision volumes because revised entries are now being handled exclusively through the more efficient *New Revision Series* mentioned below.

***CA* Original Volumes**

- 45-48 through 97-100 (14 books)
  *Cover:* Brown with black and gold trim.
- 101 through 159 (59 books)
  *Cover:* Blue and black with orange bands.
  The same as previous *CA* original volumes but with a new, simplified numbering system and new cover design.

***CA* Permanent Series**

- *CAP*-1 and *CAP*-2 (2 books)
  *Cover:* Brown with red and gold trim.
  There will be no further *Permanent Series* volumes because revised entries are now being handled exclusively through the more efficient *New Revision Series* mentioned below.

***CA* New Revision Series**

- *CANR*-1 through *CANR*-61 (61 books)
  *Cover:* Blue and black with green bands.
  Includes only sketches requiring significant changes; **sketches are taken from any previously published *CA, CAP,* or *CANR* volume**.

| If You Have: | You May Discard: |
| --- | --- |
| *CA* First Revision Volumes 1-4R through 41-44R **and** *CA Permanent Series* Volumes 1 and 2 | *CA* Original Volumes 1, 2, 3, 4 Volumes 5-6 through 41-44 |
| *CA* Original Volumes 45-48 through 97-100 **and** 101 through 159 | **NONE:** These volumes will not be superseded by corresponding revised volumes. Individual entries from these and all other volumes appearing in the left column of this chart may be revised and included in the various volumes of the *New Revision Series.* |
| *CA New Revision Series* Volumes *CANR*-1 through *CANR*-61 | **NONE:** The *New Revision Series* does not replace any single volume of *CA*. Instead, volumes of *CANR* include entries from many previous *CA* series volumes. All *New Revision Series* volumes must be retained for full coverage. |

# A Sampling of Authors and Media People Featured in This Volume

**Amiri Baraka**

Described by one critic as a writer who has "significantly affected the course of African-American literary culture," Baraka's standing as a major poet and playwright is matched by his importance as a cultural and political leader. The recipient of a PEN-Faulkner Award, a Langston Hughes medal, and numerous other awards for his work, Baraka's titles include *A Good Girl Is Hard to Find, Preface to a Twenty Volume Suicide Note, Dutchman,* and *Transbluency: The Selected Poems of Amiri Baraka/LeRoi Jones (1961-1995).*

**Samuel Beckett**

Along with the work of Eugene Ionesco, Jean Genet, and Harold Pinter, Beckett's stark plays are said to compose the "Theater of the Absurd," an avant-garde form of drama combining surrealism, existentialism, and black humor to illustrate the absurdity of the human condition. Perhaps most-often identified as the author of the classics *Waiting for Godot, Endgame, Krapp's Last Tape,* and *Happy Days,* Beckett's work has enjoyed renewed attention with the 1993 publication of his first and previously-unpublished novel, *Dream of Fair to Middling Women,* and the 1995 publications of his *Collected Poems, 1930-1989,* a new edition of *Elutheira: A Play in Three Acts,* and *Dramaticulesg.*

**Elizabeth Bishop**

Bishop's work has had the ability to make the most diverse groups of poets—those who normally disagree over themes, techniques, and forms—agree on one point: that Bishop was an admirable artist. A highly-celebrated poet and recipient of a Pulitzer Prize, a National Book Award, and a National Book Critics Circle Award, Bishop died in 1979, prompting Frank Bidart to write: "If the future is smart, surely her poems will continue to be read. Great poems don't replace one another; each does something nothing else does." Bishop's titles include *Poems: North & South, Questions of Travel,* and the recently-published *Selected Poetry, 1937-1990* and *Conversations with Elizabeth Bishop.*

**Cleanth Brooks**

From the early-1940s until his death in 1994, Brooks was, according to one critic, "one of the pillars of the American literary-critical establishment." Best remembered as one of the pioneers of the so-called "New Criticism," his titles include *The Well Wrought Urn: Studies in the Structure of Poetry* and *Understanding Poetry: An Anthology for College Students.*

**James M. Cain**

Best-known for his first novel, *The Postman Always Rings Twice,* which, according to one critic, became "one of those rarest of literary achievements in America: a phenomenal best seller that received the highest acclaim from critics," Cain has been described as "the twenty-minute egg" of the "hard-boiled" school. His other titles include *Double Indemnity, Mildred Pierce, Serenade,* and the more-recently published *The Baby in the Icebox, and Other Short Fiction* and *Career in C Major, and Other Fiction.*

**Italo Calvino**

Italian novelist and short story writer Calvino was famous for the monumental collection of Italian fables he edited as well as for the fables he wrote. Gore Vidal noted that because Calvino both edited and wrote fables he was "someone who reached not only primary school children . . . but, at one time or another, everyone who reads." Following his death in 1985, Calvino's widow oversaw the issue of new volumes of his work in English, including the 1993 edition of *The Road to San Giovanni.* Calvino's other titles include *The Path to the Nest of Spiders* and *Palomar.*

**Benjamin Capps**

Described by one critic as "one of the best writers in America today," Capps writes novels that focus on the American West and are "serious depictions of the real life on the frontier, which explore serious themes of cultures in confrontation, and recreate the people—both whites and Indians—who lived on the plains a hundred years ago." His titles include *The Trail to Ogallala, The Brothers of Uterica,* and *Woman Chief.*

**James Dickey**

Dickey was widely regarded as a major American poet because of what critics and readers identified as his unique vision and style. "It is clear," said Joyce Carol Oates, "that Dickey desires to take on 'his' own personal history as an analogue to or a microscopic exploration of twentieth-century American history, which is one of the reasons he is so important as a poet." Often focusing on what one critic described as a concern "to get back wholeness of being, to respond full-heartedly and full-bodiedly to experience," Dickey's works include *Buckdancer's Choice, Poems, 1957-1967,* and *Deliverance.*

**Will Durant**

Durant was a prize-winning historian whose chronicles of world history and civilization reached a mass audience. Perhaps his most enduring work is the eleven-volume *The Story of Civilization,* on which he collaborated with his wife, Ariel. In this collection, the pair endeavored to synthesize the developments in art, science, religion, politics, literature, and economics. Awarded a Pulitzer Prize in 1968 for *Rousseau and Revolution,* Durant's other titles include *The Lessons of History* and *Interpretations of Life.*

**Ellen Gilchrist**

The author of poems, short stories, and novels, Gilchrist opens for her readers a side door through which to view the world of the contemporary American South. Praised for her depictions of "ordinary happenings in out of the way places" and "domestic routine disrupted by violence," she has received numerous awards for her work, including an American Book Award in 1984. Occasionally compared to Carson McCullers and Tennessee Williams, Gilchrist's titles include *In The Land of Dreamy Dreams, Victory over Japan, The Anna Papers,* and *Rhoda: A Life in Stories.*

**Jan Morris**

A critically-acclaimed British journalist and travel essayist, Morris has written numerous books on travels and adventures around the world. Known to readers under the name James Morris until changing genders in a sex-change operation in 1972, Morris gained fame in the 1950s for covering the Mt. Everest climbing expedition of Sir Edmund Hillary. Her works often explore the past in the form of the rise and fall of the British Empire and include *Pax Britannica: The Climax of an Empire, The Spectacle of Empire,* and *Fisher's Face, or, Getting to Know the Admiral.*

**R. K. Narayan**

Perhaps the best-known Indian writing in English today, Narayan's long and prolific career has been marked by well-received novels, novellas, and short stories, almost all of which are set in the fictional backwater town of Malgudi and its environs. Malgudi has perhaps inevitably drawn comparisons to William Faulkner's Yoknapatawpha County, both because Narayan returns to its setting again and again, and because he uses its eccentric citizens to meditate upon the human condition in a global context. His titles include *The Bachelor of Arts, Waiting for the Mahatma, The World of Nagaraj,* and *Salt & Sawdust: Stories and Table Talk.*

**Julia O'Faolain**

Irish writer O'Faolain has garnered significant acclaim and attention for her novels, short story collections, and works of nonfiction. Drawing on her extensive foreign travels, O'Faolain has used Italy, France, Ireland, and the United States as settings for her stories. Often identified for her works that focus on women in history, including *Not in God's Image: Women in History from the Greeks to the Victorians* and *Women in the Wall,* O'Faolain also authored *No Country for Young Men, The Irish Signorina* and *The Judas Cloth.*

**Valerie Sayers**

All of Sayers' five novels have won critical acclaim as fresh reflections of modern life in the time-honored Southern literary tradition. With affectionate but unrelenting satire, Sayers has revised old Southern themes—particularly evoking the strong Southern faith in family—to accord with her view of an uncertain modern world. The forceful writing and Southern wit of the "Due East" novels, in the opinion of several critics, place Sayers in the ranks of such revered Southern writers as Eudora Welty and Flannery O'Connor. Her titles include *Due East, Who Do You Love?,* and *Brain Fever.*

**Charles Simic**

Simic, a native of Yugoslavia who immigrated to the United States during his teens, has been hailed as one of his adopted homeland's finest poets. Simic's work, which includes *Unending Blues, Walking the Black Cat,* and *Hotel Insomnia,* has won numerous prestigious awards, among them the 1990 Pulitzer Prize and the coveted MacArthur Foundation "genius grant."

# A

***Indicates that a listing has been compiled from secondary sources believed to be reliable but has not been personally verified for this edition by the author sketched.***

**ADAMS, F(rank) Ramsay 1883-1963**
**(Carl Dane)**

*PERSONAL:* Born July 7, 1883, in Morrison, IL; died October 8, 1963; son of George Bradford (an editor) and Lucy E. (Ramsay) Adams; married Hazel Leslie Judd, 1907 (died); married Lorna D. Margrave, December 1, 1931; children: Penny Adams Munroe. *Education:* University of Chicago, Ph.B., 1904. *Politics:* Republican. *Religion:* Protestant. *Avocational interests:* Vegetable gardening.

*CAREER:* Reporter for *City Press, Chicago Tribune,* and *Chicago Herald Examiner,* all Chicago, IL, 1903-04; Playhouse Theater, Whitehall, MI, manager, 1916-32; Sylvan Beach Resort Co., Whitehall, MI, president, 1916-32; Carlson-Adams Garage, Whitehall, MI, owner and operator, 1923-51. *Military service:* U.S. Army, Artillery, American Expeditionary Forces, 1916-19; became first lieutenant; received French Service Medal.

*MEMBER:* Authors League of America, Screen Writers Guild, American Society of Composers, Authors and Publishers, American Legion, Veterans of World War One, Chicago Press Vets, Masons, Phi Sigma, Delta Upsilon.

*WRITINGS:*

*Secret Attic,* Stanley Paul (London), 1930.
*The Long Night,* Stanley Paul, 1932.
*For Valor,* Stanley Paul, 1934.
*Pleasure Island,* Stanley Paul, 1936.
*Men on Foot,* Newnes (London), 1937.
*Gunsight Ranch,* Doubleday, Doran (New York City), 1939.
*Arizona Feud,* Doubleday, Doran, 1941.
*When I Come Back,* McBride (New York City), 1944.
*The Impossible Dream: A Report,* F. Adams (Camarillo, CA), 1976.

*PLAYS*

(With Will M. Hough) *His Highness, the Bey: A Musical Satire in Two Acts,* produced in Chicago, 1905.
(With Hough) *The Isle of Bong-Bong: A Musical Comedy in Two Acts,* produced in Chicago, 1905.
(With Hough) *The Land of Nod: A Musical Extravaganza with a Prologue and Two Acts,* produced in Chicago, 1905.
(With Hough) *The Time, the Place and the Girl: A Three-Act Comedy with Music,* produced in Chicago, 1906.
*Five Fridays,* Small, Maynard (Boston), 1915.
*Molly and I; or, The Silver Ring,* Small, Maynard, 1915.
*Stage Struck,* Jacobsen-Hodgkinson (New York City), 1925.
*Almost a Lady,* Jacobsen-Hodgkinson, 1927.
*Help Yourself to Happiness,* Macaulay (New York City), 1929.
*King's Crew,* Long and Richard R. Smith (New York City), 1932.

Also author of plays *Honeymoon Trail, The Flirting Princess, The Golden Girl, A Stubborn Cinderella, The Goddess of Liberty, Miss Nobody from Starland, The Prince of Tonight, The Heartbreakers, Princess April,* and *Fast and Grow Fat.*

*OTHER*

Author of screenplays *The Cowboy and the Lady, Peg o' My Heart, Trade-Winds, The Virginia Judge, She*

*Made Her Bed, The Super-Sex,* and *Scandal Street.* Contributor of short stories and serials to *Cosmopolitan, Red Book, Munsey Magazine, Black Cat, Illustrated Detective, Smart Set, MacLean's,* and *Nash's;* stories included in many textbooks and anthologies. Author of lyrics to approximately two hundred songs, including "I Wonder Who's Kissing Her Now," "Honeymoon," and "Blow the Smoke Away."

*SIDELIGHTS:* F. Ramsay Adams was a writer of plays, screenplays, song lyrics, and novels. Adams, wrote J. Fraser Cocks, III in *Twentieth-Century Western Writers,* "specialized in romantic adventure and mystery fiction featuring bright, sophisticated, articulate people engaged in witty repartee and light-hearted love affairs."

Adams began writing while still attending the University of Chicago at the turn of the century. Along with collaborator Will M. Hough, Adams wrote a number of musical comedies staged in Chicago at this time. Among their most popular works was the song "I Wonder Who's Kissing Her Now." The song earned national exposure in 1947 when George Jessel produced a film musical by the same title and the song became a nationwide hit.

Adams' novels often featured lightly humorous plots mixed with adventure or mystery. In *Five Fridays,* for example, he wrote of a young woman who takes everything she reads in the magazines seriously, to the point of following an extreme regimen of fasting for the benefit of her health. A critic for the *New York Times* claimed that "Adams tells his hilarious story with much sense of humor and with a happy faculty for quaint conceits and entertaining statement." The novel *King's Crew* combines adventure with mystery in its story of a group of young friends on vacation who encounter a Mexican bandit. A critic for *Springfield Republican* stated: "The characters are intensely alive and the dialog is gaily humorous." "Readers who enjoy a sentimental, swift-moving tale . . . will find the book to their taste," wrote a critic for the *New York Times.*

The mystery element reappears in several of Adams' other popular novels. In *Help Yourself to Happiness,* a young woman is wrongly accused of murdering a prominent artist and must flee the city. Following a train wreck, she assumes the identity of a female passenger on the train. "If," wrote a critic in the *Boston Transcript,* "you want rollicking humor and delicate satire, you will be satisfied." In a similar plot line, *Gunsight Ranch* sees the narrator on the run for bank fraud, a crime he has not committed. When a man sitting next to him at the train station suffers a fatal heart attack, the narrator assumes the dead man's identity. G. W. Harris in the *New York Times* noted that "Adams has an uncanny deftness in getting his hero into, and out of, tight places." In *Arizona Feud,* a reporter solves a murder and puts an end to a violent family feud. Harris stated that this novel portrayed a "grim and horrible tragedy" but with "lightness and dash and cleverness and wise-cracking dialogue."

*BIOGRAPHICAL/CRITICAL SOURCES:*

*BOOKS*

*Twentieth-Century Western Writers,* second edition, St. James Press (Detroit), 1991.

*PERIODICALS*

*Boston Transcript,* November 16, 1929, p. 10.
*New York Times,* July 14, 1915, p. 20; May 15, 1932, p. 6; April 30, 1939, p. 16; September 14, 1941, p. 17.
*Springfield Republican,* May 1, 1932, p. 7E.*

* * *

**ALGREN, Nelson 1909-1981**

*PERSONAL:* Given name Nelson Ahlgren Abraham; name legally changed to Nelson Algren; born March 28, 1909, in Detroit, MI; died of a heart attack, May 9, 1981, in Sag Harbor, NY; married Amanda Kontowicz, 1936 (divorced, 1939); married Betty Ann Jones, 1965 (divorced, 1967). *Education:* University of Illinois, Urbana, B.A., 1931. *Avocational interests:* Boxing, horse racing, poker and other card games.

*CAREER:* Salesperson (sold coffee door to door for a time) and migratory worker in the South and Southwest during the Depression; worked at a gas station in Rio Hondo, TX, 1933, which eventually led to the writing of his first published story; worked briefly for a Works Progress Administration writers' project; worked on venereal-disease control for the Chicago Board of Health; edited, with Jack Conroy, an experimental magazine called *The New Anvil,* Chicago, 1939-41; author and journalist, 1941-81, including coverage of the Vietnam War, 1969; columnist, Chicago *Free Press,* 1970; teacher of creative writing, University of Iowa, Iowa City, 1967, and the University of Florida, Gainesville, 1974. *Military service:* U.S. Army, 1942-45; medical corpsman.

*MEMBER:* American Academy and Institute of Arts and Letters.

*AWARDS, HONORS:* American Academy grant and Newberry Library fellow, both 1947; National Institute of Arts and Letters fellowship, 1947, and Newberry Library fellowship, both for the writing of *The Man with the Golden Arm;* National Book Award, 1950, for *The Man with the Golden Arm;* National Institute of Arts and Letters medal of merit, 1974; National Endowment for the Arts grant, 1976; "Nelson Algren fiction contest" established in author's memory by *Chicago Magazine,* 1982, continued by *Chicago Tribune,* 1986—; "PEN/Nelson Algren Fiction Award" established in author's memory by PEN American Center, 1983—.

*WRITINGS:*

*Somebody in Boots* (novel), Vanguard, 1935, reprinted with new preface, Berkley Publishing, 1965.

*Never Come Morning* (novel), Harper, 1942, reprinted, Berkley Publishing, 1968, Seven Stories Press, 1996.

*The Neon Wilderness* (short stories), Doubleday, 1947, reprinted with afterword by Studs Terkel and a 1955 *Paris Review* interview, Writing and Readers, 1986.

*The Man with the Golden Arm* (novel), Doubleday, 1949, reprinted, Robert Bentley, 1978.

*Chicago: City on the Make* (prose poem), Doubleday, 1951, University of Chicago Press, 1987.

*A Walk on the Wild Side* (novel; also see below), Farrar, Strauss, 1956, reprinted, Greenwood Press, 1978, Thunder's Mouth Press, 1990.

(With Jay Landesman, Fran Landesman and Tommy Wolf) *A Walk on the Wild Side* (three-act musical play), first produced at Crystal Palace Theatre, St. Louis, 1960.

(Author of foreword and contributor) *Nelson Algren's Own Book of Lonesome Monsters* (short story anthology), Lancer Books, 1962, Bernard Geis, 1963.

*Notes from a Sea Diary: Hemingway All the Way* (nonfiction), Putnam, 1965.

*Who Lost an American?* (nonfiction), Macmillan, 1963.

(Author of introduction) Jan I. Fortune, editor, *The True Story of Bonnie and Clyde: As Told by Bonnie's Mother and Clyde's Sister,* Signet, 1968.

*The Last Carousel* (collection of short pieces), Putnam, 1973.

*Calhoun: Roman eines Verbrechens,* edited and translated by Carl Weissner, Zweitausendeins, 1981, original English language edition published as *The Devil's Stocking,* Arbor House, 1983.

*America Eats,* University of Iowa Press (Iowa City), 1993.

*He Swung and He Missed,* Creative Education (Mankato, MN), 1993.

*The Texas Stories of Nelson Algren,* University of Texas Press (Austin), 1995.

*Nonconformity: Writing on Writing,* Seven Stories Press (New York City), 1996.

*CONTRIBUTOR TO ANTHOLOGIES*

*Galena Guide,* Works Progress Administration, 1937.

Herschell Brickell, editor, *O. Henry Memorial Award Prize Stories of 1941,* Doubleday, 1941.

Martha Foley, editor, *Best American Short Stories 1942,* Houghton, 1942.

*Modern Reading,* Wells, Gardner, Darton, 1943.

*Cross Section,* Simon & Schuster, 1947.

John Lehmann, editor, *The Penguin New Writing,* Penguin Books, 1948.

*New World Writing,* New American Library, 1956.

*Taboo,* New Classics House, 1964.

*Focus/Media,* Chandler, 1972.

*OTHER*

Contributor of short stories, essays, articles and reviews to numerous periodicals, including *Story, Nation, Life, Saturday Evening Post, American Mercury, Atlantic, Chicago Tribune, Partisan Review, Playboy,* and *Rolling Stone.* A collection of Nelson Algren's papers are at the Ohio State University Library, Columbus, OH.

*ADAPTATIONS: The Man with the Golden Arm* was produced as a film under the same title by United Artists, 1955. *A Walk on the Wild Side* was produced as a film under the same title by Columbia Pictures, 1962, and as a musical play under the same title at New York's Musical Theater Workshop and later at the Back Alley Theatre in Van Nuys, California, 1988. (Algren did not approve of the productions.)

*SIDELIGHTS:* The late Nelson Algren's casts of hopeless drifters, prostitutes, petty thieves, con men, addicts and derelicts earned him the designation "poet of the Chicago slums," but he preferred to call himself "the tin whistle of American letters." Algren's novels, including *A Walk on the Wild Side, Never Come Morning,* and the National Book Award-winning *The Man with the Golden Arm,* explore life situations in the seamy sections of town with emphasis on humanity battered by abject poverty and social indifference. As Chester E. Eisinger notes in *Fiction of the Forties,* Algren was "the poet of the jail and the whorehouse; he has made a close study of the cockroach, the drunkard, and the pimp, the garbage in the street and the spittle on the chin. He has a truly cloacal vision of the American experience." Though Algren worked as a journalist, essayist and reviewer most of his life, Eisinger suggests the author earned a reputation for writing fiction that attacked the "bluebird vision of America." According to Eisinger, the criticism in Algren's novels "is not in any sense ideological. It is a compound of resentment and perversity, of feelings; it is a conviction that the respectable classes ought to have their noses rubbed in the poverty and degradation of American life as an antidote to their self-satisfaction; it is a conviction that the poor are just as good as the rich, and more fun to boot; it is sheer sentimental sympathy for the underdog."

Critics such as Ralph J. Gleason and Sheldon Norman Grebstein feel that Algren took a singular responsibility for exploding the myths of opportunity and democracy generated by and for the American middle class. In *Rolling Stone,* Gleason writes: "Up until Algren, no American writer had really combined a poetic gift for words and a vision of truth about the textbook democracy." Grebstein elaborates in *The Forties: Fiction, Poetry, Drama,* noting that Algren's work "depicts but three milieux: life on the road or in the jails of the South-west in the 1930's; life in the slums, bars, and whorehouses of New Orleans of the '30's; life in the poorer working-class neighborhoods . . . in the Chicago of the 1930's and '40's. . . . Nowhere in Algren are there people vibrantly healthy, free of guilt, clean, fulfilled, content." Grebstein concludes that Algren's central theme is "the refutation of what has been among the hallowed official truths of American society, a truth which Algren considers the blackest lie: the belief that the individual retains the power of choice, of deciding between two alternatives, in plotting his destiny."

Kenneth G. McCollum reflects on Algren's vision of hopelessness in the *Dictionary of Literary Biography,* claiming that Algren's stories and novels are "often loose and rambling, partly because the lives of the characters are uncertain and disconnected. . . . Algren deals with man in a world of chance in a universe that is indifferent or even hostile to his microcosmic sense of himself." Eisinger likewise cites Algren's "unheroic hero who comes to a blank end in a hostile world," trapped by his own fallible nature and by social circumstances. McCollum contends that this existential viewpoint entered Algren's fiction without the author's conscious philosophical design. "Algren's works abound with manifestations of such existential terms as *dread, anxiety, despair, nothingness, alienation,* and the *absurd,*" concludes McCollum. Often an Algren protagonist finds momentary redemption or meaning through love, as George Bluestone notes in the *Western Review:* "[In] Algren's central vision, self-destruction becomes operative only after the destruction of some loved object. The moment a central character becomes responsible for such ruin, he is irrevocably doomed. That 'irrational, destructive force,' then, is the impulse to destroy love which is tantamount to death." Eisinger sees Algren as "insisting that nothing can kill the aspiration for a more meaningful life than it is possible for his people to attain. And he is insisting most of all upon the survival of love, not as the romantic passion that men die for but as the only source of warmth in the lives of the hopeless."

Algren wrote for more than forty years, but a conviction that novels require an "all out" single-minded dedication limited his output of longer fiction. In *Conversations with Nelson Algren,* the author told H. E. F. Donohue about his approach to the craft: "If you do the big book there's no way—at least I have no way—of doing a big book and doing anything else. . . . In fact you don't do much of anything but get a scene and you live within the scene and keep pushing that particular scene. . . . You've got to cut everything else out. You're never free. And you've got to do that for a couple of years before you can make a pattern or cut a scene that nobody else has touched." Algren added that he required firsthand experience of his fictional milieux in order to create a novel: "The only way I can write is to try to make something that hasn't been done before, and in order to do that you can't just take notes. You have to *be* there. You write about your own reactions to the scene. You identify yourself with the scene. And you have to get all the details that nobody knows about. You have to be specific." In their study entitled *Nelson Algren,* Martha Heasley Cox and Wayne Chatterton cite Algren for "style and language that are drawn from the world he depicts." They also record Algren's often-quoted assertion about his realistic yet poetic prose: "My most successful poetry, the lines people threw back at me years after they were written, were lines I never wrote. They were lines I heard, and repeated, usually by someone who never read and couldn't write."

Algren indeed spent a great deal of time in the company of the homeless and the illiterate. He was born in Detroit but was raised in a working-class section of Chicago, the only son of a machinist. Despite an undistinguished high school career, he enrolled in college at the University of Illinois and majored in journalism. When he graduated in 1931, work was unobtainable; he searched for a job for a year and then began to hitchhike south. The following two years were extremely difficult ones for Algren. He spent some months in New Orleans, selling coffee and bogus beauty parlor discount certificates door-to-door. For a time he accepted responsibility for an all-but-deserted gas station in Rio Hondo, Texas, until an unscrupulous partner began to abscond with the gasoline. Algren then hopped a freight train to El Paso, where he was arrested for vagrancy, thrown in jail, and fined five dollars. When he was released he moved to Alpine, Texas, and discovered that he could use the typewriters at the understaffed Alpine Teachers College without detection. He began to write short stories and letters that he mailed back to Chicago, and it was from among these Depression-era experiences that his early fiction was culled.

Eventually Algren decided to return to Chicago. He chose a typewriter from the Alpine Teachers College and attempted to mail it north. Then he jumped into a boxcar himself, but he only got as far as San Antonio before he was arrested for the theft of the typewriter. He spent the next four months in jail, awaiting trial with a circuit-riding judge. This incident involving rural law enforcement is reflected throughout Algren's fiction, most notably in *The Neon Wilderness, Somebody in Boots,* and *A Walk on the Wild Side*. After his trial, Algren left Texas immediately, riding freight trains and hitchhiking back to Chicago.

In *Conversations with Nelson Algren,* the author reminisced about why he decided to write fiction: "I wanted to be a writer in the literary sense. That is, I wanted to find a place in the literary world. . . . But the experience on the road gave me something to write about. It was just an accidental, just a fortuitous thing. I didn't go on the road in order to have something to write about. You do see what it's like, what a man in shock who is dying looks like. . . . Or you're waiting for a boxcar and it seems to be going a little too fast and some kid makes a try for it and you see him miss and then you get the smell of blood and you go over and you see it sliced off his arm. And all the whores in New Orleans. And all the tens of thousands of Americans literally milling around at that time trying to survive. . . . All these scenes, one after another, piled up into something that made me not just want to write but to really say it, to find out that this thing was all upside down."

*Somebody in Boots,* Algren's first novel, was published in 1935. The book's emphasis, writes Maxwell Geismar in *American Moderns: From Rebellion to Conformity,* lies in its "scenes of brutality which mark the life of the 'lumpen proletariat,' the social scum, the passively rotting mass of people who lie at the bottom of the social scale." The hero of *Somebody in Boots,* Cass McKay, is driven from his home in a Texas border town by violence and poverty; the narrative follows the youth's misadventures as a homeless, freight-hopping hobo. Bluestone calls the work "the most uneven and least satisfying, but in some ways the most revealing of [Algren's] books." Eisinger also finds the novel revealing in its "Marxist-angled social criticism," but he adds: "[Algren] displays an unreasoning hatred for the respectable, property-owning classes in America, but unfortunately nothing of what he says has relevance in his story. In this inability to integrate such criticism and the themes of his novel one may find a reason for Algren's surrender of the techniques of frontal attack on social issues." Bluestone likewise cites "parenthetical broadsides" in the novel that are "purely didactic intrusions," but he concludes that *Somebody in Boots* "reveals certain inclinations which will become more important later on: the choice of fallen, barely articulate characters; a narrative sensibility aware of verbal complexity; a prose appropriation of poetic devices; a piecing together of previously published pieces; . . . [and] a central concern with love and survival in the face of loneliness and death."

Much of the critical commentary on *Somebody in Boots* is retrospective, for the book was not widely reviewed or commercially successful when first released. This lack of public enthusiasm for his work led Algren to concentrate on short stories and journalism for nearly five years. He worked as a staff writer for the Works Progress Administration and helped to edit a small leftist magazine, the *New Anvil,* while publishing occasional poems in other magazines. In 1940 he returned to work on longer fiction, and the resulting novel, *Never Come Morning,* was published in 1942 to immediate critical acclaim. Set in a Polish community of the Chicago slums, the story revolves around Bruno Bicek, an aspiring boxer who turns to criminal activity and murder after allowing his street gang friends to rape his girlfriend. According to McCollum, the book's theme of physical conquest devoid of love is "symbolic of the differences between Algren's perception and the middle-class idea of what was going on in America. To Algren, niceness, purity, and fairness were part of a myth that disguised the strong taking from the weak."

*Never Come Morning* established Algren as a "Chicago novelist" as well as a practitioner of the style known as native American realism. *New Republic* contributor Malcolm Cowley writes: "It is the poetry of familiar things that is missing in the other Chicago novels and that shows the direction of Algren's talent. In spite of the violent story he tells—and tells convincingly—he is not by instinct a novelist. He is a poet of the Chicago slums, and he might well be Sandburg's successor." According to Philip Rahv in *Nation, Never Come Morning* "is pervaded by a feeling of loss rather than of bitterness or horror. And Algren's realism is so paced as to avoid the tedium of the naturalistic stereotype, of the literal copying of surfaces. He knows how to select, how to employ factual details without letting himself be swamped by them, and, finally, how to put the slang his characters speak to creative uses so that it ceases to be an element of mere documentation and turns into an element of style." Bluestone concludes that, in *Never Come Morning,* "Algren's characteristic symbolism and indirection endow the action with pity and concealed prophecy. . . . [One finds] here, woven into the matrix of the prose, those haunting images of deserted cities, symbolizing the characters' life-in-death, which becomes increasingly typical of Algren. . . . More important than any plot or character development is the general doom implicit from the start. Only, the powerful voice behind the events insists on our attention."

Algren served in the U.S. Army as a medical corpsman from 1942 until 1945. After his discharge he began his most productive decade as a fiction writer—between 1947 and 1956 he published a short story collection, *The Neon Wilderness,* a lengthy prose poem, *Chicago: City on the Make,* and two highly acclaimed novels, *The Man with the Golden Arm* and *A Walk on the Wild Side.* It was also during this period that Algren began to undertake the extensive travels that would form a basis for much of his nonfiction. Sometimes accompanied by the French novelist Simone de Beauvoir, he visited Europe, Central America, and many regions of the United States. Through de Beauvoir Algren met members of prominent Parisian literary circles, including Jean-Paul Sartre. Algren continued to reside primarily in Chicago, however, usually renting a small furnished flat in which he could write through the night.

*The Man with the Golden Arm,* published in 1949, propelled Algren to the literary forefront. He won the first National Book Award for the work, and it was also a bestseller. Once again centered in the Chicago slums, *The Man with the Golden Arm* details the downfall of Frankie Machine, a card dealer with a morphine addiction who is inevitably pursued by the law. The reaction of the book's reviewers is almost universally positive. Grebstein writes: "Not only is Algren's novel the first serious treatment in our literature of the drug addict, it is also a profoundly felt and profoundly moving book. . . . This novel marks the culmination of Algren's identification with characters the 'normal' man might think beneath or beyond his sympathies, yet such is Algren's craft that he extends the norm." *New York Times* contributor A. C. Spectorsky claims that *The Man with the Golden Arm* "is a powerful book, illuminated by flashes of Algren's grisly, antic, almost horrifying humor, by passages of finely poetic writing, and by his love and understanding, which are, at times, almost morbidly compassionate." A critic for *Time* concludes: "Readers with queasy stomachs may shrink from an environment in which the unbelievably sordid has become a way of life. They will also come away with some of Algren's own tender concern for his wretched, confused and hopelessly degenerate cast of characters. In that, writer Algren scores a true novelist's triumph."

Critics of *The Man with the Golden Arm* cite a strong portrayal of Algren's recurring theme of love, guilt and death. "The particular conflict here," Grebstein writes, "is that between self-sacrifice and self-preservation, a conflict knotted into the relationship between Frankie Machine and his wife Sophie, his friend Sparrow, and his girl Molly. These are the dynamic relationships which fluctuate with the condition of the participants. Such is Algren's version of the whole truth that his people tend to prey on one another, whether in friendship or love." McCollum likewise contends that in *The Man with the Golden Arm* "the personal interactions of the characters have more impact on the progression of the plot than does the effect of the total environment." McCollum also notes an absence of didacticism in the work despite its elucidation of the pernicious nature of slum life. "The personal tragedy of Frankie Machine," McCollum concludes, "is not death, but loneliness and isolation in an environment where everybody hustles and everybody is on the take." Bluestone offers a similar assessment: "Algren's final image, despite the humor, despite the intensity, despite the struggle to survive, is one of hopelessness and desolation. In this world, death is inescapable. What possible approaches are open to the narrator who wishes to communicate such a vision? He can laugh; or he can lament. Algren does both supremely well. But the laughter is edged with bitterness; before the reality of death, it sadly falls away."

Algren was known to recycle material, especially memorable lines and scenes. His 1956 novel, *A Walk on the Wild Side,* bears a strong thematic resemblance to *Somebody in Boots.* The protagonist of *A Walk on the Wild Side* is once again a young illiterate Texan who drifts to Depression-era New Orleans and becomes involved in a sordid sex show in a house of prostitution. In his appraisal of Algren's work, Bluestone writes: "At first glance, *A Walk on the Wild Side* seems to be a mere rewriting of *Somebody in Boots.* . . . From the point of view of Algren's entire output, however, it represents a fascinating reappraisal of his central theme. Ultimately the differences between the two books are more striking than the resemblances. The narrative alternates between a mood of savage tenderness and one of broad burlesque, but this time the comic mood is strongest. . . . Out of the poetic exploration of this marginal, half-lit world there emerges the image of a universe in which human action must inevitably seem absurd. And yet, within that world, there coexists a real belief that human action can have validity and meaning." This belief, Bluestone concludes, contrasts with the nihilistic tones and outcomes of Algren's earlier works.

Critics are divided on the quality of *A Walk on the Wild Side. New York Times* contributor Alfred Kazin states: "It is impossible to feel that [Algren] really cares about these people, that he is interested in them, that these are human beings he has observed. What I object to most in this book is the plainly contrived quality of this pretended feeling about characters whom Mr. Algren writes about not because they are 'lost,' but because they are freaks." In his *New Yorker* review, Norman Podhoretz finds the book "more in the spirit of the boozy sentimentality of the broken-down Shakespearean actor declaiming to the boys on the barroom floor than an expression of Rabelaisian exuberance." Cox and Chatterton express a different opinion in their study of Algren's work: "One of Algren's most remarkable achievements in *A Walk on the Wild Side* is his convincing, compassionate treatment of a group of characters who could, in less skillful hands, be little more than a gallery of freaks and sheer grotesques. . . . The impressive verbal mortar which binds the other stylistic properties is still the concreteness and specificity of detail; the accurate terminology of road, gutter, bar, and brothel; the keen and comprehensive ear for dialect; the eye for significant idiosyncrasies of dress and behavior; the quick grasp of obsessive quirks of thought—the ring of authority." In the *New York Herald Tribune Book Review,* Milton Rugoff concludes that the novel "is an American tradition of emotional gigantism: its comedy is farce, its joys are orgies, the feats of its characters Bunyanesque, their sexuality is prodigious, their sorrow a wild keening almost too high for ordinary ears. . . . In a period that hasn't lacked for novels of degeneracy and cruelty, . . . 'A Walk on the Wild Side' is almost without peer."

Algren's shorter works—fiction, nonfiction, and poetry—reflect many of the same concerns that motivated him to write novels. Cox and Chatterton call the author's short stories "a considerable achievement," adding: "The stories in *The Neon Wilderness* have elicited unexpected discipline from an author so often charged with looseness and with over-rhapsodizing in his novels. . . . Nowhere outside the short stories has Algren been so free to exercise his ability to construct a tale from the single, self-revelatory catch-phrase. . . . Nowhere else has he controlled so stringently his tendency to blend the sordid and poetic; as a result the short stories have largely escaped the adverse reaction which such a controversial mixture has brought against his novels." Geismar likewise writes: "Algren's powerful effects are usually in his big scenes rather than in the portrayal or development of character. He is almost at his best in . . . short stories where he can suggest the whole contour of a human life in a few terse pages."

The "blend of sordid and poetic" that Cox and Chatterton note finds further elucidation in *Chicago: City on the Make,* Algren's best-known prose poem. Commissioned by *Holiday* magazine as the lead article for a Chicago theme issue, the completed poem "was so unflattering that it was relegated to rear pages," according to Jack Conroy in the *Dictionary of Literary Biography Yearbook: 1982.* The work was subsequently published in book form in 1951. In a *Saturday Review* assessment, Emmett Dedmon states: "The qualities of Nelson Algren's prose essay on

Chicago are those of fine poetry—vivid images, richness of language, economy of form, and most importantly, poetic vision. It is necessary to go back to the 'Chicago Poems' of Carl Sandburg . . . to find a book about the city comparable to Algren's." Bluestone feels that Algren's impressions of Chicago are "typical of a new and sympathetic look at urban life which goes beyond recoil and horror. Much of what we have seen in the stories and novels appears here, too: a pervasive sense of loss and loneliness, an image of urban desolation, an eye for graphic detail, incantory prose. . . . This author knows that in urban society there is vertical as well as horizontal mobility, that Skid Row is merely the ugliest manifestation of tendencies embedded in all strata of city life."

Most of Algren's output in the 1960s and 1970s was nonfiction, some of it distilled from magazine and newspaper pieces. He published two travelogues, *Who Lost an American?* and *Notes from a Sea Diary: Hemingway All the Way,* both of which combine travel experiences with commentary on other authors and their works. Algren's most notable book from this period is *The Last Carousel,* a chrestomathy of thirty-seven pieces from 1947 to 1972, including short fiction, unpublished bits of novels, and nonfiction essays on a variety of subjects. In the *New York Times Book Review,* James R. Frakes calls *The Last Carousel* a "catch-all volume" with moments at which Algren is "at the top of his form, with his hallmark stamped on every link." Tom Carson comments in the *Voice Literary Supplement:* "Ironically, losing his sense of obligation to an audience he had decided wasn't there freed Algren; the loosened responsibilities of who-gives-a-damn product allowed him to express himself more idiosyncratically and directly than ever. And his wonderful ear, that spinning-against-the-way-it-drives colloid of highly charged poetic language and colloquial closed-mouthedness, survives in even his most occasional pieces."

In 1974 Algren was commissioned to write an article about Rubin "Hurricane" Carter for *Esquire* magazine. Carter, a former boxer who had been convicted on three counts of murder, received a second trial that year when two witnesses denied their previous testimony. Leaving Chicago behind, Algren moved to Paterson, New Jersey, where he immersed himself in the case. When Carter lost in the second trial, *Esquire* dropped the story. Algren, however, did not. As James Hardin notes in the *Dictionary of Literary Biography Yearbook: 1982,* Algren "thought of himself as a fighter, a reporter who championed the rights of the outsiders." Hardin claims additionally that "the social milieu of the case appealed to Algren, not merely the opportunity to expose an injustice." Algren eventually fictionalized the events for a novel entitled *The Devil's Stocking.* Hardin writes: "All the figures of the novel have or had their counterparts in real life, among them Algren himself. It is a world of prostitutes, gangsters, jaded barkeeps—the fringes of society—but it also describes the brief rise in the fortunes of the [boxer Ruby Calhoun] and gives a glimpse of the life that might have been, of the loser who was on the way to the big time."

*The Devil's Stocking* appeared in German translation before it was released in the United States. By the time it saw American publication in 1983, Algren had been dead for two years. Critical reaction to the work is mixed; some reviewers feel Algren would have served the material more faithfully had he maintained nonfictional accuracy. "Since most of the work is patently based on fact," Hardin contends, "it could be argued that a 'documentary'—Algren's original plan—would have been more effective, more disquieting." Hardin admits, however, that the novel "is an excellent example of unpretentious reportage. The conversations have the ring of authenticity. It is a hard-nosed piece of writing." John W. Aldridge expresses similar sentiments in the *New York Times Book Review:* "Algren . . . seems not to have aged but only matured and to be, as never before, in firm possession of his subject. His language throughout the novel is precise, controlled, almost entirely free of the lush lyrical excesses of the past, but nonetheless genuinely warm and alive. The story is recognizable as belonging in the classic Algren repertoire, yet is also freshly conceived and carried forward with an easy assurance that indicates Algren had it in him to write five or six more novels in the same vein."

Two other Algren works have been published posthumously. During the lean years of the 1930s, Algren found work with the Works Progress Administration (WPA) Writers Project in Illinois, compiling a report on Native American and ethnic food customs and recipes. Published in 1993 as *America Eats,* the manuscript, states a reviewer for *Kirkus Reviews,* "has far more style, vitality, and pat detail than the run of today's (or yesterday's) folksy foodlore." Algren wrote *Nonconformity: Writing on Writing* during another difficult time for writers—the early 1950s, when artists were being pressured by politicians to conform to anti-Communist political ideals. The original publisher rejected this book-length essay because of information it received from FBI informants stating that Algren's politics were suspect.

Algren died of a heart attack on May 9, 1981, just weeks before his formal induction into the prestigious American Academy and Institute of Arts and Letters. His eulogists, including Carson, suggest that his work has not received sufficient critical attention and respect. "Algren's story isn't that of a once-fashionable writer gone out of season," Carson states. "He never was all that fashionable. Bad timing, for one thing: a '30s novelist shouldn't do his best work in the '40s and '50s. Then there's the problem of being a Chicago novelist—Algren saw himself extending the Midwestern tradition . . . at a time when New York was establishing a near-total literary hegemony and thanking God it'd gotten the rough boys out. And after popular success finally came, Algren's reaction was to deny the worth of writing fiction at all. What that adds up to is a career spent entirely on the fringe; and the center, nettled by his sense of its irrelevance, ended up returning the favor." In a *Chicago Tribune Book World* retrospective, Budd Schulberg writes: "To his honor, Algren never denied himself the pain endured by the victims who were his heroes in book after book. . . . Nor did he deny himself the risk of failure in a fickle, success-ridden America that might reward him with fame and fortune for one book . . . and then turn its back on him because he would not play the game of the Eastern Literary Establishment, . . . the 'club' that decides from its high and haughty platforms which writers are in and which are out. Let the Eastern literati praise him, damn him, or neglect him, the Nelson Algren I knew really didn't give a damn."

If literary critics tend to ignore Algren, many of his fellow writers have accorded him a great deal of recognition. Authors such as Ernest Hemingway, Carl Sandburg, Studs Terkel and Richard Wright have praised Algren for his contribution to the body of twentieth century American letters. Hemingway, for instance, once listed Algren as one of the two most notable authors of his generation. In a foreword to *Nelson Algren: A Checklist,* Terkel suggests: "My hunch is [Algren's] writings will be read long after acclaimed works of the Academe's darlings, yellowed on coffee tables, will be replaced by acclaimed works of other Academe's darlings." Ross Macdonald also offers plaudits in the *New York Times Book Review:* "Algren's Chicago and the people who live in its shadows are still there. Algren is their tragic poet, enabling those who can read him to feel pain. . . . The intensity of his feeling, the accuracy of his thought, make me wonder if any other writer of our time has shown us more exactly the human basis of our democracy."

The author who has given American literature such memorable phrases as "monkey on my back," "Never play cards with a man named Doc," and "I'm the girl that men forget" is memorialized by two annual fiction contests that bear his name. Eisinger, who calls Algren "the twentieth century man of feeling, inexplicably caught in the city slums," contends that the writer gave his characters "yearnings for love or pride in themselves as separate and identifiable individuals—yearnings that reveal a tender concern for them as human beings." In *American Moderns,* Geismar comments: "Nelson Algren . . . represents a solid and enduring part of the American literary heritage. . . . And Algren is a writer who carries with him our hope and concern for something more than entertainment." "Algren's ambitions as a social novelist notwithstanding," Grebstein concludes, "his ambition to write 'influential' books, books that ameliorate unfair conditions, he has perhaps already accomplished something more important for literature: the scenes he has created have become part of our imaginative life, and his people are now among those we know."

*BIOGRAPHICAL/CRITICAL SOURCES:*

*BOOKS*

Algren, Nelson, *Who Lost an American?,* Macmillan, 1963.

Algren, Nelson, *Notes from a Sea Diary: Hemingway All the Way,* Putnam, 1965.

Algren, Nelson, *The Last Carousel,* Putnam, 1973.

Beauvoir, Simone de, *America Day by Day,* Duckworth, 1952, Grove, 1953.

Beauvoir, Simone de, *The Force of Circumstance,* translated by Richard Howard, Putnam, 1965.

*Contemporary Literary Criticism,* Gale, Volume 4, 1975, Volume 10, 1979, Volume 33, 1985.

Cowley, Malcolm, editor, *Writers at Work: The "Paris Review" Interviews,* Viking, 1958.

Cox, Martha H. and Wayne Chatterton, *Nelson Algren,* Twayne, 1975.

*Dictionary of Literary Biography,* Volume 9: *American Novelists 1910-1945,* Gale, 1981.

*Dictionary of Literary Biography Yearbook: 1982,* Gale, 1983.

Donohue, H. E. F., *Conversations with Nelson Algren,* Hill & Wang, 1964.

Drew, Bettina, *Nelson Algren: A Life on the Wild Side,* Putnam, 1989.

Eisinger, Chester E., *Fiction of the Forties,* University of Chicago Press, 1963.

French, Warren, editor, *The Forties: Fiction, Poetry, Drama,* Everett/Edwards, 1969.
Geismar, Maxwell, *American Moderns: From Rebellion to Conformity,* Hill & Wang, 1958.
Giles, James Richard, *Confronting the Horror: The Novels of Nelson Algren,* Kent State University Press (Kent, OH), 1989.
McCollum, Kenneth G., *Nelson Algren: A Checklist,* Gale, 1973.
Saccani, Jean-Pierre, *Nelson et Simone,* Editions du Rocher (Monaco), 1994.
Shay, Arthur, *Nelson Algren's Chicago,* University of Illinois Press (Urbana), 1988.

*PERIODICALS*

*Antioch Review,* fall, 1992, pp. 775-76.
*Atlantic,* June, 1963; October, 1964; August, 1965; October, 1983.
*Books,* April 26, 1942.
*Book Week,* November 1, 1964; August 15, 1965.
*Chicago Sun Book Week,* February 2, 1947.
*Chicago Sun-Times,* March 26, 1973.
*Chicago Tribune,* September 11, 1985.
*Chicago Tribune Book World,* August 21, 1983.
*Chicago Tribune Magazine,* September 14, 1986.
*Commonweal,* February 8, 1974.
*Critic,* October, 1965; January-February, 1973.
*Current History,* August, 1942.
*Harper's,* May, 1965.
*Kirkus Reviews,* April 1, 1992, p. 435; July 15, 1996, p. 1015.
*Library Journal,* November 1, 1995, p. 108.
*Life,* May 18, 1964.
*Los Angeles Times,* September 2, 1988.
*Los Angeles Times Book Review,* October 30, 1983.
*Nation,* April 18, 1942; October 17, 1953; June 1, 1964; September 21, 1964; October 25, 1965.
*New Republic,* July 17, 1935; May 4, 1942; May 21, 1956; January 19, 1974.
*Newsweek,* May 13, 1963; October 26, 1964; August 16, 1965.
*New Yorker,* June 2, 1956.
*New York Herald Tribune Book Review,* October 21, 1951; May 20, 1956.
*New York Herald Tribune Weekly Book Review,* September 11, 1949.
*New York Review of Books,* June 28, 1990, pp. 22-23; October 25, 1990, p. 66.
*New York Times,* April 7, 1935; May 10, 1942; February 2, 1947; September 11, 1949; October 21, 1951; May 20, 1956; August 24, 1965; August 28, 1968; November 1, 1973; October 25, 1989; July 22, 1992, p. C18.
*New York Times Book Review,* October 2, 1949; June 2, 1963; October 25, 1964; August 22, 1965; December 4, 1977; October 9, 1983; November 26, 1989, p. 18; April 29, 1990, p. 34.
*Publishers Weekly,* March 23, 1992, p. 20; May 18, 1992, p. 67; July 26, 1996, p. 81.
*Reporter,* June 11, 1959; June 20, 1963.
*Rolling Stone,* August 6, 1970.
*San Francisco Chronicle,* October 9, 1949; May 27, 1956.
*Saturday Review,* May 26, 1956.
*Saturday Review of Literature,* April 18, 1942; February 8, 1947; October 8, 1949; December 8, 1951.
*Time,* September 12, 1949; May 28, 1956; May 31, 1963.
*Times Literary Supplement,* September 29, 1966; July 30, 1993, pp. 3, 4.
*Tribune Books* (Chicago), May 10, 1987.
*Voice Literary Supplement,* November, 1983.
*Western Review,* autumn, 1957.
*Writer,* March, 1943.

*OBITUARIES:*

*BOOKS*

*Dictionary of Literary Biography Yearbook: 1982,* Gale, 1983.

*PERIODICALS*

*Detroit News,* May 17, 1981.
*Los Angeles Times Book Review,* June 7, 1981.
*New York Times,* May 10, 1981.
*Publishers Weekly,* May 22, 1981.
*Times* (London), May 1, 1981.*

* * *

**ALLEN, John**
**See PERRY, Ritchie (John Allen)**

* * *

**ALLEN, T. D.**
**See ALLEN, Terril Diener**

**ALLEN, Terril Diener 1908-
(Terry D. Allen; Gloria Diener Autry; T. D. Allen, a joint pseudonym)**

*PERSONAL:* Born August 13, 1908, in Douglas, OK; daughter of David M. (banker and real estate agent) and Clara (Cline) Diener; married Don B. Allen (a writer), June 21, 1941 (died, 1966). *Education:* Phillips University, B.A. (magnum cum laude), 1929; Yale University, B.D. (cum laude), 1935; graduate study at University of Oklahoma, 1940-41, Columbia University, 1941-42, Maren Elwood College, 1945-47, New York University, 1958-59, and University of California, Los Angeles, 1965. *Politics:* Independent. *Religion:* Presbyterian.

*ADDRESSES:* *Home*—P. O. Box 2775, Carmel-by-the Sea, CA 93921.

*CAREER:* Freelance writer. Westminster Press, Philadelphia, PA, editor, 1936-39; Young Readers' Press, New York, NY, editor, 1942-44; Institute of American Indian Arts, Santa Fe, NM, professor of creative writing, 1963-68; director of communications arts, Bureau of Indian Affairs, U.S. Government, 1968-74; University of California at Santa Cruz, lecturer and staff specialist on American Indians, 1969-74.

*MEMBER:* Authors League of America, Western Writers of America, National Association for Outlaw and Lawman History, National Council of Teachers of English.

*AWARDS, HONORS:* Distinguished Alumna Award, Phillips University, 1970.

*WRITINGS:*

*WITH HUSBAND DON B. ALLEN, UNDER JOINT PSEUDONYM T. D. ALLEN*

*Doctor in Buckskin,* Harper (New York City), 1951.
*Troubled Border,* Harper, 1954.
*Ambush at Buffalo Wallow,* Fawcett (New York City), 1956.
*Miss Alice and the Cunning Comanche,* Friendship Press (New York City), 1957.
*Prisoners of the Polar Ice,* Westminster (Philadelphia), 1962.
*Tall as Great Standing Rock,* Westminster, 1963.
*Navahos Have Five Fingers,* University of Oklahoma Press (Norman), 1963.
*Doctor, Lawyer, Merchant, Chief,* Westminster, 1965.
*Not Ordered by Men,* Rydal, 1967.

*UNDER NAME TERRY D. ALLEN*

(Co-author) *And Now Tomorrow* (screenplay), Westminster, 1952.
(With Emerson Blackhorse Mitchell) *Miracle Hill: The Story of a Navaho Boy,* University of Oklahoma Press, 1967.
(Editor) *Arrow* (anthology of children's writings), six volumes, Bureau of Indian Affairs (Washington, DC), 1969-74.
(Editor) *The Whispering Wind: Poetry by Young American Indians,* Doubleday, 1972.
*They Can Say It in English,* University of Oklahoma Press, 1981.

*OTHER*

(Under pseudonym Gloria Diener Autry) *The Color-Coded Allergy Cookbook,* Bobbs Merrill (Indianapolis), 1983.

Also author of educational materials for Presbyterian Board of Christian Education and of filmstrips and motion pictures for Family Films, 1961—. Author of screenplay, *Ambush at Buffalo Wallow,* 1960.

*SIDELIGHTS:* Terril Diener Allen, better known under the joint pseudonym T. D. Allen which she shared with her late husband, wrote a number of historical novels set in the American West. "The historical context and character outlines are accurate and there is an insistence on details of place and date," writes Christine Bold in *Twentieth-Century Western Writers.* "At the same time, fictionalized events are added and the conventions of romance affect character portrayal and the description of climactic scenes."

*Doctor in Buckskin,* the first joint effort of the husband-and-wife writing team, is based on the real-life story of Marcus Whitman, a doctor and missionary who was a pioneer in the Oregon territory. While teaching and administering to the medical needs of the Cayuse Indians, the Whitman family was massacred. As V. P. Hass wrote in the *New York Herald Tribune Book Review,* "the Allens have brought to the Whitmans something of the zeal that the Whitmans brought to their pioneering."

The Allens tackled another historical episode from the Old West in *Troubled Border,* the story of John McLoughlin, head of the Hudson Bay Company's outpost at Fort Vancouver. Richard Neuberger, writing in the *New York Times,* believed that "the description of The Company and the native tribes squares well with history." Clarence Gorchels in *Library Journal* noted that the novel "can be interesting even to the reader who does not happen to have much knowledge of history."

Besides the historical novels, the Allens also wrote nonfiction accounts of the American Indian way of life. *Navahos Have Five Fingers* tells of the couple's extended visit to a Navaho reservation and the people they met while there. J. E. Levy in *American Anthropology* dubbed the book's writing style "folksy but never maudlin" and allowed that some chapters were "remarkably perceptive." In *Miracle Hill: The Story of a Navaho Boy,* Allen presented the life story of a young Navaho boy. Begun as a class assignment, Emerson Blackhorse Mitchell's account of his life caught Allen's attention as his teacher. The two worked on the manuscript for two years before completing the book. One goal of *Miracle Hill* is to capture the distinctive Navaho thought pattern through an innovative use of written language. As Bold explained, Allen "left undisturbed linguistic irregularities in tense, verb contruction, and numbering, for she feels that this grammar translates the Navaho's sensory experience directly." D. O. Kelley in *Library Journal* called *Miracle Hill* "a unique autobiographical account" and believed that readers "will gain a better understanding of Navajo family life and will have a truer account than can be obtained from books written by so-called experts."

Allen once told *CA:* "Expecting to escape from my fifteen-year captivity by the Indians, I returned to free-lance writing and discovered an extra career in watercolor painting. Even so, I spend much of my time and a great deal of postage and telephone money in protecting Indians' literary property rights—fighting government publication without copyright, granting permissions to quote from eight volumes of student writings I've gotten published under copyright, and, finally, searching until I locate former Indian students in order to deliver royalty and permission-fee checks to them. Since no one on salaries or grants is interested in preserving their rights, even at this late date, and, since most of those writing about Indians are still exploiting them for personal gain, my volunteer work is a quiet, one-woman crusade in which I strongly believe."

*BIOGRAPHICAL/CRITICAL SOURCES:*

*BOOKS*

*Twentieth-Century Western Writers,* second edition, St. James Press (Detroit), 1991.

*PERIODICALS*

*American Anthropology,* April, 1964, p. 66.
*Library Journal,* May 15, 1954, p. 79; August, 1967, p. 92.
*New York Herald Tribune Book Review,* August 26, 1951, p. 4.
*New York Times,* June 27, 1954, p. 20.

* * *

**ALLEN, Terry D.**
**See ALLEN, Terril Diener**

* * *

**ANAND, Valerie 1937-**
**(Fiona Buckley)**

*PERSONAL:* Born July 6, 1937, in London, England; daughter of John McCormick (a proofreader) and Florence (a dressmaker; maiden name, Sayers) Stubington; married Dalip Singh Anand (a civil servant), March 26, 1970. *Education:* Attended convents and local public school. *Politics:* "Not much, as ideologies seem to me to be 'package deals' in ideas." *Avocational interests:* Horseback riding, flying, reading, cats, food, good wine, the southwest corner of England.

*ADDRESSES: Home*—Surrey, England. *Office*—Matthew Hall PLC, 7 Baker St., London W1M 1AB, England.

*CAREER:* Secretary and typist, 1956-59; *Quarry Managers Journal,* London, England, secretary and sub-editor, 1959-60; Institute of British Launderers, London, assistant public relations officer, 1960-63; *Accountancy,* London, reporter on office equipment, 1963-66; *Index to Office Equipment,* Croyden, Surrey, England, reporter and feature writer, 1966-68; E. J. Poole Associates, London, public relations officer and feature writer on business systems, 1968-71;

Heal & Son Ltd., London, assistant editor of house organ, 1971-72, editor, 1972-75; Matthew Hall PLC (engineering group), London, editor of house organ, 1975—.

*MEMBER:* British Association of Industrial Editors.

*WRITINGS:*

*HISTORICAL NOVELS, EXCEPT AS INDICATED*

*Gildenford* (first novel in "Wessex Trilogy"), Scribner (New York City), 1977.
*The Norman Pretender* (second novel in "Wessex Trilogy"), Scribner, 1979.
*The Disputed Crown* (third novel in "Wessex Trilogy"), Scribner, 1982.
*To a Native Shore: A Novel of India* (contemporary novel), Scribner, 1984.
*King of the Wood,* Headline (London), 1988, St. Martin's (New York City), 1989.
*Crown of Roses,* St. Martin's, 1989.
*The Proud Villeins,* Headline, 1990, St. Martin's, 1992.
*The Ruthless Yeoman,* Headline, 1991, St. Martin's, 1993.
*Women of Ashdon,* Headline, 1992, St. Martin's 1993.
*West of Sunset,* Hodder and Stoughton (London), 1992.
*The Faithful Lovers,* Headline, 1993, St. Martin's, 1994.
*The Cherished Wives,* St. Martin's, 1996.

Contributor of articles to *Surrey Life* and *Accountancy* and of short stories, under pseudonym Fiona Buckley, to *Evening News.*

*SIDELIGHTS:* British historical novelist Valerie Anand is critically acclaimed for her ability to paint a picture of life during various periods in English history by blending fictional material with historical fact. Her "Wessex Trilogy" is a good example of this kind of fusion. The series, which contains the novels *Gildenford, The Norman Pretender,* and *The Disputed Crown,* examines the way of life, politics, and the events that took place during the Norman Conquest of England. Anand provides readers with glimpses into the lifestyles of the English and the Normans, and explores the friction caused by the melding of the cultures during times of battle and after the English were conquered. She presents two major types of characters—those who resist the new rule and others who succumb to it. *Books and Bookmen* reviewer Cara Chanteau describes the third novel in the trilogy, *The Disputed Crown,* as "humorous, entertaining, astute and very moving." Susan Branch, writing in *Twentieth-Century Romance and Historical Writers,* proclaims that Anand's "artfulness lies in avoiding the two main downfalls of the historical novelist: creating characters who are really just 20th-century people in fancy dress, and creating characters who are totally alien to modern readers."

In 1984 Anand took a break from historical writing and produced the contemporary novel *To a Native Shore: A Novel of India.* The book is the story of Melanie Purvis, a woman who must deal with her emotions following a move from her homeland in England to a foreign land (India) with her husband, Dr. Avtar Singh. Melanie is forced to decide how she feels about her situation during a return visit to England. Branch calls *To a Native Shore* "an excellent contemporary romance."

Anand once told *CA:* "I first became interested in history at the age of fifteen when I saw MGM's film of *Ivanhoe.* I began reading history in secret, due to the fear that, if the school found out, I would be pounced on and forced to take it seriously, which would wreck the fun and sense of adventure. The deception worked. I enjoyed history on the side and my school reports complained bitterly of my lack of interest in this subject.

"I picked historical fiction as opposed to any other sort of writing, because I was in love with a bit of history. I regard a novelist's function primarily as entertainment: it doesn't matter what you write about as long as it can take someone's mind off his income tax or his influenza.

"Fiction—historical or otherwise—can be a means of exploring human dilemmas and extending situations imaginatively to see where they lead. Historical fiction in particular allows one to examine, [for instance], the position of people in an occupied country without the issues being clouded by the reader's (or the author's) own personal loyalties. In other words, you can see the problem more objectively if you write about Normans and Saxons than if you write about occupied France or Israel vs. Palestine.

"I never planned my career (my chief philosophy of life is that it's for living) but took it as it came, though with strong bias toward traditionally masculine fields. I regard ordinary women's journalism as too limiting.

"My husband is Punjabi-born, Sikh by religion. I have found the resultant introduction into Indian society an enthralling experience. It is very interesting to get 'inside' a culture other than one's own. This may have something to do with the attraction history has for me."

*BIOGRAPHICAL/CRITICAL SOURCES:*

*BOOKS*

Vasudevan, Aruna, editor, *Twentieth-Century Romance and Historical Writers,* third edition, St. James Press (Detroit), 1994.

*PERIODICALS*

*Books and Bookmen,* March, 1983, p. 34.
*British Book News,* May, 1984, p. 327.
*Kirkus Reviews,* November 1, 1979, p. 1272; November 1, 1983, p. 1134.
*New York Times Book Review,* January 22, 1984.
*Washington Post Book World,* December 5, 1982, March 4, 1984.*

* * *

**ANDERSON, Sherwood 1876-1941**
**(Buck Fever)**

*PERSONAL:* Born September 13, 1876, in Camden, OH; died of peritonitis, March 8, 1941, in Cristobal (one source says Colon), Panama Canal Zone; son of Irwin M. (a harnessmaker) and Emma (Smith) Anderson; married Cornelia Lane, 1904 (divorced, 1916); married Tennessee Mitchell, 1916 (divorced, 1924); married Elizabeth Prall, 1924 (divorced, 1932); married Eleanor Copenhaver, 1933; children: two sons, one daughter. *Education:* Attended Wittenberg Academy, 1899.

*CAREER:* Writer. Worked as copywriter for advertising firm in Chicago, 1900; president of United Factories Co., in Cleveland, OH, 1906, and of Anderson Manufacturing Co., in Elyria, OH, 1907-12; advertising copywriter in Chicago, 1913; editor of two newspapers in Marion, VA, 1927-29; lecturer. *Military service:* U.S. Army, 1899; served in Cuba.

*AWARDS, HONORS:* Prize from *Dial,* 1921.

*WRITINGS:*

*Windy McPherson's Son* (novel), John Lane, 1916, revised edition, B. W. Huebsch, 1922, reprinted, University of Illinois Press, 1993.
*Marching Men* (novel), John Lane, 1917, reprinted as *Marching Men: A Critical Text,* edited by Ray Lewis White, Press of Case Western Reserve University, 1972.
*Mid-American Chants* (poems), John Lane, 1918, reprinted, Frontier Press, 1972.
*Winesburg, Ohio: A Group of Tales of Ohio Small Town Life* (also see below), B. W. Huebsch, 1919, New American Library, 1956, reprinted with introduction by Malcolm Cowley, Viking, 1960, reprinted as *Winesburg, Ohio: Text and Criticism,* edited by John G. Ferres, Viking, 1966, reprinted as *Winesburg, Ohio: Authoritative Text, Backgrounds and Contexts, Criticism* edited by Charles E. Modlin and Ray Lewis White, Norton, 1996.
*Poor White* (novel), B. W. Huebsch, 1920, reprint, New Directions Publishing, 1993.
*The Triumph of the Egg: A Book of Impressions From American Life in Tales and Poems,* B. W. Huebsch, 1921, new edition with an introduction by Herbert Gold, Four Walls Eight Windows, 1988.
*Many Marriages* (novel), B. W. Huebsch, 1923, reprinted as *Many Marriages: A Critical Edition,* edited by Douglas G. Rogers, Scarecrow, 1978.
*Horses and Men: Tales, Long and Short,* B. W. Huebsch, 1923.
*A Story-Teller's Story: The Tale of an American Writer's Journey through His Own Imaginative World and through the World of Facts, with Many of His Experiences and Impressions among Other Writers—Told in Many Notes—in Four Books and an Epilogue,* B. W. Huebsch, 1924, reprinted as *A Story Teller's Story: A Critical Text,* edited by White, Press of Case Western Reserve University, 1968, revised edition with preface by Rideout, Viking, 1969, recent edition published as *A Story-Teller's Story,* Penguin, 1989.
*Dark Laughter* (novel), Boni & Liveright, 1925, reprinted with introduction by Howard Mumford Jones, Liveright, 1925.
*Hands and Other Stories* (selections from *Winesburg, Ohio: A Group of Tales of Ohio Small Town Life*), Haldeman-Julius, 1925.
*The Modern Writer* (nonfiction), Lantern Press, 1925, reprinted, Folcroft, 1976.
*Sherwood Anderson's Notebook: Containing Articles Written During the Author's Life as a Story Teller, and Notes of His Impressions from Life*

*Scattered through the Book,* Boni & Liveright, 1926, reprinted, P. P. Appel, 1970.

*Tar: A Midwest Childhood* (semi-autobiography), Boni & Liveright, 1926, reprinted as *Tar: A Midwest Childhood; A Critical Text,* edited by White, Press of Case Western Reserve University, 1969.

*A New Testament* (prose poems), Boni & Liveright, 1927.

*Alice* [and] *The Lost Novel,* E. Mathews & Marrot, 1929, reprinted, Folcroft, 1973.

*Hello Towns!* (collection of newspaper articles), Liveright, 1929, reprinted, Dynamic Learning, 1980.

*Nearer the Grass Roots* [and] *An Account of a Journey, Elizabethton* (essays), Westgate Press, 1929, reprinted, Folcroft, 1976.

*Perhaps Women* (essays), Liveright, 1931, reprinted, P. P. Appel, 1970.

*Beyond Desire* (novel), Liveright, 1932, reprinted with introduction by Rideout, Liveright, 1961.

*Death in the Woods, and Other Stories,* Liveright, 1933, recent edition, 1986.

*No Swank* (articles), Centaur Press, 1934, reprinted, Appel, 1970.

*Puzzled America* (articles), Scribner, 1935.

*Kit Brandon* (novel), Scribner, 1936.

*Plays: Winesburg and Others* (includes *Jaspar Deeter, a Dedication, Winesburg, The Triumph of the Egg, Mother,* and *They Married Later*), Scribner, 1937.

*Home Town* (nonfiction), Alliance Book Corp., 1940, reprinted, P. P. Appel, 1975.

*Sherwood Anderson's Memoirs,* Harcourt, 1942, reprinted as *Sherwood Anderson's Memoirs: A Critical Edition,* edited by White, University of North Carolina Press, 1969.

*The Sherwood Anderson Reader,* edited by Paul Rosenfeld, Houghton, 1947.

*The Portable Sherwood Anderson,* edited by Horace Gregory, Viking, 1949, Penguin, 1970.

*Letters of Sherwood Anderson,* edited by Rideout and Jones, Little, Brown, 1953.

*The Short Stories of Sherwood Anderson,* edited by Maxwell Geismar, Hill & Wang, 1962.

*Return to Winesburg: Selections from Four Years of Writing for a Country Newspaper,* edited by White, University of North Carolina Press, 1967.

*Buck Fever Papers* (articles), edited by Welford Dunaway Taylor, University Press of Virginia, 1971.

*A Teller's Tales,* selected and introduced by Frank Gado, Union College Press, 1983.

*Sherwood Anderson: Selected Letters,* edited by Charles E. Modlin, University of Tennessee Press, 1984.

*Letters to Bab: Sherwood Anderson to Marietta D. Finely, 1916-1933,* edited by William A. Sutton, University of Illinois Press, 1985.

*The Sherwood Anderson Diaries, 1936-1941,* edited by Hilbert H. Campbell, University of Georgia Press, 1987.

*Sherwood Anderson: Early Writings,* edited by Ray Lewis White, Kent State University Press, 1989.

*Sherwood Anderson's Love Letters to Eleanor Copenhaver Anderson,* edited by Charles E. Modlin, University of Georgia Press, 1989.

*Sherwood Anderson's Secret Love Letters,* edited by Ray Lewis White, Louisiana State University Press, 1991.

*Certain Things Last: The Selected Stories of Sherwood Anderson,* edited by Modlin, Four Walls Eight Windows, 1992.

Work represented in anthologies. Contributor to periodicals, including *Dial.*

*SIDELIGHTS:* While Sherwood Anderson did his best creative work in prose fiction, he created not only a distinctive, repetitive persona in his stories but also a public role. Giving impetus both to his fiction and to his life was a profound autobiographical need expressed in the lyrical nature of his fiction and in the creation of the public myth as well as in three major autobiographical works *A Story-Teller's Story, Tar: A Midwest Childhood,* and his *Sherwood Anderson's Memoirs.* Anderson's contributions to twentieth-century American letters are both defined and circumscribed by this need to express his intense personal vision.

Anderson's critical reputation has been a subject of much debate. However, in at least three areas his literary impact has been considerable. First, he was very active in helping other writers. For example, writer Ernest Hemingway carried Anderson's letter of introduction with him to writer Gertrude Stein's influential salon in Paris, and clearly such stories as Hemingway's "My Old Man" suggest how Hemingway found inspiration in Anderson's racetrack stories. More candid in acknowledging Anderson's influence was Nobel laureate writer William Faulkner, who in 1950 recalled how Anderson helped him publish his first novel, *Soldier's Pay* (1926), and provided an attractive example of a writer's lifestyle when they spent time together in the New Orleans French Quarter. In a statement made before he quarreled with

Anderson, writer Thomas Wolfe declared that Anderson was the only man in America who taught him anything; the pervasiveness of the "aloneness" theme in the fictions of both writers is apparent to even the most casual reader. While these instances suggest Anderson's roles in the careers of our foremost novelists, they are but a few of the many instances of how, in literally thousands of letters, lectures, and essays, Anderson promoted the craft.

Another, more elusive aspect of Anderson's influence is found in the development of the short story form. Many studies of modern story theory and short story anthologies allude to his technique in and his pronouncements about fictive form. While Anderson's statements about his art do not add up to a clear, conscious sense of design, they are consistent and can be characterized as "expressive"—focusing on the writer in his art of creation, not on the fidelity of his imitation or the response of the audience. His notion of form is central to his aesthetics; and form for him was subjective and organic.

Such an approach to artistic form can be more vulnerable to failure than is an aesthetic that is self-conscious and dependent on willed techniques. Certainly Anderson experienced many periods when form did not come—or came imperfectly—while he seemed powerless to change the imperfections.

Two important ramifications of his aesthetic stance are his views of plot and characterization. He bitterly attacked the stories of O. Henry and others for their "poison plots"—stories that sacrificed characterization and fidelity to life for the sake of striking turns of event. In an almost perverse way, Anderson expected a writer to have utter loyalty to the characters in his imagination. His typical stories, then—both unique and typically modern in eschewing strict plots—offered a compelling model for other writers.

Most importantly, Anderson was the creator of some of the finest American stories. *Winesburg, Ohio* (1919), his masterpiece, remains a durable classic, and half a dozen or more individual stories, such as "The Egg," "I Want to Know Why," "The Man Who Became a Woman," and "Death in the Woods," are among the finest products of the American short story tradition. *Winesburg, Ohio* is a hybrid form, unified by setting, theme, and character; but clearly the stories are also discreet and are further evidence that Anderson's genius lay in the short form. He wrote seven novels, but most critics agree that not one is completely satisfactory. Some of Anderson's most acclaimed writing appears in the mixed genres such as *A Story-Teller's Story* (1924) and his *Memoirs* (1942), but his lasting achievement is in his short fiction.

Because of the nature of Anderson's art, as outlined above, some survey of his life is of more than usual concern in assessing his literary achievement. The outline is familiar to most Anderson scholars: early boyhood in Ohio, mainly Clyde, Ohio; his "conventional" period when he became a businessman, husband to a better-educated, more sophisticated woman, and when he became father of three children; the break from commercial life into the greatest period of his artistic development and achievement—the decade after 1912; most of the 1920's when, despite a few exceptions and interludes of professional contentment, he struggled to maintain the level of earlier achievement; and a final period until his death in 1941, when from a base in southwestern Virginia, his writing turned increasingly toward social commentary, and he appeared to reach a state of relative equanimity, content in his fourth marriage and in the role as elder statesman in the writing community.

The richest lode of material for Anderson's best fiction was comprised of his experiences growing up in the Ohio small towns. While many of the characters in *Winesburg, Ohio* were based on people he met in an apartment house in Chicago, the fictional Winesburg is essentially Clyde, Ohio, in the 1890s. Critic Walter Rideout has shown how fully Anderson evokes the Clyde setting. Like the book's protagonist, George Willard, Anderson left his hometown after his mother's death in 1895 broke up the family, and both were budding writers. Furthermore, Tom and Elizabeth Willard are important creations in a long series of veiled portraits of and responses to Anderson's own parents. The trajectory of his coming to terms with his father's life can be traced from his first novel, *Windy McPherson's Son* (1916), through *Winesburg, Ohio* to a kind of acceptance in *A Story-Teller's Story*. His deepest feelings about his mother impel the characterizations of many of his women; but especially noteworthy are Elizabeth Willard, who figures so prominently in *Winesburg*, and, in a kind of apotheosis, the old woman in "Death in the Woods," one of his finest stories.

Anderson, like George Willard, was perhaps an incipient artist when he left his hometown, but the creative fires were banked while he pursued the American dream of business success. After short tenures as a Chicago laborer, as a soldier in the Spanish-American War, and as a student at Wittenberg Academy, he began working for a Chicago advertising firm in sales and copywriting. He did similar work in Cleveland, Ohio, and Elyria, Ohio; but despite his apparent success and growing family responsibilities—children born in 1917, 1908, and 1911—Anderson had begun to write fiction and to feel the warring claims of artistic creation and business values. Finally Anderson left the Anderson Manufacturing Company in November, 1912, as he said, in the middle of dictating a letter. He was found a few days later in a Cleveland hospital and did return briefly to the business world, but that day proved to be the great watershed of his career. When Anderson wrote of the urban settings, the business world, and businessmen in his fiction, it was usually to satirize corrupting materialism.

It was fortuitous that the Chicago to which Anderson returned provided an exciting milieu for writers—the so-called Chicago Renaissance. He met and was encouraged by such men and women as Floyd Dell, Margery Currey, Margaret Anderson, Ben Hecht, Carl Sandburg, Burton Rascoe, Lewis Galantiere, Harry Hansen, Ferdinand Schevill, and Robert Morss Lovett. He heard discourses on socialism, on the pioneering psychoanalytic theories of Sigmund Freud, and on writers such as Fedor Dostoevsky, August Strindberg, Gertrude Stein, and James Joyce. And he began playing the bohemian role not only in appearance, but also in his second, "modern" marriage to Tennessee Mitchell. More importantly, he sounded the thematic notes of his writing career and discovered the distinctive voice of his best writing.

As critic Irving Howe has noted, Anderson continued to be under great pressure, not only the pressure of guilt for failing to meet family responsibilities but also that of his sense of inadequacy. In 1919, the year that *Winesburg, Ohio* appeared, he was a forty-three-year old, ill-educated ex-salesman. But it was exhilarating to try to catch up. His first published story appeared in *Harper's,* in July, 1914; and two of the novels he had been working on in Elyria were published soon after: *Windy McPherson's Son* in 1916 and *Marching Men* in 1917.

*Windy McPherson's Son* foreshadows the materials and themes of later works. Sam McPherson, the novel's title character, rises from humble, small-town beginnings to become a business executive and to marry the boss's daughter. But in an act that recurs in Anderson's fiction and career, Sam rejects the business world to find happiness in love rather than money. Simplistic, didactic, and very awkwardly written, this first novel did not augur well for future novels. Nor is *Marching Men* a successful novel, for in addition to the book's wooden dialogue and generally inept construction and style, Anderson's notion of a marching men movement, whether suggestive of fascism or not, is a simplistic, irresponsible response to the complex problems of a materialistic world. These earlier works did little to prepare readers for the immense leap in artistic quality represented by *Winesburg, Ohio,* published in 1919.

As critic William Phillips noted, *Winesburg* was written in a burst of concentrated creation in 1915 and 1916. A number of the individual stories appeared in periodicals before 1919. But, perhaps taking a clue from Edgar Lee Masters's *Spoon River Anthology,* a collection of poetic vignettes, Anderson probably discovered in his Winesburg stories a firmer unity as the project developed, and rounded off the collection with the unifying plotting of the final three stories.

*Winesburg* is not a novel; what unity it has is often tenuous. However, the book is tied together by four important elements: the common setting, the episodic story of George Willard's development, the "aloneness" theme, and the tone. All of the stories take place in or around a small rural Ohio community in the last decade of the nineteenth century. The community of about eighteen hundred inhabitants depends on the fertile cabbage and strawberry fields of nearby farms and boasts a train depot, a hotel, fairgrounds, and a prominent Presbyterian church. But, significantly, much is missing—the stories present very little dramatization of community life or even family life; much of the action takes place at night or at least in shadowy and private surroundings; and the characters themselves are hardly typical.

George Willard appears first in "Hands," and after the death of his mother and the climactic experiences of "Sophistication," he leaves Winesburg. In his eighteen years he has learned something about women in a progression from the first furtive experience in "Nobody Knows" through the rueful lesson of "An Awakening" to tentative sophistication in the story with that title. The young *Winesburg Eagle* reporter is also the auditor of the secret stories of many of the grotesques. His teacher, Kate Swift, most directly encourages him as a writer; but others not only pour out to George their most intimate truths in therapeutic release but also want him to perpetuate their truths. Dr. Parcival, for example, wants everyone to know that all men are Christ in that their love is rejected and they are crucified. One of the most important lessons George learns is that of silence, for, alter the prodigality of his expression in, for example, "An Awakening," George seems to have learned Kate Swift's lesson, as he walks "in dignified silence" with Helen White on the fair grounds. Except that the omniscient narrator and George share virtually the same Andersonian sensibility, no trace of George emerges in a number of stories; but his development is a thread seen frequently in the *Wineburg* fabric.

A third unifying motif is the aloneness theme, a main element in the "grotesque" concept. The title of the first story written, "The Book of the Grotesque," was also a title Anderson considered for the whole book. The implication is that *Winesburg* would be a collection of brief biographical sketches of people, many of whom are grotesque. The complete titles in the table of contents suggest the approach, as for example, "Hands"—concerning Wing Biddlebaum.

Anderson's concept of the grotesque, set forth in only a limited way in "The Book of the Grotesque," has been variously interpreted by such important scholars as Irving Howe, Malcolm Cowley, Edwin Fussell, and David Anderson, but among the most searching analyses is Ralph Ciancio's. Ciancio concluded that to Anderson grotesqueness "was nothing more than a metaphor of the natural condition of man, of his being at cross-purposes with himself, of his compulsive hearkening to the infinite call of transcendence which his finitude makes impassible from the start." Some of the grotesques are, indeed, horrible; but the largest group is motivated by genuine human emotions. Included in this group of *Winesburg* characters are Wash Williams, who seeks love beyond the physical, Curtis Hartman, who strives to reconcile his religion with his erotic feelings, and Elmer Cowley, who wants to belong. Grotesqueness can thus be seen as an imbalance—not that the thrust of an individual's fanaticism is intrinsically wrong but rather that any single note sounded exclusively repels the auditor. In describing what he perceives to be common to all of the "grotesques," Malcolm Cowley stresses their inability to communicate. This view plausibly accounts for typical behavior in Winesburg, however, as the above remarks suggest, chronic, crippling failures in communication may merely be symptomatic of the ineffable aloneness dramatized hyperbolically in these twisted beings. Whatever the case, the fair-grounds scene in "Sophistication" is climactic not only in George's development, but also in suggesting that only through others can we mitigate the "sadness of sophistication," consciousness of our cosmic limitations and aloneness.

Finally, complementing and sustaining *Winesburg*'s theme is its tone. The omniscient narrator—seemingly fumbling along, arranging ill-fitting blocks of information, and complaining of his lack of art—provides a sympathetic continuo for the sad tales. This unity of feeling in the book Howe called "the accents of love."

The advance in the simplicity, directness, and evocative power of the language in *Winesburg* over the earlier work is remarkable. Gertrude Stein's stylistic experiments, as in *Tender Buttons* (1914), are often cited as a major influence on Anderson's style. In his *Memoirs* Anderson credited her example for making him conscious of his own vocabulary and how he might convey emotions through "a kind of word color, a march of simple words, simple sentence structures." The style of *Winesburg* became a staple of his best work. When he experimented with a very loose, impressionistic style in the twenties, the result compounded the blurred thinking that weakened too much of his later storytelling.

As critic Rex Burbank suggested in *Sherwood Anderson,* the stories of the hero and the heroine in *Poor White* (1920) are juxtaposed awkwardly, and too often the narrative loses effect by relying on assertion instead of dramatization. Nevertheless, *Poor White* is probably Anderson's best novel. The idea of industrialization's impact on a small Midwestern town sustains the novel when the narrative falters. Hugh McVey, one of the novel's main characters, progresses from innocence, to naive inventor in Bidwell, Ohio, to the realization that the new industrial society to which he contributes distorts community values, to a final, more fulfilling aesthetic and humane view of life. This progress is a more searching and cogent dramatization than those appearing in Anderson's first two novels. Unfortunately, the novel's parallel story of Clara Butterworth is awkwardly juxtaposed with Hugh's tale of development.

*Poor White* reflects both the influence of American writer Mark Twain and Anderson's lifelong critique of the values of the industrial society. His affinity for Twain and Twain's fiction is explained in part by Anderson's projection of his own sense of his career into the career of the older writer. For Anderson, both Twain and U.S. president Abraham Lincoln were Midwestern primitives whose innocence and integrity clashed with the intellectually more complex and morally more ambiguous Eastern culture. The very first sentence of *Poor White* conjures up the setting of Twain's classic *Huckleberry Finn,* and the early characterization of Hugh suggests the character and situation of Twain's protagonist Huck.

In *Winesburg* the "Godliness" sequence provides the context of the impact of the post-Civil War industrialism on villages such as Winesburg, but most of Anderson's best work in fiction, including *Winesburg,* is more concerned with the personal and the psychological, rather than the socio-economic issues. However, in *Poor White* the battle is engaged against the dehumanizing machine age that later in Anderson's career would command much more of his attention.

Anderson's major single work was published in 1919, and his arguably best novel in 1920. While he wrote a number of good stories during the remainder of his career, the publication of the two story collections *The Triumph of the Egg* (1921) and *Horses and Men* (1923) marked the close of his major creative period. "Death in the Woods," a story that Anderson did not publish until 1926, was created from a fragmentary version he had written on the back of the *Winesburg* manuscript possibly before the publication of *Winesburg* and it epitomizes the best of his narrative art.

The narrative point of view is one of the most distinctive features of Anderson's stories and is especially salient in "Death in the Woods." *Winesburg, Ohio* and *Poor White* are narrated in the third person. The speaking voice in each of these works is unique. For example, the speaker in *Winesburg* is a groping, seemingly artless storyteller outside the story action, who constantly invites attention to how he is crafting the story—"it needs a poet there"; "It will, however, be necessary to talk a little of young Hal so that you will get into the spirit of it." In contrast, the first-person, frustrated speaker in "I'm a Fool" is the chief character in this tale of poignant social failure. However, there is a sense in most of Anderson's stories of an oral tradition, a convention that presumes a sympathetic audience and invites the reader to share in the epistemological search for the essence of a particular character.

What needs to be underscored in "Death in the Woods" is that the narrator is not an adolescent like the youths in "I'm a Fool" and "I Want to Know Why," but a mature person who is recalling not only a striking event of his youth but also subsequent experiences that modify his understanding of the event. The story contains a double theme: the significance of the old woman's complete life *and* the nature of the artistic process.

Like the *Winesburg* stories, "Death in the Woods" is not conventionally plotted. It is fabricated of a number of related episodes, of which the chief is the course of an old woman's winter day. The woman, Ma Grimes, walks to town to trade a few eggs for "some salt pork, a little sugar, and some coffee perhaps" and liver and meat bones. Trudging home through the heavy snow, she decides to take a short cut through the woods, and there in a clearing she sits down to rest and freezes to death. The dogs which have accompanied her seize the grain bag tied to her back and drag her body into the center of the clearing. A hunter finds the body, its dress torn off, and returns to inform the town. The crowd that returns to the clearing includes the young narrator upon whose consciousness the sight of the frozen, naked woman in the middle of that scene—the men, the tracks made by the circling dogs, the white fragments of clouds above—is impressed indelibly. As he says, the scene was the "foundation for the real story I am now trying to tell." It is the epiphany, like many of those illuminated moments in *Winesburg*—such as Alice Hindman running naked in the rain, Wash Williams attacking his mother-in-law, Ray Pearson running in the fields—moments that epitomize the character because the context of the character's life has informed the epiphany.

At one level "Death in the Woods" is about Ma Grimes, whose life is so wholly concentrated on feeding animal life that it takes on mythic dimensions. Throughout her joyless life she is preyed upon, by the farmer in whose home she is a hound girl and then by her vicious husband, children, and dogs, all of whom exploit her remorselessly. She is, to a degree, grotesque; but, reinforced by the repetitive, ritualistic language of the story, the reader is led to perceive her as an earth mother, an incarnate principle of that which feeds carnal need. In unpublished statements Anderson expressed his intent to stress her fundamental role in the community. Indirectly, through the orchestration of the narrator, the reader shares the narrator's respect and awe before the absolute purity and even beauty of her unified life.

But the other important character is the narrator himself, who is a variation of the character type who appears most frequently in Anderson's fiction: the artistic man. To be sure, as William Scheick has emphasized, an element of sexual guilt or at least sexual ambivalence exists in the narrator's make up—this, too, is a familiar motif in many of Anderson's stories that may contribute to his anxiety. However, at a level that respects the full data of the story, the source of the narrator's frustration is, more plausibly, his struggle for artistic expression. He is driven to tell the story. He has collected all of the experiences—the epiphany scene, gossipy stories about Ma Grimes, and even more oblique experiences such as the time when he saw dogs running in the circle—and he seeks to bring them all to artistic form. What he and the story say about the significance of Ma Grimes's life is a truth, "music heard from far off"; but both the "mystery of life" and artistic perfection lie beyond human grasp.

A few stories, including "Death in the Woods" and *Winesburg, Ohio,* then, created during the decade after he left his Elyria paint business, appear to be Anderson's most durable achievements; but he would go on to write four more novels and a number of good stories. One need not agree with Anderson's harshest critics, who stress a precipitous decline in his career after 1923, to nevertheless recognize that Anderson struggled often unsuccessfully with his craft in the later 1920s. He had received recognition: the *Dial* award in 1921 and growing praise for his fiction both in the United States and abroad. But he was never to be secure financially; he was forced to depend on advertising writing through most of the period of his greatest achievements and then on lecturing, a generous allowance from publisher and theatre producer Horace Liveright, and the patronage of Burton Emmett to supplement his income in the 1920s. Furthermore, since income and status came with success in writing novels, Anderson directed much of his energies to a form uncongenial with his artistic gifts. The bizarre fable of *Many Marriages* (1923) alienated critics, publishers, and general readers; while *Dark Laughter* (1925) was the only commercial success among his novels, it did little to restore his critical reputation and even inspired Hemingway's parody *Torrents of Spring.*

In 1923, a year in which he was dissolving his second marriage in Reno, Nevada, Anderson's fourth novel, *Many Marriages,* appeared. Rex Burbank has called this story of a man's rebellion against puritan repression of sexual expression "irresponsible," despite the validity of Anderson's motive and thesis. The acts of John Webster, the book's main character, are grotesque in a negative sense, featuring a scene with the naked Webster, his wife, and daughter that in length, symbolism, and muddled thought illustrates the novel's chief weaknesses. *Dark Laughter* also concerns sexual repression and reflects, as Burbank and Howe have shown, the influence of D. H. Lawrence and James Joyce. Anderson was not only again assaying the longer form but also seeking to generate subject matter beyond that of his earlier successes. However, *Dark Laughter* is not much better than *Many Marriages* in execution, flawed again by the unconvincing analysis of the conflict between middle-class values and the primitive expression of feelings and additionally by the Joycean stream-of-consciousness style, which in this novel and in his later writings seems pretentious and serves to exacerbate the problems of his intellectual analysis.

More successful during this period of his career were Anderson's two fictional autobiographies. *A Story-Teller's Story* is in the tradition of mythic works or parables. Not interested in telling the whole biographical truth, the book presents stories to illustrate an argumentative position or moral. Anderson was in his element in writing this book, for he was writing both about the personality and role that is ubiquitous in his fiction and about settings and plot rooted in fact. The book is loose in form and episodic, but the stories that make up his life are often intrinsically interesting and finally unified by the narrator's personality. The exploration of such issues as craftsmanship in literature, business and artistic ethics, the impact of industrialism on human life, and the role of the American artist make *A Story-Teller's Story* profitable reading for students of American literature.

The second fictional autobiography, *Tar: A Midwest Childhood* (1926), focuses on the earliest stage of the author's life, the boyhood years when he was growing up in Clyde, Ohio. The text includes a version of "Death in the Woods" and other effective passages, but the book repeats much of the material of *A Story-Teller's Story,* and the stylistic mannerisms that seek to reflect the boy's sensibility are unsuccessful. Anderson's intent was to recapture the boyhood scenes and ideals in tales projected to be published as a series in *The Woman's Home Companion,* and, indeed, six installments were published in this magazine. His decisions about how *Tar* would be written might have been influenced by his sense of the *Companion* readers.

In 1927, Anderson's career took an unexpected turn when he bought two newspapers in Marion, Virginia, and became a country editor. For two years these papers absorbed his energies, and apparently he found the business, the reporting, and the writing to his liking. However, his newspaper writings, some of them gathered in *Hello Towns!* (1929), could not sustain the self-esteem of one who had tasted international acclaim only a few years before. Critics Walter

Rideout and Welford Taylor have examined this epoch in Anderson's career with subtlety and depth. In 1929, he turned over the papers to his son Robert, during the same year that his third marriage broke up.

While we may designate the period from 1930 to Anderson's death in 1941 as the final phase, we do so because of his developing relationship with Eleanor Copenhaver and his growing interest in the industrial South that his association with her fostered. This connection signaled a new direction in his life and career toward greater personal contentment and toward writing which reflected his developing interest in the contemporary economic, political, and social scene, a dominant but not exclusive direction for his final years.

But Anderson did not stop writing fiction. Indeed, *Death in the Woods,* published in 1933, is a story collection that includes not only "Brother Death" and the title story first published in 1926, but also other stories that give evidence that his creative power in the shorter forms was diminished but intact. The conflicts in "Brother Death," between the values represented by the younger brother who dies but maintains his freedom and those of the older brother who surrenders his spiritual freedom to secure the legacy of the farm, are quite effective symbolically but the important theme obtrudes as that element does not in the greater, earlier stories. It is important to note that Anderson's final collection of stories appeared in the middle of the Great Depression and that the bankruptcy of his publisher Liveright permitted only a technical publication of the book, without the marketing that might have bolstered Anderson's bank account and his morale.

In addition, Anderson wrote two novels in the 1930s. Divided into four books, *Beyond Desire* (1932) is Anderson's dramatization of the New South, stressing especially the southern mill workers' struggle against the established power behind the machines. Anderson's growing interest in socio-economic conflict and even his attraction to aspects of Communism lie behind the story, though Anderson's *real* concern remains, as always, with the relationships among people. Unfortunately, in structure and style the novel is confused and awkwardly written.

*Kit Brandon* (1936), his last published novel, is in many ways more satisfactory than *Beyond Desire.* Heroically, in the sixtieth year of his life, Anderson sought, as he told Maxwell Perkins, to be "more objective," to exercise greater control over the form. Despite technical problems in handling point of view and transitions, the novel may be, in David Anderson's words, "the best constructed of any of Anderson's long works." He published thirteen stories with a similar Appalachian setting that stressed a similar social pattern, but *Kit Brandon* is his only full treatment of the hill setting and bootlegging. The sense of place is established well, and the episodes and characters encountered as the novel traces Kit's career are effective in themselves and for what they reveal about the human cost of the mechanized culture. Kit is a southern mountain girl who is raised on a poverty-ridden farm where the chief "crop" is moonshine. She leaves her moonshining family at sixteen to take a mill job and then marries the weak son of a powerful bootlegger. After the marriage fails, Kit joins the bootleg gang and becomes a wealthy, notorious runner. Her obsession with the powerful cars she drives provides a short-lived compensation for the failures of the men she encounters. Although at the novel's end Kit has not found fulfillment, she has learned the emptiness of pursuing mere wealth and adventure, the same lesson Windy McPherson learned in Anderson's first published novel.

*Beyond Desire* and *Kit Brandon* deserve emphasis because Anderson's reputation resides not solely but primarily on his fiction; however, in addition to the posthumously published *Sherwood Anderson's Memoirs,* he wrote a number of journalistic pieces and four other nonfiction books during the last decade of his life: *Perhaps Women* (1931), *No Swank* (1934), *Puzzled America* (1935), and *Home Town* (1940). While Irving Howe and David Anderson, two astute critics of Anderson's social criticism, offered essentially contrasting evaluations of Anderson's social analyses, even the more adversely critical Howe found insights buried within "untenable" theses and admiration for Anderson's unique gifts. For example, Howe wrote, "*Puzzled America* is one of the few books that convey a sense of what it meant to live in depression America."

Appropriately Anderson's last important work was his *Memoirs,* published first in 1942 but more dependably edited by Ray Lewis White in 1969. This is appropriate first because, like *Winesburg, Ohio, A Story-Teller's Story,* and *Tar,* it is another maverick form: fact and fiction, biographical and mythic, unified and fragmented. Secondly, *Memoirs* is written in the natural style of his most successful works. The mannerisms of *Tar* are gone, and Anderson's "voice" is steady, informed, and mature. Finally, the *Memoirs,* though unfinished, is unified once more by the Anderson myth. One last time he has put on record the anecdotal parable of the life of an American artist. Beyond the aesthetic issues, the *Memoirs* is also the record of a sensitive American who experienced the coming of the modern industrial world, its factories and advertising, and—measuring that world by the criteria of craftsmanship, brotherhood, and love—often found it wanting. In the *Memoirs* Anderson judged himself harshly: "For all my egotism I know I am but a minor figure." Some have chosen to underscore the word minor, but such ratings can distort value. One may, as did T. S. Eliot, prefer Italian renaissance poet Dante Alighieri to William Shakespeare, but the value of such judgments should be to honor and foster what is valuable in writings of both. Sherwood Anderson wrote much that will not stand close scrutiny; however, in *Winesburg, Ohio,* in a number of short stories, and in at least parts of such works as *A Story-Teller's Story* and *Poor White,* Anderson's literary achievement is impressive.

Since his death, Anderson's diaries, early works, and letters have been published in collections. Jotted in the free desk calendars provided by an insurance company, the entries in *The Sherwood Anderson Diaries, 1936-1941* record Anderson's frequent trips, his writings and submissions, and other notes about his daily life, especially the weather, his health, and his fourth and last wife, Eleanor Copenhaver. "We do not come away with a second sight into Anderson's works," concluded Yolanda Butts in *The Georgia Review.* "What does emerge is an aging writer in the inglorious trappings of daily life-enough, I think, for a true portrait of the man." Reviewer Tom Williams observed in Chicago *Tribune Books*: "Always coming through in bits and pieces is the sadness of a writer in his 60s looking for something, anything, to bring back the remembered fervor and ease of mood that might enable him to write the grand masterpiece he never gave up trying to do."

Editor Ray Lewis White collected sixty-six short prose pieces written by Anderson between 1902 and 1916 for inclusion in *Sherwood Anderson: Early Writings.* The pieces include articles written for magazines, short stories, and essays. "White's collection traces the author's developing narrative and literary voice, technique, and philosophic orientation to advertising, materialism, and literature," noted Philip A. Greasley in *Modern Fiction Studies.* J. J. Patton acknowledged in *Choice* that the selections "evidence characteristics of [Anderson's] later fictional style," including his "sharp eye for the telling detail." Concluded Greasley: "This book is valuable to anyone seeking to understand Sherwood Anderson, the evolution of twentieth-century fiction, and even America's growing sense of self in the early twentieth century."

The three volumes of letters published between 1985 and 1991 brought to five the number of books offering an epistolary look at Anderson. *Letters to Bab: Sherwood Anderson to Marietta D. Finley, 1916-1933* contains letters Anderson wrote to his longtime friend and benefactor during the period he was writing his major fiction. The letters have stories and poems worked into them. "The letters are of interest as a record of Anderson's preoccupations—with writing (both stories and ad copy), women, and modern America-at a crucial time in his career," remarked *New York Review of Books* writer Christopher Benfey. Eugene T. Carroll expressed a similar view in *Modern Fiction Studies*: "[T]he letters reveal a frank and subjective portrait of a steady craftsman whose concerns about war, industrialization, women, and the literary figures of the time parallel his fictive writings. . . . However, the letters are not affectionate; they completely obscure whatever relationship he and Finley had for each other, and although they demonstrate personal feelings for or against a particular social or political event, they inevitably show the craftsmanship, the cameralike precision of the right word for the right moment."

The other two volumes of letters were written to Eleanor Copenhaver. Every day of 1932 Anderson wrote a letter to Eleanor, whom he would make his wife in 1933 despite a twenty-year difference in their ages and the discouragement of her family. He hid the letters in a cupboard of his home, where she discovered them after his death. They are collected in *Sherwood Anderson's Secret Love Letters.* Jack B. Moore wrote in *Studies in Short Fiction*: "While the letters contain a great deal of knee jerk lamentation, they also depict Anderson's sadly impossible desires midway through his fifties." A reviewer for *American Literature* found that "the letters not only detail Anderson's daily activities and give insights into his character but also show him at his descriptive best, whether he is writing of his love or recording how ordinary Americans are struggling through the worst year of the Great Depression." The second epistolary volume, *Sherwood Anderson's Love Letters to Eleanor Copenhaver Anderson,* contains a selection of the some 1400 letters written by Anderson to Eleanor between 1929 and 1941. "[T]his volume is often engaging, partly because Anderson acknowledges his faults and makes no attempt to conceal them, and partly because the letters reveal a man who refused to let his passion for life be diminished by age or doubt," Greg Johnson summed up in the *New York Times Book Review.*

*BIOGRAPHICAL/CRITICAL SOURCES:*

*BOOKS*


Anderson, David D., *Sherwood Anderson: An Introduction and Interpretation,* Holt, 1967.

Anderson, David D., editor, *Sherwood Anderson: Dimensions of His Literary Art,* Michigan State University Press, 1976.

Anderson, David D., editor, *Critical Essays on Sherwood Anderson,* G. K. Hall, 1981.

Anderson, Sherwood, *Winesburg, Ohio,* introduction by Malcolm Cowley, Viking, 1960, new edition edited by John G. Ferres, Viking, 1966.

Anderson, Sherwood, *Beyond Desire,* introduction by Walter B. Rideout, Liveright, 1961.

Anderson, Sherwood, *Poor White,* introduction by Walter B. Rideout, Viking, 1966.

Bridgman, Richard, *The Colloquial Style in America,* Oxford University Press, 1966.

Burbank, Rex, *Sherwood Anderson,* Twayne, 1964.

*Dictionary of Literary Biography,* Gale, Volume 4: *American Writers in Paris, 1920-1939,* 1980, Volume 9: *American Novelists, 1910-1945,* 1981, Volume 86: *American Short-Story Writers, 1910-1945, First Series,* 1989.

*Dictionary of Literary Biography Documentary Series,* Volume 1, Gale, 1982.

Geismar, Maxwell David, *The Last of the Provincials: The American Novel, 1915-1925,* Houghton, 1947.

Howe, Irving, *Sherwood Anderson,* William Sloane Associates, 1951, reprinted, Stanford University Press, 1966.

Kazin, Alfred, *On Native Grounds,* Reynal & Hitchcock, 1942.

Rideout, Walter B., editor, *Sherwood Anderson: A Collection of Critical Essays,* Prentice-Hall, 1974.

Rosenfeld, Paul, *Port of New York,* Harcourt, 1924.

Schevill, James, *Sherwood Anderson: His Life and Work,* University of Denver Press, 1951.

Small, Judy Jo, *A Reader's Guide to the Short Stories of Sherwood Anderson,* G. K. Hall, 1994.

Sutton, William A., *Exit to Elsinore,* Ball State University Press, 1967.

Sutton, William A., *The Road to Winesburg: A Mosaic of the Imaginative Life of Sherwood Anderson,* Scarecrow, 1972.

Taylor, Welford Dunaway, *Sherwood Anderson,* Ungar, 1977.

Townsend, Kim, *Sherwood Anderson,* Houghton, 1988.

Trilling, Lionel, *The Liberal Imagination: Essays on Literature and Society,* Viking, 1950.

*Twentieth-Century Literary Criticism,* Gale, Volume 1, 1978, Volume 10, 1983.

Walcutt, Charles C., *American Literary Naturalism: A Divided Stream,* University of Minnesota Press, 1956.

Weber, Brom, *Sherwood Anderson,* University of Minnesota Press, 1964.

White, Ray Lewis, editor, *The Achievement of Sherwood Anderson,* University of North Carolina Press, 1966.


*PERIODICALS*


*Accent,* Volume 16, number 2, 1956.

*American Literature,* Volume 23, number 1, 1951; Volume 40, number 1, 1968; Volume 41, number 1, 1969; December, 1989, p. 731; December, 1991, p. 781.

*American Quarterly,* Volume 20, number 4, 1968.

*Antioch Review,* spring, 1988, p. 278; fall, 1989, p. 505.

*Choice,* January, 1990, p. 794.

*Esquire,* September, 1992.

*Georgia Review,* spring, 1988, p. 208.

*Hudson Review,* Volume 10, number 4, 1957-58.

*Journal of English and Germanic Philology,* Volume 54, number 4, 1955.

*Los Angeles Times Book Review,* May 26, 1991, p. 8.

*Mark Twain Journal,* Volume 11, number 2, 1960.

*MidAmerica,* Volume 1, 1974.

*Midcontinent American Studies Journal,* Volume 3, 1962.

*Modern Fiction Studies,* Volume 5, number 2, 1959; Volume 5, number 4, 1959-60; summer, 1986, p. 273; winter, 1990, p. 533, 557.

*National Review,* June 5, 1987, p. 44; May 31, 1985, p. 42.

*New Statesman & Society,* September 29, 1989.

*New York Review of Books,* January 30, 1986, p. 16.

*New York Times Book Review,* July 10, 1988; February 25, 1990, p. 25; December 20, 1992.

*PMLA,* Volume 74, number 3, 1959; Volume 80, number 4, 1965; Volume 87, number 5, 1972.

*Studies in Short Fiction,* Volume 4, number 3, 1967; Volume 11, number 2, 1974; fall, 1991, p. 572.

*Tribune Books* (Chicago), September 13, 1987, p. 10.

*University of Chicago Magazine,* January, 1955.

*Wilson Library Bulletin,* November, 1989, p. 110.

*Winesburg Eagle,* 1975—.
*World Literature Today,* spring, 1988, p. 286.*

* * *

**ANDREWS, Lucilla (Mathew)**
**(Diana Gordon, Joanna Marcus)**

*PERSONAL:* Born in Suez, Egypt; married a doctor, 1947 (husband died, 1954); children: one daughter. *Education:* Studied nursing at St. Thomas's Hospital, London.

*ADDRESSES: Office*—c/o Heinemann, Michelin House, 81 Fulham Road, London SW3 6RB, England.

*CAREER:* Nurse and author.

*WRITINGS:*

NONFICTION

*No Time for Romance: An Autobiographical Account of a Few Moments in British and Personal History,* Harrap (London), 1977.

ROMANCE NOVELS

*The Print Petticoat,* Harrap, 1954, reprinted, Corgi (London), 1979.
*The Secret Armour,* Harrap, 1955, reprinted, Corgi, 1980.
*The Quiet Wards,* Harrap, 1956, reprinted, Corgi, 1980.
*The First Year,* Harrap, 1957, reprinted, Century, 1984.
*A Hospital Summer,* Harrap, 1958, reprinted, Corgi, 1980.
*My Friend, the Professor,* Harrap, 1960.
*Nurse Errant,* Harrap, 1961, reprinted, Severn House (London), 1984.
*The Young Doctors Downstairs,* Harrap, 1963, reprinted, Severn House, 1983.
*Flowers for the Doctor,* Harrap, 1963.
*The New Sister Theatre,* Harrap, 1964.
*The Light in the Ward,* Harrap, 1965.
*A House for Sister Mary,* Harrap, 1966.
*Hospital Circles,* Harrap, 1967.
*Highland Interlude,* Harrap, 1968.
(Under pseudonym Diana Gordon) *A Few Days in Endel,* Corgi, 1968, reprinted under pseudonym Joanna Marcus, Barrie & Jenkins (London), 1978.
*Highland Interlude,* Harrap, 1968.
*The Healing Time,* Harrap, 1969.
*The Edinburgh Excursion,* Harrap, 1970.
*Ring o' Roses,* Harrap, 1972.
*Silent Song,* Harrap, 1973.
*In Storm and in Calm,* Harrap, 1975.
*Busman's Holiday,* Corgi, 1977.
*The Crystal Gull,* Harrap, 1978.
*The Lucilla Andrews Omnibus* (includes *My Friend, the Professor, Highland Interlude,* and *Ring o' Roses*), Harrap, 1979.
*One Night in London,* Corgi, 1979.
(Under pseudonym Joanna Marcus) *Marsh Blood,* Hutchinson (London), 1980.
*A Weekend in the Garden,* Heinemann (London), 1981.
*In an Edinburgh Drawing Room,* Heinemann, 1983.
*After a Famous Victory,* Heinemann, 1984.
*The Lights of London,* Heinemann, 1985.
*The Phoenix Syndrome,* Heinemann, 1987.
*Front Line,* Heinemann, 1990.
*The Africa Run,* Heinemann, 1993.
*The Sinister Side,* Heinemann, 1996.

*SIDELIGHTS:* British author Lucilla Andrews has achieved recognition for her hospital fiction set both during World War II and the years following the war. A former nurse, Andrews applies much of her personal experience to her work. She expounds on her wartime experience as a nurse for the British during World War II in her 1977 autobiography *No Time for Romance: An Autobiographical Account of a Few Moments in British and Personal History.* The book traces Andrews's life from her secure years in private schools to her unlucky love life and her struggle as a writer. Andrews also describes the pain and suffering she witnessed as she tended the wounds of soldiers and civilians, at times even under fire herself. P. D. James, writing in the *Times Literary Supplement,* lauds Andrews's writing in *No Time for Romance:* "Always the writing is honest, direct and vivid; often it rises to something more."

Andrews's novels are written from the vantage point of a nurse, describing romance in the hospital milieu. The novels set during World War II, such as *One Night in London, After a Famous Victory,* and *The Phoenix Syndrome,* give attention to the abhorrent effects of the war, especially the insecurity and urgency that envelops the wartime relationships. The novels that are set after the war, such as *In Storm and in Calm*—while still set in a hospital—are more lighthearted and focus mainly on romance. Writing in *Twentieth-Century Romance and Historical Writers,* contributor Naya Quinn concludes that Andrews's "obvious respect for her profession make her books extremely readable and well loved by her fans."

*BIOGRAPHICAL/CRITICAL SOURCES:*

*BOOKS*

*Twentieth-Century Romance and Historical Writers,* third edition, St. James Press (Detroit), 1994.

*PERIODICALS*

*Books and Bookmen,* July, 1984, p. 28.
*Times Literary Supplement,* July 27, 1977, p. 922.*

* * *

**ANTSCHEL, Paul 1920-1970**
**(Paul Celan)**

*PERSONAL:* Born November 23, 1920, in Cernowitz, Romania; committed suicide by drowning, sometime in April, 1970, in France; married Gisele de Lestrange (an artist), 1950; children: Eric. *Education:* Earned licence es lettres in Paris, 1950. *Religion:* Jewish.

*CAREER:* Poet and translator. Lecturer at L'Ecole Normale Superieure of University of Paris, 1959-70.

*AWARDS, HONORS:* Literary Prize of City of Bremen, 1958; Georg Buechner Prize, German Academy of Language and Literature, 1960.

*WRITINGS:*

*POETRY; UNDER PSEUDONYM PAUL CELAN*

*Der Sand aus den Urnen,* Sexl (Vienna), 1948.
*Mohn und Gedaechtnis: Gedichte* (title means "Poppy and Memory"), Deutsche Verlags-Anstalt (Stuttgart), 1952.
*Von Schwelle zu Schwelle: Gedichte* (title means "From Threshold to Threshold"), Deutsche Verlags-Anstalt, 1955.
*Sprachgitter,* S. Fischer, 1959, translation by Joachim Neugroschel published as *Speech-Grille and Selected Poems,* Dutton, 1971.
*Gedichte: Eine Auswahl,* edited by Klaus Wagenbach, S. Fischer, 1959.
*Der Meridian: Rede anlaesslich der Verleihung des Georg-Buechner-Preises, Darmstadt, a, 22. Oktober 1960,* S. Fischer, 1961.
*Die Niemandsrose* (title means "The No Man's Rose"), S. Fischer, 1963.
*Atemkristall,* Brunidor, 1965.
*Gedichte* (title means "Poetry"), Moderner Buch-Club, 1966.
*Atemwende: Gedichte,* Suhrkamp (Frankfurt am Main), 1967; published in English as *Breathturn,* Sun & Moon Press (Los Angeles), 1995.
*Fadensonnen,* Suhrkamp, 1968.
*Ausgewaehlte Gedichte: Zwei Reden,* Suhrkamp, 1968.
*Lichtzwang,* Suhrkamp, 1970.
*Schneepart,* Suhrkamp, 1971.
*Strette. Suivis du Meridien et d'Entretien dans la montagne,* Mercure de France, 1971.
*Nineteen Poems,* translation by Michael Hamburger, Carcanet Press, 1972.
*Selected Poems,* translation by Hamburger and Christopher Middleton, Penguin, 1972.
*Gedichte: In zwei Banden,* Suhrkamp, 1975.
*Zeitgehoeft: Spaete Gedichte aus dem Nachlass,* Suhrkamp, 1976.
*Poesie/Paul Celan; a cura di Moshe Kahne e Marcella Bagnasco,* A. Mondadori (Italy), 1976.
*Paul Celan: Poems,* translation by Hamburger, Persea Books, 1980, published as *Poems of Paul Celan,* 1989.
*Gesammelte Werke in fuenf Baenden,* 5 volumes, Suhrkamp, 1983.
*Todesfuge,* Edition Gunnar A. Kaldewey, 1984.
*65 Poems,* Raven Arts Press (Dublin), 1985.
*Last Poems,* translation by Katherine Washburn and Margret Guillemin, North Point Press, 1986.
*Eingedunkelt: und Gedichte aus dem Ukreis von Eingedunkelt,* Suhrkamp, 1991.
*Meridianen: bij Paul Celan en De Niemandroos,* Picaron Editions (Amsterdam), 1991.

Also author of *Breath Crystal: Translations of Paul Celan,* translation by Walter Billeter, Ragman Productions (Australia), and of *Conversation in the Mountains,* translation by Rosmarie Waldrop.

*OTHER; UNDER PSEUDONYM PAUL CELAN*

*Edgar Jene und der Traum vom Traume,* Agathon (Vienna), 1948.
*Paul Celan: Prose Writings and Selected Poems,* translation by Walter Billeter, Paper Castle (Victoria, Australia), 1977.

*Collected Prose,* translation by Rosemarie Waldrop, Carcanet Press, 1986.

(With Harrison Birtwistle) *White and Light* (musical score), Universal Edition (London), 1989.

(With Gerhard Hoehme) *Gerard Hoehme, 1920-1989: Engfeuhrung, Hommage a Paul Celan und eine Folge von Tuschzeichnungen aus den Hahren 1969 bis 1978,* Das Museum (Neuss), 1990.

(With Manfred de La Motte and Georg Nothelfer) *Die Weurde und der Mut: L'Art Moral,* Galerie Georg Nothelfer (Berlin), 1991.

(With Gerhard Steabler) *Fallen, Fallen —Und Liegen und Fallen: Geseange zu Gedichten von Paul Celan: Feur Sopran (Alt), Akkordeon, Tuba und Vierkanaliges Tonband, 1989* (musical score), Ricord (Meunchen), 1991.

(With Jan Vriend) *Three Songs for (Mezzo) Soprano and Orchestra, 1991* (musical score), Donemus (Amsterdam), 1992.

*Paul Celan, Nelly Sachs: Briefwechsel,* Suhrkamp, 1993.

*Paul Celan, Franz Wurm: Briefwechsel,* Suhrkamp, 1995.

Translator of numerous works into German. Also author of works represented in anthologies, including *Modern German Poetry, 1910-1960,* edited by Hamburger and C. Middleton, 1962, *Twentieth-Century German Verse,* edited by P. Bridgewater, 1963, and *Modern European Poetry,* edited by W. Barnstone, 1966.

*SIDELIGHTS:* Paul Antschel, best known under his pseudonym Paul Celan, was regarded as one of the most important poets to emerge from post-World War II Europe. According to one critic, he "made a more original and substantial contribution to modern poetry than any other German-language poet of his generation." His work bears the influence of both the French surrealists and Rainer Maria Rilke in terms of poetic devices and linguistic stylization. His thematic obsession, however, is the extermination of the Jews during World War II. A writer for the *Times Literary Supplement* wrote that Celan "makes us aware of the horror of our age in a way that is the more powerful for being oblique. The humble and familiar images . . . combine with others that suggest blinding, mutilation and empaling, burning, whipping and shooting, hunting down and shutting in with walls and barbed wire—festering memories of Auschwitz which are relevant not only to Germany and not only to an era that ended in 1945."

Born in Romania in 1920, Celan was the son of German-speaking Jews. He learned several languages as a child and studied for a time in France, but he was in Romania when World War II began. After the Nazis overran his hometown in 1941, Celan was transported to a Nazi labor camp; his parents were killed. His experiences during the war would serve as perhaps the primary thematic concern of Celan's later poetry.

Celan began writing poetry shortly after the war, when he lived for a time in Bucharest, Romania, and Vienna, Austria, before settling for good in Paris, France. His first book, published in 1947, caused little stir in the German literary community. His second collection, *Mohn und Gedaechtnis* ("Poppy and Memory"), received much more critical attention, and Celan quickly became a reputable poet. Among his most popular poems is "Death Fugue," a stark recreation of activities at Auschwitz which was featured in both of the early collections. Paul Auster called it "literally a fugue composed of words, and the incessant, rhythmical repetitions and variations of phrases evoke a nightmare more devastating than any forthright description could." This description is exemplified in the stanza which includes the lines "death is a master from Germany / his eye is blue / he shoots you with bullets of lead / his aim is true / a man lives in the house your / golden hair Margarete / he sets his hounds on us he gives / us a grave in the air he plays with the serpent and / dreams death is a master from / Germany." Despite its high regard, "Death Fugue" was later refuted by Celan as, according to Auster, "too obvious and superficially realistic," and he disallowed its inclusion in collections.

Celan spent the 1950s and 1960s getting his university degree and teaching German language and literature at L'Ecole Normale Superieure of the University of Paris. During this period he also continued to develop his poetic technique. As Celan progressed, his poetry became increasingly inaccessible. "The poems grow shorter," observed John Hollander, "denser and less easily rewarding toward the end of the poet's career, and more starkly impressive." His poetry also became less depressing. One critic wrote, "The worst, we are made to feel, has been faced, and out of despair has come a new beauty which *is* truth." The same reviewer added that the collection *Atemwende,* first published in 1967 and then in English translation as *Breathturn* in 1995, "shows a poet projecting his breath into emptiness and feeling it return . . . charged with a numinous power." Aside from its rather positive stance, *Atemwende* was also noted for its attention to the language itself. "The author of *Atemwende* is obsessed by words and obsessed by forms," contended a writer for the *Times Literary Supplement*. The critic attributed Celan's brighter outlook to his new interest in words. "And this new reality has been uniquely embodied in language," the critic claimed, "language, in fact, has helped not just to shape it, but to bring it life."

Celan pursued his interest in economy of form in *Lichtzwang,* a collection published the same year as his death. A reviewer for the *Times Literary Supplement* wrote that "his poems are very much word-sculptures." Jerry Glenn believed that Celan was moving towards a union of his early realist style with his later structure-conscious poems. He also noted in a review of *Lichtzwang,* "There are some fine poems here, poems which will justly become a part of the permanent legacy of German literature."

Celan committed suicide by drowning in 1970. In a eulogy, Auster called him "one of the truly great poets of our time." In the same article, he observed that by reading the collected works, one could perceive a developing sense of despair within Celan. Referring to the poems, Auster wrote, "One feels both a shrinking and an expansion in them, as if, by traveling to the inmost recesses of himself, Celan had somehow vanished, joining with the greater forces beyond him, and at the same time sinking more deeply into his terrifying sense of isolation." *New York Review of Books* critic J. M. Cameron remarked, "Despite the difficulties his work offers the reader, he is a public poet, a writer concerned with the great events of the time." Celan once revealed, "I have tried to write poetry in order to acquire a perspective of reality for myself." Perhaps he forecast his own fate when he wrote, "You were my death: / you I could hold / when all fell away from me."

*BIOGRAPHICAL/CRITICAL SOURCES:*

*BOOKS*

Block, Haskell M., *The Poetry of Paul Celan: Papers from the Conference at the State University of New York at Binghamton,* October 28-29, 1988, P. Lang (New York City), 1991.

Borkowska, Ewa, *From Donne to Celan: Logo(theo)-logical Patterns in Poetry,* Wydawn (Katowice), 1994.

Buhr, Gerhard, *Paul Celan, "Atemwende": Materialen,* Keonigshausen & Neumann (Weurzburg), 1991.

Celan, Paul, *Speech-Grille and Selected Poems,* Dutton, 1971.

Celan, Paul, *Selected Poems,* Penguin, 1972.

Chalfen, Israel, *Paul Celan: Eine Biographie seiner Jugend,* Suhrkamp, 1979; published in English as, *Paul Celan: A Biography of His Youth,* Persea Books (New York City), 1991.

Colin, Amy D., *Paul Celan: Holograms of Darkness,* Indiana University Press (Bloomington), 1991.

*Contemporary Literary Criticism,* Gale, Volume 10, 1979, Volume 19, 1981, Volume 82, 1994.

*Dictionary of Literary Biography,* Volume 69: *Contemporary German Fiction Writers,* first series, Gale, 1988.

Felstiner, John, *Paul Celan: Poet, Survivor, Jew,* Yale University Press (New Haven), 1995.

Fioretos, Aris, *Word Traces: Readings of Paul Celan,* Johns Hopkins University Press (Baltimore), 1994.

Glenn, Jerry, *Paul Celan,* Twayne, 1973.

Meinecke, Dietlind, editor, *Uber Paul Celan,* Suhrkamp, 1973.

Neumann, Peter Horst, *Zur Lyrik Paul Celans,* Vandenhoeck & Ruprecht, 1968.

Samuels, Clarise, *Holocaust Visions: Surrealism and Existentialism in the Poetry of Paul Celan,* Camden House (Columbia, SC), 1993.

Wolosky, Shira, *Language Mysticism: The Negative Way of Language in Eliot, Beckett, and Celan,* Stanford University Press (Stanford, CA), 1995.

*PERIODICALS*

*Books Abroad,* spring, 1971.

*Chicago Review,* Volume 29, number 3, 1978.

*Commentary,* February, 1976.

*Library Journal,* September 1, 1995, p. 181.

*New Republic,* October 30, 1995, p. 35A.

*New York Review of Books,* January 18, 1990, p. 3.

*New York Times Book Review,* July 18, 1971.

*Present Tense,* January-February, 1990, p. 59.

*Publishers Weekly,* May 4, 1990, p. 59; July 31, 1995, p. 73.

*Studies in Twentieth Century Literature,* fall, 1983.

*Times Literary Supplement,* December 7, 1967, September 18, 1970, September 29, 1984.*

* * *

**ARNEY, James**
**See RUSSELL, Martin**

**AUDEN, W(ystan) H(ugh) 1907-1973**

*PERSONAL:* Born February 21, 1907, in York, England; came to the United States in 1939, became U.S. citizen in April, 1946; died September 28, 1973, in Vienna, Austria; son of George Augustus (a medical officer) and Constance Rosalie (a nurse; maiden name, Bicknell) Auden; married Erika Mann (a writer; daughter of Thomas Mann), 1935, in order to provide her with a British passport (divorced). *Education:* Attended Christ Church, Oxford, 1925-28. *Religion:* Episcopal.

*CAREER:* Poet, playwright, librettist, critic, editor, and translator. Larchfield Academy, Helensburgh, Scotland, and Downs School, Colwall, near Malvern, England, schoolmaster, 1930-35; with Rupert Doone, Robert Medley, and others, founded the Group Theatre, 1932; worked with General Post Office film unit, 1935, collaborating on such films as *Night Mail* and *Coal-Face*; made trip to Iceland with Louis MacNeice, 1936; went to Spain as stretcher-bearer for Loyalists during Spanish Revolution, 1937; made trip to China with Christopher Isherwood, 1938; taught at St. Mark's School, Southborough, MA, 1939-40; faculty member of American Writers League Writers School, 1939; taught at New School for Social Research, 1940-41 and 1946-47; faculty member of University of Michigan, 1941-42, Swarthmore College, 1942-45, Bryn Mawr College, 1943-45, Bennington College, 1946, and Barnard College, 1947; with Lionel Trilling and Jacques Barzun, founded The Reader's Subscription Book Club, 1951, associated with Club until 1959, wrote occasionally for its publication, *The Griffin,* 1951-58; Smith College, Northampton, MA, W. A. Neilson Research Professor, 1953; Oxford University, Oxford, England, professor of poetry, 1956-61; with Jacques Barzun and Lionel Trilling, established the Mid-Century Book Society, 1959, wrote occasionally for its periodical, *The Mid-Century,* 1959-63.

*MEMBER:* American Academy of Arts and Letters.

*AWARDS, HONORS:* King's Gold Medal for poetry, 1937; Guggenheim fellowships, 1942 and 1945; Award of Merit Medal, American Academy of Arts and Letters, 1945; Pulitzer Prize in Poetry, 1948, for *The Age of Anxiety;* Bollingen Prize in Poetry, 1954; National Book Award, 1956, for *The Shield of Achilles;* Feltrinelli Prize (Rome), 1957; Alexander Droutzkoy Memorial Award, 1959; shared Guiness Poetry Award (Ireland) with Robert Lowell and Edith Sitwell, 1959; honored on Chicago Poetry Day, 1960; Honorary Student (Fellow), Christ College, Oxford University, 1962-73; Austrian State Prize for European Literature, 1966; National Medal for Literature of National Book Committee, 1967, for total contributions to literature; Gold Medal of National Institute of Arts and Letters, 1968.

*WRITINGS:*

COLLECTED WORKS

*The English Auden: Poems, Essays, and Dramatic Writings*, edited by Mendelson, Faber, 1977, Random House, 1978.

*Complete Works of W. H. Auden*, Princeton University Press, 1989.

POETRY

*Poems*, hand printed by Stephen Spender, 1928, Faber, 1930, 2nd edition, 1933, Random House, 1934, revised edition, Faber, 1960, revised, with new foreword by Spender, for Elliston Poetry Foundation of the University of Cincinnati, 1965.

*The Orators: An English Study* (includes prose), Faber, 1932, revised edition with new foreword, Random House, 1967.

*Look, Stranger!*, Faber, 1936, published as *On This Island*, Random House, 1937.

(With Louis MacNeice) *Letters from Iceland*, Random House, 1937, revised edition, 1969.

*Selected Poems*, Faber, 1938.

(With Christopher Isherwood) *Journey to a War*, Random House, 1939, reprinted, Hippocrene Books, 1972, revised edition, Faber, 1973.

*Another Time*, Random House, 1940.

*Some Poems*, Random House, 1940.

*Three Songs for St. Cecilia's Day*, privately printed, 1941.

*The Double Man*, Random House, 1941 (published in England as *New Year Letter*, Faber, 1941).

*For the Time Being*, Random House, 1944.

*The Collected Poetry of W. H. Auden*, Random House, 1945.

*The Age of Anxiety: A Baroque Eclogue* (performed Off-Broadway at the Attic Theatre, March 18, 1954), Random House, 1947.

*Collected Shorter Poems, 1930-1944*, Random House, 1951.

*The Shield of Achilles*, Random House, 1955.

*The Old Man's Road*, Voyages Press, 1956.

*A Gobble Poem* ("snatched from the notebooks of W. H. Auden and now believed to be in the Morgan Library"), [London], 1957.

*Selected Poetry*, Modern Library, 1959, 2nd edition, Vintage, 1971.

*Homage to Clio*, Random House, 1960.

*W. Auden, A Selection*, with notes and critical essay by Richard Hoggart, Hutchinson, 1961.

*The Common Life* (written in German), translation by Dieter Leisegang, Blaeschke, 1964.

*The Cave of the Making* (written in German), translation by Leisegang, Blaeschke, 1965.

*Half-Way*, limited edition, Lowell-Adams House Printers, 1965.

*About the House*, Random House, 1965.

*The Platonic Blow*, [New York], 1965.

*Collected Shorter Poems, 1927-57*, Faber, 1966, Random House, 1967.

*Portraits*, Apiary Press, 1966.

*Marginalia*, Ibex Press, 1966.

*A Selection by the Author*, Faber, 1967.

*Selected Poems*, Faber, 1968, revised edition, Random House, 1979.

*Two Songs*, Phoenix Book Shop, 1968.

*Collected Longer Poems*, Faber, 1968, Random House, 1969.

*City without Walls, and Many Other Poems*, Random House, 1969.

*Academic Graffiti*, Faber, 1971, Random House, 1972.

(With Leif Sjoeberg) *Selected Poems*, Pantheon, 1972.

*Epistle to a Godson, and Other Poems*, Random House, 1972.

*Poems and Lithographs*, edited by John Russell, British Museum, 1974.

*Poems*, lithographs by Henry Moore, edited by Vera Lindsay, Petersburg Press, 1974.

*Thank You Fog: Last Poems*, Random House, 1974.

*Collected Poems*, edited by Edward Mendelson, Random House, 1976.

*Sue*, Sycamore Press, 1977.

*'The Map of All My Youth': Early Works, Friends, and Influences,* edited by Katherine Bucknell and Nicholas Jenkins, Oxford, 1990.

(With Bucknell, Katherine, editor) *Juvenilia: Poems, 1922-1928,* Princeton University Press (Princeton, NJ), 1994.

PLAYS

*The Dance of Death* (produced in London, 1934; produced in New York City, 1935; produced in Poughkeepsie, N.Y., as *Come Out into the Sun*, 1935), Faber, 1933, 2nd edition, 1935.

(With Isherwood) *The Dog Beneath the Skin; or, Where Is Francis?* (also see below; produced in London, 1936; revised version produced in New York City, 1947), Faber, 1935, reprinted, Random House, 1968.

*The Ascent of F6: A Tragedy in Two Acts* (also see below; produced in London, 1931; produced in New York City, 1939), Faber, 1936, 2nd edition, 1957, published as *The Ascent of F6*, Random House, 1937, 2nd edition, 1956.

(Adaptor with Edward Crankshaw) Ernst Toller, *No More Peace! A Thoughtful Comedy* (produced in London, 1936; produced in New York City, 1937), Farrar & Rinehart, 1937.

*On the Frontier: A Melodrama in Three Acts* (produced in London, 1939), Random House, 1938.

(With Isherwood) *Two Great Plays* (contains *The Dog Beneath the Skin* and *The Ascent of F6*), Random House, 1959.

(With Isherwood) *Plays and Other Dramatic Writings by W. H. Auden, 1928-1938,* edited by Edward Mendelson, Faber, 1989.

Also author of documentary screenplays in verse, including *Night Mail,* 1936, *Coal-Face,* 1936, and *The Londoners,* 1938; author of radio plays, including *Hadrian's Wall,* 1937, *The Dark Valley,* 1940, and *The Rocking-Horse Winner* (adapted from the short story by D. H. Lawrence).

CRITICISM AND ESSAYS

(With T. C. Worley) *Education, Today, and Tomorrow*, Hogarth, 1939.

*Address on Henry James* (booklet), [New York], 1947.

*The Enchafed Flood or, The Romantic Iconography of the Sea*, Random House, 1950.

*Making, Knowing, and Judging*, Clarendon Press, 1956.

*The Dyer's Hand, and Other Essays*, Random House, 1962.

*Louis MacNeice* (memorial address), Faber, 1963.

*Shakespeare, Fuenf Augsaetze*, [Frankfurt am Main], 1964.

*Selected Essays*, Faber, 1964.

*Secondary Worlds* (T. S. Eliot Memorial Lectures at University of Kent, 1967), Faber, 1968, Random House, 1969.

*A Certain World: A Commonplace Book* (annotated personal anthology), Viking, 1970.

*Forewords and Afterwords*, edited by Mendelson, Random House, 1973.

EDITOR

(With Charles Plumb) *Oxford Poetry, 1926*, Basil Blackwell, 1926.

(With C. Day Lewis) *Oxford Poetry, 1927*, Appleton, 1927.

(With John Garrett) *The Poet's Tongue*, G. Bell, 1935.

(With Arthur Elton) *Mechanics*, Longmans, Green, 1936.

(And author of introduction) *Oxford Book of Light Verse*, Oxford University Press, 1938.

(And author of introduction) *A Selection of the Poems of Alfred Lord Tennyson*, Doubleday, 1944 (published in England as *Tennyson: An Introduction and a Selection*, Phoenix House, 1946).

(And author of introduction) Henry James, *American Scene*, Scribner, 1946.

(And author of introduction) John Betjeman, *Slick but Not Streamlined*, Doubleday, 1947.

(And author of introduction) *The Portable Greek Reader*, Viking, 1948.

(And author of introduction) Edgar Allan Poe, *Selected Prose and Poetry*, Rinehart, 1950, revised edition, 1957.

(With Norman Holmes Pearson) *Poets of the English Language*, Viking, 1950, reprinted, Penguin, 1977, Volume 1: *Medieval and Renaissance Poets: Langland to Spenser*, Volume 2: *Elizabethan and Jacobean Poets: Marlowe to Marvell*, Volume 3: *Restoration and Augustan Poets: Milton to Goldsmith*, Volume 4: *Romantic Poets: Blake to Poe*, Volume 5: *Victorian and Edwardian Poets: Tennyson to Yeats*.

(And author of introduction) *The Living Thoughts of Kierkegaard*, McKay, 1952 (published in England as *Kierkegaard*, Cassell, 1955).

(With Marianne Moore and Karl Shapiro) *Riverside Poetry 1953: Poems by Students in Colleges and Universities in New York City*, Association Press, 1953.

(With Chester Kallman and Noah Greenberg) *An Elizabethan Song Book: Lute Songs, Madrigals, and Rounds*, Doubleday, 1956, published as *An Anthology of Elizabethan Lute Songs, Madrigals, and Rounds*, Norton, 1970.

(And author of introduction) *Selected Writings of Sydney Smith*, Farrar, Straus, 1956.

(And author of introduction) *The Criterion Book of Modern American Verse*, Criterion, 1956 (published in England as *The Faber Book of Modern American Verse*, Faber, 1956).

*Van Gogh: A Self Portrait* (selected letters), New York Graphic Society, 1961.

Joseph Jacobs, *The Pied Piper, and Other Fairy Tales*, Macmillan, 1963.

(With Louis Kronenberger) *The Viking Book of Aphorisms*, Viking, 1963 (published in England as *The Faber Book of Aphorisms*, Faber, 1964).

Walter de la Mare, *A Choice of de la Mare's Verse*, Faber, 1963.

*Selected Poems of Louis MacNeice*, Faber, 1964.

(And author of introduction) *Nineteenth Century British Minor Poets*, Delacorte, 1966 (published in England as *Nineteenth Century Minor Poets*, Faber, 1967).

(With John Lawlor) *To Nevill Cognill from Friends*, Faber, 1966.

*Selected Poetry and Prose of George Gordon, Lord Byron*, New American Library, 1966.

MacNeice, *Persons from Porlock, and Other Plays for Radio*, BBC Productions, 1969.

*G. K. Chesterton: A Selection from His Non-Fictional Prose*, Faber, 1970.

*George Herbert*, Penguin, 1973.

(And author of preface) *Selected Songs of Thomas Campion*, Godine, 1973.

Also editor and author of foreword of *Yale Series of Younger Poets*, 1947-59. Coeditor of "The Looking Glass Library" series of children's books.

*CONTRIBUTOR*

Clifton Fadiman, editor, *I Believe*, Simon & Schuster, 1939, revised edition, G. Allen, 1941.

Donald A. Stauffer, editor, *The Intent of the Critic*, Princeton University Press, 1941.

Rudolf Arnheim, editor, *Poets at Work*, introduction by Charles D. Abbott, Harcourt, 1948.

Marvin Halvorsen, editor, *Religious Drama*, Volume 1, Peter Smith, 1957.

Igor Stravinsky, *Memories and Commentaries* (letters), Faber, 1960.

Raymond Mortimer, compiler, *The Seven Deadly Sins*, Sunday Times Publications, 1962.

Norman Davis and C. C. Wrenn, editors, *English and Medieval Studies* (tribute to J. R. R. Tolkien), Allen & Unwin, 1962.

A. Ostroff, editor, *The Contemporary Poet as Artist and Critic*, Little, Brown, 1964.

Eric W. White, editor, *Poems by W. H. Auden and Others*, Poetry Book Society, 1966.

C. B. Cox and A. E. Dyson, editors, *Word in the Desert*, Oxford University Press, 1968.

G. F. Kennan, editor, *Democracy and the Student Left*, Little, Brown, 1968.

Contributor to periodicals, including *Botteghe Obscure, Poetry, New Verse, New Republic, The Griffin, Trace, Listener, Times Literary Supplement, New Statesman, Mid-Century, Texas Quarterly, Nation, New York Times Book Review, Atlantic, Spectator,*

*Kenyon Review, Reporter, Horn Book, New Yorker, Harper's, Mademoiselle, Partisan Review, Christian Scholar, Encounter, Vogue, Tulane Drama Review, Esquire, Delos, New York Review of Books,* and *Quest.*

*AUTHOR OF INTRODUCTION OR AFTERWORD*

(With others) Robert Frost, *Selected Poems of Robert Frost,* J. Cape, 1936.
Baudelaire, *Intimate Journals,* Methuen, 1949.
Charles Williams, *The Descent of the Dove,* Meridian Books, 1956.
Iwan Goll, *Jean sans Terre,* Yoseloff, 1958.
William Shakespeare, *Romeo and Juliet,* edited by Francis Fergusson, Dell, 1958.
John Hollander, *A Crackling of Thorns,* Yale University Press, 1958, reprinted, AMS Press, 1974.
Phyllis McGinley, *Times Three: Selected Poems From Three Decades,* Viking, 1960.
Henrik Ibsen, *Brand,* Anchor, 1960.
Konstantinos P. Kabaphes, *The Complete Poems of Cavafy,* Harcourt, 1961.
M. F. K. Fisher, *The Art of Eating,* Faber, 1963.
William Burto, editor, *Shakespeare: The Sonnets,* New American Library, 1964.
Anne Fremantle, editor, *The Protestant Mystics,* Little, Brown, 1964.
Oscar Wilde, *De Profundis and The Ballad of Reading Gaol,* Avon, 1964.
B. C. Bloomfield, *W. H. Auden: A Bibliography,* University Press of Virginia, 1964.
Sister Mary Immaculate, *The Tree and the Master: An Anthology of Literature on the Cross of Christ,* Random House, 1965.
Victor Yanovsky, *No Man's Time* (novel), Weybright & Talley, 1967.
George McDonald, *The Golden Key,* Farrar & Straus, 1967.
G. Handley-Taylor and T. d'A. Smith, compilers, *Cecil Day Lewis, The Poet Laureate,* St. James Press, 1968.
Eugen Rosenblock-Huessy, *I Am an Impure Thinker,* Argo Books, 1970.

*TRANSLATOR*

(With others) *Adam Mickiewicz, 1798-1855: Selected Poems,* Noonday Press, 1956.
Jean Cocteau, *The Knights of the Round Table,* 1957, published in *The Infernal Machine, and Other Plays,* New Directions, 1973.
(With Kallman) Bertolt Brecht and Kurt Weill, *The Seven Deadly Sins* (ballet cantata), performed at New York City Center, 1959.
(With others) Brecht, *The Caucasian Chalk Circle,* published in *Bertolt Brecht Plays,* Volume 1, Methuen, 1960.
St. John Perse (pseudonym of Alexis Saint-Leger Leger) *On Poetry,* Pantheon, 1961, also published in *Two Addresses* (also see below).
(With Elizabeth Mayer) Johann Wolfgang von Goethe, *Italian Journey,* Pantheon, 1962.
(With Sjoeberg, and author of foreword) Dag Hammarskjoeld, *Markings,* Knopf, 1964.
Perse, *Two Addresses,* Pantheon, 1966.
(With others, and author of foreword) Andrei Voznesenski, *Antiworlds,* Basic Books, 1966, bilingual edition including additional Voznesenski work published as *Antiworlds, and the Fifth Ace,* 1967.
(With Paul Beekman Taylor) *Voeluspa: The Song of the Sybil,* Windhover Press, 1968.
(With Taylor) Edda Saemundar, *The Elder Edda: A Selection,* Random House, 1969.
Perse, *Collected Poems,* Princeton University Press, 1971.
Goethe, *The Sorrows of Young Werther,* Random House, 1971.
(With Sjoeberg) Gunnar Ekeloef, *Selected Poems,* Pantheon, 1972.
(With Sjoeberg) Paer Lagerkvist, *Evening Land,* Wayne State University Press, 1975.
(With Kallman) Brecht, *The Rise and Fall of the City of Mahagonny,* Godine, 1976.
(with Paul B. Taylor) *Norse Poems,* Athlone Press, 1981.

Also translator, with Kallman, of opera libretto *The Magic Flute* (music by Wolfgang Amadeus Mozart), Random House, 1956, and (with others) *The Great Operas of Mozart,* Grossett, 1962.

*LIBRETTOS AND LYRICS*

*Our Hunting Fathers*, music by Benjamin Britten, Boosey & Hawkes, 1936.
*Fish in the Unruffled Lakes*, music by Britten, Boosey & Hawkes, 1937.
*On This Island*, music by Britten, Boosey & Hawkes, 1937.
*Two Ballads*, Boosey & Hawkes, 1937.
*Now through the Night's Caressing Grip*, music by Britten, Boosey & Hawkes, 1938.
*Ballad of Heroes*, music by Britten, Boosey & Hawkes, 1939.
*Hymn to St. Cecilia for S.S.A.T.B.*, music by Britten, Boosey & Hawkes, 1942.

*For the Time Being: A Christmas Oratorio* (first produced at Carnegie Hall, New York, December 7, 1959), music by Marvin David Levy, [New York], 1944.

(With Brecht and H. R. Hays) *The Duchess*, music by John Webster, performed in New York, 1946.

(With Kallman) *The Rake's Progress*, music by Igor Stravinsky, Boosey & Hawkes, 1951.

(With Kallman) *Delia; or, A Masque of Night*, published in *Botteghe Obscure*, 1953.

(With Greenberg) *The Play of Daniel: A Thirteenth Century Musical Drama*, Oxford University Press, 1959.

*Five Poems* (produced in New York, March, 1959), music by Lennox Berkeley, J. & W. Chester, 1960.

(With Kallman) *Elegy for Young Lovers*, music by Hans Werner Henze, Schott (Mainz), 1961.

(Adapter with Kallman) Lorenzo Da Ponte, *Don Giovanni*, music by Mozart, Schirmer, 1961.

*Elegy for J.F.K.*, music by Stravinsky, Boosey & Hawkes, 1964.

*The Twelve: Anthem for the Feast Day of Any Apostle*, music by William Walton, Oxford University Press, 1966.

(With Kallman) *The Bassarids* (based on Euripides' *The Bacchae;* produced in German at Salzburg Festival, 1966; produced in Santa Fe, N.M., August, 1966), Schott, 1966.

*Moralities: Three Scenic Plays from Fables by Aesop*, music by Henze, Schott, 1969.

(With Kallman) *Love's Labour's Lost* (adapted from the play by William Shakespeare), music by Nicholas Nabokov, first performed at 25th Edinburgh International Festival, Scotland, 1971.

*Paul Bunyan* (performed at Columbia University, New York, 1941), music by Britten, Faber, 1976.

(With Chester Kallman) *Libretti and Other Dramatic Writings by W. H. Auden, 1939-1973,* edited by Edward Mendelson, Princeton, 1993.

*OTHER*

(With others) *Time Cycle, for Soprano and Orchestra,* performed by New York Philharmonic, directed by Leonard Bernstein, at Carnegie Hall, New York, October 21, 1960.

(Adapter with Kallman) *Arcifanfano, King of Fools,* for its first performance since 1778, held at Town Hall, New York, November, 1965.

*The Prolific and the Devourer,* Ecco Press (Hopewell, NJ), 1994.

(With Bucknell, Katherine and Nicholas Jenkins, editors), *The Language of Learning and the Language of Love: Uncollected Writing , New Interpretations,* Oxford University Press (New York City), 1994.

(With Edward Mendelson) *As I Walked Out One Evening: Songs, Ballads, Lullabies, Limericks, and Other Light Verse,* Vintage Books (New York City), 1995.

(With Bucknell, Katherine and Nicholas Jenkins, editors), *In Solitude, for Company: W. H. Auden after 1940, Unpublished Prose and Recent Criticism* (also see below), Oxford University Press (New York City), 1995.

(With Edward Mendelson) *Prose and Travel Books in Prose and Verse,* Princeton University Press (Princeton, NJ), 1996.

Also composed narrative for "The Ballad of Barnaby" (adapted from Anatole France's version of "Our Lady's Juggler"), for music written by students of Wykeham Rise School under the direction of Charles Turner, first performed at St. John's Episcopal Church, Washington, Conn., May, 1969.

*SIDELIGHTS:* W. H. Auden exerted a major influence on the poetry of the twentieth century. Much of his poetry is concerned with moral issues and evidences a strong political, social, and psychological context. While the teachings of Marx and Freud weigh heavily in his early work, they later give way to religious and spiritual influences. Some critics have called Auden an "antiromantic"—a poet of analytical clarity who sought for order, for universal patterns of human existence. Auden's poetry is considered versatile and inventive, ranging from the tersely epigrammatic to book-length verse, and incorporating a vast range of scientific knowledge. Throughout his career, he collaborated with Christopher Isherwood and Louis MacNeice, and also frequently joined with Chester Kallman to create libretti for musical works by Benjamin Britten, Stravinsky, and Mozart.

Auden was born and raised in a heavily industrial section of northern England. His father, a prominent physician with an extensive knowledge of mythology and folklore, and his mother, a strict Anglican, both exerted strong influences on Auden's poetry. Auden's early interest in science and engineering earned him a scholarship to Oxford University, where his fascination with poetry led him to change his field of study to English. His attraction to science never completely waned, however, and scientific references are frequently found in his poetry. While at Oxford, Auden became familiar with modernist poetry, particularly that of T. S. Eliot. It was also at Oxford that Auden became the pivotal member of a group of writers called the "Oxford Group" or the "Auden Generation," which included Stephen Spender, C. Day Lewis, and Louis MacNeice. The group adhered to various Marxist and anti-fascist doctrines and addressed social, political, and economic concerns in their writings. Auden's first book of poetry, *Poems,* was privately printed by Stephen Spender in 1928. Critics have noted that Auden's early verse suggests the influences of Thomas Hardy, Laura Riding, Wilfred Owen, and Edward Thomas. Stylistically, the poems are fragmentary and terse, relying on concrete images and colloquial language to convey Auden's political and psychological concerns.

Auden's poems from the second half of the 1930s evidence his many travels during this period of political turmoil. "Spain," one of his most famous and widely anthologized pieces, is based upon his experiences in that country during its civil war of 1936 to 1939. *Journey to War,* a book of the period written by Auden with Christopher Isherwood, features Auden's sonnet sequence and verse commentary "In Time of War." The first half of the sequence recounts the history of humanity's move away from rational thought, while the second half addresses the moral problems faced by humankind on the verge of another world war. It was W. H. Auden who characterized the thirties as "the age of anxiety." His poem by that title (composed in 1947), wrote Monroe K. Spears in his *Poetry of W. H. Auden,* was a "sympathetic satire on the attempts of human beings to escape, through their own efforts, the anxiety of our age." Auden struck an extraordinarily receptive chord in readers with his timely treatment of the moral and political issues that directly affected them. Harold Bloom suggested in the *New Republic* that "Auden [was] accepted as not only a great poet but also a Christian humanist sage not because of any conspiracy among moralizing neo-Christian academicians, but because the age require[d] such a figure."

Some critics have suggested that Auden's unusual writing style germinated in the social climate of his childhood. Robert Bloom, writing in *PMLA,* commented that in Auden's writing in 1930 "the omission of articles, demonstrative adjectives, subjects, conjunctions, relative pronouns, auxiliary verbs—form a language of extremity and urgency. Like telegraphese . . . it has time and patience only for the most important words." In his *W. H. Auden as a Social Poet,* Frederick Buell identified the roots of this terse style in the private, codified language in which Auden and his circle of schoolboy friends conversed. Buell quoted Christopher Isherwood, one of those friends and later a collaborator with Auden, who described a typical conversation between two members of the group: "We were each other's ideal audience; nothing, not the slightest innuendo or the subtlest shade of meaning, was lost between us. A joke which, if I had been speaking to a stranger, world have taken five minutes to lead up to and elaborate and explain, could be conveyed by the faintest hint. . . . Our conversation would have been hardly intelligible to anyone who had happened to overhear it; it was a rigamarole of private slang, deliberate misquotations, bad puns, bits of parody, and preparatory school smut." Peter E. Firchow felt that the nature of Auden's friendships affected not only his style but also his political views. In *PMLA,* Firchow noted that Auden thought of his friends "as a 'gang' into which new members were periodically recruited," pointing out that Auden, "while never a Fascist, came at times remarkably close to accepting some characteristically Fascist ideas, especially those having to do with a mistrust of the intellect, the primacy of the group over the individual, the fascination with a strong leader (who expresses the will of the group), and the worship of youth."

Auden left England in 1939 and became a citizen of the United States. His first book written in America, *Another Time,* contains some of his best-known poems, among them "September 1, 1939" and "Musee des Beaux Arts," which was inspired by a Breughel painting. The volume also contains elegies to A. E. Housman, Matthew Arnold, and William Butler Yeats, whose careers and aesthetic concerns had influenced the development of Auden's artistic credo. A famous line from "In Memory of W. B. Yeats" is "Poetry makes nothing happen"—suggesting Auden's complete rejection of romantic ideals. Some critics have suggested that Auden's concentration on ethical concerns in *Another Time* was influenced by his reconversion to Christianity, which he had previously abandoned at age fifteen. Others, such as John G. Blair (author of *The Poetic Art of W. H. Auden*), however, have cautioned against reading Auden's personal sentiments into his poetry: "In none of his poems can one feel sure that the speaker is Auden himself. In the course of his career he has demonstrated impressive facility in speaking through any sort of dramatic persona; accordingly, the choice of an intimate, personal tone does not imply the direct self-expression of the poet."

Following several noted publications, *The Double Man, For the Time Being,* and *The Sea and the Mir-*

*ror,* Auden's next volume of verse, *The Collected Poetry,* helped to solidify his reputation as a major poet. He won the Pulitzer Prize for his following book, *The Age of Anxiety: A Baroque Eclogue,* which features four characters of disparate backgrounds who meet in a New York City bar during World War II. Written in the heavily alliterative style of Old English literature, the poem explores the attempts of the protagonists to comprehend themselves and the world in which they live. Auden's next major work, *Nones,* includes another widely anthologized piece, "In Praise of Limestone," which asserts a powerful connection between the landscape depicted and the psychology of Auden's characters.

Auden possessed a formidable technique and an acute ear. In her book *Auden,* Barbara Everett commented on the poet's facility: "In his verse, Auden can argue, reflect, joke, gossip, sing, analyse, lecture, hector, and simply talk; he can sound, at will, like a psychologist on a political platform, like a theologian at a party, or like a geologist in love; he can give dignity and authority to nonsensical theories, and make newspaper headlines sound both true and melodious." Jeremy Robson noted in *Encounter:* "The influence of music on Auden's verse . . . has always been salient: even his worst lines often 'sound' impressive." Everett found that a musical sensibility marked Auden's work from the very beginning, and she felt that when "he turned more and more, in the latter part of his career, to the kind of literary work that demands free exercise of verbal and rhythmic talent—for instance, to the writing of libretti—[he developed] that side of his artistic nature which was from the beginning the strongest."

Auden's linguistic innovations, renowned enough to spawn the adjective "Audenesque," were described by Karl Shapiro in his *In Defense of Ignorance* as "the modernization of diction, [and] the enlarging of dictional language to permit a more contemporary-sounding speech." As his career progressed, however, Auden was more often chastised than praised for his idiosyncratic use of language. James Fenton wrote in the *New Statesman:* "For years—for over forty years—the technical experimentation started by Auden enlarged and enriched the scope of English verse. He rediscovered and invented more than any other modern poet. . . . And yet there grew up . . . a number of mannerisms, such as the use of nouns as verbs, or the employment of embarrassingly outdated slang, or the ransacking of the OED [Oxford English Dictionary], which became in the end a hindrance to his work."

The extent to which Auden believed in various political theories is still debated; what is clear to some critics, though, is that Auden habitually revised his writing to accommodate any shifts in faith. Hannah Arendt considered Auden's changes of heart to be a natural response to the flux of the times. She wrote in the *New Yorker:* "In the Forties, there were many who turned against their old beliefs. . . . They simply changed trains, as it were; the train of Socialism and Communism had been wrong, and they changed to the train of Capitalism or Freudianism or some refined Marxism." Auden apparently changed trains frequently. In the case of his poem *"Spain 1937,"* a denouncement of Fascism in the Spanish Civil War, Auden later wrote that "it would have been bad enough if I had ever held this wicked doctrine [of Marxism], but that I should have stated it simply because it sounded to me rhetorically effective is quite inexcusable." Although in *Yale Review* Frank Kermode acknowledged that Auden "denied that his revision and rejections had an ideological motive," Kermode asserted that "his earlier rhetoric failed later ethical tests." Robert Greacen supported the latter claim, noting in *Books and Bookmen* that the poems of *Journey to a War* were "extensively revised because Auden was 'shocked to discover how carelessly [he] had written them.'" Greacen reported that Auden had found his work "preachy," and had commented that "if he were to preach the same sermon today he would do it in a very different way."

Buell drew a parallel between the political activism of Auden and that of playwright Bertolt Brecht, noting that both men were "attempting to find an artistic voice for a left-wing polemic." Arendt supported Buell's assertion, writing that "[Auden] once mentioned as a 'disease' his 'early addiction to German usages,' but much more prominent than these, and less easy to get rid of, was the obvious influence of Bertolt Brecht with whom he had more in common than he was ever ready to admit. . . . What made this influence possible was that [Auden and Brecht] both belonged to the post-First World War generation, with its curious mixture of despair and *joie de vivre.*" Buell found stylistic as well as political similarities: "The techniques of Brecht's epic theatre and Verfremdungseffekt [alienation-effect; a method of dramatic presentation calculated to alert the audience to the unreality of a performance and to jolt them to political activism] correlate with a number of Auden's specific rhetorical practices: Auden's own propensity to quick changes in and explosions of poetic mood, his use of a wide range of rhetoric and diction that calls attention to itself as such, and his cultivation of a poetic structure that is intentionally nonorganic would be the most important examples."

Bernard Bergonzi, writing in *Encounter,* contended that ideologies were only tools to serve Auden's foremost interest: understanding the workings of the world. For Auden, said Bergonzi, Marxism and psychoanalysis alike were "attractive as techniques of explanation." Bergonzi posited that Auden perceived reality as "actually or potentially known and intelligible, without mysteries or uncertainty," and that he considered experience to be a complex entity which could be "reduced to classifiable elements, as a necessary preliminary to diagnosis and prescription." Auden expressed his desire for order in his preface to *Oxford Poetry 1927:* "All genuine poetry is in a sense the formation of private spheres out of a public chaos." Bergonzi was one of many critics who felt that Auden succeeded in giving his readers a feeling of the well-ordered "private sphere." He wrote: "At a time of world economic depression there was something reassuring in Auden's calm demonstration, mediated as much by style as by content, that reality was intelligible, and could be studied like a map or a catalogue, or seen in temporal terms as an inexorable historical process. . . . It was the last time that any British poet was to have such a global influence on poetry in English."

In his later years, Auden wrote three major volumes: *City without Walls, and Many Other Poems, Epistle to a Godson, and Other Poems,* and the posthumously published *Thank You, Fog: Last Poems.* While all three works are noted for their lexical range and humanitarian content, Auden's later poems often received mixed, and sometimes unenthusiastic, reviews. Commenting on *Thank You, Fog,* Howard Moss of *The New York Times Book Review* argued that the collection is "half the ghost of what it might have been. Writers, being human, are not in a position to choose their monuments. This one is more Audenesque than Auden, hardly fitting as the final words, the summing up of a man who set his mark on an age."

Since Auden's death in 1973, numerous anthologies of his works have been published, leading to revaluations (and in some respects, the critical rehabilitation) of the poet's career. Edited by Edward Mendelson, *W. H. Auden and Chester Kallman: Libretti and Other Dramatic Writings by W. H. Auden, 1939-1973,* for example, presents a compilation of Auden's opera libretti, radio plays, film narratives, liturgical dramas, and adaptations of Euripides and Shakespeare, many of which were written in collaboration with his companion Chester Kallman. While the collection points to Auden's diverse musical and dramatic interests, "the libretti are rightly the focus of the book," observed J. D. McClatchy for *The New Republic.* McClatchy continued: "[The opera libretto] *The Rake's Progress* remains [Auden's and Kallman's] masterpiece. Simplest verse is the hardest to write, because it is most exposed, and Auden's spare style here achieves both elegance and speechliness." Highlighting Auden's writing partnership with Christopher Isherwood during the early years of their career is Mendelson's *W. H. Auden and Christopher Isherwood: Plays and Other Dramatic Writings by W. H. Auden 1928-1938,* which contains plays, documentary film-scripts, as well as scripts for a radio play and a cabaret act. The plays in the volume, such as *The Dance of Death* and *The Dog beneath the Skin,* reveal Auden's early desire to eschew dramatic realism in favor of the more ritualistic and communal dramatic forms that characterized the Mystery plays of the Middle Ages. The subject-matter of the plays nevertheless demonstrates their modern orientation, as political and psychological commentary are of central importance. In *The Ascent of F 6,* for example, a man embarks upon a dangerous mountain climb only to discover that his true longing is for his mother. "[T]he plays suggest that politics, which both authors came consciously to take as their topic, almost always functions as a metaphor for a violent and uncomprehended world which could just as easily be, which quite often is, psychological or domestic," asserted Michael Wood in *Times Literary Supplement.* The collection received praise for illuminating the nature of the collaborative writing process between Isherwood and Auden, as well as for its presentation of some of Auden's lesser-known works. "This outstanding edition is faithful to the spirit in which the contents were written, taking us inside the workshop," observed Sean French in *New Statesman & Society.* "There was no such thing as a clinically completed text. Plays and scripts were written, rewritten, abandoned and then cannibalised in order to make new plays."

Edited by Katherine Bucknell and Nicholas Jenkins (co-founders of the W. H. Auden society), *'The Map of All My Youth': Early Works, Friends and Influences* contains several previously unpublished works by Auden, including six poems from the 1930s and an essay by Auden titled "Writing." The first in a planned series of scholarly books dedicated "not only to Auden but also [to] his friends and contemporaries, those who influenced him, and those by whom he was influenced," the volume also contains correspondence between Auden and Stephen Spender, as well as critical essays on Auden by contemporary scholars.

Auden's career has undergone much reevaluation in recent decades. While some critics have contended that he wrote his finest work when his political sentiments were less obscured by religion and philosophy, others defend his later material as the work of a highly original and mature intellect. Many critics echo the assessment of Auden's career by the National Book Committee, which awarded him the National Medal for Literature in 1967: "[Auden's poetry] has illuminated our lives and times with grace, wit and vitality. His work, branded by the moral and ideological fires of our age, breathes with eloquence, perception and intellectual power."

*BIOGRAPHICAL/CRITICAL SOURCES:*

*BOOKS*

Aisenberg, Katy, *Ravishing Images: Ekphrasis in the Poetry and Prose of William Wordsworth, W. H. Auden, and Philip Larkin,* P. Lang (New York City), 1995.

Auden, W. H., *A Certain World: A Commonplace Book,* Viking, 1970.

(With Bucknell, Katherine and Nicholas Jenkins, editors) Auden, W. H., *In Solitude, for Company: W. H. Auden after 1940, Unpublished Prose and Recent Criticism,* Oxford University Press (New York City), 1995.

Bahlke, G. W., *The Later Auden,* Rutgers University Press, 1970.

Beach, Joseph Warren, *The Making of the Auden Canon,* University of Minnesota Press, 1957.

Blair, J. G., *The Poetic Art of W. H. Auden,* Princeton University Press, 1965.

Bloom, Harold, *Ringers in the Tower: Studies in Romantic Tradition,* University of Chicago Press, 1971.

Bloomfield, B. C., *W. H. Auden: A Bibliography,* University Press of Virginia, 1964, 2nd edition, 1972.

Brophy, J. D., *W. H. Auden,* Columbia University Press, 1970.

Buell, Frederick, *W. H. Auden as a Social Poet,* Cornell University Press, 1973.

Callan, Edward, *An Annotated Check List of the Works of W. H. Auden,* A. Swallow, 1958.

*Contemporary Literary Criticism,* Gale, Volume 1, 1973, Volume 2, 1974, Volume 3, 1975, Volume 4, 1975, Volume 6, 1976, Volume 9, 1978, Volume 11, 1979, Volume 14, 1980, Volume 43, 1987.

Davenport-Hines, R. P. T., *Auden,* Pantheon Books (New York City), 1995.

Davidson, D., *W. H. Auden,* Evans, 1970.

*Dictionary of Literary Biography,* Gale, Volume 10: *Modern British Dramatists, 1940-45,* 1982, Volume 20, *British Poets, 1914-1945,* 1983.

Everett, Barbara, *Auden,* Oliver & Boyd, 1964.

Fuller, J., *A Reader's Guide to W. H. Auden,* Thames & Hudson, 1970.

Greenberg, Herbert, *Quest for the Necessary: W. H. Auden and the Dilemma of Divided Consciousness,* Harvard University Press, 1969.

Hoggart, Richard, *Auden: An Introductory Essay,* Yale University Press, 1951.

Mitchell, Donald, *Britten and Auden in the Thirties,* Faber, 1981.

Nelson, G., *Changes of Heart: A Study of the Poetry of W. H. Auden,* University of California Press, 1969.

Osborne, Charles, *W. H. Auden: The Life of a Poet,* M. Evans and Co. (New York City), 1995.

Osborne, C. W. H., *W. H. Auden,* Harcourt, 1979.

Pike, James Albert, editor, *Modern Canterbury Pilgrims,* Morehouse, 1956.

*Poetry Criticism,* Volume 1, Gale, 1991.

Replogle, J. M., *Auden's Poetry,* Methuen, 1969, University of Washington Press, 1971.

Scarfe, Francois, *Auden and After,* Routledge, 1942, reprinted, Norwood, 1978.

Shapiro, Karl, *In Defense of Ignorance,* Random House, 1960.

Spears, Monroe K., *The Poetry of W. H. Auden: The Disenchanted Island,* Oxford University Press, 1963.

Spender, Stephen, *W. H. Auden,* Macmillan, 1975.

Srivastava, N., *W. H. Auden: A Poet of Ideas,* Chand, 1978.

Untermeyer, Louis, *Lives of the Poets,* Simon & Schuster, 1959.

Wright, G. T. W., *W. H. Auden,* Twayne, 1969.

*PERIODICALS*

*Agenda,* autumn, 1994, p. 273.

*American Scholar,* spring, 1994, p. 287.

*Atlantic Monthly,* August, 1966.

*Books and Bookmen,* June, 1969.

*Carleton Miscellany,* fall, 1969.

*Chicago Tribune Book World,* January 18, 1981.

*Choice,* April, 1972.

*Christian Science Monitor,* January 8, 1970; December 30, 1976.

*Commentary,* July, 1968.
*Comparative Literature,* spring, 1970.
*Encounter,* January, 1970; February, 1975.
*Harper's,* April, 1970.
*Holiday,* June, 1969.
*Hudson Review,* spring, 1968.
*Life,* June 30, 1970.
*Listener,* March 17, 1966; May 4, 1967; November 9, 1967; May 28, 1970; December 24, 1970.
*London Magazine,* January, 1961; March, 1968; February, 1969; October, 1969.
*London Review of Books,* January 11, 1990, p. 9; September 8, 1994, p. 12; November 16, 1995, p. 3.
*Nation,* February 9, 1970; March 19, 1978.
*New Leader,* October 27, 1969.
*New Republic,* April 23, 1956.
*New Statesman,* January 28, 1956; June 9, 1956; July 19, 1958; December 13, 1968; September 26, 1969; September 27, 1974.
*Newsweek,* May 20, 1968; July 28, 1969; September 28, 1981, p. 92.
*New Republic,* November 29, 1993, p. 40.
*New Yorker,* August 4, 1956.
*New York Review of Books,* January 17, 1991; November 3, 1994, p. 52.
*New York Times,* October 26, 1967; January 24, 1970; December 27, 1988.
*New York Times Book Review,* February 15, 1968; July 20, 1969; March 18, 1973; April 29, 1979.
*Observer* (London), June 28, 1970; May 2, 1971; October 24, 1993, p. 18.
*Opera News,* February 19, 1994, p. 40.
*Parnassus,* February, 1994, p. 36.
*Philological Quarterly,* January, 1960.
*Playboy,* December, 1970.
*PMLA,* June, 1968.
*Poetry,* March, 1961; January, 1969; July, 1995, p. 226.
*Prairie Schooner,* summer, 1970.
*Publishers Weekly,* October 15, 1973; August 11, 1975.
*Punch,* October 1, 1969.
*Reporter,* January 31, 1963.
*Review of English Studies,* May, 1993, p. 283.
*Shenandoah,* winter, 1967.
*Spectator,* September 24, 1994, p. 40.
*Time,* May 3, 1960; May 31, 1968; January 26, 1970; July 6, 1970.
*Times Literary Supplement,* June 7, 1963; December 7, 1967; January 23, 1969; June 26, 1969; February 15, 1980; November 21, 1980; February 25, 1982, p. 205; August 4-10, 1989, p. 849; February 15, 1991; November 5, 1993, p. 9; August 19, 1994; May 5, 1995, p. 25; October 27, 1995, p. 3.
*Twentieth Century,* September, 1960.
*Twentieth Century Literature,* January, 1970.
*Variety,* July 26, 1972.
*Village Voice,* February 10, 1972.
*Virginia Quarterly Review,* spring, 1966; spring, 1969.
*Washington Post Book World,* November 19, 1967; July 27, 1969; November 26, 1972.
*Yale Review,* autumn, 1968.

* * *

**AUTRY, Gloria Diener**
**See ALLEN, Terril Diener**

# B

**BALLARD, K. G.**
**See ROTH, Holly**

* * *

**BANKS, Iain**
**See BANKS, Iain M(enzies)**

* * *

**BANKS, Iain M(enzies) 1954-**
**(Iain Banks)**

*PERSONAL:* Born February 16, 1954, in Fife, Scotland; son of Thomas Menzies (an admiralty officer) and Euphemia (an ice skating instructor; maiden name, Thomson) Banks. *Education:* University of Stirling, B.A., 1975. *Politics:* Socialist. *Religion:* Atheist. *Avocational interests:* "Hillwalking, eating and drinking, and talking to friends."

*ADDRESSES: Home*—31 South Bridge, Flat 3, Edinburgh EH1 1LL, Scotland. *Agent*—c/o Mac-millan Publishers Ltd., 4 Little Essex St., London WC2R 3LF, England.

*CAREER:* Writer. Nondestructive testing technician in Glasgow, Scotland, 1977; International Business Machines Corp. (IBM), Greenock, Scotland, expediter-analyzer, 1978; solicitor's clerk in London, 1980-84.

*MEMBER:* Amnesty International, Campaign for Nuclear Disarmament.

*WRITINGS:*

*UNDER NAME IAIN BANKS*

*The Wasp Factory,* Houghton (Boston), 1984.
*Walking on Glass,* Macmillan (London), 1985, Houghton, 1986.
*The Bridge,* Macmillan, 1986.
*Espedair Street,* Macmillan, 1987.
*Canal Dreams,* Doubleday (New York City), 1991.
*Complicity,* Doubleday, 1995.
*Whit, or Isis amongst the Unsaved,* Little, Brown (London), 1995.
*The Crow Road,* Little, Brown, 1996.
*A Song of Stone,* Villard (New York City), 1998.

*SCIENCE FICTION; UNDER NAME IAIN M. BANKS*

*Consider Phlebas,* St. Martin's (New York City), 1987.
*The Player of Games,* Macmillan, 1988, St. Martin's, 1989.
*The State of the Art,* M.V. Ziesing (Willimantic, CT), 1989.
*Use of Weapons,* Bantam, 1992.
*Against a Dark Background,* Spectra, 1993.
*Feersum Endjinn,* Bantam (New York City), 1995.
*Excession,* Orbit, 1996, Bantam, 1997.

*SIDELIGHTS:* Scottish novelist Iain M. Banks has sparked considerable controversy in British and American literary circles with his unique and highly imaginative brand of fiction. While the author is credited with crossing and redefining the boundaries of the thriller, fantasy, and science fiction genres, he is probably best known for his macabre tales of horror, which have been compared by reviewers to the psychologically probing fiction of Franz Kafka and Edgar Allan Poe. Although Banks's books have received widely mixed reviews, most critics have conceded that the writer possesses a distinctive talent for structuring bold and compelling stories.

Banks first captured the attention of the critics in 1984 with his highly acclaimed novel, *The Wasp Factory.* A bizarre tale of murder and perversity, *The Wasp Factory* centers on Frank Cauldhame, a disturbed adolescent who narrates the sordid story of his life. Living on a remote Scottish island with his reclusive ex-professor father, Frank has developed a taste for killing children and ritualistically mutilating animals and insects. The book's plot turns on the escape from an asylum of Frank's insane half-brother, Eric, who was committed for his sadistic indulgences, which included setting dogs on fire and choking babies with maggots. Eric's return to the Cauldhame cottage and Frank's revelation of his father's ghastly secret bring the novel to its climax.

*The Wasp Factory* takes its title from a device that Frank concocted specifically for the systematic torture and execution of wasps, a process which, according to Frank, can reveal the future if correctly interpreted. In the novel Frank muses, "Everything we do is part of a pattern we at least have some say in. . . . The Wasp Factory is part of the pattern because it is part of life and—even more so—part of death. Like life it is complicated, so all the components are there. The reason it can answer questions is because every question is a start looking for an end, and the Factory is about the End—death, no less."

Some critics were outraged by the sadistic streak that runs through Banks's narrator. Commenting on the apparent delight Frank takes in his ghoulish acts of cruelty, Patricia Craig, writing in the *Times Literary Supplement,* deemed the book "a literary equivalent of the nastiest brand of juvenile delinquency." But in an article for *Punch,* Stanley Reynolds defended Banks's novel as "a minor masterpiece. . . . red and raw, bleeding and still maybe even quivering . . . on the end of the fork." Much controversy surrounds the question of the author's intent in composing such a grizzly and fantastic tale; critics have attributed Banks's motivation to several varied forces, including the desire to expose the dark side of humanity, to experiment in the avant-garde, or simply to shock and revolt readers. Reynolds suggested that *The Wasp Factory* "is not an indictment of society" but "instead a toy, a game." But this assessment was disputed by several other critics, including *Washington Post Book World* contributor Douglas E. Winter, who judged the novel "a literate, penetrating examination of the nature of violence and the dwindling value of life in the modern world."

Reviewers generally considered Banks's skillful use of black humor and mesmerizingly evocative narrative power more than enough compensation for the novel's few cited structural flaws, mainly the implausibility of plot and character. Winter felt that "Banks indulges too often in . . . insight beyond the years of his young narrator." Rosalind Wade echoed that sentiment in *Contemporary Review,* claiming that the tale "strain[s] credulity to the breaking point"; she nevertheless dubbed *The Wasp Factory* "a first novel of unusual promise."

Banks's second novel, *Walking on Glass,* consists of three separate but ultimately interwoven stories, each of which, upon interpretation, sheds light upon the others. Two of the tales are set in London, the first detailing young Graham Park's obsessive pursuit of the mysterious Sara ffitch and the second focusing on temperamental former pothole filler Steven Grout's paranoid belief that "They" are out to get him. The last story concerns Quiss and Ajayi, prisoners in a surreal castle who are doomed to play "One-Dimensional Chess" and "Spotless Dominoes" until they can correctly answer the riddle, "What happens when an unstoppable force meets an immovable object?" Banks ties the three narratives together in the book's closing pages, making *Walking on Glass* "a brilliant mind-boggler of a novel . . . [with] real kick," according to Jack Sullivan in the *Washington Post Book Review.* Critics once again praised the author for his skillfully crafted, continually unfolding story lines and the firm grip on mood and tone evidenced in his writings. M. George Stevens considered *Walking on Glass* another example of "the almost frighteningly well-structured, willfully perverse novelistic machinery of Iain Banks."

Banks followed *Walking on Glass* with another complexly designed story called *The Bridge,* about an amnesiac's fantasy life. Following an accident, Orr (the central character, whose real name is Alexander Lennox), awakens in the world of the "Bridge," a land of social segregation arranged around an expansive railway that literally divides the classes. Dream and reality clash as Orr tries to make his escape. While some critics faulted Banks for his sketchy account of the narrator's life prior to the accident, the author was once again praised for his technical acumen. *The Bridge* drew comparisons to what Justin

Wintle, in an article for *New Statesman,* termed "Banks's Kafka-Orwellian polity." Wintle further ventured that through his writings, the author strives "to make a point of pointlessness."

In 1987 Banks published his first science fiction novel, *Consider Phlebas,* one of two books released that year. He refined his skill for the genre with his follow-up novel, *The Player of Games,* in 1988. Although a few reviewers characterized both of these novels as overly extravagant, Tom Hutchinson, writing in the London *Times,* called *The Player of Games* "tremendous."

Gerald Jonas, a critic for the *New York Times Book Review,* noted that Banks's "passion for overwriting" was evident in another science fiction offering, *Use of Weapons,* but admitted that the flashback-laden narrative was worth reading just to get to the surprising denouement. Yet another science fiction novel, *Feersum Endjinn,* featured sections narrated by a character who can only spell phonetically, leading to sentences such as "Unlike evrybody els I got this weerd wirin in mi brane so I cant spel rite, juss - 2 do eveythin foneticly." Gerald Jonas, again writing in the *New York Times Book Review,* explained: "I confess that I groaned inwardly each time this narrator took over. But despite the effort required, I was so caught up in the story and so eager to solve the puzzle that I never for a moment considered giving up." *Analog* reviewer Tom Easton similarly noted that at times the book is "irritating," but went on to declare that "Banks proves quite convincingly that his imagination can beggar anyone else's. Wow. . . . If you can stand orthographic-phonetic-rebus overkill, yool find a grate deel hear 2 luv." Carl Hays concluded in *Booklist:* "Banks' skill at high-tech speculation continues to grow. Every page of this, his most ingenious work yet, seems to offer more dazzling, intriguing ideas." Summarizing Banks's work in the science fiction genre, Charles Shaar Murray wrote in *New Statesman:* "What comes through most clearly is just how much Banks loves SF. . . . He stuffs each novel to bursting point with everything he adores about the genre, and with everything his literary ancestors unaccountably left out. [His work proves] that 'fun' SF doesn't need to be either dumb or reactionary."

As his career has progressed, Banks's mainstream work has drawn increasingly positive reviews, despite his continued use of brutality and labyrinthine plots. In *Canal Dreams,* for example, he starts with a Japanese concert cellist whose fear of flying leads her to travel on her world tours by such unusual means as oil tankers. On one such cruise, she is caught in the middle of a terrorist action, raped, and transformed into a grenade-carrying warrior. A *Publishers Weekly* writer called *Canal Dreams* a "stunning, hallucinatory, semi-surreal fable" and a "wrenching story, which can be read as a parable of the feminine principle reasserting itself and taking revenge on earth-destroying males." *Booklist* contributor Peter Robertson was so impressed with Banks's achievement in *Canal Dreams* that he declared, "Banks joins Martin Amis and Ian McEwan among the vanguard of the new British subversive novelist."

Banks once told *CA:* "I want to make people laugh and think, though not necessarily in that order."

For an interview with Banks, see *Contemporary Authors,* Volume 128.

*BIOGRAPHICAL/CRITICAL SOURCES:*

*BOOKS*

*Contemporary Literary Criticism,* Volume 34, Gale (Detroit), 1985.

*PERIODICALS*

*Analog,* December, 1995, pp. 183-84.
*Booklist,* August, 1991, p. 2097; July, 1995, p. 1865.
*Books and Bookmen,* February, 1984, pp. 22-23.
*British Book News,* April, 1984, p. 238.
*Contemporary Review,* April, 1984, pp. 213-24.
*Globe and Mail* (Toronto), October 19, 1985.
*Library Journal,* August, 1991, p. 150; June 15, 1995, p. 98.
*Los Angeles Times,* August 19, 1984; February 5, 1986.
*Los Angeles Times Book Review,* September 15, 1991, p. 6.
*New Scientist,* March 20, 1993.
*New Statesman,* April 5, 1985; July 18, 1986; July 26, 1996, pp. 47-48.
*New Statesman and Society,* August 12, 1988; April 24, 1992; September 3, 1993.
*New York Times Book Review,* March 2, 1986; May 3, 1992, p. 38; February 19, 1995, p. 26; September 10, 1995, p. 46; January 7, 1996, p. 32.
*Observer* (London), March 10, 1985; July 13, 1986; August 23, 1987.
*Publishers Weekly,* June 28, 1991, p. 88.
*Punch,* February 29, 1984, p. 42.
*Sunday Times* (London), February 12, 1984.

*Times* (London), February 16, 1984; March 7, 1985; September 24, 1988.
*Times Literary Supplement,* March 16, 1984; November 13, 1987; June 14, 1996.
*Voice Literary Supplement,* April, 1986.
*Washington Post,* March 17, 1986.
*Washington Post Book World,* September 9, 1984; July 31, 1988; October 29, 1989, p. 8; February 19, 1995, p. 7.*

* * *

**BARAKA, Amiri 1934-**
**(LeRoi Jones)**

*PERSONAL:* Born October 7, 1934, in Newark, NJ; original name Everett LeRoi Jones; name changed to Imamu ("spiritual leader") Ameer ("blessed") Baraka ("prince"); later modified to Amiri Baraka; son of Coyette Leroy (a postal worker and elevator operator) and Anna Lois (Russ) Jones; married Hettie Roberta Cohen, October 13, 1958 (divorced, August, 1965); married Sylvia Robinson (Bibi Amina Baraka), 1966; children: (first marriage) Kellie Elisabeth, Lisa Victoria Chapman; (second marriage) Obalaji Malik Ali, Ras Jua Al Aziz, Shani Isis, Amiri Seku, Ahi Mwenge. *Education:* Attended Rutgers University, 1951-52; Howard University, B.A., 1954; Columbia University, M.A. in philosophy; New School for Social Research, M.A. in German literature.

*ADDRESSES: Office*—Department of Africana Studies, State University of New York, Long Island, NY 11794-4340. *Agent*—Joan Brandt, Sterling Lord Agency, 660 Madison Ave., New York, NY 10021.

*CAREER:* State University of New York at Stony Brook, assistant Professor, 1980-83, associate professor, 1983-85, professor of African Studies, 1985—. Instructor, New School for Social Research, New York City, 1962-64; Visiting professor, University of Buffalo, summer, 1964, Columbia University, fall, 1964, and 1966-67, San Francisco State University, 1967, Yale University, 1977-78, George Washington University, 1978-79, and Rutgers University, 1988. Founded *Yugen* magazine and Totem Press, 1958; co-editor and founder of *Floating Bar* magazine, 1961-63; editor of *The Black Nation.* Founder and director, 1964-66, of Black Arts Repertory Theatre (disbanded, 1966); director of Spirit House (a black community theater; also known as Heckalu Community Center), 1965-75, and head of advisory group at Treat Elementary School, both in Newark. Founder, Congress of African People, 1970-76. Member, Political Prisoners Relief Fund, and African Liberation Day Commission. Candidate, Newark community council, 1968. *Military service:* U.S. Air Force, 1954-57; weather-gunner; stationed for two and a half years in Puerto Rico with intervening trips to Europe, Africa, and the Middle East.

*MEMBER:* All African Games, Pan African Federation, Black Academy of Arts and Letters, National Black Political Assembly (secretary general; co-governor), National Black United Front, Congress of African People (co-founder, chairperson), Black Writers' Union, League of Revolutionary Struggle, United Brothers (Newark), Newark Writers Collective.

*AWARDS, HONORS:* Longview Best Essay of the Year award, 1961, for "Cuba Libre"; John Whitney Foundation fellowship for poetry and fiction, 1962; Obie Award, Best American Off-Broadway Play, 1964, for *Dutchman;* Guggenheim fellowship, 1965-66; Yoruba Academy fellow, 1965; second prize, International Art Festival, Dakar, 1966, for *The Slave;* National Endowment for the Arts grant, 1966; Doctorate of Humane Letters, Malcolm X College, Chicago, IL, 1972; Rockefeller Foundation fellow (drama), 1981; Poetry Award, National Endowment for the Arts, 1981; New Jersey Council for the Arts award, 1982; American Book Award, Before Columbus Foundation, 1984, for *Confirmation: An Anthology of African-American Women;* Drama Award, 1985; PEN-Faulkner Award, 1989; Langston Hughes Medal, 1989, for outstanding contribution to literature; Ferroni Award, Italy, and Foreign Poet Award, 1993; Playwright's Award, Black Drama Festival, Winston-Salem, NC, 1997.

*WRITINGS:*

*UNDER NAME LEROI JONES UNTIL 1967; PLAYS*

*A Good Girl Is Hard to Find,* produced in Montclair, NJ, at Sterington House, 1958.
*Dante* (one act; an excerpt from the novel *The System of Dante's Hell;* also see below), produced in New York at Off-Bowery Theatre, 1961; produced again as *The Eighth Ditch,* at the New Bowery Theatre, 1964.
*Dutchman,* (also see below; produced Off-Broadway at Village South Theatre, 1964; produced Off-Broadway at Cherry Lane Theater, 1964; produced in London, 1967), Faber & Faber, 1967.

*The Baptism: A Comedy in One Act* (also see below; produced Off-Broadway at Writers' Stage Theatre, 1964, produced in London, 1970-71), Sterling Lord, 1966.

*The Toilet* (also see below; produced with *The Slave: A Fable* Off-Broadway at St. Mark's Playhouse, 1964; produced at International Festival of Negro Arts at Dakar, Senegal, 1966), Sterling Lord, 1964.

*J-E-L-L-O* (one act comedy; also see below; produced in New York by Black Arts Repertory Theatre, 1965), Third World Press, 1970.

*Experimental Death Unit #1* (one act; also see below), produced Off-Broadway at St. Mark's Playhouse, 1965.

*The Death of Malcolm X* (one act), produced in Newark at Spirit House, 1965, published in *New Plays from the Black Theatre,* edited by Ed Bullins, Bantam, 1969.

*A Black Mass* (also see below), produced in Newark at Proctor's Theatre, 1966.

*Slave Ship* (also see below; produced as *Slave Ship: A Historical Pageant* at Spirit House, 1967; produced in New York City, 1969), Jihad, 1967.

*Madheart: Morality Drama* (one act; also see below), produced at San Francisco State College, May, 1967.

*Arm Yourself, or Harm Yourself, A One-Act Play* (also see below; produced at Spirit House, 1967), Jihad, 1967.

*Great Goodness of Life (A Coon Show)* (one act; also see below), produced at Spirit House, 1967; produced Off-Broadway at Tambellini's Gate Theater, 1969.

*Home on the Range* (one act comedy; also see below), first produced at Spirit House, 1968; produced in New York City at a Town Hall rally, 1968.

*Junkies Are Full of SHHH . . . ,* produced at Spirit House, 1968; produced with *Bloodrites* (also see below) Off-Broadway at Henry Street Playhouse, 1970.

*Board of Education* (children's play), produced at Spirit House, 1968.

*Resurrection in Life* (one act pantomime) produced under the title *Insurrection* in Harlem, NY, 1969.

*Black Dada Nihilism* (one act), produced Off-Broadway at Afro-American Studio, 1971.

*A Recent Killing* (three acts), produced Off-Broadway at the New Federal Theatre, 1973.

*Columbia the Gem of the Ocean,* produced in Washington, DC, by Howard University Spirit House Movers, 1973.

*The New Ark's A-Moverin,* produced in Newark, February, 1974.

*The Sidnee Poet Heroical, in Twenty-Nine Scenes,* (one act comedy; also see below; produced Off-Broadway at the New Federal Theatre, 1975), Reed & Cannon, 1979.

*S-1: A Play with Music in 26 Scenes* (also see below), produced in New York at Washington Square Methodist Church, 1976, produced at Afro-American Studio, August, 1976.

(With Frank Chin and Leslie Siko) *America More or Less* (musical), produced in San Francisco at Marine's Memorial Theater, 1976.

*The Motion of History* (four acts; also see below), produced at New York City Theatre Ensemble, 1977.

*What Was the Relationship of the Lone Ranger to the Means of Production?: A Play in One Act,* (also see below; produced in New York at Ladies Fort, 1979), Anti-Imperialist Cultural Union, 1978.

*Dim Cracker Party Convention,* produced in New York at Columbia University, 1980.

*Boy and Tarzan Appear in a Clearing,* produced Off-Broadway at New Federal Theatre, 1981.

*Money: Jazz Opera,* produced Off-Broadway at La Mama Experimental Theatre Club, 1982.

*Song: A One Act Play about the Relationship of Art to Real Life,* produced in Jamaica, NY, 1983.

Also author of the play *Police,* published in *Drama Review,* summer, 1968; *Rockgroup,* published in *Cricket,* December, 1969; *Black Power Chant,* published in *Drama Review,* December, 1972; *The Coronation of the Black Queen,* published in *Black Scholar,* June, 1970; *Vomit and the Jungle Bunnies,* unpublished; *Revolt of the Moonflowers,* 1969, lost in manuscript; *Primitive World,* 1991; *Jackpot Melting,* 1996; *Election Machine Warehouse,* 1996; *Meeting Lillie,* 1997; *Biko,* 1997; and *Black Renaissance in Harlem,* 1998.

*PLAY COLLECTIONS*

*Dutchman* [and] *The Slave: A Fable,* Morrow, 1964.

*The Baptism* [and] *The Toilet,* Grove, 1967.

*Four Black Revolutionary Plays: All Praises to the Black Man* (contains *Experimental Death Unit #1, A Black Mass, Great Goodness of Life (A Coon Show),* and *Madheart*), Bobbs-Merrill, 1969.

(Contributor) Woodie King and Ron Milner, editors, *Black Drama Anthology* (includes *Bloodrites* and *Junkies Are Full of SHHH . . .*), New American Library, 1971.

(Contributor) Rochelle Owens, editor, *Spontaneous Combustion: Eight New American Plays* (includes *Ba-Ra-Ka*), Winter House, 1972.

*The Motion of History and Other Plays* (contains *Slave Ship* and *S-1: A Play with Music in 26 Scenes*), Morrow, 1978.
*Selected Plays and Prose of Amiri Baraka/LeRoi Jones,* Morrow, 1979.

*SCREENPLAYS*

*Dutchman,* Gene Persson Enterprises, Ltd., 1967.
*Black Spring,* Jihad Productions, 1968.
*"A Fable"* (based on *The Slave: A Fable*), MFR Productions, 1971.
*Supercoon,* Gene Persson Enterprises, Ltd., 1971.

*POETRY*

*April 13* (broadside Number 133), Penny Poems (New Haven), 1959.
*Spring & So Forth* (broadside Number 141), Penny Poems, 1960.
*Preface to a Twenty Volume Suicide Note,* Totem/Corinth, 1961.
*The Disguise* (broadside), [New Haven], 1961.
*The Dead Lecturer* (also see below), Grove, 1964.
*Black Art* (also see below), Jihad, 1966.
*Black Magic* (also see below), Morrow, 1967.
*A Poem for Black Hearts,* Broadside Press, 1967.
*Black Magic: Sabotage; Target Study; Black Art; Collected Poetry, 1961-1967,* Bobbs-Merrill, 1969.
*It's Nation Time,* Third World Press, 1970.
*Spirit Reach,* Jihad, 1972.
*Afrikan Revolution: A Poem,* Jihad, 1973.
*Hard Facts: Excerpts,* People's War, 1975, 2nd edition, Revolutionary Communist League, 1975.
*Spring Song,* Baraka, 1979.
*AM/TRAK,* Phoenix Bookship, 1979.
*Selected Poetry of Amiri Baraka/Leroi Jones* (includes *Poetry for the Advanced*), Morrow, 1979.
*In the Tradition: For Black Arthur Blythe,* Jihad, 1980.
*Reggae or Not! Poems,* Contact Two, 1982.
*LeRoi Jones—Amiri,* Thunder's Mouth Press, 1991.
*Transbluency: The Selected Poems of Amiri Baraka/LeRoi Jones (1961-1995),* Marsilio, 1995.
*Funk Lore: New Poems, 1984-1995,* Sun & Moon Press, 1996.

*ESSAYS*

*Cuba Libre,* Fair Play for Cuba Committee (New York City), 1961.
*Blues People: Negro Music in White America,* Morrow, 1963, reprinted, Greenwood Press, 1980, published in England as *Negro Music in White America,* MacGibbon & Kee, 1965.
*Home: Social Essays* (contains "Cuba Libre," "The Myth of a 'Negro Literature,'" "Expressive Language," "the legacy of malcolm x, and the coming of the black nation," and "state/meant"), Morrow, 1966, Ecco Press (Hopewell, NJ), 1998.
*Black Music,* Morrow, 1968, reprinted, Greenwood Press, 1980.
*Raise, Race, Rays, Raze: Essays since 1965,* Random House, 1971.
*Strategy and Tactics of a Pan-African Nationalist Party,* Jihad, 1971.
*Kawaida Studies: The New Nationalism,* Third World Press, 1972.
*Crisis in Boston!,* Vita Wa Watu People's War, 1974.
*Daggers and Javelins: Essays, 1974-1979,* Morrow, 1984.
(With wife, Amina Baraka) *The Music: Reflections on Jazz and Blues,* Morrow, 1987.

Also contributor of essays to Lorraine Hansberry, *A Raisin in the Sun; and, The Sign in Sidney Brustein's Window,* Vintage Books (New York City), 1995.

*EDITOR*

*January 1st 1959: Fidel Castro,* Totem, 1959.
*Four Young Lady Poets,* Corinth, 1962.
(And author of introduction) *The Moderns: An Anthology of New Writing in America,* 1963, published as *The Moderns: New Fiction in America,* 1964.
(And co-author) *In-formation,* Totem, 1965.
Gilbert Sorrentino, *Black & White,* Corinth, 1965.
Edward Dorn, *Hands Up!,* Corinth, 1965.
(And contributor) *Afro-American Festival of the Arts Magazine,* Jihad, 1966, published as *Anthology of Our Black Selves,* 1969.
(With Larry Neal and A. B. Spellman) *The Cricket: Black Music in Evolution,* Jihad, 1968, published as *Trippin': A Need for Change,* New Ark, 1969.
(And contributor, with Larry Neal) *Black Fire: An Anthology of Afro-American Writing,* Morrow, 1968.
*A Black Value System,* Jihad, 1970.
(With Billy Abernathy under pseudonym Fundi) *In Our Terribleness (Some Elements of Meaning in Black Style),* Bobbs-Merrill, 1970.
(And author of introduction) *African Congress: A Documentary of the First Modern Pan-African Congress,* Morrow, 1972.
(With Diane Di Prima) *The Floating Bear, A Newsletter, No.1-37, 1961-1969,* McGilvery, 1974.

(With Amina Baraka) *Confirmation: An Anthology of African-American Women,* Morrow, 1983.

*OTHER*

(Contributor) Herbert Hill, editor, *Soon, One Morning,* Knopf, 1963.
*The System of Dante's Hell* (novel; includes the play *Dante*), Grove, 1965.
(Author of introduction) David Henderson, *Felix of the Silent Forest,* Poets Press, 1967.
*Striptease,* Parallax, 1967.
*Tales* (short stories), Grove, 1967.
(Author of preface) *Black Boogaloo (Notes on Black Liberation),* Journal of Black Poetry Press, 1969.
*Focus on Amiri Baraka: Playwright LeRoi Jones Analyzes the 1st National Black Political Convention* (sound recording), Center for Cassette Studies, 1973.
*Three Books by Imamu Amiri Baraka (LeRoi Jones),* (contains *The System of Dante's Hell, Tales,* and *The Dead Lecturer* ), Grove, 1975.
*The Autobiography of LeRoi Jones/Amiri Baraka,* Freundlich, 1984, Lawrence Hill Books (Chicago), 1997.
(Author of introduction) Martin Espada, *Rebellion is the Circle of a Lover's Hand,* Curbstone Press, 1990.
(Author of introduction) Eliot Katz, *Space, and Other Poems,* Northern Lights, 1990.
*LeRoi Jones/Amiri Baraka Reader,* Thunder's Mouth Press, 1991.
*Thornton Dial: Images of the Tiger,* Harry N. Abrams, 1993.
*Jesse Jackson and Black People,* Third World Press, 1994.
*Shy's Wise, Y's: The Griot's Tale,* Third World Press, 1994.
(With Charlie Reilly) *Conversations with Amiri Baraka* (also see below), University Press of Mississippi (Jackson), 1994.
*Eulogies,* Marsilio Publishers (New York City), 1996.

Works represented in more than seventy-five anthologies, including *A Broadside Treasury, For Malcolm, The New Black Poetry, Nommo,* and *The Trembling Lamb.* Contributor to *Evergreen Review, Poetry, Downbeat, Metronome, Nation, Negro Digest, Saturday Review,* and other periodicals. Editor with Diane Di Prima, *The Floating Bear,* 1961-63.

Baraka's works have been translated into Japanese, Norwegian, Italian, German, French, and Spanish.

*SIDELIGHTS:* Amiri Baraka (known as LeRoi Jones until 1967) is a major author whose strident social criticism and incendiary style have made it difficult for audiences and critics to respond with objectivity to his works. His art stems from his African-American heritage. His method in poetry, drama, fiction and essays is confrontational, calculated to shock and awaken audiences to the political concerns of black Americans. Baraka's own political stance has changed several times, each time finding expression in his plays, poems, and essays so that his works can be divided into periods; a member of the avant garde during the 1950s, Baraka became a black nationalist, and later a Marxist with socialist ideals. Critical opinion has been sharply divided between those who feel, with *Dissent* contributor Stanley Kaufman, that Baraka's race and political moment account for his fame, and those who feel that Baraka stands among the most important writers of the age. In *American Book Review,* Arnold Rampersad counts Baraka with Phyllis Wheatley, Frederick Douglass, Paul Laurence Dunbar, Langston Hughes, Zora Neale Hurston, Richard Wright, and Ralph Ellison "as one of the eight figures . . . who have significantly affected the course of African-American literary culture."

Baraka did not always identify with radical politics, nor did he always train his writing to be their tool. He was born in Newark, New Jersey, and enjoyed a middle-class education. During the 1950s he attended Rutgers University and Howard University. Then he spent two years in the Air Force, stationed for most of that time in Puerto Rico. When he returned to New York City, he attended Columbia University and the New School of Social Research. He lived in Greenwich Village's lower east side where his friends were the Beat poets Allen Ginsberg, Frank O'Hara, and Gilbert Sorrentino. The white avant garde—primarily Ginsberg, O'Hara, and leader of the Black Mountain poets Charles Olson—and Baraka believed that writing poetry is a process of discovery rather than an exercise in fulfilling traditional expectations of what poems should be. Baraka, like the projectivist poets, believed that a poem's form should follow the shape determined by the poet's own breath and intensity of feeling. In 1958 Baraka founded *Yugen* magazine and Totem Press, important forums for new verse. His first play, *A Good Girl Is Hard to Find,* was produced at Sterington House in Montclair, New Jersey, that same year.

*Preface to a Twenty Volume Suicide Note,* Baraka's first published collection of poems, appeared in 1961. M. L. Rosenthal writes in *The New Poets: American and British Poetry* that these poems show Baraka's "natural gift for quick, vivid imagery and spontaneous humor." The reviewer also praised the "sardonic or sensuous or slangily knowledgeable passages" that fill the early poems. While the cadence of blues and many allusions to black culture are found in the poems, the subject of blackness does not predominate. Throughout, rather, the poet shows his integrated, Bohemian social roots. For example, the poem "Notes for a Speech" states, "African blues / does not know me . . . Does / not feel / what I am," and the book's last line is "You are / as any other sad man here / american."

With the rise of the civil rights movement, however, Baraka's works took on a more militant tone, and he began a reluctant separation from his Bohemian beginnings. His trip to Castro's Cuba in July of 1959 marked an important turning point in his life. His view of his role as a writer, the purpose of art, and the degree to which ethnic awareness deserved to be his subject changed dramatically. In Cuba he met writers and artists from Third World countries whose political concerns included the fight against poverty, famine, and oppressive governments. They felt he was merely being self-indulgent, "cultivating his soul" in poetry while there were social problems to solve in America. In *Home: Social Essays,* Baraka explains how he tried to defend himself against these accusations, and was further challenged by Jaime Shelley, a Mexican poet, who had said, "'In that ugliness you live in, you want to cultivate your soul? Well, we've got millions of starving people to feed, and that moves me enough to make poems out of.'" Soon Baraka began to identify with Third World writers and to write poems and plays that had strong ethnic and political messages.

*Dutchman,* a play of entrapment in which a white woman and a middle-class black man both express their murderous hatred on a subway, was first performed Off-Broadway in New York City in 1964. The one-act play makes many references to sex and violence and ends in the black man's murder. While other dramatists of the time were using the techniques of naturalism, Baraka used symbolism and other experimental techniques to enhance the play's emotional impact. Lula, the white woman, represents the white state, and Clay, the black man in the play, represents ethnic identity and non-white manhood. Lula kills Clay after taunting him with sexual invitations and insults such as "You ain't no nigger, you're just a dirty white man. Get up, Clay. Dance with me, Clay." The play established Baraka's reputation as a playwright and has been often anthologized and performed. Considered by many to be the best play of the year, it won the *Village Voice* Obie Award in 1964. Later, Anthony Harvey adapted it for a film made in Britain, and in the 1990s it was revived for several productions in New York City. Darryl Pinckney comments in the *New York Times Book Review* that *Dutchman* has survived the test of time better than other protest plays of the 1960s due to its economic use of vivid language, its surprise ending, and its quick pacing.

The plays and poems following *Dutchman* expressed Baraka's increasing disappointment with white America and his growing need to separate from it. Baraka wrote in *Cuba Libre* that the Beat generation had become a counterculture of drop-outs, which did not amount to very meaningful politics. Baraka felt there had to be a more effective alternative to disengagement from the political, legal, and moral morass that the country had become. In *The Dead Lecturer,* Baraka explored the alternatives, finding that there is no room for compromise: if he identifies with an ethnic cause, he can find hope of meaningful action and change; but if he remains in his comfortable assimilated position, writing "quiet" poems, he will remain "a dead lecturer." The voice in these poems is more sure of itself, led by a "moral earnestness" that is wedded to action, Baraka wrote in a 1961 letter to Edward Dorn. Critics observed that as the poems became more politically intense, they left behind some of the flawless technique of the earlier poems. *Nation* review contributor Richard Howard comments, "These are the agonized poems of a man writing to save his skin, or at least to settle in it, and so urgent is their purpose that not one of them can trouble to be perfect."

To make a clean break with the Beat influence, Baraka turned to writing fiction in the mid-1960s. He wrote *The System of Dante's Hell,* a novel, and *Tales,* a collection of short stories. The novel echoes the themes and structures found in earlier poems and plays. The stories, like the poems in *Black Magic,* also published in 1967, are "'fugitive narratives' that describe the harried flight of an intensely self-conscious Afro-American artist / intellectual from neo-slavery of blinding, neutralizing whiteness, where the area of struggle is basically within the mind," Robert Eliot Fox writes in *Conscientious Sorcerers: The Black Post-Modernist Fiction of LeRoi Jones/Baraka, Ishmael Reed, and Samuel R. Delany.* The role of violent action in achieving political change is more prominent in these stories. Unlike Shakespeare's

Hamlet, who deliberates at length before taking violent action, during this period Baraka sought to stand with "the straight ahead people, who think when that's called for, who don't when they don't have to," he wrote in *Tales*. The role of music in black life is seen more often in these books, also. In the story "Screamers," the screams from a jazz saxophone galvanize the people into a powerful uprising.

Baraka's classic history *Blues People: Negro Music in White America,* published in 1963, traces black music from slavery to contemporary jazz. The blues, a staple of black American music, grew out of the encounter between African and American cultures in the South to become an art form uniquely connected to both the African past and the American soil. Finding indigenous black art forms was important to Baraka at this time, for he was searching for a more authentic ethnic voice for his own poetry. In this important study, Baraka became known as an articulate jazz critic and a perceptive observer of social change. As Clyde Taylor states in *Amiri Baraka: The Kaleidoscopic Torch* edited by James B. Gwynne, "The connection he nailed down between the many faces of black music, the sociological sets that nurtured them, and their symbolic evolutions through socio-economic changes, in *Blues People,* is his most durable conception, as well as probably the one most indispensable thing said about black music."

Baraka will also be long remembered for his other important studies, *Black Music,* which expresses black nationalist ideals, and *The Music: Reflections on Jazz and Blues,* which expresses his Marxist views. In *Black Music,* John Coltrane emerges as the patron saint of the black arts movement, for replacing "weak Western forms" of music with more fluid forms learned from a global vision of black culture. Though some critics feel that Baraka's essay writing is not all of the same quality, Lloyd W. Brown comments in *Amiri Baraka* that his essays on music are flawless: "As historian, musicological analyst, or as a journalist covering a particular performance Baraka always commands attention because of his obvious knowledge of the subject and because of a style that is engaging and persuasive even when the sentiments are questionable and controversial."

After Black Muslim leader Malcolm X was killed in 1965, Baraka moved to Harlem and became a black nationalist. He founded the Black Arts Repertory Theatre/School in Harlem and published the collection *Black Magic.* Poems in *Black Magic* chronicle Baraka's divorce from white culture and values and display his mastery of poetic techniques. In *Amiri Baraka: The Kaleidoscopic Torch,* Taylor observes, "There are enough brilliant poems of such variety in *Black Magic* and *In Our Terribleness* to establish the unique identity and claim for respect of several poets. But it is beside the point that Baraka is probably the finest poet, black or white, writing in this country these days." There was no doubt that Baraka's political concerns superseded his just claims to literary excellence, and the challenge to critics was to respond to the political content of the works. Some critics who felt the best art must be apolitical, dismissed his new work as "a loss to literature." Kenneth Rexroth writes in *With Eye and Ear,* "In recent years [Baraka] has succumbed to the temptation to become a professional Race Man of the most irresponsible sort. . . . His loss to literature is more serious than any literary casualty of the Second War." In 1966 he moved back to Newark, New Jersey, and a year later changed his name to the Bantuized Muslim appellation Imamu ("spiritual leader," later dropped) Ameer (later Amiri, "blessed") Baraka ("prince").

A new aesthetic for black art was being developed in Harlem and Baraka was its primary theorist. Black American artists should follow "black," not "white" standards of beauty and value, he maintained, and should stop looking to white culture for validation. The black artist's role, he wrote in *Home: Social Essays,* was to "aid in the destruction of America as he knows it." Foremost in this endeavor was the imperative to portray society and its ills faithfully so that the portrayal would move people to take necessary corrective action.

By the early 1970s Baraka was recognized as "a teacher of great talent" by Broadside Press publisher Dudley Randall and many others. Randall notes in *Black World* that younger black poets Nikki Giovanni and Don. L. Lee (now Haki R. Madhubuti) were "learning from LeRoi Jones, a man versed in German philosophy, conscious of literary tradition . . . who uses the structure of Dante's *Divine Comedy* in his *System of Dante's Hell* and the punctuation, spelling and line divisions of sophisticated contemporary poets." More importantly, Rampersad writes in the *American Book Review,* "More than any other black poet, however, he taught younger black poets of the generation past how to respond poetically to their lived experience, rather than to depend as artists on embalmed reputations and outmoded rhetorical strategies derived from a culture often substantially different from their own."

After coming to see black nationalism as a destructive form of racism, Baraka denounced it in 1974 and became a Third World Socialist. Hatred of non-whites, he declared in the *New York Times,* "is sickness or criminality, in fact, a form of fascism." Since 1974 he has produced a number of Marxist poetry collections and plays. His new political goal is the formation of socialist communities and a socialist state. *Daggers and Javelins* and the other books produced during this period lack the emotional power of the works from the black nationalist period, say the American critics. However, critics who agree with his new politics such as exiled Filipino leftist intellectual E. San Juan praise his work of the late 1970s. San Juan writes in *Amiri Baraka: The Kaleidoscopic Torch* that Baraka's 1978 play *Lone Ranger* was "the most significant theatrical achievement of 1978 in the Western hemisphere." Joe Weixlmann responds in the same source to the tendency to categorize the radical Baraka instead of analyze him: "At the very least, dismissing someone with a label does not make for very satisfactory scholarship. Initially, Baraka's reputation as a writer and thinker derived from a recognition of the talents with which he is so obviously endowed. The assaults on that reputation have, too frequently, derived from concerns which should be extrinsic to informed criticism."

In recent years, recognition of Baraka's impact on contemporary American culture has taken the form of two anthologies of his literary oeuvre. In 1991 *The LeRoi Jones/Amiri Baraka Reader* presented a thorough overview of the writer's development, covering the period from 1957 to 1983. The volume presents Baraka's work from four different periods and emphasizes lesser-known works rather than the author's most-famous writings. Although criticizing the anthology for offering little in the way of original poetry, *Sulfur* reviewer Andrew Schelling terms the collection "a sweeping account of Baraka's development." A *Choice* contributor also praises the volume, calling it "a landmark volume in African American literature." *Transbluency: The Selected Poems of Amiri Baraka/ LeRoi Jones (1961-1995),* published in 1995, is hailed by Daniel L. Guillory in *Library Journal* as "critically important." And Donna Seaman, writing in *Booklist,* commends the "lyric boldness of this passionate collection."

Baraka's standing as a major poet is matched by his importance as a cultural and political leader. His influence on younger writers has been so significant and widespread that it would be difficult to discuss American literary history without mentioning his name. As leader of the Black Arts movement of the 1960s, Baraka did much to define and support black literature's mission into the twenty-first century. His experimental fiction of the 1960s is yet considered some of the most significant contribution to black fiction since that of Jean Toomer, who wrote during the Harlem Renaissance of the 1920s. Writers from other ethnic groups credit Baraka with opening "tightly guarded doors" in the white publishing establishment, notes Native American author Maurice Kenney in *Amiri Baraka: The Kaleidoscopic Torch.* Kenny adds, "We'd all still be waiting the invitation from the *New Yorker* without him. He taught us how to claim it and take it."

*BIOGRAPHICAL/CRITICAL SOURCES:*

*BOOKS*

Allen, Donald M., and Warren Tallman, editors, *Poetics of the New American Poetry,* Grove, 1973.

Baraka, Amiri, *Tales,* Grove, 1967.

Baraka, and Larry Neal, editors, *Black Fire: An Anthology of Afro-American Writing,* Morrow, 1968.

Baraka, *Black Magic: Sabotage; Target Study; Black Art; Collected Poetry, 1961-1967,* Bobbs-Merrill, 1969.

Baraka, *The Autobiography of LeRoi Jones/Amiri Baraka,* Freundlich Books, 1984.

Baraka and Charlie Reilly, *Conversations with Amiri Baraka,* University Press of Mississippi (Jackson), 1994.

Benston, Kimberly A., editor, *Baraka: The Renegade and the Mask,* Yale University Press, 1976.

Benston, *Imamu Amiri Baraka (LeRoi Jones): A Collection of Critical Essays,* Prentice-Hall, 1978.

Bigsby, C. W. E., *Confrontation and Commitment: A Study of Contemporary American Drama, 1959-1966,* University of Missouri Press, 1968.

Bigsby, editor, *The Black American Writer, Volume II: Poetry and Drama,* Everett/Edwards, 1970, Penguin, 1971.

Bigsby, *The Second Black Renaissance: Essays in Black Literature,* Greenwood Press, 1980.

Birnebaum, William M., *Something for Everybody Is Not Enough,* Random House, 1972.

*Black Literature Criticism,* Gale, 1991.

Brown, Lloyd W., *Amiri Baraka,* Twayne, 1980.

*Concise Dictionary of American Literary Biography,* Volume 1: *The New Consciousness,* Gale, 1987.

*Contemporary Literary Criticism,* Gale, Volume 1, 1973, Volume 2, 1974, Volume 3, 1975, Volume

5, 1976, Volume 10, 1979, Volume 14, 1980, Volume 33, 1985.

Cook, Bruce, *The Beat Generation,* Scribner, 1971.

Dace, Letitia, *LeRoi Jones (Imamu Amiri Baraka): A Checklist of Works by and about Him,* Nether Press, 1971.

Dace, and Wallace Dace, *The Theatre Student: Modern Theatre and Drama,* Richards Rosen Press, 1973.

Debusscher, Gilbert, and Henry I. Schvey, editors, *New Essays on American Drama,* Rodopi, 1989.

*Dictionary of Literary Biography,* Gale, Volume 5: *American Poets since World War II,* 1980, Volume 7: *Twentieth Century American Dramatists,* 1981, Volume 16: *The Beats; Literary Bohemians in Postwar America,* 1983, Volume 38: *Afro-American Writers after 1955: Dramatists and Prose Writers,* 1985.

Dukore, Bernard F., *Drama and Revolution,* Holt, 1971.

Elam, Harry Justin, *Taking It to the Streets: The Social Protest Theater of Luis Valdez and Amiri Baraka,* University of Michigan Press (Ann Arbor), 1997.

Ellison, Ralph, *Shadow and Act,* New American Library, 1966.

Emanuel, James A., and Theodore L. Gross, editors, *Dark Symphony: Negro Literature in America,* Free Press, 1968.

Fox, Robert Elliot, *Conscientious Sorcerers: The Black Post-modernist Fiction of LeRoi Jones/Baraka, Ishmael Reed and Samuel R. Delany,* Greenwood Press, 1987.

Frost, David, *The Americans,* Stein & Day, 1970.

Gayle, Addison, editor, *Black Expression: Essays by and about Black Americans in the Creative Arts,* Weybright & Talley, 1969.

Gayle, *The Way of the New World: The Black Novel in America,* Anchor/Doubleday, 1975.

Gwynne, James B., editor, *Amiri Baraka: The Kaleidoscopic Torch,* Steppingstones Press, 1985.

Hall, Veronica, *Chicorel Theater Index to Plays in Anthologies, Periodicals, Discs and Tapes,* Chicorel Library Publishing, 1970.

Harris, William J., *The Poetry and Poetics of Amiri Baraka: The Jazz Aesthetic,* University of Missouri Press, 1985.

Haskins, James, *Black Theater in America,* Crowell, 1982.

Hatch, James V., *Black Image on the American Stage: A Bibliography of Plays and Musicals, 1770-1970,* Drama Book Specialists, 1970.

Hatch, editor, *Black Theatre,* U.S.A., Free Press, 1974.

Henderson, Stephen E., *Understanding the New Black Poetry: Black Speech and Black Music as Poetic References,* Morrow, 1973.

Hill, Herbert, *Soon, One Morning,* Knopf, 1963.

Hill, editor, *Anger, and Beyond: The Negro Writer in the United States,* Harper, 1966.

Hudson, Theodore, *From LeRoi Jones to Amiri Bar-aka: The Literary Works,* Duke University Press, 1973.

Inge, M. Thomas, Maurice Duke, and Jackson R. Bryer, editors, *Black American Writers: Bibliographic Essays; Richard Wright, Ralph Ellison, James Baldwin, and Amiri Baraka,* St. Martin's, 1978.

*International Authors and Writers Who's Who, 1991-1992,* International Biographical Centre, 1991.

Jones, LeRoi, *Preface to a Twenty Volume Suicide Note,* Totem Press/Corinth Books, 1961.

Jones, *Blues People: Negro Music in White America,* Morrow, 1963.

Jones, *The Dead Lecturer,* Grove, 1964.

Jones, *Home: Social Essays,* Morrow, 1966.

Keil, Charles, *Urban Blues,* University of Chicago Press, 1966.

King, Woodie, and Ron Milner, editors, *Black Drama Anthology,* New American Library, 1971.

Knight, Arthur and Kit Knight, editors, *The Beat Vision,* Paragon House, 1987.

Kofsky, Frank, *Black Nationalism and the Revolution in Music,* Pathfinder, 1970.

Lacey, Henry C., *To Raise, Destroy, and Create: The Poetry, Drama, and Fiction of Imamu Amiri Baraka (LeRoi Jones),* The Whitson Publishing Company, 1981.

Lewis, Allan, *American Plays and Playwrights,* Crown, 1965.

Littlejohn, David, *Black on White: A Critical Survey of Writing by American Negroes,* Viking, 1966.

O'Brien, John, *Interviews with Black Writers,* Liveright, 1973.

Olaniyan, Tejumola, *Scars of Conquest/Masks of Resistance: The Invention of Cultural Identities in African, African-American, and Caribbean Drama,* Oxford University Press (New York City), 1995.

Ossman, David, *The Sullen Art: Interviews with Modern American Poets,* Corinth, 1963.

Rexroth, Kenneth, *With Eye and Ear,* Herder and Herder, 1970.

Rosenthal, M. L., *The New Poets: American and British Poetry since World War II,* Oxford University Press, 1967.

Sollors, Werner, *Amiri Baraka/LeRoi Jones: The Quest for a "Populist Modernism,"* Columbia University Press, 1978.

Stepanchev, Stephen, *American Poetry since 1945,* Harper, 1965.
Weales, Gerald, *The Jumping-Off Place: American Drama in the 1960s,* Macmillan, 1969.
Whitlow, Roger, *Black American Literature: A Critical History,* Nelson Hall, 1973.
*Who's Who in America, 1992,* Marquis, 1992.
Williams, Martin, *The Jazz Tradition,* New American Library, 1971.
Williams, Sherley Anne, *Give Birth to Brightness: A Thematic Study in Neo-Black Literature,* Dial, 1972.

*PERIODICALS*

*American Book Review,* February, 1980; May-June, 1985.
*Atlantic,* January, 1966; May, 1966.
*Avant Garde,* September, 1968.
*Black American Literature Forum,* spring, 1980; spring, 1981; fall, 1982; spring, 1983; winter, 1985.
*Black World,* Volume 29, number 6, April, 1971; December, 1971; November, 1974; July, 1975.
*Booklist,* January 1, 1994, p. 799; February 15, 1994, p. 1052; October 15, 1995, p. 380.
*Book Week,* December 24, 1967.
*Book World,* October 28, 1979.
*Boundary 2,* number 6, 1978.
*Chicago Defender,* January 11, 1965.
*Chicago Tribune,* October 4, 1968.
*Commentary,* February, 1965.
*Contemporary Literature,* Volume 12, 1971.
*Detroit Free Press,* January 31, 1965.
*Detroit News,* January 15, 1984; August 12, 1984.
*Dissent,* spring, 1965.
*Ebony,* August, 1967; August, 1969; February, 1971.
*Educational Theatre Journal,* March, 1968; March, 1970; March, 1976.
*Esquire,* June, 1966.
*Essence,* September, 1970; May, 1984; September, 1984; May, 1985.
*Jazz Review,* June, 1959.
*Journal of Black Poetry,* fall, 1968; spring, 1969; summer, 1969; fall, 1969.
*Library Journal,* January, 1994, p. 112; November, 1995, pp. 78-9.
*Los Angeles Free Press,* Volume 5, number 18, May 3, 1968.
*Los Angeles Times,* April 20, 1990.
*Los Angeles Times Book Review,* May 15, 1983; March 29, 1987.
*Nation,* October 14, 1961; November 14, 1961; March 13, 1964; April 13, 1964; January 4, 1965; March 15, 1965; January 22, 1968; February 2, 1970.
*Negro American Literature Forum,* March, 1966; winter, 1973.
*Negro Digest,* December, 1963; February, 1964; Volume 13, number 19, August, 1964; March, 1965; April, 1965; March, 1966; April, 1966; June, 1966; April, 1967; April, 1968; January, 1969; April, 1969.
*Newsweek,* March 13, 1964; April 13, 1964; November 22, 1965; May 2, 1966; March 6, 1967; December 4, 1967; December 1, 1969; February 19, 1973.
*New York,* November 5, 1979.
*New Yorker,* April 4, 1964; December 26, 1964; March 4, 1967; December 30, 1972.
*New York Herald Tribune,* March 25, 1964; April 2, 1964; December 13, 1964; October 27, 1965.
*New York Post,* March 16, 1964; March 24, 1964; January 15, 1965; March 18, 1965.
*New York Review of Books,* January 20, 1966; May 22, 1964; July 2, 1970; October 17, 1974; June 11, 1984; June 14, 1984.
*New York Times,* April 28, 1966; May 8, 1966; August 10, 1966; September 14, 1966; October 5, 1966; January 20, 1967; February 28, 1967; July 15, 1967; January 5, 1968; January 6, 1968; January 9, 1968; January 10, 1968; February 7, 1968; April 14, 1968; August 16, 1968; November 27, 1968; December 24, 1968; August 26, 1969; November 23, 1969; February 6, 1970; May 11, 1972; June 11, 1972; November 11, 1972; November 14, 1972; November 23, 1972; December 5, 1972; December 27, 1974; December 29, 1974; November 19, 1979; October 15, 1981; January 23, 1984; February 9, 1991.
*New York Times Book Review,* January 31, 1965; November 28, 1965; May 8, 1966; February 4, 1968; March 17, 1968; February 14, 1971; June 6, 1971; June 27, 1971; December 5, 1971; March 12, 1972; December 16, 1979; March 11, 1984; July 5, 1987; December 20, 1987.
*New York Times Magazine,* February 5, 1984.
*Salmagundi,* spring-summer, 1973.
*Saturday Review,* April 20, 1963; January 11, 1964; January 9, 1965; December 11, 1965; December 9, 1967; October 2, 1971; July 12, 1975.
*Studies in Black Literature,* spring, 1970; Volume 1, number 2, 1970; Volume 3, number 2, 1972; Volume 3, number 3, 1972; Volume 4, number 1, 1973.
*Sulfur,* spring, 1992.
*Sunday News* (New York), January 21, 1973.

*Time,* December 25, 1964; November 19, 1965; May 6, 1966; January 12, 1968; April 26, 1968; June 28, 1968; June 28, 1971.
*Times Literary Supplement,* November 25, 1965; September 1, 1966; September 11, 1969; October 9, 1969; August 2, 1991.
*Tribune Books,* March 29, 1987.
*Village Voice,* December 17, 1964; May 6, 1965; May 19, 1965; August 30, 1976; August 1, 1977; December 17-23, 1980; October 2, 1984.
*Washington Post,* August 15, 1968; September 12, 1968; November 27, 1968; December 5, 1980; January 23, 1981; June 29, 1987.
*Washington Post Book World,* December 24, 1967; May 22, 1983.

* * *

**BARBETTE, Jay**
**See SPICER, Bart**

* * *

**BAUSCH, Richard (Carl) 1945-**

*PERSONAL:* Born April 18, 1945, in Fort Benning, GA; son of Robert Carl and Helen (Simmons) Bausch; married Karen Miller (a photographer), May 3, 1969; children: Wesley, Emily, Paul, Maggie, Amanda. *Education:* George Mason University, B.A., 1974; University of Iowa, M.F.A., 1975; also attended Northern Virginia Community College. *Politics:* Democrat. *Religion:* Roman Catholic. *Avocational interests:* Singing and songwriting.

*ADDRESSES: Home*—Fairfax, VA. *Office*—Department of English, George Mason University, 4400 University Dr., Fairfax, VA 22030-4443. *Agent*—Harriet Wasserman, Russell & Volkening, Inc., 551 Fifth Ave., New York, NY 10017.

*CAREER:* Worked as singer-songwriter and comedian. George Mason University, Fairfax, VA, professor of English and Heritage chair of creative writing, 1980—. Visiting professor at University of Virginia—Charlottesville, 1985, 1988, and Wesleyan University, 1986, 1990, 1992, 1993. *Military service:* U.S. Air Force, survival instructor, 1966-69.

*MEMBER:* Associated Writing Programs.

*AWARDS, HONORS:* PEN/Faulkner Award nominations, 1982, for *Take Me Back,* and 1988, for *Spirits and Other Stories;* National Endowment for the Arts grant, 1982; Guggenheim fellowship, 1984; Lila Wallace Reader's Best Writer's Award, Lila Wallace Fund, 1992; AAAL Award in Literature, 1993.

*WRITINGS:*

*NOVELS*

*Real Presence,* Dial (New York City), 1980.
*Take Me Back,* Dial, 1981.
*The Last Good Time,* Dial, 1984.
*Mr. Field's Daughter,* Linden Press/Simon & Schuster (New York City), 1989.
*Violence,* Houghton Mifflin/Seymour Lawrence (Boston), 1992.
*Rebel Powers,* Houghton Mifflin/Seymour Lawrence, 1993.
*Good Evening Mr. and Mrs. America, and All the Ships at Sea,* HarperCollins (New York City), 1996.

*SHORT STORY COLLECTIONS*

*Spirits and Other Stories,* Linden Press/Simon & Schuster, 1987.
*The Fireman's Wife and Other Stories,* Linden Press, 1990.
*Rare & Endangered Species* (novella and stories), Houghton Mifflin/Seymour Lawrence, 1994.
*The Selected Stories of Richard Bausch,* Random House (New York City), 1996.

*OTHER*

Work represented in numerous anthologies and contributor to various periodicals, including *Ploughshares, Esquire, Atlantic,* and the *New Yorker.*

*SIDELIGHTS:* "My vital subjects are family, fear, love, and anything that is irrecoverable and *missed,*" Richard Bausch once told *CA,* "but I'll dispense with all of that for a good story. . . . I grew up listening to my father tell stories—he is a great story-teller, and all the Bauschs can do it." Bausch added that he has no literary creed: "My only criterion is that fiction make feeling, that it deepen feeling. If it doesn't do that it's not fiction." Bausch's works are true to his self-description: dealing with the ordinary tragedies of American family life in our time, they spring from feeling and, at their best, create it.

Bausch's first novel, *Real Presence,* examines the crisis of faith of an aging priest, Monsignor Vincent Shepherd. Bitter, withdrawn, recovering from a heart attack, Shepherd is assigned to a West Virginia parish whose beloved previous priest is a hard act to follow. He is shaken from his doldrums by the arrival of a down-and-out family, the Bexleys, which includes the terminally ill war veteran and ex-convict, Duck, and his wife, Elizabeth, who is pregnant with her sixth child. The Bexleys test Shepherd's ability to live up to his symbolic surname, and Elizabeth succeeds in reaching him. After Duck is killed, and while Elizabeth is in labor, Shepherd declares his desire to leave the priesthood and replace Duck as the surviving Bexleys' father figure. In an *America* review, Thomas M. Gannon criticized the novel's ending, saying, "The abrupt disregard for the emotional and physical limitations the author has previously imposed on this character is a serious defect in Bausch's otherwise careful effort." Scott Spencer, however, reviewing the novel for the *New York Times Book Review,* called the ending "moving and even satisfying" but also "a foregone conclusion." Other reviewers praised Bausch's first effort, including *Washington Post Book World*'s Doris Grumbach, who found *Real Presence* distinguished by "its distance from the customary first novel subjects." A *Critic* reviewer called it "excellently crafted," and the *Los Angeles Times Book Review*'s Dick Roraback found it an "exquisite, excruciating novel" and concluded, "Bausch has written a book that disturbs; sometimes it is good to be disturbed."

Bausch wrote his second novel, *Take Me Back,* in four months of fifteen-hour days. Set in a low-rent area of Virginia, the novel dissects the lives of Gordon Brinhart, an unsuccessful and hard-drinking insurance salesman, his wife Katherine, a former rock musician, and Katherine's illegitimate son Alex, as well as a neighboring family which includes Amy, a thirteen-year-old who is dying of leukemia. Gordon goes on a binge, loses his job, and sleeps with a seventeen-year-old neighbor; in response Katherine attempts suicide, and Alex witnesses it all. "Telling the story skillfully from the alternating points of view of the three members of the [Brinhart] family, Bausch has us suffer through the whole ordeal right along with them," wrote Bruce Cook in *Washington Post Book World.* Cook added, "*Take Me Back* isn't pretty. It is, however, as well written as any novel I have read in a while. . . . Richard Bausch has captured something essential in the quality of American life today in these pages." The *New York Times Book Review*'s Richard P. Brickner gave a nod to the novel's "uncanny skillfulness in dialogue and atmosphere" but objected to its "smallness of vision," finding in it "no evident conviction beyond the glum one that life stinks."

Bausch's third novel, *The Last Good Time,* was again the product of mere months of work. It is about two men, seventy-five-year-old Edward Cakes and eighty-nine-year-old Arthur Hagood, into whose lives the twenty-four-year-old Mary Virginia Bellini arrives by chance. Mary makes love to Edward in exchange for friendship and material support; meanwhile Arthur, bedridden in a hospital and learning of the events through Edward's visits, is jealous. On Mary's departure, Edward takes up with Ida Warren, the elderly woman upstairs whose phonograph records have been keeping him awake. "Bausch makes them all believable," wrote Art Seidenbaum in the *Los Angeles Times.* "These are little people at work here . . . what stamps them as human is the novelist's gift of character." In the *Washington Post Book World,* Stephen Dobyns had high praise for Bausch's style, and despite "shortcomings" of plot, structure, and character believability, called *The Last Good Time* "quite a good novel." *New York Times Book Review* critic Nancy Forbes called particular attention to the way Bausch's narrative relates the elderly's experience of time, and remarked that the book "has a way of being superlatively funny and disturbing by turns, but the experience that emerges most strongly is that of spending an interesting time getting to know the sort of people whose lives we take for granted."

While strengthening his reputation as a novelist, Bausch also wrote numerous short stories. His 1987 collection, *Spirits and Other Stories,* won considerable critical praise. Michael Dorris, in the *Washington Post Book World,* called Bausch "a master of the short story," while Madison Smartt Bell in the *New York Times Book Review* termed the book a "thoughtful, honest collection" and remarked upon the absence of "superfluous stylistic flash." Thomas Cahill, writing in *Commonweal,* praised the stories' narrative magnetism and the author's ability to imagine his characters in all their details, and asserted, "It is my deep, perverse suspicion that, when I am an old man . . . all of Bausch . . . will be in print, and names like Updike, Roth, Bellow will have faded from view."

In *Mr. Field's Daughter,* Bausch's next novel, James Field, a sixty-something widower and loan officer, leads a household that includes his widowed sister Ellen, his daughter Annie, and Annie's daughter

Linda. Linda's father, the cocaine-snorting Cole Gilbertson, soon arrives, wielding a .22 pistol. Opting for realistic drama rather than melodrama, Bausch fashioned from these familiar narrative ingredients and from the conventional thoughts of his characters a work that Jonathan Yardley of the *Washington Post Book World* called "exceptionally mature and satisfying" as well as "original and immensely affecting." "Strong characters sustain a family story line as a gifted novelist mines the universal in a pit of the mundane," summarized *Los Angeles Times Book Review*'s Seidenbaum. Gene Lyons, in the *New York Times Book Review,* called Bausch "an author of rare and penetrating gifts, working at the height of his powers."

Bausch published a second short story collection, *The Fireman's Wife,* in 1990. Bette Pesetsky noted in the *New York Times Book Review* that the stories "are all about relationships; they are all about redemption through understanding," and asserted, "We are fortunate to have [*The Fireman's Wife*] with which to explore and search for the meaning of how we live today." The *Los Angeles Times*'s Richard Eder found "Consolation," in which a young widow takes her baby to visit her dead husband's parents, the best story in *The Fireman's Wife,* "subtle and moving—with a fine comic turn by the widow's bossy and self-centered sister—even if the warmth at the end is a shade overinsistent."

*Violence,* Bausch's 1992 novel, continued the author's tradition of dealing realistically with the troubles of ordinary Americans. Charles Connally, in the grip of an emotional crisis, wanders into a Chicago convenience store where a robbery is taking place, saves the life of a woman, and is treated as a hero by the press. In the aftermath, he succumbs to depression, dropping out of college and questioning his marriage to dental hygienist Carol. "This is a sad and daring book," Carolyn See commented in the *Washington Post Book World.* The *New York Times Book Review*'s Susan Kenney called the novel "masterly" for Bausch's realistic exploration of "both the public and private manifestations of violence with persistence as well as sensitivity. And he does so with a redeeming grace of language and detail that goes beyond mere witnessing, straight to the heart."

Another novel, *Rebel Powers,* drew mixed comment from reviewers. *Tribune Books* contributor Joseph Coates started his assessment of the novel by calling Bausch "one of our most talented writers"; yet went on to say that this book "never engages its subject and amounts to one long denouement that fizzles out in anticlimax," because it is wholly concerned with a woman's refusal to face her emotions. That main character, Connie, defies her father by marrying Daniel Boudreaux, an Air Force daredevil who dreams of getting rich from Alaskan oil. His tour of duty in Vietnam robs him of the reckless bravery that attracted Connie to him, however, and their marriage deteriorates into violent fighting. Their son, Thomas, narrates the tale. Although Coates rated the book a failed effort, Elizabeth Tallent was much more positive in her assessment, writing in the *New York Times Book Review:* "As a narrator, Thomas is willing to qualify his perceptions, to admit incomprehension, to examine and even reverse his judgments. Indeed, the originality of Mr. Bausch's novel lies in its unapologetic devotion to the process of perception. Obsession usually censors the peripheral, but Thomas's intense concentration on the unraveling of his family is richly generous and accommodating. There are savage rages here, and great loss, but grievance, irritation, foolishness and the range of little daily miseries occupy psychic space in a way that is common in real life but rare in fiction."

In *Good Evening Mr. and Mrs. America, and All the Ships at Sea,* Bausch treats the details of daily life with his usual style and also explores the socio-political issues of the early 1960s. The story revolves around Walter, who is nineteen years old in 1964. Sweet, devoutly Catholic, and idealistic, Walter is devastated by the assassination of John F. Kennedy, participates in civil rights sit-ins, and generally has his consciousness raised throughout the course of the book. According to Sybil S. Steinberg of *Publishers Weekly,* "Bausch is a wily and subtle writer," and "Walter's slide from idealism to disillusionment is revealed through brilliant passages of mundane (but revealing) conversations, hilarious comic moments and characters' poignant attempts to communicate with one another." "Mr. Busch spins this intricate and delicious story with a wondrously tender touch," reported Richard Bernstein in the *New York Times.* "There is an intermingling of the comic and the dangerous in the qualities and foibles of his characters, well-formed, resistant to simplification, stubbornly individualistic. . . . Walter exists on that narrow patch of ground in American history between reverence and disillusionment." *Booklist* contributor Donna Seaman stated of *Good Evening Mr. & Mrs. America, and All the Ships at Sea:* "Bausch's brilliant dialogue, quicksilver comedy, and perception into the nature of innocence give this vivacious novel a George Cukor-like dazzle, and you can't get much better than that."

Seaman also applauded the collection *The Selected Stories of Richard Bausch,* declaring that in it, the "ever-inventive" author "presents fresh takes on his favorite theme, the failure to communicate. His complex and troubled characters talk at cross-purposes and misinterpret one another, often to rather painful or violent ends." *Dictionary of Literary Biography* contributor Paul R. Lilly, Jr., summarized Bausch's themes in this way: "Bausch's concerns are moral; his subject matter is the self in conflict with the need to discover or invent a better version of itself and a need to hold on to a haunted, often unhappy past. Bausch's stories probe this tension between self and selfishness in the form of tormented sons whose fathers have been alcoholic or violent, wives who repress their anger at husbands who fail to do the right thing, and daughters who are crippled by the memory of their parents' silent combats of will."

*BIOGRAPHICAL/CRITICAL SOURCES:*

*BOOKS*

*Contemporary Authors Autobiography Series,* Volume 14, Gale (Detroit), 1992.

*Contemporary Literary Criticism,* Volume 51, Gale, 1989.

*Dictionary of Literary Biography,* Volume 130: *American Short-Story Writers since World War II,* Gale, 1993.

*PERIODICALS*

*America,* August 23, 1980, pp. 77-78; May 14, 1994, p. 7.

*Atlanta Journal-Constitution,* May 9, 1993, p. N8; October 20, 1996, p. L10.

*Booklist,* August, 1994, p. 2020; August, 1996, p. 1880.

*Chicago Tribune,* February 21, 1995, section 5, p. 3.

*Commonweal,* October 9, 1987, pp. 568-69.

*Critic,* September, 1980, p. 8.

*Library Journal,* July, 1994, p. 131; August, 1996, p. 109.

*Los Angeles Times,* August 20, 1980; May 14, 1981; November 9, 1984; August 16, 1990; August 30, 1994, p. E5.

*Los Angeles Times Book Review,* August 20, 1980; July 12, 1987, p. 7; May 7, 1989; September 9, 1991; January 26, 1992; April 25, 1993, p. 3; November 12, 1995, p. 11.

*New York Times,* July 18, 1987; September 25, 1996, p. C15.

*New York Times Book Review,* September 7, 1980, pp. 13, 38; April 26, 1981, p. 14; December 23, 1984, p. 25; April 26, 1987, p. 16; June 14, 1987, p. 16; August 27, 1989, p. 14; August 19, 1990, p. 9; January 26, 1992, p. 7; May 16, 1993, p. 9; August 14, 1994, p. 6; October 27, 1996, p. 15.

*Publishers Weekly,* August 10, 1990, pp. 425-26; July 4, 1994, p. 52; July 15, 1996, pp. 52-53.

*Time,* September 22, 1980, p. E4.

*Tribune Books* (Chicago), July 29, 1990; April 11, 1993, p. 6.

*Washington Post,* March 26, 1982, pp. C1, C6; November 1, 1996, p. D2.

*Washington Post Book World,* June 15, 1980, p. 4; May 3, 1981, p. 5; December 11, 1984; June 28, 1987, p. 6; April 30, 1989, p. 3; August 21, 1990; December 29, 1991; April 11, 1993, p. 8; August 7, 1994, p. 7.*

* * *

**BEAUVOIR, Simone (Lucie Ernestine Marie Bertrand) 1908-1986**

*PERSONAL:* Born January 9, 1908, in Paris, France; died April 14, 1986, of a respiratory ailment in Paris, France; daughter of Georges Bertrand (an advocate to the Court of Appeal, Paris) and Francoise (Brasseur) de Beauvoir; children: (adopted) Sylvie Le Bon. *Education:* Sorbonne, University of Paris, licencie es lettres and agrege des lettres (philosophy), 1929. *Religion:* Atheist.

*CAREER:* Philosopher, novelist, autobiographer, nonfiction writer, essayist, editor, lecturer, and political activist. Instructor in philosophy at Lycee Montgrand, Marseilles, France, 1931-33, at Lycee Jeanne d'Arc, Rouen, France, 1933-37, at Lycee Moliere and Lycee Camille-See, both Paris, France, 1938-43. Founder and editor, with Jean-Paul Sartre, of *Les Temps modernes,* beginning 1945.

*MEMBER:* International War Crimes Tribunal, Ligue du Droit des Femmes (president), Choisir.

*AWARDS, HONORS:* Prix Goncourt, 1954, for *Les Mandarins;* Jerusalem Prize, 1975; Austrian State Prize, 1978; Sonning Prize for European Culture, 1983; LL.D. from Cambridge University.

*WRITINGS:*

*L'Invitee* (novel), Gallimard, 1943, reprinted, 1977, translation by Yvonne Moyse and Roger Senhouse published as *She Came to Stay,* Secker & Warburg, 1949, World Publishing, 1954, reprinted, Flamingo, 1984.

*Pyrrhus et Cineas* (philosophy; also see below), Gallimard, 1944.

*Les Bouches inutiles* (play in two acts; first performed in Paris), Gallimard, 1945, translation published as *Who Shall Die?,* River Press, 1983.

*Le Sang des autres* (novel), Gallimard, 1946, reprinted, 1982, translation by Moyse and Senhouse published as *The Blood of Others,* Knopf, 1948, reprinted, Pantheon, 1984.

*Tous les hommes sont mortel* (novel), Gallimard, 1946, reprinted, 1974, translation by Leonard M. Friedman published as *All Men Are Mortal,* World Publishing, 1955.

*Pour une morale de l'ambiguite* (philosophy; also see below), Gallimard, 1947, reprinted, 1963, translation by Bernard Frechtman published as *The Ethics of Ambiguity,* Philosophical Library, 1948, reprinted, Citadel, 1975.

*Pour une morale de l'ambiguite* [and] *Pyrrhus et Cineas,* Schoenhof's Foreign Books, 1948.

*L'Existentialisme et la sagesse des nations* (philosophy; title means "Existentialism and the Wisdom of the Ages"), Nagel, 1948.

*L'Amerique au jour le jour* (diary), P. Morihien, 1948, translation by Patrick Dudley published as *America Day by Day,* Duckworth, 1952, Grove, 1953.

*Le Deuxieme Sexe,* two volumes, Gallimard, 1949, translation by H. M. Parshley published as *The Second Sex,* Knopf, 1953, reprinted, Random House, 1974 (Volume 1 published in England as *A History of Sex,* New English Library, 1961, published as *Nature of the Second Sex,* 1963).

*The Marquis de Sade* (essay; translation of *Faut-il bruler Sade?*; also see below; originally published in *Les Temps modernes*), translation by Annette Michelson Grove, 1953 (published in England as *Must We Burn de Sade?,* Nevill, 1953, reprinted, New English Library, 1972).

*Les Mandarins* (novel), Gallimard, 1954, reprint published in two volumes, French and European, 1972, translation by Friedman published as *The Mandarins,* World Publishing, 1956, reprinted, Flamingo, 1984.

*Privileges* (essays; includes *Faut-il bruler Sade?*), Gallimard, 1955.

*La Longue Marche: Essai sur la Chine,* Gallimard, 1957, translation by Austryn Wainhouse published as *The Long March,* World Publishing, 1958.

*Memoires d'une jeune fille rangee* (autobiography), Gallimard, 1958, reprinted, 1972, translation by James Kirkup published as *Memoirs of a Dutiful Daughter,* World Publishing, 1959, reprinted, Penguin, 1984.

*Brigitte Bardot and the Lolita Syndrome,* translated by Frechtman, Reynal, 1960, published with foreword by George Amberg, Arno, 1972.

*La Force de l'age* (autobiography), Gallimard, 1960, reprinted, 1976, translation by Peter Green published as *The Prime of Life,* World Publishing, 1962.

(With Gisele Halimi) *Djamila Boupacha,* Gallimard, 1962, translation by Green published under same title, Macmillan, 1962.

*La Force des choses* (autobiography), Gallimard, 1963, reprinted, 1977, translation by Richard Howard published as *The Force of Circumstance,* Putnam, 1965.

*Une Mort tres douce* (autobiography), Gallimard, 1964, reprinted with English introduction and notes by Ray Davison, Methuen Educational, 1986, translation by Patrick O'Brian published as *A Very Easy Death,* Putnam, 1966, reprinted, Pantheon, 1985.

(Author of introduction) Charles Perrault, *Bluebeard and Other Fairy Tales of Charles Perrault,* Macmillan, 1964.

(Author of preface) Violette Leduc, *La Batarde,* Gallimard, 1964.

*Les Belles Images* (novel), Gallimard, 1966, translation by O'Brian published under same title, Putnam, 1968, reprinted with introduction and notes by Blandine Stefanson, Heinemann Educational, 1980.

(Author of preface) Jean-Francois Steiner, *Treblinka,* Simon & Schuster, 1967.

*La Femme rompue* (three novellas; includes *L'Age de discretion*), Gallimard, 1967, translation by O'Brian published as *The Woman Destroyed* (includes *Age of Discretion* and *Monologue*), Putnam, 1969, reprinted, Pantheon, 1987.

*La Vieillesse* (nonfiction), Gallimard, 1970, translation by O'Brian published as *The Coming of Age,* Putnam, 1972 (published in England as *Old Age,* Weidenfeld & Nicolson, 1972).

*Tout compte fait* (autobiography), Gallimard, 1972, translation by O'Brian published as *All Said and Done,* Putnam, 1974.

*Quand prime le spirituel* (short stories), Gallimard, 1979, translation by O'Brian published as *When Things of the Spirit Come First: Five Early Tales,* Pantheon, 1982.

*Le Ceremonie des adieux: Suivi de entretiens avec Jean-Paul Sartre* (reminiscences), Gallimard, 1981, translation published as *Adieux: A Farewell to Sartre,* Pantheon, 1984.

(Contributor with Jean-Paul Sartre; also editor) *Lettres au Castor et a quelques autres,* Gallimard, 1983, Volume 1: *1926-1939,* Volume 2: *1940-1963.*

*Lettres a Sartre,* French and European Publications, 1990, Volume 1: *1930-1939,* Volume 2: *1940-1963.*

*Journal de guerre, septembre 1939-janvier 1941,* Gallimard, 1990.

(Editor) *Witness to My Life: The Letters of Jean-Paul Sartre to Simone de Beauvoir,* translated by Norman MacAfee and Lee Fahnestock, Macmillan, 1992.

*ADAPTATIONS: The Mandarins* was adapted for film by Twentieth Century-Fox in 1969; *The Blood of Others* was adapted for film by Home Box Office starring Jodie Foster in 1984.

*SIDELIGHTS:* At Simone de Beauvoir's funeral on April 19, 1986, flowers from all over the world filled the corner of the Montparnasse cemetery where she was laid to rest next to Jean-Paul Sartre (1905-1980). Banners and cards from the American-based Simone de Beauvoir Society, women's studies groups, women's health centers and centers for battered women, diverse political organizations, and publishing houses attested to the number of lives that the author had touched during her seventy-eight years. Five thousand people, many of them recognizable figures from the political, literary, and film worlds, made their way along the boulevard du Montparnasse past her birthplace, past the cafes where she, Sartre, and their friends had discussed their ideas and written some of their manuscripts, to the cemetery.

Beauvoir was a perceptive witness to the twentieth century, a witness whose works span the period from her early childhood days before World War I to the world of the 1980s. Born in Paris in 1908, in the fourteenth "arrondissement" or district where she continued to live throughout most of her life, Beauvoir was raised by a devoutly Catholic mother from Verdun and an agnostic father, a lawyer who enjoyed participating in amateur theatrical productions. The contrast between the beliefs of the beautiful, timid, provincial Francoise de Beauvoir and those of the debonair Parisian Georges de Beauvoir led the young Simone to assess situations independently, unbiased by the solid parental front presented by the more traditional families of many of her classmates. As family finances dwindled during World War I, Beauvoir observed the uninspiring household chores that fell upon her mother and decided that she herself would never become either a homemaker or a mother. She had found such pleasure in teaching her younger sister Helene everything she herself was learning at school that she decided to pursue a teaching career when she grew up.

Beauvoir and her best friend Zaza "Mabille" (Beauvoir often assigned fictional names to friends and family members described in her autobiographical writings) sometimes discussed the relative merits of bringing nine children into the world, as Zaza's mother had done, and of creating books, an infinitely more worthwhile enterprise, the young Beauvoir believed. As the girls matured, Beauvoir observed the degree to which Zaza's mother used her daughter's affection and commitment to Christian obedience to manipulate Zaza's choice of career and mate. When Zaza, tormented by her parents' refusal to grant her permission to marry Maurice Merleau-Ponty, the "Jean Pradelle" of the memoirs, died at twenty-one, Beauvoir felt that her friend had been assassinated by bourgeois morality. Many of Beauvoir's early fictional writings attempted to deal on paper with the emotions stirred by her recollection of the "Mabille" family and of Zaza's death. Only many years later did she learn that Merleau-Ponty, who became a well-known philosopher and writer and remained a close friend of Beauvoir's and Sartre's, was unacceptable to the "Mabilles" because he was an illegitimate child.

Despite her warm memories of going to early morning mass as a little girl with her mother and of drinking hot chocolate on their return, Beauvoir gradually pulled away from the traditional values with which Francoise de Beauvoir hoped to imbue her. She and her sister began to rebel, for example, against the restrictions of the Cours Adeline Desir, the private Catholic school to which they were being sent. Weighing the pleasures of this world against the sacrifices entailed in a belief in an afterlife, the fifteen-year-old Beauvoir opted to concentrate on her life here on earth. Her loss of faith erected a serious barrier to communication with her mother.

Beauvoir was convinced during several years of her adolescence that she was in love with her cousin Jacques Champigneulles ("Jacques Laiguillon" in her memoirs), who introduced her to books by such French authors as Andre Gide, Alain-Fournier, Henry de Montherlant, Jean Cocteau, Paul Claudel, and Paul

Valery; these books scandalized Beauvoir's mother, who had carefully pinned together pages of volumes in their home library that she did not want her daughters to read. Jacques Champigneulles, however, seemed unwilling to make a commitment either to Beauvoir or to anything else, and the Beauvoir sisters were totally disillusioned when this bright bohemian opted to marry the wealthy and generously dowried sister of one of his friends.

Because family finances did not allow Georges de Beauvoir to provide dowries, his daughters became unlikely marriage prospects for young middle-class men, and both Simone and Helene were delighted to have this excuse for continuing their studies and pursuing careers. Even as a young girl, Beauvoir had a passion for capturing her life on paper. In the first volume of her autobiography, *Memoires d'une jeune fille rangee* (*Memoirs of a Dutiful Daughter*), she looked back with amusement at her determination, recorded in her adolescent diary, to "tell all"; yet her memoirs, her fiction, her essays, her interviews, and her prefaces do indeed record events, attitudes, customs, and ideas that help define approximately seven decades of the twentieth century.

It was through Rene Maheu, a Sorbonne classmate called "Andre Herbaud" in the memoirs, that Beauvoir first met Jean-Paul Sartre in a study group for which she was to review the works and ideas of German philosopher Gottfried Wilhelm von Leibniz. In Sartre, Beauvoir found the partner of whom she had dreamed as an adolescent. As she remarked in *Memoirs of a Dutiful Daughter,* "Sartre corresponded exactly to the ideal I had set for myself when I was fifteen: he was a soulmate in whom I found, heated to the point of incandescence, all of my passions. With him, I could always share everything." And so she did, for fifty-one years, from the time they became acquainted at the Sorbonne in 1929 until his death on April 15, 1980.

Together Sartre and Beauvoir analyzed their relationship, deciding that they enjoyed an indestructible essential love but that they must leave themselves open to "contingent loves" as well, to expand their range of experience. Although marriage would have enabled them to receive a double teaching assignment instead of being sent off to opposite ends of the country, they were intent upon escaping the obligations that such a "bourgeois" institution would entail. That neither had a particular desire for children was an added reason to avoid marriage. A daring and unconventional arrangement during the early 1930s, their relationship raised consternation in conservative members of Beauvoir's family.

Except for a brief period during World War II, Beauvoir and Sartre never lived together but spent their days writing in their separate quarters and then came together during the evenings to discuss their ideas and to read and criticize one another's manuscripts. As both became well-known figures in the literary world, they found it increasingly difficult to maintain their privacy; as *La Force des choses* (*The Force of Circumstance*) records, they had to alter their routine and avoid certain cafes during the years after the war in order to protect themselves from the prying eyes of the public.

Sartre's autobiography, *Les Mots* (*The Words*), published in 1963, dealt only with the early years of his life. Beauvoir's autobiographical writings provide a much more complete and intimate account of the adult Sartre. In several volumes of reminiscences, Beauvoir described their mutual reluctance to leave their youth behind and become part of the adult world, their struggles to set aside adequate time for writing, the acceptance of their works for publication, their travels, their friendships, their gradually increasing commitment to political involvement; her final autobiographical volume, *Le Ceremonie des adieux: Suivi de entretiens avec Jean-Paul Sartre* (*Adieux: A Farewell to Sartre*), recreates her anguish in witnessing the physical and mental decline of a lifelong companion who had been one of the most brilliant philosophers of the twentieth century.

For Beauvoir, writing was not only a way of preserving life on paper but also a form of catharsis, a means of working out her own problems through fiction. Her early short stories, written between 1935 and 1937 and originally rejected by two publishers, were brought out by Gallimard in 1979. The tales in *Quand prime le spirituel* (*When Things of the Spirit Come First: Five Early Tales*) captured Beauvoir's infatuation with Jacques, the tragedy of Zaza's death, the young philosophy teacher's ambivalence about the impact her ideas and her life-style might have on her impressionable lycee students in Marseille and Rouen, and her sense of excitement as she saw the world opening up before her. Beauvoir identified strongly with her central character Marguerite who, in the final paragraphs of the book, perceives the world as a shiny new penny ready for her to pick up and do with as she wishes. Terry Keefe's *Simone de Beauvoir: A Study of Her Writings* provides a detailed discussion of each of the five stories that make up this collection.

Experimenting with nontraditional relationships, Sartre and Beauvoir had formed a trio with Beauvoir's lycee student Olga Kosakiewicz in 1933. The anguish experienced by Beauvoir as a result of this intimate three-way sharing of lives led to the writing of her first published work, *L'Invitee* (*She Came to Stay*). In this novel, the author relived the hothouse atmosphere generated by the trio, and she chose to destroy the judgmental young intruder, the fictional Xaviere, on paper, but to dedicate her novel to Olga. The real life situation resolved itself less dramatically after Olga became interested in Jacques-Laurent Bost, a former student of Sartre's, and broke away from the trio; the four principals remained lifelong friends, however. In her 1986 study, *Simone de Beauvior,* Judith Okely suggests that *She Came to Stay* reflects not only the Beauvoir-Sartre-Olga trio but also the young Simone's rivalry with her mother for her father's affections.

With World War II Beauvoir's attention shifted from the concerns and crises of her personal life to a broader spectrum of philosophical, moral, and political issues. In the short essay "Pyrrhus et Cineas," written during a three-week period in 1943, she launched an inquiry into the value of human activity, examining questions of freedom, communication, and the role of the other in the light of the existentialist ideas presented in Sartre's *L'Etre et le neant: Essai d'ontologie phenomenologique* (*Being and Nothingness: Essay on Phenomenological Ontology*). In his 1975 monograph, *Simone de Beauvoir,* Robert Cottrell discusses *Pyrrhus et Cineas* as "a popularization of existentialist thought."

Beauvoir's second novel, *Le Sang des autres* (*The Blood of Others*), focused on the dilemma of dealing with the consequences of one's acts. The liberal Jean Blomart, shaken by the accidental death of a young friend he inspired to participate in a political demonstration, struggles throughout much of the narrative to avoid doing anything that may inadvertently harm another human being, his "search for a saintly purity," as Carol Ascher labels it in *Simone de Beauvoir: A Life of Freedom.* The female protagonist, Helene Bertrand, intent on protecting her own happiness in a world turned upside down by war and the German Occupation, is shaken out of her inertia by the cries of a Jewish mother whose small daughter is being wrenched away from her by the Gestapo. Helene seeks an active and ultimately fatal involvement in terrorist Resistance activities orchestrated by Jean Blomart, who has decided finally that violence is perhaps the only rational response to Hitler's insanity. Infused with the euphoria of Resistance camaraderie, the novel highlights a question that is also central to Sartre's play *Les Mains sales* (*Dirty Hands*)—the relationship between intellectuals and violence.

Moral and ethical issues continued to dominate Beauvoir's works in the 1940s. Caught up in the success of Sartre's play *Les Mouches* (*The Flies*) during the Occupation, she decided that she too would like to write for the theatre. *Les Bouches inutiles* (*Who Shall Die?*), based on a historical incident which took place in the fourteenth century, reprises the main theme of *The Blood of Others,* examining the consequences of a young man's determination to remain pure and blameless by not taking part in the decisions of the town council. The play also protests the assumption that able-bodied young men are the only truly useful citizens in a besieged community. Beauvoir frankly related in her memoirs dramatist Jean Genet's criticism of her theatrical sense, confessing that he sat beside her shaking his head disapprovingly throughout the entire opening night performance. She never again attempted to write for the theatre, although Keefe notes the dramatic potential of her plot and the "spare and sharp" quality of the dialogue in Act I.

One of the most difficult aspects of the war years for Beauvoir and her friends was the often senseless deaths of their contemporaries. In *Simone de Beauvoir: Encounters with Death,* Elaine Marks focuses on the preoccupation with death permeating the writer's works and on what Marks labels her evasions of confrontation with death. For Beauvoir, death was an outrage, a scandal, and in 1943, she began to write a third novel, *Tous les hommes sont mortel* (*All Men Are Mortal*), for which she created a hero who has become immortal and who therefore meanders from his thirteenth-century birthplace in Italy on through to the twentieth century. Because Raymond Fosca's alternating attempts to seize political power and to establish peace on earth all result in disappointment and frustration, the reader concludes that immortality would be a curse rather than a blessing, that life's value is derived from sharing experiences with one's contemporaries and from a willingness to take the risks implicit in human mortality. According to *The Force of Circumstance,* this novel was Beauvoir's attempt to deal with her own feelings and anxieties about death. Konrad Bieber, in his 1979 study *Simone de Beauvoir,* senses the presence of "the philosopher behind the novelist" throughout the book yet also notes "long moments of drama, of genuine poignancy, that bring to the fore all that is human."

As Beauvoir's works and Sartre's became better known, the label "existentialist" was regularly attached to them. At first Beauvoir resisted the use of the term, but she and Sartre gradually adopted it and began to try to explain existentialist philosophy to the public. In *Pour une morale de l'ambiguite* (*The Ethics of Ambiguity*), published in 1947, Beauvoir defined existentialism as a philosophy of ambiguity, one which emphasized the tension between living in the present and acting with an eye to one's mortality; she also attempted to answer critics who had accused existentialists of wallowing in absurdity and despair. In the four essays published the following year as *L'Existentialisme et la sagesse des nations* ("Existentialism and the Wisdom of the Ages"), Beauvoir argued for the importance of a philosophical approach to modern life. Here she defended existentialism against accusations of frivolity and gratuitousness and explained that existentialists considered man neither naturally good nor naturally bad: "He is nothing at first; it is up to him to make himself good or bad depending upon whether he assumes his freedom or denies it." Emphasizing the fact that man can be "the sole and sovereign master of his destiny," Beauvoir insisted that existentialist philosophy was essentially optimistic; in *Simone de Beauvoir and the Limits of Commitment,* however, Anne Whitmarsh sees the author's existentialism as "a stern ethical system."

With the end of the war came the opportunity to travel again. Beauvoir spent four months in the United States in 1947, lecturing on college campuses throughout the country about the moral problems facing writers in postwar Europe. She recorded her impressions through journal entries dating from January 25 to May 19, 1947, in *L'Amerique au jour le jour* (*America Day by Day*), which was dedicated to black author Richard Wright and his wife Ellen. Her perceptive eye took in a great variety of detail but saw everything through a lens whose focus was influenced by certain preconceived notions. Keefe finds the value of the book in the record it presents of Beauvoir's "excitement and disappointment at a historical moment when many Europeans knew little about America and were eager to expose themselves to its impact, for better or worse." Consistently critical of capitalist traditions and values, *America Day by Day* can be paired with Beauvoir's account of her 1955 trip to China, *La Longue Marche: Essai sur la Chine* (*The Long March*), in which she euphorically accepts everything in communist China. While praising Beauvoir's ability to evoke settings and glimpses of life in China, Keefe sees *The Long March* as "first and foremost a long, extremely serious attempt to explain the situation of China in 1955-56 and justify the direction in which the new regime [was] guiding the country."

Ready after the war to begin her purely autobiographical works, Beauvoir realized that she first needed to understand the extent to which being born female had influenced the pattern of her life. She therefore spent hours at the Bibliotheque Nationale (National Library) in Paris seeking documentation for each section of the book that was to become the battle cry of feminism in the latter half of the twentieth century. When *Le Deuxieme Sexe* (*The Second Sex*) appeared in 1949, reactions ranged from the horrified gasps of conservative readers to the impassioned gratitude of millions of women who had never before encountered such a frank discussion of their condition. The opening statement of the section on childhood, "One is not born a woman, one becomes one," has become familiar throughout the world, and the book advises women to pursue meaningful careers and to avoid the status of "relative beings" implied, in its author's view, by marriage and motherhood. Donald L. Hatcher's 1984 study, *Understanding "The Second Sex,"* provides valuable information about the philosophical framework of what is undoubtedly Beauvoir's best-known work.

Before turning to her memoirs, Beauvoir wrote the novel that won her the prestigious Goncourt Prize. *Les Mandarins* (*The Mandarins*) presents the euphoria of Liberation Day in Paris and the subsequent disillusionment of French intellectuals who had been temporarily convinced that the future was theirs to fashion as they saw fit, but who found themselves gradually dividing into factions as the glow of Resistance companionship and of victory over the Nazis dimmed. Beauvoir always denied that *The Mandarins* was a roman a clef, with Robert Dubreuilh, Henri Perron, and Anne Dubreuilh representing Sartre, Albert Camus, and herself; nonetheless, echoes of the developing rift between Sartre and Camus, of the discussions of staff members of *Les Temps modernes* (the leftist review founded by Sartre, Beauvoir, and their associates), and of the concern of French intellectuals over the revelation of the existence of Soviet work camps are clearly audible throughout the novel. Moreover, Lewis Brogan is certainly a fictionalized portrait of Chicago author Nelson Algren, who became one of Beauvoir's "contingent loves" during her 1947 trip to the States and to whom the novel is dedicated. Whether or not the work is a roman a clef, it is generally regarded, in Ascher's words, as Beauvoir's "richest, most complex, and most beautifully wrought novel."

The first volume of Beauvoir's autobiography appeared in 1958. In *Memoirs of a Dutiful Daughter,* the author chronicled the warmth and affection of the early years of her life, her growing rebellion against bourgeois tradition, her sense of emancipation when she moved from the family apartment on the rue de Rennes to a rented room at her grandmother's. Highlighted in these pages are her close association with her sister—"I felt sorry for only children," she declared, her relationship with Zaza, her infatuation with Jacques. Jean-Paul Sartre appears only in the concluding pages of this volume. In *Simone de Beauvoir on Woman,* Jean Leighton focuses on the portrait of Zaza in *Memoirs of a Dutiful Daughter,* finding that she "epitomizes . . . traditional feminine qualities. Next to Simone de Beauvoir she is the most vivid person in the book."

Beauvoir dedicated the second volume of her autobiography, *La Force de l'age* (*The Prime of Life*), to Sartre. The first half of the narrative tells the story of their lives from 1929 to 1939, recounting the exhilarating sense of freedom they experienced as they pooled their money to travel throughout France and to London, Italy, Germany, and Greece. Here the memoir looks back on the experiment of the trio, on the illness which put Beauvoir in a clinic for several weeks, on her insistence upon living in the present and trying to ignore the menacing news filtering through from Hilter's Germany. The second half of the book begins in 1939, as the German occupation of France was about to begin, and ends with Liberation Day in Paris in August 1944. These pages provide one of the most vivid accounts of life in France during World War II, as the reader witnesses the lines of people waiting for gas masks, the sirens and descents into metro stations during air raids, and the struggle to find enough food to survive. These were the years when leftist intellectuals remained in close contact with one another, when Albert Camus, actress Maria Casares, writers Michel Leiris and Raymond Queneau, theatrical director Charles Dullin, and artist Pablo Picasso joined Beauvoir, Sartre, Olga, and Bost in "fiestas" that provided occasional nights of relaxation amidst the bombings and the anticipation of the Allied landing. The emotions of Liberation Day were unforgettable for Beauvoir, who asserted: "No matter what happened afterward, nothing would take those moments away from me; nothing has taken them away; they shine in my past with a brilliance that has never been tarnished."

What did become tarnished, however, were Beauvoir's hopes of participating in the creation of a brave new world, preferably one in which socialism would solve the problems of society. The third volume of autobiography, *The Force of Circumstance,* begins with the Liberation and covers the period from 1944 to early 1963. Despite the success of her many books that were published during those years, despite her extensive travels and increasing political involvement, *The Force of Circumstance* was written with a heavy heart because of the anguish associated with the Algerian war. These were also the years during which Beauvoir began to reflect upon aging and death, began to realize that there were certain activities in which she was engaging for perhaps the last time. The final sentence in the memoir's epilogue has been widely discussed: "I can still see . . . the promises with which I filled my heart when I contemplated that gold mine at my feet, a whole life ahead of me. They have been fulfilled. However, looking back in amazement at that gullible adolescent I once was, I am stupefied to realize to what extent I have been cheated." She felt cheated because the goals she had set for herself did not lead to the sense of fulfillment that she had anticipated; she also felt cheated because all human activity, no matter how successful, leads uncompromisingly to the same impasse, the death of the individual. For Konrad Bieber, *The Force of Circumstance* is "a remarkable monument to the crucial years of the cold war. . . . A whole era, with its ups and downs, its hopes and disillusionments, is seen through the temperament of a highly gifted writer."

Nineteen sixty-three was a time of personal crisis for Beauvoir both because of her vision of the state of the modern world and because of the death of her mother. Deeply affected by watching her mother valiantly struggle against cancer, Beauvoir shared with her readers the anxiety of knowing more about her mother's condition than she could reveal to her, the dilemma of how far to authorize heroic medical measures, the pain of helplessly watching a life ebb away. In the moving pages of *Une Mort tres douce* (*A Very Easy Death*), a slender volume dedicated to her sister, the author recaptured the warmth of her childhood relationship with her mother and reactivated her admiration for this woman who had always "lived against herself" yet could still appreciate a ray of sunlight or the song of the birds in the tree outside her hospital window. Looking back at her interaction with her mother, Beauvoir realized the full impact of Francoise de Beauvoir's unhappy childhood, of the unfortunate social restraints that kept her mother from finding a satisfying outlet for the energy and vitality which she had passed on to her daughters but which she had never been able to use appropriately herself. Sartre considered *A Very Easy Death* Beauvoir's best work; Marks, who has commented on its "excruciating lucidity," calls the book the only one of the author's writings "in which the hectic rhythm which she projects on the world is abruptly interrupted and the interruption prolonged."

*Tout compte fait* (*All Said and Done*), dedicated to Sylvie Le Bon whom Beauvoir later adopted, covers the decade following the publication of *The Force of Circumstance.* Here Beauvoir abandons the chronological treatment of events employed in the earlier volumes of memoirs; instead she devotes one section to speculation about what might have happened *if* she had been born into a different family, she had not met Sartre at the Sorbonne, or had married her cousin Jacques, for example; other sections explore her dreams and provide accounts of her trips to places such as Japan, the U.S.S.R., Israel, and Egypt. After expressing a sense of satisfaction about her ability to communicate the tone of her life to her readers, she leaves it to them to draw whatever conclusions they wish from this particular volume of her autobiography.

*Adieux: A Farewell to Sartre,* a companion piece to *A Very Easy Death,* records Beauvoir's efforts to cope with the anguish of watching age and illness take their toll on her companion of fifty years. It is dedicated to "those who have loved Sartre, who love him and who will love him." Beauvoir's subsequent publication of Sartre's *Lettres au Castor et a quelques autres* further attempts to share the quality of their relationship with her readers. "Castor" was a nickname invented by her Sorbonne classmate Rene Maheu, who noted the similarity between the name Beauvoir and the English word "beaver" (castor in French) and who considered it an appropriate appellation for the hard-working Beauvoir. The two volumes of Sartre's letters cover a period from 1926 to 1963 and include quite detailed references to his involvements with other women. Some feminist criticism has seen *Adieux,* with its rather graphic account of Sartre's mental and physical decline, as Beauvoir's revenge on her partner for the pain inflicted upon her by his numerous "contingent" affairs. In an essay appearing in *Philosophy and Literature,* Hazel Barnes disagrees, considering these passages "both factual reporting and a tribute" and noting "the profound respect which Sartre and Beauvoir had for each other, something deeper than the obvious affection, companionship and commonality of values, more bedrock than love."

Beauvoir's own correspondence to Sartre was published in 1990 in the volume, *Letters to Sartre,* providing readers with what Jerome Charyn in the *Los Angeles Times Book Review* termed "an incredible gift." Beauvoir herself had claimed these letters were lost, but they were found stashed away in a cupboard in her apartment after her death. The letters are explicit in their detail of Beauvoir's relationship with Sartre as well as with several women who were also Sartre's lovers. Their graphic portrayal of Beauvoir's unconventional personal life led some critics to posit their damage to her reputation as a dedicated feminist. "This is nonsense," stated Elaine Showalter in the *London Review of Books.* "Beauvoir's feminist credentials come from her writing, and from her years of staunch, courageous and generous support of abortion legislation, battered women's shelters, women's publishing, and the cause of women's liberation around the world. . . . To have had a less-than-perfect personal life weighs no more against her intellectual achievements than it would against those of a man."

During the mid-1960s Beauvoir had also returned to fiction with a novel, *Les Belles Images.* Dedicated to Claude Lanzmann, one of the younger staff writers for *Les Temps modernes* and a "contingent love" of Beauvoir's from 1952 to 1958, *Les Belles Images* describes a milieu quite alien to Beauvoir, that of the mid-century technocrats. The novel centers on a bright, attractive career woman, comfortably married and the mother of two daughters, who suddenly finds herself caught between two generations as she attempts to help her estranged mother cope with the loss of her wealthy lover and to answer the probing questions of her own ten-year-old daughter about poverty and misery. As she gradually develops sensitivity she has been taught by her mother to restrain, Laurence despairs of ever changing anything in her own life, yet vows in the concluding lines of the novel that she will raise her daughters to express their feelings, to allow themselves to be moved by the plight of undernourished children in Third World countries, of factory workers shackled to uninspiring jobs. Laurence is an incarnation of the contemporary superwoman who attempts to juggle her commitments to her career, her husband, her children, her aging parents, even her lover, until she eventually falls apart under the strain of such responsibilities.

The three novellas in the 1967 collection *La Femme rompue* (*The Woman Destroyed*) reflect the degree to which Beauvoir had been listening to the women who wrote and spoke to her about the problems of their more traditional lives. One of the novellas, *Age of Discretion,* focuses on a recently retired woman professor, author of several books, for whom life seems to lose all meaning when her son abandons academia for a more lucrative business job and when critics suggest that her latest book merely repeats ideas presented in earlier ones. *Monologue* takes the reader through a New Year's Eve of neurotic ranting by the twice-divorced Murielle, whose possessiveness has driven her sixteen-year-old daughter to suicide and who wants to force her son and her second husband to live with her once again so that she will regain her social status as a wife and mother. The title story highlights the plight of the middle-aged Monique, who abandoned her medical studies in order to marry and have children and who suddenly discovers that her husband is having an affair with a younger and more independent woman. In each case the protagonist has allowed herself to be relegated to the status of a "relative being" dependent upon others for her sense of identity. According to Mary Evans in *Simone de Beauvoir: A Feminist Mandarin,* the setting of both *Les Belles Images* and *The Woman Destroyed* is "the culture in which people become objects, but the objects least able to manipulate their fate are women."

In the late 1960s Beauvoir turned her attention to an important study of old age, a companion piece to *The Second Sex.* She gave her book, published in 1970, the straightforward title *La Vieillesse* ("Old Age"), but the title was euphemistically translated as *The Coming of Age* in the United States. The work focuses upon the generally deplorable existence of most elderly people, and along with a film entitled *Promenades au pays de la vieillesse* ("Wandering through the Pathways of Old Age"), in which Beauvoir appeared, this book defines one of the as yet unresolved dilemmas of the late twentieth century. Bieber sees in *The Coming of Age* an example of Beauvoir's "boundless empathy" and of her understanding of human frailty; Ascher, in contrast, finds it "shocking for its lack of feeling for the special plight of old women" and asserts that for the author the universal is male, at least among the elderly.

Several critics have taken Beauvoir to task for her apparently negative presentation of women and their values. Leighton sees the women of Beauvoir's fiction as "finely etched portraits of various types of femininity [that] personify in a compelling way the pessimistic and anti-feminine bias of *The Second Sex.*" Ascher's personal letter to Beauvoir in the middle of her *Simone de Beauvoir: A Life of Freedom* speaks of "my resistance to accepting your grim view of women's condition." For Evans there is an assumption in Beauvoir's works that "traditionally male activities (the exercise of rationality, independent action, and so on) are in some sense superior, and are instances almost of a higher form of civilization than those concerns—such as child care and the maintenance of daily life—that have traditionally been the preserve of women." Whitmarsh is critical of the author's confining her political commitment to the ethical and the literary rather than extending her activities to the practical aspects of everyday politics. Okely finds that many of Beauvoir's generalizations are based on her limited experience in a small Parisian intellectual circle and do not apply as readily to cultures that are neither western, white, nor middle class.

A substantial number of interviews granted by Beauvoir gave her the opportunity to clarify many of her ideas and to answer her critics. Speaking with Francis Jeanson in an interview published as *Simone de Beauvoir ou l'entreprise de vivre,* she elaborated on her childhood, on her relationship with both her parents, on her conviction that being a woman had never hindered her progress toward the goals she had set for herself. At that particular time (the mid-1960s), she defined feminism as a way of living individually and of fighting collectively and strongly opposed any tendency to consider men as the enemy. Literature, in her opinion, should serve to make people more transparent to one another. She acknowledged a puritanical strain in herself caused by her early upbringing and spoke with Jeanson about what she labeled her "schizophrenia," a determination to throw herself wholeheartedly into any project she undertook and an accompanying unwillingness to deviate from her original plan even when intervening circumstances made it no longer practical.

Betty Friedan's *It Changed My Life* contains a dialogue with Beauvoir, to whom Friedan looked for answers to the questions raised by the American feminist groups that were forming in the 1970s. In her introduction to this dialogue, Friedan acknowledges her debt to Beauvoir: "I had learned my own existentialism from her. It was *The Second Sex* that introduced me to that approach to reality and political responsibility that . . . led me to whatever original analysis of women's existence I have been able to contribute." When they spoke, however, she and

Beauvoir disagreed completely about the viability of motherhood for women seeking their independence and about the possibility of providing salaries for housewives in order to enhance their self-image. In *It Changed My Life,* Friedan expressed disappointment over what she saw in Beauvoir as detachment from the lives of real women, and concluded: "I wish her well. She started me out on a road on which I'll keep moving. . . . There are no gods, no goddesses. . . . We need and can trust no other authority than our own personal truth."

Who was Simone de Beauvoir for others? The newspaper and magazine articles that appeared after her death provide a variety of answers to that question. For many women, she was the person who led the way, who opened up horizons and suggested possibilities of breaking out of the mold society had previously forged for them. The caption on the front page of *Le Nouvel Observateur,* taken from an article by philosophy professor Elisabeth Badinter, proclaimed, "Women, you owe her everything!" According to American feminist Kate Millett, quoted in London's *Observer,* "She had opened a door for us. All of us . . . women everywhere, their lives touched and illumined ever after." In the *New York Times* Gloria Steinem remarked that "More than any other single human being, she's responsible for the current international women's movement," and Betty Friedan labeled her "an authentic heroine in the history of womanhood." Despite her determination never to have children of her own, she became the "symbolic mother" of several generations of women. Josyane Savigneau declared in *Le Monde* that women in responsible positions today are "the descendants of this woman without children . . . who, obstinately, for more than sixty years . . . affirmed that there was nothing wrong with being born a woman."

Most appraisals of Beauvoir's writings focused on *The Second Sex,* called by Philip Wylie in the *New York Times* "one of the few great books of our era." However, Bertrand Poirot-Delpech, who noted in *Le Monde* that Beauvoir was "a much less minor novelist than one might think," described *The Mandarins* as one of the best sources of documentation on the committed intellectuals of the cold war period. Millett pronounced *The Woman Destroyed* "a literary masterpiece" and Beauvoir's books on aging and death great social documents. Michel Contat, writing for *Le Monde,* saw the 1946 novel *All Men Are Mortal* as Beauvoir's most powerful philosophical work, "the most daring, the most scandalous and the most strangely passionate interrogation launched by this great rationalist intellectual against the human condition."

Still other French newspapers highlighted Beauvoir's intelligence and underlined the fact that at twenty-one she was the youngest student ever to receive the "agregation" degree in philosophy. Friends emphasized, however, that her keen mind was accompanied by sincere concern for other people. Jean Cathala noted in *Le Monde* that "her remarkable intelligence was inseparable from her remarkable hearts"; Millett cited her "endless generosity and patience" in giving of herself and her time to others; singer Juliette Greco recalled in *Le Monde* Beauvoir's "generosity, human tenderness and . . . ability to listen." Equally praised in the press was Beauvoir's tireless commitment to causes in which she believed. Contacted by *Le Monde* for his reaction to the author's death, Jack Lang, former Minister of Culture under Francois Mitterrand, described Beauvoir as "a generous human being who never hesitated to defend the cause of the oppressed." Claudine Serre recorded in *Le Monde Aujourd'hui* that to the last days of her life, Beauvoir remained "a free woman opposed to servitude, and nothing ever appeased her anger. . . . Her commitment . . . did not diminish with age."

*BIOGRAPHICAL/CRITICAL SOURCES:*

*BOOKS*

Ascher, Carol, *Simone de Beauvoir: A Life of Freedom,* Beacon Press, 1981.

Bergoffen, Debra B., *The Philosophy of Simone de Beauvoir: Gendered Phenomenologies, Erotic Generosities,* State University of New York Press (Albany), 1996.

Bieber, Konrad, *Simone de Beauvoir,* Twayne, 1979.

Bree, Germaine, *Women Writers in France: Variations on a Theme,* Rutgers University Press, 1973.

Brombert, Victor, *The Intellectual Hero,* Lippincott, 1961.

Brophy, Brigid, *Don't Never Forget: Collected Views and Reviews,* Holt, 1966.

*Contemporary Literary Criticism,* Gale, Volume 1, 1973, Volume 2, 1974, Volume 4, 1975, Volume 8, 1978, Volume 14, 1980, Volume 31, 1985, Volume 44, 1987, Volume 50, 1988, Volume 71, 1992.

Corbin, Laurie, *The Mother-Mirror: Self-Representation and the Mother-Daughter Relation in Colette, Simone de Beauvoir, and Marguerite Duras,* P. Lang (New York City), 1996.

Cottrell, Robert D., *Simone de Beauvior,* Ungar, 1975.

Dayan, Josee and Malka Ribowska, *Simone de Beauvoir, un film,* Gallimard, 1979.

*Dictionary of Literary Biography,* Volume 72: *French Novelists, 1930-1960,* Gale, 1988.

*Dictionary of Literary Biography Yearbook: 1986,* Gale, 1987.

Evans, Mary, *Simone de Beauvoir: A Feminist Mandarin,* Tavistock, 1985.

Francis, Claude and Fernande Gontier, *Les Ecrits de Simone de Beauvoir,* Gallimard, 1979.

Francis, Claude and Fernande Gontier, *Simone de Beauvoir: A Life . . . A Love Story,* Librairie Academique Perrin, 1985.

Friedan, Betty, *It Changed My Life,* Random House, 1976.

Fullbrook, Kate and Edward, *Simone de Beauvoir and Jean-Paul Sartre: The Remaking of a Twentieth-Century Legend,* Basic Books (New York City), 1994.

Hatcher, Donald L., *Understanding "The Second Sex,"* P. Lang, 1984.

Jeanson, Francis, *Simone de Beauvoir ou l'entreprise de vivre,* Editions du Seuil, 1966.

Keefe, Terry, *Simone de Beauvoir: A Study of Her Writings,* Barnes, 1983.

Lamblin, Bianca, *A Disgraceful Affair: Simone de Beauvoir, Jean-Paul Sartre, and Bianca Lamblin,* Northeastern University Press (Boston), 1996.

Leighton, Jean, *Simone de Beauvoir on Woman,* Associated University Presses, 1975.

Lundgren-Gothlin, Eva, *Sex and Existence: Simone de Beauvoir's "The Second Sex,"* Wesleyan University Press (Hanover, NH), 1996.

Madsen, Axel, *Hearts and Minds: The Common Journey of Simone de Beauvoir and Jean-Paul Sartre,* Morrow, 1977.

Marks, Elaine, *Simone de Beauvior: Encounters with Death,* Rutgers University Press, 1973.

Moi, Toril, *Simone de Beauvoir: The Making of an Intellectual Woman,* Blackwell (Cambridge, MA), 1994.

Nedeau, Maurice, *The French Novelist since the War,* Methuen, 1967.

Okely, Judith, *Simone de Beauvoir,* Pantheon, 1986.

Sartre, Jean-Paul, *The Words,* translation by Bernard Fechtman, Braziller, 1964.

Schwarzer, Alice, *After "The Second Sex": Conversations with Simone de Beauvoir,* Pantheon Books, 1984.

Simons, Margaret A., *Feminist Interpretations of Simone de Beauvoir,* Pennsylvania State University Press (University Park), 1995.

Vintges, Karen, *Philosophy as Passion: The Thinking of Simone de Beauvoir,* Indiana University Press (Bloomington), 1996.

Whitmarsh, Anne, *Simone de Beauvoir and the Limits of Commitment,* Cambridge University Press, 1981.

Zephir, Jacques J., *Le Neo-Feminisme de Simone de Beauvoir,* Denoel/Gonthier, 1982.

*PERIODICALS*

*Antioch Review,* Volume 31, number 4, 1971-72.

*Booklist,* September 15, 1990, p. 143.

*Catholic Forum,* October, 1965.

*Chicago Tribune Book World,* March 20, 1983.

*Contemporary French Civilization,* spring, 1984.

*Dalhousie Review,* autumn, 1970.

*Feminist Studies,* summer, 1979.

*Fontaine,* October, 1945.

*Forum for Modern Languages Studies,* April, 1975.

*France-Dimanche,* April 27, 1986.

*French Review,* April, 1979.

*Globe & Mail* (Toronto), April 19, 1986.

*Hecate,* Volume 7, number 2, 1981.

*Journal de la Ligue des Droits de l'Homme,* number 33, 1984.

*La Vie en Rose,* March 16, 1984.

*Le Monde,* March 20, 1948, April 16, 1986.

*Le Nouvel Observateur,* April 18-24, 1986.

*L'Express,* November 7, 1963.

*London Review of Books,* June 14, 1990, p. 6.

*Los Angeles Times,* April 25, 1984.

*Los Angeles Times Book Review,* May 24, 1992, p. 2.

*Nation,* June 8, 1958; June 27, 1959; June 14, 1975.

*New Statesman,* June 6, 1959; January 5, 1968; December 13, 1991.

*Newsweek,* June 8, 1959; February 9, 1970.

*New Yorker,* February 22, 1947.

*New York Review of Books,* July 20, 1972.

*New York Times,* June 2, 1974; May 6, 1984; April 15, 1986.

*New York Times Book Review,* May 18, 1958; June 7, 1959; March 3, 1968; February 23, 1969; July 21, 1974; November 7, 1982; May 24, 1987; July 19, 1992; January 9, 1994.

*Paris-Match,* April 25, 1986.

*Paris Review,* spring/summer, 1965.

*Philosophy and Literature,* Volume 9, number 1, 1985.

*Saturday Review,* May 22, 1956.

*Time,* March 20, 1966; May 22, 1972.

*Times* (London), January 21, 1982; August 12, 1982; May 11, 1984.

*Times Literary Supplement,* June 5, 1959; May 5, 1966; March 30, 1967; April 4, 1980; December 25, 1981; July 30, 1982; January 21, 1983; September 14, 1990, p. 963.

*Washington Post Book World,* August 18, 1974; May 20, 1984.

*OBITUARIES:*

*PERIODICALS*

*Chicago Tribune*, April 15, 1986.

*Detroit Free Press*, April 15, 1986.

*Figaro,* April 20, 1986.

*Le Monde Aujourd'hui,* April 20-21, 1986.

*Los Angeles Times*, April 15, 1986.

*Newsweek*, April 28, 1986.

*New York Times*, June 2, 1974.

*Observer,* April 20, 1986.

*Publishers Weekly,* May 2, 1986.

*Time,* April 28, 1986.

*Times* (London), April 15, 1986.

*USA Today*, April 15, 1986.

*Washington Post*, April 15, 1986.*

* * *

**BECKETT, Samuel (Barclay) 1906-1989**

*PERSONAL:* Born April 13, 1906, in Foxrock, Dublin, Ireland; died of respiratory failure, December 22, 1989, in Paris, France; son of William Frank (a quantity surveyor) and Mary Jones (an interpreter for the Irish Red Cross; maiden name, Roe) Beckett; married Suzanne Dechevaux-Dumesnil (a pianist), March 25, 1961. *Education:* Attended Portora Royal School, County Fermanagh, Ireland; Trinity College, Dublin, B.A. (French and Italian), 1927, M.A., 1931.

*CAREER:* Ecole Normale Superieure, Paris, France, lecturer in English, 1928-30; Trinity College, University of Dublin, Dublin, Ireland, lecturer in French, 1930-32 (resigned because "he could not bear the absurdity of teaching to others what he did not know himself"). During the early 1930s he, among others, helped James Joyce, who was then nearly blind, by taking dictation and by copying out parts of *Finnegans Wake.* (Beckett never served as secretary to Joyce as many believe. A. J. Leventhal, writing for Beckett, stated that "there was never any question of a formal position. . . . It's very hard to kill this story.") From 1932 to 1936 Beckett traveled extensively in England and Europe, residing briefly in London and in several European cities. He settled permanently in Paris in 1937. From about 1940 to 1943, Beckett was involved with the French resistance movement and had to hide from the Germans. He spent these years working as a farmhand near Roussillon, an isolated region in southeast France. From the early 1940s on, Beckett devoted most of his time to writing. *Military service:* Storekeeper and interpreter for Irish Red Cross Hospital, St. Lo, France, 1945-46; decorated.

*MEMBER:* Modern Language Association of America (honorary fellow, 1966), American Academy of Arts and Letters (fellow, 1968); American Academy of Arts and Sciences (honorary member).

*AWARDS, HONORS:* Hours Press (Paris) award for the best poem concerning time, 1930, for *Whoroscope: Poem on Time; London Evening Standard* Award for Most Controversial Play, 1955, for *Waiting for Godot;* Italia Prize, 1957, for *All That Fall,* and 1959, for *Embers; Village Voice* Off-Broadway (Obie) awards for best new play, 1958, for *Endgame,* and 1964, for *Play,* for distinguished play, 1960, for *Krapp's Last Tape,* and for best foreign play, 1962, for *Happy Days;* Litt.D., Trinity College, Dublin, 1959; International Publishers prize, 1961 (shared with Jorge Luis Borges), for all literary work, especially *Molloy, Malone meurt, L'Innommable,* and *Comment c'est*; Prix Filmcritice, 1965, and Tours Film Prize, 1966, both for *Film;* Nobel Prize for Literature, 1969; Grand Prix National du Theatre (France), 1975.

*WRITINGS:*

*NOVELS*

*Murphy* (written in English), Routledge & Kegan Paul (London), 1938, Grove (New York City), 1957, French translation by Beckett, Bordas (Paris), 1947.

*Molloy* (fragment of an earlier version published in *transition,* number 6, 1950, together with an early fragment of *Malone Dies* under collective title, "Two Fragments"; also see below), Editions de Minuit, 1951, English translation by Beckett and Patrick Bowles, Grove, 1955.

*Malone meurt,* Editions de Minuit, 1951, English translation by Beckett published as *Malone Dies,* Grove, 1956.

*Watt* (written in English), Olympia Press (Paris), 1953, Grove, 1959, rewritten, and translated into French by the author, Editions de Minuit, 1968.

*L'Innommable,* Editions de Minuit, 1953, English translation by Beckett published as *The Unnamable,* Grove, 1958.

*Three Novels: Molloy, Malone Dies, [and] The Unnamable,* Grove, 1959.

*Comment c'est,* Editions de Minuit, 1961, English translation by Beckett published as *How It Is,* Grove, 1964 (excerpts published in *X* [a London magazine], number 1, 1959, and, under title "From an Unabandoned Work," in *Evergreen Review,* September-October, 1960).

*Imagination morte imaginez* (although only 14 pages long, Beckett called this work a novel), Editions de Minuit, 1965, English translation by Beckett published as *Imagination Dead Imagine,* Calder & Boyars, 1965.

*Mercier et Camier,* Minuit, 1970, translation by Beckett published as *Mercier and Camier,* Calder & Boyars, 1974, Grove, 1975.

*Dream of Fair to Middling Women,* edited by Eoin O'Brien and Edith Fournier, Arcade Publishing in association with Riverrun Press (New York City), 1993, reissued, 1996.

*Nohow On: Three Novels,* edited by S. E. Gontarski, Grove Press, 1996.

*SHORT FICTION*

*More Pricks Than Kicks* (ten short stories, written in English), Chatto & Windus, 1934, special edition, Calder & Boyars, 1966.

*Nouvelles et textes pour rien* (fiction; contains "L'Expulse," "Le Calmant," and "La Fin," and thirteen monologues), Editions de Minuit, 1955, translation by Beckett and others published in England as *No's Knife: Collected Shorter Prose, 1947-1965* (also includes "From an Abandoned Work," "Enough," *Imagination Dead Imagine,* and *Ping;* also see below), Calder & Boyars, 1967, published as *Stories and Texts for Nothing,* Grove, 1967.

*Assez,* Editions de Minuit, 1966.

*Ping,* Editions de Minuit, 1966.

*Tete-mortes* (includes *Imagination morte imaginez, bing, Assez,* and a new novella, *Tete-mortes*), Editions de Minuit, 1967.

*L'Issue,* Georges Visat, 1968.

*Sans,* Editions de Minuit, 1969, translation by Beckett published as *Lessness,* Calder & Boyars, 1971.

*Sejour,* Georges Richar, 1970.

*Premier amour,* Editions de Minuit, 1970, translation by Beckett published as *First Love,* Calder & Boyars, 1973.

*The North,* Enitharmon Press, 1972.

*First Love and Other Shorts,* Grove, 1974.

*Fizzles,* Grove, 1976.

*For to End Yet Again and Other Fizzles,* Calder, 1976.

*All Strange Away,* Gotham Book Mart, 1976.

*Four Novellas,* Calder, 1977, published as *The Expelled and Other Novellas,* Penguin, 1980.

*Six Residua,* Calder, 1978.

*Mal vu mal dit,* Editions de Minuit, 1981, translation by Beckett published as *Ill Seen Ill Said,* Grove, 1982, variorum edition edited by Charles France, Garland, 1996.

*Worstward Ho,* Grove, 1983.

*As the Story Was Told,* Riverrun Press, 1990.

*Stirrings Still,* Blue Moon Books, 1991.

*Nohow On* (novella), Riverrun Press, 1993.

*Collected Shorter Prose, 1945-1988,* Riverrun Press, 1995.

*Samuel Beckett, The Complete Short Prose, 1929-1989,* edited and with introduction by S. E. Gontarski, Grove Press, 1995.

Also author of the short story "Premier amour" which was perhaps intended to complete a quartet begun with "L'Expulse," "Le Calmant," and "La Fin."

*PLAYS*

*Le Kid,* produced in Dublin, 1931.

*En Attendant Godot* (first produced in Paris at Theatre de Babylone, January 5, 1953), Editions de Minuit, 1952, English translation by Beckett entitled *Waiting for Godot* (first premiered at Arts Theatre Club, London, August, 1955; U.S. premiere in Miami Beach, FL, at Coconut Grove Playhouse, January, 1956; produced on Broadway at John Golden Theatre, April, 1956), Grove, 1954, with a revised text, Grove Press (New York City), 1994.

*All That Fall* (radio play written in English; produced in London for BBC Third Programme, January 13, 1957), Grove, 1957, updated for American radio, 1968-69, French translation by Robert Pinget and Beckett published as *Tous ceux qui tombent,* Editions de Minuit, 1957.

*Fin de partie* (a play in one act; first produced with *Acte sans paroles* in London at Royal Court Theatre, April 3, 1957), French & European Publications, 1957, English translation by Beckett produced as *Endgame* in New York at Cherry Lane Theatre, 1958.

*Acte sans paroles* (a mime for one player, with music by John Beckett), first produced with *Fin de partie* in London at Royal Court Theatre, April 3,

1957), English translation by Beckett produced as *Act without Words*, produced in New York at Living Theatre, 1959.

*From an Abandoned Work* (written in English; produced in London for BBC Third Programme, 1957), first published in *Evergreen Review*, Volume 1, number 3, 1957, Faber & Faber, 1958, published in French as *D'un ouvrage abandonne*, 1967.

*Krapp's Last Tape* (written in English), first produced in London at Royal Court Theatre, October 28, 1958, then at Provincetown Playhouse, 1960, French translation as *Le Derniere Bande*, French & European Publications, 1960.

*Embers* (written in English), first produced in London for BBC Third Programme, June 24, 1959.

*Acte sans paroles II*, produced at Institute of Contemporary Arts, London, 1960, English translation as *Act without Words II.*

*Happy Days* (written in English; first produced in New York at Cherry Lane Theatre, September 17, 1961), Grove, 1961, French translation by Beckett as *Oh les beaux jours* (produced in Paris, 1963), Editions de Minuit, 1963, 2nd edition, French & European Publications, 1975.

*Spiel*, German translation by Elmar Tophoven, produced in Germany, 1963, produced in English as *Play*, London, 1964, produced in French as *Comedie*, Paris, 1964.

*Film* (22-minute mime adaptation, by Mariu Karmitz, of *Play*), directed by Alan Schneider for Evergreen Theatres, and starring Buster Keaton, M. K. Productions, 1966.

*Eh, Joe? and Other Writings* (written in English for television; first produced by New York Television Theatre, 1966; also see below), Faber & Faber, 1967.

*Va et vient* (121-word "dramaticule," produced in Berlin, 1966), published in *Comedie et actes divers*, Calder & Boyars, 1967, English version produced as *Come and Go*, Dublin, 1968.

*Breath*, produced in Oxford, England, 1970.

*Le Depeupleur*, French & European Publications, 1970, translation by Beckett published as *The Lost Ones* (produced in New York, 1975), Grove, 1972.

*Not I* (produced at Lincoln Center, New York, 1972), Faber, 1971.

*That Time* (produced in London, 1976), Faber, 1976.

*Footfalls* (produced in London, 1976), Faber, 1976.

*A Piece of Monologue*, produced in New York, 1979.

*Company* (monologue), Grove, 1980.

*Rockabye*, produced in Buffalo, NY, 1981.

*Texts for Nothing*, produced in New York, 1981.

*Ohio Impromptu*, produced in Columbus, OH, 1981.

*Eleutheria* (new edition), Editions de Minuit (Paris), 1995, published in English as *Eleutheria: A Play in Three Acts*, Foxrock (New York City), 1995.

*OMNIBUS EDITIONS OF PLAYS*

*Fin de partie* [and] *Acte sans paroles*, Editions de Minuit, 1957, English translation by Beckett published as *Endgame* [and] *Act without Words*, Grove, 1958.

*Krapp's Last Tape* [and] *Embers*, Faber & Faber, 1959, published as *Krapp's Last Tape and Other Dramatic Pieces* (also contains *All that Fall*, *Act without Words [I]*, and *Act without Words II* [written in English]), Grove, 1960.

*Dramatische Dichtungen* (trilingual edition of dramatic works originally published in French; German translations by Tophoven), Suhrkamp Verlag, 1963-64.

*Play and Two Short Pieces for Radio* (written in English; contains *Play*, *Words and Music* [first published in *Evergreen Review*, November-December, 1962], and *Cascando* [first published in *Dublin Magazine*, October-December, 1936; also see below]), Faber & Faber, 1964.

*Comedie et actes divers* (contains *Comedie*, *Va et vient*, *Cascando*, *Paroles et musiques* [French translation by Beckett of *Words and Music*], *Dis Joe* [French translation by Beckett of *Eh, Joe?*; also see below], and *Acte sans paroles II*), Editions de Minuit, 1966.

*Cascando and Other Short Dramatic Pieces*, Grove, 1968.

*Breath and Other Shorts*, Faber, 1971.

*Ends and Odds: Eight New Dramatic Pieces*, Faber, 1977.

*Rockabye and Other Short Pieces*, Grove, 1981.

*Catastrophe et autres dramaticules: Cette fois, Solo, Berceuse, Impromptu d'Ohio*, Editions de Minuit, 1982.

*Three Occasional Pieces*, Faber, 1982.

*Collected Shorter Plays*, Grove, 1984.

*Ohio Impromptu, Catastrophe, and What Where*, Grove, 1984.

*The Complete Dramatic Works*, Faber, 1986.

*Samuel Beckett's Company-Compagnie and a Piece of Monologue—Solo: A Bilingual Variorum Edition*, Garland, 1993.

*Dramaticulesg*, Riverrun Press, 1995.

*OTHER*

(Contributor) *Our Exagmination round His Factification for Incamination of Work in Progress* (on

James Joyce and *Finnegans Wake*), Shakespeare & Co. (Paris), 1929, New Directions, 1939, 2nd edition, 1962.

*Whoroscope: Poem on Time* (written in English), Hours Press (Paris), 1930.

*Proust* (criticism, written in English), Chatto & Windus, 1931, Grove, 1957.

*Echo's Bones and Other Precipitates* (poems, written in English), Europa Press (Paris), 1935.

*A Samuel Beckett Reader,* edited by John Calder, Calder & Boyars, 1967.

(With Georges Duthuit and Jacques Putnam) *Bram van Velde* (criticism of the painter's work), Falaise (Paris), 1958, English translation by Olive Chase and Beckett, Grove, 1960.

*Henri Hayden,* Waddington Galleries, 1959.

*Gedichte* (in French and German; contains "Echo's Bones" and 18 poems written between 1937 and 1949), German translations by Eva Hesse, Limes Verlag (Wiesbaden), 1959.

*Poems in English,* Calder & Boyars, 1961, Grove, 1962.

(With Georges Duthuit) *Proust and Three Dialogues* (criticism), Calder & Boyars, 1965.

*Poemes,* Editions de Minuit, 1968.

*Abandonne,* Georges Visat, 1972.

*Au loin un oiseau,* Double Elephant Press, 1973.

*An Examination of James Joyce*, M.S.G. House, 1974.

*Pour finir encore*, French and European Publications, 1976.

*I Can't Go On: A Selection from the Works of Samuel Beckett,* edited by Richard Seaver, Grove Press, 1976.

*Collected Poems in English and French,* Grove, 1977, revised edition published as *Collected Poems, 1930-1978,* Calder, 1984.

*Disjecta: Miscellaneous Writings and a Dramatic Fragment,* edited by Ruby Cohn, Calder, 1983, Grove, 1984.

*Collected Shorter Prose, 1945-1980,* Calder, 1984.

*Happy Days: The Production Notebook,* edited by James Knowlson, Faber, 1985, Grove, 1986.

(Translator with Edouard Roditi and Denise Levertov) Alain Bosquet, *No Matter No Fact,* New Directions, 1988.

*Collected Poems in English,* Grove/Atlantic, 1989.

*Endgame: Production Notebook,* revised edition, Grove, 1993.

*Collected Poems, 1930-1989,* Riverrun Press, 1995.

Contributor to *transition, New Review, Evergreen Review, Contempo, Les Temps Modernes, Merlin, Spectrum,* and other periodicals.

*ADAPTATIONS:* Many of Beckett's works have been adapted for radio and television broadcast.

*SIDELIGHTS:* "He wanders among misty bogs turned surreal, he talks to the wee folk of his own bad dreams, he files reports on introspected black visions with a kind of blarney eloquence. Like an actress cradling a doll for her stage baby, his language keens and croons about tales that are not quite there." Melvin Maddocks is talking about Samuel Beckett, a literary legend of the twentieth century. "It is neither night nor morning. A man must find himself without the support of groups, or labels, or slogans," writes R. D. Smith. And Beckett, by removing his characters from nearly all recognizable contexts, Smith continues, is "engaged in finding or saving" himself. Martin Esslin writes: "What is the essence of the experience of being? asks Beckett. And so he begins to strip away the inessentials. What is the meaning of the phrase 'I am myself'? he asks . . . and is then compelled to try to distinguish between the merely accidental characteristics that make up an individual and the essence of his self." A *Time* reviewer noted: "Some chronicle men on their way up; others tackle men on their way down. Samuel Beckett stalks after men on their way out." Such is the tone of most discussions of Beckett's work. But no single reviewer could communicate the unique power of Beckett's writing, his use of "a language in which the emptiness of conventional speech is charged with new emotion." "While [his] lesser colleagues work in rhetoric," writes Smith, Beckett produces poetry. "Well," says Harold Pinter, "I'll buy his goods, hook, line, and sinker, because he leaves no stone unturned and no maggot lonely. He brings forth a body of beauty. His work is beautiful." Leo Bersani, somewhat less politely, writes: "I know of no writer who has come closer than Beckett in his novels to translating the rhythms of defecation into sentence structure."

Along with the work of Eugene Ionesco, Jean Genet, and Harold Pinter, Beckett's stark plays are said to compose the "Theatre of the Absurd." But to so label Beckett's work is to disqualify one of his own first premises—that, since no human activity has any intrinsic meaning, it is pointless to ascribe traditional or categorical significance to the existence of an object or the performance of a deed. George Wellwarth discusses Beckett's concept of a protean reality: "What all these things—the sameness of human beings and their actions, the vanity of human ambition, the uselessness of thought—amount to is a pessimism deeper than any that has ever been put into words before. Throughout Beckett's work we can find evidence of his conviction that everything is hopeless, meaningless, purposeless, and, above all, agonizing to endure. Beckett's people are leveled off and merged into each other by being all more or less physically disabled—as if this were really the common condition on earth. . . . Beckett is a prophet of negation and sterility. He holds out no hope to humanity, only a picture of unrelieved blackness; and those who profess to see in Beckett signs of a Christian approach or signs of compassion are simply refusing to see what is there." Perhaps Beckett himself stated his dilemma most succinctly in *L'Innommable:* "Dans ma vie, puisqu'il faut l'appeler ainsi, il y eut trois choses, l'impossibilite de parler, l'impossibilite de me taire, et la solitude." ("One must speak; man cannot possibly communicate with his fellows, but the alternative—silence—is irreconcilable with human existence.")

Smith and Esslin, however, insist that Beckett did not intend to express unqualified despair, but that, by stripping significance from the world, he showed us the one way to achieve redemption (although any salvation, according to Beckett's essentially deterministic philosophy, is necessarily only a respite). Smith writes: "Beckett's characters remain at their darkest moments anguished human beings: Beckett, when intellectually at his most pitiless, feels and suffers with them." Esslin states that Beckett's message "is anything but gloomy or despairing." He writes: "On the contrary: the starkness of [his] reminders of the evanescence of life and the certainty of death, [his] uncompromising rejection of any easy solution or cheap illusion of comfort ultimately has a liberating effect; such is the nature of man that in the very act of facing up to the reality of his condition his dignity is enhanced; we are only defeated by things by which we are taken unawares; what we know and have faced up to we can master." Alec Reid also believes that Beckett's message must be interpreted optimistically. "Beckett's world," he writes, "is one of darkness, of disembodied voices, of ignorance, impotence, and anguish. But even as he insists that he knows nothing, can know nothing, Beckett reminds us of an astronaut, a human surrounded by nothing, walking on nothing. Our spacemen are no cause for despair; no more are Mr. Beckett's explorations." But then, according to *Time* magazine, "Beckett's champions argue that his threnodies in dusky twilight represent the existential metaphor of the human condition, that the thin but unwavering voices of his forlorn characters speak the ultimate statement of affirmation, if only because the merest attempt at communication is itself affirmation."

But in case the reader of Beckett criticism should come to regard this question as the black and white one of "despair" versus "optimism," Richard N. Coe adds new terms to the argument: "To class Beckett himself as the simple incarnation of 'despair' is a drastic oversimplification. To begin with, the concept of 'despair' implies the existence of a related concept 'hope,' and 'hope' implies a certain predictable continuity in time—which continuity Beckett would seriously question. 'Despair,' with all its inherent moral overtones, is a term which is wholly inadequate to describe Beckett's attitude towards the human condition; nor is this condition, in the most current sense of the definition, 'absurd.' It is literally and logically impossible. And in this central concept of 'impossibility,' his thought has most of its origins—as does also his art."

Although John Gassner was not happy with the scholarly complexity of the critical response to Beckett's work (he wrote: "To a parvenu intelligentsia, it would seem that a work of art exists not for its own sake but only for the possibilities of interpreting it"), some critics believe that Beckett's theater is most meaningful when considered within the context of a recognizable literary tradition. Kenneth Allsop writes: "His harsh, desolate, denuded style is entirely and unmistakably his own, but his literary 'form,' the stream-of-consciousness device which most young British writers wouldn't dream of using nowadays for fear of being thought quaint, derives from his years [working with] . . . James Joyce. That is only a partial explanation. He is in a monolithic way the last of the Left Bank Mohicans of the Twenties; the others of the *avant-garde* died or deserted or prospered, but Beckett was a loyal expatriate." Esslin, J. D. O'Hara, and John Fletcher prefer to align Beckett with the philosophers. "Although Beckett himself [was] not aware of any such influence," Esslin writes, "his writings might be described as a literary exposition of Sartre's Existentialism." O'Hara sees his work as exponential to the philosophy of Descartes: "In Beckett's world of post-Cartesian dualism, the mind has no connection to the body, its values worth nothing there, and so it cannot logically concern itself with the body's problems." Fletcher concludes that "whatever the truth of the matter, one thing is certain. Beckett has ranged freely among the writings of the philosophers, where he has found confirmation and justification of the metaphysical obsessions that haunt his work: the gulf set between body and mind, the epistemological incertitude. His genius has achieved the transmutation of such speculative problems into art." But, according to Coe, one must keep in mind that "Beckett has renounced his claim to erudition. The main theme of his work is impotence, of mind just as much as of body."

The problem of analyzing and interpreting Beckett's work, on the other hand, has been met with a somewhat surprising amount of scholarship and erudition. But David Hesla's criticism, in which the novels are considered as the expression of Beckett's personal enigma, is equally effective. Hesla notes that the dilemma which confronts the contemporary writer, according to Beckett, "is constituted . . . by the fact that the writer must take seriously two opposed and apparently irreconcilable claims to his allegiance. On the one hand, he must recognize that the principal fact about modern man's life is that it is a 'mess,' a 'confusion,' a 'chaos.' On the other hand, the writer, as artist, has an obligation to form. But to admit the 'mess' into art is to jeopardize the very nature of art; for the mess 'appears to be the very opposite of form and therefore destructive of the very thing that art holds itself to be.'" Hesla quotes Beckett as saying: "It only means that there will be a new form; and that this form will be of such a type that it admits the chaos and does not try to say that the chaos is really something else. The form and the chaos remain separate. The latter is not reduced to the former. That is why the form itself becomes a preoccupation, because it exists as a problem separate from the material it accommodates. To find a form that accommodates the mess, that is the task of the artist now." Hesla notes that with *Watt,* "Beckett [began] a process of removing from his artificial world those tangibles by which the reader usually is able to orient himself in time and space, and those causal relationships amongst the incidents of the plot by which the reader is able to discern the conditions of necessity and probability which—be they never so strained or extraordinary—determine in part the structural coherence and the 'meaning' of the story. . . . In *Watt* he has found the form which permits 'the mess' to enter art without destroying it. He has developed a literary method—the negative way—which is capable of accommodating chaos without reducing it to form. Furthermore, in developing this method he has developed an instrument of greater precision for the explication of a world-view which was only roughly sketched out in *Murphy*. Beckett's work after *Watt* has, in a certain sense, consisted largely in refining and adapting both the manner and the matter of his new art."

Most critics agree that it was the 1954 English-language publication of *Waiting for Godot* that established Beckett's prominence in the United States. Many, in fact, still consider this play to be his most important work. H. A. Smith calls it "the most comprehensively and profoundly evocative play of the last thirty years," and William R. Mueller and Josephine Jacobsen write: *"Waiting for Godot,* of all of Beckett's dramatic works, expresses most clearly and explicitly the fundamental tension—to wait or not to wait—which is found to a lesser degree in his other writings. The human predicament described in Beckett's first [major, staged] play is that of man living on the Saturday after the Friday of the crucifixion, and not really knowing if all hope is dead or if the next day will bring the new life which has been promised." Allsop found the play's message less ambiguous. He writes: "*Godot* is a hymn to extol the moment when the mind swings off its hinges. . . . Beckett is unconcerned with writing requiems for humanity, for he sees life as polluted and pointless: he merely scrawls its obituary, without bitterness or compassion because he cannot really believe it is worth the words he is wasting." Gassner also found the play to be a straightforward pronouncement, but he did not accept it as a prediction of certain doom. "To all this tohu and bohu about the profundity and difficulty of the play," he wrote, "my reply is simply that there is nothing painfully or exhilaratingly ambiguous about *Waiting for Godot* in the first place. It presents the view that man, the hapless wanderer in the universe, brings his quite wonderful humanity—his human capacity for hope, patience, resilience, and, yes, for love of one's kind, too, as well as his animal nature—to the weird journey of existence. He is lost in the universe and found in his own heart and in the hearts of his fellow men." Bert O. States adds parenthetically: "Convicts and children love it!"

Kenneth Tynan believes that the implications of *Waiting for Godot* are significant not only in themselves, but for all of contemporary theater. He writes: "A special virtue attaches to plays which remind the drama of how much it can do without and still exist. By all known criteria, Beckett's *Waiting for Godot* is a dramatic vacuum. Pity the critic who seeks a chink in its armour, for it is all chink. It has no plot, no climax, no *denouement;* no beginning, no middle, and no end. Unavoidably, it has a situation, and it might be accused of having suspense. . . . *Waiting for Godot* frankly jettisons everything by which we recognise theatre. It arrives at the custom-house, as it were, with no luggage, no passport, and nothing to declare; yet it gets through, as might a pilgrim from Mars. It does this, I believe, by appealing to a definition of drama much more fundamental than any in the books. A play, it asserts and proves, is basically a means of spending two hours in the dark without being bored. . . . It forced me to re-examine the rules which have hitherto governed the drama; and, having done so, to pronounce them not elastic enough."

Some critics found 1957's *Endgame* to be an even more powerful expression of Beckett's negativism. Gassner wrote: "Nothing happens in *Endgame* and that nothing is what matters. The author's feeling about nothing also matters, not because it is true or right but because it is a strongly formed attitude, a felt and expressed viewpoint. . . . The yardsticks of dialectical materialism and moralism are equally out in appraising the play. Dialectical materialism could only say that *Endgame* is decadent. Moralism and theology would say that the play is sinful, since nothing damns the soul so much as despair of salvation. Neither yardstick could tell us that this hauntingly powerful work of the imagination is art."

Although critics discuss his plays more frequently than his novels, Beckett himself was said to have considered his novels to be his major works. Alec Reid notes: "For Beckett each novel is a journey into the unknown, into an area of utter lawlessness." And a *Times Literary Supplement* reviewer, in his discussion of *Imagination Dead Imagine,* summarizes Beckett's work thus: "[This novel] certainly describes two people in an imaginary situation and it is equally certainly a work of large implications and a desolate, cruel beauty. It might not seem so, however, if it had not been apparent for some time that Mr. Beckett's prose narratives compose a single, long saga of exclusion and heroic relinquishment as well as of the desperate, perhaps unavailing, pursuit of finality." A. I. Leventhal writes: "When Beckett changes to writing his novels in French he leaves behind him much of the humour, grim as it was, in his previous work. He has less interest in making his characters indulge in games to pass the time as in *Waiting for Godot.* They are now concentrating on their *penible* task of dying." Frank Kermode offers this analysis of the novels: "In Beckett's plays the theatrical demand for communicable rhythms and relatively crude satisfactions has had a beneficent effect. But in the novels he yields progressively to the magnetic pull of the primitive, to the desire to achieve, by various forms of decadence and deformation, some Work that eludes the intellect, avoids the spread nets of habitual meaning. Beckett is often allegorical, but he is allegorical in fitful patches, providing illusive toeholds to any reader scrambling for sense." Bersani hasn't discovered the toeholds (and laughs behind his hand at those who have), nor does he think he will, if, as he says, he continues to take Beckett "seriously." Bersani writes: "The most interesting fact about Samuel Beckett's novels is that they are, at their best, almost completely unreadable." Bersani, citing Beckett's expressed desire to fail (to be an artist, for Beckett, is to fail), finds his "extreme attempt to render literature autonomous" to be not only "an ironic reminder of the ultimate dependence of literature on life," but also a generally suspicious undertaking. "The attempt to eliminate 'occasion' from art," he writes, "is in itself an occasion, and insofar as this attempt is a process of what [Ruby] Cohn has called progressive 'retrenchment,' the process rather than the achievement becomes the subject of Beckett's work."

The fact that most of Beckett's important work was originally written in French is far more than coincidentally significant to his stylistic achievement. Coe explains: "Beckett, in the final analysis, is trying to say what cannot be said; he must be constantly on his guard, therefore, never to yield to the temptation of saying what the words would make him say. Only when language is, as it were, defeated, bound hand and foot; only when it is so rigorously disciplined that each word describes exactly and quasiscientifically the precise concept to which it is related and no other, only then, by the progressive elimination of that which precisely is, is there a remote chance for the human mind to divine the ultimate reality which is not. And this relentless, almost masochistic discipline, which reaches its culmination in *Comment c'est,* Beckett achieves by writing in a language which is not his own—in French." John Barth explains, however, that Beckett's denuded French is yet only another step in his creative process and must not be construed as a total achievement. Barth writes: "Beckett has become virtually mute, musewise, having progressed from marvelously constructed English sentences through terser and terser French ones to the unsyntactical, unpunctuated prose of *Comment c'est* and 'ultimately' to wordless mimes. One might extrapolate a theoretical course for Beckett: language, after all, consists of silence as well as sound, and the mime is still communication, . . . but by the language of action. But the language of action consists of rest as well as movement, and so in the context of Beckett's progress immobile, silent figures still aren't altogether ultimate. . . . For Beckett [in the 1960s, toward the end of his writing career], to cease to create altogether would be fairly meaningful: his crowning work, his 'last word.' What a convenient corner to paint yourself into!"

In 1967 the Firehouse Theatre of Minneapolis, directed by Marlow Hotchkiss, performed *Act without Words I* and *Act without Words II* simultaneously. Also in 1967, Jack Emery composed and performed an hour-long, one-man program consisting of "a selection of the desperate reveries and furious tirades of half a dozen of Samuel Beckett's dying heroes," including Malone, Hamm, and the Unnamable. A *Punch* reviewer writes: "Many of the passages are fatiguing to follow in the original novels but so conversational are the rhythms of Beckett's language and so eloquently does Mr. Emery speak them (except when he essays a scream) that the effect in a dark, hushed theatre of this grim gallows humour is electrifying. There is more to life than talking of waiting for death, but Beckett has phrases—'Vent the pent!'—that resound in the mind with the urgency of great poetry." Emery's program, which premiered at Arts Theatre, London, was also produced in Glasgow, Edinburgh, and Exeter.

Although unpublished for sixty years, Beckett's first novel, *Dream of Fair to Middling Women,* finally made it into print in the United States in 1993. The author composed the book as a young man of twenty-six during a summer spent in Paris. The protagonist of *Dream* is the adventurous Belacqua, and the story centers on his varied experiences in Dublin and Paris. Beckett's style here, according to Colm Toibin in the *London Review of Books,* "is a rambling stream of consciousness, full of asides and associations, with a tone of half-seriousness and oblique mockery. . . . The writing is self-conscious: it reads as though the writer wrote it merely to read it himself." Beckett himself described *Dream* as "the chest into which I threw my wild thoughts." And, as J. D. O'Hara comments in the *New York Times Book Review,* "he reused them, often word for word." In the end, George Craig asserts in the *Times Literary Supplement,* "this is Beckett's earliest venture, and it shows. . . . But . . . something important is going on: the search for [his] voice."

Similarly, Beckett's first play, *Eleutheria* (the title means "freedom" in Greek), collected dust in the author's trunk for nearly fifty years before being published in 1995. The dark, three-act comic piece concerns a privacy-obsessed writer who tries in vain to escape from his family and friends, spending most of the play fighting off their efforts to mend what's left of his life. *Eleutheria* was written just prior to *Waiting for Godot,* but it demanded rather complex staging (seventeen characters and two sets, both which are shown simultaneously in the first two acts before one disappears into the orchestra pit in the final act) and so was not produced in the 1950s when *Godot* burst onto the contemporary theatrical scene.

"No one . . . disputes that Beckett did not want *Eleutheria* published," explains Jonathan Kalb in an article for the *Village Voice.* Its publication in 1995 prompted considerable controversy among members of the literary establishment, with opponents appalled at the thought of the author's final request for its suppression—from his deathbed, no less—being ignored. Kalb notes that the play is neither "a hidden masterpiece" nor "a catastrophe," but rather "a fascinating, rare instance of Beckettian excess. . . . At times windy, redundant, even confusing, it will certainly take its proper place as a minor, formative work that is bouyed by eloquent and hilarious passages and the tantalizing seeds of great themes, devices, and characters to come." As Mel Gussow puts it in the *New York Times Book Review,* "*Waiting for Godot* is revolutionary; *Eleutheria* is evolutionary."

Few critics have discussed Beckett's ideas (or the man himself) apart from their manifestation in his work. And Beckett would doubtless have it so. As Robert Wernick writes, "so striking is the personality that emerges from [his] gloomy plays and so striking [was] the occasionally glimpsed, gaunt pterodactylous face of the real-life Samuel Beckett that many people assume[d] the two [were] identical. A whole folklore of anecdote has grown up around Beckett, in which he appears as a fanatic solitary, brooding eternally . . . on the black mystery of the human race. . . . It is true that he . . . built a wall around his country house, but he denie[d] that he built it, as people contend, to shut out the view. It is true he avoid[ed] all the trappings of the celebrity life, [gave] no interviews, attend[ed] no cultural congresses. But then, why should he [have]?" Alec Reid met Beckett in New York during the making of *Film* and described him as "a close-knit person, all of a piece." Reid says that Beckett "believe[d] that physical movement conveys at least as much as the words. . . . Once the initial reserve . . . evaporated Beckett reveal[ed] a genius for companionship, a remarkable ability to make those around him feel the better for his presence."

*BIOGRAPHICAL/CRITICAL SOURCES:*

*BOOKS*

Abbott, H. Porter, *Beckett Writing Beckett: The Author in the Autograph,* Cornell University Press (Ithaca, NY), 1996.

Allsop, Kenneth, *The Angry Decade,* Copp, 1958.
Armstrong, William A., and others, editors, *Experimental Drama,* G. Bell, 1963.
*Beckett at Sixty* (a festschrift by twenty-four of his friends), Calder & Boyars, 1967.
Brater, Enoch, *The Drama in the Text: Beckett's Late Fiction,* Oxford University Press (New York City), 1994.
Butler, Lance St. John, *Critical Essays on Samuel Beckett,* Ashgate Publishing Co. (Brookfield, VT), 1994.
Coe, Richard N., *Beckett,* Oliver & Boyd, 1964.
Cohn, Ruby, *Samuel Beckett: The Comic Gamut,* Rutgers University Press, 1962.
*Contemporary Literary Criticism,* Gale (Detroit), Volume 1, 1973, Volume 2, 1974, Volume 3, 1975, Volume 4, 1975, Volume 6, 1976, Volume 9, 1978, Volume 10, 1979, Volume 11, 1979, Volume 14, 1980, Volume 18, 1981, Volume 29, 1984, Volume 57, 1990, Volume 59, 1990, Volume 83, 1994.
Cronin, Anthony, *Samuel Beckett: The Last Modernist,* HarperCollins, 1996.
Danziger, Marie A., *Text/Countertext: Fear, Guilt, and Retaliation in the Postmodern Novel,* Peter Lang (New York City), 1996.
Davies, Paul, *The Ideal Real: Beckett's Fiction and Imagination,* Associated University Presses (Cranbury, NJ), 1994.
*Dictionary of Literary Biography,* Gale, Volume 13: *British Dramatists since World War II,* 1982, Volume 15: *British Novelists, 1930-1959,* 1983.
Dillon, Brian, *Beckett's Blurry Signature,* Department of Liberal Arts, Nova University (Ft. Lauderdale, FL), 1995.
Esslin, Martin, *The Theatre of the Absurd,* Doubleday-Anchor, 1961.
Fletcher, John, *Samuel Beckett's Art,* Barnes & Noble, 1967.
Gassner, John, *Theatre at the Crossroads,* Holt, 1960.
Gordon, Lois G., *The World of Samuel Beckett, 1906-1946,* Yale University Press (New Haven), 1996.
Guicharnaud, Jacques, and June Beckelman, *Modern French Theatre from Giraudoux to Beckett,* Yale University Press, 1961.
Harding, James M., *Adorno and "A Writing of the Ruins": Essays on Modern Aesthetics and Anglo-American Literature and Culture,* State University of New York Press (Albany), 1997.
Hoffman, Frederick J., *Samuel Beckett: The Language of Self,* Southern Illinois University Press, 1962.
Kenner, Hugh, *Samuel Beckett,* J. Calder, 1962.
Kenner, Hugh, *A Reader's Guide to Samuel Beckett,* Syracuse University Press (Syracuse, NY), 1996.
Kermode, Frank, *Puzzles and Epiphanies,* Chilmark, 1962.
Kim, Hwa Soon, *The Counterpoint of Hope, Obsession, and Desire for Death in Five Plays by Samuel Beckett,* P. Lang (New York City), 1996.
Knowlson, James, *Damned to Fame: The Life of Samuel Beckett,* Bloomsbury, 1996.
Kostelanetz, Richard, editor, *On Contemporary Literature,* Avon, 1954.
Lumley, Frederick, *New Trends in Twentieth-Century Drama,* Oxford University Press, 1967.
Minihan, John and Aidan Higgins, *Samuel Beckett: Photographs,* George Braziller (New York City), 1996.
Murphy, P. J., *Critique of Beckett Criticism: A Guide to Research in English, French, and German,* Camden House (Columbia, SC), 1994.
Oppenheim, Lois, *Directing Beckett,* University of Michigan Press (Ann Arbor), 1994.
Oppenheim, Lois, Marius Buning and The International Beckett Symposium, *Beckett On and On,* Farleigh Dickinson University Press (Madison, NJ), 1996.
Piette, Adam, *Remembering and the Sound of Words: Mallarmae, Proust, Joyce, Beckett,* Clarendon Press (New York City), 1996.
Pilling, John, *The Cambridge Companion to Beckett,* Cambridge University Press (New York City), 1994.
Pultar, Geoneul, *Technique and Tradition in Beckett's Trilogy of Novels,* University Press of America (Lanham, MD), 1996.
Simpson, Alan, *Beckett and Behan and a Theatre in Dublin,* Routledge & Kegan Paul, 1962.
Smith, H. A., and R. D. Smith, contributors, *Contemporary Theatre,* Stratford-upon-Avon Studies 4, edited by John Russell Brown and Bernard Harris, Edward Arnold, 1962.
Tindall, William York, *Samuel Beckett,* Columbia University Press, 1964.
Tynan, Kenneth, *Curtains,* Atheneum, 1961.
Wellwarth, George, *Theatre of Protest and Paradox,* New York University Press, 1964.
Wolosky, Shira, *Language Mysticism: The Negative Way of Language in Eliot, Beckett, and Celan,* Stanford University Press (Stanford, CA), 1995.

*PERIODICALS*

*American Scholar,* winter, 1992, p. 124.
*Atlantic,* August, 1967.
*Carleton Miscellany,* winter, 1967.

*Christian Science Monitor,* July 27, 1967.
*Comparative Literature,* winter, 1965.
*Connoisseur,* July, 1990, p. 56.
*Critique,* spring, 1963; winter, 1964-65.
*Economist,* January 6, 1990, p. 90.
*Esquire,* September, 1967; May, 1990, p. 87.
*Hudson Review,* spring, 1967.
*Kenyon Review,* March, 1967.
*Kirkus Reviews,* February 15, 1993, p. 162.
*Life,* February 2, 1968.
*Listener,* August 3, 1967.
*Livres de France,* January, 1967.
*London Magazine,* August, 1967.
*London Review of Books,* November 9, 1989, p. 26; April 8, 1993, p. 14.
*Manchester Guardian,* April 21, 1966.
*Nation,* October 3, 1987, p. 349; December 19, 1988, p. 26; April 30, 1990, p. 611; May 6, 1996, p. 16.
*New Republic,* December 12, 1988, p. 26; October 22, 1990, p. 30.
*New Statesman,* February 14, 1964; March 25, 1966; July 14, 1967.
*New Statesman & Society,* July 6, 1990, p. 46; October 11, 1991, p. 22; January 8, 1993, p. 42.
*New York,* September 28, 1987, p. 133; July 11, 1988, p. 46.
*New York Review of Books,* March 19, 1964; December 7, 1967; December 8, 1988, p. 30; August 13, 1992, p. 17; December 16, 1993, p. 42.
*New York Times,* July 21, 1964; February 27, 1966; April 19, 1966; July 20, 1967; September 14, 1967.
*New York Times Book Review,* June 12, 1988, p. 18; June 13, 1993, p. 11; April 17, 1994, p. 24; June 25, 1995, p. 9; May 26, 1996, p. 4.
*Observer* (London), July 16, 1967; July 15, 1990, p. 53; July 22, 1990, p. 52; November 1, 1992, p. 62.
*Partisan Review,* spring, 1966.
*Publishers Weekly,* September 26, 1994, p. 12.
*Punch,* August 2, 1967.
*Saturday Review,* October 4, 1958.
*Time,* July 14, 1967; November 21, 1988, p. 58.
*Times Literary Supplement,* December 21, 1962; January 30, 1964; June 30, 1966; July 20, 1990, p. 782; November 27, 1992, p. 25.
*Tri-Quarterly,* winter, 1967.
*Tulane Drama Review,* summer, 1967.
*Village Voice,* April 6, 1967; July 13, 1967; June 20, 1995, p. 69.
*Washington Post Book World,* May 23, 1993, p. 8.
*World Literature Today,* winter, 1994, p. 125; autumn, 1995, p. 761.

*OBITUARIES:*

*PERIODICALS*

*Chicago Tribune,* December 27, 1989.
*Los Angeles Times,* December 27, 1989.
*Maclean's,* January 8, 1990, p. 47.
*Newsweek,* January 8, 1990, p. 43.
*New York Times,* December 27, 1989.
*People,* January 8, 1990, p. 46.
*Time,* January 8, 1990, p. 69.*

* * *

**BELLAH, James Warner 1899-1976**

*PERSONAL:* Born September 14, 1899, in New York, NY; died in 1976; son of James Warner (a merchant) and Harriette (Johnson) Bellah; married Helen Lasater Hopkins, October 22, 1942; children: James II, Ann Power, John Lasater, Stephen Hopkins. *Education:* Wesleyan University, Middletown, CT, student, 1919-22; Columbia University, A.B., 1923; Georgetown University, M.A., 1945; University of Pennsylvania, postgraduate study. *Politics:* Republican. *Religion:* Episcopalian. *Avocational interests:* Bellah held epee and sabre championships in France and the United States and was a competitor in Atlantic ocean sailing races.

*CAREER:* Advertising copywriter, New York City, 1923-26; Columbia University, New York City, instructor in English, 1923-26; *Aero Digest,* correspondent in Europe and Far East, 1927-30; freelance writer, 1930-76. James Warner Bellah, Inc., president; Lancaster & Chester Railroad, vice-president. Licensed as pilot, Federation Aeronautique Internationale, 1918; member of Pan-American Airways crew on first regular mail plane, Miami to Panama, 1929. Lecturer in United States and Canada, 1947-49. Civil War Centennial Commission, member of national advisory committee and of California executive committee. *Military service:* Royal Air Force, pilot, 1917-19; became second lieutenant. U.S. Army, Infantry and General Staff Corps, 1939-45; graduate of Army Command and General Staff College, 1940, with 1st and 80th Infantry Divisions, 1942-43, at headquarters, Southeast Asia Command, 1943-44; became colonel. Decorations for service in both World Wars include Legion of Merit, Bronze Star Medal, Air Medal, Commendation Pendant,

Combat Infantry Badge, Combat Glider Badge, Imperial Russian Order of St. Nicholas.

*MEMBER:* Sons of the Revolution, Society of Colonial Wars, American Legion, Columbia University Club (New York), Royal Air Force Club (London), British United Services Club (Los Angeles).

*AWARDS, HONORS:* Knopf Prize for *Sketch Book,* 1923; *Time* Award for best western film of 1961 for *A Thunder of Drums;* Western Heritage Award for outstanding western film of 1962 for *The Man Who Shot Liberty Vance;* Georgetown University 175th Anniversary Medal of Honor, 1963.

*WRITINGS:*

*Sketch Book of a Cadet from Gascony,* Knopf (New York City), 1923.
*These Frantic Years,* Appleton (New York City), 1927.
*The Sons of Cain,* Appleton, 1928.
*Gods of Yesterday,* Appleton, 1928.
*Dancing Lady,* Farrar & Rinehart (New York City), 1932.
*White Piracy,* Farrar & Rinehart, 1933.
*South by East a Half East,* privately published, 1936.
*The Brass Gong Tree,* Appleton, 1936.
*This Is the Town,* Appleton, 1937.
*Seven Must Die,* Appleton, 1938.
*The Bones of Napoleon,* Appleton, 1940.
*Ward Twenty,* Doubleday (New York City), 1946.
*Irregular Gentleman,* Doubleday, 1948.
*Massacre,* Lion Books (New York City), 1950.
*Rear Guard,* Popular Library (New York City), 1950.
*The Apache,* Gold Medal (New York City), 1951.
*Divorce,* Popular Library, 1952.
*The Valiant Virginians,* Ballantine (New York City), 1953.
*Ordeal at Blood River,* Ballantine, 1959.
*Sergeant Rutledge,* Bantam (New York City), 1960.
*A Thunder of Drums,* Bantam, 1961.
*Soldiers Battle—Gettysburg,* McKay (New York City), 1962.
*Reveille,* Gold Medal, 1962.
*Fighting Men USA,* Regnery (Evanston, IL), 1963.
*The Journal of Colonel De Lancey,* Chilton (Philadelphia), 1967.

*SCREENPLAYS*

*Dancing Lady,* 1933.
*Fort Apache,* 1948.
*She Wore a Yellow Ribbon,* 1949.
*Rio Grande,* 1950.
(With others) *Ten Tall Men,* 1952.
(With John Twist) *The Sea Chase,* 1955.
(With Sam Rolfe) *Target Zero,* 1956.
(With Willis Goldbeck) *Sergeant Rutledge,* 1960.
(With Tony Lazzarino) *X-15,* 1961.
*A Thunder of Drums,* 1961.
(With Goldbeck) *The Man Who Shot Liberty Vance,* 1962.

Author of dialogue for film *This Is Korea.*

*OTHER*

Contributor to magazines, including *Saturday Evening Post* and *Holiday.* Stories included in twenty-five anthologies. Bellah's novels were translated into fifteen languages. Bellah's literary files have been presented to the Boston University Library.

*SIDELIGHTS:* James Warner Bellah wrote adventure novels, Westerns, romantic mysteries and such well-known screenplays as *Fort Apache, Rio Grande* and *She Wore a Yellow Ribbon*—all filmed by director John Ford. Jon Tuska in *Twentieth-Century Western Writers* claimed that "Bellah wrote a vivid, hard prose and his plots were almost always structured with unusual precision."

Beginning as a magazine writer, Bellah quickly switched to writing a variety of novels during the 1920s and 1930s. His early work often featured military situations. *These Frantic Years,* for example, tells of a wounded aviator who must go through rehabilitation following the First World War. The critic for the *Boston Transcript* called the novel "a brilliant piece of post-war literature," while the reviewer for the *Independent* found that "Bellah handles the fast-moving plot with the verve which has made his short stories so popular." *Gods of Yesterday* contains stories of the air corps during the war, including Bellah's story "Fear" which the *New York Times* critic called "beautifully written, psychologically sound, . . . a splendid rendering of the loyalty and high courage which . . . characterized the members of the British flying units."

By the 1930s, Bellah's novels had moved from a wartime setting to America's high society. *White Piracy,* for example, focuses on a wealthy Maryland family and their carefree lifestyle. The *Saturday Review of Literature* critic found the novel "written in the quick, sparkling patter of a Broadway show." Lisle Bell in *Books* praised the novel's "vivid personalities—frank in speech and rash in action. Their emotions and what they do about them are presented in a deft and colorful narrative." In *This Is the Town* Bellah writes of a Southern girl coming to New York City to make a fortune and falling in with the theatrical crowd. Charlotte Dean in the *New York Times* called the story "spontaneous, real and likable. . . . It is the bright insularity of Manhattan's theatre crowd talking nonsense that gives the book distinction."

Bellah also wrote several adventure novels during the 1930s, often set in Southeast Asia. *Brass Gong Tree* concerns the assassination of two top Japanese statesmen and the efforts of American newsman Sturgis Hammond to uncover the real story. The reviewer for the *New York Times* described the book as a "rapid-fire tale" enlivened by "the intensity and color of Mr. Bellah's descriptive writing." *Seven Must Die* follows the South Seas search for a missing ship loaded with pearls. Dean found the story to be "smoothly written. The people talk like real people, the characters are sharply defined."

After serving in the Second World War (he had already served as a Royal Air Force pilot in the First World War), Bellah wrote *Ward Twenty,* a novel set in a veterans' hospital. Noted for its stark realism, the novel drew praise from a number of critics for its frank account of those damaged by war and the conditions they must endure. E. D. Branch of *Book Week* called the novel "vivid, poignant, beautiful. . . . There's hardly a book in the fiction of World War II that you can mention in the same breath." James McBride in the *New York Times* believed that Bellah's "book is a grim reminder of the price American youth has paid—and must go on paying—for today's fumble at a decent world." A. Q. Maisel in the *Saturday Review of Literature* described *Ward Twenty* as "a shocking book . . . because it admits frankly the facts that most of us would avoid facing."

Bellah's Western screenplays earned him a lasting place in cinematic history. Director John Ford's adaptations of three Bellah stories, often referred to as Ford's "cavalry trilogy," starred John Wayne and are ranked among the best work by that film team. Despite this success, Tuska believed that in his Western screenplays and novels, Bellah exhibited "a combination of white supremacy and social Darwinism." Indian characters in Bellah's work, Tuska believed, are often portrayed in unflattering terms. Citing Bellah's screenplay *A Thunder of Drums,* Tuska claimed that it "celebrated male celibacy, misogyny, and devotion to military life."

In his autobiography *Irregular Gentleman,* Bellah gathered together a number of his favorite anecdotes and reminiscences to tell of a life of wide travel and famous friends. The *Kirkus* reviewer described the book as "a potpourri of an adventurous life," while Thomas Sugrue in the *New York Times* claimed that "if there was a dull page in the manuscript, someone removed it before publication. . . . There is no continuity, no chronology, no particular pattern to the anecdotes as Mr. Bellah relates them, but they build in detail the picture of a man, a man with a large appetite for living."

*BIOGRAPHICAL/CRITICAL SOURCES:*

*BOOKS*

Bellah, James Warner, *Irregular Gentleman,* Doubleday, 1948.

*Twentieth-Century Western Writers,* second edition, St. James Press (Detroit), 1991.

*PERIODICALS*

*Annals of the American Academy,* March, 1963, p. 346.

*Bookman,* May 28, 1928, p. 67.

*Books,* October 29, 1933, p. 10; September 20, 1936, p. 16; August 8, 1937, p. 8; January 30, 1938, p. 12; June 30, 1940, p. 14.

*Book Week,* January 6, 1946, p. 1.

*Boston Transcript,* June 11, 1927, p. 4; March 7, 1928, p. 2.

*Independent,* May 7, 1927, p. 22.

*Kirkus,* November 1, 1945, p. 13; December 15, 1947, p. 15.

*Library Journal,* December 15, 1945, p. 70; July, 1962, p. 86.

*New Yorker,* January 12, 1946, p. 21.

*New York Herald Tribune Books,* November 4, 1928, p. 20.

*New York Times,* February 19, 1928, p. 18; November 18, 1928, p. 34; September 27, 1936, p. 17; August 15, 1937, p. 17; February 6, 1938, p. 20; June 30, 1940, p. 14; January 13, 1946, p. 6; February 22, 1948, p. 7.

*San Francisco Chronicle,* April 18, 1948, p. 16.

*Saturday Review,* December 29, 1962, p. 45.

*Saturday Review of Literature,* May 12, 1928, p. 4; October 21, 1933, p. 10; June 29, 1940, p. 22; February 9, 1946, p. 29; May 22, 1948, p. 31.

*Springfield Republican,* February 3, 1946, p. 4D.

*Times Literary Supplement,* March 8, 1928, p. 168.

*U.S. Quarterly Booklist,* September, 1946, p. 2.
*Weekly Book Review,* January 13, 1946, p. 2.*

* * *

## BELLE, Pamela 1952-

*PERSONAL:* Born June 16, 1952, in Ipswich, England; daughter of Brian Henry (a teacher) and Sylvia (a homemaker; maiden name, Wilkinson) Belle; married Alan David Fincher, July 3, 1976 (divorced, 1983); married Stephen Thomas, August 6, 1990; children: Hugh. *Education:* Ipswich School of Art, 1969-70; Ipswich Civic College, 1970-71; University of Sussex, Brighton, B.A.(with honors), 1975; Coventry College of Education, postgraduate certificate in education, 1976. *Politics:* "Slightly left of center." *Religion:* None.

*ADDRESSES:* *Home*—184 Melksham Lane, Broughton Gifford, Melksham, Wiltshire SN12 8LN, England. *Agent*—Vivienne Schuster, John Farquharson Ltd., 162-168 Regent St., London W1R 5TB, England.

*CAREER:* Hemel Hempstead, Hertfordshire, England, library assistant, 1976-77; Hemel Hempstead, Tring and Berkhamsted, Hertfordshire, primary school teacher, 1977-78; Northchurch St. Mary's First School, Berkhamsted, primary school teacher, 1978-85. Writer, 1985—.

*MEMBER:* National Union of Teachers, Richard III Society.

*WRITINGS:*

ROMANCE AND HISTORICAL NOVELS

*The Moon in the Water* (first novel in the "Goldhayes Trilogy"), Berkley Publishing (New York City), 1984.
*The Chains of Fate* (second novel in the "Goldhayes Trilogy"), Berkley Publishing, 1984.
*Alathea* (third novel in the "Goldhayes Trilogy"), Berkley Publishing, 1985.
*The Lodestar,* St. Martin's (New York City), 1988.
*Wintercombe* (first novel in the "Wintercombe" series), St. Martin's, 1988.
*Herald of Joy* (second novel in the "Wintercombe" series), St. Martin's, 1989.
*A Falling Star* (third novel in the "Wintercombe" series), St. Martin's, 1990.
*Treason's Gift* (fourth novel in the "Wintercombe" series), St. Martin's, 1993.

*SIDELIGHTS:* Pamela Belle is a British author of romance and historical fiction, whose novels frequently take place in the seventeenth century and involve large families and hard-earned love. Critics have praised her characterizations of children, women, and villains, in addition to her realistic depictions of historical time periods. In *Twentieth-Century Romance and Historical Writers,* contributor Pamela Cleaver lauds that "the thoughts and attitudes of [Belle's] characters always ring true to their time."

Belle's first three novels, *The Moon in the Water, The Chains of Fate,* and *Alathea,* form the "Goldhayes Trilogy." These books feature the many branches of the Heron family. Thomazine Heron is the protagonist of the first two books; her daughter, Alathea, is the main character in the third title.

The first "Goldhayes" book, *The Moon in the Water,* called a "fetching romance" by a *Booklist* reviewer takes place in Elizabethan England and revolves around the orphaned Thomazine Heron who is being raised by her uncle with her five cousins on the Goldhayes Estate. In time, Thomazine falls in love with her quixotic cousin Francis. However, Thomazine's uncle has promised her to a different cousin, Sir Dominic Drakelon. Unhappy about the proposed marriage, Thomazine breaks the engagement upon her uncle's death. Thomazine and Francis, however, are not reunited. Francis is thrown in jail as a traitor, and Thomazine believes he has been killed. The marriage plans for Thomazine and the villainous Drakelon are reinstated, and eventually a child is born into their loveless marriage. The novel concludes with Thomazine leaving her husband and son in search of Francis after she discovers that he is still alive. A *Publishers Weekly* reviewer deems *The Moon in the Water* "a top-drawer historical romance."

*The Chains of Fate* picks up where *The Moon in the Water* ends. Thomazine makes her way to Francis, who is thought to be close to the Scottish border fighting in a civil war. She finds him with a group of Royalist supporters. After a bit of resistance, Francis admits he still cares for Thomazine, yet again they separate. Eventually, Drakelon dies and Thomazine is reunited with her son. At long last, when Thomazine and Francis are married, they have a baby girl, Alathea, and settle down at Goldhayes. A writer for

*Kirkus Reviews* assesses the novel as "a hard-working, unobjectionable amalgam of high-strung romance, family-saga woes, and potted history."

Following the "Goldhayes Trilogy," Belle wrote *The Lodestar,* which goes further back in time to portray the Herons and Drakelons of the fifteenth century. The story is told using the seventeenth century as a frame for the fifteenth-century story. The first two titles of the "Wintercombe" series focus on Silence St Barbe, an unhappily married woman who becomes pregnant during an extramarital affair. The next two "Wintercombe" novels feature the love between Alexander St Barbe and Louise Chevalier. Overall, Cleaver summarizes that Belle's novels "can be confidently recommended to all who enjoy a romantic story, forceful characters and fast-moving action."

Belle once told *CA:* "Originally I wrote purely for my own enjoyment. Successful publication was a bonus! I have no particular viewpoint to put forth or axe to grind, although I tend to fill my books with all the things I find enjoyable: poetry, music, magic, food, animals, children, humor, and the fascination of entering a world long vanished. My characters also tend to reflect my own beliefs and prejudices on the equality of women and the importance of love, tolerance, and compassion, my distrust of organized religion, and my love of the world of imagination. Nevertheless, my main concern is to tell my story entertainingly and convincingly, and more serious considerations are by the way. I would rather have my books read and enjoyed by many and ignored by serious reviewers than write more difficult and obscure works that, like many 'classics,' people think they ought to read, but haven't.

"I do, however, place great importance on proper historical research. I think this is because my characters seem so real to me that I cannot bear to destroy the illusion by falsifying the picture. Everything I write about *could* have happened or existed, even if it never did in reality. I want my characters to be sufficiently real and alive to lead my readers into my own enjoyment and study of history."

*BIOGRAPHICAL/CRITICAL SOURCES:*

*BOOKS*

*Twentieth-Century Romance and Historical Writers,* edited by Aruna Vasudevan, St. James Press (Detroit), 1994.

*PERIODICALS*

*Booklist,* August, 1984, p. 1596.
*Kirkus Review,* June 15, 1984, p. 533; August 15, 1984, pp. 761-62.
*Publishers Weekly,* June 29, 1984, p. 102.
*Washington Post,* October 9, 1984.
*Washington Post Book World,* November 6, 1988, p. 8.*

* * *

## BETTELHEIM, Bruno 1903-1990

*PERSONAL:* Born August 28, 1903, in Vienna, Austria; came to United States in 1939, naturalized citizen in 1944; committed suicide after long illness, March 13, 1990, in Silver Springs, MD; son of Anton and Paula (Seidler) Bettelheim; married Gertrud Weinfeld (a teacher and researcher; died, 1984), May 14, 1941; children: Ruth, Naomi, Eric. *Education:* University of Vienna, Ph.D., 1938. *Politics:* Democrat. *Religion:* Jewish.

*CAREER:* Progressive Education Association, Chicago, IL, research associate, 1939-41; Rockford College, Rockford, IL, associate professor of psychology, 1942-44; University of Chicago, Chicago, assistant professor, 1944-47, associate professor, 1947-52, professor of educational psychology, 1952-73, Stella M. Rowley Distinguished Service Professor of Education, and professor of psychology and psychiatry, 1963-73, head of Sonia Shankman Orthogenic School, 1944-73; writer, 1973-90. Diplomate of American Psychological Association. Fellow of Center for Advanced Studies in the Behavioral Sciences, 1971-72. Former member of Chicago Council for Child Psychology.

*MEMBER:* American Psychological Association (fellow), American Orthopsychiatric Association (fellow), American Philosophical Association, American Association of University Professors, American Sociological Association, American Academy of Education (founding member), American Academy of Arts and Sciences, Chicago Psychoanalytical Society, Quadrangle Club.

*AWARDS, HONORS:* D.H.L. from Cornell University; National Book Award and National Book Critics Circle Award, both 1977, both for *The Uses of Enchantment: The Meaning and Importance of Fairy*

*Tales; Los Angeles Times* current interest prize nominee, 1983, for *Freud and Man's Soul.*

*WRITINGS:*

(With Morris Janowitz) *Dynamics of Prejudice: A Psychological and Sociological Study of Veterans,* Harper, 1950.

*Love Is Not Enough: The Treatment of Emotionally Disturbed Children,* Free Press, 1950.

*Overcoming Prejudice* (booklet), Science Research Associates, 1953.

*Symbolic Wounds: Puberty Rites and the Envious Male,* Free Press, 1954, revised edition, Collier Books, 1962.

*Truants from Life: The Rehabilitation of Emotionally Disturbed Children,* Free Press, 1955.

*The Informed Heart: Autonomy in a Mass Age,* Free Press, 1960.

*Paul and Mary: Two Case Histories from "Truants from Life,"* Doubleday-Anchor, 1961.

(With others) *Youth: Change and Challenge* (proceedings of the American Academy of Arts and Sciences), American Academy of Arts and Sciences, 1961.

*Dialogues with Mothers,* Free Press, 1962.

*Child Guidance, a Community Responsibility: An Address, with a Summary of Public Provisions for Child Guidance Services to Michigan Communities,* Institute for Community Development and Services, Continuing Education Service, Michigan State University, 1962.

(With Janowitz) *Social Change and Prejudice: Including Dynamics of Prejudice,* Free Press, 1964.

*Art: As the Measure of Man,* Museum of Modern Art, 1964.

*The Empty Fortress: Infantile Autism and the Birth of the Self,* Free Press, 1967.

*Mental Health in the Slums: Preliminary Draft,* Center of Policy Study, University of Chicago, 1968.

*The Children of the Dream,* Macmillan, 1969, reprinted as *The Children of the Dream: Communal Childrearing and American Education,* Avon, 1970, published in England as *The Children of the Dream: Communal Child-Rearing and Its Implications for Society,* Paladin, 1971.

*Food to Nurture the Mind,* Children's Foundation (Washington, DC), 1970.

*Obsolete Youth: Toward a Psychograph of Adolescent Rebellion,* San Francisco Press, 1970.

(With others) *Moral Education: Five Lectures,* Harvard University Press, 1970.

*A Home for the Heart,* Knopf, 1974.

*The Uses of Enchantment: The Meaning and Importance of Fairy Tales,* Knopf, 1976.

*Surviving, and Other Essays,* Knopf, 1979, reprinted with a new introduction as *Surviving the Holocaust,* Flamingo, 1986.

(With Karen Zelan) *On Learning to Read: The Child's Fascination with Meaning,* Knopf, 1982.

*Freud and Man's Soul,* Knopf, 1982.

(With Anne Freedgood) *A Good Enough Parent: A Book on Child-Rearing,* Knopf, 1987.

*Freud's Vienna and Other Essays,* Knopf, 1990.

(With Nathan M. Szajnberg) *Educating the Emotions: Bruno Bettelheim and Psychoanalytic Development* (also see below), Plenum Press (New York City), 1992.

(With Alvin A. Rosenfeld) *The Art of the Obvious,* Knopf (New York City), 1993.

Columnist for *Ladies' Home Journal.* Contributor to professional and popular journals, including *New Yorker* and *New York Times Book Review.*

*SIDELIGHTS:* Bruno Bettelheim was a world authority on the treatment of childhood emotional disorders, especially autism and juvenile psychosis. Himself a survivor of debilitating experiences in concentration camps at Dachau and Buchenwald, Bettelheim brought to his work firsthand knowledge of the acute anxiety engendered by extreme situations; his efforts with mentally ill children reflect his sensitivity to their often-unarticulated fears. Bettelheim's writings have found an audience beyond the psychoanalytic community, as he seeks to explain psychological phenomena without resorting to professional jargon. In books such as *Love Is Not Enough: The Treatment of Emotionally Disturbed Children, Truants from Life: The Rehabilitation of Emotionally Disturbed Children,* and *The Empty Fortress: Infantile Autism and the Birth of the Self,* he described the pioneering efforts of staff at the Sonia Shankman Orthogenic School of the University of Chicago, where he presided from 1944 until 1973. He also wrote two penetrating works on the Nazi death camps, *The Informed Heart: Autonomy in a Mass Age* and *Surviving, and Other Essays,* both of which explore the psychological legacy of the camp experience. After his retirement from the University of Chicago, Bettelheim undertook other projects aimed at specialists and general readers alike. He sounded a call for childhood intellectual stimulation in *The Uses of Enchantment: The Meaning and Importance of Fairy Tales* and *On Learning to Read: The Child's Fascination with Meaning,* and he discussed the implications of mistranslation in *Freud and Man's Soul. Spectator* contributor Anthony Storr believes that Bettelheim's writings bear witness to a "long and fruitful life" celebrating "the fact that the human spirit can sometimes triumph over Hell itself."

*New York Times Book Review* correspondent Paul Roazen observes that Bettelheim "stands as one of Freud's genuine heirs in our time. Fearlessly independent and yet working within Freud's great discoveries, Bettelheim has sought to think through all of human psychology for himself." To a certain extent, Bettelheim's life paralleled that of the "father of psychoanalysis." Both Bettelheim and Freud grew up in Vienna; both chose to work and live there until Nazi atrocities forced them to go elsewhere. As a young student forty-seven years Freud's junior, Bettelheim was strongly influenced by psychoanalytic theory and was frankly awed by Freud's accomplishments. In a piece for the *New York Times Book Review,* Bettelheim recalled passing the apartment building where Freud lived and worked: "I used to walk on this street, more often than not choosing to use this hilly, unattractive way to get where I was going only because Freud lived there." Having received a Ph.D. in psychology from the University of Vienna in 1938—and having undergone psychoanalysis—Bettelheim set himself on a career dedicated to "a distinctive vein of Freudian orthodoxy, free of the scholasticism that has settled like dust over psychoanalytic literature," according to Joseph Featherstone in *The New Republic.* Like Freud, Bettelheim undertook clinical work that had lasting implications for his writings. Featherstone claims: "In his hands, orthodox concepts are metaphors for real experiences, not abstractions leading bloodless lives of their own."

The Nazis annexed Austria in 1938, just after Bettelheim had finished his degree requirements. Later that same year, Bettelheim, a Jew, was arrested and sent first to Dachau and then to Buchenwald. He endured the camps for one year, and when he was released, he drew upon his harrowing experiences there to form his professional positions. Storr notes that, while incarcerated, Bettelheim "was able to use his psychoanalytic experience and insight to distance himself from the impact of what surrounded him, and that made it possible for him to come through. Bettelheim was not only able to survive, but also to make positive use of his experience." In fact, Bettelheim conducted research in the camps and observed the impact of the life-threatening and dehumanizing environment on numerous individuals. After being freed and moving to the United States, he summarized these observations in a landmark article, "Individual and Mass Behavior in Extreme Situations." Ironically, the article, which was the first by a scholar to detail Nazi methods, was rejected by numerous periodicals until 1943, when it appeared in *The Journal of Abnormal and Social Psychology.* As the death camps were liberated, revealing Bettelheim's assertions and conclusions to be true, his article gained worldwide renown and became required reading for all officers in the United States military service.

Bettelheim's camp experiences are explored in more depth in *The Informed Heart* and *Surviving, and Other Essays.* "Although Bettelheim's contribution to our understanding of psychotic children is important," Storr writes, "it is by his account of the concentration camps that he will be remembered. . . . *The Informed Heart* has long been famous. . . . What he has to say is of such signal importance to our understanding of human nature that it cannot be too often repeated." *New York Review of Books* contributor Charles Rycroft describes *The Informed Heart* as "largely an analysis of what decided whether a person lived or died in a concentration camp. In it [ Bettelheim] was concerned not so much with the physical capacity to survive brutality and torture as with the psychological factors determining whether a person will be able to resist demoralization in a setting in which he has ceased to be in any way a free agent a setting, moreover, which is designed to reduce him to a nonentity and, indeed, has no wish that he should go on living." Critics have found much to praise in *The Informed Heart.* In his *New York Times Book Review* assessment, Franz Alexander remarks: "This is a dignified book, convincing because it is not derived from textbook knowledge, but from insights gained in the laboratory of the author's own life. In it reason and life experiences are closely integrated." *New Statesman* essayist Maurice Richardson contends that the book "gives you the impression of being lit from within by a humanist glow. [Bettelheim's] clinical but by no means cold detachment from the horrors, both factual and social of the camps is moving and impressive."

Almost twenty years separate the publication dates of *The Informed Heart* and *Surviving, and Other Essays.* The latter work represents Bettelheim's retrospective attempts to understand not only the burden of experience he bears, but also the lasting legacy of guilt and commitment borne by all survivors. "The experience had to be confronted," Clara Claiborne Park declares in the *Nation,* "not because it could be denied or left behind . . . but because only by confronting it, not once but over and over again, could meaning be found. The full heroism of that early objectivity [in

*The Informed Heart*] can be measured only after reading the later essays." In a *New York Times Book Review* assessment of *Surviving, and Other Essays,* Paul Robinson writes: "Among Bettelheim's many virtues are intellectual humility, analytic skill and unfailing clarity of expression. He is altogether compelling when he recounts his experiences as a camp inmate and survivor. He's not merely persuasive, but moving when he tells that he was able to retain his identity within the camps because, in his earlier life, he had cultivated the powers of observation and analysis. . . . In his survival, one witnesses the triumph of civilization, of mind, of inner culture against almost impossible odds, and the prospect is exhilarating." *New York Review of Books* essayist Rosemary Dinnage adds that the collection exposes Bettelheim's two great strengths: "his totally realistic acceptance of the satanic in human beings and of the gross disintegrations of personality this can impose on others, and his simultaneous unshaken confidence in order and mutuality and reconstruction." Claiborne Park similarly concludes that in *Surviving, and Other Essays,* "it is finally to the humanity of society that Bettelheim has survived to bear witness."

According to Richard Rhodes in the *Chicago Tribune Book World,* Bettelheim's identity as a psychologist and teacher is closely linked to his identity as a survivor of the Holocaust. Bettelheim's experimental approach at the Orthogenic School "was directly a result of his camp experience," Rhodes states. "He saw at Dachau that a total environment is a far more powerful instrument of personality change than the partial environment of classical psychoanalysis. . . . He realized that camp victims and psychotic children have much in common—that both became what they became by adapting to extreme situations. He designed his school, then, as a total environment that might reverse in the direction of healing and of hope the total environments of extremity that he had experienced and studied. By design and by the sheer force of its director's compassion, the school has salvaged and restored to function children of whom all other agencies had despaired, which for Bettelheim must be a profoundly gratifying experience of humane revenge." Indeed, Elsa First reports in the *New York Review of Books* that Bettelheim was driven "to create a therapeutic environment which in each detail of everyday life would create an existence that he envisioned as the exact opposite of the dehumanization so systematically engineered by the camps." Choosing his staff and even the decor with great care, Bettelheim created "probably the most remarkable mental institution in the country," in the words of a *New Yorker* reviewer. The Orthogenic School, with its humane, deinstitutionalized approach, has had an unprecedented eighty-five per cent cure rate among children thought to be far beyond help.

*Love Is Not Enough, Truants from Life, The Empty Fortress,* and *A Home for the Heart* all document events at the Orthogenic School and outline Bettelheim's educational and therapeutic philosophy. In *The Empty Fortress,* for instance, Bettelheim advances his theory of autism and reviews the case histories of three autistic children who were patients at the school. Central to Bettelheim's treatment approach is the belief that autistic behavior occurs when a child perceives that none of his acts have any effect on the outside world. Therapy therefore must have as its goal the development of autonomy in the child's social perception. A *Scientific American* reviewer of *The Empty Fortress* finds Bettelheim's strategy in the clinic even more convincing than his theories: "The pragmatic argument of successful therapy is generally powerful in medicine, but the humanity, intelligence, self-sacrifice and endurance of the therapy given by Dr. Bettelheim and his devoted staff seem to outweigh the specific content of any theory." *New Republic* contributor Robert Coles feels that the author is "modest, sensible and unpretentious when he tries to specify the particulars that make for autism."

Bettelheim's 1974 overview of his professional stance, *A Home for the Heart,* also received critical acclaim. Elsa First writes: "Bettelheim's myth of the embattled child served to inspire a powerful amount of goodness within the fortress of his school. His clinical intuitiveness and resourcefulness and the unfailing respect he showed his psychotic children were remarkable. . . . There are many useful lessons to be learned from Bettelheim's retrospective look at his life's work." Elizabeth Janeway expresses a similar view in the *New York Times Book Review:* "Bettelheim combines a capacity for lucid speech with a mind of rare strength and subtlety, as his readers well know. He is a natural parabolist, capable of seeing the universe in a grain of sand and passing the vision on. . . . Those who get most from Bettelheim will be those who read him with eyes open and minds alert to the nuances and vistas of this thought."

During the 1970s and 1980s, Bettelheim focused much of his attention on the nurturing of healthy children. In *The Children of the Dream: Communal Child-Rearing and American Education* he discussed the ramifications of a childhood spent in an Israeli kibbutz. Both *The Uses of Enchantment* and *On*

*Learning to Read* offer strident calls for reform in American early childhood education through the use of traditional fairy tales and other more stimulating reading matter. Bettelheim believed fantasy, even violent fantasy, necessary for children and that fairy tales often offer healthy outlets for subconscious wishes and anxieties. As Richard Todd notes in an *Atlantic* review of *The Uses of Enchantment,* Bettelheim "makes plain that the [fairy] tales are supple, many-layered things, and that different children may find in the same story quite different, even contradictory, forms of psychic comfort. . . . He is sincere in his urgency about the irreplaceableness of these traditional tales, so many of which are now effectively forgotten, or adulterated into Disneyesque good cheer." *New York Review of Books* essayist Harold Bloom calls *The Uses of Enchantment* "a splendid achievement, brimming with useful ideas, with insights into how young children read and understand, and most of all overflowing with a realistic optimism and with an experienced and therapeutic good will." In his *New York Times Book Review* assessment of *The Uses of Enchantment,* John Updike hails the work as "a charming book about enchantment, a profound book about fairy tales. . . . What is new, and exciting, is the warmth, humane and urgent, with which Bettelheim expounds fairy tales as aids to the child's growth."

In 1982 Bettelheim published his controversial book *Freud and Man's Soul,* a short study of how standard English translations of Freud misrepresent Freud's intentions. Storr explains in the *New Republic:* "[Bettelheim] believes that the effect of the English translation of Freud's ideas was to make them into an abstract intellectual system, something that might be applied to the understanding of others in a cerebral fashion, but that was not easily applicable to the study of one's own unconscious." *Los Angeles Times Book Review* contributor Harvey Mindess further contends that Bettelheim sees the results of these expositional misrepresentations as having produced "an impression of Freud as far more impersonal than he was, and to define psychoanalysis as a medical specialty when its founder intended it to be 'a part of psychology' and an inquiry into the nature of the soul."

Opinions on the validity of Bettelheim's thesis vary widely. *Voice Literary Supplement* reviewer Walter Kendrick asserts that Bettelheim's "desire to make Freud sweet and cuddly has caused him to write a stupid, dangerous little book." Frank Kermode likewise notes in the *New York Times Book Review* that it is "salutary to have instruction in what we have lost [through translation]. But on the evidence here presented, Bettelheim has treated rather harshly a huge labor of translation, carried out with devotion and skill, and has unfairly visited the failings of American psychoanalytic practice on that translation." Storr, on the other hand, finds Bettelheim's concern "to resuscitate Freud as a humanist . . . an understandable aspiration," and in the London *Times,* A. S. Byatt concludes: "We need books like Bettelheim's to keep us alert and supple, to remind us of the complex nature of language and translation, culture and history, the limitations of their power, the power of their limitations."

Bettelheim examines the topics of psychoanalysis, children, and the Holocaust in *Freud's Vienna and Other Essays.* The essays reflect Bettelheim's cultural experiences. "Everywhere in the book," remarks *Chicago Tribune* reviewer Joseph Costes, "we see the shrewd shrink's grasp of the sometimes petty human circumstance behind the grand achievement." William J. McGrath writes in the *New York Times Book Review* that Bettelheim "allows his life and work to speak directly to the reader on a personal level. The result is a volume in which both the life and the work emerge in a strikingly sympathetic and humane light."

*The Art of the Obvious* contains the edited discussions of the cases of psychiatrists, researchers, and psychotherapists. Notes David Adams in the *New York Times Book Review,* "Bettelheim clearly identifies strongly with children who he believes are being subjected to oppression, takes their side in any conflict of opinion, advocates a degree of permissiveness and indulgence which alarms his audience, and has a moral repugnance for research methods in which children are placed in frustrating situations." However some former patients have made accusations since Bettelheim's suicide that his treatment of children at the Orthogenic School was in practice abusive rather than empathetic.

Both Bettelheim's clinical accomplishments and his body of writing reflect a half century's devotion to improving the human condition. *New York Times* correspondent James Atlas suggests that life itself "has provided Professor Bettelheim with ample opportunities to witness human behavior in all its terrifying variety, and to nurture what is valuable in it while remorselessly condemning what is dangerous." To *Washington Post Book World* critic William McPherson, Bettelheim is "renowned in his field and acclaimed throughout the world" because he is "a survivor who bears witness" not only to the disintegration of the personality but also to the resurgence and resilience of the human spirit. Rosemary Dinnage also contends that Bettelheim's experiences have strengthened, not shaken, his faith in cooperation between individuals. "Bettelheim's achievement," Dinnage concludes, "is that while his professional life has been concerned with the distress of others, he has also been able to teach us through the writings—objective rather than passionate—that are based on his own distresses and endurance. Those experiences are the basis of his special understanding both of the growth and the destruction of what makes a person human."

Close friends of Bettelheim speculate that loneliness—his wife died in 1984—and an ailing body—he had suffered two strokes and congestive heart failure—prompted him to end his life in March, 1990, while in a retirement home in Silver Springs, Maryland.

*BIOGRAPHICAL/CRITICAL SOURCES:*

*BOOKS*

Bettelheim, Bruno, *The Informed Heart: Autonomy in a Mass Age,* Free Press, 1960.
Bettelheim, Bruno, *A Home for the Heart,* Knopf, 1974.
Bettelheim, Bruno, *Surviving, and Other Essays,* Knopf, 1979, reprinted with a new introduction as *Surviving the Holocaust,* Flamingo, 1986.
*Contemporary Literary Criticism,* Gale (Detroit), Volume 79.
Goldsmith, Jerome M. and Jacquelyn Seevak Sanders, *Milieu Therapy: Significant Issues and Innovative Applications,* Haworth Press (New York City), 1993.
Sutton, Nina, *Bettelheim, A Life and a Legacy,* Basic Books (New York City), 1996.
Szajnberg, Nathan M. and Bruno Bettelheim, *Educating the Emotions: Bruno Bettelheim and Psychoanalytic Development,* Plenum Press (New York City), 1992.

*PERIODICALS*

*America,* August 7, 1976.
*American Academy of Political and Social Science: Annals,* July, 1950; November, 1950; September, 1961.
*American Journal of Sociology,* May, 1961; July, 1969.
*American Political Science Review,* June, 1961.
*American Sociological Review,* August, 1950; October, 1955; June, 1961.
*Atlantic,* June, 1976.
*Book World,* April 27, 1969.
*Chicago,* August, 1991, p. 82.
*Chicago Sunday Tribune,* July 16, 1950.
*Chicago Tribune Book World,* April 29, 1979; February 21, 1982.
*Choice,* October, 1967; October, 1974; October, 1976.
*Christian Century,* December 6, 1967; June 23-30, 1976.
*Commentary,* October, 1990, p. 26.
*Critic,* October-December, 1974.
*Harper's,* June, 1976.
*Harvard Educational Review,* fall, 1967.
*Journal of Home Economics,* October, 1955; November, 1962.
*Los Angeles Times,* October 16, 1983; October 12, 1986; November 12, 1987; January 24, 1990; April 3, 1990.
*Los Angeles Times Book Review,* January 23, 1983.
*Nation,* June 24, 1950; July 30, 1955; April 1, 1961; May 12, 1979; February 12, 1983.
*National Review,* May 10, 1974; August 20, 1976.
*New Leader,* March 31, 1969.
*New Perspectives Quarterly,* summer, 1990, p. 46.
*New Republic,* May 22, 1961; March 4, 1967; May 24, 1969; April 20, 1974; May 29, 1976; December 31, 1982.
*New Statesman,* March 17, 1961; September 26, 1969; June 7, 1974.
*New Statesman & Society,* February 16, 1990, p. 36.
*Newsweek,* January 10, 1983; September 10, 1990.
*New Yorker,* April 22, 1974; January 25, 1982.
*New York Review of Books,* May 4, 1967; May 30, 1974; July 15, 1976; April 19, 1979; April 1, 1982.
*New York Times,* February 12, 1950; September 17, 1950; May 29, 1955; March 24, 1969; August 15, 1979; December 21, 1982; December 27, 1989.
*New York Times Book Review,* October 8, 1961; February 26, 1967; April 6, 1969; March 17, 1974; May 23, 1976; January 2, 1977; April 29, 1979; January 31, 1982; February 6, 1983; January 21, 1990; March 21, 1993, p. 18.
*San Francisco Chronicle,* March 26, 1950; July 16, 1950.
*Saturday Review,* July 8, 1961; June 9, 1962; May 17, 1969; May 15, 1976.
*Scientific American,* July, 1967.
*Society,* March-April, 1991, p. 61.
*Spectator,* October 23, 1976, April 1, 1978, August 11, 1979, March 20, 1982.

*Time,* May 3, 1976; January 8, 1990, p. 74.
*Times* (London), December 22, 1983.
*Times Literary Supplement,* October 9, 1969; August 2, 1974; October 1, 1976; July 29, 1983; August 15, 1986; April 2, 1993, p. 22.
*Tribune Books,* December 24, 1989, p.5.
*Voice Literary Supplement,* February, 1983; December, 1985.
*Washington Post,* December 17, 1989.
*Washington Post Book World,* June 13, 1976; May 13, 1979; January 3, 1982; December 17, 1989, p. 1.

*OBITUARIES:*

*PERIODICALS*

*Chicago Tribune,* March 14, 1990.
*Current Biography,* May, 1990, p. 61.
*Los Angles Times,* March 14, 1990.
*Newsweek,* March 26, 1990, p. 49.
*New York Times,* March 14, 1990.
*People,* April 2, 1990, p. 51.
*Time,* March 26, 1990, p. 65.
*Times* (London), March 16, 1990.
*Washington Post,* March 14, 1990.*

* * *

**BISHOP, Elizabeth 1911-1979**

*PERSONAL:* Born February 8, 1911, in Worcester, MA; died October 6, 1979, of a cerebral aneurysm, in Boston, MA; daughter of William Thomas (a builder) and Gertrude (Bulmer) Bishop. *Education:* Vassar College, A.B., 1934. *Avocational interests:* Travel, sailing.

*CAREER:* Poet, author of prose, and translator. Library of Congress, Washington, DC, consultant in poetry, 1949-50, honorary consultant in American Letters, beginning in 1958. University of Washington, Seattle, poet in residence, 1966; also taught at Harvard University and Massachusetts Institute of Technology.

*MEMBER:* National Institute of Arts and Letters, Academy of American Poets (chancellor, beginning in 1966).

*AWARDS, HONORS:* Houghton Mifflin Poetry Award, 1946, for *North & South;* Guggenheim fellowship, 1947; American Academy of Arts and Letters grant, 1951; awarded the first Lucy Martin Donnelly fellowship, Bryn Mawr College, 1951; Shelley Memorial Award, 1952; Academy of American Poets Award, 1955; *Partisan Review* fellowship, 1956; Pulitzer Prize in poetry, 1956, for *Poems: North & South* [and] *A Cold Spring;* Amy Lowell traveling fellowship, 1957; Chapelbrook fellowship, 1962; Academy of American Poets fellowship, 1964; Rockefeller Foundation grant, 1967; Merrill Foundation Award, 1969; National Book Award in poetry, 1970, for *The Complete Poems;* Order Rio Branco (Brazil), 1971; LL.D., Rutgers University and Brown University, both 1972; Harriet Monroe Award for Poetry, 1974; Neustadt International Prize for Literature, 1976; National Book Critics Circle Award in poetry, 1977, for *Geography III.*

*WRITINGS:*

*POETRY*

(Contributor) *Trial Balances* (anthology of young poets), edited by Ann Winslow, Macmillan, 1935.
*North & South* (also see below), Houghton, 1946, reprinted, 1964.
*Poems: North & South* [and] *A Cold Spring,* Houghton, 1955, abridged edition published as *Poems,* Chatto & Windus, 1956.
*Questions of Travel,* Farrar, Straus, 1965.
*Selected Poems,* Chatto & Windus, 1967.
*The Ballad of the Burglar of Babylon,* Farrar, Straus, 1968.
*The Complete Poems,* Farrar, Straus, 1969.
*Geography III,* Farrar, Straus, 1976.
*The Complete Poems, 1927-1979,* Farrar, Straus, 1983.

Poems anthologized in numerous collections.

*OTHER*

(Translator from the Portuguese) Alice Brant, *The Diary of "Helena Morley,"* Farrar, Straus, 1957, reprinted, Ecco Press, 1977.
(With the editors of Life) *Brazil,* Time, Inc., 1962.
(Editor with Emanuel Brasil) *An Anthology of Twentieth-Century Brazilian Poetry,* Wesleyan University Press, 1972.
(Translator with G. Aroul) Octavio Paz, *Selected Poems of Octavio Paz,* New Directions, 1984.
*The Collected Prose,* edited and introduced by Robert Giroux, Farrar, Straus, 1984.

(With Lee Hoiby) *Three Ages of Woman: For High Voice and Piano* (musical score), Southern Music (New York City), 1994.

(Translator) De Melo Neto, Joao C., *Selected Poetry, 1937-1990,* University Press of New England, 1995.

(William Benton, editor) *Exchanging Hats: Thirty-Nine Paintings,* Farrar, Straus & Giroux (New York City), 1996.

(With George Monteiro) *Conversations with Elizabeth Bishop* (interviews), University Press of Mississippi (Jackson), 1996.

Also translator, with others, of *Travelling in the Family* by Carlos Drummond. Contributor of poetry and fiction to periodicals, including *Kenyon Review, New Republic, Partisan Review,* and *Poetry*. Co-founder of *Con Spirito,* Vassar College.

*SIDELIGHTS:* Elizabeth Bishop's refusal to settle for easy answers to life's problems, her handling of both ordinary and exotic topics, her precise yet relaxed technique, and in particular her extraordinary perception all revealed her supreme control over her craft and marked her poetry as major. Bishop's work has had the ability to make the most diverse groups of poets—those who normally disagree over themes, techniques, forms, in short the ideology informing a poem—agree on one point: that she was an admirable artist. As William Meredith put it in his "Invitation to Miss Elizabeth Bishop," reprinted in Lloyd Schwartz and Sybil P. Estess's *Elizabeth Bishop and Her Art:* "[Bishop] will yet civilize and beguile us from our silly schools. The [Charles] Olsons will lie down with the [Richard] Wilburs and the Diane Wakoskis dance quadrilles with the J. V. Cunninghams and the Tooth Mother will suckle the rhymed skunk kittens of [Robert] Lowell."

Only months after Bishop's birth her father died, and her mother suffered a nervous breakdown from which she never recovered. For her first six years, Bishop lived with her mother's family in Great Village, Nova Scotia, and then moved to the home of her father's parents in Worcester, Massachusetts. The memories of these early traumatic years surface occasionally in poems like "Sestina" or "In the Waiting Room" and the story "In the Village." A lonely child in Great Village and Worcester, a shy orphan with asthma and bronchitis, Bishop found "a much more congenial and sympathetic world for herself in books," according to Anne Stevenson in *Elizabeth Bishop*. In a 1966 *Shenandoah* interview with Ashley Brown, Bishop recollected that while her relatives were not literary, they did own many books, that she started reading poetry when she was eight years old, and that she was also "crazy about fairy tales—Andersen, Grimm, and so on." In "Influences," a memoir published in the *American Poetry Review,* she remembered how old English ballads, nursery rhymes, fairy tales, and riddles affected her as a child and later as a poet. Bishop told Brown during the 1966 interview that when she was thirteen she discovered Walt Whitman; at about the same time, she encountered Emily Dickinson, H. D. (Hilda Doolittle), Joseph Conrad, and Henry James. Soon after she first read some of Gerard Manley Hopkins's poetry, which captivated her. Later at Vassar College she wrote a piece for the *Vassar Review* entitled "Gerard Manley Hopkins: Notes on Timing in His Poetry," and her poem "A Cold Spring," collected in the volume of the same title, begins with an epigraph from Hopkins and is in part a response to Hopkins's perceptions of spring. Bishop also discovered the work of another favorite poet, George Herbert, by the time she was fourteen. Herbert scholar Joseph Summers recalled in the *George Herbert Journal* that when he first met Bishop during the mid-1940s "she knew Herbert's poems better than anyone I had ever met before."

At sixteen, Bishop entered Walnut Hill boarding school in Natick, Massachusetts. Robert Giroux has included the recollection of one of Bishop's schoolmates, Frani Muser, in his introduction to *The Collected Prose:* "When I arrived at the Walnut Hill School in Natick in 1927, I met a most remarkable girl. . . . She had read more widely and deeply than we had. But she carried her learning lightly. She was very funny. She had a big repertory of stories she could tell, not read, and of wonderful songs she could sing, like ballads and sea chanteys. And if some school occasion called for a new song, or a skit, it would appear overnight like magic in her hands. Her name was Elizabeth Bishop. We called her 'Bishop,' spoke of her as 'the Bishop,' and we all knew with no doubt whatsoever that she was a genius." In the interview with Brown, Bishop herself remembered her activities and early work on poetry: "I was on the staff of the literary magazine at school and published some poems there. I had a good Latin teacher and a good English teacher at Walnut Hill. . . . I now wish I'd studied nothing but Latin and Greek in college. In fact I consider myself badly educated. Writing Latin prose and verse is still probably the best possible exercise for a poet."

Bishop began Vassar with the thought of studying music, but as she told Elizabeth Spires in a *Paris*

*Review* interview, the thought of public piano recitals so terrified her that she changed her major to English. Among Bishop's Vassar classmates were some promising writers: "It was a very literary class. Mary McCarthy was a year ahead of me. Eleanor Clark was in my class. And Muriel Rukeyser, for freshman year. We started a magazine you may have heard of, *Con Spirito.* I think I was a junior then. There were six or seven of us—Mary, Eleanor Clark and her older sister, my friends Margaret Miller and Frani Blough, and a couple of others. . . . Most of us had submitted things to the *Vassar Review* and they'd been turned down. It was very old-fashioned then. . . . After [*Con Spirito*'s] third issue the *Vassar Review* came around and a couple of our editors became editors on it and then they published things by us," Bishop told Spires.

The poems "The Flood," "A Word with You," "Hymn to the Virgin," and "Three Sonnets for Eyes" appeared in *Con Spirito,* and "Some Dreams They Forgot," "Valentine," and "Valentine II" were first published in the *Vassar Review;* all of these early works have been collected and reprinted in *The Complete Poems, 1927-1979.* Stevenson has called these poems "exceptionally mature" and technically proficient; Alan Hollinghurst in a 1983 *Poetry Review* article has noted in them "a relished collision of colloquial tone and high formal artifice," finding particularly in "The Flood" an attempt "to create a world free from personalities . . . related to an abiding concern with detachment." Hollinghurst has maintained that this pattern persisted throughout Bishop's work, ultimately forming a body of work "noticeably characterized by its more abstract, questing and, in a way, cerebral poems."

Other readers, however, view "The Flood" in a different relationship to Bishop's canon. Instead of being an early indication of a persistent pattern, the poem, they feel, possibly presents only one segment of a fluctuating tendency to shift between the poles of detachment and involvement, and, in theme, to move increasingly toward the latter position. Robert Lowell sensed that most of the poems in Bishop's first collection *North & South* form a "single symbolic pattern," although one a bit elusive to characterize, as he said in an early *Sewanee Review* assessment; he isolated "two opposing factors," one of which he called "something in motion," and the other "a terminus." More recently, in the *American Poetry Review,* Robert Pinsky has identified what he considers Bishop's great subject: "[The] dual nature of the art [of poetry], its physical reminder of our animal privacy and its formal reminder of our communal dealings. . . . To put the idea a bit differently, her great subject is the contest—or truce, or trade-agreement—between the single human soul on one side and, on the other side, the contingent world of artifacts and other people." And in the 1966 interview with Brown, Bishop herself admitted to the shift between solitary and communal concerns, when she stated that she was "much more interested in social problems and politics now than I was in the '30's."

In many ways poet Marianne Moore was Bishop's mentor. Meeting Bishop while she was still at Vassar, Moore encouraged the younger woman to write, discouraged her from attending medical school, offered editorial and poetic advice during Bishop's early career, and continued a friendship which Bishop recounted with humor and affection both in her poem "Invitation to Miss Marianne Moore," and in her prose piece "Efforts of Affection: A Memoir of Marianne Moore." Throughout their friendship the two poets maintained an active correspondence. They discussed their reading, exchanged books they were eager to have the other read, mailed postcards from exotic places, and sent whimsical little gifts. Bishop solicited Moore's opinions on poems in progress and sometimes mentioned in her letters people or places that later appeared in poems, for instance, the description of a Cuban sitting room that then became part of "Jeronimo's House."

Perhaps because of this friendship and because Moore helped get Bishop's work published in the anthology *Trial Balances,* the introduction of which included Moore's appreciative statements on Bishop, early reviewers continually linked Bishop's poetry with Moore's. They noticed that both poets often described animals and emphasized a visual quality in their work. In a review later collected in *Poetry and the Age,* Randall Jarrell wrote of a poem in *North & South,* "When you read Miss Bishop's 'Florida,' a poem whose first sentence begins, 'The state with the prettiest name,' and whose last sentence begins, 'The alligator, who has five distinct calls: / friendliness, love, mating, war, and warning,' you don't need to be told that the poetry of Marianne Moore was, in the beginning, an appropriately selected foundation for Miss Bishop's work." Less enthusiastically, Louise Bogan noted in a 1946 *New Yorker* review Bishop's "slight addiction to the poetic methods of Marianne Moore."

Aside from continually invoking Moore, whose influence Bishop increasingly questioned as her own reputation grew, most early reviewers voiced respect or praise. Moore herself, in the *Nation,* emphasized Bishop's tasteful poetics, her tactful handling of material, and finally her control of tension and emotion. Bogan declared that the poems of *North & South* "strike no attitudes and have not an ounce of superfluous emotional weight, and they combine an unforced ironic humor with a naturalist's accuracy of observation." In *Pleasure Dome: On Reading Modern Poetry,* Lloyd Frankenberg pointed new readers to the very first poem in *North & South,* "The Map," as a reference point from which to begin reading Bishop's poetry. He felt that this work, as well as the rest of the poetry in the collection, possessed a "surface clarity [which] is deceptive. Its effect is so natural, we are hardly aware how much is being described: the map itself, the seacoast it suggests, and a particular way of seeing and relating both. . . . The method is direct, reticent and gracious." Jarrell found Bishop to be morally attractive because in certain of her poems "she understands so well that the wickedness and confusion of the age can explain and extenuate other people's wickedness and confusion, but not, for you, your own," that individual morality "is usually a small, personal, statistical, but heartbreaking or heartwarming affair of omissions and commissions." Lowell praised Bishop's "unrhetorical, cool, and beautifully thought out poems" and labeled her "one of the best craftsmen alive."

A few reviewers did criticize. Oscar Williams declared in the *New Republic* that Bishop had "possibly overeducated herself in what is, or rather was, going on in the best circles, and hasn't trusted enough in her own psyche. She has listened every once in a while to certain cliques which are trying to palm off academic composition as poetic perception." And in a *Partisan Review* assessment of Bishop's *Poems: North & South* [and] *A Cold Spring,* Edward Honig argued that Bishop's poems "arrest one by their brilliant surfaces and transparency. But underneath is a curious rigidity, a disturbing lack of movement and affective life, betraying a sprained and uneasy patience. [The poems] frequently resemble the fish in her most anthologized poem of that name: caught half-dead, the fight knocked out of it, '. . . a grunting weight, battered and venerable and homely,' achieving in the end, a pyrrhic victory by being thrown back into the sea." Like Frankenberg, Honig regarded "The Map" as emblematic of the volume *North & South,* but unlike Frankenberg, he criticized it and then the volume as "a plan for suppressing rather than compressing contours, dimension, tonality, emotion. A slow hard gaze moves behind the deliberately drawn-out ironies." The poems of *North & South* may indeed prove unsatisfactory in the several ways Honig mentions, yet such shortcomings must be studied, because they reveal an important pattern in Bishop's canon. While the poems surely function to suppress, as Honig suggests, much feeling and movement do exist beneath their surfaces. The poems suppress emotion, not to stifle it, but to transform it into something shaped and artful, something which both contains and embodies change. While Bishop often tended to comfortably deny change, she also knew she needed to accommodate it in order to exist as a person and grow as an artist. Thus she vacillated between the two states throughout her canon.

Bishop's vacillation manifested itself in several ways. She sometimes completely retracted what seemed a decisive judgment, she varied forms and styles, she experimented with tone and diction, and she explored a wide variety of subjects. Inconsistent precisely because it moved back and forth between many different styles ranging from traditional to surreal, *North & South* reflected Bishop's meditation on her own art, her efforts to see what it was, how it affected her, how it would affect her readers. The volume also revealed her questioning how far she should follow already established poetic traditions and how much she should strike out on her own. As a young artist she worried that her comfort with a tradition, with past ideas and forms, might also stifle her own uniqueness. Finding herself breathing what Calvin Bedient has called in a *Parnassus* essay "the awful, sweet ether of tradition," she struggled in her early poetry to find a pure air for nurturing her own style and to change what no longer suited her purpose. *North & South* recorded the beginnings of what would be a life-long effort to merge successfully with a tradition so that her individuality ultimately would shine forth.

*North & South* was chosen from among 843 manuscripts for the Houghton Mifflin Poetry Award in 1945. In 1949, Bishop was named poetry consultant to the Library of Congress and moved to Washington, D.C. She admitted, however, to both Anne Stevenson and Elizabeth Spires, that she did not enjoy the year: as she told Spires, "There were so many government buildings that looked like Moscow. There was a very nice secretary . . . [who] did most of the work. I'd write something and she'd say, 'Oh, no, that isn't official,' so then she'd rewrite it in gobbledegook. We used to bet on the horses. She and I would sit there reading the Racing Form when poets came to call." Still more awards were forthcoming: the

American Academy of Arts and Letters Award in 1950, the Lucy Martin Donnelly Fellowship from Bryn Mawr College in 1951, and the Shelley Memorial Award in 1952.

In 1955 Bishop published *Poems,* which contained both her new volume, *A Cold Spring,* and a reprint of the by then out-of-print *North & South.* In a *Hudson Review* assessment, Anthony Hecht praised Bishop's work generally but regarded the poems in *A Cold Spring* as "not quite up to the level of [Bishop's] earlier work; though it is a little hard to say why. . . . Perhaps it is that . . . [her] attitude . . . is distant . . . and uncommitted." Writing in *Dublin Magazine,* Padraic Fallon, also critical, felt that language had "over-awed the person" and that the reader remained unmoved because "in the process of making poetry [Bishop] herself seems to be unmoved." Astutely pointing out that "the rise of the Imagist movement—in England, at least—coincided with the enfranchisement of women," A. Alvarez in the *Kenyon Review* then criticized Bishop for her feminine poetic qualities. Alvarez linked Bishop to Imagism and, like the earlier reviewers of *North & South,* to Marianne Moore's influence. But he ultimately disliked Imagism ("the first full-scale feminist movement in poetry"); he felt Bishop's descriptive powers were overpraised after she wrote *North & South* and considered these powers "little more than an obscure fussiness" conveying a "finicky air" that seemed "improvised and not quite to the point." Alvarez preferred a more masculine style, which he found in "poets like, say, Richard Eberhart, whose language makes you jump to his meaning . . . [and whose] language has a kind of physical complexity."

Ironically, Eberhart himself reviewed Bishop's *Poems* in the *New York Times Book Review,* finding the best poems of *A Cold Spring* to be "as good as anything she has done, but with a difference. The difference is that they seem looser woven, more confessional. . . . [Bishop] has a strong grip on her own realities. She gives the reader a rich world of slow, curious, strong discoveries, uniquely seen and set." Still another poet, Howard Nemerov, writing in *Poetry,* praised Bishop's reluctance to moralize openly and singled out "At the Fishhouses" as the collection's most beautiful poem: "Its slow-paced and intricate visual development seems justly completed by a serious eloquence." Donald Hall in the *New England Quarterly* observed that Bishop's poems show "a desperate hanging on to the object as if in refuge from the self," a crucial tension reiterated by later critics. Declaring that "Elizabeth Bishop is a partisan in the world," Wallace Fowlie in *Commonweal* contended that "the observation and the intuition in [the double sonnet 'The Prodigal'] are equivalent to partisan action in the world." Fowlie also commented on Bishop's language, calling it "even more simple and more unmannered than it was in the early poems. It has become more immediate and more direct . . . more aphoristic, more concise, more energetic . . . more serious, more grave." Yet as Alan Williamson has shown in an essay collected in *Elizabeth Bishop and Her Art,* Bishop tended in the love poems of *A Cold Spring* to distance emotion because feelings such as despair, loneliness, and apprehension were dialectically uncontrollable through reason or, in poetry, through structure. These poems, for him, "betray an immense anxiety about the adjustments between inner and outer worlds" and an obsession with the distance between human beings.

One important tension in Bishop's canon emerged clearly in *A Cold Spring:* the fierce need to settle into absolutes—securities—checked by an equally fierce resistance to this need. Bishop half wished to accept those dogmas, theologies, or poetic schools that had existed as the tradition for many years, but this wish encountered a fierce opponent in her own resistance, stirred mainly by her brutally clear sight. What she saw often rendered tradition unacceptable because, simply, her perceptions offered another story.

Another important tension in *A Cold Spring* occurred between nature and people. In the earlier poems nature was often more closely associated with the mind, with the imagination, than with human interaction, and Bishop frequently used the lure of nature to signify the lure of the mind and the imagination. In "The Imaginary Iceberg," for example, the title object is an ice mountain of the imagination, a mountain that the poet initially prefers to the ship full of companions in travel. But when she favors nature over society, it becomes siren-like, its chief danger an abstract, romantic self-destruction. For Bishop, withdrawal from people thus signified a tragically empty and impoverished life; she foresaw deadly consequences if at any time she employed nature as a means of withdrawal from others rather than as a constant reminder of her moral obligation to maintain and nurture connections with those others, despite the pain involved in such connections.

Although *A Cold Spring* actually contained no clear "resolution" to the split between a self-involving nature and people, no one answer for a way to exist, Bishop did hint at what an answer might be. What remained constant through *A Cold Spring* was the tension between the two conditions Bishop had posited as polar opposites. Being a person alive in the world of this volume thus involved in the uneasy trading back and forth between poles; trying to control the mind, yet appreciating its imagination; accepting the past and what it offered, yet growing enough oneself to see clearly; accepting the fact that the life human beings see might be "awful," yet having the courage to face it cheerfully. In 1956, the year after its publication, *Poems: North & South* [and] *A Cold Spring* won the Pulitzer Prize for poetry.

In his book *American Poetry since 1945: A Critical Survey,* Stephen Stepanchev made observations about *North & South* and *A Cold Spring* that apply to the rest of Bishop's canon. He declared that Bishop's "At the Fishhouses" "tells brilliantly what Miss Bishop thinks of human knowledge, which is always undermined by time, by change. It is obvious that change is the most disturbing principle of reality for her." Bishop was, for him, "a poet who, early in her career, chose to avoid politics and public issues without, at the same time, abandoning the objective realities that constitute the otherness of the world. She believes in that world, especially when it shocks or baffles her, and she renders it with precision and clarity. By 1955 the interchange between self and scene deepens in her poems, and her love of geography takes her, as tourist and everyman, to many places on many roads."

Although Stepanchev exaggerated Bishop's avoidance of politics and public issues, he was correct about her feelings for change and about geography taking her on many roads, for in late November 1951, Bishop traveled to South America on a cruise. But then, as Ashley Brown described it in a 1977 *Southern Review* essay, "Elizabeth ate some item of fruit . . . that disagreed horribly with her; she was laid up for an extended recovery and her ship sailed on without her. But she had friends in Brazil whom she had known in New York during an earlier period; she liked the country, and she stayed." One poem from *A Cold Spring,* "Arrival at Santos," then was reprinted in her next collection, *Questions of Travel,* where it fit in more exactly with the rest of the poems.

Ten years passed between the publication of *A Cold Spring* and *Questions of Travel,* a period also marked by the appearance of a pictorial history, *Brazil,* which Bishop wrote with the editors of *Life.* Her perception of herself and her world changed recognizably during these years. There she found a culture that contrasted in values and priorities with the North American culture she had known. It is no wonder that the poems in *Questions of Travel* often explored previously unfelt or rediscovered emotions set vibrating by this exotic, emotional culture. She also began to perceive the flaws of her North American culture and to realize that a kind of provincial blindness as emotional paralysis had settled over her.

In the *New Republic,* Frank J. Warnke noted that "*Questions of Travel* is impressively varied in its forms and modes, ranging from the irregular but firmly controlled metrics of many of the Brazilian pieces to such strict forms as the folk ballad . . . and the sestina." Warnke found "the Brazilian half of the book more exciting," but did point out the technical achievement of "Visits to St. Elizabeth's," which recounted the poet's responses to Ezra Pound, who had been confined to a mental hospital for his pro-Mussolini broadcasts during World War II. Irvin Ehrenpreis wrote in the *Virginia Quarterly Review* that in this poem, "one of the masterpieces of this collection, . . . [Bishop's] own presence, on the series of occasions when she saw Pound, is never mentioned; . . . the form is the incremental-refrain structure of 'this is the House that Jack Built.' But by varying or modulating the epithets to reflect with unwavering fidelity the mixture of her feelings toward that great, corrupted poet, she produces a strength of pathos that will make those who read this poem aloud weep."

Remarking, like Howard Moss, on the revolutionary quality of Bishop's verse, Willard Spiegelman in the *Centennial Review* found a "natural hero" in Bishop's work, a hero who "occupies a privileged position which is unattainable by the super—or unnatural—exploits of masculine achievement which the poetry constantly debunks." To illustrate "Bishop's habitual tactic of diminution or undercutting" with which "certain ideas of masculine greatness are filed down or eroded to their essential littleness," Spiegelman cited several poems from this volume, including "'The Burglar of Babylon' [which] deprives its eponymous hero of his glory by recounting, in childlike ballad quatrains, his life as a petty criminal sought by a whole army of police who finally, and unceremoniously, kill him."

While critics twenty years later would see that Bishop was strongly involved with the world, most contemporary reviewers of *Questions of Travel* missed this characteristic amid the more spectacularly dramatic political movements and poetry of the time.

Stepanchev, among others, felt that "public events, political issues, or socioeconomic ideology" did not inspire Bishop and that her poetry left readers unaware of Hitler and World War II: "Unlike many of her Auden-influenced contemporaries, she distrusts history, with its melodramatic blacks and whites, and prefers geography, with its subtle gradations of color."

In 1985 Robert von Hallberg, however, offered another point of view about two of the poems in *Questions of Travel,* "Arrival at Santos," and "Brazil, January 1, 1502." Writing in *American Poetry and Culture, 1945-1980,* von Hallberg declared the latter poem "about the Portuguese colonization of Brazil," in that it focused on the way the Portuguese projected the imaginative structures of a Christian, imperialistic ideology onto the foreign landscape they encountered. He felt that Bishop intended to implicate herself in the actions of the Portuguese by setting up these two poems as "the coordinates of Brazilian history. . . . She comes out of a culture that reaches right back to those Christian imperialists. Horrifying as their actions were . . . she can understand their way of seeing." Von Hallberg also argued that as a poet she sensed the attraction of expansion, and because she did, she became critical; implicating herself, she subtly criticized the expansionist, imperialist position.

*Questions of Travel*'s form openly reflected a point of view hinted at in *North & South* and implied in *A Cold Spring.* The collection's division into two sections, "Brazil" and "Elsewhere," was more than a convenient sorter for poems about different countries; it reflected the mind organizing the volume. Divisions in all parts of life—between past and present, for instance, or one country and another, even between a person like Bishop and the poor peasants in Brazil—seemed more pronounced than earlier but reflected a lessening of naivete and idealism and, oddly enough, a trust that change, though difficult, was possible. While both of her previous poetry collections also tended to sift into two styles and subject matters, in her third collection, Bishop found a truer metaphor in her Brazilian experience for the apparently unbridgeable gaps she perceived.

Poet Adrienne Rich has said in the *Boston Review* that at first Bishop's exalted reputation "made her less, rather than more available to me. The infrequency of her public appearances and her geographic remoteness—living for many years in Brazil, with a woman as it happened, but we didn't know that—made her an indistinct and problematic life-model for a woman poet." But, "given the times and customs of the 1940s and 1950s Bishop's work now seems . . . remarkably honest and courageous," embodying her need to come to terms "with a personal past, with family and class and race, with her presence as a poet in cities and landscapes where human suffering is not [simply] a metaphor."

Having returned to the United States from Brazil, by 1976 Bishop no longer treated that country in her poetry. The lush, colorful, and sometimes humorous dimensions that Brazil seemed to inspire in her verse therefore disappeared, and *Geography III,* which was published eleven years after *Questions of Travel,* possessed a much more subdued form, tone, and emphasis. While part of *Questions of Travel*'s thematic preoccupation had been the struggle for vision and its ensuing perceptions, *Geography III* seemed to take that vision for granted and to concentrate instead on observing the world with an unfaltering, unclouded eye.

Since *Geography III* was Bishop's fourth book of poetry and followed the premature *The Complete Poems,* which won the National Book Award in 1970, most of her reviewers felt that they now had the perspective to assess *Geography III* in relation to the earlier three books. In *Canto,* J. D. McClatchy, for instance, noted the increasingly autobiographical, intimate quality of the work, an opinion confirmed by Harold Bloom of the *New Republic:* "The poet who gave us meditations like 'The Monument,' 'Roosters,' and 'At the Fishhouses,' comparable to the most memorable poems of [Robert] Frost and [Wallace] Stevens, gives us now work of a curious immediacy, comparable to some of the abrupt lyrics of [Emily] Dickinson, at nearly their most intense. Where the language of personal loss was once barely suggested by Bishop, it now begins to usurp the meditative voice. An oblique power has been displaced by a more direct one, by a controlled pathos all the more deeply moving for having been so long and so nobly postponed."

In *Geography III* Bishop focused her art on what it meant to be human, what people felt living on the earth; the physical world more clearly became a metaphor for her self. While she examined the lives and cares of human beings, the poems sometimes revealed her wondering what those lives and cares had, ultimately, to do with such an apparently impractical activity as creating art, with such an apparently useless craft as poetry. This volume recorded her journey as a geographer of the self and her decisions about art's relevance to life. Loosely outlining a music career, *Geography III* suggested that poetry might ultimately offer knowledge useful in alleviating the pain caused by being human but that it should never become the artist's retreat.

In the villanelle "One Art," perhaps the volume's climax, themes introduced by Bishop elsewhere converged in a perfect lyric indirectly revealing poetry ("Write it!") as one art that could provide some sense of comfort and wholeness in what the collection suggested was a desolate, fragmented, spiritually bankrupt time. But the poems following "One Art" reflected a spirit almost defeated by the world's chaos and cruelty, and Bishop continued musing over her desire to retreat, as in "The End of March" which flirted with her recurring wish to take refuge in a perfect dream house. The final poem, "Five Flights Up," began on a note close to "The End of March," with a mind burdened by consciousness, by time, by the knowledge of what terrible things people can do to each other, but it concluded with the speaker quietly confronting that world, determined to face what she must.

A consistent moral character thus developed in Bishop's poetry, one that faced up to life's difficulties despite its fervent wish to avoid them and always chose to remain involved with a changing world. The constant struggle between Bishop's Dickinsonian wish to withdraw from the world and her desire to confront the world's sorrows and people was apparent early in Bishop's life—if readers take "In the Waiting Room" as any indication—and it certainly showed up in such early works as "The Imaginary Iceberg" or "The Prodigal." Bishop shied from complete connection with others partly because of her acute lifelong awareness that human beings are always eventually faced with their own solitude. Yet she also realized that being human meant making connections between the self and the world; for in the solitude of old age, what mattered were the pacts people had made with life, the treaties they had managed to negotiate in that war between self and world, and the terrain they had been able to map out to help their friends along their ways.

While known mainly for her poetry, Bishop also published in other genres. Preceding her 1962 text for the pictorial history of Brazil, Bishop's translation, *The Diary of "Helena Morley,"* an account of a young girl's experiences in a nineteenth-century Brazilian mining town, appeared in 1957. In 1972 Bishop co-edited with Emanuel Brasil *An Anthology of Twentieth-Century Brazilian Poetry*. In their introduction to this volume, Bishop and Brasil noted the esteem that poets and poetry enjoyed in Brazil, discussed the difficulties of Portuguese versification, and also gave brief highlights of Brazilian poetry—shifts in movements and styles—from the nineteenth century to the time of their volume. Bishop also wrote short stories and memoirs, but these remained uncollected, and many of them unpublished, until the 1984 appearance of *The Collected Prose,* edited by Robert Giroux.

Several of Bishop's readers have lamented the nature of the criticism treating her work. McClatchy has suggested that because most critics have treated Bishop to "an essentially rhetorical reading" with occasional thematic speculations, their approach is "shortsighted" because "it ignores or distorts or reduces the true power of her work and career." Similarly, in a 1985 *Contemporary Literature* essay, Lee Edelman has noted that many critics "have cited [Bishop's poetry] . . . as exemplary of precise observation and accurate detail, presenting us with an Elizabeth Bishop who seems startlingly like some latter-day 'gentle Jane'. . . . Viewing it as a species of moral anecdote, even admirers of Bishop's work have tended to ignore the rigor of her intellect, the range of her allusiveness, the complexity of her tropes." Lynn Keller and Cristanne Miller in a *New England Quarterly* article have observed that the critical tendency to trivialize Bishop's literary contribution represents a failure by many male reviewers to understand that she employed "as a central poetic strategy techniques of indirection available from both literary tradition and women's speech. . . . In [her] work, tools traditionally used by women in speech to control situations without appearing to control, to hide strength while exercising it, complement the more conventional poetic tools that express shades of emotion. . . . Characteristically, in a . . . Bishop poem, subtle manipulations of language create a subtext that contrasts with the direct statement of the poem to reveal a more daring and more intensely personal involvement of the poet with her subject that the surface of the poem suggests or to present a socially disruptive, often feminist, perspective." Moreover, in a *Grand Street* essay, David Kalstone, a longtime friend of Bishop and a major commentator on her work, has persuasively attacked the frequently held assumption that Bishop's work was excessively influenced by Marianne Moore.

Bishop was a prolific letter-writer, as evidenced by the approximately 3,000 letters she left behind. Five hundred of these were collected and published by

Robert Giroux, Bishop's lifelong friend, in *One Art: Letters of Elizabeth Bishop,* titled after the villanelle of the same name. Beyond developing her reputation as a prolific writer (which she was not known as, nor did she consider herself one), as Gail Mazur noted in the Chicago *Tribune Books,* these letters also provide insight into Bishop's personal life. It is interesting to note, too, that Bishop once taught a seminar "Personal Correspondence, Famous and Infamous" at Harvard. In any case, the publication of these letters provided readers with additional insight into Bishop's personal anxiety and guilt about her drinking and her relationships with her Brazilian lover Lota de Macedo Soares as well as the writers Marianne Moore and Robert Lowell. Mazur commented: "Autobiography is often unsatisfying in its deliberately molded presentation of self and often inspired by a need for self-justification. Bishop's letters, no less a presentation, are so immediate in texture, so various, so mood-driven, so vibrant with intelligence, that they create a truly authentic testament of art and life as she lived it."

Several reviewers appreciated the intimacy and casual style of the letters, which contrast with Bishop's more formal and restrained poetry. As Helen Vendler noted in the *New York Review of Books,* "Bishop was a natural writer, but she wrote poems slowly, painstakingly, and with an almost disabling perfectionism; the great relief of letters was that they could be written off the cuff, with amusement, with relaxation, abundantly. Often her pen . . . seems to fly over the page." In the *Observer,* Lorna Sage commented on Bishop's longstanding correspondences: "No wonder so many of her correspondents became epistolary intimates for life: she made letters into a living landscape, with the humans only one item in the menagerie." J. D. McClatchy in the *New York Times Book Review* found Bishop's letters to have a tragic undercurrent, despite their conversational style. "The routines of daily life have rarely seemed so fascinating, nor the great events of the day more comic, than in her accounts of them. And beneath all the enchanting detail one senses—without their ever being dwelt upon—the anxieties, the losses, the suffering."

Elizabeth Bishop died in 1979, leaving behind an impressive canon of poetry and prose. Among the tributes to Bishop reprinted in *Elizabeth Bishop and Her Art* are those by Richard Wilbur and Frank Bidart. Wilbur recalled, "She attended to her art, but she also attended to other people and to the things of every day. James Merrill put this happily, in a recent reminiscence, when he spoke of her 'life-long impersonation of an ordinary woman.' Well, she was an incomparable poet and a delectable person; we loved her very much." "If the future is smart," Bidart declared, "surely her poems will continue to be read. Great poems don't replace one another; each does something nothing else does. The pathos and intimacy in her work deepened until the very end of her life. On October 6, 1979, we ran out of luck."

*BIOGRAPHICAL/CRITICAL SOURCES:*

*BOOKS*

Bishop, Elizabeth, *The Collected Prose,* edited and introduced by Robert Giroux, Farrar, Straus, 1984.

Bishop, Elizabeth, and George Monteiro, *Conversations with Elizabeth Bishop* (interviews), University Press of Mississippi (Jackson), 1996.

Blasing, Mutlu Konuk, *Politics and Form in Postmodern Poetry: O'Hara, Bishop, Ashbery, and Merrill,* Cambridge University Press (New York City), 1995.

*Contemporary Authors Bibliographical Series,* Volume 2: *American Poets,* Gale, 1986.

*Contemporary Literary Criticism,* Gale, Volume 1, 1973, Volume 4, 1975, Volume 9, 1978, Volume 13, 1980, Volume 15, 1980, Volume 32, 1985.

*Contemporary Poetry in America,* edited by Robert Boyers, Schocken, 1974.

*Dictionary of Literary Biography,* Volume 5: *American Poets since World War II,* Gale, 1980.

*Elizabeth Bishop and Her Art,* edited by Lloyd Schwartz and Sybil P. Estess, University of Michigan Press, 1983.

Fountain, Gary and Peter Brazeau, *Remembering Elizabeth Bishop: An Oral Biography,* University of Massachusetts Press (Amherst), 1994.

Frankenberg, Lloyd, *Pleasure Dome: On Reading Modern Poetry,* Houghton, 1949.

Fussell, *Abroad: British Literary Travelling between the Wars,* Oxford University Press, 1980.

Jarrell, Randall, *Poetry and the Age,* Random House, 1953.

Jarrell, Randall, *Third Book of Criticism,* Farrar, Straus, 1969.

Kalstone, David, *Five Temperaments: Elizabeth Bishop, Robert Lowell, James Merrill, Adrienne Rich, John Ashbery,* Oxford University Press, 1977.

Lombardi, Marilyn May, *The Body and the Song: Elizabeth Bishop's Poetics,* Southern Illinois University (Carbondale), 1995.

*Elizabeth Bishop: A Bibliography, 1927-1979,* compiled by Candace MacMahon, University Press of Virginia, 1980.

Mazzaro, Jerome, *Postmodern American Poetry,* University of Illinois Press, 1980.

McCabe, Susan, *Elizabeth Bishop: Her Poetics of Loss,* Pennsylvania State University Press (University Park), 1994.

Molesworth, Charles, *The Fierce Embrace: A Study of Contemporary American Poetry,* University of Missouri Press, 1979.

Pinsky, Robert, *The Situation of Poetry,* Princeton University Press, 1976.

*Poet's Choice,* edited by Paul Engle and Joseph Langland, Dial, 1962.

Rosenthal, M. L., *The Modern Poets,* Oxford University Press, 1960.

Shigley, Sally Bishop, *Dazzling Dialectics: Elizabeth Bishop's Resonating Feminist Reality,* Peter Lang (New York City), 1997.

Stepanchev, Stephen, *American Poetry since 1945: A Critical Survey,* Harper, 1965.

Stevenson, Anne, *Elizabeth Bishop,* Twayne, 1966.

*Trial Balances,* edited by Ann Winslow, Macmillan, 1935.

*Twentieth Century Literature in Retrospect,* edited by Reuben A. Brower, Harvard University Press, 1971.

Vendler, Helen, *Part of Nature, Part of Us: Modern American Poets,* Harvard University Press, 1980.

von Hallberg, Robert, *American Poetry and Culture, 1945-1980,* Harvard University Press, 1985.

Wylie, Diana E., *Elizabeth Bishop and Howard Nemerov: A Reference Guide,* G. K. Hall, 1983.

*PERIODICALS*

*America,* February 19, 1994, p. 21.

*American Literature,* March, 1982; October, 1983.

*American Poetry Review,* March/April, 1978; January/February, 1980; January/February, 1985.

*Antaeus,* winter/spring, 1981.

*Antioch Review,* summer, 1981.

*Arizona Quarterly,* Volume 32, 1976; winter, 1982.

*Atlantic,* January, 1966.

*Bloomsbury Review,* November/December, 1996, p. 5.

*Books Abroad,* winter, 1967.

*Book Week,* February 20, 1966.

*Book World,* April 27, 1969.

*Boston Review,* April, 1983.

*Canadian Poetry,* fall/winter, 1980.

*Canto,* winter, 1977.

*Centennial Review,* winter, 1978; winter, 1981.

*Chicago Review,* Volume 18, numbers 3-4, 1966.

*Chicago Tribune Book World,* April 1, 1984.

*Christian Science Monitor,* January 6, 1966.

*College English,* February, 1959.

*Commonweal,* February 15, 1957.

*Contemporary Literature,* winter, 1971; fall, 1984; summer, 1985.

*Dublin Magazine,* January-March, 1957.

*Encounter,* December, 1983.

*Field,* fall, 1984.

*George Herbert Journal,* spring, 1982.

*Grand Street,* autumn, 1983.

*Hollins Critic,* February, 1977.

*Hudson Review,* autumn, 1956.

*Iowa Review,* winter, 1979.

*Kenyon Review,* Volume 19, number 2, 1957; Volume 28, number 2, 1966.

*Life,* July 4, 1969.

*Listener,* November 30, 1967; June 2, 1983.

*London Magazine,* March 1968.

*London Review of Books,* May 7, 1984.

*Los Angeles Times Book Review,* April 17, 1983; February 19, 1984.

*Massachusetts Review,* autumn, 1970; autumn, 1982; summer, 1983.

*Michigan Quarterly Review,* winter, 1977.

*Modern Poetry Studies,* winter, 1975; spring, 1977; winter, 1977.

*Nation,* September 28, 1946.

*New England Quarterly,* June, 1956; December, 1984.

*New Leader,* December 6, 1965; May 9, 1994, p. 14.

*New Republic,* October 21, 1946; April 9, 1966; February 5, 1977; November 10, 1979; April 4, 1983; March 19, 1984; August 8, 1994, p. 29.

*New Statesman,* April 6, 1984.

*Newsweek,* January 31, 1977; March 14, 1982; February 13, 1984.

*New Yorker,* October 5, 1946; October 8, 1955; May 29, 1978; September 30, 1991, p. 85; March 28, 1994, p. 82.

*New York Herald Tribune Book Review,* September 4, 1955.

*New York Review of Books,* October 12, 1967; June 9, 1977; January 13, 1994, p. 15; June 9, 1994, p. 39.

*New York Times,* January 22, 1977; February 12, 1983; January 5, 1984.

*New York Times Book Review,* July 17, 1955; May 5, 1968; January 7, 1973; February 6, 1977; December 3, 1978; February 27, 1983; January 15, 1984; April 17, 1994, p. 1.

*Observer* (London), April 8, 1984; April 24, 1995, p. 24.

*Paris Review,* summer, 1981.
*Parnassus,* spring/summer, 1973; fall/winter, 1976; spring/summer, 1977.
*Partisan Review,* winter, 1956; spring, 1970.
*Ploughshares,* Volume 2, number 4, 1975; Volume 3, numbers 3 and 4, 1977; Volume 5, number 1, 1979; Volume 6, number 2, 1980.
*PN Review,* February, 1984.
*Poetry,* December, 1955; March, 1979; December, 1990, p. 159t.
*Poetry Review,* June, 1983.
*Publishers Weekly,* July 7, 1945.
*Raritan,* summer, 1984.
*Salmagundi,* summer/fall, 1974.
*Saturday Review,* January 18, 1958.
*Sewanee Review,* summer, 1947; spring, 1978.
*Shenandoah,* Volume 17, number 2, 1966; Volume 33, number 1, 1981-82.
*South Atlantic Quarterly,* summer, 1983.
*South Carolina Review,* November, 1977.
*Southern Review,* autumn, 1977.
*Time,* April 25, 1994, p. 82.
*Times Literary Supplement,* November 23, 1967; March 7, 1980; August 28, 1981; June 3, 1983; April 27, 1984.
*Tribune Books* (Chicago), April 24, 1994, p. 19.
*Twentieth Century Literature,* Volume 11, number 4, 1966; Volume 28, number 4, 1982.
*Vanity Fair,* June, 1983.
*Virginia Quarterly Review,* spring, 1966; autumn, 1969; spring, 1984.
*Washington Post Book World,* February 20, 1983; May 1, 1994, p. 5.
*World Literature Today,* winter, 1977.
*Young Readers Review,* September, 1968.

*OBITUARIES:*

*PERIODICALS*

*Chicago Tribune,* October 9, 1979.
*New York Times,* October 8, 1979.
*Publishers Weekly,* October 22, 1979.
*Time,* October 22, 1979.*

* * *

## BLACKWOOD, Caroline 1931-1996

*PERSONAL:* Born Lady Caroline Hamilton-Temple-Blackwood, July 16, 1931, in Northern Ireland; died February 14, 1996, of cancer; daughter of the Marquis and Marchioness of Dufferin and Ava; married Lucien Freud (a painter; divorced); married Israel Citkowitz (a pianist; divorced); married Robert Lowell (a poet), 1972 (died September 12, 1977); children: (with Citkowitz) three daughters (one deceased); (with Lowell) Robert Sheridan.

*CAREER:* Essayist, short story writer, and novelist.

*WRITINGS:*

*For All That I Found There* (short stories and nonfiction), Duckworth, 1973, Braziller, 1974.
*The Stepdaughter* (novel), Duckworth, 1976, Scribner, 1977.
*Great Granny Webster* (novel), Duckworth, 1977, Scribner, 1978.
(With Anna Haycraft) *Darling, You Shouldn't Have Gone to So Much Trouble* (cookbook), Cape, 1980.
*The Fate of Mary Rose* (novel), Summit, 1981.
*Goodnight Sweet Ladies* (short stories), Heinemann, 1983.
*Corrigan* (novel), Heinemann, 1984, Viking, 1985.
*On the Perimeter* (nonfiction), Heinemann, 1984, Penguin, 1985.
*In the Pink: Caroline Blackwood on Hunting* (nonfiction), Bloomsbury, 1987.
*The Last of the Duchess,* Pantheon Books (New York City), 1995.

*SIDELIGHTS:* Well known in England as a novelist and nonfiction writer, Caroline Blackwood evoked unusual praise from a variety of critics during her career. As Priscilla Martin notes in a *Dictionary of Literary Biography* article on the author, "Her material is anguish, dementia, and despair—injuries of all kinds, insanity, rape, murder, internecine marriages, a disastrous face-lift, suicidal isolation. Her distinctive power is to direct an unflinching gaze at the intolerable and convey it in elegant, witty, and dispassionate prose." Such subject matter seems initially unlikely for a woman born Lady Caroline Hamilton-Temple-Blackwood, heiress to an Irish peerage, as well as a descendent of the eighteenth-century dramatist Richard Brinsley Sheridan. "She grew up in the beautiful, crumbling, leaky ancestral mansion, Clandeboye, in County Down, the basis for the white elephant of a stately home in [Blackwood's novel] *Great Granny Webster,*" adds Martin. Educated in boarding schools, Blackwood avoided college and instead dabbled in journalism and writing book reviews. She met and married the painter Lucien Freud, the first of three marriages. She was later married to

Israel Citkowitz, with whom she had three daughters, and the poet Robert Lowell, with whom she had a son. During her marriages she lived mostly in the United States, spending time both in Los Angeles and New York City.

Blackwood's first writing collection, *For All That I Found There,* reflects on her youth around Ulster, Northern Ireland, where "The Troubles" plagued others. This book "is odd because it's split into three parts: Fiction, Fact, and Ulster," reports *London Magazine* writer Digby Durrant. "But it's not the hopscotch that makes it sound. In fact, this curious dividing . . . is revealing. For the excellent short story writer she is turns into an equally excellent journalist with such smoothness there seems little difference."

With *The Stepdaughter* Blackwood moved into the kind of psychological drama that characterizes the best of her style. The anti-heroine of this first novel has been abandoned by her husband in Manhattan and left with "his grotesquely fat child bloated by rejection and a magnificent apartment with dizzy views through plexiglass," as Duncan Fallowell describes it in a *Spectator* review. There is also a howling infant, the product of their marriage, who is being cared-for by an unhappy *au pair.* The stepmother, known only as "K," fumes constantly and quietly through letters as she plots a way out of her unhappy lot. "Like all [of Blackwood's] novels, *The Stepdaughter* can be seen as a modern variation on an established form," notes Martin. "It is a miniature epistolary novel whose arena is . . . the conscience of a threatened and isolated woman." With its "unblinking view of man's selfishness and woman's dependence *The Stepdaughter* is a notable contribution to the women's movement," finds *Encounter* reviewer James Price. "It is also, I should hazard, a philosophical and religious novel. It begins with a cry of pain, which can be seen to be a philosophical position. It ends with a sense of loss, which can be seen to be a religious one. It is an unusual and affecting experience."

The title character of Blackwood's second novel, *Great Granny Webster,* "is enormously wealthy [but] stingy with a vengeance," as Carol Greenberg Felsenthal puts it in *Chicago Tribune Book World.* Granny is "nearly as old-fashioned as she is stingy, but there is absolutely nothing charming or even eccentric about her aversion to modern conveniences," writes Felsenthal, who adds that "no matter what the season, her manor is cold and damp." Since Granny outlives all her friends and enemies, her eventual death is noted only by her great-granddaughter (the book's narrator) and Richards, her "trampled maid," as described by *New York Review of Books* critic Karl Miller. As Granny's history unfolds, it becomes apparent that "the women of the dynasty have been inclined to go mad," Miller offers. The critic goes on to say that in England, where *Great Granny Webster* was first published, "the tale has gone down well [since there] the appetite for the eccentricities and sufferings of the privileged never sleeps. But there is another reason for its doing well, which has to do with the appetite of its writer. Without being, in any extensive way, artless or careless, it reads like a long and colorful letter, and has the force of an eager unburdening."

Among Blackwood's other novels, *Corrigan* gained favorable notices as a gothic satire in the author's tradition. It centers on the unlikely romance between Devina, a widow wasting away from ennui, and Corrigan, the wheelchair-bound man who rejuvenates her. "Meanwhile, Devina's daughter, Nadine, discovers that she loathes her journalist husband, madly envies her mother, and feels savage ill will toward Corrigan," Laurie Stone observes in a *Village Voice* column. "What Nadine discovers about the mysterious Corrigan and his complex relationship with her mother at the end of her life provides a denouement filled with surprises and irony," *New York Times Book Review* writer Carolyn Gaiser explains. To this reviewer, the author's "sly wit and her affection for her characters brings a glow to these pages, a sunniness that manages to be believable without ever becoming sentimental. [Blackwood] has written a charming tour de force."

Departing from fiction, Blackwood co-wrote a cookbook with the arresting title *Darling, You Shouldn't Have Gone to So Much Trouble,* as well as an examination of the British passion for fox hunting and its equally passionate anti-hunting foes. *In the Pink: Caroline Blackwood on Hunting* didn't garner the praise that Blackwood's novels have—"It cannot be said that Lady Caroline knows much about the vast and boring literature on this touchy subject," finds *Spectator* critic Raymond Carr—but the author continued to be cherished in England as a stringent social critic.

Blackwood's final book before her death in 1996 was *The Last of the Duchess,* a nonfiction work about Wallis Simpson, the American woman whom King Edward VIII of England relinquished his crown to marry. The book grew out of a failed attempt to interview the Duchess of Windsor. Prevented from seeing the ailing Duchess by her attorney and protector, Suzanne Blum, Blackwood instead interviewed many of the Duchess's friends and acquaintances. The result is a sobering look at royalty and old age that most critics responded to with praise. Chicago *Tribune Books* contributor Amanda Vaill calls the book "a marvelously loopy narrative" and notes that "if 'The Last of the Duchess' lacks something as critical biography, it is brilliant—and brilliantly entertaining—journalism." Zoe Heller, writing in the *London Review of Books,* criticizes the "speculation and gossip" that Blackwood uses to supplement her story in the absence of first-hand information from the Duchess about her life. Nevertheless, Heller concedes that Blackwood's "trawl through the nursing homes and sick-beds of various, ancient, aristocratic ladies yields some fascinating fragments of oral history and some wonderfully sad vignettes of old age."

*BIOGRAPHICAL/CRITICAL SOURCES:*

*BOOKS*

*Contemporary Literary Criticism,* Gale, Volume 6, 1976, Volume 9, 1978.
*Dictionary of Literary Biography,* Volume 14: *British Novelists since 1960,* Gale, 1983.

*PERIODICALS*

*Chicago Tribune Book World,* September 10, 1978.
*Encounter,* September, 1976.
*London Magazine,* October/November, 1974.
*London Review of Books,* July 20, 1995, p. 18.
*Los Angeles Times Book Review,* July 28, 1985.
*New Statesman,* November 30, 1973; June 4, 1976.
*New York Review of Books,* September 15, 1977; November 9, 1978; March 23, 1995, p. 18.
*New York Times Book Review,* July 26, 1981; July 14, 1985; December 1, 1985; March 19, 1995, p. 22.
*New York Times Magazine,* April 2, 1995, p. 32.
*Spectator,* June 5, 1976; September 17, 1977; December 13, 1980; March 7, 1981; October 15, 1983; October 10, 1987.
*Times Literary Supplement,* April 5, 1974; September 2, 1977; November 14, 1980; February 27, 1981; September 21, 1984; October 19, 1984; September 25, 1987.
*Tribune Books* (Chicago), April 2, 1995, p. 3.
*Village Voice,* June 25, 1985.
*Vogue,* March, 1995, p. 280.
*Washington Post Book World,* June 2, 1974; October 16, 1977; July 10, 1981; June 30, 1985.

*OBITUARIES:*

*PERIODICALS*

*New York Times,* February 15, 1996, p. 16.
*Time,* February 26, 1996, p. 19.*

* * *

**BLOM, Jan**
**See BREYTENBACH, Breyten**

* * *

**BLOOM, Amy 1953-**

*PERSONAL:* Born June 18, 1953, in New York, NY; daughter of Murray (a journalist and author) and Sydelle (a writer, teacher, and group therapist) Bloom; married Donald Moon (a professor), August 21, 1977; children: Alexander (stepson), Caitlin, Sarah. *Education:* Wesleyan University, B.A., 1975; Smith College, M.S.W., 1978.

*ADDRESSES: Office*—Middletown, CT. *Agent*—Phyllis Wender, Rosenstone/Wender, 3 East 48th St., New York, NY 10077.

*CAREER:* Private practice of psychotherapy, Middletown, CT, 1981—; writer.

*AWARDS, HONORS:* National Book Award nomination, 1993, for *Come to Me;* O. Henry Award for story "Semper Fidelis," 1994.

*WRITINGS:*

*Come to Me* (stories; includes "Faultlines," "Hyacinths," "Love Is Not a Pie," "Only You," "Semper Fidelis," "The Sight of You," "Silver Water," and "Sleepwalking"), HarperCollins (New York City), 1993.
*Love Invents Us* (novel), Random House (New York City), 1996.

Work represented in anthologies, including *Best American Short Stories, 1991,* edited by Alice Adams, Houghton, 1991, and *Best American Short Stories, 1992,* edited by Robert Stone and Katrina Kenison,

Houghton, 1992. Contributor to periodicals, including *New Yorker.*

*WORK IN PROGRESS:* A novel; nonfiction.

*SIDELIGHTS:* Practicing psychotherapist Amy Bloom demonstrates her knowledge of the human condition in her first book, *Come to Me,* a collection of twelve short stories. In *Come to Me,* Bloom delves into the emotional states and mental illnesses of her characters, ranging from Rose, a schizophrenic woman whose family tries to come to terms with her illness in "Silver Water," to an adulterous pianist whose story is related in "The Sight of You." "Although her stories may be full of tragic implications, Ms. Bloom's characters possess extraordinary dignity that lifts them beyond pity," Barbara Kaplan Lane notes in the *New York Times.* "Those whom circumstances might otherwise define as victims or villains reveal heroic potential in the author's skillful, empathic hands." "What Bloom manages to do in story after story is vary her voice . . . , alternate the point of view, change the cadence," writes Ruth Coughlin in the *Detroit News.* "But throughout—always, always—she is able to maintain an extraordinarily high level of emotion and a piercingly sharp intelligence." According to *New York Times Book Review* contributor Anne Whitehouse, Bloom "has created engaging, candid and unorthodox characters, and has vividly revealed their inner lives." Coughlin calls *Come to Me* "a remarkable collection, an exhilarating display of a talent both large and luminous," and Elizabeth Benedict, reviewing the collection in the *Los Angeles Times Book Review,* writes: "*Come to Me* is so rich, moving and gracefully written, it's hard to believe [Bloom] hasn't been doing this all her life."

Bloom's first novel, *Love Invents Us,* emerges in part from a story that appeared in the collection *Come to Me.* The larger novel format enables the author to develop her characters in greater detail and explore their lives over a longer span of time, without losing what Donna Seaman describes in the *Chicago Tribune* as "her arresting economy and pointed poignancy."

In the novel, the protagonist Elizabeth Taube tells her story in her own words, the story of an unattractive, awkward child searching for love and affection long denied. Her urban Jewish parents are cold and distant, her classmates hostile and cruel. "To compensate for this agonizing combination of indifference and malice," writes Gary Krist in the *Washington Post,* "Elizabeth is forced to find warmth wherever she can." Not surprisingly, the lonely child does not always make the wisest choices.

Among Elizabeth's discoveries is Mr. Klein, the furrier from the story "Light Breaks Where No Sun Shines," who encourages her to model his furs in her underwear in the back room of his shop and gives Elizabeth the esteem-building praise and warmth that was missing from her life. Another discovery is Mrs. Hill, an elderly, disabled member of a black church who engages Elizabeth's services as a companion and caretaker, and whose genuine interest in the young woman provides a parent-substitute that inspires Elizabeth's "loyalty unto death," as Marion Winik comments in the *Los Angeles Times.* A more "unhealthy" discovery, according to Krist, is English teacher Max Stone, "a pitiful character, a married father tortured by his scandalous desire for a girl who could be his daughter."

These encounters prepare Elizabeth for her own true love, who turns out to be a black high school basketball player. With Huddie Lester, Krist writes, "Elizabeth gets her first glimpse of a passion unmuddied by complexities and shame, and it's in these scenes that *Love Invents Us* truly comes into its own." Seaman comments: "Elizabeth narrates . . . in a voice as notable for its matter-of-factness in the face of trauma as for its nimble wit, a style that makes each complex scene shimmer."

If the first part of the novel represents discovery, then the second acknowledges loss. Huddie's father exiles him to Alabama, and Mrs. Hill dies. Max, who has become less a lover and more a friend, is afflicted by a series of tragedies that ruin his ability to proffer the love that Elizabeth continues to seek. Huddie's long-delayed return proves anticlimactic. As Winik reports, "it seems the characters are helpless against the assaults of destiny." The final part of the book suggests reconciliation. Winik writes that "things are turning out . . . not perfectly, but hopefully, with . . . the suggestion, if not the assurance, of a happy ending."

Bloom's critics are full of praise for this first novel. Winik writes: "It is a quiet book . . . you almost don't notice how brave it is." Seaman concludes: "Bloom's precise, sensual and heartbreaking tale reminds us that the most exquisite of pleasures can be wedded to the most searing of sorrows" and "we are both scarred and strengthened by the ordeal." Krist summarizes: "Although her book is not flawless . . . its intelligence and passion never flag." Bloom has, Krist concludes, "[shown] us that while love may take many different and surprising forms, there's never enough of it to go around."

Bloom grew up in Long Island, New York, and spent a great deal of her time in her local library. After earning a degree in government and theater, she received her master's degree in social work and went into private practice. "I became a therapist because I am not judgmental," Bloom explained to Lane. "People have always liked to tell me their stories. Even when I was seventeen, taking the Long Island Rail Road to a summer job, the conductor sat down to tell me his life story."

*BIOGRAPHICAL/CRITICAL SOURCES:*

*PERIODICALS*

*Belles Lettres,* winter, 1993, p. 28.
*Booklist,* December 15, 1996, p. 708.
*Chicago Tribune,* January 26, 1997, p. 14-3.
*Detroit News,* August 4, 1993, p. 3F.
*Harper's Bazaar,* January, 1997, p. 54.
*Hudson Review,* winter, 1994, pp. 770-771.
*Library Journal,* January, 1994, p. 200; December, 1996, p. 141.
*Los Angeles Times Book Review,* June 13, 1993, pp. 3, 12; January 12, 1997, p. 8.
*New Statesman and Society,* April 15, 1994, p. 38.
*New York Times,* June 20, 1993, section CN, p. 14; August 16, 1993, p. C18.
*New York Times Book Review,* July 18, 1993, p. 16; January 19, 1997, p. 23.
*People,* February 24, 1997, p. 32.
*Studies in Short Fiction,* fall, 1994, p. 694.
*U.S. News and World Report,* January 27, 1997, p. 69.
*Voice Literary Supplement,* December, 1993, p. 10.
*Washington Post Book World,* February 23, 1997, p. 3.

* * *

**BLOUNT, Roy (Alton), Jr. 1941-**
**(Noah Sanders, C. R. Ways)**

*PERSONAL:* Surname rhymes with "punt"; born October 4, 1941, in Indianapolis, Ind.; son of Roy Alton (a savings and loan executive) and Louise (Floyd) Blount; married Ellen Pearson, September 6, 1964 (divorced March, 1973); married Joan Ackerman, 1976 (separated); children: (first marriage) Ennis Caldwell, John Kirven. *Education:* Vanderbilt University, B.A. (magna cum laude), 1963; Harvard University, M.A., 1964. *Politics:* "Dated white Southern liberalism, with healthy undertones of redneckery and anarchism; nostalgia for Earl Long." *Religion:* "Lapsed Methodist."

*ADDRESSES: Home*—Mill River, MA; and New York, NY.

*CAREER: Decatur-DeKalb News,* Decatur, GA, reporter and sports columnist, 1958-59; *Morning Telegraph,* New York City, reporter, summer, 1961; *New Orleans Times-Picayune,* New Orleans, LA, reporter, summer, 1963; *Atlanta Journal,* Atlanta, GA, reporter, editorial writer, and columnist, 1966-68; *Sports Illustrated,* New York City, staff writer, 1968-74, associate editor, 1974-75; freelance writer, 1975—. Occasional performer for American Humorists' Series, American Place Theatre, 1986, and 1988, and has appeared on *A Prairie Home Companion, The CBS Morning Show, The Tonight Show, The David Letterman Show, Austin City Limits, All Things Considered,* and many other radio and television programs. Instructor at Georgia State College, 1967-68. Member of usage panel, American Heritage Dictionary. Has lectured at Manhattan Theatre Club, San Diego Forum, Washington State University, Wyoming Bar Association, and others. *Military service:* U.S. Army, 1964-66; became first lieutenant.

*MEMBER:* Phi Beta Kappa.

*WRITINGS:*

*About Three Bricks Shy of a Load,* Little, Brown, 1974, revised edition published as *About Three Bricks Shy—and the Load Filled Up: The Story of the Greatest Football Team Ever,* Ballantine (New York City), 1989.
*Crackers: This Whole Many-Sided Thing of Jimmy, More Carters, Ominous Little Animals, Sad-Singing Women, My Daddy and Me,* Knopf, 1980.
*One Fell Soup; or, I'm Just a Bug on the Windshield of Life,* Little, Brown, 1982.
*What Men Don't Tell Women,* Atlantic-Little, Brown, 1984.
*Not Exactly What I Had in Mind,* Atlantic Monthly Press, 1985.
*It Grows on You: A Hair-Raising Survey of Human Plumage,* Doubleday, 1986.
*Roy Blount's Happy Hour and a Half* (one-man show), produced Off-Broadway at American Place Theatre, January 22-February 7, 1986.

*Soupsongs/Webster's Ark* (double book of verse), Houghton, 1987.

*Now, Where Were We?,* Villard (New York City), 1989, audio cassette version, Sound Editions (Holmes, PA), 1989.

*First Hubby,* Villard, 1990.

*Camels Are Easy, Comedy's Hard,* Villard, 1991.

*Roy Blount's Book of Southern Humor,* Norton (New York City), 1994.

Also author of two one-act plays produced at Actors Theater of Louisville, KY, November, 1983, and fall, 1984. Contributor to anthologies, including *The Best of Modern Humor,* 1983, *Laughing Matters,* 1987, *The Norton Book of Light Verse,* 1987, *The Oxford Book of American Light Verse, The Ultimate Baseball Book, Classic Southern Humor,* and *Sudden Fiction.* Columnist, *Atlanta Journal,* 1967-70. Contributor of articles, short stories, poems, crossword puzzles, and drawings, sometimes under pseudonyms Noah Sanders and C. R. Ways, to 92 very different publications, including *Sports Illustrated, New Yorker, Atlantic, New York Times, Magazine, Esquire, Playboy, Rolling Stone, GQ, Conde Nast Traveler, Spy,* and *Antaeus.* Contributing editor, *Atlantic,* 1983—.

*WORK IN PROGRESS:* Lyrics for musical comedy, *Murder at Elaine's,* book by Nora Ephron.

*SIDELIGHTS:* Roy Blount, Jr., "is Andy Rooney with a Georgia accent, only funnier," declares Larry L. King in the *Washington Post Book World.* Like Rooney, Blount has entertained the American public not only through his multitudinous magazine publications (his articles have appeared in nearly 100 different magazines) and his books, but also through other media—he has performed on radio and television shows ranging from Minnesota Public Radio's *A Prairie Home Companion* to TV's *David Letterman Show.* "The unceasing drip-drip-drip of bizarre images, intricate wordplay, droll asides and crazy ideas disorients the reader," states Patrick F. McManus in the *New York Times Book Review,* "until Mr. Blount finally has him at his mercy." His work has been compared to that of Mark Twain, and his "light touch and sense of bemusement," declares Eric Zorn in the *Chicago Tribune,* "combine with arch intellect to give him the versatility to publish in *Organic Gardening* and *Country Journal* one day and *Harvard Magazine* the next."

Blount's books, says Leslie Bennetts in the *New York Times,* "attest to the breadth of his interests, from 'One Fell Soup, or I'm Just a Bug on the Windshield of Life' (which is also the name of one of the original songs Mr. Blount sings 'unless I'm forcibly deterred') to 'What Men Don't Tell Women' to 'It Grows on You,' a volume about hair." His first book, *About Three Bricks Shy of a Load,* "did for the Pittsburgh Steelers roughly what Sherman did for the South," states Donald Morrison in *Time,* and it "remains the most comic treatise on professional football extinct or extant," reports King. *New York Times Book Review* contributor Robert W. Creamer calls *About Three Bricks Shy of a Load* "a terrific book," and he concludes, "I have never read anything else on pro football, fiction or nonfiction, as good as this."

With his second book, *Crackers: This Whole Many-Sided Thing of Jimmy, More Carters, Ominous Little Animals, Sad-Singing Women, My Daddy and Me,* Blount established his reputation as a humorist. *Crackers* examines the presidency of Jimmy Carter, a Georgian like Blount, and concludes that what the Carter administration needed was a more down-to-earth, redneck approach to the business of governing the country. "If *Crackers* reveals an overarching thesis, it is that contemporary America, like its president, is too emotionally constrained, too given to artifice, too Northern," explains Morrison. The book was a critical success; Harry Crews, writing in the *Washington Post Book World,* calls *Crackers* "the funniest book I've read in a decade," and labels it "a triumph over subject, proving—if it needed proving again—that there are no dull subjects, only dull writers."

Blount has also achieved success in collections of his magazine articles, including *One Fell Soup; or, I'm Just a Bug on the Windshield of Life, What Men Don't Tell Women, Not Exactly What I Had in Mind, It Grows on You: A Hair-Raising Survey of Human Plumage,* and *Now, Where Were We?* Gathered from sources as diverse as *Esquire,* the *New Yorker,* and *Eastern Airlines Pastimes,* the collections prove Blount's "ability to be amusing on a diversity of topics," according to Beaufort Cranford of the *Detroit News.* After all, he asks, "what other source can prove the existence of God by considering the testicle?"

Although some critics—like *Los Angeles Times* contributor Taffy Cannon, who calls Blount's stories "considerably funnier in a bar at midnight than spread at meandering and pointless length across the printed page"—find that Blount's later works aren't as successful as his earlier ones, many others celebrate his collections. "It gives me great pleasure," King declared after reading *One Fell Soup,* "to here officially designate [Blount ] . . . a semi-genius at the very least. I have been reading his stuff for years and he seldom fails to break me up." Ron Givens, writing in *Newsweek,* declares, "It's downright refreshing, then, to read somebody who has taste, intelligence, style and, oh, bless you, wit—qualities that Roy Blount Jr. . . . [has] in abundance."

Blount has also attracted attention as a versifier and songwriter. Despite his claims to be "singing impaired," Blount has performed both his stories and his verses in his one-man show, *Roy Blount's Happy Hour and a Half,* and on radio programs such as *A Prairie Home Companion.* A recent collection of the comic's verse, *Soupsongs/Webster's Ark,* "contains odes to beets, chitlins, barbeque sauce, catfish and grease ('I think that I will never cease / To hold in admiration grease')," explains Bennetts, "along with a 'Song Against Broccoli' that reads in its entirety: 'The neighborhood stores are all out of broccoli, / Loccoli.'" "Blount's verses may resemble Burma Shave's more than Byron's," declares the *Chicago Tribune*'s Jim Spencer, "but they are bodaciously funny."

Blount continued to strike literary gold with a string of well-reviewed books published in 1989, 1990, and 1991—*Now, Where Were We?, First Hubby,* and *Camels Are Easy, Comedy's Hard,* respectively. The first and most lauded of these, *Now, Where Were We?,* is a collection of the author's previously published essays. "The genre of earnest, plain-spoken bumpkinhood," writes Deborah Mason in the *New York Times Book Review,* "forms one of the primal pools of American humor. . . . These pieces are brilliantly loopy, reassuringly subversive, and they put Mr. Blount in serious contention for the title of America's most cherished humorist." Indeed, *Washington Post Book World* contributor Jonathan Yardley goes so far as to say that "a half dozen [of the essays] are likely to cause guttural eruptions, five are moderately dangerous to one's health—and one may be, for those with weak constitutions, terminally fatal."

Blount's debut novel, *First Hubby,* was generally considered a credible first effort in the longer genre. The story hinges on a major political event: the first female vice-president of the United States becomes president after the elected chief executive is killed by a huge falling fish. The narrator of *First Hubby* is none other than the frustrated writer-husband of the nation's new president, and he expounds upon his life and times with familiar Blountian humor. "Dialogue, internal and external, is Blount's forte," states Christopher Hitchens in *Washington Post Book World.* And the author's ability to recognize good dialogue when he reads it put *Roy Blount's Book of Southern Humor* at the top of the critics' picks in late 1994. Blount chose short southern writings from over one hundred artists—Flannery O'Connor, Edgar Allan Poe, Alice Walker, Louis Armstrong, and Lyle Lovett among them—and collected them in one of the most acclaimed volumes of its kind.

Critics have tried to define with varying success the sources of Blount's sense of humor. "I can't tell you what makes Roy Blount such a funny writer," confesses *Washington Post Book World* reviewer Dennis Drabelle, "—perhaps a dose of comic afflatus administered by the gods." Another contributing factor, suggests Givens, "derives from his off-center perceptions." Kenneth Turan of *Time* calls Blount's work "in the tradition of the great curmudgeons like H. L. Mencken and W. C. Fields." And the comic "is not of the punch-line school of humor writing," declares McManus. "His humor is cumulative in effect, like Chinese water torture. When you can bear it no longer, you collapse into a spasm of mirth, often at a line that taken by itself would provoke no more than a smile."

Roy Blount, Jr., summed up his life for *CA,* saying, "Raised in South by Southern parents. Couldn't play third base well enough so became college journalist. Ridiculed cultural enemies. Boosted integration. Decided to write, teach. Went to Harvard Graduate School. Didn't like it. Went back to journalism. Liked it. Got a column. Ridiculed cultural enemies. Wrote limericks. Boosted integration. Wanted to write for magazines. Took writing job at *Sports Illustrated.* Have seen country, met all kinds of people, heard all different kinds of talk. Like it. Ready now to write a novel that sums it all up."

For an interview with Blount, see *Contemporary Authors New Revisions,* Volume 28.

*BIOGRAPHICAL/CRITICAL SOURCES:*

*BOOKS*

Brown, Jerry Elijah, *Roy Blount, Jr.,* Twayne (Boston), 1990.

*PERIODICALS*

*Books of the Times,* December, 1980.
*Chicago Tribune,* November 4, 1982; December 24, 1987.

*Detroit News,* October 17, 1982.
*Globe and Mail* (Toronto), July 14, 1984.
*Kirkus Reviews,* January 1, 1989, p. 23; April 15, 1990, p. 512; July 15, 1991, p. 900.
*Library Journal,* October 1, 1994, p. 80.
*Los Angeles Times,* December 13, 1985.
*Los Angeles Times Book Review,* September 30, 1990, p. 14.
*Newsweek,* September 17, 1984; December 5, 1994, p. 74.
*New York Times,* September 27, 1980; November 1, 1982; April 28, 1984; January 25, 1988; January 26, 1988; June 25, 1990, p. 58.
*New York Times Book Review,* December 1, 1974; September 28, 1980; May 13, 1984; November 17, 1985; February 7, 1988; March 26, 1989; April 2, 1989, p. 9; June 10, 1990, p. 7; October 7, 1990, p. 38; December 29, 1991, p. 16.
*People,* April 24, 1989, p. 32; June 25, 1990, p. 33; November 21, 1994, p. 41.
*Publishers Weekly,* June 8, 1990, p. 37; July 5, 1991, p. 54; September 5, 1994, p. 88.
*Sports Illustrated,* February 10, 1969; June 18, 1973; April 15, 1974; August 5, 1974.
*Time,* October 20, 1980; June 4, 1984; June 25, 1990, p. 72; April 15, 1991, p. 4; October 23, 1995, p. 43.
*Times Literary Supplement,* June 3, 1983.
*Tribune Books* (Chicago), February 26, 1989, p. 9; September 23, 1990, p. 8; October 13, 1991, p.8.
*Washington Post,* June 19, 1984.
*Washington Post Book World,* September 28, 1980; November 2, 1980; January 23, 1983; October 13, 1985; February 19, 1989, p. 3; June 17, 1990, p. 9; October 20, 1991, p. 13.*

* * *

**BOLAND, Eavan (Aisling) 1944-**

*PERSONAL:* Born September 24, 1944, in Dublin, Ireland; daughter of Frederick Boland (a diplomat) and Frances (a painter; maiden name, Kelly); married Kevin Casey (a novelist), 1969; children: Sarah Margaret and Eavan Frances. *Education:* Trinity College, Dublin, B.A., 1966; University of Iowa, International Writing Programme, 1979.

*CAREER:* Trinity College, Dublin, lecturer, 1967-68; School of Irish Studies, Dublin, lecturer, 1968—; writer.

*MEMBER:* Irish Academy of Letters.

*AWARDS, HONORS:* Irish Arts Council Macauley Fellowship, 1967, for *New Territory;* Poetry Book Society Choice, 1987, for *The Journey;* Irish American Cultural Award, 1983.

*WRITINGS:*

POETRY

*23 Poems,* Gallagher (Dublin), 1962.
*New Territory,* Allan Figgis (Dublin), 1967.
*The War Horse,* Gollancz, 1975, Arlen House (Dublin), 1980.
*In Her Own Image,* Arlen House, 1980.
*Introducing Eavan Boland,* Ontario Review Press, 1981.
*Night Feed,* Arlen House, 1982, Marion Boyars, 1982.
*The Journey,* Gallery Press, 1983, Deerfield Press, 1983.
*The Journey and Other Poems,* Carcanet, 1987.
*Selected Poems,* Carcanet, 1989.
*Outside History: Selected Poems, 1980-90,* Norton, 1990.
*In a Time of Violence,* Norton, 1994.
*Collected Poems,* Carcanet, 1995, published in the United States as *An Origin Like Water: Collected Poems, 1967-1987,* Norton (New York City), 1996.

Work represented in anthologies, including *Faber Anthology of Irish Verse, Penguin Anthology of Irish Verse, Pan Anthology of Irish Verse,* and *Sphere Anthology of Irish Verse.*

OTHER

(With Michael MacLiammoir) *W. B. Yeats and His World,* Thames & Hudson, 1971, Viking, 1972.
*A Kind of Scar: The Woman Poet in a National Tradition,* Attic Press (Dublin), 1989.
*A Dozen Lips,* Attic Press, 1994.
*Object Lessons: The Life of the Woman and the Poet in Our Time,* Norton, 1995.

Regular contributor to *Irish Times.* Contributor to *Irish Press, Spectator, American Poetry Review,* and *Soundings.*

*SIDELIGHTS:* Irish poet Eavan Boland's poetry often focuses on the central experiences of ordinary women. Presenting such activities as motherhood and domestic life as vital elements of the Irish nation and civilization in general, she challenges the opinion that such topics are mundane or inappropriate for literature. Many of her poems express a sense of anger and imprisonment associated with the constricted or unrealistic expectations placed upon women by Irish society. Marilyn Hacker asserted: "Boland has set herself no less a task than giving words, giving music to that half of human endeavor which has been routinely erased, silenced, or passed by word of mouth, not by word of text; from mother to daughter, neighbor to neighbor, friend to friend. . . ."

The youngest of five children, Boland was born in Dublin. She has acknowledged her parents' influence on her artistic development: her father was a medievalist in law and the classics at Trinity College in Dublin and a diplomat who served in London and with the United Nations, and her mother was a painter who abhorred the academic in art. When Boland was six years old, her family moved to London, where she attended a convent school. Her childhood experiences in England, where she often encountered anti-Irish hostility, strongly influenced her perception of her homeland: "My image-makers as a child were just refractions of my exile: conversations overheard, memories and visitors. I listened and absorbed. Long before Ireland was my country, therefore, it had become my nation." Her sense of isolation continued when her family moved to New York City in 1956, where she attended another Catholic school. Several years later, she returned to Dublin to attend the Holy Child Convent, where she found the solitude and peace of her surroundings beneficial for writing poetry. After graduating, she worked as a housekeeper, and self-published a pamphlet titled *23 Poems.* Most critics (including Boland herself) consider the work ambitious but far inferior to her later collections. Following her completion of an English degree at Trinity College, she held a position as a lecturer there, but resigned when she found the highly structured academic environment threatening to her creativity. However, she has continued to teach at the School of Irish Studies in Dublin, and frequently contributes reviews and articles to the *Irish Times.*

Boland's early poems are formal in structure and tone, and frequently focus on political and academic subjects. In her collection *The War Horse,* for example, Boland addresses political turmoil in Northern Ireland and comments on such literary figures as Horace, Herodotus, and Vladimir Mayakovsky. Although some critics considered the work overly mannered and restrained, many praised the collection's title poem, in which Boland compares her perception of a distant war to the vision of a horse trampling flowers outside a window: "You might say, only a crocus, its bulbous head / Blown from growth, onc of the screamless dead. / But we, we are safe, our unformed fear / Of fierce commitment gone; why should we care?" *The War Horse* also examines the theme of entrapment—a central motif of Boland's work. In "Ode to Suburbia," she laments the passivity and lethargy of a housewife confined by her culture's limited expectations of women: "By this creature drowsing now in every house, / The same lion who tore stripes / Once off zebras, who now sleeps / Small beside the coals. . . . " Her following collection, *In Her Own Image,* also focuses on themes of limitation, but departs from the subdued tone of *The War Horse,* addressing the victimization of women in an angry, often shocking manner in such poems as "Mastectomy," "Menses," and "Anorexic." "In His Own Image" graphically depicts domestic violence: "He splits my lip with his fist, / shadows my eyes with a blow, / knuckles my neck to its proper angle. / What a perfectionist!" Amy Klauke observed: "[These] poems are at times confessional, jumping into an uncomfortable intimacy with the reader, who is both repelled and fascinated with their revelations of the degraded self."

Boland's poetry often reflects her effort to restructure a poetic tradition that has largely simplified or excluded the genuine experiences of women. In her essay "The Woman Poet in a National Tradition," she explained: "Inexorably, I wrote my way into my own reality. Inevitably, Irishness, womanhood, things which had remained safely at the edges of the poem moved dangerously to its centre." Much of her collection *Night Feed* focuses on motherhood, emphasizing nurturance and growth. In an interview, Boland explained her decision to write poetry about familiar domestic experiences: "I was there with two small children in a house and I could see what was potent and splendid and powerful happening everyday in front of me and I wanted to express that." Her following book, *The Journey,* also presents a heightened perspective on routine household work through detailed images of color and texture, as reflected in such poems as "The Bottle Garden:" "I decanted them—feather mosses, fan-shaped plants, / asymmetric greys in the begonia— / into this globe. . . ." Many critics praised the collection's blending of common experience with elements of myth. The title poem, for example, begins with the mother of an ill child contemplating the need for a poem to the antibiotic. The traditionally-structured verse of "The Journey" then diverges into a mythical dream sequence descending into the underworld and building into a dark vision of "the children of the plague." Commending the poem's understated depiction of the suffering of mothers and children throughout history, Anthony Libby asserted, "I have a feeling that this moving poem may be one for the ages."

Boland's 1994 book of poetry, *In a Time of Violence,* continues her focus on political and personal themes. The title does not refer to the political violence in Ireland but rather to Boland's perception of "violence" in issues such as the "marginalization" of poetry in society and of women in poetry. Critics, however, praised Boland's masterful command of poetic structure and syntax rather than her themes. James Scruton, writing for the *Irish Literary Supplement* reminded readers that "It is not . . . the inquiry into history and violence and gender and myth that defines poetry . . . but line-break and an audible syntactic, syllabic music: the poet's voice rather than the novelist's or the essayist's." Under this scrutiny, Scruton found Boland's poetry to be "of the highest order." Mark Wormald of the *Times Literary Supplement* was of a similar mind: "It's for the details of the ingenious, unpredictable and sometimes startlingly beautiful 'cadences of change' . . . that *In a Time of Violence* is so memorable." Reviewers were somewhat divided in their opinions on Boland's ability to fully engage in her subject matter. Calvin Bedient in *Poetry* found her to be too distant from her work, stating "There are times when pathos excuses Boland from getting serious." Noting unfavorable comparisons of her to Adrienne Rich as being "deserved," Bedient continued, "She's like an iconoclastic photographer who casts a professional-at-work shadow in the picture, but, in her case, the picture is more and more the shadow itself, the rest becoming merely accompanying matter." Denis Donoghue in the *New York Review of Books* faulted Boland's voice as overly self-conscious in its politics: "She tends to see herself in a dramatic and representative light, such that her censoriousness is to be understood as exemplary, her moods as universally significant. Her representative 'suburban woman' has only to stand in a garden in Dundrum to feel the whole natural world ministering to her disposition as if the fate of nations hung upon it." He continued, citing his preference for work such as "The Pomegranate," "Eavan Boland's best poems seem to me those in which she writes without apparent fuss or political flourish. She gets on with it, writes the poem, and leaves the ideological significance of it to be divined."

*Object Lessons,* subtitled *The Life of the Woman and the Poet in Our Time,* is defined as a "prose memoir." It contains Boland's reflections on her childhood, her early years as a poet, Irish poetry and women's place within the poetic history of Ireland, and other personal pieces. In this volume, Boland "weaves autobiography into analysis . . . spinning an object lesson made of her self and her 'story,'" commented Carol Muske in *The Nation.* Reviewers were mixed in their opinions of this work. "While some of its material will be of interest to critics and scholars . . . on the whole it is a disappointing venture for a writer so widely and rightfully admired," noted Scruton in his review for the *Irish Literary Supplement.* He found Boland to "merely rework in diluted terms" the ideas of others, ineffectually combining the historical with the personal, and making "pronouncements that seem unexamined and indefensible" thereby "reducing and simplifying rather than extending or illuminating" her own poetry. However, he concluded, readers will find "plenty that is worthwhile." Bernard O'Donoghue summarized in the *Times Literary Supplement* that "it is not this book's concern to develop arguments or to demonstrate," citing the result to be "within its carefully set limits . . . a masterpiece." Ailbhe Smyth, writing for the *Women's Review of Books,* stated: "I value *Object Lessons* as a rare record, one that tells of the dilemmas and defiances of a woman and a poet striving for truth in her life and work." Muske concluded: "Boland is clearly a woman who does not fear controversy. . . . It is not like any other book in memory: inspired, relentless, deliberately and eloquently hand-drawn."

*An Origin Like Water: Collected Poems 1967-1987* covers Boland's work and life from her days as a young poet following graduation from Trinity College through her marriage to novelist Kevin Casey and as mother of two children. The collection reflects that progression: Boland's early poetry as influenced by Yeats, Keats, and Irish myth, her later work focused on marriage and motherhood, and finally, unification of these themes in Boland's examination of the role of women in Irish poetry and society. A contributor to *Publishers Weekly* noted this progression and its connection to *Object Lessons,* stating "Readers of that work will recognize—and relish—the way this collection charts a life's course." Ray Olson, writing for *Booklist,* called Boland's poetry "Forceful . . . and evocative, provocative, and powerful, too." "Boland's gift is that she is always accessible, never elitist, but intelligent, striving and inclusive," declared Sue Hubbard in the *New Statesman & Society.*

Deborah McWilliams Consalvo placed Boland firmly in Irish literary history, commenting in the *Irish Literary Supplement,* "The keening of Boland's poetic voice has, indeed, shattered the looking-glass ideal of literary elitism . . . [her] creativity has yielded and forged new territory within the context of literary Ireland."

*BIOGRAPHICAL/CRITICAL SOURCES:*

*BOOKS*

*Contemporary Literary Criticism,* Gale, Volume 40, 1986, Volume 67, 1992.

*Dictionary of Literary Biography,* Volume 40: *Poets of Great Britain and Ireland since 1960,* Gale, 1985.

Haberstroh, Patricia Boyle, *Women Creating Women: Contemporary Irish Women Poets,* Syracuse University Press (Syracuse, NY), 1996.

*PERIODICALS*

*Booklist,* March 15, 1994, p. 1322; February 15, 1996, p. 983.

*Commonweal,* November 4, 1988, p. 595.

*Irish Literary Supplement,* fall, 1994, p. 23; fall, 1995, p. 8; spring, 1996, p. 30.

*Library Journal,* November 15, 1990, p. 74; March 1, 1994, p. 90.

*Nation,* June 6, 1994, p. 798; April 24, 1995, p. 564.

*New Statesman & Society,* January 26, 1996, p. 40.

*New York Review of Books,* May 26, 1994, p. 25.

*New York Times Book Review,* April 21, 1991, p. 40.

*Poetry,* July, 1990, p. 236; October, 1994, p. 41.

*Publishers Weekly,* October 26, 1990, p. 62; December 18, 1995, p. 51.

*Times Literary Supplement,* August 5, 1994, p. 19; September 8, 1995, p. 28.

*Women's Review of Books,* September, 1995, p. 7.*

* * *

## BOYLE, Kay 1902-1992

*PERSONAL:* Born February 19, 1902, in St. Paul, MN; died December 27, 1992, in Mill Valley, CA; daughter of Howard Peterson and Katherine (Evans) Boyle; married Richard Brault, June 24, 1923 (divorced); married Laurence Vail, April 2, 1931 (divorced, 1943); married Baron Joseph von Franckenstein, February 20, 1943 (died, 1963); children: Sharon Walsh; (second marriage) Apple-Joan, Kathe, Clover; (third marriage) Faith Carson, Ian Savin. *Education:* Studied architecture at Parson's School of Fine and Applied Arts in New York and Ohio Mechanics Institute in Cincinnati, 1917-19; took courses at Columbia University, East Washington University, 1982, and studied violin at Cincinnati Conservatory of Music. *Politics:* Democrat. *Avocational interests:* Riding horses and climbing mountains.

*CAREER:* Writer. Taught night school course in writing, Nyack, NY, 1941-43; teacher at Miss Thomas's School in Connecticut during fifties and early sixties; San Francisco State College (now San Francisco State University), San Francisco, CA, member of English faculty, 1963-79. Member of workshop in the short story, New School for Social Research, 1962; lecturer and writer in residence at various colleges and universities, including Northwestern State University, Spokane, WA, 1981, and Bowling Green State University, Bowling Green, OH, 1986. Fellow at Wesleyan University, Middletown, CT, 1963, and Radcliffe Institute for Independent Study, 1965.

*MEMBER:* National Institute of Arts and Letters, American Academy.

*AWARDS, HONORS:* Guggenheim fellowships, 1934 and 1961; O. Henry Memorial Award for best short story of the year, 1934, for "The White Horses of Vienna," and 1941, for "Defeat"; D. Litt., Columbia College, 1971, Skidmore College, 1977, Southern Illinois College, 1982, and Bowling Green State University, 1986; California Literature Medal Award, 1971, for *Testament for My Students;* San Francisco Art Commission Award, 1978; National Endowment for the Arts Fellowship, 1980, for "extraordinary contribution to American literature over a lifetime of creative work"; American Book Award, Before Columbus Foundation, 1984, for lifetime achievement; Robert Kirsch Award, *Los Angeles Times,* 1986; French-American Foundation Translation prize, 1986, for "distinguished contribution to French and American letters as author and translator"; nominated for *Los Angeles Times* Book Award in poetry, 1986, for *This Is Not a Letter and Other Poems*; Lannan Foundation Award, 1991; Fred Cody Award, 1992.

*WRITINGS:*

*NOVELS*

*Plagued by the Nightingale,* Cape & Smith, 1931, new edition, Southern Illinois University Press,

1969, reprinted with new introduction by the author, Virago, 1981.

*Year before Last,* H. Smith, 1932, new edition, Southern Illinois University Press, 1969.

*Gentlemen, I Address You Privately,* Smith & Haas, 1933.

*My Next Bride,* Harcourt, 1934, reprinted with new introduction by Doris Grumbach, Virago, 1986.

*Death of a Man,* Harcourt, 1936.

*Monday Night,* Harcourt, 1938, reprinted, P. P. Appel, 1977.

*The Crazy Hunter: Three Short Novels* (also see below; includes *The Crazy Hunter, The Bridegroom's Body,* and *Big Fiddle*), Harcourt, 1940 (published in England as *The Crazy Hunter and Other Stories,* Faber, 1940), reprinted with introduction by Margaret Atwood, Penguin, 1982.

*Primer for Combat,* Simon & Schuster, 1942.

*Avalanche,* Simon & Schuster, 1944.

*A Frenchman Must Die,* Simon & Schuster, 1946.

*1939,* Simon & Schuster, 1948.

*His Human Majesty,* Whittlesey House, 1949.

*The Seagull on the Step,* Knopf, 1955.

*Three Short Novels* (includes *The Crazy Hunter, The Bridegroom's Body,* and *Decision*), Beacon 1958.

*Generation without Farewell,* Knopf, 1960.

*The Underground Woman,* Doubleday, 1975.

*Winter Night,* Creative Education (Mankato, MN), 1993.

*SHORT STORIES*

*Short Stories,* Black Sun (Paris), 1929.

*Wedding Day and Other Stories,* Cape & Smith, 1930, reprinted, Books for Libraries Press, 1972.

*The First Lover and Other Stories,* Random, 1933.

*The White Horses of Vienna and Other Stories,* Harcourt, 1936.

*Thirty Stories,* Simon & Schuster, 1946.

*The Smoking Mountain: Stories of Post-War Germany,* McGraw, 1951.

*Nothing Ever Breaks Except the Heart,* Doubleday, 1966.

*Fifty Stories,* Doubleday, 1980.

*Life Being the Best and Other Stories,* New Directions, 1988.

*POETRY*

*A Statement,* Modern Editions Press, 1932.

*A Glad Day,* New Directions, 1938.

*American Citizen: Naturalized in Leadville, Colorado* (long poem), Simon & Schuster, 1944.

*The Lost Dogs of Phnom Pehn,* Two Windows (Berkeley), 1968.

*Testament for My Students and Other Poems,* Doubleday, 1970.

*A Poem for February First 1975,* Quercus Press, 1975.

*Collected Poems of Kay Boyle,* Copper Canyon, 1995.

*JUVENILE*

*The Youngest Camel,* Little, Brown, 1939, revised edition published as *The Youngest Camel: Reconsidered and Rewritten,* Harper, 1959.

*Pinky, the Cat Who Liked to Sleep,* Crowell-Collier, 1966.

*Pinky in Persia,* Crowell-Collier, 1968.

*NONFICTION*

*Breaking the Silence: Why a Mother Tells Her Son about the Nazi Era* (pamphlet), Institute of Human Relations Press (New York City), 1962.

*The Long Walk at San Francisco State and Other Essays,* Grove, 1970.

(With others) *Four Visions of America,* Capra, 1977.

*Words that Must Somehow Be Said: Selected Essays of Kay Boyle, 1927-1984,* North Point Press, 1985.

*TRANSLATOR FROM THE FRENCH*

Joseph Delteil, *Don Juan,* Cape & Smith, 1931.

Rene Crevel, *Mr. Knife Miss Fork,* Black Sun, 1931.

Raymond Radiguet, *Devil in the Flesh,* H. Smith, 1932.

(And author of afterword) Crevel, *Babylon,* North Point Press, 1985.

*GHOST WRITER*

Gladys Palmer Brooke, *Relations & Complications: Being the Recollections of H. H. the Dayang Muda of Sarawak,* Lane, 1929.

Bettina Bedwell, *Yellow Dusk,* Hurst & Blackett, 1937.

*EDITOR*

*Poems and Sonnets by Ernest Walsh,* Harcourt, 1934.

(With former husband Laurence Vail and Nina Conarain) *365 Days,* Harcourt, 1936.

*The Autobiography of Emanuel Carnevali,* Horizon Press, 1967.

(And contributor of supplementary chapters) Robert McAlmon, *Being Geniuses's Together, 1920-1930*

(memoirs), Doubleday, 1968, revised edition with new afterword by Boyle, Northpoint Press, 1984.
(With Justine Van Gundy) *Enough of Dying! Voices for Peace,* Laurel, 1972.

*OTHER*

(Author of foreword) Herbert Kubly, *At Large,* Gollancz, 1963, Doubleday, 1964.
(Author of afterword) McAlmon, *A Hasty Bunch,* Southern Illinois University Press, 1977.

Contributor to anthologies, including numerous volumes of *Best American Short Stories,* edited by Edward O'Brien. On staff of *Broom* magazine, 1922; foreign correspondent in Germany for *New Yorker,* 1946-53. Regular contributor to *transition, Saturday Evening Post, Harper's,* and *Nation.*

*ADAPTATIONS: The Crazy Hunter,* was adapted for television by Desilu Productions, 1958; the short story, "The Ballet of Central Park," was adapted and filmed as a short subject in 1972; the short story, "Maiden, Maiden," was made into a full-length feature film by Highland Films, 1980.

*SIDELIGHTS:* "The older I grow," novelist, short story writer, poet, and essayist Kay Boyle commented in an interview with Kay Mills of the *Los Angeles Times,* "the more I feel that all writers should be more committed to their times and write of their times and of the issues of their times." According to Mills, both Boyle's narrative style and themes reflect the writer's commitment to her times. Boyle's largely autobiographical fiction was her major vehicle for social commentary. Her short stories—which critics such as Robert E. Kroll in *Prairie Schooner* and Theodore L. Gross in *Saturday Review* described as her best work—illustrate both the writer's noteworthy style and what Gross called, "her intention to measure [in her fiction] . . . the central issues of our time."

From the publication of Boyle's first volume of short fiction to her anthology of nearly forty years of writing, *Fifty Stories,* her mastery of style interested critics. When Katherine Anne Porter examined Boyle's early work in a 1931 review (included in *The Critic as Artist: Essays on Books, 1920-1970),* she noted Boyle's involvement with the experimental Parisian literary monthly, *transition,* and the journal's effect on Boyle's writing. According to Porter, Boyle's prose "sums up the salient qualities of [those writers who regularly contributed to *transition*]: a fighting spirit, freshness of feeling, curiosity, the courage of her own attitude and idiom, a violently dedicated search for the meanings and methods of art."

Critical comment on Boyle's style also came from other sources, including Richard C. Carpenter and Vance Bourjaily. Both compared Boyle's work to that of more well-known writers of the same period. In *Critique: Studies in Modern Fiction,* Carpenter commented: "Like Faulkner or Virginia Woolf or Joyce, Kay Boyle works largely with interior monologue, sometimes with a stream of consciousness, thus setting the internal states of her characters in contrast to the outer world, or complementary to it." In Bourjaily's *New York Times Book Review* essay the critic found *Fifty Stories* "a wonderful exhibit of . . . techniques and themes [introduced by writers living in Paris in the twenties] in evolution. Among the techniques we have grammatical simplification, rhythmic repetition, the mixing in of vernacular, stream of consciousness, density of impressions, radical imagery and experiments with surrealism that may have originated with Gertrude Stein and James Joyce but became community property of the group."

Like the others members of the American literary set that flourished in Paris during the early years of the twentieth century, Boyle was committed to resisting traditional forms of writing. But, although her writing may have been her first act of defiance against authority, it wasn't her last. During the fifties she fought the accusations and subsequent black-listing brought against her husband, Joseph von Franckenstein, and herself, by Communist-hunters Senator Joseph McCarthy and the House Un-American Activities Committee (HUAC). She continued to speak out against injustice throughout her life no matter how unpopular her views, speaking out in the sixties against the war in Vietnam and in the eighties protesting the U.S. bombing of Libya.

Like the stylistic elements of her fiction, Boyle's most important theme, which *Saturday Review* contributor Carole Cook cited as "the individual's moral responsibility," dates back to some of her earliest writing. For example, in his introduction to *Fifty Stories* David Daiches noted this moral function in particular in Boyle's stories written during World War II. The stories "read as though they have been *lived through*. . . ," he remarked. "But they are far from being merely 'on the spot' reporting, nor are they 'war stories' in the conventional sense. Their object is not to describe either horror or heroism, but to explore the core of human meaning in desperate situations." Earl Rovit found the same theme in Boyle's stories. He noted in his *Nation* essay, "A steady passionate concern for social justice and an equally unswerving compassion for the poignancies of human suffering are powerful and noble weapons in any artist's arsenal—and to these Kay Boyle can justly lay claim." *Chicago Tribune Book World* contributor Cyra McFadden similarly noted the "strong moral center" illustrated by Boyle's fiction.

This same vein of outspoken passion for social justice is echoed in Boyle's poems, many of which are included in *Collected Poems of Kay Boyle,* published in 1991, a year before Boyle's death. The poems display Boyle's defense of women and minorities; her opposition to anti-Semitism; and her avowed support for gays and lesbians. Writing in *Western American Literature,* Charles Daughaday remarked that with this collection "the poetry of an important American writer will achieve a more deserved reading to match that which already exists for her short stories."

Despite general critical approval for Boyle's work, she never enjoyed wide-spread popularity. *Dictionary of Literary Biography* contributor David V. Koch theorized that Boyle was "so busy writing and acting upon her beliefs . . . that she . . . had little time to cultivate a following. Indeed seeking literary fame would be contrary to Boyle's beliefs, for she . . . consistently sought to speak for those who could not speak for themselves."

Boyle's papers and manuscripts are at the Morris Library, Southern Illinois University, Carbondale.

*BIOGRAPHICAL/CRITICAL SOURCES:*

*BOOKS*

Bell, Elizabeth S., *Kay Boyle: A Study of the Short Fiction,* Twayne (New York City), 1992.

Boyle, Kay, *Fifty Stories,* with introduction by David Daiches, Doubleday, 1980.

Boyle, Kay, *Life Being the Best & Other Stories,* edited and with an introduction by Sandra Whipple Spanier, New Directions, 1988.

*Contemporary Authors Autobiography Series,* Volume 1, Gale, 1984.

*Contemporary Literary Criticism,* Gale, Volume 1, 1973, Volume 5, 1976, Volume 19, 1978, Volume 58, 1990.

*Dictionary of Literary Biography,* Gale, Volume 4: *American Writers in Paris, 1920-1939,* 1980, Volume 9: *American Novelists, 1910-1945,* 1981, Volume 48, *American Poets, 1880-1945, Second Series,* 1986, Volume 86: *American Short Story Writers, 1910-1945, First Series,* 1989.

Elkins, Marilyn Roberson, *Metamorphosizing the Novel: Kay Boyle's Narrative Innovations,* P. Lang (New York City), 1993.

Madden, Charles F., *Talks with Authors,* Southern Illinois University Press, 1968.

Mellen, Joan, *Kay Boyle: Author of Herself,* Farrar, Straus & Giroux (New York City), 1994.

Moore, Harry T., *Age of the Modern and Other Literary Essays,* Southern Illinois University Press, 1971.

Porter, Katherine Anne, *The Critic as Artist: Essays on Books, 1920-1970,* edited by Gilbert A. Harrison, Liveright, 1972.

*Short Story Criticism,* Volume 5, Gale, 1990.

Spanier, Sandra Whipple, *Kay Boyle: Artist and Activist,* Southern Illinois University Press, 1986.

Wilson, Edmund, *Classics and Commercials: A Literary Chronicle of the Forties,* Farrar, Straus, 1950.

Yalom, Marilyn, editor, *Women Writers of the West Coast,* Capra Press, 1983.

*PERIODICALS*

*Antioch Review,* fall, 1992, p. 780.

*Bookman,* June, 1932.

*Book World,* June 9, 1968.

*Chicago Tribune Book World,* October 12, 1980.

*Christian Science Monitor,* January 5, 1971; November 10, 1980.

*College English,* November, 1953.

*Critique: Studies in Modern Fiction,* winter, 1964-65.

*English Journal,* November, 1953.

*Harper's Bazaar,* April, 1994, p. 229.

*Kenyon Review,* spring, 1960.

*Library Journal,* November 15, 1990, p. 100; August, 1991, p. 105; June 1, 1992, p. 188.

*London Review of Books,* April 15, 1982.

*Los Angeles Times,* December 10, 1980; June 18, 1984; October 12, 1986.

*Los Angeles Times Book Review,* August 4, 1985; September 29, 1985; April 13, 1986.

*Ms.,* August, 1985.

*Nation,* December 24, 1930; October 24, 1936; June 8, 1970; June 15, 1970; April 26, 1971; June 26, 1972; March 22, 1975; September 27, 1980.

*New Republic,* April 22, 1931; July 13, 1932; December 13, 1933; October 21, 1936; January 24, 1970; February 8, 1975.

*Newsweek,* January 25, 1960; January 13, 1975.

*New Yorker,* January 20, 1975.

*New York Herald Tribune Books,* November 12, 1933; February 9, 1936; March 10, 1940.
*New York Times,* November 16, 1930; March 26, 1933; November 12, 1933; October 11, 1936; December 1, 1946; June 21, 1966.
*New York Times Book Review,* July 10, 1966; June 9, 1968; February 2, 1975; September 28, 1980; July 15, 1984; August 25, 1985; September 22, 1985; November 16, 1986; July 3, 1988.
*Poetry,* November, 1971; May 5, 1991, p. 25.
*Prairie Schooner,* summer, 1963; winter, 1966-67.
*Publishers Weekly,* October 17, 1980; March 11, 1988; December 21, 1990, p. 49; June 28, 1991, p. 97.
*Saturday Review,* March 25, 1933; November 4, 1933; November 30, 1946; April 9, 1949; April 21, 1951; July 16, 1966; January 7, 1978; September, 1980.
*Times Literary Supplement,* November 30, 1967; April 17, 1981; September 27, 1985.
*Washington Post Book World,* October 19, 1980; October 5, 1986.
*Western American Literature,* summer, 1993, p. 166.
*Wilson Library Bulletin,* January, 1932.

*OBITUARIES:*

*PERIODICALS*

*New York Times,* December 29, 1992, p. A13.
*Time,* January 11, 1993, p. 15.
*Washington Post,* December 30, 1992, p. B6.*

* * *

**BRADSHAW, John 1933-**

*PERSONAL:* Born June 29, 1933, in Houston, TX; son of John McCullough (a railroad clerk) and Norma (Eliot) Bradshaw; married Nancy Isaacs (a counselor), 1969 (divorced); children: John, Brenda (stepchild). (theology), 1958, degree in philosophy, 1963; Rice University, degree in religion, 1969, and degree in psychology, 1972. *Education:* Attended Basilian Fathers Seminary, 1955-63; University of Toronto, B.A. *Avocational interests:* Collecting antiques, Indian artifacts, and wizard figurines.

*ADDRESSES: Home—* Houston, TX.

*CAREER:* Author, lecturer, and counselor. Worked variously as a high school teacher and a pharmaceutical salesman; counselor in private practice, 1969-88; stress management consultant to major corporations, 1977-83; addiction counselor at Los Angeles chapter of Palmer Drug Abuse Program, 1981-85. Creator and host of ten-part television series *Bradshaw On—The Family: A Revolutionary Way of Self-Discovery,* Public Broadcasting System (PBS-TV), 1986; creator of numerous self-help tapes.

*AWARDS, HONORS:* Cardinal Mercier Gold Medal in Philosophy; Trustees' Gold Medal for academic excellence.

*WRITINGS:*

*Bradshaw On—The Family: A Revolutionary Way of Self-Discovery* (print adaptation of Bradshaw's television program), Health Communications, 1988.
*Healing the Shame That Binds You,* Health Communications, 1988.
*Homecoming: Reclaiming and Championing Your Inner Child,* Bantam (New York City), 1990.
*Creating Love: The Next Great Stage of Growth,* G. K. Hall (Boston), 1992.
*Family Secrets: What You Don't Know Can Hurt You,* Bantam, 1995.

*ADAPTATIONS:* Material from *Homecoming: Reclaiming and Championing Your Inner Child* was adapted as a ten-hour series of the same title for PBS-TV, 1990-91. Bradshaw's writings have been released on audiotape.

*SIDELIGHTS:* John Bradshaw has been called a "pop" psychologist and has also been described as a leader in the field of self-help. Through his books, television appearances, and numerous touring workshops, Bradshaw has spread his message to the emotionally and psychologically wounded: each person possesses the power to heal themselves. Millions of people believe in Bradshaw's methods and credit his techniques as a major force in overcoming their physical, psychological, and emotional addictions.

Bradshaw had a tumultuous childhood and early adulthood, one that led him through a series of unfulfilling jobs and eventually into alcoholism. After checking into a hospital, he was able to control his drinking and began a career as a counselor. Bradshaw enjoyed considerable success with his counseling practice, which included work with the renowned Palmer Drug Abuse Program, but he still felt empty. The root of his problem, he discovered, ran back to his childhood. As he told Victoria Balfour in *People:* "As a child I was not allowed to express my feelings, so I had to go back through therapy and express the child's pain." Not only would this realization help Bradshaw achieve peace with himself, it would also become the focus of his writing and counseling, as well as the major source of his success.

Bradshaw's first exposure to a wide audience was through a ten-part Public Broadcasting System (PBS) series that he created and hosted—without a script. *Bradshaw On—The Family* first aired on PBS in 1986 and was accompanied by a book of the same title. In the book and series, Bradshaw examines his own dysfunctional family and provides insight into the familial problems of others. As Bradshaw told Balfour in *People,* his methods attack these problems and are aimed at "helping people to see they are all about the child's loss of emotions and about shame." Bradshaw further addressed childhood trauma in his next book, *Healing the Shame That Binds You.*

Bradshaw's third book, *Homecoming: Reclaiming and Championing Your Inner Child,* became his most successful venture. The book was adapted into a series for PBS, and its subject matter became the focus for Bradshaw's increasingly popular workshops. In the book, Bradshaw depicts adult addictions as outgrowths of childhood deprivation. He states that by overcoming their youthful feelings of loss, people can resolve the problems that plague their adult life. "The goal of this work is to get you to come to peace with the past and finish it," he was quoted as saying in *Time.* Bradshaw's approach involves an internal separation of adult and child, with the adult self becoming the champion for the child self's needs and thus healing the wounds of both.

Bradshaw continued his project of "reclaiming the inner child" with a joint book and PBS television series entitled *Creating Love: The Next Stage of Growth.* This work attempts to analyze the culturally generated confusions regarding the nature of love and to replace these with what the author terms "soulful love," an emotion that successfully integrates the facts of reality with the need for creativity and play. While some reviewers acknowledged that *Creating Love* contained numerous insights, others judged that the work was damaged by a superficial and saccharine tone.

In addition to his books, television series, and personal appearances, Bradshaw also touts his programs through a series of self-help tapes. His market has expanded, and he reaches millions of people each year. Along with his success has come criticism. Some psychology professionals have complained that Bradshaw's methods provide people with an all-too-convenient escape from accepting responsibility for their adult failures. Dr. Gerald Goodman, an associate professor of psychology at the University of California in Los Angeles, criticized Bradshaw's technique as oversimplified, stating in *Time:* "The way it sounds, if only we had got more hugs in our infancy, we'd be fine." Others have pointed out that Bradshaw's style is really just bits and pieces of theories stolen rom the prominent minds of psychology. As Bradshaw explained to Balfour in *People,* however, he views his methods differently: "My job has been to translate the more abstract theories so the people can understand. What I really am is a teacher." Regardless of the criticism leveled at him, Bradshaw continues to be successful, and his followers truly believe in his abilities. Many have praised his facility in taking complex psychological issues and fashioning them into a modern and accessible presentation. Emily Mitchell, writing in *Time,* described Bradshaw and his technique as "Dr. Freud meets the New Age."

*BIOGRAPHICAL/CRITICAL SOURCES:*

*PERIODICALS*

*Commonwealth,* September 9, 1994, p. 21.
*Kirkus Reviews,* October 15, 1992, p. 1287-88.
*Los Angeles Magazine,* April, 1992, p. 76.
*People,* May 28, 1990, pp. 73-76.
*Publishers Weekly,* November 2, 1992, p. 61; April 10, 1995, p. 49.
*Redbook,* January, 1992, p. 48.
*Time,* November 25, 1991, pp. 82-83.*

* * *

**BREYTENBACH, Breyten 1939(?)-**
**(Jan Blom)**

*PERSONAL:* Born September 16, 1939 (one source says 1940), in Bonnievale (one source says Wellington), South Africa; naturalized French citizen; married Yolande Ngo Thi Hoang Lien, 1964. *Education:* Attended University of Cape Town until 1959.

*ADDRESSES: Home*—Paris, France.

*CAREER:* Political activist, painter, and writer.

*AWARDS, HONORS:* A. P. B. Literary Prize for *Die ysterkoei moet sweet* and Afrikaans Press Corps Prize for *Die ysterkoei moet sweet* and *Katastrofes,* both 1964; South African Central News Agency prizes, 1967, for *Die huis van die dowe,* 1969, for *Kouevuur,* and 1970, for *Lotus;* Lucie B. and C. W. Van der Hoogt prize from Society of Netherlands Literature, 1972, for *Skryt;* prize from Perskor newspaper group, 1976, for *Voetskrif;* Pris des Sept (international publisher's prize to provide funding for six foreign translations of Breytenbach's work), 1977; Hertzog Prize from South African Academy of Science and Arts, 1984; Rapport Prize for Literature from Afrikaans newspaper *Rapport,* 1986, for *YK.*

*WRITINGS:*

*Die ysterkoei moet sweet* (poetry; title means "The Iron Cow Must Sweat"), Afrikaanse Pers-Boekhandel (Johannesburg, South Africa), 1964.
*Katastrofes* (short stories), Afrikaanse Pers-Boekhandel, 1964.
*Die huis van die dowe* (poetry; title means "House of the Deaf"), Human & Rousseau (Cape Town, South Africa), 1967.
*Kouevuur* (poetry; title means "Gangrene"), Buren-Uitgewers (Cape Town), 1969.
(Under pseudonym Jan Blom) *Lotus* (poetry), Buren-Uitgewers, 1970.
*Om te vlieg: 'N opstel in vyf ledemate en 'n ode,* Buren-Uitgewers, 1971.
*Skryt: Om 'n sinkende skip blou te verf* (title means "Sky/Write: To Paint a Sinking Ship Blue"), Meulenhoff Nederland (Amsterdam), 1972.
*Met ander woorde: Vrugte van die droom van stilte* (poetry; title means "In Other Words"), Buren (Cape Town), 1973.
*Voetskrif* (poetry; title means "Footscript"), Perskor (Johannesburg), 1976.
*'N seisoen in die Paradys* (poetry and prose), [South Africa], 1976, translation by Rike Vaughan published as *A Season in Paradise*, introduction by Andre Brink, Persea Books, 1980.
(Under name Breyten Breytenbach and pseudonym Jan Blom) *Blomskryf: Uit die gedigte van Breyten Breytenbach en Jan Blom* (selected poetry; title means "Flower Writing"), introduction by A. J. Coetzee, Taurus (Emmarentia, South Africa), 1977.
*Sinking Ship Blues* (selected poetry), Oasis (Toronto), 1977.
*And Death White as Words: An Anthology of the Poetry of Breyten Breytenbach*, edited with an introduction by Coetzee, Collings (London), 1978.
*In Africa Even the Flies Are Happy: Selected Poems, 1964-1977*, English translation by Denis Hirson, J. Calder (London), 1978, Riverrun Press, 1982.
*Miernes* (short stories), Taurus, 1980.
*Eklips*, Taurus, 1983.
*Mouroir: Bespieeelende notas van 'n roman* (sketches in English and Afrikaans), Taurus, 1983, complete English translation published as *Mouroir: Mirrornotes of a Novel*, Farrar, Straus, 1984.
*The True Confessions of an Albino Terrorist*, Taurus, 1984, Faber, 1984, Farrar, Straus, 1985.
*YK* (poetry), Meulenhoff (Amsterdam), 1985.
*Lewendoad*, Taurus, 1985.
*End Papers: Essays, Letters, Articles of Faith, Workbook Notes*, Farrar, Straus, 1986.
*Boek: Dryfpunt* (essays), Taurus, 1987.
*Judas Eye* (poetry and essays), Penguin, 1988.
*Soos Die So,* Taurus (Bramley), 1990.
(With Marilet Sienaert) *Breyten: Breytenbach: Painting the Eye,* D. Philip (Cape Town), 1993.
*Return to Paradise,* Harcourt (New York City), 1993.
*A Season in Paradise,* translation by Rike Vaughan, Harcourt, 1994.
*The Memory of Birds in Times of Revolution,* Harcourt, 1996.

Also author of *Oorblyfsels* (title means "Remnants"), 1970. Contributor to periodicals, including *Poetry International* and *Raster.*

*SIDELIGHTS:* At the height of his literary acclaim, Breyten Breytenbach, South Africa's leading Afrikaner poet, was imprisoned by the government of his fellow Afrikaners for clandestine activities against its apartheid system of racial laws. Although he was released in December, 1982, and lives in Paris, Breytenbach remains an outspoken critic of the oppression of blacks and other minorities. Much of his writing is in his native Afrikaans, the language evolved from the Dutch spoken by the first white settlers in South Africa and the first language of three million white Afrikaners—the group that ruled South Africa from 1948 until the early 1990s.

Descended from a distinguished old Cape Province family—the Breytenbachs were among the early settlers of the seventeenth century who called themselves Afrikaners—Breytenbach graduated from high school in the Afrikaner heartland. He became interested in art and poetry, and, impressed by the reputation of the fine arts faculty of the University of Cape Town, he enrolled in that English-language university instead of Stellenbosch University, the traditional center of Afrikaner higher education. At the age of twenty, however, Breytenbach left school and set out for Europe, drifting into a variety of jobs in England and on the Continent. In 1961 he settled in Paris, where he painted, wrote, and taught English, and where he married Yolande Ngo Thi Hoang Lien, who was born in Vietnam. In 1964 Breytenbach published *Die ysterkoei moet sweet,* his first book of poems, followed by *Die huis van die dowe* in 1967, *Kouevuur* in 1969, and, under the pseudonym Jan Blom, *Lotus* in 1970.

When Breytenbach wanted to return to South Africa to collect awards he had won in 1967 and 1969, his wife was refused an entry visa as a "non-white" and Breytenbach was told he could face arrest under the Immorality Act, which made interracial marriage a crime. Then in 1973, when *Met ander woorde* was published, the Breytenbachs were both issued three-month visas to visit South Africa. That journey back to his homeland after twelve years of exile in Paris both rekindled warm childhood memories and reinforced his anger at the violence and injustice of apartheid. Breytenbach recorded his homecoming impressions in what Richard Rathbone described in the *Times Educational Supplement* as "an inspired and sometimes ecstatic book" published in a censored version in South Africa in 1976 as *'N seisoen in die Paradys* and in English translation in 1980 as *A Season in Paradise.* According to *Washington Post Book World* contributor Stanley Uys, the book, a mixture of poetry and prose, is "an intensely personal narrative, nostalgic and bitter at the same time. The images of South Africa—of friends and familiar places—are vivid. [Breytenbach] gazes upon everything with the heightened perception of the artist and leaves the reader to make what he can of it." *Los Angeles Times Book Review* critic Malcolm Boyd called *A Season in Paradise* "an ode to freedom, an existential work about the tension between belonging and transcendence" in which Breytenbach reveals himself as "angry, sensuous, ironical."

By the end of his three-month stay, Breytenbach had so exasperated authorities with his scathing public criticism of the Afrikaner nationalist government that authorities told him not to come back. Upon his return with his wife to Paris, Breytenbach, however, lost no time renewing his ties with anti-apartheid groups. Ultimately he founded—with other white South Africans in exile—an anti-apartheid organization called Okhela. They decided that Breytenbach should travel incognito to South Africa to contact sympathetic whites and some black spokesmen in order to channel money from European church groups to black trade unionists in South Africa.

In August, 1975, with the help of a French anti-apartheid organization that supplied a forged French passport, Breytenbach shaved off his beard and flew to Johannesburg under an assumed name. But the French group had apparently been infiltrated, because from the time Breytenbach obtained his visa the South African security police had him under surveillance. The police shadowed the poet in Johannesburg and Cape Town, noting his contacts, before arresting him and charging him under the Terrorist Act. Initially Breytenbach was not unduly concerned about his imprisonment because he believed he had not done anything more illegal than use a false passport. But he was sentenced to nine years in prison for the intent with which he had entered the country. The court took the view that trade union campaigns against apartheid constituted a threat to the safety of the state.

In November, 1975, Breytenbach began his solitary confinement in Pretoria's maximum security section. Then he was brought to trial under the Terrorism Act for a second time in June, 1977. Breytenbach, however, was acquitted of all charges except smuggling letters out of prison, for which he was fined the equivalent of fifty dollars.

The poet was taken a thousand miles, from Pretoria to Pollsmoor Prison, near Cape Town, where he spent the next five years of his captivity. During this period the French Government brought diplomatic pressure to bear on Pretoria, pressure that intensified when the socialist government of Francois Mitterand came to power. In December, 1982, the South African Government finally relented and commuted Breytenbach's sentence from nine years to seven, to which the South African authorities attached no conditions beyond requiring that he leave the country. He was allowed a brief visit with his father, then flown with his wife to Johannesburg and on to Paris.

While he was in prison, Breytenbach managed to write the semifictional pieces subsequently published and translated under the title *Mouroir: Mirrornotes of a Novel.* Not really a novel at all, the book is a series of loosely connected stories or sketches that present an imagistic, surreal portrait of Breytenbach's psyche as a prisoner. *New York Times Book Review* contributor John Wideman called *Mouroir* a "complex, demanding, haunting book" that "contains characters, themes and images which occur and reoccur, creating the illusion of narrative, continuity, reality unfolding." Fellow South African writer Nadine Gordimer, an *Atlantic Monthly* contributor, lauded its images as "exquisite, chilling, aphoristic, witty," and Grace Ingoldby, reviewing *Mouroir* for *New Statesman,* judged it "a beautifully written, grappling, difficult book" in which "the mirror images both elucidate and confuse; at times it is too obscure to be successful, at others, far too plain to be forgotten." Other critics likewise found *Mouroir* difficult to read. "Breytenbach's writing . . . is astonishingly vigorous and agile," noted Neal Ascherson in *New York Review of Books*. "It can also become lush, indigestible." Similarly, Judy Cooke observed in the *Times Educational Supplement, "Mouroir* is an uneven, fragmentary, unforgettable piece of writing."

On his release from prison Breytenbach felt compelled to publish a more direct account of his experiences. The result was *The True Confessions of an Albino Terrorist,* in which Breytenbach recounts how he was trapped by his captors, describes his years of physical and psychological deprivation, and outlines the prospects for South Africa's future as he sees them. Breytenbach's narrative of his prison experiences was disturbing to several critics. Among them were Malcolm Boyd, whose *Los Angeles Times Book Review* article described Breytenbach's book as "a harrowing, unrelenting, searing account of a writer's survival in an experience of hell" and *Detroit News* contributor Charles R. Larson, who remarked, "I've read a lot from journals of people who have been jailed for their political beliefs, and a lot of South African literature as well. But nothing I have read in either category upset me as much as Breytenbach's account of his imprisonment. The details of bestiality, crime and murder, ritual cannibalism and even the daily routines of prison life have never been as revolting as they are here."

According to Joseph Lelyveld, writing in the *New York Times Book Review,* the memoir tells the story of Breytenbach's "personal misadventure in revolutionary politics and the nightmarish quality of the South African penal system." The book, Lelyveld added, also represents "the final stage of a major cultural rupture, the poet's apostasy from the creed of an Afrikaner nationalism. This did not begin in prison but, inevitably, it was completed there." Lelyveld further speculated that Breytenbach's "confessions" are "an important contribution to a corpus of South African prison literature that has been steadily, painfully accumulating over the last quarter-century; and they are especially important since his is the first such memoir to have been written by an Afrikaner."

Rob Nixon, writing in *American Book Review,* came to a similar conclusion. In the confessions themselves, he posited, Breytenbach "meticulously recreates his spell in prison, interrogating with undiminished insight, not only his own shifting selves but also his jail-mates and the motley flunkeys of apartheid whose job it was to ensure that he remained solitary but not private." Like Lelyveld, Nixon viewed *The True Confessions of an Albino Terrorist* as an important document in South Africa's rich "traditions of prison literature . . . partly because Breyten Breytenbach is firstly an established writer and only secondarily a political activist . . . and partly because he is a rare and important defector from Afrikanerdom." Continued Nixon, "the book is largely an account of the unmaking of an Afrikaner. . . . Some of the finest passages evoke the pathos of being a poet born into a policeman's language and of having to concede," the critic quoted Breytenbach, that "'To be an Afrikaner in the way *they* define it is to be a living insult to whatever better instincts we human beings possess.'"

Several critics commented as well on the literary merits of *The True Confessions of an Albino Terrorist.* For example, *New York Times* reviewer John Gross remarked: "Given the ordeal it chronicles, 'The True Confessions of an Albino Terrorist' could hardly fail to make a powerful impression, but it displays considerable artistry as well. The writing is sharp, restless, often raspingly sarcastic; a little mannered here and there, perhaps, but no matter—Mr. Breytenbach succeeds brilliantly in depicting the horror and squalor and near-madness . . . of the prison world into which he was thrust." *Observer* contributor Bernard Levin underscored the influence of Breytenbach's background as a poet in what the critic called "the savage rhythms and psychedelic colours of his prose." And Robert Cox, reviewing *The True Confessions of an Albino Terrorist* for the *Washington Post Book World,* was particularly generous in his praise. He called the book "a testament of suffering and exultation—a powerful document, full of humanity, expressing a limitless love for life," averring that Breytenbach's "literary achievement is so considerable that the political impact of *The True Confessions of an Albino Terrorist* is like the blast of a truck bomb. He holds up a mirror to the South African penal system, which in turn reflects the self-destructive madness of apartheid." In conclusion, Cox pronounced Breytenbach "a remarkable man" and *The True Confessions of an Albino Terrorist* "a magnificent book."

Breytenbach insists that his prison experiences have scarred him forever. "Resistance," Nixon quoted the activist's words in *The True Confessions of an Albino Terrorist,* "if that is what you want to call survival, is made up of a million little compromises and humiliations, so subtle that the human eye cannot perceive them." Yet, to the astonishment of those familiar with his history, Breytenbach returned to South Africa in the spring of 1986 to receive the *Rapport* prize for literature. But more importantly, as he has stated, he returned because he identified with the struggle of South Africans for liberation.

Breytenbach's 1993 memoir, *Return to Paradise* chronicles his 1991 return visit to his homeland. According to the author, this title, along with *A Season in Paradise* and *The True Confessions of an Albino Terrorist,* are meant to be read as a series comprising the writer's intercessions with South Africa: "exile, incarnation, and return," noted Lynn Freed in the *Washington Post Book World.* Breytenbach finds South Africa in a state of turmoil, surrounding the fall of F. W. De Klerk and the white-controlled government. J. M. Coetzee, a fellow South African novelist, writing in the *New York Review of Books,* decried Breytenbach's analysis as "not . . . original." However, along with other reviewers, he praised Breytenbach's narrative: "An immensely gifted writer, he is able to descend effortlessly into the Africa of the poetic unconscious and return with the rhythm and the words, the words in the rhythm, that give life." Freed also lauded the author's writing, noting of his descriptions in particular, "Breytenbach's portraits themselves are extraordinary, resonant." About Breytenbach's emotional ties to his subject, Freed averred, "The book is written with a wild heart and an unrelenting eye, and is fueled by the sort of rage that produces great literature." Adam Kuper in the *Times Literary Supplement* concurred, "The best parts of this book have nothing to do with politics. They are the occasional descriptions of landscapes, rendered with the intensity of a painter, and the portraits of his Afrikaner friends." William Finnegan, in *The New York Times Book Review,* noted that "purposeful reporting is not Mr. Breytenbach's forte" but declared the book to be "protean, funny, bitchy, beautifully written and searingly bleak."

*The Memory of Birds in Times of Revolution,* published in 1996, is a collection of Breytenbach's essays and talks on apartheid, South Africa, and writing. While a *Kirkus Reviews* critic found it "an outdated, awkward collection . . . [lacking] the saving humanism and insight . . . that would have kept them otherwise readable and trenchant," other reviewers were more charitable. A *Library Journal* reviewer declared it to be "an important addition to his narrative essays." "Though . . . he is not above the political cliches and moral posturing for which he criticizes others, Breytenbach's passionate desire to know and serve the truth . . . is deeply admirable," concluded Bruce Bawer in the *Washington Post Book World.*

*BIOGRAPHICAL/CRITICAL SOURCES:*

*BOOKS*

Breytenbach, Breyten, *The True Confessions of an Albino Terrorist,* Farrar, Straus, 1985.

Breytenbach, Breyten with Marilet Sienaert, *Breyten Breytenbach: Painting the Eye,* D. Philip (Cape Town), 1993.

*Contemporary Literary Criticism,* Gale, Volume 23, 1983, Volume 37, 1986.

Golz, Hans-Georg, *Staring at Variations: The Concept of 'Self' in Breyten Breytenbach's "Mouroir: Mirrornotes of a Novel,"* P. Lang (New York City), 1995.

Jolly, Rosemary Jane, *Colonization, Violence, and Narration in White South African Writing: Andre Brink, Breyten Breytenbach, and J. M. Coetzee,* Ohio University Press (Athens), 1995.

*PERIODICALS*

*American Book Review,* January/February, 1983; January/February, 1986.

*Atlantic Monthly,* July, 1984.

*Best Sellers,* September, 1984.

*Detroit News,* March 31, 1985.

*Globe and Mail* (Toronto), October 8, 1988.

*Kirkus Reviews,* December 1, 1995, p. 1677.

*Library Journal,* February 15, 1996, p. 152.

*Los Angeles Times,* June 27, 1984.

*Los Angeles Times Book Review,* February 10, 1985; August 17, 1986.

*New Statesman,* October 3, 1980; May 4, 1984.

*New York Review of Books,* October 25, 1984; November 23, 1993, p. 3.

*New York Times,* February 5, 1985.

*New York Times Book Review,* March 30, 1980; April 13, 1980; February 10, 1985; April 6, 1986; November 22, 1987; November 28, 1993, p. 3.

*Times Educational Supplement,* July 13, 1984; December 20, 1985; June 24, 1988.
*Times Literary Supplement,* December 24, 1993, p. 22.
*Washington Post,* February 9, 1985.
*Washington Post Book World,* April 20, 1980; June 24, 1984; May 5, 1985; April 6, 1986; November 28, 1993, p. 4; May 5, 1996, p. 5.
*World Literature Today,* spring, 1977; winter, 1978; summer, 1978; autumn, 1978; winter, 1979; summer, 1981; winter, 1982; summer, 1984; summer, 1987.*

* * *

**BRINKLEY, Joel (Graham) 1952-**

*PERSONAL:* Born July 22, 1952, in Washington, DC; son of David McClure (a television commentator) and Ann (Fischer) Brinkley. *Education:* University of North Carolina at Chapel Hill, A.B., 1975.

*ADDRESSES: Home*—1334 Cherokee Rd., Louisville, KY 40204. *Office—New York Times,* 1000 Connecticut Ave. N.W., Washington, DC 20036-5302.

*CAREER:* Associated Press (AP), Charlotte, NC, reporter, 1975; *Richmond News Leader,* Richmond, VA, reporter, 1975-78; *Louisville Courier-Journal,* Louisville, KY, reporter, 1978-83; *New York Times,* New York City, Washington correspondent and editor, 1983-87, White House correspondent, 1987—, also served as chief of Jerusalem bureau. Notable assignments include coverage of the Cambodian crisis and a year-long investigation of Kentucky's nursing home industry that prompted major reforms.

*MEMBER:* Society of Professional Journalists, Investigative Reporters, and Editors.

*AWARDS, HONORS:* Pulitzer Prize for international reporting, 1980, for *Courier-Journal* series, "Living the Cambodian Nightmare"; named National Citizen of the Year, National Association of Social Workers, 1981; Roy W. Howard Award, public service reporting, Scripps-Howard Foundation, 1981, 1982; consumer reporting awards, National Press Foundation, 1981, 1983; grand prize, Investigative Reporters and Editors Awards, 1982; Clarion Award, 1982; Heywood Broun Award, Newspaper Guild, 1982; National Headliner Award, public service reporting, 1983; William S. Miller Enterprise Reporting Award, 1983; Penney-Missouri Consumer Reporting Award, 1983; George Polk Award, 1995.

*WRITINGS:*

(Editor and author of introduction, with Stephen Engelberg) *Report of the Congressional Committees Investigating the Iran-Contra Affair: With the Minority Views,* abridged edition, Times Books (New York City), 1988.
*The Circus Master's Mission* (novel), Random House (New York City), 1989.
*Defining Vision: The Battle for the Future of Television,* Harcourt (New York City), 1997.

*SIDELIGHTS: New York Times* correspondent Joel Brinkley is a Pulitzer Prize-winning journalist who has also written a novel, *The Circus Master's Mission,* based on his experiences in Washington and a nonfiction account of the future of television, *Defining Vision: The Battle for the Future of Television.* Brinkley is the son of NBC news commentator David Brinkley.

On his first overseas assignment, Brinkley was sent to report on the war-torn nation of Cambodia. Shortly after returning to the United States, he was stricken with typhoid fever; nevertheless, he continued to work on "Living the Cambodian Nightmare," a series of articles describing the war in Cambodia and the desperate plight of hundreds of thousands of refugees.

Brinkley told *CA:* "My stories from Cambodia contained few revelations; most of what I wrote had already been reported elsewhere. The stories were successful, I think, because of vivid writing. And that's a point journalists everywhere ought to note. Fewer and fewer people are inclined to read newspapers these days. So newspaper writing has to improve. It will have to become more creative and entertaining, if newspapers are to keep their readers."

Brinkley's first novel draws upon his own experience as White House correspondent for the *New York Times.* A tale of government, politics, and intrigue, *The Circus Master's Mission* is a fictional exploration, as David Traxel writes in the *New York Times Book Review,* "about power, about the way the lines of authority run in Washington and what happens when they are controlled by unscrupulous hands." John Krich tells readers of the *New York Times:* "Joel Brinkley has asked—and attempted to answer—the doubly intribuing question of how and why the circumstances might be created for a full-scale United States invasion of Nicaragua."

The novel features reporter Christopher Eaton, "whose ambition," Traxel suggests, "is goaded by his second-string standing in the profession" and "his lover, Leslie DeSalles, who works for the National Security Council." The team uncovers a conspiracy within a conspiracy. The fictional president of the United States has assigned a young foreign service officer named Terry Ascher to develop a pre-election policy for using "contra" activities to promote a resolution to, or improvement of, the Nicaragua issue. Ascher in turn relies on the help of a Central Intelligence Agency contra coordinator and a U.S. embassy attache in Nicaragua to accelerate the intensity of military activity in the region. These two, however, are secretly planning to pursue a far more sinister directive, one that they hope will lead to a full-scale invasion.

Barbara Conaty comments in *Library Journal:* "Brinkley brings to his first novel an admirable eye for crystalline detail and a keen ear for a journalist's persistence." In his review, Krich faults Brinkley's character development, but adds that the author's "expertise shines through in two areas: military hardware and the working habits of the Washington press corps." Yet Traxel concludes: "Mr. Brinkley has engineered his plot with great care, so that the action flows smoothly . . . and he has filled the novel with just the kind of realistic detail . . . that convinces the reader that he knows what he is writing about. Most of the characters are fully dimensional, especially, for some reason, the minor ones."

In *Defining Vision: The Battle for the Future of Television,* Brinkley describes the race to develop the high-definition, digital television technology that will radically alter the way Americans watch television. It is a story that begins and ends in politics and economic greed. "Brinkley," writes Jonathan Storm in the *Chicago Tribune,* "shows not only the diligence and inspiration that moves technology forward but the greed and deceit of the business interests that seek to control it, and the frequent ineptitude (not to mention occasional greed and deceit) of some of the people who are supposedly in government to watch out for you and me." Timothy Ferris tells *New York Times* readers: "As Joel Brinkley reports . . . the process of arriving at a high-definition standard involved a sweaty, greed-drenched struggle that spanned two Administrations and three F.C.C. commissioners and left nobody unblemished. Least attractive are the broadcasters."

"If not for Brinkley's exhaustive reporting," comments *Los Angeles Times* reviewer Marshall Jon Fisher, "the world might never have known that digital television arose from a greedy ruse to fool the FCC." He refers to the secure grip of the broadcast communications industry on air space available from the Federal Communications Commission (FCC) and a potential threat from the growing mobile communications industry. A solution appeared in the hands of Japanese electronics experts who, in 1987, demonstrated their new, analog, high-definition television (HDTV) system. The system would require substantially more broadcast air space, which could enable the broadcasting industry to retains its dominance of the air waves, a victory over both the mobile communications industry and the growing cable television networks.

To the government, however, this boon carried with it a new threat. "A wave of xenophobia crashed over Washington," writes Fisher, "and HDTV became the newest national crusade" to revive the languishing U.S. consumer electronics industry. The FCC announced a competition for proposals and the result, after much tribulation, was the adoption in December, 1996, of a new HDTV standard. Tim Jones reports in the *Chicago Tribune* that Brinkley "describes in rich and dramatic detail the almost all-consuming passion to develop a TV with the picture quality of film. . . . [He] takes us through arguments, deceit, testing trials, successes and many, many failures." Ferris comments that Brinkley "tells the HDTV story with clarity, verve and an engaging bemusement at the broadcasters' more than occasional venalities."

*Defining Vision* is, according to Ferris, "a sordid, bewildering and always entertaining tale." He adds that the book is "a superior work of journalism. Brinkley has fun with the endless litany of obstacles and enemies to the process of approving the new digital standard. . . . The emphasis here is on politics and intrigue, and there's enough of both to rival John le Carre."

*BIOGRAPHICAL/CRITICAL SOURCES:*

*PERIODICALS*

*Booklist,* June 15, 1989, p. 1738; December 15, 1996, p. 695.

*Kirkus Reviews,* June 1, 1989, p. 784.
*Library Journal,* July, 1989, p. 105.
*Los Angeles Times,* March 2, 1997, p. 11.
*New York Times,* August 12, 1989, p. A14; February 19, 1997, p. C15.
*New York Times Book Review,* July 2, 1989, p. 10; February 2, 1997, p. 25.
*Publishers Weekly,* June 9, 1989, p. 52; December 16, 1996, p. 52.
*Tribune Books* (Chicago), July 16, 1989, p. 4; February 3, 1997, p. 3; March 11, 1997, p. 3.
*Video Magazine,* February-March, 1997, p. 14.
*Washington Post Book World,* July 2, 1989, p. 9.

* * *

**BROOKE, Rupert (Chawner) 1887-1915**

*PERSONAL:* Born August 3, 1887, in Rugby, Warwickshire, England; died of blood poisoning, April 23, 1915, near the island of Skyros, Greece; son of William Parker (a secondary school teacher) and Mary Ruth (Cotterill) Brooke. *Education:* King's College, Cambridge, B.A. (with second-class honors), 1909.

*CAREER:* Writer. Schoolmaster at Rugby School, 1909-10. Traveled to Germany, 1912; traveled to America, 1913, contributing articles to the *Westminster Gazette* and the *New Statesman;* traveled to the South Pacific, 1913-14. *Military service:* Royal Navy Volunteer Reserve, 1914-15; became sub-lieutenant.

*AWARDS, HONORS:* Fellowship from King's College, Cambridge, c. 1911.

*WRITINGS:*

*Poems* (also see below), Sidgwick & Jackson, 1911.
(Editor with Edward Marsh, and contributor) *Georgian Poetry, 1911-1912* (includes "The Old Vicarage, Grantchester"), Poetry Bookshop, 1912.
*Nineteen Fourteen, and Other Poems* (also see below), Doubleday, 1915.
*The Collected Poems of Rupert Brooke* (includes *Poems* and *Nineteen Fourteen, and Other Poems*), introduction by George Edward Woodberry, John Lane, 1915.
*Lithuania: A Drama in One Act,* Chicago Little Theatre, 1915.
*Letters From America* (essays; first published in *Westminster Gazette* and *New Statesman*), preface by Henry James, Scribner, 1916.
*John Webster and the Elizabethan Drama* (thesis), John Lane, 1916.
*The Collected Poems of Rupert Brooke,* edited and with a memoir by Edward Marsh, Sidgwick & Jackson, 1918, revised edition, 1942.
*The Poetical Works of Rupert Brooke,* edited by Geoffrey Keynes, Faber, 1946.
*Democracy and the Arts* (nonfiction), Hart-Davis, 1946.
*The Prose of Rupert Brooke,* edited and introduced by Christopher Hassall, Sidgwick & Jackson, 1956.
*The Letters of Rupert Brooke,* edited by Geoffrey Keynes, Harcourt, 1968.
*Rupert Brooke: A Reappraisal and Selection from His Writings, Some Hitherto Unpublished,* edited by Timothy Rogers, Barnes & Noble, 1971.
*Letters from Rupert Brooke to His Publisher, 1911-1914,* Octagon Books, 1975.
*Song of Love: The Letters of Rupert Brooke and Noel Olivier, 1909-1915,* edited by Pippa Harris, Crown, 1991.

*SIDELIGHTS:* Few writers have provoked as much excessive praise and scornful condemnation as English poet Rupert Brooke. Handsome, charming, and talented, Brooke was a national hero even before his death in 1915 at the age of twenty-seven. His poetry, with its unabashed patriotism and graceful lyricism, was revered in a country that was yet to feel the devastating effects of two world wars. Brooke's early death only solidified his image as "a golden-haired, blue-eyed English Adonis," as Doris L. Eder notes in the *Dictionary of Literary Biography,* and among those who lauded him after his death were writers Virginia Woolf and Henry James and British statesman Winston Churchill. In the decades after World War I, however, critics reacted against the Brooke legend by calling his verse foolishly naive and sentimental. Despite such extreme opinions, most contemporary observers agree that Brooke—though only a minor poet—occupies a secure place in English literature as a representative of the mood and character of England before World War I.

Brooke's early years were typical of virtually every English boy who was a member of a well-to-do family. He attended a prestigious boarding school—Rugby, where his father was a headmaster—studied Latin and Greek, and began to write poetry. It was taken for granted that Brooke would go on to one of the great English universities, and accordingly he entered Cambridge in 1906.

During his three years at Cambridge, Brooke became a visible figure in English intellectual circles, counting among his acquaintances Virginia Woolf, writer Lytton Strachey, economist John Maynard Keynes and his brother Geoffrey (later to become Brooke's bibliographer), and poet William Butler Yeats. Brooke also continued to write poetry, although his poems from this period are, as Eder comments, "highly derivative, facile literary exercises." In *The Neo-Pagans: Rupert Brooke and the Ordeal of Youth,* Paul Delany gives an example of Brooke's verse from his Cambridge years. Written in 1909, "The Voice," like most of his early poetry, dwells on the themes of love and nature: "Safe in the magic of my woods / I lay, and watched the dying light / . . . The three that I loved, together grew / One, in the hour of knowing, / Night, and the woods, and you." Although his early work is thought to be of little significance, Brooke by this time was considered a serious though unaccomplished poet. In addition, he was an increasingly conspicuous figure in literary circles—a fame fueled without doubt by his charm and good looks.

Between his graduation from Cambridge in 1909 and the start of World War I in 1914, Brooke spent most of his time writing and traveling. His poetry during this period, which still emphasized the themes of love and nature, resembled that of most of the poets of his generation, including D. H. Lawrence, John Drinkwater, and Walter de la Mare. These poets came to be known as Georgian poets (named after England's king at the time); their verse reflects an idealistic preoccupation with rural, youthful motifs. In fact, Brooke and many of his friends enjoyed spending time in the countryside, bathing nude in local streams and sleeping on the ground; such activities earned them the nickname "neo-pagans." Eder points out that "Georgian verse now seems faded and pseudopastoral, a poetry of suburbia written by city dwellers celebrating cozy weekends in flower-wreathed country cottages." At the time, though, such poetry was fashionable and respected, and the first collection of poems by these writers, *Georgian Poetry, 1911-1912,* was extremely successful.

"The Old Vicarage, Grantchester" was Brooke's contribution to *Georgian Poetry,* and it remains one of his most popular poems. Grantchester is a small village near Cambridge where Brooke lived for a time after 1909. Brooke, however, wrote the poem later in a cafe in Germany. The poem's nostalgia for an England far away—"And laughs the immortal river still / Under the mill, under the mill / . . . Stands the Church clock at ten to three / And is there honey still for tea?," as quoted by Delany in *The Neo-Pagans*—reflects "patriotism and homesickness at their most endearing," writes Eder. After Brooke's death, Henry James wrote that the poem was "booked for immortality." Christopher Hassall, in his introduction to *The Prose of Rupert Brooke,* offers a perhaps more realistic analysis when he comments that "The Old Vicarage, Grantchester"—though one of Brooke's most personal and original statements—is nonetheless a "lightweight poem."

"The Old Vicarage, Grantchester" was written in mid-1912, one of the most turbulent periods in Brooke's life. According to Delany, Brooke had experienced a sexual crisis—confusion about homosexual impulses and frustration caused by the rejections of a woman with whom he was in love. *Song of Love: The Letters of Rupert Brooke and Noel Olivier, 1909-1915* portrays Brooke's impulsive nature and emotional confusion during this period. Though Olivier was only one of numerous women that Brooke fell in and out of love with in the pre-war years, she elicited "extravagant declarations of love" from Brooke in his letters to her, notes Michael Shelden in the *Washington Post Book World.* In fact, avers Delany in a review of the letters in the *London Review of Books,* "His love for Noel was never a thing in itself, but only a half-love; the other half was the figure, male or female, who was the current object of his sensual desires."

In early 1912, Brooke's emotional turbulence culminated in a nervous breakdown. He spent several months in rehabilitation, during which he was not allowed to write poetry. By summer, though, he had recovered enough to travel to Germany, a trip that marked the beginning of almost three years of constant travel. In May of 1913, he traveled to the United States, where he spent four months before sailing to the South Pacific. Of the seven months that Brooke stayed in the Pacific, three were spent in Tahiti, where, as Delany states, he wrote "the best of his poems, and [experienced] probably the most unbroken happiness of his life."

Several of the poems that Brooke wrote during this period are considered to be among his most effective, including "Tiare Tahiti" and "The Great Lover." Delany notes that the first poem's inspiration was a woman called "Taatamata," whom Brooke met and became intimate with in Tahiti. Not surprisingly, the poem is a love poem, a tribute to an exotic land and carefree love: "Hasten, hand in human hand, / Down the dark, the flowered way, / . . . And in the water's soft caress, / Wash the mind of foolishness, / Mamua, until the day." "The Great Lover" is a list "of the hundred and one everyday things that gave [the poet] joy," writes A. C. Ward in *Twentieth-Century Literature: 1901-1950.* "He invested this domestic catalogue with significance and beauty, and turned the commonplace into the strangely new," praises Ward. Similarly, John Lehmann in *Rupert Brooke: His Life and His Legend* remarks on "the precise and vivid images with which in *The Great Lover* [Brooke] enumerates the concrete things that evoke his love in recollection."

Despite the apparent happiness that Brooke found in Tahiti, he decided to return to England in the spring of 1914. Within a few months of his return, World War I began. Like most men of his age and class, Brooke immediately volunteered for service in the war. He joined the Royal Navy Volunteer Reserve; the group's first destination was Antwerp, Belgium, where it stayed through the beginning of 1915. The area around Antwerp was not volatile at this time, though, and the Reserve saw no military action during its entire stay in Belgium. The lull in fighting turned into a fruitful period for Brooke, for it was then that he produced his best-known poetry, the group of five war sonnets titled "Nineteen Fourteen."

Written during late 1914, these sonnets express the hopeful idealism and enthusiasm with which Britain entered the war. In the first sonnet, "Peace," Brooke rejoices in the feeling that the war is a welcome relief to a generation for whom life had been empty and void of meaning. As quoted by Bernard Bergonzi in *Heroes' Twilight: A Study of the Literature of the Great War,* Brooke wrote: "God be thanked Who has matched us with His hour, / And caught our youth, and wakened us from sleeping, / With hand made sure, clear eye, and sharpened power, / To turn, as swimmers into cleanness leaping, / Glad from a world grown old and cold and weary." In the second sonnet, "Safety," Brooke continues to revel in the coming of war by comparing death to a shelter that protects its refugees from the horrors of life.

The third and fourth sonnets are both titled "The Dead," but it is the second of the two that has enjoyed more popularity and more critical acclaim. In this fourth sonnet, Brooke again paints death as a positive, pristine state. For Brooke, death is like an infinite frost that "leaves a white / Unbroken glory, a gathered radiance, / A width, a shining peace, under the night," as quoted by Eder. Finally, Brooke ends the sonnet sequence with "The Soldier," his most famous and most openly patriotic poem. He imagines his own death, but rather than conveying sadness or fear at such an event, he accepts it as an opportunity to make a noble sacrifice by dying for his country. As quoted by Delany, Brooke wrote: "If I should die, think only this of me, / That there's some corner of a foreign field / That is forever England."

The "Nineteen Fourteen" sonnets were immediately famous. On Easter Sunday in 1915, the dean of St. Paul's Cathedral in London, William Ralph Inge, read aloud "The Soldier." Brooke's death three weeks later insured that his name would always be intertwined with the war sonnets, and with "The Soldier" in particular. As A. C. Ward comments, "The Soldier" "became the one poem inseparably linked with Rupert Brooke's name. It is, for all time, his epitaph—beautiful and tranquil." The events surrounding Brooke's death were a significant factor in the success of "Nineteen Fourteen." In February of 1915, Brooke had been ordered to sail to the Dardanelles—a strait between Europe and Turkey—for the Gallipoli campaign that would begin that spring. During the journey, however, Brooke contracted blood poisoning from an insect bite; he died on April 23 on a ship in the Aegean Sea and was buried in an olive grove on the Greek island of Skyros. Such a death and burial, notes Delany, fueled the myth that the handsome poet had provoked the wrath of angry, jealous gods. "Rupert's death was first reported as caused by sunstroke," writes Delany, "and had not Phoebus Apollo, the golden-haired god of poetry, struck down Marsyas for boasting that he could sing as well as the god?" Furthermore, Brooke died in a part of the world long associated with another famous English poet, George Gordon, Lord Byron. As Delany says, "Now another Cambridge poet, who had loved to swim in Byron's Pool, had shared Byron's fate."

Brooke's death was felt throughout his country; Eder states that "all England mourned the poet-soldier's death." In his tribute to Brooke for the London *Times* as quoted by Delany, Winston Churchill praised Brooke's "classic symmetry of mind and body." "He was all that one would wish England's noblest sons to be," added Churchill, "in days when no sacrifice but the most precious is acceptable." Since the war was still in its early stages, such sentiment could still be cherished. After the staggering number of deaths that the English incurred during the trench warfare of 1916 and 1917, however, such patriotic feeling was viewed—like Brooke's poetry—as foolish and naive. As John Lehmann comments, "What soldier, who had experienced the meaningless horror and foulness of the Western Front stalemate in 1916 and 1917, could think of it as a place to greet 'as swimmers into cleanness leaping' or as a welcome relief 'from a world grown old and cold and weary'?"

A more realistic poetry grew out of the war's latter stages and supplanted Brooke's verse as the most important literary expression of the war. Poets such as Wilfred Owen, Siegfried Sassoon, and Robert Graves captured the terror and tragedy of modern warfare; next to their poetry, Brooke's war sonnets seem "sentimental and unrealistic," notes Lehmann. For several decades after his death Brooke's poetry—though always popular—was dismissed by critics responding both to the consequences of two world wars and to the pessimistic poetry that dominated the age, of which T. S. Eliot's *The Waste Land* is the prime example. But more recent critics, while admitting that Brooke's poetry lacks depth, maintain that his verse does have significance. In *Rupert Brooke: The Man and the Poet,* Robert Brainard Pearsall does not deny the "slightness in mass and idea" of Brooke's work but avers that "all technical criticism droops before the fact that his verse was lyrical, charming, and companionable." Other critics, including Eder and Edward A. McCourt, argue that Brooke's poetry—especially the "Nineteen Fourteen" sequence—is important as a barometer of England between 1910 and 1915. As Eder states, "Brooke's war sonnets perfectly captured the mood of the moment."

Several observers, both past and present, have speculated as to what Brooke—and his poetry—might have achieved had the poet lived longer. Woolf, who wrote in the *Times Literary Supplement* that Brooke's "poetry was the brilliant by-product of energies not yet turned upon their object," speculated that Brooke might have become prime minister. Lehmann, referring to the legend that continues to surround Brooke—that of the angelic, idealistic, naive young poet—notes that "perhaps, if [Brooke] had survived into 1917 and 1918, he would have dismissed the legend himself more ruthlessly than anyone else." As it is, Brooke left only the legacy of a poetry that reflects his brief, fascinating life. "It is not," writes Timothy Rogers in *Rupert Brooke,* "for flights of fancy or for the deeper philosophic insights that we may read him; rather, for his sensitive response to a short but vivid life."

*BIOGRAPHICAL/CRITICAL SOURCES:*

*BOOKS*

Bergonzi, Bernard, *Heroes' Twilight: A Study of the Literature of the Great War,* Constable, 1965.

Brooke, Rupert, *The Prose of Rupert Brooke,* edited and introduced by Christopher Hassall, Sidgwick & Jackson, 1956.

Brooke, *The Letters of Rupert Brooke,* edited by Geoffrey Keynes, Harcourt, 1968.

Cheason, Denis, *The Cambridgeshire of Rupert Brooke,* privately printed, 1980.

*Concise Dictionary of British Literary Biography,* Volume 6: *Modern Writers, 1914-1945,* Gale, 1991.

de la Mare, Walter, *Rupert Brooke and the Intellectual Imagination,* Sidgwick & Jackson, 1919.

Delany, Paul, *The Neo-Pagans: Rupert Brooke and the Ordeal of Youth,* Free Press, 1987.

*Dictionary of Literary Biography,* Volume 19: *British Poets, 1880-1914,* Gale, 1983.

Hall, Roger and Sandra Martin, editors, *Rupert Brooke in Canada,* PMA Books, 1978.

Hassall, Christopher, *Rupert Brooke: A Biography,* Harcourt, 1964.

Hastings, Michael, *The Handsomest Young Man in England: Rupert Brooke,* Michael Joseph, 1967.

James, Henry, *The Letters of Henry James, Volume II,* edited by Percy Lubbock, Scribner, 1920.

Keynes, Geoffrey, *A Bibliography of Rupert Brooke,* Hart-Davis, 1959.

Laskowski, William E., *Rupert Brooke,* Twayne (New York City), 1994.

Lehmann, John, *Rupert Brooke: His Life and His Legend,* Weidenfeld & Nicolson, 1980.

Pearsall, Robert Brainard, *Rupert Brooke: The Man and the Poet,* Humanities Press, 1975.

Rogers, Timothy, editor, *Rupert Brooke: A Reappraisal and Selection from His Writings, Some Hitherto Unpublished,* Barnes & Noble, 1971.

Stringer, Arthur, *Red Wine of Youth: A Life of Rupert Brooke,* Bobbs-Merrill, 1948.

*Twentieth-Century Literary Criticism,* Gale, Volume 2, 1979, Volume 7, 1982.

*World Literature Criticism,* Gale, 1992.

*PERIODICALS*

*Dalhousie Review,* summer, 1944.

*London Review of Books,* February 27, 1992, p. 23.

*Los Angeles Times Book Review,* September 6, 1992, p. 2.

*New York Times Book Review,* November 24, 1968.

*Times Literary Supplement,* August 8, 1918; July 18, 1968; November 27, 1987.
*Voice Literary Supplement,* June, 1988.
*Washington Post Book World,* September 6, 1992, p. 11.*

* * *

**BROOKS, Cleanth 1906-1994**

*PERSONAL:* Born October 16, 1906, in Murray, KY; died of cancer of the esophagus, May 10, 1994, in New Haven, CT; son of Cleanth (a Methodist minister) and Bessie Lee (Witherspoon) Brooks; married Edith Amy Blanchard, September 12, 1934 (died, October 1, 1986). *Education:* Vanderbilt University, B.A., 1928; Tulane University, M.A., 1929; Oxford University, Rhodes scholar, 1929-32, B.A. (with honors), 1931, B.Litt., 1932. *Politics:* Independent Democrat. *Religion:* Episcopalian.

*CAREER:* Louisiana State University, Baton Rouge, 1932-47, began as lecturer, became professor of English, visiting professor, 1970 and 1974; Yale University, New Haven, CT, professor of English, 1947-60, Gray Professor of Rhetoric, 1960-75, professor emeritus, 1975-94. Visiting professor of English at University of Texas, summer, 1941, University of Michigan, summer, 1942, University of Chicago, 1945-46, Kenyon School of English, summer, 1948 (fellow, 1948-94), University of Southern California, summer, 1953, Breadloaf School of English, summer, 1963, University of South Carolina, 1975, Tulane University, 1976, University of North Carolina, 1977 and 1979, and University of Tennessee, 1978 and 1980; research professor with Bostick Foundation, 1975; Lamar Lecturer, 1984; Jefferson Lecturer, 1985. *Southern Review,* Baton Rouge, LA, Co-Managing Editor, 1932-41, Co-Editor, 1941-42. Member of advisory committee for Boswell Papers, 1950-94; Library of Congress, fellow, 1953-63, member of council of scholars, 1984-87; American Embassy, London, England, cultural attache, 1964-66; National Humanities Center, senior fellow, 1980-81.

*MEMBER:* Modern Language Association of America, American Academy of Arts and Sciences, National Institute of Arts and Letters, American Philosophical Society, American Association of University Professors, Royal Society of Literature, Phi Beta Kappa, Athenaeum (London), Fellowship of Southern Writers (chancellor 1986-91).

*AWARDS, HONORS:* Guggenheim fellowship, 1953 and 1960; senior fellowship, National Endowment for the Humanities, 1975; Explicator Award, c. 1980, for *William Faulkner: Toward Yoknapatawpha and Beyond;* honorary B. A., 1931, and B. Litt., 1932 from Oxford University; D.Litt. from Upsala College, 1963, University of Kentucky, 1963, University of Exeter, 1966, Washington and Lee University, 1968, Tulane University, 1969, University of the South, 1975, Newberry College, 1979, and Indiana State University, 1992; L.H.D. from University of St. Louis, 1968, Centenary College, 1972, Oglethorpe University, 1976, St. Peter's College, 1978, Lehigh University, 1980, Millsaps College, 1983, University of New Haven, 1984, University of South Carolina, 1984, and Adelphi University, 1992.

*WRITINGS:*

*EDITOR*

(With others) *An Approach to Literature,* Louisiana State University Press, 1936, 5th edition, Prentice-Hall, 1975.
(With Robert Penn Warren, and coauthor) *Understanding Poetry,* Holt, 1938, 4th edition, 1975, transcript of tape recording to accompany 3rd edition entitled *Conversations on the Craft of Poetry: Cleanth Brooks and Robert Penn Warren, with Robert Frost, John Crowe Ransom, Robert Lowell, and Theodore Roethke,* Holt, 1961.
(With Warren) *Understanding Fiction,* F. S. Crofts, 1943, 3rd edition, Prentice-Hall, 1979, abridged edition published as *The Scope of Fiction,* 1960.
(General editor with A. F. Falconer and David Nichol Smith) *The Percy Letters,* 1944-88, Volumes 1-6, Louisiana State University Press, Volumes 7-9, Yale University Press; special editor of Volume 2: *The Correspondence of Thomas Percy and Richard Farmer* and Volume 7: *The Correspondence of Thomas Percy and William Shenstone.*
(With Robert Heilman) *Understanding Drama,* Holt, 1945.
(With John Edward Hardy) *The Poems of John Milton* (1645 edition), Harcourt, 1951.
(With Warren) *An Anthology of Stories from the "Southern Review,"* Louisiana State University Press, 1953.
*Tragic Themes in Western Literature: Seven Essays by Bernard Knox (and Others),* Yale University Press, 1956.
(With Warren and R. W. B. Lewis) *American Literature: The Makers and the Making,* two volumes,

St. Martin's, 1973, paperbound edition published in four volumes, 1974.

*Southern Review*, managing editor with Robert Penn Warren, 1935-41, editor with Warren, 1941-42; member of advisory board, *Kenyon Review*, 1942-60.

*OTHER*

*The Relation of the Alabama-Georgia Dialect to the Provincial Dialects of Great Britain*, Louisiana State University Press, 1935.

*Modern Poetry and the Tradition*, University of North Carolina Press, 1939.

*The Well Wrought Urn*, Reynal & Hitchcock, 1947, Harcourt, 1956.

(With Warren) *Modern Rhetoric*, Harcourt, 1949, 4th edition, 1979, abridged edition, 1961.

(With Warren) *Fundamentals of Good Writing*, Harcourt, 1950.

(Contributor) *Humanities: An Appraisal*, University of Wisconsin Press, 1950.

(With William K. Wimsatt) *Literary Criticism: A Short History*, Knopf, 1957.

*Metaphor and the Function of Criticism*, Institute for Religious and Social Studies, c. 1957.

*The Hidden God: Studies in Hemingway, Faulkner, Yeats, Eliot and Warren*, Yale University Press, 1963.

*William Faulkner: The Yoknapatawpha Country*, Yale University Press, 1963.

*A Shaping Joy: Studies in the Writer's Craft*, Harcourt, 1972.

*William Faulkner: Toward Yoknapatawpha and Beyond*, Yale University Press, 1978.

(Contributor) Louis D. Dollarhide and Ann J. Abadie, editors, *Eudora Welty: A Form of Thanks*, University Press of Mississippi, 1979.

*Cleanth Brooks at the United States Air Force Academy, April 11-12, 1978* (lectures), edited by James A. Grimshaw, Jr., Department of English, U.S. Air Force Academy, 1980.

*William Faulkner: First Encounters*, Yale University Press, 1983.

*The Language of the American South*, University of Georgia Press, 1985.

*On the Prejudices, Predilections, and Firm Beliefs of William Faulkner*, Louisiana State University Press, 1987.

*Historical Evidence and the Reading of Seventeenth Century Poetry*, University of Missouri Press, 1991.

*Community, Religion, and Literature: Essays*, University of Missouri Press (Columbia), 1995.

Also author of recorded lectures on works by William Faulkner. Contributor of articles and reviews to literary journals.

*SIDELIGHTS:* From the early 1940s until his death in 1994, Cleanth Brooks was "one of the pillars of the American literary-critical establishment," to quote Brian Stonehill in the *Los Angeles Times*. Brooks is best remembered as one of the pioneers of the so-called "New Criticism," a scholarly approach that examines literary works to discover internal tensions and abiding ironies that enable them to stand free of personal, religious, and historical circumstances. *Southern Review* essayist Rene Wellek describes the erudite Brooks as an "eminently fair-minded, text-oriented, conscientious examiner of ideas who is rarely openly polemical." Wellek adds that Brooks "is convinced that the amalgamation and confusion of literary theory with morals, politics, and religion has been at the root of many difficulties of critical theory."

From his base at Yale University, Brooks wrote and edited a number of volumes that aimed to enlarge a reader's understanding of seminal works of literature. His best-known books, including *The Well Wrought Urn: Studies in the Structure of Poetry* and (with Robert Penn Warren) *Understanding Poetry: An Anthology for College Students* "revolutionized literary pedagogy by employing the criterion of shared aesthetic properties, rather than subject, author, or chronology, to organize poems," according to *Dictionary of Literary Biography* contributor James J. Sosnoski. Long before his retirement from Yale in 1975, Brooks had turned to an in-depth examination of William Faulkner's fiction, becoming "*the* most important Faulkner critic," to quote a *Washington Post Book World* reviewer.

Sosnoski writes of Brooks: "Not only was he considered to be *the* critic of his generation of critics but also. . . he was critical of other critics. During the 1940s and 1950s he was widely regarded as the most lucid and instructive close reader of literary texts." Unlike his associates Warren, Allen Tate, and John Crowe Ransom, Brooks wrote little poetry or fiction of his own. Instead he concentrated on criticism, revealing undervalued or unsuspected complexity in poetry from Shakespeare to William Butler Yeats. In *The Possibilities of Order: Cleanth Brooks and His Work*, Monroe K. Spears notes: "Far from being the irresponsible aesthete or technician that his opponents have represented him as (in the polemics of literary journals and seminar rooms), Brooks is . . . distinguished among critics precisely by his strong sense of responsibility. This is not his only distinction; aside from such obvious gifts as perceptiveness, imagination, and intelligence, his critical integrity, his sense of proportion, and his instinct for the centrally human are rare qualities indeed. But responsibility is primary."

Brooks was born in Kentucky in 1906, the son of a Methodist clergyman. During his childhood the family moved often, going from town to town in Tennessee. Brooks's father was a scholarly man who encouraged his son to read works of world literature. Later Brooks attended the McTyeire School, a small classical academy where students became well acquainted with Greek and Latin in addition to a standard curriculum.

In 1924 Brooks entered Vanderbilt University, the seat of an important 1920s literary group known as the Fugitives. The Fugitives—including Ransom, Donald Davidson, Tate, and Warren—wrote and discussed modern literature and "laid the theoretical groundwork for the New Critical movement," according to Sosnoski. Brooks's exposure to the Fugitives changed the direction of his career. He had planned to become a lawyer, but he opted instead to pursue the study of literature. He is quoted in the *Dictionary of Literary Biography* as saying: "The thing that I got most out of Vanderbilt was to discover suddenly that literature was not a dead thing to be looked at through the glass of a museum case, but was very much alive."

After graduating from Vanderbilt in 1928, Brooks continued his studies at Tulane University, receiving his M.A. in 1929. Tulane nominated him for a prestigious Rhodes scholarship that sent him to Exeter College at Oxford University in England. There—at Exeter College—he earned another B.A. with honors and was accorded a graduate degree in 1932. He returned to the United States the same year and began teaching literature at Louisiana State University. Robert Penn Warren was also hired by LSU shortly after Brooks arrived, and the two men continued a close personal and professional relationship that had begun in their Vanderbilt days. Together, in 1939, they founded the *Southern Review,* one of the nation's most important critical quarterlies.

As college professors, Brooks and Warren found the existing textbooks for the study of literature grossly inadequate. They determined to develop their own, editing *An Approach to Literature: A Collection of Prose and Verse with Analyses and Discussions, Understanding Poetry,* and *Understanding Fiction.* Sosnoski notes of these works that the editors "tried to deal with what they considered a widespread problem, namely to get students to do a close analyses of the literary works. Therefore, they provided model analyses as well as questions that might provoke students to do their own analyses. This approach was quite controversial." Indeed, some opponents of Brooks's approach accused him of neglecting such "essentials" as the author's background and the poem's place in cultural history. Brooks, on the other hand, saw himself merely as a proponent of a more text-oriented criticism.

In *The Well Wrought Urn,* published in 1947, Brooks applied this text-oriented New Criticism to ten English language poems, some of them centuries old. *New York Times Book Review* correspondent R. P. Blackmur notes of the work: "Mr. Brooks gives us intensive and exciting readings of his chosen poems. . . . He wants to liberate—to bring out into the open air of the poems themselves—a way in which the poems grow together and grow into life which we can recognize as related to our own practice. His readings suggest something much more important: that, at least from Shakespeare to Yeats, English poetry has an identity of inner or conceptual forms; and that even more important, we can learn the scope of our own practice, and stretch it, too, better from old models than our own."

From works such as *The Well Wrought Urn,* Brooks earned a reputation as a "close reader" of literary texts—in his own words, an examiner of "what the poem says as a poem." In *Southern Renascence: The Literature of the Modern South,* John Edward Hardy remarks of Brooks's method: "Commentary is never allowed to get in the way of the poem. Whatever the other risks involved in the style he has chosen, Brooks avoids the greatest danger that the 'inspired' critic faces, that of having his critique become a rival or substitute poem for the one supposedly being investigated." Sosnoski writes: "In combining aesthetic formalism with linguistic self-reflexivity, Brooks's readings mark a real turning point in the development of poetic theory, one that (to Brooks's chagrin) could be claimed to lead to deconstructionist practices. On the other hand, Brooks also thus moves even further from the kind of political or social or cultural criticism so many called for in the troubled decades of the 1930s and 1940s."

Like many other writers, Brooks found the labels attached to him—"New Critic," "close reader"—quite confining. In *A Shaping Joy: Studies in the Writer's Craft,* Brooks commented on his position in the academic community. "The pigeonhole assigned to me carries the label 'The New Criticism,'" he wrote. "Now, it is bad enough to live under any label, but one so nearly meaningless as 'The New Criticism'—it is certainly not *new*—has peculiar disadvantages. For most people it vaguely signifies an anti-historical bias and a fixation on 'close reading.'" Brooks called this reaction to his intentions "an overshadowing generalization."

Brooks moved to Yale University in 1947 and remained there until his retirement in 1975. He also served as a visiting professor at numerous universities and even worked as a cultural attache at the American embassy in London. As a Southerner himself, Brooks was perhaps inevitably drawn to William Faulkner's fiction, and he spent nearly three decades analyzing Faulkner's difficult but rewarding texts.

Yale University Press published Brooks's *William Faulkner: The Yoknapatawpha Country* in 1963. The book considers Faulkner as a product of his Southern milieu with its particular ethical and religious heritage and then explores the themes and characters in Faulkner's Yoknapatawpha novels. *Yale Review* contributor Joseph Blotner calls the work "the best single critical work on the novels of Faulkner's fictional saga," praising Brooks for his "remarkable erudition, broad historical consciousness, penetrating insight, sympathetic sensitivity, blessed common sense, and the ability to express them in a flexible prose that is clear, straightforward, and persuasive." Blotner concludes that Brooks "leads the reader through Faulkner's complexities and intricacies, not only making them more easily understandable but also showing how they function in the novel's ultimate meaning."

In 1978 Brooks published a companion volume, *William Faulkner: Toward Yoknapatawpha and Beyond,* a study of Faulkner's development as a writer with a discussion of novels not set in Yoknapatawpha County. Critics also found favor with a 1983 Brooks work, *William Faulkner: First Encounters.* The volume, intended principally for undergraduates and general readers interested in Faulkner, assists in unraveling the great writer's most difficult novels. *Washington Post* columnist Jonathan Yardley writes of *First Encounters* that, for the reader coming to Faulkner for the first time, "this slender volume provides the keys to the kingdom." Yardley concludes: "*First Encounters* can be read with profit by the scholar, for it is a distillation of our most important Faulkner critic's views of Faulkner's most enduring work. But the reader who will value it most is the daunted but determined one who wants to gain admission to one of the great bodies of work in the English language."

Many of Brooks's books were inspired by lectures he gave to students over the years. He also published two volumes on Southern dialect and its relationship to speech patterns in the south of England. "Brooks has always seemed to think of his criticism as simply an extension of his teaching, exactly the same in nature and purpose," Spears notes. ". . .It appears never to have occurred to him to think of his criticism as autotelic; assuming its role to be obviously ancillary to that of literature itself but nevertheless vitally important, he has been concerned chiefly with its practical effectiveness upon its audience—mostly students and teachers, with some general readers. Through collaborative textbooks and editing, as well as through reviewing, lecturing, and criticism proper, Brooks has devoted himself single-mindedly to the aim of improving this audience's understanding of literature and hence its power of discrimination."

Sosnoski offers a similar assessment of Brooks's career. "Brooks's accomplishments are considerable," Sosnoski writes. "He has been in every respect an exemplary literary scholar. Despite his. . . disclaimer, he is important in the history of criticism as a 'close reader' of complex modern literary texts. His two greatest achievements are that he made difficult modern writers accessible to a generation of scholars for whom it was inconceivable that a great writer could exist in the twentieth century, and he taught the next generation of critics how to read closely. He has never regarded himself as a theorist, but he has been a sensitive reader of contemporary literary theory and has articulated an approach to literature that made excellent sense to students of literature in the 1950s and 1960s."

Brooks's death in 1994 inspired additional reflection on his lifelong dedication and highly influential contributions to the study of literature. Former student and friend Judith Farr writes in a *Dictionary of Literary Biography Yearbook: 1994* tribute to Brooks: "Cleanth's vision was that the critic, however magisterial, however brilliant, essentially served the artist: he was never a rival presence but an adroit commentator, the most willing of willing, informed, knowledgeable readers, prepared to assist the public in achieving the richest possible understanding of the artist's work. There was a modesty implicit in this point of view, and I always felt Cleanth's reverence for true writers, though he could certainly be savage in his controlled fashion to a false or poor one." A London *Times* reviewer adds, "To his students, Brooks appeared a gentle, quietly spoken man, with enormous authority."

Commenting on Brooks's persistent effort to reconcile competing social, political, and historical forces in both literary creation and interpretation, Carol M. Andrews writes in an essay for *The Vanderbilt Tradition,* "Brooks solves this conflict to his own satisfaction by seeing his traditional values as universal, inhering in human experience itself and therefore quite rightly represented in a work of art that separates itself from historical flux." According to Brooks, as quoted by Monroe K. Spears in the *New York Review of Books,*: "Genuine literature . . . 'is not a luxury commodity but neither is it an assembly-line product. It cannot be mass produced. It has to be hand made, fashioned by a genuine craftsman out of honest human emotions and experiences, in the making of which the indispensable material is our common language, in all its variety, complexity, and richness.'"

As Michael L. Hall notes in *Sewanee Review,* "Brooks intends to demonstrate, finally, that his method of historical reading is not antiquarian but serves a larger purpose, and part of that purpose is to remind us why we would want to read these old poems, or any other works of literature, in the first place: 'No one has ever doubted that poems (and novels and plays) are products of the culture out of which they came, and consequently at some level they must reflect that culture. But that fact does not prevent our assessing these literary documents on other levels, including what they can tell us about the universal human condition.'"

For an interview with Brooks, see *Contemporary Authors New Revisions,* Volume 35.

*BIOGRAPHICAL/CRITICAL SOURCES:*

*BOOKS*

Bryher, Jackson R., editor, *Sixteen Modern American Authors,* Norton, 1973.

*Contemporary Literary Criticism,* Gale, Volume 24, 1983; Volume 86, 1995.

*Dictionary of Literary Biography,* Volume 63: *Modern American Critics, 1920-1955,* Gale, 1988.

*Dictionary of Literary Biography Yearbook: 1994,* Gale, 1995.

Crane, R. S., editor, *Critics and Criticism: Ancient and Modern,* University of Chicago Press, 1952.

Cutrer, Thomas W., *Parnassus on the Mississippi: The Southern Review and the Baton Rouge Literary Community,* Louisiana State University Press, 1984.

Krieger, Murray, *The New Apologists for Poetry,* University of Minnesota Press, 1956.

Littlejohn, David, *Interruptions,* Grossman, 1970.

*Poems and Essays,* Vintage, 1955.

Price, Reynolds, *Things Themselves: Essays and Scenes,* Atheneum, 1972.

Pritchard, John Paul, *Criticism in America,* University of Oklahoma Press, 1956.

Rubin, Louis D., and Robert D. Jacobs, editors, *Southern Renascence: The Literature of the Modern South,* Johns Hopkins University Press, 1953.

Simpson, Lewis P., editor, *The Possibilities of Order: Cleanth Brooks and His Work,* Louisiana State University Press, 1975.

Vanderbilt, Kermit, *American Literature and the Academy: The Roots, Growth, and Maturity of a Profession,* University of Pennsylvania Press, 1986.

Walsh, John Michael, *Cleanth Brooks: An Annotated Bibliography,* Garland, 1990.

Wellek, Rene, *Concepts of Criticism,* Yale University Press, 1963.

Wellek, Rene, *Discriminations,* Yale University Press, 1970.

Wellek, Rene, *History of Modern Criticism, 1750-1950,* Volume 6, 1986.

Winchell, Mark Royden, *A Blossoming Labor: Cleanth Brooks and the Rise of Modern Criticism,* University Press of Virginia (Charlottesville), 1996.

Winchell, Mark Royden, editor, *The Vanderbilt Tradition: Essays in Honor of Thomas Daniel Young,* Louisiana State University Press, 1991.

*PERIODICALS*

*American Scholar,* Volume 53, 1983; spring, 1995, p. 257.

*Books,* July 28, 1963.

*Encounter,* December, 1971.

*Georgia Review,* winter, 1973.

*Globe and Mail* (Toronto), February 25, 1984.

*Los Angeles Times,* November 18, 1983.

*New Republic,* February 5, 1940; July 29, 1978.

*New York Herald Tribune Books,* July 28, 1963.

*New York Review of Books,* January 9, 1964; May 7, 1987, p. 38; March 7, 1991, p. 48.
*New York Times Book Review,* June 8, 1947; December 10, 1972; May 21, 1978; November 13, 1983; November 15, 1987.
*Sewanee Review,* fall, 1947; Volume 87, 1979; spring, 1992.
*Southern Review,* winter, 1974.
*Times* (London), May 16, 1994, p. 19.
*Times Literary Supplement,* March 30, 1984.
*Washington Post,* August 31, 1983.
*Washington Post Book World,* March 10, 1985.
*Yale Review,* October, 1978.

*OBITUARIES:*

*PERIODICALS*

*Chicago Tribune,* May 12, 1994, p. 11.
*Facts on File,* May 19, 1994, p. 372.
*Los Angeles Times,* May 14, 1994, p. A26.
*New York Times,* May 12, 1994, p. B14.
*Washington Post,* May 13, 1994, p. C4.*

* * *

**BUCKLEY, Fiona**
**See ANAND, Valerie**

# C

## CAIN, James M(allahan) 1892-1977

*PERSONAL:* Born July 1, 1892, in Annapolis, MD; died October 27, 1977, of a heart attack in University Park, MD; son of James William (a former president of Washington College) and Rose Cecilia (Mallahan) Cain; married Mary Rebekah Clough, 1920 (divorced); married Elina Sjosted Tyszecka, 1927 (divorced); married Aileen Pringle, 1944 (divorced); married Florence Macbeth Whitwell (an opera singer), 1947 (deceased). *Education:* Washington College, A.B., 1910, A.M., 1917. *Politics:* Democrat. *Avocational interests:* Music.

*CAREER:* Journalist and writer. *Baltimore American,* Baltimore, MD, staff member, 1917-18; *Baltimore Sun,* Baltimore, reporter, 1919-23; St. John's College, Annapolis, MD, professor of journalism, 1923-24; *New York World,* New York City, editorial writer, 1924-31; *New Yorker,* New York City, managing editor, beginning 1931; screenwriter in Hollywood, CA, 1932-48. *Military service:* U.S. Army, American Expeditionary Forces, 1918-19; served as editor in chief of *Lorraine Cross,* official newspaper of the 79th Division.

*AWARDS, HONORS:* Grand Masters Award, Mystery Writers of America, 1970.

*WRITINGS:*

*NOVELS*

*The Postman Always Rings Twice* (also see below), Knopf, 1934, reprinted, Lightyear, 1981.

*Serenade* (also see below), Knopf, 1937, reprinted AMS Press, 1981.

*Mildred Pierce* (also see below), Knopf, 1941, reprinted, Lightyear, 1981.

*Love's Lovely Counterfeit* (also see below), Knopf, 1942, reprinted, Vintage Books, 1979.

*Double Indemnity* (also see below), Avon, 1943, reprinted Random House, 1989.

*The Embezzler* (also see below), New Avon Library, 1944.

*Past All Dishonor* (also see below), Knopf, 1946.

*The Butterfly* (also see below), Knopf, 1947, reprinted, Vintage Books, 1979.

*The Sinful Woman* (also see below), Avon, 1947, reprinted, Creative Arts Books, 1989.

*The Moth,* Knopf, 1948, abridged edition, New American Library, 1950.

*Jealous Woman* (also see below), Avon, 1950, reprinted, Creative Arts Books, 1989.

*Galatea,* Knopf, 1953.

*The Root of His Evil,* R. Hale, 1954, reprinted, Creative Arts Books, 1989, published as *Shameless,* Avon, 1979.

*Mignon,* Dial, 1962.

*The Magician's Wife,* Dial, 1965, reprinted, Carnegie Mellon, 1985.

*Rainbow's End,* Mason/Charter, 1975.

*The Institute,* Mason/Charter, 1976.

*OMNIBUS EDITIONS*

*Three of a Kind: Career in C Major, The Embezzler, Double Indemnity* (*Career in C Major* originally titled *Two Can Sing,* 1938), Knopf, 1943.

*Cain Omnibus: The Postman Always Rings Twice, Serenade, Mildred Pierce,* World, 1946.

*The Embezzler* [and] *Double Indemnity,* Triangle Books, 1948.

*Three of Hearts: Love's Lovely Counterfeit, The Butterfly, Past All Dishonour,* Hale, 1949.
*Jealous Woman* [and] *Sinful Woman,* R. Hale, 1955.
*Cain x 3: Three Novels* (contains *The Postman Always Rings Twice, Mildred Pierce,* and *Double Indemnity;* a Book-of-the-Month Club selection), introduction by Tom Wolfe, Knopf, 1969.
*Three Novels by James M. Cain: Double Indemnity, The Postman Always Rings Twice, Serenade,* Bantam, 1973.
*Hard Cain* (contains *Sinful Woman, Jealous Woman,* and *The Root of His Evil*), introduction by Harlan Ellison, Gregg, 1980.
*The Baby in the Icebox, and Other Short Fiction* ("The Baby in the Icebox" first published in *American Mercury,* 1933), edited by Roy Hoopes, Holt, 1981.
*Career in C Major, and Other Fiction,* McGraw, 1986.
*Three by Cain: Serenade, Love's Lovely Counterfeit, The Butterfly,* McKay, 1989.
*Three Complete Novels* (includes *The Postman Always Rings Twice, Double Indemnity,* and *Mildred Pierce*), Wings (New York City), 1994.

*OTHER*

*Our Government* (sketches), Knopf, 1930.
*The Postman Always Rings Twice* (play based on his novel of the same title), first produced on Broadway, February 25, 1936.
(Editor) *For Men Only: A Collection of Short Stories,* World, 1944.
*The Institute,* Dorchester, 1982.
*Cloud Nine,* Mysterious Press, 1984.
*The Enchanted Isle,* Mysterious Press, 1986.

Also author of short plays, including, "Hero," "Hemp," "Red, White, and Blue," "Trial by Jury," "Theological Interlude," "Citizenship," "Will of the People," published in *American Mercury,* 1926-29. Author of uncollected stories, including "Dead Man," published in *American Mercury,* 1936, "The Birthday Party," published in *Ladies' Home Journal,* 1936, "The Girl in the Story," published in *Liberty,* 1940, and "Visitor," published in *Esquire,* 1961.

*ADAPTATIONS:* Cain's short story "The Baby in the Icebox" was filmed as *She Made Her Bed,* by Paramount in 1934; *Career in C Major* was filmed as *Wife, Husband, Friend,* by Twentieth Century Fox in 1938; *The Embezzler* was filmed as *Money and the Woman* by Warner Bros. in 1940; *Double Indemnity* was filmed by Paramount in 1944; *Mildred Pierce* was filmed by Warner Bros. in 1945; *Serenade* was filmed by Warner Bros. in 1956; *Loves' Lovely Counterfeit* was filmed as *Slightly Scarlet* by Benjamin Beaugeus in 1956; *The Root of His Evil* was filmed as *Interlude* by Universal in 1957. In 1938 an authorized version of *The Postman Always Rings Twice* was made in France by Gladiator Films, with the title *Le Dernier Tourant,* because Metro-Goldwyn-Mayer, the American owner of the film rights, decided that the film could not be released in the United States. In 1939, G. Musso of Italy released *Obsessione* (a Cocinor-Marcean release of ICI Productions), also based on *The Postman Always Rings Twice.* MGM and Gladiator Films then filed a joint suit against the Italian producers, charging plagiarism. In 1946 the U.S. censorship of the film was lifted and the MGM production was released. Critics agreed, however, that the Italian version was superior to both the American and the French efforts. A Lorimar production of *The Postman Always Rings Twice* was also released in the United States in 1981. In addition, *Postman* was adapted and performed as opera by the Opera Theatre of St. Louis, 1982, and revived by the Washington Opera of Washington, D.C., in 1989. *Butterfly* was adapted for the screen by John Goff and Matt Climber and released in 1982.

*WORK IN PROGRESS:* An autobiography.

*SIDELIGHTS:* When James M. Cain moved to Hollywood to become a screenwriter, he had already run the gamut of writing careers. Behind him lay stints as a newspaper reporter, a professor of journalism at St. John's College, an editorial writer for Walter Lippmann, and the managing editor of the *New Yorker* magazine. And yet none of his efforts had fully taken hold; his career in journalism had been "fragmented and inconclusive," according to Kevin Starr, who reported in *New Republic* that Cain "was on the way to becoming just another hard-drinking Irish-American journalist with baffled aspirations in the direction of literature." And then, in 1934, having been fired by Paramount Pictures and in desperate need of money, the 42-year-old writer published his first novel, *The Postman Always Rings Twice.* Described by Cain biographer Roy Hoopes as "one of those rarest of literary achievements in America: a phenomenal best seller that received the highest acclaim from critics," *Postman* brought Cain "out of obscurity and into the literary limelight where he remained for fourteen years."

After *Postman,* Cain wrote *Double Indemnity, Mildred Pierce,* and *Serenade.* These four books earned him a reputation as a "tough-guy" writer or, as David Madden called him in *James M. Cain,* "the twenty-minute egg" of the "hard-boiled" school. "Cain and other hard-boiled writers," Madden explained in his critical study, "wrote not only about but mainly to the masses, giving violent impetus to their forbidden dreams, dramatizing their darkest temptations and their basic physical drives." His protagonists were the kind of people you read about "almost every day in the newspapers," according to William Rose Benet in *Saturday Review.* "They are chiefly stupid, slightly pathetic, capable of rape, arson, or murder in a sort of dumb, driven way. They have glimmers of decency, passions that overcome them, and are chiefly selfish and morally composed of gelatin while being big, husky brutes to outward view."

Cain resented such categorization. "I don't know what they're talking about—'tough,' 'hard-boiled.' I tried to write as 'people talk,'" he told David Zinsser of *Paris Review.* When asked to describe his work, he said: "I, so far as I can sense the pattern of my mind, write of the wish that comes true, for some reason a terrifying concept, at least to my imagination. I think my stories have some quality of the opening of a forbidden box." What Cain's "forbidden box" contains, according to W. M. Frohock in his *The Novel of Violence in America: 1920-1950,* "invariably turns out to be sex, experienced with perfect animal intensity, sometimes with a little hint of the abnormal or the forbidden about it." Though Cain repeatedly insisted to Zinsser and other interviewers that he took no interest in violence, Frohock argued that "sex, so conceived, is inseparable from violence. Violence is at once associated with the sexual act itself, and made an inevitable accompaniment of anything which tends to frustrate the sexual experience. In addition violence stimulates sexual activity, as in the scene of Nick's murder [in *The Postman Always Rings Twice*]. For Cain, sex and violence are not so much subjects as necessary accessories of the plot." And plot, Frohock continued, is "the essence of the Cain novel."

*Chicago Tribune Book World* critic David Mamet observed that "the understanding of plot that Cain embraced goes back . . . to Aristotle: Cain discovered the dramatic/tragic plot—discarding narration, exposition, and characterization in favor of event." But unlike the Greek dramas, Cain's books, Frohock argued, do not strike a tragic note "because the violence in them is not endowed with any sort of moral significance. We are aware of his violence not as something which we must accept because it is a part of Man's Fate, but as something for a clever writer to play tricks with." For these reasons, Frohock maintained that "nothing he has ever written has been entirely out of the trash category." But Ross Macdonald, writing in the *New York Times Book Review,* disagreed. Citing Cain's ability to transmute "blood into symbol" as the "stuff of art," he concluded that Cain was "a conscious and deliberate artist" whose novel *The Postman Always Rings Twice* had "moral and symbolic overtones."

James T. Farrell in his *Literature and Morality* expressed still another point of view: "Writers like Cain stand between the work of a serious and tragic character which has been fathered in America by such men as [Theodore] Dreiser and the work derived from the more-or-less forgotten writings of Robert W. Chambers, Gene Stratton-Porter, or Harold Bell Wright. And in this in-between, neither-fish-nor-fowl literary medium, James M. Cain has become the master. He is a literary thrill producer who profits by the reaction against the sentimentality of other years and, at the same time, gains from the prestige of more serious and exploratory writing."

While the argument over the seriousness of Cain's work continues, so too does his popularity. *Cain x 3,* a 1969 reprint of his most popular works, *Postman, Double Indemnity,* and *Mildred Pierce,* found a wide audience, as Macdonald observed. "There is," he said, "a new generation of readers for Cain's stories—*Cain x 3* should make its way into the universities." And Frohock wrote that "in spite of the cheapness which sooner or later finds its way into his novels, an inordinate number of intelligent and fully literate people have read him. He has been translated in many parts of the world, and writers whose stature makes him look stunted have paid him the compliment of imitating him as Albert Camus did, for example, in *The Stranger.*"

In his *Nation* review of *Cain x 3,* Kenneth Lamott explained Cain's continued appeal: "There is the remembered tautness of structure, the absolute control of the well-articulated plot, the cold eye for the essential truth about men and women. The language is spare and clean, only occasionally breaking down into cliche. It is hardly an original observation, but watching Cain at work can still give the reader that particular pleasure that comes from watching a master craftsman, a cabinetmaker fitting a joint, or a potter throwing a pot. I would not go as far as Tom Wolfe, who in his introduction to this book suggests that Norman Mailer might well sit at Cain's feet to learn how to become a real novelist, but the spirit of the suggestion is not without merit."

Despite the success of what Mamet called the "California novels," Cain experienced many bouts of failure in his fiction-writing career. His first effort to write a novel, for example, was a vain attempt as Cain explained to *Paris Review:* "In 1922 when I was still on the *Baltimore Sun,* I took the winter off to go down and work in the mines. I tried to write the Great American Novel, and wrote three of them, none of them any good. I had to come slinking back to work admitting that the Great American Novel hadn't been written."

Six years passed before Cain sold his first piece of fiction—a short story published by H. L. Mencken in the *American Mercury*. Entitled "Pastorale," it was a humorous rendering of a grisly murder, told—according to Hoopes—in the Ring Lardner manner and significant for reasons which he outlined in his *Chicago Tribune Book World* review: "In the first place, Cain now found that he could tell a story in the first person, preferably in the voice of some 'lowlife character,' as his mother called that type. [And in the second,] he also found his favorite theme: Although two people may get away with committing a crime, they cannot live with it." Encouraged by the success of "Pastorale," Cain continued to write short fiction and his name eventually came to the attention of several Hollywood producers who invited him to California. Since he was unhappy in New York, Cain accepted the offer, moving west in 1931. But his efforts at screenwriting were failures and, as Hoopes reported in his introduction to *The Baby in the Icebox, and Other Short Fiction,* "within six months of his arrival in Hollywood, Cain was out of a job in the middle of the Depression, forty years old, and supporting a second wife and her two young children."

Unwilling to return east, Cain took up free-lance writing and, Hoopes reported, "as he drove around in his 1932 Ford roadster, he began to feel more and more that California and its people provided a natural milieu for his writing. And there was one gas station, where he regularly stopped, that provided a spark that would eventually ignite Cain's phenomenal career as a writer of controversial best-sellers. 'Always this bosomy looking thing comes out—commonplace, but sexy, the kind you have ideas about,' he later told an interviewer. 'We always talked while she filled up my tank. One day I read in the paper where a woman who runs a filling station knocked off her husband. Can it be this bosomy thing? I go by and sure enough the place is closed. I inquire. Yes, she's the one—this appetizing but utterly commonplace woman.'

"He began to think: What about a novel in which a woman and a typical California automobile tramp kill the woman's husband to get his gas station and car? Cain and [his wife] Elina discussed the idea for months, but he was still not ready for a long story. At the same time, he only felt comfortable in his writing when he pretended to be someone else, telling his story in the first person, in the manner of Ring Lardner. . . . So Cain put his idea for a novel in the back of his mind and decided to try another short story. The result was 'The Baby in the Icebox,' and like 'Pastorale,'. . . it was written in the first person, Ring Lardner style. But unlike his earlier stories, 'The Baby in the Icebox' was set in the West and had characters who were western in origin. Suddenly Cain found something happening in his fiction." As Cain reported to *Paris Review,* "Out there in California I began writing in the local idiom. Everything broke for me."

Paramount bought the movie rights to "Icebox" and produced the story as *She Made Her Bed,* the first in a succession of nine Cain stories and novels that would be adapted to the screen. Meanwhile, in New York, H. L. Mencken had shown "Icebox" to Alfred A. Knopf, a prominent publisher, who liked it so much that he encouraged Cain to try his hand at a novel. Cain did, and just six months later, in June 1933, he had a 159-page manuscript that would eventually become *The Postman Always Rings Twice.*

In an interview with *Paris Review,* Cain discussed the origins of the story: "It was based on the Snyder-Grey case, which was in the papers about then. . . . Grey and this woman Snyder killed her husband for the insurance money. Walter Lippmann went to that trial one day and she brushed by him. . . . Walter said it seemed very odd to be inhaling the perfume or being brushed by the dress of a woman he knew was going to be electrocuted. So the Snyder-Grey case provided the basis. The bit influence in how I wrote *The Postman Always Rings Twice* was this strange guy, Vincent Lawrence, who had more effect on my writing than anyone else. He had a device which he thought was so important—the 'love rack' he called it. . . . What he meant by the 'love rack' was the poetic situation whereby the audience felt the love between the characters. He called this 'the one, the two, and the three.'"

One time, reported Hoopes in the *Washington Post,* "when Lawrence was talking about his 'love rack,' Cain asked: 'Why couldn't the whole thing be a love rack; why such attention to the one episode where they fall in love?' Cain asked why every episode in the story could not be written with a view to its effect on the love story. Lawrence thought that this had possibilities." So Cain wrote a story about Frank Chambers, a young drifter, who wanders into a diner run by a Greek named Nick and his restless wife, Cora, who is disgusted by Nick's "greasiness." After seeing Cora, Frank agrees to work in the restaurant and they become lovers. Soon Cora convinces Frank to help her murder Nick so that she will inherit his property. Although the first attempt is unsuccessful, their second effort succeeds. But, according to Hoopes, "the murder eventually becomes their love rack, and they are brought to justice when Cora is killed in an automobile accident and Frank is wrongly found guilty of her murder."

The first version of the story was called *Bar-B-Q,* and Knopf turned it down. "At that point," Cain told *Publishers Weekly,* "Lippmann wanted to see the book. He thought he could do something with it. He took it to Macmillan and Macmillan turned it down. Then Lippmann took it back to Knopf and they decided to publish it." But there was one final problem—Knopf did not like the title and wanted it changed. In his *Washington Post* article, Hoopes explained how *Bar-B-Q* was renamed: "Around this time Cain and Lawrence were musing about the agony of sweating out the publication of a first novel and Lawrence told him about sending his first play to a New York producer. Lawrence had been living in Boston then and would go to the window every day to watch for the postman; when he could not stand the waiting, he would go into the back yard, but always listening for the ring. 'And no fooling about that ring. The son-of-a-bitch always rang twice, so you'd know it was the postman.'" Lawrence's story reminded Cain of the old Irish tradition that the postman must always ring or in olden days, knock twice. He turned to Lawrence and said, "Vincent, I think I've got my title," Hoopes reported. And Vincent Lawrence's response to Cain's suggestion of *The Postman Always Rings Twice* was "Hey, that is a title. He sure did ring twice for [Frank] Chambers, didn't he?" (Though Chambers did kill Nick, his first attempt was unsuccessful, thus exemplifying how, as Macdonald notes, "everything that happens in this novel happens twice, the first time with a twist [the cat dies instead of the Greek], the second time with a reverse twist.")

Like "Icebox," *Postman* was sold to a movie studio, though it was not filmed for more than ten years. "Mr. Cain's subject matter at the time he wrote was shocking," explained *New York Times* critic John Leonard. "The book was tried for obscenity in Boston, and his own Hollywood did not dare make a movie of it until 10 years after publication, with Lana Turner and John Garfield. And the movie makers dared only after the box-office successes of *Double Indemnity,* directed by Billy Wilder, and *Mildred Pierce,* for which Joan Crawford won an Academy Award. Though the success of *Postman* got Cain back into the studios as a writer, he was never invited to do the adaptations of his own books. Furthermore, he considered his efforts totally unsuccessful: "I want it understood that I consider I have a record of failure unmatched in Hollywood's history," he told *Publishers Weekly.*

In the early 1940s, Cain attempted to establish an authority headed by what he called "a tough mug," to whom authors would turn over their copyrights. "The authority," explained Leonard, "would have protected authors' rights in courts and legislative halls, represented writers in litigation, negotiated contracts, and lobbied in Washington." While Leonard believed that Cain may have been motivated by the discrepancy between the $12 million that Hollywood made on his books and the $100,000 he received, some of Cain's contemporaries interpreted the project as a "Communist plot" or a "totalitarian attempt to control and manipulate creative talent." Cain's efforts failed.

Shortly afterwards, in 1947, Cain returned to Maryland, where he lived until his death in 1977. "During those twenty-nine years," reported Joe Flaherty in the *New York Times Book Review,* "he wrote nine novels. Three found a publisher; none found a public. Why he left California (he called it El Dorado) and went back to the Eastern Shore is a psychological mystery." In assessing his contribution to modern literature, Madden, writing in his *James M. Cain,* concluded: "Certainly Cain's art, more than anything else, moves even the serious reader to almost complete emotional commitment to the traumatic experiences Cain renders; and this artistic control convinces me that without his finest novels—*The Postman, Serenade, Mildred Pierce,* and *The Butterfly*—the cream of our twentieth-century fiction would be thinner. Straddling realism and expressionism, he often gives us a vivid account of life on the American scene as he has observed and experienced it; and, in his best moments, he provides the finer vibrations afforded by the esthetic experience. Cain takes us through experiences whose special quality is found in no other writer's work."

Several of Cain's novels were published posthumously, including the thriller *Cloud Nine*. Published in 1984, it harkens back to Cain's earlier work in its tale of vengeance. Sonya, only sixteen, is brutally raped by Burl. Pregnant, she is comforted by Burl's half-brother Graham, who marries her against the wishes of his admirer, an older woman. The results are murder, jealousy, and revenge. Critics were mixed in their reviews of the work. While some reviewers such as a *Booklist* critic found *Cloud Nine* to be a "minor masterpiece and a publishing event of some note," others such as a *Kirkus Reviews* contributor deemed it "an unwise posthumous publication." Still other reviewers scolded the author's dated treatment of his subject manner: "archaic attitudes toward women and sex," commented Lynette Friesen in *Library Journal*. Charles Shibuk in the *Armchair Detective* noted that the storyline "may often strain credulity" but declared *Cloud Nine* was "definitely worth reading."

*BIOGRAPHICAL/CRITICAL SOURCES:*

*BOOKS*

*Authors in the News*, Volume 1, Gale, 1976.
*Contemporary Literary Criticism*, Gale, Volume 3, 1975, Volume 11, 1979, Volume 28, 1984.
Farrell, James T., *Literature and Morality*, Vanguard, 1947.
Fine, Richard, *James M. Cain and the American Authors' Authority*, University of Texas Press (Austin), 1992.
Frohock, W. M., *The Novel of Violence in America: 1920-1950*, University Press in Dallas, 1950.
Hoopes, Roy, *Cain: The Biography of James M. Cain*, Holt, 1982.
Madden, David, editor, *Tough Guy Writers of the Thirties*, Southern Illinois University Press, 1968,
Madden, David, *James M. Cain*, Twayne, 1970.
Marling, William, *The American Roman Noir: Hammett, Cain, and Chandler*, University of Georgia Press (Athens), 1995.
Wilson, Edmund, *Classics and Commercials*, Farrar, Straus, 1950.

*PERIODICALS*

*Armchair Detective*, Fall, 1987, p. 441.
*Booklist*, June 15, 1984, p. 1409.
*Chicago Tribune Book World*, October 4, 1981.
*Kirkus Reviews*, July 15, 1984, p. 656.
*Library Journal*, July, 1984, p. 1351.
*Nation*, May 22, 1943; June 16, 1969.
*New Republic*, October 6, 1941.
*New Yorker*, January 8, 1966.
*New York Times*, February 5, 1982; January 26, 1989.
*New York Times Book Review*, August 8, 1965; March 2, 1969; April 22, 1976; December 13, 1981.
*Publishers Weekly*, July 24, 1972; June 8, 1984, p. 58.
*Saturday Review*, October 4, 1941; August 14, 1965.
*Time*, August 27, 1965.
*Village Voice*, April 8-14, 1981.
*Washington Post*, January 19, 1969; November 8, 1981.*

* * *

## CALVINO, Italo 1923-1985

*PERSONAL:* Born October 15, 1923, in Santiago de Las Vagas, Cuba; grew up in San Remo, Italy; died following a cerebral hemorrhage, September 19, 1985, in Siena, Italy; son of Mario (a botanist) and Eva (a botanist; maiden name, Mameli) Calvino; married Chichita Singer (a translator), February 19, 1964; children: Giovanna. *Education:* University of Turin, graduated, 1947.

*CAREER:* Writer. Member of editorial staff of Giulio Einaudi Editore, 1947-83; lecturer. *Military service:* Italian Resistance, 1943-45.

*AWARDS, HONORS:* Viareggio Prize, 1957; Bagutta Prize, 1959, for *I racconti*; Veillon Prize, 1963; Premio Feltrinelli per la Narrative, 1972; honorary member of the American Academy and Institute of Arts and Letters, 1975; Oesterreichiches Staatspreis fuer Europaeische Literatur, 1976; *Italian Folktales* was included on the American Library Association's Notable Book List for 1980; Grande Aigle d'Or du Festival du Livre de Nice (France), 1982; honorary degree from Mt. Holyoke College, 1984; Premio Riccione (Italy), for *Il sentiero dei nidi de ragno*.

*WRITINGS:*

*FICTION*

*Il sentiero dei nidi di ragno*, Einaudi (Turin, Italy), 1947, translation by Archibald Colquhoun published as *The Path to the Nest of Spiders*, Collins, 1956, Beacon Press, 1957.

*Ultimo viene il corvo* (short stories; title means "Last Comes the Crow"; also see below), Einaudi, 1949.

*Il visconte dimezzato* (novel; title means "The Cloven Viscount"; also see below), Einaudi, 1952.

*L'entrata en guerra* (short stories; title means "Entering the War"), Einaudi, 1954.

*Il barone rampante* (novel; also see below), Enaudi, 1957, translation by Colquhoun published as *The Baron in the Trees*, Random House, 1959, original Italian text published under original title with introduction, notes and vocabulary by J. R. Woodhouse, Manchester University Press, 1970.

*Il cavaliere inesistente* (novel; title means "The Nonexistent Knight"; also see below), Einaudi, 1959.

*La giornata d'uno scutatore* (novella; title means "The Watcher"; also see below), Einaudi, 1963.

*La speculazione edilizia* (novella; title means "A Plunge into Real Estate"; also see below), Einaudi, 1963.

*Ti con zero* (stories), Einaudi, 1967, translation by William Weaver published as *T Zero*, Harcourt, 1969 (published in England as *Time and the Hunter*, J. Cape, 1970).

*Le cosmicomiche* (stories), Einaudi, translation by Weaver published as *Cosmicomics*, Harcourt, 1968.

*La memoria del mondo* (stories; title means "Memory of the World"), Einaudi, 1968.

(Contributor) *Tarocchi*, F. M. Ricci (Parma), 1969, translation by Weaver published as *Tarots: The Viscount Pack in Bergamo and New York* (limited edition), F. M. Ricci, 1975.

*La citta invisibili* (novel), Einaudi, 1972, translation by Weaver published as *Invisible Cities*, Harcourt, 1974.

*Il castello dei destini incrociati* (includes text originally published in *Tarocchi*), Einaudi, 1973, translation by Weaver published as *The Castle of Crossed Destinies*, Harcourt, 1976.

*Marcovaldo ovvero le stagioni in citta*, Einaudi, 1973, translation by Weaver published as *Marcovaldo: or, The Seasons in the City*, Harcourt, 1983.

*Se una notte d'inverno un viaggiatore* (novel), 1979, translation by Weaver published as *If on a winter's night a traveler*, Harcourt, 1981.

*Palomar* (novel), Einaudi, 1983, translation by Weaver published as *Mr. Palomar*, Harcourt, 1985.

*Cosmicomiche vecchie e nuove* (title means "Cosmicomics Old and New"), Garzanti, 1984.

*Sotto il sole giaguaro* (stories), Garzanti, 1986, translation by Weaver published as *Under the Jaguar Sun*, Harcourt, 1988.

*Numbers in the Dark and Other Stories*, Pantheon (New York City), 1995.

*OMNIBUS VOLUMES*

*Adam, One Afternoon and Other Stories* (contains translation by Colquhoun and Peggy White of stories in *Ultimo viene il corvo* and "La formica argentina"; also see below), Collins, 1957.

*I racconti* (title means "Stories"; includes "La nuvola de smog" and "La formica argentina"; also see below), Einaudi, 1958.

*I nostri antenati* (contains *Il cavaliere inesistente, Il visconte dimezzato*, and *Il barone rampante*; also see below), Einaudi, 1960, translation by Colquhoun with new introduction by the author published as *Our Ancestors*, Secker & Warburg, 1980.

*The Nonexistent Knight and The Cloven Viscount: Two Short Novels* (contains translation by Colquhoun of *Il visconte dimezzato* and *Il cavaliere inesistente*), Random House, 1962.

*La nuvola de smog e La formica argentina* (also see below), Einaudi, 1965.

*Gli amore dificile* (contains stories originally published in *Ultimo viene il corvo* and *I racconti*), Einaudi, 1970, translation by Weaver, Colquhoun, and Wright published as *Difficult Loves*, Harcourt, 1984, translation by Weaver and D. C. Carne-Ross published with their translations of "La nuvola de smog" and *La speculazione edilizia* under same title (also see below), Secker & Warburg.

*The Watcher and Other Stories* (contains translations by Weaver, Colquhoun, and Wright of *La giornata d'uno scutatore,* "La nuvola de smog," and "La formica argentina"), Harcourt, 1971.

*EDITOR*

Cesare Pavese, *La letteratura americana e altri saggi*, Einaudi, 1951.

(And reteller) *Fiabe italiane: Raccolte della tradizione popolare durante gli ultimi cento anni e transcritte in lingua dai vari dialetti*, Einaudi, 1956, translation by Louis Brigante of selections published as *Italian Fables*, Orion Press, 1959, translation by George Martin of complete text published as *Italian Folktales*, Harcourt, 1980.

Pavese, *Poesie edite e inedite*, Einaudi, 1962.

Pavese, *Lettere* (with Lorenzo Mondo and Davide Lajolo) Volume I: *1924-1944*, (sole editor) Volume II: *1945-1950*, Einaudi, 1966.

*Vittorini: Progettazione e letteratura*, All'insegno del pesce d'oro, 1968.

(And reteller) Ludovico Ariosto, *Orlando furioso*, Einaudi, 1970.

Jakob Ludwig Karl Grimm and Wilhelm Karl Grimm, *Fiabe*, Einaudi, 1970.

*L'uccel belverde e altre fiabe italiane*, Einaudi, 1972, translation by Sylvia Mulcahy of selections published as *Italian Folk Tales*, Dent (London), 1975.

*Il principe granchio e altre fiabe italiane*, Einaudi, 1974.

*Racconti fantastici dell'Ottocento*, Mondadori (Milan), 1983, translation published as *Fantastical Tales*, Pantheon, 1994.

Also editor of fiction series "Cento Pagi" for Einaudi.

*OTHER*

*Una pietra sopra: Discorsi di letteratura e societa*, Einaudi, 1980, translation by Patrick Creagh published as *The Uses of Literature: Essays*, Harcourt, 1986.

*Collezione di sabbia: Emblemi bizzarri e inquietanti del nostro passato e del nostro futuro gli og getti raccontano il mondo* (articles), Garzanti, 1984.

*Six Memos for the Next Millenium* (lectures), originally published as *Sulla fiaba*, translation by Creagh, Harvard University Press, 1988.

*The Road to San Giovanni* (autobiographical essays), originally published as *ITA*, translation by Tim Parks, Pantheon, 1993.

Co-editor with Elio Vittorini of literary magazine, *Il Menabo,* 1959-66.

*SIDELIGHTS:* Italian novelist and short story writer Italo Calvino was famous for the monumental collection of Italian fables he edited as well as for the fables he wrote. Commenting in the *New York Times Book Review,* for example, novelist John Gardner called Calvino "one of the world's best fabulists." Although he wrote in what Patchy Wheatley referred to in the *Listener* as a "dazzling variety of fictional styles," his stories and novels were all fables for adults. Gore Vidal noted in a *New York Review of Books* essay that because Calvino both edited and wrote fables he was "someone who reached not only primary school children . . . but, at one time or another, everyone who reads."

Calvino's theory of literature, established very early in his career, dictated his use of the fable. For Calvino, to write any narrative was to write a fable. In *Guide to Contemporary Italian Literature: From Futurism to Neorealism,* Sergio Pacifico quoted a portion of Calvino's 1955 essay "Il midollo del leone" ("The Lion's Marrow") in which the novelist wrote: "The mold of the most ancient fables: the child abandoned in the woods or the knight who must survive encounters with beasts and enchantments remains the irreplaceable scheme of all human stories."

To understand Calvino, therefore, one must first understand the fable. Calvino "portrayed the world around him," Sara Maria Adler noted in *Calvino: The Writer as Fablemaker,* "in the same way it is portrayed in the traditional fable. In all his works, the nature of his narrative coincides with those ingredients which constitute the underlying structure of the genre."

A traditional fable, Adler explained, is told from a child's point of view and usually has a young protagonist. Although not all of Calvino's protagonists or narrators are young, John Gatt-Rutter maintained in the *Journal of European Studies,* "The childlike psychology is characteristic of all [of them], whatever their supposed age." The presence of such a youthful narrator/protagonist in Calvino's work lent a fanciful touch to his fiction because, according to Pacifici, "only a youngster possesses a real sense of enchantment with nature, a sense of tranquility and discovery of the mysteries of life."

Another aspect of the fable is what Adler called "the basic theme of tension between character and environment." A typical tale might have a child lost in the woods, for example. Such tension is also a constant in Calvino's fiction. Adler noted, "No matter what the nature of the author's fantasy may be, in every case his characters are faced with a hostile, challenging environment [over] which they are expected to triumph." In "The Argentine Ant," for instance, a family moves to a house in the country only to find it inhabited by thousands of ants. In a more comic example from *Mr. Palomar,* the title character must decide how to walk by a sunbather who has removed her bathing suit top—without appearing either too interested or too indifferent.

Calvino began his career as a fabulist in the late 1940s while still under the influence of the leading writers of postwar Italy. These authors, who had been kept from writing about the world around them by government censorship, now turned whole-heartedly to their everyday life for themes and action for their narratives. Together they formed the neorealist literary movement and, according to Nicholas A. DeMara in the *Italian Quarterly,* drew "material directly from life and . . . reproduce[d] faithfully real situations through traditional methods."

Conceived in this milieu, Calvino's first novel, *The Path to the Nest of Spiders,* and his short story collections, *Adam, One Afternoon* and *L'entrata in guerra* ("Entering the War"), are all realistic. A *Times Literary Supplement* reviewer noted, for example, that the narratives were "sometimes based on autobiography, and mainly set against the background of recent Italian history and politics." But even while the three works portrayed the realities of war, Calvino's imagination was the dominant element.

The Italian novelist Cesare Pavese was one of the first to note the appearance of fantasy in Calvino's work. Adler reported that, in a 1947 review of *The Path to the Nest of Spiders,* Pavese praised the book's originality, noting "the shrewdness of Calvino, squirrel of the pen, has been this, to climb upon the plants, more in play than out of fear, and to observe . . . life like a fable of the forest, noisy, multi-colored, [and] 'different.'"

Following the standard form of a fable, *The Path to the Nest of Spiders* has a young protagonist, an adolescent boy named Pin. According to critics DeMara and Adler, Calvino's choice of Pin as his protagonist allowed the novelist to add fanciful elements to an otherwise realistic story. "In [*The Path to the Nest of Spiders*]," DeMara stated, "Calvino portray[ed] an essentially realistic world, but through the use of the adolescent figure he [was] frequently able to inject into the work a sense of fantasy." Pin is nearly a child, and he describes his world as many children do, using a combination of real and imaginary elements. A fable-like quality is added to the novel, Adler observed, because "seen through the boy's own eyes . . . [everything] is thus infused with a fanciful and spirited attitude toward life. . . . The countryside may be as lyrical as an animated cartoon, while at other times it may assume the proportions of a nightmare."

Calvino's childlike imagination and sense of playfulness filled his work with fantasy but also served another purpose. According to J. R. Woodhouse in *Italo Calvino: A Reappraisal and Appreciation of the Trilogy,* "Calvino's description of child-like candour is often a very telling way of pointing to an anomaly, a stupidity in society, as well as providing a new and refreshing outlook on often well-worn themes." In this way Calvino added another fable-like dimension to his work, that of moral instruction.

Young people play prominent roles in all three of the novels in Calvino's *Our Ancestors* trilogy: *The Cloven Viscount, The Baron in the Trees,* and *The Nonexistent Knight.* The "tension between character and environment" and the moral intent are also clear in the three works. They demonstrate the reasoning behind JoAnn Cannon's assertion in *Modern Fiction Studies* that "the fantastic in Calvino is not a form of escapism, but is grounded in a persistent sociopolitical concern."

The narrator of *The Baron in the Trees,* for instance, is the younger brother of the twelve-year-old baron of the title who ascends into the trees to avoid eating snail soup. In *Books Abroad,* Pacifici noted that *The Baron in the Trees* stands for man "who, by choosing and acting an extraordinarily eccentric role, tries to fulfill a certain aspiration of diversity apparently denied to man in our age." And in his introduction to *Our Ancestors,* Calvino explained the meaning of *The Cloven Viscount,* a narrative about a soldier split in half by a cannonball during a crusade: "Mutilated, incomplete, an enemy to himself is modern man; Marx called him 'alienated,' Freud 'repressed'; a state of ancient harmony is lost, [and] a new state of completeness aspired to."

Calvino's ability to fuse reality and fantasy captured the imagination of critics on both sides of the Atlantic. For example, in the *New York Times Book Review* Alan Cheuse wrote about Calvino's "talent for transforming the mundane into the marvelous," and in the *London Review of Books* Salman Rushdie referred to Calvino's "effortless ability of seeing the miraculous in the quotidian." According to *New York Times* reviewer Anatole Broyard, the books in which Calvino perfected this tendency were three later works: *Cosmicomics, Invisible Cities,* and *If on a winter's night a traveler.* With their juxtaposition of fantasy and reality these books led critics such as John Updike and John Gardner to compare Calvino with two other master storytellers noted for using the same technique in their fiction: Jorge Luis Borges and Gabriel Garcia Marquez.

The stories in *Cosmicomics*—as well as most of the stories in *T Zero* and *La memoria del mondo* (*Memory of the World*)—chronicle the adventures of Qfwfq, a strange, chameleon-like creature who was present at the beginning of the universe, the formation of the stars, and the disappearance of the dinosaurs. In a playful scene typical of Calvino—and reminiscent of the comic episodes of Garcia Marquez's *One Hundred Years of Solitude*—Qfwfq describes how time began: According to his story, all the universe was contained in a single point until the day one of the inhabitants of the point, Mrs. Ph(i)Nko, decided to make pasta for everyone. Rushdie explained, "The explosion of the universe outwards . . . is precipitated by the first generous impulse, the first-ever 'true outburst of general love,' when . . . Mrs. Ph(i)Nko cries out: 'Oh, if I only had some room, how I'd love to make some noodles for you boys.'"

Even as his fiction became more and more fantastic in the Qfwfq stories, Calvino continued to maintain the moral and social overtones present in his earlier work. In *Science-Fiction Studies,* Teresa de Lauretis observed that while Calvino's fiction acquired a science-fiction quality during the 1960s and 1970s due to its emphasis on scientific and technological themes, it was still based on specific human concerns. "The works," she commented, "were all highly imaginative, scientifically informed, funny and inspired meditations on one insistent question: What does it mean to be human, to live and die, to reproduce and to create, to desire and to be?"

In a *New Yorker* review Updike made a similar observation about the seriousness underlying Calvino's fantasies. Updike wrote: "Calvino is . . . curious about the human truth as it becomes embedded in its animal, vegetable, historical, and comic contexts; all his investigations spiral in upon the central question of *How shall we live?*"

*Invisible Cities* was the book which Calvino called his "most finished and perfect" in a *Saturday Review* interview with Alexander Stille. It was also, according to Lorna Sage in the *Observer,* "the book that first brought him large-scale international acclaim."

*Invisible Cities* relates an imaginary conversation between the thirteenth-century explorer Marco Polo and the emperor Kublai Khan in which Polo describes fifty-five different cities within the emperor's kingdom. Critics applauded the book for the beauty of Calvino's descriptions. In the *New Republic,* for instance, Albert H. Carter III called it "a sensuous delight, a sophisticated literary puzzle," while in the *Chicago Tribune* Constance Markey judged it "a fragile tapestry of mood pieces." Perhaps the most generous praise came from *Times Literary Supplement* contributor Paul Bailey, who observed, "This most beautiful of [Calvino's] books throws up ideas, allusions, and breathtaking imaginative insights on almost every page."

*Invisible Cities* is another fable with a youthful Marco Polo and a moral to be pondered. Adler explained: "Polo's task is that of teaching the aging Kublai Khan to give a new meaning to his life by challenging the evil forces in his domain and by insuring the safety of whatever is just. . . . [Polo's] observations . . . are a general explanation of the world—a panoramic view where rich and poor, the living and the dead, young and old, are challenged by the complex battles of existence."

In the *Hudson Review,* Dean Flower compared *Invisible Cities* with one of Calvino's later novels, *The Castle of Crossed Destinies,* calling them both "less novels than meditations on the mysteries of fictive structures." This statement could also be applied to Calvino's most experimental novel, *If on a winter's night a traveler. The Castle of Crossed Destinies,* like *The Nonexistent Knight,* is a chivalric tale filled with knights and adventure. *If on a winter's night a traveler,* however, is not only different from Calvino's previous work, it is also marked by a complexity that makes it his least fable-like book.

In *If on a winter's night a traveler,* Calvino parodied modern fictional styles in a complicated novel-within-a-novel format. But even this novel included at least one element of the fable. In *Newsweek* Jim Miller noted that in Calvino's introduction to *Italian Folktales* the novelist wrote, "There must be present [in the . . . tale] the infinite possibilities of mutation, the unifying element in everything: men, beasts, plants, things." While the fable explores mutation in nature, in *If on a winter's night a traveler* Calvino explored the "infinite possibilities of mutation" within the novel.

After his death, Calvino's widow oversaw the issue of new volumes of his work in English. *The Road to San Giovanni* is a compilation of several essays or "memory exercises" that are the closest Calvino ever came to writing an autobiography. These works span his development as a writer from his boyhood in San Remo during the 1930s, through his work in the Italian Resistance during World War II, to his experience as an expatriate in Paris during the 1960s. "The Calvino that emerges here is extremely self-conscious, offering finely observed evocations of the Italian landscape or a Parisian suburb, but also a running metacommentary on the act of writing a biography," wrote Lawrence Venuti in the *New York Times Book Review.* "A Cinema-Goers Autobiography" details Calvino's adolescent obsession with the movies, particularly American movies with their popular movie stars. Movies, for Calvino, helped him satisfy his craving for fantasy, which would show up later in his work. "Memories of Battle" chronicles a part of Calvino's resistance activities during the war, and also, the vagaries of memory as he tries to recall it. The title essay tells of Calvino's rift with his father, who wanted him to continue in the family business of farming. John Updike commented in the *New Yorker* that "through this small, scattered, posthumous book, we draw closer to the innermost Calvino than we have before."

*Numbers in the Dark and Other Stories,* also published after Calvino's death, gave English-speaking audiences a chance to read some of the author's earlier short stories, as well as a few that had not been translated into English. These tales span his development from a 1943 story on a Communist brigade to a later work about a man who goes to get ice for his whisky and finds his apartment, upon return, turned into an icy world. "The earliest stories present a Calvino still preoccupied with the war and the impact of fascism," wrote Aamer Hussein in *New Statesman and Society.* "He demonstrates his belief—still prevalent among writers resisting dictatorships—in the fable as the best vehicle for veiled protest." Calvino moved from his early interest in communism to later esoteric works in which he conducts imaginary interviews with historical figures such as Montezuma, Henry Ford, and a Neanderthal. "This collection brings American readers a somewhat different Calvino, more the product of his cultural and political origins in Italy, but as ever a writer of fantasies that possess extraordinary precision and beauty," concluded Lawrence Venuti in the *New York Times Book Review.*

Calvino's childlike imagination allowed him to leave the tenets of neorealism behind and opened up infinite possibilities for his fiction. He imaginatively used the traditional fable form to write non-traditional fiction. Although he was a fabulist, according to Pacifici in *A Guide to Modern Italian Literature,* Calvino's works were "not . . . flights from reality but [came] from the bitter reality of our twentieth century. They are the means—perhaps the only means left to a writer tired of a photographic obsession with modern life—to re-create a world where people can still be people—that is, where people can still dream and yet understand."

*BIOGRAPHICAL/CRITICAL SOURCES:*

*BOOKS*

Adler, Sara Maria, *Calvino: The Writer as Fablemaker,* Ediciones Jose Porrua Turanzas, 1979.

*Contemporary Literary Criticism,* Gale, Volume 5, 1976, Volume 8, 1978, Volume 11, 1979, Volume 22, 1982, Volume 33, 1984, Volume 39, 1986, Volume 73, 1993.

Gatt-Rutter, John, *Writers and Politics in Modern Italy,* Holmes & Meier, 1978.

Mandel, Siegfried, editor, *Contemporary European Novelists,* Southern Illinois University Press, 1986.

Pacifici, Sergio, *A Guide to Contemporary Italian Literature: From Futurism to Neorealism,* World, 1962.

Re, Lucia, *Calvino and the Age of Neorealism: Fables of Estrangement,* Stanford University Press, 1990.

Woodhouse, J. R., *Italo Calvino: A Reappraisal and an Appreciation of the Trilogy,* University of Hull, 1968.

*PERIODICALS*

*Atlantic,* March, 1977.

*Chicago Tribune,* November 10, 1985.

*Commonweal,* November 8, 1957; June 19, 1981; June 2, 1989, p. 339.

*Globe and Mail* (Toronto), July 7, 1984; January 25, 1986.

*Hudson Review,* summer, 1984.

*Italian Quarterly,* winter, 1971; winter-spring, 1989, pp. 5-15, 55-63.

*Journal of European Studies,* December, 1975.

*Listener,* February 20, 1975; March 17, 1983, p. 24.

*London Review of Books,* September 30, 1981; March 26, 1992, pp. 20-21.

*Los Angeles Times Book Review,* November 27, 1983; October 6, 1985; October 20, 1985, p. 15.

*Modern Fiction Studies,* spring, 1978.

*Nation,* February 19, 1977; May 23, 1981; December 29, 1984-January 5, 1985.

*New Criterion,* December, 1985.

*New Leader,* May 16, 1988, p. 5; January 9, 1989, p. 19.
*New Republic,* October 17, 1988, pp. 38-43.
*New Statesman,* April 3, 1987, p. 27.
*New Statesman and Society,* February 21, 1992, p. 40; December 1, 1995, p. 38.
*Newsweek,* February 14, 1977; November 17, 1980; June 8, 1981; November 28, 1983; October 8, 1984; October 21, 1985.
*New Yorker,* February 24, 1975; April 18, 1977; February 23, 1981; August 3, 1981; September 10, 1984; October 28, 1985, pp. 25-27; November 18, 1985; May 30, 1994, p. 105.
*New York Review of Books,* November 21, 1968; January 29, 1970; May 30, 1974; May 12, 1977; June 25, 1981; December 6, 1984; November 21, 1985; October 8, 1987, p. 13; September 29, 1988, p. 74; July 14, 1994, p. 14.
*New York Times,* October 11, 1959; August 6, 1968; January 13, 1971; May 5, 1981; November 9, 1983, p. C20; September 25, 1984; November 26, 1984; September 26, 1985.
*New York Times Book Review,* November 8, 1959; August 5, 1962; August 12, 1968; August 25, 1968; October 12, 1969; February 7, 1971; November 17, 1974; April 10, 1977; October 12, 1980; June 21, 1981; January 22, 1984, p. 8; October 7, 1984; March 20, 1988, pp. 1, 30; October 23, 1988, p. 7; October 10, 1993, p. 11; November 26, 1995, p. 16.
*New York Times Magazine,* July 10, 1983.
*PMLA,* May, 1975.
*Saturday Review,* December 6, 1959; November 15, 1969; May, 1981; March/April, 1985.
*Science-Fiction Studies,* March, 1986, pp. 97-98.
*Spectator,* February 22, 1975; May 14, 1977; August 15, 1981; September 24, 1983, pp. 23-24; November 20, 1993, p. 46.
*Time,* January 31, 1977; October 6, 1980; May 25, 1981; October 1, 1984; September 23, 1985; November 14, 1988, p. 95.
*Times* (London), July 9, 1981; September 1, 1983; October 3, 1985.
*Times Literary Supplement,* April 24, 1959; February 23, 1962; September 8, 1966; April 18, 1968; February 9, 1973; December 14, 1973; February 21, 1975; January 9, 1981; July 10, 1981; September 2, 1983; July 12, 1985; September 26, 1986; March 11, 1994, p. 29.
*Village Voice,* December 16, 1981.
*Voice Literary Supplement,* October, 1986.
*Washington Post,* January 13, 1984.
*Washington Post Book World,* April 25, 1971; October 12, 1980; June 7, 1981; November 18, 1984; September 22, 1985; November 16, 1986.

*OBITUARIES:*

*PERIODICALS*

*Chicago Tribune,* September 21, 1985.
*Detroit Free Press,* September 20, 1985.
*Listener,* September 26, 1985, p. 9.
*Los Angeles Times,* September 21, 1985, part IV, p. 7.
*Newsweek,* September 30, 1985.
*New York Times,* September 20, 1985, p. A20.
*Observer,* September 22, 1985, p. 25.
*Times* (London), September 20, 1985.
*Washington Post,* September 20, 1985.*

* * *

**CAMPBELL, Joseph 1904-1987**

*PERSONAL:* Born March 26, 1904, in New York, NY; died October 30, 1987, in Honolulu, HI; son of Charles William (a hosiery importer and wholesaler) and Josephine (Lynch) Campbell; married Jean Erdman (a dancer and choreographer), May 5, 1938. *Education:* Canterbury School, graduated 1921; attended Dartmouth College, 1921-22; Columbia University, A.B., 1925, M.A., 1927, additional graduate study, 1927-28, 1928-29; graduate study at the University of Paris, 1927-28, and the University of Munich, 1928-29.

*CAREER:* Independent study of mythology, 1929-32; Canterbury School, New Milford, CT, teacher of French, German, and ancient history, 1932-33; Sarah Lawrence College, Bronxville, NY, member of literature department faculty, 1934-72. Lecturer, Foreign Service Institute, U.S. Department of State, 1956-73, and at Columbia University, 1959. President, Creative Film Foundation, 1954-63, and of Foundation for the Open Eye, beginning 1973. Trustee, Bollingen Foundation, 1960-69.

*MEMBER:* American Folklore Society, American Oriental Society, American Society for the Study of Religion (president, 1972-75), American Academy of Psychotherapists (honorary member), American Institute of Arts and Letters, Society for Arts, Religion and Contemporary Culture, Century Club, New York Athletic Club.

*AWARDS, HONORS:* Proudfit fellow, 1927-28, 1928-29; grants-in-aid for editing Zimmer volumes, 1946-

55; National Institute of Arts and Letters grant in literature, 1949, for *The Hero with a Thousand Faces;* Distinguished Scholar Award, Hofstra University, 1973; D.H.L., Pratt Institute, 1976; Melcher Award for contribution to religious liberalism, 1976, for *The Mythic Image;* National Arts Club medal of honor for literature, 1985; elected to the American Academy of Arts and Letters, 1987.

*WRITINGS:*

(With Maud Oakes and Jeff King) *Where the Two Come to Their Father: A Navaho War Ceremonial,* Pantheon, 1943.

(With Henry Morton Robinson) *A Skeleton Key to "Finnegans Wake,"* Harcourt, 1944.

*The Hero with a Thousand Faces,* Pantheon, 1949, revised edition, Princeton University Press, 1980.

*The Masks of God,* Viking, Volume 1: *Primitive Mythology,* 1959, Volume 2: *Oriental Mythology,* 1962, Volume 3: *Occidental Mythology,* 1964, Volume 4: *Creative Mythology,* 1968, published together, Arkana (New York City), 1991.

*The Flight of the Wild Gander,* Viking, 1969, published as *The Flight of the Wild Gander: Explorations in the Mythological Dimension,* HarperPerennial (New York City), 1990.

*Myths to Live By,* Viking, 1972.

(With M. J. Abadie) *The Mythic Image,* Princeton University Press, 1974.

(With Richard Roberts) *Tarot Revelations,* Alchemy Books, 1980, 2nd edition, Vernal Equinox, 1982.

*Historical Atlas of World Mythology,* Van der Marck, Volume 1: *The Way of the Animal Powers,* 1983, revised edition published in two parts, Part 1: *Mythologies of the Primitive Hunters and Gatherers,* 1988, Part 2: *Mythology of the Great Hunt,* 1988, Volume 2: *The Way of the Seeded Earth,* Part 1: *The Sacrifice,* 1988.

*The Inner Reaches of Outer Space: Metaphor as Myth and as Religion,* Van der Marck, 1986.

(With Bill Moyers) *The Power of Myth* (also see below; interviews), Doubleday, 1988.

*Renewal Myths and Rites of the Primitive Hunters and Planters,* Spring Publications (Dallas), 1989.

*Transformations of Myth through Time,* Perennial Library (New York City), 1990.

(With Phil Cousineau and Stuart L. Brown) *The Hero's Journey: The World of Joseph Campbell: Joseph Campbell on His Life and Work,* HarperSanFrancisco, 1990.

(With Michael Toms) *An Open Life: Joseph Campbell in Conversation with National Public Radio's "New Dimensions" Host Michael Toms,* edited by John M. Maher, and Dennis Briggs, Perennial Library, 1990.

*The Universal Myths: Heroes, Gods, Tricksters, and Others,* edited by Alexander Eliot and Mircea Eliade, New American Library (New York City), 1990.

*A Joseph Campbell Companion: Reflections on the Art of Living,* edited by Diane K. Osbon, HarperCollins (New York City), 1991.

*Mythic Worlds, Modern Words: On the Art of James Joyce,* edited by Edmund L. Epstein, HarperCollins, 1993.

(With Fraser Boa) *The Way of Myth: Talking with Joseph Campbell,* Shambhala (Boston), 1994.

*EDITOR*

Heinrich Robert Zimmer, *Myths and Symbols in Indian Art and Civilization,* Pantheon, 1946.

Zimmer, *The King and the Corpse: Tales of the Soul's Conquest of Evil,* Pantheon, 1948.

Zimmer, *Philosophies of India,* Pantheon, 1951.

*The Portable Arabian Nights,* Viking, 1952.

(General editor) *Papers from the Eranos Yearbooks,* Princeton University Press, Volume 1: *Spirit and Nature,* 1954, Volume 2: *The Mysteries,* 1955, Volume 3: *Man and Time,* 1957, Volume 4: *Spiritual Disciplines,* 1960, Volume 5: *Man and Transformation,* 1964, Volume 6: *The Mystic Vision,* 1969.

Zimmer, *The Art of Indian Asia,* Pantheon, 1955, two-volume 2nd edition, Princeton University Press, 1960.

*Myths, Dreams, and Religion,* Dutton, 1970.

*The Portable Jung,* Viking, 1972.

Rato K. Losang, *My Life and Times: The Story of a Tibetan Incarnation,* Dutton, 1977.

(With Charles Muses) *In All Her Names: Explorations of the Feminine in Divinity,* HarperSanFrancisco, 1991.

Also editor of *The Mountainy Singer* by Seosamh MacCathmhaoil, AMS Press. General editor of "Myth and Man" series, Thames & Hudson, 1951-54.

*CONTRIBUTOR*

*The Complete Grimm's Fairy Tales,* Pantheon, 1944.

*James Joyce: Two Decades of Criticism,* Vanguard, 1948.

*Psychoanalysis and Culture,* International Universities Press, 1951.

*Basic Beliefs,* Sheridan, 1959.

*Culture in History,* Columbia University Press, 1960.

*Myth and Mythmaking,* Braziller, 1960.
*Myths,* McGraw, 1974.

Contributor of articles to publications.

*ADAPTATIONS: The Power of Myth* was adapted as a six-part television series, Public Broadcasting Service (PBS), 1988; *Transformations of Myth through Time* was adapted as a thirteen-part television series, PBS, 1990; *The Hero's Journey* was adapted as a television film, PBS.

*SIDELIGHTS:* One of the world's leading authorities on mythology and folklore and a prominent figure in the New Age movement of the 1980s and 1990s, Joseph Campbell believed that all myth has a common source in the biology of humans. Mythology is "a production of the human imagination," he told D. J. R. Bruckner of the *New York Times Book Review,* "which is moved by the energies of the organs of the body operating against each other. These are the same in human beings all over the world and this is the basis for the archetypology of myth." Campbell saw the world's myths, religions, and rituals to be humanity's explanations for the essential mystery of creation. "God," Garry Abrams of the *Los Angeles Times* quoted Campbell explaining, "is a metaphor for a mystery that absolutely transcends all categories of human thought. . . . It's as simple as that." Jeffrey Hart of the *National Review* explained that Campbell "sought out the great overarching patterns of human perception that underlie the stories human beings tell about themselves, that inform the works of art they create and the rites they perform." For modern man, Campbell advocated a new mythology, "a modern, planetary myth," he told Chris Goodrich of *Publishers Weekly,* "not one of this group or that group." Campbell's work made him "known among an avid circle of friends and admirers as the Western world's foremost authority on mythology," K. C. Cole wrote in *Newsweek.* Hart called Campbell "a great modern anthropologist, . . . a great modern artist, . . . [and] one of the last survivors of the heroic age of twentieth-century modernism. Like Goethe, whom he worshipped, he combined science and art."

Born in 1904 into a staunch Roman Catholic family, as a young boy in New York City, Campbell was first drawn to mythology by his interest in Native Americans. After a visit to Buffalo Bill's Wild West Show at Madison Square Garden, Campbell invaded his local library and read every book they had about Indian tribes. He spent his spare time touring the American Museum of Natural History with his brother and sister, enthralled by the Indian exhibits there. In school he studied the primitive cultures of the South Pacific and by the time he entered college, Campbell had a wide knowledge of folklore and mythology. Majoring in English and earning a degree in medieval literature, he dropped out of Columbia University's doctoral program when told that mythology was not a fit subject for his thesis.

Campbell disagreed, and spent the remainder of his career proclaiming the validity of myth, and warning of the results of its loss from the common literacy. As he would explain to Bill Moyers many years later in *The Power of Myth,* Classical literature—Greek and Roman writings, readings from the Bible—were the mainstay of education up until the early twentieth century. When the study of such "great books" was discontinued, a fact bemoaned by many scholars, among them Allan Bloom in his *The Closing of the American Mind,* "a whole tradition of Occidental mythological information was lost," according to Campbell. "It used to be that these stories were in the minds of people. When the story is in your mind, then you see its relevance to something happening in your own life. . . . These bits of information from ancient times, which have to do with the themes that have supported human life, built civilizations, and informed religions over the millennia, have to do with deep inner problems, inner mysteries, inner thresholds of passage." Such stories, myths, provide each individual with "guidesigns," or "clues to the spiritual potentialities of the human life" that gives meaning to existence on Earth.

For several years after his exodus from Columbia University, Campbell studied mythology on his own. A stay in California allowed him to accompany a scientific expedition along the Alaskan coast. For a year and a half he lived in a cabin in rural Woodstock, New York, reading scholarly works on mythology, legends, and folklore. In 1932 he was offered a teaching position with his old preparatory school, the Canterbury School, in New Milford, Connecticut. Two years later he moved to Sarah Lawrence College, where he taught literature until 1972.

During his years as a teacher, Campbell produced a massive body of work in the fields of comparative mythology, folklore, and religion. He began during the 1940s by editing the works of the late Heinrich Zimmer, a friend of his who was also a noted Indologist at Columbia University. With Henry Morton Robinson, Campbell also wrote a literary interpretation of James Joyce's novel *Finnegans Wake* in which the story's archetypical origins are explained. The book, *A Skeleton Key to "Finnegans Wake,"* is, Andrew Klavan recounted in the *Village Voice,* "still a standard textbook 44 years after its publication." Campbell's interest in Joyce would extend throughout his career; in 1993 a collection of his speeches and essays on the Irish writer and his work were edited by Edmund L. Epstein as *Mythic Worlds, Modern Words: On the Art of James Joyce.* Containing a memorable review of playwright Thorton Wilder's *The Skin of Our Teeth,* which Campbell condemned as *Finnegans Wake* rewritten for Americans, the collection includes his analysis of the mythic origins of several of Joyce's major written works.

Campbell's first book as sole author, *The Hero with a Thousand Faces,* took him four years to write. Campbell felt "that the four years he put into *The Hero* were sublime madness, a passage of joyous creativity he has not matched since," Donald Newlove reported in *Esquire. The Hero with a Thousand Faces* attempts to unite the world's mythologies into what Campbell called a *monomyth,* the single underlying story which all the myths tell. This story outlines the proper way for humans to live. "In Campbell's view," Cole said of the book's thesis, "the myths are not merely entertaining tales, but are allegorical instructions that seek to teach us, as he put it, nothing less than 'how to live a human lifetime under any circumstances.'"

*The Hero with a Thousand Faces* focuses on the many tales of heroes who overcome great odds to perform impossible tasks. Campbell discerns a consistent pattern in these tales: The hero is called to an adventure which he accepts; he is given charms or magical weapons by a protective figure who is older and wiser; the hero then journeys into an unknown land where he meets demons and undergoes great suffering; the hero triumphs over the menace and is reborn in the process; he then returns to his homeland enriched with new insights that will benefit his people. Campbell saw this story as primarily an inner battle in which the hero undergoes a kind of self-psychotherapy, confronts his own darker side, and gains a greater understanding of himself and his culture in the process.

Early reviewers of *The Hero with a Thousand Faces* were put off by Campbell's almost mystical tone. "It is all presented," complained Max Radin of the *New York Times Book Review,* "in the mystical and pseudo-philosophical fog of Jung." H. A. Reinhold of *Commonweal* found the book to be "full of inconclusive tales, vague and shadowy parallels pressed into service, as if they were solid proofs, and also complete misunderstandings assembled from an alphabetic register in the back of books eagerly looted by a man obsessed with a faith." A *New Yorker* critic judged *The Hero with a Thousand Faces* to be "one of the most fascinating and maddening books of the season." Despite such critical misgivings, the book was awarded a grant-in-literature from the National Institute of Arts and Letters and went on to sell several hundred thousand copies.

In the four-volume work *The Masks of God,* Campbell surveyed the world's mythology, arguing on behalf of his idea of the monomyth. The first volume, *Primitive Mythology,* begins with the religious ideas of the Bronze Age, when prehistoric men were still hunters and gatherers. At this time, Campbell believed, humankind was stamped with a basic set of religious beliefs, a coda of responses to his questions about the nature of the universe. These beliefs grew from the daily life of early man, a life that consisted of hunting for food, constant migration, and the observance of the cosmos. Because of this experience, peoples throughout the world developed common rituals and beliefs revolving around the hunt, astronomy, and the cycles of nature.

*Primitive Mythology,* according to *Library Journal* reviewer Joseph Bram, is "truly thought-provoking and in some ways path breaking and should be welcomed as a real contribution to the ancient science of mythology." But other critics were less sure about the book's importance. S. P. Dunn, in his review for *American Anthropologist,* claimed that "Campbell has written a stimulating, disturbing, often quite exasperating book." M. E. Opler of the *New York Herald Tribune Book Review* found himself "alternately exhilarated and puzzled. . . . But if Campbell seems sometimes wrong, he is never dull." Philip Rieff of the *American Sociological Review* called *Primitive Mythology* "highly readable, almost too much so. Campbell cannot resist telling a good story. . . . Not all are necessary to his argument." "This work," a *Kirkus* reviewer commented, "is one of enormous scholarship."

The second volume of *The Masks of God,* titled *Oriental Mythology,* turns to the East, covering the myths of Egypt, Japan, China, and India. Campbell discusses the particularly Asian ideas of reincarnation and transcendence of the ego, tracing their historical emergence in Eastern culture. Alan Watts, reviewing the book for *Saturday Review,* called it "the first time that anyone has put the rich complexities of Asian mythology into a clear historical perspective. . . . What Mr. Campbell is offering here is not so much a mythological encyclopedia as a thoroughly documented discussion of the development of myth and of its function in human cultures. It is a bold, imaginative, deeply stimulating work."

Campbell followed the same historical approach in *Occidental Mythology,* the third volume in the series. Beginning with the prehistoric belief in a mother-goddess, he follows the course of Western religious belief down through the centuries. A strong contrast in attitude is shown between the beliefs of the East and West, a difference that Campbell felt was due to environment. The harsher landscape of the West "challenged man to shape his own destiny," explained Bram, "whereas India and the Far East have always fostered the attitudes of passivity, resignation, and fatalism." Watts, reviewing the book for *New Republic,* thought it to be "the best and richest" volume in the series.

*The Masks of God* concludes with the volume *Creative Mythology,* in which Campbell shifts his attention from the myths of the past, created by anonymous authors, to those of the present, which have been created by such artists and writers as Dante, Joyce, and T. S. Eliot. He argues that a new mythology is needed, one that speaks to the entire human race in modern terms, and one that is created by the individual artist from his own life. The book, the *New Yorker* critic summarized, "deals with the modern 'secular' use of myth to express individual experience." Gerald Sykes of the *New York Times Book Review* saw a "major implication" of the book to be that "although we were once given our myths by the group that nurtured us, now we must mine them painfully from the depths of our own experience." Newlove claimed that in *Creative Mythology* Campbell "is out to show the face of God burning away the received masks of culture and to herald the birth within." A *Choice* reviewer called *Creative Mythology* "a landmark in its field," while Bram concluded that it was "a major work of inspired scholarship that no student of mythology will be able to ignore."

In 1974's *The Mythic Image* Campbell turned to the origins of myth, arguing that man's unconscious mind, particularly his dreams, formed the basis of all mythology. Through the use of four hundred illustrations drawn from all over the world, and ranging from prehistoric cave paintings to the avant-garde works of the present day, he showed how the relationship between myth and dream was evident in humankind's artistic creations. Peter S. Prescott of *Newsweek* described the book as "an iconography of the human spirit." Although he felt that psychologist Carl Jung had raised the same point earlier with his theory of the universal unconscious, Winthrop Sargeant of the *New Yorker* nonetheless believed that the idea "has never before been given such a clear and splendid demonstration " as in *The Mythic Image.* Prescott concluded that the book's premise "is convincing, and elegantly supported by hundreds of excellent reproductions of art."

In 1983 Campbell published the first of a planned six-volume series titled *Historical Atlas of World Mythology,* a work meant to relate the world's mythological history in a single, all-encompassing narrative. The initial volume, *The Way of the Animal Powers,* covers the beginnings of human culture and examines the early myth of the Great Hunt, a story common to many prehistoric hunting peoples. Combining an authoritative text with an extensive collection of relevant artwork, *The Way of the Animal Powers* is "a beautiful and informative volume by a world-renowned scholar," as C. Robert Nixon commented in *Library Journal.* Wendy O'Flaherty of the *New York Times Book Review* claimed that "no one but Joseph Campbell could conceive of such a scheme or carry it out as boldly as he does in this extraordinary book. . . . It is an exhilarating experience." Hart concluded that *The Way of the Animal Powers* is "one of the great works of our time."

The second volume in the *Historical Atlas of World Mythology, The Way of the Seeded Earth,* moves forward in time, focusing on the mythology of the first agricultural communities and contrasting the beliefs of that time with the earlier beliefs of nomadic hunting cultures. As Campbell explained to Goodrich: "In *The Way of the Animal Powers,. . .* people are killing animals all the time; that's where the base of the culture rests. This second book is about women's magic—birth and nourishment. The myth shifts from the male-oriented to the gestation-oriented, and the image is of the plant world." Women-centered mythology would serve as the focus of *In All Her Names: Explorations of the Feminine in Divinity,* a collection of essays coedited by Campbell and Charles Muses and published in 1991. The collection contains "The Mystery Number of the Goddess," the last work Campbell completed before his death in 1987. The intended six volumes of the *Historical Atlas of World Mythology* were never completed.

In addition to his writing, Campbell's last project was a number of interviews with Bill Moyers for a special Public Broadcasting Service (PBS) television program titled *The Power of Myth.* These interviews were broadcast in 1988 as a six-part series, drawing an audience of some 2.5 million people per episode. A best-selling book based on the television program was also released. *The Power of Myth* allowed Campbell to range over a host of topics, including the mythology of many cultures, the role of myth in modern society, and the possibilities for myth-making in the future. "Intermittently provocative and ponderous, the conversations are a rambling, serendipitous intellectual journey," explained Clifford Terry in the *Chicago Tribune.* A second PBS television program, *Transformations of Myth through Time,* a collection of thirteen lectures on the evolution of myth, was also collected in book form in 1989. While praised by Campbell's many fans, Steve Weingartner took exception to the author's approach in *Booklist,* contending that the "guru of myth. . . . very typically displays his peculiar mix of cultural relativism and a pronounced bias against the Judeo-Christian cornerstone of our civilization."

Campbell's influence has extended far beyond his death; since 1987, several volumes of interviews, essays, and other works have been collected. *An Open Life: Joseph Campbell in Conversation with National Public Radio's "New Dimensions" Host Michael Toms* is the transcription of ten years' worth of interviews on such diverse subjects as the lost continent of Atlantis and the psychology of the individual in which Campbell "stresses the need to integrate the message of mythology into everyday life," according to a *Los Angeles Times Book Review* piece. Drawing on the focus of his entire career, the mythologist stresses the need for society to relinquish provincial attitudes, religious and political dogmatism, and welcome a multicultural, multiethnic world. A more intimate collection of interviews is contained in *The Hero's Journey: Joseph Campbell on His Life and Work,* which includes discussions with both friends and family members.

Because of his exposure via PBS, Campbell became known to more people after his death than knew him while he was alive, transformed into "one of the world's great scholars and teachers of mythology," Terry reported. As Cole remarked, "Campbell has become the rarest of intellectuals in American life: a serious thinker who has been embraced by the popular culture." Among his most fervent disciples has been filmmaker George Lucas, who credited Campbell with inspiring his movie *Star Wars.* "If it hadn't been for him," Lucas told Wolfgang Saxon of the *New York Times,* "it's possible I would still be trying to write 'Star Wars' today." Some critics have maintained a more cautious approach to Campbell's musings, contending that his cultural relativism has become "lost in the clamor of New Agers looking for a religion to sanctify their self-preoccupation," in the words of *Booklist* reviewer Stuart Whitwell. In addition, in 1989, biographer Brendan Gill attacked Campbell as a closet racist and anti-Semite and condemned the mythologist's "follow your bliss" dictum as defending the principles of anti-humanitarianism promoted by such philosophers as Ayn Rand. "For what is this condition of bliss, as Campbell has defined it?," asked Gill in an essay in the *New York Review of Books.* "If it is only to do whatever makes one happy, then it sanctions selfishness on a colossal scale—a scale that has become deplorably familiar . . . in [the] post-Reagan years." Gill went on to contend that following one's bliss was "bound to interfere sooner or later with another precept that many Americans were brought up to believe in . . . that we are our brother's keeper." Gill contended that throughout his teachings, Campbell's meanings were often misconstrued, that terms like "bliss" and "happiness" remained unclear, while "good" and "evil" were but two sides of the same coin. "From which it can be argued," maintained Gill, "that selfishness and unselfishness, like good and evil, though contradictory in appearance are identical in nature, and may therefore serve equally well as a source of happiness."

While the late mythologist's works and methodology have continued to be studied and debated, his supporters remain steadfast. Sir Lauren van der Post, writing in the London *Times,* cited Campbell for his efforts to "rediscover for a deprived world the fundamental mythological pattern of the human spirit. . . . He has done more than any scholar of our time to reconnect modern man to a reality which his mind and spirit were rejecting at great peril to his well-being and sanity." And Joseph Coates of the *Chicago Tribune* called Campbell "that rare scholar with something really useful to say about how life should be lived."

*BIOGRAPHICAL/CRITICAL SOURCES:*

*BOOKS*

Campbell, Joseph, and Bill Moyers, *The Power of Myth,* Doubleday, 1988.

Campbell, Joseph, Phil Cousineau, and Stuart L. Brown, *The Hero's Journey: The World of Joseph Campbell: Joseph Campbell on His Life and Work,* HarperSanFrancisco, 1990.

Campbell, Joseph, and Diane K. Osbon, *A Joseph Campbell Companion: Reflections on the Art of Living,* HarperCollins, 1991.

Campbell, Joseph, and Fraser Boa, *The Way of Myth: Talking with Joseph Campbell,* Shambhala, 1994.

*Contemporary Literary Criticism,* Volume 69, Gale, 1992.

Frost, William P., *Following Joseph Campbell's Lead in the Search for Jesus' Father,* E. Mellen Press (Lewiston, NY), 1991.

Golden, Kenneth L., *Uses of Comparative Mythology: Essays on the Work of Joseph Campbell,* Garland (New York City), 1992.

Larsen, Stephen, and Robin Larsen, *A Fire in the Mind: The Life of Joseph Campbell,* Doubleday, 1991.

Madden, Lawrence J., *The Joseph Campbell Phenomenon: Implications for the Contemporary Church,* Pastoral Press (Washington, DC), 1992.

Manganaro, Marc, *Myth, Rhetoric, and the Voice of Authority: A Critique of Frazer, Eliot, Frye, and Campbell,* Yale University Press (New Haven), 1992.

Noel, Daniel C., *Paths to the Power of Myth: Joseph Campbell and the Study of Religion,* Crossroad (New York City), 1990.

Sartore, Richard L., *Joseph Campbell on Myth and Mythology,* University Press of America (Lanham, MD), 1993.

Snyder, Thomas Lee, *Myth Conceptions: Joseph Campbell and the New Age,* Baker Books (Grand Rapids, MI), 1995.

Tigue, John W., *The Transformation of Consciousness in Myth: Integrating the Thought of Jung and Campbell,* P. Lang (New York City), 1994

*PERIODICALS*

*America,* February 20, 1993, p. 12.

*American Anthropologist,* December, 1960.

*American Scholar,* summer, 1990, p. 429.

*American Sociological Review,* December, 1960.

*Booklist,* January 15, 1990, p. 959; February 15, 1990, p. 1123.

*Chicago Tribune,* May 23, 1988.

*Choice,* December, 1968; July/August 1989, p. 1824; October, 1990, p. 292.

*Christian Century,* July 5, 1989, p. 652; April 4, 1990, p. 332.

*Christianity Today,* July 14, 1989, p. 61.

*Christian Science Monitor,* October 9, 1969.

*Commentary,* December, 1969.

*Commonweal,* July 8, 1949; April 21, 1989, p. 231.

*Esquire,* September, 1977.

*Kirkus,* August 15, 1959; December 1, 1989, p. 1742.

*Library Journal,* September 1, 1959; January 15, 1964; February 15, 1968; January, 1984; December, 1988, pp. 126-27; February 15, 1990, p. 193; May 15, 1990, p. 82; October 1, 1991, p. 108.

*Los Angeles Times,* May 27, 1987.

*Los Angeles Times Book Review,* May 20, 1990, p. 14.

*National Catholic Reporter,* November 9, 1990, p. 24.

*National Review,* July 13, 1984.

*New Republic,* June 27, 1964; August 3, 1992, p. 29.

*Newsweek,* March 31, 1975; November 14, 1988.

*New Yorker,* May 7, 1949; February 1, 1969; July 21, 1975.

*New York Herald Tribune Book Review,* November 22, 1959.

*New York Review of Books,* September 28, 1989, pp. 16, 18-19; November 9 , 1989, p. 57.

*New York Times,* June 26, 1949; March 22, 1987.

*New York Times Book Review,* May 18, 1969; December 18, 1983.

*People,* November 27, 1989, p. 25.

*Publishers Weekly,* August 23, 1985; April 13, 1990, p. 50; October 11, 1993, p. 81.

*Saturday Review,* June 2, 1962.

*Tikkun,* May-June, 1989, p. 23.

*Times* (London), July 12, 1984.

*Utne Reader,* November-December, 1989, p. 102; March-April, 1990 , p. 38.

*Village Voice,* August 1, 1968; May 24, 1988.

*Washington Post Book World,* January 2, 1994.

*OBITUARIES:*

*PERIODICALS*

*Chicago Tribune,* November 5, 1987.

*New York Times,* November 3, 1987.

*Time,* November 16, 1987.

*Washington Post,* November 4, 1987.*

* * *

**CANETTI, Elias 1905-1994**

*PERSONAL:* Born July 25, 1905, in Russe, Bulgaria; died 1994; son of Jacques (in business) and Mathilde

(Arditti) Canetti; married Venetia Taubner-Calderon, February 26, 1934 (died May 1, 1963); married, wife's name Hera; children: (second marriage) Johanna. *Education:* Attended schools in England, Austria, Switzerland, and Germany; University of Vienna, Dr. Philosophy, 1929. *Religion:* Jewish. *Avocational interests:* Canetti gave *CA* the following list: anthropology, history, psychiatry, history of religions, philosophy, sociology, psychology, and the civilizations of Egypt, Sumer, Greece, Rome, Persia, India, China, Japan, Mexico, Maya, Inca. He added: "It is ridiculous to have so many; but they are all equally important to me and have cost me years and decades of study."

*CAREER:* Writer and lecturer.

*AWARDS, HONORS:* Prix International (Paris), 1949, for *Die Blendung*; Deutscher der Stadt (Vienna), 1966; Deutscher Kritikerpreis (Berlin), 1967; Grosser Oesterreichischer Staatspreis (Vienna), 1968; George Buechner Prize (Darmstadt), 1972; Franz Nabl Prize (Graz), 1975; Nelly Sachs Prize (Dortmund), 1975; Gottfried Keller Pries (Zurich), 1977; Order Pour le merito (Bonn), 1979; Johann Peter Hebel Preis, 1980; Premio Europa Prato (Italy), 1980; Kafka Prize and Nobel Prize for literature, both 1981; Order of Merit, Federal Republic of Germany; D.Litt., University of Manchester; Dr. Philosophy, University of Munich.

*WRITINGS:*

*Hochzeit* (play; first produced in Braunschweig, West Germany, February 6, 1965), [Berlin], 1932, reprinted, Hanser Verlag, 1981, English translation by Gitta Honegger published as *The Wedding*, PAJ Publications, 1986.

*Die Blendung* (novel; title means "The Deception"), H. Reichner, 1935, English translation, under the personal supervision of Canetti, by C. V. Wedgwood published as *Auto-da-fe*, J. Cape, 1946, published as *The Tower of Babel*, Knopf, 1947, reprint published as *Auto-da-fe,* Stein & Day, 1964, reprinted, Seabury, 1979.

*Fritz Wotruba* (criticism), Brueder Rosenbaum, 1955.

*Masse und Macht* (nonfiction), Claassen Verlag, 1960, English translation by Carol Stewart published as *Crowds and Power*, Viking, 1962, reprinted, Seabury, 1978.

*Welt im Kopf,* edited and with an introduction by Erich Fried, Stiasny Verlag, 1962.

*Komoedie der Eitelkeit* (three-part play, written 1933-34; first produced in Braunschweig, November 3, 1965), Hanser Verlag, 1964, Sessler (Munich), 1976, English translation by Honegger published as *Comedy of Vanity and Life-Terms*, PAJ Publications, 1983.

*The Numbered* (play; first produced at Oxford Playhouse, Oxford, England, November 5, 1956), published as *Die Befristeten*, Hanser Verlag, 1964, published as *The Numbered,* Marion Boyars, 1984.

*Dramen* (contains *Hochzeit, Komoedie der Eitelkeit,* and *Die Befristeten*), Hanser Verlag, 1964.

*Aufzeichnungen, 1942-1948* (notebooks), Hanser Verlag, 1965.

*Die Stimmen von Marrakesch* (travel), Hanser Verlag, 1968, English translation by J. A. Underwood published as *The Voices of Marrakesh: A Record of a Visit*, Seabury, 1978.

*Der Andere Prozess*, Neue Rundschau, 1968, English translation by Christopher Middleton published as *Kafka's Other Trial: The Letters to Felice*, Schocken, 1974.

*Macht und Ueberleben: Drei Essays*, Literarische Colloquium, 1972.

*Die Gespaltene Zukunft: Aufsaetz und Gesppraeche*, Hanser Verlag, 1972.

*Die Provinz des Menschen: Aufzeichnungen 1942-1972*, Hanser Verlag, 1973, English translation by Joachim Neugroschel published as *The Human Province*, Seabury, 1978.

(Author of commentary) Alfred Hrdlicka, *Graphik*, Propylaeen (Berlin), 1973.

*Der Ohrenzeuge: 50 Charaktere*, Hanser Verlag, 1974, English translation by Neugroschel published as *Earwitness: Fifty Characters*, Seabury, 1979.

*Das Gewissen der Worte: Essays*, Hanser Verlag, 1975, English translation by Neugroschel published as *The Conscience of Words*, Seabury, 1979.

*Die Gerettete Zunge: Geschichte einer Jugend* (autobiography), Hanser Verlag, 1977, English translation by Neugroschel published as *The Tongue Set Free: Remembrance of a European Childhood,* Seabury, 1979.

*Die Fackel im Ohr: Lebensgeschichte 1921-1931* (autobiography), Hanser Verlag, 1980, English translation by Neugroschel published as *The Torch in My Ear*, Farrar, Straus, 1982.

*Das Augenspiel: Lebensgeschichte 1931-1937* (autobiography), Hanser Verlag, 1985, English translation by Ralph Manheim published as *The Play of the Eyes*, Farrar, Straus, 1986.

*The Agony of Flies: Notes and Notations,* translated by H. F. Broch de Rothermann, Farrar, Straus, 1994.

*SIDELIGHTS:* Nobel Prize-winner Elias Canetti achieved a considerable literary reputation primarily on the strength of two works—his 1935 novel *Die Blendung* (published in English as *Auto-da-fe* and *The Tower of Babel*) and his 1960 psycho-sociological study of crowd behavior, *Masse und Macht* (translated as *Crowds and Power*). These two books established Canetti's position "among the most distinguished writers in contemporary German literature," according to Sidney Rosenfeld in *World Literature Today*. Long admired as a profound thinker in Europe, Canetti was largely overlooked in English-speaking countries until he won the Nobel Prize in 1981. As Susan Sontag notes in the *New York Review of Books*, Canetti's work "has never lacked admirers, and yet aside from scattered reviews he has not been much written about." A recent and aggressive translation program has brought English readers access to most of Canetti's writing, thereby extending his audience beyond the bounds of the literary establishment. Sontag feels that the author's effort "has been to stand apart from other writers and he has succeeded. Shunning the modern means by which a writer gains an audience, he long ago decided that he would, he must, live long enough for his audience to come to him. Canetti is, both literally and by his own ambitions, a writer in exile."

The literal exile to which Sontag alludes began early in Canetti's childhood. Born in Bulgaria to parents whose Jewish forebears were driven from Spain by the Inquisition, Canetti lived in Austria, Switzerland, Germany, and England. Nazi anti-Semitism compelled him to move to England in 1939, and it was in that country—writing in German—that he composed most of his works. *New Yorker* contributor George Steiner suggests that the "wild hazards" of Canetti's own fate have produced "the stoic force that gives to his writings their compelling edge." Although as Rosenfeld notes, Canetti was a writer "whose sensibilities are keenly attuned to the most critical problems of the modern epoch," Sontag and others credit Canetti with a sophisticated perception of the human psyche that transcends the twentieth century and even the modern age. "Canetti is not Eurocentric—one of his large achievements as a mind," writes Sontag. "Conversant with Chinese as well as with European thought, with Buddhism and Islam as with Christianity, Canetti enjoys a remarkable freedom from reductive habits of thinking. He seems incapable of using psychological knowledge in a reductive way."

Several essential ideas intrigued Canetti throughout his working career. His novel *Auto-da-fe* explores one of these, "the destructiveness of paranoia. His great theme is the fascism of the soul, the tendency of the human mind to fortify itself with aggressive power plays," in the words of *Voice Literary Supplement* contributor Gary Giddins. *Chicago Review* essayist Ian Watson contends that in *Auto-da-fe* Canetti uses the minutiae of lunatic delusions to expose "the obsessions and fantasies of everyday life, raised to a new pitch of intensity, where they possess the exaggerated savagery of a cartoon strip." In the *Times Literary Supplement*, Idris Parry comments that Canetti is "a specialist in the observation of fixed ideas. . . . He is fascinated by the delusions of people who live in capsules." Canetti was also associated with a strident rejection of death and an energetic support of life and intellectual growth. Sontag notes: "Canetti insists that death is really unacceptable; unassimilable, because it is what is outside life; unjust, because it limits ambition and insults it." She continues: "Canetti does not justify his yearning for longevity with any appeal to its greater scope for good works. So large is the value of the mind that it alone is used to oppose death."

The theme most closely associated with Canetti, however, is that of the psychology of crowd phenomena, a study that consumed the author for more than thirty years. According to Giddins, Canetti's "fidelity to the study of crowd behavior, . . . surely constitutes one of the most stubborn devotions in contemporary scholarship." In *Crowds and Power*, which he considered his "life's work," Canetti exhaustively explores crowd pathology from historical, psychological, and even biological perspectives, locating its impetus—"the yearning for power—in the very mitosis and cellular colonization from which life derives," to quote Giddins.

Through these and other provocative reflections, Canetti stimulated his own thought and offered his readers intense challenges. *Spectator* correspondent Iris Murdoch claims that Canetti's work produces "that rare sense of being 'let out' into an entirely new region of thought. Canetti has done what philosophers ought to do, and what they used to do: he has provided us with new concepts." In *Modern Austrian Literature*, Marion E. Wiley offers similar praise. Wiley writes: "[The] critic accustomed to the desperate confusion reflected in the literature of the later twentieth century may be moved to note that the reflective writing of Canetti is a stimulating and complementary addition to contemporary prose. It is stimulating to share ideas with an author who verbalizes his thoughts with clarity, frequent wit, and appropriate compassion. It is also encouraging to encounter the refutation of inevitability and the advocacy of spirited inquiry. In this respect Canetti is the antipode to the writer who records primarily the spiritual malnutrition of contemporary society and the resulting loss of illusions. Canetti possesses a view of life which impels him to search for alternative approaches to existence."

Much is known about Canetti's early life by virtue of his three autobiographical volumes, translated from the original German as *The Tongue Set Free: Remembrance of a European Childhood, The Torch in My Ear*, and *The Play of the Eyes*. In these works covering the first third of his life, Canetti recounts the many influences on his emotional and intellectual growth—the polyglot culture into which he was born, the demands of his exacting mother, and the inspiration offered by teachers and European literati. Canetti was born in Russe, Bulgaria, a Danube port city where it was common to hear seven or eight languages spoken every day. In his home, his parents addressed him in Ladino, a Spanish dialect of Sephardic exiles; the servants spoke Bulgarian. Additionally, Canetti's parents used German to communicate private thoughts to one another, "and from this association with secrecy the language seemed to him a vehicle of magical incantation," according to Parry. Sontag also notes that Canetti's family example "and the velocity of his childhood all facilitated an avid relation to language." By the time he turned ten, Canetti knew four languages, including the English he learned during a year his family spent in Manchester. It was German, however, that captured his imagination, even though his mother's methods of teaching it were particularly severe. "I was reborn under my mother's influence to the German language, and the spasm of that birth produced the passion tying me to both the language and my mother," Canetti claims in *The Tongue Set Free*. "Without these two, basically one and the same, the further course of my life would have been senseless and incomprehensible."

From 1913 to 1921, Canetti attended school in Vienna and Zurich, pursuing his greatest interests, literature and writing. His father had died and his mother was consumed with concern that a literary bent would cause her son to become "soft." Determined to expose Canetti to harsh reality, she moved him from Zurich to Frankfurt, a city struggling with the ravages of World War I. Canetti finished his secondary schooling there in 1924 and returned to Vienna to study chemistry—at his mother's insistence—even though he was determined to be a writer. Although chemistry held little appeal for him, he obtained a doctorate in the subject from the University of Vienna in 1929. Canetti's college years in Vienna were made more pivotal by his interest in the work of Viennese satirist Karl Kraus, a sensational orator, critic, and author of the journal *Die Fackel* (*The Torch*). *New York Review of Books* contributor S. S. Prawer suggests that Kraus' public readings left a "profound and lasting impression" on the young Canetti. During that period Canetti also met Bertolt Brecht, Geroge Grosz, and Isaac Babel, and he especially enjoyed a productive working relationship with Babel.

In *The Torch in My Ear*, Canetti describes the "most crucial day" in his life, July 15, 1927. On that day he was enveloped by and "dissolved" into a crowd of irate workers who burned down Vienna's Palace of Justice in protest over a controversial verdict. In that experience, contends Parry, Canetti "found both theme and image for his life's work. . . . From that moment he resolved to dedicate his energies to the study of crowds and mass phenomena." An idea for fiction also came to Canetti in 1927, according to Parry, but the novel was influenced more by Canetti's impressions of paintings—most notably Rembrandt's "The Blinding of Samson" and Breughel's "The Triumph of Death"—as well as his fascination with the grotesque and the power of the fixed idea. At the age of twenty-four, Canetti began to write what he thought would be the first of eight novel-length sketches of monomaniac characters—his tale of the "Book Man's" descent into self-immolation, *Auto-da-fe*.

First published in 1935 as *Die Blendung*, the novel *Auto-da-fe* took on "the monumentality of a classic" almost overnight in Germany, according to Steiner. Its popularity was short-lived, however, because Nazi censors removed it from circulation. After the Second World War, the book slowly began to draw more readers; it was reissued in Germany and an authorized English translation by C. V. Wedgwood appeared in 1946. Modern critics are generous in their praise of the work; some consider it one of the most important novels of the twentieth century. Steiner contends that *Auto-da-fe* "remains a classic study of the violence subtly but steadily present in abstract thought, of the pathological element in pure scholarship." Calling it "uncompromising and brilliant," *Critique* contributor Mark Sacharoff finds the novel the most "obsessional portrayal of obsessive characters in all of literature . . . . *Auto-da-fe*, long buried by a combination of unfavorable circumstances, has again come to light and now has a chance to be re-evaluated."

In *Harper's*, Jeffrey Burke writes that *Auto-da-fe* "describes the descent into madness of a world-renowned but reclusive sinologist whose scholarly life disintegrates at the hands of three vulgar, brutish characters. . . . It is the professor who dominates the novel. Canetti creates him out of the quirks and compulsions of a strong mind steeped in erudition." Sacharoff suggests that all of the four major characters are "driven from minute to minute by a central preoccupation and by all the speculations which radiate from it. . . . Thus, if we are to speak of Canetti's originality, a good starting-point would be the singularity and unswerving purpose with which he has pursued his characters' warped preoccupations." *Spectator* reviewer Kate O'Brien cites the work for its agonizingly slow detail and its sophisticated method: "With dessicated, pedantic caution, [Canetti] reflects fantasy against fact, merges nightmare with routine, cupidity with fanatical innocence, and so establishes his forces as one great hell. . . . All in a curiously dry writing, where no detail is spared, and while asking the most detached patience for phantasmagoria beyond comparable echo. . . . There is no light. Only vileness enthroned, and reason nobly flying to its own obliteration. A mad, magnificent work which we are not able to endure, which perhaps we are right not to accept, but of which we dare not deny the genius or the justification."

In Steiner's view of *Auto-da-fe*, "the holocaust to come somehow cast its hungry shadow on the entire fable." Parry likewise contends that "the destructive fires of history and the ritual fires of mythology" seem to converge in the novel. Parry adds that in the fate of Kien, the central character, "we sense both a timeless human declension into death and a contemporary reference to individuality lost in the forest of flags and figures at Nuremburg, that ordered system of savagery." Whether or not the book prefigured the rise of European fascism, its author certainly foresaw the destruction to come in Germany. Canetti left for Paris in 1938 and moved to England in 1939. Nazism and its extreme measures strengthened Canetti's resolve to delve into the psychology of crowds; however, he retained a loyalty to German culture and continued to write in German, attuned, in Sontag's words, to "the higher cosmopolitanism. . . . With this decision, not the one made by most Jewish intellectuals who were refugees from Hitler, Canetti chose to remain unsullied by hatred, a grateful son of German culture who wants to help make it what one can continue to admire. And he has."

*Masse und Macht*, translated as *Crowds and Power*, is the culmination of more than thirty years' work for Canetti. According to Bruce Cook in the *Washington Post Book World*, the book "astonished the intellectual world—not just with its scholarship, some of it from the most recondite sources, but also with its insights, which are packed into gnomic essays . . . that can be read independently but stand as building blocks of the whole work." Cook adds: "It is a book that is not easily summarized, ranging as it does over the whole of human history to examine every conceivable aspect of mass psychology. . . . Its style, anecdotal and accessible, slyly implies the author's attitude of skepticism toward human institutions and his contempt for the men whom historians hold great. *Crowds and Power* is the nearest thing to a book of wisdom we are likely to get in the 20th century." Murdoch feels that to deal adequately with the work, "one would have to be, like its author, a mixture of historian, sociologist, psychologist, philosopher and poet. One is certainly confronted here with something large and important: an extremely imaginative, original and massively documented theory of the psychology of crowds."

When evaluating *Crowds and Power*, critics stress its unique blend of historical/psychological discourse and poetic anecdotage. In an essay for *MOSAIC: A Journal for the Comparative Study of Literature and Ideas*, Dagmar Barnouw suggests that Canetti "does not judge crowds directly . . . from a particularly 'elitist' position, or indirectly like the stoical Freud who finds them frighteningly alien and therefore keeps them at bay. He demonstrates their destructive potential, their deadly interaction with systems of power whose operators know, as Hitler for instance showed very clearly, that the member of a mass society which is, of course, a hierarchically structured group of a great number of individuals, is willing to forget the sting of death . . . if he can rid himself, through temporary immersion in the crowd, of the sting of isolation." Burke notes: "Having made the uncommon choice of so common a fact of life as crowds, [Canetti] then supplies his own definitions, arrives at conclusions, and supports his findings with references from decades of reading in world literature, myth, history, and anthropology. In doing so, he arrives at a level of discourse that is less convincing than it is cerebrally poetic." Despite this objection, Burke claims that *Crowds and Power* "is capable of engaging a willing mind." Murdoch calls the book "marvelously rewarding . . . even if one were to read it without any theoretical interests at all. It is written in a simple, authoritative prose, . . . and it is radiant with imagination and humor. . . . We need and we shall always need the visions of great imaginers and solitary men of genius."

"Since the publication of *Crowds and Power*, Canetti has written several . . . works that encircle the major works like satellites," writes Giddins. "But taken together they also suggest a new and less isolated stage in Canetti's devotion to writing." Canetti's other publications include volumes of essays and aphorisms, plays, criticism, a travelogue, a highly regarded study of a portion of Franz Kafka's letters, and the three volumes of autobiography. Cook feels that as each piece of Canetti's work receives translation, the author "is more clearly defined as the important figure in European literature that he certainly is." Giddins sees a common thread that unites all of Canetti's disparate works. The critic comments: "As novelist, philosopher, and autobiographer, Canetti, the intransigent moral witness, offers no moral codes, utopian dreams, or escape hatches for 'our monstrous century.' The only code to which he adheres absolutely—a writer's code—is to stand in undaunted opposition to his time. . . . At 60, Canetti was essentially a two-book writer. His subsequent work can be read as an attempt to integrate the writer into the vision, to demonstrate that 'the representative writer of this age' can personally exemplify the virtues—diligence, disaffection, scholarship, realism—that make grace possible in an insane world."

One of these publications, *The Agony of Flies: Notes and Notations,* contains Canetti's original German counterpointed by its English translation. The work is a collection of Canetti's impressions and adages. For a *Kirkus Reviews* contributor, however, the "shards . . . read like diary entries ripped prematurely from their notebooks." A reviewer for the *Washington Post Book World* finds some of the observations "cryptic" but others "while elliptical, seem like the very answer to our prayers." Other critics note profound insight in *The Agony of Flies,* such as T. L. Cooksey in *Library Journal,* who remarks, "Like the Confucian *Analects,* which deeply influenced Canetti, these are the fragments of a wise teacher."

Canetti eschewed the publicity surrounding his choice as a Nobel Prize recipient, and continued to live and write far from the public eye. As William Gass observes in *New Republic,* Canetti "achieved such fame as to be unknown all over the world. His obscurity is a part of his character, and is a credit to him, for he might be more widely recognized if his thought were sly and riddling, got up in a seductive lingo all its own so as to seem complex and problematic, not simply, plainly, and vertiginously deep." *Spectator* contributor Paul Theroux offers concurrent praise. "Canetti's reputation has been so formidable as to be off-putting"; Theroux contends, "and the less a person like Canetti is read the more grotesque he seems, until at last he becomes merely a terrifying presence. . . . The strange thing is that Canetti sometimes seems so original as to be an invented figure, yet no single mind could have invented this man, unless it were Canetti himself. . . . My feeling is that Canetti has been associated (unfairly) with gloom—long lugubrious tomes written at the Wailing Wall. That is such an unfair impression of a mind so nimble, imaginative and humane." According to Marion E. Wiley, Canetti's reflective prose "attests to the success of his intellectual exploration. In respect to this achievement his prose is a unique contribution to contemporary writing, and his belated reception . . . is a noteworthy entry for a history of German literary reception."

*BIOGRAPHICAL/CRITICAL SOURCES:*

*BOOKS*

Best, Alan and Hans Wolfschuetz, *Modern Austrian Writing: Literature and Society after 1945*, B & N Imports, 1980.

Canetti, Elias, *Die Gerettete Zunge: Geschichte einer Jugend*, Hanser Verlag, 1977, English translation by Joachim Neugroschel published as *The Tongue Set Free: Remembrance of a European Childhood,* Seabury, 1979.

Canetti, Elias, *Die Fackel im Ohr: Lebensgeschichte 1921-1931*, Hanser Verlag, 1980, English translation by Neugroschel published as *The Torch in My Ear*, Farrar, Straus, 1982.

Canetti, Elias, *Das Augenspiel: Lebensgeschichte 1931-1937*, Hanser Verlag, 1985, English translation by Ralph Manheim published as *The Play of the Eyes*, Farrar, Straus, 1986.

*Contemporary Literary Criticism*, Gale, Volume 3, 1975, Volume 14, 1980, Volume 25, 1983, Volume 75, 1993, Volume 86, 1995.

Elbaz, Robert and Lea Hadomi, *Elias Canetti, or, The Failing of the Novel,* P. Lang (New York City), 1995.

*Elias Canetti*, R. Boorberg (Stuttgart), 1970.

Foell, Kristie A., *Blind Reflections: Gender in Elias Canetti's "Die Blendung,"* Ariadne Press (Riverside, CA), 1994.

Murphy, Harriet, *Canetti and Nietzsche: Theories of Humor in "Die Blendung,"* State University of New York Press (Albany), 1996.

Schultz, Uwe, editor, *Das Tagebuch und der Moderne Autor*, Hanser Verlag, 1965.

Sontag, Susan, *Under the Sign of Saturn*, Farrar, Straus, 1980.

*PERIODICALS*

*Books Abroad,* autumn, 1965.

*Book Week,* May 29, 1966.

*Canadian Forum,* April, 1947.

*Chicago Review,* May, 1969.

*Chicago Tribune Book World,* January 6, 1980.

*Critique: Studies in Modern Fiction,* Volume XIV, number 1, 1972.

*Globe and Mail* (Toronto), October 4, 1986.

*Harper's,* January, 1980.

*Kirkus Reviews,* June 15, 1994, p. 835.

*Library Journal,* August, 1994, p. 85.

*Los Angeles Times Book Review,* June 6, 1982; October 3, 1982; August 31, 1986.

*Manchester Guardian,* May 10, 1946.

*Modern Austrian Literature,* Volume XII, number 2, 1979.

*MOSAIC: A Journal for the Comparative Study of Literature and Ideas,* winter, 1974.

*New Republic,* November 8, 1982.

*Newsweek,* October 26, 1981.

*New Yorker,* May 19, 1980; November 22, 1982.

*New York Herald Tribune Book Review,* February 23, 1947.

*New York Review of Books,* September 25, 1980; February 4, 1982; November 4, 1982; July 17, 1986.

*New York Times,* October 16, 1981; February 27, 1982; March 20, 1982; September 17, 1982; July 1, 1986; August 10, 1986.

*New York Times Book Review,* April 29, 1979; September 19, 1982.

*Publishers Weekly,* October 31, 1981; July 25, 1994, p. 53.

*San Francisco Chronicle,* March 9, 1947.

*Saturday Review,* December, 1978.

*Saturday Review of Literature,* March 8, 1947.

*Spectator,* May 24, 1946; September 7, 1962; November 30, 1985; April 19, 1986.

*Sunday Times* (London), August 15, 1982.

*Time,* October 26, 1981.

*Times* (London), February, 18, 1982.

*Times Literary Supplement,* July 8, 1965; October 31, 1968; January 15, 1971; January 25, 1974; January 10, 1975; February 28, 1975; December 22, 1975; January 9, 1981; October 23, 1981; July 26, 1985.

*Voice Literary Supplement,* March, 1982; October, 1982.

*Washington Post,* October 16, 1981.

*Washington Post Book World,* September 26, 1982; November 13, 1994, p. 13.

*World Literature Today,* winter, 1978; spring, 1979; autumn, 1979; spring, 1981; winter, 1985; May 20, 1984.

*OBITUARIES:*

*PERIODICALS*

*Chicago Tribune,* August 20, 1994, sec. 2, p. 17.

*Los Angeles Times,* August 19, 1994, p. A20.

*New York Times,* August 19, 1994, p. A25.

*Times* (London), August 19, 1994, p. 19.*

* * *

**CAPPS, Benjamin (Franklin) 1922-**

*PERSONAL:* Born June 11, 1922, in Dundee, TX; son of Benjamin Franklin (a cowboy) and Ruth Kathleen (a teacher; maiden name, Rice) Capps; married Millie Marie Thompson (a nurse), December 12, 1942; children: Benjamin F., Jr., Kathleen Marie, Mark Victor. *Education:* Attended Texas Technological College (now Texas Tech University), 1938-39; University of Texas, B.A., 1948, M.A., 1949. *Politics:* Independent. *Avocational interests:* Folk music, country music, bluegrass music, "pick the mandolin and guitar with amateur musician friends."

*ADDRESSES: Home*—366 Forrest Hill Lane, Grand Prairie, TX 75051. *Agent*—A. L. Hart, The Fox Chase Agency, Inc., 419 East 57th St., New York, NY 10022.

*CAREER:* Surveyor, Civilian Conservation Corps., 1940-41, and Corps. of Engineers, 1941-42; Northeastern State College, Tahlequah, OK, began as instructor, became assistant professor of English and journalism, 1949-51; tool and die maker for various companies, 1951-61; freelance writer, 1961—. Writer-in-residence, University of Texas, Arlington, 1976. *Military service:* U.S. Army Air Forces, 1942-45; became first lieutenant; participated in Pacific campaigns; received three battle stars.

*MEMBER:* Western Writers of America, Western Literature Association (honorary lifetime member), Texas Folklore Society, Phi Beta Kappa.

*AWARDS, HONORS:* Spur Award of Western Writers of America, for best western novel of 1964, Levi Strauss Golden Saddleman Award, for best western writing of 1964, selection by National Association of Independent Schools as one of ten best books of 1964 for pre-college readers, and selection by American Booksellers Association for White House library, all for *The Trail to Ogallala;* Spur Award of Western Writers of America, for best western novel of 1965, for *Sam Chance,* and for best historical novel of 1969, for *The White Man's Road;* Wrangler Award of Western Heritage Center, 1969, for *The White Man's Road,* and 1974, for *The Warren Wagontrain Raid;* American Book Award nomination, 1980, for *Woman Chief;* also received Wrangler Award of Cowboy Hall of Fame.

*WRITINGS:*

*NOVELS*

*Hanging at Comanche Wells,* Ballantine (New York City), 1962.

*The Trail to Ogallala,* Duell, Sloan, & Pearce (New York City), 1964.

*Sam Chance,* Duell, Sloan, & Pearce, 1965, revised edition, Southern Methodist University Press (Dallas).

*A Woman of the People,* Duell, Sloan, & Pearce, 1966.

*The Brothers of Uterica,* Meredith (New York City), 1967.

*The White Man's Road,* Harper (New York City), 1969.

*The True Memoirs of Charley Blankenship,* Lippincott (Philadelphia), 1972.

*Woman Chief,* Doubleday (New York City), 1978.

*The Heirs of Franklin Woodstock,* Texas Christian Press (Fort Worth, TX), 1989.

*NONFICTION*

(With the editors of Time-Life) *The Indians,* Time-Life (New York City), 1973.

*The Warren Wagontrain Raid,* Dial (New York City), 1974, revised edition, Southern Methodist University Press, 1989.

(With the editors of Time-Life) *The Great Chiefs,* Time-Life, 1975.

(Co-editor) *Duncan Robinson: Texas Teacher and Humanist,* University of Texas at Arlington, 1976.

A collection of Capps' manuscripts is housed at the University of Texas at Arlington Library.

*SIDELIGHTS:* Benjamin Capps, according to James W. Lee in *Twentieth-Century Western Writers,* "is one of the best writers in America today." Capps' novels focus on the American West of the late nineteenth century and are, Lee writes, "serious depictions of the real life on the frontier, which explore serious themes of cultures in confrontation, and recreate the people—both whites and Indians—who lived on the plains a hundred years ago."

In *The Trail to Ogallala* Capps writes of one of the last great cattle drives, before the spread of fenced-in ranches and the railroads ended that era of Western history. The novel tells of Billy Scott, who brings a herd of three thousand cattle some 1,800 miles to market. According to G. E. Grauel in *Best Sellers,* the novel is "stylistically adequate without achieving brilliance, [but] is significant as history, sociology, and regional literature." R. D. Spector in *Book Week* finds that *The Trail to Ogallala* is "honest in characterization, accurate in historical and technical details, [Capps'] novel lacks genuine dramatic power, but it presents a significant story with appropriate dignity." H. E. Smith in *Library Journal* calls the novel an "excellent Western" with "exceptional character development."

Capps' novel *Sam Chance* follows the title character from his move to Texas at the end of the Civil War to his death in 1922, when he is a wealthy cattleman who has withstood the onslaughts of urbanization. Grauel describes Sam Chance as "a striking figure set in a far-above-average story" and praises Capps as "one of our leading portrayers of the West that really was." J. K. Hutchens, writing in *Saturday Review,* states: "Almost before he knows it, Benjamin Capps is going to be in the first rank of novelists chronicling the world of the old Southwestern cattlemen."

With *A Woman of the People,* Capps presents a look at the lifestyle of the Comanches. When two white girls are kidnapped and raised by a Comanche tribe, the elder of the two girls resists indoctrination into their way of life. "It takes years for Helen to realize—suddenly and startlingly—that she too has become an Indian," Lee writes. Her realization comes just as the tribe is being forced onto a reservation where their lives will be forever different. Lee concludes that "*A Woman of the People* is an American classic."

Reservation life again appears in *The White Man's Road,* a novel about a young Comanche boy on a reservation who yearns to live in the freedom his ancestors enjoyed. To taste some adventure, he joins with some other youths to steal horses and head for the open plains. The reviewer for *Publishers Weekly* calls it "a vigorous and appealing portrait of a young Comanche." The *Booklist* critic describes *The White Man's Road* as "a perceptive portrayal of the Comanche Indians as the white man closes in on them in the late 1800s."

*Woman Chief* draws on a real historical figure for its plot. Sweet Thunder Woman began as a young slave captured from a neighboring tribe by the Crow Indians. As she grew older, she rose to become the tribe's warrior chief. Even though she is renowned for her military skills, Sweet Thunder Woman was also known for her kindness and affection for children. Capps' account of her life, according to the *Publishers Weekly* reviewer, "is told with simple grace" and is "both poignant and informative." The *Booklist* critic calls *Woman Chief* "accurate and moving; it contains the elements both of good storytelling and of verifiable fact."

Lee explains what makes Capps' novels of Indian life so effective: "The author is sympathetic to the Indians but does not sentimentalize and patronize them. By treating the Indians as humans whose culture is different but not inferior to that of the whites, Capps gives an authentic picture of life among the Plains Indians."

Capps once told *CA:* "My ideal in literature is that writing which has deep roots in a particular time and place and way of life, and has at the same time universal value and meaning. I love the land of New Mexico, Texas, Oklahoma, Colorado."

*BIOGRAPHICAL/CRITICAL SOURCES:*

*BOOKS*

*Benjamin Capps and the South Plains,* University of North Texas Press (Denton), 1990.

Speck, Ernest B., *Benjamin Capps,* Boise State University Press (Boise, ID), 1981.

*Twentieth-Century Western Writers,* second edition, St. James Press (Detroit), 1991.

*PERIODICALS*

*Best Sellers,* May 15, 1964, p. 71; March 15, 1965, p. 24; October 15, 1969.

*Booklist,* January 15, 1970, pp. 598-599; October 15, 1979, p. 30.

*Publishers Weekly,* July 21, 1969, p. 52; July 16, 1979, p. 57.

*Saturday Review,* March 27, 1965, p. 48.

* * *

## CARRIER, Roch 1937-

*PERSONAL:* Born May 13, 1937, in Sainte-Justine-de-Dorchester, Quebec, Canada; son of Georges (in sales) and Marie-Anna (Tanguay) Carrier; married Diane Gosselin, 1959; children: two daughters. *Education:* Attended College Saint-Louis; received B.A. from L'Universite de Montreal, M.A., 1961; further study at the Sorbonne, University of Paris, 1961-64.

*ADDRESSES: Home*—Montreal, Quebec, Canada.

*CAREER:* Novelist, poet, dramatist, screenwriter, and author of short fiction. Has held teaching positions at College Militaire Royal de Saint-Jean, Quebec, and at L'Universite de Montreal, Montreal, Quebec; lecturer. Theatre du Nouveau Monde, Quebec, secretary-general, 1970—; chair, Salon du Livre, Montreal.

*AWARDS, HONORS:* Prix Litteraire de la Province de Quebec, 1964, for *Jolis deuils: Petites tragedies pour adultes;* Grand Prix Litteraire de la Ville de Montreal, 1981.

*WRITINGS:*

*TRANSLATED WORKS; NOVELS*

*La Guerre, Yes Sir!,* Editions du Jour, 1968, translation by Sheila Fischman published under the same title, Anansi, 1970.

*Floralie, ou es-tu?,* Editions du Jour, 1969, translation by Fischman published as *Floralie, Where Are You?,* Anansi, 1971.

*Il est par la, le soleil,* Editions du Jour, 1970, translation by Fischman published as *Is It the Sun, Philibert?,* Anansi, 1972.

*Le Deux-millieme etage,* Editions du Jour, 1973, translation by Fischman published as *They Won't Demolish Me!,* Anansi, 1974.

*Le Jardin des delices,* Editions la Press, 1975, translation by Fischman published as *The Garden of Delights,* Anansi, 1978.

*Il n'y a pas de pays sans grand-pere,* Stanke, 1979, translation by Fischman published as *No Country without Grandfathers,* Anansi, 1981.

*La Dame qui avait des chaines aux chevilles,* Stanke, 1981, translation by Fischman published as *Lady with Chains,* Anansi, 1984.

*De l'amour dans la ferraille,* Stanke, 1984, translation by Fischman published as *Heartbreaks along the Road,* Anansi, 1987.

*Prieres d'un enfant tres tres sage,* Stanke, 1988, translation by Fischman published as *Prayers of a Very Wise Child,* Penguin, 1991.

*Fin,* Stanke (Montreal), 1992, translation by Fischman published as *The End,* Viking (New York City), 1994.

*TRANSLATED WORKS; FOR CHILDREN*

*Les Enfants du bonhomme dans la lune,* Stanke, 1979, translation by Fischman published as *The Hockey Sweater, and Other Stories,* Anansi, 1979.

*Un Champion,* translation by Fischman published as *The Boxing Champion,* illustrated by Sheldon Cohen, Tundra Books, 1991.

*Un Bonne et heureuse annee* (juvenile), published as *A Happy New Year's Day,* illustrated by Gilles Pelletier, Tundra Books, 1991.

*Canada je t'aime—I Love You,* illustrated by Miyuki Tanobe, Tundra Books, 1991.

*Le Plus Long Circuit,* Tundra Books, 1993, translation by Fischman published as *The Longest Home Run,* illustrated by Cohen, Tundra Books, 1993.

*UNTRANSLATED WORKS*

*Les Jeux incompris* (poems), Editions Nocturne, 1956.

*Cherche tes mots, cherche tes pas,* Editions Nocturne, 1958.

*Jolis deuils: Petites tragedies pour adultes* (stories), Editions du Jour, 1964.

*L'Aube d'acier* (poem), illustrated by Maurice Savoie, Les Auteurs Reunis, 1971.

*Les Fleurs vivent-elles ailleurs que sur la terre,* Stanke, 1980.

*Les Voyageurs de l'arc-en-ciel,* illustrations by Francois Olivier, Stanke, 1980.

*Le Cirque noir,* Stanke, 1982.

*Ne faites pas mal a l'avenin* (juvenile), Les Editions Paulinas, 1984.

*L'Ours et le kangourou,* Stanke, 1986.

*Un Chameau en jordanie,* Stanke, 1988.

*Enfants de la planete,* Paulines, 1989.

*L'Homme dans le placard* (mystery), Stanke, 1991.

Contributor of short stories to periodicals, including *Etudes francaises* and *Ellipse.* Contributor of articles to periodicals, including *Ecrits du Canada francais.*

*PLAYS*

*La Guerre, Yes Sir!* (four-act; adapted from Carrier's novel of the same title; produced in Montreal, 1970; English-language version produced in Stratford, Ontario, 1972), Editions du Jour, 1970, revised edition, 1973.

*Floralie* (adapted from Carrier's novel *Floralie, ou es-tu?*; produced in Montreal, 1974), Editions du Jour, 1974.

*Il n'y a pas de pays sans grand-pere* (adapted from Carrier's novel of the same title), produced in Montreal, 1978.

*La Celeste bicyclette* (produced in Montreal, 1979; translation produced in Toronto as *The Celestial Bicycle,* 1982), Stanke, 1980.

*SCREENPLAYS*

*Le Martien de Noel,* National Film Board of Canada, 1970.

*The Ungrateful Land,* National Film Board of Canada, 1972.

*The Hockey Sweater* (short subject), animated by Cohen, National Film Board of Canada, 1980.

*SIDELIGHTS:* Quebec writer Roch Carrier is considered one of French Canada's most important novelists. With the translation of many of his works into English, he has also become one of the most widely read Quebecois writers in North America and England. Carrier first earned recognition with a trilogy of novels—*La Guerre, Yes Sir!; Floralie, Where Are You?;* and *Is It the Sun, Philibert?*—that together span about fifty years of Quebec's history. He has established a reputation for his sensitive portrayal of the often-turbulent misunderstandings that exist between French-and English-speaking Canadians. Carrier incorporates dark humor, dense allegory, and political satire into the fictional confrontations his characters enact in small Quebec towns. Describing his style as "[combining] the classical poise of Voltaire with the burly gusto of Rabelais," Mark Abley writes in *Saturday Night* that Carrier "stylizes and heightens the speech of rural Quebec." Nancy Wigston agrees in the Toronto *Globe and Mail,* proclaiming Carrier "one of Quebec's . . . geniuses of the written word."

Carrier published several short stories and poems during the 1950s and 1960s. However, it was not until publication of *La Guerre, Yes Sir!* in 1968—and its translation into English two years later—that he began to earn substantial acclaim. Set in a small Quebec town during World War II, the novel focuses on the wake of a village boy whose coffin is carried into town by English soldiers. To the villagers, the dead boy becomes a challenge to the living; the wake is at first a rowdy, good-natured celebration. But the underlying bitterness the villagers feel at the return of so many dead from European battlefields—the result of an *anglais* war that they feel should not involve their largely French-speaking province—transforms their initial boisterousness to hostility toward the English soldiers who are present. The festivity turns violent; ultimately one of the soldiers is killed. "Despite [the villagers'] unanimous opposition to the war," summarizes Philip Stratford in *Dictionary of Literary Biography,* "it visits them one grotesque night characterized by absurdity and nightmare."

*La Guerre* was enthusiastically received. "[This] is a first novel of staggering sophistication and control, proving that there now exists in Montreal a major international writer," declares Robert J. Green in *Journal of Commonwealth Literature.* Commending Carrier for his "fine, demanding talent," Mark Levene in *Canadian Forum* praises the author's "brilliant sense of narrative pace" and his ability to move "between the comic and the grotesque, between the realistic and the nightmarish." In *Saturday Night,* Andy Wainwright calls *La Guerre* "a black comedy of devastating effect . . . strewn with humour [and] bitter irony."

Although published as the second novel of what would be Carrier's trilogy, the events in *Floralie, Where Are You?* precede those of *La Guerre;* the book centers on the wedding night of the parents of the dead boy of the first novel. After their wedding feast, Anthyme and Floralie Corriveau hastily drive towards home through thick woods. Unable to control his mounting passion, Anthyme stops in the forest to consummate the marriage, after which he suspects his wife of having had another lover. Floralie confesses that she is not a virgin, and, depressed, the couple separates from one another in the woods. They each encounter misadventures while wandering through the dark until they finally reunite. Exhausted, the couple falls asleep; awakened by the still-feasting wedding guests, Anthyme and Floralie wonder if they had merely dreamed their traumatic night.

Although critics were impressed with *Floralie, Where Are You?,* the book was generally deemed less successful than Carrier's first novel. "Despite the considerable power of the early sections," writes Levene, "*Floralie, Where Are You?* possesses little of the overall control and intensity which mark his other work." Ronald Sutherland in *Canadian Literature* agrees, but nonetheless finds *Floralie* "another impressive accomplishment . . . filled with boisterous, ribald humour and stylistic fireworks." Sutherland concludes that *Floralie, Where Are You?* "is rich in amusing dialogue and incident. It is entertainment of a high order. There can be no doubt that here is a major talent . . . capable of producing a great deal more and very likely to do so."

*Is It the Sun, Philibert?* is the concluding novel in Carrier's trilogy. Focusing on Philibert, the son of a gravedigger who appeared in *La Guerre,* the novel records the young man's experiences after he leaves his rural village to travel to Montreal. Although demoralized while living in a city he finds ugly and hostile, Philibert remains optimistic, and his ability to love prevails—even at his death—over his bleak surroundings. Like Carrier's first two novels, *Is It the Sun, Philibert?* has been praised for its raucous humor, rich symbolism, and dark images. "It is not so much plot or character that are memorable in Carrier's trilogy," Stratford notes of Carrier's three novels, "as it is a series of original, kaleidoscopic images, made virtually indelible by their explosive violence, shot through with grim humor, and set against the little, down-trodden man's faith . . . that life should be beautiful."

Carrier has written several other novels that have been popular with his growing readership in both the original French version and in English translation. *They Won't Demolish Me!,* first published in French in 1973, captures what Brian Vintcent in *Saturday Night* labels "Roch Carrier's world" of the "bizarre, folkloric, [and] brawling." In the book, a comic cast of characters try unsuccessfully to save their rotting tenement building from being razed—a symbolic representation of the struggle between the disadvantaged and large and powerful capitalist concerns. *Garden of Delights* depicts an ex-convict who, while visiting a pub in a rural Quebec town, claims he wants to buy the rights to mine gold along a local river. When this news spreads, almost the entire town greedily tries to buy into the enterprise, resulting in a chaotic scene that ends in tragedy. More political in tone is Carrier's *No Country without Grandfathers,* possibly the author's most anti-English work. Centering on an elderly Quebecois man who muses about the injustices of the past from the confines of his rocking chair, the novel culminates in a final demonstration of freedom as the man takes action against his country's English rule.

*Lady with Chains* appeared in English translation in 1984. Set in the 1860s, the novel centers on a young pioneer couple, Victor and Virginie. When Victor's negligence causes the tragic death of their child, Virginie is unable to forgive him and falls mute, consumed with vengeful fantasies of murdering her husband. "When she finally decides to turn her fantasies into reality," explains Paul Stuewe in *Books in Canada,* "her actions set in motion a bizarre but believable chain of events that culminates in a cathartic revelation." *Lady with Chains* was widely praised as a powerful and compelling tale. Wigston deems the novel "a strange . . . exploration of a young woman's psyche," adding that "Carrier's tale unfolds in supple, incantatory rhythms that capture . . . loneliness and despair." Proclaiming the work "supremely moving literature," Stuewe declares that *Lady with Chains* "finds one of [Canada's] most talented authors writing at the top of his form."

Carrier's 1987 novel, *Heartbreaks along the Road,* is considered by critics to be his most ambitious work. A satire, it is based on the controversial regime, during the 1950s, of Maurice Duplessis, a corrupt premier of Quebec popularly known as "Le Chef." The work portrays Le Chef, hoping to earn votes, following through on a campaign promise to build roads in rural towns in an effort to bolster employment. The roads, however, lead to nowhere, and they are dismantled immediately following their construction, thus creating more jobs. Embracing a large cast of characters, the novel outlines how the people of Quebec fall prey to the unscrupulous politician. The novel elicited mixed reviews—although criticized for being digressive and overly long, the book earned acclaim for its robust humor and biting political satire. Brent Ledger in *Books in Canada,* for example, is "baffled by the endless parade of characters and the plethora of incident," but praises parts of the book as "powerful bits of writing" and "deeply impressive." Similarly, while *Canadian Forum* contributor Jeannette Urbas finds the novel uneven and repetitious, she adds that these weaknesses are "offset by the successful creation of a panoramic fresco of the Quebec rural scene." More enthusiastic about the book, Stratford thinks that *Heartbreaks along the Road* "displays Carrier's humor and compassion at their inventive best." And, in high praise of the work, Mark Abley of *Saturday Night* feels that in its ability to "transform and illuminate a fragment of the visible world with the grace and force of myth," *Heartbreaks along the Road* "is Carrier's best novel and one of the most important Canadian books of our time."

Carrier has written numerous books in his native French, as well as adapted several of his novels for the stage. In addition, he is the author of several works about and for children. Carrier's illustrated short story collection entitled *The Hockey Sweater* exhibits his characteristic political overtones on such topics as French Canadian nationalism, fear of the English, and the English-French language barrier. Told mostly from the perspective of Roch, a young boy growing up in rural Quebec, the stories have been acclaimed for their poetic and allegorical nature. *The Hockey Sweater* is "a gem of a book," writes Michael Benazon in *Canadian Forum;* "it is Roch Carrier at his best, his most personal work of prose fiction thus far." As a companion to *The Hockey Sweater,* Carrier published *The Boxing Champion* featuring the same young protagonist as he leaves behind his passion for hockey in an attempt to become a champion in the boxing ring. Young Roch also appeared in another book, *A Happy New Year's Day.* As with the two books before it, it is a memoir, viewing the events of childhood from the naivete of youth and the understanding that comes with age. Set on New Year's Day in 1941, the memoir features Carrier's memories of the day, including numerous details about his large, extended family. "Carrier has filled his story with humour and an eye for the sort of clever details that many think children miss," remarks Linda Granfield in *Quill & Quire.*

In *The Longest Home Run,* Carrier infuses a seemingly simple story with complex, adult-oriented themes. Set in 1940s Quebec, the story features a boys' baseball game that is interrupted by a girl named Adeline, who asks to join in the game. She promptly hits the longest home run that any of the boys have ever witnessed; when asked who she is, the girl gives her name and divulges that she is a magician with a traveling theater act visiting the area. The boys later attempt to visit the girl and witness her magic act but are told by her father that she is gone; he has made her disappear. While some reviewers criticized the lack of coherent plot, others praised the author's portrayals of small-town adults and remarked favorably on the story's wry comment about the societal forces that attempt to make strong females invisible.

*Prayers of a Very Wise Child,* while not written explicitly for children, nevertheless features a seven-year-old narrator whose brief prayers form the basis of the book. Once again set in the author's home terrain of rural Quebec, this autobiographical work portrays a child's pious simplicity, his puzzlement at the presence of evil-the child wonders why God "kills" little children and allows wars to happen-and his growing awareness of the differences between boys and girls. Writing in *Quill & Quire,* Daniel Jones notes that "*Prayers of a Very Wise Child* succeeds by its richly comic invention." *Canadian Literature* reviewer John Lennox avers that "Carrier is skilled at underlining the characteristics of human community and in using the child to illustrate the potential and limitations of human understanding."

*BIOGRAPHICAL/CRITICAL SOURCES:*

*BOOKS*

Cameron, Donald, *Conversations with Canadian Novelists,* Macmillan of Canada, 1973, pp. 13-29.

*Contemporary Literary Criticism,* Gale (Detroit), Volume 13, 1980; Volume 78, 1994.

*Dictionary of Literary Biography,* Volume 53: *Canadian Writers since 1960, First Series,* Gale, 1986.

Northey, Margot, *The Haunted Wilderness: The Gothic and Grotesque in Canadian Fiction,* University of Toronto Press, 1976, pp. 79-87.

Sutherland, Ronald, *Second Image: Comparative Studies in Quebec/Canadian Literature,* New Press (Toronto), 1971.

*PERIODICALS*

*Antigonish Review,* autumn, 1981, pp. 91-94.

*Books in Canada,* November, 1979, p. 10; February, 1982, pp. 9-10; December, 1984; December, 1987; November, 1991, p. 48; September, 1993, p. 57.

*Canadian Children's Literature,* fall, 1994, p. 77; winter, 1995, p. 90.

*Canadian Forum,* September, 1970, p. 220; June, 1971; July, 1971, p. 36; May-June, 1974; September, 1979, p. 30; March, 1980, pp. 36-37; December, 1987, pp. 41-42.

*Canadian Literature,* spring, 1967, pp. 86-87; spring, 1970; autumn, 1971, pp. 87-88; spring, 1979, pp. 120-31; spring, 1985, pp. 24-33; autumn-winter, 1989, pp. 209-11; autumn, 1992, p. 174.

*Essays on Canadian Writing,* spring, 1990, pp. 32-39.

*French Review,* April, 1979, pp. 789-90.

*Globe and Mail* (Toronto), August 11, 1984; October 13, 1984; October 17, 1987.

*Horn Books,* May/June, 1992, p. 371.

*Journal of Canadian Fiction,* summer, 1972, pp. 43-47.

*Journal of Commonwealth Literature,* June, 1972.

*Kirkus Reviews,* June 1, 1993, p. 716.

*Quill & Quire,* October, 1991, p. 27; November, 1991, p. 26; April, 1993, p. 34.

*Saturday Night,* May, 1970, pp. 42-43; August, 1974; October, 1987, pp. 59-62.

*School Library Journal,* February, 1992, p. 71; December, 1993, p. 85.

*Studies in Canadian Literature,* Volume 17, number 2, 1992-93, pp. 92-108.

*Studies in Twentieth Century Literature,* fall, 1982, pp. 59-76.

*Variety,* August 23, 1972.

*World Literature Today,* winter, 1980, p. 67.*

* * *

## CARTER, Angela (Olive) 1940-1992

*PERSONAL:* Born May 7, 1940, in London, England; died of cancer, February 16, 1992, in London, England; daughter of Hugh Alexander (a journalist) and Olive (Farthing) Stalker; married Paul Carter, September 10, 1960 (divorced, 1972). *Education:* University of Bristol, B.A., 1965. *Politics:* Left. *Religion:* None.

*CAREER:* Novelist, short story writer, teacher, and critic. Journalist for papers in Croyden, Surrey, England, 1958-61.

*AWARDS, HONORS:* John Llewllyn Rhys Prize, 1968, for *The Magic Toyshop;* Somerset Maugham Award, 1969, for *Several Perceptions;* Cheltenham Literary Festival Award, 1979, for *The Bloody Chamber and Other Stories;* Kust Maschler Award, 1982, for *Sleeping Beauty and Other Favorite Fairy Tales;* James Tait Black Memorial Prize, 1986, for *Nights at the Circus.*

*WRITINGS:*

*NOVELS*

*Shadow Dance,* Heinemann, 1966, published as *Honeybuzzard,* Simon & Schuster, 1967.

*Several Perceptions,* Heinemann, 1968, Simon & Schuster, 1969.
*Heroes and Villains,* Heinemann, 1969, Simon & Schuster, 1970.
*Love,* Hart-Davis, 1971.
*The Infernal Desire Machines of Doctor Hoffman,* Hart-Davis, 1972, published as *The War of Dreams,* Harcourt, 1974.
*Passion of New Eve,* Harcourt, 1977.
*War of Dreams,* Avon, 1983.
*Nights at the Circus,* Viking, 1985.
*Come unto These Yellow Sands,* Bloodaxe, 1985.
*Saints and Strangers,* Penguin, 1987.
*Old Wives' Fairy Tale Book,* Random House, 1990.
*Wise Children,* Chatto & Windus (London), 1991, Farrar Straus Giroux (New York City), 1992.

*JUVENILE*

*The Magic Toyshop* (also see below), Heinemann, 1967, Simon & Schuster, 1968.
*Miss Z, the Dark Young Lady,* Simon & Schuster, 1970.
*The Donkey Prince,* Simon & Schuster, 1970.
(Translator) *Fairy Tales of Charles Perrault,* Gollancz, 1977.
*Comic and Curious Cats,* illustrated by Martin Leman, Gollancz, 1979.
(With Leslie Carter) *The Music People,* Hamish Hamilton, 1980.
*Moonshadow,* David & Charles, 1984.
(Editor) *Sleeping Beauty and Other Favorite Fairy Tales,* Schocken, 1984.
*The Second Virago Book of Fairy Tales,* Virago Press (London), 1992, published as *Strange Things Sometimes Still Happen: Fairy Tales from Around the World,* Faber and Faber (Boston), 1993.
*American Ghosts & Old World Wonders,* Chatto & Windus (London), 1993.

*OTHER*

*Unicorn* (poetry), Location Press, 1966.
*Fireworks: Nine Profane Pieces,* Quartet Books, 1974, published as *Fireworks: Nine Stories in Various Guises,* Harper, 1981.
*The Sadeian Woman and the Ideology of Pornography,* Pantheon, 1979, published in England as *The Sadeian Woman and the Ideology of Pornography,* Virago, 1979.
*The Bloody Chamber and Other Stories,* Gollancz, 1979, Harper, 1980.
*Black Venus's Tale,* Faber-Text, 1980.
*Nothing Sacred: Selected Journalism,* Virago, 1982.
(With Neil Jordan) *The Company of Wolves* (screenplay), ITC Entertainment, 1985.
(Editor) *Don't Bet on the Prince: Contemporary Feminist Fairy Tales in North America and Europe,* Routledge, Chapman & Hall, 1987.
*The Magic Toyshop* (screenplay; based on novel of same title), Granada Television Productions, 1989.
(Editor) *Wayward Girls and Wicked Women: An Anthology of Subversive Women,* Penguin, 1989.
*Expletives Deleted: Selected Writings,* Chatto & Windus (London), 1992.
*Burning Your Boats: The Complete Short Stories,* H. Holt & Co. (New York City), 1996.

Also author of radio scripts, including *Vampirella,* 1976; *Come Unto These Sands,* 1979; *The Company of Wolves,* 1980; *Puss in Boots,* 1982. Contributor to periodicals, including *New Society* and *Vogue.*

*SIDELIGHTS:* Angela Carter combined a number of literary genres into a unique style that makes her work "difficult to place," observes Lorna Sage in the *Dictionary of Literary Biography.* Critics note four recurring elements in Carter's fiction: lush prose, violence, Gothic suspense, and eroticism. Although sometimes faulted during her life for an extravagant prose style, Carter is now highly regarded as an imaginative and uncommon stylist.

Carter's first novel, *Shadow Dance,* published in the United States as *Honeybuzzard,* is set in an English junk shop that sells newly fashionable Victorian antiques. Morris, the owner of the shop, and his girlfriend Honeybuzzard prowl condemned houses at night, stripping them of items to sell in their shop. "The fantasy motifs lurking in the background in *Shadow Dance* come into their own in Magic Toyshop [Carter's second novel]," writes Sage. *The Magic Toyshop* is a "Freudian fairy tale," according to Sage, complete with "something of a fairy-tale's happy-ever-after promise."

Carter won the Somerset Maugham Award for her third novel, *Several Perceptions.* Set in England during the late 1960s, the novel tells the story of Joseph Harker, a young man whose attempted suicide fails. Plagued by hallucinations and macabre images, Harker gradually comes to terms with his life through his interaction with his eccentric neighbors. With *Heroes and Villains,* Carter abandoned the English settings that had characterized her previous novels for science fiction. Set in a post-World War III world of barbarians and scattered remnants of civilization, the novel is largely a fable about the nature of "civilized" society. "The fantasy is made to work through the use of detail and the firmly established individuality of the characters," notes a reviewer in the *Times Literary Supplement*. John S. Philipson, writing in *Bestsellers,* comments that "one could call [the book] a commentary on tomorrow's world, with nihilistic implications."

Carter's interest in mythology and fantasy is apparent in such novels as *The War of Dreams* and in story collections such as *The Bloody Chamber,* which includes adult retellings of fairy tales like *Snow White* and *Little Red Riding Hood.* Carter also edited fairy tale collections for children, including *Sleeping Beauty and Other Fairy Tales* and *The Fairy Tales of Charles Perrault.* Carter's "retelling of European folk and fairy tales has the power, not only to cause us to think again, and deeply, . . .but to plunge us into hackle-raising speculation about aspects of our human/animal nature," remarks Susan Kennedy in the *Times Literary Supplement.* With her ability to blend reality with the bizarre to create imaginary worlds, Carter's oeuvre stretches the boundaries of contemporary fiction. As James Brockway comments in *Books and Bookmen,* Carter, "like all geniuses . . . walks the tightrope on one side of which yawns the chasm of madness, and the other the chasm of bathos. . . . Our Lady Edgar Allan Poe."

Critics have emphasized Carter's concern with gender roles and feminist themes in such works as her novel *The Passion of New Eve* and the nonfiction work *The Sadeian Woman and the Ideology of Pornography.* The latter is a feminist study of pornography in which Carter argues that the Marquis de Sade created in his pornographic novels truthful portraits of the status of women in society. What makes Sade unusual as a pornographer, and of special interest to feminists, according to Carter, was his "claiming rights of free sexuality for women, and in installing women as beings of power in his imaginary worlds. This sets him apart from all other pornographers at all times and most other writers of his period." Feminist themes are also significant in Carter's last novel, *Wise Children,* which depicts a pair of twins who have made their living first as vaudeville performers and later as actresses in Hollywood. The novel satirically parallels many of the conventions of Shakespearean comedy, such as mistaken identity and a benevolently happy ending. "Carter sets herself to demonstrate that the jungle law of the casting couch and the tawdry world of stage and screen can nonetheless be pure at heart, peopled not by tigers but by does and fauns, creatures who may be grotesque but are also endearing," summarizes John Bayley in *New York Review of Books.* Sage finds that although Carter won several literary awards, "her preoccupations as a writer—deepened and defined over the years—remain radically at odds with the puritanism and the conventional realism that characterize much of British fiction." Carter, who regarded the fantasy element of her work as "social satire" or "social realism of the unconscious," explained in a *Publisher's Weekly* interview, "I have always felt that one person's fantasy is another person's everyday life. It has its own logic as well. I got more and more into it as I got older, because it's a genre with its own rigorous logic."

Carter's numerous short stories have been collected in a single volume titled *Burning Your Boats: The Complete Short Stories.* Distinguishing the style of Carter's stories from the realism that characterizes much contemporary fiction, *Publishers Weekly* observes that Carter's short fiction consists of "tales, legends, [and] variations on mythic themes." "What becomes ever clearer as one reads these tales . . . is that short fiction was a laboratory in which [Carter] remade herself over and over again," comments Roz Kaveney in *New Statesman & Society.* Carter's literary essays are collected in *Expletives Deleted: Selected Writings.* The volume articulates her feminist perspective and highlights her incisive commentary on a wide variety of books. "Angela Carter writes with wild grace, like a dandy, as is demonstrated by the best . . . of these articles. She can never forego the wicked pleasures of a joke, of a literary reference, of dancing on the pomposities of dullards." Another posthumous volume titled *American Ghosts & Old World Wonders* presents several of Carter's previously uncollected stories and prose writings, each of which is concerned in some way with the subject of myths and legends. While discussions and renderings of fairy tales inform such pieces as "Ashputtle or The Mother's Ghost," in which Carter expounds upon the story of Cinderella, "[s]ome of the most fertile ground in this collection is found . . . where American ghosts and Old World wonders meet, where the 'mirth, anarchy and terror' of Europe clash with the airy, mysterious promise of the New World," asserts Candice Rodd in *Times Literary Supplement.*

*BIOGRAPHICAL/CRITICAL SOURCES:*

*BOOKS*

Carter, Angela, *The Sadeian Woman and the Ideology of Pornography,* Pantheon, 1979.

*Contemporary Issues in Criticism,* Volume 1, Gale, 1982.
*Contemporary Literary Criticism,* Gale, Volume 5, 1976, Volume 41, 1987.
*Dictionary of Literary Biography,* Volume 14: *British Novelists since 1960,* 2 parts, Gale, 1983.
Michael, Magali Cornier, *Feminism and the Postmodern Impulse: Post-World War II Fiction,* State University of New York Press (Albany), 1996.
Robinson , Sally, *Engendering the Subject: Gender and Self-Representation in Contemporary Women's Fiction,* State University of New York Press (Albany), 1991.
Sage, Lorna, *Angela Carter,* Northcote House in association with the British Council (Plymouth, U. K.), 1994.
Sage, Lorna, editor, *Flesh and the Mirror: Essays on the Art of Angela Carter,* Virago Press (London), 1994.

*PERIODICALS*

*Books and Bookmen,* February, 1975.
*Chicago Tribune,* April 22, 1985; September 26, 1986; February 23, 1992, section 2, p. 6.
*Listener,* May 20, 1971; September 26, 1974.
*Literature and History,* spring, 1984.
*London Review of Books,* June 13, 1991, p. 3.
*Los Angeles Times Book Review,* March 16, 1980.
*Nation,* April 20, 1992, p. 526.
*New Review,* June/July, 1977.
*New Statesman,* July 8, 1968; November 14, 1969; August 16, 1974; March 25, 1977; May 25, 1979; October 18, 1985.
*New Statesman & Society,* April 10, 1992, p. 38; July 31, 1992; July 21, 1995, pp. 39-40.
*New York Review of Books,* April 23, 1992, p. 9.
*New York Times Book Review,* January 19, 1992, p. 7; May 19, 1996, p. 11.
*Observer,* January 31, 1993.
*Publishers Weekly,* January 14, 1985; June 17, 1986; January 8, 1996, p. 57.
*Saturday Review,* February 18, 1967.
*Spectator,* March 26, 1977.
*Times Literary Supplement,* August 1, 1968; November 20, 1969; June 18, 1974; February 8, 1980; July 4, 1981; September 28, 1984; October 18, 1985; June 19, 1992, p. 5; April 2, 1993, p. 20; August 4, 1995, p. 20.
*Washington Post Book World,* August 18, 1974; February 24, 1980; June 28, 1981; February 3, 1985.
*Yale Review,* April, 1992, p. 227.

*OBITUARIES:*

*PERIODICALS*

*Chicago Tribune,* February 17, 1992, section 1, p. 10.
*Los Angeles Times,* February 22, 1992, p. A22.
*New York Times,* February 19, 1992, p. D21.
*Times* (London), February 17, 1992, p. 15.
*Washington Post,* February 18, 1992, p. B4.*

* * *

**CARVER, Raymond 1938-1988**

*PERSONAL:* Born May 25, 1938, in Clatskanie, OR; died of lung cancer, August 2, 1988, in Port Angeles, WA; son of Clevie Raymond (a laborer) and Ella Beatrice (maiden name, Casey; a homemaker) Carver; married Maryann Burk (a teacher), June 7, 1957 (divorced, October, 1983); married Tess Gallagher (a poet), June 17, 1988; children: Christine LaRae, Vance Lindsay. *Education:* Humboldt State College (now California State University, Humboldt), A.B., 1963; University of Iowa, M.F.A., 1966. *Avocational interests:* Travel.

*CAREER:* Writer. Manual laborer, c. late 1950s-early 1960s; Science Research Associates, Inc., Palo Alto, CA, editor, 1967-70. University of California, Santa Cruz, lecturer in creative writing, 1971-72; University of California, Berkeley, lecturer in fiction writing, 1972-73; Syracuse University, Syracuse, NY, professor of English, 1980-83. Visiting professor of English, Writers Workshop, University of Iowa, 1973-74; member of faculty writing program, Goddard College, 1977-78; visiting distinguished writer, University of Texas at El Paso, 1978-79.

*MEMBER:* International PEN (member of executive board), Authors Guild.

*AWARDS, HONORS:* National Endowment for the Arts Discovery Award for poetry, 1970; Joseph Henry Jackson Award for fiction, 1971; Wallace Stegner Creative Writing Fellowship, Stanford University, 1972-73; National Book Award nomination in fiction, 1977, for *Will You Please Be Quiet, Please?;* Guggenheim fellowship, 1977-78; National Endowment for the Arts Award in fiction, 1979; Carlos Fuentes Fiction Award, for short story "The Bath"; Mildred and Harold Strauss Living Award, American

Academy and Institute of Arts and Letters, 1983; National Book Critics Circle Award nomination in fiction, 1984, and Pulitzer Prize nomination for fiction, 1985, both for *Cathedral;* Levinson Prize for poetry, 1985; Los Angeles Times book prize, 1986, for *Where Water Comes Together with Other Water;* inducted into American Academy and Institute of Arts and Letters, 1988; Creative Arts Award citation, Brandeis University, 1988; National Book Critics Circle Award nomination in fiction, 1988, and Pulitzer Prize nomination for fiction, 1989, both for *Where I'm Calling From: New and Selected Stories.* Honorary degree from University of Hartford, 1988.

*WRITINGS:*

*Near Klamath* (poems), Sacramento State College, 1968.
*Winter Insomnia* (poems), Kayak, 1970.
*Put Yourself in My Shoes* (short stories), Capra, 1974.
*Will You Please Be Quiet, Please?* (short stories), McGraw, 1976.
*At Night the Salmon Move* (poems), Capra, 1976.
*Furious Seasons* (short stories), Capra, 1977.
*What We Talk about When We Talk about Love* (short stories), Knopf, 1981.
*Two Poems,* Scarab Press, 1982.
*The Pheasant* (short stories), Metacom, 1982.
*Fires: Essays, Poems, Stories, 1966-1982,* Capra, 1983.
(Author of foreword) John Gardner, *On Becoming a Novelist,* Harper, 1983.
(Author of introduction) William Kittredge, *We Are Not in This Together,* Greywolf Press, 1984.
*Cathedral* (short stories), Knopf, 1984.
*If It Please You* (short stories), Lord John, 1984.
*Dostoevsky: The Screenplay,* Capra, 1985.
*The Stories of Raymond Carver,* Picador, 1985.
*Where Water Comes Together with Other Water* (poems), Random House, 1985.
*This Water* (poems), Ewert, 1985.
*Ultramarine* (poems), Random House, 1986.
(Editor with Shannon Ravenel) *The Best American Short Stories 1986,* Houghton, 1986.
*In a Marine Light: Selected Poems,* Harvill, 1987.
*Saints,* Random House, 1987.
(Editor with Tom Jenks) *American Short Story Masterpieces,* Delacorte, 1987.
*Elephant, and Other Stories,* Harvill, 1988.
*Where I'm Calling From: New and Selected Stories,* Atlantic Monthly Press, 1988.
*A New Path to the Waterfall* (poems), Atlantic Monthly Press, 1989.
*Carver Country,* Scribner (New York City), 1990.
*No Heroics, Please: Uncollected Writings* (essays and short stories), Random House, 1992.
*Short Cuts: Selected Stories,* Vintage, 1993.
*All of Us: The Collected Poems,* Harvil, 1997.

Also author, with Michael Cimino, of script "Purple Lake." Guest editor, *The Best American Short Stories,* 1986. Contributor to anthologies, including *The Best American Short Stories,* 1967, 1982, and 1983, *Short Stories from the Literary Magazines, Best Little Magazine Fiction,* 1970 and 1971, *Prize Stories: The O. Henry Awards,* 1973, 1974, 1975, and 1983, *Pushcart Prize Anthology,* 1976, 1981, 1982, and 1983, *New Voices in American Poetry,* and *The Generation of 2000: Contemporary American Poets.*

Contributor of poems and stories to national periodicals, including *Esquire, New Yorker, Atlantic,* and *Harper's,* and to literary journals, including *Antaeus, Georgia Review, Ohio Review, Paris Review,* and *Poetry.* Editor, *Quarry* (magazine), 1971-72; editor, *Ploughshares,* Volume 9, number 4, 1983.

*ADAPTATIONS:* Several of Carver's short stories were adapted into a screenplay and released as the motion picture *Short Cuts,* directed by Robert Altman.

*SIDELIGHTS:* Raymond Carver was one of a handful of contemporary short story writers credited with reviving what was once thought of as a dying literary form. His stories mainly take place in his native Pacific Northwest region; they are peopled with the type of lower-middle-class characters the author was familiar with while he was growing up. In a *New York Review of Books* article, Thomas R. Edwards describes Carver's fictional world as a place where "people worry about whether their old cars will start, where unemployment or personal bankruptcy are present dangers, where a good time consists of smoking pot with the neighbors, with a little cream soda and M & M's on the side. . . . Carver's characters are waitresses, mechanics, postmen, high school teachers, factory workers, door-to-door salesmen. [Their surroundings are] not for them a still unspoiled scenic wonderland, but a place where making a living is as hard, and the texture of life as drab, for those without money, as anywhere else."

Carver's own life paralleled that of one of his characters. Born in an Oregon logging town, the author was married and the father of two before he was twenty years old. Also like his characters, Carver worked at a series of low paying jobs: he "picked tulips, pumped gas, swept hospital corridors, swabbed toilets, [and] managed an apartment complex," according to Bruce Weber in a *New York Times Magazine* profile of the author. Carver's wife at the time, continues Weber, "worked for the phone company, waited tables, [and] sold a series of book digests door-to-door." Not coincidentally, "of all the writers at work today, Carver may have [had] the most distinct vision of the working class," as Ray Anello observes in a *Newsweek* article. Carver taught creative writing in California and produced two books of poetry before his first book of short stories, *Will You Please Be Quiet, Please?,* was published in 1976.

In introducing readers to his world of the desperation of ordinary people, Carver created tales that are "brief . . . but by no means stark," notes Geoffrey Wolff in his *New York Times Book Review* piece on *Will You Please Be Quiet, Please?* Continues the critic: "They imply complexities of action and motive and they are especially artful in their suggestion of repressed violence. No human blood is shed in any of these stories, yet almost all of them hold a promise of mayhem of some final, awful breaking from confines, and breaking through to liberty." The theme of breaking from confines is central to one of the stories, "Neighbors," in which Bill and Arlene Miller agree to feed their neighbors' cat while the neighbors, the Stones, are on vacation. With access to the Stones' home, the Millers find themselves increasingly taken with their friends' clothes, furniture, and other belongings. Bill and Arlene, in fact, begin to assume the identities of the Stones; "each finds this strangely stimulating, and their sex life prospers, though neither can find anything much to say about it at all," reports Edwards. The end of the story finds the Millers clinging to the Stones' door as their neighbors return, knowing that their rich fantasy life will soon end.

The author's "first book of stories explored a common plight rather than a common subject," notes *New York Times Book Review* critic Michael Wood. "His characters were lost or diminished in their own different ways. The 17 stories in [Carver's third collection, *What We Talk about When We Talk about Love*], make up a more concentrated volume, less a collection than a set of variations on the themes of marriage, infidelity and the disquieting tricks of human affection." "The first few pieces seem thin and perfunctory," Adam Mars-Jones writes in the *Times Literary Supplement,* "and there is a recurring pattern . . . of endings which lurch suddenly sideways, moving off in a direction that seems almost random." Anatole Broyard finds such endings frustrating. In his *New York Times* review of *What We Talk about When We Talk about Love,* Broyard criticizes what he calls "the most flagrant and common imposition in current fiction, to end a story with a sententious ambiguity that leaves the reader holding the bag."

"Perhaps there is a reason for this," says Mars-Jones. "Endings and titles are bound to be a problem for a writer like Carver, since readers and reviewers so habitually use them as keys to interpret everything else in a story. So he must make his endings enigmatic and even mildly surrealist, and his titles for the most part oblique. Sometimes he over- compensates." And *Newsweek's* Peter S. Prescott feels that all seventeen stories in Carver's third collection "are excellent, and each gives the impression that it could not have been written more forcefully, or in fewer words."

Prescott also notes that the author was concerned "with the collapse of human relationships. Some of his stories take place at the moment things fall apart; others, after the damage has been done, while the shock waves still reverberate. Alcohol and violence are rarely far removed from what happens, but sometimes, in another characteristic maneuver, Carver will nudge the drama that triggers a crisis aside to show that his story has really been about something else all along." "Carver's is not a particularly lyrical prose," says Weber in his *New York Times Magazine* article: "A typical sentence is blunt and uncomplicated, eschewing the ornaments of descriptive adverbs and parenthetical phrases. His rhythms are often repetitive or brusque, as if to suggest the strain of people learning to express newly felt things, fresh emotions. Time passes in agonizingly linear fashion, the chronology of a given scene marked by one fraught and simple gesture after another. Dialogue is usually clipped, and it is studded with commonplace observations of the concrete objects on the table or on the wall rather than the elusive, important issues in the air."

Of Carver's 1984 short fiction collection, *Cathedral,* "it would be hard to imagine a more dispirited assortment of figures," declares David Lehman in a *Newsweek* review. In each story, a "note of transcendent indifference, beyond resignation or fatigue, is sounded," adds Lehman, cautioning, "fun to read they're not." But, the critic stresses, "it's impossible to ignore Carver's immense talent." In *Cathedral,* Carver rewrites the ending of one of his most acclaimed stories from *What We Talk about When We Talk about Love.* The original story, "The Bath," is about a mother who orders a special cake for her eight-year-old son's birthday—but the boy is hit by a car on that day and is rushed to the hospital, where he lingers in a coma. The baker, aware only that the parents haven't picked up their expensive cake, badgers them with endless calls demanding his money. As the story ends, the boy's fate is still unknown, and the desperate parents hear the phone ring again. In *Cathedral,* the author retells this story (now titled "A Small, Good Thing") up to the final phone ring. At this point, ambiguity vanishes; Carver reveals that the boy has died, and the call is from the irate baker. But this time the parents confront the baker with the circumstances, and the apologetic man invites them over to his bakery. There he tells the parents his own sad story of loneliness and despair and feeds them fresh coffee and warm rolls, because "eating is a small, good thing in a time like this."

"In revising 'The Bath' into 'A Small, Good Thing,' Carver has indeed gone into [what he describes as] 'the heart of what the story is about,' and in the process has written an entirely new story—has created, if you will, a completely new world," declares Jonathan Yardley in the *Washington Post Book World.* "The first version is beautifully crafted and admirably concise, but lacking in genuine compassion; the mysterious caller is not so much a human being as a mere voice, malign and characterless. But in the second version that voice becomes a person, one whose own losses are, in different ways, as crippling and heartbreaking as the one suffered by the grieving parents." As Broyard writes in a *New York Times* review of *Cathedral,* "It is typical of Mr. Carver's stories that comfort against adversity is found in incongruous places, that people find improbable solace. The improbable and the homely are [the author's] territory. He works in the bargain basement of the soul." Yardley maintains that "'The Bath' is a good short story," while "'A Small, Good Thing' comes breathtakingly close to perfection."

*New Republic* reviewer Dorothy Wickenden agrees that "A Small, Good Thing" and the story "Cathedral" "are astute, even complex, psychological dramas," but remarks that "a touch of sentimentality, an element previously foreign to Carver's work, has crept into these stories. Perhaps because he doesn't quite trust the sense of hope with which he leaves his characters, the writing at the end becomes self-consciously simple and the scenes of resolution contrived." Yet "compared with his previous two collections of stories," Broyard concludes, "[*Cathedral*] shows an increase in vitality. Like a missionary, Mr. Carver seems to be gradually reclaiming or redeeming his characters."

According to *New York Times Book Review* critic Irving Howe, Carver's stories evoke "strong American literary traditions. Formally, they summon remembrances of Hemingway and perhaps Stephen Crane, masters of tightly packed fiction. In subject matter they draw upon the American voice of loneliness and stoicism, the native soul locked in this continent's space. [The author's] characters, like those of many earlier American writers, lack a vocabulary that can release their feelings, so they must express themselves mainly through obscure gesture and berserk display." And Paul Gray, writing about *Cathedral* in *Time,* says that "Carver's art masquerades as accident, scraps of information that might have been overheard at the supermarket check-out or local beer joint. His most memorable people live on the edge: of poverty, alcoholic self-destruction, loneliness. Something in their lives denies them a sense of community. They feel this lack intensely, yet are too wary of intimacy to touch other people, even with language."

Such appraisals of his writing left Carver himself a little wary. He told Weber: "Until I started reading these reviews of my work, praising me, I never felt the people I was writing about were so bad. . . . The waitress, the bus driver, the mechanic, the hotel keeper. God, the country is filled with these people. They're good people. People doing the best they could."

Carver's 1988 short fiction collection *Where I'm Calling From,* released shortly before his death, combines new and previously published stories. The entire volume is colored by Carver's standard themes of alienation, failed relationships, and death, but critics generally considered the newer contributions softer and more rambling than the author's earlier, more intense pieces. *Where I'm Calling From* was nominated for both a Pulitzer Prize and a National Book Critics Circle Award.

Carver also wrote extensively as a poet. A collection of his poetry, including some works being written shortly before his death, was published in *A New Path to the Waterfall.* Although he had already released a volume of his collected verse, the diagnosis of lung cancer inspired him to write another volume. These poems are characterized by a reliance on sentence-sounds and a structure steeped in storytelling. Edna Longley comments in the *London Review of Books* that "all his writing tends toward dramatic monologue, present-tense soliloquy that wears the past like a hairshirt." He explores tortured marriages and strained familial relationships, all of which lead him bravely into discussing his own terminal illness. Longley praises Carver for his ability to forge solid beginnings and endings: "A Carver poem instantly establishes its presence." Fred Chappell, writing in the *Kenyon Review,* takes a much different view of the book. He admits that he had reservations in reviewing the it: "My personal impression has been that Carver desiccated the short story and that his effort to trivialize the form has been as irrelevant as it was unsuccessful. . . . the poems here are pretty bad. In fact, it is difficult to think of these productions as poems; they stand in relation to poetry rather as iron ore does to Giacometti sculpture."

In 1992 a collection of Carver's early works was published. *No Heroics, Please: Uncollected Writings* contains poems, essays, book reviews, and other pieces that Carver had chosen not to include in any of his other collected work. Several of the short stories included had only been published before in student literary magazines. Of interest was the fact that in these stories Carver uses literary devises such as flashbacks and experimentation with verb tenses—techniques he shunned in his later work. Alan Davis comments in the *Hudson Review* that "the artfulness of Carver, the way he consciously chisels a world out of workaday detail, becomes quickly apparent after perusing his earliest stories."

Several of Carver's previously published short stories received attention when acclaimed film director Robert Altman turned them into a motion picture. Although Altman took some liberties in adapting these stories for the screen, they remained essentially true to Carver's ideas. The stories were collected into the book *Short Cuts,* which bears the same name as the movie. In one story, a couple becomes entranced with their neighbor's life when they are left to cat-sit for a weekend. In "So Much Water So Close to Home," a wife learns that the source of her marital disharmony is the fact that her husband found a drowned woman while on a fishing trip and took days before reporting his find to the police. "Jerry and Molly and Sam" chronicles the life of a disgruntled husband and father who thinks ditching the family pet will relieve some of his stress.

"I never figured I'd make a living writing short stories," Carver told Penelope Moffet in a *Publishers Weekly* interview only a few months before he died. "How far in this world are you going to get writing short stories? I never had stars in my eyes. I never had the big-score mentality." Astonished by his literary prominence, Carver told Moffet that fame "never ceases to amaze me. And that's not false modesty, either. I'm pleased and happy with the way things have turned out. But I was surprised."

*BIOGRAPHICAL/CRITICAL SOURCES:*

*BOOKS*

Carver, Raymond, *Cathedral,* Knopf, 1984.

*Contemporary Literary Criticism,* Gale, Volume 22, 1982, Volume 26, 1983, Volume 53, 1989, Volume 55, 1989.

*Dictionary of Literary Biography Yearbook: 1984,* Gale, 1985, *Dictionary of Literary Biography Yearbook: 1988,* 1989.

*Dictionary of Literary Biography,* Volume 130: *American Short-Story Writers since World War II,* Gale, 1993.

Gentry, Marshall Bruce, and Stull, William L., editors, *Conversations with Raymond Carver,* University Press of Mississippi, 1990.

Halpert, Sam, *Raymond Carver: An Oral Biography,* University of Iowa Press (Iowa City), 1995.

Lohafer, Susan, *Coming to Terms with the Short Story,* Louisiana State University Press, 1983.

Meyer, Adam, *Raymond Carver,* Twayne (New York City), 1994.

Nesset, Kirk, *The Stories of Raymond Carver: A Critical Study,* Ohio University Press (Athens), 1995.

*Short Story Criticism,* Gale, Volume 8, 1991.

Weaver, Gordon, editor, *The American Short Story, 1945-1980,* Twayne, 1983.

*PERIODICALS*

*Akros Review,* spring, 1984.

*Antioch Review,* spring, 1984.

*Atlantic,* June, 1981.

*Booklist,* June 1, 1994, p. 1775.

*Books,* March, 1994, p. 13.

*Boston Globe,* July 17, 1983.

*Canto,* Volume 2, number 2, 1978.

*Chariton Review,* spring, 1984.

*Chicago Tribune,* October 28, 1986.

*Chicago Tribune Book World,* October 2, 1983.

*Commonweal,* December 1, 1989.

*Contemporary Literature,* winter, 1982.

*Detroit News,* October 2, 1983.

*Economist,* January 4, 1992.

*Eureka Times-Standard* (Eureka, CA), June 24, 1977.

*Georgia Review,* fall, 1982; winter, 1993, pp. 820-21.
*Globe and Mail* (Toronto), November 24, 1984; July 2, 1988.
*Harper's Bookletter,* April 26, 1976.
*Hollins Critic,* December, 1987.
*Hudson Review,* summer, 1976; autumn, 1981; spring, 1984; winter, 1993, pp. 653-8.
*Iowa Review,* summer, 1979.
*Kenyon Review,* summer, 1990, pp. 168-79.
*London Review of Books,* February 2-15, 1984; March 22, 1990, pp. 22-3; March 10, 1994, p. 19.
*Los Angeles Times,* May 25, 1988.
*Los Angeles Times Book Review,* May 24, 1981; October 2, 1983; July 28, 1985; October 26, 1986; December 28, 1986; January 31, 1988; June 26, 1988; July 19, 1992, p. 1.
*Nation,* July, 1981.
*New Republic,* April 25, 1981; November 14, 1983.
*New Statesman & Society,* August 19, 1988; February 16, 1990; December 6, 1991.
*Newsweek,* April 27, 1981; September 5, 1983.
*New York,* April 20, 1981.
*New York Review of Books,* November 24, 1983; November 18, 1993, p. 66.
*New York Times,* April 15, 1981; September 5, 1983; May 11, 1988; May 31, 1988.
*New York Times Book Review,* March 7, 1976; April 26, 1981; February 9, 1986; June 7, 1987; May 15, 1988; July 19, 1992.
*New York Times Magazine,* June 24, 1984.
*Paris Review,* summer, 1983.
*People,* November 23, 1987.
*Philological Quarterly,* winter, 1985.
*Publishers Weekly,* May 27, 1988; April 20, 1990, p. 70; August 16, 1993, p. 100.
*Saturday Review,* April, 1981; October, 1983.
*Studies in Short Fiction,* winter, 1984; summer, 1985; summer, 1986.
*Time,* April 6, 1981; September 19, 1983.
*Times* (London), January 21, 1982; April 17, 1985; May 16, 1985.
*Times Literary Supplement,* January 22, 1982; February 17, 1984; May 24, 1985; September 15, 1989; February 28, 1992, p. 16; January 24, 1997.
*Tribune Books* (Chicago), November 9, 1986; May 8, 1988; September 4, 1994, p. 12.
*Village Voice,* September 18, 1978.
*Washington Post,* August 4, 1988.
*Washington Post Book World,* May 3, 1981; September 4, 1983; May 15, 1988; July 9, 1989; January 27, 1991, p. 15.

*OBITUARIES:*

*PERIODICALS*

*Chicago Tribune,* August 3, 1988; August 7, 1988.
*Los Angeles Times,* August 4, 1988.
*New York Times,* August 3, 1988.
*Times* (London), August 4, 1988.
*Washington Post,* August 4, 1988.*

* * *

**CELAN, Paul**
**See ANTSCHEL, Paul**

* * *

**CHARYN, Jerome 1937-**

*PERSONAL:* Born May 13, 1937, in New York, NY; son of Sam (a furrier) and Fannie (Paley) Charyn; married Marlene Phillips (a writer), January 24, 1965 (divorced). *Education:* Columbia College, B.A. (cum laude), 1959.

*ADDRESSES: Home*—302 West 12th St., Apt. 10-C, New York, NY 10014; 1 rue Boulard, Paris 75014, France. *Office*—Creative Writing Program, Princeton University, Princeton, NJ 08544. *Agent*—Georges Borchardt, 136 East 57th St., New York, NY 10022; Mic Cheetham, Anthony Sheil Associates, 43 Doughty St., London WC1N 2LF, England.

*CAREER:* Recreation leader, Department of Parks, New York City, early 1960s; High School of Music and Art, and School of Performing Arts, New York City, English teacher, 1962-64; City College of the City University of New York, New York City, lecturer in English, 1965; Stanford University, Stanford, CA, assistant professor of English, 1965-68; Herbert Lehman College of the City University of New York, Bronx, NY, assistant professor, 1968-72, associate professor, 1972-78, professor of English, 1978-80; Princeton University, Princeton, NJ, visiting professor, 1980, and lecturer in creative writing, 1981-85; City College of New York, visiting distinguished professor of English, 1988-89; Rice University, Houston, TX, Mellon Visiting Professor of English, 1989; The American University of Paris, adjunct professor of film studies, 1995—.

*MEMBER:* PEN American Center (member of executive board, 1984—); International Association of Crime Writers (executive board, 1988—); Mystery Writers of America (executive board, 1989—), Playwright/Director Unit (1986—), Actors Studio, Phi Beta Kappa.

*AWARDS, HONORS:* Grants from National Endowment for the Arts, 1979 and 1984; Richard and Hinda Rosenthal Foundation Award from American Academy and Institute of Arts and Letters, 1981, for *Darlin' Bill;* Guggenheim grant, 1982; Chevalier, Order of Arts and Letters, 1989; Deanville Film Festival Fiction Award, 1995.

*WRITINGS:*

*Once upon a Droshky,* McGraw (New York City), 1964.
*On the Darkening Green,* McGraw, 1965.
*The Man Who Grew Younger and Other Stories,* Harper (New York City), 1967.
*Going to Jerusalem,* Viking (New York City), 1967.
*American Scrapbook,* Viking, 1969.
*Eisenhower, My Eisenhower,* Holt (New York City), 1971.
*The Tar Baby,* Holt, 1972.
*Blue Eyes* (part of *Isaac Quartet* tetralogy; also see below), Simon & Schuster (New York City), 1975.
*The Education of Patrick Silver* (part of *Isaac Quartet* tetralogy; also see below), Arbor House (New York City), 1976.
*Marilyn the Wild* (part of *Isaac Quartet* tetralogy; also see below), Arbor House, 1976.
*The Franklin Scare,* Arbor House, 1977.
*Secret Isaac* (part of *Isaac Quartet* tetralogy; also see below), Arbor House, 1978.
*The Seventh Babe,* Arbor House, 1979; reprinted with an afterword by Neil D. Isaacs, University Press of Mississippi (Jackson), 1996.
*The Catfish Man: A Conjured Life,* Arbor House, 1980.
*Darlin' Bill: A Love Story of the Wild West,* Arbor House, 1980.
*Panna Maria,* Arbor House, 1982.
*Pinocchio's Nose,* Arbor House, 1983.
*The Isaac Quartet* (contains *Blue Eyes, Marilyn the Wild, The Education of Patrick Silver,* and *Secret Isaac*), Zomba (London), 1984.
*War Cries Over Avenue C,* Donald I. Fine (New York City), 1985.
*Metropolis: New York as Myth, Marketplace, and Magical Land* (nonfiction), Putnam (New York City), 1986.
*The Magician's Wife* (comic book), Casterman (Tournai, Belgium), 1986; Catalan Communications (New York City), 1988.
*Paradise Man,* Donald I. Fine (New York City), 1987.
*Movieland: Hollywood and the Great American Dream Culture* (nonfiction), Putnam, 1989.
*The Good Policeman,* Mysterious Press (New York City), 1990.
*Margot in Badtown,* Tundra Publishing with Comics USA (Northampton, MA), 1991.
*Elsinore,* Mysterious Press, 1991.
*Maria's Girls,* Mysterious Press, 1992.
*Montezuma's Man,* Mysterious Press, 1993.
*Back to Bataan,* Farrar, Straus (New York City), 1993.
*Little Angel Street,* Mysterious Press, 1994.
*Family Man,* with art by Joe Staton, Paradox Press (New York City), 1995.
*El Bronx,* Mysterious Press (New York City), 1997.

Also author of screenplay, "Crayola Detective," 1971. Contributor of short stories to *Commentary, Mademoiselle,Transatlantic Review,* and other publications.

*EDITOR*

*The Single Voice: An Anthology of Contemporary Fiction,* Collier (New York City), 1969.
*The Troubled Vision: An Anthology of Contemporary Short Novels and Passages,* Collier, 1970.
*The New Mystery: The International Association of Crime Writers' Essential Crime Writing of the Late 20th Century,* Dutton (New York City), 1993.

Founding editor, *Dutton Review,* 1970-72; executive editor, *Fiction,* 1970-75.

*SIDELIGHTS:* Jerome Charyn writes unconventional novels both within and outside the realm of mystery. "I do not think of myself as a 'genre' writer," Charyn told the *St. James Guide to Crime and Mystery Writers.* "My own crazy wanderings have led me toward the crime novel. Where else could I go? New York is my heartland, and the heart of New York is crime."

Critics often have called Charyn's prose brilliant and have characterized his novels as antirealist, wild, satirical, experimental, and surreal. James Walt of the *Washington Post* terms Charyn "a sophisticated writer" and "extraordinarily gifted." *St. James Guide* contributor William Malloy describes Charyn as "a prose poet who writes crime novels."

Charyn's focus on crime has come in the latter part of his career. His works outside this genre have much in common with his mystery novels, though; they tend to be set in New York City, and they display a sense of the fantastic and bizarre. His earliest efforts, however, are conventionally organized and written. "Charyn's talent at the outset," writes Albert J. Guerard of *Tri-Quarterly,* "was traditional in a fine uninhibited way: Dickensian, but within a New York Jewish world." Guerard sees Charyn's Dickensian tendency in "the richly loquacious, irrepressible caricatures." Reviewing *The Man Who Grew Younger, and Other Stories* for *Saturday Review,* Samuel I. Bellman discovers "a freshness and yet a face-slapping impact . . . that one won't find in most slick or academic magazines, and it is also this quality of differentness that makes Charyn's collection unusually forceful and artistically successful."

In his first three books—*Once Upon a Droshky, On the Darkening Green,* and *The Man Who Grew Younger*—Charyn used a typical narrative structure, something Guerard believes "tended to limit rather than encourage Charyn's natural impulse to the fabulous." Although these early works were successful, Charyn did something different in *Going to Jerusalem,* beginning the novel in a traditional manner but slowly transforming it into a more and more fantastic story. What begins as a fairly plausible tour by a chess prodigy becomes a wild odyssey across America. Critical reaction has been mixed. Stephen Wall of the *Observer Review* finds that *Going to Jerusalem* "illustrates the increasing American recourse to fantastical modes," but judges the book "an arbitrary accumulation of irrational incidents." Writing in the *Saturday Review,* Bellman describes the novel as a "wild, zany melange of sketches, revelations, and epistles. . . . Too disorganized for the narrow, conventional taste, this novel calls up moods and responses below the threshold of consciousness." Guerard holds that "*Going to Jerusalem* is a novel full of fictional ideas, rich in Dickensian geniality and comic life, admirable in its effort to achieve a freer form; finally boring."

It was not until *Eisenhower, My Eisenhower* that Charyn left the conventional novel entirely behind him. The book, Guerard writes, is "Charyn's first genuinely antirealist, mythologizing extravaganza and first major effort to reflect the absurd aspects of contemporary urban violence." *Eisenhower, My Eisenhower* is about the Azazians, a race of gypsies living in modern America. They are discriminated against by the Anglos, the dominant group in society, and so engage in urban guerrilla warfare against the Anglos, using a wide variety of absurd disguises and stratagems. Although named in the title, President Eisenhower does not appear as a character in the novel. Critics praised Charyn's humor and intensity but criticized his lack of structure and coherence. "Here," Paul Theroux of the *Washington Post Book World* avows, "is the novel simplified to a freakish cartoon, with enough obscurities and flourishes to pass as serious writing. . . . Charyn's fluency and humor is apparent, but it is entirely a glib surface horror; there is not a coherent thought anywhere." "This comic distortion of contemporary American reality," writes Robert Scholes of *Saturday Review,* "is certainly amusing, and sometimes the satire bites pleasantly." But Scholes finds that "something is lacking in the work of this talented young man. . . . The problem is, in the broadest sense, structural. . . . The ingenuity of the parts is greater than the intelligibility of the whole."

Charyn's subsequent novels have continued in the antirealist vein, violating conventional expectations in narrative structure, characters, and subject matter. Guerard believes that although Charyn's work is experimental, "one discovers certain constants in book after book: the irrepressible comic impulse and the delight in playful inventive language." These elements can be seen in *The Franklin Scare,* for example, a fantasy concerning the presidency of Franklin Roosevelt. Although reference is made to the important events during Roosevelt's administration, the focus of the novel is on Oliver Beebe, a sailor befriended by Roosevelt and given a room in the White House attic. John Leonard of the *New York Times* explains some of the novel's plot this way: "[Beebe] eats Tootsie Rolls and dreams of sleeping with his sister; his sister is actually sleeping with a Spanish Chancellery official on the payroll of the Federal Bureau of Investigation; a Trotskyite poet from Charleston, S.C., plots to assassinate Eleanor Roosevelt with a penknife; the Wild Man of Tangiers, naked in a closet, is hiding from the Secret Service, and the Empress of Bulgaria is dying." Charyn "takes apparently factual details, . . . but he dwells upon them so that they become 'magical' and distorted," Irving Malin observes in his review of the book for the *Hollins Critic.* "Charyn continually stresses the unexpected. . . . His plot refuses to adhere to any 'sane' arrangement. . . . I believe that the world Charyn presents is so *arbitrary*—but deliberately so!—

that it is, to use his title-word, 'scary.'" Leonard claims that Charyn "has tamed his prose and makes it perform tricks. It is a New York prose, street-smart, sly and full of lurches, like a series of subway stops on the way to hell." Malin concludes that *The Franklin Scare* is "a wonderfully enjoyable, instructive novel."

Flamboyant characters and stunning prose are recurring elements in Charyn's novels, several critics note. Charyn, writes LeAnne Schreiber of *Time,* "endows his most grotesque characters with a certain beauty. His kinkiest people—an albino Negro pyromaniac, a senile, one-eyed dishwasher—are the imaginings of a major talent." Melvin Maddocks of the *Christian Science Monitor* thinks that "at their worst, Charyn's characters are eccentrics for eccentricity's sake. At their best, they are imagination-releasing examples of the infinitely varied ways human beings try to fulfill themselves." In *The Catfish Man,* Charyn uses himself as a character. The novel, writes Steven Kosek of the *Chicago Tribune Book World,* is "a humorously idiosyncratic vision of the author's life, not as he remembers it but as he imagines it. . . . The author undergoes a series of physical, sexual, and psychological transformations, rendered as cartoon-like adventures. Together, they comprise a lively, clever, and entertaining story."

Charyn's crime stories, like his other efforts, contain many elements of the bizarre. "He is a writer of police fantasies, not procedurals," remarks Malloy in the *St. James Guide. Washington Post Book World* contributor Paul Skenazy adds that "Charyn has been remaking the detective story into a kind of Ebbetts Field bleachers where no one's quite kosher, everyone's schmoozing with someone they've barely met, and a fight's about to break out."

Several of Charyn's crime novels center on a character named Isaac Sidel, initially a New York deputy police commissioner, later commissioner, and eventually mayor. This character is featured in the volumes that make up *The Isaac Quartet* and in some subsequent novels. Sidel displays "the sort of idiosyncrasies that link him to the the great tradition of eccentric detective heroes," Malloy asserts. For instance, after criminals infect Sidel with a tapeworm, he keeps a bottle of milk handy to satisfy it. *Armchair Detective* critic Norma J. Shattuck, in a review of *Montezuma Man,* pronounces Sidel "decidedly outre (and possibly certifiable)." Sidel's adventures are as peculiar as he is. Skenazy notes that in *Little Angel Street* "issues of historical preservation mingle with tales of old baseball players; the art of ping-pong blends with Dostoyevsky and Dickens; gruesome murders and illegal adoptions share the page with bad jokes, men with metal shards in their brains and blind ambulance drivers."

Skenazy finds Charyn's frenetically paced storytelling a bit hard to take at times, but concludes that "the Sidel stories are great literary farce, a satiric hothouse of fast talk and low life." Malloy calls Charyn's work "an acquired taste" but one worth developing: "Once the adventurous reader allows himself to enter Charyn's dangerously enchanted 'forest' of New York City, he will find fruit unlike any other in crime fiction."

Charyn's body of work also includes nonfiction books and a juvenile novel. His nonfiction efforts are *Metropolis: New York as Myth, Marketplace, and Magical Land* and *Movieland: Hollywood and the Great American Dream Culture.* The former is a book of essays about the varied social, cultural, historical, and ethnic aspects of New York City. In the latter, Charyn examines the history of American cinema, pointing out ways in which the movie industry has influenced American culture. His novel for youth is *Back to Bataan.* It tells the story of 11-year-old Jack Dalton; grieving over his father's death in World War II and frustrated by being a poor boy in a rich boys' school, he joins a criminal gang.

Critical reaction to Charyn's work has varied, but it usually has been anything but indifferent. Maddocks describes Charyn's prose as "a special kind of 20th-century whimsy—whistfully fey, in graceful but hard-pressed retreat before history's current brutalities." Emphasizing the energy of Charyn's writing, Malin states that Charyn "uses short sentences which startle us; we are shaken by their bursts of energy and juxtaposition. . . . The sentences are charged; the details move so swiftly and surprisingly that we are unbalanced." Writing in the *New York Times Book Review,* William Plummer states: "Charyn is one of our most consistently daring and interesting writers."

*BIOGRAPHICAL/CRITICAL SOURCES:*

*BOOKS*

*Contemporary Literary Criticism,* Gale (Detroit), Volume 5, 1976, Volume 8, 1978, Volume 18, 1981.

*Dictionary of Literary Biography Yearbook: 1983,* Gale, 1984.

*St. James Guide to Crime and Mystery Writers,* St. James Press (Detroit), 1996.

*PERIODICALS*

*Armchair Detective,* fall, 1993, pp. 20, 92; spring, 1994, p. 31.
*Atlantic,* November, 1977.
*Chicago Tribune,* May 19, 1985; September 7, 1986.
*Chicago Tribune Book World,* April 20, 1980; February 8, 1981.
*Christian Science Monitor,* October 5, 1967; July 24, 1969; May 7, 1993, p. 10.
*Columbia College Today,* winter-spring, 1971.
*Commonweal,* April 21, 1967; March 26, 1976.
*Globe and Mail* (Toronto), July 6, 1985.
*Hollins Critic,* October, 1977.
*Hudson Review,* summer, 1971.
*Library Journal,* December 1, 1974.
*Life,* June 6, 1969.
*Los Angeles Times,* December 19, 1980; September 24, 1982; July 2, 1986.
*Los Angeles Times Book Review,* February 7, 1988; June 4, 1989.
*Midstream,* October, 1969.
*New Republic,* April 10, 1976.
*Newsweek,* June 9, 1969.
*New York Review of Books,* July 22, 1971.
*New York Times,* June 3, 1969; January 23, 1975; November 19, 1977; June 18, 1979.
*New York Times Book Review,* September 17, 1967; March 28, 1971; May 2, 1976; September 5, 1976; January 21, 1979; May 6, 1979; April 20, 1980; December 7, 1980; July 16, 1989, p. 17; August 5, 1990, p. 29.
*Observer Review,* June 30, 1968.
*Partisan Review,* winter, 1968.
*Playboy,* March, 1993, p. 30.
*Publishers Weekly,* April 26, 1985; December 7, 1990, p. 79; March 8, 1991, p. 68; March 16, 1992, p. 67; June 14, 1993, p. 63; September 19, 1994, p. 53.
*Punch,* July 10, 1968.
*Rolling Stone,* October 18, 1979.
*Saturday Review,* January 14, 1967; September 9, 1967; August 23, 1969; June 5, 1971.
*School Library Journal,* June, 1993, p. 126.
*Time,* July 4, 1969; April 19, 1976; October 30, 1978.
*Tri-Quarterly,* spring, 1974.
*Village Voice,* April 21, 1980.
*Village Voice Literary Supplement,* May, 1982.
*Virginia Quarterly Review,* summer, 1973.
*Washington Post,* June 21, 1969; December 6, 1980; September 5, 1983; May 3, 1989.
*Washington Post Book World,* June 6, 1971; November 20, 1994, p. 6.*

* * *

**CHASE, James Hadley**
**See RAYMOND, Rene (Brabazon)**

* * *

## COBURN, Walt(er J.) 1889-1971

*PERSONAL:* Born October 23, 1889, in White Sulphur Springs, MT; died May 24, 1971; son of Robert (a cattleman) and Mary (Blessing) Coburn; married Blake Beck (divorced); married Mina Acheson Evans, July 7, 1927. *Education:* Attended Manzinata Hall Preparatory School, 1910. *Religion:* Roman Catholic.

*CAREER:* Cattleman; freelance writer, 1922-71. *Military service:* U.S. Army Air Service, Signal Corps, 1917-19; became sergeant first class.

*MEMBER:* Westerners, Montana Historical Society, Arizona Historical Society, Arizona Cattle Growers, Prescott Press Club.

*WRITINGS:*

*WESTERN NOVELS*

*The Ringtailed Rannyhans,* Century (New York City), 1927.
*Mavericks,* Century, 1929.
*Barb Wire,* Century, 1931.
*Walt Coburn's Action Novels* (contains *The Four Aces, Cartridges Free, Paths to Glory* and *The Maverick League*), Fiction House (New York City), 1931.
*Law Rides the Range,* Century, 1935.
*Sky-Pilot Cowboy,* Appleton (New York City), 1937, published as *The Kansas Killers,* Lancer (New York City), 1966.
*Pardners of the Dim Trails,* Lippincott (Philadelphia), 1951, published as *Tough Texan,* Lancer, 1966.
*The Way of a Texan,* Star Guidance (New York City), 1953.

*Drift Fence,* Hammond (London), 1953, Berkley (New York City), 1959.

*The Burnt Ranch,* Hammond, 1954, Macfadden (New York City), 1970, published as *Dark and Bloody Ground,* Chivers (Bath, England), 1986.

*Gun Grudge,* Hammond, 1954, Lancer, 1963.

*Wet Cattle,* Hammond, 1955, published as *Violent Maverick,* Avon (New York City), 1956.

*The Square Shooter,* Hammond, 1955, Macfadden, 1970.

*The Renegade,* Harlequin (Toronto), 1956.

*Cayuse,* Hammond, 1956.

*Border Jumper,* Hammond, 1956, Pyramid (New York City), 1961.

*Beyond the Wild Missouri,* Arcadia House (New York City), 1956.

*One Step Ahead of the Posse,* Ace Books (New York City), 1956.

*The Night Branders,* Ace Books, 1957.

*Fear Branded,* Hammond, 1957, Avon, 1971.

*Buffalo Run,* Hammond, 1958.

*Guns Blaze on Spiderweb Range,* Avon, 1958.

*Free Rangers,* Hammond, 1959.

*Branded,* Avon, 1959.

*Fast Gun,* Avon, 1959.

*Feud Valley* [and] *Sleeper-Marked: Two New Westerns,* Hammond, 1960, *Feud Valley* published separately, Lancer, 1964.

*The Ramrod* [and] *Sons of Gunfighters: Two New Westerns,* Hammond, 1960.

*La Jornada,* Consul (London), 1961, Avon, 1971.

*Invitation to a Hanging,* Avon, 1963.

*An Avon Triple Western: Renegade Legions, The Lightning Brand, Kilbourne Brothers, Wolf Hunters,* Avon, 1965.

*Man from Montana,* Lancer, 1966.

*El Hombre,* Belmont (New York City), 1967.

*Reckless!,* Belmont, 1968.

*SCREENPLAYS*

(With Isadore Bernstein) *The Black Trail,* 1924.

(With William E. Wing) *No Man's Land,* 1925.

(With Frank L. Inghram) *Pals in Peril,* 1927.

(With Inghram) *The Desert of the Lost,* Pathe, 1927.

(With Inghram) *The Ridin' Rowdy,* 1927.

*OTHER*

*Stirrup High* (autobiography), Messner (New York City), 1957.

*Pioneer Cattleman: The Story of the Circle C Ranch,* University of Oklahoma Press (Norman), 1968.

*Walt Coburn, Western Word Wrangler: An Autobiography,* Northland Press (Flagstaff, AZ), 1973.

Contributor to anthologies, including *Popular Book of Western Stories,* Popular Library (New York City), 1948; *Gunpoint,* Pyramid, 1960; *Great Stories of the West,* Doubleday (New York City), 1971; and *Westerns of the Forties,* Bobbs Merrill (Indianapolis), 1977. Contributor of over eight hundred novelettes and short stories to *Western Story, Adventure, Cowboy Story, North-West Stories, Argosy, Romance, West, Complete Story, All Western,* and *Star Western.* Two pulp magazines were at one time published as *Walt Coburn's Action Novels* and *Walt Coburn's Western Magazine.*

*ADAPTATIONS:* A number of Coburn's stories have been adapted for film, including *Fighting Fury,* Universal, 1924, *Between Dangers,* Pathe, 1927, *The Fightin' Comeback,* Pathe, 1927, *Silent Men,* Columbia, 1933, *Rusty Rides Alone,* Columbia, 1933, *The Westerner,* Columbia, 1934, and *Return of Wild Bill,* Columbia, 1940.

*SIDELIGHTS:* Walt Coburn was a prolific author of Western stories, producing over 800 novelettes for the pulp magazines during a thirty-year period. His working method, according to John D. Flanagan in *Twentieth-Century Western Writers,* "was to write four hours each day, six days a week, usually with a bottle of 'hooch' beside the typewriter." Coburn explained that he never began a story with a plot in mind, preferring to let the characters interact as he developed the story. This free-style approach, Flanagan noted, often produced "uneven and sometimes remarkably bad" stories. But Coburn's stories always displayed his authentic, firsthand knowledge of the American West. "These stories," Flanagan admitted, "do have an authentic middle ground of ranching practice, hardware, and slang."

Coburn's stories often dealt with a rough kind of frontier justice. In *Mavericks,* for example, Lance Mansfield must fight local cattle rustlers who have framed him. His efforts involve escaping jail, joining the Army for an overseas tour, and returning home to Montana to beat the rustlers and win his sweetheart. The critic for *Boston Transcript* claimed that "courage of the finest type is exemplified and the rascals and villains get becoming results." The *New York Times* reviewer observed that the novel is "told in a rushing, careless style that is intent only on keeping the reader on edge for the next happening." In 1957 Coburn published *Stirrup High,* an account of his childhood on the Montana range and his subsequent career as a Western writer. Aimed at a young audience, the book recounts Coburn's remembrances of working on his father's ranch at the turn of the century. Although Pauline Winnick in *Library Journal* called the book "of dubious moral value" because Coburn recalls aiding a local train robber escape the law, H. B. Lent in the *New York Times* found that "for sheer excitement this autobiography is superb. Men were men in the turn-of-the-century West, and young Walt Coburn learned why the hard way."

Speaking of Coburn's enormous output of Western fiction, Flanagan noted that "Coburn's West is an adolescent fantasy landscape of violence where the gun rules and all good women are virgins. No one dies of old age here, but always from the bullet, the knife, or the rope. And the one true measure of a man is the size of his fist."

Coburn once gave this summary of his life to *CA:* "I started writing Western stories in 1922 and after two years of rejection slips I sold around 900 novelettes to 37 different pulp paper magazines and had the cover and feature story in each magazine over those years. The pulps folded around 1950 and since then I have been writing novels.

"I do little research. I knew the early day cow country about which I write, cowmen, cowpunchers, sheepmen, outlaws, Indians, freighters, et al, before barbwire fenced the free range.

"I have never read another Western author's work in my lifetime of writing. I work four or five hours a day, in the mornings. I take Sundays off and a day or two between stories. I ride horseback for relaxation, and swim when I am near the ocean.

"Born and raised in the cattle business, both in Montana and Arizona, I am still interested in the cattle industry. I am proud to say I have many friends among the cattlemen and old time cowhands who are fast becoming a vanishing breed of man.

"As for myself, I have lived a full life and taken my share of hard knocks along with the good fortune that is my writing career. As the late lamented cowboy artist, Charlie Russell, who was my good friend and neighbor in Great Falls, Montana, from the time I was six years old, once remarked; 'If I cash in my chips tonight, I'm ahead of the game.' I feel the same way."

*BIOGRAPHICAL/CRITICAL SOURCES:*

*BOOKS*

Matzen, Madeline, *Writers' Markets and Methods,* [Hollywood], 1939.

*Twentieth-Century Western Writers,* second edition, St. James Press (Detroit), 1991.

*PERIODICALS*

*Booklist,* December, 1931, p. 28; October 1, 1937, p. 34.

*Books,* December 15, 1929, p. 20; September 6, 1931, p. 12; May 23, 1937, p. 18.

*Boston Transcript,* October 11, 1929, p. 2; July 10, 1937, p. 4.

*Denver Post,* July 4, 1948.

*Kirkus,* August 1, 1957, p. 25.

*Library Journal,* February 15, 1958, p. 83.

*New York Times,* December 29, 1929, p. 7; May 30, 1937, p. 15; November 24, 1957, p. 36.

*Phoenix Republic,* October 19, 1952.

*Publishers Weekly,* May 1, 1967, p. 57.

*Saturday Review of Literature,* November 14, 1931, p. 8.*

* * *

**CONNOLLY, Cyril (Vernon) 1903-1974**

*PERSONAL:* Born September 10, 1903, in Coventry, England; died November 26, 1974; son of Matthew (an army major) and Muriel (Vernon) Connolly; married Jean Bakewell; Barbara Skelton, 1950; Deirdre Craig, 1959; children: one son, one daughter. *Education:* Attended Balliol College, Oxford.

*CAREER:* Writer for the *New Statesman* and other periodicals, 1927-74; *Horizon,* London, founder, editor, and writer, 1939-50; *Observer,* London, literary editor, 1942-43; weekly contributor to the *Sunday Times,* 1951-74.

*MEMBER:* Royal Society of Literature (fellow), White's, Pratt's, Beefsteak Clubs.

*AWARDS, HONORS:* Chevalier de la Legion d'Honneur; Brackenbury scholar; D.Litt., Trinity College, Dublin; Companion of Honour, L'Academie Francaise; knighted; Commander of the Order of the British Empire, 1972.

*WRITINGS:*

*The Rock Pool* (fiction), Scribner, 1936.

*Enemies of Promise,* Routledge & Kegan Paul, 1938, Little, Brown, 1939, revised edition, Macmillan, 1948.

(Editor) *Horizon Stories,* Faber, 1943, Vanguard, 1946.

(Translator) Jean Bruller (writing under pseudonym Vercors), *Silence of the Sea,* Macmillan, 1944 (published in England as *Put Out the Light,* Macmillan, 1944).

(Under pseudonym Palinurus) *The Unquiet Grave: A Word Cycle,* Horizon (London), 1944, Harper, 1945, revised edition, Hamish Hamilton, 1945.

*The Condemned Playground* (essays), Routledge & Kegan Paul, 1945, Macmillan, 1946.

*The Missing Diplomats,* Queen Anne Press, 1952.

*Ideas and Places,* Harper, 1953.

*The Golden Horizon,* Weidenfeld & Nicolson, 1953, University Books, 1955.

(Editor and author of introduction) *Great English Short Novels,* Dial, 1953.

(With Jerome Zerbe) *Les Pavillons: French Pavilions of the Eighteenth Century,* Macmillan, 1962.

*Previous Convictions: Selected Writings of a Decade,* Harper, 1963.

*The Modern Movement: 100 Key Books from England, France, and America,* Deutsch, 1965, Atheneum, 1966.

(Translator with Simon W. Taylor) Alfred Jarry, *The Ubu Plays* (contains *Ubu Rex, Ubu Cuckolded,* and *Ubu Enchained*), Grove, 1969.

*The Evening Colonnade,* Harcourt, 1975.

*The Selected Essays of Cyril Connolly,* edited by Peter Quennell, Persea Books, 1984.

(With Peter Levi) *Shade Those Laurels,* Pantheon (New York City), 1990.

Contributor of article to *Art and Literature.*

*SIDELIGHTS:* Cyril Connolly was a respected literary critic and essayist who was at the center of the English literary scene for much of his life. He related his "Georgian boyhood" in Eton College in the last part of his formidable work *Enemies of Promise.* He believed that he was a spoiled child who suffered all the miseries of the English public school caste system while managing to acquire an excellent education. With a sharp tongue he wasn't afraid to use, he was at times a critic of the literary world, at times a self-critic. Remembering a "very nasty review" he had written on Ernest Hemingway's *Green Hills of Africa,* Connolly remarked that "the first time I met Hemingway I was introduced to him, just after I had reviewed this book, in Sylvia Beach's bookshop in Paris. When he realised who I was, he turned to Sylvia Beach and he said: 'This is a very bad moment for both of us.' That, I think, is a lovely remark: you see, he forgave me, because I was minding terribly the tactlessness of being introduced to him after writing this review, and he showed that he minded the review. We had dinner together and we became great friends, because after all I had liked his earlier books and said so."

The *New Yorker* critic found *Enemies of Promise* to be "a collection of searching and idea-packed literary essays, precisely noting the temper of current writing and pointing out the pitfalls that beset the beginning or the successful author." To Geoffrey Grigson, the complete book was most interesting, sociologically, "as a specimen [and] as a piece from the war between the ninety per cent art-gentlemen and his gentility. It is good to see conscience at work in an art-gentleman." James Stern reflected that "had I a son, whether destined for Eton, Dalton or the dogs, I would place a copy of *Enemies of Promise* in his hands at an early age. For this book is an education, a warning, an encouragement, a preparation for the literary life."

Connolly wrote one complete novel, *The Rock Pool,* published in 1936. After Connolly's death, Peter Levi, a longtime friend and admirer, completed *Shade Those Laurels,* a second novel that Connolly had worked on for nearly forty years before he died; three early parts of the novel, a murder mystery, were included in the magazine *Encounter* in the 1950s. Frank Kermode wrote in the *London Review of Books* that Connolly left "it unfinished for what must have come to seem good reasons—for example, that his talents were for silvery prose and high-spirited parody rather than for sustained narrative." He stated that "Peter Levi has a good try at keeping up the tone," but indicated the book should have been left uncompleted. Charlotte Innes gave a similar opinion in the *New York Times Book Review*: "Mr. Levi does a stylish job of rounding out a flimsily structured novel that at times threatens to keel over under the weight of its literary and gastronomic obsessions."

In 1968, responding to questions about the whole of his own "literary life" and the things which influenced it, Connolly told interviewer Richard Kershaw that his own family "would have liked me most of all, I think, to go into the Foreign Office; failing that, they'd have liked me to take some kind of nice job, like a clerk in the House of Commons, or perhaps the Lords, or anything but the thing that I did do—which was to waste a lot of time and be very extravagant and get so into debt that I spent years trying to get out of it."

Kershaw queried Connolly if involvement in politics had prevented him from doing writing he ought to have done, to which Connolly replied: "I would say only myself has prevented me doing the writing I ought to have done. A writer ought to have politics, but when it comes to the executive side of politics, standing for Parliament, speaking at a lot of meetings, being on committees, writing a lot of pamphlets, unless you're that kind of writer it must be bad for you. A writer has a vintage product which is him. He produces his little *vin ordinaire* called Chateau Connolly or whatever it is. Well, that wine results from his personality being kept in a certain condition, a certain temperature, a certain soil; and if you take him too far away from that, he becomes indistinguishable from other products of the new political soil. The Spanish war produced its best work from writers who were not involved in the running of the war but who made private sorties into it." Connolly attested, "I could never do more than write for some political cause. But I was political. So were Auden and Spender and Isherwood, of the people I knew who were slightly younger than me, and many people of my own age. But for us, the Spanish war was the crux of everything, and it was such a disaster to our hopes: it was so awful to see the side we were convinced was right totally defeated, with the democracies looking on, either sadly or cheering. It made one feel nothing could be done by politics. You had to give up all that side. And then go back into the ivory tower."

To the Virginia Woolf idea that it is essential for a writer to have a room of his own and a private income, Connolly responded: "Well, I think the room of one's own—don't forget, half of one's life one is married and hasn't got a room of one's own, unless you have a large study of your own—is a great help. There is no doubt that one's best thoughts come reading at night when you have gone to bed. If you can't read half the night your tank doesn't fill up for the next day. And a private income is very, very good too, if it isn't too big or too small. [T. S.] Eliot had a tiny income, which was no good to him. When he was offered to leave the bank where he worked, in return for a fixed income of 250 pounds a year subscribed by his admirers, he refused to leave: 'With that income I would still have to work for my living. I would do just as much journalism as if I didn't have an income at all. I'd rather stay in the bank.' Which he did for another few years . . . A good writer rises above everything and it's an alibi to say: 'I can't write, I haven't got a room of my own . . .' 'I can't write, I haven't got a private income . . .' 'I can't write, I'm a journalist,' and so on. Those are all alibis. But I have seen in my contemporaries a great many who could have been much better if it hadn't been for two or three things: social climbing, drink and unhappy love affairs, due to flaws in themselves which made their love affairs go on for too long, or become too unhappy. All novelists," Connolly reflected, "have got to be social animals, I think. You can't write a novel if you don't go to parties. And even poets have got to take a lot of their material from daily life or from things they do."

Kershaw asked Connolly if he thought psychoanalyst Sigmund Freud, political philosopher Karl Marx, politicians, and great mass movements had destroyed the ability to be a writer in the sense that Connolly wished to be thirty or forty years ago, when he had started. Connolly answered: "Each has made it harder. Freud has made it very much harder. For a critic Freud is invaluable as a tool to help you to understand other writers and the processes derived from their childhood. But in yourself Freud is a blocker: the moment you know enough Freud you know your own motives. Take, for instance, condemnation. Part of a critic's professional talent is his ability to abuse other people, especially if he can do it with moral indignation. Well, when you read Freud, who says, 'Whatever you blame you wish to do yourself,' you cannot blame in the same way. . . . I think nowadays [that the 'enemies of promise' are] the pressure of instant success, the enormous sums to be made by one book and the pathetically small ones to be made by the other ninety-nine. And, of course, the general visual impact of the television world—that is very bad for the writer, who has based himself for 2,000 years on the idea of the private person writing in his lavatory for someone who is going to read him in their lavatory. The totally private life of the writer," Connolly observed, "has become economically impossible. The cottage in the country where the Georgian poet did his own cooking and wrote his imitation Elizabethan sonnets—all that has become rather ridiculous. You couldn't live like that now. You'd get nothing but a lot of brown envelopes from the Income Tax." Connolly felt strongly "that all human beings are sentenced to death and that as the sentence will never be commuted, we are all entitled to the amenities of the condemned cell."

*BIOGRAPHICAL/CRITICAL SOURCES:*

*BOOKS*

Enright, D. J., *Conspirators and Poets,* Dufour, 1966.
Fisher, Clive, *Cyril Connolly: The Life and Times of England's Most Controversial Literary Critic,* St. Martin's Press (New York City), 1996.
Martin, Kingsley, editor, *New Statesman Profiles,* Phoenix House, 1958.
Shelden, Michael, *Friends of Promise: Cyril Connolly and the World of Horizon,* Harper & Row (New York City), 1989.

*PERIODICALS*

*Boston Transcript,* October 10, 1936.
*Encounter,* February, 1964.
*Listener,* April 11, 1968.
*London Review of Books,* January 24, 1991, pp. 20.
*Manchester Guardian,* December 13, 1938.
*New Republic,* July 15, 1946; January 31, 1948.
*New Statesman and Nation,* May 30, 1953.
*New Yorker,* April 8, 1939, October 27, 1945; January 29, 1996, p. 84.
*New York Herald Tribune Weekly Book Review,* February 27, 1949.
*New York Times Book Review,* October 11, 1936, October 7, 1945; October 20, 1991, p. 36.
*Spectator,* November 12, 1938.
*Time,* March 25, 1966.*

* * *

**COUSINS, Norman 1915-1990**

*PERSONAL:* Born June 24, 1915, in Union Hill, NJ; died November 30, 1990; son of Samuel and Sara Barry (Miller) Cousins; married Ellen Kopf, June 23, 1939; children: Andrea, Amy Loveman, Candis Hitzig, Sara Kit. *Education:* Attended Teachers College, Columbia University.

*CAREER:* *New York Evening Post,* New York City, educational editor, 1934-35; *Current History,* New York City, 1935-40, began as book critic, became literary editor and managing editor; *Saturday Review of Literature* (after 1972, *Saturday Review*), New York City, executive editor, 1940-42, editor, 1942-78, editor emeritus, 1980-82; *World,* New York City, editor, 1972-73; *Saturday Review/World,* New York City, editor, 1973-74; University of California, Los Angeles, professor of medical humanities and affiliated with Brain Research Institute. McCall's Corp., New York City, vice president and director, 1961-90.

U.S. Government diplomat and lecturer in India, Pakistan, and Ceylon, 1951; Japan-America exchange lecturer, Japan, 1953. Chair of board of directors of National Educational Television, 1969-70; member of Commission to Study Organized Peace; member of board of directors of Freedom House and Willkie Memorial Foundation; member of board of directors of Columbia University Conference on Science, Philosophy, and Religion. Chair of Connecticut Fact Finding Commission on Education, 1948-52; founder and president of United World Federalists, 1952-54, honorary president, 1954-56; co-chair of National Committee for a Sane Nuclear Policy, 1957-63; served on Mayor's Task Force on Air Pollution, New York City, from 1966. *Military service:* Office of War Information, Overseas Bureau, member of editorial board, 1943-45; co-chair of national campaign board of 1943 Victory Book Campaign.

*MEMBER:* American Council of Learned Societies (member-at-large), National Planning Association, National Academy of Sciences (member of committee on international relations), Hiroshima Peace Center Association, Menninger Foundation, Ruth Mott Foundation, Charles F. Kettering Foundation (trustee), United Nations Association (director of U.S. Division), World Association of World Federalists, Council on Foreign Relations, National Press Club, Overseas Press Club (member of board of governors), PEN (vice president of American Center, 1952-55), Century Club, Coffee House (New York City).

*AWARDS, HONORS:* Thomas Jefferson Award for the Advancement of Democracy in Journalism, 1948; Tuition Plan award for outstanding service to American education, 1951; Benjamin Franklin citation in magazine journalism, 1956; Wayne State University award for national service to education, 1958; New York State Citizens Education Commission award, 1959; John Dewey Award for Education, 1959; New York State Citizens Education Community award, 1959; Eleanor Roosevelt Peace award, 1963; Publius award, United World Federalists, 1964; Overseas Press Club award, 1965; Distinguished Citizen award, Connecticut Bar Association, 1965; New York Academy of Public Education award, 1966; Family of Man award, 1968; Annual award, Aquinas College, 1968; national magazine award, Association of Deans of Journalism Schools, 1969.

Peace medal, United Nations, 1971; Sarah Josepha Hale award, 1971; Carr Van Anda award for contributions to journalism, Ohio State University, 1971; Gold medal for literature, National Arts Club, 1972; Journalism Honor award, University of Missouri School of Journalism, 1972; Irita Van Doren book award, 1972; award for service to the environment, Government of Canada, 1972; Henry Johnson Fisher award as magazine publisher of the year, Magazine Publishers Association, 1971; Human Resources award, 1977; Convocation medal, American College of Cardiology, 1978; Author of the Year award, American Society of Journalists and Authors, 1981; American Book Award nomination in paperback nonfiction, 1982, for *Anatomy of an Illness as Perceived by the Patient;* Niwano Peace Award (Japan), 1990; Physicians for Social Responsibility Award, 1990; Albert Schweitzer Peace Prize, John Hopkins University, 1990.

Also recipient of nearly fifty honorary doctorate degrees, including: Litt.D., American University, 1948, Syracuse University, 1956, Temple University, 1961, Michigan State University, 1969; L.H.D. from Colgate University, 1959, Brandeis University, 1969; L.L.D. from Washington and Jefferson College, 1956 and George Washington University, 1982; honorary M. D. from New Haven County Medical Association/ Connecticut State Medical Society, 1984.

*WRITINGS:*

*The Good Inheritance: The Democratic Chance,* Coward, 1942.
(Editor) *A Treasury of Democracy,* Coward 1942.
*Modern Man Is Obsolete,* Viking, 1945.
(Editor with William Rose Benet) *An Anthology of the Poetry of Liberty,* Modern Library, 1945.
(Editor) *Writing for Love or Money: Thirty-Five Essays Reprinted from the Saturday Review of Literature,* Longmans, Green, 1949.
(Contributor) John W. Chase, editor, *Years of the Modern,* Longmans, Green, 1949.
(With Jawaharlal Nehru) *Talks with Nehru,* Day, 1951.
*Who Speaks for Man?,* Macmillan, 1953.
*Amy Loveman, 1881-1955, A Eulogy* (pamphlet), Overbrook Press, 1956.
*The Religious Beliefs of the Founding Fathers,* 1958.
(Editor) *In God We Trust,* Harper, 1958.
(Editor) Francis March, *Thesaurus Dictionary,* Doubleday, 1958.
*The Rejection of Nothingness* (pamphlet), Pacific School of Religion, 1959.
*Dr. Schweitzer of Lambarene,* Harper, 1960.
*In Place of Folly,* Harper, 1961, revised edition, Washington Square Press, 1962.
*Can Cultures Co-Exist?* (symposium), Ministry of Scientific Research & Cultural Affairs (New Delhi), 1963.
(With others) *". . . Therefore Choose Life, That Thou Mayest Live, Thou and Thy Seed,"* Center for the Study of Democratic Institutions, 1965.
(Editor) *Profiles of Nehru: America Remembers a World Leader,* Indian Book Co., 1966.
(Editor) *Great American Essays,* Dell, 1967.
*Present Tense: An American Editors Odyssey,* McGraw, 1967.
(With others) *Issues: 1968,* University Press of Kansas, 1968.
*Profiles of Gandhi: America Remembers a World Leader,* Indian Book Co., 1969.
*The Improbable Triumvirate: John F. Kennedy, Pope Paul, Nikita Khruschev: An Asterisk to the History of a Hopeful Year, 1962-1963,* Norton, 1972.
*The Celebration of Life: A Dialogue on Immortality and Infinity,* Harper, 1974, published as *The Celebration of Life: A Dialogue on Hope, Spirit, and the Immortality of the Soul,* Bantam (New York City), 1991.
*The Quest for Immortality,* Harper, 1974.
(Editor with Mary L. Dimond) *Memoirs of a Man: Grenville Clark,* Norton, 1975.
*Anatomy of an Illness as Perceived by the Patient: Reflections on Healing and Regeneration,* G. K. Hall, 1979.
*Reflections on Healing and Regeneration,* G. K. Hall, 1980.
*Human Options: An Autobiographical Notebook,* Norton, 1981.
*The Physician in Literature,* Saunders, 1981.
*Healing and Belief,* Mosaic Press, 1982.
*The Healing Heart: Antidotes to Panic and Helplessness,* Norton, 1983.
*The Trial of Dr. Mesmer: A Play,* Norton, 1984.
*Albert Schweitzer's Mission: Healing and Peace,* Norton, 1985.
*The Human Adventure: A Camera Chronicle,* Saybrook, 1986.
*The Pathology of Power,* Norton, 1987.
(Editor) *The Republic of Reason: The Personal Philosophies of the Founding Fathers,* Harper, 1988.
(Author of commentary) *Jason Sitwell's Book of Spoofs,* Dutton, 1989.
*Head First: The Biology of Hope,* Dutton, 1989, published as *Head First: The Biology of Hope and the Healing Power of the Human Spirit,* Penguin (New York City), 1990.

Also author of *The Last Defense in a Nuclear Age,* 1960. Also featured in sound recording *Betting One's Life on the Future of Print,* Development Digest, 1973. Editor *U. S. A.*, 1943-45; member of board of editors, *Encyclopaedia Britannica;* editorial supervisor, *March's Dictionary-Thesaurus,* 1980.

*ADAPTATIONS: Anatomy of an Illness as Perceived by the Patient* was adapted as the television movie *Anatomy of an Illness* starring Ed Asner, Columbia Broadcasting System, 1984. *Head First* was recorded on audio cassette, Nightingale-Conant Corporation (Chicago), 1990.

*SIDELIGHTS:* "I get a kick out of challenging the odds," Norman Cousins once told *Publishers Weekly* interviewer Lisa See. His life and career gave him ample opportunity to do just that. While serving as longtime editor of *Saturday Review,* where Cousins bolstered that magazine's circulation to 650,000, he also served as a diplomat during three presidential administrations, became a professor of medical humanities, and produced numerous books on political and social issues. In the process, Cousins fended off a life-threatening disease and a massive coronary, both times using his own regimen of nutritional and emotional support systems as opposed to traditional methods of treatment. These experiences would be later chronicled in two books, *Anatomy of an Illness as Perceived by the Patient: Reflections on Healing and Regeneration* and *The Healing Heart: Antidotes to Panic and Helplessness.*

Cousins was often described as the man who laughed his way to health, a simplified explanation of the controversial healing method the author/editor employed when he was diagnosed in the mid-1960s as having ankylosing spondylitis, a degenerative disease causes the breakdown of collagen, the fiberous tissue that binds together the body's cells. Almost completely paralyzed and given only a few months to live, Cousins ordered himself checked out of the hospital where he had spent weeks undergoing tests. He moved into a hotel room and began taking extremely high doses of vitamin C, counting on the ascorbic acid to oxygenate his bloodstream and thereby counteract the effects of the illness. At the same time, intent on maintaining a positive mental outlook, Cousins exposed himself to equally high doses of humor—old "Candid Camera" tapes, Marx Brothers movies, and books by P. G. Wodehouse and Robert Benchley.

This unusual regimen started to work: "I made the joyous discovery that ten minutes of genuine belly laughter had an anesthetic effect and would give me at least two hours of pain-free sleep," wrote Cousins in *Anatomy of an Illness.* Slowly, the patient regained use of his limbs. As his condition steadily improved over the following months, Cousins resumed his busy life, eventually returning to work full-time at the *Saturday Review.*

As Cousins noted in his book, "the will to live is not a theoretical abstraction, but a physiologic reality with therapeutic characteristics." While agreeing that a positive attitude may certainly help a patient through his illness, some of the author's critics questioned the nature of Cousins' ailment and the healing methods he began to swear by. In a *Commentary* article Florence A. Ruderman took exception to the author's case history as related in *Anatomy of an Illness.* Questioning the role that positive emotions play in health, Ruderman questioned whether Cousins' treatment could be adapted by the general public—and if it should be at all. "Should *all* patients have the same rights and freedom that Cousins had?," she wrote. "If not, why is it inspiring that such rights and deference were accorded to Cousins? Under what circumstances should doctors allow patients to choose their own drugs, invent their own routines and regimens—in effect, direct their doctors?. . . How was it possible for so many doctors to greet [the author's] account with enthusiasm, and ignore every substantive and ethical issue in it?" Responding to Ruderman's charge in *Publishers Weekly,* Cousins maintained that "she didn't see the medical reports and didn't interview the doctors." He also answered another criticism: "the *Mt. Sinai Journal of Medicine,* . . . said that I might have had a nominal remission. That may be right, but the doctors didn't think so at the time."

Others found more to recommend in *Anatomy of an Illness.* Daphne Abeel suggested in *New Republic* that Cousins' story was "a tribute to what may be achieved by the individual. It is not a brief for self-cure in any and all circumstances, as he is quick to point out. And it must be said that not every patient will possess Cousins' unusual curiosity and knowledge about medicine. Still, his example of gumption and faith will offer hope to many." And *Washington Post* critic Richard Restak called the book "an entertaining and instructive example of an inspired participation on the part of a patient in his own treatment."

In 1980, some fifteen years after winning his bout with ankylosing spondylitis, Cousins suffered a near-fatal heart attack while on a teaching assignment in California. Again faced with the challenge of restoring his health, he responded by telling his doctors at the UCLA Intensive Care unit that they were "looking at what is probably the darndest healing machine that has ever been wheeled into the hospital," according to Joel Elkes's *Saturday Review* article on *The Healing Heart.* "As before," Elkes continued, Cousins used his body as "a personal laboratory. . . . He refuses morphine; he asks for a change in the visiting routine to ensure rest. Gradually he improves."

One major obstacle Cousins faced during his recovery was the treadmill test, designed to chart the progress of his heart rate. The patient was "scared stiff at *being* exercised, at an accelerating pace, on a moving band over which he had no control," explained Elkes. "He tries to suppress his fear, but fails and has to stop. He tries again and cannot manage." Quickly realizing that fear was the factor slowing his progress, Cousins adopted a more relaxed life style, changed his diet, and avoided stressful situations. Eventually, he was able to manage the treadmill test successfully.

Publishing these findings in *The Healing Heart,* Cousins again met with mixed reaction. *Los Angeles Times* contributor Fred Rosenfelt, for instance, while acknowledging that the author's "opinion of the salutary effects of positive emotion was widely accepted," nevertheless wondered "how many patients have the fortitude to disagree with their physicians and follow an alternative recovery program after a major heart attack? Furthermore, if a large number of individuals do so, how many will improve or worsen?" Elkes, on the other hand, argued that *The Healing Heart* is not a medical textbook, but a study of "awareness, listening, trust, choice, and intention, and about the intelligent use of a benevolent, centering will. It is about communication and partnership between the healer and the healed. It addresses as complementary the art of medicine and the science of medicine, the person and the institution, and freedom of choice and professional responsibility. [The book] affirms hope and belief as biologically constructive forces: not as blind faith, but as belief guided by knowledge and tempered by reason. It asserts that the quality of a person's life is the sum of the quality of his days."

Cousins' most popular book of the late 1980s was almost certainly *Head First: The Biology of Hope and the Healing Power of the Spirit,* a further elucidation of his beliefs and concerns regarding medicine and doctor-patient relations. Focusing on what *Washington Post Book World* critic Fitzhugh Mullan called "the great mind-body debate," *Head First* summarizes Cousins' work after his publication of *Anatomy of an Illness* resulted in an invitation to join UCLA's Medical School faculty in the late 1970s. Working as both a teacher and a consultant over the following decade, Cousins grew concerned that the pressures of the traditional education in medicine that most young doctors received had resulted in a decline in the humanistic component of healing. As the author later maintained in *Head First,* of utmost importance in healing is "the doctor's role beyond the prescription pad, and, in particular, his ability to invoke the patient's own bodily resources." Indeed, the greatest portion of *Head First* is a discussion of Cousin's belief in what he dubbed "psychoneuroimmunology"—the affect of a patient's emotional attitude upon his ability to get well.

*Head First* directly addresses one of the more controversial aspects of Cousins' claims—that the mind is to some extent capable of controlling the body. As Mullan put it, "If some of us can take credit for mastering our psycho-biology, are others to blame for failing to succeed in their efforts?" And Melvin Konner, Ph.D, M.D., noted of Cousins' contribution to the advancement of the psychological dimension of human illness that although he has contributed much to the discussion, "there is nothing like clinical experience to make you realize how complex and difficult the battle against illness is—and how capriciously it defies our pieties, including these new ones about hope." Continuing to address the issue of hope, both through his medical writing and in such works as 1987's *The Pathology of Power,* wherein he addressed the issue of world peace, Cousins remained an active literary force up until his death in 1990 at age seventy-five.

*BIOGRAPHICAL/CRITICAL SOURCES:*

*BOOKS*

Cousins, Norman, *Present Tense: An American Editor's Odyssey,* McGraw, 1967.

Cousins, Norman, *Anatomy of an Illness as Perceived by the Patient: Reflections on Healing and Regeneration,* G. K. Hall, 1979.

Cousins, Norman, *Human Options: An Autobiographical Notebook,* Norton, 1981.

Cousins, Norman, *The Healing Heart: Antidotes to Panic and Helplessness,* Norton, 1983.

Cousins, Norman,*Head First: The Biology of Hope,* Dutton, 1989.

*Dictionary of Literary Biography,* Volume 137: *American Magazine Journalists, 1900-1960,* Gale, 1994.

*PERIODICALS*

*American Health,* January-February, 1990, p. 106.
*Chicago Tribune,* December 26, 1979.
*Commentary,* May, 1980.
*Detroit News,* June 22, 1980.
*Esquire,* February, 1980.
*Journal of the American Medical Association,* April 17, 1996, p. 1209.
*Los Angeles Times,* September 29, 1983.
*Los Angeles Times Book Review,* December 13, 1981; October 24, 1982; December 3, 1989, p. 1.
*National Review,* April 30, 1982; December 9, 1983.
*New England Journal of Medicine,* April 26, 1990, p. 1240.
*New Republic,* September 29, 1979; December 10, 1990, p. 10.
*New Statesman,* October 3, 1980.
*New York Times,* June 22, 1972; September 15, 1979; May 8, 1984; May 15, 1984.
*New York Times Book Review,* January 1, 1984.
*People,* June 1, 1979.
*Publishers Weekly,* September 23, 1983.
*Saturday Review,* September-October, 1983.
*Time,* August 30, 1982.
*Times Literary Supplement,* March 30, 1984.
*Washington Post,* October 9, 1979; November 9, 1981.
*Washington Post Book World,* April 12, 1987; November 5, 1989, p. 11.

*OBITUARIES:*

*PERIODICALS*

*Current Biography,* January, 1991, p. 58.
*National Review,* December 31, 1990, p. 14.
*Time,* December 10, 1990, p. 77.*

* * *

**CULP, John H(ewett, Jr.) 1907-**

*PERSONAL:* Born August 31, 1907, in Meridian, MS; son of John Hewett and Nelle (Hoyle) Culp; married Elizabeth Price, June 25, 1934 (deceased). *Education:* University of Oklahoma, A.B., 1934.

*ADDRESSES: Home and office*—1805 North Louisa, Shawnee, OK 74801.

*CAREER:* Teacher in public schools of Norman, OK, 1934-41; owner of music store in Admore, OK, 1941-42, and Shawnee, OK, 1946-68; freelance writer, 1968—. *Military service:* U.S. Army Air Forces, 1943-45; became sergeant.

*MEMBER:* Phi Beta Kappa.

*WRITINGS:*

*Born of the Sun,* Sloane (New York City), 1959.
*The Men of Gonzales,* Sloane, 1960.
*The Restless Land,* Sloane, 1962.
*The Bright Feathers,* Holt (New York City), 1965.
*A Whistle in the Wind,* Holt, 1968.
*Timothy Baines,* Holt, 1969.
*The Treasure of the Chisos,* Holt, 1971.
*Oh, Valley Green!,* Holt, 1972.

*SIDELIGHTS:* John H. Culp, in his novels of the American West, "breathes life into an era, and creates characters who can recapture a reader's mind and heart," according to R. E. Briney in *Twentieth-Century Western Writers.*

In *Born of the Sun,* Culp tells the story of the early Texas cattle drives of the 1870s from the viewpoint of young Martin Cameron, an orphan who accompanies one such drive. The tale is continued in *The Restless Land.* These two books, according to Briney, "tell of [Martin's] painful and adventurous passage to maturity against the background of post-Civil War Texas." Speaking of *Born of the Sun,* Lon Tinkle in the *Chicago Sunday Tribune* calls it "a triumph of narrative invention" containing "the characters and the episodes and the inventiveness that first class westerns display to the delight of millions." Donald Wetzel noted in the *New York Herald Tribune Book Review* that Culp shows "a genuine knowledge and love of the West and its history. . . . The author has written boldly and with vigor of a bold land and a vigorous people."

*The Men of Gonzales* is a fictional account of the thirty-two Texans who answered the call for help at the Alamo and lost their lives in attempting to fight off the Mexican army. Wetzel states: "Both [Culp's] love of the land and his knowledge of the times . . . are obviously abundant. In the field of romantic historical fiction dealing with the early American West and Southwest Mr. Culp has clearly established a unique and respectable place for himself."

*The Treasure of the Chicos* follows the quest by a young man to make his fortune in the old west after receiving a land grant from his dying grandfather. Colin O'Reiley travels down the Mississippi from St. Louis on a whiskey-runner and then heads into the Texas Indian country, all the while stalked by a stranger who wants to steal his land. The *Publishers Weekly* critic calls the book a "rather naive, good-natured adventure story [with] a certain rollicking charm." Janet Strothman in *Library Journal* finds the book "a pleasure to read, with much background on the Old West tucked in." The reviewer for *Booklist* notes that "the character of the country and the people of the era . . . is well conveyed."

*Oh, Valley Green!* tells the story of a family migrating westward over the Santa Fe Trail in 1842. Son Carey "who captains the caravan, rises to each new challenge, triumphing over adversity and tragedy," writes the reviewer for *Publishers Weekly*. "The author," writes Lee Sullenger in *Library Journal*, "apparently intends only escape entertainment, and knows how to write it." Briney finds that, "as in all of Culp's novels, it is the human story in the foreground that holds the attention and stirs the emotions."

Briney concludes that "Culp's novels are mixtures of myth-making and history, marked by a scrupulous fidelity to the nature of the people, the times, and the country about which he writes."

*BIOGRAPHICAL/CRITICAL SOURCES:*

*BOOKS*

*Twentieth-Century Western Writers*, second edition, St. James Press (Detroit), 1991.

*PERIODICALS*

*Best Sellers*, August 15, 1968, p. 28.
*Booklist*, June 15, 1971, p. 853.
*Chicago Sunday Tribune*, June 21, 1959, p. 3.
*Christian Science Monitor*, May 5, 1960, p. 5.
*Library Journal*, July, 1971, p. 2376; April 1, 1972, p. 1345.
*New York Herald Tribune Book Review*, June 21, 1959, p. 8; May 22, 1960, p. 7.
*New York Times Book Review*, July 5, 1959, p. 12; April 8, 1960, p. 43; June 23, 1968, p. 33.
*Publishers Weekly*, January 11, 1971, p. 61; January 17, 1972, pp. 56-57.

**CURRY, Peggy Simson 1911-1987**

*PERSONAL:* Born December 30, 1911, in Dunure, Ayrshire, Scotland; died after a long illness, January 20, 1987, in Casper WY; daughter of William Andrew (a rancher) and Margaret (Anderson) Simson; married William Seeright Curry (an educator), July 21, 1937; children: Michael Munro. *Education:* University of Wyoming, B.A., 1936. *Politics:* Republican. *Religion:* Presbyterian.

*CAREER:* Casper College, Casper, WY, instructor in creative writing, 1951-87. Poet-in-residence, State of Wyoming poetry-in-schools program, 1970-87. Lecturer at various colleges and writers' conferences.

*MEMBER:* Western Writers of America, Kappa Kappa Gamma, P.E.O. Sisterhood.

*AWARDS, HONORS:* Spur Award for short stories, Western Writers of America, 1957, 1970; Kappa Kappa Gamma Distinguished Alumni award, 1964; University of Wyoming Distinguished Alumni award, 1968; poet laureate of Wyoming, 1981.

*WRITINGS:*

*Fire in the Water* (novel), McGraw (New York City), 1951.
*Red Wind of Wyoming* (poetry), Sage (Denver), 1955, revised edition, Spirit Mound Press (Fairbanks, AK), 1977.
*So Far from Spring* (novel), Viking (New York City), 1956.
*The Oil Patch* (novel), McGraw, 1959.
*Creating Fiction from Experience*, Writer (Boston), 1964, revised edition, 1975.
*A Shield of Clover* (juvenile novel), McKay (New York City), 1970.
(Editor) *Western Romances*, Fawcett (New York City), 1973.
*Summer Range* (poetry), Dooryard Press (Story, WY), 1981.

Contributor to anthologies, including *Twenty-Two Stories about Horses and Men*, Coward (New York City), 1953; *Colt's Law*, Bantam (New York City), 1957; *Frontiers West*, Doubleday (New York City), 1959; *Spurs West*, Doubleday, 1960; *Women Poets of the West*, Boise State University, 1979; *The West*, Doubleday, 1980; and *Westward the Women*, Doubleday, 1984. Contributor to *New York Times*, *Saturday Evening Post*, *Christian Science Monitor*, *Collier's*, *American Magazine*, *Reader's Digest*, *Good*

*Housekeeping,* and *Boys' Life.* Author of weekly poet's column in *Chicago Sunday Tribune* and in other publications.

*SIDELIGHTS:* Peggy Simson Curry wrote several collections of poetry and two novels which focus on "her adopted western homeland" of Wyoming, as Robert J. Barnes stated in *Twentieth-Century Western Writers.* Curry was named Wyoming's Poet Laureate for her lyrics about the state. Her novels *So Far from Spring* and *The Oil Patch* are realistic portrayals of ranch life in Wyoming, while her juvenile novel *A Shield of Clover* tells of a runaway boy who takes refuge in rural Wyoming.

Curry's *So Far from Spring* is the autobiographical story of Kelsey Cameron, a Scottish man who brings his family to the American West in hopes of making his fortune. The novels follows Cameron's daughter Heather as she grows up in Wyoming's open spaces. "We see [Heather] growing up and maturing emotionally and intellectually," Barnes noted. "But what is most impressive here is the realistic detail about the cattle industry. . . . Curry tells us how it feels to muck a stable, ride a cow pony, dig a ditch or a post hole, and feed, breed, and brand cattle. She knows about grass, about droving, and about natural hazards: wind, drought, blizzards. It is a first-class performance."

In *The Oil Patch* Curry tells the story of a newly-married couple working in a Wyoming oil camp of the 1930s. "Curry," Barnes wrote, "is at her best . . . in depicting the workaday world of the oil field and the pipeline, the dreary company houses, the rules and the impersonality of the oil company."

Curry's juvenile novel *A Shield of Clover* is the story of 17-year-old Chris, a runaway from Illinois who ends up working on a ranch in Wyoming. During the course of the summer, Chris "comes to a better understanding of life and of himself," as Judith L. Schwarz wrote in *Library Journal.* The *Publishers Weekly* critic noted that it is "the ever-present wisdom of adults and the boy's own moral strength that forces him to face up to the realities from which he has tried to escape." The story, Schwarz concluded, "is handled subtly and skillfully." Barnes admired how Curry "competently evokes the presence of the vibrant, brooding land, and the necessity of honest endeavor."

*BIOGRAPHICAL/CRITICAL SOURCES:*

*BOOKS*

*Twentieth-Century Western Writers,* second edition, St. James Press (Detroit), 1991.

*PERIODICALS*

*Library Journal,* January 15, 1971, p. 265.
*Publishers Weekly,* January 11, 1971, p. 63.

*OBITUARIES:*

*PERIODICALS*

*Baltimore Sun,* January 22, 1987.
*Detroit Free Press,* January 23, 1987.
*Seattle Times,* January 25, 1987.
*Washington Post,* January 24, 1987.*

# D

**DANE, Carl**
**See ADAMS, F(rank) Ramsay**

* * *

**DARLINGTON, David 1951-**

*PERSONAL:* Born March 14, 1951, in Houston, TX; son of David A. (in sales) and Patricia (a legal secretary and homemaker; maiden name, Houser) Darlington. *Education:* Attended Yale University, 1974.

*ADDRESSES: Home and office*—Berkeley, CA. *Agent*—Frederick Hill Associates, 1842 Union St., San Francisco, CA 94123.

*CAREER:* Freelance writer, 1974—. *Amador Progress News,* Ione, CA, reporter, 1977-78; copywriter for Banana Republic (clothing retailer), 1985-87.

*WRITINGS:*

*In Condor Country,* Houghton (Boston, MA), 1987, published as *In Condor Country: A Portrait of a Landscape, Its Denizens, and Its Defenders,* Holt (New York City), 1991.
*Angels' Visits: An Inquiry into the Mystery of Zinfandel,* Holt, 1991.
*The Mojave: A Portrait of the Definitive American Desert,* Holt, 1996.

Columnist for *East Bay Express,* 1983-85. Contributor to periodicals, including *California, Life,* and *Outside.*

*WORK IN PROGRESS:* Research on nature, outdoor, environmental, and geographical topics.

*SIDELIGHTS:* David Darlington writes about the natural environment and those who care about—and for—it. His books are based on extended personal observations of the land, its flora and fauna, and its human residents, as well as explorations of the historical rise and fall of the habitats about which he writes. Often he selects one or more local mentors who can provide a wealth of background information, guide the direction of Darlington's research, and enrich or inform the focus from which the author's perspective grows.

*In Condor Country* is the story of the California condor and the government effort to preserve the vanishing species by relocating the surviving condors to zoos, where they would live in safety and with the support of current scientific technology. Darlington's mentors were brothers Ian and (especially) Eben McMillan, eighty-year residents of the condor country around San Luis Obispo, California. These farmer-conservationists had conducted an Audubon Society study of condors in the 1960s. Over a five-year period, reports Dennis Drabelle in the *Washington Post Book Review,* "they educated Darlington about a wide spectrum of environmental issues." These included the contrasting positions of biologists who believed, according to *Los Angeles Times Book Review* reviewer David Graber, "that the birds should not be molested in any way" and those who wanted "to capture birds in order to obtain physiological information" and ultimately to confine the condors in captive breeding areas. The last of the thirty-odd free condors was captured in April, 1987. "Darlington is a fine storyteller and a vivid writer," Drabelle concludes, and of the author's relationship with Eben McMillan, he suggests that "the result is an affectionate portrait of a man living in harmony with an environment most of his peers regard as begging to be tamed." In *Publishers Weekly,* Genevieve Stuttaford calls *In Condor Country* "an authoritative account of the controversy . . . and the final days of the wild California condor."

*Angels' Visits: An Inquiry into the Mystery of Zinfandel* "belongs on the shelf of anyone who likes to read about and/or drink wine," states Karen Stabiner in the *Los Angeles Times Book Review.* Frank J. Prial comments in the *New York Times Book Review* that the book "weaves history, geography, wine and some of the fascinating people who make it into a downright enthralling tale." The reviewer concludes: "Mr. Darlington writes with wit and clarity. He knows his wine but carries his erudition lightly."

Darlington's third book represents a return to the wilderness. *The Mojave: A Portrait of the Definitive American Desert* is, in the words of *Los Angeles Times Book Review* critic Frank Levering, "a first-person portrait of the region both remarkably broad and fair-minded, encompassing huge swaths of natural and cultural history." In it, writes Donna Seaman in *Booklist,* Darlington "defines the Mojave's distinct ecological niche and summarizes the politics of its environmental issues, especially the battle over the desert tortoise." The subject of the book, Janet Lembke tells *New York Times Book Review* readers, is "the wide-ranging impact of the human presence on a region that appears to be rugged but is perilously fragile and vulnerable." Levering comments that "what a reader will remember longest are Darlington's vivid portraits, often laced with irony and dark humor." "It is," contributes Lembke, "in this respect,—giving faces, voices and passion to an otherwise immense complexity—that Mr. Darlington succeeds most brilliantly." Stuttaford calls the book "a sparkling narrative" and "a gem." Levering recommends that "traveling deep into the Mojave with David Darlington will prove as satisfying as a cool drink of water in the desert sun."

*BIOGRAPHICAL/CRITICAL SOURCES:*

*PERIODICALS*

*American Heritage,* July-August, 1996, p. 107.
*American West,* February, 1988, p. 42.
*Audobon,* July, 1996, p. 108.
*Booklist,* April 15, 1996, p. 1410.
*Los Angeles Times Book Review,* May 24, 1987, p. 9; June 2, 1991, p. 6; April 14, 1996, p. 3.
*New York Times Book Review,* March 17, 1991, p. 11; April 12, 1992, p. 32; September 1, 1996, p. 14.
*Publishers Weekly,* April 10, 1987, p. 86; February 26, 1996, p. 70.
*Sierra,* July, 1987, p. 71.
*Washington Post Book World,* April 26, 1987, p. 7.
*Western American Literature,* spring, 1988, p. 82.
*Wilderness,* fall, 1987, p. 61.
*Wine Spectator,* June 15, 1991, p. 40.

* * *

**de MAN, Paul (Adolph Michel) 1919-1983**

*PERSONAL:* Born December 6, 1919, in Antwerp, Belgium; immigrated to United States, 1947; died of cancer, December 21, 1983, in New Haven, CT; son of Robert (a manufacturer of X-ray equipment) and Magdalena (de Brey) de Man; married Anaide Baraghian, 1943 (marriage ended); married Patricia Kelley, 1950; children: (first marriage) Hendrik, Robert, Marc; (second marriage) Patricia, Michael. *Education:* University of Brussels, Candidature, 1942; Harvard University, M.A., 1958, Ph.D., 1960.

*CAREER: Le Soir* (daily newspaper), Brussels, Belgium, writer, 1940-42; worked as a translator and in publishing business in Brussels and Antwerp, Belgium, 1942-47; affiliated with faculty of University of Zurich, Zurich, Switzerland; Bard College, Annandale-on-Hudson, NY, teacher of French literature, 1949-51; Berlitz School, Boston, MA, French teacher, beginning in 1951; Harvard University, Cambridge, MA, lecturer, c. 1955-60; Cornell University, Ithaca, NY, teacher, 1960-67; Johns Hopkins University, Baltimore, MD, professor of humanistic studies, 1967-1970; Yale University, New Haven, CT, 1970-83, became Sterling Professor of Humanities and chair of department of comparative literature.

*WRITINGS:*

(Translator) Paul Alverdes, *Le Double Visage,* Editions de la Toison d'Or (Brussels), 1942.
(Translator) Filip de Pillecyn, *Le Soldat Johan,* Editions de la Toison d'Or, 1942.
(Translator) Albert Erich Brinckmann, *Esprit des nations,* Editions de la Toison d'Or, 1943.

(Translator) Herman Melville, *Moby Dick,* Helicon, Kipdorp (Antwerp), 1945.

(Editor and translator) Gustave Flaubert, *Madame Bovary: Backgrounds and Sources; Essays in Criticism,* Norton, 1965.

*Field of Comparative Literature: Analysis of Needs,* [Ithaca, NY], 1967.

*Blindness and Insight: Essays in the Rhetoric of Contemporary Criticism,* Oxford University Press, 1971, 2nd edition, revised, with introduction by Wlad Godzich, University of Minnesota Press (Minneapolis), 1983.

(Editor) Ranier Maria Rilke, *Oeuvres,* Editions du Seuil, 1972.

*Allegories of Reading: Figural Language in Rousseau, Nietzsche, Rilke, and Proust,* Yale University Press, 1979.

(With Harold Bloom, Jacques Derrida, Geoffrey H. Hartman, and J. Hillis Miller) *Deconstruction and Criticism,* Seabury Press, 1979.

*The Rhetoric of Romanticism,* Columbia University Press, 1984.

*The Resistance to Theory,* foreword by Wlad Godzich, University of Minnesota Press, 1986.

*Aesthetic Ideology,* edited by Andrzej Warminski, University of Minnesota Press, 1988.

*Fugitive Writings,* edited by Lindsay Waters, University of Minnesota Press, 1988.

*Wartime Journalism, 1939-1943,* University of Nebraska Press, 1988.

Lindsay Waters, editor, *Critical Writings, 1953-1978,* University of Minnesota Press, 1989.

(With E. S. Burt and others) *Romanticism and Contemporary Criticism: The Gauss Seminar and Other Papers,* Johns Hopkins University Press (Baltimore), 1993.

Also author of foreword to Carol Jacobs's *The Dissimulating Harmony,* 1978. Contributor to American, Flemish, and French periodicals, including *Critical Inquiry, Critique, Het Vlaamsche Land, Les Cahiers du libre examen, Monde nouveau, Preuves,* and *Revue internationale de philosophie.*

*SIDELIGHTS:* "Venerated as a teacher and scholar, [Paul de Man] was the originator of a controversial theory of language that some say may place him among the greatest thinkers of his age," a *New York Times* reporter professed. De Man and French philosopher Jacques Derrida revolutionized literary criticism in America by devising deconstructionism, a theory that emphasizes the uncertainty of meaning caused by the imprecision of language. But after de Man's death in 1983, his work was clouded in controversy when a student compiling a bibliography of his works uncovered numerous articles that he had written for a pro-Nazi and anti-Semitic newspaper, *Le Soir,* in his native Belgium between 1940 and 1942.

Born in Antwerp and graduated from the University of Brussels, de Man immigrated to the United States following World War II and took his master's degree and doctorate at Harvard University. He subsequently taught at Cornell and Johns Hopkins universities before settling at Yale University in 1970, where he stayed until his death in 1983. His presence at Yale, as well as the presence of other outstanding deconstructive critics including J. Hillis Miller and Geoffrey Hartman, brought great prestige to the school, which subsequently became known as the seat of deconstructive theory in the United States.

During his second year at Yale, de Man published *Blindness and Insight: Essays in the Rhetoric of Contemporary Criticism,* a collection of articles that previously appeared in journals during de Man's tenure at Harvard and Cornell. Revised in 1983 with five additional essays, *Blindness and Insight* is considered by scholars to be the best introduction to de Man's early academic work. The volume includes such essays as "Criticism and Crisis," "Literary History and Literary Modernity," and an English translation of de Man's 1956 article "Impasse de la critique formaliste," which introduced French readers to New Criticism, an Anglo-American literary theory that was considered radical at the time. The New Critics maintained that a text's meaning could be discovered by reconciling its ambiguities and contradictions, disregarding the influences of an author's psychology, biography, culture, and politics on the text's meaning.

"To write critically about critics," de Man wrote in *Blindness and Insight,* "becomes a way to reflect on the paradoxical effectiveness of a blinded vision that has to be rectified by means of insights that it unwittingly provides," Jonathan Culler quoted the author in the *Dictionary of Literary Biography.* In *Blindness and Insight* de Man explains the principle behind a deconstructive reading: a scholar, when closely reading a text, can uncover many of the author's unstated philosophical, cultural, and linguistic assumptions by exposing contradictions that appear in the language of a text. In turn, a subsequent critic can discover the hidden assumptions in that scholar's analysis. Thus deconstruction posits the radical notion that the meaning of the text resides as much in the act of interpretation as in the words of the text itself.

*Blindness and Insight* contains deconstructive readings of texts such as "Heidegger's Exegesis of Holderlin," in which de Man critiques German philosopher Martin Heidegger's study of works by German poet Friedrich Holderlin. Also included is an essay on Hungarian Marxist philosopher and critic Gyorgy Lukacs's reading of French novelist Gustave Flaubert's *Education sentimentale,* as well as what many consider de Man's most influential work, an analysis of Derrida's criticism of writings by French author Jean-Jacques Rousseau. Articles such as these by de Man and other deconstructive scholars often brought scorn upon the new school of criticism; its detractors, such as *New York Review of Books* contributor Denis Donoghue, discounted the system as "mainly a commentary written in the margin of other philosophical and literary texts." Nonetheless, Culler attests, with *Blindness and Insight* scholars began reading literary criticism with the kind of attention that was only given previously to literary and philosophical works.

*Allegories of Reading: Figural Language in Rousseau, Nietzsche, Rilke, and Proust,* de Man's second collection of essays, consists of works published in journals during the 1970s. A volume of dense and difficult close readings of works by French and German writers, it contains analyses of Rousseau's novel *La Nouvelle Heloise* and *Discourse on the Origin of Language,* Friedrich Nietzsche's philosophical treatise *The Birth of Tragedy,* many of Ranier Maria Rilke's poems, and Marcel Proust's epic novel *Remembrance of Things Past.* In *Allegories of Reading* de Man pays extremely close attention to the use of language in these works, dissecting allegories and metaphors to answer the questions "precisely whether a literary text is *about* that which it describes, represents, or states," Anthony Thorlby cited de Man in the *Times Literary Supplement,* or "whether *all* language is about language."

The main assertion of *Allegories of Reading* (and of deconstructive theory) is that language cannot be taken literally. Because all language is metaphorical, where one set of signs are only substitutions for another, there is no reconcilability or oneness between a word and the idea of the specific object. Robert Alter in *New Republic* explained that deconstruction professes "the relation between word and referent, signifier and signified, is inevitably an arbitrary and conventional one. . . . [W]hat appears to be literal is necessarily metaphorical; what is proffered as reality is in fact fiction." Thus when language uses metaphors to be most authoritative it undermines its own intent by clearly revealing its fictive nature. Furthermore, when studying a literary text the reader cannot reconcile the difference between the opposing literal and the figurative meanings of the work, thus the text is considered "unreadable."

Yet, if de Man's theory is true, *Allegories of Reading* itself—relying on written language—is an unreadable text, according to *Washington Post Book World* contributor Julia Epstein. She observed that in the work "de Man presents a system of figurative language and literary structure. Then, as systematically, he unravels his own system." Indeed, de Man admits that his own theory is disputable. In *Allegories of Reading,* cited by Thorlby, he writes: "A text . . . although it presents itself legitimately as a demystification of literary rhetoric remains entirely literary, rhetorical, and deceptive itself."

A major complaint of deconstructionism's critics is that the theory attacks language's ability to represent reality. Thorlby remarked, "de Man is knowingly condescending towards anyone who . . . enjoys 'a literal or thematic reading that takes the value assertions of the text at their word.'" Epstein, another detractor, stated: "Where other interpreters look for referential meaning, substance, values, truth . . . deconstructors see the traditional quest for meaning as a naive search for the nonexistent." Deconstructionist Culler admits that "De Man's writing grants great authority to texts—a power of illumination which is a power of disruption—but little authority to meaning. . . . His works celebrate great literary and philosophical texts for their insightful undoings of the meanings that usually pass for their value." Thus a work must be read "as though it referred primarily to itself," Thorlby explained de Man's process.

Mark Edmundson, in a *Harper's* article titled "A Will to Cultural Power," echoed Thorlby and Epstein's concerns, stating that "one result of [deconstructive] reading is to place in doubt the myth of the author as a shaping deity. To the deconstructor the author appears to be more a relay point for language than its sovereign authority." Likewise, Denis Donoghue, in a *New York Review of Books* critique of *Deconstruction and Criticism,* a 1979 offering de Man wrote with Harold Bloom, Derrida, Hartman, and Miller, asserts that de Man, in his deconstructive reading of Percy Bysshe Shelley's "The Triumph of Life," denies the poet any active role in the writing process, ascribing to language and grammar what is normally ascribed to the author. Donoghue opined, "If [deconstruction] were to prevail, it would surround with anxiety and misgiving not only the reading of poems but the negotiation of every major theme in Western literature and philosophy."

The first volume of de Man's essays collected after the author's death in 1983 was published the following year. *The Rhetoric of Romanticism,* compiled from articles written after 1956 and two never before issued, is considered an indispensable tool by scholars of romanticism. In this strictly linguistic approach to romantic and postromantic themes de Man studies the course toward greater concreteness in poetic diction (especially when writing of nature), the shift from the use of allegorical to symbolic language, and the development of the study of the union of imagination and nature. He writes on individual romantics, including Rousseau, William Wordsworth, Shelley, William Butler Yeats, and Holderlin, and examines the general relationship among German, French, and English trends in romanticism. Culler reflected that *The Rhetoric of Romanticism* was extremely influential; it forced literary critics to reassess the place of European romantic writings in the canon of world literature.

Three other collections of de Man's academic essays have been published posthumously. Both *The Resistance to Theory,* consisting of six recent essays focusing on contemporary literary criticism, and *Aesthetic Ideology,* featuring essays on German philosophers Immanuel Kant and Georg Hegel and German writer Friedrich von Schiller, explore the incompatibility of a linguistically oriented and an aesthetic approach to literature. *Fugitive Writings,* also published in 1988, is a group of essays on literary criticism de Man wrote during the 1950s for the French periodicals *Critique* and *Monde nouveau.*

In December, 1987, the *New York Times* revealed that from 1940 until 1942 de Man, under his own name, wrote more than one hundred articles for *Le Soir,* a pro-Nazi and strongly anti-Semitic daily newspaper in his native Belgium, then occupied by the German army. A Belgian graduate student, Ortwin de Graef, came across these essays and book and music reviews when compiling a list of de Man's works. The uncovering of de Man's writings for *Le Soir*—which have been collected in *Wartime Journalism, 1939-1943*—shocked many who knew de Man, for his colleagues considered him an unbiased and affable man. These articles "seem so at odds with the sense of the person I knew later on," reflected Neil Hertz, one of de Man's friends, quoted in the *New York Times.* Shochana Felman, a student of de Man's at Yale, added that she thought he was "almost entirely without prejudice," claiming de Man "took an ethical stance in all his daily life." Peter Brooks, with whom de Man worked at Yale, in a letter to the editor of the *New York Times,* claimed that he and many of de Man's friends and colleagues "wish to testify that [de Man's] life and character, as we knew them, suggested a complete repudiation of the hateful things he wrote in a sordid time."

Many scholars agree that in only one of the articles, "Jews in Contemporary Literature," does de Man take an overtly anti-Semitic stance. In the piece he states that Jews "pollute" modern fiction and that their influence in modern letters is negligible. However, some of de Man's detractors detect anti-Semitic sentiments in his other articles, including reviews of works by Austrian writer Franz Kafka and French historian Daniel Halevy. The revelation increased the existing controversy surrounding deconstruction theory, which the *New York Times* reporter alleged "always reflects the biases of its users." But Hartman, writing in the *New Republic,* rebutted the *New York Times* article, stating that de Man's "position is the very opposite of an idealism that confuses intellect and action, ideology and political praxis." De Man, Hartman asserted, stressed "the non-identity of these realms."

This revelation about de Man continues to color critics' views of his work. This was commented on by Leon S. Roudiez in *World Literature Today,* "it would seem impossible to read the mature works as one did earlier." *Critical Writings,* published posthumously in 1989, includes around two dozen essays selected by de Man and Lindsay Waters from those written between 1953 and 1978. As a result of de Man's infamous writings, many reviewers commented as much on Waters's biographical chapter on de Man as they did on the essays. The essays themselves, noted Frank Kermode in the *London Review of Books,* "have that air of quiet, even tolerant authority which, despite occasional severities and bursts of ill temper, was of the essence of de Man's personality." Denis Donoghue remarked drily in *The New York Review of Books* that the essays "show, by the way, that he could write just as lucidly as the next critic, when he chose to." However, he concluded, "I do not imply that when his style was obscure the opacity is sufficiently explained by his having something to hide: the themes in hand were often intractable."

*Romanticism and Contemporary Criticism: The Gauss Seminars and Other Papers* is another posthumous collection of de Man's writings, including the Gauss seminars on Romanticism which he delivered at Princeton in 1967. David Bromwich in the *London Review of Books* stated that as the volume "is the latest and probably the last of several posthumous volumes of de Man's; touching as it does his central concerns, it makes inevitable some assessment of the impact of his work." Bromwich's assessment was that de Man "brought to light and established the worth of one kind of [critical] attention. It is a major quality in a critic." He continued, "With it, at least in his dealings with English poetry, went an odd deficiency of verbal tact . . . in reading him one is apt to respond to the drive toward persuasion rather than the exact propriety of any detail." Michael Sprinkler in the *Times Literary Supplement* found "no startling revelations" in this collection but a "de Man . . . already familiar from the essays collected in *Blindness and Insight*." He concluded, "The principal interest of these texts is twofold . . . in their relationship to the long mediation on Rousseau that comprises the second half of *Allegories of Reading*, and in the way they illuminate the turn towards rhetoric that . . . was the decisive factor enabling his mature work."

David P. Haney in *Southern Humanities Review* also used the collection to review de Man's impact on criticism. Haney stated that while *Romanticism and Contemporary Criticism* "will probably not change the terms of the debate about his politics or criticism . . . it may help put us back in touch with de Man's romantic origins." Haney appreciated the "informal, often rough nature of these essays," as it "gives us a different, less guarded, and in some ways more complex de Man than we find in . . . previously published work." Haney concluded, "Despite (and perhaps even through) de Man's notoriously selective reading of texts and his suspect past, his criticism opens a window on our relation to romanticism that must be looked through, for better or worse."

*BIOGRAPHICAL/CRITICAL SOURCES:*

*BOOKS*

de Man and others, editors, *Responses: On Paul de Man's Wartime Journalism*, University of Nebraska Press (Lincoln), 1989.

Derrida, Jacques, *Memoires: Lectures for Paul de Man*, translated by Cecile Lindsay, Jonathan Culler, and Eduardo Cadava, Columbia University Press, 1986.

*Dictionary of Literary Biography*, Volume 67: *Modern American Critics since 1955*, Gale, 1988.

Eagleton, Terry, *Literary Theory: An Introduction*, University of Minnesota Press, 1983.

Graef, Ortwin de, *Serenity in Crisis: A Preface to Paul de Man, 1939-1960*, University of Nebraska (Lincoln), 1993.

Graef, Ortwin de, *Titanic Light: Paul de Man's Post-Romanticism, 1960-1969*, University of Nebraska Press (Lincoln), 1995.

Herman, Luc, Kris Humbeeck, and Geert Lernout, editors, *(Dis)continuities: Essays on Paul de Man*, Rodopi (Atlanta), 1989.

Lehman, David, *Signs of the Times: Deconstruction and the Fall of Paul de Man*, Poseidon Press (New York City), 1991.

Loesberg, Jonathan, *Aestheticism and Deconstruction: Pater, Derrida, and de Man*, Princeton University Press (Princeton, NJ), 1991.

Morrison, Paul, *The Poetics of Fascism: Ezra Pound, T. S. Eliot, Paul de Man*, Oxford University Press (New York City), 1996.

*Responses*, University of Nebraska Press, 1989.

Rosiek, Jan, *Figures of Failure: Paul de Man's Criticism 1953-1970*, Aarhaus University Press (Denmark), 1992.

Waters, Lindsay and Wlad Godzich, editors, *Reading de Man Reading*, University of Minnesota Press (Minneapolis), 1989.

*PERIODICALS*

*Critical Inquiry*, spring, 1982, summer, 1986.

*Harper's*, July, 1988.

*Insight on the News*, January 23, 1989, p. 61.

*London Review of Books*, March 16, 1989, p. 3; October 7, 1993, p. 22.

*Modern Language Notes*, December, 1993, p. 953.

*Nation*, January 9, 1988, April 9, 1988.

*New Republic*, April 25, 1983, July 7, 1986, March 7, 1988; March 6, 1989, p. 30.

*Newsweek*, February 15, 1988.

*New York Review of Books*, June 12, 1980; June 29, 1989, p. 32; October 12, 1989, p. 69.

*New York Times*, December 1, 1987, August 28, 1988, October 2, 1988, January 25, 1989.

*New York Times Book Review*, May 24, 1992, p. 1.

*Southern Humanities Review*, spring, 1994, p. 169.

*Times Literary Supplement*, February 29, 1980, January 17, 1986, November 6, 1987; December 24, 1993, p. 19.

*Village Voice Literary Supplement*, April, 1988.

*Washington Post Book World*, February 24, 1980.

*World Literature Today*, spring, 1990, p. 370.

*OBITUARIES:*

*PERIODICALS*

*New York Times,* December 31, 1983.*

* * *

**DEWITT, Addison**
**See NEWMAN, Kim (James)**

* * *

**DICKEY, James (Lafayette) 1923-1997**

*PERSONAL:* Born February 2, 1923, in Buckhead, GA, died January 19, 1997, in Columbia, SC, of complications from lung disease; son of Eugene (a lawyer) and Maibelle (Swift) Dickey; married Maxine Syerson, November 4, 1948 (died October 28, 1976); married Deborah Dodson, December 30, 1976; children: (first marriage) Christopher Swift, Kevin Webster; (second marriage) Bronwen Elaine. *Education:* Attended Clemson College (now University), 1942; Vanderbilt University, B.A. (magna cum laude), 1949, M.A., 1950.

*CAREER:* Poet, novelist, and essayist. Instructor in English at Rice Institute (now Rice University), Houston, TX, 1950 and 1952-54, and University of Florida, Gainesville, 1955-56; worked in advertising, 1956-60, first as copywriter for McCann-Erickson, New York City, then as official for Liller, Neal, Battle & Lindsey and Burke Dowling Adams, both in Atlanta, GA; poet in residence at Reed College, Portland, OR, 1963-64, San Fernando Valley State College (now California State University, Northridge), Northridge, CA, 1964-65, University of Wisconsin—Madison, 1966, University of Wisconsin—Milwaukee, 1967, and Washington University, St. Louis, MO, 1968; Georgia Institute of Technology, Atlanta, Franklin Distinguished Professor of English, 1968; University of South Carolina, Columbia, professor of English and poet in residence, 1969-97. Library of Congress, consultant in poetry, 1966-68, honorary consultant in American Letters, 1968-71; Yale Younger Poets contest, judge, 1989-1994. *Military service:* U.S. Army Air Forces, served in World War II, flew 100 combat missions in 418th Night Fighter Squadron. U.S. Air Force, served in Korean War; awarded Air Medal.

*MEMBER:* American Academy of Arts and Sciences, American Academy of Arts and Letters, National Advisory Council on the Arts, National Institute of Arts and Letters, Fellowship of Southern Writers, South Carolina Academy of Authors, Writer's Guild of America, Phi Beta Kappa.

*AWARDS, HONORS: Sewanee Review* poetry fellowship, 1954-55; *Poetry* magazine, Union League Civic and Arts Foundation Prize, 1958, Vachel Lindsay Prize, 1959, and Levinson Prize, 1982; Guggenheim fellowship, 1961-62; National Book Award for poetry and Melville Cane Award of Poetry Society of America, both 1966, for *Buckdancer's Choice;* National Institute of Arts and Letters grant, 1966; Medicis prize for best foreign book of the year (Paris), 1971, for *Deliverance;* invited to read poem "The Strength of Fields" at Inauguration of U.S. President Jimmy Carter, 1977; *New York Quarterly* Poetry Day Award, 1977; invited to read poem "For a Time and Place" at second inauguration of Richard Riley, governor of South Carolina, 1983.

*WRITINGS:*

*POETRY*

*Into the Stone, and Other Poems,* Scribner (New York City), 1960.
*Drowning with Others* (also see below), Wesleyan University Press (Middletown, CT), 1962.
*Helmets* (also see below), Wesleyan University Press, 1964.
*Two Poems of the Air,* Centicore Press (Portland, OR), 1964.
*Buckdancer's Choice,* Wesleyan University Press, 1965.
*Poems, 1957-1967* (selections issued as miniature edition prior to publication), Wesleyan University Press, 1968.
*The Eye-Beaters, Blood, Victory, Madness, Buckhead, and Mercy,* Doubleday (Garden City, NY), 1970.
*Exchanges,* Bruccoli Clark (Columbia, SC), 1971.
*The Zodiac* (long poem; based on Hendrik Marsman's poem of the same title), Doubleday and Bruccoli Clark, 1976.
*The Strength of Fields* (poem; also see below), Bruccoli Clark, 1977.
*Tucky the Hunter* (for children), Crown (New York City), 1978.

*The Strength of Fields* (collection; title poem previously published separately), Doubleday, 1979.

*Head Deep in Strange Sounds: Improvisations from the UnEnglish,* Palaemon Press (Winston-Salem, NC), 1979.

*Scion,* Deerfield Press (Deerfield, MA), 1980.

*The Early Motion: "Drowning with Others" and "Helmets,"* Wesleyan University Press, 1981.

*Falling, May Day Sermon, and Other Poems,* Wesleyan University Press, 1981.

*The Eagle's Mile* (also see below), Bruccoli Clark, 1981.

*Puella,* Doubleday, 1982.

*Vaermland: Poems Based on Poems,* Palaemon Press, 1982.

*False Youth: Four Seasons,* Pressworks (Dallas, TX), 1983.

*The Central Motion,* Wesleyan University Press, 1983.

(With Sharon Anglin Kuhne) *Intervisions: Poems and Photographs,* Visualternatives, 1983.

*Veteran Birth: The Gadfly Poems, 1947-1949,* Palaemon Press, 1983.

*Bronwen, the Traw, and the Shape Shifter: A Poem in Four Parts* (for children), illustrations by Richard Jesse Watson, Harcourt, 1986.

*Of Prisons and Ideas,* Harcourt, 1987.

*Summons,* Bruccoli Clark, 1988.

*The Eagle's Mile* (collection), Wesleyan University Press, 1990.

*The Whole Motion: Collected Poems, 1945-1992,* Wesleyan University Press, 1992.

Poems represented in many anthologies, including: *Contemporary American Poetry,* edited by Donald Hall, Penguin, 1962; *Where Is Viet Nam? American Poets Respond,* edited by Walter Lowenfels, Doubleday, 1967; *The Norton Anthology of Poetry,* revised shorter edition, edited by Alexander W. Allison, Herbert Barrows, Caesar R. Blake, Arthur J. Carr, Arthur M. Eastman, and Hubert M. English, Jr., Norton, 1975; *The Norton Anthology of American Literature,* Volume 2, edited by Ronald Gottesman, Laurence B. Holland, William H. Pritchard, and David Kalstone, Norton, 1979.

*PROSE*

*The Suspect in Poetry* (criticism), Sixties Press (Madison, MN), 1964.

*A Private Brinksmanship* (lecture given at Pitzer College, June 6, 1965), Castle Press (Pasadena), 1965.

*Spinning the Crystal Ball: Some Guesses at the Future of American Poetry* (lecture given at Library of Congress, April 24, 1967), Library of Congress (Washington, DC), 1967.

*Metaphor as Pure Adventure* (lecture given at Library of Congress, December 4, 1967), Library of Congress, 1968.

*Babel to Byzantium: Poets and Poetry Now* (criticism), Farrar, Straus (New York City), 1968.

*Deliverance* (novel; Literary Guild selection; excerpt entitled "Two Days in September" published in *Atlantic Monthly,* February, 1970; also see below), Houghton (Boston), 1970.

*Self-Interviews* (informal monologues; excerpt entitled "The Poet Tries to Make a Kind of Order" published in *Mademoiselle,* September, 1970), recorded and edited by Barbara Reiss and James Reiss, Doubleday, 1970.

*Sorties: Journals and New Essays,* Doubleday, 1971.

(With Hubert Shuptrine) *Jericho: The South Beheld* (Book-of-the-Month Club alternate selection), Oxmoor (Birmingham, AL), 1974.

(With Marvin Hayes) *God's Images: The Bible, a New Vision,* Oxmoor, 1977.

*The Enemy from Eden,* Lord John Press (Northridge, CA), 1978.

*In Pursuit of the Grey Soul,* Bruccoli Clark, 1978.

*The Water Bug's Mittens* (Ezra Pound Lecture at University of Idaho), Bruccoli Clark, 1980.

*The Starry Place between the Antlers: Why I Live in South Carolina,* Bruccoli Clark, 1981.

*Night Hurdling: Poems, Essays, Conversations, Commencements, and Afterwords,* Bruccoli Clark, 1983.

*Alnilam* (novel), Doubleday, 1987.

*Wayfarer: A Voice from the Southern Mountains,* Oxmoor House, 1988.

*Southern Light,* with photography by James Valentine, Oxmoor House, 1991.

*To the White Sea* (novel), Houghton, 1993.

Contributor to books, including *Modern Southern Literature in Its Cultural Setting,* edited by Louis D. Rubin, Jr., and Robert D. Jacobs, Doubleday, 1961; *Poets on Poetry,* edited by Howard Nemerov, Basic Books, 1966; *Pages: The World of Books, Writers, and Writing,* Volume 1, Gale, 1976; *Conversations with Writers,* Volume 1, Gale, 1977; *Dictionary of Literary Biography,* Volume 5: *American Poets since World War II,* Gale, 1980; and *From the Green Horseshoe: Poems by James Dickey's Students,* University of South Carolina Press, 1987.

*OTHER*

(Adapter with others of English version) Evgenii Evtushenko, *Stolen Apples: Poetry,* Doubleday, 1971.

*Deliverance* (screenplay; based on Dickey's novel of the same title; produced by Warner Bros., 1972), Southern Illinois University Press (Carbondale), 1982.

(With Charles Fries) *Call of the Wild* (screenplay; based on the novel by Jack London), produced by National Broadcasting Co. (NBC-TV), 1976.

*Striking In: The Early Notebooks of James Dickey,* edited by Gordon Van Ness, University of Missouri Press (Columbia), 1996.

Also author of screenplays *To Gene Bullard* and *The Sentence.* Contributor of poems, essays, articles, and reviews to more than thirty periodicals, including *Atlantic Monthly, Harper's, Hudson Review, Nation, New Yorker, Paris Review, Poetry, Sewanee Review, Times Literary Supplement,* and *Virginia Quarterly Review.*

*SIDELIGHTS:* James Dickey was widely regarded as a major American poet because of what critics and readers identified as his unique vision and style. "It is clear," said Joyce Carol Oates in her *New Heaven, New Earth: The Visionary Experience in Literature,* "that Dickey desires to take on 'his' own personal history as an analogue to or a microscopic exploration of twentieth-century American history, which is one of the reasons he is so important a poet." Winner of both the 1966 National Book Award and the Melville Cane Award for *Buckdancer's Choice,* Dickey was called an expansional poet, not only because the voices in his work loomed large enough to address or represent facets of the American experience, but also because his violent imagery and eccentric style exceeded the bounds of more traditional norms, often producing a quality he described as "country surrealism."

One of Dickey's principal themes, usually expressed through a direct confrontation between or a surreal juxtaposition of the world of nature and the world of civilized man, was the need to intensify life by maintaining contact with the primitive impulses, sensations, and ways of seeing suppressed by modern society. It was a theme made explicit in his internationally bestselling novel *Deliverance* and was one given much attention in critical reviews. Through his poetry and prose, Dickey came to be known as a shaman of contemporary culture, for as Joan Bobbitt wrote in *Concerning Poetry,* he "sees civilization as so far removed from nature, its primal antecedent, that only [grotesque] aberrations can aptly depict their relationship and, as he implies, possibly restore them to harmony and order."

Although he started writing poetry in 1947 at the age of twenty-four, Dickey did not become a full-time poet until thirteen years later. After earning a master's degree in 1950, he taught and lectured at several colleges for six years, but when some of his poems were construed to be obscene, he decided to forsake academic life for the advertising business. "I thought if my chosen profession, teaching, was going to fall out to be that sort of situation," he said in *Conversations with Writers,* "I'd rather go for the buck and make some damn dough in the market place. I had the confidence of Lucifer in myself by that time, and I was beginning to appear all over the place in the *Hudson Review, Partisan* [*Review*], *Sewanee* [*Review*], *Kenyon* [*Review*], and so on. I figured that the kind of thing that an advertising writer would be able to write, I could do with the little finger of the left hand, and they were getting paid good dough for it. I happened to have been right."

Dickey got a job with McCann-Erickson, the biggest ad agency in New York at the time, and wrote jingles for its Coca-Cola account. Later, he went to Liller, Neal, Battle & Lindsey in Atlanta, GA, for twice the salary, working on potato chips and fertilizer accounts, and then jumped agencies again for still another increase, becoming an executive with Burke Dowling Adams, where his primary concern was the Delta Airlines account. Robert W. Hill reported in *Dictionary of Literary Biography* that by the late 1950s, Dickey was earning enough to have a secure future in the business. But after his first book, *Into the Stone, and Other Poems,* was published in 1960, Dickey left advertising to devote all his time to poetry. "There could have been no more unpromising enterprise or means of earning a livelihood than that of being an American poet," he admitted in *Conversations with Writers.* "It's different now. They're still having a relatively rocky road, but it ain't like it was when I used to give readings sometimes for maybe ten or fifteen dollars, where there would be five people in the audiences, three of them relatives."

Dickey's emotional attachment to his craft—obviously great enough to lead him to abandon a lucrative career in advertising—surfaced early in his writing career. "I came to poetry with no particular qualifications," he recounted in Howard Nemerov's *Poets on Poetry.* "I had begun to suspect, however, that there is a poet—or a kind of poet—buried in every human being like Ariel in his tree, and that the people whom we are pleased to call poets are only those who have felt the need and contrived the means to release this spirit from its prison."

In seeking the means to liberate his poetic spirit, Dickey concentrated at first on rhythms, on anapests and iambs. "Although I didn't care for rhyme and the 'packaged' quality which it gives even the best poems," he said in *Poets on Poetry,* "I did care very much for meter, or at least rhythm." With his prize-winning collection, *Buckdancer's Choice,* he began using the split line and free verse forms that came to be associated with his work. But perhaps the most recognizable feature of his stylistic development was his ambitious experimentation with language and form—inverted or odd syntax, horizontal spaces within lines, spread-eagled and ode-like shaped poems. Dickey's poems, wrote Paul Zweig in the *New York Times Book Review,* "are like richly modulated hollers; a sort of rough, American-style bel canto advertising its freedom from the constraints of ordinary language. Dickey's style is so personal, his rhythms so willfully eccentric, that the poems seem to swell up and overflow like that oldest of American art forms, the boast."

According to David Kalstone in another *New York Times Book Review* article, Dickey's "achievement has been to press the limit of language and, in his criticism, to point up the strengths of other writers who do: Hart Crane, [D. H.] Lawrence, [Theodore] Roethke." L. M. Rosenberg expressed a similar sentiment in the *Chicago Tribune Book World.* Claiming that for "sheer beauty and passion we have no greater spokesman, nor do we have any poet more powerfully, naturally musical [than Dickey]," Rosenberg maintained that Dickey's "experiments with language and form are the experiments of a man who understands that one of the strangest things about poetry is the way it looks on the page: It just isn't normal. The question of how to move the reader's eye along the page, particularly as it makes an unnatural jump from line to line . . . how to slow the reader down or speed him up, how to give words back their original, almost totemic power—that's something any poet thinks a lot about, and it's something Dickey works with almost obsessively."

Dickey's stylistic endeavors, however, only partially explain why he was, in the minds of several critics, the most frequently discussed American poet of his generation. As noted above in *Poets on Poetry,* Dickey admitted that he considered style subordinate to the spirit of poetry, the "individually imaginative" vision of the poet, and, according to William Meredith in the *New York Times Book Review,* he consequently looked "for shapes and rhythms that correspond exactly to the kind of testimony his poems have always been. When he is testifying to an experience that declares its shape and meaning eloquently—'The Shark's Parlor' and 'Falling' are examples of this—the poems have form in [Ezra] Pound's phrase, as a tree has form." But, said William Heyen in the *Southern Review,* in addition to the unity of form and content, there is in Dickey's poetry and criticism "an emphasis on the humanism, or the morality or larger concerns of poetry. There's the idea that what the poet has to reach for is not necessarily affirmation, but, yes, a kind of affirming of values."

A primary thematic concern of Dickey's, one well served by his vigorous style, was the need "to get back wholeness of being, to respond full-heartedly and full-bodiedly to experience," observed Anatole Broyard of the *New York Times.* In *Poets on Poetry,* Dickey recalled that the subject matter of his early poems came from the principal incidents of his life, "those times when I felt most strongly and was most aware of the intense reality of the objects and people I moved among. If I were to arrange my own poems in some such scheme, chronologizing them, they would form a sort of story of this kind."

Despite the many allusions to his own life which he included in his poetry, Dickey "is able to assimilate and report the experiences of others and himself, coming to that kind of peculiarly Dickeyesque fusion of selves so powerfully worked in 'Drinking from a Helmet,' 'Slave Quarters,' and 'The Firebombing,'" claimed Hill. "This aesthetic viewpoint, with the speaker self-consciously observing, knowing that he has a perspective that is momentary and unique, that the time and the place are special, that the voice of the visionary observer is the only one to deal with the striking matter before him, emphasizes Dickey's dedication to art, to the exploration of the creative process, especially with regard to the use of narrative voice under special, extreme conditions."

Extreme conditions permeated Dickey's work. "To make a radical simplification," wrote Monroe K. Spears in *Dionysus and the City: Modernism in Twentieth-Century Poetry,* "the central impulse of Dickey's poetry may be said to be that of identifying with human or other creatures in moments of ultimate confrontation, of violence and truth. A good example is [the poem] 'Falling,' which imagines the thoughts and feelings of an airline stewardess, accidentally swept through an emergency door, as she falls thousands of feet to her death" in a field in Kansas. Alive as she hurtles through space, she strips and imagines making love "in a furious, death-defying motion toward fertile farms and sensuous people who must in their blood understand even such a strange, naked ritual," explained Robert W. Hill. "Hers is a dance all the way to death; she makes a poem of her last life and a fertility prayer of her last breath: 'AH, GOD—.'"

Many of Dickey's poems explored moments of being as known by horses, dogs, deer, bees, boars, and other inhabitants of non-human worlds. In "The Sheep Child," for example, a creature half child and half sheep (the result of boys coupling with sheep) speaks out from a jar of formaldehyde. The poem "attains very nearly the power of mythic utterance," maintained Hill, for the sheep child "shows its magnified view of the truth of two worlds," the fusion of man and nature, with an "eternal, unyielding vision." In Hill's opinion, "The Sheep Child" is "the most radical expression of Dickey's sense of transcendence in fusing man and nature to achieve 'imperishable vision,'" but it is not the only such expression.

"Everywhere in [Dickey's] body of writing in-touchness with 'the other forms of life' stands forth as a primary value," asserted Benjamin DeMott in *Saturday Review*. "The strength of this body of poetry lies in its feeling for the generative power at the core of existence. A first-rate Dickey poem breathes the energy of the world, and testifies to the poet's capacity for rising out of tranced dailiness—habitual, half-lived life—into a more intense physicality, a burly appetitive wanting-ness of being. To read him is, for an instant, to share that capacity." Richard Tillinghast, writing in the *Southern Review,* agreed: "Alone among his contemporaries, Dickey has a quality of exuberance that one must go back to [Walt] Whitman to see equaled. . . . This exuberance has hurt Dickey among critics, just as it has hurt Whitman; with Randall Jarrell in his praising mood a notable exception, a critic almost by nature dislikes exuberance and rejects it when he sees it."

Along with DeMott, critics generally agreed that by pressing "the neglected natural nerve in humanness" through shockingly bizarre or surreal images, Dickey sought to depict man's proper relationship with nature. "It is rarely or never so simple as this," cautioned Nemerov in *Reflexions on Poetry and Poetics,* "yet the intention seems often enough this, a feeling one's way down the chain of being, a becoming the voice which shall make dumb things respond, sometimes to their hurt or deaths, a sensing of alien modes of experience, mostly in darkness or in an unfamiliar light; reason accepting its animality; a poetry whose transcendences come of its reconciliations. Salvation is this: apprehending the continuousness of forms, the flowing of one energy through everything." "Dickey makes it clear," suggested Bobbitt, "that what seems to be unnatural is only so because of its context in a civilized world, and that these deviations actually possess a vitality which modern man has lost."

In an interview with William Heyen in the *Southern Review,* Dickey commented on the necessity for man to make some sort of connection with animal life: "I remember a quotation from D. H. Lawrence to the effect that we are in the process of losing the cosmos. We dominate it, but in a sense we've lost it or we're losing it. It's the sense of being part of what Lovejoy called 'the great chain of being.' Randall Jarrell, one of my favorite critics and poets, was a great punster, and he said that we have substituted for the great chain of being 'the great chain of buying,' which is, maybe, something that's diametrically opposed, and will be the ruination of everything."

Dickey was widely praised for having what Herbert Leibowitz in the *New York Times Book Review* called "a shrewd and troubled knowledge of the 'primal powers'" of nature, as well as "a dramatic skill in presenting the endless beauty of instinct, the feel of icy undertows and warm shallows, the bloodlettings which are a regular part of nature's law." But because a Dickey poem centers on "moments of ultimate confrontation," as Spears said, and because that confrontation often seems to involve a conflict with the norms of civilized society, Dickey was criticized for what some saw as an inherent preoccupation with violence that led to a castigation of modern society. Zweig, for example, maintained that Dickey's "imagination rides the edge of violence," and James Aronson claimed in the *Antioch Review* that this characteristic gave Dickey a reputation as "a kind of primitive savage" who extolled the virtues of uncivilized life.

Although Dickey's images were often primitive, many reviewers considered it a mistake to see him as a spokesman for a return to savagery. Oates wrote that Dickey, "so disturbing to many of us, must be seen in a larger context, as a kind of 'shaman,' a man necessarily at war with his civilization because that civilization will not, cannot, understand what he is saying." A writer in the *Virginia Quarterly Review* observed that at the heart of Dickey's work lay a "desperate insistence that every human experience, however painful or ugly, be viewed as a possible occasion for the renewal of life, [and] with Dickey any renewal inevitably requires struggle."

According to Hill and Aronson, a typical case of misinterpretation involved "The Firebombing," the first poem in *Buckdancer's Choice.* In part a result of Dickey's own experiences in the air force as a fighter-pilot, the poem presents a speaker who, in a momentary flashback, recalls that twenty years ago he was dropping 300-gallon tanks filled with napalm and gasoline on neighborhoods much like his own. Aronson reported that some readers believe the poem portrays the "joy of destroying" experienced by men at war, or even suggests that destruction itself is natural, when actually the poem expresses the complex emotion of "guilt at the inability to feel guilt." Hill concurred: "The moral indignation that might flood so readily for artists and thinkers flows less surely and less fleetingly for one whose life has depended upon a certain screening out of moral subtleties in times of actual combat. The 'luxury' of moral pangs seems to come upon the fighter-pilot in 'The Firebombing' only after his war is over, his safety and his family's restored to allow the contemplation of distant and not-to-be-altered acts of horrible proportion."

Noting the characteristic power of Dickey's vision and the intensity of his language, Oates called "The Firebombing" the central poem of his work. "It is," she wrote, "unforgettable, and seems to me an important achievement in our contemporary literature, a masterpiece that could only have been written by an American, and only by Dickey. Having shown us so convincingly in his poetry how natural, how inevitable, is man's love for all things, Dickey now shows us what happens when man is forced to destroy, forced to step down into history and be an American ('and proud of it'). In so doing he enters a tragic dimension in which few poets indeed have operated."

In Dickey's internationally bestselling novel *Deliverance,* critics generally saw a thematic continuity with his poetry. A novel about how decent men kill, it is also about the bringing forth, through confrontation, of those qualities in a man that usually lie buried. Simply put, *Deliverance* is the story of four Atlanta suburbanites on a back-to-nature canoe trip that turns into a terrifying test of survival. Dickey, who made a number of canoe and bow-hunting trips in the wilds of northern Georgia, told Walter Clemons in the *New York Times Book Review* that much of the story was suggested by incidents that had happened to him or that he had heard about through friends. All those experiences, according to Dickey, shared the feeling of excitement and fear that "comes from being in an unprotected situation where the safeties of law and what we call civilization don't apply, they just don't. A snake can bite you and you can die before you could get treatment. There are men in those remote parts that'd just as soon kill you as look at you. And you could turn into a counter-monster yourself, doing whatever you felt compelled to do to survive."

"In writing *Deliverance,*" said the *New York Times*'s Christopher Lehmann-Haupt, "Dickey obviously made up his mind to tell a story, and on the theory that a story is an entertaining lie, he has produced a double-clutching whopper." Three ill-prepared businessmen join Lewis Medlock, an avid sportsman who constantly lectures about the purity of nature and the corruption of civilization, on a weekend escape from the banality of suburban living. Canoeing down a wild and difficult stretch of the Cahulawassee River, the men experience only the natural hazards of the river on the first day. Their idyllic sense of community with nature and of masculine camaraderie is shattered on the second, however, when two members of the party, resting from the unaccustomed strain, are surprised by two malicious strangers coming out of the woods. Ed Gentry, the novel's narrator, is tied to a tree while Bobby Trippe is held at gunpoint and sexually assaulted by one of the mountain men. Before the attack can go much further, Lewis catches up, kills one of the assailants by shooting an arrow into his back—thereby partially avenging the homosexual rape—and scares off the other. Fearing a trial conducted by city-hating hicks, the canoeists decide to bury the body and continue down the river. But after Drew, the sole member of the party to advocate informing the authorities, accidentally drowns, and Lewis suffers a broken leg, Ed must kill the other assailant who is gunning them from the cliffs above the Cahulawassee.

Critical reactions to *Deliverance* helped explain its popular success. "The story is absorbing," wrote Evan S. Connell, Jr., in the *New York Times Book Review,* "even when you are not quite persuaded Dickey has told the truth. He is effective and he is deft, with the fine hand of an archer." Lehmann-Haupt gave the book similar praise, stating that Dickey "has succeeded in hammering out a comparatively lean prose style (for a man in the habit of loading words with meaning) and built the elements of his yarn into its structure. And except for one blind lead and an irritating logical discrepancy, he has built well. Best of all, he has made a monument to tall stories."

Though Christopher Ricks, critiquing the novel in the *New York Review of Books,* believed *Deliverance* was "too patently the concoction of a situation in which it will be morally permissible—nay, essential—to kill men with a bow and arrow," Charles Thomas Samuels pointed out in the *New Republic* that Dickey "himself seems aware of the harshness of his substructure and the absurdity of some of his details" and overcomes these deficiencies through his stylistic maneuvers: "Such is Dickey's linguistic virtuosity that he totally realizes an improbable plot. How a man acts when shot by an arrow, what it feels like to scale a cliff or to capsize, the ironic psychology of fear: these things are conveyed with remarkable descriptive writing. His publishers are right to call *Deliverance* a *tour de force.*"

Much more than a violent adventure tale, *Deliverance* is a novel of initiation that, according to William Stephenson in the *Georgia Review,* "has the potential of becoming a classic." As a result of their experience, Lewis and Ed come to a realization of the natural savagery of man in nature, said C. Hines Edwards in *Critique.* "In three days they have retraced the course of human development and have found in the natural state not the romantic ideal of beauty in nature coupled with brotherhood among men but beauty in nature coupled with the necessity to kill men, coolly and in the course of things." In line with this view, Samuels and other critics noted that *Deliverance* alludes to Joseph Conrad's *Heart of Darkness.*

In *American Visionary Fiction: Mad Metaphysics as Salvation Psychology* Richard Finholt suggested that there are other literary allusions: "Ed Gentry, the quintessential contemporary American, a soft and overweight suburbanite, finds himself nonetheless [among the chosen] of Lewis. If this is not exactly the honor of being chosen by Odysseus to man the voyage to Ithaca, it is at least as good as being asked by [Ernest Hemingway] himself to join him on the 'tragic adventure' of fishing the swamp on the big two-hearted river. And since Lewis's river happens to flow through just such a dreaded underworld, his weekend canoe trip takes on an epical significance demanding an American-bred heroism that is at least Hemingwayesque, if not Homeric." Finholt considered the novel a return to a time when "the final difference between meaning and meaninglessness was the hero's ability, versus his inability, to act when the necessary time came. This is the nature of Ed's discovery after undergoing an initiation rite into heroism on the death climb up the cliff."

Consistent with this interpretation of *Deliverance* as epic, a *Times Literary Supplement* reviewer claimed Lewis and Ed "are not horrified by what has happened, they are renewed by it; it was, once it became inevitable, indispensable to them. This shockingly credible insight is the central point of the book, and James Dickey reveals it with an appropriate and rewarding subtlety."

Donald W. Markos, discussing the novel in the *Southern Review,* observed that while the book "is in an obvious sense a celebration of an anachronistic concept of manhood," it is more complex than that. "It does not propose that all men embark on canoe trips or undergo a regimen of weight lifting and archery in order to salvage their manhood. An interesting conversation between Medlock and the narrator prior to the outing reveals that masculine prowess is not the primary norm of the book." Oates echoed this sentiment, noting that *Deliverance* is "about our deep, instinctive needs to get back to nature, to establish some kind of rapport with primitive energies; but it is also about the need of some men to do violence, to be delivered out of their banal lives by a violence so irreparable that it can never be confessed." Oates called the book "a fantasy of a highly civilized and affluent society, which imagines physical violence to be transforming in a mystical—and therefore permanent—sense, a society in which rites of initiation no longer exist. . . . Dickey's work is significant in its expression of the savagery that always threatens to become an ideal, when faith in human values is difficult to come by or when a culture cannot accommodate man's most basic instincts."

Edward Doughtie concluded in the *Southwest Review* that through *Deliverance,* "Dickey shows art to be a necessary mediator between nature—both the exterior nature of woods and rivers and the interior nature of man's drives and dreams—and modern urban 'civilized' life. . . . The positive elements of nature can be stifled by civilization; but without civilization the darker, destructive natural forces may get out of hand. Art is a product of civilization, and a civilizing force, yet for Dickey genuine art never loses touch with the primitive: in short, art embraces both Dionysus and Apollo."

*Deliverance* represented only one of Dickey's ventures outside the realm of poetry. He not only adapted the novel for the screen but also appeared in the box-office smash as the redneck Sheriff Bullard, whom the canoeists face at the end of their journey. In addition to criticism, Dickey published a retelling of several biblical stories, *God's Images: The Bible, a New Vision,* as well as *Jericho: The South Beheld,* an exploration of "the rich prose language and sensual impressions of the American South, which Dickey has publicly championed," wrote Hill. "Like Whitman or [Mark] Twain," said Michael Dirda in the *Washington Post Book World,* "Dickey seems in a characteristic American tradition, ever ready to light out for new territories."

Dickey told *Publishers Weekly* that he spent thirty-six years working on his lengthy World War II novel *Alnilam,* which was published in 1987. Named for the central star in the belt of the constellation Orion, *Alnilam* concerns the recently blinded Frank Cahill's search for his son, Joel, whom he has never met. Cahill slowly discovers that his son, an extraordinary pilot thought to have been killed in an aircraft-training accident, had been the leader of a mysterious, dictatorial military training cult known as Alnilam. By interviewing anyone who knew Joel, Cahill forms an impressionistic and sometimes contradictory portrait of this unusual young man. Describing the novel to R. Z. Sheppard of *Time* magazine, Dickey said, "I've tried to do for the air what [Herman] Melville did for water." Sheppard elaborated: "Flying, in the mechanical as well as transcendental sense, is basic to the action, which is surprisingly abundant for a book that is shaped by poetic impulses rather than plot."

The novel received mixed reviews, with most critics comparing it unfavorably to the powerful *Deliverance.* As Erling Friis-Baastad put it in the Toronto *Globe and Mail, Alnilam* "is an awkward and overworked book, but the touch of a master poet can still be experienced periodically throughout . . . at least by those who can endure the uphill read." Robert Towers, writing in the *New York Times Book Review,* said that *Alnilam* "is, for better and worse, very much a poet's novel, Mr. Dickey's extended hymn to air, light, wind and the ecstasies of flight." Although he found Cahill an engaging character, Towers faulted Dickey for the "inordinately slow pacing" of the novel. He noted that one of Dickey's innovative devices interrupts the flow of the already slow-moving narrative. Wrote Towers, "On many of its pages, the symbolic contrasts between blindness and sight, between darkness and light, are typographically rendered. The page is split down the middle into two columns. The left, which represents Cahill's internal sensations and thoughts, is printed in dark type; the right, which contains the objective narration of speech and events, is printed in ordinary type. Such a device has, of course, the effect not only of dividing one's attention, but also of modifying the degree of one's involvement in what is taking place."

Although the situations in *Alnilam* sometimes seemed implausible to critics, Henry Taylor believed that Dickey was able to write so convincingly that he overcame many of these problems. In the *Los Angeles Times Book Review,* Taylor commented, "One of Dickey's great strengths as a poet has been his extraordinary ability to give plausibility to nearly incredible situations and events." Taylor concluded by saying, "There are a few brief passages in which the style becomes self-conscious, or where the intensity seems too laboriously worked up. But Dickey's ear for Southern talk, his understanding of the sensations involved in flying, and his interest in a wide array of minor characters, make the novel rich and rewarding reading. *Alnilam* is a solid achievement."

In his final novel, *To the White Sea,* published in 1993, Dickey returned to the themes of his earlier novels. The book's one character, Muldrow, is an Air Force tail gunner whose plane is shot down over Tokyo during World War II. During the early stages of the novel, Muldrow endures supremely difficult circumstances as he struggles for survival. Fleeing Tokyo and heading north to the island of Hokkaido-whose cold and wintry climate appeals to his own childhood experiences growing up in Alaska-Muldrow kills several people in search of food and clothing. "Initially one identifies with . . . [Muldrow's] unbelievable courage and control in the face of almost hopeless odds," noted Steve Brzezinski in *The Antioch Review.* However, as the novel progresses, Muldrow's actions grow increasingly violent and shocking, as he enjoys his murderous actions. "His 'heart of ice' proves to be another heart of darkness," commented John Melmoth in the *Times Literary Supplement.* "Things take an apocalyptic turn and end in a welter of blood and feathers." During his journey, Muldrow comes to identify with the animals he encounters in the wilderness and seeks to transform himself into a facet of the harsh landscape around him.

As with *Alnilam,* critical reaction to *To the White Sea* was mixed, with critics praising Dickey's prose style but recoiling at the novel's disturbing plot. "Dickey takes language as far as it will go and sometimes overdoes it," remarked Melmoth, who added that "some of the writing has an eerie brilliance." While commending Dickey's "haunting" imagery and stylistic achievement, Brzezinski averred that *To the White Sea* "is a bleak and unsettling book." In the end, concluded Ronald Curran in a *World Literature Today* review, "however the reader conceives of Muldrow's musings about his adaptive identifications with animals or his eventual transcendence into weather itself, the success of *To the White Sea* depends upon whether or not empathetic identification can be fostered" among readers.

Despite his excursions into other genres, Dickey's main concern was always poetry, he admitted in the *New York Times*. "In poetry you have the utmost concentration of meaning in the shortest space." In a 1981 *Writer's Yearbook* interview, Dickey elaborated on his devotion to verse: "Poetry is, I think, the highest medium that mankind has ever come up with. It's language itself, which is a miraculous medium which makes everything else that man has ever done possible." In 1992, a major collection of Dickey's poems was published as *The Whole Motion: Collected Poems, 1945-1992.*

Dickey once told *CA:* "I'm the same way about novels as I am about anything I write. I build them very slowly. I work on the principle that the first fifty ways I try to write a novel or a critical piece or a poem or a movie are going to be wrong. But you get a direction in some way or other. Keep drafting and redrafting and something emerges eventually. If the subject is intense, if you are intense about it, something will come. In my case, at least, the final work is nothing like what I started out with; generally I don't have a very good idea at first. But something begins to form in some unforeseen, perhaps unforeseeable, shape. It's like creating something out of nothing—creation ex nihilo, which is said to be impossible. God must have done it, I guess, but nobody else can—except poets."

*BIOGRAPHICAL/CRITICAL SOURCES:*

*BOOKS*

*Authors in the News,* Gale (Detroit), Volume 1, 1976, Volume 2, 1976.

Baughman, Ronald, editor, *The Voiced Connections of James Dickey: Interviews and Conversations,* University of South Carolina Press (Columbia), 1989.

Boyars, Robert, editor, *Contemporary Poetry in America,* Schocken (New York City), 1974.

Bruccoli, Matthew J., and Judith S. Baughman, *James Dickey: A Descriptive Bibliography,* University of Pittsburgh Press (Pittsburgh), 1990.

Calhoun, Richard J., editor, *James Dickey: The Expansive Imagination,* Everett/Edwards (DeLand, FL), 1973.

Carroll, Paul, *The Poem in Its Skin,* Follett, 1968.

*Contemporary Authors Bibliographical Series,* Volume 2, *American Poets,* Gale, 1986.

*Contemporary Literary Criticism,* Gale, Volume 1, 1973, Volume 2, 1974, Volume 4, 1975, Volume 7, 1977, Volume 10, 1979, Volume 15, 1980, Volume 47, 1988.

*Conversations with Writers,* Volume 1, Gale, 1977.

De La Fuente, Patricia, editor, *James Dickey: Splintered Sunlight,* School of Humanities, Pan American University, 1979.

Dickey, James, *Self-Interviews,* recorded and edited by Barbara Reiss and James Reiss, Doubleday, 1970.

*Dictionary of Literary Biography,* Volume 5: *American Poets since World War II,* Gale, 1980.

*Dictionary of Literary Biography Documentary Series,* Volume 7, Gale, 1989.

*Dictionary of Literary Biography Yearbook: 1982,* Gale, 1983, *Dictionary of Literary Biography Yearbook: 1993,* 1994.

Elledge, J., *James Dickey: A Bibliography, 1947-1974,* Scarecrow (Metuchen, NJ), 1979.

Finholt, Richard, *American Visionary Fiction: Mad Metaphysics as Salvation Psychology,* Kennikat (Port Washington, NY), 1978.

Garrett, George, editor, *The Writer's Voice: Conversations with Contemporary Writers,* Morrow (New York City), 1973.

Glancy, Eileen, *James Dickey: The Critic as Poet,* Whitston Publishing (Troy, NY), 1971.

Hill, Robert and Calhoun, *James Dickey,* Twayne, 1983.

Howard, Richard, *Alone with America: Essays on the Art of Poetry in the United States since 1950,* Atheneum (New York City), 1969.

Kirschten, Robert, *Critical Essays on James Dickey,* G.K. Hall (Boston), 1994.

Lieberman, Laurence, editor, *The Achievement of James Dickey,* Scott, Foresman (Glenview, IL), 1968.

Lieberman, *Unassigned Frequencies: American Poetry in Review, 1964-77,* University of Illinois Press (Champaign), 1978.

Nemerov, Howard, editor, *Poets on Poetry,* Basic Books (New York City), 1966.

Nemerov, *Reflexions on Poetry and Poetics,* Rutgers University Press (New Brunswick, NJ), 1972.

Oates, Joyce Carol, *New Heaven, New Earth: The Visionary Experience in Literature,* Vanguard, 1974.

*Pages: The World of Books, Writers, and Writing,* Volume 1, Gale, 1976.

Rosenthal, M. L., *The New Poets: American and British Poetry since World War II,* Oxford University Press, 1967.

Shaw, Robert B., editor, *American Poetry since 1960: Some Critical Perspectives,* Carcanet, 1973.

Spears, Monroe K., *Dionysus and the City: Modernism in Twentieth-Century Poetry,* Oxford University Press, 1970.

Stepanchev, Stephen, *American Poetry since 1945,* Harper (New York City), 1965.

Vernon, John, *The Garden and the Map: Schizophrenia in Twentieth-Century Literature and Culture,* University of Illinois Press, 1973.

Walsh, Chad, *Today's Poets,* Scribner, 1964.

Weigl, Bruce, and Terry Hummer, editors, *James Dickey: The Imagination of Glory,* University of Illinois Press, 1984.

*Writer's Yearbook,* Writer's Digest (Cincinnati), 1981.

*PERIODICALS*

*Agenda,* winter-spring, 1977.

*Alaska,* February, 1994, p. 75.

*American Literature,* June, 1990, p. 370.

*Antioch Review,* fall-winter, 1970-71; spring, 1994, p. 358.

*Atlantic Monthly,* October, 1967; November, 1968; December, 1974; February, 1980.

*Best Sellers,* April 1, 1970.

*Booklist,* July 15, 1971.

*Book World,* June 30, 1968; March 15, 1970; December 6, 1970; April 25, 1971.

*Bulletin of Bibliography,* April-June, 1981, pp. 92-100; July-September, 1981, pp. 150-155.

*Chicago Review,* November 1, 1966.

*Chicago Tribune,* May 10, 1987.

*Chicago Tribune Book World,* January 27, 1980.

*Christian Science Monitor,* December 3, 1964; November 12, 1970; February 20, 1980.

*Commonweal,* December 1, 1967; February 19, 1971; September 29, 1972; December 3, 1976.

*Concerning Poetry,* spring, 1978.

*Contemporary Literature,* summer, 1975.

*Critic,* May, 1970.

*Critique,* Volume 15, number 2, 1973.

*English Journal,* November, 1990, p. 84; January, 1992, p. 27.

*Esquire,* December, 1970.

*Georgia Review,* spring, 1968; summer, 1969; spring, 1974; summer, 1978; fall, 1993, p. 603.

*Globe and Mail* (Toronto), August 15, 1987.

*Hudson Review,* spring, 1966; autumn, 1967; autumn, 1968; spring, 1993, p. 223; spring, 1994, p. 133.

*James Dickey Newsletter,* 1984—.

*Life,* July 22, 1966; July, 1987, p. 35.

*Literary News,* May-June, 1967.

*Los Angeles Times,* May 19, 1968; February 26, 1980; July 9, 1987; December 8, 1987.

*Los Angeles Times Book Review,* June 27, 1982; January 18, 1987, p. 8; June 7, 1987, p. 1.

*Mademoiselle,* September, 1970; August, 1972.

*Milwaukee Journal,* March 20, 1966.

*Modern Fiction Studies,* summer, 1975.

*Mother Earth News,* March-April, 1990.

*Nation,* June 20, 1966; April 24, 1967; March 23, 1970; April 6, 1970; February 5, 1983.

*National Review,* November 15, 1993, p. 64.

*New Leader,* May 22, 1967; May 20, 1968.

*New Republic,* September 9, 1967; June 29, 1968; April 18, 1970; December 5, 1970; August 5, 1972; November 30, 1974; November 20, 1976; January 5, 1980; January 12, 1980.

*New Statesman,* September 11, 1970.

*Newsweek,* March 30, 1970; August 7, 1972; December 6, 1976; January 31, 1977; August 30, 1993, p. 54.

*New Yorker,* May 2, 1970; August 5, 1972; September 27, 1993, p. 101.

*New York Review of Books,* April 23, 1970.

*New York Times,* March 16, 1966; September 10, 1966; March 27, 1970; December 17, 1971; July 31, 1972; August 20, 1972; January 22, 1977; June 1, 1987; May 19, 1988; October 27, 1990, p. 16; March 23, 1997.

*New York Times Book Review,* January 3, 1965; February 6, 1966; April 23, 1967; March 22, 1970; June 7, 1970; November 8, 1970; December 6, 1970; January 23, 1972; February 9, 1975; November 14, 1976; December 18, 1977; July 15, 1979; January 6, 1980; June 3, 1984, p. 23; February 15, 1987; March 8, 1987, p. 31; June 21, 1987, p. 7; September 19, 1993.

*Paris Review,* spring, 1976.

*Partisan Review,* summer, 1966.

*People,* July 6, 1987, p. 16; October 11, 1993, p. 29; January 31, 1994, p. 80.

*Playboy,* May, 1971; September, 1993, p. 78.

*Poetry,* October, 1966; March, 1968; July, 1971.

*Publishers Weekly,* May 29, 1987, p. 62; October 19, 1990, p. 52; June 7, 1993, p. 65; June 21, 1993, p. 82.

*Rapport,* Volume 17, number 5, 1993, p. 31.

*Salmagundi,* spring-summer, 1973.
*Saturday Review,* May 6, 1967; March 11, 1970; March 28, 1970; March 11, 1972.
*Saturday Review of Science,* August 5, 1972.
*Sewanee Review,* winter, 1963; summer, 1966; spring, 1969; summer, 1971.
*Sixties,* winter, 1964; spring, 1967.
*Southern Review,* winter, 1971; summer, 1971; winter, 1973; spring, 1973; spring, 1981; autumn, 1992, p. 971.
*Southwest Review,* spring, 1979.
*Time,* December 13, 1968; April 20, 1970; August 7, 1972; June 29, 1987; October 11, 1993, p. 88.
*Times* (London), February 3, 1990.
*Times Literary Supplement,* October 29, 1964; May 18, 1967; September 11, 1970; May 21, 1971; December 2, 1983, p. 1342; January 24, 1986, p. 95; May 10, 1991, p. 22; February 11, 1994, p. 21.
*Tribune Books* (Chicago), November 16, 1986, p. 4; May 24, 1987, p. 3.
*Triquarterly,* winter, 1968.
*Village Voice,* February 4, 1980.
*Virginia Quarterly Review,* autumn, 1967; autumn, 1968; winter, 1971; spring, 1990, p. 66; summer, 1991, p. 100; winter, 1994, p. 23.
*Washington Post,* March 31, 1987; May 24, 1987; December 8, 1987.
*Washington Post Book World,* November 21, 1976; December 30, 1979; May 24, 1987, p. 1; November 22, 1992, p. 8.
*World Literature Today,* summer, 1991, p. 489; spring, 1993, p. 384; autumn, 1994, p. 809.
*Yale Review,* October, 1962; December, 1967; winter, 1968; October, 1970.

*OBITUARIES:*

*PERIODICALS*

*New York Times,* January 21, 1997, p. C27.*

* * *

**DOCHERTY, James L.**
**See RAYMOND, Rene (Brabazon)**

* * *

**DOWNES, Quentin**
**See HARRISON, Michael**

**DR. ALPHABET**
**See MORICE, Dave**

* * *

**DUFRESNE, John 1948-**

*PERSONAL:* Born January 30, 1948, in Worcester, MA; son of Bernard V. (an electric company supervisor) and Doris (an office worker; maiden name, Berard) Dufresne; married Marilyn Virbasius, 1971 (divorced, 1978); married Cindy Chinelly (an adjunct professor), May 18, 1985; children: Tristan Jude. *Education:* Worcester State College, B.A., 1970; University of Arkansas, M.F.A., 1984; attended State University of New York at Binghamton, 1987-88. *Politics:* "Ramshackle Socialist Victory Party." *Religion:* "Lapsed Catholic." *Avocational interests:* Running, reading, travel.

*ADDRESSES: Home*—1299 Southeast Seventh Ave., No. 102, Dania, FL 33004. *Office*—Department of English, Florida International University, North Miami, FL 33181. *Agent*—Richard P. McDonough, P.O. Box 1950, Boston, MA 02130.

*CAREER:* Northeast Louisiana University, Monroe, instructor in composition and creative writing, 1984-87; Augusta College, Augusta, GA, instructor in composition, creative writing, and humanities, 1988-89; Florida International University, North Miami, began as instructor, became associate professor of creative writing, 1989—. Has also worked as a social worker and crisis intervention counselor; served as a draft counselor during the Vietnam War. Has worked variously as a cab driver, bartender, janitor, house painter, and in a plastics factory.

*MEMBER:* National Council of Teachers of English, Associated Writing Programs, Popular Culture Association in the South.

*AWARDS, HONORS: Transatlantic Review* Award, 1983; PEN Syndicated Fiction Award, 1984; *Yankee Magazine* Fiction Award, 1988; Florida State Arts Council grant, 1992.

*WRITINGS:*

*The Way That Water Enters Stone* (short stories), Norton (New York City), 1991.

*Louisiana Power & Light* (novel), Norton, 1994.
*Love Warps the Mind a Little* (novel), Norton, 1997.

*WORK IN PROGRESS:* Editing *A Place in the Heart* (tentative title), a collection of essays about place in fiction.

*SIDELIGHTS:* John Dufresne is the author of short stories and novels which have received critical praise for their parodic mixing of humor and pain. Richard Bernstein comments in the *New York Times* that Dufresne "is an abundantly talented storyteller with a habit for droll, self-referential parody."

Dufresne's *The Way That Water Enters Stone* is a collection of short stories set in New England and the deep South. Many of the pieces deal with relationships and loss, and a number of characters are adults whose spouses have left them, or they are children of broken marriages. In the title story, a teacher's marriage disintegrates as his children grow up and leave home. "Surveyors" concerns a boy, his grandfather, and their vegetable garden, which is soon to be destroyed by developers. In "A Long Line of Dreamers," a former priest is dying of cancer, and his family struggles to say good-bye. *Sun-Sentinel* contributor Chauncey Mabe called the stories in the collection "spare and elegant and carefully constructed," and termed the author a "born storyteller." Josephine Humphreys, writing in the *New York Times Book Review,* commented that Dufresne writes "the kind of story that grabs the heart and won't let go."

Dufresne's first novel, *Louisiana Power & Light,* is described by *New York Times Book Review* contributor Jill McCorkle as "a tragicomic example of self-fulfilling prophecy." It is the story of the ill-fated and gene-cursed Fontana family, who appeared earlier in the story collection *The Way That Water Enters Stone.* Billy Wayne Fontana drives a truck for Louisiana Power and Light. He had planned to become a priest, believing that his celibacy would ensure the extinction of genetic flaws that had afflicted his family for generations. Instead, he ends up marrying twice and fathering a series of children to carry on the Fontana heritage.

Billy tells the story in his own meandering words, in what McCorkle calls his "perfectly pitched Southern vernacular," darting into the past, rebounding into the future, confusing some readers, but surprising and enchanting others. McCorkle writes: "He offers a plot line as complex as the network of backwoods roads these people and their ancestors have committed to memory. The miraculous beauty of his tale-telling is that dead ends simply do not exist."

When Billy begins to hear voices in his head, misfortune strikes, and one pitiful event leads to another until the accumulated pile of grief is almost overpowering. A *New Yorker* reviewer comments: "Billy Wayne's story assumes the immediacy of revelation as the self-destruction running through the Fontana past . . . becomes his own inescapable reality."

Favorable reviews of *Louisiana Power & Light* point to the charming vignettes and asides that fill the novel to the brim. McCorkle reports: "Though many of the asides are not directly related to the story at hand . . . there isn't a single one that isn't well worth the time." Moreover, she adds, "these bits of local color . . . are firmly held in place by a story that is much bigger than that of Billy Wayne Fontana."

In *Booklist,* reviewer John Ott calls *Louisiana Power & Light* "a beguiling mix of Faulkner and Barry Gifford," in which Dufresne "takes this nearly surrealistic story of southern-style squalor well beyond parody." Albert E. Wilhelm comments in *Library Journal* that Dufresne "distills high comedy from intense pain, philosophical insight from bayou murkiness." McCorkle concludes: "From wildly funny lines to achingly sad turns, Mr. Dufresne brings Monroe, La., and every road that leads there, into a much-deserved light."

For his second novel, Dufresne returns to his native New England. *Love Warps the Mind a Little* is set in Worcester, Massachusetts. It is filled with characters of "French ancestry and Catholic upbringing," writes Dennis Drabelle in the *Washington Post.* These include Laf Proulx, a fiction writer who narrates the story that, according to Drabelle, "seems to have been not so much written as taken down while it was happening," Laf's girlfriend Judi and "her magnificently disturbed family," and a host of other eccentrics. There is Laf's father, whose eyes often see things upside down or backward, and Mr. Lesperence, whose job is to soften synthetic hair to be used in wigs for dolls, and Pozzo Beckett, a boy convinced that he is the sun.

In this staunchly Catholic community, "Laf is no believer," Drabelle reports. "He muddles along without the Church or God, trying to make sense of an unmoored world." He has left his wife of many years for a girlfriend who is dying of cancer. He works as a cook, sells a few stories now and then, and documents the lives of his friends and neighbors in meticulous and often amusing detail.

Dufresne told *CA:* "I think it is a great privilege to be able to write, to spend the day thinking about whatever it is I think is important at that moment, be it homelessness, separation, apartheid, love, or blood-sucking capitalists. What more could I ask?

"Place shapes characters in a story and it also shapes the writer of the story. The most important influence on my writing was the neighborhood in Worcester, Massachusetts, where I grew up—and the people who lived there. The neighborhood is where I heard my first stories around my grandmother's kitchen table—stories about my grandfather's latest drinking bout; about the motorcycle boys at the Jay-Dee Grille who looked just like the Everly Brothers; about the people we'd seen that morning at mass and the no-good they were up to. They are the people I write for, as well as about."

*BIOGRAPHICAL/CRITICAL SOURCES:*

*PERIODICALS*

*Bloomsbury Review,* November, 1995, p. 3.
*Booklist,* July, 1994, pp. 1921-1922.
*Kirkus Reviews,* May 1, 1994, p. 574.
*Library Journal,* June 1, 1994, p. 156.
*New Yorker,* July 25, 1994, p. 81.
*New York Times,* February 7, 1997, p. C33.
*New York Times Book Review,* April 21, 1991, p. 10; June 9, 1991, p. 34; July 31, 1994, p. 9; February 16, 1997, p. 11.
*Sun-Sentinel* (Fort Lauderdale, FL), July 28, 1991.
*Tribune Books* (Chicago), August 10, 1994, p. 5; January 19, 1997, p. 3.
*Washington Post Book World,* February 9, 1997, p. 6.

* * *

**DURANT, Will(iam James) 1885-1981**

*PERSONAL:* Born November 5, 1885, in North Adams, MA; died November 7, 1981, in Los Angeles, CA, of heart failure; son of Joseph (a superintendent of a Du Pont branch) and Marie (Allors) Durant; married Ariel Kaufman (a writer and researcher), October 31, 1913; children: Ethel Benvenuta (Mrs. Stanislas Kwasniewski), Louis R. (adopted). *Education:* St. Peter's College (Jersey City, N.J.), B.A., 1907, M.A., 1908; Columbia University, Ph.D., 1917. *Religion:* "Agnostic, formerly Catholic."

*CAREER:* Seton Hall College (now University), South Orange, NJ, instructor in Latin and French, 1907-11; Ferrer Modern School, New York City, teacher, 1911-13; Labor Temple School, New York City, director and lecturer, 1914-27; Columbia University, New York City, instructor in philosophy, 1917; University of California, Los Angeles, professor of philosophy, 1935; full-time writer. Reporter, *New York Evening Journal,* 1908. Lecturer.

*MEMBER:* National Institute of Arts and Letters.

*AWARDS, HONORS:* L.H.D., Syracuse University, 1930; with wife, Ariel K. Durant, Huntington Hartford Foundation award for literature, 1963, for *The Age of Louis XIV;* with A. K. Durant, Pulitzer Prize, 1968, for *Rousseau and Revolution;* with A. K. Durant, California Literature Medal Award, 1971, for *Interpretations of Life;* with A. K. Durant, Medal of Freedom, 1977.

*WRITINGS:*

*Philosophy and the Social Problem,* Macmillan, 1917.
*The Story of Philosophy,* Simon & Schuster, 1926, revised edition, 1933.
*Transition: A Sentimental Story of One Mind and One Era* (autobiographical novel), Simon & Schuster, 1927, reprinted, 1978.
(Editor) Arthur Schopenhauer, *Works,* Simon & Schuster, 1928, revised edition, Ungar, 1962.
*Mansions of Philosophy: A Survey of Human Life and Destiny,* Simon & Schuster, 1929, published as *The Pleasures of Philosophy: A Survey of Human Life and Destiny,* 1953.
*The Case for India,* Simon & Schuster, 1930.
*Adventures in Genius* (essays and articles; also see below), Simon & Schuster, 1931.
*A Program for America,* Simon & Schuster, 1931.
*On the Meaning of Life* (correspondence), R. R. Smith, 1932.
*Tragedy of Russia: Impressions from a Brief Visit,* Simon & Schuster, 1933.
*100 Best Books for an Education* (excerpt from *Adventures in Genius*), Simon & Schuster, 1933.
*Great Men of Literature* (excerpt from *Adventures in Genius*), Simon & Schuster, 1936.
*The Story of Civilization,* Simon & Schuster, Volume 1: *Our Oriental Heritage* (also see below), 1935, Volume 2: *The Life of Greece,* 1939, Volume 3: *Caesar and Christ: A History of Roman Civiliza-*

*tion from Its Beginnings to A.D. 337,* 1944, Volume 4: *The Age of Faith,* 1950, Volume 5: *The Renaissance,* 1953, Volume 6: *The Reformation,* 1957, Volume 7: (with wife, Ariel K. Durant) *The Age of Reason Begins,* 1961, Volume 8: (with A. K. Durant) *The Age of Louis XIV,* 1963, Volume 9: (with A. K. Durant) *The Age of Voltaire,* 1965, Volume 10: (with A. K. Durant) *Rousseau and Revolution,* 1967, Volume 11: (with A. K. Durant) *The Age of Napoleon,* 1975.

*The Foundations of Civilization* (introduction to Volume 1 of *The Story of Civilization*), Simon & Schuster, 1936.

(With A. K. Durant) *The Lessons of History,* Simon & Schuster, 1968.

(With A. K. Durant) *Interpretations of Life,* Simon & Schuster, 1970.

(With A. K. Durant) *A Dual Autobiography,* Simon & Schuster, 1977.

*SIDELIGHTS:* Will Durant was a prize-winning historian and philosopher whose chronicles of world history and civilization reached a mass audience. Perhaps his most enduring work is the eleven-volume *The Story of Civilization,* on which he collaborated in part with his wife, Ariel. In this collection, the pair endeavored to synthesize the developments in art, science, religion, politics, literature, and economics. It was an unusual approach, according to Bernard A. Weisberger in the *Washington Post Book World,* as these subjects and their progress are "usually treated separately." The Durants' purpose was to popularize history, to make a large and varied amount of information accessible and comprehensible to the average reader. Though their efforts were popular bestsellers, professional historians often insisted, as Weisberger reports, "that the attempt to handle sixty centuries of human history resulted fatally and inevitably in shallowness and error."

However, Weisberger contends that, notwithstanding the scholars' criticism, "the Durants fill a spiritual vacuum." He believes that "the key" to the popularity and success of *The Story of Civilization* was "[Will] Durant's late 19th-century faith in the simple concepts of history and civilization," his belief in "patterns and structures, tides and movements in history." The reviewer explains: "Somehow, out of chaos, civilizations emerged, and if one unravelled and went under in a civil war or a barbarian incursion, another painfully emerged. . . . People appear to need this assurance that there is a purposeful flow in the life of the whole human race; that their instant of existence matters in an overall scheme."

A *Time* critic argues that "the charge that [the Durants] are popularizers is meaningless. Of course they are popularizers—and great ones." Durant himself responded to his detractors in a *Publishers Weekly* interview with John F. Baker: "We're amateurs. . . . We want to make history meaningful for ordinary readers. . . . We need specialists who devote their time to research, and who work from first-hand materials, sure, but I reject the notion that only university professors can write history. There's room for an integral view, which looks at every aspect of an age—its art, its manners and morals, its philosophy, even its architecture—and shows how they all interrelate. That's how history works—it's not all in separate compartments."

The Durants wrote *The Lessons of History* as a follow-up to *The Story of Civilization.* In short thematic essays, they reflect on the changes humankind has undergone through history and draw conclusions about its achievements, conduct, and prospects.

*Interpretations of Life* contains some two dozen sketches by the Durants on notable twentieth-century American, British, and European writers. In the book's introduction Durant admits he is not a critic and finds authors more interesting than their works. Nonetheless, several critics note that the essays are interesting but provide few insights about the writers.

In *A Dual Autobiography,* the Durants share letters to each other and from well-known contemporaries, press clippings, book reviews, and alternate accounts of their life together. The pair met while Ariel was a student at the New York school where Will taught. They married when she was fourteen and he seventeen. Besides collaborating with his wife on books, Durant was a lecturer on topical subjects and philosophers and debated such eminent persons as Clarence Darrow on stage. Alden Whitman says in the *New York Times Book Review* that the Durants mention the numerous well-known people they met during their lives in their accounts, which are written in ordinary language, but reveal nothing of their own character and personality. He states, "The puzzle of *A Dual Autobiography* is that it recites the trivial and scants the substantial. It is all surface, and even that does not glitter very brightly."

The Durants garnered several important awards for their writings, including a Pulitzer Prize in 1968 for *Rousseau and Revolution.* Will Durant died in 1981 in Los Angeles, California.

*BIOGRAPHICAL/CRITICAL SOURCES:*

*BOOKS*

Durant, Will, and A. K. Durant, *A Dual Autobiography,* Simon & Schuster, 1977.
Frey, Raymond, *William James Durant: An Intellectual Autobiography,* E. Mellen Press (Lewiston, NY), 1991.

*PERIODICALS*

*Book Week,* September 15, 1963; October 10, 1965.
*Christian Science Monitor,* October 28, 1965; November 30, 1967.
*Forbes,* March 27, 1995, p. 26.
*Life,* October 18, 1963.
*National Review,* January 16, 1968.
*New Republic,* October 2, 1965.
*Newsweek,* September 16, 1957; September 11, 1961; September 16, 1963.
*New York Herald Tribune Book Review,* October 25, 1953.
*New York Times Book Review,* September 15, 1963; September 19, 1965; October 15, 1967; February 5, 1978.
*Publishers Weekly,* November 24, 1975.
*Reader's Digest,* October, 1969.
*Saturday Review,* September 9, 1961; September 21, 1963; October 23, 1965; September 23, 1967.
*Time,* September 28, 1953; September 27, 1963; August 13, 1965; October 8, 1965; October 6, 1967.
*Washington Post Book World,* November 27, 1977.
*Yale Review,* December, 1963.

*OBITUARIES:*

*PERIODICALS*

*Chicago Tribune,* November 10, 1981.
*Detroit News,* November 15, 1981.
*Kirkus Reviews,* June 1, 1968, p. 627.
*Newsweek,* November 23, 1981.
*New York Times,* November 10, 1981.
*Publishers Weekly,* November 20, 1981.
*Time,* November 23, 1981.
*Times* (London), November 10, 1981.*

# E

**EDELMAN, Marian Wright 1939-**

*PERSONAL:* Born June 6, 1939, in Bennettsville, SC; daughter of Arthur J. and Maggie (Bowen) Wright; married Peter Benjamin Edelman, July 14, 1968; children: Joshua Robert, Jonah Martin, Ezra Benjamin. *Education:* Attended University of Paris and University of Geneva, 1958-59; Spelman College, B.A., 1960; Yale University, LL.B., 1963.

*ADDRESSES: Office—* Children's Defense Fund, 122 C St. N.W., Washington, DC 20001.

*CAREER:* National Association for the Advancement of Colored People (NAACP), Legal Defense and Education Fund, Inc., New York City, staff attorney, 1963-64, director of office in Jackson, MS, 1964-68; partner of Washington Research Project of Southern Center for Public Policy, 1968-73; Children's Defense Fund, Washington, DC, founder and president, 1973—. W. E. B. Du Bois Lecturer at Harvard University, 1986. Member of Lisle Fellowship's U.S.-U.S.S.R. Student Exchange, 1959; member of executive committee of Student Non-Violent Coordinating Committee (SNCC), 1961-63; member of Operation Crossroads Africa Project in Ivory Coast, 1962; congressional and federal agency liaison for Poor People's Campaign, summer, 1968; director of Harvard University's Center for Law and Education, 1971-73. Member of Presidential Commission on Americans Missing and Unaccounted for in Southeast Asia (Woodcock Commission), 1977, United States-South Africa leadership Exchange Program, 1977, National Commission on the International Year of the Child, 1979, and President's Commission for a National Agenda for the Eighties, 1979; member of board of directors of Carnegie Council on Children, 1972-77, Aetna Life and Casualty Foundation, Citizens for Constitutional Concerns, U.S. Committee for UNICEF, and Legal Defense and Education Fund of the NAACP; member of board of trustees of Martin Luther King, Jr., Memorial Center, and Joint Center for Political Studies.

*MEMBER:* Council on Foreign Relations, Delta Sigma Theta (honorary member).

*AWARDS, HONORS:* Merrill scholar in Paris and Geneva, 1958-59; honorary fellow of Law School at University of Pennsylvania, 1969; Louise Waterman Wise Award, 1970; Presidential Citation, American Public Health Association, 1979; Outstanding Leadership Award, National Alliance of Black School Educators, 1979; Distinguished Service Award, National Association of Black Women Attorneys, 1979; National Award of Merit, National Council on Crime and Delinquency, 1979; named Washingtonian of the Year, 1979; Whitney M. Young Memorial Award, Washington Urban League, 1980; Professional Achievement Award, Black Enterprise magazine, 1980; Outstanding Leadership Achievement Award, National Women's Political Caucus and Black Caucus, 1980; Outstanding Community Service Award, National Hookup of Black Women, 1980; Woman of the Year Award, Big Sisters of America, 1980; Award of Recognition, American Academy of Pedodontics, 1981; Rockefeller Public Service Award, 1981; Gertrude Zimand Award, National Child Labor Committee, 1982; Florina Lasker Award, New York Civil Liberties Union, 1982; Anne Roe Award, Graduate School of Education at Harvard University, 1984; Roy Wilkins Civil Rights Award,

National Association for the Advancement of Colored People (NAACP), 1984; award from Women's Legal Defense Fund, 1985; Hubert H. Humphrey Award, Leadership Conference on Civil Rights, 1985; fellow of MacArthur Foundation, 1985; Grenville Clark Prize from Dartmouth College, 1986; Compostela Award of St. James Cathedral, 1987; Gandhi Peace Award, 1989; Fordham Stein Prize, 1989; Murray-Green-Meany Award, AFL-CIO, 1989; Frontrunner Award, Sara Lee Corporation, 1990; Jefferson Award, American Institute for Public Service, 1991; more than thirty honorary degrees.

*WRITINGS:*

*Families in Peril: An Agenda for Social Change,* Harvard University Press, 1987.

*The Measure of Our Success: A Letter to My Children and Yours,* Beacon Press (Boston, MA), 1992.

*Guide My Feet: Prayers and Meditations on Loving and Working for Children,* Beacon Press, 1995.

Also author of *School Suspensions: Are They Helping Children?,* 1975, and *Portrait of Inequality: Black and White Children in America,* 1980. Contributor to books, including *Raising Children in Modern America: Problems and Prospective Solutions,* edited by Nathan B. Talbot, Little, Brown, 1975; *Toward New Human Rights: The Social Policies of the Kennedy and Johnson Administrations,* edited by David C. Warner, Lyndon B. Johnson School of Public Affairs, University of Texas at Austin, 1977.

*SIDELIGHTS:* Dubbed "the 101st Senator on children's issues" by Senator Edward Kennedy, Marian Wright Edelman left her law practice in 1968, just after the assassination of civil rights leader Martin Luther King, Jr., to work toward a better future for American children. She was the first black woman on the Mississippi bar and had been a civil rights lawyer with the National Association for the Advancement of Colored People (NAACP). "Convinced she could achieve more as an advocate than as a litigant for the poor," wrote Nancy Traver in *Time,* Edelman moved to Washington, DC, and began to apply her researching and rhetorical skills in Congress. She promotes her cause with facts about teen pregnancies, poverty, and infant mortality and—with her Children's Defense Fund—has managed to obtain budget increases for family and child health care and education programs. In *Ms.* magazine Katherine Bouton described Edelman as "the nation's most effective lobbyist on behalf of children . . . an unparalleled strategist and pragmatist."

Edelman's book, *Families in Peril: An Agenda for Social Change,* was judged "a powerful and necessary document" of the circumstances of children by *Washington Post* reviewer Jonathan Yardley, and it urges support for poor mothers and children of all races. The book is based on the 1986 W. E. B. Du Bois Lectures that Edelman gave at Harvard University. In making her case for increased support for America's children, Edelman offers numerous statistics that paint a grim portrait of life for the country's poor. Don Wycliff, reviewing the book for the *New York Times Book Review,* questioned Edelman's solutions as overly dependent on government support and neglectful of parental responsibility for children: "Governmental exertions . . . are indispensable. But . . . Edelman doesn't satisfactorily address how [parents] can be induced to behave wisely and responsibly *for their child's benefit.*" A *Kirkus Review* contributor, however, termed the book "graphic and eloquent."

In *Measure of Our Success: A Letter to My Children and Yours,* Edelman again deals with the problems and possible solutions of poverty and the neglect of children, in part by discussing her own experience as a parent. The book is divided into five sections: "A Family Legacy"; "Passing on the Legacy of Service"; "A Letter to My Sons"; "Twenty-five Lessons for Life"; and "Is the Child Safe?" Writing in the *New York Times Book Review* about the "Twenty-five Lessons for Life" chapter, Clifton L. Taulbert commented, "In the 25 lessons for life that she presents here, she issues a call for parental involvement, a commitment of personal time on behalf of others, the primacy of service over self, and the assumption of individual responsibility for our nation's character."

Edelman once commented: "I have been an advocate for disadvantaged Americans throughout my professional career. The Children's Defense Fund, which I have been privileged to direct, has become one of the nation's most active organizations concerned with a wide range of children's and family issues, especially those which most affect America's children: our poorest Americans.

"Founded in 1968 as the Washington Research Project, the Children's Defense Fund monitors and proposes improvements in federal, state, and local budgets, legislative and administrative policies in the areas of child and maternal health, education, child care, child welfare, adolescent pregnancy prevention, youth employment, and family support systems.

"In 1983 the Children's Defense Fund initiated a major long-term national campaign to prevent teenage pregnancy and provide positive life options for youth. Since then, we have launched a multimedia campaign that includes transit advertisements, posters, and television and radio public service announcements, a national prenatal care campaign, and Child Watch coalitions in more than seventy local communities in thirty states to combat teen pregnancy.

"The Children's Defense Fund also has been a leading advocate in Congress, state legislatures, and courts for children's rights. For example, our legal actions blocked out-of-state placement of hundreds of Louisiana children in Texas institutions, guaranteed access to special education programs for tens of thousands of Mississippi's children, and represented the interests of children and their families before numerous federal administrative agencies."

*BIOGRAPHICAL/CRITICAL SOURCES:*

*PERIODICALS*

*Ebony,* July, 1987.
*Harper's,* February, 1993, p. 154.
*Kirkus Reviews,* February 1, 1987, p. 189.
*Library Journal,* March 1, 1987, p. 66.
*Ms.,* July/August, 1987.
*New Republic,* March 4, 1996, p. 33.
*Newsweek,* June 10, 1996, p. 32.
*New York Times Book Review,* June 7, 1987, p. 12; August 23, 1992, p. 13.
*Psychology Today,* July-August, 1993, p. 26.
*School Library Journal,* September, 1992, p. 290; December, 1992, p. 29.
*Time,* March 23, 1987.
*Washington Post,* March 4, 1987.
*Washington Post Book World,* April 19, 1992, p. 13.*

* * *

**EDGAR, David 1948-**

*PERSONAL:* Born February 26, 1948, in Birmingham, England; son of Barrie (a TV producer) and Joan (Burman) Edgar. *Education:* Manchester University, B.A. (with honors), 1969. *Politics:* Socialist. *Religion:* None.

*ADDRESSES: Agent*—Michael Imison, 81 Shaftesbury Ave., London W1, England.

*CAREER:* Playwright. Leeds Polytechnic, Leeds, England, fellow in creative writing, 1972-74; Birmingham Repertory Theatre, Birmingham, England, resident playwright, 1974-75.

*MEMBER:* Association of Cinematograph, Television and Allied Technicians, Writers' Guild, Theatre Writers' Union.

*AWARDS, HONORS:* United Kingdom/United States Bicentennial Arts fellow, 1978-79; John Whiting Award, Arts Council of Great Britain for *Destiny*; Society of West End Theatres award for best play, Antoinette Perry ("Tony") Award, and New York Drama Critics Circle award for best play, all 1982, for *The Life and Adventures of Nicholas Nickleby*; Emmy Award nomination, Academy of Television Arts and Sciences, 1983, for the television production of *The Life and Adventures of Nicholas Nickleby*; *Maydays* was named best new play by a number of periodicals, including *Plays and Players, Punch, The Stage*, and *Daily Express*; London Drama Award, 1995, for *Pentecost.*

*WRITINGS:*

*PLAYS*

*Two Kinds of Angel* (one-act), first produced in Bradford, England, 1970, produced in London, 1971.
*A Truer Shade of Blue*, first produced in Bradford, 1970.
*Bloody Rosa*, first produced in Bradford, 1970, produced in Edinburgh, Scotland, 1971.
*Still Life: Man in Bed*, first produced in Edinburgh, 1971, produced in London, 1972.
*Acid*, first produced in Bradford, 1971, produced in Edinburgh, 1971.
*The National Interest* (one-act), produced by General Will (theatre company), 1971.
*Conversation in Paradise*, first produced in Edinburgh, 1971.
*Tedderella*, first produced in Edinburgh, 1971, produced in London, 1973.
*The Rupert Show* (one-act), first produced in Bradford, produced by General Will, 1972.
*The End*, first produced in Bradford, 1972.
*Excuses Excuses* (two-act), first produced in Coventry, England, 1972, produced in London, 1973, produced as *Fired* by Second City Theatre Co., 1975.
*Rent: Or, Caught in the Act*, produced by General Will, 1972, produced in London, 1972.

*State of Emergency* (one-act), first produced by General Will, 1972, produced in London, 1972.

(With Tony Bicat, Howard Brenton, Brian Clark, Francis Fichs, David Hare, and Snoo Wilson) *England's Ireland*, first produced in Amsterdam, Netherlands, 1972, produced in London, 1972.

*Road to Hanoi*, first produced by Paradise Foundry (theatre company), 1972.

*Not with a Bang But a Whimper*, first produced in Leeds, England, 1972.

*Death Story*, first produced in Birmingham, England, 1972, produced in New York, 1975.

(With Brenton) *A Fart for Europe* (one-act), produced in London, 1973.

(With others) *Up Spaghetti Junction*, first produced in Birmingham, 1973.

*Gangsters* (also see below), produced in London, 1973.

*Baby Love* (one-act; also see below), first produced in Leeds, 1973, produced in London, 1973, published in *Shorts,* 1989.

*Liberated Zone*, produced in Bingley, England, 1973.

*The Case of the Workers' Plane* (two-act), produced in Bristol, England, 1973, revised play produced as *Concorde Cabaret* (also see below), by Avon Touring Co., 1975.

*Operation Iskra* (three-act), produced by Paradise Foundry, 1973.

*The Eagle Has Landed* (also see below), produced in Liverpool, England, 1973.

*The Dunkirk Spirit*, produced by General Will, 1974.

*Dick Deterred* (two-act; produced in London, 1974, produced in New York, 1983), Monthly Review Press, 1974.

*The All-Singing All-Talking Golden Oldie Rock Revival Ho Chi Minh Peace Love and Revolution Show*, produced in Bingley, 1974.

*Man Only Dines*, produced in Leeds, 1974.

*O Fair Jerusalem*, produced in Birmingham, 1975, published in *Plays 1,* 1987.

*Summer Sports*, first produced in Birmingham, 1975, produced in London, 1975, produced as *Blood Sports* in London, 1976.

*The National Theatre*, produced in London, 1975, published in *Shorts,* 1989.

*Events Following the Closure of a Motorcycle Factory*, produced in Birmingham, 1976.

*Saigon Rose* (also see below), produced in Edinburgh, 1976, produced in New York, 1982, published in *Plays 1,* 1987.

*Destiny* (also see below; first produced in Stratford, England, 1976, produced on the West End, 1977), Eyre Methuen, 1976.

*The Perils of Bardford*, produced in Bradford, 1976.

*Wreckers* (first produced in Exeter, England, 1977, produced in London, 1977), Eyre Methuen, 1977.

*Our Own People*, first produced by Pirate Jenny (theatre company), 1977, produced in London, 1978, published in *Plays 3,* 1991.

*Ball Boys*, Pluto Press, 1978.

(Adapter) *The Jail Diary of Albie Sachs* (also see below; produced in London, 1978, produced in New York, 1979), Collings, 1978.

(Adapter) *Mary Barnes* (first produced in Birmingham, 1978, produced in London, 1979, produced in New York, 1983), Eyre Methuen, 1979.

*Teendreams* (produced in Bristol, 1979), Eyre Methuen, 1979.

(Adapter) *The Life and Adventures of Nicholas Nickleby* (also see below; based on the Charles Dickens novel; first produced on the West End by Royal Shakespeare Co., 1980, produced on Broadway, 1981), Dramatists Play Service, 1982.

*Maydays* (produced in London, 1983), Eyre Methuen, 1983.

*Entertaining Strangers: A Play for Dorchester* (produced in Dorchester, England, 1985; revised version produced in London, 1987), Methuen, 1986.

*That Summer* (produced in London, 1987), Methuen, 1987.

*Plays 1* (includes *The Jail Diary of Albie Sachs, Mary Barnes, Saigon Rose, O Fair Jerusalem,* and *Destiny*), Methuen, 1987.

*Shorts: Short Plays* (includes *Blood Sports with Ball Boys, Baby Love, The National Theatre,* and *The Midas Connection*), Hern, 1989.

(With Stephen Bill and Anne Devlin) *Heartlanders* (produced in Birmingham, 1989), Hern, 1989.

*The Shape of the Table* (produced in London, 1990), Hern, 1990.

*Plays 2* (includes *Ecclesiastes, The Life and Adventures of Nicholas Nickleby,* and *Entertaining Strangers*), Methuen, 1990.

*Plays 3* (includes *Our Own People, Teendreams, Maydays,* and *That Summer*), Methuen, 1991.

*The Strange Case of Dr. Jekyll and Mr. Hyde* (adapted from Robert Louis Stevenson's novel), Hern, 1991.

*Pentecost,* produced in London at the Other Place, 1994.

*SCREENPLAYS*

*The Eagle Has Landed* (based on play of the same title), Granada Television, 1973.

*Sanctuary* (based on the author's play *Gangsters*), Scottish Television, 1973.

*I Know What I Meant*, Granada Television, 1974.

*Baby Love* (based on play of the same title), British Broadcasting Corp. (BBC), 1974.

*Concorde Cabaret* (based on play of the same title), Harlech Television, 1975.

(With Robert Muller and Hugh Whitemore) *Censors*, BBC, 1975.

*The Midas Touch*, BBC, 1975.

*Ecclesiastes* (radio play), BBC Radio 4, 1977.

*Destiny* (based on play of the same title), BBC, 1978.

*Saigon Rose* (radio play; based on play of the same title), BBC Radio 3, 1979.

*The Jail Diary of Albie Sachs* (based on play of the same title), BBC, 1980.

*The Life and Adventures of Nicholas Nickleby* (based on play of the same title), Channel Four, 1982, syndicated in America by Mobil Showcase Theatre, 1983.

(With Neil Grant) *Vote for Them* (broadcast by BBC, 1989), BBC Publications, 1989.

Also author of *Lady Jane*, for Paramount.

*OTHER*

*The Second Time as Farce: Reflections on the Drama of Modern Times*, Lawrence & Wishart, 1988.

Contributor to *The London Fringe Theatre*, edited by V. E. Mitchell, Burnham House, 1975; *Workers and Writers*, edited by Wilfrid van der Will, Department of German, Birmingham University, 1975; *Contemporary Dramatists*, St. James Press, 1977; *Best Short Plays of 1982*, edited by Ramon Delgado, Chilton, 1982; and *The Changing World of Charles Dickens*, edited by Robert Giddings, Barnes & Noble, 1983.

Also contributor to periodicals, including *Plays and Players*, *New Edinburgh Review*, and *Socialist Review*.

*SIDELIGHTS:* Although best known as the adapter of Charles Dickens's *The Life and Adventures of Nicholas Nickleby* into the highly publicized theatre event of the 1980-81 season, David Edgar is more notable as one of the most outspoken—and prolific—playwrights of Britain's New Left. Since 1970, when *Two Kinds of Angel* premiered, Edgar has seen more than forty subsequent plays and musicals successfully staged.

Most of Edgar's work reflects his interest in the "agitprop" (extremely liberal) politics of Britain's counterculture; his dramatic style often draws from the encompassing, audience-involving mode popularized by Bertolt Brecht. One scene from *The Jail Diary of Albie Sachs*, for instance, calls for the audience to join the political-prisoner title character in remaining absolutely quiet for two minutes. This gesture "actually conveys the nature of prison solitude," says Michael Billington in the *New York Times*. "The relief with which the audience shuffles and coughs at the end of that period says a lot about the torture of confinement."

The theme of imprisonment is also explored in Edgar's adaptation *Mary Barnes*, the true story of a woman's harrowing treatment for schizophrenia at an East London "therapy community." The play, according to Stanley Weintraub in his *Dictionary of Literary Biography* article, examines "not only what constitutes madness by societal standards but also whether or not society is guilty of complicity in the maladjustment of a talented human being, whether or not the mind's potential is wasted in order to seize easy solutions for controlling a 'mad' person, and whether or not one can even talk of sanity in a less-than-sane society."

In a lighter vein, the playwright created a musical farce, *Dick Deterred*, which compares the Nixon administration to the court of the corrupt King Richard III. This work features such characters as H. R. (Bob) Buckingham, the king's chief of staff, and Eugene McClarence, "duke and Senator from Minnesota, [who] is done in by Richard, Mayor of Chicago," as Richard F. Shepard writes in a *New York Times* review. With another comedy, *Rent: Or, Caught in the Act*, Edgar prefigured his success with adapting *Nicholas Nickleby* by giving his characters Dickensian names like Mr. Devious (of the legal firm of Devious, Devious, and Downright Dishonest) and Honest Tom Hard-Done-By, the corruptible hero of the piece. *State of Emergency* and *Operation Iskra* constitute two more titles of what Weintraub calls the author's "agitprop cartoons."

Running eight and one half hours, Edgar's *Nicholas Nickleby* set transatlantic records as the longest play ever produced and, in New York, for the most expensive theatre ticket price ever legally set. While many objected to the one-hundred dollar price for the two evenings of entertainment (hardier playgoers could opt to see the entire show in one day), *Time* magazine critic Richard Corliss points out that at twenty cents per minute, *Nicholas Nickleby* was one of Broadway's biggest bargains. In adapting Dickens's book, Edgar observes to Corliss, the author faced "a twofold challenge: to convert a rambling, complexly plotted novel into a play in a few months, and to respond to ideas from the two directors [Trevor Nunn and John Caird], from Designer John Napier, from Composer Stephen Oliver and all those actors." The challenge was met with overwhelming success: *Nicholas Nickleby* went on to win several theatre awards in both artistic and technical categories. The production also captured praise such as the kind Bernard Levin writes in the *Times*. Levin describes the event as "a celebration of love and justice that is true to the spirit of Dickens's belief that those are the fulcrums on which the universe is moved, and the consequence is that we come out not merely delighted but strengthened, not just entertained but uplifted, not only affected but changed."

In the 1990s Edgar has written several plays dealing with the changing face of Europe after the fall of the Soviet Empire and the crumbling of the Berlin Wall, including 1990's *The Shape of the Table* and 1994's *Pentecost*. The latter work is set in an unnamed eastern European country and deals with issues of art history and nationality, as a British art historian sets out to discover whether a fresco in an old church is a modern work or an authentic fresco produced more than 600 years ago. Writing in the *New Statesman & Society*, Andy Lavender states that the play "is more subtly comic and ironic than anything [Edgar has done] to date" and adds that *Pentecost*'s ". . . ambition is undeniable and its metaphors eloquent."

Edgar told *CA:* "The aim of my work is to create a theatre of public life, as a counter to the domestic drama which dominates theatre and television on both sides of the Atlantic. I have recently become interested in adaptation of historical and contemporary works in pursuit of this aim."

*BIOGRAPHICAL/CRITICAL SOURCES:*

*BOOKS*

*Dictionary of Literary Biography*, Volume 13: *British Dramatists since World War II*, Gale, 1982.
Hayman, Ronald, *British Theatre since 1955*, Oxford University Press, 1979.
Itzin, Catherine, *Stages in the Revolution*, Eyre Methuen, 1980.
Swain, Elizabeth, *David Edgar, Playwright and Politician*, Peter Lang, 1986.
Trussler, Simon, editor, *New Theatre: Voices of the Seventies*, Eyre Methuen, 1981.
Trussler, Simon, editor, *File on Edgar*, Methuen, 1991.

*PERIODICALS*

*New Statesman & Society*, October 21, 1994, p. 34.
*Newsweek*, October 12, 1981.
*New York Times*, March 18, 1979; March 6, 1980; October 5, 1981; January 10, 1982; November 30, 1982; January 24, 1983.
*Time*, October 5, 1981.
*Times* (London), July 8, 1980; October 22, 1983.*

* * *

**ELLMANN, Richard (David) 1918-1987**

*PERSONAL:* Born March 15, 1918, in Highland Park, MI; died May 13, 1987, of pneumonia brought on by amyotrophic lateral sclerosis (Lou Gehrig's disease) in Oxford, England; son of James I. (a lawyer) and Jeanette (Barsook) Ellmann; married Mary Donahue (a writer), August 12, 1949; children: Stephen, Maud, Lucy. *Education:* Yale University, B.A., 1939, M.A., 1941, Ph.D., 1947; Trinity College, Dublin, B.Litt., 1947; Oxford University, England, M.A., 1970.

*CAREER:* Harvard University, Cambridge, MA, instructor, 1942-43, 1947-48, Briggs-Copeland Assistant Professor of English Composition, 1948-51; Northwestern University, Evanston, IL, professor of English, 1951-63, Franklin Bliss Snyder Professor, 1963-68; Yale University, New Haven, CT, professor of English, 1968-70; Oxford University, Oxford, England, Goldsmiths' Professor of English Literature, 1970-1984, New College, fellow, 1970-84, honorary fellow, 1984-87; Wolfson College, extraordinary fellow, 1984-87. Frederick Ives Carpenter Visiting Professor, University of Chicago, 1959, 1967, and 1975-77; Emory University, visiting professor, 1978-81, Woodruff Professor of English, 1982-87. Member of United States/United Kingdom Educational Commission, 1970-85. Consultant to "The World of James Joyce," Public Broadcasting Service, 1983. *Military service:* U.S. Navy and Office of Strategic Services, 1943-46.

*MEMBER:* British Academy (fellow), Modern Language Association of America (chairman of English Institute, 1961-62; member of executive council, 1961-65), English Institute (chairman, 1961-62), Royal Society of Literature (fellow), American Academy and Institute of Arts and Letters (fellow), American Academy and Institute of Arts and Letters (fellow), Phi Beta Kappa, Chi Delta Theta, Athenaeum, Elizabethan Club, Signet.

*AWARDS, HONORS:* Rockefeller Foundation fellow in humanities, 1946-47; Guggenheim fellow, 1950, 1957-58, and 1970; grants from American Philosophical Society and Modern Language Association of America, 1953; *Kenyon Review* fellowship in criticism, 1955-56; School of Letters fellow, Indiana University, 1956 and 1960, senior fellow, 1966-72; National Book Award for nonfiction, Friends of Literature Award in biography, Thormond Monson Award from Society of Midland Authors, and Carey-Thomas Award for creative book publishing to Oxford University Press, all for *James Joyce,* 1960, and Duff Cooper Prize and James Tair Black Prize for new and revised edition, 1982; George Polk Memorial Award, 1970, for *The Artist As Critic: Critical Writings of Oscar Wilde;* New College fellow, Oxford University, 1970-84, honorary fellow, 1984-87; Extraordinary fellow, Wolfson College, 1984-87; National Book Critics Circle Award for best biography/autobiography, 1989, for *Oscar Wilde.* D.Litt. from National University of Ireland, 1975, Emory University, 1979, Northwestern University, 1980, and McGill University, 1986; National Endowment for the Humanities research grant, 1977; Ph.D., University of Gothenburg (Sweden), 1978; D.H.L. from Boston College and University of Rochester, both 1979;

*WRITINGS:*

*Yeats: The Man and the Masks,* Macmillan, 1948, reprinted, Norton, 1978, corrected edition with new preface, Oxford University Press, 1979.

*The Identity of Yeats,* Oxford University Press, 1954, 2nd edition, 1964, reprinted, 1985.

*James Joyce,* Oxford University Press, 1959, new and revised edition with corrections, 1982.

*Edwardians and Late Victorians,* Columbia University Press, 1960.

(With E. D. H. Johnson and Alfred L. Bush) *Wilde and the Nineties: An Essay and an Exhibition,* edited by Charles Ryskamp, Princeton University Library, 1966.

*Eminent Domain: Yeats among Wilde, Joyce, Pound, Eliot, and Auden,* Oxford University Press, 1967.

*Ulysses on the Liffey,* Oxford University Press, 1972, corrected edition, Faber and Faber, 1984.

*Golden Codgers: Biographical Speculations,* Oxford University Press, 1973.

(With John Espey) *Oscar Wilde: Two Approaches* (Papers Read at a Clark Library Seminar, April 17, 1976), Williams Andrews Clark Memorial Library, 1977.

*The Consciousness of Joyce,* Oxford University Press, 1977.

*Four Dubliners: Wilde, Yeats, Joyce, and Beckett,* U.S. Government Printing Office, 1986.

*Oscar Wilde,* Hamish Hamilton, 1987, Knopf, 1988.

*a long the riverrun: Selected Essays,* Knopf (New York City), 1989.

*EDITOR*

(And translator, and author of introduction) Henri Michaux, *Selected Writings,* Routledge & Kegan Paul, 1952.

Stanislaus Joyce, *My Brother's Keeper: James Joyce's Early Years,* Viking, 1958.

(With others) *English Masterpieces,* 2nd edition, two volumes, Prentice-Hall, 1958.

Arthur Symons, *The Symbolist Movement in Literature,* Dutton, 1958.

(With Ellsworth Mason) *The Critical Writings of James Joyce,* Faber and Faber, 1959, reprinted, 1979.

(With Charles Feidelson, Jr.) *The Modern Tradition: Backgrounds of Modern Literature,* Oxford University Press, 1965.

James Joyce, *Letters of James Joyce,* Volumes 2-3, Viking, 1966.

(Of corrected holograph) James Joyce, *A Portrait of the Artist As a Young Man,* drawings by Robin Jacques, Cape, 1968.

Oscar Wilde, *The Artist As Critic: Critical Writings of Oscar Wilde,* Random House, 1969.

*Oscar Wilde: A Collection of Critical Essays,* Prentice-Hall, 1969.

(With Robert O'Clair) *The Norton Anthology of Modern Poetry,* Norton, 1973, second edition published as *Modern Poems: A Norton Introduction,* Norton (New York City), 1989.

James Joyce, *Selected Letters of James Joyce,* Viking, 1975.

(With O'Clair) *Modern Poems: An Introduction to Poetry,* Norton, 1976.

*The New Oxford Book of American Verse,* Oxford University Press, 1976.

(And author of introduction) Oscar Wilde, *The Picture of Dorian Gray and Other Writings,* Bantam, 1982.

*OTHER*

(Contributor of "A Chronology on the Life of James Joyce") James Joyce, *Letters,* Volume 1, edited by Stuart Gilbert, Viking, 1957.

*Ulysses the Divine Nobody* (monograph), Yale University Press, 1957, reprinted, 1981.

*Joyce in Love* (monograph), Cornell University Library, 1959.

(Contributor of "Overtures to Wilde's Salome") *Twentieth Anniversary, 1968,* Indiana University School of Letters, 1968.

(Author of introduction and notes) James Joyce, *Giacomo Joyce,* Faber, 1968, reprinted, 1984.

(Contributor of "Ulysses: A Short History") James Joyce, *Ulysses,* Penguin, 1969.

*James Joyce's Tower* (monograph), Eastern Regional Tourism Organisation (Dublin), 1969.

*Literary Biography* (monograph; inaugural lecture, University of Oxford, May 4, 1971), Clarendon Press, 1971.

*The Poetry of Yeats* (phono tape), BFA Educational Media, 1974.

*James Joyce's Hundredth Birthday, Side and Front Views* (monograph), Library of Congress, 1982.

*Oscar Wilde at Oxford* (monograph), Library of Congress, 1984.

(Author of introduction) Michael Moscato and Leslie LeBlanc, *The United States of America vs. One Book Entitled Ulysses by James Joyce; Documents and Commentary: 50-Year Retrospective,* University Publications of America, 1984.

*Henry James among the Aesthetes* (lectures), Longwood Publishing Group, 1985.

*W. B. Yeats' Second Puberty* (monograph), Library of Congress, 1985.

*Samuel Beckett, Nayman of Noland* (monograph), Library of Congress, 1986.

Also author of monographs *Wallace Stevens' Ice-Cream,* 1957, and *The Background of Joyce's The Dead,* 1958.

*SIDELIGHTS:* A renowned biographer, literary critic, and educator, Richard Ellmann held professorial posts at such universities as Harvard, Northwestern, and Yale before becoming the first American to teach English literature at Oxford University, a position he held for many years. Ellmann devoted most of his distinguished academic career to the study of the Irish literary renaissance. "It is difficult to think of the great writers of Irish literature—W. B. Yeats, James Joyce, or Oscar Wilde—without thinking of Ellmann," remarked Steven Serafin in a *Dictionary of Literary Biography Yearbook: 1987* essay. Ellmann's scholarship on Yeats remains a standard reference, and he is widely acknowledged as having been the foremost authority on Joyce. His much heralded, National Book Award-winning biography *James Joyce,* not only represents the definitive work on the artist but, in the opinion of many, casts its shadow as the best literary biography ever written. Referring to him as "an extraordinary individual of rare and exceptional talent," Serafin believed that "Ellmann essentially redefined the art of biography." And in a *Times Literary Supplement* review of Ellmann's National Book Critics Circle Award-winning final work, the biography *Oscar Wilde,* Gore Vidal deemed him "our time's best academic biographer."

Ellmann's scholarship sought the literary influences upon and connections among writers and their work. Calling Ellmann "particularly sensitive to the impingement of one talent upon another," Denis Donoghue added in a *New York Times Book Review* essay about *Eminent Domain: Yeats among Wilde, Joyce, Pound, Eliot, and Auden:* "As critics we look for corresponding moments in the work, moments of representative force and definition. Mr. Ellmann is a keen student of these epiphanies in life and art. He finds them more often than not in the pressure of one mind upon another, and he delights in these occasions." In Ellmann's *Eminent Domain,* "Yeats's greatness as a poet is seen as illustrated by his gift for expropriating or confiscating, from youth to age, ideas or tactics from other writers," stated a *Times Literary Supplement* contributor.

Ellmann, whose work on Yeats "set the tone of much subsequent criticism," stated Kevin Sullivan in *Nation* review of *Eminent Domain,* believed that as "a young poet in search of an aesthetic," Yeats was significantly indebted to Wilde, whose "professional reputation rested . . . on his skill as a talker before all else." Yeats "pillaged freely" of this talk during their London meetings and believed that "Wilde's dazzling conversation was an aristocratic counterpart to the oral culture that had persisted among the Irish peasantry at home," explained Sullivan. "But what really attracted him was Wilde's easy assumption of the superiority of imagination to reason and intellect, and the corollary that followed almost at once upon that assumption—the primacy and autonomy of art." And about the relationship between Yeats and Joyce, the *Times Literary Supplement* contributor noted that while "Joyce's attitude to Yeats was that of a rebel in the Irish literary movement," according to Sullivan, Ellmann believed that "Joyce turned from verse to prose out of an awareness of Yeats's unchallengeable mastery as a poet." Praised by Sullivan for describing "a wide and graceful arc that encompasses many of the major developments in English poetry during a full half-century," *Eminent Domain* was labeled "lucid, perceptive, urbane, in itself a graceful occasion" by Donoghue.

*James Joyce,* Ellmann's masterwork, was hailed with critical superlatives. "This immensely detailed, massive, completely detached and objective, yet loving biography, translates James Joyce's books back into his life," wrote Stephen Spender in the *New York Times.* "Here is the definitive work," assessed Dwight Macdonald in *New Yorker,* "and I hope it will become a model for future scholarly biographies." And according to Mark Schorer in the *San Francisco Chronicle,* "This is not only the most important book that we have had on James Joyce until now (and the only reliable biography), it is also, almost certainly, one of the great literary biographies of this century, a book that will last for years, probably for generations." A few critics, however, faulted the biography for the enormity of its detail. A *Times Literary Supplement* contributor, for example, contended that "much of the difficulty with Mr. Ellmann's book is in seeing the wood for the trees." But in the *Saturday Review,* Stuart Gilbert echoed the widely shared critical recognition that Ellmann performed commendably, calling *James Joyce* "a masterpiece of scholarly objectivity and exact research, in which the facts are marshaled and set forth with fine lucidity, and the imposing mass of detail never clogs the analysis."

In 1982, more than twenty years after the publication of *James Joyce,* Ellmann marked the centennial year of Joyce's birth with a new and revised edition of his biography. Having had access to Joyce's private library and other previously unavailable material, Ellmann was able to define the influences upon Joyce's art, especially *Ulysses.* "Ellmann's task was a dual one," wrote Thomas Flanagan in the *Washington Post Book World.* "He re-created for the reader what had become one of the exemplary lives of modern literature, conveying its color and its textures, its characterizing movements and stances, by the adroit but unobtrusive deployment of many thousands of details." The *New York Time*'s Christopher Lehmann-Haupt, who felt that this minutely detailed new material was "entirely appropriate and desirable, considering the obsessive sort of attachment that Joyce's art inspires," remarked: "And the effect of this experience is fairly stunning, not alone because of the remarkable wealth of details that the author has gathered up and artfully pieced together. What also strikes the reader is the number of those details that wound up in Joyce's fiction, or, to put it the other way around, the degree to which Joyce's art was grounded in actuality."

Although *Newsweek*'s Peter S. Prescott regarded it "a pleasure to salute this masterly book as it marches past again," critics such as Hugh Kenner in the *Times Literary Supplement* acknowledged the book's achievement while pondering its veracity. Kenner suggested that because much of Ellmann's data was based upon interviews with those who claimed a link to Joyce, it was essentially unreliable, citing in particular Ellmann's use of "Irish Fact, definable as anything you get told in Ireland, where you get told a great deal." Kenner further maintained: "'Definitive' in 1959, was a word that got thrown around rather thoughtlessly by reviewers stunned beneath an avalanche of new information. But there can be no 'definitive' biography. Biography is a narrative form: that means, a mode of fiction. Many narratives can be woven from the same threads. Biography incorporates 'facts', having judged their credibility. Its criteria for judgment include assessment of sources . . .and, pervasively, assessment of one's man." Moreover, Kenner also questioned whether Ellmann's detachment from his subject was sufficient: "Tone is a delicate matter; we don't want a hagiography. We'd like, though, to feel the presence of the mind that made the life worth writing and makes it worth reading." Conversely, Flanagan concluded that it was "because of the unsparing scrupulousness of his own methods," that Ellmann wrote "the kind of book which has become unhappily rare—a work of exacting scholarship which is also a humane and liberating document. Joyce found the proper biographer, and there can be no higher praise." John Stallworthy concurred in the *Times Literary Supplement,* "Speaking with his master's voice, his master's elegance, and his master's wit, Ellmann has produced a biography worth its place on the shelf beside *Dubliners, Ulysses,* and *Finnegans Wake.*"

*James Joyce* marked a turning point for Ellmann, even though he was encouraged by its critical reception, said Serafin: "Shortly after its publication he ruminated about the future of his career: 'There really aren't any other modern writers that measure up to Yeats or Joyce. I can't think of anyone else I'd want to work on the way I've worked on them.'" Vidal suggested that "since Ellmann had already written magisterial works on two of the four [subjects of his essays, *Four Dubliners: Wilde, Yeats, Joyce, and Beckett*], symmetry and sympathy plainly drew him to a third." Ellmann spent the last twenty years of his life working on *Oscar Wilde.* Suffering from Lou Gherig's disease, "during the last weeks of his life, with the help of small machines on which he typed out messages that were then printed on a screen or on paper, he made final revisions on his long-awaited biography," reported Walter Goodman in the *New York Times*.

"While the literary world will continue to mourn his passing, we must all be grateful that he lived long enough to complete his magnificent life of Oscar Wilde . . . ," wrote Robert E. Kuehn in *Tribune Books*. "Like his earlier life of James Joyce, this book is biography on the grand scale: learned, expansive, judicious, magnanimous, and written with care and panache." Ellmann perceived Wilde, said Michael Dirda of the *Washington Post Book World,* "chiefly as a fearless artist and social critic who, like a kamikaze pilot, used himself as the bomb to explode the bourgeois values, pretentions and hypocrisies of late Victorian society." Likening Wilde's fate to that of "a hero of classic tragedy [who] plummeted from the heights of fame to utter ruin," Dirda pointed out that although Wilde has been the subject of several biographies, "they cannot compete with this capacious, deeply sympathetic and vastly entertaining new life of Richard Ellmann."

"There's no question that *Oscar Wilde* is brilliant," declared Walter Kendrick in the *Voice Literary Supplement;* "its posthumous publication splendidly caps Ellmann's career and, like his *James Joyce,* it belongs on the short shelf of biographies correctly labeled definitive." Although praising Ellmann as "a masterful biographer," Eslpeth Cameron continued in the Toronto *Globe and Mail* that "no biography is definitive, and this one is not without its flaws. Ellmann's intellectual grasp of Wilde is firmer than his comprehension of Wilde's emotional life." However, Kuehn found that "when it comes to interpretation, the psychological patterns he traces tend to be all the more persuasive for his refusal to overstate the case." Declaring that "Oscar Wilde is not easily led," Richard Eder acknowledged in the *Los Angeles Times Book Review* that "Ellmann does everything a biographer could do, and some things that few biographers have the courage and talent to do. He refuses to net the butterfly Wilde; he flies with him instead."

Regarding Ellmann as "unusually intelligent, a quality seldom found in academe or, indeed, on Parnassus itself," Vidal felt that Wilde did "not quite suit his schema or his talent." Wilde does not require "explication or interpretation," assessed Vidal. "He needs only to be read, or listened to." Noting that "Wilde provides little occasion for Ellmann's formidable critical apparatus," Vidal added that "where Ellmann showed us new ways of looking at Yeats and, above all, at Joyce, he can do nothing more with Wilde than fit him into a historical context and tell, yet again, the profane story so well known to those who read." Concluding, however, that "nobody could do better than Ellmann," Eder questioned how does one "deliver up a figure who lived and wrote under such polymorphous signs of evasion?"

In Serafin's estimation, Ellmann's *Oscar Wilde* has "rekindled interest in both the subject and the biographer. Virtually assured a permanent position in the history of literary biography, Ellmann has given new and sustained meaning to an ancient art." Serafin also credited Ellmann with "establishing a standard of excellence in the art of contemporary life writing" by fulfilling "'the ideal of sympathetic intuition' in recreating and virtually reliving the lives of his subjects." As Seamus Heaney observed in *Atlantic,* "There is an overall sense of Wilde's being tolerantly supervised by an intelligence at once vigilant and dignified." Remarking that "Joyce as well as his Irish compatriot Oscar Wilde might have agonized less in knowing Ellmann would write the story of his life," Serafin recalled: "It was Wilde who professed every great man has his disciples, and it is usually Judas who writes the biography. Surely no Judas, Ellmann would neither deceive nor deny."

"He loved language as he loved life," said Serafin, "and never failed in his work, as Anthony Burgess would astutely observe, 'to stimulate, instruct, amuse, and, for this writer, reawaken a sleeping belief in the glory of making literature.'" Critics and colleagues alike unanimously admired Ellmann's intelligence as well as his humility. "He carries much learning with lightness and illumination," wrote Stephen Spender in a *New York Review of Books* piece on Ellmann's book of essays, *Golden Codgers: Biographical Speculations.* And in the *Chicago Sun Times,* Bob Hergath observed: "The nice thing about Ellmann, for all his scholarship and erudition, he was a regular guy. He had a terrific sense of humor." Referring to Ellmann's "notable sense of humor and a donnishly droll way with a punchline," Goodman remarked that "his wit remained intact throughout his illness; with speech difficult, he typed out jokes and repartee with visitors." As his brother, William Ellmann, is quoted in the *Detroit Free Press,* "Dick Ellmann was a literary giant whose first question might be, 'How are the Tigers doing?'"

At the time of his death, Ellmann was planning to collect many of his own essays for publication. While he was unable to complete this task, his family gathered a number of Ellmann's essays and published them as *a long the riverrun: Selected Essays* in 1989. The title phrase refers to the words that link the beginning and ending sections of Joyce's *Finnegans Wake*. Consisting of twenty essays, all but one of which were previously published, the volume finds Ellmann ruminating on a wide range of literary subjects, from the authors—Joyce, Wilde, Yeats—whose lives he chronicled to the discipline of literary biography. "These twenty essays testify to Ellmann's versatility and interests," commented Kark Beckson in the *Times Literary Supplement,* adding that the work inspires many re-readings: "when one turns the last page of this volume, one is impelled to begin again." According to *World Literature Today* reviewer John L. Brown, despite the numerous writers that Ellmann discusses in the collection, "the leading man in the cast . . . remains Yeats." *New York Times Book Review* contributor Angeline Goreau termed the volume "witty, ironic, [and] unfailingly astute" and remarked that it "offers one final glimpse of a matchless literary mind at work, unearthing the 'mysterious armature' (as Mallarme called it) that binds the life of writing to its creation, fiction."

*BIOGRAPHICAL/CRITICAL SOURCES:*

*BOOKS*

*Contemporary Literary Criticism,* Volume 50, Gale, 1988.

*Dictionary of Literary Biography,* Volume 103: *American Literary Biographers, First Series,* Gale, 1991.

*Dictionary of Literary Biography Yearbook: 1987,* Gale, 1988.

Heaney, Seamus, *The Place of Writing,* Scholars Press (Atlanta), 1989.

Schroeder, Horst, *Additions and Corrections to Richard Ellmann's Oscar Wilde,* H. Schroeder (Braunschweig), 1989.

*PERIODICALS*

*Antioch Review,* spring, 1972; winter, 1978.

*Chicago Sun Times,* May 15, 1987.

*Contemporary Literature,* winter, 1969.

*Detroit Free Press,* May 14, 1987.

*English Journal,* January, 1995, p. 116.

*Globe and Mail* (Toronto), December 26, 1987.

*Guardian,* October 30, 1959.

*Hudson Review,* spring, 1968.

*Los Angeles Times,* May 16, 1987.

*Los Angeles Times Book Review,* November 14, 1982; February 14, 1988.

*Maclean's,* December 21, 1987.

*Nation,* October 17, 1959; November 13, 1967; June 23, 1969; June 19, 1972; November 20, 1982; February 13, 1988.

*New Republic,* June 3, 1972; February 15, 1988.

*Newsweek,* September 27, 1982.

*New Yorker,* December 12, 1959; March 21, 1988.

*New York Review of Books,* August 26, 1965; October 18, 1973; September 19, 1974; October 13, 1977; February 18, 1988.

*New York Times,* October 25, 1959; January 1, 1968; October 25, 1969; November 25, 1969; May 17, 1972; December 15, 1975; June 1, 1977; September 21, 1982; May 14, 1987.

*New York Times Book Review,* December 10, 1967; January 21, 1968; May 14, 1972; June 19, 1977; April 19, 1981; February 21, 1988; March 19, 1989, p. 21.

*Publishers Weekly,* January 27, 1989, p. 461.

*San Francisco Chronicle,* November 1, 1959.

*Saturday Review,* October 24, 1959; May 24, 1969; March 28, 1970; May 13, 1972.

*Sewanee Review,* winter, 1969.

*South Atlantic Quarterly,* winter, 1968; winter, 1973, summer, 1978.

*Spectator,* November 13, 1959; February 12, 1977; October 23, 1982.

*Time,* January 4, 1988.

*Times* (London), November 20, 1959; January 5, 1967; July 25, 1968; March 17, 1972; February 18, 1977; October 8, 1987.

*Times Literary Supplement,* December 30, 1965; July 25, 1968; April 2, 1970; March 17, 1972; October 26, 1973; January 24, 1975; December 17, 1982; March 23, 1984; November 14, 1986; October 2-8, 1987; November 4, 1988, p. 1234.

*Tribune Books* (Chicago), February 7, 1988.

*Virginia Quarterly Review,* spring, 1968.

*Washington Post Book World,* May 21, 1972; March 29, 1981; October 31, 1982; October 30, 1983; January 24, 1988.

*World Literature Today,* winter, 1979; summer, 1983; winter, 1990, p. 114.

*OBITUARIES:*

*PERIODICALS*

*Cincinnati Post,* May 14, 1987.

*Detroit Free Press,* May 14, 1987.

*International Herald Tribune,* May 16-17, 1987.

*Los Angeles Times,* May 16, 1987.

*Newsday,* May 15, 1987.
*Newsweek,* May 25, 1987.
*New York Times,* May 14, 1987.
*Sun-Times* (Chicago), May 15, 1987.
*Time,* May 25, 1987.
*Times* (London), May 15, 1987.*

* * *

**EMPSON, William 1906-1984**

*PERSONAL:* Born September 27, 1906, in Yokefleet, Howden, East Yorkshire, England; died April 15, 1984, in London, England; son of A. R. and Laura (Micklethwait) Empson; married Hester Henrietta Crouse, 1941; children: William Hendrick Mogador, Jacobus Arthur Calais. *Education:* Winchester College, 1920-25; Magdalen College, Cambridge, B.A., 1929, M.A., 1935.

*CAREER:* Bunrika Daigaku, Tokyo, Japan, chair of English literature, 1931-34; Peking National University (then part of South-Western Combined Universities), Peking, China, professor of English literature, 1937-39; British Broadcasting Co. (BBC), London, England, editor in monitoring department, 1940-41, Chinese editor, 1941-46; Peking National University, Peking, China, professor of English, 1947-52; Sheffield University, Sheffield, England, professor of English literature, 1953-1971, became professor emeritus. Visiting fellow, Kenyon College, Gambier, Ohio, summers, 1948, 1950, and 1954; visiting professor, University of Toronto, 1973-74, and Pennsylvania State University, University Park, 1974-75.

*AWARDS, HONORS:* Ingram Merrill Foundation Award for Literature, 1968; D.Litt., from University of East Anglia, Norwich, 1968, University of Bristol, 1971, and University of Sheffield, 1974; knighted, 1979.

*WRITINGS:*

*Letter IV* (poems), privately printed, 1929.
*Seven Types of Ambiguity: A Study of its Effects on English Verse* (criticism), Chatto & Windus, 1930, revised edition, 1947, Meridan, 1957.
*Poems,* privately printed, 1934, Chatto & Windus, 1935.
*Some Versions of Pastoral,* Chatto & Windus, 1935, New Directions, 1950, published as *English Pastoral Poetry,* Norton, 1938, reprinted, Books for Libraries, 1972.
(Editor and translator from technical into basic English) John Haldane, *Outlook of Science,* Routledge & Kegan Paul, 1935.
(Editor and translator from technical into basic English) Haldane, *Science and Well-Being,* Routledge & Kegan Paul, 1935.
(With George Garrett) *Shakespeare Survey,* Brendin Publishing Co., 1937.
*The Gathering Storm* (poems), Faber, 1940.
*Collected Poems of William Empson,* Harcourt, 1949, enlarged edition, 1961.
*The Structure of Complex Words,* New Directions, 1951, 3rd edition, Rowman, 1979.
(Contributor) Derek Hudson, *English Critical Essays: Twentieth Century, Second Series,* Oxford University Press, 1958.
*Milton's God,* Chatto & Windus, 1961, New Directions, 1962, enlarged edition, Cambridge University Press, 1981.
(Author of introduction) John R. Harrison, *The Reactionaries: Yeats, Lewis, Pound, Eliot, Lawrence,* Schocken, 1967.
(Editor) *Shakespeare's Poems,* New American Library, 1969.
(Editor with David Pirie) *Coleridge's Verse: A Selection,* Faber, 1972, Schocken, 1973.
*Using Biography* (criticism), Harvard University Press, 1984.
*Essays on William Shakespeare,* edited by Pirie, Cambridge University Press, 1986.
*The Royal Beasts and Other Works,* edited by John Haffenden, Chatto & Windus, 1986.
*Faustus and the Censor: The English Faust-Book and Marlowe's Dr. Faustus,* edited by John Henry Jones, Basil Blackwell, 1987.
*Argufying: Essays on Literature and Culture,* edited by Haffenden, Chatto & Windus, 1988.
*Essays on Renaissance Literature,* Cambridge University Press, Volume 1: *Donne and the New Philosophy,* 1993, Volume 2: *The Drama,* 1994.

*SIDELIGHTS:* Sir William Empson, professor of English literature at Sheffield University for nearly twenty years, "revolutionized our ways of reading a poem," notes a London *Times* writer. The school of literary criticism known as New Criticism gained important support from Empson's *Seven Types of Ambiguity: A Study of Its Effects on English Verse.* This work, together with his other published essays, has become "part of the furniture of any good English or American critic's mind," G. S. Fraser remarks in *Great Writers of the English Language: Poets.*

Empson will also be remembered for "the peculiar, utterly original and startling tenor of his works," says the *Times* writer. Radically different from the romantic poetry produced by Dylan Thomas and Empson's other peers, Empson's poetry employed a more objective, nonsentimental language that reflected his competence as a mathematician and his reverence for science. The *Times* article relates that his first collection, *Poems,* "made an immediate deserved and explosive impact such as the literary scene in Britain knows only two or three times in a century."

John Gross of the *New York Times Book Review* relates, "An essentially positive critic, [Empson] had the gift of being able to show you qualities in a work you would never have seen without him, and the even more important gift of enlarging your imagination, encouraging you to go on looking for yourself." This new approach to poetry appreciation centered on the reader's close attention to the properties of poetic language opened up a new field of literary criticism—a remarkable accomplishment, considering that Empson did so without proposing to alter previous methods of criticism; neither did he revise the standards by which literature is traditionally judged, nor did he invent new ways to reclassify well-known works of literature, Hugh Kenner points out in *Gnomon: Essays on Contemporary Literature.* Empson's explanations of how meaning is carried in poetic language have made poetry accessible to hundreds of readers, Kenner observes.

Perhaps most helpful to erstwhile readers of poetry is Empson's first book-length work of criticism, *Seven Types of Ambiguity.* In general usage, a word or reference is deemed ambiguous if it has more than one possible meaning. In *Seven Types,* Empson wrote, "I propose to use the word in an extended sense, and shall think relevant to my subject any verbal nuance, however slight, which gives room for alternative reactions to the same piece of language." Empson's seven types are briefly defined in the table of contents: "First-type ambiguities arise when a detail is effective in several ways at once. . . . In second-type ambiguities two or more alternative meanings are fully resolved into one. . . . The condition for the third type ambiguity is that two apparently unconnected meanings are given simultaneously. . . . In the fourth type the alternative meanings combine to make clear a complicated state of mind in the author. . . . The fifth type is a fortunate confusion, as when the author is discovering his idea in the act of writing . . . or not holding it in mind all at once. . . . In the sixth type what is said is contradictory or irrelevant and the reader is forced to invent interpretations. . . . The seventh type is that of full contradiction, marking a division in the author's mind."

Ambiguity impedes communication when it results from the writer's indecision, Empson wrote in *Seven Types:* "It is not to be respected in so far as it is due to weakness or thinness of thought, obscures the matter at hand unnecessarily . . . or when the interest of the passage is not focussed upon it, so that it is merely an opportunism in the handling of the material, if the reader will not understand the ideas which are being shuffled, and will be given a general impression of incoherence." However, the protean properties of words—their ability to carry multiple meanings in a variety of ways—are a major component of poetic language, and being aware of how this facet of language operates is one of the pleasures of poetry, said Empson. "*Seven Types* is primarily an exercise intended to help the reader who has already felt the pleasure understand the nature of his response," a *Contemporary Literary Critics* contributor suggests.

"Some of Empson's early critics felt that he had simply written himself a license to search for multiple meanings with no awareness of the controlling context in which the local ambiguity appears," reports the same contributor. On the contrary, Empson guides critics to consider "purpose, context and person" in addition to "the critical principles of the author and of the public he is writing for" when explicating meaning. *Hudson Review* contributor Roger Sale believes that the book has been too harshly judged in many reviews. He writes, "Most discussions have picked on its least interesting aspects, its use of the word 'ambiguity' and its ranging of the 'types' along a scale of 'advancing logical disorder.' But these matters are really minor. . . . The book, [Empson] says, is not philosophical but literary, and its aim is to examine lines Empson finds beautiful and haunting. . . . But in at least fifteen places Empson shows that the aim of analysis is not so much understanding lines as uncovering whole tracts of the mind, and the book is studded with the right things said about a poet or an historical period." In fact, concludes Robert M. Adams in the *New York Review of Books,* "Already certain passages of Empsonian exegesis . . . have attained classic status, so that the text can't be intelligently considered without them. . . . I think he had, though in lesser measure, Dr. Johnson's extraordinary gift for laying his finger on crucial literary moments; and that alone is likely to ensure him a measure of permanence."

*Some Versions of Pastoral* addresses the modern propensity to express nostalgia for idyllic world views that belong to the past. According to Empson, pastoral literature implied "a beautiful relation between rich and poor [ and made] . . . simple people express strong feelings. . . in learned and fashionable language (so that you wrote about the best subject in the best way)." Empson maintains that contemporary expressions of the pastoral are for the most part pretenses: "in pastoral you take a limited life and pretend it is the full and normal one." Writing in *Modern Heroism: Essays on D. H. Lawrence, William Empson, and J. R. R. Tolkien,* Sale contends that by examining a series of leader/heroes from the sixteenth century forward, Empson means to say that the moieties that used to bind leaders to their people no longer exist—in Sales's words, "the people have become a mob and the hero painfully alienated"—and that, therefore, the role of hero or Christ-figure is not attainable.

Sale believes that *Some Versions of Pastoral* is Empson's best book, although it too has been misjudged as a literary work and misused as a critical tool. Sale notes that "in [this book] he can move from the work at hand to his vision with almost no shoving of the evidence, so even though his prose and organization may seem difficult on first reading, he turns with almost indescribable grace from the smallest particular to the largest generalization and then back to various middle grounds. When one becomes used to the book and begins to hear the massive chords of its orchestrations supporting even the most irrelevant aside, the effect is one only the greatest books can produce—it envelopes and controls such large areas of the imagination that for a while one is willing to admit it is the only book ever written. As a modern work of persuasion it is unrivaled."

*Milton's God* is "a diatribe against Christianity which Empson feels has had a monopoly on torture-worship, sexual repression and hypocrisy," the *Contemporary Literary Critics* essayist relates. Milton's God, Empson maintains, seems to want to set aside the cruelty of his absolute rule, and "has cut out of Christianity both the torture-horror and the sex-horror, and after that the monster seems almost decent." Questioning Milton's orthodoxy on these grounds, Empson presents Milton as a humanist—a view that raised a "furor" among the "entrenched Miltonic establishment," says Adams. It was, he says, the eccentric professor's "last raid on the academic chicken coop" before his retirement from the University of Sheffield in 1971.

Empson's own humanism accounts in part for his open-minded approach to the topic of meaning in literature. Kenner notes: "'The object of life, after all,' [Empson] tells us late in *Ambiguity,* 'is not to understand things, but to maintain one's defenses and equilibrium and live as well as one can; it is not only maiden aunts who are placed like this.'" In *Milton's God,* he declared his agreement with philosopher Jeremy Bentham "that the satisfaction of any impulse is in itself an elementary good, and that the practical ethical question is how to satisfy the greatest number." Empson's poetry and criticism are the natural extensions of his views. Empson offers "not a theory of literature or a single method of analysis but a model of how to read with pleasure and knowledge," notes *New Statesman* reviewer Jon Cook. In *Using Biography,* for example, he demonstrates how familiarity with an author's life helps the critic to empathize with the author, allowing the critic to apply corresponding personal experiences to see into an author's intentions. The resulting insights on Andrew Marvell and W. B. Yeats, says James Fenton in the London *Times,* owe more to Empson's speculations and free associations than to systematic analysis of biographical detail. According to Cook, Empson makes it clear that it is far worse to succumb to "the critical habit of pressing literary works into the service of authoritarian and repressive ideologies, all this, of course, under the comforting guise that to receive authority in this way does us good."

Some reviewers aver that Empson, after *Milton's God,* "decline[d] into isolated crankiness during the two decades prior to his death," writes Tyrus Miller in *Modern Language Notes.* Nevertheless, even after his death in 1984 Empson's ideas continued to impact the field of literary criticism, as several of his unfinished, uncollected, or unpublished writings were posthumously published. These include *Argufying: Essays on Literature and Culture, Faustus and the Censor,* and the two-volume *Essays on Renaissance Literature.* A collection of previously published reviews and essays, *Argufying* is divided into five sections, covering such topics as poetry, fiction, and Western vs. Far Eastern cultural perspectives. Much of the collection is taken up with Empson's verbal sparring with fellow critics, prompting Miller to comment on "the imminently polemical tone with which Empson pursues even the friendliest review or comment." *Faustus and the Censor* is a critical study of Christopher Marlowe's *Dr. Faustus.*

Empson's two-volume *Essays on Renaissance Literature,* like *Argufying,* was edited by Empson's authorized biographer, John Haffenden. Volume 1, *Donne and the New Philosophy,* is a collection of essays about the man whose poetry greatly influenced Empson. Volume 2 includes miscellaneous essays focusing on Shakespeare's *A Midsummer Night's Dream* as well as a host of other Renaissance writers including Christopher Marlowe and Ben Jonson. "Empson was a true miracle-worker in his criticism; he made the dead live again and gave the silenced speech. Fielding comes alive when Empson writes about him, as Donne's poems do under the critic's deftly charitable hands," notes Eric Griffiths in a *Times Literary Supplement* review of Volume 1. Stephen Greenblatt, however, reviewing Volume 2 in the *London Review of Books,* states that "None of this is close to the level of Empson's major work." While Charles Rosen, writing in the *New York Review of Books,* admits that Empson was "wrong . . . often enough" as a critic, he contends that "Empson's achievement here as elsewhere comes from the generosity of spirit which made him consistently a great critic."

Although Empson is best known for his criticism, *Preliminary Essays* author John Wain writes: "It may well be that criticism will be read and remembered while poetry is forgotten, for criticism breeds fresh criticism more easily than poetry breeds fresh poetry; but in Empson's case it would be a pity if he were known simply as the 'ambiguity' man, and not as a poet." A. Alvarez writes in *Stewards of Excellence,* "The poetry of William Empson has been more used [as a model] than that of any other English poet of our time." As the upheavals of World War II threatened to render romanticism and pastoralism obsolete, poets were challenged to find language and forms equal to the age. "Empson's verse was read with an overwhelming sense of relief after the brash and embarrassed incoherence of wartime and post-war poetry," notes Alvarez, who elaborates, "there is something in his work which encourages other writers to use it for their own ends. It has, I think, an *essential* objectivity. . . . In the later poems what goes in as strong personal feeling comes out as something more general; whilst in the earlier work all the personal energy goes into a particularly impersonal business."

In addition, Empson's best verses "have a quality of mystery and incantation which runs quite counter to his professed rationalism," notes Robert Nye in the London *Times.* The poems, says a writer for the London *Times,* were perceived by some critics to be like "exercises: ingenious, resembling staggeringly clever crossword puzzles, abstruse, riddling—in a word, over-intellectual. But as Edwin Muir and other shrewder readers noted, their real keynote was passion. They represent, as Empson put it in one of the most famous of them, a style learned from a despair. The subject matter of the great ones . . . is the nature of sexual passion and the nature of political passion." Writers found in Empson's verse the balance between intense emotion and detachment that seemed appropriate to describe life in the contemporary world.

Alvarez believes that Empson's poetry depends on his control over a large range of ideas: "[Empson] is less interested in saying his own say than in the agility and skill and variety with which he juggles his ideas. So it is a personal poem only at a remove: the subject is impersonal; the involvement is all his effort to make as much as he can out of the subject, and in the accomplishment with which he relates his manifold themes so elegantly together. Empson's, in short, is a poetry of wit in the most traditional sense. . . . And, like most wit, the pleasure it gives is largely in the immaculate performance, which is a rare pleasure but a limited one."

In tracing the development of Empson's poetry, Alvarez says of the early poems: "In his sardonic way, Empson made his polish and inventiveness seem like a personal claim for sanity, as though he saw everything in a fourth and horrifying dimension but was too well-mannered to say so. Hence the wry despair and vigorous stylishness seemed not at all contradictory." He notes that "It is as a stylist of poetry and ideas that, I think, Empson is most important. He took over all [T. S.] Eliot's hints about what was most significant in the English tradition, and he put them into practice without any of the techniques Eliot had derived from the French and Italians. And so his poetry shows powerfully and with great purity the perennial vitality of the English tradition; and in showing this it also expresses the vitality and excitement of the extraordinarily creative moment when Empson began writing."

While Empson focused on poetry when he was not writing criticism, he did attempt several fictional works during his lifetime. *The Royal Beasts and Other Works,* edited by Haffenden, collects several of Empson's unpublished fictional works, including poems, a satirical fable, and the outline for a ballet. The title of the collection comes from Empson's fable, *The Royal Beasts,* written while Empson was teaching in China in 1937. This work "explores the possibility of a race of apelike creatures, the Wurroos, who by a quirk of evolution evolved rational capacities of thought," notes Tyrus Miller in *Modern Language*

*Notes*. The ballet sketch, also inspired by Empson's stint in the Far East, examines both Eastern and Western religious myths.

Before his death, Empson was knighted by Queen Elizabeth. His most-lasting legacy will likely be as a critic. "Empson's critical achievement has nothing to do with paralysing theories," notes Jim McCue in *Agenda*. "It is an empirical investigation of how to read, think and perhaps live better."

*BIOGRAPHICAL/CRITICAL SOURCES:*

*BOOKS*

Alvarez, A., *Stewards of Excellence,* Scribner, 1958.
Constable, John, *Critical Essays on William Empson,* Ashgate (Brookfield, VT), 1993.
*Contemporary Literary Criticism,* Gale, Volume 3, 1975, Volume 8, 1981, Volume 19, 1981, Volume 33, 1985, Volume 34, 1985.
*Contemporary Literary Critics,* St. James, 1977.
Crane, R. S., *Critics and Critics: Ancient and Modern,* University of Chicago Press, 1952.
*Dictionary of Literary Biography,* Volume 20: *British Poets, 1914-1945,* Gale, 1983.
Fry, Paul H., *William Empson: Prophet Against Sacrifice,* Routledge (New York), 1991.
Gill, Roma, editor, *William Empson: The Man and His Work,* Routledge & Kegan Paul, 1974.
Hamilton, Ian, editor, *The Modern Poet: Essays from "The Review,"* MacDonald, 1968.
Hyman, Stanley Edgar, *The Armed Vision: A Study in the Methods of Modern Literary Criticism,* Knopf, 1948, revised edition, 1955.
Kenner, Hugh, *Gnomon: Essays in Contemporary Literature,* McDowell, 1958.
*Makers of Modern Culture,* Facts on File, 1981.
Norris, Christopher, *William Empson and the Philosophy of Literary Criticism,* Athlone Press, 1978.
Norris, Christopher and Nigel Mapp, *William Empson: The Critical Achievement,* Cambridge University Press (New York City), 1993.
Sale, Roger, *Modern Heroism: Essays on D. H. Lawrence, William Empson, and J. R. R. Tolkien,* University of California Press, 1973.
Untermeyer, Louis, *Lives of the Poets,* Simon & Schuster, 1959.
Vinson, James, editor, *Great Writers of the English Language: Poets,* St. Martins, 1979.
Wain, John, *Preliminary Essays,* Macmillan (London), 1957.
*William Empson: The Man and His Work,* Routledge & Kegan Paul, 1974.
Wills, J. H., *William Empson,* Columbia University Press, 1969.

*PERIODICALS*

*Agenda,* winter, 1994, p. 309.
*Criticism,* fall, 1966.
*Hudson Review,* spring, 1952; autumn, 1966.
*London Review of Books,* July 22, 1993, p. 15; October 20, 1994, p. 31.
*Modern Language Notes,* December, 1988, p. 1155.
*Nation,* June 16, 1962.
*New Statesman,* October 12, 1984; April 19, 1996, p. 39.
*New York Review of Books,* April 11, 1985; October 21, 1993, p. 72.
*New York Times Book Review,* May 20, 1984.
*Observer,* September 30, 1984.
*Review of English Studies,* November, 1989, p. 551.
*Scrutiny,* Volume 2, number 3, December, 1933.
*Southern Review,* autumn, 1938.
*Time,* April 18, 1949; August 10, 1962.
*Times* (London), October 25, 1984; February 8, 1985; November 13, 1986.
*Times Literary Supplement,* November 14, 1986; January 1, 1988; February 26, 1988; July 30, 1993, p. 6.
*Washington Post Book World,* May 19, 1985.
*Yale Review,* June, 1962.

*OBITUARIES:*

*PERIODICALS*

*Chicago Tribune,* April 18, 1984.
*Times* (London), April 16, 1984.
*Washington Post,* April 17, 1984.*

# F

**FARRELL, James T(homas) 1904-1979**
**(Jonathan Titulescu Fogarty, Esq.)**

*PERSONAL:* Born February 27, 1904, in Chicago, IL; died of a heart attack, August 22, 1979, in New York, NY; son of James Francis and Mary (Daly) Farrell; married Dorothy Patricia Butler, 1931 (divorced); married Hortense Alden (divorced September, 1955); remarried Dorothy Butler Farrell, September, 1955 (separated, 1958); children: (with second wife) Kevin. *Education:* Attended night classes at De Paul University, one semester, 1924-25; attended University of Chicago, eight quarters, until 1929; attended New York University, one semester. *Avocational interests:* Baseball.

*CAREER:* Writer. Worked wrapping shoes in a chain store in Chicago, IL; as a clerk for the American Railway Express Co. in Chicago; a filling-station attendant; a cigar store clerk in New York City; an advertising salesman for Donnelly's *Red Book* in Queens, NY; in an undertaking parlor in Chicago; as a campus reporter for the *Chicago Herald Examiner;* and, for two weeks, as a scenario writer in Hollywood, CA. Served as chair of the national board, Workers Defense League, New York City, and as a member of the Spanish Refugee Aid Committee.

*MEMBER:* National Institute of Arts and Letters, Authors League of America, American Civil Liberties Union, Overseas Press Club.

*AWARDS, HONORS:* Guggenheim fellowship for creative writing, 1936; Book-of-the-Month Club prize, 1937, for *Studs Lonigan: A Trilogy;* Messing Award, St. Louis University Library Association; honorary degrees from Miami University, Oxford University, Ohio State University, Columbia University, University of Chicago, and Glassboro State College.

*WRITINGS:*

*Young Lonigan: A Boyhood in Chicago Streets* (also see below), Vanguard, 1932, reprinted with new introduction, World Publishing, 1943, published as *Young Lonigan: The Studs Lonigan Story,* Avon, 1972.

*Gas-House McGinty,* Vanguard, 1933.

*Calico Shoes, and Other Stories* (also see below), Vanguard, 1934 (published in England as *Seventeen, and Other Stories,* Panther, 1959).

*The Young Manhood of Studs Lonigan* (also see below), Vanguard, 1934, reprinted with new introduction, World Publishing, 1944, reprinted, Avon, 1973.

*Judgment Day,* Vanguard, 1935, reprinted with new introduction, World Publishing, 1945, reprinted, Avon, 1973.

*Studs Lonigan: A Trilogy* (contains *Young Lonigan, The Young Manhood of Studs Lonigan,* and *Judgment Day*), Vanguard, 1935, reprinted with new introduction, Modern Library, 1938, published with an introduction and a new epilogue by the author, Vanguard, 1978.

*Guillotine Party, and Other Stories* (also see below), Vanguard, 1935.

*A World I Never Made,* Vanguard, 1936, reprinted with new introduction, World Publishing, 1947.

*A Note on Literary Criticism,* Vanguard, 1937, Columbia University Press (New York City), 1992.

*Fellow Countrymen: Collected Stories,* Vanguard, 1937.

*Can All This Grandeur Perish?, and Other Stories* (also see below), Vanguard, 1937.

*The Short Stories of James T. Farrell* (contains *Calico Shoes, and Other Stories, Guillotine Party, and Other Stories,* and *Can All This Grandeur Perish?, and Other Stories*), Vanguard, 1937.

*No Star Is Lost,* Vanguard, 1938, reprinted with new introduction, World Publishing, 1947, reprinted, Popular Library, 1961.

*Father and Son,* Vanguard, 1940, reprinted with new introduction, World Publishing, 1947 (published in England as *Father and His Son,* Routledge & Kegan Paul, 1943).

*Ellen Rogers,* Vanguard, 1941.

*Short Stories,* Blue Ribbon Books, 1941.

*$1000 a Week, and Other Stories* (also see below), Vanguard, 1942.

*My Days of Anger,* Vanguard, 1943, reprinted with new introduction, World Publishing, 1947.

*Fifteen Selected Stories,* Avon, 1943.

*To Whom It May Concern, and Other Stories,* Vanguard, 1944 (also see below), published as *More Stories,* Sun Dial Press, 1946.

*Twelve Great Stories,* Avon, 1945.

*The League of Frightened Philistines, and Other Papers,* Vanguard, 1945.

*When Boyhood Dreams Come True,* Vanguard, 1946, published as *Further Short Stories,* Sun Dial Press, 1948.

*More Fellow Countrymen,* Routledge & Kegan Paul, 1946.

*Bernard Clare,* Vanguard, 1946, published as *Bernard Carr,* New American Library, 1952.

*The Fate of Writing in America,* New Directions, 1946.

*The Life Adventurous, and Other Stories* (also see below), Vanguard, 1947.

*Literature and Morality,* Vanguard, 1947.

*A Hell of a Good Time, and Other Stories,* Avon, 1947.

*Yesterday's Love, and Eleven Other Stories,* Avon, 1948.

*The Road Between,* Vanguard, 1949.

*A Misunderstanding,* House of Books, 1949.

*An American Dream Girl, and Other Stories,* Vanguard, 1950.

(Under pseudonym Jonathan Titulescu Fogarty, Esq.) *The Name Is Fogarty: Private Papers on Public Matters,* Vanguard, 1950.

*This Man and This Woman,* Vanguard, 1951.

(Contributor of "The Frontier and James Whitcomb Riley") *Poet of the People,* Indiana University Press, 1951.

*Yet Other Waters,* Vanguard, 1952.

*The Face of Time,* Vanguard, 1953.

*Reflections at Fifty, and Other Essays,* Vanguard, 1954.

*French Girls Are Vicious, and Other Stories,* Vanguard, 1955.

(Author of introduction) Theodore Dreiser, *Best Short Stories,* World Publishing, 1956.

*An Omnibus of Short Stories* (contains *$1000 a Week, and Other Stories, To Whom It May Concern, and Other Stories,* and *The Life Adventurous, and Other Stories*), Vanguard, 1956.

*My Baseball Diary,* A. S. Bames, 1957.

*A Dangerous Woman, and Other Stories,* Vanguard, 1957.

*Saturday Night, and Other Stories,* Hamish Hamilton, 1958.

*It Has Come to Pass,* T. Herzl Press, 1958.

(Editor) H. L. Mencken, *Prejudices,* Vintage, 1958.

*The Girl at the Sphinx* (collection of short stories previously published by Vanguard), Hamish Hamilton, 1959.

(With others) *Dialogue on John Dewey,* edited by Corliss Lamont and Mary Redmer, Horizon, 1959.

*Boarding House Blues,* Paperback Library, 1961.

*Side Street, and Other Stories,* Paperback Library, 1961.

*Sound of a City* (short stories), Paperback Library, 1962.

*The Silence of History* (first of a projected 29-volume series), Doubleday, 1963.

*Selected Essays,* edited by Luna Wolf, McGraw, 1964.

*What Time Collects,* Doubleday, 1964.

*The Collected Poems of James T. Farrell,* Fleet, 1965.

*Lonely for the Future,* Doubleday, 1966.

*When Time Was Born* (prose poem), The Smith, 1966.

*The Letters to Theodore Dreiser,* The Smith, 1966.

*New Year's Eve, 1929,* The Smith, 1967.

*A Brand New Life* (novel), Doubleday, 1968.

*Childhood Is Not Forever,* Doubleday, 1969.

*Judith* (also see below), Duane Schneider Press, 1969.

*Invisible Swords,* Doubleday, 1971.

(Contributor) Ray Boxer and Harry Smith, editors, *The Smith-Fourteen,* The Smith, 1972.

*Judith, and Other Stories,* Doubleday, 1973.

*The Dunne Family,* Doubleday, 1976.

*Literary Essays, 1954-1974,* edited by Jack Alan Robbins, Kennikat Press, 1976.

*Olive and Maryanne,* Stonehill Publishing, 1977.

*The Death of Nora Ryan,* Doubleday, 1978.

*Eight Short Stories and Sketches,* Arts End, 1981.

*On Irish Themes,* University of Pennsylvania Press (Philadelphia), 1982.

*Sam Holman: A Novel,* Prometheus Books (Buffalo), 1983.

*Hearing Out James T. Farrell: Selected Lectures,* edited by Donald Phelps, The Smith (New York City), 1985.

(With Alain Dugrand) *Trotsky in Mexico,* Carcanet (Manchester), 1992.

Also author of *Tommy Gallagher's Crusade,* 1939, and editor of *A Dreiser Reader,* 1962. Contributor to magazines and to the Asian press.

*ADAPTATIONS: Studs Lonigan* was filmed by United Artists in 1960.

*SIDELIGHTS:* In 1941, Joseph Warren Beach described James T. Farrell's writing as "perhaps the plainest, soberest, most straightforward of any living novelist," thus citing the basis of both the criticism and praise of Farrell's work. Farrell is most often recognized as a naturalistic writer, a school to which he adhered even during the 1930s when symbolism was increasingly popular. In *Reflections at Fifty,* Farrell wrote: "I have been called a naturalist and I have never denied it. However, my own conception of naturalism is not that which is usually attributed to me. By naturalism I mean that whatever happens in this world must ultimately be explainable in terms of events in this world, in terms of natural origins rather than of extranatural or supernatural origins." In *The Modern Novel in Britain and the United States,* Walter Allen wrote: "James T. Farrell, for all his indebtedness to Joyce, began as a naturalist and has remained one, unrepentant and defiant. He is the true heir of Dreiser. If he lacks Dreiser's tragic sense, he has an icily relentless passion that transforms his best work into a formidable indictment of society."

In *American Fiction, 1920-1940,* Beach wrote: "Farrell's type of naturalism is not a kind to appeal to the common run of readers. It has little to offer those who go to fiction for light entertainment, the glamour of the stage, or the gratification of their bent for wishful thinking. There is no reason why the squeamish or tender-minded should put themselves through the ordeal of trying to like his work. But there will always be a sufficient number of those whom life and thought have ripened and disciplined, who have a taste for truth, however unvarnished, provided it be honestly viewed, deeply pondered, and imaginatively rendered. For many such it may well turn out that James T. Farrell is the most significant of American novelists writing in 1940."

Farrell's ambition and direction as a writer, as well as his thematic material, sprang directly from his own youth in Chicago's South Side. Blanche Housman Gelfant noted in *The American City Novel* that, although the South Side was a slum, without variety, beauty, or surprise, "it provided Farrell with the substance of his art and his purpose as a city novelist. . . . Few city writers are as much the insider as he; and of the writers who have the same kind of inmost knowledge of manners, none has exploited his material to such powerful effect." Beach added: "His literary performance is determined by his pity and loathing for all that was mean, ugly, and spiritually poverty stricken in the mores and culture to which he was born. All his work is a representation, patient, sober, feeling, tireless, pitiless, of a way of living and a state of mind which he abhors, and from which he has taken flight as one flees from the City of Destruction."

Beach contended that "the main theme of all this writing is a state of mind widely diffused in the world [Farrell] knows best—a social state of mind highly unfavorable to the production of full and happy lives, to beauty of thought and sentiment or any of those spiritual values that characterize human civilization at its best." The state of mind is the product of the environment; the environment, in turn, is "defined in its effect upon the inner man," wrote Gelfant. The development of the individual is thus shown as a cumulative process of assimilating these environmental influences. Gelfant noted that Farrell once said: "The conditions of American life create alienated and truncated personalities" because the individual is forced to rely on himself in the face of chaos and "his inner experience becomes one of loneliness, alienation, and unfulfillment." It was Farrell's purpose, according to Gelfant, to utilize the novel to "establish communication between people who in real life had become lost in their private inner worlds and were no longer able to reach out towards each other." And although "the emotional drive behind Farrell's art was anger," he proceeded by objectively considering those problems which are characteristically rooted in emotional involvement. His method was to develop a cinematic sequence of self-contained episodes (each "significant as a revelation of individual character, as well as of a total way of life," noted Gelfant) that would best portray the lack of orientation and the fragmented nature of life in the South Side.

Beach said of the novels: "These are linguistic documents, as they are social documents, of high seriousness and value, but not slavishly photographic. Farrell is obviously more concerned with the spirit than the letter of truth. The documentation is really prodigious, but it did not require the author's going beyond the limits of experience and memory. [Scenes] spring like geysers from the seething burdened depths of the author's being. The appeal is first to the imagination, and only in retrospect to the mind and conscience. In so far as anything is lacking it is some principle of relief." Gelfant stated: "And in the vision of life projected in Farrell's novels this lack of relief is an essential and fundamental quality." Without this relief the world created by Farrell becomes a dynamic oppressive force with which the individual must unsuccessfully contend. Gelfant summarized: "Although Farrell's style has been severely criticized, it is an effective medium through which milieu and character come to life. As a city novelist, Farrell was keenly aware of the inappropriateness of a lyrical manner to the materials of everyday urban life. He adopted the language of his characters as his aesthetic medium, and his versatility as a stylist is revealed in the variety of distinctive speech patterns he recreated."

During the 1930s, Farrell decided that certain literary critics were "perpetrating error and should be exposed before they could do further damage," noted Walter B. Rideout in *The Radical Novel in the United States, 1900-1954.* In 1936 Farrell published *A Note on Literary Criticism,* which, according to Rideout, was the "only extended discussion of Marxist aesthetics written from a Marxist standpoint in the United States during the thirties." Rideout contended that "the book constitutes a simultaneous attack and defense. The attack is directed against both 'revolutionary sentimentalism,' as represented by [Michael] Gold, and 'mechanical Marxism,' as represented by [Granville] Hicks. Since each of these two 'Leftist' tendencies in literary criticism has, in its extreme emphasis on the functional ('use-value') aspect of literature, ignored the aesthetic aspect, they have together, Farrell argued, kept Marxist criticism weak, because they substitute measurement for judgment. Hence, the critic's task, which is ultimately one of judgment, of evaluation, has been avoided." Rideout added later: "If Farrell's own statement of the critic's function is not strikingly original, if his dissection of the deficiencies of proletarian literature and criticism is, stylistically speaking, performed as much with a meat ax as with a scalpel, still the dissection itself was a thorough one." Farrell, in fact, aroused so much critical feeling with this work that *The New Masses* summarized his comments, and those of his supporters, with the arguments of his opponents under the heading "The Farrell Controversy."

Rideout believed that Farrell was prompted, to some extent, to write the criticism by the demands of "several extremist reviewers [who] had called for the display of more 'class-consciousness' in the un-class-conscious characters of whom he wrote." But Farrell also believed that critics were essentially redefining literature as a socially effective instrument. Gelfant wrote: "Farrell's definition of literature as an 'instrument of social control,' makes clear his belief that fiction could not be directly a 'means of solving problems' within society. Rather it was 'a means of helping people to discover more about themselves and about the condition of life about them.' As literature brought the reader to a sharper awareness, it was . . . instrumental in social reform, for it is awareness that produces the pressing sense of concern that moves man finally to act. In order to make the reader more sensitive to his world, literature must exploit fully its aesthetic potentialities." And in 1967 Farrell told the *New York Times:* "I don't think literature should include partisan thinking. I don't believe in things like political commitment in novels." He admitted that he had been in "political campaigns of all kinds" though, and he once bought Russian Communist leader Leon Trotsky a typewriter. "Why? Because he needed it."

Farrell's was not a simple separation of art from propaganda, however. Gelfant noted: "He distinguished between the two by defining literature as a form of revelation, and propaganda as a form of political action. The implicit assumption underlying Farrell's theory is that knowledge will make us free. Whatever the artist has to add to our experience and understanding of the world about us, of any part of it, can be of social consequences."

Many critics believed that Farrell's Studs Lonigan trilogy was extremely successful as a work of "social consequence." Rideout contended that Farrell was the only writer who succeeded in chronicling "with great zest and passion the slow downward spiral of what [was then] considered both a dull and ideologically unimportant class. [Farrell succeeded] because setting down the minutely detailed degradation of Studs Lonigan represented for [Farrell] an angry act of catharsis." Rideout believed that the Studs Lonigan trilogy is one of the "most durable achievements of the radical novel of the thirties."

Farrell's later work, however, received less critical acclaim. James R. Frakes wrote of *Lonely for the Future:* "At this late date Farrell's style reads like vicious self-parody. In this world of human wrecks and pointless waste, James T. Farrell continues to chronicle his bleak Chicago inferno like a bleeding

Virgil." Although the *Time* reviewer called Farrell "the most heroic figure in modern American letters," he wrote in his review of *When Time Was Born:* "Farrell calls his latest literary enterprise a prose poem. It is neither prose nor poem, but it appears to be an attempt to rewrite the first chapters of the Book of Genesis. The first sentence blithers and blathers and blunders along for five pages and 1,390 words. Reading it can only be likened to the experience of a man who, having lost an election bet, has undertaken to eat a pad of Brillo and is wondering which is the more unpalatable—the steel-wool structure or the pink soapy filling." But Beach summarized: "The best single test for a writer of fiction is the creation of characters that live in the imagination. Farrell has brought to life an unusual number of such living characters. Studs Lonigan, Jim O'Neill, Al O'Flaherty, Aunt Margaret, and grandmother O'Flaherty are among the memorable people in English fiction."

Farrell's last novel was *Sam Holman,* which tells the story of a young and brilliant encyclopedia editor in New York City in the 1930s. The work has been disparaged for concentrating mainly on Sam's sexual exploits and his ponderous philosophical disquisitions with his fellow overly earnest Communist Party members. John W. Aldridge wrote in *The New York Times Book Review*—summing up his feelings about *Sam Holman* and Farrell's career—that the novel "contains all the faults for which Farrell has always been famous, but here they are unredeemed by the presence of his former virtues. From the beginning Farrell was a peculiarly graceless and tone-deaf writer whose prose often appeared to have been laid on the page with a dump truck and shovel. Yet in the best of his early work one sensed a current of evangelical rage that gained special authenticity from being expressed with bludgeoning artlessness."

To comment on his life's work, Farrell borrowed a line from Yeats: "I, too," said Farrell, "spit into the face of time, even though I am aware that this is merely a symbolic expression of a mood: Time slowly transfigures me. . . . Joy and sadness, growth and decay, life and death are all part of the transfiguration of time. To look into the Face of Time, and to master its threat to us—this is one of the basic themes and purposes of art and literature."

Farrell once told *CA* that his works have been translated into about twenty-five languages. A Farrell archive is maintained at the University of Pennsylvania.

*BIOGRAPHICAL/CRITICAL SOURCES:*

*BOOKS*

Allen, Walter, *The Modern Novel in Britain and the United States,* Dutton, 1965.

Beach, Joseph Warren, *American Fiction, 1920-1940,* Macmillan, 1941.

Branch, Edgar Marquess, *A Bibliography of James T. Farrell's Writings, 1921-1957,* University of Pennsylvania Press, 1959.

Branch, *James T. Farrell,* University of Minnesota Press, 1963.

Branch, *Studs Lonigan's Neighborhood and the Making of James T. Farrell,* Arts End Books (Newton, MA), 1996.

*Contemporary Literary Criticism,* Gale, Volume 1, 1973, Volume 4, 1975, Volume 8, 1978, Volume 11, 1979, Volume 66, 1991.

*Conversations with Writers,* Volume 2, Gale, 1978.

*Dictionary of Literary Biography,* Gale, Volume 4: *American Writers in Paris, 1920-1939,* 1980, Volume 9: *American Novelists, 1910-1945,* 1981, Volume 86: *American Short-Story Writers, 1910-1945,* 1989.

*Dictionary of Literary Biography Documentary Series,* Volume 2, Gale, 1982.

Farrell, James T., *Reflections at Fifty, and Other Essays,* Vanguard, 1954.

Fried, Lewis, *Makers of the City,* University of Massachusetts Press (Amherst), 1990.

Gelfant, Blanche Housman, *The American City Novel,* University of Oklahoma Press, 1954.

Kazin, Alfred, *On Native Grounds,* Harcourt, 1942.

Rideout, Walter B., *The Radical Novel in the United States, 1900-1954,* Harvard University Press, 1956.

Walcutt, Charles Child, editor, *Seven Novelists in the American Naturalist Tradition,* University of Minnesota Press, 1974.

Wald, A. M., *James T. Farrell,* New York University Press, 1978.

*PERIODICALS*

*American Book Collector,* May, 1967.

*American Book Review,* December, 1993-January, 1994.

*American Heritage,* April, 1995, pp. 135, 150.

*American Quarterly,* winter, 1977.

*Best Sellers,* May 15, 1971.

*Esquire,* December, 1962.

*Harper's,* October, 1954.

*The Humanist,* November-December, 1983.

*Literary Times,* April, 1965.
*Nation,* June 3, 1968; October 16, 1976.
*National Observer,* June 29, 1964.
*New Yorker,* March 18, 1974.
*New York Herald Tribune Book Week,* February 27, 1966.
*New York Times,* December 3, 1967.
*New York Times Book Review,* August 12, 1962; January 7, 1968; July 14, 1968; January 19, 1969; November 25, 1973; September 16, 1979; October 9, 1983.
*People,* March 12, 1979.
*Prairie Schooner,* spring, 1967.
*Saturday Review,* June 20, 1964.
*Time,* May 27, 1966.
*Twentieth Century Literature,* February, 1976.
*Washington Post,* September 11, 1968.

*OBITUARIES:*

*PERIODICALS*

*AB Bookman's Weekly,* October 22, 1979.
*Chicago Tribune,* August 23, 1979.
*Detroit News,* August 26, 1979.
*New York Times,* August 23, 1979.
*Time,* September 3, 1979.
*Washington Post,* August 23, 1979.*

* * *

**FAY, Stephen (Francis John) 1938-**

*PERSONAL:* Born August 14, 1938, in Littleborough, England; son of Gerard (a journalist) and Alice Mary (Bentley) Fay; married Prudence Butcher, August 29, 1964; children: Matthew, Susanna. *Education:* University of New Brunswick, B.A., 1958, M.A., 1959; London School of Economics and Political Science, graduate study, 1959-60.

*ADDRESSES: Home*—17 College Cross, London N.1, England.

*CAREER:* Canadian Atlantic Provinces Office (diplomatic and trade representatives), London, England, economist, 1959-61; *Glasgow Herald,* Glasgow, Scotland, leader writer and industrial correspondent in Glasgow and London, 1961-64; *Sunday Times,* London, various editorial posts, 1964-84; *Business Magazine,* London, editor, 1986-89; associate editor, *Independent on Sunday,* 1989—.

*WRITINGS:*

(With Lewis Chester and Hugo Young) *The Zinoviev Letter,* Heinemann, 1967, Lippincott (Philadelphia, PA), 1968.
*Measure for Measure: Reforming the Unions,* Chatto & Windus, 1970.
(With Chester and Magnus Linklater) *Hoax: The Inside Story of the Clifford Irving-Howard Hughes Affair,* Viking (New York City), 1972.
(With Phillip Knightley) *The Death of Venice,* Praeger (New York City), 1976.
*Beyond Greed: The Hunts and Their Silver Bubble,* Viking, 1982 (published in England as *The Great Silver Bubble,* Hodder & Stoughton, London, 1982).
(With Roger Wood) *The Ring: Anatomy of an Opera,* with photographs by Roger Wood, Secker & Warburg (London, England), 1984, Longwood (Dover, NH), 1985.
*Portrait of an Old Lady: Turmoil at the Bank of England,* Viking, 1987.
*Power Play: The Life and Times of Peter Hall,* Hodder & Stoughton, 1995.
*The Collapse of Barings,* Norton (New York City), 1997.

*SIDELIGHTS:* Stephen Fay has written several nonfiction studies of colorful business executives whose careers have attracted worldwide attention. His *Beyond Greed: The Hunts and Their Silver Bubble* tells the story of an attempt at cornering the world silver market; *Power Play: The Life and Times of Peter Hall* focuses on the successful director of the Royal Shakespeare Company; and *The Collapse of Barings* examines the destruction of one of England's most prestigious banks.

In 1979 and 1980, a small group of investors, led by the Hunt brothers of Texas, attempted to control the silver market by buying large quantities of the metal and driving up prices. "The tale of how the Hunts and their shadowy international consorts moved toward the peak of the silver mountain and how they were toppled on the verge has been mined with great skill by Stephen Fay, a British journalist with an engaging manner, a respect for the line between fact and surmise, and an ability to convey his own fascination with the commodities market and its denizens," summarizes Walter Goodman in the *New York Times Book Review.* In *Beyond Greed: The Hunts and Their Silver Bubble,* Fay "provides essential explanations of how the market is supposed to work and how it really works, the difference between bullion and bull. . . .

He hops about the globe, offering sharp sketches of rascals and respectables, though it is not always easy to tell them apart." In addition, notes economist John Kenneth Galbraith in the *Atlantic,* "Fay writes with a justifiable awe of the large sums—always in the tens and often in the hundreds of millions— that were involved in the silver caper . . . [and] also with a pleasant absence of indignation." "Mr. Fay has made it all seem . . . simple and straightforward," observes the *New York Times*'s Christopher Lehmann-Haupt. "And this is quite remarkable when you consider the numbers involved."

*Times Literary Supplement* contributor Richard Lambert similarly states that Fay's account "makes gripping reading when it deals with matters of public record," in addition to giving "a very clear and comprehensive explanation of the extremely complicated way in which the commodity markets operate." Nevertheless, the critic faults Fay for being "occasionally driven to flights of fancy and to rather irritating *Dallas*-style writing" in relating the history of the Hunts and their collaborators. In contrast, Lehmann-Haupt believes that "what with the secrecy of the Hunt brothers—or perhaps one should say, what with their selective lapses of memory when they were finally investigated . . . —it is impressive how much Mr. Fay has managed to dig up. Only once does he resort to pure speculation," continues the critic, "and this involves only a relatively minor passage of events." *Beyond Greed* "is well written and admirably researched," remarks Galbraith, "some minor errors notwithstanding. Mr. Fay is an Englishman, an exponent of the modern British art form that consists in taking some subject of current interest, not necessarily one involving criminal intent, tracking down all details and ramifications, and presenting the results in wholly literate fashion," the critic concludes. "This he has done with the Hunts and the silver bubble."

Peter Hall, the subject of Fay's 1995 book, is the colorful director who has been credited with a major role in the development of London's National Theatre and the Royal Shakespeare Company. *Power Play: The Life and Times of Peter Hall* is his "authorized" biography. Stephen Fay was given free access to Hall's diaries, letters, colleagues, and friends. James Saynor reports in the *Observer Review* that Fay "stays largely in step with the official version of Hall's life, while providing a thorough and highly absorbing audit."

The "audit" covers Hall's professional and private life, candidly discussing the director's several marriages, extravagant lifestyle, and immoderate spending habits. "Fay stresses Hall's cunning and extravagance," Saynor writes, "without turning them into vices. There's [also] much new material on his private life." "What Mr. Fay has attempted," contributes John Bowen of the *Spectator,* "is an objective assessment."

When this assessment focuses on Hall's professional accomplishments, a *Times Literary Supplement* reviewer suggests: "Neutrality is the key to Stephen Fay's biographical style." Without a personal background in the theater, Fay reports the historical events, "but he shies away from interpreting the facts he so assiduously collects." Fay documents Hall's contribution to the foundation of subsidized theater in England through his work at the National Theatre. He also discusses Hall's role, not only in the development of the Royal Shakespeare Company, but in the creation of what Bowen calls "a style of playing Shakespeare" that Saynor claims "has preserved the Bard on his international plinth and sustained British acting's claim to be the keeper of his flame."

Though the *Times Literary Supplement* refers to *Power Play* as a "laborious chronicling of spats, strikes, and sackings," the reviewer also notes that the book "provides a useful account of the changing landscape of post-war British theatre and of the part Hall played in [it]."

In *The Collapse of Barings,* Fay's background in financial journalism bolsters his account of the scandalous ruin of one of England's most prestigious banking firms. The focus of Fay's study is Nick Leeson, the bold young clerk-turned-trader whose losses cost the bank nearly 150-million British pounds in a single day. By February, 1995, the accumulated loss was more than 869-million pounds, a catastrophe that even Barings, the Queen's bankers, could not survive.

According to Fay's account, Leeson ventured into questionable trading operatings at the Barings office in Singapore. A series of losses prompted him to establish "Error Account No. 88888" to conceal the results of his errors and foster the illusion of "balanced books." As the losses continued to escalate, Leeson began taking greater and riskier chances in an attempt to recover the money he had lost, and the "Five Eights" account grew so large that its discovery was inevitable. Even then, it was only Leeson's sudden resignation and flight from Singapore that alerted Barings to impending disaster. In assessing blame, Fay "is dismissive of Leeson's attempts to play down his guilt," writes Martin Vander Weyer in the *Spectator,* but he also "highlights the staggering incompetence of [Barings] managers in London and Singapore in their failure, over 32 months, to carry out the elementary checks which would have revealed what Leeson was doing."

Michael Lewis comments in the *New Yorker:* "I doubt whether anyone can read [this book] without feeling that the upper reaches of English society have given themselves over entirely to the American way of life—or, at least, to their own peculiar interpretation of it." He writes that the whole scandal "represents what happens when Englishmen imitate American financiers without really understanding what American financiers do." Of *The Collapse of Barings, Times Literary Supplement* reviewer John Chown writes: "Stephen Fay's book provides an approachable and informed, if provisional, account of what happened to Barings." Vander Weyer states that Fay "provides an entertaining account. . . . He is particularly good on the enfeebled state of the Barings dynasty . . . and on the workings of the Bank of England."

*BIOGRAPHICAL/CRITICAL SOURCES:*

*PERIODICALS*

*Atlantic,* May, 1982.
*Booklist,* February 15, 1997, p. 983.
*Economist,* February 24, 1996, p. 90.
*Forbes,* May 6, 1996, p. 18.
*New Yorker,* June 17, 1996, pp. 97-99.
*New York Times,* May 15, 1972; December 21, 1982.
*New York Times Book Review,* June 25, 1972; November 21, 1976; April 18, 1982.
*Observer Review,* May 21, 1995, p. 19.
*Spectator,* June 19, 1982; May 20, 1995, p. 36; February 24, 1996, pp. 29-30.
*Times* (London), August 23, 1984.
*Times Literary Supplement,* August 4, 1972; December 17, 1976; August 6, 1982; December 15, 1995, p. 28; April 19, 1996, p. 7.
*Washington Post,* May 21, 1982.

* * *

**FISH, Robert L(loyd) 1912-1981**
**(Robert L. Pike, Lawrence Roberts)**

*PERSONAL:* Born August 21, 1912, in Cleveland, OH; died of a heart attack, February 24, 1981, in Trumbull, CT; son of David and Sarah (Osserman) Fish; married Mamie Kates, December 26, 1935; children: Ruth (Mrs. David Stillson), Catherine Ann. *Education:* Case Institute of Technology (now Case Western Reserve University), B.S., 1933. *Politics:* Independent. *Religion:* Jewish.

*CAREER:* Consulting engineer to the plastics industry. Consulting engineer to plastics industry in Brazil, 1952-62; writer, 1962-81. *Military service:* Member of National Guard, Ohio 37th Division, three years.

*MEMBER:* Society of Plastics Engineers, Mystery Writers of America (president, 1978), Authors Guild, Authors League of America, Crime Writers Association, Crime Club of England.

*AWARDS, HONORS:* Edgar Allan Poe Award from Mystery Writers of America, 1962, for *The Fugutive,* 1963, for *Isle of the Snakes,* and 1972, for short story, "Moonlight Gardner"; Ohioana Book Award, 1970, for *The Xavier Affair.*

*WRITINGS:*

*The Fugitive,* Simon & Schuster (New York City), 1962.
*Isle of the Snakes,* Simon & Schuster, 1963.
*Assassination Bureau* (completed from notes of Jack London), McGraw (New York City), 1963.
*Shrunken Head,* Simon & Schuster, 1963.
*Brazilian Sleigh Ride,* Simon & Schuster, 1965.
*The Diamond Bubble,* Simon & Schuster, 1965.
*The Incredible Schlock Homes,* Simon & Schuster, 1966.
*Always Kill a Stranger,* Putnam (New York City), 1967.
*The Hochmann Miniatures,* New American Library (New York City), 1967.
*The Murder League,* Simon & Schuster, 1968.
*The Bridge That Went Nowhere: A Captain Jose da Silva Novel,* Putnam, 1968.
(Editor and author of foreword) *With Malice Toward All: An Anthology of Mystery Stories,* Putnam, 1968.
*The Xavier Affair: A Jose da Silva Novel,* Putnam, 1969.
*Whirligig,* New American Library, 1970.
*Rub-A-Dub-Dub,* Simon & Schuster, 1971, published as *Death Cuts the Deck,* Ace Books (New York City), 1972.
*The Green Hell Treasure,* Putnam, 1971.
*The Tricks of the Trade: A Kek Huuygens Novel,* Putnam, 1972.

(With Henry Rothblatt) *A Handy Death,* Simon & Schuster, 1973.
*The Wager: A Kek Huuygens Novel,* Putnam, 1974.
*The Memoirs of Schlock Homes: A Bagel Street Dozen,* Bobbs-Merrill (Indianapolis), 1974.
*Trouble in Paradise: A Captain Jose de Silva Novel,* Doubleday (New York City), 1975.
(Editor) *Every Crime in the Book,* Putnam, 1975.
*Kek Huuygens, Smuggler,* Mysterious Press (New York City), 1976.
(With Pele) *My Life and the Beautiful Game: The Autobiography of Pele,* Doubleday, 1977.
*Pursuit: A Novel,* Doubleday, 1978.
*Find One Happy Moment* (poetry), Dorrance, 1979.
*A Gross Carriage of Justice,* Doubleday, 1979.
*The Gold of Troy,* Doubleday, 1980.

*UNDER PSEUDONYM ROBERT L. PIKE*

*Mute Witness,* Doubleday, 1963.
*The Quarry,* Doubleday, 1964.
*Police Blotter,* Doubleday, 1965.
*Reardon,* Doubleday, 1970.
*The Gremlin's Grampa,* Doubleday, 1972.
*Bank Job,* Doubleday, 1974.
*Deadline 2 A.M.,* Doubleday, 1976.

*OTHER*

Contributor to anthologies and to *Ellery Queen's Mystery Magazine. The Diamond Bubble* has been translated into French.

*ADAPTATIONS:* The motion picture *Bullitt* was based on *Mute Witness* and filmed by Warner Brothers Studio-Seven Arts Productions Ltd. in 1968; *The Assassination Bureau* was filmed by Paramount Picture Corp. in 1969.

*SIDELIGHTS:* Robert L. Fish was a prolific American author best known for his mystery thrillers, including *The Assassination Bureau,* a novel left unfinished by Jack London at the time of his death and completed by Fish. Writing in the *St. James Guide to Crime and Mystery Writers,* Mary Ann Grochowski praised "the quality and versatility of [Fish's] talents. Ranging from Sherlockian parodies to fascinatingly realistic police procedural novels, Fish's short stories and novels are witty and well-plotted, alternating between expertly crafted humor and breathtaking suspense."

Jack London wrote some 40,000 words of *The Assassination Bureau* before giving up the book. He apparently felt the story, based on an idea he had purchased from the then-unknown Sinclair Lewis, was not worth finishing. It had also become so complicated that London was at a loss at to how to resolve the plot. Fish's completed version of the story, drawing largely from London's few remaining notes, tells the tale of a socialist millionaire who gets entangled with the Assassination Bureau, an underground organization killing those it deems to be detrimental to society. Critics split on their evaluation of the novel. The critic for the *Times Literary Supplement* found *The Assassination Bureau* "a thoroughly poor novel" and "Fish's ending, though stylistically and dramatically adequate, does not suffice to make the story worth reading." But Anthony Boucher in the *New York Times Book Review* called it a "delight—the grandest thriller in years."

In the series of mystery novels featuring Captain Jose Maria Carvalho Hantos da Silva, a Brazilian police officer, Fish created a number of exotic stories set in South America. Da Silva, Grochowski observed, is an "intuitive, witty, romantic, and extremely courageous character." Drawing on his own years as an engineer in Brazil, Fish vividly recreated the tropical locale while spinning fast-moving plots. Speaking of *The Diamond Bubble,* in which da Silva is on the trail of diamond smugglers, John Dickson Carr in *Harper* noted that "again the scene is Rio in a heat haze, with every atmosphere detail skillfully evoked." Anthony Boucher in the *New York Times Book Review* remarked on the same book that it possessed "vivid color and plentiful excitement . . . all narrated with vim and relish."

Fish's adventures of Schlock Homes, his parody version of Sherlock Holmes, employ, according to Grochowski, "hilarious puns, extremely astute misobservations, and outrageously illogical solutions." Reviewing in *Book Week* the collection *The Incredible Schlock Homes,* D. B. Hughes observed that "you don't need to have been exposed to the prototype to chortle over his alter ego."

*BIOGRAPHICAL/CRITICAL SOURCES:*

*BOOKS*

*St. James Guide to Crime and Mystery Writers,* fourth edition, St. James Press (Detroit), 1996.

*PERIODICALS*

*Book Week,* August 14, 1966, p. 10.
*Harper,* July, 1965, p. 106.

*New York Times Book Review,* December 8, 1963, p. 49; March 21, 1965, p. 22; May 31, 1970; June 28, 1970; February 7, 1971; March 12, 1972.
*Times Literary Supplement,* December 3, 1964, p. 1101; August 6, 1982.
*Village Voice,* February 10, 1975.
*Washington Post Book World,* September 4, 1975.

*OBITUARIES:*

*PERIODICALS*

*AB Bookman's Weekly,* July 27, 1981.
*New York Times,* February 25, 1981.
*Publishers Weekly,* March 13, 1981.*

* * *

## FLOOK, Maria 1952-

*PERSONAL:* Born July 9, 1952, in Ontario, Canada; daughter of George and Elise (Felix) Bruce; children: Kate. *Education:* Roger Williams College, B.A., 1973; University of Iowa, M.F.A., 1979.

*ADDRESSES:* *Office*—Department of English, Rhode Island College, Providence, RI 02908.

*CAREER:* Iowa Security Medical Facility, Oakdale, corrections officer, 1978-79; Roger Williams College, Bristol, RI, adjunct professor of English, 1981—. Adjunct professor at Rhode Island College, 1982—.

*AWARDS, HONORS:* Fellow at Fine Arts Work Center, Provincetown, MA, 1980-81; Great Lakes Award, 1983, for *Reckless Wedding.*

*WRITINGS:*

*Reckless Wedding* (poems), Houghton (Boston), 1982.
*Dancing with My Sister Jane* (stories), Ampersand Press (Bristol, RI), 1987.
*Sea Room* (poems), Wesleyan University Press (Middletown, CT), 1990.
*Family Night* (novel), Pantheon (New York City), 1993.
*Open Water* (novel), Pantheon, 1994.
*You Have the Wrong Man* (stories), Pantheon, 1996.

Contributor to magazines, including *Poetry, American Poetry Review, Agni Review, Antioch Review, Iowa Review,* and *Iron-wood.*

*SIDELIGHTS:* Maria Flook has proven herself to be an accomplished writer of poetry, short stories, and novels. Her first book, *Reckless Wedding,* revealed her to be "a poet with many points to make," according to a *Booklist* reviewer, who further noted that "Flook works by indirection, her seemingly impulsive leaps in imagery usually matched by her intuitive grasp of human experience." *New York Times Book Review* contributor Alan Williamson criticized *Reckless Wedding* for containing "some of the mannerisms of a generic writing-workshop style," but praised the "powerful, if slightly oblique, family poems" in the collection. Discussing Flook's second volume of poetry, *Sea Room, Booklist* reviewer Pat Monaghan called Flook's writing "breathlessly intense, full of strained power created by surprising juxtapositions," and declared that *Sea Room* is proof that her work "grows stronger with each reading."

Flook's poetic sensibility was evident in her first novel, *Family Night,* according to many critics. The story concerns Margaret, her often-cruel lover, Tracy, and her stepbrother Cam. The trio embarks together on a search for Cam's father, whom he has never seen. Emily White observed in the *Village Voice* that Flook has produced a dark novel, often filled with powerful language. However, she admitted that she "didn't particularly care for Margaret, Tracy, or Cam; their shallowness undermines a story hinged on a deep erotic current even as the descriptions of sex are near-perfect." Michiko Kakutani of the *New York Times* also noted that "none of [Flook's] characters are terribly likable individuals," but went on to say that "while we might never really empathize with any of these characters, it is a measure of Ms. Flook's skill and poise as a writer that she makes us understand these people and the sad, tumbling row of emotional dominoes that has brought them to this place in their lives. She has written a fierce, nervous and highly accomplished novel." *New York Times Book Review* contributor Daniel Woodrell was also impressed with *Family Night,* calling it "a potent, richly realized novel with sentences that cut, and cut cleanly, revealing hearts tormented by regret and desire. Ms. Flook's gifts as a writer of prose are extravagant and apparent on every page. Her style is spare, subtle, ethereal and erotic, comparable with the best of James Salter."

In *Open Water,* Flook again examines the effects of family experience on individuals. In this novel, the protagonist is Willis, a lost soul who, as a child, watched his mother die in a freak choking accident caused by his father. As an adult, Willis becomes a morphine addict who displays "a mixture of spiritual lunacy and animal frenzy," in the words of *New York Times Book Review* writer Ralph Lombreglia, who noted that, in light of Flook's poetic roots, "it's no surprise that her pages are filled with striking images, with fresh figures of speech." Lombroglia found, however, that the author's facility with words could be a fault, causing her characters to "banter in a witty but unlikely way." Yet, he concluded, any shortcomings in the book "arise from large ambitions and talent, and they fail to diminish the accomplishment of a novel that manages to be not only literary but suspenseful too." Kakutani described *Open Water* as "disturbing. . . . A strange, original and fully absorbing novel."

The eccentric characters and bizarre situations that mark her novels appeared again in *You Have the Wrong Man,* Flook's first short-story collection. "Ms. Flook . . . seems drawn to characters who can best be called exotic," stated Gary Krist in a *New York Times Book Review* article on *You Have the Wrong Man.* "A grotesquely scarred medical student, a reluctant transsexual, a despondent office worker given to asphyxial masturbation—these are the types of marginalized individuals who populate the eight stories in this collection." Krist complained that "the stories are too often hobbled by slack pacing and a surprising carelessness in the storytelling," but allowed that "Ms. Flook is clearly an accomplished stylist. Her writing never succumbs to cliche, and there is a metaphorical opulence to her prose that succeeds . . . more often than it founders."

*BIOGRAPHICAL/CRITICAL SOURCES:*

*PERIODICALS*

*Booklist,* December 1, 1982, p. 479; October 15, 1990, p. 411; November 1, 1994, p. 477; March 1, 1996, p. 1120.

*Chicago Tribune,* February 4, 1993.

*Library Journal,* August, 1994, p. 168; January, 1995, p. 136; February 15, 1996, p. 177.

*Los Angeles Times Book Review,* February 7, 1993, p. 8; March 26, 1995, p. 13.

*New York Times,* January 19, 1993, p. C17; January 31, 1995, p. C16.

*New York Times Book Review,* May 1, 1983, pp. 15, 34; February 21, 1993, p. 8; March 5, 1995, p. 18; January 21, 1996; March 10, 1996, p. 25.

*Poetry,* December, 1983, p. 325.

*Publishers Weekly,* November 7, 1994, p. 65; January 22, 1996, p. 60.

*Tribune Books,* January 22, 1995, p. 3.

*Village Voice,* March 23, 1993, p. 83.*

*    *    *

**FOGARTY, Jonathan Titulescu, Esq.**
**See FARRELL, James T(homas)**

# G

## GAITSKILL, Mary 1954-

*PERSONAL:* Born November 11, 1954, in Lexington, KY; daughter of Lawrence Russell (a teacher) and Dorothy Jane (a social worker and homemaker; maiden name, Mayer) Gaitskill. *Education:* University of Michigan, B.A., 1981. *Avocational interests:* Aikido.

*ADDRESSES: Home*—5 1/2 Jane St., New York, NY 10014. *Agent*—Curtis Brown, 10 Astor Place, New York, NY 10003.

*CAREER:* Writer.

*AWARDS, HONORS:* Jule and Avery Hopwood Award from University of Michigan, 1981, for "The Women Who Knew Judo and Other Stories."

*WRITINGS:*

*Bad Behavior* (short stories), Poseidon Press (New York City), 1988.

*Two Girls, Fat and Thin* (novel), Poseidon Press, 1991.

*Because They Wanted To* (short stories), Simon & Schuster (New York City), 1997.

*SIDELIGHTS:* "Mary Gaitskill isn't for everyone," writes Carolyn See in the opening lines of her *Washington Post* review of Gaitskill's latest book, *Because They Wanted To,* "She's got a reputation as a rowdy and a reprobate whose ideas about sex are—to say the least—startlingly innovative." Certainly, Gaitskill's books, one novel and two short story collections, concern a certain "sexual pathology." Her characters' actions generally center on abuse they have given or abuse they have suffered. These warped sexualities go on to infect the core of their lives. Gaitskill told *CA,* about her first book, *Bad Behavior:* "My characters' apparent interest in sadomasochistic sex is more a confusion of violation with closeness than a desire to be hurt. I will continue to work with both of these themes in my novel." Gaitskill's lives up to this promise in her ensuing novel and short story collection.

In Gaitskill's first collection of stories, *Bad Behavior,* she portrays the seamy side of New York City and the troubled characters who inhabit it. Martin Waxman in the Toronto *Globe and Mail* wrote that "her characters are outsiders whose behavior is 'bad' in that it is different, . . . unexpected." Often their behavior is self-destructive. Quoting from the story "Daisy's Valentine," Waxman wrote: "Joey felt that his romance with Daisy might ruin his life . . . it had been a long time since he felt his life was in danger of further ruin and it was fun to think it was still possible." In Gaitskill's stories a would-be writer becomes a prostitute to support herself, a secretary submits to being molested by her boss, and, in the ironic "Romantic Weekend," a nervous young woman spends a weekend with a married man who tries to humiliate her.

These characters abuse drugs, themselves, or other people, often in a misguided effort to realize their dreams, according to *New York Times* critic Michiko Kakutani. For example, Kakutani noted, in "Something Nice" a veterinarian offers a young prostitute five hundred dollars to "take the night off so they can 'have time to really act like people in a relationship.'" According to Kakutani, these incidents are believable and not "merely perverse" because

"Gaitskill writes with such authority, such radar-perfect detail, that she is able to make even the most extreme situations seem real." Kakutani added that Gaitskill's detailed treatment of the characters results in "fierce portraits of individuals rather than a gallery of eccentric types." Similarly, Waxman praised Gaitskill's fiction as honest, original, and memorable, and called her "a gifted writer whose prose sparkles with wit and surprises."

Gaitskill's novel, *Two Girls, Fat and Thin,* centers on the relationship between Justine Sade and Dorothy Never. Thin Justine is a freelance journalist who meets fat Dorothy while working on a story about an Ayn Rand-like philosophical/literary figure. The two women seem to be complete opposites—Justine is a sexually promiscuous sadomasochist, while Dorothy treasures complete solitude and has no friends or lovers. But the two women are drawn together over a shared history of sexual abuse: 13-year-old Dorothy at the hands of her father; 5-year-old Justine first by a colleague of her father, and in ensuing years, by other men. Lesley A. Rimmel, writes in the *Women's Review of Books,* "Rarely has a work so sensitively portrayed the pain, anguish and isolation caused by the trauma of this abuse, and of the resulting desperate quest for solace and dignity." Jane Smiley writes in *Tribune Books* of another important aspect of the book, that it offers a "potent picture of an America promoted by advertising—a place where physical looks, good or bad, are paramount, where adolescent hell is life's central episode and one that lasts much longer than high school, but where, if luck holds, strength can be drawn from facing up to, and seeking to understand, early experiences of cruelty and fear."

"It is a credit to Ms. Gaitskill's skillful prose," writes Ginger Danto in the *New York Times Book Review,* "with its fine storyteller's pace and brilliant metaphors, that we are drawn along, loath to abandon this grim story." Indeed, the novel resolves on a more optimistic note, with Justine and Dorothy poised on forging what has been unknown to them before—a caring relationship. Roz Kaveney, in the *Times Literary Supplement,* calls *Two Girls, Fat and Thin* an "assured first novel" and notes that it has the "same polish [as *Bad Behavior*] in a longer and more complex form." Some critics have complained that Gaitskill's style in the novels can be overwritten and even "clunky." But Sarah Schulman declares in *Advocate* that "Readers must pick and choose what information they will retain, because the clues are buried in this text as they would be in real life. But even this use of banality cannot hide certain cruelties: "'You are an argument for abortion,' said [Dororthy's] father. 'If I had known you were going to happen, I never would have had a child.'" And Katie Roiphe points out in *Harper's Magazine* the impact of Gaitskill's writing: "You have to feel sympathy, horror, and the breathless panic of the thirteen-year-old being molested by her father."

*Because They Wanted To* offers a cast of depressed and sometime depraved characters, similar to those found in *Bad Behavior.* Again, Gaitskill tends to focus on sexual relations between women and men or women and women. A rape fantasy willingly played out between a couple gets taken too far, a man confides to his airplane seatmate of his involvement in a gang rape of a drunk girl at a college party. Such stories enlighten Gaitskill's point, writes Craig Seligman in the *New York Times Book Review,* that "sex is never simple—it's always complicated." "The Dentist" finds Jill developing an obsession with her dentist, who insists on sending out mixed signals. Richard Eder writes in the *Los Angeles Time Book Review,* "Jill is neither victim nor fool; she is also both. The signals of the modern sexual game and of modern life in general are so balefully inscrutable that each step is a trap." Gaitskill herself has said that her characters are searching for "a carnality full of honor and truth."

David Gates of *Newsweek* finds in *Because They Wanted To* Gaitskill's true subject: her characters' "essential disconnectedness and their sometimes pathetic, sometimes heroic solitude." Rather than seeing Gaitskill as many others do, as a "dark" presence in contemporary literature, Gates explains, "Gaitskill seems to have a vision rather than a career agenda." Carolyn See also finds in the novella that ends the collection—about a bisexual woman "too old for the standard run of Gaitskill shenanigans"—the question of how to find love. "Gaitskill's answer," writes See, "though tentative, is affectionate, charming, thoughtful, tender." *Because They Wanted To* is filled with such complex characters who both seek a connection and remain alone—characters are like those in *Bad Behavior* who, Gaitskill told *CA,* "don't know how to be intimate, whose efforts to be intimate are painfully thwarted by their ignorance." Gates enthuses, "*Because They Wanted To* is too rich to read at a sitting—too many good lines, too much precision about too many complex emotions—yet it's too compelling *not* to." Seligman, as well, writes, "A lot of these stories are just about perfect."

Gaitskill's works to date all showcase her strengths: according to Valerie Miner of *Tribune Books,* "her unflinching flirtation with taboo, her clear-eyed used of seamy detail and her talent in portraying sometimes-creepy people as vulnerable and endearing." Sex functions as a common thread. As Jill says in "The Dentist," "Sex . . . connects to the dirt within, and there's just too much dirt." Seligman writes of Gaitskill and all of her writings, "'The dirt within' is what she's after, because she recognizes it as the secret of personality—the core of our humanity."

Gaitskill once told *CA:* "Many articles have, in various tones of voice, chronicled my 'troubled' adolescence, the time spent in mental institutions, the fact that I ran away from home at age sixteen and became a stripper, and so on. This background is of limited relevance to my writing except for one thing: my experience of life as essentially unhappy and uncontrollable taught me to examine the way people, including myself, create survival systems and psychologically 'safe' places for themselves in unorthodox and sometimes apparently self-defeating ways. These inner worlds, although often unworkable and unattractive in social terms, can have a unique beauty and courage. One of my desires in writing *Bad Behavior* was to elucidate these worlds (or at least one or two of them) rather than to shock people or to portray 'losers,' as a few unintelligent critics have suggested."

*BIOGRAPHICAL/CRITICAL SOURCES:*

*BOOKS*

*Contemporary Literary Criticism,* Volume 69, Gale (Detroit), 1991.

*PERIODICALS*

*Advocate,* May 21, 1991, p. 90.
*American Book Review,* July-August, 1989, pp. 12, 19.
*Booklist,* January 1, 1997, p. 818.
*Entertainment Weekly,* August 14, 1992, p. 56.
*Globe and Mail* (Toronto), September 10, 1988.
*Harper's Magazine,* November, 1995, p. 65.
*Interview,* January, 1991, p. 54.
*Library Journal,* February 1, 1991, p. 102; January, 1997, p. 152.
*Los Angeles Times,* January 19, 1997, p. 2.
*Los Angeles Times Book Review,* February 24, 1991, p. 3.
*Michigan Quarterly Review,* summer, 1989, pp. 450-458.
*Mother Jones,* January, 1991, p. 73.
*Nation,* December 30, 1991, p. 858.
*New Leader,* May 6, 1991, p. 18.
*New Statesman & Society,* July 5, 1991, p. 38.
*Newsweek,* April 8, 1991, p. 63; January 20, 1997, p. 57.
*New York Times,* May 21, 1988, p. 17.
*New York Times Book Review,* August 21, 1988, p. 3; February 17, 1991, p. 1; February 9, 1997.
*People,* February 11, 1991, p. 21; January 27, 1997, p. 33.
*Publishers Weekly,* January 4, 1991, p. 56; November 25, 1996, p. 57.
*Time,* April 22, 1991, p. 94.
*Times Literary Supplement,* June 28, 1991, p. 19.
*Tribune Books* (Chicago), June 21, 1992; March 9, 1997, p. 9.
*Village Voice,* June 14, 1988, p. 64.
*Voice Literary Supplement,* January-February, 1989, p. 42; February, 1991, p. 17; November, 1992, p. 30.
*Washington Post,* March 14, 1997, p. G3.
*Washington Post Book World,* February 17, 1991, p. 3.
*Women's Review of Books,* July, 1991, p. 19.

* * *

## GILCHRIST, Ellen 1935-

*PERSONAL:* Born February 20, 1935, in Vicksburg, MS; daughter of William Garth (an engineer) and Aurora (Alford) Gilchrist; children: Marshall Peteet Walker, Jr., Garth Gilchrist Walker, Pierre Gautier Walker. *Education:* Millsaps College, B.A., 1967; University of Arkansas, postgraduate study, 1976. *Avocational interests:* Love affairs (mine or anyone else's), all sports, children, inventions, music, rivers, forts and tents, trees.

*ADDRESSES: Home and office*—Fayetteville, AK.

*CAREER:* Author and journalist. *Vieux Carre Courier,* contributing editor, 1976-79. National Public Radio, Washington, DC, commentator on *Morning Edition* (news program), 1984-85.

*MEMBER:* Authors Guild, Authors League of America.

*AWARDS, HONORS:* Poetry award, Mississippi Arts Festival, 1968; poetry award, University of Arkansas, 1976; craft in poetry award, *New York Quarterly,* 1978; National Endowment for the Arts grant in fiction, 1979; Pushcart Prizes, Pushcart Press, 1979-80, for the story "Rich," and 1983, for the story "Summer, An Elegy"; fiction award, *Prairie Schooner,* 1981; Louisiana Library Association Honor book, 1981, for *In the Land of Dreamy Dreams;* fiction awards, Mississippi Academy of Arts and Science, 1982 and 1985; Saxifrage Award, 1983; American Book Award for fiction, Association of American Publishers, 1984, for *Victory over Japan;* J. William Fulbright Award for literature, University of Arkansas, 1985; literature award, Mississippi Institute of Arts and Letters, 1985, 1990, 1991; national scriptwriting award, National Educational Television Network, for the play *A Season of Dreams*; D. Litt., Millsaps College, 1987; L. H. D., University of Southern Illinois, 1991.

*WRITINGS:*

*SHORT STORIES*

*In the Land of Dreamy Dreams,* University of Arkansas Press, 1981, reissued, Little, Brown (Boston), 1985.
*Victory over Japan: A Book of Stories,* Little, Brown, 1984.
*Drunk with Love,* Little, Brown, 1986.
*Two Stories: "Some Blue Hills at Sundown" and "The Man Who Kicked Cancer's Ass,"* Albondocani Press, 1988.
*Light Can Be Both Wave and Particle: A Book of Stories,* Little, Brown, 1989.
*I Cannot Get You Close Enough,* Little, Brown, 1990.
*The Age of Miracles: Stories,* Little, Brown, 1995.
*Rhoda: A Life in Stories,* Little, Brown, 1995.
*The Courts of Love: A Novella and Stories,* Little, Brown, 1996.

*NOVELS*

*The Annunciation,* Little, Brown, 1983.
*The Anna Papers,* Little, Brown, 1988.
*Net of Jewels,* Little, Brown, 1992.
*Starcarbon: A Meditation of Love,* Little, Brown, 1994.
*Anabasis: A Journey to the Interior,* University of Mississippi, 1994.

*OTHER*

*The Land Surveyor's Daughter* (poetry), Lost Roads (Fayetteville, AK), 1979.
*Riding out the Tropical Depression* (poetry), Faust, 1986.
*Falling through Space: The Journals of Ellen Gilchrist,* Little, Brown, 1987.

Also author of *A Season of Dreams* (play; based on short stories by Eudora Welty), produced by the Mississippi Educational Network. Work represented in anthologies, including *The Pushcart Prize: Best of the Small Presses,* Pushcart, 1979-80, 1983. Contributor of poems, short stories, and articles to magazines and journals, including *Atlantic Monthly, California Quarterly, Cincinnati Poetry Review, Cosmopolitan, Iowa Review, Ironwood, Kayak, Mademoiselle, New Laurel Review, New Orleans Review, New York Quarterly, Poetry Northwest, Pontchartrain Review, Prairie Schooner,* and *Southern Living.*

*WORK IN PROGRESS:* A novel; short stories; a play; a screenplay.

*SIDELIGHTS:* The author of poems, numerous short stories, and several novels, Ellen Gilchrist opens for her readers a side door through which to view the world of the gracious, upscale South. With a prose steeped in the traditions of her native Mississippi, Gilchrist's fiction is unique: As Sabine Durrant commented in the London *Times,* her writing "swings between the familiar and the shocking, the everyday and the traumatic." "She writes about ordinary happenings in out of the way places, of meetings between recognizable characters from her other fiction and strangers, above all of domestic routine disrupted by violence." The world of her fiction is awry; the surprise ending, although characteristic of her works, can still shock the reader. "It is disorienting stuff," noted Durrant, "but controlled always by Gilchrist's wry tone and gentle insight."

With the publication of her first short story collection in 1981, Gilchrist gained the attention of literary critics, publishers, and, most importantly, the reading public. In its first few months in print, *In the Land of Dreamy Dreams* sold nearly ten thousand copies in the Southwest alone, a phenomenon particularly impressive since the book was published by a small university press, unaccompanied by major promotional campaigns. The book's popular appeal continued to spread, generating reviews in major newspapers, until it reached the attention of Little, Brown & Co. which offered Gilchrist a cash advance on both a novel and a second collection of short stories. In the meantime, the critical review of *In the Land of Dreamy Dreams* reflected that of the public. As Susan Wood remarked in a review for the *Washington Post Book World,* "Gilchrist may serve as prime evidence for the optimists among us who continue to believe that few truly gifted writers remain unknown forever. And Gilchrist is the real thing alright. In fact," added Wood, "it's difficult to review a first book as good as this without resorting to every known superlative cliche—there are, after all, just so many ways to say 'auspicious debut.'"

*In the Land of Dreamy Dreams* is a collection of fourteen short stories. Most are set in the city of New Orleans and many focus on the lives and concerns of young people. They are "traditional stories" according to Wood, "full of real people to whom things really happen—set, variously, over the last four decades among the rich of New Orleans, the surviving aristocracy of the Mississippi Delta, and Southerners transplanted . . . to southern Indiana." The main characters in the stories, many of them adolescents, exhibit such flaws of character as envy, lust, and avarice; however Wood noted that more positive motivations lay underneath the surface: "It is more accurate to say that *In the Land of Dreamy Dreams* is about the stratagems, both admirable and not so, by which we survive our lives." Jim Crace, in a *Times Literary Supplement* review of *In the Land of Dreamy Dreams,* indicated that Gilchrist's text "is obsessively signposted with street names and Louisiana landmarks. . . . But *In the Land of Dreamy Dreams* cannot be dismissed as little more than an anecdotal street plan. . . . The self-conscious parading of exact Southern locations is a protective screen beyond which an entirely different territory is explored and mapped. Gilchrist's 'Land of Dreamy Dreams' is Adolescence."

The adolescent struggle to come to terms with the way one's dreams and aspirations are limited by reality figures largely in these fourteen stories. Gilchrist introduces her readers to a variety of characters: an eight-year-old girl who delights in masquerading as an adult and commiserates with a newly widowed wartime bride; a girl who fantasizes about the disasters that could befall the brothers who have excluded her from their Olympic-training plans; a young woman who gains her father's help in obtaining an abortion; another girl who discovers the existence of her father's mistress; and an unruly teenager who disrupts the order of her adoptive father's world, challenges his self-esteem, and so aggravates him that he finally shoots her and then commits suicide. "Domestic life among the bored, purposeless, self-indulgent and self-absorbed rich" is the author's central focus, according to reviewer Jonathan Yardley in the *Washington Post Book World.* But domestic is not to be confused with tame. As Yardley observed, the "brutal realities that Gilchrist thrusts into these lives are chilling, and so too is the merciless candor with which she discloses the emptiness behind their glitter." And John Mellors similarly remarked in the *Listener:* "*In the Land of Dreamy Dreams* has many shocks. The author writes in a low, matter-of-fact tone of voice and then changes key in her dramatic, often-bloody endings."

Gilchrist completed her second collection of short stories, *Victory over Japan,* three years later. Winner of the 1984 American Book Award for fiction, *Victory over Japan* was hailed by reviewers as a return to the genre, style, and several of the characters of *In the Land of Dreamy Dreams.* Beverly Lowry, critiquing *Victory over Japan* in the *New York Times Book Review,* commented: "Those who loved *In the Land of Dreamy Dreams* will not be disappointed. Many of the same characters reappear. . . . Often new characters show up with old names. . . . These crossovers are neither distracting nor accidental. . . . Ellen Gilchrist is only changing costumes, and she can 'do wonderful tricks with her voice.'" *Drunk with Love,* published in 1987, and *Light Can be Both Wave and Particle,* released two years later, expanded the author's exploration of her characters' many facets. While continuing to praise her voice, critics have found Gilchrist's later work to be of a more "uneven" quality than her early writing. Reviewing the volume in the *Chicago Tribune,* Greg Johnson noted that Gilchrist "seems to get carried away with her breezy style and verbal facility. The stories read quickly and are often enjoyable, but they lack the thought and craft that make for memorable fiction." However, Roy Hoffman praised the book in the *New York Times Book Review* as full of "new energy" and noted of the title story that "it brings together lovers from different cultures more spiritedly than any past Gilchrist story."

Indeed, the "voice" and characters that Gilchrist employs throughout her fiction are the hallmarks of her work. David Sexton remarked of her voice in a *Times Literary Supplement* review of *Victory over Japan* that it had its roots in the "talk of the Mississippi Delta," adding that "the drawly 'whyyyyy not' world of the modern South which she creates is a great pleasure to visit." Equally important within her prose are the characters who appear time and time again throughout her writing. "Without much authorial manicuring or explanation, [Gilchrist] allows her characters to emerge whole, in full possession of their considerable stores of eccentricities and passion," commented reviewer Lowry. The central characters in her works are usually women; whether they are young, as in *The Land of Dreamy Dreams,* or more mature, they are usually spirited, spoiled, and fighting their way out of poverty or out of a bad relationship. "Ms. Gilchrist's women . . . are unconventional, nervy, outspoken," noted Hoffman. "As grown-ups they are passionate to the point of recklessness, romantic in the midst of despair. As youngsters they vex adults."

Eight of the sixteen short stories in *The Age of Miracles,* a collection published in 1995, feature Rhoda Manning, a familiar character who appeared as a child in *Victory over Japan* and as a wife and mother in *Net of Jewels.* In this collection Gilchrist portrays Rhoda as a divorced and matured writer in midlife with failed relationships and drinking problems behind. Julia Glass observed in a *Chicago Tribune* review, "As always, [Rhoda's] adventures are brazen and self-indulgent, seedy yet oddly heroic." In one story, "A Statue of Aphrodite," Gilchrist describes a burgeoning romance between Rhoda and a wealthy doctor who attempts to persuade Rhoda to accompany him to his daughter's wedding dressed in a prim Laura Ashley dress. Though noting that this collection is not Gilchrist's best, Bharat Tandon wrote in a *Times Literary Supplement* review, "there are in this new collection moments of more profound and graceful achievement than she has shown before." While critical of Rhoda's overbearing personae and tendency toward irrelevance, critics praised Gilchrist for several pieces that do not include her character. In "Madison at 69th, a Fable," Gilchrist describes how a woman's facelift is averted when her children kidnap her and talk her out of the procedure. Glass commented that the story is "a wholly original comedy that enfolds a dark tangle of fears and betrayed obligations," highlighted by the mother's wish to regain youth while her children revolt against novelty. Diane Cole concluded in the *New York Times Book Review,* "at her best [Gilchrist] blends a sense of poignancy with an often outrageously Gothic humor."

In 1983, Gilchrist's first novel, *The Annunciation,* was published. It recounts the life of Amanda McCarney, from her childhood on a Mississippi Delta plantation where she falls in love with and, at the age of fourteen, has a child by her cousin Guy, to her marriage to a wealthy New Orleans man and a life of high society and heavy drinking. Eventually rejecting this lifestyle, Amanda returns to school where she discovers a gift for languages that has lain dormant during the forty-some years of her life and is offered the chance to translate the rediscovered poetry of an eighteenth-century Frenchwoman. She divorces her husband and moves to a university town in Arkansas to pursue her translating where, in addition to her work, Amanda finds love and friendship among a commune of hippie-type poets and philosophers in the Ozarks. *The Annunciation* received mixed reviews from critics. Yardley, critiquing the book in the *Washington Post Book World,* asserted that for most of its length "*The Annunciation* is a complex, interesting, occasionally startling novel; but as soon as Gilchrist moves Amanda away from the conflicts and discontents of New Orleans, the book falls to pieces." Yardley agreed, noting that once Amanda moves to the Ozarks *The Annunciation* "loses its toughness and irony. Amid the potters and the professors and the philosopher-poets of the Ozarks, Amanda McCarney turns into mush." However Frances Taliaferro, reviewing *The Annunciation* in *Harper's,* deemed Gilchrist's novel "'women's fiction' par excellence" and described the book as "a cheerful hodgepodge of the social and psychological fashions of the past three decades." Taliaferro explained that "Amanda is in some ways a receptacle for current romantic cliches, but she is also a vivid character of dash and humor . . . . Even a skeptical reader pays her the compliment of wondering what she will do next in this surprisingly likable novel." Taliaferro concluded that, despite some tragedy, the "presiding spirit of this novel is self-realization, and Amanda [in the end] has at last made her way to autonomy."

Gilchrist has gone on to write several more books in the novel or novella genre. *The Anna Papers* takes as its start the short story "Anna, Part I" that concluded *Drunk with Love.* Published in 1988, the novel begins with the suicide of 43-year-old Anna Hand, who decides to conclude her life after being diagnosed with cancer. The work deals with the aftermath of her death as family and friends are left to the influence of Anna's legacy; the recollection of her full and joyous, yet unconventional, life. Although the critical reception of the novel was mixed, *The Anna Papers* was praised for both the quality of its prose and the complexity of Gilchrist's fictional characters. Ann Vliet ascribed to its author "a stubborn dedication to the uncovering of human irony, a tendency, despite temptations toward glamour and comfort, to opt for the harder path, often using 'poorly disguised' autobiographical fiction, usually the short story, to dredge up the order in messy human relationships" in a review in the *Washington Post Book World. I Cannot Get You Close Enough,* published in 1991, is a continuation of

*The Anna Papers* in the form of three novellas, each taking as its focus one of the characters of the previous book. Ilene Raymond of the *Washington Post Book World* praised the work. "Not since J. D. Salinger's Glass family has a writer lavished so much loving attention on the eccentricities and activities of an extended clan," Raymond commented, adding that the novellas were not "easy tales, but stories rich with acrimony, wisdom, courage and, finally, joy."

In *Starcarbon: A Meditation of Love,* Gilchrist returns to the Hand family of North Carolina, whose various members appeared in *The Anna Papers, I Cannot Get You Close Enough* and *Net of Jewels.* Prefaced by an extensive genealogical chart that includes some forty-five names, the novel recounts the summer excursions of several members, including Olivia de Havilland Hand, a half-Cherokee college freshman who visits her maternal grandparents in Oklahoma; Jessie, her half-sister who prepares for the birth of her first child in New Orleans; their Aunt Helen, who leaves her marriage and children to pursue an Irish poet in Boston; and Daniel, brother of Helen and wealthy father of Olivia and Jessie, who remains in North Carolina to wallow in midlife crisis and drink. "Ellen Gilchrist's writing tumbles and spills off the page, seemingly without effort, like a voluble cousin breathlessly bringing you up to date on the liaisons and adventures of various members of a sprawling family," wrote *Chicago Tribune* reviewer Victoria Jenkins. Offering tempered praise, Trev Broughton commented in the *Times Literary Supplement,* "The novel's ageing roues and their gold-digging mistresses, the psychiatrists, even the horses are crisply drawn." *Kirkus Reviews* noted that "*Starcarbon* is soap at its most elegant." Sarah Ferguson concluded in the *New York Times Book Review,* "Ms. Gilchrist has blended these resolutely individual voices to create a richly textured family fugue."

With *Anabasis: A Journey to the Interior* Gilchrist ventures away from the Deep South to create a novel set in ancient Greece during the Peloponnesian War (431-404 B.C.). Inspired by the storytelling of her mother, Gilchrist conceived this book about a literate Greek slave girl as a child. The main character, an orphaned slave named Auria, receives an early education from renowned healer Philokrates, then escapes her cruel master, adopts his abandoned newborn daughter, and joins a band of runaway slaves who retreat into the mountains to plot rebellion. Among the rebels, Auria finds love and marries Meion, the grandnephew of Pericles, and plies her skills as healer and teacher. A *Publishers Weekly* review described the work as a "richly textured but overly idealized historical novel." Similarly critical of the novel's improbable plot, Margaret A. Robinson noted in the *New York Times Book Review,* "Such fiction demands suspension of disbelief, and Auria, an appealing heroine, often makes that faith possible."

Gilchrist explained to Wendy Smith her evolution from short-story writer to novelist in an interview for *Publishers Weekly:* "The thing about the short story form is that in order to do a good job with it you've got to concentrate on no more than two characters; you've got to pretend that nobody has any children or parents." The novel provides her with a larger canvas on which to set forth her fictional world. "I think that in order to serve the vision I currently have of reality, I'm going to have to have at least five or six characters interplaying," she noted. However, Gilchrist has found that the novel format presents its own set of problems. As she told Walker, "You can't go back to the easy fix you learn as a short story writer, where you kill somebody off or get somebody laid to create a climax. What I'm trying to do now is make a study of existence—that's the high ground, but I perceive it as that. I want it to be as true to what I know about human beings as it can be." Commenting on her novel, *Net of Jewels,* Gilchrist explained that the more she writes about a character in a short story or a novel, the more she discovers about that character. She decided to "serve that knowledge" in *Net of Jewels,* an account of character Rhoda Manning's emotional growth in college and beyond, as her young protagonist becomes involved with a succession of other characters through situations that influence her, sometimes indulge her innate willfulness, and shape her personality. "This is the difference between writing novels and writing short stories," commented Gilchrist, "there aren't any tricks."

In 1987 Gilchrist published *Falling through Space,* a collection of brief journal excerpts. Originally intended as segments of her National Public Radio commentary, the book's segments reflect the life of a working writer. "I write to learn and to amuse myself and out of joy and because of mystery and in praise of everything that moves, breathes, gives, partakes, is," Gilchrist once told *CA.* "I like the feel of words in my mouth and the sound of them in my ears and the creation of them with my hands. If that sounds like a lot of talk, it is. What are we doing here anyway, all made out of stars and talking about everything and telling everything? The more one writes the clearer it all becomes and the simpler and more divine. A friend once wrote to me and ended the letter by saying: 'Dance in the fullness of time.' I write that in the books I sign. It may be all anyone needs to read."

Critics have repeatedly praised Gilchrist for her subtle perception, unique characters, and sure command of her writer's voice. Yardley remarked of *In the Land of Dreamy Dreams,* "Certainly it is easy to see why reviewers and readers have responded so strongly to Gilchrist; she tells home truths in these stories, and she tells them with style." Crace concluded that her "stories are perceptive, her manner is both stylish and idiomatic—a rare and potent combination." Miranda Seymour, reviewing her first short story collection for the London *Times,* noted that "Gilchrist's stories are elegant little tragedies, memorable and cruel" and compared her writing to that of fellow southerners Carson McCullers and Tennessee Williams in that all three writers share "the curious gift for presenting characters as objects for pity and affection." And Wood observed: "Even the least attractive characters become known to us, and therefore human, because Gilchrist's voice is so sure, her tone so right, her details so apt."

*BIOGRAPHICAL/CRITICAL SOURCES:*

*BOOKS*

*Contemporary Literary Criticism,* Gale, Volume 34, 1985, Volume 48, 1988, pp. 114-22.

*PERIODICALS*

*Booklist,* January 15, 1994; September 1, 1994.
*Chicago Tribune,* October 14, 1986; October 9, 1987; October 2, 1988; October 1, 1989; May 22, 1994; June 11, 1995.
*Harper's,* June, 1985.
*Kirkus Reviews,* February 15, 1994, p. 162; July 1, 1994, p. 867.
*Library Journal,* March 1, 1994; August, 1994, p. 128.
*Listener,* January 6, 1983.
*Los Angeles Times Book Review,* September 14, 1986; November 27, 1988.
*Ms.,* June, 1985.
*New Statesman,* March 16, 1984.
*Newsweek,* January 14, 1985; February 18, 1985.
*New Yorker,* November 19, 1984.
*New York Times Book Review,* September 23, 1984; October 5, 1986; January 3, 1988; January 15, 1989; October 22, 1989; November 4, 1990; October 13, 1991; April 12, 1992; June 19, 1994, p. 33; October 30, 1994, p. 48; May 21, 1995.
*Observer,* November 24, 1991.
*Publishers Weekly,* March 2, 1992; January 31, 1994; August 8, 1994, p. 382.
*Times* (London), November 25, 1982; June 7, 1990; November 21, 1991.
*Times Literary Supplement,* October 15, 1982; April 6, 1984; May 24, 1985; March 6, 1987; October 27, 1989; November 29, 1991; September 7, 1990; July 1, 1994, p. 21; October 20, 1995, p. 23.
*Vogue,* May, 1994, p. 184.
*Washington Post,* September 12, 1984; September 28, 1986; December 31, 1987; October 20, 1988; December 15, 1989.
*Washington Post Book World,* January 24, 1982; March 21, 1982; May 29, 1983; December 31, 1987; December 16, 1990; September 3, 1995, p. 6.*

* * *

**GILES, Kris**
**See NIELSEN, Helen Berniece**

* * *

**GORDON, Diana**
**See ANDREWS, Lucilla (Mathew)**

* * *

**GOYTISOLO, Juan 1931-**

*PERSONAL:* Born January 5, 1931, in Barcelona, Spain; immigrated to France, 1957. *Education:* Attended University of Barcelona and University of Madrid, 1948-52.

*CAREER:* Writer. Worked as reporter in Cuba, 1965; associated with Gallimard Publishing Co., France. Visiting professor at universities in the United States.

*AWARDS, HONORS:* Received numerous awards for *Juegos de Manos;* Premio Europalia, 1985.

*WRITINGS:*

*NOVELS*

*Juegos de manos,* Destino, 1954, recent edition, 1975, translation by John Rust published as *The Young Assassins,* Knopf, 1959.

*Duelo en el paraiso,* Planeta, 1955, Destino, 1981, translation by Christine Brooke-Rose published as *Children of Chaos,* Macgibbon & Kee, 1958.

*El circo* (title means "The Circus"), Destino, 1957, recent edition, 1982.

*Fiestas,* Emece, 1958, Destino, 1981, translation by Herbert Weinstock published as *Fiestas,* Knopf, 1960.

*La resaca* (title means "The Undertow"), Club del Libro Espanol, 1958, J. Mortiz, 1977.

*La isla,* Seix Barral, 1961, reprinted, 1982, translation by Jose Yglesias published as *Island of Women,* Knopf, 1962 (published in England as *Sands of Torremolinos,* J. Cape, 1962).

*Senas de identidad,* J. Mortiz, 1966, translation by Gregory Rabassa published as *Marks of Identity,* Grove, 1969.

*Reivindicacion del Conde don Julian,* J. Mortiz, 1970, Catedra, 1985, translation by Helen R. Lane published as *Count Julian,* Viking, 1974.

*Juan sin tierra,* Seix Barral, 1975, translation by Lane published as *Juan the Landless,* Viking, 1977.

*Makbara,* Seix Barral, 1980, translation by Lane published as *Makbara,* Seaver Books, 1981.

*Paisajes despues de la batalla,* Montesinos, 1982, translation by Lane published as *Landscapes after the Battle,* Seaver Books, 1987.

*Quarantine,* translated by Peter Bush, Dalkey Archive Press, 1994.

Also author of novels *Las virtudes del parajo solitario,* 1988, published as *The Virtues of the Solitary Bird,* 1993; and *La cuarentena,* 1991.

*SHORT STORIES*

*Para vivir aqui* (title means "To Live Here"), Sur, 1960, Bruguera, 1983.

*Fin de fiesta: Tentativas de interpretacion de una historia amorosa,* Seix Barral, 1962, translation by Yglesias published as *The Party's Over: Four Attempts to Define a Love Story,* Weidenfeld & Nicolson, 1966, Grove, 1967.

*TRAVEL NARRATIVES*

*Campos de Nijar,* Seix Barral, 1960, Grant & Cutler, 1984, translation by Luigi Luccarelli published as *The Countryside of Nijar* in *The Countryside of Nijar* [and] *La chanca,* Alembic Press, 1987.

*La Chanca,* Libreria Espanola, 1962, Seix Barral, 1983, translation by Luccarelli published in *The Countryside of Nijar* [and] *La chanca,* Alembic Press, 1987.

*Pueblo en marcha: Instantaneas de un viaje a Cuba* (title means "People on the March: Snapshots of a Trip to Cuba"), Libreria Espanola, 1963.

*Cronicas sarracinas* (title means "Saracen Chronicles"), Iberica, 1982.

*OTHER*

*Problemas de la novela* (literary criticism; title means "Problems of the Novel"), Seix Barral, 1959.

*Las mismas palabras,* Seix Barral, 1963.

*Plume d'hier: Espagne d'aujourd'hui,* compiled by Mariano Jose de Larra, Editeurs francais reunis, 1965.

*El furgon de cola* (critical essays; title means "The Caboose"), Ruedo Iberico, 1967, Seix Barral, 1982.

*Spanien und die Spanien,* M. Bucher, 1969.

(Author of prologue) Jose Maria Blanco White, *Obra inglesa,* Formentor, 1972.

*Obras completas* (title means "Complete Works"), Aguilar, 1977.

*Libertad, libertad, libertad* (essays and speeches), Anagrama, 1978.

(Author of introduction) Chukri, Mohamed, *El pan desnudo* (title means For Bread Alone), translation from Arabic by Abdellah Djibilou, Montesinos, 1982.

*Coto vedado* (autobiography), Seix Barral, 1985, translation by Peter Bush published as *Forbidden Territory: The Memoirs of Juan Goytisolo,* North Point Press, 1989.

(Author of commentary) Omar Khayyam, *Estances,* translation into Catalan by Ramon Vives Pastor, del Mall, 1985.

*Contracorrientes,* Montesinos, 1985.

*En los reinos de taifa* (autobiography; title means "Realms of Strife: The Memoirs of Juan Goytisolo, 1956-1982"), Seix Barral, 1986.

*Space in Motion* (essays), translation by Lane, Lumen Books, 1987.

Also author of *Disidencias* (essays), 1977. Work represented in collections and anthologies, including *Juan Goytisolo,* Ministerio de Cultura, Direccion General de Promocion del Libro y la Cinematografia, 1982. Contributor to periodicals.

*SIDELIGHTS:* "Juan Goytisolo is the best living Spanish novelist," wrote John Butt in the *Times Literary Supplement.* The author, as Butt observed, became renowned as a "pitiless satirist" of Spanish society during the dictatorship of Francisco Franco, who imposed his version of conservative religious values on the country from the late 1930s until his death in 1975. Goytisolo, whose youth coincided with the rise of Franco, had a variety of compelling reasons to feel alienated from his own country. He was a small child when his mother was killed in a bombing raid, a casualty of the civil war that Franco instigated to seize power from a democratically elected government. The author then grew up as a bisexual in a country dominated, in Butt's words, by "frantic machismo." Eventually, said Goytisolo in his memoir *Coto Vedado* (*Forbidden Territory*), he became "that strange species of writer claimed by none and alien and hostile to groups and categories." In the late 1950s, when his writing career began to flourish, he left Spain for Paris and remained in self-imposed exile until after Franco died.

The literary world was greatly impressed when Goytisolo's first novel, *Juegos de manos* (*The Young Assassins*), was published in 1954. David Dempsey found that it "begins where the novels of a writer like Jack Kerouac leave off." Goytisolo was identified as a member of the Spanish "restless generation" but his first novel seemed as much akin to Fedor Dostoevski as it did to Kerouac. The plot is similar to Dostoevski's *The Possessed:* a group of students plot the murder of a politician but end up murdering the fellow student chosen to kill the politician. Dempsey wrote, "Apparently, he is concerned with showing us how self-destructive and yet how inevitable this hedonism becomes in a society dominated by the smug and self-righteous."

*Duelo en el paraiso* (*Children of Chaos*) was seen as a violent extension of *The Young Assassins.* Like Anthony Burgess's *A Clockwork Orange* and William Golding's *Lord of the Flies, Children of Chaos* focuses on the terror wrought by adolescents. The children have taken over a small town after the end of the Spanish Civil War causes a breakdown of order.

*Fiestas* begins a trilogy referred to as "The Ephemeral Morrow" (after a famous poem by Antonio Machado). Considered the best volume of the trilogy, it follows four characters as they try to escape life in Spain by chasing their dreams. Each character meets with disappointment in the novel's end. Ramon Sender called *Fiestas* "a brilliant projection of the contrast between Spanish official and real life," and concluded that Goytisolo "is without doubt the best of the young Spanish writers."

*El circo*, the second book in "The Ephemeral Morrow," was too blatantly ironic to succeed as a follow-up to *Fiestas.* It is the story of a painter who manages a fraud before being punished for a murder he didn't commit. The third book, *La resaca*, was also a disappointment. The novel's style was considered too realistic to function as a fitting conclusion to "The Ephemeral Morrow."

After writing two politically oriented travelogues, *Campos de Nijar* (*The Countryside of Nijar*) and *La Chanca,* Goytisolo returned to fiction and the overt realism he'd begun in *La resaca.* Unfortunately, critics implied that both *La isla* (*Island of Women*) and *Fin de Fiesta* (*The Party's Over*) suffered because they ultimately resembled their subject matter. *The Party's Over* contains four stories about the problems of marriage. Although Alexander Coleman found that the "stories are more meditative than the full-length novels," he also observed, "But it is, in the end, a small world, limited by the overwhelming ennui of everything and everyone in it." Similarly, Honor Tracy noted, "Every gesture of theirs reveals the essence of the world, they're absolutely necessary, says another: we intellectuals operate in a vacuum. . . . Everything ends in their all being fed up."

Goytisolo abandoned his realist style after *The Party's Over.* In *Senas de identidad* (*Marks of Identity*), wrote Barbara Probst Solomon, "Goytisolo begins to do a variety of things. Obvious political statement, he feels, is not enough for a novel; he starts to break with form—using a variety of first, second and third persons, he is looking and listening to the breaks in language and. . . he begins to break with form—in the attempt to describe what he is really seeing and feeling, his work becomes less abstract." Robert J. Clements called *Marks of Identity* "probably his most personal novel," but also felt that the "most inevitable theme is of course the police state of Spain." Fusing experimentation with a firm political stance, Goytisolo reminded some critics of James Joyce while others saw him elaborating his realist style to further embellish his own sense of politics.

*Reivindicacion del Conde don Julian* (*Count Julian*), Goytisolo's next novel, is widely considered to be his masterpiece. In it, he uses techniques borrowed from Joyce, Celine, Jean Genet, filmmaker Luis Bunuel, and Pablo Picasso. Solomon remarked that, while some of these techniques proved less than effective in many of the French novels of the 1960s, "in the hands of this Spanish novelist, raging against Spain, the results are explosive." *Count Julian* is named for a legendary Spanish nobleman who betrayed his country to Arab invaders in the Middle Ages. In the shocking fantasies of the novel's narrator, a modern Spaniard living as an outcast in Africa, Julian returns to punish Spain for its cruelty and hypocrisy. Over the course of the narration, the Spanish language itself gradually transforms into Arabic. Writing in the *New York Times Book Review,* Carlos Fuentes called *Count Julian* "an adventure of language, a critical battle against the language appropriated by power in Spain. It is also a search for a new/old language that would offer an alternative for the future."

With the publication of *Juan sin tierra* (*Juan the Landless*), critics began to see Goytisolo's last three novels as a second trilogy. However, reviews were generally less favorable than those for either *Marks of Identity* or *Count Julian.* Anatole Broyard, calling attention to Goytisolo's obsession with sadistic sex and defecation, remarked, "Don Quixote no longer tilts at windmills, but toilets." A writer for *Atlantic* suggested that the uninformed reader begin elsewhere with Goytisolo.

Even after the oppressive Franco regime was dismantled in the late 1970s, Goytisolo continued to write novels that expressed deep alienation by displaying an unconventional, disorienting view of human society. *Makbara,* for example, is named for the cemeteries of North Africa where lovers meet for late-night trysts. "What a poignant central image it is," wrote Paul West in *Washington Post Book World,* "not only as an emblem of life in death. . . but also as a vantage point from which to review the human antic in general, which includes all those who go about their daily chores with their minds below their belts." "The people [Goytisolo] feels at home with," West declared, "are the drop-outs and the ne'er do wells, the outcasts and the misfits." In *Paisajes despues de la batalla* (*Landscapes after the Battle*), the author moved his vision of alienation to Paris, where he had long remained in exile. This short novel, made up of seventy-eight nonsequential chapters, displays the chaotic mix of people—from French nationalists to Arab immigrants—who uneasily coexist in the city. "The Paris metro map which the protagonist contemplates. . . for all its innumerable permutations of routes," wrote Abigail Lee in the *Times Literary Supplement,* "provides an apt image for the text itself." *Landscapes* "looked like another repudiation, this time of Paris," Butt wrote. "One wondered what Goytisolo would destroy next."

Accordingly, Butt was surprised to find that the author's memoir of his youth, published in 1985, had a markedly warmer tone than the novels that had preceded it. "Far from being a new repudiation," Butt observed, *Forbidden Territory* "is really an essay in acceptance and understanding. . . . Gone, almost, are the tortuous language, the lurid fantasies, the dreams of violation and abuse. Instead, we are given a moving, confessional account of a difficult childhood and adolescence." Goytisolo's recollections, the reviewer concluded, constitute "a moving and sympathetic story of how one courageous victim of the Franco regime fought his way out of a cultural and intellectual wasteland, educated himself, and went on to inflict a brilliant revenge on the social system which so isolated and insulted him."

In *The Virtues of the Solitary Bird* Goytisolo explores the Christian, Jewish, and Moorish heritage of Spain and the hybrid mysticism that emerged from the intermingling of the three religions, particularly as expressed in the writings of Saint John of the Cross and Arabian poet Ibn al Farid. Goytisolo juxtaposes the persecution of Saint John with a contemporary narrator who entertains imaginary conversations with the sixteenth century saint while living in exile and suffering from AIDS. Mirroring the author's own political oppression and departure from Franco's Spain, the book "is also the story of the independent thinker throughout history, flushed out by those fearful of 'contaminating ideas,'" observed a *Publishers Weekly* reviewer. Jack Byrne noted in the *Review of Contemporary Fiction* that Goytisolo's version of the martyred saint's verse "modernize[s], while not sanitizing, the horror of heresy—theological, political, social, moral—wherever and whenever it appears." Amanda Hopkinson wrote in the *Times Literary Supplement,* "Goytisolo expects to be read as a parable of our time, with all its complexities and obscurities. This is not prose, at least as conventionally punctuated, it is poetry full of rhapsodic psalms and oriental mysticism."

*Quarantine,* another complex, experimental novel, follows the spiritual wandering of a recently deceased female writer whose soul, according to Islamic tradition, must embark on a forty day journey to eternal rest. Through an unnamed narrator, Goytisolo likens the spiritual quarantine to the creative writing process, whereby an author remains in isolation for a time to summon memory and the imagination. In effect, the fictional author's meditations on death and writing become the story itself as he imagines his own death, encounters the soul of his dead friend among angels and a Sufi mystic, and considers parallels to Dante's *Divine Comedy*. Jack Shreve noted in a *Library Journal* review that Goytisolo "multiplies levels of interpretation in order to 'destabilize' the reader." Goytisolo also interjects a strong antiwar theme through surreal news reports that describe the carnage of the Persian Gulf War.

*BIOGRAPHICAL/CRITICAL SOURCES:*

*BOOKS*

Amell, Samuel, editor, *Literature, the Arts, and Democracy: Spain in the Eighties,* Fairleigh Dickinson University Press, 1990.
*Contemporary Literary Criticism,* Gale, Volume 5, 1976, Volume 10, 1979, Volume 23, 1983.
Epps, Bradley S., *Significant Violence: Oppression and Resistance in the Later Narrative of Juan Goytisolo,* Clarendon (New York City), 1996.
Gazarian Gautier, Marie-Lise, *Interviews with Spanish Writers,* Dalkey Archive Press, 1991.
Goytisolo, Juan, *Forbidden Territory,* translation by Peter Bush, North Point Press, 1989.
Pope, Randolph D., *Understanding Juan Goytisolo,* University of South Carolina Press (Columbia), 1995.
Schwartz, Kessel, *Juan Goytisolo,* Twayne, 1970.
Schwartz, Ronald, *Spain's New Wave Novelists 1950-1974: Studies in Spanish Realism,* Scarecrow Press, 1976.

*PERIODICALS*

*Atlantic,* August, 1977.
*Best Sellers,* June 15, 1974.
*Journal of Spanish Studies,* winter, 1979, pp. 353-364.
*Kirkus Reviews,* March 1, 1994, p. 234.
*Lettres Peninsulares,* fall-winter, 1990, pp. 259-278.
*Library Journal,* October 1, 1990, p. 89; March 1, 1994, p. 117.
*Los Angeles Times Book Review,* January 22, 1989.
*Nation,* March 1, 1975.
*New Republic,* January 31, 1967.
*New Statesman & Society,* July 19, 1991, p. 38; December 17, 1993, p. 46.
*New York Times Book Review,* January 22, 1967; May 5, 1974; September 18, 1977; June 14, 1987; July 3, 1988; February 12, 1989.
*Publishers Weekly,* November 30, 1992, p. 48; March 7, 1994, p. 55.
*Review of Contemporary Fiction,* fall, 1993, p. 213.
*Saturday Review,* February 14, 1959; June 11, 1960; June 28, 1969.
*Texas Quarterly,* spring, 1975.
*Times Literary Supplement,* May 31, 1985; September 9, 1988; May 19, 1989; November 17, 1989; July 12, 1991, p. 18.
*Washington Post Book World,* January 17, 1982; June 14, 1987.
*World Press Review,* April, 1994. p. 51.*

* * *

**GRANT, Ambrose**
**See RAYMOND, Rene (Brabazon)**

* * *

**GREENE, Graham (Henry) 1904-1991**

*PERSONAL:* Born October 2, 1904, in Berkhamsted, Hertfordshire, England; died of a blood disease, April 3, 1991, in Vevey, Switzerland; son of Charles Henry (headmaster of Berkhamsted School) and Marion Raymond Greene; married Vivien Dayrell Browning, 1927; children: one son, one daughter. *Education:* Attended Berkhamsted School; Balliol College, Oxford, B.A., 1925. *Religion:* Catholic convert, 1926.

*CAREER:* Writer. *Times,* London, England, sub-editor, 1926-30; film critic for *Night and Day* during the 1930s; *Spectator,* London, England, film critic, 1935-39, literary editor, 1940-41; with Foreign Office in Africa, 1941-44; Eyre & Spottiswoode Ltd. (publishers), London, England, director, 1944-48; Indo-China correspondent for *New Republic,* 1954; Bodley Head (publishers), London, England, director, 1958-68. Member of Panamanian delegation to Washington for signing of Canal Treaty, 1977.

*AWARDS, HONORS:* Hawthornden Prize, 1940, for *The Labyrinthine Ways* (published in England as *The Power and the Glory*); James Tait Black Memorial Prize, 1949, for *The Heart of the Matter;* Catholic Literary Award, 1952, for *The End of the Affair;* Boys' Clubs of America Junior Book Award, 1955, for *The Little Horse Bus;* Pietzak Award (Poland), 1960; D.Litt., Cambridge University, 1962; Balliol

College, Oxford, honorary fellow, 1963; Companion of Honour, 1966; D.Litt., University of Edinburgh, 1967; Shakespeare Prize, 1968; Legion d'Honneur, chevalier, 1969; John Dos Passos Prize, 1980; medal of the city of Madrid, 1980; Jerusalem Prize, 1981; Grand Cross of the Order of Vasco Nunez de Balboa (Panama), 1983; named commander of the Order of Arts and Letters (France), 1984; named to British Order of Merit, 1986; named to the Order of Ruben Dario (Nicaragua), 1987; Royal Society of Literature Prize; honorary doctorate, Moscow State University, 1988.

*WRITINGS:*

FICTION, EXCEPT AS INDICATED

*Babbling April* (poems), Basil Blackwell, 1925.

*The Man Within,* Doubleday, 1929.

*The Name of Action,* Heinemann, 1930, Doubleday, 1931.

*Rumour at Nightfall,* Heinemann, 1931, Doubleday, 1932.

*Orient Express,* Doubleday, 1932 (published in England as *Stamboul Train,* Heinemann, 1932).

*It's a Battlefield,* Doubleday, 1934, reprinted with new introduction by author, Heinemann, 1970.

*The Basement Room, and Other Stories,* Cresset, 1935, title story revised as "The Fallen Idol" and published with *The Third Man* (also see below), Heinemann, 1950.

*England Made Me,* Doubleday, 1935, published as *The Shipwrecked,* Viking, 1953, reprinted under original title with new introduction by author, Heinemann, 1970.

*The Bear Fell Free,* Grayson & Grayson, 1935.

*Journey without Maps* (travelogue; also see below), Doubleday, 1936, 2nd edition, Viking, 1961.

*This Gun for Hire,* Doubleday, 1936 (also see below; published in England as *A Gun for Sale,* Heinemann, 1936).

*Brighton Rock,* Viking, 1938, reprinted with new introduction by author, Heinemann, 1970, reprinted, 1981.

*The Confidential Agent* (also see below), Viking, 1939, reprinted with new introduction by author, Heinemann, 1971.

*Another Mexico,* Viking, 1939, reprinted, 1982 (published in England as *The Lawless Roads,* Longmans, Green, 1939; also see below).

*The Labyrinthine Ways,* Viking, 1940 (published in England as *The Power and the Glory,* Heinemann, 1940), reprinted under British title, Viking, 1946, reprinted under British title with new introduction by author, Heinemann, 1971, reprinted, Viking, 1982.

*British Dramatists* (nonfiction), Collins, 1942, reprinted, Folcroft, 1979.

*The Ministry of Fear* (also see below), Viking, 1943.

*Nineteen Stories,* Heinemann, 1947, Viking, 1949, later published with some substitutions and additions as *Twenty-one Stories,* Heinemann, 1955, Viking, 1962.

*The Heart of the Matter,* Viking, 1948, reprinted with new introduction by author, Heinemann, 1971.

*The Third Man* (also see below), Viking, 1950, reprinted, 1983.

*The Lost Childhood, and Other Essays,* Eyre & Spottiswoode, 1951, Viking, 1952.

*The End of the Affair,* Viking, 1951.

*The Living Room* (two-act play; produced in London, 1953), Heinemann, 1953, Viking, 1957.

*The Quiet American,* Heinemann, 1955, reprinted, Viking, 1982.

*Loser Takes All,* Heinemann, 1955, Viking, 1957.

*The Potting Shed* (three-act play; produced in New York, 1957, and in London, 1958), Viking, 1957.

*Our Man in Havana* (also see below), Viking, 1958, reprinted with new introduction by author, Heinemann, 1970.

*The Complaisant Lover* (play; produced in London, 1959), Heinemann, 1959, Viking, 1961.

*A Burnt-Out Case,* Viking, 1961.

*In Search of a Character: Two African Journals,* Bodley Head, 1961, Viking, 1962.

*Introductions to Three Novels,* Norstedt (Stockholm), 1962.

*The Destructors, and Other Stories,* Eihosha Ltd. (Japan), 1962.

*A Sense of Reality,* Viking, 1963.

*Carving a Statue* (two-act play; produced in London, 1964, and in New York, 1968), Bodley Head, 1964.

*The Comedians,* Viking, 1966.

(With Dorothy Craigie) *Victorian Detective Fiction: A Catalogue of the Collection,* Bodley Head, 1966.

*May We Borrow Your Husband?, and Other Comedies of the Sexual Life,* Viking, 1967.

(With Carol Reed) *The Third Man: A Film* (annotated filmscript), Simon & Schuster, 1968.

*Collected Essays,* Viking, 1969.

*Travels with My Aunt,* Viking, 1969.

(Author of introduction) Al Burt and Bernard Diederich, *Papa Doc,* McGraw, 1969.

*A Sort of Life* (autobiography), Simon & Schuster, 1971.

*Graham Greene on Film: Collected Film Criticism, 1935-1940,* Simon & Schuster, 1972 (published in

England as *The Pleasure Dome,* Secker & Warburg, 1972).

*The Portable Graham Greene* (includes *The Heart of the Matter,* with a new chapter; *The Third Man;* and sections from eight other novels, six short stories, nine critical essays, and ten public statements), Viking, 1972, updated and revised, Penguin (New York City), 1994.

*The Honorary Consul,* Simon & Schuster, 1973.

*Collected Stories,* Viking, 1973.

*Lord Rochester's Monkey, Being the Life of John Wilmot, Second Earl of Rochester,* Viking, 1974.

*The Return of A. J. Raffles* (three-act comedy based on characters from E. W. Hornung's *Amateur Cracksman;* produced in London, 1975), Simon & Schuster, 1976.

*The Human Factor,* Simon & Schuster, 1978.

*Dr. Fischer of Geneva; or, The Bomb Party,* Simon & Schuster, 1980.

*Ways of Escape,* Simon & Schuster, 1981.

*Monsignor Quixote,* Simon & Schuster, 1982.

*J'accuse: The Dark Side of Nice,* Bodley Head, 1982.

*Yes and No* [and] *For Whom the Bell Chimes* (comedies; produced together in Leicester, England, at Haymarket Studio, March, 1980), Bodley Head, 1983.

*Getting to Know the General: The Story of an Involvement,* Simon & Schuster, 1984.

*The Tenth Man,* Bodley Head, 1985.

(Author of preface) *Night and Day* (selections from London periodical), edited by Christopher Hawtree, Chatto & Windus, 1985.

*Granta 17,* Penguin, 1986.

*Collected Short Stories,* Penguin, 1988.

*The Captain and the Enemy,* Viking, 1988.

*Yours, etc.: Letters to the Press, 1945-1989,* edited by Hawtree, Reinhardt, 1989.

*Reflections* (essays), Viking, 1990.

*The Graham Greene Film Reader: Reviews, Essays, Interviews & Film Stories,* Applause Theatre Book Publishers (New York City), 1994.

*A World of My Own: A Dream Diary,* Reinhardt (New York City), 1994.

*OMNIBUS VOLUMES*

*3: This Gun for Hire; The Confidential Agent; The Ministry of Fear,* Viking, 1952, reprinted as *Three by Graham Greene: This Gun for Hire; The Confidential Agent; The Ministry of Fear,* 1958.

*Three Plays,* Mercury Books, 1961.

*The Travel Books: Journey Without Maps* [and] *The Lawless Roads,* Heinemann, 1963.

*Triple Pursuit: A Graham Greene Omnibus* (includes *This Gun for Hire, The Third Man,* and *Our Man in Havana*), Viking, 1971.

Works also published in additional collections.

*JUVENILE*

*This Little Fire Engine,* Parrish, 1950, published as *The Little Red Fire Engine,* Lothrop, Lee & Shepard, 1952.

*The Little Horse Bus,* Parrish, 1952, Lothrop, Lee & Shepard, 1954.

*The Little Steamroller,* Lothrop, Lee & Shepard, 1955.

*The Little Train,* Parrish, 1957, Lothrop, Lee & Shepard, 1958.

*EDITOR*

*The Old School* (essays), J. Cape, 1934.

H. H. Munro, *The Best of Saki,* 2nd edition, Lane, 1952.

(With brother, Hugh Greene) *The Spy's Bedside Book,* British Book Service, 1957.

(Author of introduction) Marjorie Bowen, *The Viper of Milan,* Bodley Head, 1960.

*The Bodly Head Ford Madox Ford,* Volumes 1 and 2, Bodley Head, 1962.

(And author of epilogue) *An Impossible Woman: The Memories of Dottoressa, Moor of Capri,* Viking, 1976.

(With brother, Hugh Greene) *Victorian Villainies,* Viking, 1984.

*CONTRIBUTOR*

*24 Short Stories,* Cresset, 1939.

*Alfred Hitchcock's Fireside Book of Suspense,* Simon & Schuster, 1947.

*Why Do I Write?,* Percival Marshall, 1948.

Contributor to *Esquire, Commonweal, Spectator, Playboy, Saturday Evening Post, New Statesman, Atlantic, London Mercury, New Republic, America, Life,* and other publications.

*ADAPTATIONS:* Screenplays based on his books and stories: *Orient Express,* 1934; *This Gun for Hire,* 1942; *The Ministry of Fear,* 1944; *The Confidential Agent,* 1945; *Brighton Rock,* screenplay by Greene and Terrence Rattigan, 1947; *The Smugglers,* 1948; *The Fallen Idol* (based on Greene's 1935 short story

"The Basement Room"), screenplay by Greene, 1949; *The Third Man,* screenplay by Greene, 1950; *The Heart of the Matter,* 1954; *The End of the Affair,* 1955; *Loser Takes All,* 1957; *The Quiet American,* 1958; *Across the Bridge,* 1958; *Our Man in Havana,* screenplay by Greene, 1960; *The Power and the Glory,* 1962; *The Comedians,* screenplay by Greene, 1967; *The Living Room,* 1969; *The Shipwrecked,* 1970; *May We Borrow Your Husband?,* 1970; *The End of the Affair,* 1971; *Travels with My Aunt,* 1973; *England Made Me,* 1973; *A Burned-Out Case,* 1973; *The Human Factor,* screenplay by Tom Stoppard, directed by Otto Preminger, 1980; *Beyond the Limit,* 1983; *Strike It Rich* (based on Greene's 1955 novella *Loser Takes All*), 1990.

*SIDELIGHTS:* Graham Greene is among the most widely read of all major English novelists of the twentieth century. Yet Greene's popular success—which David Lodge in *Graham Greene* holds partly responsible for a "certain academic hostility" towards Greene—came neither quickly nor easily. Of Greene's initial five novels, the first two were never published; and two others, *The Name of Action* and *Rumour at Nightfall* sold very poorly and have never been reprinted. In his first autobiographical volume, *A Sort of Life,* Greene lamented that, in his earliest novels, he did not know "how to convey physical excitement:" the ability to write a "simple scene of action . . . was quite beyond my power to render exciting." Even as late as 1944, Greene confessed in his introduction to *The Tenth Man,* he had "no confidence" in sustaining his literary career.

Greene's string of literary failures drove him to write *Stamboul Train,* a thriller that Greene hoped would appeal to film producers. The novel, filmed two years later as *Orient Express,* is recognized by critics as Greene's coming-of-age work. Writing in a taut, realistic manner, Greene set *Stamboul Train* in contemporary Europe; gathered a train load of plausibly motivated characters; and sent them on their journey. Retaining such stock melodramatic devices as cloak-and-dagger intrigue, flight and pursuit, hair-breadth escapes, and a breakneck narrative pace, Greene shifted the focus away from the conventional hero—the hunter—and onto the villain and/or ostensible villain. What emerged was less a formula than a set of literary hardware that Greene would be able to use throughout the rest of his career, not just to produce further entertainments, but to help give outward excitement to his more morally centered, more philosophical novels.

*Stamboul Train* was the first of several thrillers Greene referred to as "entertainments"—so named to distinguish them from more serious novels. In his next two such entertainments, *A Gun for Sale* (published in the United States as *This Gun for Hire*) and *The Confidential Agent,* Greene incorporated elements of detective and spy fiction, respectively. He also injected significant doses of melodrama, detection, and espionage into his more serious novels *Brighton Rock, The Power and the Glory* (published in the United States as *The Labyrinthine Ways*),*The Heart of the Matter, The End of the Affair, The Quiet American, A Burnt-Out Case, The Comedians, The Honorary Consul,* and *The Human Factor.* Indeed, so greatly did Greene's entertainments influence his other novels that, after 1958, he dropped the entertainment label.

Intrigue and contemporary politics are key elements of Greene's entertainments. In at least two of his thrillers Greene eulogized the tranquility of European life before the First World War. "It was all so peaceful," Dr. Hasselbacher muses about Germany in *Our Man in Havana,* "in those days. . . . Until the war came." And Arthur Rowe, dreaming in *The Ministry of Fear,* notes that his mother, who "had died before the first great war, . . . could [not] have imagined" the blitz on London of the second. He tells his mother that the sweet Georgian twilight—"Tea on the lawn, evensong, croquet, the old ladies calling, the gentle unmalicious gossip, the gardener trundling the wheelbarrow full of leaves and grass"—"isn't real life any more." He continues: "I'm hiding underground, and up above the Germans are methodically smashing London to bits all round me. . . . It sounds like a thriller, doesn't it, but the thrillers are like life . . . spies, and murders, and violence . . . that's real life."

Suffering, seediness, and sin are also recurring motifs that typify the tone of Greene's work. When, in one of the very early novels Greene later disowned, a character moans, "I suffer, therefore I am," he defines both the plight and the habit of mind of many protagonists who would follow him. In *A Burnt-Out Case* Dr. Colin sees suffering as a humanizing force: "Sometimes I think that the search for suffering and the remembrance of suffering are the only means we have to put ourselves in touch with the whole human condition." And he adds—what none of Greene's other characters would dispute—"suffering is not so hard to find."

Greene's characters inhabit a world in which lasting love, according to the narrator of the story "May We

Borrow Your Husband?," means the acceptance of "every disappointment, every failure, every betrayal." By Greene's twenty-second novel, *Doctor Fischer of Geneva; or, The Bomb Party,* suffering had become a sufficient cause for having a soul. When the narrator of *Doctor Fischer* tells his wife, "If souls exist you certainly have one," and she asks "Why?," he replies, "You've suffered." This statement may well sound masochistic—"Pain is part of joy," the whiskey priest asserts in *The Power and the Glory,* "pain is a part of pleasure"; but as Greene wrote in the essay "Hans Anderson," it is really the "Catholic ideal of the acceptance of pain for a spiritual benefit." This ideal is behind the saintly Sarah's striking statement in *The End of the Affair*: "How good You [God] are. You might have killed us with happiness, but You let us be with You in pain."

According to Kenneth Allott and Miriam Farris in their 1951 study *The Art of Graham Greene,* "seediness . . . seems to Greene the most honest representation of the nature of things." One typical recurring character, for example, appeared as early as the opening chapters of *The Man Within.* From the "shambling," bored priest in that novel who sniffles his way through the burial service for Elizabeth's guardian; to the wheezing old priest smelling of eucalyptus at the end of *Brighton Rock*; to the whiskey priest in *The Power and the Glory*; to the broken-down Father Callifer in *The Potting Shed* with his "stubbly worn face," "bloodshot eyes," and "dirty wisp of a Roman collar," Greene anointed a small cathedral of seedy priests. Francis Wyndham summarizes an objection whose validity each reader must judge for himself: "Some find [Greene's] continual emphasis on squalor and seediness . . . overdone."

Also typical of Greene's characters is their predilection for sin. Greene "seems to have been born with a belief in Original Sin," John Atkins suggests in *Graham Greene,* and certainly his characters have been tainted by it. Raven in *A Gun for Sale* is but one of many Greene protagonists who "had been marked from birth." Another is the whiskey priest's illegitimate daughter in *The Power and the Glory*: "The world was in her heart already, like the small spot of decay in the fruit." Likewise, D. the "confidential agent:" "Give me time," he thinks, "and I shall infect anything." Atkins "can almost hear [Greene's] teeth gnashing at those who omitted to sleep with someone else's wife or husband . . . it is difficult to read Greene's fiction without sensing a contempt for sinlessness." Atkins concludes: Greene's "concern with sin has become so intense he finds a life without sin to be devoid of meaning." But George Orwell's witty complaint about Greene in *The Collected Essays, Journalism and Letters of George Orwell* is the best known. Labeling his subject the leader of the "cult of the sanctified sinner," Orwell declares that Greene shows a Catholic's "snobbishness" about sin: "there is something *distingue* in being damned; Hell is a sort of high-class nightclub, entry to which is reserved for Catholics only."

Although Greene's Catholicism has generated the most intense critical debate, only five or six of his more than twenty novels actually focus on the religion: *Brighton Rock, The Power and the Glory, The Heart of the Matter* (the so-called "Catholic trilogy" analyzed by R. W. B. Lewis in *The Picaresque Saint* and by Marie-Beatrice Mesnet in *Graham Greene and the Heart of the Matter*), *The End of the Affair, Monsignor Quixote,* and, perhaps, *A Burnt-Out Case.* In exploring Catholicism in his fiction, Greene eschewed propaganda. He noted in *Ways of Escape,* his second volume of autobiography, that he was "not a Catholic writer but a writer who happens to be a Catholic." That is, Catholicism did not provide a dogma he wished to promulgate in his novels but instead supplied a framework within which he could measure the human situation. "I'm not a religious man," Greene told *Catholic World* interviewer Gene D. Phillips, "though it interests me. Religion is important, as atomic science is."

Despite the attention paid his Catholicism, Greene told Phillips that religion occupied only "one period" of his writing career: "My period of Catholic novels was preceded and followed by political novels." Greene's first successful novels were written in the 1930s, a decade G. S. Fraser in *The Modern Writer and His World* has said "forced the writer's attention back on the intractable public world around him." In *Ways of Escape* Greene defined the mid-1930s as "clouded by the Depression in England . . . and by the rise of Hitler. It was impossible in those days not to be committed, and it is hard to recall details of ones' private life as the enormous battlefield was prepared around us." Greene's earlier political novels are set in Europe, usually in England (Smith calls *It's a Battlefield,* published in 1934, and *England Made Me,* published in 1935, "condition-of-England" novels); but the later political novels move from one third-world trouble spot to another, even as they explore the themes found throughout Greene's work: commitment, betrayal, corruption, sin, suffering, and the nature of human sexuality, often against a backdrop of Catholicism.

In both religion and politics Greene opposed the dogmatic and the doctrinaire, sided against those who sacrifice the corrupt but living human spirit for a grand but bloodless thesis. For example, in *Monsignor Quixote,* however much the good-natured priest and the equally good-natured communist politician quibble, both reject the intellectual rigidities of those whose commitment to their respective causes is ideologically absolute. Politics and religion, then, are closely related. *Monsignor Quixote* is at once political and religious in nature; and, while nobody denies that *The Power and the Glory* is one of Greene's Catholic works, it can also be studied as a political novel.

Not only a novelist, Greene wrote in more than a dozen other genres, including novellas, short stories, plays, radio plays, screenplays, essays, memoirs, biographies, autobiographies, travel books, poetry, and children's literature. This remarkable output, Smith says, testifies "to a creative energy that has sought to explore the forms open to the literary imagination, and to the fact that Greene is a writer in the deepest, as well as the widest, sense of the term." Although Greene made his mark primarily in the novel, at least his stories, plays, and nonfiction prose, as well as his work in film, deserve consideration.

About the short story genre, Greene wrote in *Ways of Escape*: "I remain in this field a novelist who happens to have written short stories." Unfailingly modest in appraising his own literary efforts, Greene said in a note to his collection *Nineteen Stories,* "I am only too conscious of the defects of these stories. . . . The short story is an exacting form which I have not properly practised." His stories, he said, are "merely . . . the by-products of a novelist's career." However true this evaluation might be for *Nineteen Stories,* and however correct Lodge might be in calling the short story a "form in which [Greene] has never excelled," some of Greene's stories do merit reading. Even John Atkins, who in *Graham Greene* concurs with Lodge that the "short story is not one of Greene's successful forms," concedes that the four newer works in *Twenty-One Stories* "show an improvement" over those in the earlier volume. And in *Ways of Escape* Greene registered contentment with "The Destructors," "A Chance for Mr. Lever," "Under the Garden," and "Cheap in August": "I have never written anything better than" these works, he declared.

Less distinguished than his fiction, Greene's dramas provided him with, if nothing else, diversion. He recorded, almost bragged about, his life-long attempt to escape depression and boredom, starting with Russian roulette as a teenager and culminating in a career as a restless, wandering novelist who, when his mainstay got boring, tried to escape by shifting genres. Writing plays, he declared in *Ways of Escape,* "offered me novelty, an escape from the everyday:" "I needed a rest from novels."

As with his short stories, critics have not been enthusiastic about Greene's plays. *The Complaisant Lover,* however, has attracted applause. Stratford calls it an "outstanding and original achievement," and to Atkins it is as "vital as many of the Restoration comedies." But Smith is acute in pointing to a "curious lack in the plays, that of memorable characters"—certainly not a problem in Greene's novels. On the whole most critics would agree with Lodge's assessment: "it does not seem likely that Greene will add a significant chapter to the history of British drama."

Greene's nonfiction prose, though not widely analyzed, has been more appreciated. Metaphorical and speculative, the travel books are distinctly literary; Greene's narratives record spiritual no less than physical journeys. Greene's first travel book, *Journey without Maps,* is representative of his work in the genre. Believing Africa to be "not a particular place, but a shape, . . . that of the human heart," Greene imagined his actual trip as, simultaneously, a descent, with Freud as guide, into the collective soul of humanity in quest of "those ancestral threads which still exist in our unconscious minds." Greene found in Africa "associations with a personal and racial childhood;" and when in the end he returned to civilization, the conclusion he drew about his experience affirmed the "lost childhood" theme about which he so frequently wrote: "This journey, if had done nothing else, had reinforced a sense of disappointment with what man had made out of the primitive, what he had made out of childhood."

Other essay collections include *Reflections,* which brings together various nonfiction pieces such as film reviews, travel essays, and examinations of communism, Catholicism, and major literary figures; and *A World of My Own: A Dream Diary,* which presents dreams Greene recorded throughout his life. Malcolm Bradbury, writing in *The New York Times Book Review,* concludes of the latter volume: "It's not surprising that the strange tales told here—and they do emerge as tales, not as random notes on disconnected, chaotic events—are as powerful as his fiction, and interweave with it. Greene's *World of My Own*—a carefully organized and edited selection from his dream diaries, which he made and introduced himself, just before his death—is equally the world of his novels, his distinctive, adventurous life as an author, his enigmatic character as a man"

Not surprisingly, commentators frequently turn to Greene's nonfiction pieces to aid their understanding of his fiction; "Fresh and stimulating," as Wyndham says, the essays throw "much light on [Greene's] own work as a novelist." But the essays are worth reading in their own right. Atkins contends that "When Greene's criticism is gathered together we realize how very good it is," that Greene "has unerring good judgment in all literary matters. He can always be relied upon to see through falsity and to detect the ring of truth in others." And Atkins offers a startling evaluation: Greene's "criticism is much more free of fault than his fiction."

Many critics believe that, among serious novelists, Greene had the closest contact with film. From 1935 to 1940 he wrote film reviews for the *Spectator* and in 1937 for *Night and Day*. All of these are collected in *The Graham Greene Film Reader,* which also includes reviews of film books, interviews, lectures, letters, scripts he wrote for short documentaries, film stories, and film treatments. "What provides pleasure in these musings on the movies," notes Pat Dowell in the *Washington Post Book World,* is the glittering nuggets of a prose stylist who writes of the young Bette Davis's 'corrupt and phosphorescent prettiness' or pens a hilariously exasperated description of the unintentionally magnificent surrealism of 'The Garden of Allah.'" Writing in the *New Republic* Stanley Kauffmann comments, "Overall, this assemblage of Greene's criticism is a boon."

In addition, more than twenty of his own novels and stories have been filmed, some with his own screenplays. Furthermore, Greene wrote original screenplays, including the 1949 classic *The Third Man.* It is, then, understandable that to the *Paris Review* interviewers he called himself a "film man."

At least since 1945, when James Agee in *The Nation* noticed that "Greene achieves in print what more naturally belongs in films, and in a sense does not write novels at all, but verbal movies," critics have been discussing the cinema's impact on Greene's fiction. To Evelyn Waugh, in a review printed in both *The Tablet* and *Commonweal, The Heart of the Matter* seems to have been created "out of an infinite length of film" from which "sequences had been cut": "The writer has become director and producer. Indeed, the affinity to the film is everywhere apparent . . . the cinema . . . has taught a new habit of narrative." Fraser picks up this point: "Greene is present in his novels as a producer is present in a film. . . . He cuts, like a film director, from episode to episode."

Greene's cinematic prose method is evident in his first successful novel, *Stamboul Train.* In creating this work with an eye on the film camera, Greene interspersed passages of extended narrative with brief cuts from one character or group of characters to another. This device both sustains the novel's full-throttle pace by generating a sense of motion—appropriate to a story whose center is a speeding express train—and, with great economy, evokes the stew of humanity thrown together at a railway station or on a train. The union of film and fiction is even pondered in *Stamboul Train* by the character Q. C. Savory, who seems to describe Greene's own ambition to incorporate aspects of film into his fiction: "One thing the films had taught the eye, Savory thought, the beauty of the landscape in motion, how a church tower moved behind and above the trees, how it dipped and soared with the uneven human stride, the loveliness of a chimney rising towards a cloud and sinking behind the further cowls. That sense of movement must be conveyed in prose."

Although acclaimed for his work in various genres, it is as a novelist that he is most respected. Some critics even recognize him as the leading English novelist of his generation. In Lodge's words, among the British novelists who were Greene's contemporaries, "it is difficult to find his equal." Smith's evaluation that Greene's was "one of the more remarkable careers in twentieth-century fiction" is understated, especially alongside the judgment of the anonymous *Times Literary Supplement* reviewer who wrote that Greene is the "principal English novelist now writing in [the 'great'] tradition" of Henry James, Joseph Conrad, and Ford Madox Ford. But it was, perhaps, Wyndham who came closest to explaining Greene's sustained popularity when he stated, simply, that "everything [Greene wrote] is readable."

*BIOGRAPHICAL/CRITICAL SOURCES:*

*BOOKS*

Allain, Marie-Francoise, *The Other Man: Conversations with Graham Greene,* Bodley Head, 1983.

Allen, Walter, *The Modern Novel,* Dutton, 1965.

Allott, Kenneth, and Miriam Farris Allott, *The Art of Graham Greene,* Hamish Hamilton, 1951, Russell & Russell, 1965.

Atkins, John, *Graham Greene,* Roy, 1958.

*Bestsellers 89,* Issue 4, Gale, 1989.

Boardman, Gwenn R., *Graham Greene: The Aesthetics of Exploration,* University of Florida Press, 1971.

Cassis, A. F., *Graham Greene: An Annotated Bibliography of Criticism,* Scarecrow, 1981.

*Contemporary Literary Criticism,* Gale, Volume 1, 1973, Volume 3, 1975, Volume 6, 1976, Volume 9, 1978, Volume 14, 1980, Volume 18, 1981, Volume 27, 1984, Volume 37, 1986, Volume 70, 1992, Volume 72, 1992.

Crawford, Fred D., *Mixing Memory and Desire: The Waste Land and British Novels,* Pennsylvania State University Press, 1982, pp. 103-23.

DeVitis, L. A., *Graham Greene,* Twayne, 1964.

*Dictionary of Literary Biography,* Gale, Volume 13: *British Dramatists since World War II,* 1982, Volume 15: *British Novelists, 1930-1959,* 1983, Volume 77: *British Mystery Writers, 1920-1939,* 1989.

*Dictionary of Literary Biography Yearbook: 1985,* Gale, 1986.

Duraan, Leopoldo, *Graham Greene: An Intimate Portrait by His Closest Friend and Confidant,* Harper (San Francisco), 1994.

Duraan, *Graham Greene: Friend and Brother,* HarperCollins (London), 1994.

Evans, R. O., editor, *Graham Greene: Some Critical Considerations,* University of Kentucky Press, 1963.

Falk, Quentin, *Travels in Greeneland: The Cinema of Graham Greene,* Quartet, 1984.

Greene, Graham, *The Graham Greene Film Reader: Reviews, Essays, Interviews & Film Stories,* Applause Theatre Book Publishers (New York City), 1994.

Greene, Graham with A. F. Cassis, *Graham Greene: Man of Paradox,* Loyola University Press (Chicago), 1994.

Hynes, Samuel, editor, *Graham Greene: A Collection of Critical Essays,* Prentice-Hall, 1973.

Kermode, Frank, *Puzzles and Epiphanies,* Chilmark, 1962.

Kunkel, Francis L., *The Labyrinthine Ways of Graham Greene,* Sheed, 1959.

*Living Writers,* Sylvan Press, 1947.

Lodge, David, *Graham Greene,* Columbia University Press, 1966.

Mauriac, Francois, *Great Men,* Rockliff, 1952.

Mesnet, Maire-Beatrice, *Graham Greene and the Heart of the Matter,* Cresset, 1954.

Miller, Robert H., *Graham Greene: A Descriptive Catalog,* University of Kentucky Press, 1979.

Mueller, Walter R., *The Prophetic Voice in Modern Fiction,* Association Press, 1959.

Newby, P. H., *The Novel: 1945-1950,* Longmans, Green, 1951.

O'Faolain, Dean, *The Vanishing Hero,* Atlantic Monthly Press, 1956.

Pendleton, Robert, *Graham Greene's Conradian Masterplot: The Arabesques of Influence,* St. Martin's Press (New York City), 1996.

Prescott, Orville, *In My Opinion,* Bobbs-Merrill, 1952.

Reed, Henry, *The Novel since 1939,* Longmans, Green, 1947.

Rostenne, Paul, *Graham Greene: Temoin des temps tragiques,* Julliard, 1949.

Shelden, Michael, *Graham Greene: The Enemy Within,* Random House (New York City), 1994.

Sherry, Norman, *The Life of Graham Greene,* Viking, Volume 1: *1904-1939,* 1989, Volume 2: *1939-1955,* 1995.

Stratford, Philip, *Faith and Fiction,* University of Notre Dame Press, 1964.

Vann, Jerry Donn, *Graham Greene: A Checklist of Criticism,* University of Kentucky Press, 1970.

Wobbe, R. A., *Graham Greene: A Bibliography and Guide to Research,* Garland, 1979.

Wyndham, Francis, *Graham Greene,* Longmans, Green, 1955.

Zabel, Morton Dauwen, *Craft and Character in Modern Fiction,* Viking, 1957.

*PERIODICALS*

*America,* January 25, 1941.

*Catholic World,* December, 1954, pp. 172-75; August, 1969, pp. 218-21.

*College English,* October, 1950, pp. 1-9.

*Globe and Mail* (Toronto), September 29, 1984.

*Life,* February 4, 1966.

*London Magazine,* June-July, 1977, pp. 35-45.

*Los Angeles Times,* September 25, 1980; January 2, 1981; March 20, 1985.

*Los Angeles Times Book Review,* October 23, 1988; October 23, 1994.

*Modern Fiction Studies,* autumn, 1957, pp. 249-88.

*New Republic,* December 5, 1994, p. 30.

*New Yorker,* April 11, 1994, p. 46.

*New York Review of Books,* March 3, 1966; June 8, 1995; June 22, 1995.

*New York Times,* February 27, 1978; May 19, 1980; January 18, 1981; September 24, 1982; October 25, 1984; March 4, 1985; June 6, 1985; October 17, 1988; January 17, 1995.

*New York Times Book Review,* January 23, 1966; January 8, 1995.

*Playboy,* November, 1994, p. 32.
*Southwest Review,* summer, 1956, pp. 239-50.
*Time,* September 20, 1982.
*Times* (London), September 6, 1984; September 7, 1984; March 14, 1985; February 5, 1990.
*Times Literary Supplement,* January 27, 1966; March 28, 1980; March 15, 1985.
*Washington Post,* April 3, 1980; September 20, 1988.
*Washington Post Book World,* May 18, 1980; October 16, 1988; March 12, 1995.
*World Press Review,* December, 1981, pp. 31-2; April, 1983, p. 62.

*OBITUARIES:*

*PERIODICALS*

*Detroit Free Press,* April 4, 1991.*

# H-K

**HALEY, Alex(ander Murray Palmer) 1921-1992**

*PERSONAL:* Born August 11, 1921, in Ithaca, NY; died of cardiac arrest, February 10, 1992, in Seattle, WA; son of Simon Alexander (a professor) and Bertha George (a teacher; maiden name, Palmer) Haley; married Nannie Branch, 1941 (divorced, 1964); married Juliette Collins, 1964 (divorced); children: (first marriage) Lydia Ann, William Alexander; (second marriage) Cynthia Gertrude. *Education:* Attended Alcorn Agricultural & Mechanical College (now Alcorn State University); attended Elizabeth City Teachers College, 1937-39.

*CAREER:* U.S. Coast Guard, 1939-59, retiring as chief journalist; freelance writer, 1959-92. Founder and president of Kinte Corporation, Los Angeles, CA, 1972-92. Board member of New College of California, 1974; member of King Hassan's Royal Academy. Script consultant for television miniseries *Roots, Roots: The Next Generations,* and *Palmerstown, U.S.A.;* has lectured extensively and appeared frequently on radio and television; adviser to African American Heritage Association, Detroit, MI.

*MEMBER:* Authors Guild, Society of Magazine Writers.

*AWARDS, HONORS:* Litt.D. from Simpson College, 1971, Howard University, 1974, Williams College, 1975, and Capitol University, 1975; honorary doctorate from Seton Hall University, 1974; special citation from National Book Award committee, 1977, for *Roots;* special citation from Pulitzer Prize committee, 1977, for *Roots;* Spingarn Medal from NAACP, 1977; nominated to Black Filmmakers Hall of Fame, 1981, for producing *Palmerstown, U.S.A.,* 1981.

*WRITINGS:*

(With Malcolm X) *The Autobiography of Malcolm X,* Grove, 1965.

*Roots: The Saga of an American Family,* Doubleday, 1976.

*Alex Haley Speaks* (recording), Kinte Corporation, 1980.

*A Different Kind of Christmas,* Doubleday, 1988, abridged edition, Literacy Volunteers of New York City, 1991.

*Alex Haley: The Playboy Interviews* (edited with an introduction by Murray Fisher), Ballantine Books, 1993.

(With David Stevens) *Queen* (screenplay adapted from dictation tapes), Columbia Broadcasting System (CBS-TV), 1993.

Author of forewords, *Somerset Homecoming,* by Dorothy Redford and Michael D'Orso, Anchor/Doubleday, 1988; *Marva Collins' Way: Returning to Excellence in Education,* by Marva Collins, J. P. Tarcher, 1990; and *They That Go Down to the Sea: A Bicentennial Pictorial History of the United States Coast Guard,* by Paul A. Powers, United States Coast Guard Chief Petty Officers Association, 1990. Initiated "Playboy Interviews" feature for *Playboy,* 1962. Contributor to periodicals, including *Reader's Digest, New York Times Magazine, Smithsonian, Harper's,* and *Atlantic.*

*ADAPTATIONS:* *Roots* was adapted as two television miniseries by American Broadcasting Companies (ABC), as *Roots,* 1977, and *Roots: The Next Genera-*

*tions* (also known as *Roots II*), 1979; Haley served as script consultant for both productions. Filmmaker Spike Lee used *The Autobiography of Malcolm X* as the source for his 1992 film biography *Malcolm X. Queen,* a novel based an outline and research left by Haley, was published by Morrow in 1993.

*WORK IN PROGRESS:* Haley was working on the following projects at the time of his death: *My Search for Roots,* an account of how *Roots* was researched and written; a study of Henning, Tennessee, where Haley was raised.

*SIDELIGHTS:* Alex Haley's reputation in the literary world rests upon his much acclaimed historical novel, *Roots: The Saga of an American Family.* Haley's tracing of his African ancestry to the Mandinka tribe in a tiny village in Juffure of the Gambia region of West Africa, spawned one of the most ambitious American television productions ever undertaken and inspired a generation of ancestry-seeking Americans. Eleven years prior to the appearance of *Roots,* Haley had gained recognition for writing Malcolm X's "as-told-to" autobiography, which was released shortly after the charismatic leader was gunned down while giving a speech in New York. After Spike Lee released the movie *Malcolm X* in 1992, bookstore owners had difficulty keeping the autobiography in stock.

Haley was born in 1921 in Ithaca, New York, and reared in the small town of Henning, Tennessee. He was the eldest of three sons born to Bertha George Palmer and Simon Alexander Haley, and when he was born, both his parents were in their first years of graduate school—his mother at the Ithaca Conservatory of Music, and his father at Cornell University. After finishing school, his parents took young Alex to Henning, where he grew up under the influence of his grandmother and aunts Viney, Mathilda, and Liz, who perpetuated stories about his African ancestor Kunte Kinte. These stories became the impetus for *Roots,* with which hundreds of thousands of African Americans would identify.

Before Haley became famous for this autobiographical work, however, he earned his living as a journalist. He was the first interviewer for *Playboy* magazine, and the volume *Alex Haley: The Playboy Interviews* collects eleven of his conversations with notable and controversial public figures, including Miles Davis, Muhammad Ali, Dr. Martin Luther King, Jr., George Lincoln Rockwell—a leader of the American Nazi Party—and Malcolm X. The interview with Malcolm X predates and resulted in the book *The Autobiography of Malcolm X. The Playboy Interviews* also includes an excerpt from *Roots.*

Although it took Haley twelve years to research and write *Roots,* success quickly followed its publication. Recipient of numerous awards, including a citation from the judges of the 1977 National Book Awards and the Pulitzer Prizes, the book is recognized as one of the most successful bestsellers in American publishing history, having sold millions of copies worldwide in 37 languages. Combined with the impact of the televised miniseries, *Roots* has become a "literary-television phenomenon" and a "sociological event," according to *Time.* By April, 1977, almost 2 million people had seen all or part of the first eight-episode series; and seven of those eight episodes ranked among the top ten shows in TV ratings, attaining an average of 66 percent of audience share.

Although critics generally lauded Haley for his accomplishment, they seemed unsure whether to treat *Roots* as a novel or as a historical account. While it is based on factual events, the dialogue, thoughts, and emotions of the characters are fictionalized. Haley himself described the book as "faction," a mixture of fact and fiction. Most critics concurred and evaluated *Roots* as a blend of history and entertainment. And despite the fictional characterizations, Willie Lee Rose suggested in the *New York Review of Books* that Kunta Kinte's parents Omoro and Binte "could possibly become the African proto-parents of millions of Americans who are going to admire their dignity and grace." *Newsweek* found that Haley's decision to fictionalize was the right approach: "Instead of writing a scholarly monograph of little social impact, Haley has written a blockbuster in the best sense—a book that is bold in concept and ardent in execution, one that will reach millions of people and alter the way we see ourselves."

Some concern was voiced, especially at the time of the first television series, that racial tension in America would be aggravated by *Roots.* But while *Time* reported several incidents of racial violence following the telecast, it commented that "most observers thought that in the long term, *Roots* would improve race relations, particularly because of the televised version's profound impact on whites. . . . A broad consensus seemed to be emerging that *Roots* would spur black identity, and hence black pride, and eventually pay important dividends." Some black leaders viewed *Roots* "as the most important civil rights event since the 1965 march on Selma," according to *Time.* Vernon Jordan, executive director of the National Urban League, called it "the single most spectacular educational experience in race relations in America."

Haley has heard only positive comments from both blacks and whites. He told William Marmon in a *Time* interview: "The blacks who are buying books are not buying them to go out and fight someone, but because they want to know who they are. *Roots* is all of our stories. It's the same for me or any black. It's just a matter of filling in the blanks—which person, living in which village, going on what ship across the same ocean, slavery, emancipation, the struggle for freedom. . . . The white response is more complicated. But when you start talking about family, about lineage and ancestry, you are talking about every person on earth. We all have it; it's a great equalizer. . . . I think the book has touched a strong, subliminal chord."

But there was also concern, according to *Time,* that "breast-beating about the past may turn into a kind of escapism, distracting attention from the present. Only if *Roots* turns the anger at yesterday's slavery into anger at today's ghetto will it really matter." And James Baldwin wrote in the *New York Times Book Review:* "*Roots* is a study of continuities, of consequences, of how a people perpetuate themselves, how each generation helps to doom, or helps to liberate, the coming one—the action of love, or the effect of the absence of love, in time. It suggests, with great power, how each of us, however unconsciously, can't but be the vehicle of the history which has produced us. Well, we can perish in this vehicle, children, or we can move on up the road."

For months after the publication of *Roots* in October, 1976, Haley signed at least 500 books daily, spoke to an average of 6,000 people a day, and traveled round trip coast-to-coast at least once a week, according to *People.* Stardom took its toll on Haley. *New Times* reported that on a trip to his ancestral village in Africa, Haley complained: "You'll find that people who celebrate you will kill you. They forget you are blood and flesh and bone. I have had days and weeks and months of schedules where everything from my breakfast to my last waking moment was planned for me. . . . Someone has you by the arm and is moving you from room to room. Then people *grab* at you. You're actually pummeled—hit with books—and you ask yourself, My God, what *is* this?"

*Roots* was so successful that ABC produced a sequel, *Roots: The Next Generations,* a $16.6-million production that ran for 14 hours. The story line of *Roots II,* as it was called, begins in 1882, twelve years after the end of the *Roots I,* and it concludes in 1967. During the 85-year span, Haley's family is depicted against the backdrop of the Ku Klux Klan, world wars, race riots, and the Great Depression; the commonalities between black and white middle-class life are dramatized as well.

Haley also researched his paternal heritage; and in 1993, CBS aired a three-episode miniseries, *Queen,* about his paternal great-grandmother, Queen, the daughter of a mulatto slave girl and a white slave owner. Writing in the *New York Times,* John J. O'Connor noted that although "the scope is considerably more limited . . . the sense of unfolding history, familial and national, is still compelling." Accusations surfaced about the historical accuracy of *Queen,* though, which recalled the charges of plagiarism and authenticity leveled at *Roots* by the author of *The Africans,* Harold Courtlander, who was subsequently paid $650,000 in an out-of-court settlement. Critics questioned whether a romance had actually existed between Queen and her slave-owning master. According to Melinda Henneberger in the *New York Times,* the tapes left by Haley did not mention a romance between his paternal great-grandparents, and David Stevens, who worked with Haley's research and outline, recalled Haley's intent to soften the relationship. Producer Mark Wolper indicated that "Haley had become convinced by his later inquiries . . . that his great-grandparents had actually been in love," wrote Henneberger, adding that "several scholars, all of whom said they would never contradict Haley's research into his own family, added that consensual, lifelong relationships between slaves and owners were exceedingly rare." Esther B. Fein noted in the *New York Times* that the book was published as a novel "partly because Mr. Haley could not verify all the family folklore that inspired it and died before the project was completed."

In 1985, Haley was working on a novel set in the Appalachian culture that he had researched extensively. The novel was centered around the relationships among a mountain father, son, and grandson. Because this book was not about blacks but primarily about whites, Haley said of the project, "I think one of the most fascinating things you can do after you learn about your own people is to study something about the history and culture of other people." Haley also planned to write a book detailing the life of Madame C. J. Walker and her daughter A'Lelia. Haley had signed a three-book contract with Ballantine for its new multicultural publishing program, for which his first title was to be a comprehensive history of his hometown, Henning. Those who knew Haley well say his research on Henning predated the writing of *Roots*. Haley was buried on the grounds of his Henning homestead, but in 1992, his estate auctioned off virtually all his possessions to pay a $1.5 million debt.

*BIOGRAPHICAL/CRITICAL SOURCES:*

*BOOKS*

*The Black Press U.S.A.*, Iowa State University Press, 1990.
*Contemporary Literary Criticism,* Gale, Volume 8, 1978, Volume 12, 1980, Volume 76, 1993.
*Dictionary of Literary Biography,* Volume 38: *Afro-American Writers After 1955: Dramatists and Prose Writers,* Gale, 1985.
Gonzales, Doreen, *Alex Haley: Author of Roots,* Enslow Publishers (Hillside, NJ), 1994.
Shirley, David, *Alex Haley,* Chelsea House (New York City), 1994.
Williams, Sylvia B., *Alex Haley,* Abdo & Daughters (Edina, MN), 1996.

*PERIODICALS*

*Black Collegian,* September/October, 1985.
*Booklist,* July, 1993, p. 1938.
*Christianity Today,* May 6, 1977.
*Ebony,* April, 1977.
*Forbes,* February 15, 1977.
*Library Journal,* June 1, 1993, p. 144.
*Los Angeles Times Book Review,* December 25, 1988, p. 1.
*Ms.*, February, 1977.
*National Review,* March 4, 1977.
*Negro History Bulletin,* January, 1977.
*New Republic,* March 12, 1977.
*Newsweek,* September 27, 1976, February 14, 1977.
*New Yorker,* February 14, 1977.
*New York Review of Books,* November 11, 1976.
*New York Times,* October 14, 1976; February 12, 1993, p. C34; February 14, 1993, p. H1; March 3, 1993, p. C18.
*New York Times Book Review,* September 26, 1976, January 2, 1977, February 27, 1977.
*People,* March 28, 1977.
*Publishers Weekly,* September 6, 1976; March 2, 1992; October 12, 1992, p. 10.
*San Francisco Review of Books,* February-March, 1994.
*Saturday Review,* September 18, 1976.
*Time,* October 18, 1976, February 14, 1977; February 19, 1979.
*Today's Educator,* September, 1977.
*Washington Post Book World,* July 25, 1993, p. 12.

*OBITUARIES:*

*PERIODICALS*

*Chicago Tribune,* February 11, 1992, sec. 1, pp. 1, 10; February 16, 1992, sec. 2, p. 10.
*Essence,* February, 1992, pp. 88-92.
*New York Times,* February 11, 1992, p. B8.
*Times* (London), February 11, 1992, p. 15.
*Washington Post,* February 11, 1992, pp. A1, A10, and p. E1.*

* * *

**HARRISON, Michael 1907-**
**(Quentin Downes)**

*PERSONAL:* Born April 25, 1907, in Milton, Kent, England; son of George (an insurance broker) and Veronica (Downes) Harrison; married Maryvonne Aubertin, May 4, 1950 (died August 9, 1977); children: Jacqueline, Grancoise (stepchildren). *Education:* Attended King's College, London, School of Oriental and African Studies, London, and North Kent College of Art. *Politics:* "Nil." *Religion:* Church of England. *Avocational interests:* "I am deeply interested in the history and development of languages, and I have made some important contributions to both etymology and philology."

*ADDRESSES: Home*—5A Palmeira Court, 31-33 Palmeira Square, Hove, Sussex BN3 2JP, England. *Agent*—Jonathan Clowes Ltd., 22 Prince Albert Rd., London NW1 75ST, England.

*CAREER:* Writer. Worked as journalist, editor, and creative director of an advertising agency; managing editor of Trade News Ltd.; co-director of Common Market Publicity Ltd. and Lemon Promotion Ltd. *Military service:* Served in British Military Intelligence, 1943.

*MEMBER:* Society of Authors, Crime Writers Association, Baker Street Irregulars of New York, Sherlock Holmes Society of London, Society of Sussex Authors, Sherlock Holmes Club of Denmark, "and numerous other Sherlockian 'Scion societies' in Europe and America."

*AWARDS, HONORS:* Occident Prize for best non-Italian novel from Rome, 1934, for *Weep for Lycidas;* named Duke of Sant'Estrella by Kingdom of Redonda, 1951, for "services to literature"; award for best advertisement idea from British Industrial Advertising Association, 1964, for Midland Silicones Ltd.; named Irregular Shilling by Baker Street Irregulars of New York, 1964, for "distinguished services in the cause of keeping green the Master's memory."

*WRITINGS:*

*NOVELS*

*Weep for Lycidas,* Barker (London), 1934.
*Spring in Tartarus: An Arabesque,* Barker, 1935.
*All the Trees Were Green,* Barker, 1936.
*What Are We Waiting For?* Rich & Cowan (London), 1939.
*Vernal Equinox,* Collins (London), 1939.
*Battered Caravanserai,* Rich & Cowan, 1942.
*Reported Safe Arrival: The Journal of a Voyage to Port X,* Rich & Cowan, 1943.
*So Linked Together,* Macdonald (London), 1944.
*Higher Things,* Macdonald, 1945.
*The House in Fishergate,* Macdonald, 1946.
*Treadmill,* Langdon Press (London), 1947.
*Sinecure,* Laurie (London), 1948.
*There's Glory for You!* Laurie, 1949.
*Thing Less Noble: A Modern Love Story,* Laurie, 1950.
*Long Vacation,* Laurie, 1951.
*The Brain,* Cassell (London), 1953.
*The Dividing Stone,* Cassell, 1954.
*A Hansom to St. James's,* Cassell, 1954.

*OTHER*

*Transit of Venus* (short stories), Fortune Press (London), 1936.
*Dawn Express: There and Back* (travelogue), Collins (London), 1938.
(Editor) *Under Thirty* (anthology of short stories), Rich & Cowan, 1939.
*Gambler's Glory: The Story of John Law of Lauriston,* Rich & Cowan, 1940.
*Count Cagliostro: Nature's Unfortunate Child,* Rich & Cowan, 1942.
*They Would Be King* (historical essays), Somers (London), 1947.
*Post Office Mauritius, 1847: The Tale of Two Stamps,* Stamp Collecting Ltd. (London), 1947.
*The Story of Christmas: Its Growth and Development from Earliest Times,* Odhams Press (London), 1951, revised edition published as *Saturnalia,* Skoob Books (London), 1990.
*The Darkened Room,* Home & Van Thal, 1952.
*Airborne at Kitty Hawk: The Story of the First Heavier-Than-Air Flight Made by the Wright Brothers,* Cassell (London), 1953.
*Charles Dickens: A Sentimental Journey in Search of an Unvarnished Portrait,* Cassell, 1953, Haskell House (New York City), 1976.
(With Douglas Armstrong) *A New Approach to Stamp Collecting,* Batsford (London), 1953, Hanover House (New York City), 1954.
*Beer Cookery: 101 Traditional Recipes,* Spearman-Calder (London), 1954.
*Peter Cheyney, Prince of Hokum: A Biography,* Spearman, 1954.
*In the Footsteps of Sherlock Holmes,* Cassell, 1958, Fell (New York City), 1960, revised edition, David & Charles (Newton Abbot, Devon), 1971, Drake (New York City), 1972.
*The History of the Hat,* Jenkins (London), 1960, Berkeley (New York City), 1974.
*London Beneath the Pavement,* Peter Davies (London), 1961, revised edition, 1971.
*Rosa* (biography of Rosa Lewis), Peter Davies, 1962.
*Painful Details: Twelve Victorian Scandals,* Parrish (London), 1962.
*London by Gaslight: 1861-1911,* Peter Davies, 1963.
*London Growing: The Development of a Metropolis,* Hutchinson (London), 1965.
*Mulberry: The Return in Triumph,* W. H. Allen (London), 1965.
*Lord of London: A Biography of the Second Duke of Westminster,* W. H. Allen, 1966.
*Technical and Industrial Publicity,* Business Publications (London), 1968.
*The London That Was Rome: The Imperial City Created by the New Archaeology,* Allen & Unwin (London), 1971.
*Fanfare of Strumpets,* W. H. Allen, 1971.
*Clarence: The Life of H.R.H., the Duke of Clarence and Avondale,* W. H. Allen, 1972, published as *Clarence: Was He Jack the Ripper?,* Drake, 1974.
*The London of Sherlock Holmes,* Drake, 1972.

*The Roots of Witchcraft,* Muller (London), 1973, Citadel (Secaucus, NJ), 1974, revised edition, Skoob Books, 1990.

*The World of Sherlock Holmes,* Muller, 1973, Dutton (New York City), 1975.

*Theatrical Mr. Holmes: The World's Greatest Consulting Detective, Considered Against the Background of the Contemporary Theatre,* Convent Garden Press (London), 1974.

(Editor and contributor) *Beyond Baker Street: A Sherlockian Anthology,* Bobbs-Merrill, 1976.

*Fire From Heaven; or, How Safe Are You from Burning?,* Sidgwick & Jackson (London), 1976, 2nd revised edition, Skoob Books, 1990.

*I, Sherlock Holmes,* Dutton, 1977.

*Vanishings,* New English Library (London), 1981.

*Immortal Sleuth: Sherlockian Musings and Memories,* Gasogene Press (Dubuque, IA), 1983.

*A Study in Surmise: The Making of Sherlock Holmes,* Gaslight (Bloomington, IN), 1984.

*A Sheaf of Sherlock,* Gasogene Press, 1990.

*UNDER PSEUDONYM QUENTIN DOWNES*

*No Smoke No Flame* (novel), Wingate (London), 1952, Roy (New York City), 1956.

*Heads I Win* (novel), Wingate, 1953, Roy, 1955.

*They Hadn't a Clue* (novel), Arco (London), 1954.

*The Exploitations of the Chevalier Dupin* (stories), Mycroft & Moran (Sauk City, WI), 1968, expanded edition published as *Murder in the Rue Royale,* Stacey (London), 1972.

Contributor to periodicals, including *Ellery Queen's Mystery Magazine.*

*SIDELIGHTS:* Michael Harrison has earned a reputation as a scholar of the adventures of the literary detective Sherlock Holmes and as a writer of mysteries of his own, based on the Edgar Allan Poe character C. Auguste Dupin. Edward D. Hoch, writing in the *St. James Guide to Crime and Mystery Writers,* believes that "Harrison's major contribution has been his short stories, with a series of excellent pastiches of Edgar Allan Poe's detective C. Auguste Dupin. Mystery readers who have long bemoaned the fact that Poe wrote only three Dupin tales can take heart from the work of Michael Harrison, who created 12 new adventures."

Harrison's studies of Sherlock Holmes began with *In the Footsteps of Sherlock Holmes,* a comprehensive look at Arthur Conan Doyle's stories about the famous detective and his sleuthing partner, Dr. John Watson. Harrison dissects the stories for clues about the pair. As S. B. Bellows in *Christian Science Monitor* explains, "Every word, every move, of the famous pair becomes significant in establishing conclusions as to their families, their backgrounds, their incomes, dress and deportment—all rationally deducible between-the-lines information." Harrison also tracks down the actual London locations of the Holmes' adventures and how those locations look today and how they must have looked in the 1890s. Charles Poore in the *San Francisco Chronicle* finds this side of the book to be "an amazing guide to changing England." The critic for the *New York Times Book Review* admits that Harrison's book is "rambling and unorganized," and yet finds it "wonderful" and Harrison to be "communicative and enthralling." E. F. Walbridge in *Library Journal* calls *In the Footsteps of Sherlock Holmes* "amiable, discursive and knowledgable" and "a masterful work," while Roger Fulford in *Manchester Guardian* calls Harrison "an agreeable guide" to Holmes' London who "draws back the curtain to reveal some strange scenes."

Harrison told *CA:* "My interest in Sherlock Holmes began because I am, by nature, a puzzle-solver; and in the case of Holmes, I wished to discover who—and what—Conan Doyle had in mind when he began the character of Holmes in *A Study in Scarlet.* Four full-size Holmes books have consolidated my 'Sherlockian' position, and I am by no means finished with the production of Holmes books. I do think, however, that we could do without some of the more trivial works which have been written, it seems, simply to 'cash in' on the fashionable Holmes cult."

Of Harrison's stories featuring C. Auguste Dupin, a French detective character created by Edgar Allan Poe, Hoch claims that "at least six deserve special mention. 'The Vanished Treasure' finds Dupin solving a 50-year-old mystery involving missing Spanish gold. The discovery of some old Roman ruins masks a crime in 'The Man in the Blue Spectacles.' 'The Fires in the Rue Honore' reveals an ingenious method of arson. A diplomat who vanishes in an empty street provides the mystery in 'The Facts in the Case of the Missing Diplomat.' Another type of seemingly impossible crime is presented in 'The Assassination of Sir Ponsonby Brown.' 'The Clew of the Single Word' is a clever spy tale."

Speaking to *CA,* Harrison spoke of how he first turned to writing nonfiction titles: "The economic blizzard which hit British publishing around 1950 caused me to turn from novels (that no publisher would commission) to nonfiction. And as the only book that I have ever written without having been commissioned was my first novel, I have written nonfiction since 1954. Almost all my nonfiction works have been of a 'detective' quality. Each now sets out clearly the problem to be solved; the suspected or hypothesized fact to be demonstrated as fact. This does not make my writing, or my approach to my writing, unique: every author is impelled by a didactic impulse, even when he or she is writing novels. Lord Byron's cynicism and the flourishing modern 'vanity publishing' industry apart, all 'serious' writers feel the need to write because they feel that they have something new to say or something new to say about old things. Writing, in its essence, is the result of a compulsion to explain to others. In that respect my own writing is no different from that of the many other researchers, except, perhaps, that I do try to set out my aims a little more clearly. In *The London That Was Rome,* I explained at the very beginning of the book what I was setting out to do: to re-map the Roman city of London by the use of an archaeological method of my own invention. The reader was left in no doubt of my rather ambitious aim, and could follow my vindication of my method step by step throughout the book.

"Now that I am a widower, I do not travel as much as I did, but I still visit Europe fairly frequently, always with some research in view. I have had a long and, on the whole, productive life, and I hope that I may be spared to add to my long list of writings—there are still many subjects to be tackled."

*BIOGRAPHICAL/CRITICAL SOURCES:*

*BOOKS*

*St. James Guide to Crime and Mystery Writers,* fourth edition, St. James Press (Detroit), 1996.

*PERIODICALS*

*Booklist,* June 15, 1960, p. 622.
*Choice,* December, 1972, p. 1292.
*Christian Science Monitor,* June 2, 1960, p. 11.
*Economist,* July 10, 1971, p. 62; April 8, 1972, p. 243.
*Library Journal,* July, 1960, p. 2593.
*Manchester Guardian,* January 9, 1959, p. 6.
*New York Times Book Review,* September 4, 1960, p. 13; February 4, 1973, p. 14.
*San Francisco Chronicle,* July 21, 1960, p. 31.
*Times Literary Supplement,* April 7, 1972, p. 391.

* * *

**HOLLAND, Joyce**
**See MORICE, Dave**

* * *

**HUBBARD, P(hilip) M(aitland) 1910-1980**

*PERSONAL:* Born November 9, 1910, in Reading, Berkshire, England; died March 17, 1980, in Scotland; separated; children: one son, two daughters. *Education:* Jesus College, Oxford, B.A., 1933, M.A., 1940.

*CAREER:* Civil servant in British India, mainly in northwest India (now Pakistan), 1934-47; worked for the British Council, 1948-51; freelance writer, 1951-55; worked for the National union of Manufacturers, 1955-60; freelance writer, 1960-80.

*WRITINGS:*

*SUSPENSE NOVELS*

*Flush as May,* British Book Centre (New York City), 1963.
*Picture of Millie,* British Book Centre, 1964.
*A Hive of Glass,* Atheneum (New York City), 1965.
*The Holm Oaks,* M. Joseph (London), 1965, Atheneum, 1966.
*The Tower,* Atheneum, 1967.
*The Country of Again,* Atheneum, 1967, published as *The Custom of the Country,* Bles (London), 1969.
*Cold Waters,* Atheneum, 1969.
*High Tide,* Atheneum, 1970.
*The Dancing Man,* Atheneum, 1971.
*The Whisper in the Glen,* Atheneum, 1972.
*A Rooted Sorrow,* Atheneum, 1973.
*A Thirsty Evil,* Atheneum, 1974.
*The Graveyard,* Atheneum, 1975.
*The Causeway,* Macmillan (London), 1976, Doubleday (New York City), 1978.
*The Quiet River,* Doubleday, 1978.
*Kill Claudio,* Doubleday, 1979.

*OTHER*

*Ovid Among the Goths* (poems), Blackwell (Oxford, England), 1933.
*Anna Highbury* (children's fiction), Cassell (London), 1963.
*Rat Trap Island* (children's fiction), Cassell, 1964.
*Dead Man's Bay* (radio play), 1966.

Work represented in anthologies, including *Dream of Fair Woman,* edited by Charlotte Armstrong, A. & C. Black, 1966. Contributor of several hundred poems and stories to magazines, including *Punch.*

*SIDELIGHTS:* As Mary Helen Becker noted in the *St. James Guide to Crime and Mystery Writers,* "P. M. Hubbard produced a fine suspense novel almost every year. His writing is singular in its simplicity and elegance. A survey of his crime fiction reveals that there is, in fact, quite a variety of settings and situations, but an impression remains of almost mythic conflict between few characters, of elemental struggle acted out in a lonely world of brooding landscapes and cold waters. Protagonists, some merely odd or whimsical, others clearly abnormal, are driven by their compulsions."

Hubbard's writing was different from that found in most novels of suspense. As Newgate Callendar explained in the *New York Times Book Review:* "What sets Hubbard's writing far above most is his understated and almost poetic style. . . . His kind of literary sensitivity is far removed from the normal punchy prose of mystery writing." Despite the sensitivity of Hubbard's prose, his stories were able to deliver sufficient chills for the reader. Anthony Boucher, writing in the *New York Times Book Review* of *A Hive of Glass,* explained that "the novel, set in a decaying English seaside town, has a curious dank Gothic feel to it, and should provide, for all its irony and wit, a few genuine shudders."

"Hubbard," Becker wrote, "is easily one of the best contemporary writers of suspense fiction. His 'thrillers' are, in psychological complexity and literary quality, comparable to the novels of Patricia Highsmith. His fascination with water, sailing, and adventure invites comparison with Andrew Garve's, but while Garve is basically optimistic and upbeat, Hubbard deals with darker aspects of these subjects. Most crime novels are quickly read and as quickly forgotten, but P. M. Hubbard's books linger in the memory and in the imagination."

*BIOGRAPHICAL/CRITICAL SOURCES:*

*BOOKS*

*St. James Guide to Crime and Mystery Writers,* fourth edition, St. James Press (Detroit), 1996.

*PERIODICALS*

*Best Sellers,* April 15, 1971, p. 48.
*Books,* June, 1970.
*Book World,* May 5, 1968.
*Library Journal,* August, 1963, p. 2933; October 1, 1965, p. 4116; July, 1970, p. 2522.
*New Yorker,* May 23, 1970.
*New York Herald Tribune Books,* August 4, 1963, p. 11.
*New York Times Book Review,* July 21, 1963, p. 19; September 5, 1965, p. 21; April 3, 1966, p. 30; May 28, 1967; April 20, 1970, p. 46; August 1, 1971, p. 16.
*Punch,* May 7, 1969.
*Spectator,* March 28, 1970.
*Times Literary Supplement,* March 11, 1965, p. 201; April 23, 1970; October 22, 1971, p. 1340; August 27, 1976.

*OBITUARIES:*

*PERIODICALS*

*London Times,* March 19, 1980.*

* * *

**HUNCKE, Herbert E(dwin) 1915-1996**

*PERSONAL:* Name rhymes with "junkie"; born January 9, 1915, in Greenfield, MA; died of congestive heart failure, August 8, 1996, in New York; son of Herbert Spencer (a machine parts distributor) and Marguerite (Bell) Huncke.

*ADDRESSES:* c/o Contact/Two Publications, P.O. Box 451, Bowling Green Station, New York, NY 10004.

*CAREER:* Writer. Instructor of writing at Naropa Institute; lecturer.

*WRITINGS:*

*Huncke's Journal,* illustrations by Erin Matson, Poets Press (New York City), 1965.

*Elsie John and Joey Martinez,* Pequod Press, (New York City) 1979.

*The Evening Sun Turned Crimson,* introduction by Allen Ginsberg, Cherry Valley Editions (Cherry Valley, NY), 1980.

*Guilty of Everything: The Autobiography of Herbert Huncke,* foreword by William S. Burroughs, Paragon House (New York City), 1990.

*The Herbert Huncke Reader,* edited by Benjamin J. Schafer, foreword by William S. Burroughs, introduction by Raymond Foye, Morrow (New York City), 1997.

Also contributor of short story "Alvarez" to *Playboy,* 1968.

*SIDELIGHTS:* Herbert E. Huncke is rated a second-class writer by many critics, but he was undeniably a highly significant figure in the literary movement known as the Beat Generation. Beat luminaries such as Jack Kerouac, Allen Ginsberg, and William S. Burroughs were inspired by Huncke's unconventional street life, and it is said that he was the originator of the term "Beat." He was first and foremost a hustler, drug addict, and petty criminal, and he would probably never have written any books if not for his association with his literary colleagues. Still, his famous friends—and some critics—found much to admire in his writing, which, with its frequent use of pauses and dashes, mirrored the sense of ephemerality, loss, and weariness that characterized his Bohemian lifestyle.

Huncke was born in Greenfield, Massachusetts, but the family moved to Detroit when he was just four years old, and two years later relocated once again to Chicago. His family was unremarkably middle-class, but his rejection of societal norms began early. He began using drugs when he was only twelve years old, and by the time he was in his early teens, he was spending much of his time on the street, "acquiring a lifelong passion for drugs and discovering the joys—and lucrative possibilities—of sex with men," reported Robert McG. Thomas, Jr. in a *New York Times* obituary. Thomas quoted Huncke as stating that he was only modestly successful as a prostitute, however, because he was "always falling in love." He worked as a runner for gangster Al Capone in Chicago, and later worked independently as a thief. He also served briefly with the Civilian Conservation Corps during the Great Depression, but that was one of the few legitimate jobs he ever held in his lifetime. "I always followed the road of least resistance," he once commented to Michael T. Kaufman of the *New York Times.*

He had first visited New York City when he was about seventeen years old; in 1939, he made it his permanent base of operations. He continued to support himself by stealing, dealing drugs, and selling sex. He also made a little money describing his unusual sex life to researcher Alfred Kinsey, and procuring other subjects for Kinsey's landmark studies. In 1945, Huncke's roommate was approached by an elegantly-dressed man who wanted to sell a sawed-off shotgun and some morphine Syrettes. Huncke was at first suspicious of the man, believing him to be an FBI agent or other law enforcer. It was, in fact, William S. Burroughs, and the two soon developed a fast friendship. Huncke introduced Burroughs to heroin; he would eventually serve as the title character in Burroughs's first book, the Beat classic *Junkie.*

It was through Burroughs that Huncke met the other writers who would eventually be known as the core of the Beat Generation, including Allen Ginsberg and Jack Kerouac. Ginsberg was still a student at Columbia University at the time, and Kerouac was a recent dropout. Disillusioned with what they considered to be the flat, hypocritical world of middle-class, postwar America, these young writers found Huncke's underworld enthralling. "Though it seemed strange to some people that such a wide array of literary figures found Mr. Huncke so enchanting, he was always more than he seemed," mused Thomas. "For all his disreputable pursuits, he had elegant, refined manners and a searing honesty. He was also uncommonly well read for someone who had never been to high school, and such a natural and affecting storyteller that he could keep a table of admirers enthralled until the wee hours."

Kaufman wrote that Huncke "knew that he was not a great criminal artist like Francois Villon or Jean Genet, but he wasn't just a dope fiend thief either." He quoted Huncke as saying: "I had read all my life and I had known writers and painters before I came into contact with the Beats. . . . When I did meet them I was delighted that they had writing inclinations because I had decided that I could never write a great work, which is one of the things I had wanted to do." In his view, he served as a catalyst to the developing Beats. He stated: "I was more of a hipster than they were. They were college kids holding collegiate discussions. To say that I was as hip as someone like Charlie Parker would be really stupid but I was pretty hip for a white guy. They were going around saying 'hep' until I came along. I brought a whole new lexicon and they were interested in language. Take the word 'beat.' I would use it a lot. Eventually, it got to be used to describe the group as beatific. But when I used it, I meant tired, exhausted, beat down to your socks."

Huncke was immortalized under his own name in many of Ginsberg's poems. He appeared as "Ancke" in John Clellon Holmes's 1952 novel *Go.* He made many appearances in the Kerouac canon: he was Junkey, the dominant figure in the urban half of Kerouac's debut novel *The Town and the City;* he was "Elmo Hassel" in the book many consider the pinnacle of Beat writing, *On the Road;* and he also appeared as "Huck" in Kerouac's *Visions of Cody* and *Book of Dreams.* Huncke too had begun writing, using the men's room in a New York subway station as his office. But while his friends went on to fame and notoriety for their writing, Huncke soon found himself in prison. Over the course of his lifetime, he spent more than eleven years behind bars for drug-related offenses and petty crime. He also spent some time in psychiatric hospitals.

Discussing Huncke's accomplishments as a writer, *Dictionary of Literary Biography* contributor Arthur Winfield Knight commented that his style takes the "automatic writing" method recommended by Kerouac to its highest form. Knight further commented that "it is virtually impossible to imagine anyone's work being more intensely personal, more honest, than Huncke's." "Johnnie 1," a memoir, is "one of Huncke's most successful," asserted Knight. "The frequent use of dashes makes the reader feel how weary Huncke must have been. Brilliantly describing his life on Forty-second Street, Huncke has to pause frequently to find the energy to continue." Huncke's range of subject is "remarkable"; in *Huncke's Journal,* for example, he covers everything "from his early sexual experiences in Chicago to a lyrical description of Ponderosa Pine country in Idaho." Knight found that Huncke's writing also revealed a "goodness" within its author, "easily . . . seen in a number of pieces, such as one in which he describes how he talked a man out of shooting another man ('A Story—New York') and another ('Hallowe'en') in which he makes a plea for a more loving, benevolent universe."

Not all critics were so kind in their assessment of Huncke's efforts. Penelope Mesic could find only "a kind of low-down fascination" in *The Evening Sun Turned Crimson,* but in *Small Press Review,* Knight defended the book as "brilliantly" evoking the street life, and mentioned the author's "almost uncanny ability . . . to empathize with others." He further noted: "Loneliness, shame and guilt are the emotions Huncke experiences most often, yet he never loses the ability to transcend his anguish; even in his most perverse or desperate moments, he feels love or compassion for others." A later memoir, *Guilty of Everything,* was dismissed in *Publishers Weekly* as "guilty of inducing boredom," and as a "sordid, ill-written memoir." But Alan Ansen, evaluating the same book in *Review of Contemporary Fiction,* found that "beyond the sordidness and the apologetics there is a sense of his having found in the literary life something beyond envy, hatred and malice, something akin to the flowers and stars that occasionally cheer the bleakness."

Whatever the merits of his own writing, "Huncke's impact on counterculture history is inestimable," declared *High Times* writer Chris Eudaley. "Would Burroughs have ever written *Junkie* had he not met Huncke? Would Kerouac have been able to pen *On the Road* in a seven-day writing binge without the help of Benzedrine, which Huncke turned him onto?" Looking back on his own life, Huncke reflected to Kaufman: "I didn't weigh or balance things. I started out this way and I never really changed. . . . All I really think is this: If people are going to do things, they should just do it. Don't apologize. Don't constantly cop a plea. This is what you wanted, you did it."

*BIOGRAPHICAL/CRITICAL SOURCES:*

*BOOKS*

*Dictionary of Literary Biography,* Volume 16, *The Beats: Literary Bohemians in Postwar America,* Gale (Detroit), 1983.

Huncke, Herbert, *Guilty of Everything: The Autobiography of Herbert Huncke,* foreword by William S. Burroughs, Paragon House (New York City), 1990.

*PERIODICALS*

*Booklist,* December 1, 1980, p. 499.

*Chicago Tribune,* March 4, 1993, section 5, p. 11B.

*Library Journal,* April 1, 1990, pp. 114-16.

*New York Times,* December 9, 1992, p. B3.
*New York Times Book Review,* June 10, 1990, p. 22.
*Publishers Weekly,* March 23, 1990, p. 72.
*Review of Contemporary Fiction,* fall, 1990, pp. 227-28.
*Small Press Review,* May, 1981, p. 11.
*unspeakable visions of the individual,* 3, nos. 1-2, 1973, pp. 3-15.

*OBITUARIES:*

*PERIODICALS*

*High Times,* December, 1996.
*New York Times,* August 9, 1996, p. B7.
*Washington Post,* August 10, 1996, p. B4.*

* * *

**HURSTON, Zora Neale 1903-1960**

*PERSONAL:* Born January 7, 1891, in Eatonville, FL; died January 28, 1960, in Fort Pierce, FL; daughter of John (a preacher and carpenter) and Lucy (a seamstress; maiden name, Potts) Hurston; married Herbert Sheen, May 19, 1927 (divorced, 1931); married Albert Price III, June 27, 1939 (divorced). *Education:* Attended Howard University, 1923-24; Barnard College, B.A., 1928; graduate study at Columbia University.

*CAREER:* Writer and folklorist. Collected folklore in the South, 1927-31; Bethune-Cookman College, Daytona, FL, instructor in drama, 1933-34; collected folklore in Jamaica, Haiti, and Bermuda, 1937-38; collected folklore in Florida for the Works Progress Administration, 1938-39; Paramount Studios, Hollywood, CA, staff writer, 1941; collected folklore in Honduras, 1946-48; worked as a maid in Florida, 1950; freelance writer, 1950-56; Patrick Air Force Base, FL, librarian, 1956-57; writer for *Fort Pierce Chronicle* and part-time teacher at Lincoln Park Academy, both in Fort Pierce, FL, 1958-59. Librarian at the Library of Congress, Washington, DC; professor of drama at North Carolina College for Negroes (now North Carolina Central University), Durham; assistant to writer Fannie Hurst.

*MEMBER:* American Folklore Society, American Anthropological Society, American Ethnological Society, Zeta Phi Beta.

*AWARDS, HONORS:* Guggenheim fellowship, 1936 and 1938; Litt.D. from Morgan College, 1939; Annisfield Award, 1943, for *Dust Tracks on a Road.*

*WRITINGS:*

(With Clinton Fletcher and Time Moore) *Fast and Furious* (musical play), published in *Best Plays of 1931-32,* edited by Burns Mantle and Garrison, Sherwood, 1931.
(With Langston Hughes) *Mule Bone: A Comedy of Negro Life in Three Acts,* HarperPerennial, 1931, reprint, 1991.
*Jonah's Gourd Vine* (novel), with an introduction by Fanny Hurst, Lippincott, 1934, reprinted with a new introduction by Rita Dove, Perennial, 1990.
*Mules and Men* (folklore), with an introduction by Franz Boas, Lippincott, 1935, reprinted with a new foreword by Arnold Rampersad, Perennial, 1990.
*Their Eyes Were Watching God* (novel), Lippincott, 1937, reprinted, University of Illinois Press, 1991.
*Tell My Horse* (nonfiction), Lippincott, 1938, reprinted, Turtle Island Foundation, 1981, published as *Voodoo Gods: An Inquiry into Native Myths and Magic in Jamaica and Haiti,* Dent, 1939, reprint published as *Tell My Horse: Voodoo and Life in Haiti and Jamaica,* with an introduction by Ishmael Reed, Perennial, 1990.
*Moses, Man of the Mountain* (novel), Lippincott, 1939, reprint, HarperPerennial, 1991.
*Dust Tracks on a Road* (autobiography), Lippincott, 1942, reprinted with an introduction by Neal, 1971, reprinted with a foreward by Maya Angelou, HarperPerennial, 1991.
(With Dorothy Waring) *Stephen Kelen-d'Oxylion Presents Polk County: A Comedy of Negro Life on a Sawmill Camp with Authentic Negro Music* (three-act play), [New York], c. 1944.
*Seraph on the Suwanee* (novel), Scribner, 1948, reprint, HarperPerennial, 1991.
*I Love Myself When I Am Laughing . . . And Then Again When I Am Looking Mean And Impressive,* edited by Alice Walker, Feminist Press, 1979.
*The Sanctified Church,* Turtle Island Foundation, 1983.
*Spunk: The Selected Stories of Zora Neale Hurston,* Turtle Island Foundation, 1985, reprint, Dramatists Play Service, 1992.
*The Gilded Six-Bits,* Redpath Press, 1986.
*The Complete Stories,* HarperCollins, 1994.

*Folklore, Memoirs, and Other Writings,* Library of America, 1995.

*Novels and Stories,* Library of America, 1995.

Also author of *The First One* (one-act play), published in *Ebony and Topaz,* edited by Johnson, and of *Great Day* (play). Work represented in anthologies, including *Black Writers in America,* edited by Barksdale and Kinnamon; *Story in America,* edited by E. W. Burnett and Martha Foley, Vanguard, 1934; *American Negro Short Stories,* edited by Clarke; *The Best Short Stories by Negro Writers,* edited by Hughes; *From the Roots,* edited by James; *Anthology of American Negro Literature,* edited by Watkins. Contributor of stories and articles to periodicals, including *American Mercury, Negro Digest, Journal of American Folklore, Saturday Evening Post,* and *Journal of Negro History.*

*SIDELIGHTS:* Zora Neale Hurston is considered one of the greats of twentieth-century African-American literature. Although Hurston was closely associated with the Harlem Renaissance and has influenced such writers as Ralph Ellison, Toni Morrison, Gayl Jones, Alice Walker, and Toni Cade Bambara, interest in her has only recently been revived after decades of neglect. Hurston's four novels and two books of folklore are important sources of black myth and legend. Through her writings, Robert Hemenway wrote in *The Harlem Renaissance Remembered,* Hurston "helped to remind the Renaissance—especially its more bourgeois members—of the richness in the racial heritage; she also added new dimensions to the interest in exotic primitivism that was one of the most ambiguous products of the age."

Hurston was born and raised in the first incorporated all-black town in America, and was advised by her mother to "jump at de sun." At the age of thirteen she was taken out of school to care for her brother's children. At sixteen, she joined a traveling theatrical troupe and worked as a maid for a white woman who arranged for her to attend high school in Baltimore. Hurston later studied anthropology at Barnard College and Columbia University with the anthropologist Franz Boas, which profoundly influenced her work. After graduation she returned to her hometown for anthropological study. The data she collected would be used both in her collections of folklore and her fictional works.

"I was glad when somebody told me: 'You may go and collect Negro folklore,'" Hurston related in the introduction to *Mules and Men.* "In a way it would not be a new experience for me. When I pitched headforemost into the world I landed in the crib of Negroism. From the earliest rocking of my cradle, I had known about the capers Br'er Rabbit is apt to cut and what the Squinch Owl says from the housetop. But it was fitting me like a tight chemise. I couldn't see it for wearing it. It was only when I was off in college, away from my native surroundings, that I could see myself like somebody else and stand off and look at my garment. Then I had to have the spyglass of anthropology to look through at that."

Hurston was an ambiguous and complex figure. She embodied seemingly antipodal traits, and Hemenway described her in his *Zora Neale Hurston: A Literary Biography* as being "flamboyant yet vulnerable, self-centered yet kind, a Republican conservative and an early black nationalist." Hurston was never bitter and never felt disadvantaged because she was black. Henry Louis Gates, Jr., explained in the *New York Times Book Review:* "Part of Miss Hurston's received heritage—and perhaps the traditional notion that links the novel of manners in the Harlem Renaissance, the social realism of the 30s, and the cultural nationalism of the Black Arts movement—was the idea that racism had reduced black people to mere ciphers, to beings who react only to an omnipresent racial oppression, whose culture is 'deprived' where different, and whose psyches are in the main 'pathological'. . . . Miss Hurston thought this idea degrading, its propagation a trap. It was against this that she railed, at times brilliantly and systematically, at times vapidly and eclectically."

Older black writers criticized Hurston for the frequent crudeness and bawdiness of the tales she told. The younger generation criticized her propensity to gloss over the injustices her people were dealt. According to Judith Wilson, Hurston's greatest contribution was "to all black Americans' psychic health. The consistent note in her fieldwork and the bulk of her fiction is one of celebration of a black cultural heritage whose complexity and originality refutes all efforts to enforce either a myth of inferiority or a lie of assimilation." Wilson continued, "Zora Neale Hurston had figured out something that no other black author of her time seems to have known or appreciated so well—that our home-spun vernacular and street-corner cosmology is as valuable as the grammar and philosophy of white, Western culture."

Hurston herself wrote in 1928: "I am not tragically colored. There is no great sorrow dammed up in my soul, nor lurking behind my eyes. I do not mind at all. I do not belong to the sobbing school of Negrohood who hold that nature somehow has given them a lowdown dirty deal and whose feelings are all hurt about it. . . . No, I do not weep at the world—I am too busy sharpening my oyster knife."

*Their Eyes Were Watching God* is generally acknowledged to be Hurston's finest work of fiction. Still, it was controversial. Richard Wright found the book to be "counter-revolutionary" in a *New Masses* article. June Jordan praised the novel for its positiveness. She declared in a *Black World* review: "Unquestionably, *Their Eyes Were Watching God* is the prototypical Black novel of affirmation; it is the most successful, convincing, and exemplary novel of Blacklove that we have. Period. But the book gives us more: the story unrolls a fabulous, written-film of Blacklife freed from the constraints of oppression; here we may learn Black possibilities of ourselves if we could ever escape the hateful and alien context that has so deeply disturbed and mutilated our rightly efflorescence—*as people.* Consequently, this novel centers itself on Blacklove—even as *Native Son* rivets itself upon white hatred."

Hurston's autobiography, *Dust Tracks on a Road,* was reissued in 1985 with many chapters that had been deleted restored. The publication of this book coincided with the rediscovery by many contemporary black writers-especially Alice Walker—of the excellence of Hurston's work. The work is lengthy and tends to ramble; Hurston organized the tome around several visions she had that signified her life as an artist. In the work she delves into her childhood, when the death of her mother sent her to a boarding school where she was ignored by her family. The autobiography also traces Hurston's out-of-fashion views of racial issues, such as her opposition to desegregation and her belief that blacks should not consider themselves victims of racism. At the time of the original release of this book in 1942, she was soundly criticized for these views from leading black authors of the day, including Richard Wright, a fact which perhaps led to her fading popularity. However, with the new material in this book, Hurston is able to explain further many of her ideas.

"*Dust Tracks on a Road* suffers from weak structure, a tone that is too conciliatory, too many concessions to the publisher and an anticipated audience, and not enough concern with narrative development and proportion," commented Joanne M. Braxton in the *Women's Review of Books.* While Henry Louis Gates, Jr., noted in the *New York Times Book Review* that there were flaws in the book, namely with Hurston's clever prose overshadowing the interesting details of her life, he related that "Hurston's achievement in *Dust Tracks* is twofold. First, she gives us a *writer's* life—rather than an account of 'the Negro Problem'—in a language [that is] dazzling. . . . [And] a verbal analogue of her double experiences as a woman in a male-dominated world and as a black person in a non-black world—strikes me as her second great achievement." He concluded that "black male writers caricatured Hurston as the fool. For protection, she made up significant parts of herself."

Hurston's collection of short stories, *Spunk,* was published in 1985. She entered the title story in an *Opportunity* (the publication most central to the Harlem Renaissance) contest and won second prize. It concerns the huge and intimidating Spunk Banks, a man who has power over an entire town because of his intimidation. Banks has a public affair with Lena Kanty. Her husband, Joe, seeks revenge on Banks and attempts to kill him, but is shot to death by Banks instead. Eventually, Banks is haunted by a black bobcat, which many of the townspeople suspect is the ghost of Joe Kanty. Finally, Banks is killed in a grisly accident at the town mill, and the villagers quickly forget his reign of terror. In "Muttsy," another *Opportunity* contest winner, the tragic relationship of sheltered Pinkie and worldly Muttsy Owens is chronicled. Pinkie has been forced to live in a brothel after she runs away from home; after seeing her in the brothel, Muttsy falls for her immediately. Pinkie tries to change Muttsy's gambling addiction, forcing him to get a job before she'll become romantically involved with him. While he does get a respectable job and the two marry, Muttsy eventually resumes his gambling. Grace Ingoldby, writing in *New Statesman,* praised the collection, saying that "the stories in *Spunk* transcend the particular without any sense that Hurston knows how far she's leaping: unselfconscious, exuberant, tragi-comic, they are, to wipe the grime of overuse from a good word, brilliant."

In 1995, the Library of America collected and combined much of Hurston's writings into two volumes: *Folklore, Memoirs, and Other Writings,* and *Novels and Stories.* Critics commented that her inclusion into this prestigious collection of American writers has done much to cement her work in the minds of Americans. "That we remember her today is due, of course, to the untiring work of women like Alice Walker and the literary critic Mary Helen Washington," remarked David Nicholson in the *Washington*

*Post Book World.* "Black women reclaimed her. Now, with her inclusion in the Library of America, Zora Neale Hurston belongs to all of us." Joyce Irene Middleton commended both works in the *Women's Review of Books:* "a sustained reading of the chronology of her life . . . in this beautiful, two-volume Library of America collection, reanimates the complex cultural and political forces that shaped the world in which we see Zora Hurston laughing and lying, fighting and loving, speaking and writing."

"She was full of sidesplitting anecdotes, humorous tales, and tragicomic stories," Langston Hughes wrote of Hurston, "remembered out of her life in the South as a daughter of a traveling minister of God. She could make you laugh one minute and cry the next. . . . But Miss Hurston was clever, too—a student who didn't let college give her a broad 'a' and who had great scorn for all pretensions, academic or otherwise. That is why she was such a fine folklore collector, able to go among the people and never act as if she had been to school at all. Almost nobody else could stop the average Harlemite on Lenox Avenue and measure his head with a strange-looking, anthropological device and not get bawled out for the attempt, except Zora, who used to stop anyone whose head looked interesting, and measure it."

*BIOGRAPHICAL/CRITICAL SOURCES:*

*BOOKS*


*Black Literature Criticism,* Gale, 1992.

Bloom, Harold, editor, *Zora Neale Hurston,* Chelsea House, 1986.

Bone, Robert, *Down Home: A History of Afro-American Short Fiction from Its Beginnings to the End of the Harlem Renaissance,* Putnam, 1975.

Carter-Sigglow, Janet, *Making Her Way With Thunder: A Reappraisal of Zora Neale Hurston's Narrative Art,* P. Lang (New York City), 1994.

*Contemporary Literary Criticism,* Gale, Volume 7, 1977, Volume 30, 1984; Volume 61, 1990.

Davis, Arthur P., *From the Dark Tower,* Howard University Press, 1974.

*Dictionary of Literary Biography,* Gale, Volume 51: *Afro-American Writers From the Harlem Renaissance to 1940,* 1987; Volume 86:*American Short-Story Writers, 1910-1945,* 1989.

Harris, Trudier, *The Power of the Porch: the Storyteller's Craft in Zora Neale Hurston, Gloria Naylor, and Randall Kenan,* University of Georgia Press (Athens), 1996.

Hemenway, Robert E., *Zora Neale Hurston: A Literary Biography,* University of Illinois Press, 1977.

Hill, Lynda Marion, *Social Rituals and the Verbal Art of Zora Neale Hurston,* Howard University Press (Washington, DC), 1996.

Howard, Lillie P., *Zora Neale Hurston,* G. K. Hall, 1980.

Hughes, Langston, *The Big Sea,* Knopf, 1940.

Hughes, Langston and Arna Bontemps, editors, *The Harlem Renaissance Remembered,* Dodd, 1972.

Hurston, Zora Neale, *Dust Tracks on a Road* (autobiography), Lippincott, 1942.

Johnson, Yvonne, *The Voices of African American Women: The Use of Narrative and Authorial Voice in the Works of Harriet Jacobs, Zora Neale Hurston, and Alice Walker,* P. Lang (New York City), 1996.

Kaplan, Carla, *The Erotics of Talk: Women's Writing and Feminist Paradigms,* Oxford University Press (New York City), 1996.

Karanja, Ayana I., *Zora Neale Hurston: Dialogue in Spirit and in Truth,* P. Lang (New York City), 1996.

Lowe, John, *Jump at the Sun: Zora Neale Hurston's Cosmic Comedy,* University of Illinois Press (Urbana), 1994.

Plant, Deborah G., *Every Tub Must Sit on Its Own Bottom: The Philosophy and Politics of Zora Neale Hurston,* University of Illinois Press (Urbana), 1995.

Turner, Darwin T., *In a Minor Chord: Three Afro-American Writers and Their Search for Identity,* Southern Illinois University Press, 1971.

Wall, Cheryl A., *Women of the Harlem Renaissance,* Indiana University Press (Bloomington), 1995.

Witcover, Paul, *Zora Neale Hurston,* Melrose Square (Los Angeles), 1994.

Yannuzzi, Della A., *Zora Neale Hurston: Southern Storyteller,* Enslow (Springfield, NJ), 1996.


*PERIODICALS*


*African American Review,* summer, 1994, p. 283; spring, 1995, p. 17.

*Black World,* August, 1972; August, 1974.

*Entertainment Weekly,* March 17, 1995, p. 82.

*Ms.,* March, 1975; June, 1978.

*National Review,* April 3, 1995, p. 58.

*Negro American Literature Forum,* spring, 1972.

*Negro Digest,* February, 1962.

*New Masses,* October 5, 1937.

*New Republic,* February 11, 1978; July 3, 1995, p. 30.

*New Statesman,* July 3, 1987, pp. 29-30.
*New York Times Book Review,* February 19, 1978; April 21, 1985, p. 43, 45.
*Observer,* February 16, 1986.
*Times Literary Supplement,* May 2, 1986, p. 479.
*Village Voice,* August 17, 1972.
*Washington Post Book World,* July 23, 1978; May 12, 1985, p. 10; March 5, 1995, p. 4.
*Women's Review of Books,* July, 1985, p. 5; November, 1995, p. 28.

*OBITUARIES:*

*PERIODICALS*

*Newsweek,* February 15, 1960.
*New York Times,* February 5, 1960.
*Publishers Weekly,* February 15, 1960.
*Time,* February 15, 1960.
*Wilson Library Bulletin,* April, 1960.*

* * *

**JANCE, J(udith) A(nn) 1944-**

*PERSONAL:* Born October 27, 1944, in Watertown, SD; daughter of Norman (in insurance sales) and Evelyn (Anderson) Busk; married Jerry Joseph Teale Janc, January 29, 1967 (divorced, 1980); married William Alan Schilb, 1985; children: (first marriage) Jeanne Teale, Josh Mikki; (second marriage) two stepsons and one stepdaughter. *Education:* University of Arizona, B.A., 1966, M.Ed., 1970; American College, Bryn Mawr, PA, C.L.U., 1980.

*ADDRESSES: Home*—P.O. Box 766, Bellevue, WA 98009. *Agent*—Alice Volpe, Northwest Literary Agency, 4500 108th NE, Kirkland, WA 98033.

*CAREER:* Pueblo High School, Tucson, AZ, teacher, 1966-68; Indian Oasis Schools, Sells, AZ, librarian, 1968-73; Equitable Life Assurance Society, New York, NY, life insurance salesperson, 1974-84. Writer, 1985—.

*MEMBER:* Denny Regrade Business Association (president, 1983-84).

*WRITINGS:*

*J. P. BEAUMONT SERIES; MYSTERY NOVELS*

*Until Proven Guilty,* Avon (New York City), 1985.
*Injustice for All,* Avon, 1986.
*Trial by Fury,* Avon, 1987.
*Improbable Cause,* Avon, 1987.
*A More Perfect Union,* Avon, 1988.
*Dismissed with Prejudice,* Avon, 1989.
*Minor in Possession,* Avon, 1990.
*Payment in Kind,* Avon, 1991.
*Without Due Process,* Morrow (New York City), 1992.
*Failure to Appear,* Morrow, 1993.
*Lying in Wait,* Morrow, 1994.
*Name Withheld,* Morrow, 1995.

*JOANNA BRADY SERIES; MYSTERY NOVELS*

*Desert Heat,* Avon, 1993.
*Tombstone Courage,* Morrow, 1994.
*Shoot/Don't Shoot,* Avon, 1995.
*Dead to Rights,* Avon, 1997.
*Skeleton Canyon,* Avon, 1997.

*OTHER NOVELS*

*Hour of the Hunter,* Morrow, 1991.

*BOOKS FOR CHILDREN*

*It's Not Your Fault,* Charles Franklin (Edmonds, WA), 1985.
*Dial Zero for Help: A Story of Parental Kidnapping,* Charles Franklin, 1985.
*Welcome Home, Stranger: A Child's View of Family Alcoholism,* Charles Franklin, 1986.

*POETRY*

*After the Fire,* Lance Publications, 1984.

*SIDELIGHTS:* J. A. Jance is best known for her mystery novels, especially the eleven books that depict the adventures of Seattle police detective J. P. Beaumont. The first Beaumont tale, *Until Proven Guilty,* was published in 1985 in paperback. It establishes Beaumont's wealth, the outcome of a relationship with a woman named Anne Corley. This and later titles reveal Beaumont as a resentful, morose man who is battling alcoholism and an unstable love life. Critics find him a decent enough character, however. Jennifer A. Strus in *Armchair Detective* points out that Beaumont "is . . . a delight; he is tough on the outside but is truly a soft touch."

Jance became interested in police work following an incident in which her husband was driven home from work, unknowingly, by a serial killer who later began stalking them. The police investigation that followed inspired Jance to depict police procedures in her work. The Beaumont series has been praised by critics for its accurate descriptions of Seattle as well as for well-drawn characterizations. In a review of *Dismissed with Prejudice,* a *Publishers Weekly* contributor praises "the dexterous characterizations that have become the hallmarks of [Jance's] mysteries."

In 1991 Jance, a former librarian on a Native American reservation, switched gears from the Beaumont series to produce *Hour of the Hunter,* a novel set on a reservation in Arizona. The novel features a recently released killer who seeks revenge against a woman who was instrumental in putting him behind bars. Bill Farley, writing in *St. James Guide to Crime & Mystery Writers,* lauds this novel as "Jance's most complex and compelling work to date." Liz Currie of *Armchair Detective* suggests that "Jance skillfully brings everything—and everyone—together in a climax that is guaranteed to leave readers breathless."

Jance continued to write stories set in Arizona, including *Desert Heat* and *Tombstone Courage*—two titles that feature protagonist Joanna Brady. The first book in the Joanna Brady series concludes with the murder of Brady's husband, during his campaign for sheriff of Cochise County. Following her husband's death, Brady decides to run for sheriff herself. *Tombstone Courage* begins with Brady winning the election. This book depicts Brady's experiences as the first female sheriff in Arizona. Farley comments on both Beaumont and Brady series: "They are written (told) in easily accessible, compulsively readable, sometimes overly sentimental prose, without literary pretension."

Jance once told *CA:* "Writing has provided a means of rewriting my own history, both in terms of the children's books and the murder thrillers. The children's books confront difficult issues—sexual molestation, parental kidnapping, and a child's view of family alcoholism. The murder thrillers are escapist fare with no redeeming social value."

*BIOGRAPHICAL/CRITICAL SOURCES:*

*BOOKS*

*St. James Guide to Crime & Mystery Writers,* 4th edition, St. James Press (Detroit), 1996.

*PERIODICALS*

*Armchair Detective,* winter, 1990, p. 97; winter, 1991, p. 113; spring, 1992, p. 232.

*Booklist,* December 1, 1991, p. 677.

*Publishers Weekly,* April 28, 1989, pp. 72-3; March 2, 1990, p. 79.

* * *

**JONES, LeRoi**
**See BARAKA, Amiri**

* * *

**JONES, Robert F(rancis) 1934-**

*PERSONAL:* Born May 26, 1934, in Milwaukee, WI; son of Charles F. (a banker) and Rose Mary (Pueringer) Jones; married Louise Tyor (a writer), October 21, 1956; children: Leslie Ellen, Benno Francis. *Education:* University of Michigan, B.A., 1956. *Politics:* Independent. *Religion:* None. *Avocational interests:* Hunting, fishing, skindiving, gardening.

*ADDRESSES:* *Home*—West Rupert, VT 05776. *Agent*—John Boswell, 45 East 51st St., Suite 301, New York, NY 10022.

*CAREER:* Time, Inc., New York, NY, associate editor and writer for *Time* (magazine), 1960-68, writer for *Sports Illustrated,* beginning in 1968. *Military service:* U.S. Navy, 1956-59; became lieutenant junior grade.

*MEMBER:* Hudson River Fishermen's Association, Kappa Tau Alpha.

*WRITINGS:*

*NOVELS*

*Blood Sport: A Journey up the Hassayampa,* Simon & Schuster (New York City), 1974.

*The Diamond Bogo: An African Idyll,* Prentice-Hall (Englewood Cliffs, NJ), 1977.

*Wolfslade's Glacier,* Simon & Schuster, 1980.

*Blood Tide,* Atlantic Monthly Press (New York City), 1990.

*Tie My Bones to Her Back,* Farrar, Straus (New York City), 1996.

*NONFICTION*

*Upland Passage: A Field Dog's Education,* Farrar, Straus, 1992.

*Jake: A Labrador Puppy at Work and Play* (juvenile), Farrar, Straus, 1992.

*The Fishing Doctor,* Villard (New York City), 1992.

*Dancers in the Sunset Sky: The Musings of a Bird Hunter,* Lyons & Burford (New York City), 1996.

*OTHER*

Contributor of articles and reviews to *Washington Post* and *New York Times Sunday Magazine.*

*SIDELIGHTS:* Robert F. Jones lists his primary writing motivations as a boyhood spent hunting and fishing in the upper Midwest, wide travel in the Western Pacific, and further travel in Africa, Eastern Europe, Central America, and New Zealand. Jones's appreciation of hunting is expressed in some of his nonfiction works, including *Dancers in the Sunset Sky: The Musings of a Bird Hunter* and *Upland Passage: A Field Dog's Education.* His interest in sport and travel is further reflected in his novels. *Blood Sport,* for example, tells the story of two men, father and son, who "leave the world of women to travel upriver in search of fish, game, danger, masculinity," according to *Newsweek*'s Peter Prescott. The river of *Blood Sport* is a mythical waterway, the Hassayampa, that encompasses such actual settings as China, Wisconsin, and New York, and provides dangers—in the forms of bear, outlaws, marlin, and mastodons—and challenges, in unicorns to be captured and miniature girls in sunken taxicabs to be rescued.

This farcical re-telling of what Prescott calls the "masculine mystique" is not entirely successful, according to Michael Mewshaw of the *New York Times Book Review.* Although he praises Jones's "considerable talent and accomplishment," Mewshaw states that "some of the potential remains unrealized while Jones indulges himself in aimless digressions, indigestible brews of fact and fantasy, and incessant puns and word plays." Prescott also finds problems in the novel, calling it "ambitious to the point of foolhardiness. . . . Sensing that this story can no longer be played straight he gives us a yarn far gone (but not entirely) into self-parody, with all the mythic elements . . . dredged up and kicked around for laughs." Yet, Prescott concludes, "it's worth it. Jones writes very well, can often be very funny." John Skow of *Time* is more positive in his reaction to *Blood Sport.* He writes: "Half liar, half believer, spinning yarns out of racial memory and the L. L. Bean catalogue, Jones has created the great rarity—a new myth. What is surprising, considering the opportunities he has given himself to waft off into artiness, is that he has also written a good boots-in-the-mud hunting story whose textures are as natural to the touch as the worn stock of an old rifle."

Hunting of a sort provides the basis for *Blood Tide*—but in this novel, the quarry is human. The plot follows a charter boat skipper and her Vietnam veteran father on a cruise to Southeast Asia in search of revenge. A *Library Journal* reviewer warns some readers about the graphic violent content, but goes on to advise that "this is a compelling adventure tale that in some ways recalls [Joseph] Conrad's *Heart of Darkness.*" "There is never a dull moment in 'Blood Tide,'" concurs Newgate Callendar in *New York Times Book Review.* "Mr. Jones is a superior writer who can turn a telling phrase and who—when he writes about the sea—has a pronounced streak of poetry. His characters, too, are beautifully developed." A *Kirkus Reviews* contributor gives a lighter assessment of *Blood Tide,* calling it an "up-to-date swashbuckler. Swords in the teeth, wind in the sails, and it all works. Great fun."

Violence was again an issue in *Tie My Bones to Her Back,* a novel about a brother and sister caught up in the government-sanctioned slaughter of the great buffalo herds of the American West. A reviewer for *Washington Post Book World* calls it an "unsentimental and unflinching tale." In graphic detail, Jones described the gruesome carnage of the buffalo hunt and the brutality of those involved in it. His fiction was based on his extensive investigation into the events of the late 1800s, and the reviewer finds that "occasionally Jones's prodigious research—on everything from the invention of the Gatling gun to the intricacies of the Cheyenne language—bogs down the narrative. . . . Even so, this is a worthy novel that ultimately becomes the kind of crimson-soaked morality play that's at the heart of so many immortal cowboy and Indian sagas." *New York Times* contributor Richard Bernstein praises *Tie My Bones to Her Back* as "the product of a serious attempt to understand and evoke a special, central episode of American history," but he also professes to being somewhat overwhelmed by the research that provided the foundation for the book. "One almost wishes . . . that Mr. Jones had written a history of the slaughter of the buffalo and its terrible effect on Indian life rather than trying to use it as the backdrop for a work of fiction," he comments.

Addressing the gory nature of the story, Linda Barrett Osborne notes that although it sometimes made for difficult reading, it is well-handled. She writes in the *New York Times Book Review,* "Jones . . . portrays the thrill of the hunt, animal or human, with a lyricism that is often unnerving and a realism that belies the glamour of conquest and adventure." A *Publishers Weekly* writer sums up: "It would be hard to find a more brutal and unsentimental portrait of the American West than the one offered in this bleak yet beautifully written novel."

*BIOGRAPHICAL/CRITICAL SOURCES:*

*BOOKS*

*Contemporary Literary Criticism,* Volume 7, Gale (Detroit), 1977.

*PERIODICALS*

*Booklist,* March 15, 1990, p. 1416; October 19, 1992, p. 81; November 1, 1992, p. 508; August 9, 1996, pp. 1874, 1882.
*Kirkus Reviews,* January 15, 1990, p. 71.
*Library Journal,* February 1, 1990, pp. 106-107.
*Newsweek,* May 20, 1974, p. 111, 114.
*New York Times,* July 17, 1996, p. C14.
*New York Times Book Review,* May 19, 1974, pp. 4-5; July 22, 1990, p. 22; September 1, 1996, p. 16.
*Publishers Weekly,* February 21, 1977; January 26, 1990, p. 403; May 20, 1996, p. 237.
*Time,* May 27, 1974, pp. 93, E3.
*Washington Post Book World,* October 6, 1996, p. 8.*

**KIDDER, Tracy 1945-**

*PERSONAL:* Born November 12, 1945, in New York, NY; son of Henry Maynard (a lawyer) and Reine (a high school teacher; maiden name, Tracy) Kidder; married Frances T. Toland, January 2, 1971; children: a boy and a girl. *Education:* Harvard University, A.B., 1967; University of Iowa, M.F.A., 1974.

*ADDRESSES: Agent*—Georges Borchardt, Inc., 136 East 57th St., New York, NY 10022.

*CAREER:* Writer, 1974—. Contributing editor, *Atlantic Monthly,* Boston, 1982—. *Military service:* U.S. Army, 1967-69, served in intelligence in Vietnam; became first lieutenant.

*AWARDS, HONORS:* Atlantic First Award, *Atlantic Monthly,* for short story "The Death of Major Great"; Sidney Hillman Foundation Prize, 1978, for article, "Soldiers of Misfortune"; Pulitzer Prize and American Book Award, 1982, both for *The Soul of a New Machine;* National Book Critics Circle nomination (nonfiction), 1986, for *House;* Christopher Award and National Book Critics Circle Award nomination (nonfiction), 1989, Robert F. Kennedy Award and Ambassador Book Award, 1990, all for *Among Schoolchildren;* New England Book Award, 1994, for *Old Friends.*

*WRITINGS:*

*NONFICTION*

*The Road to Yuba City: A Journey into the Juan Corona Murders,* Doubleday (New York City), 1974.
*The Soul of a New Machine,* Little, Brown (Boston), 1981, revised edition, Modern Library (New York City), 1997.
*House,* Houghton Mifflin (Boston), 1985.
*Among Schoolchildren,* Houghton Mifflin, 1989.
*Old Friends,* Houghton Mifflin, 1993, large print edition, Wheeler, 1993.

*OTHER*

Contributor to newspapers and magazines, including the *New York Times Book Review, Atlantic Monthly,* and *Country Journal.*

*SIDELIGHTS:* In several critically acclaimed and award-winning nonfiction books, Tracy Kidder has combined meticulous research and reportial skills to produce fascinating portrayals of subjects as diverse as elementary education, homebuilding, and nursing homes. Kidder's *The Soul of a New Machine* proved by its critical reception that technical subjects can be comprehensible and intriguing to laymen when they are skillfully presented. The book details the eighteen-month-long struggle of engineers at Data General Corporation to create a competitive super-mini computer. Kidder, a newcomer to this highly technical world, spent months in a basement laboratory at the corporation's Massachusetts headquarters observing teams of young engineers at work: the hardware specialists, or "Hardy Boys," who put the computer's circuitry together, and the "Micro-kids," who developed the code that fused the hardware and software of the system. In telling the story of the assembly, setbacks, and perfection of the thirty-two "bit" prototype computer, the Eagle, Kidder exposes the inner workings of a highly competitive industry, illustrates both concentrated teamwork and moments of virtuosity on the part of the project's brilliant engineers, and produces what reviewer Edward R. Weidlein, in the *Washington Post Book World,* judged "a true-life adventure" and "compelling entertainment."

Many critics cited Kidder's masterful handling of the complex subject matter in *The Soul of a New Machine* as one of the book's strongest features. "Even someone like this reviewer," wrote Christopher Lehmann-Haupt of the *New York Times,* "who barely understood the difference between computer hardware and software when he began *The Soul of a New Machine,* was able to follow every step of the debugging mystery, even though it involves binary arithmetic, Boolean algebra, and a grasp of the difference between a System Cache and an Instruction Processor." Weidlin concurred, observing that Kidder "offers a fast, painless, enjoyable means to an initial understanding of computers, allowing us to understand the complexity of machines we could only marvel at before."

Kidder's portraits of the Eagle's engineers were applauded by critics as well. A *New Yorker* reviewer proclaimed that Kidder "gives a full sense of the mind and motivation, the creative genius of the computer engineer." And a *Saturday Review* critic claimed that *The Soul of a New Machine* "tells a human story of tremendous effort." Critics also lauded *The Soul of a New Machine* for its departure from the standard journalistic approach to nonfiction. Jeremy Bernstein, writing in the *New York Review of Books,* declared, "I strongly recommend Tracy Kidder's book. I do not know anything quite like it. It tells a story far removed from our daily experience, and while it may seem implausible, it has the ring of truth."

Following the working style he established in *The Soul of a New Machine,* Kidder immersed himself once again in the workaday world of a diverse group of individuals for his next book, *House.* Documenting the construction of a new home from blueprints to finished product, *House* presents the pleasures and pitfalls that occur at all phases of the building process. The book allows the reader to view that process through the eyes of the seven adults involved: architect and "Renaissance man in delirium" Bill Rawn, the quartet of counterculturist builders known as the Apple Corps, and the prospective homeowners, Jonathan and Judith Souweine. Kidder, who spent six months observing all aspects of the construction, as well as the lives of the people involved, traces their combined efforts to design, finance, and build the house, and places special emphasis on the parties' abilities to forge relationships under somewhat trying circumstances.

Reviewers noted that the theme of *House* centers on the building of these relationships, and of the lines of trust and communication necessary for the relationships to occur. Writing in the *Los Angeles Times,* Esther McCoy noted: "*House* . . . essentially is concerned with the people who build the house and their interaction with clients and architect." The ties do not come easily, however, as the participants haggle and argue about the various problems that arise. A rift develops between the Souweines and the Apple Corps over the final $660 of the $146,660 construction cost; in another instance, the builders are at odds with Rawn over his underdeveloped designs for a staircase. Commenting on the give-and-take nature of these dealings, Paul Goldberger of the *New York Times Book Review* stated: "The clients, the architect and the builders form a kind of triangle . . . and they push and pull each other in every possible way." Jonathan Yardley, writing in the *Washington Post Book World,* agreed, adding, "The construction of a house is an undertaking that puts human beings in an odd relationship of cooperation and conflict, a relationship that begins as business but invariably acquires intensely personal overtones."

To some reviewers, these "personal overtones" were also reflected in Kidder's quiet observations of the differences in the characters' social positions and the tensions that exist as those distinctions become more and more apparent. Though three members of the Apple Corps "had upbringings more white collar than blue collar," Goldberger wrote, "they are aware that their lives are different from those of people like Mr. and Mrs. Souweine." Kidder approached the situation democratically, claimed R. Z. Sheppard in *Time,* giving "equal time to client, architect and builders." Sheppard went on to find that "the interplay between confident professionals and self-conscious craftsmen conveys much about misunderstandings and bad feelings in a society stratified by education and status."

*House* does more than chronicle the relationships that developed over the course of the home's construction; it is also a nuts-and-bolts account of the construction itself. In addition, Kidder fills the book with a collection of short essays on topics as varied as the history of nails and a cost analysis of Henry Thoreau's Walden Pond shelter, so that *House* becomes more a study of architectural lore than a how-to of homebuilding. "The book keeps opening out into discourses on welcome, unexpected subjects," stated *Newsweek* reviewer David Lehman, "Kidder's book is filled with this kind of unobtrusive information." Affirming Kidder's inclusion of these asides, Adele Freedman of the Toronto *Globe and Mail* claimed: "After reading *House,* no one will ever take the design of a staircase or the installation of a window for granted."

As with *The Soul of a New Machine,* Kidder earned praise for his clear presentation of unfamiliar terms and operations. Christopher Lehmann-Haupt of the *New York Times* found Kidder "a master at the difficult art of describing complex objects and processes." Citing the parallels in style between *The Soul of a New Machine* and *House, Chicago Tribune* reviewer Max J. Friedman declared that Kidder wrote *House* "with the same thoroughness, attention to detail and technical explanation that marked the earlier work. . . . Kidder's careful, precise reportage and brand of literary verite take us on a remarkable journey into the technical, mechanical and emotional world of housebuilding." Finally, Goldberger summarized the feelings of many critics with his statement that *House* "is told with such clarity, intelligence and grace it makes you wonder why no one has written a book like it before."

Kidder changed his subject matter but retained his reportorial methods for *Among Schoolchildren,* a record of the nine months he spent observing a Holyoke, Massachusetts, elementary school classroom. The book follows thirty-four-year-old Chris Zajac and her class of twenty fifth-grade students from their first day together at Kelly School to their last. In order to gather his material, Kidder placed himself at a desk in the front of the classroom, right next to Mrs. Zajac's own. He remained there, a silent observer on the scene, for nearly 180 schooldays. "I missed two days all year," Kidder told *Publishers Weekly* interviewer Amanda Smith. "One I just played hooky, and the other one, I was sick." The author eventually took over 10,000 pages of notes, compiled from his own observations and his frequent talks with Mrs. Zajac, which he then assembled, edited, and reworked into the finished book.

Written from Zajac's point of view, *Among Schoolchildren* serves as an account of the teacher's thoughts and feelings about her day-to-day teaching decisions and provides a first-hand look at what occurs in an American classroom. Kidder drew praise for his portrayals of the diminutive, energetic Zajac and her "fragile rubber raft of children," as *New York Times Book Review* contributor Phyllis Theroux called them. Students like the hyperactive, destructive Clarence, the barely literate Pedro, who was "born and raised with my grandmother, because I was cryin' too much," and the intelligent, introverted Judith test the limits of Zajac's teaching skills and patience. Because of his proximity to the participants, especially Zajac, Kidder was able to get "inside her head and inside the heads of the children," reflected Gerald Grant in the Chicago *Tribune Books,* adding that the author's "close observations of the children in their many moods tie us into the emotional networks that make up classroom life." Those thoughts were echoed by *New York Times* reviewer Eva Hoffman, who asserted: "By the end of the book, we appreciate Mrs. Zajac's skills and strengths, and we come to care about the children's small hurts and triumphs."

Aside from providing insights into these characters, *Among Schoolchildren* also tackles some of the difficult issues facing the American educational system. Talking about the progress of reform with Smith, Kidder noted that "most efforts at reform usually are conducted independently of the experience, knowledge, wishes of teachers. And that's a *terrible* mistake, of course, since, for better or worse, education *is* what happens in these little rooms." Several reviewers found Kidder's observations worthy of praise. "Kidder writes with sensitivity . . . of the need for educational reform," a *Publishers Weekly* reviewer judged. "We see Kelly School as a compelling microcosm of what is wrong—and right—with our educational system." Grant concurred, adding: "Tracy Kidder has written a wonderful, compassionate book about teaching. While we have some cause for despair about the operation of the system, we have grounds for hope if his book helps draw more Mrs. Zajacs into our classrooms." And Phillip Lopate in the *Washington Post Book World* stressed: "At a time when public education seems to be fair game for attacks from all sides, Tracy Kidder has written a celebration of the work of one good schoolteacher."

Kidder's next book was a foray into the world of a nursing home. With much the same technique he used in his other "journalistic" works, in *Old Friends* Kidder spent a year observing the lives of the residents of Linda Manor, a nursing home near Northampton, Massachussets. The residents of the nursing home are a diverse group, including the former actress Eleanor, who at eighty years of age is running the facility's theater program; Ted, a former morse-code operator who still drums the code on the arms of his chair; Winifred, who because of her obesity must be winched into her wheelchair every day; and Fleur, a ninety-two-year-old who is convinced she is still at summer camp. The narrative focuses, however, on Joe Torchio and Lou Freed, two reluctant roommates forced together out of economic necessity. After living together, their friendship grows, despite their apparent differences. A well-educated former probation officer, Joe was incapacitated by a stroke in his early fifties. Now, at seventy-two, he is young enough to be Lou's son. Lou, ninety-two, is a retired machinist whose beloved wife has just died. During the book's course, Kidder shows their happiness at being able-bodied enough to live on the top floor (the one requiring the least assistance), their thoughts about life and death, and their hopes and disappointments. Paul Hemphill related in the *Los Angeles Times* that the book shows "that behind those doors and inside those wasted bodies there are hearts and souls still lusting to go around the block one more time, no matter how reduced the circumstances."

David L. Kirp, writing in the *Nation* found fault with the book, calling the writing "mainly treacly, and that evinces another, related kind of failed vision, another misuse of authorial omniscience." He believed that the book "emphasizes the superficial and noncontroversial," and stays away from important, yet untidy, aspects of the clients lives. However, Reeve Lindbergh, writing in the *Washington Post Book World* commented that Kidder has a "breathtaking writer's skill," adding that "the real tour de force here . . . is the author's ability to look so closely and unsentimentally at the sufferings of age, and yet with such unwavering affection for the individual aged." Lindbergh concluded that "this beautifully written and remarkably compassionate book, my own favorite in Tracy Kidder's impressive body of work, shows us the way."

In his best-known books, Tracy Kidder has shown himself to be adept at creating works of nonfiction that, as he told Smith, "do a lot of the things that novels do." By using similar research and writing techniques for all of his works, Kidder has discovered a formula for success, yet his books are far from formulaic. Critics have complimented Kidder's ability to transform the ordinary and everyday into something fascinating, a talent that Friedman termed Kidder's "penchant . . . for taking the reader on a journey into undiscovered knowledge." But as informative and entertaining as those journeys may be, the focus of Kidder's energy is on the people who inhabit his books. Speaking of his writing to Smith, Kidder admits that one of his purposes is "to bring people to life on the page." According to reviewers, who agree with Theroux's summation that Kidder's works are "full of the author's genuine love, delight and celebration of the human condition," he does so successfully.

*BIOGRAPHICAL/CRITICAL SOURCES:*

*PERIODICALS*

*Business Week,* November 1, 1993, p. 18.
*Chicago Tribune,* September 29, 1985.
*Globe and Mail* (Toronto), December 14, 1985.
*Los Angeles Times,* November 12, 1985; September 12, 1993, p. 1, 9.
*Nation,* April 11, 1994, p. 490.
*New Leader,* September 6, 1993, p. 18.
*New Statesman,* May 20, 1994, p. 39.
*Newsweek,* October 28, 1985.
*New Yorker,* October 19, 1981.
*New York Review of Books,* October 8, 1981.
*New York Times,* August 11, 1981; September 5, 1985; October 3, 1985; August 30, 1989.
*New York Times Book Review,* August 23, 1981; November 29, 1981; October 6, 1985; September 17, 1989; October 3, 1993, p. 1.

*Publishers Weekly,* July 21, 1989; September 15, 1989; July 26, 1993, p. 50; October 10, 1994, p. 67.
*Saturday Review,* December, 1981.
*Time,* October 14, 1985; October 11, 1993, p. 86.
*Tribune Books* (Chicago), August 13, 1989.
*Washington Post Book World,* September 9, 1981; October 6, 1985; September 3, 1989; September 19, 1993, p. 4.

* * *

## KIS, Danilo 1935-1989

*PERSONAL:* Surname is pronounced "kish"; born February 22, 1935, in Subotica, Yugoslavia; died of cancer, October 15, 1989; son of Eduard and Milica (Dragicevic) Kis. *Education:* University of Belgrade, B.A., 1958.

*CAREER:* Writer. Teacher of Serbo-Croation and Yugoslavian at University of Strasbourg, Strasbourg, France, 1961-63, and in Bordeaux, France, 1973-76, and Lille, France, 1979-83.

*AWARDS, HONORS:* Award from *NiN,* 1972, for *Pescanik;* Ivan Goran Kovacic Award from *Vjesnik* (Zagreb, Yugoslavia), 1977, for *Grobnica za Borisa Davidovica;* Grand Aigle d'Or from the City of Nice, 1980, for body of work; Award Ivo Andric, 1984, for *Enciklopedija mrtvih.*

*WRITINGS:*

*IN ENGLISH*

*Basta, pepeo* (novel), Prosveta, 1965, translation from the Serbo-Croatian by William J. Hannaher published as *Garden, Ashes,* Harcourt, 1978, reprinted, 1994.
*Grobnica za Borisa Davidovica* (stories), Liber, 1976, translation by Duska Mikic-Mitchell published as *A Tomb for Boris Davidovich,* Harcourt, 1978.
*Homo Poetics: Essays and Interviews,* Farrar, Straus, 1995.

*IN SERBO-CROATIAN*

*Mansarda* (novel; title means "Attic"), Kosmos, 1962.
*Psalam 44* (novel; title means "Psalm 44"), Kosmos, 1962.
*Rani jadi* (stories; title means "Youthful Grief"), Nolit, 1970.
*Pescanik,* Prosveta, 1972, reprinted as *Hourglass,* Farrar, Straus, 1990.
*Po-etika* (essays), Volume 1, Nolit, 1972, Volume 2, Ideje, 1974.
*Cas anatomije* (essays; title means "The Anatomy Lesson"), Nolit, 1978.
*Enciklopedija mrtvih* (stories), Globus/Prosveta, 1983, reprinted as *The Encyclopedia of the Dead,* Farrar, Straus, 1989, reprinted, Penguin, 1991.
*Djela Danila Kisa* (selected works), ten volumes, Globus/Prosveta, 1983.

Also author of plays, including "Elektra," "Noc i magla," "Papagaj," and "Drveni sanduk Tomasa Vulfa" (for television). Translator of poems from French, Hungarian, and Russian. Contributor to periodicals, including *Delo, Knizevnost, New York Times Book Review,* and *Vidici.*

*SIDELIGHTS:* Many critics consider Danilo Kis to be one of the most important Yugoslavian writers of the twentieth century. He first came to the attention of Western readers with *Garden, Ashes,* a short novel about an East European family during World War II. The story is narrated by the son, Andreas Scham, who relates how the war forced his family from their comfortable home on a tree-lined street to a hovel in an abandoned railyard. Young Scham also recounts how the Holocaust claimed his father, a railroad official given to poetry and alcohol. Although much of *Garden, Ashes* is conveyed in a realistic manner, it ends rather mystically, with Scham's father, an apparent victim of Nazi terrorism, possibly surviving the war to live out his final years under various disguises and pseudonyms.

Ernst Pawel, reviewing *Garden, Ashes* in *Nation* after the novel was reprinted in 1978, described Kis's work as "a singularly moving evocation of being a child without childhood, and of a family trying to survive the end of the world." Pawel, who remarked that the novel is somewhat autobiographical—Kis's family fled Yugoslavia during the war, and his father presumably died in a concentration camp—praised Kis's ability to transform "childhood and exile into an original vision of exceptional force and beauty." Pawel was particularly impressed with Kis's style, which he described as a "potent blend of lyrical poignancy and sardonic irreverence," and he deemed the novel "superb."

Equally impressive to many reviewers was *A Tomb for Boris Davidovich,* Kis's cycle of short stories about anti-Semitism and the Stalin purges. Notable among the book's seven tales is the title work, in which Davidovich's defiance before his Communist interrogators leads to the systematic assassination of other prisoners and eventually compels him to a ghastly suicide. Another disturbing tale concerns one of Davidovich's fourteenth-century ancestors, a Jew whose refusal to repent his faith results in a grisly bloodbath. Kis's depiction of these and other horrifying events prompted many critical comments like those of Zora Devrnja Zimmerman, who wrote in *World Literature Today* that *A Tomb for Boris Davidovich* was "a stunning statement on political persecution."

Some critics accorded special attention to Kis's technique of poetic journalism in *A Tomb for Boris Davidovich.* Zimmerman noted Kis's "gaunt, stark prose" and added that the "descriptions of interior worlds are given as though they were reports, as though Kis had transcribed secret confidences from informants." Joseph Brodsky, in his introduction to a later printing of *Boris Davidovich,* lauded Kis's unique method, in which "his emphasis on imagery and detail . . . puts his horrific subject matter into the most adequate perspective." Brodsky attributed the book's impact to its unusual form and contended, "It is not that the thought is felt but, rather, that the feeling is thought."

Although *A Tomb for Boris Davidovich* brought Kis acclaim in the West, its initial publication proved less rewarding in his native Yugoslavia, where the writers union, reacting to the book's anti-Stalinism, sought to besmirch Kis by accusing him of plagiarizing writers such as Alexander Solzhenitsyn and James Joyce. Kis responded by publishing *Cas anatomije,* which Ernst Pawel described as "a 344-page polemic counterblast." Pawel added that *Cas anatomije* proved "quite successful" in Yugoslavia, but Kis eventually moved to France.

Besides *Gardens, Ashes* and *A Tomb for Boris Davidovich,* Kis's *Encyclopedia of the Dead* and *Hourglass* have been translated into English. According to Brendon Lemon in *The Nation,* the stories in *Encyclopedia* are concerned with the disappearance of Eastern European Jews. Lemon stated: "A Kis chronology can be postwar or imperial, biblical or contemporary, as precise as a stopwatch or as indeterminate as a dream. . . . He is a master of indirectly rendered emotion." The title story in *Encyclopedia* relates a woman's dream about a book containing the biographies of everyone who ever lived who was not listed in another reference work. Through devices such as the inclusion of footnotes, Kis gave the stories a documentary feel. Angela Carter noted in the *New York Times Book Review* that Kis's stories are fiction that are also about fiction: "Everywhere in these stories the correspondence among what is real, what might be real, and the mediation of the written word between these conditions, reverberates on many levels."

*Hourglass* reflects the illusory image stamped on a Bakelite surface, one that may be perceived as a vase, an hourglass, a human face. The story unfolds through dialogue between the chief investigator and the witnesses and suspect in a murder that occurred during World War II, as well as through various literary devices, including a real letter written by Kis's father. Some critics remarked that Kis's use of unusual literary devices rendered the book ineffective, but others praised the author's technique. For instance, Stanislaw Baranczak proclaimed in *The New Republic* that this book is Kis's "most perfect work, in which the all-pervading mirror motif serves the purposes of the story and shapes the way it is narrated," while John Bayley in the *New York Review of Books* asserted, "Probably no other novelist has succeeded better than Kis in making a densely stylistic pattern out of such a nightmare, conveying with gruesome but also aesthetically beautiful effect the interrelation in such a life at such a time of the quotidian and the apocalyptic, the combination of the sense of trivia with the sense of doom."

*BIOGRAPHICAL/CRITICAL SOURCES:*

*BOOKS*

*Contemporary Literary Criticism,* Volume 57, Gale, 1989.

*PERIODICALS*

*Christian Science Monitor,* September 22, 1975.
*Cross Currents 3,* 1984.
*Nation,* September 16, 1978; March 6, 1989, p. 313.
*New Leader,* August 7, 1989, p. 18.
*New Republic,* January 6, 1979; April 10, 1989, p. 36; October 22, 1990, p. 38.
*New Statesman,* December 19, 1975.

*New Statesman & Society,* January 18, 1991, p. 38.
*New York Review of Books,* October 26, 1989, p. 18; April 11, 1991, p. 45.
*New York Times Book Review,* April 23, 1989, p. 14; October 7, 1990, p. 14.
*Review of Contemporary Fiction,* Spring, 1994, p. 145, p. 161.
*Times Literary Supplement,* October 30, 1989, p. 713; January 11, 1991, p. 71.
*World Literature Today,* summer, 1977; winter, 1977; autumn, 1979.

*OBITUARIES:*

*PERIODICALS*

*Chicago Tribune,* October 17, 1989.
*Los Angeles Times,* October 18, 1989.
*New York Times,* October 17, 1989.*

* * *

**KIYOTA, Minoru 1923-**

*PERSONAL:* Born October 12, 1923, in Seattle, WA; son of Ishisaku and Ine (Aoyagi) Kiyota; married Noriko Motoyoshi; children: Noreen, Eileen. *Education:* University of California, Berkeley, B.A., 1950; Tokyo University, M.A., Ph.D., 1963. *Politics:* "No preference." *Religion:* "No preference." *Ethnicity:* "Japanese-American."

*ADDRESSES:* *Home*—2422 Chamberlain Ave., Madison, WI 53705. *Office*—Department of Kinesiology, University of Wisconsin—Madison, Madison, WI 53706.

*CAREER:* University of Wisconsin—Madison, assistant professor, 1962-68, associate professor, 1968-78, professor of East Asian languages and literature and South Asian studies, beginning 1978, chair of Buddhist studies program, beginning 1978, member of faculty in department of kinesiology, 1986—.

*WRITINGS:*

(Editor) *Mahayana Buddhist Meditation: Theory and Practice,* University Press of Hawaii (Honolulu), 1978.
*Shingon Buddhism: Theory and Practice,* Buddhist Books International, 1978.
*Tantric Concepts of Bodhicitta: A Buddhist Experiential Philosophy,* Center for South Asian Studies, University of Wisconsin—Madison, 1982.
*Gedatsukai: Its Theory and Practice; a Study of a Shinto-Buddhist Syncretic School in Contemporary Japan,* Buddhist Books International, 1982.
(Editor) *Japanese Buddhism: Its Tradition, New Religions and Interaction with Christianity,* Buddhist Books International, 1987.
(Editor with Hideaki Kinoshita) *Japanese Martial Arts and American Sports: Cross-Cultural Perspectives on Means to Personal Growth,* Nihon University Press, 1990.
*Nikkei hangyakuji: minken jurin to hakugai no kiroku,* Nihon Hanbaisha (Tokyo), 1990, translation published as *Beyond Loyalty: The Story of a Kibei,* University of Hawaii Press, 1997.
*Kendo: Its Philosophy, History and Means to Personal Growth,* Kegan Paul (London), 1995.
(Editor and compiler with Jordon Lee) *Personal Growth Through Martial Arts: Studies in Kendo, Fencing and Indian Sword-fighting,* Center for South Asian Studies and Department of Kinesiology, University of Wisconsin—Madison, 1997.

# L

**LEE, Dennis (Beynon) 1939-**

*PERSONAL:* Born August 31, 1939, in Toronto, Ontario, Canada; son of Walter and Louise (Garbutt) Lee; married Donna Youngblut, June 24, 1962 (divorced); married Susan Perly, October 7, 1985; children: (first marriage) two daughters, one son. *Education:* University of Toronto, B.A., 1962, M.A., 1964.

*ADDRESSES:* *Agent*—Sterling Lord Associates, 10 St. Mary's St., Suite 510, Toronto, Ontario, Canada M4Y 1P9.

*CAREER:* Writer. University of Toronto, Victoria College, Toronto, Ontario, lecturer in English, 1964-67; Rochdale College (experimental institution), Toronto, self-described "research person," 1967-69; Artist-in-Residence, Trent University, Peterborough, Ontario, 1975; House of Anansi Press, Toronto, cofounder and editor, 1967-72. Editorial consultant, Macmillan of Canada, 1973-78; poetry editor, McClelland & Stewart, 1981-84. Lyricist for television series *Fraggle Rock,* 1982-86.

*MEMBER:* Officer of the Order of Canada, 1994.

*AWARDS, HONORS:* Governor-General's Award for Poetry, 1972, for *Civil Elegies;* Independent Order of Daughters of the Empire award, 1974; Canadian Association of Children's Librarians Best Book Medals, 1974 and 1977, and English Medal, 1975, all for *Alligator Pie;* named to Hans Christian Andersen Honour List and recipient of Canadian Library Association award, both 1976, both for *Alligator Pie;* Ruth Swartz Award, 1978; Philips Information Systems Literary Award, 1984; Vicky Metcalf Award, Canadian Authors' Association, 1986, for body of work for children; Mr. Christie's Book Award, 1991.

*WRITINGS:*

*POETRY*

*Kingdom of Absence,* House of Anansi (Toronto), 1967.

*Civil Elegies,* House of Anansi, 1968, revised edition published as *Civil Elegies and Other Poems,* 1972.

*Not Abstract Harmonies But,* Kanchenjunga Press (Vancouver and San Francisco), 1974.

*The Death of Harold Ladoo,* Kanchenjunga Press, 1976.

*Miscellany,* privately printed (Toronto), 1977.

*The Gods,* Kanchenjunga Press, 1978.

*The Gods* (collection of revised versions of *Not Abstract Harmonies But, The Death of Harold Ladoo,* and *The Gods*), McClelland and Stewart (Toronto), 1979.

*Riffs,* Brick (London, Ontario), 1993.

*Nightwatch: New and Selected Poems, 1968-1996,* McClelland and Stewart, 1996.

*JUVENILE*

(With illustrator Charles Pachter) *Wiggle to the Laundromat,* New Press (Toronto), 1970.

(With illustrator Frank Newfield) *Alligator Pie,* Macmillan (Toronto), 1974, reprinted, Houghton Mifflin (Boston), 1975.

(With illustrator Frank Newfield) *Nicholas Knock and Other People,* Macmillan, 1974, reprinted, Houghton Mifflin, 1975.

*The Ordinary Bath,* McClelland & Stewart, 1977.

(With illustrator Frank Newfield) *Garbage Delight,* Macmillan, 1977, reprinted, Houghton Mifflin, 1978.

(With illustrator Juan Wijngaard) *Jelly Belly,* Macmillan, 1983, reprinted, Blackie (London), 1983.

(With illustrator Marie-Louise Gay) *Lizzy's Lion,* Stoddart (Toronto), 1984, Hodder & Stoughton (London), 1984.

(With illustrator Barb Klunder) *The Dennis Lee Big Book* (anthology), Gage (Toronto), 1985.

*The Difficulty of Living on Other Planets* (some poems previously published in *Nicholas Knock and Other People* and *The Gods*), Macmillan, 1987.

(With illustrator David McPhail) *The Ice Cream Store,* HarperCollins (Toronto), 1991, reprinted, Scholastic (New York), 1992.

*Ping and Pong,* HarperCollins (Toronto), 1993.

*OTHER*

(Co-editor with R. A. Charlesworth) *An Anthology of Verse,* Oxford University Press (Toronto), 1964.

(Co-editor with Charlesworth) *The Second Century Anthologies of Verse 2,* Oxford University Press, 1967.

(Co-editor with Howard Adelman) *The University Game* (essays), House of Anansi, 1968.

(Editor) *T.O. Now: The Young Toronto Poets* (poetry anthology), House of Anansi, 1968.

*Savage Fields: An Essay in Cosmology and Literature,* House of Anansi, 1977.

(Editor and author of introduction) *New Canadian Poets, 1970 1985* (poetry anthology), McClelland & Stewart, 1985.

(Co-author of story with Jim Henson) *Labyrinth* (screenplay adapted by Terry Jones) Henson Associates Inc./Lucasfilm Ltd., 1985.

(Co-editor with Charlesworth) *A New Anthology of Verse,* Oxford University Press, 1989.

Also contributor to periodicals such as *Descant, Open Letter, Saturday Night,* and *Quarry.*

*RECORDINGS*

*Alligator Pie and Other Poems,* Caedmon, 1978.

*Fraggle Rock,* Muppet Music, 1984.

*SIDELIGHTS:* In a speech delivered at the 1975 Loughborough Conference in Toronto and reprinted in *Canadian Children's Literature,* Canadian author Dennis Lee examines the way his attitude toward children's verse evolved. As an adult and parent, he contemplates Mother Goose and discovers: "The nursery rhymes I love . . . are necessarily exotic. . . . But they were in no way exotic to the people who first devised them and chanted them. . . . The air of far-off charm and simpler pastoral life which now hangs over Mother Goose was in no way a part of those rhymes' initial existence. . . . The people who told nursery rhymes for centuries would be totally boggled if they could suddenly experience them the way children do here and now, as a collection of references to things they never see or do, to places they have never heard of and may never visit, told in words they will sometimes meet only in those verses."

Out of concern that his own children were learning that "the imagination leads always and only to the holy city of elsewhere," Lee decided to build his imaginary "city" from the language of familiar objects—elements of contemporary life made extraordinary by their unique use and sound in verse. Maintaining that "you are poorer if you never find your own time and place speaking words of their own," he believes the "fire hydrants and hockey sticks" of today can be the stuff of nursery rhymes, much like the "curds and whey" of a previous time. Thus, he says, "to look for living nursery rhymes in the hockey-sticks and high-rises that [children know] first-hand [is not] to go on a chauvinistic trip, nor to wallow in a fad of trendy relevance. It [is] nothing but a rediscovery of what Mother Goose [has been] about for centuries."

While Lee's poetic narratives, tongue-twisters, and riddles have been called nonsense verse, he often emphasizes the here-and-now objects of daily life in his work—things children may or may not recognize. Canadian places, history, politics, and colloquial diction, as well as purely invented words, all play a part in his pieces. Many critics feel the readability and repeatability of the poems—rather than references to far-away places—are what fascinates young children, as represented by the poems in *Alligator Pie* which evoke the Canadian landscape, and attempt, as Sheila Egoff writes in *The Republic of Childhood,* "to give Canadian children . . . a sense of their particular time and space." More recent works, however, like *The Ice Cream Store,* as Carolyn Phelan notes in *Booklist,* have expanded his focus so that "the scope is worldwide, with a consciously multicultural slant to the text and the art alike." Still, as Betsy English writes in *In Review: Canadian Books for Children,* the strong rhythms, rhymes, and other sound devices produce "a sense of gaiety, an appeal that shouts for reading aloud," making Lee's work appealing to both adults and children alike. As a result, Lee, who has been compared by critics to Lewis Carroll, A. A. Milne, Edward Lear, and Shel Silverstein, has even been called "a Canadian Mother Goose."

In addition to his nearly one dozen children's books, and his nearly as many anthologies, Lee is also a successful writer of serious adult poetry. He has, as John Robert Colombo writes in *Contemporary Poets,* "played a transitional role in the evolution of literary thinking in Canada, linking the humanistic concerns of the 1950's with the nationalistic and cultural aspirations of the 1960's and 1970's. His range of awareness is wide enough to encompass the academy, the marketplace, and the antiestablishment." Bruce Meyer, writing in *Books in Canada,* calls Lee "grandiloquent," since "his profound sense of rhetoric gives his poetry a wonderful flavour," and "his aphorisms, often cryptic, are stabbing attempts at philosophical wit and axiom."

*Kingdom of Absence* (1967), Lee's first book, received mixed reviews for what critics cited as its lack of a consistent and authentic voice and of formal mastery. Still, as Douglas Barbour notes in *Dictionary of Literary Biography,* this book identifies "a sense of alienation that separates the poet from others and from his own most deeply rooted self," which becomes the "central problem to which Lee returns again and again in his work."

*Civil Elegies and Other Poems* (1972), expanded from an earlier 1968 version, is Lee's set of elegiac meditations on living in Canada in the late 1960s. Using a new free-form line which Colombo believes "contrasts throwaway allusions and tough talk" and which "verges on 'free prose,'" Lee finds a more flexible instrument for his voice. "Using Nathan Phillips Square in Toronto as his base," according to Barbour, "Lee sends his thoughts coursing out through space and time in an attempt to discover what it means to be a Canadian." Colombo calls *Civil Elegies and Other Poems* Lee's "most impressive and influential publication," since the poet defines himself in "sociopolitical terms as a liberal leftist or cultural and social activist." This theme in Lee's work is considered to be inspired by Canadian philosopher George Grant, who saw Canada as "a conservative country on a liberal continent trapped in the economic and electronic web of modern technology." In the "Coming Back" section of the book, Lee candidly explores his roles as husband, father, teacher, editor, lover, idealist, and writer. *Civil Elegies and Other Poems,* called by Barbour "a testament to Lee's hunger for authenticity," won him the Governor General's Award for poetry.

*The Gods* (1979) collected three previously published works (*Not Abstract Harmonies But, The Death of Harold Ladoo,* and *The Gods*) and is cited by Barbour for its "jangly creative sense of exploration, of engaging, continually changing process," and for "the continual shifts from one level of discourse to another that occur in any attempt to speak truly." *Not Abstract Harmonies But* displays an attitude of acceptance of living in the present, despite all the ideologies which pull at an individual on a regular basis. *The Gods* wrestles with the notion of a traditional god in an era of increasing technology. *The Death of Harold Ladoo* is an elegy dedicated to Lee's friend, the Trinidad novelist who was murdered when he returned to his native island in 1973, which Barbour calls a "painfully honest exploration" that "resolutely affirms life."

*Riffs* (1993), a meditation upon a love affair, shows that Lee has discovered a new voice. A sequence of eighty-eight sections, the same as the number of keys on a piano, takes its title from the jazz term for a repeated phrase underlying an improvised solo. As Colombo notes, "improvisation is certainly a good word to describe the tone and style of the whole suite of poems. . . . The author's verbal resources permit him to encompass monologue, dialogue, many levels of diction, meditation, contemplation, and even swear words" which effectively capture "the urban idiom of an educated literary person living in North America." Though the poems appear to be spontaneously written, Lee told John Bemrose in a *Maclean's* review that he spent over ten years composing "thousands of pages" to complete the book. The result, as Sandra Nicholls calls it in *Books in Canada,* is "true jazz" which "resurrects the music of Dylan Thomas [and] the wordplay of e.e. cummings."

*Nightwatch: New and Selected Poems, 1968-1996,* which collected the best of Lee's work, has been called by Bruce Meyer of *Books in Canada* "something of a landmark, or rather a benchmark, in Canadian literature," since it is the work of a poet "whose works have had an impact not only on a generation of poets but also on one of critics. . . . [It is] a record, a chronicle of a career and its various leitmotifs and themes." As Bemrose states, "There have always been at least two Dennis Lees; the children's poet and the more intellectual author of the adult poetry collections." Lee has been successful in both of these areas, as well as in his work over the years as an anthologist. What perhaps makes Lee stand out most significantly, however, is his dedication to helping define and shape a distinctly Canadian literature.

*BIOGRAPHICAL/CRITICAL SOURCES:*

*BOOKS*

Bennett, Donna, Russell Brown, and Karen Mulhallen, editors, *Task of Passion: Dennis Lee at Mid-Career,* Descant (Toronto), 1982.

*Children's Literature Review,* Volume 3, Gale (Detroit), 1978.

*Contemporary Poets,* sixth Edition, St. James Press (Detroit), 1996.

Davey, Frank, *From There to Here,* Press Porcepic (Erin, Ontario), 1974.

*Dictionary of Literary Biography,* Volume 53: *Canadian Writers Since 1960, Second Series,* Gale, 1986.

Egoff, Sheila, *The Republic of Childhood: A Critical Guide to Canadian Children's Literature in English,* second Edition, Oxford University Press (Toronto), 1975.

Middlebro, T. G., *Dennis Lee and His Works,* ECW Press (Toronto), 1985.

*PERIODICALS*

*Books,* August, 1988, p. 11.

*Booklist,* May 15, 1985, p. 1334; November 15, 1992, p. 602.

*Books for Young Children,* summer, 1988, p. 7.

*Books for Young People,* April, 1987, p. 1.

*Books in Canada,* February, 1980, p. 21; December, 1984, p. 12; October, 1985, p. 30; December, 1993, p. 37; summer, 1996, pp. 19-21.

*Brick,* winter, 1981, pp. 8-12.

*Canadian Children's Literature,* number 4, 1976, pp. 25-58; number 33, 1984, p. 15; number 41, 1986, p. 74; number 42, 1986, p. 55, 56, 103; number 52, 1988, p. 56; number 63, 1991, p. 61-71; number 67, 1992, p. 102.

*Canadian Forum,* February, 1986, p. 38.

*Canadian Literature,* autumn, 1978, pp. 53-58; autumn, 1989, p. 228; spring, 1996, p. 143.

*Canadian Materials,* March, 1988, p. 58; May, 1988, p. 103; March, 1992, p. 86; March-April, 1994, p. 46.

*Center for Children's Books—Bulletin,* December, 1992, p. 116.

*Childhood Education,* summer, 1993, p. 244.

*Children's Book News,* fall, 1991, p. 35.

*Children's Book Review Service,* spring, 1985, p. 126; December, 1992, p. 40.

*Children's Literature Association Quarterly,* winter, 1990, p. 216.

*Choice,* May, 1995, p. 1506.

*Christian Science Monitor,* October 5, 1984, p. 88.

*CV,* autumn, 1980, pp. 14-17.

*Descant,* Winter, 1982.

*Emergency Librarian,* November, 1984, p. 20; May, 1985, p. 12; January, 1989, p. 51; January, 1992, p. 50; March, 1992, p. 15, 50.

*Essays on Canadian Writing,* Spring, 1988, p. 110-122; spring, 1994, p. 126-131.

*Horn Book Guide,* spring, 1993, p. 134.

*Horn Book Magazine,* December, 1975; December, 1977, p. 675; May, 1986, 354.

*In Review: Canadian Books for Children,* spring, 1971, winter, 1975.

*Instructor,* November-December, 1992, p. 36.

*Maclean's,* December 10, 1984, p. 12; August 12, 1985, p. 55; October 25, 1993, p. 61.

*New Yorker,* December 1, 1975, p. 184.

*New York Times Book Review,* November, 1977, p. 47.

*Poetry,* February, 1970, p. 353.

*Publishers Weekly,* September 5, 1977, p. 73; October 12, 1992, p. 76.

*Quill & Quire,* November, 1983, p. 25; November, 1984, p. 11; August, 1985, p. 44; fall, 1991, p. 35; October, 1993, p. 28.

*Reference and Research Book News,* May, 1995, p. 6.

*Saturday Night,* January, 1978, p. 74; November, 1979, p. 61.

*Saturday Review,* November 29, 1975, p. 33.

*School Library Journal,* December, 1975, p. 47; December, 1985, p. 77; September 1992, p. 221.

*Times Educational Supplement,* May 13, 1988, p. B3.

*Times Literary Supplement,* December 13, 1985, p. 1435.*

*—Sketch by Robert Miltner*

* * *

**LEINER, Katherine 1949-**

*PERSONAL:* Born January 28, 1949, in Washington, DC; daughter of Stanley (a lawyer and executive) and Julia Jeanette (a model, actress, and homemaker; maiden name, Schubach) Gewirtz; married Michael Rodney Leiner, November, 1970 (divorced); married Miles Budd Goodman (a film composer), 1973; children: Dylan Leiner, Makenna Goodman. *Education:* Attended Emerson College. *Politics:* Democrat. *Religion:* Buddhist.

*ADDRESSES: Office*—11812 San Vicente Blvd. #200, Los Angeles, CA 90049.

*CAREER:* Writer. Member of Heal the Bay, Pesticide Watch, Mothers against Drunk Driving, and Los Angeles Commission of Assaults against Women.

*MEMBER:* PEN, Society of Children's Book Writers and Illustrators, Authors Guild.

*WRITINGS:*

CHILDREN'S BOOKS

*Ask Me What My Mother Does,* photos by Michael Arthur, F. Watts (New York City), 1978.
*The Real Flash Gordon,* illustrated by Michael Arthur, Oak Tree (San Diego), 1980.
*The Greatest Show on Earth,* photos by Michael Arthur, Oak Tree, 1980.
*The Steam Engine Lady,* Oak Tree, 1981.
*Both My Parents Work,* photos by Steve Sax, F. Watts, 1986.
*Between Old Friends,* photos by Michael Arthur, F. Watts, 1987.
*The New Adventures of Pippi Longstocking,* Viking (New York City), 1988.
*Something's Wrong in My House,* illustrated by Chuck Gardner, F. Watts, 1988.
*Halloween,* Atheneum, 1993.
*First Children: Growing Up in the White House,* illustrated by Katie Keller, Tambourine, 1995.

Also author, with Astrid Lindgren, of *Pippi Longstocking, VII,* 1991.

OTHER

Also author of poems and short stories for adults.

*WORK IN PROGRESS:* Research for a novel and a cookbook.

*SIDELIGHTS:* Katherine Leiner writes books about and for children, often emphasizing the ways in which they cope in difficult situations. In such works as *Ask Me What My Mother Does* and *Both My Parents Work,* Leiner addresses the topic of two working parents and the effects of this arrangement on children, including additional responsibilities for young people in the home. In *Something's Wrong in My House* Leiner portrays the emotional, psychological, and sometimes physical toll taken on eight children who have one parent or more addicted to alcohol, and provides resources to help children of alcoholics. *First Children,* a historical look at children who have lived in the White House, shows both the sorrowful and the more joyous occasions in the lives of the children and grandchildren of seventeen American presidents. Typically illustrated with photographs of models portraying the situations she explores, Leiner's books are sometimes faulted for having an ambiguous layout or an uneven writing style. Her books are often praised, however, for providing a rarely seen or much needed look at how ordinary children cope in extraordinary circumstances.

In *Ask Me What My Mother Does,* seventeen women are depicted in photographs and drawings at work in a variety of paying jobs, including manual, clerical, and professional posts, accompanied by text that describes the work. Betsy Hearne of *Booklist* noted that *Ask Me What My Mother Does* "makes a good kickoff for very early career and role discussions." The response to *Both My Parents Work,* which surveys the children of ten families in which both parents work outside the home, was more positive. While it was noted that Leiner does not make clear whether the text is comprised of direct quotes or paraphrases from interviews, or indeed whether the people in the photographs are models or actual subjects, "youngsters in the same boat may enjoy hearing about other children and how they cope," maintained Denise M. Wilms in *Booklist.* And a critic for *Bulletin of the Center for Children's Books* called *Both My Parents Work,* "a good choice for family or classroom discussion."

In *Something's Wrong in My House,* Leiner uses the same format as *Ask Me What My Mother Does* and *Both My Parents Work* to present life among families of alcoholics from the children's perspective. Eight children of various ages are featured in situations that convey "the emotional effects of alcohol and validate children's feelings," according to Heide Piehler in *School Library Journal.* Critics praised the author's emphasis on urging children in this situation to seek out support, particularly in the form of Alateen meetings, the twelve-step program for children of alcoholics that is associated with Alcoholics

Anonymous. The reviewer for *Bulletin of the Center for Children's Books,* however, cited the limitations of *Something's Wrong in My House,* including its failure to address the causes of alcoholism, and objected to its seeming portrayal of alcoholic parents as "moral failure[s]." Piehler, on the other hand, while admitting that the book's photographs in particular "detract from [its] impact," nonetheless concluded, "this title should be purchased for its content."

*First Children* is a departure from Leiner's earlier works in that it offers a historical perspective on the lives of children. Seventeen U.S. presidents and the children who lived in the White House during their terms of office are featured in brief essays illustrated by contemporary photographs and a modern-day drawing. "Many chapters draw effectively on diaries, correspondence, and news accounts, while tidbits of valuable social history are incorporated throughout," remarked a *Kirkus Reviews* commentator. "Ms. Leiner couldn't ask for richer material, and she handles her facts with careful consideration," observed Nathalie op de Beeck in the *New York Times Book Review.* Although some critics complained of contrivance in instances where the inner thoughts of Leiner's subjects are conjectured, a reviewer for *Publishers Weekly* concluded: "This assiduously researched volume is a great way to bring American history to life for young readers."

Leiner once commented: "I feel quite strongly that the more children are exposed to nature and the natural elements, the greater the chance that their involvement in the environment will be positive and caring and that they will become resilient adults. I spent the first forty years of my life exploring cities, and I intend to spend the next forty years exploring the mountains and valleys and natural hideaways of the world."

*BIOGRAPHICAL/CRITICAL SOURCES:*

*PERIODICALS*

*Booklist,* May 1, 1978, pp. 1434-1435; May 1, 1986, p. 1313; May 1, 1988, p. 1526; April 15, 1996, p. 1436.

*Bulletin of the Center for Children's Books,* May, 1986, p. 172; May, 1988, p. 182.

*Horn Book,* spring, 1994, p. 104.

*Kirkus Reviews,* March 1, 1996, p. 376.

*New York Times Book Review,* May 19, 1996, p. 30.

*Publishers Weekly,* January 23, 1981, p. 124; April 1, 1996, p. 78.

*School Library Journal,* April, 1981, p. 114; September, 1986, p. 124; January, 1988, p. 73; June-July, 1988, p. 111; December, 1993, p. 106; May, 1996, p. 124.

*Science Books and Films,* November, 1986, p. 107.

* * *

## LESCROART, John T. 1948-

*PERSONAL:* Surname is pronounced *Les*-qua; born January 14, 1948, in Houston, TX; son of Maurice E. and Loretta (a homemaker; maiden name, Gregory) Lescroart; married Leslee Ann Miller, June 13, 1976 (divorced July, 1979); married Lisa M. Sawyer (an architect), September 2, 1984; children: (second marriage) one daughter and one son. *Education:* University of California, Santa Cruz, 1966; College of San Mateo, 1967; University of San Francisco, 1967-68; University of California, Berkeley, B.A. (with honors) in English literature, 1970.

*ADDRESSES: Home and office*—129 C Street, Suite 3, Davis, CA 95616. *Agent*—Barney Karpfinger, The Karpfinger Agency, 357 W. 20th St., New York City, NY 10011.

*CAREER:* Computer room supervisor, 1970-72; professional singer and guitarist in Los Angeles and San Francisco, CA, 1972-77; *Guitar Player,* Cupertino, CA, editor and advertising director, 1977-79; Guardians of the Jewish Homes for the Aging, Los Angeles, associate director, 1979-83; A. T. Kearney, Inc. (consulting firm), Alexandria, VA, technical writer and associate consultant, 1982-85; Pettit & Martin (law firm), Los Angeles, word processor and legal administrator, 1985-1991. Writer, 1991—.

*MEMBER:* Mystery Writers of America.

*AWARDS, HONORS:* Joseph Henry Jackson Award from San Francisco Foundation, 1978, for novel *Sunburn.*

*WRITINGS:*

(Editor) Craig Anderton, *Home Recording for Musicians,* GPI Publications, 1975.

(Editor) Rusty Young, *The Pedal Steel Handbook,* GPI Publications, 1976.

*Sunburn* (novel), Pinnacle Books, 1982.

*Son of Holmes* ("Auguste Lupa" series; also see below), Donald I. Fine (New York City), 1986, Curley (South Yarmouth, MA), 1991.

*Rasputin's Revenge: The Further Startling Adventures of Auguste Lupa—Son of Holmes* ("Auguste Lupa" series, see also below), Donald I. Fine, 1987.

*Dead Irish* ("Dismas Hardy" series), Donald I. Fine, 1989, Headline (London, England), 1996.

*The Vig* ("Dismas Hardy" series), Donald I. Fine, 1990, Headline, 1997.

*Hard Evidence* ("Dismas Hardy" series), Donald I. Fine, 1993, Headline, 1997.

*The 13th Juror* ("Dismas Hardy" series), Donald I. Fine and G. K. Hall (Thorndike, ME), 1994.

*A Certain Justice* ("Abe Glitsky" series), Donald I. Fine, 1995, G. K. Hall, 1996.

*Son of Holmes and Rasputin's Revenge: The Early Works of John T. Lescroart,* Donald I. Fine, 1995.

*Guilt* ("Abe Glitsky" series), Delacorte Press (New York City) and Wheeler Pub. (Accord, MA), 1997.

*The Mercy Rule* ("Dismas Hardy" series), Delacourt Press, in press.

*WORK IN PROGRESS:* A contemporary mystery novel, as yet untitled, featuring Dismas Hardy.

*SIDELIGHTS:* John T. Lescroart once told *CA:* "I have always been intrigued with the written word. I viewed my creative writing assignments as early as the sixth grade as great fun, and I continue to feel pretty much the same way. After experimenting with short stories, poetry, and song lyrics (and continuing to do so), when I was twenty-two I took the plunge and began my first novel, which no one will ever see.

"Six years later, my novel *Sunburn* won the Joseph Henry Jackson Award from the San Francisco Foundation. That award gave me the confidence to continue my pursuit of novel-writing as a career. Though it hasn't to this day proven especially lucrative, I still love writing books. I work daily first thing in the morning for two to four hours and also work full-time (currently as a word processor, though I have done the proverbial 'everything' they say every writer needs to do, from singing to bartending to housepainting to consulting). I don't consider this an ideal situation, and I would very much like to be able to devote more time to writing. Still, I have finished two novels in the past year and continue to keep busy and hopeful. I am blessed with my wife Lisa, who is incredibly and consistently supportive of my pursuit of my dreams and my art.

"My heroes, disparate though they may be, are Ernest Hemingway, Lawrence Durrell, and John Fowles. I like Larry McMurtry and James Clavell. I am also a big fan of several mystery writers, including Arthur Conan Doyle, Rex Stout, John D. MacDonald, P. D. James, and Elmore Leonard. And I continue to believe, naively I'm sure, that if more people would read quality fiction, it would do more good for them and for the world than all the how-to and self-help books ever published."

Richard G. La Porte, writing in *St. James Guide to Crime & Mystery Writers,* says, "After a Joseph Henry Jackson Award-winning and veiled autobiographical *Sunburn,* . . . Lescroart went on to a two-step experiment in the creation of a literary linkage between the Sherlock Holmes/Irene Adler liaison and Nero Wolfe called John Hamish Adler-Holmes who appears in *Son of Holmes* and *Rasputin's Revenge: The Further Startling Adventures of Auguste Lupa—Son of Holmes* as Auguste Lupa. Lupa, a British Secret Service agent with a penchant for Roman Imperial aliases works for Mycroft Holmes the original "M" of the Service but carries an American passport. After The Great War Lupa retired to New York City and apparently took up orchid culture. Both of these relatively brief novels are well planned and researched and are believable pastiches. Lescroart is not, of course, the first to determine Nero Wolfe's parentage."

Lescroart's second series feature the wayward Dismas Hardy of San Francisco's corporate culture. "In *Dead Irish,*" states La Porte, Dismas Hardy is "a failed cop, husband, lawyer, and parent. He [is] a part-time barkeep, nursing his Guinness and darts in the Little Shamrock, catty-cornered across 9th and Lincoln from the Hall of Flowers in Golden Gate Park." A *Library Journal* review deems the book "a full-bodied, substantive, and stylistic effort of the first order [with] full attention to character, . . . a sympathetic protagonist, and a satisfying conclusion." Peter Robertson, writing in *Booklist,* calls it "An unusual and powerful mystery."

In the same *Booklist* review of *The Vig* ("vig" or "vigorish" is street slang for the interest a loan shark charges), Robertson says, "Details are all in Lescroart's compelling vision of a world made up of dark bars, dark drinks, and dark lives."

A *Publishers Weekly* review of *The 13th Juror* states: "The story gets off to a slow start, . . . and [Lescroart]. . . comes close to telegraphing the solution to the mystery, and much of his writing about characters' personal lives is hamfisted. Despite these flaws, however, an intricate story and satisfying courtroom scenes carry the day." Dan Bogey, writing in *Booklist,* calls the novel: "Very readable . . . with engaging characters and a riveting plot that fans of Scott Turow and John Grisham will love."

Regarding the protagonist of Lescroart's most recent series novels, *A Certain Justice* and *Guilt,* La Porte summarizes: "Back before *Dead Irish* when Hardy was a cop, his partner was Abe Glitsky. Abe stayed in the SFPD and is on his way up the promotional ladder with its treacherous snakes of political reform. Affirmative action policies posed a double-ended problem to Abe. Glitsky senior is an orthodox Jew and Abe's mother was black. Although his appearance is strongly African-American, his commitments are not."

Dawn L. Anderson, writing in *Library Journal,* calls *A Certain Justice* a "heart-stopping thriller" that "will keep readers riveted to their chairs." *Chicago Tribune* reviewer Chris Petrakos agrees, noting that "Lescroart does a masterly job juggling politics and justice, demonstrating along the way that the two rarely mix." A *Kirkus Reviews* critic surmises that it is not as humorous as Tom Wolfe's *Bonfire of the Vanities,* but it is "just as mordant and electric."

Steve Brewer, writing in *Mostly Murder,* calls *Guilt* "a blockbuster of a trial. . . . [Lescroart] establishes the main characters carefully."

La Porte states: "Although the Hardy/Glitsky books are part of the mystery/detection genre, they are far more fully developed than most of the earlier series character studies. For one thing, the greater length gives Lescroart more time for detailing the fauna and flora of the mean streets of San Francisco and their effects on the people in the story. For another, they are primarily plot-driven, character-development studies. They are not stories of how the protagonist, The Master Detective, brings his acute powers to bear on a single problem but more the reverse. The crime and its manifestations are brought to bear on the protagonist forcing him to rise, change and challenge himself to prove his beliefs."

La Porte summarizes: "All of this [writing] is done with a smooth literary style with a padding of truth and a verisimilitude that makes you feel that you are right there where it is happening. There may not be an old bar with its dartboard on that corner of 9th and Lincoln but it seems as if there should be one. This is one of the strongest points in Lescroart's writing; the believability, not only the places, but also the people."

*BIOGRAPHICAL/CRITICAL SOURCES:*

*BOOKS*

*St. James Guide to Crime & Mystery Writers,* St. James Press (Detroit), 1996.

*PERIODICALS*

*Booklist,* January 15, 1990, p. 804, p. 976; September 1, 1994, p. 27.
*Chicago Tribune,* July 16, 1995, Section 14, p. 6.
*Kirkus Reviews,* June 1, 1995, p. 731.
*Library Journal,* January, 1990, p. 151; July, 1994, p. 127; July, 1995, p. 121.
*Mostly Murder,* May/June, 1997.
*Publishers Weekly,* June 20, 1994, p. 93-94.

* * *

**LESLIE, O. H.**
**See SLESAR, Henry**

* * *

**LESTER, Mark**
**See RUSSELL, Martin**

* * *

**LEVI, Primo 1919-1987**
**(Damiano Malabaila)**

*PERSONAL:* Born July 31, 1919, in Turin, Italy; died from a fall down a stairwell in an apparent suicide attempt, April 11, 1987, in Turin, Italy; son of Cesare (a civil engineer) and Ester (Luzzati) Levi;

married Lucia Morpurgo (a teacher), September 8, 1947; children: Lisa, Renzo. *Education:* University of Turin, B.S. (summa cum laude), 1941. *Religion:* Jewish.

*CAREER:* Chemist and author. Partisan in Italian Resistance, 1943; deported to Auschwitz Concentration Camp in Oswiecim, Poland, and imprisoned there, 1943-45; SIVA (paints, enamels, synthetic resins), Settimo, Turin, Italy, technical executive, 1948-77.

*AWARDS, HONORS:* Premio Campiello (Venice literary prize), 1963 for *La Tregua,* and 1982, for *Se non ora, quando?;* Premio Bagutta (Milan literary prize), 1967, for *Storie Naturali;* Premio Strega (Rome literary prize), 1979, for *La chiave stella;* Premio Viareggio (Viareggio literary prize), 1982, for *Se non ora, quando?;* co-recipient (with Saul Bellow) of Kenneth B. Smilen fiction award from Jewish Museum in New York, 1985; Present Tense/ Joel H. Cavior literary award, 1986, for *The Periodic Table.*

*WRITINGS:*

*Se Questo e un Uomo,* F. de Silva (Turin), 1947, 15th edition, Einaudi (Turin), 1975, translation by Stuart Woolf published as *If This Is a Man,* Orion Press (New York City), 1959, published as *Survival in Auschwitz: The Nazi Assault on Humanity,* Collier, 1961 (also see below), new edition, 1966 (published in England as *If This Is a Man,* Bodley Head, 1966), dramatic version in original Italian (with Pieralberto Marche), Einaudi, 1966.

*La Tregua,* Einaudi, 1958, 8th edition, 1965, translation by Woolf published as *The Reawakening,* Little, Brown, 1965 (also see below; published in England as *The Truce: A Survivor's Journey Home From Auschwitz,* Bodley Head, 1965).

(Under pseudonym Damiano Malabaila) *Storie Naturali* (title means "Natural Histories"; short story collection), Einaudi, 1967.

(With Carlo Quartucci) *Intervista Aziendale* (radio script), Radiotelevisione Italiana, 1968.

*Vizio di Forma* (title means "Technical Error"; short story collection), Einaudi, 1971.

*Il sistema periodico,* Einaudi, 1975, translation by Raymond Rosenthal published as *The Periodic Table,* Schocken, 1984, reprinted, Knopf, 1996.

*Abruzzo forte e gentile: Impressioni d'occhio e di cuore,* edited by Virgilio Orsini, A. Di Cioccio, 1976.

*Shema: Collected Poems,* Menard, 1976.

*La chiave a stella* (novel), Einaudi, 1978, translation by William Weaver published as *The Monkey's Wrench,* Summit Books, c. 1986.

*La Ricerca della radici: Antologia personale,* Einaudi, c. 1981.

*Lilit e altri racconti,* Einaudi, 1981, translation by Ruth Feldman published as *Moments of Reprieve,* Summit Books, c. 1986.

*Se non ora, quando?* (novel), Einaudi, 1982, translation by Weaver published as *If Not Now, When?,* introduction by Irving Howe, Summit Books, c. 1985.

(Translator) Franz Kafka, *Il processo* (title means "The Trial"), c. 1983.

*L'altrui mestiere,* Einaudi, c. 1985.

*Survival in Auschwitz* [and] *The Reawakening: Two Memoirs,* Summit Books, 1986, reprinted, 1993.

*Autoritratto di Primo Levi,* Garzanti (Milan), 1987.

*Sommersi e i salvati* (originally published in 1986), translation by Rosenthal published as *The Drowned and the Saved,* Summit Books, 1988.

*The Collected Poems of Primo Levi,* translation by Feldmand and Brian Swann, Faber & Faber, 1988.

*The Mirror Maker,* translation by Rosenthal, Schocken, 1989.

(With Tullio Regge) *Dialogo,* Princeton University Press, 1989.

*Other People's Trades,* translation by R. Rosenthal, Summit Books (New York City), 1989.

*The Sixth Day, and Other Tales,* Summit Books, 1990, Penguin, 1990.

*Conversazione con Primo Levi,* Garzanti (Milano), 1991.

*SIDELIGHTS:* Italian author Primo Levi earned significant acclaim and numerous awards during his forty-year writing career. Levi once told *CA:* "My uncommon experience as a concentration camp inmate and as a survivor has deeply influenced my later life and has turned me into a writer. The two books [*Se Questo un Uomo* and *La Tregua*] are a chronicle of my exile and an attempt to understand its meaning."

*If This Is a Man* and *The Reawakening,* the English translations of *Se Questo un Uomo* and *La Tregua,* have been widely praised for their portrayal of Levi's imprisonment and subsequent return home. W. J. Cahnman, for example, reviewing *If This Is a Man* in *American Journal of Sociology,* writes: "Here is literally a report from hell: the detached, scientific, unearthly story of a man who descended to the nether world at Auschwitz and returned to the land of the living." Levi's "lack of personal bitterness is almost unnatural, especially when it is realised that he wrote so soon after the German retreat brought him his freedom," notes G. F. Seddon in the *Manchester Guardian.* "Levi's more outstanding virtue is his compassionate understanding of how in these conditions men cease to be men, either give up the struggle or in devious ways win it, usually at the expense of their fellow men." In a 1985 interview published in the *Los Angeles Times,* Levi defended his scientific approach to recounting the horrors of the Holocaust: "It was my duty not to behave as a victim, not to wail and weep, but to be a witness, to give readers material for judgment. This is Divine Law, to be a witness, not to overstate or distort but to deliver and furnish facts. The final judge is the reader."

Sergio Pacifici points out in *Saturday Review* that like *If This Is a Man, The Reawakening,* which chronicles the author's return to Italy, is more than an intimate and accurate diary. "It is a plea for self-restraint and generosity in human relations that may well be heeded in our own critical times," he says. "Levi's lucid and wise reflections on the nature of man deserve more than a mere hearing. *The Reawakening* must take its honored place next to Carlo Levi's *Christ Stopped at Eboli,* Andre Schwartz-Bart's *The Last of the Just,* and *The Diary of Anne Frank.*"

After the successful publication of these first two memoirs, Levi continued to write about the Jewish Holocaust in a variety of works, including two award-winning novels, *La chiave a stella* (published in English as *The Monkey's Wrench*) and *Se non ora, quando?* (published in English as *If Not Now, When?*). Toward the mid-1980s, however, Levi became progressively despondent over what he felt was a general disregard for the immense suffering and loss the Jews experienced during World War II. For reasons not clearly understood, Levi ended his life in 1987 when he jumped down a stairwell in his native town of Turin, Italy. Levi's friend Italian newspaper editor Lorenzo Mundo told Steve Kellerman of the *New York Times* that during the months preceding his death, Levi "would come to visit me and his face looked so discouraged and helpless. He kept saying he was tired, physically and mentally. And he was terribly pessimistic about the destiny of the world and the fate of the spirit of man." Since Levi's death a number of his works have been translated into English, including *The Collected Poems of Primo Levi, The Mirror Maker, The Sixth Day, and Other Stories, Other People's Trades,* and *The Drowned and the Saved.*

*Other People's Trades* presents forty-three essays on a variety of diverse scientific and personal subjects ranging from insect behaviors to computers to the patterns of human memory. Critics have praised the impressive range of knowledge, insight, and originality evidenced by the essays, often noting that the volume provides insight into Levi as a talented writer apart from his role as a witness of the Holocaust. Christopher Lehmann-Haupt of the *The New York Times* notes that "the prevalent themes of these essays are the behavior of matter, its independence of human desires and the extent to which we project our fears onto the behavior of animals that are more or less indifferent to us." Leonard Michaels, writing in *New York Times Book Review,* emphasizes the sense of alienation that characterizes Levi's contemplation of the universe and humankind's relationship to the cosmos in *Other People's Trades.*

*The Sixth Day and Other Tales* surprised many readers who were familiar with Levi's nonfiction; the volume contains fantastical short fables that reveal the influence of futurism and surrealism. Writing in Chicago *Tribune Books,* Constance Markey argues that Levi's fiction is weak in comparison with his nonfiction writings about the Holocaust. She comments: "Rich in imagination, Levi is nonetheless uncomfortable with fiction, not to mention comedy." Richard Eder of the *Los Angeles Times,* however, notes the limitations of Levi's short fiction but also praises the stories as imaginative vehicles of social commentary that suggest both the influence of Levi's experience of the Holocaust and his scientific training.

*The Mirror Maker* combines both essays and stories, many of which Levi wrote during the last twenty years of his life for the newspaper *La Stampa* in Turin. Like *Other People's Trades,* the volume contains essays on a variety of scientific topics as well as stories that reveal Levi's interest in science fiction and the fantastic. Discussing *The Mirror Maker* in *The Sewanee Review,* Gabriel Motola comments: "Levi's most engaging stories and essays remain those that address ethical and moral questions raised by political considerations and by his literary readings and scientific studies." Levi's suicide remains the subject of speculative discussion; many critics examine his later writings in hopes of finding evidence of the author's motivation to kill himself.

Critics such as Isa Kapp and Michiko Kakutani, for example, perceive a note of darkness and pessimism concerning the human condition in some of the later pieces included in *The Mirror Maker.* Kapp, writing in *The New York Times Book Review,* suggests that "Levi had many reasons for faith in humanity, for feeling himself lucky. Yet perhaps he imagined that the impact of his warnings, of his moral force, was evaporating."

*BIOGRAPHICAL/CRITICAL SOURCES:*

*BOOKS*

Patruno, Nicholas, *Understanding Primo Levi,* University of South Carolina Press, 1995.
Sodi, Risa B., *A Dante of Our Time: Primo Levi and Auschwitz,*P. Lang (New York City), 1990.

*PERIODICALS*

*American Journal of Sociology,* May, 1960.
*American Scholar,* winter, 1990, p. 142.
*Los Angeles Times Book Review,* June 17, 1990, p. 3; May 14, 1993, p.8
*Manchester Guardian,* April 22, 1960; February 12, 1965.
*New Statesman & Society,* October 19, 1990, p. 32.
*New York Times,* May 22, 1989, p. C18.
*New York Times Book Review,* November 7, 1965; February 4, 1990, p. 15; May 7, 1989, p. 14.
*Observer,* January 26, 1965; October 22, 1989, p. 49; November 11, 1990, p. 67.
*Publishers Weekly,* May 11, 1990, p. 246.
*Saturday Review,* January 2, 1960; May 15, 1965.
*Sewanee Review,* Summer, 1990, pp. 506-14.
*Technology Review,* April, 1990, p. 77.
*Times Literary Supplement,* April 15, 1960; December 3, 1982.
*Tribune Books* (Chicago), July 5, 1990.

*OBITUARIES:*

*PERIODICALS*

*Chicago Tribune*, April 13, 1987.
*Cincinnati Post*, April 14, 1987.
*Detroit Free Press*, April 12, 1987.
*Fresno Bee*, April 12, 1987.
*Internatonal Herald Tribune*, April 13, 1987.
*Los Angeles Times*, April 12, 1987.
*New York Daily News*, April 12, 1987.
*New York Times*, April 12, 1987, April 14, 1987.
*Times*, April 20, 1987.
*Times* (London), April 13, 1987.
*Wall Street Journal*, April 13, 1987.
*Washington Post*, April 12, 1987.*

* * *

**LIPPMANN, Walter 1889-1974**

*PERSONAL:* Born September 23, 1889, in New York, NY; died December 14, 1974, in New York, NY; son of Jacob (a clothing manufacturer) and Daisy (Baum) Lippmann; married Faye Albertson, May 24, 1917 (divorced, 1938); married Helen Byrne Armstrong, March 26, 1938. *Education:* Harvard University, A.B. (cum laude), 1909, graduate study, 1909-10. *Politics:* Independent.

*CAREER:* Worked for *Everybody's Magazine* as Lincoln Steffens's secretary, 1910, became associate editor within a year; executive secretary to George R. Lunn, Socialist mayor of Schenectady, NY, during four months in 1912; with Herbert Croly, founded the *New Republic,* 1914, served as associate editor until 1917, returned to magazine, 1919; assistant to U.S. Secretary of War Newton D. Baker, 1917; secretary to a governmental organization, 1917, was one of the authors of President Woodrow Wilson's Fourteen Points; *The Inquiry,* secretary, 1917-18; *New York World,* New York City, editorial staffmember, 1921-29, editor, 1929-31; *New York Herald Tribune,* New York City, columnist ("Today and Tomorrow"), 1931-62, column syndicated by *Washington Post* and *Los Angeles Times* syndicates, 1963-67; also syndicated in over 275 papers around the world; fortnightly columnist, *Newsweek,* beginning 1962. Member of board of overseers, Harvard University, 1933-39; member of board of directors, Fund for the Advancement of Education, beginning 1951. *Military service:* U.S. Army Military Intelligence, 1918-19; commissioned a captain; attached to General Pershing's headquarters.

*MEMBER:* National Institute of Arts and Letters, American Academy of Arts and Letters (fellow), National Press Club, Phi Beta Kappa (senator, 1934-40), Sigma Delta Chi (fellow, 1950); Cosmos Club, Metropolitan Club, Army-Navy Country Club (all Washington, DC); Century Club, River Club, Harvard Club, Coffee House Club (all New York City); Harvard Club, Tavern Club (both Boston).

*AWARDS, HONORS:* Commander, Legion of Honor (France), 1946; Commander, Legion of Honor, Officer of Order of Leopold (Belgium), 1947; Knight's Cross of Order of St. Olav (Norway), 1950; Commander, Order of Orange Nassau (Netherlands), 1952; Overseas Press Club Award, 1953, 1955, and 1959; Pulitzer Prizes, 1958 and 1962; George Foster Peabody Award, 1962; Presidential Medal of Freedom, 1964, for "profound interpretation of his country and the affairs of the world"; Gold Medal, National Academy of Arts and Letters, 1965; Bronze Medallion, City of New York, 1974. LL.D., Wake Forest College, 1926, University of Wisconsin, 1927, University of California and Union College, 1933, Wesleyan University and University of Michigan, 1934, George Washington University and Amherst College, 1935, University of Rochester, 1936, College of William and Mary and Drake University, 1937, University of Chicago, 1955, New School for Social Research, 1959; Litt.D. from Dartmouth College and Columbia University, 1932, Oglethorpe College, 1934, Harvard University, 1944.

*WRITINGS:*

*A Preface to Politics,* Mitchell Kennerly, 1913.

*Drift and Mastery: An Attempt to Diagnose the Current Unrest,* Mitchell Kennerly, 1914, new edition with an introduction and notes by William E. Leuchtenberg, Prentice-Hall, 1961.

*The Stakes of Diplomacy,* Holt, 1915, 2nd edition, 1917.

*The World Conflict in Its Relation to American Democracy* (originally published in *Annals of the American Academy of Political Science,* July, 1917), U.S. Government Printing Office, 1917.

*The Political Scene: An Essay on the Victory of 1918,* Holt, 1919.

*Liberty and the News* (portion originally published in *Atlantic*), Harcourt, 1920.

*France and the European Settlement* (pamphlet), Foreign Policy Association, 1922.

*Public Opinion,* Harcourt, 1922.

*Mr. Kahn Would Like to Know* (pamphlet; originally published in *New Republic,* July 4, 1923), Foreign Policy Association, 1923.

*The Phantom Public,* Harcourt, 1925, published as *The Phantom Public: A Sequel to "Public Opinion,"* Macmillan, 1930.

*H. L. Mencken* (pamphlet; originally published in *Saturday Review,* December 11, 1926), Knopf, 1926.

*Men of Destiny,* drawings by Rollin Kirby, Macmillan, 1927, revised edition with an introduction by Richard Lowitt, University of Washington Press, 1969.

*American Inquisitors: A Commentary on Dayton and Chicago,* Macmillan, 1928.

*A Preface to Morals,* Macmillan, 1929, published with a new introduction by Sidney Hook, Time, 1964.

*Notes on the Crisis* (pamphlet; originally published in *New York Herald Tribune,* September, 1931), John Day, 1931.

(With W. O. Scroggs and others) *The United States in World Affairs: An Account of American Foreign Relations, 1931,* Harper, Volume I, 1932, Volume II, 1933.

*Interpretations, 1931-1932,* edited by Allan Nevins, Macmillan, 1932.

*A New Social Order* (pamphlet), John Day, 1933.

*The Method of Freedom,* Macmillan, 1934.

(With G. D. H. Cole) *Self-Sufficiency: Some Random Reflections* [and] *Planning International Trade* (the former by Lippmann, the latter by Cole), Carnegie Endowment for International Peace, 1934.

*The New Imperative* (portions originally published in *Yale Review,* June, 1935), Macmillan, 1935.

*Interpretations, 1933-1935,* edited by Nevins, Macmillan, 1936.

(Editor with Nevins) *A Modern Reader: Essays on Present-day Life and Culture,* Heath, 1936, 2nd edition, 1946.

*An Inquiry into the Principles of the Good Society,* Little, Brown, 1937, new edition, 1943, published as *The Good Society,* Allen & Unwin (London), 1938.

*The Supreme Court: Independent or Controlled?,* Harper, 1937.

*Some Notes on War and Peace,* Macmillan, 1940.

*U.S. Foreign Policy: Shield of the Republic,* Little, Brown, 1943.

*U.S. War Aims,* Little, Brown, 1944.

*In the Service of Freedom* (pamphlet), Freedom House, c. 1945.

*The Cold War: A Study in U.S. Foreign Policy,* Harper, 1947.

*Commentaries on American Far Eastern Policy* (pamphlet), American Institute of Pacific Relations, 1950.

*Isolation and Alliances: An American Speaks to the British,* Little, Brown, 1952.

*Public Opinion and Foreign Policy in the United States* (lectures), Allen & Unwin, 1952.

*Essays in the Public Philosophy,* Little, Brown, 1955, published as *The Public Philosophy,* Hamish Hamilton (London), 1955).

*America in the World Today* (lecture), University of Minnesota Press, 1957.

*The Communist World and Ours,* Little, Brown, 1959.

*The Confrontation* (originally published in column "Today and Tomorrow," September 17, 1959), Overbrook Press, 1959.

(With Clarence C. Little) *Speeches of Walter Lippmann and Clarence C. Little,* [Cambridge], 1960.

*The Coming Tests with Russia,* Little, Brown, 1961.

*The Nuclear Era: A Profound Struggle* (pamphlet), University of Chicago Press, 1962.

*Western Unity and the Common Market,* Little, Brown, 1962.

*The Essential Lippmann: A Political Philosophy for Liberal Democracy,* edited by Clinton Rossiter and James Lave, Random House, 1963.

(Author of introduction) *Fulbright of Arkansas: The Public Positions of a Private Thinker,* edited by Karl E. Meyer, Luce, 1963.

*A Free Press* (pamphlet), Berlingske Bogtrykkeri (Copenhagen), c. 1965.

*Conversations with Walter Lippmann* (CBS Reports television program), introduction by Edward Weeks, Little, Brown, 1965.

(Author of introduction) Carl Sandburg, *The Chicago Race Riots, July, 1919,* Harcourt, 1969.

*Early Writings,* introduction by Arthur Schlesinger, Jr., Liveright, 1971.

*Public Persons,* edited by Gilbert A. Harrison, Liveright, 1976.

*Public Philosopher: Selected Letters of Walter Lippmann,* edited by John Morton Blum, Ticknor & Fields (New York City), 1985.

Also author of *American Trade Policy* (originally published in *Sunday Times* [London]), 1943; editor of *The Poems of Paul Mariett,* 1913.

*CONTRIBUTOR*

Arno Lehman Bader, Theodore Hornberger, Sigmund K. Proctor, and Carlton Wells, editors, *Prose Patterns,* Harcourt, 1933.

Edward Simpson Noyes, editor, *Readings in the Modern Essay,* Houghton, 1933.

Albert Craig Baird, editor, *Essays and Addresses Toward a Liberal Education,* Ginn, 1934.

Joseph Bradley Hubbard and others, editors, *Current Economic Policies: Selected Discussions,* Holt, 1934.

Frank Howland McCloskey and Robert B. Dow, editors, *Pageant of Prose,* Harper, 1935.

Frank Luther Mott and Ralph D. Casey, editors, *Interpretations of Journalism: A Book of Readings,* F. S. Crofts, 1937.

Hillman M. Bishop and Samuel Hendel, editors, *Basic Issues of American Democracy: A Book of Readings,* Appleton, 1948, 6th edition, 1969.

William Ebenstein, editor, *Modern Political Thought: The Great Issues,* Rinehart, 1954, 2nd edition, 1960.

Robert U. Jamison, editor, *Essays Old and New,* Harcourt, 1955.

H. J. Rockel, editor, *Reflective Reader: Essays for Writing,* Holt, 1956.

Alan P. Grimes and Robert Horwitz, editors, *Modern Political Ideologues,* Oxford University Press, 1959.

C. Wright Mills, editor, *Images of Man,* Braziller, 1960.

Harry K. Girvetz, editor, *Contemporary Moral Issues,* Wadsworth, 1963.

Arthur A. Ekirch, editor, *Voices in Dissent: An Anthology of Individualistic Thought in the U.S.,* Citadel, 1964.

D. L. Larson, editor, *The Puritan Ethic in United States Foreign Policy,* Van Nostrand, 1966.

Anthologized in numerous volumes, including *Roots of Political Behavior,* edited by Richard Carlton Snyder and H. Herbert Wilson, American Book Co., 1949; *State of the Social Sciences,* edited by L. D. White, University of Chicago Press, 1956; *Conflict and Cooperation among the Nations,* edited by Ivo D. Duchacek and K. W. Thompson, Holt, 1960; and *Power and Civilization: Political Thought in the Twentieth Century,* edited by David Cooperman and E. V. Walter, Crowell, 1962. Contributor to many periodicals, including *Atlantic, Yale Review, New Republic, Life,* and *Harper's.*

Lippmann's writings have been collected at Yale University Library, Yale University, New Haven, CT.

*ADAPTATIONS:* Some of Lippmann's books have been translated into French, German, Italian, Spanish, and Chinese.

*SIDELIGHTS:* "Anything that makes the world more humane and more rational is progress," political journalist Walter Lippmann once said. "That's the only measuring stick we can apply to it." This statement exemplifies the attitude that characterized Lippmann's career: from long-running columnist and founder and editor of the *New Republic* in 1914 to advisor to politicians as eminent as President Woodrow Wilson, for whom Lippmann helped to author the historic Fourteen Points. Although he was always fully cognizant of the occurrences of the day, in books such as *A Preface to Politics, Public Opinion,* and *An Inquiry into the Principles of the Good Society* Lippmann also attempted to place current political events within a larger time perspective in his effort to make reason out of the seeming chaos. "I have led two lives," he once stated. "One of books and one of newspapers. Each helps the other. The philosophy is the context in which I write my columns. The column is the laboratory or clinic in which I test the philosophy and keep it from becoming too abstract."

This objective viewing of current events as though they were already part of history made Lippmann unique. Norman Podhoretz, in *Doings and Undoings: The Fifties and After in American Writing,* recognized this quality in Lippmann, although he believed that it had its disadvantages. Podhoretz wrote in 1964: "His main fault, I think, is a tendency toward pomposity which showed itself even in his most youthful efforts and which, if anything, has been encouraged by the veneration that his advancing years . . . have brought upon him. Presidents come and go; Congressmen and Senators come, and even they eventually go; but Walter Lippmann stays on in Washington forever—the last articulate representative of the political ambience of an older America, our last remaining link to the ethos of the Federalist Papers. He is, apparently, heeded and feared in Washington in a way that no other writer is, for his judgment of a government official, or of a policy, or of a bill seems to carry with it all the authority of the basic intentions of the American political system. When he speaks, it is as though the true Constitution were speaking, or as though Jefferson and Madison and Hamilton were communicating a mystical consensus through him—so thoroughly has he steeped himself in their spirit, and with such authenticity is he capable of recapturing the accents of their intellectual style. This, I suspect, is the secret source of his unique power to make the mighty listen: Walter Lippmann's opinion is the closest they can ever come to the judgment of history upon them. Under these circumstances, it is no wonder that Lippmann should occasionally be given to delivering himself of portentous platitudes without being aware that platitudes are what they are. The wonder is that he should be capable of anything else at all."

Podhoretz's comparison of Lippmann to the founding fathers is characteristic of many other analyses of Lippmann's philosophy and writing. In *A Continuing Journey,* Archibald MacLeish described Lippmann's attitude toward freedom in a democracy as one which closely paralleled the idealism of the leaders of the American Revolution: "True freedom, to Mr. Lippmann, is not the freedom of the liberal democracies. True freedom was founded on the postulate that there was a universal order on which all reasonable men were agreed: within that public agreement on the fundamentals and on the ultimates, it was sage to permit, and it would be desirable to encourage, dissent and dispute. True freedom for Mr. Lippmann, in other words, is freedom to think as you please and say as you think provided what you say and think falls within the periphery of what all reasonable men agree to be fundamentally and ultimately true." For Lippmann rationality was not only the highest ideal, but the possible savior of modern society. He once said: "The world will go on somehow, and more crises will follow. It will go on best, however, if among us there are men who have stood apart, who refused to be anxious or too much concerned, who were cool and inquiring, and had their eyes on a longer past and longer future."

It was in the field of foreign affairs that Lippmann revealed the principles central to his view of man and the modern world. In a *New York Times Magazine* interview, Lippmann stated that U.S. foreign policy was most responsible for the political unrest and social crises of the 1960s: "I ascribe the essence of the failure [of the United States to solve its internal problems] to miscalculation, to misunderstanding our post-World War II position in the world. That has turned our energies away from our real problems. The error is not merely the trouble in Vietnam, but the error lies in the illusion that the position occupied in the world by the United States at the end of the war was a permanent arrangement of power in the world. It wasn't. The United States was victorious; but by then all the imperial structures which set the bounds of American power had been destroyed: the German Reich, the Japanese empire. The result is that we flowed forward beyond our natural limits and the cold war is the result of our meeting the Russians with no buffers between us. That miscalculation, which was made by my generation, has falsified all our other calculations—what our power was, what we could afford to do, what influence we had to exert in the world."

One of Lippmann's chief concerns was that lack of reasonable attitudes toward other nations and domestic dissenters would continue to lead to an illogical disregard for the truly significant issues with which U.S. leaders must deal. "You have only to look at the Senate of the United States," Lippmann wrote in 1912, "to see how that body is capable of turning itself into a court of preliminary hearings for the Last Judgment, wasting its time and our time and absorbing public enthusiasm and newspaper scareheads. For a hundred needs of the nation it has no thought, but about the precise morality of an historical transaction eight years old there is a meticulous interest . . . enough to start the Senate on a protracted man-hunt. Now if one half of the people is bent upon proving how wicked a man is and the other half is determined to show how good he is, neither half will think very much about the nation." Lippmann also applied this disparagement of emotional politics to the passionate anti-Communists: "The reactionary radicals, who would like to repeal the twentieth century, are, so they tell us, violently opposed to Communism. But Communism also belongs to the twentieth century and these reactionary radicals do not understand it and do not know how to resist it."

Lippmann believed that it was his ultimate role as a journalist to reveal the absurdity of these emotional diversions. With this goal he hoped to influence the people to accept his creed; he objectified events so that the populace could comprehend them. "If the country is to be governed with the consent of the governed, then the governed must arrive at opinions about what their governors want them to consent to. How do they do this? They do it by hearing on the radio and reading in the newspapers what the corps of correspondents tells them is going on in Washington and in the country at large and in the world. Here we perform an essential service . . . we do what every sovereign citizen is supposed to do, but has not the time or the interest to do for himself. This is our job. It is no mean calling, and we have a right to be proud of it."

Perhaps even more than his many columns for such periodicals as the *New Republic, Vanity Fair,* and *New York World,* Lippmann's beliefs can be distilled from his letters. Collected and published in 1985 as *Public Philosopher: Selected Letters of Walter Lippmann,* the journalist's correspondences with a variety of fellow journalists, politicians, readers, and members of the business community extend from 1907 to 1969, five years before their author's death. Gleaned by editor John Morton Blum from a collection of over twenty thousand letters assembled at Yale University, *Public Philosopher* reveals a man whose "vaunted realism masked an impractical ideal as old as Plato's," according to Warren F. Kimball, who details Lippmann's ideal in his review for the *New York Times Book Review* as "a belief in a priesthood of wise realists, aided by technocrats, who would replace traditional leaders. . . . Only occasionally did Lippmann confront the difficulty of reconciling the ideal and the practical worlds, and then his letters indicated frustration with [such] reform-in-the-trenches" movements as Chicago's Hull House experiments. In the *Times Literary Supplement,* David Seideman contends, in fact, that *Public Philosopher* views its subject through *too* narrow a lens: "Blum's decision to publish 'significant' letters about 'politics and political ideas' to the deliberate exclusion of the 'routine and intimate' means that only one dimension of Lippmann is presented. The private person behind the dispassionate commentary remains mostly hidden. Through much of his life, Lippmann appears cold, unsympathetic and completely obsessed with professional advancement."

John Gross, commenting on *Public Philosopher* in the *New York Times* notes that while the volume has significance as a documentation of twentieth-century history, readers may well begin "wishing that [Lippmann's] tone was less detached and his perspective less lofty—the air on Olympus is sometimes rather thin—but there can be no denying the intellectual breadth that he brought to his trade. His letters no less than his books and journalism reveal a constant effort to penetrate beyond the confusion of the hour to basic issues and underlying patterns." "Lippmann was the century's great journalistic insider," adds Michael Kirkhorn in *Dictionary of Literary Biography,* "a man who sought—testing and dismissing one president after another—the great disinterested leader who would rescue the people from themselves and the century from its turmoil. The leader never appeared, but Lippmann's search was an adventure worthy of that invisible figure."

*BIOGRAPHICAL/CRITICAL SOURCES:*

*BOOKS*

*Authors in the News,* Volume 1, Gale, 1976.

Brown, John Mason, *Through These Men: Some Aspects of Our Passing History,* Harper, 1956.

Cary, F. C., *The Influence of Walter Lippmann, 1914-1944,* State Historical Society of Wisconsin, 1967.

Childs, Marquis, and James Reston, editors, *Walter Lippmann and His Times,* Harcourt, 1959.

Cohen, Felix S., *The Legal Conscience,* Yale University Press, 1960.
Commager, Henry Steele, *The American Mind,* Yale University Press, 1950.
*Dictionary of Literary Biography,* Volume 29: *American Newspaper Journalists, 1926-1950,* Gale, 1984.
Forcey, Charles B., *The Crossroads of Liberalism: Croly, Weyl, Lippmann, and the Progressive Era, 1900-1925,* Oxford University Press, 1961.
Forsee, Aylesa, *Headliners: Famous American Journalists,* Macrae, 1967.
Lerner, Max, *Actions and Passions: Notes on the Multiple Revolution of Our Time,* Simon & Schuster, 1949.
MacLeish, Archibald, *A Continuing Journey,* Houghton, 1967.
Morgenthau, Hans J., *The Restoration of American Politics,* University of Chicago Press, 1962.
Podhoretz, Norman, *Doings and Undoings: The Fifties and After in American Writing,* Farrar, Straus, 1964.
Schapsmeier, Edward L., and Frederick H. Schapsmeier, *Walter Lippmann: Philosopher, Journalist,* Public Affairs Press, 1969.
Schlesinger, Arthur, Jr., *The Politics of Hope,* Houghton, 1963.
Sevareid, Eric, *Conversations with Eric Sevareid,* Public Affairs Press, 1976.
Steel, Ronald, *Walter Lippmann and the American Century,* Atlantic/Little, Brown, 1980.
Stewart, Kenneth Norman, and John Tibbel, *Makers of Modern Journalism,* Prentice-Hall, 1952.
Syed, Anwar H., *Walter Lippmann's Philosophy of International Politics,* University of Pennsylvania Press, 1964.
Weingast, David E., *Walter Lippmann: A Study in Personal Journalism,* Rutgers University Press, 1949.
Wellborn, Charles, *Twentieth Century Pilgrimage: Walter Lippmann and the Public Philosophy,* Louisiana State University Press, 1969.

*PERIODICALS*

*Chicago Tribune Book World,* December 22, 1985.
*New Republic,* October 31, 1994, p. 11.
*New York Times,* December 3, 1985, p. C24.
*New York Times Book Review,* December 22, 1985, p. 14.
*New York Times Magazine,* September 14, 1969.
*Times Literary Supplement,* December 6, 1985.
*Washington Post Book World,* November 24, 1985, p. 1.*

**LORENZ, Konrad Zacharias 1903-1989**

*PERSONAL:* Born November 7, 1903, in Vienna, Austria; died February 27, 1989, in Vienna (some sources say Altenburg), Austria; son of Adolf (an orthopedic surgeon) and Emma (Lecher) Lorenz; married Margarethe Gebhardt (a gynecologist), June 24, 1927; children: Thomas, Agnes (Lorenz von Cranach), Dagmar. *Education:* Attended Columbia University, 1922; University of Vienna, M.D., 1928, Ph.D. (zoology), 1933.

*CAREER:* University of Vienna, Vienna, Austria, lecturer in comparative anatomy and animal psychology, 1937-40, university lecturer, 1940; University of Koenigsberg, Koenigsberg, Germany, professor and head of the department of general psychology, 1940-42; Institute of Comparative Ethology, Altenburg, Austria, director, 1949-51; Max Planck Society for the Advancement of Science, Institute for Marine Biology, head of research station for physiology of behavior in Buldern, Germany, 1951-55, Institute for Behavior Physiology, Seewiesen, Germany, co-founder, 1955-58, co-director, 1958-61, director, 1961-73; Austrian Academy of Science, Institute of Comparative Ethology, Vienna, director of department of animal sociology, 1973-82; Konrad-Lorenz Insitute, Austrian Academy of Science, Altenburg, Austria, director, 1982-89. Honorary professor at University of Muenster, 1953, University of Munich, 1957, University of Vienna, and University of Salzburg, beginning in 1974. Lecturer at numerous educational institutions worldwide, including University of Colorado, Denver. *Military service:* German Army, physician, 1942-44; captured in Russia and returned to Austria, 1948.

*MEMBER:* Pour le Merite for Arts and Science, Austrian Academy of Sciences, Bavarian Academy of Sciences, American Philosophical Society, Association for the Study of Animal Behaviour, American Ornithology Union, Deutsche Akademie der Naturforscher Leopoldina, Royal Society (foreign member), National Academy of Sciences (foreign associate).

*AWARDS, HONORS:* Gold Medal from Zoological Society of New York, 1955; City of Vienna Prize, 1959; Gold Boelsche Medal, 1962; Austrian Distinction for Science and Art, 1964; Prix Mondial, Cino de Duca, 1969; Kalinga Prize from UNESCO, 1970; Nobel Prize for Physiology or Medicine, 1973; Cervia Amniente Naturschutzpreis; Ehrenmedaille d. Katholischen Universitet Mailand, Bayer;

Maximiliansorden. Honorary degrees from University of Leeds, 1962, University of Basel, 1966, Yale University, 1967, Oxford University, 1968, University of Chicago, 1970, University of Durham, 1972, University of Birmingham, 1974, Grosses Verdienstkreuz der Bundesrepublik Deutschland, 1974, and Bayerischer Verdienstorden, 1974.

*WRITINGS:*

*Er redete mit dem Vieh, den Voegeln, und den Fischen,* Borotha-Schoeler (Vienna), 1949, 17th edition, 1958, U.S. edition, edited by Eva Schiffer, Scott, Foresman, 1968, translation by Marjorie Kerr Wilson, with illustrations by the author and foreword by Sir Julian Huxley, published as *King Solomon's Ring: New Light on Animal Ways,* Crowell, 1952, P. Smith, 1988.

*So kam der Mensch auf den Hund,* Borotha-Schoeler, 1950, translation by Wilson, with illustrations by the author and Annie Eisenmenger, published as *Man Meets Dog,* Methuen, 1954, Houghton, 1955, reprinted, Penguin, 1988, reprinted, Kodansha (New York), 1994.

(Contributor) Claire H. Schiller, editor and translator, *Instinctive Behavior: The Development of a Modern Concept,* International Universities Press, 1957.

*Das sogenannte Boese: Zur Naturgeschichte der Aggression,* Borotha-Schoeler, 1963, translation by Marjorie Latzke, with foreword by Sir Julian Huxley, published as *On Aggression,* Methuen, 1966, translation by Wilson published under same title, Harcourt, 1966.

*Gestaltwahrnehmung als Quelle wissenschaftlicher Erkenntnis* (title means "Gestalt Perception as a Source of Scientific Knowledge"), Wissenschaftliche Buchgesellschaft (Darmstadt), 1964.

*Darwin hat recht gesehen* (title means "Darwin Saw the Truth"), Neske (Pfullingen), 1965.

*Ueber tierisches and menschliches Verhalten,* R. Piper (Munich), 1965, selections published as *Vom Weltbild des Verhaltensforschers,* Deutscher Taschenbuch-Verlag (Munich), 1968, translation of unabridged edition by Robert Martin published as *Studies in Animal and Human Behavior,* two volumes, Harvard University Press, 1970-71.

*Evolution and Modification of Behavior,* University of Chicago Press, 1965, reprinted, 1986.

*Der Vogelflug* (title means "Bird Flight"), Neske, 1965.

(With Paul Leyhausen) *Antriebe tierischen and menschlichen Verhaltens,* R. Piper, 1968, translation by B. A. Tonkin published as *Motivation of Human and Animal Behavior: An Ethological View,* Van Nostrand, 1973.

*Die acht Todsuenden der zivilisierten Menschheit,* R. Piper, 1973, translation by Wilson published as *Civilized Man's Eight Deadly Sins,* Harcourt, 1974.

*Die Rueckseite des Spiegels: Versuch einer Naturgeschichte menschlichen Erkennens,* R. Piper, 1973, translation by Ronald Taylor published as *Behind the Mirror: A Search for a Natural History of Human Knowledge,* Harcourt, 1978.

*The Foundations of Ethology,* Springer, 1981 (published in German as *Grundeagen der Ethologie*).

*The Waning of Humaneness,* Little, Brown, 1987.

*Hier bin ich—wo bist du—Ethologie der Graugans,* R. Piper, 1988, reprinted as *Here Am I—Where Are You?: The Behavior of the Greylag Goose,* Harcourt Brace Jovanovich, 1991.

*On Life and Living: Konrad Lorenz in Conversation with Kurt Meundl,* St. Martin's Press, 1991.

*The Natural Science of the Human Species: An Introduction to Comparative Behavioral Research: the "Russian Manuscript,"* MIT Press, 1996.

Also author of *The Year of the Graylag Goose,* 1980. Contributor of articles to numerous journals in his field. Co-editor of *Zeitschrift fuer Tierpsychologie* (occasional periodical of Deutsche Gesellschaft fuer Tierpsychologie), 1937-89.

*SIDELIGHTS:* The acknowledged father of modern ethology, Konrad Zacharias Lorenz contributed toward a greater understanding of human behavioral patterns through the study of animals in their natural environment. Working with Oskar Heinroth, he identified the early biological learning process of imprinting, which, although the cybernetics are not understood, has been successfully applied in psychoanalysis and psychiatry. "As well as gaining the Nobel Prize for his efforts, he also won a large readership [throughout his career]," noted Andrew Motion in the *Observer,* "partly because he went out of his way to cheer up dull science by interspersing his plain observations with jolly intuitions."

Of his work, Maxine Kingston wrote in *English Journal:* "Lorenz integrates poetry and science by describing animal behavior with accuracy and beauty. A zoologist who sometimes seems to take flight with his jackdaws, ravens, and greylag geese,

Lorenz, perhaps believing his own delightful use of language merely scientific," often uses the classical English poets and Goethe . . . to "help him introduce chapters and to culminate both scientific and philosophical speculations."

The books are more controversial in the scientific community. In answer to the criticism that his work is speculative and anthropomorphic, Lorenz once said: "If in an octopus or a squid I find an eye, with lens, an iris, a nerve—I need not even observe the animal—I need only to state these formal analogies to know it is an eye, which has evolved to see with. It has the same formation as my eye, my vertebrate eye, which has evolved independently of the octopus eye, but a detailed similarity informs me it has the same function, and nobody balks at calling it an eye. . . . Construct a computer model of an animal being jealous—one system having a social relationship with another, resenting a third one doing the same, and interacting with both and trying to break up their relationship. This function would presuppose an enormous complication, much more so than the functioning of an eye. You can speak of jealousy with respect to dogs and ganders, certainly. Assertions that these are false analogies or anthropomorphizations betray a lack of understanding of functional conceptions. To call the animal jealous is just as legitimate as to call an octopus' eye an eye or a lobster's leg a leg."

Lorenz's posthumously published book *Here Am I—Where Are You?* presents the author's observations of a colony of greylag geese, analyzing their social behavior and communication patterns while also asserting connections between human behavior and that of geese. "We learn how geese fall in love, how they hate, how they maintain long-term relationships or divorce," commented Bernd Heinrich in *New York Times Book Review.* Reviewers emphasized Lorenz's lifelong interest in ducks and geese and noted his passion for the subject of his study. "I cannot claim that rational considerations alone determined the course of my studies," affirmed Lorenz in his introduction to the work.

With *The Natural Science of the Human Species: An Introduction to Comparative Behavioral Research: the "Russian Manuscript"*, Lorenz identified the fundamental principles of what later became the field of ethology. In the work, Lorenz explained how "[t]he route to an understanding of humans leads just as surely through an understanding of animals as the evolutionary pathway of humans had led through animal precursors." Originally written immediately after World War II, during a period when Lorenz was being held in a Soviet prison camp, the book's scientific principles are now less revolutionary than they were at the time of their conception. "[*The Natural Science of the Human Species* was a] pioneering work in its field, now interesting primarily as a historical document and the first great work of an unusually literate scientist," commented a reviewer for *Kirkus Reviews.* Before his death in 1989, Lorenz worked with journalist Kurt Mundl on a book of memoirs, published as *On Life and Living.* Generally praised by reviewers, the volume recollects Lorenz's lifelong work with animals and articulates his criticisms of modern life, most of which concern man's negative impact on the environment.

*BIOGRAPHICAL/CRITICAL SOURCES:*

*PERIODICALS*

*English Journal,* January, 1973.
*Harper's,* May, 1968.
*Newsweek,* August 6, 1973; October 22, 1973.
*New Yorker,* March 8, 1969.
*New York Times Book Review,* February 16, 1992, p. 19.
*Psychology Today,* November, 1974.
*Publishers Weekly,* July 25, 1991, p. 45.
*Science,* November 2, 1973.
*Time,* October 22, 1973.
*Zeitschrift fuer Tierpsychologie,* 1963.

*OBITUARIES:*

*PERIODICALS*

*Chicago Tribune,* March 1, 1989; March 5, 1989.
*Los Angeles Times,* March 2, 1989.
*New York Times,* March 1, 1989.
*Times* (London), March 1, 1989.
*Washington Post,* March 1, 1989.*

* * *

**LOVELL, Marc**
**See MCSHANE, Mark**

**LYONS, Arthur (Jr.) 1946-**

*PERSONAL:* Born January 5, 1946, in Los Angeles, CA; son of Arthur and Shirley (Hamilton) Lyons; married Barbara. *Education:* University of California, Santa Barbara, B.A., 1967.

*ADDRESSES: Home*—646 Morongo Rd., Palm Springs, CA 92264.

*CAREER:* Writer. Former proprietor of a restaurant in Palm Springs, CA; former mayor pro tem, Palm Springs; energy consultant for the city of Palm Springs.

*WRITINGS:*

*FICTION*

*The Dead Are Discreet,* Mason/Charter (New York City), 1974.
*All God's Children,* Mason/Charter, 1975.
*The Killing Floor,* Mason/Charter, 1976.
*Dead Ringer,* Mason/Charter, 1977.
*Castles Burning,* Holt (New York City), 1980.
*Hard Trade,* Holt, 1981.
*At the Hands of Another,* Holt, 1983.
*Three with a Bullet,* Holt, 1985.
*Fast Fade,* Mysterious Press (New York City), 1987.
*Jacob Asch Mystery,* Mysterious Press, 1987.
(With Thomas Noguchi) *Unnatural Causes,* Putnam (New York City), 1988.
*Other People's Money,* Mysterious Press, 1989.
(With Noguchi) *Physical Evidence,* Putnam, 1990.
*False Pretenses,* Mysterious Press, 1994.

*NONFICTION*

*The Second Coming: Satanism in America,* Dodd (New York City), 1970 (published in England as *Satan Wants You: The Cult of Devil Worship,* Hart Davis [London], 1971).
(With Marcello Truzzi) *The Blue Sense,* Mysterious Press, 1991.

*SIDELIGHTS:* Arthur Lyons' fiction is firmly rooted in the hard-boiled detective genre pioneered by Dashiell Hammet and Raymond Chandler. Most of his novels feature an ongoing protagonist, California private eye Jacob Asch, who in many ways resembles Hammet's Sam Spade and Chandler's Phillip Marlowe. Like his literary antecedents, Asch generally operates alone and casts a sardonic eye on the world about him. At the same time his actions reveal an underlying moral strength that betrays his cynical posture. Steven R. Carter in the *St. James Guide to Crime and Mystery Writers* describes Asch as a character with "integrity, courage, and concern for others."

Lyon's first novel, *The Dead Are Discreet,* also marked Jacob Asch's debut. Set in the world of California's oddball religious cults, it makes use of some of the same material Lyon researched for *The Second Coming: Satanism in America,* his study of Satanism and the occult. Although *Booklist* praises *The Dead Are Discreet* as "a smoothly fabricated detective novel," a reviewer in *Library Journal* states: "There doesn't seem to be any way to give the California private eye a decent burial. . . . The same old hash rehashed. . . . The plot is creaky and the effect not unlike a second-rate movie." However, as Carter notes, even if the Asch novels began as merely an updated version of the Hammet-Chandler genre, offering "little new in form or content," they have gained in strength and quality and taken on a distinctive individuality as the series has progressed. Carter attributes this improvement to the fact that Lyons has consistently strived to give his novels variety, not only in terms of the subcultures and social issues explored, but with regard to the diverse aspects of Asch's character that have surfaced in each successive book.

*Castles Burning* takes place in the exclusive world of Palm Springs and explores the theme of rebellious youth. According to Robin Winks in the *New Republic,* it "will keep you bolt upright." *Hard Trade,* described by Carter as "the best political study in detective fiction since Hammet's *The Glass Key,"* delves into pornography and drug addiction. In *The Killing Floor* Asch confronts the conflicts inherent in his own Jewish-Episcopalian background. In *At the Hands of Another,* which *Library Journal* calls "a sexy action-filled tale full of switchbacks and confusions," he must examine his unresolved feelings toward a woman he loved and lost years earlier.

Newgate Callendar in the *New York Times Book Review* feels that what sets Lyons apart from his literary predecessors "is the pungency of his style, the neat planning, and the avoidance of hokum." Winks states that Lyons has "his own point of view and a special toughness that Chandler often denied to himself." Carter believes that Lyons arrived fully as "a master in his own right—and a model for others," with *Other People's Money,* the tenth book in the Asch series, which pays homage to one of Lyons' primary influences. Carter describes the novel as "a continuously fascinating tribute to [Hammet's] *The Maltese Falcon"* and yet at the same time "new and rivetingly suspenseful."

*BIOGRAPHICAL/CRITICAL SOURCES:*

*BOOKS*

*St. James Guide to Crime and Mystery Writers,* fourth edition, St. James Press (Detroit, MI), 1996.

*PERIODICALS*

*Booklist,* July 15, 1974, p. 1132; April 15, 1981, p. 1140; September 1, 1983, p. 31.

*Chicago Tribune,* March 24, 1985.

*Library Journal,* May 1, 1974, p. 1331; May 1, 1981, p. 995; July, 1983, p. 1386.

*Los Angeles Times Book Review,* April 24, 1988.

*New Republic,* April 12, 1980.

*New York Times Book Review,* September 14, 1975, p. 39; January 16, 1977; February 3, 1980, p. 22; May 10, 1981; July 30, 1989.

*Times* (London), May 6, 1989; March 17, 1990.

*Washington Post,* February 4, 1985.

# M

## MacBETH, George (Mann) 1932-1992

*PERSONAL:* Born January 19, 1932, in a mining village in Scotland; died of motor neuron disease, February 17, 1992, in Tuam, County Galway, Ireland; son of George and Amelia Morton Mary (Mann) MacBeth. *Education:* New College, Oxford, Litt. Hum. (first class honours), 1955.

*CAREER:* Writer. British Broadcasting Corp (BBC), London, England, 1955-76, producer, Overseas Talks Department, 1957-58, producer, Talks Department, 1958-76.

*AWARDS, HONORS:* Co-recipient of Sir Geoffrey Faber Award, 1964.

*WRITINGS:*

*A Form of Words* (poems), Fantasy Press (England), 1954.

*Lecture to the Trainees* (poems), Fantasy Press, 1962.

*The Broken Places* (poems), Scorpion Press (England), 1963, Walker & Co., 1968.

(Editor) *The Penguin Book of Sick Verse,* Penguin (London), 1963, Penguin (Baltimore), 1965.

(With Edward Lucie-Smith and Jack Clemo) *Penguin Modern Poets VI* (anthology), Penguin (London), 1964.

*A Doomsday Book: Poems and Poem-Games,* Scorpion Press, 1965.

(Editor) *The Penguin Book of Animal Verse,* Penguin (London), 1965.

*The Calf: A Poem,* Turret Books (London), 1965.

*The Humming Birds: A Monodrama,* Turret Books, 1965.

*Missile Commander,* Turret Books, 1965.

*The Twelve Hotels* (poems), Turret Books, 1965.

*Noah's Journey* (a long poem in four parts, for children), Viking, 1966.

*The Castle,* privately printed, 1966.

(Editor) *Poetry 1900-1965,* Longmans, Green, 1967.

*The Colour of Blood* (poems), Atheneum, 1967.

*The Screens,* Turret Books, 1967.

*The Night of Stones* (poems), Macmillan, 1968, Atheneum, 1969.

(Editor) *The Penguin Book of Victorian Verse,* Penguin, 1968.

*A War Quartet* (poems), Macmillan, 1969.

*Jonah and the Lord* (long poem for children), Macmillan, 1969, Holt, 1970.

*A Death,* Sceptre Press, 1969.

*Zoo's Who,* privately printed, 1969.

*The Burning Cone* (poems), Macmillan, 1970.

*The Bamboo Nightingale,* Sceptre Press, 1970.

*Poems,* Sceptre Press, 1970.

*The Hiroshima Dream,* Academy Editions, 1970.

*Two Poems,* Sceptre Press, 1970.

(Editor) *The Falling Splendor: Poems of Alfred Lord Tennyson,* Macmillan, 1970.

*Collected Poems: 1958-70,* Macmillan, 1971, Atheneum, 1972.

*The Orlando Poems,* Macmillan, 1971.

*A Prayer, Against Revenge,* Sceptre Press, 1971.

*A Farewell,* Sceptre Press, 1972.

*Lusus: A Verse Lecture,* Fuller d'Arch Smith, 1972.

*A Litany,* Sceptre Press, 1972.

*Transformation,* Gollancz, 1972.

*Shrapnel* (poems), Macmillan, 1972.

*Prayers,* Aquila, 1973.

*My Scotland: Fragments of a State of Mind* (prose poems), Macmillan, 1973.

*The Poet's Year,* Gollancz, 1973.

*The Vision,* Sceptre Press, 1973.

*Elegy for the Gas Dowsers,* Sceptre Press, 1974.

*Shrapnel, and A Poet's Year,* Atheneum, 1974.

*In the Hours Waiting for Blood to Come,* Gollancz, 1975.

*Samurai,* Harcourt, 1975.

*Trespassing: Poems from Ireland,*Hutchinson, 1991.

*The Testament of Spencer,* A. Deutsch, 1992.

*The Patient,* Hutchinson, 1992.

*PLAYS*

*The Doomsday Show* (first produced in London, 1964), published in *New English Dramatists 14,* Penguin, 1970.

*The Scene-Machine* (first produced in Kassel, Germany, 1971; produced in London, 1972), B. Schott's Soehne (Germany), 1971.

Editor, *Poet's Voice,* 1958-65, *New Comment,* 1959-64, and *Poetry Now,* 1965-76.

*SIDELIGHTS:* A prolific and prominent poet and novelist, George MacBeth was a member of a loose-knit group of British poets known as The Group. D. M. Thomas wrote: "George MacBeth's poems in *The Colour of Blood* move in the post-Einstein world where Time and the Ego are fluid, past slides and merges into present and future, mind slides into mind: the kind of neo-Christian world—all of us, in the space-time continuum, members of one body—that Lawrence Durrell symbolizes in the city Alexandria." Similarly, Peter Bland found a certain fluence in the poems composing *The Night of Stones* which, he said: "liberates the imagination . . . in an unusual and yet recognizable way. Recognizable, I think, because MacBeth's imagination is often cinematic." "MacBeth directs," Bland continued, a "constantly changing 'non-picture' with consummate skill, cutting back and forth between various states of mind and creating a world where normal oppositions between fantasy and reality cease to exist."

Several critics, however, agreed with Thomas Kinsella, who noted that many of MacBeth's poems "suffer under their formal intricacies and a cumulative rhythmic dullness." MacBeth, wrote Kinsella, "is chameleon poet only in his agile attempts to compensate for an essentially technical obscurity."

But many more critics, particularly the Americans who read MacBeth's poems for the first time in the Atheneum edition of *The Colour of Blood,* were favorably impressed. "*The Colour of Blood* gives us a poet in full stride," said a *Virginia Quarterly Review* writer, "seeing with a clear eye and commanding a language rich in metaphor and alive with sound. Dream poems and rituals, a bright and witty discourse on metre and even some amazing 'Chinese synopses,' all give this book a vitality and vibrancy that has so long been lacking in English poetry (although MacBeth *is* Scottish). Wit and violence, elegance and a grand lack of restraint, he has them all, can look at the blood that spills around us and find the strength and the wisdom to make his songs fly far and high. This is an exciting collection of poems."

While reviewing *A War Quartet,* Peter Porter wrote: "George MacBeth is a poet who rarely writes without a consciously chosen and pursued form. For all his diversity of interests and many changes of style, he remains true to one aspect of his first collection—called appropriately *A Form of Words*—the ordering of feeling by means of rules and regulations. The principles of construction he uses are not merely the traditional ones of metre, rhyme and stanza pattern; they can also be instructions to the reader, rules of a game, mathematical divisions or patterns on the page. He is not a characteristic member of an avant-grade, though he likes a lot of its work. In a very real sense, MacBeth is a public poet. He can be obscure and recondite and yet every poem he writes is open to the audience. There is a direct appeal to the common reader—in this sense he is the opposite of a guildpoet like Graves; he doesn't want his washing taken in only by other professionals. The pop side of the avant-grade has attracted him most, because they are the ones who are making it with the public. But he would never allow himself to be as rhapsodic or sloppy as they can be. Ever since *The Broken Places,* which is still his finest book, he has been seeking new ways of combining approachableness (the sine qua non of our poetic renaissance) with the lapidary skill of the Victorians he admires."

MacBeth's life was cut short by motor neuron disease, which completely debilitated him before his death in 1992. In one of his final poetry collections, the posthumously published *The Patient,* MacBeth catalogued his illness in verse that is both moving and wry. "Nothing in [MacBeth's] collections has quite prepared the reader for the painful candour and unadorned quality of the verse that this last volume contains," remarked Stephen Knight in the *Times Literary Supplement.* Several reviewers commented on a sequence of sixteen sonnets in *The Patient* in which the poet chronicles the stages of his illness and the heartbreak of his wife: "The sequence of 16 sonnets which depict and explore their shared and separate torments is piercingly moving in its honesty and unhistrionic courage," declared *Specatator* reviewer Vernon Scannell. Concluded Scannell, "In his poems . . . George MacBeth has created his own, I believe enduring, monument."

*BIOGRAPHICAL/CRITICAL SOURCES:*

*BOOKS*

*Contemporary Literary Criticism,* Gale, Volume 2, 1974, Volume 5, 1976, Volume 9, 1978.
*Dictionary of Literary Biography,* Volume 40: *Poets of Great Britain and Ireland since 1960,* Gale, 1985.

*PERIODICALS*

*Books and Bookmen,* November, 1967.
*Book World,* December 24, 1967; November 9, 1969.
*Hudson Review,* winter, 1967-68.
*Kenyon Review,* November, 1967.
*Listener,* July 6, 1967.
*London Magazine,* May, 1967; October, 1968; January, 1970.
*New York Times Book Review,* October 16, 1966.
*Observer,* May 14, 1967; November 15, 1992, p. 64; January 3, 1993, p. 36.
*Poetry Review,* summer, 1967.
*Punch,* July 5, 1967.
*Spectator,* November 21, 1992, p. 50.
*Times Literary Supplement,* June 22, 1967; September 27, 1991, p. 27; February 5, 1993, p. 24.
*Virginia Quarterly Review,* winter, 1968; summer, 1969.

*OBITUARIES:*

*PERIODICALS*

*Chicago Tribune,* February 17, 1992, section 1, p. 10.
*Times* (London), February 18, 1992, p. 15.*

* * *

**MacLEAN, Alistair (Stuart) 1922(?)-1987**
**(Ian Stuart)**

*PERSONAL:* Born 1922 (some sources say 1923), in Glasgow, Scotland; died of heart failure following a stroke, February 2, 1987, in Munich, West Germany (now Germany); married Gisela Hinrichsen (divorced, 1972); married Mary Marcelle Georgeus (a film production company executive), October 13, 1972 (divorced, 1977); children: Lachlan, Michael, and Alistair; Curtis (stepson). *Education:* University of Glasgow, M.A., 1953. *Avocational interests:* Science and astronomy.

*CAREER:* Writer, 1955-87. Former teacher of English and history at Gallowflat Secondary School in Glasgow, Scotland. *Military service:* Royal Navy, 1941-46; served as torpedo man on convoy escorts.

*WRITINGS:*

*NOVELS*

*H.M.S. Ulysses*, Collins, 1955, Doubleday, 1956.
*The Guns of Navarone* (also see below), Doubleday, 1957.
*South by Java Head*, Doubleday, 1958.
*The Secret Ways*, Doubleday, 1959 (published in England as *The Last Frontier*, Collins, 1959).
*Night without End*, Doubleday, 1960.
*Fear Is the Key*, Doubleday, 1961.
*The Golden Rendezvous* (also see below), Doubleday, 1962.
*Ice Station Zebra*, Doubleday, 1963.
*When Eight Bells Toll* (also see below), Doubleday, 1966.
*Where Eagles Dare* (also see below; Companion Book Club and Readers' Book Club selections), Doubleday, 1967, published in large print, Eagle Large Print, 1994.
*Force 10 from Navarone* (also see below), Doubleday, 1968.
*Puppet on a Chain* (also see below), Doubleday, 1969.
*Caravan to Vaccares* (also see below), Doubleday, 1970.
*Bear Island*, Doubleday, 1971.
*The Way to Dusty Death*, Doubleday, 1973.
*Breakheart Pass* (also see below), Doubleday, 1974.
*Circus*, Doubleday, 1975.
*The Golden Gate*, Doubleday, 1976.
*Seawitch*, Doubleday, 1977.
*Goodbye, California*, Collins, 1977, Doubleday, 1978.
*Athabasca*, Doubleday, 1980.
*River of Death*, Collins, 1981, Doubleday, 1982.
*Partisans*, Collins, 1982, Doubleday, 1983.
*Floodgate*, Collins, 1983, Doubleday, 1984.

*San Andreas*, Collins, 1984, Doubleday, 1985.
*Santorini*, Collins, 1986, Doubleday, 1987.

*OMNIBUS VOLUMES*

*Five War Stories*, Collins, 1978.
*Four Great Adventure Stories*, Collins, 1981.

*UNDER PSEUDONYM IAN STUART*

*The Black Shrike*, Scribner, 1961 (published in England as *The Dark Crusader*, Collins, 1961, published under name Alistair MacLean, Collins, 1963).
*The Satan Bug*, Scribner, 1962.

*SCREENPLAYS*

*The Guns of Navarone* (based on novel of same title), Columbia, 1959.
*Where Eagles Dare* (based on novel of same title), Metro-Goldwyn-Mayer, 1969.
*When Eight Bells Toll* (based on novel of same title), Rank, 1971.
*Puppet on a Chain* (based on novel of same title), Scotia-Barber, 1971.
*Caravan to Vaccares* (based on novel of same title), Rank, 1974.
*Breakheart Pass* (based on novel of same title), United Artists, 1976.
*The Golden Rendezvous* (based on novel of same title), Rank, 1977.
*Force 10 from Navarone* (based on novel of same title), American-International, 1978.

Also author of *Deakin.*

*OTHER*

*Lawrence of Arabia* (juvenile), Random House, 1962 (published in England as *All About Lawrence of Arabia*, W. H. Allen, 1962).
*Captain Cook* (nonfiction), Doubleday, 1972.
*Alistair MacLean Introduces Scotland*, McGraw-Hill, 1972.
(With John Denis) *Hostage Tower*, Fontana, 1980.
(With Denis) *Air Force One Is Down*, Fontana, 1981.
*The Lonely Sea* (story collection), Collins, 1985, Doubleday, 1986.

Also author of *A Layman Looks at Cancer*, for the British Cancer Council.

*ADAPTATIONS: South by Java Head* was filmed by Twentieth Century-Fox, 1959; *The Secret Ways* was filmed by Universal, 1961; *The Satan Bug* was filmed by United Artists, 1964; *Ice Station Zebra* was filmed by Metro-Goldwyn-Mayer, 1968; *Fear Is the Key* was filmed by Metro-Goldwyn-Mayer—EMI, 1972. *H.M.S. Ulysses* and *Bear Island* were also filmed.

*SIDELIGHTS:* Alistair MacLean once claimed that he wrote fast, taking only thirty-five days to complete a novel, because he disliked writing and didn't want to spend much time at it. He also claimed never to reread his work once it was finished and to never read reviews of his books. According to the *New York Post,* MacLean once explained: "I'm not a novelist, I'm a storyteller. There's no art in what I do, no mystique." Despite his disclaimers, MacLean's many adventure novels sold over 30 million copies and were translated into a score of languages. He was, Edwin McDowell noted in the *New York Times,* "one of the biggest-selling adventure writers in the world."

MacLean's first success as a writer came while he was teaching school in his native Glasgow, Scotland, in the mid-1950s. A local newspaper, the *Glasgow Herald,* sponsored a story contest and MacLean's entry about a fishing family in the West Highlands won first prize. The story attracted the interest of an editor at the publishing house of William Collins & Sons when he noticed his wife crying over a short story in the local newspaper and asked to see it for himself. It was MacLean's winning entry. The editor, Ian Chapman, enjoyed the story so much that he called MacLean and suggested that he try his hand at a novel. MacLean agreed. Over the next three months he worked evenings on the novel, *H.M.S. Ulysses,* drawing upon his years as a torpedo man in the Royal Navy. The novel came out in September of 1955 and sold a record 250,000 copies in hardcover in its first six months. It was to be the first in a long string of best-selling novels.

*H.M.S. Ulysses* is based on MacLean's own experiences during World War II. For much of the war he worked on convoy ships delivering much-needed supplies to Britain, the Soviet Union, and other Allied nations. The work was perilous. MacLean was wounded twice by the Nazis and captured by the Japanese. The Japanese tortured him, pulling out his teeth "without benefit of anesthetic," as MacLean once remarked. The ordeal, Bob McKelvey noted in the *Detroit Free Press,* "left him bearing a grudge against the Japanese until his death."

The pain and hardship of the war at sea is evident in *H.M.S. Ulysses,* the story of a convoy in the North Atlantic which battles German submarines as well as the treacherous weather. "Even in his first novel," Robert A. Lee wrote in his *Alistair MacLean: The Key Is Fear,* "MacLean has an acute sense of plot and structure, and it is clear that he understands quite well the consequences of action as defined by the necessities of story-telling." Reviewers of the time found faults with MacLean's work, citing a melodramatic tendency, for example, but saw the novel as a forceful and realistic portrayal of the war at sea. E. B. Garside of the *New York Times* claimed that "this novel is a gripping thing. . . . Mr. MacLean, former torpedoman, now a Scottish schoolmaster, has caught the bitter heart of the matter." Writing in the *Saturday Review,* T. E. Cooney maintained that "Mr. MacLean's true achievement [is] that of setting down in print the image of war, so that any reader, regardless of his experience, can say, That is what is was like."

This "first and greatest work," as Martin Sieff of the *Washington Times* called *H.M.S. Ulysses,* was MacLean's personal favorite and the novel which he believed was his best work. It also set the pattern for much of his later novels. Its emphasis on men battling the elements as well as the immoral machinations of other men was to recur in all of MacLean's later books. Speaking of the clear demarcation between good and evil to be found in MacLean's work, Sieff explained that MacLean's "novels are imbued with a powerful, uncompromising moral vision—that there is wickedness in the world and that it must be recognized and fought to the death, come what may."

Despite the success of his first novel, MacLean was too cautious to leave his teaching job. He suspected that the book's success might prove to be only a fluke. It wasn't until his second novel, *The Guns of Navarone,* appeared in 1957 to popular acclaim that he became a full-time writer. This novel, telling of a mission to destroy an enemy gun installation during the Second World War, proved to be "MacLean's most famous and popular novel," as Lee observed. It is, William Hogan remarked in the *San Francisco Chronicle,* "a tense, compelling, extraordinarily readable adventure." The book sold some 400,000 copies in its first six months and is still a worldwide best-seller. In 1959, it was adapted as a successful motion picture starring Gregory Peck and David Niven and produced by Carl Forman.

After the success of *The Guns of Navarone,* MacLean moved to Switzerland, where he found the climate and tax laws to his liking. For a time he wrote one new novel every year. His usual writing schedule began early in the morning and lasted until early afternoon, working away on an IBM electric typewriter. "He never rewrote anything," Caroline Moorehead revealed in the London *Times,* "and resisted, with considerable stubbornness, even minor editorial changes proposed by [his publisher] Collins." MacLean's faith in his work proved to be justified. Once, after receiving the manuscript for a MacLean novel and judging it unsatisfactory, his publisher dispatched a representative to speak with MacLean about rewriting it. By the time the agent arrived in Switzerland, however, film rights to the book had already been sold and the rewrite idea was quietly shelved. "I don't write the first sentence," MacLean told Moorehead, "until I have the last in mind. . . . I don't even re-read. One draft and it's away." MacLean never kept copies of any of his books, preferring to give them away to friends and admirers. "I don't think any are very good," he explained to Moorehead. "I'm slightly dissatisfied with all of them. I'm pleased enough if at the end of the day I produce a saleable product—and that I do."

By the early 1970s, MacLean's books had sold over 20 million copies and had been made into several popular films. He was one of the top ten best-selling writers in the world and arguably the one whose books were most often adapted for the screen. MacLean made enough money from his writing that at one point in the 1960s he gave it up and went into business as a hotelier, buying the famous Jamaica Inn and three other hotels. But he found running a hotel chain too boring. When a filmmaker offered him the chance to write a screenplay in 1967, MacLean accepted. The resulting work, *Where Eagles Dare,* was a bestseller and a successful film and MacLean returned to his book-a-year schedule again.

MacLean's final novels were in the same vein as his first. *San Andreas,* published in 1984, features a British Merchant Navy ship under seige by a German U-boat during World War II. *Santorini,* MacLean's last novel, is set during the present and offers the story of a British spy ship commander attempting to stop the detonation of a wayward atomic bomb near the island of Santorini. The book was published in 1986, a year before MacLean's death.

The enormous amount of money that his adventure novels earned him never seemed to alter MacLean's lifestyle. Several observers noted that he lived frugally, content with few of the luxuries one might associate with such a successful writer. MacLean's frugality was in part the result of his innate caution. He had been raised in poverty and was always aware that his wealth might prove to be transitory. And, as Moorehead noted, he always felt "that it is morally wrong to earn so much." A writer for the London *Times* claimed that MacLean's "vast wealth lay uncomfortably on his conscience." At the time of his death in 1987, MacLean was living in a modest apartment in Switzerland, where he bought his own food and prepared his own meals.

Evaluations of MacLean's career are often colored by the sheer popularity of his books, which moved some critics to see him as nothing more than a writer who catered to mass tastes. And MacLean's flippant dismissals of his work abet this view. One such critic is Reg Gadney. Writing in *London Magazine,* Gadney described a typical MacLean adventure as "a hero, a band of men, hostile climate, a ruthless enemy. . . . The pace of the narrative consists in keeping the hero or heroes struggling on in the face of adversity. There's little time for reflection upon anything which does not contribute to the race: no characterization, merely the odd caricature; no subtlety of ploy, anything other than a fatuous one would get in the way. So the refinements are discarded and the narrative is a sprint from start to finish."

Yet, at his best, MacLean moved other critics to praise his work. Tim Heald of the London *Times* called him the "Yarnspinner Laureate" and "one of the country's most distinguished old thriller writers." Heald affectionately explained that MacLean "is at his best on the bridge of an indomitable British craft fighting its way through stupendous seas. The crew—and part of the plot—will resemble one of those stories in which an Englishman, a Scotsman, an Irishman, and a Welshman say or do something incredibly characteristic. They will be united, not only against the appalling gale, but also against a number of perfectly filthy foreigners." According to Sieff, MacLean's strong points included his "unmatched narrative drive, his complex plots and his—in the earlier novels—powerfully compelling characters." Sieff maintained that MacLean "was also a master of black, biting wit—a quality for which he was seldom given credit."

Most reviewers did credit MacLean with writing absorbing adventure novels, a task he performed with particular skill in such books as *H.M.S. Ulysses, The Guns of Navarone, Ice Station Zebra,* and *Where Eagles Dare.* In a review of *Ice Station Zebra,* the story of a nuclear submarine in peril under the Arctic ice cap, a *Times Literary Supplement* critic maintained that "the story evolves in a succession of masterful puzzles as astonishing as they are convincing. . . . There is so much swift-moving action, so much clever innuendo and such a feeling for relevant detail that one cannot help but be fascinated by the mind at work here." Speaking of *Where Eagles Dare,* Anthony Boucher of the *New York Times Book Review* described it as "a real dazzler of a thriller, with vivid action, fine set pieces of suspense, and a virtuoso display of startling plot twists."

Despite such appreciation of his work, MacLean always dismissed the value of his accomplishment. According to McKelvey, the author once claimed: "I am just a journeyman. I blunder along from one book to the next, always hopeful that one day I will write something really good." This appraisal of his work was not shared by Sieff, who ranked MacLean's *H.M.S. Ulysses* with "Nicholas Montsarrat's 'The Cruel Sea' as the greatest novel to come out of the maritime war." Lee concluded that "MacLean's books work best when he allies evil and the natural forces of violence, when he makes the structure of his novels an undulation of tension, release, and tension, when he manages to twist his plots in such a way as to reveal parts of the mystery bit by bit, until a final stunning denouement at the end. When all these elements mesh together in one harmonious whole, the result is adventure writing at its best." MacLean, according to Linda Bridges of the *National Review,* was "one of the best suspense writers around."

*BIOGRAPHICAL/CRITICAL SOURCES:*

*BOOKS*

*Contemporary Literary Criticism,* Gale, Volume 3, 1975, Volume 13, 1980, Volume 50, 1988, Volume 63, 1990.

Lee, Robert A., *Alistair MacLean: The Key Is Fear,* Borgo Press, 1976.

*PERIODICALS*

*Books and Bookmen,* May, 1968; November, 1971.

*British Book News,* March, 1985; April, 1986; February, 1987.

*Glasgow Herald,* March 6, 1954; September 27, 1955.
*Kirkus Reviews,* April 1, 1986.
*Library Journal,* October 15, 1992; November 1, 1991; March 15, 1989; February 1, 1987.
*Life,* November 26, 1971.
*London Magazine,* December-January, 1972-73.
*National Review,* January 31, 1975.
*New Statesman,* February 20, 1976.
*New York Times,* January 15, 1956; March 2, 1984.
*New York Times Book Review,* December 31, 1967; March 12, 1978; October 20, 1985; June 15, 1986; March 7, 1987; March 28, 1987.
*Publishers Weekly,* January 23, 1987.
*San Francisco Chronicle,* February 3, 1957.
*Saturday Review,* January 14, 1956.
*Spectator,* January 22, 1977.
*Time,* February 16, 1987.
*Times* (London), September 8, 1983; December 13, 1984; October 7, 1985; December 4, 1986.
*Times Literary Supplement,* August 9, 1963; September 14, 1973.
*Variety,* February 4, 1987.
*Washington Post,* March 6, 1982; March 12, 1984.

*OBITUARIES:*

*PERIODICALS*

*AB Bookman's Weekly,* February 23, 1987.
*Chicago Sun-Times,* February 3, 1987.
*Chicago Tribune,* February 3, 1987.
*Detroit Free Press,* February 3, 1987.
*Los Angeles Times,* February 3, 1987.
*New York Post,* February 3, 1987.
*New York Times,* February 3, 1987.
*San Francisco Examiner,* February 3, 1987.
*Times* (London), February 3, 1987.
*Variety,* February 21, 1994, p. 168.
*Washington Post,* February 3, 1987.
*Washington Times,* February 3, 1987.

* * *

**MacNEICE, (Frederick) Louis 1907-1963**
**(Louis Malone)**

*PERSONAL:* Born September 12, 1907, in Belfast, Ireland; died of pneumonia, September 4, 1963, in London, England; son of John Frederick (a Protestant bishop) and Elizabeth Margaret (Clesham) MacNeice; married Giovanna Marie Therese Babette Ezra, 1930 (divorced, 1936); married Hedli Anderson (a singer), April, 1942 (separated, 1960); children: (first marriage) Dan; (second marriage) Corinna. *Education:* Attended Merton College, Oxford University, 1926-30.

*CAREER:* University of Birmingham, Birmingham, England, lecturer in classics, 1930-36; University of London, Bedford College, London, England, lecturer in Greek, 1936-40; British Broadcasting Corp. (BBC), London, feature writer and producer, 1940-49 and 1950-63. Special lecturer in English, Cornell University, spring, 1940; director, British Institute, Athens, Greece, 1949-50, assistant representative, 1951.

*AWARDS, HONORS:* Commander of the Order of the British Empire, 1957.

*WRITINGS:*

*POETRY*

*Blind Fireworks,* Gollancz, 1929.
(Editor with Stephen Spender) *Oxford Poetry: 1929,* Oxford University Press, 1929.
*Poems,* Faber, 1935, Random House, 1937.
*The Earth Compels: Poems,* Faber, 1938.
*Autumn Journal,* Random House, 1939.
*Poems 1925-1940,* Random House, 1940.
*Selected Poems,* Faber, 1940.
*The Last Ditch,* Cuala Press (Dublin), 1940.
*Plant and Phantom,* Faber, 1941.
*Springboard: Poems, 1941-1944,* Faber, 1944, Random House, 1949.
*Holes in the Sky: Poems, 1944-1947,* Faber, 1948, Random House, 1949.
*Collected Poems, 1925-1948,* Faber, 1949.
*Ten Burnt Offerings,* Faber, 1952.
*Autumn Sequel: A Rhetorical Poem,* Faber, 1954.
*The Other Wing,* Faber, 1954.
*Visitations,* Faber, 1957, Oxford University Press (New York City), 1958.
*Eighty-five Poems,* Faber, 1959.
*Solstices,* Oxford University Press, 1961.
*The Burning Perch,* Faber, 1963.
*Round the Corner,* Faber, 1963.
*Selected Poems,* selected by W. H. Auden, Faber, 1964.
*The Collected Poems of Louis MacNeice,* edited by E. R. Dodds, Faber, 1966, Oxford University Press, 1967.
*The Revenant: A Song Cycle for Hedli Anderson,* Cuala Press, 1975.

*Selected Poems,* edited by Michael Longley, Faber, 1989.

*Selected Prose of Louis MacNeice,* Oxford University Press, 1993.

*STAGE PLAYS*

(Translator) *The Agamemnon of Aeschylus* (first produced in London by the English Group Theatre, 1936), Faber, 1936.

*Station Bell,* first produced at Birmingham University, 1937.

*Out of the Picture: A Play in Two Acts* (first produced in London by the English Group Theatre), Faber, 1937, Harcourt, 1938.

*Traitors in Our Way,* first produced at Lyric Theatre, Belfast, 1957.

*One for the Grave: A Modern Morality Play* (first produced at Abbey Theatre, Dublin, October, 1966), Faber, 1968, Oxford University Press, 1968.

Also author of *The March Hare Reigns,* published in *The Smith,* 1959.

*RADIO PLAYS*

*Christopher Columbus* (produced on BBC-Radio, October 12, 1942), Faber, 1944.

*He Had a Date,* produced on BBC-Radio, June 28, 1944.

*Sunbeams in His Hat* (also see below), produced on BBC-Radio, July 16, 1944.

*The Dark Tower* (also see below), music by Benjamin Britten, produced on BBC-Radio, January 21, 1946.

*Enter Caesar* (also see below), produced on BBC-Radio, September 20, 1946.

*The Dark Tower and Other Radio Scripts* (includes *The Dark Tower, Sunbeams in His Hat, The Nosebag,* and *The March Hare Saga*), Faber, 1948, Random House, 1949.

*The Queen of Air and Darkness,* produced on BBC-Radio, March 28, 1949.

(Translator with E. L. Stahl) *Goethe's Faust* (produced on BBC-Radio, October 30, 1949), Faber, 1951, Oxford University Press, 1953.

*Prisoner's Progress,* produced on BBC-Radio, April 27, 1954.

*The Waves* (adapted from the novel by Virginia Woolf), produced on BBC-Radio, March 18, 1955.

*East of the Sun and West of the Moon* (also see below), produced on BBC-Radio, July 25, 1959.

*They Met on Good Friday* (also see below), produced on BBC-Radio, September 8, 1959.

*The Administrator* (also see below), produced on BBC-Radio, March 10, 1961.

*The Mad Islands* (also see below), produced on BBC-Radio, April 4, 1962.

*Persons from Porlock* (also see below), produced on BBC-Radio, August 30, 1963.

*The Mad Islands [and] The Administrator,* Faber, 1964.

*Persons From Porlock and Other Plays for the Radio* (includes *Persons from Porlock, Enter Caesar, East of the Sun and West of the Moon,* and *They Met on Good Friday*), BBC, 1969.

*Selected Plays of Louis MacNeice,* Oxford University Press, 1993.

*OTHER*

(Under pseudonym Louis Malone) *Roundabout Way* (novel), Putnam, 1932.

(With W. H. Auden) *Letters From Iceland,* Random House, 1937.

*I Crossed the Minch,* Longmans, Green, 1938.

*Modern Poetry: A Personal Essay,* Oxford University Press, 1938.

*Zoo,* M. Joseph, 1938.

*The Poetry of W. B. Yeats,* Oxford University Press, 1941.

*Meet the U.S. Army,* Ministry of Information (London), 1943.

*Louis MacNeice Reading His Own Poetry* (sound recording with commentary), Harvard College Library, 1953.

*Collected Poems* (sound recording), Harvard College Library, 1953.

*The Penny That Rolled Away,* Putnam, 1954 (published in England as *The Sixpence That Rolled Away,* Faber, 1956).

*Astrology,* edited by Douglas Hill, Doubleday, 1964.

*Varieties of Parable,* Cambridge University Press, 1965.

*The Strings Are False: An Unfinished Autobiography,* Faber, 1965, Oxford University Press, 1966.

Contributor to numerous periodicals, including *Spectator, New Statesman and Nation, London Mercury, Criterion, Times Literary Supplement,* and *New Verse.*

*SIDELIGHTS:* In the 1930s, Louis MacNeice was associated with the group of English poets that included W. H. Auden, Stephen Spender, and C. Day Lewis. Theirs was a Freudian Marxian verse that shared, in M. L. Rosenthal's words in *Chief Modern Poets of England and America,* "a sense of the historical moment that was sometimes as violent as a physical sensation." They also shared a discursive, allusive and, at the same time, pointed manner. Yet MacNeice is distinguished from these 30s poets: his tone was more colloquial than that of the others, his manner more casual. In addition, he refrained from following in his poetry the dictates of any political party. As Martin S. Day explained in *History of English Literature, 1837 to the Present,* MacNeice remained "the sensitive intellectual protesting the world's disorder but offering no panacea."

During the 40s and 50s, MacNeice's youthful poetic energy lagged. In 1959, Anthony Thwaite wrote in *Contemporary English Poetry:* "His work is very readable, he is never boring, he is an excellent craftsman, and has many of the virtues of a good journalist—a 'reporter of experience' with sharp, vivid, precise phrases. But he seldom has much depth or penetration." Thus has MacNeice's reputation suffered, for it is only recently that critics have begun again to see his work and his attention to detail as more than poetic journalism.

Thomas Blackburn insisted in *The Price of an Eye* that MacNeice was not a shallow writer. He "is always implicated in whatever he writes about. He is not the detached reporter . . . but a poet who writes with open heart and mind . . . [about] his own humanity." In *The Poetry of Louis MacNeice* Donald Best Moore counted among the poet's gifts "an acute sensory, and especially visual, perception" that is an integral part of the emotional or intellectual feeling being poetically expressed: "Colour, shape, light and shade, sound, smell, touch and taste, lend to his verse an immediacy closely connected with time and place."

Furthermore, in *Louis MacNeice: Sceptical Vision,* Terence Brown recognized MacNeice's maturity and assurance of voice: "His poetic contribution to our literature is the embodiment of a creative scepticism in a verse, and therefore in a voice, which is nearly always recognisably and maturely his own." John Press, writing in *Louis MacNeice,* even ranked MacNeice with Shakespeare, Jenson, Herrick, Burns, Byron, Tennyson and Browning, the few poets who "have managed to make poetry out of the enjoyment which they have distilled from the minor pleasures of life."

In addition to his poetry, MacNeice wrote numerous stage, radio, and television plays; his radio and television plays were produced as a result of his association with the BBC. Eight of MacNeice's BBC plays-seven radio plays and one television play-were collected and published as *Selected Plays of Louis MacNeice.* Critics agree that MacNeice's dramatic masterpiece was 1946's *The Dark Tower,* which features an allegorical quest story. Writing in the *Observer,* Andrew Motion remarked, "MacNeice was right to feel that his plays were products of a particular historical moment. . . . But he was wrong to worry that their appeal might fade as times changed." Motion concluded: "[The plays] are always original and invariably surprising."

*BIOGRAPHICAL/CRITICAL SOURCES:*

*BOOKS*

Blackburn, Thomas, *The Price of an Eye,* Longmans, Green, 1961.

Brown, Terence, *Louis MacNeice: Sceptical Vision,* Barnes & Noble, 1975.

*Contemporary Literary Criticism,* Gale, Volume 1, 1973, Volume 4, 1975, Volume 10, 1979, Volume 53, 1989.

David, Dan, *Closing Time,* Oxford University Press, 1975.

Day, Martin S., *History of English Literature, 1837 to the Present,* Doubleday, 1964.

*Dictionary of Literary Biography,* Gale, Volume 10: *Modern British Dramatists, 1900-1945,* 1982, Volume 20: *British Poets, 1914-1945,* 1983.

Moore, Donald Best, *The Poetry of Louis MacNeice,* Leicester University Press, 1972.

Press, John, *Louis MacNeice,* Longmans, Green, 1965.

Rosenthal, M. L., *Chief Modern Poets of England and America,* Volume 1, MacMillan, 1966.

Southworth, J., *Sowing the Spring,* Oxford University Press, 1940.

Stallworthy, Jon, *Louis MacNeice,* W. W. Norton, 1995.

Stanford, Derek, *MacNeice, Spender, Day Lewis: The Pylon Poets,* Erdmans, 1969.

Thwaite, Anthony, *Contemporary English Poetry,* Heinemann, 1959.

*PERIODICALS*

*Encounter,* August, 1972.

*New Statesman & Society,* August 3, 1990, p. 45.

*New York Times,* September 22, 1963.

*Observer,* January 23, 1994, p. 20.
*Review of English Studies,* August, 1992, p. 436; May, 1995, p. 300.
*Times Literary Supplement,* October 28, 1949; January 6-12, 1989; July 8, 1994, p. 27.*

* * *

**MALABAILA, Damiano**
**See LEVI, Primo**

* * *

**MALONE, Louis**
**See MacNEICE, (Frederick) Louis**

* * *

**MANUSHKIN, Fran(ces) 1942-**

*PERSONAL:* Surname is pronounced Ma-*nush*-kin; born November 2, 1942, in Chicago, IL; daughter of Meyer (a furniture salesman) and Beatrice (Kessler) Manushkin. *Education:* Attended University of Illinois and Roosevelt University; Chicago Teachers College, North Campus (now Northeastern Illinois University), B.A., 1964. *Avocational interests:* Swimming, bird watching, cat watching, reading, book collecting, snorkeling, movie and theatergoing.

*ADDRESSES: Home and office*—121 East 88th St., Apt. 4C, New York, NY 10128; *Email*—franm@pipeline.com. *Agent*—Amy Berkower, Writers House, 21 West 26th St., New York, NY 10010.

*CAREER:* Writer. Elementary teacher in Chicago, 1964-65; Lincoln Center for Performing Arts, New York City, tour guide, 1966; Holt, Rinehart & Winston, New York City, secretary to college psychology editor, 1967-68; Harper & Row Publishers, New York City, secretary, 1968-72, associate editor of Harper Junior Books, 1973-78; Random House, New York City, editor of Clubhouse K-2 (student paperback book club), 1978-80.

*MEMBER:* PEN, Author's League of America, National Audubon Society.

*WRITINGS:*

*CHILDREN'S BOOKS*

*Baby,* illustrated by Ronald Himler, Harper (New York City), 1972, published as *Baby, Come Out!,* 1984.
*Bubblebath!,* illustrated by Himler, Harper, 1974.
*Shirleybird,* illustrated by Carl Stuart, Harper, 1975.
*Swinging and Swinging,* illustrated by Thomas DiGrazia, Harper, 1976.
*The Perfect Christmas Picture,* illustrated by Karen A. Weinhaus, Harper, 1980.
*Annie Finds Sandy,* illustrated by George Wildman, Random House (New York City), 1981.
*Annie Goes to the Jungle,* illustrated by Wildman, Random House, 1981.
*Annie and the Desert Treasure,* illustrated by Wildman, Random House, 1982.
*Annie and the Party Thieves,* illustrated by Wildman, Random House, 1982.
*Moon Dragon,* illustrated by Geoffrey Hayes, Macmillan (New York City), 1982.
*The Tickle Tree,* illustrated by Yuri Salzman, Houghton (Boston), 1982.
*The Roller Coaster Ghost,* illustrated by Dave Ross, Scholastic (New York City), 1983.
*Hocus and Pocus at the Circus,* illustrated by Geoffrey Hayes, Harper, 1983.
*The Adventures of Cap'n O. G. Readmore: To the Tune of "The Cat Came Back,"* illustrated by Manny Campana, Scholastic, 1984.
*Buster Loves Buttons,* illustrated by Dirk Zimmer, Harper, 1985.
*Jumping Jacky,* illustrated by Carolyn Bracken, Golden Books, 1986.
(With Lucy Bate) *Little Rabbit's Baby Brother,* illustrated by Diane de Groat, Crown (New York City), 1986.
*Ketchup, Catch Up!,* illustrated by Julie Durrell, Golden Books, 1987.
*Beach Day,* illustrated by Kathy Wilburn, Western Publishing (New York City), 1988.
*Puppies and Kittens,* illustrated by Ruth Sanderson, Golden Books, 1989.
*Latkes and Applesauce: A Hanukkah Story,* illustrated by Robin Spowart, Scholastic, 1990.
(Compiler) *Glow in the Dark Mother Goose,* illustrated by Mary Grace Eubank, Western Publishing, 1990.
(With Lucy Bate) *Be Brave, Baby Rabbit,* illustrated by Diane de Groat, Crown, 1990.

(Adaptor) *Walt Disney Pictures Presents: The Prince and the Pauper* (based on the film), illustrated by Russell Schroeder and Don Williams, Western Publishing, 1990.

*Hello World: Travel Along with Mickey and His Friends,* illustrated by Juan Ortiz and Phil Bliss, Disney Press, 1991.

*Walt Disney's 101 Dalmatians: A Counting Book,* illustrated by Russell Hicks, Disney Press, 1991.

*The Best Toy of All,* illustrated by Robin Ballard, Dutton (New York City), 1992.

*My Christmas Safari,* illustrated by R. W. Alley, Dial (New York City), 1993.

(Compiler) *Somebody Loves You: Poems of Friendship and Love,* illustrated by Jeff Shelly, Disney Press, 1993.

*Let's Go Riding in Our Strollers,* illustrated by Benrei Huang, Hyperion (New York City), 1993.

*Peeping and Sleeping,* illustrated by Jennifer Plecas, Clarion (New York City), 1994.

*The Matzah That Papa Brought Home,* illustrated by Ned Bittinger, Scholastic, 1995.

*Starlight and Candles: The Joys of the Sabbath,* illustrated by Jacqueline Chwast, Simon & Schuster (New York City), 1995.

*Miriam's Cup: A Passover Story,* illustrated by Bob Dacey, Scholastic, 1998.

*"ANGEL CORNERS" SERIES*

*Rachel, Meet Your Angel,* Puffin (New York City), 1995.

*Toby Takes the Cake,* Puffin, 1995.

*Lulu's Mixed-Up Movie,* Puffin, 1995.

*Val McCall, Ace Reporter?,* Puffin, 1995.

*WORK IN PROGRESS: Daughters of Fire: Heroines of the Bible,* for Browndeer Press/Harcourt Brace.

*SIDELIGHTS:* Noted for her whimsical imagination and her lovingly drawn characters, Fran Manushkin has written such entertaining picture books as *Baby, Moon Dragon,* and *The Tickle Tree* to novels like *Lulu's Mixed-Up Movie* and *Val McCall, Ace Reporter?,* both part of her "Angel Corners" series for girls. In addition, she is the author of several books that portray children and their parents celebrating both Jewish and Christian holidays. In a writing career that has spanned over two decades, Manushkin has provided young children with a window on a world where even the simplest things are transformed into joyous events.

Manushkin's first book, *Baby,* was published in 1972; proving perennially popular with readers, it was reissued as *Baby, Come Out!* in 1984, and translated into eight other languages. *Baby* is the lighthearted story of a not-quite-yet-born baby who decides that Mom's tummy suits her just fine—until Daddy comes home promising kisses that she can't feel. *Horn Book* reviewer Sidney D. Long praised Manushkin's first effort as a "special book for mothers-to-be to share with their other children."

"My stories tend to grow from a single image," Manushkin once told *CA.* "*Baby,* for example, blossomed from an image I had in my head of a mother communicating with her newborn baby. That image metamorphosed into a mother communicating with the child she is carrying in her womb. When the child said, 'I don't want to be born,' it just happened. I did not plan it. I didn't have a plot in mind." Before she became a writer herself, Manushkin believed that books "existed in a pure state in author's heads," with their endings perfectly well thought out. "That simply isn't true," she explained. "Books develop according to their own time. You cannot dictate that a book be born; neither can you dictate to a book. Listen," she added, "really listen, and your book will speak."

*Baby* was the first of many imaginative books that Manushkin has written for children, each one evolving out of an image or idea. In *Swinging and Swinging,* a young girl on a swing soon finds that she has passengers; first a soft puffy cloud, then the cheery sun, the moon, and a rain of stars join her. As she drifts into a drowsy half-sleep the moon and stars climb back up into the sky and night falls. In *The Tickle Tree* a young squirrel in the mood for a belly-grabbing tickle gets his friends to stack up and help him reach the top of a feather-leafed palm tree—which causes such a giggle that the animal tower soon topples like a laughing house of cards.

"Whether you know it or not, every book you write is about yourself," Manushkin explained. "*Hocus and Pocus at the Circus,* for example, is about my sister and myself—but I'm not telling who the nice sister is!" Geared for beginning readers, *Hocus and Pocus* is about two witches—one mean, the other nice—who are busy laying plans for Halloween night. While Hocus plots to cause havoc at a circus, Pocus misspeaks her spells and ends up adding to the circusgoers' fun by turning rubber balls into puppies, herself into a squealing baby pig, and ends the evening by shooting her sister out of a cannon (harmlessly, of course!) A world where magic is possible also figures in *Moon Dragon,* a trickster tale wherein a tiny mouse devises a way to fool a huge, fire-breathing dragon who has eaten everything in sight and now wants the mouse for desert. Noting that the author's "magic touch invests all her stories," a *Publishers Weekly* reviewer writes that *Moon Dragon* "is one of [Manushkin's] best."

Manushkin has also written a number of well-received picture books for preschoolers, including her *Let's Go Riding in Our Strollers* and *Peeping and Sleeping*. Featuring a lively, rhyming verse text, *Let's Go Riding in Our Strollers* presents all of the excitement of the urban outdoors through the eyes of toddlers in strollers on their adventurous trip to the park. *Booklist* reviewer Ilene Cooper praised Manushkin's "exuberant text" in *Let's Go Riding in Our Strollers,* concluding the book "fun to look at and to read." *Peeping and Sleeping* centers on a peeping noise that is keeping little Barry awake. Barry's father takes the young child out to the pond to investigate, and soon his fears turn to curiosity and wonder at the busy activities of nocturnal creatures. *School Library Journal* contributor Lisa Wu Stowe praised "Manushkin's wonderfully realistic dialogue and evocative descriptions of a warm spring night's walk" in *Peeping and Sleeping.* A *Publishers Weekly* reviewer maintained: "Especially well captured is the trembling mixture of fear and giddiness that accompanies children's nighttime excursions." In another favorable estimation, *Booklist* reviewer Hazel Rochman asserted: "Although rooted in reality, the story with its gentle reversals creates a sense of hidden wonder, of magic and mischief in a hushed nighttime landscape."

For older readers, Manushkin has created the "Angel Corners" series, which takes place in the town of Angel Corners and also has guardian angels as characters. In *Rachel, Meet Your Angel,* the first book of the series, a lonely fifth grader who finds herself friendless after a move to a new town suddenly finds Merribel, a guardian-angel apprentice, looking over her shoulder. Things start to improve for Rachel; she meets three friends and together the girls find a way to raise the money needed to repair the town clock. "Middle-grade girls whose taste in novels runs to the fanciful will find the inaugural novel in the Angel Corners series a fun—if flighty—read," asserted a *Publishers Weekly* commentator. Other books in the series, each of which feature a different girl and her guardian angel, include *Toby Takes the Cake* and *Lulu's Mixed-Up Movie.*

In addition to her purely fictional tales, Manushkin has written several books that spin warm, joyous imagery around tradition-based religious holidays. Among these are *Starlight and Candles: The Joys of the Sabbath, Latkes and Applesauce: A Hanukkah Story, The Matzah That Papa Brought Home,* and *My Christmas Safari,* a retelling of the "Twelve Days of Christmas" using African jungle motifs. Reviews of *The Matzah That Papa Brought Home* characterize the favorable critical reception of these works. A cumulative Passover tale for preschoolers and beginning readers, *The Matzah* was dubbed "a unique, lively offering" by *School Library Journal* contributor Marcia Posner. Stephanie Zvirin of *Booklist* maintained that "what the book actually does best is convey the feeling of closeness and community engendered by the celebration." An earlier work, 1980's *The Perfect Christmas Picture,* which finds perplexed photographer Mr. Green attempting to get his whole family together for a holiday snapshot, "is about my family—the way I wish my family had been," the author told *CA.* "I suppose the 'message' in that book has to do with acceptance in a rather odd, madcap family." The Green family is indeed madcap; the picture-taking process lasts a full nine months, thwarted by giggling, pinching, blinking eyes, and countless other minor disasters. *Horn Book* reviewer Mary M. Burns praised Manushkin for the "pleasant, unhackneyed lilt" she brings to the book's text.

Combining writing with her job as an editor means that Manushkin's life pretty much revolves around books. "It's hard to generalize about how long it takes me to write [each one]," Manushkin told *CA.* "Some of my best books were written very quickly, almost in one sitting. *Baby* was one, as was *Swinging, Swinging,* about a little girl on a swing. *Hocus and Pocus* and *The Perfect Christmas Picture* took longer. In early drafts of both books, I had episodes my editor felt were too 'outrageous,' 'implausible,' or just literally impossible. Plot has never been my strong suit; my imagination is too wild, I guess, to readily adapt itself to constricting stories." Her advice for young writers-to-be? "In my years as a writer and editor I have learned a few things I would like to pass on: don't give up on a book even if lots of editors reject it, keep sending it around . . . and don't be nervous if you've started writing something but don't know where it is going—be willing to discover the book as it evolves."

*BIOGRAPHICAL/CRITICAL SOURCES:*

*PERIODICALS*

*Booklist,* July, 1993, p. 1971; June 1, 1993, p. 1858; June, 1994, p. 1841; January 15, 1995, p. 937.
*Bulletin of the Center for Children's Books,* April, 1972, p. 127; September, 1980, p. 16; September, 1982, p. 16; February, 1983, p. 113; November, 1990, pp. 64-65.
*Horn Book,* June, 1972, p. 261; December, 1980, p. 626.
*Junior Bookshelf,* August, 1978, p. 188.
*Kirkus Reviews,* March 15, 1972, p. 321; May 1, 1974, p. 476; August 15, 1982, p. 935; October 15, 1993, p. 1332; July 15, 1995, p. 1028.
*Publishers Weekly,* April 30, 1982, p. 59; July 25, 1986, p. 186; September 14, 1990, p. 123; September 20, 1993, p. 34; April 25, 1994, p. 77; February 6, 1995, p. 86.
*Quill and Quire,* December, 1990, p. 19.
*School Library Journal,* November, 1976, p. 50; June, 1992, p. 99; October, 1992, p. 46; June, 1994, p. 110; February, 1995, p. 76.

* * *

**MARCUS, Joanna**
**See ANDREWS, Lucilla (Mathew)**

* * *

**MARSHALL, Raymond**
**See RAYMOND, Rene (Brabazon)**

* * *

**MARTINES, Julia**
**See O'FAOLAIN, Julia**

* * *

**MAXWELL, Gavin 1914-1969**

*PERSONAL:* Born July 15, 1914, in Mochrum, Scotland; died September 7, 1969, in Inverness, Scotland; son of Aymer Edward Maxwell (an Army officer) and Lady Mary Percy; married Lavinia Joan Lascelles, February 1, 1962 (divorced 1964). *Education:* Attended Stowe School, Buckinghamshire, England; Hertford College, Oxford University, M.A.

*CAREER:* Freelance journalist, c. 1937-39; portrait painter, 1949-52; writer, beginning 1952. Soay Shark Fisheries, Hebridies, Scotland, owner, 1944-49. Member of advisory committee, Wildlife Youth Service of the World Wildlife Fund; trustee, Danilo Dolci Trust. *Military service:* Scots Guards, 1939-41, Special Operations Executive, 1941-44; disabled, 1944; became major.

*MEMBER:* International Institute of Arts and Letters (fellow), Royal Society for Literature (fellow), Royal Geographic Society (fellow), Zoological Society (scientific fellow), American Geographical Society (fellow), PEN, Fauna Preservation Society, Wildfowl Trust (honorary life member), Special Forces Club, Guards Club, Puffin Club, Third Guards Club, Household Brigade Yacht Club.

*AWARDS, HONORS:* Heinemann Award, Royal Society for Literature, 1957, for *A Reed Shaken by the Wind.*

*WRITINGS:*

*Harpoon Venture,* Viking (New York City), 1952, published as *Harpoon at a Venture,* Hart-Davies (London), 1952.
*Bandit,* Dutton (New York City), 1956, published as *God Protect Me from My Friends,* Longmans, Green (London), 1956.
*People of the Reeds,* Dutton, 1957, published as *A Reed Shaken by the Wind,* Longmans, Green, 1957.
*The Ten Pains of Death,* Longmans, Green, 1959.
*Ring of Bright Water* (first book in "Camusfearna" trilogy), Dutton, 1960, adapted for children as *The Otter's Tale,* Dutton, 1962, adaptation for children by Dorothy Welchman published under original title, Hutchinson (London), 1981.
*The Rocks Remain* (second book in "Camusfearna" trilogy), Dutton, 1962.
(Contributor) J. Montgomery, editor, *The Pan Book of Animal Stories,* Pan Books, 1964.
*The House of Elrig,* (autobiography), Dutton. 1965.
*Lords of the Atlas: The Rise and Fall of the House of Glaoua, 1893-1956,* Dutton, 1966.
(With John Stidworthy and David Williams) *Seals of the World,* Houghton, 1967.

*Raven Seek Thy Brother* (third book in "Camusfearna" trilogy), Longmans, Green, 1968, Dutton, 1969.

Contributor of poetry and travel stories to periodicals, including *New Statesman, Saturday Review, Twentieth Century, National Geographic, American Magazine of Natural History,* and *Observer.* Member of advisory panel, *Animals* Magazine.

*Lords of the Atlas* has been translated into Spanish

*ADAPTATIONS: Ring of Bright Water* was released as a film in 1969.

*SIDELIGHTS:* Up until the 1960 publication of his novel *Ring of Bright Water,* Scottish author Gavin Maxwell was primarily known for well-researched works of detective fiction or melodrama. The story of the author's life in the West Highlands of Scotland with his pet otters, *Ring of Bright Water* won the affections of readers and critics alike, extending its popularity to younger audiences after it was made into a feature motion picture in 1969. The popularity of the novel inspired Maxwell to write several other novels based on his life with animals, quickly gaining him a reputation as a nature writer.

Born in southwestern Scotland in 1914, Maxwell was raised by his aristocratic mother—his father had been killed in World War I—in the family home, *Elrig,* which was located in the country. Educated, along with his three siblings, by governesses, the author lacked the company of other children, and soon began to develop the reclusive nature that would eventually characterize him as an adult. He would later recount his childhood in 1965's *The House of Elrig,* praising the natural splendor of his rural surroundings on the Scottish moors while also bemoaning his childhood isolation. Calling *The House of Elrig* "the story of sunshine and shadow," a *Times Literary Supplement* reviewer remarked that Maxwell's account of his traumatic public school experiences "demonstrat[es] again that it is the misfits of the British public school system who often become the most interesting personalities in later life."

Young Maxwell's lonely childhood did inspire a love of nature, which would sustain his later career as a writer. A childhood illness diagnosed when Maxwell was sixteen resulted in several months of bedrest, during which time he began to write stories. After graduating from Hertford College, Oxford, he channelled his writing skills into a job as a journalist, while also indulging in his love of nature. When World War II began, Maxwell joined the Scots guards, but the spectacle of death and destruction that surrounded him on an almost daily basis only fueled his anti-social tendencies, and after the war he drew away from social interaction and more and more into the world of animals and writing. In 1944 the author went so far as to purchase his own island in the Scottish Hebridies; his efforts to found a shark fishery there would provide the subject matter of his first book, 1952's *Harpoon Venture.*

*Ring of Bright Water* also grew out of Maxwell's personal experiences, based as it is on his life in *Camusfearna,* a cottage located in the remote northwest corner of Scotland. An affectionate tale of the otters Mijbil, Teko, and Edal, who provided the author with companionship, *Ring of Bright Water* depicts the growing bond and unspoken forms of communication that can develop between man and animal. Gerald Durrell praised the work in the *New York Times Book Review* as "an enchanting, beautifully written, and, above all, a very funny book."

*Ring of Bright Water,* which received widespread critical acclaim, was followed by two other novels—*The Rocks Remain* and *Raven Seek Thy Brother*—which together make up Maxwell's "Camusfearna" trilogy. In *Raven Seek Thy Brother,* which was published in 1969, Maxwell recounts his travels to Greece, Spain, and to an eider duck colony in Iceland (without the otters) as well as of a series of homebound disasters, the upset from which his relationship with his pet otters did much to transcend. The book can be seen as the "fall of his fortunes," according to a *Times Literary Supplement* reviewer, who characterized the book as "almost hypochondriac." Indeed, it was a dismal set of ills that plagued the author's later years at his cottage retreat: a disabling injury resulting from a car accident; fears of cancer, founded upon years of heavy cigarette smoking; oversights that resulted in economic difficulties; and the confinement, due to a change in their personalities brought on by neglect, of the otters that had once been free to roam the area. Ultimately, Maxwell says goodbye to *Camusfearna,* which was destroyed by fire, and to his otters, one of which perished in the flames.

In addition to his autobiographical writings, Maxwell was also the author of several volumes of non-fiction. *Lords of the Atlas: The Rise and Fall of the House of Glaoua, 1893-1956* chronicles the history of the aristocratic, tribal Glaoua family, which lived near Marrakesh and whose leaders, the brothers Madani and T'hami, held sway over Moroccan politics during the early part of the twentieth century, responsible even for the deposition of the sultan of Morocco in 1953. While not a scholarly work of history, Maxwell's book was praised for its vivid characterization of individuals—Alden Whitman dubbed it "a fascinating study in the 'unmodernity' of modern man" in his *New York Times* review—and its spirited style. Often cited as a writer who studies and knows his subjects thoroughly, Maxwell spent time in northwestern Africa, not only combing through published and unpublished sources, but personally visiting people who still recalled the family and their exploits. Praising the work, a *Times Literary Supplement* critic called *Lords of the Atlas* an "achievement" and cited the author for having "brought the Glaoua heyday . . . splendidly to life again with all its gore and glory and a lot of unintentional comedy as well. His is a most satisfying book."

In addition to history, Maxwell also wrote several other books featuring the natural world, including *Seals of the World,* which provides a detailed reference to thirty-two species of not only seals but their cousins the sea lions and walruses as well. Prompted by the author's concern over the plight of Great Britain's Gray Seal, the book was written for the World Wildlife Fund in 1968. A year after its publication, Maxwell succumbed to the lung cancer that had haunted his later years; he died, age fifty-five, on September 6, 1969. Described by John Lister-Kay as "a half-poet with a hyper-sensitive temperament" in Lister-Kay's *The White Island,* Maxwell was remembered primarily for his early works, including the beloved *Ring of Bright Water.* As reviewer Peter Quennell concluded of Maxwell in the London *Times:* "To each subject he has brought the same intelligence, the same love of natural beauty and the same gift of unfolding a lively and exciting tale."

*BIOGRAPHICAL/CRITICAL SOURCES:*

*BOOKS*

Frere, Richard, *Maxwell's Ghost: An Epilogue to Gavin Maxwell's Camusfearna,* Verry, 1976.
Lister-Kay, John, *The White Island,* Longman, Green, 1972.

*PERIODICALS*

*Atlantic,* August, 1968.
*Best Sellers,* March 1, 1969.
*Book Week,* January 30, 1966.
*Books and Bookmen,* December, 1967.
*Christian Science Monitor,* December 15, 1966.
*Home,* February, 1963.
*Library Journal,* March 15, 1956; April 1, 1969, p. 1487.
*New Republic,* June 16, 1952.
*New Statesman and Nation,* June 7, 1952.
*New York Times,* January 27, 1967, p. 43.
*New York Times Book Review,* February 26, 1961, p. 22; November 21, 1965, p. 69; March 30, 1969, p. 14.
*Publishers Weekly,* May 6, 1968, p. 42.
*Saturday Review,* July 26, 1952.
*Spectator,* March 30, 1956.
*Time,* February 28, 1969.
*Times Literary Supplement,* February 3, 1966, p. 80; December 22, 1966, p. 1182; March 14, 1968, p. 277; January 30, 1969, p. 112; September 9, 1994, p. 28.
*Washington Post Book World,* January 24, 1988, p. 13.

*OBITUARIES:*

*PERIODICALS*

*New York Times,* September 9, 1969.
*Publishers Weekly,* October 13, 1969.
*Times* (London), September 8, 1969.*

* * *

**McCARTHY, Barry (Wayne) 1943-**

*PERSONAL:* Born September 7, 1943, in Chicago, IL; son of Edward J. (a contractor) and Dorothy (Small) McCarthy; married Emily Jeannette McCabe (a writer), November 19, 1966; children: Mark, Kara Dawn, Paul T. *Education:* Loyola University at Chicago, B.A., 1965; Southern Illinois University at Carbondale, Ph.D., 1969. *Politics:* Democrat. *Religion:* Roman Catholic.

*ADDRESSES:* *Office*—Washington Psychological Center, 4201 Connecticut Ave. N.W., Suite 602, Washington, DC 20008; fax: 202-364-0561. *Agent*—Ellen Levine Literary Agency, Inc., 15 East 26th St., Suite 1801, New York, NY 10010.

*CAREER:* American University, Washington, DC, instructor, 1969-70, assistant professor, 1970-74, associate professor, 1974-78, professor of psychology, 1978—, counselor at Counseling Center, 1969-76, associate director of training for Peer Counseling Program, 1973-76. Private practice of psychology, 1971—; partner of Washington Psychological Center, 1977—.

*MEMBER:* American Psychological Association, American Association of Sex Educators, Counselors, and Therapists, Association for the Advancement of Behavior Therapy, Behavior Research and Therapy Association (clinical fellow), American Association for Marriage and Family Therapy (clinical member), Society for Sex Therapy and Research.

*WRITINGS:*

(With Mary Ryan and Fred Johnson) *Sexual Awareness: A Practical Approach,* Boyd & Fraser, 1975.
*What You (Still) Don't Know about Male Sexuality,* Crowell (New York City), 1977.
(With wife, Emily J. McCarthy) *Sex and Satisfaction after Thirty,* Prentice-Hall (Englewood Cliffs, NJ), 1981.
(With E. J. McCarthy) *Sexual Awareness: Sharing Sexual Intimacy,* Carroll & Graf (New York City), 1984, tenth anniversary edition, 1993.
*Male Sexual Awareness: Increasing Sexual Pleasure,* Carroll & Graf, 1988.
(With E. J. McCarthy) *Female Sexual Awareness: Achieving Sexual Fulfillment,* Carroll & Graf, 1989.
(With E. J. McCarthy) *Couple Sexual Awareness,* Carroll & Graf, 1990.
(With E. J. McCarthy) *Intimate Marriage,* Carroll & Graf, 1992.
(With E. J. McCarthy) *Confronting the Victim Role,* Carroll & Graf, 1993.

*SIDELIGHTS:* Barry McCarthy told *CA:* "I am a clinical psychologist and sex therapist. Most of my time is spent doing clinical work with some teaching and presenting professional workshops.

"For me, writing is a way to inform the public of new findings in the human sexuality field and hopefully to prevent sexual problems. For too many people, sex is seen as a performance where you have to prove yourself to your partner. In my opinion, sexuality is best perceived as a cooperative, sharing experience in giving and receiving pleasure.

"Writing books with my wife is particularly enjoyable, and we are trying to decide if the next project will be on sexuality or focus more broadly on psychological well-being."

* * *

**McGERR, Patricia 1917-1985**

*PERSONAL:* Born December 26, 1917, in Falls City, NE; died of cancer, May 11, 1985, in Bethesda, MD; daughter of Patrick Thomas and Catherine (Dore) McGerr. *Education:* Attended Trinity College, 1933-34; University of Nebraska, A.B., 1936; Columbia University, M.S., 1937. *Politics:* Democrat. *Religion:* Roman Catholic.

*CAREER:* American Road Builders' Association, Washington, DC, publicity director, 1937-43; *Construction Methods* magazine, New York, NY, assistant editor, 1943-48; freelance writer, 1948-85. Lecturer and consultant, Georgetown University Writers' Conference, beginning 1960.

*MEMBER:* Mystery Writers of America (member of board of directors, 1959-62, 1965-69, 1977-81), Catholic Interracial Council of Washington (treasurer, 1950-60), Northwest Washington Fair Housing Association (treasurer, 1964-66).

*AWARDS, HONORS:* First prize, Catholic Press Association short story contest, 1950; Grand Prix de Litterature Policiere, France, 1952; *Ellery Queen's Mystery Magazine,* short story contest, second prize, 1962, first prize, 1967.

*WRITINGS:*

*Pick Your Victim,* 1946.
*The Seven Deadly Sisters,* 1947.
*Catch Me If You Can,* 1948.
*Save the Witness,* 1949.
*Follow, As the Night,* 1950, published as *Your Loving Victim,* Collins (London), 1951.
*Death in a Million Living Rooms,* 1951, published as *Die Laughing,* Collins, 1952.
*The Missing Years,* 1953.
*Fatal in My Fashion,* 1954.
*Martha, Martha,* Kenedy (New York City), 1960.
*My Brothers, Remember Monica,* Kenedy, 1964.
*Is There a Traitor in the House?,* 1964.
*Murder Is Absurd,* 1967.

*Stranger with My Face,* Luce (Washington), 1968.
*For Richer, for Poorer, til Death,* Luce, 1969.
*Legacy of Danger,* Luce, 1970.
*Daughter of Darkness,* Popular Library (New York City), 1974.
*Dangerous Landing,* Dell (New York City), 1975.

Contributor of short stories and book reviews to *Ellery Queen's Mystery Magazine, This Week* and other magazines. Work appears in anthologies, including *Alfred Hitchcock Presents: Sinister Spies,* Random House (New York City), 1966; *Murder Most Foul,* Walker (New York City), 1971; and *The Year's Best Mystery and Suspense Stories 1983,* Walker, 1983. Collections of McGerr's manuscripts are held at the Institute of Popular Culture at Bowling Green State University and at Trinity College in Washington, DC.

*ADAPTATIONS: Follow, As the Night* was filmed in 1954 under the title *One Step to Eternity; The Missing Years* was adapted for radio and television; *Fatal in My Fashion* was adapted for television; *Catch Me If You Can* was adapted for radio; the short story "Johnny Lingo" was adapted for film.

*SIDELIGHTS:* Patricia McGerr once commented in the *St. James Guide to Crime and Mystery Writers* that in her first mystery novel "I named the murderer on page one and centered the mystery around the identity of the victim. In my next book I carried that idea a little farther by asking the reader to discover both murderer and victim and then, in the third, presented a murderer whose problem was to pierce the disguise of the detective. A witness to the crime was the unknown element in the fourth book and in the fifth, having exhausted the possibilities, I returned to the design of my first crime with the question mark again beside the name of the corpse. Since then I've been writing more conventional mysteries, but in all of them I've tried to make the development of character as interesting as the puzzle."

James R. McCahery in the *St. James Guide to Crime and Mystery Writers* admitted that McGerr "is perhaps best known for her creative genius and technical skill in producing . . . the 'whodun*in*?' wherein the victim of the crime, rather than the culprit, is unknown. Her forte, indeed, her major contribution to the genre, is the mystery with this completely new twist." McGerr first employed this twist in her first novel, *Pick Your Victim,* which McCahery termed a "widely acclaimed tour de force." The story is set in the Aleutian Islands off the Alaskan coast where a group of Marines, having read a newspaper story about a murder in Washington, DC, attempt to figure out the victim's identity—the section of the newspaper containing that vital information being unavailable to them. Isaac Anderson in the *New York Times* called the book "long range detection with a vengeance, presented in an amusing manner." Anthony Boucher in the *San Francisco Chronicle* maintained that *Pick Your Victim* "would stand up excellently as a satiric novel" while the "unique towhomdunit angle makes it the find of the season."

McGerr's second mystery novel follows Sally Bowen as she tries to uncover which of her seven aunts has murdered her husband. "In many respects superior to its predecessor, this novel entails the unmasking of victim and culprit alike," McCahery observed. The *New Yorker* critic found the novel "a tricky one at best, [but] doesn't stand up as well" as McGerr's first book.

"The very nature of these early puzzlers," McCahery noted, "demands close character studies, a skill at which Miss McGerr excels—indeed, she is at her very best with a large and assorted cast of characters, all of whom she manages to define and individualize with the utmost ease and care." Speaking of the novel *Follow, as the Night,* Elizabeth Bullock in the *New York Times* noted that "McGerr etches the lines of her merciless portrait with skill and builds her story just as expertly." In a review of the same novel, the critic for the *New York Herald Tribune Book Review* praised the "excellent job" McGerr did of "building up the various characters who must be understood in order to solve this particular riddle."

In addition to her mystery novels, McGerr offered character studies in several mainstream novels as well. In *The Missing Years,* she tells the story of a man who has abandoned his wife and children and, after twelve years, returns unexpectedly to them. Ethel Dexter in the *Springfield Republican* called *The Missing Years* "a serious novel, finely written," while Andrea Parke in the *New York Times* maintained that "McGerr understands the kind of people she is writing about." David Tilden, in his review for the *New York Herald Tribune Book Review,* wrote that "McGerr explores the nature of the diversity of human beings and their compulsions. . . . Beneath the surface of a fictional pattern that occasionally runs into the oversentimental, she has some wise and stimulating things to say."

In *Martha, Martha* McGerr wrote a novel featuring the Biblical characters Martha, Mary and Lazarus. Drawing on the scant information found in the Bible, McGerr fleshed out her characters to create what Riley Hughes in *Catholic World* called "three-dimensional people instead of pious shadows." The reviewer for *Kirkus* found *Martha, Martha* to be "an exceptionally interesting Biblical novel" and stated that "the author displays unusual imaginative skill, psychological perceptiveness and accurate knowledge of the region and customs into which her characters fit." Hughes summed up that the book's pivotal scene, the raising of Lazarus from the dead, "is brilliantly drawn. . . . *Martha, Martha* succeeds strikingly where so many Biblical novels fail."

*BIOGRAPHICAL/CRITICAL SOURCES:*

*BOOKS*

*Authors in the News,* Volume 1, Gale (Detroit), 1976.
*St. James Guide to Crime and Mystery Writers,* fourth edition, St. James Press (Detroit), 1996.

*PERIODICALS*

*Book Week,* April 11, 1965, p. 10.
*Catholic World,* August, 1950, p. 171; April, 1960, p. 191.
*Chicago Sun,* November 25, 1949, p. 51.
*Kirkus,* March 15, 1960, p. 28.
*Library Journal,* February 15, 1960, p. 85.
*New Yorker,* December 21, 1946, p. 22; August 16, 1947, p. 30.
*New York Herald Tribune Book Review,* November 13, 1949, p. 34; July 9, 1950, p. 12; December 16, 1951, p. 12; October 25, 1953, p. 21; October 31, 1954, p. 14.
*New York Times,* December 8, 1946, p. 48; July 16, 1950, p. 19; August 16, 1953, p. 12.
*San Francisco Chronicle,* January 5, 1947, p. 14; June 18, 1950, p. 14; November 28, 1954, p. 31.
*Springfield Republican,* October 11, 1953, p. 6C.

*OBITUARIES:*

*PERIODICALS*

*Washington Post,* May 14, 1985.
*Washington Times,* May 15, 1985.*

**McILVANNEY, William 1936-**

*PERSONAL:* Born November 25, 1936, in Kilmarnock, Ayrshire, Scotland; son of William Angus (a miner) and Helen (Montgomery) McIlvanney; married Moira Watson, March 23, 1961; children: Siobhan, Liam. *Education:* University of Glasgow, M.A. (honors), 1959. *Politics:* "Socialism." *Religion:* Agnosticism.

*ADDRESSES:* *Office*—c/o Mainstream Publishing, 7 Albany St., Edinburgh EH1 3UG, Scotland. *Agent*—George Greenfield, John Farquharson Ltd., 162-168 Regent St., London W1R 5TB, England.

*CAREER:* Ravenspark Academy, Irvine, Ayrshire, Scotland, housemaster, beginning 1960. Tutor in English literature and creative writing, University of Grenoble, 1970-71; teacher of English, Irvine Royal Academy, 1971-72; creative writing fellow, University of Strathclyde, 1972-73; assistant rector, Greenwood Academy, Irvine, 1973-75.

*AWARDS, HONORS:* Geoffrey Faber Memorial Award of Faber & Faber Ltd., 1966, for *Remedy Is None;* Scottish Arts Council publication award, 1968, for *A Gift from Nessus;* Whitbread Fiction Award, 1975, and Scottish Arts Council Award, 1976, both for *Docherty.*

*WRITINGS:*

*NOVELS*

*Remedy Is None,* Eyre & Spottiswoode (London), 1966.
*A Gift from Nessus,* Eyre & Spottiswoode, 1968.
*Docherty,* Allen & Unwin (London), 1975.
*Laidlaw,* Pantheon (New York City), 1977.
*The Papers of Tony Veitch,* Pantheon, 1983.
*The Big Man,* Morrow (New York City), 1985.

*POETRY*

*The Longships in Harbour,* Eyre & Spottiswoode, 1970.
*Landscapes and Figures,* Circle Press (Surrey, England), 1973.
*Weddings and After,* Mainstream (Edinburgh), 1984.
*In Through the Head,* Mainstream, 1988.

*OTHER*

(Contributor) Karl Miller, editor, *Memoirs of a Modern Scotland,* Faber, 1969.

*Glasgow, 1956-1989: Shades of Grey . . . and Some Light Too,* Mainstream, 1987.
*Walking Wounded* (stories), Hodder & Stoughton, 1989.
*Dreaming* (screenplay), 1990.

*SIDELIGHTS:* William McIlvanney has written mainstream novels, poetry and detective novels. Because of his work in more serious fiction, when he turns to detective fiction, McIlvanney's "attitude to the popular form is unusually complex," writes Ian A. Bell in the *St. James Guide to Crime and Mystery Writers.* "His highly regarded detective stories, *Laidlaw* and *The Papers of Tony Veitch,* recount specific murder mysteries, but in each case the author surrounds a particular enquiry with elaborate probings into wider concerns of truth, integrity and justice, and he situates the narrative in a meticulously realized and evocative urban setting." A "writer of solid talent and sensitive intelligence," according to a *Times Literary Supplement* critic. "[McIlvanney] writes in prose of great verve and sensitivity."

*Laidlaw* is set in a dreary, gray Glasgow where the policeman Laidlaw enlists the help of the criminal underworld in his search for a sex killer. "The identity of the murderer," Bell recounts, "is never in doubt, and the novel concentrates on the philosophical and moral issues which arise in the course of the murder hunt." Newgate Callendar in the *New York Times Book Review* explains that "this book has a literary style far beyond that of most books in the genre. . . . McIlvanney has the ability to create real people. . . . Everything in *Laidlaw* rings true. It is a tough novel, with an exciting ending, and it is superbly written." Robin Winks in *New Republic* states: "Every figure is carefully realized, every line serves the purpose of motion and explication at once, every scene rings true. It has been a long time since I have read a first mystery as good as this one."

In *The Papers of Tony Veitch,* Bell writes, "Laidlaw searches for the elusive central character, finding him too late. The dying words of a wino have raised the possibility of crime. Only Laidlaw seems to care about the possible murder of this wretched character, and once again the book compares his doggedness and insistence with the more physical toughness of the criminal underworld. Through the convoluted plot, the respectable and the criminal, the innocent and the guilty are brought into discomforting proximity, and Laidlaw's own personal problems lend substance to his apparently involuntary quest after truth."

Bell sums up: "McIlvanney's fictional world is much messier than the orderly world of more conventional crime writing, and although the cases in both novels are in one obvious sense solved, the more fundamental mysteries concerning the human capacity for evil remain."

*BIOGRAPHICAL/CRITICAL SOURCES:*

*BOOKS*

Bell, Ian A. and Graham Daldry, editors, *Watching the Detectives: Essays on Crime Fiction,* Macmillan (London), 1990.
*St. James Guide to Crime and Mystery Writers,* fourth edition, St. James Press (Detroit), 1996.

*PERIODICALS*

*Books and Bookmen,* September, 1968.
*Economist,* October 22, 1977, p. 265.
*Library Journal,* July, 1977, p. 102.
*Listener,* August 8, 1968.
*New Republic,* September 24, 1977, p. 177.
*New York Times Book Review,* July 31, 1977, p. 30.
*Time,* June 27, 1977, p. 109.
*Times Literary Supplement,* September 19, 1968.

* * *

**McLUHAN, (Herbert) Marshall 1911-1980**

*PERSONAL:* Born July 21, 1911, in Edmonton, Alberta, Canada; died after a long illness, December 31, 1980, in Toronto, Ontario, Canada; son of Herbert Ernest (a real estate and insurance salesman) and Elsie Naomi (an actress and monologuist; maiden name, Hall) McLuhan; married Corinne Keller Lewis, August 4, 1939; children: Eric, Mary McLuhan Colton, Teresa, Stephanie, Elizabeth, Michael. *Education:* University of Manitoba, B.A., 1932, M.A., 1934; Cambridge University, B.A., 1936, M.A., 1939, Ph.D., 1942. *Religion:* Roman Catholic.

*CAREER:* University of Wisconsin—Madison, instructor, 1936-37; St. Louis University, St. Louis, MO, instructor in English, 1937-44; Assumption University, Windsor, Ontario, associate professor of English, 1944-46; University of Toronto, St. Michael's College, Toronto, Ontario, associate professor, 1946-52, professor of English, 1952-80, creator (by appointment) and director of Center for Culture and Technology, 1963-80. Lecturer at numerous universities, congresses, and symposia in the United States and Canada; Albert Schweitzer Professor of Humanities at Fordham University, 1967-68. Chair of Ford Foundation seminar on culture and communications, 1953-55; director of media project for U.S. Office of Education and National Association of Educational Broadcasters, 1959-60. Appointed by Vatican as consultor of Pontifical Commission for Social Communications, 1973. Consultant to Johnson, McCormick & Johnson Ltd. (public relations agency), Toronto, 1966-80, and to Responsive Environments Corp., New York City, 1968-80.

*MEMBER:* Royal Society of Canada (fellow), Modern Language Association of America, American Association of University Professors.

*AWARDS, HONORS:* Governor General's Literary Award for critical prose, 1963, for *The Gutenberg Galaxy: The Making of Typographic Man;* Fordham University Communications Award, 1964; D.Litt. from University of Windsor, 1965, Assumption University, 1966, Grinnell College, 1967, Simon Fraser University, 1967, St. John Fisher College, 1969, University of Edmonton, 1972, and University of Western Ontario, 1972; Litt.D. from University of Manitoba, 1967; Molson Prize of Canada Council for outstanding achievement in the social sciences, 1967; Carl-Einstein-Preis, German Critics Association, 1967; Companion of the Order of Canada, 1970; Institute of Public Relations President's Award (Great Britain), 1970; LL.D. from University of Alberta, 1971; Christian Culture Award, Assumption University, 1971; Gold Medal Award, President of the Italian Republic, 1971, for original work as philosopher of the mass media; President's Cabinet Award, University of Detroit, 1972.

*WRITINGS:*

*"Henry IV": A Mirror for Magistrates* (originally published in *University of Toronto Quarterly*), [Toronto], 1948.

*The Mechanical Bride: Folklore of Industrial Man,* Vanguard, 1951, reprinted, Beacon Press, 1967.

*Counterblast,* privately printed, 1954, revised and enlarged edition, designed by Harley Parker, Harcourt, 1969.

(Editor and author of introduction) Alfred Lord Tennyson, *Selected Poetry,* Rinehart, 1956.

(Editor with Edmund Carpenter) *Explorations in Communication* (anthology), Beacon Press, 1960.

*The Gutenberg Galaxy: The Making of Typographic Man,* University of Toronto Press, 1962, New American Library, 1969.

*Understanding Media: The Extensions of Man* (originally written as a report to U.S. Office of Education, 1960), McGraw, 1964, reprinted, MIT Press, 1994.

(Compiler and author of notes and commentary with Richard J. Schoeck) *Voices of Literature* (anthology), two volumes, Holt (Toronto), 1964-65, Volume 1 published as *Voices of Literature: Sounds, Masks, Roles,* 1969.

(With Quentin Fiore) *The Medium Is the Massage: An Inventory of Effects* (advance excerpt published in *Publishers Weekly,* April 3, 1967), designed by Jerome P. Agel, Random House, 1967.

(With V. J. Papanek and others) *Verbi-Voco-Visual Explorations* (originally published as Number 8 of *Explorations*), Something Else Press, 1967.

(With Fiore) *War and Peace in the Global Village: An Inventory of Some of the Current Spastic Situations That Could Be Eliminated by More Feedforward* (excerpt entitled "Fashion: A Bore War?" published in *Saturday Evening Post,* July 27, 1968), McGraw, 1968.

(With Parker) *Through the Vanishing Point: Space in Poetry and Painting,* Harper, 1968.

*The Interior Landscape: The Literary Criticism of Marshall McLuhan, 1943-1962,* edited and compiled by Eugene McNamara, McGraw, 1969.

*Culture Is Our Business,* McGraw, 1970.

(With Wilfred Watson) *From Cliche to Archetype,* Viking, 1970.

(With Barrington Nevitt) *Executives—Die-Hards and Dropouts: Management Lore in the Global Village,* Harcourt, 1971.

(With Nevitt) *Take Today: The Executive as Dropout,* Harcourt, 1972.

(Author of introduction) Harold Adams Innis and Mary Quale, editors, *Empire and Communications,* University of Toronto Press, 1972.

(Author of foreword) Willy Blok Hanson, *The Pelvic Tilt: Master Your Body in Seven Days,* McClelland & Stewart, 1973.

(With Sorel Etrog) *Spiral,* Fitzhenry & Whiteside, 1976.

(With Robert Logan) *Libraries without Shelves,* Bowker, 1977.

(With son, Eric McLuhan, and Kathy Hutchon) *City as Classroom: Understanding Language and Media,* Book Society of Canada, 1977.

(With Pierre Babin) *Autre homme, autre chretien a l'age electronique,* Chalet, 1978.

(With E. McLuhan and Hutchon) *Media, Messages, and Language: The World as Your Classroom,* preface and introduction by David A. Sohn, National Textbook Co., 1980.

*Letters of Marshall McLuhan,* edited by Matie Molinaro, Corinne McLuhan, and William Toye, Oxford University Press, 1988.

(With E. McLuhan) *Laws of Media: The New Science,* University of Toronto Press, 1989.

*The Essential McLuhan,* edited by Eric McLuhan and Frank Zingrone, Basic Books, 1996.

Contributor of chapters to books, including *Mass Culture,* edited by Bernard Rosenberg and David Manning White, Free Press of Glencoe, 1957; *The Compleat "Neurotica," 1948-1951,* edited by G. Legman, Hacker Art Books, 1963; *The Electronic Revolution* (published as a special issue of *American Scholar,* spring, 1966), United Chapters of Phi Beta Kappa, 1966; *McLuhan—Hot and Cool: A Primer for the Understanding of and a Critical Symposium with a Rebuttal by McLuhan,* edited by Gerald Emanuel Stearn, Dial, 1967; *The Meaning of Commercial Television,* (University of Texas-Stanford University seminar held in Asilomar, CA, 1966), University of Texas Press, 1967; *Beyond Left and Right: Radical Thoughts for Our Times,* edited by Richard Kostelanetz, Morrow, 1968; *Innovations,* edited by Bernard Bergonzi, Macmillan, 1968; *Exploration of the Ways, Means, and Values of Museum Communication with the Viewing Public* (seminar held at the Museum of the City of New York, October 9-10, 1967), Museum of the City of New York, 1969; and *Mutacoes em educacao Segundo McLuhan,* Editora Vozes, 1971.

Author of a multimedia bulletin, *The Marshall McLuhan Dew-Line Newsletter,* published monthly by Human Development Corp., beginning 1968. General editor, with Ernest Sirluck and Schoeck, of "Patterns of Literary Criticism" series, seven volumes, University of Chicago Press and University of Toronto Press, 1965-69. Contributor of articles and essays to numerous periodicals, including *Times Literary Supplement, Vogue, American Scholar, Kenyon Review, Sewanee Review, Family Circle, Encounter,* and *Daedalus. Explorations,* co-editor with Carpenter, 1954-59, editor, beginning 1964; member of editorial board, *Media and Methods,* beginning 1967.

*ADAPTATIONS:* A happening entitled "McLuhan Megillah," based on *Understanding Media* and *The Gutenberg Galaxy* and combining dance, film, painting, poetry, sculpture, and other art forms, was produced at Al Hansen's Third Rail Time/Space Theatre in Greenwich Village in January of 1966. A McLuhan television special based on *The Medium Is the Massage* was produced on NBC-TV, March 19, 1967. In September of 1967, Columbia Records released a four-track LP based on *The Medium Is the Massage* and produced by Jerome P. Agel.

*SIDELIGHTS:* "The medium is the message," quipped Marshall McLuhan, and the world took notice. Symbolized by this aphorism, McLuhan's novel insights into the functions of mass media and their implications for the future of our technological culture earned him both international acclaim and vitriolic criticism. He was variously called a prophet, a promoter, a poet, a prankster, an intellectual madhatter, a guru of the boob tube, a communicator who could not communicate, and a genius on a level with Newton, Darwin, Freud, Pavlov, and Einstein. Considered the oracle of the electronic age by advertising, television, and business executives who often admitted not understanding much of what he said, McLuhan made pronouncements on a vast range of contemporary issues, including education, religion, science, the environment, politics, minority groups, war, violence, love, sex, clothing, jobs, music, computers, drugs, television, and automobiles; all these pronouncements, however, were based on his belief that human societies have always been shaped more by the nature of the media used to communicate than by the content of the communication. Although he expressed his ideas in an abstruse style that reflected a predilection for puns, in books that declared the book obsolete, his influence was, and is, unmistakable. "One must admit regardless of whether he agrees with McLuhanism," observes Richard Kostelanetz in *Master Minds,* that McLuhan was "among the great creative minds—'artists'—of our time."

Contrary to his public image, McLuhan was by training a man of letters. At the University of Manitoba, he first studied engineering because of an avowed "interest in structure and design," notes Kostelanetz, but later changed his major to English literature and philosophy. After earning his first M.A. in 1934 with a thesis on "George Meredith as a Poet and Dramatic Parodist," McLuhan pursued medieval and Renaissance literature abroad at Cambridge University, ultimately producing a doctoral thesis on the rhetoric of Elizabethan writer Thomas Nashe. His writing career began with a critical study of Shakespeare's "Henry IV," and his contributions to professional journals included essays on T. S. Eliot,

Gerard Manley Hopkins, John Dos Passos, and Alfred Lord Tennyson. Kostelanetz points out that even after McLuhan became known as a communications theorist, "academic circles regard[ed] him as 'one of the finest Tennyson critics.'"

A combination of circumstances, however, gradually led McLuhan to transcend his literary upbringing. The lectures of I. A. Richards and F. R. Leavis at Cambridge initiated an interest in popular culture that blossomed when McLuhan, a Canadian whose first two teaching jobs were in the United States, found himself "confronted with young Americans I was incapable of understanding," he said in *Newsweek.* "I felt an urgent need to study their popular culture in order to get through."

McLuhan's first published exploration of the effects of mass culture on those engulfed in it was *The Mechanical Bride: Folklore of Industrial Man.* The book deals with "the pop creations of advertising and other word-and-picture promotions as ingredients of a magic potion, 'composed of sex and technology,' that [is] populating America with creatures half woman, half machine," writes Harold Rosenberg in the *New Yorker.* Exposing the effects of advertising on the unconscious, the book describes the "mechanical bride" herself as that peculiar mixture of sex and technology exemplified in attitudes toward the automobile.

Kostelanetz believes that while the book was "sparsely reviewed [in 1951] and was quickly remaindered, *The Mechanical Bride* has come to seem in retrospect a radical venture in the study of American mass culture. Previous to McLuhan, most American critics of integrity were disdainfully horrified at the growing proliferation of mass culture—the slick magazines, the comic books, the Hollywood movies, radio, television. . . . McLuhan, in contrast, was probably the first North American critic to inspect carefully the forms the stuff in the mass media took and then wonder precisely how these forms influenced people; and while he was still more scornful than not, one of his more spectacular insights identified formal similarities, rather than differences, between mass culture and elite art."

Specifically, McLuhan noticed the abrupt apposition of images, sounds, rhythms, and facts in modern poems, symphony, dance, and newspapers. Discontinuity, he concluded in *The Mechanical Bride,* is a central characteristic of the modern sensibility: "[It] is in different ways a basic concept of both quantum and relativity physics. It is the way in which a Toynbee looks at civilization, or a Margaret Mead at human cultures. Notoriously, it is the visual technique of a Picasso, the literary technique of James Joyce."

Following *The Mechanical Bride* and his promotion to full professor at St. Michael's College of the University of Toronto, McLuhan expanded his study of the relationship between culture and communication. From 1953 to 1955 he directed a Ford Foundation seminar on the subject and, with anthropologist Edmund Carpenter, founded a periodical called *Explorations* to give seminar members an additional forum for their ideas. By the late 1950s, his reputation as a communications specialist extended into the United States, earning him an appointment as director of a media project for the U.S. Office of Education and the National Association of Educational Broadcasters. The University of Toronto acknowledged his growing importance by naming him the first director of its Center for Culture and Technology, founded in 1963 to study the psychic and social consequences of technology and the media.

McLuhan's work during this period culminated in what many regard as his two major books, *The Gutenberg Galaxy: The Making of Typographic Man*—which in 1963 won Canada's highest literary honor, the Governor General's Award—and *Understanding Media: The Extensions of Man,* which eventually brought him worldwide renown. Drawing on his own impressive erudition, the analytical techniques of modern art criticism, and the theories of, among others, political economist Harold Adams Innis, McLuhan presented in these books his view of the history of mass media as central to the history of civilization in general. Borrowing Buckminster Fuller's metaphor that a tool of man's is essentially an extension of man, McLuhan claimed that the media not only represent extensions of the human senses but that they, by their very nature as determinants of knowledge, dictate "the character of perception and through perception the structure of mind," summarizes James P. Carey in *McLuhan: Pro and Con.* "The medium"—more than the content—"is the message" because it shapes human perception, human knowledge, human society.

Thus, according to McLuhan in *The Gutenberg Galaxy,* the rise of the printing press revolutionized Western civilization. By placing an overemphasis on the eye, rather than the ear of oral cultures, print reshaped the sensibility of Western man. Human beings came to see life as they saw print—as linear, often with causal relationships. Print accounted for such phenomena as linear development in music, serial thinking in mathematics, the liberal tradition, nationalism, individualism, and Protestantism (the printed book encouraged thinking in isolation; hence, individual revelation). By giving man the power to separate thought from feeling, it enabled Western man to specialize and to mechanize, but it also led to alienation from the other senses and, thus, from other men and from nature itself.

The theme of alienation was "central to the argument of Innis," notes Carey, "[but McLuhan went] beyond this critique and argue[d] that the reunification of man, the end of his alienation, the restoration of the 'whole' man will result from autonomous developments in communications technology." The electronic media of the modern era—telegraph, radio, television, movies, telephones, computers—according to McLuhan in *Understanding Media,* are reshaping civilization by "moving us out of the age of the visual into the age of the aural and tactile." Because electronic media create a mosaic of information reaching us simultaneously through several senses, our sensibility is being radically transformed as evidenced, for example, by the revolution in modern art. This redistribution and heightening of sensory awareness signifies a return to our tribal roots, where communication was multisensory and immediate. United by electronic media, the world is rapidly becoming a "global village" in which the ends of the earth are within one's reach.

From this view of history, branded "informational technological determinism" by Kostelanetz, McLuhan extrapolated numerous ideas in *The Gutenberg Galaxy, Understanding Media,* and subsequent books about the effects of education (the book is passe; one needs to be "literate" in many media), the concept of childhood, the landscape of social organization, the problem of personal privacy, war and propaganda, moral relativism, "hot" and "cool" media (a "cool" medium requires more sensory and mental participation than a "hot" one), the generation gap, television (those who worry about the programs on TV—a "cool" medium—are missing its true significance), modern art, and other topics. "McLuhan's performance was breathtaking," writes John Leonard in the *New York Times.* "He ranged from physics to Cezanne, from Africa to advertising, from the Moebius strip to Milman Parry's treatise on the oral character of Yugoslav epic poetry. Euclidean space, chronological narrative, artistic perspective, Newtonian mechanics, and capitalist economics were all called into question. They were lies of the dislocating eye."

McLuhan's ideas, however, were not as neatly nor as modestly presented as this brief summary might suggest, for he considered his books "probes"—invitations to explore—rather than carefully articulated arguments. McLuhan, notes Kostelanetz, believed "more in probing and exaggerating—'making discoveries'—than in offering final definitions, as well as raising . . . critical discourse to a higher level of insight and subtlety. For this reason, he [would] in public conversation rarely defend any of his statements as absolute truths, although he [would] explain how he developed them. 'I don't agree or disagree with anything I say myself' [was] his characteristic rationale."

To further dramatize his "probes," McLuhan eschewed the traditional, print-age, linear, expository structure of introduction, development, elaboration, and conclusion, attempting instead "to imitate in his writing the form of the TV image, which he describe[d] as 'mosaic,'" says Rosenberg. A typical McLuhan book or paragraph, according to Kostelanetz, "tends to make a series of analytic statements, none of which become an explicitly encompassing thesis, though all of them approach the same body of phenomena from different angles or examples. These become a succession of exegetical glosses on a mysterious scriptural text, which is how McLuhan analogously regard[ed] the new electronic world. . . . This means that one should not necessarily read his books from start to finish—the archaic habit of print-man. True, the preface and first chapter of *The Mechanical Bride* . . . really do *introduce* the themes and methods of the book; but beyond that, the chapters can be read in any order. The real introduction to *The Gutenberg Galaxy* is the final chapter, called 'The Galaxy Reconfigured;' even McLuhan advise[d] readers to start there; and the book itself is all but a galaxy of extensive printed quotations."

In addition to these stylistic features, McLuhan had a "predilection for positively blood-curdling puns," says a *New Republic* contributor, as well as a penchant for aphorisms. Deliberately punning on his famous dictum "The medium is the message," for example, McLuhan titled his 1967 photo-montage *The Medium Is the Massage: An Inventory of Effects* to convey his belief that instead of neutrally presenting content, "all media work us over completely.

They are so pervasive in their personal, political, esthetic, psychological, moral, ethical, and social consequences that they leave no part of us untouched, unaffected, unaltered. The medium is the massage." He said the 1967 book was designed to clarify the ideas in *Understanding Media* by depicting "a collide-oscope of interfaced situations."

McLuhan's habitual, mosaic mixture of fact and theory, pun and picture, came to be characterized as "McLuhanese," which George P. Elliott describes in *McLuhan—Hot and Cool* as "deliberately antilogical: circular, repetitious, unqualified, gnomic, outrageous." The late Dwight Macdonald refers to "McLuhanese" in *Book Week* as "impure nonsense, nonsense adulterated by sense," and in another *Book Week* article Arthur M. Schlesinger, Jr. calls it "a chaotic combination of bland assertion, astute guesswork, fake analogy, dazzling insight, hopeless nonsense, shockmanship, showmanship, wisecracks, and oracular mystification, all mingling cockily and indiscriminately in an endless and random monologue . . . , [which] contains a deeply serious argument."

The novelty of McLuhan's ideas coupled with their unconventional presentation gave rise by the late 1960s "to an ideology . . . and a mass movement producing seminars, clubs, art exhibits, and conferences in his name," reports James P. Carey. One of the most frequently quoted intellectuals of his time, McLuhan became, in Carey's words, "a prophet, a phenomenon, a happening, a social movement." Advertising and television executives hailed him as the oracle of the electronic age, though as Alden Whitman states in the *New York Times,* "he did not think highly of the advertising business. 'The hullabaloo Madison Avenue creates couldn't condition a mouse,' he said." In 1965, avant-garde composer John Cage visited him in Toronto to discuss his insights. Publisher William Jovanovich later invited him to collaborate on a study of the future of the book. McLuhanisms soon appeared everywhere, including the popular American television show "Rowan and Martin's Laugh-In." And in 1977, Woody Allen persuaded him to make a cameo appearance in the Oscar-winning film *Annie Hall* to defend his theories.

Despite winning a great deal of admiration, McLuhan was also feared and rejected, "especially . . . by journalists and television personalities who saw themselves threatened by his analyses because they did not understand either him or his equally important sources," says E. C. Wheeldon in the London *Times.* He was often denounced as a fakir, a charlatan, and—because he considered TV the most influential medium of the electronic age—a guru of the boob tube. Critics charged him with oversimplification, faulty reasoning, inconsistency, confusion of myth and reality, as well as undermining the entire humanist tradition, and these charges continue to be leveled.

John Simon, writing in *McLuhan: Pro and Con,* considers McLuhan's "worst failing" to be "the wholesale reinterpretation of texts to prove his preconceived argument," and others scoff at McLuhan's attempt to explain virtually every social and cultural phenomenon in terms of the media. "For McLuhan," writes Harold Rosenberg, "beliefs, moral qualities, social action, even material progress play a secondary role (if that) in determining the human condition. The drama of history is a crude pageant whose inner meaning is man's metamorphosis through the media. As a philosophy of cultural development, *Understanding Media* is on a par with theories that trace the invention of the submarine to conflicts in the libido."

In the *New York Review of Books,* D. W. Harding praises McLuhan's "probes" as maneuvers that try "to break free from self-inhibition and sterile dispute," yet he believes they are ultimately self-defeating: "How in the face of independent common sense could McLuhan get away with, for example, his claim that primitive cultures are oral and auditory and ours is visual? Questionable even in the limited context of the psychiatrist's article he bases it on, the notion as a generalization is wildly implausible. The American Indians' skill in tracking, the bedouins' astonishing capacity for reading camel spoor, these are ordinary instances of the familiar fact that in many habitats the survival of a primitive people depended on constant visual alertness, acute discrimination, and highly trained inference from visual data. . . . One is left with the truism that we read a lot and preliterates don't. The implications of that fact are well worth exploring, but we get no help from stories of alteration in some physiologically and psychologically undefined 'sensory ratio.'"

"McLuhan is a monomaniac who happens to be hooked on something extremely important," concludes Tom Nairn in the *New Statesman,* "but the colossal evasiveness, the slipshod reasoning, and weak-kneed glibness accompanying the mania make him dangerous going. . . . Capable of the most brilliant and stimulating insight into relationships other historians and social theorists have ignored, he systematically fails to develop this insight critically. Consequently, his view of the connection between media and society is an unbelievable shambles: his dream-logic turns necessary conditions into sufficient conditions, half-truths into sure things, the possible into a *fait accompli.*"

The overriding source of irritation for many readers is McLuhan's intricate style. John Fowles, for example, finds *From Cliche to Archetype* "as elegant and as lucid as a barrel of tar." The book, according to Fowles in *Saturday Review,* "makes one wonder whether Marshall McLuhan's celebrated doubts over the print medium don't largely stem from a personal incapacity to handle it. Perhaps the graceless style, the barbarously obscuring jargon, the incoherent hopping from one unfinished argument into the middle of the next are all meant to be subtly humorous. But the general effect is about as subtle and humorous as a Nazi storm trooper hectoring the latest trainload of Jews. It is all barked fiat: off with your head if you dare to disagree."

David Myers suggests in *Book World* that, ultimately, it is "as a poet and only as a poet that McLuhan can be read without exasperation." Others seem to agree. Kenneth Burke maintains in the *New Republic* that McLuhan "transcends the distinction . . . between 'prove' and 'probe,' both from the Latin *probare.* 'Proof' requires a considerable sense of continuity; 'probing' can be done at random, with hit-and-run slogans or titles taking the place of sustained exposition. And in the medium of books, McLuhan with his 'probing' has 'perfected' a manner in which the non sequitur never had it so good." "Even at his worst," insists Tom Wolfe in *Book World,* "McLuhan inspires you to try to see and understand in a new way, and in the long run this may prove to be his great contribution."

The aim of McLuhan's "poetry," however, remains a matter of dispute. James P. Carey, who considers McLuhan "a poet of technology," claims his work "represents a secular prayer to technology, a magical incantation of the gods, designed to quell one's fears that, after all, the machines may be taking over. . . . McLuhan himself is a medium and that is his message." But McLuhan maintained that rather than predicting the future of our technological age, he was merely extrapolating current processes to their logical conclusions. "I don't approve of the global village," he once told a *Playboy* interviewer, "I say we live in it." Writing in *McLuhan: Pro and Con,* John Culkin supports the detachment of McLuhan's viewpoint: "Too many people are eager to write off Marshall McLuhan or to reduce him to the nearest and handiest platitude which explains him to them. He deserves better. . . . He didn't invent electricity or put kids in front of TV sets; he . . . merely [tried] to describe what's happening out there so that it can be dealt with intelligently. When someone warns you of an oncoming truck, it's frightfully impolite to accuse him of driving the thing."

Richard Kostelanetz, moreover, believes that McLuhan was "trenchantly a humanist." He quotes McLuhan as saying, "By knowing how technology shapes our environment, we can transcend its absolutely determining power. . . . My entire concern is to overcome the determination that results from people trying to ignore what is going on. Far from regarding technological change as inevitable, I insist that if we understand its components we can turn it off any time we choose. Short of turning it off, there are lots of moderate controls conceivable."

Whether McLuhan was a poet of technology, a detached observer, or a trenchant humanist, "what remain paramount are his global standpoint and his zest for the new," concludes Harold Rosenberg. "As an artist working in a mixed medium of direct experience and historical analogy, he [gave] a needed twist to the great debate on what is happening to man in this age of technological speedup. [Whereas] other observers . . . [repeated] criticisms of industrial society that were formulated a century ago, . . . McLuhan, for all his abstractness, . . . found positive, humanistic meaning and the color of life in supermarkets, stratospheric flight, the lights blinking on broadcasting towers. In respect to the maladies of de-individuation, he . . . dared to seek the cure in the disease, and his vision of going forward into primitive wholeness is a good enough reply to those who would go back to it."

Even after McLuhan's death in 1980, critical opinion on his work remained intense. In 1988, a collection of his letters, *Letters of Marshall McLuhan,* were published. Containing selections from 1931 until the author's death, the collection serves as a window to McLuhan's life and work. Writing in the *London Review of Books,* Frank Kermode notes: "the letters seem to show that McLuhan felt an increasing need to convince not just enthusiasts but everybody, and a natural failure in this respect gave him an increasing sense of isolation. He repeatedly insists that he is misunderstood because he is very deliberately not thinking in the old linear rationalistic way." The following year saw the publication of *Laws of Media: The New Science,* consisting of notes and writings collected and arranged by McLuhan's son, Eric, who was working with his father on the project at the time of McLuhan's death and who is listed as co-author. Ostensibly a sequal of sorts to McLuhan's earlier *Understanding Media,* the book offers four "laws," presented as questions, with which any medium can be analyzed. As quoted by John Sturrock in the *New York Times Book Review,* the laws are: "What does [the medium] enhance or intensify? What does it render obsolete or displace? What does it retrieve that was previously obsolesced (sic)? What does it produce or become when pressed to an extreme?" Several reviewers criticized the volume as inaccessible and unconvincing. As Sturrock notes, "It would be charitable to overlook this late, rather desperate effort at restating his case." And *Quill & Quire* reviewer Paul Roberts comments that the book is "at times dense to the point of incomprehensibility, at times banal." Nevertheless, Roberts commends McLuhan's life and work and his "agile, eclectic mind." "He wasn't telling us *what* to think so much as that we *should* think."

*BIOGRAPHICAL/CRITICAL SOURCES:*

*BOOKS*

*Contemporary Literary Criticism,* Volume 37, Gale, 1986; Volume 83, 1994.

Crosby, Harry H. and George R. Bond, compilers, *The McLuhan Explosion* (casebook on McLuhan and *Understanding Media*), American Book Co., 1968.

Duffy, Dennis, *Marshall McLuhan,* McClelland & Stewart, 1969.

Fekete, John, *The Critical Twilight: Explorations in the Ideology of Anglo-American Literary Theory from Eliot to McLuhan,* Routledge & Kegan Paul, 1978.

Finkelstein, Sidney Walter, *Sense and Nonsense of McLuhan,* International Publishers, 1968.

Fiore, Quentin and Marshall McLuhan, *The Medium Is the Massage: An Inventory of Effects,* Bantam, 1967.

Gross, Theodore L., *Representative Men,* Free Press, 1970.

Kostelanetz, Richard, *Master Minds: Portraits of Contemporary American Artists and Intellectuals,* Macmillan, 1969.

McLuhan, *The Mechanical Bride: Folklore of Industrial Man,* Vanguard, 1951.

McLuhan, *The Gutenberg Galaxy: The Making of Typographic Man,* University of Toronto Press, 1962.

McLuhan, *Understanding Media: The Extensions of Man,* McGraw, 1964.

Miller, Jonathan, *Marshall McLuhan,* Viking, 1971.

Rosenthal, Raymond, editor, *McLuhan: Pro and Con,* Funk, 1968.

Stearn, Gerald Emanuel, editor, *McLuhan—Hot and Cool: A Primer for the Understanding of and a Critical Symposium with a Rebuttal by McLuhan,* Dial, 1967.

Theall, Donald F., *The Medium Is the Rear View Mirror: Understanding McLuhan,* McGill-Queens University Press, 1971.

*PERIODICALS*

*American Dialog,* autumn, 1967.

*Antioch Review,* spring, 1967.

*Books,* September, 1965, January, 1967.

*Books and Bookmen,* March, 1971.

*Book Week,* June 7, 1964; March 19, 1967.

*Book World,* October 29, 1967; September 15, 1968; July 27, 1969; November 30, 1969; December 6, 1970.

*Canadian Forum,* February, 1969.

*Chicago Tribune,* January 1, 1981.

*Christian Science Monitor,* May 17, 1972.

*Commentary,* January, 1965.

*Commonweal,* January 20, 1967; June 23, 1967.

*Critic,* August, 1967.

*Esquire,* August, 1966.

*Globe and Mail* (Toronto), December 24, 1988.

*Harper's,* November, 1965; June, 1967.

*Kenyon Review,* March, 1967.

*L'Express,* February 14-20, 1972.

*Life,* February 25, 1966.

*Listener,* September 28, 1967; October 19, 1967.

*London Review of Books,* March 17, 1988.

*Los Angeles Times Book Review,* June 4, 1989.

*Maclean's Magazine,* January 7, 1980; March 17, 1980.

*Nation,* October 5, 1964; May 15, 1967; December 4, 1967; December 8, 1969.

*National Review,* November 19, 1968.

*New Republic,* February 7, 1970; June 10, 1972.

*New Statesman,* December 11, 1964; September 22, 1967.

*Newsweek,* February 28, 1966; March 6, 1967; September 23, 1968; January 12, 1981.

*New Yorker,* February 27, 1965.

*New York Review of Books,* August 20, 1964; November 23, 1967; January 2, 1969.
*New York Times,* October 21, 1951; February 27, 1967; September 7, 1967; January 1, 1981.
*New York Times Book Review,* May 1, 1966; March 26, 1967; September 8, 1968; December 21, 1969; July 12, 1970; December 13, 1970; February 26, 1989.
*New York Times Magazine,* January 29, 1967.
*Observer,* March 6, 1988.
*Partisan Review,* summer, 1968.
*Playboy,* March, 1969.
*Publishers Weekly,* January 23, 1981.
*Quill & Quire,* October, 1988.
*Saturday Night,* February, 1967; September, 1994, p. 51.
*Saturday Review,* November 26, 1966; March 11, 1967; May 9, 1970; November 21, 1970.
*Sewanee Review,* spring, 1969.
*Time,* July 3, 1964; March 3, 1967; January 12, 1981.
*Times* (London), January 2, 1981.
*Times Literary Supplement,* August 6, 1964; September 28, 1967; May 6, 1988; August 25, 1989.
*Twentieth-Century Literature,* July, 1970.
*Village Voice,* May 12, 1966; December 26, 1970.
*Vogue,* July, 1966.
*Western Humanities Review,* autumn, 1967.

*OBITUARIES:*

*PERIODICALS*

*AB Bookman's Weekly,* January 19, 1981.
*Chicago Tribune,* January 1, 1981.
*Newsweek,* January 12, 1981.
*New York Times,* January 1, 1981.
*Publishers Weekly,* January 23, 1981.
*Time,* January 12, 1981.
*Times* (London), January 2, 1981.*

* * *

**McSHANE, Mark 1930-**
**(Marc Lovell)**

*PERSONAL:* Born November 28, 1930, in Sydney, Australia; son of Mark (a merchant) and Albereda (Fowler) McShane; married Pamela Rosemarie Armstrong, October 5, 1963; children: Rebecca, Marcus Aurelius, Damon, Todd (deceased). *Education:* Attended Technical College, Blackpool, Lancashire, England. *Politics:* Liberal. *Religion:* Humanist.

*ADDRESSES:* *Home*—Can Tumi, La Cabaneta, Mallorca, Spain. *Agent*—Collier Associates, 2000 Flat Run Rd., Seaman, OH 45679.

*CAREER:* Professional writer.

*AWARDS, HONORS:* *Seance* was nominated for the Mystery Writers of America Edgar Allan Poe Award ("Edgar") in 1962 and for the Grand Prize of French Police Literature in 1963.

*WRITINGS:*

*The Straight and the Crooked,* John Long (London), 1960.
*Seance on a Wet Afternoon,* Cassell (London), 1961, published as *Seance,* Doubleday (New York City), 1962.
*The Passing of Evil,* Cassell, 1961.
*Untimely Ripped,* Cassell, 1962, Doubleday, 1963.
*The Girl Nobody Knows,* Doubleday, 1965.
*Night's Evil,* Doubleday, 1966.
*The Crimson Madness of Little Doom,* Doubleday, 1966.
*The Way to Nowhere,* R. Hale (London), 1967.
*Ill Met by a Fish Shop on George Street,* Doubleday, 1968.
*The Singular Case of the Multiple Dead,* Putnam (New York City), 1969.
*The Man Who Left Well Enough,* McCall (New York City), 1970.
*Seance for Two,* Doubleday, 1972.
*The Othello Complex,* Gallimard (Paris), 1974.
*The Headless Snowman,* Gallimard, 1974.
*Lashed but Not Leashed,* Doubleday, 1976.
*Lifetime,* Manor (New York City), 1977.
*The Hostage Game,* Zebra (New York City), 1979.
*The Halcyon Way,* Manor, 1979.
*Just a Face in the Dark,* Doubleday, 1987.
*Once Upon a Fairy Tale,* Doubleday, 1990.
*Mourning Becomes the Hangman,* Doubleday, 1991.

*UNDER PSEUDONYM MARC LOVELL*

*The Ghost of Megan,* Doubleday, 1968, published as *Memory of Megan,* Ace (New York City), 1970.
*The Imitation Thieves,* Doubleday, 1971.
*A Presence in the House,* Doubleday, 1972.
*An Enquiry into the Existence of Vampires,* Doubleday, 1974, published as *Vampires in the Shadows,* R. Hale, 1976.

*Dreamers in a Haunted House,* Doubleday, 1975.
*The Blind Hypnotist,* Doubleday, 1976.
*The Second Vanetti Affair,* Doubleday, 1977.
*The Guardian Spectre,* Manor, 1977.
*Fog Sinister,* Manor, 1977.
*A Voice from the Living,* Doubleday, 1978.
*And They Say You Can't Buy Happiness,* R. Hale, 1979.
*Hand Over Mind,* Doubleday, 1979.
*Shadows and Dark Places,* R. Hale, 1980.
*The Spy Game,* Doubleday, 1980.
*The Spy with His Head in the Clouds,* Doubleday, 1982.
*The Last Seance,* R. Hale, 1982.
*Spy on the Run,* Doubleday, 1982.
*Apple Spy in the Sky,* Doubleday, 1983.
*Apple to the Core,* Doubleday, 1983.
*Looking for Kingford,* Rowohlt (Berlin), 1983.
*How Green Was My Apple,* Doubleday, 1984.
*The Only Good Apple in a Barrel of Spies,* Doubleday, 1984.
*The Spy Who Got His Feet Wet,* Doubleday, 1985.
*The Spy Who Barked in the Night,* Doubleday, 1986.
*Good Spies Don't Grow on Trees,* Doubleday, 1986.
*That Great Big Trenchcoat in the Sky,* Doubleday, 1987.
*The Spy Who Fell Off the Back of a Bus,* Doubleday, 1988.
*Ethel and the Naked Spy,* Doubleday, 1989.
*Comfort Me with Spies,* Doubleday, 1990.

All the McShane novels have been published in France and Germany. Collections of McShane's manuscripts are housed at the Mugar Memorial Library, Boston University, at the University of Wyoming, Laramie, and at Sydney University, Sydney, Australia.

*ADAPTATIONS: Seance on a Wet Afternoon* was filmed in 1964; *The Passing of Evil* was filmed by Mel Chaitlin under the title *The Grasshopper,* National General, 1970; *Apple Spy in the Sky* was filmed under the title *Trouble with Spies,* 1985.

*SIDELIGHTS:* Mark McShane writes what Steven R. Carter in the *St. James Guide to Crime and Mystery Writers* calls "odd crime novels." "McShane's penchant for the offbeat," Carter explains, "has enabled him to invent plots that are fascinating because the oddity of his characters makes their behaviour and its outcome nearly unpredictable. It has also led him to explore seldom observed corners of the mind and hence discover new angels of vision (it should be noted that he likes punning). In addition, it has inspired him to enrich the mystery genre with both mordant and extravagant humor."

In *Seance* (published in England as *Seance on a Wet Afternoon*), McShane tells the story of a woman trying to earn a reputation as a medium. She schemes a kidnapping with her husband, and then predicts the event to make it seem as if she can see into the future. Esther Howard in the *Spectator* calls the book "a proper horror story, rare in these days." Anthony Boucher praises *Seance* in the *New York Times Book Review:* "The tale is strong, terse, acutely plotted, and it excels most fantasy or science fiction as a believable study in parapsychology." James Sandoe of the *New York Herald Tribune Book Review* finds the novel written "with a sharp-edged thrust of phrase." *Seance* was nominated for the Edgar Allan Poe Award in 1962 and for the Grand Prize of French Police Literature in 1963.

Under the pseudonym Mark Lovell, McShane has written several books about Appleton Porter—nicknamed Apple—an abnormally tall spy whose adventures provide their author with ample opportunity for punning titles. "The series," writes Carter, "plays Apple's idealism, decency (leavened a bit by horniness), and highly romanticized view of spying against the cynicism, calculation, and coldhearted "realism" of his boss, Angus Watkin. Apple is always ruthlessly manipulated by Watkin throughout, though his decency always manages a small triumph in the end."

McShane told *CA* he began writing "to prove to myself that even without previous experience I could produce something better than most of the garbage on the market. Result was accepted, path was clear. . . . Would like to lift the crime novel to a more respected level, above mere forgettable entertainment. Contiguous interests are in criminal psychology and psychic research. No longer care for travel after having lived in, up to the age of thirty, working backwards, Canada, Australia, England, the United States (four years), Canada, France, the United Kingdom, South Africa, British West Indies, the Argentine, New Zealand, Australia. Now firmly established in Majorca."

*BIOGRAPHICAL/CRITICAL SOURCES:*

*BOOKS*

*St. James Guide to Crime and Mystery Writers,* fourth edition, St. James Press (Detroit), 1996.

*PERIODICALS*

*Best Sellers,* February 1, 1966, p. 25; March 1, 1968, p. 27.
*Guardian,* November 24, 1961, p. 14.
*Kirkus,* May 1, 1962, p. 30.
*Library Journal,* March 1, 1966, p. 91; February 1, 1968, p. 93.
*New York Herald Tribune Book Review,* July 15, 1962, p. 11.
*New York Times Book Review,* July 15, 1962, p. 20; January 16, 1966, p. 35; February 25, 1968, p. 34.
*Saturday Review,* August 25, 1962, p. 45; May 28, 1966, p. 49; May 25, 1968, p. 51.
*Spectator,* November 10, 1961, p. 676.

* * *

**MENNINGER, Karl A(ugustus) 1893-1990**

*PERSONAL:* Born July 22, 1893, in Topeka, KS; died of cancer, July 18, 1990, in Topeka, KS; son of Charles Frederick (a physician) and Flora Vesta (a teacher; maiden name, Knisely) Menninger; married Grace Gaines, September 9, 1916 (divorced, 1941); married Jeanetta Lyle (editor of *Bulletin of the Menninger Clinic*), September 8, 1941; children: (first marriage) Julia (Mrs. A. H. Gottesman), Martha (Mrs. William Nichols), Robert Gaines; (second marriage) Rosemary Jeanetta Karla. *Education:* Attended Washburn College (now Washburn University of Topeka), 1910-12, and Indiana University, summer, 1910; University of Wisconsin, Madison, A.B., 1914, B.S., 1915; Harvard Medical School, M.D. (cum laude), 1917. *Religion:* Presbyterian.

*CAREER:* The Menninger Foundation (formerly the Menninger Clinic), Topeka, KS, partner with father, Charles Frederick Menninger, 1919-25, chief of staff, 1925-46, director of education, 1946-70, chair of board of trustees, 1954-70, member of education committee, 1967-70. Kansas City General Hospital, Kansas City, MO, intern, 1917-18; Harvard Medical School, Cambridge, MA, instructor in neuropathology, 1918-20; Boston Psychopathic Hospital, Boston, assistant physician, 1918-20; Tufts Medical School, Medford, MA, assistant in neurology, 1919-20; Christ's Hospital and St. Francis Hospital, Topeka, staff member, 1919-90; Winter Veterans Administration Hospital, Topeka, manager, 1945-48, chair of dean's committee and senior consultant, 1948-55; Menninger School of Psychiatry, Topeka, founder, 1946, dean, 1946-70; University of Kansas City (now University of Missouri—Kansas City) Medical School, clinical professor of psychiatry, 1946-62; Topeka Institute of Psychoanalysis, Topeka, 1960-90; University of Kansas, Lawrence, professor of medicine, 1970-76, professor at large, 1976-90. Visiting professor, University of Cincinnati Medical School. Trustee, Albert Deutsch Memorial Foundation, 1961, and Aspen Institute for Humanistic Studies, 1961-64. Advisor to the Surgeon General, U.S. Army, 1945; consultant, Veteran Administration Hospital, Topeka, 1948-90; consultant in psychiatry to State of Illinois Department of Welfare, and Governor of Illinois, 1953-54; consultant, Office of Vocational Rehabilitation, Department of Health, Education, and Welfare, 1953-55; consultant, Bureau of Prisons, Department of Justice, 1956-90; consultant, Forbes Air Force Base Hospital and Stone-Brandel Center, 1958-90; member of advisory committee, International Survey of Correctional Research and Practice, California, 1960-90; consultant to various other institutes and associations.

*MEMBER:* International Association for Suicide Prevention, World Society of Ekistics, Masons, Central Neuropsychiatric Association (co-founder; secretary, 1922-32; president, 1932-33), Central Psychiatric Hospital Association, American Orthopsychiatric Association (secretary, 1926-27; president, 1927-28), American Psychiatric Association (life fellow; counselor, 1928-29, 1941-43), American Psychological Association, American Psychoanalytic Association (life member; president, 1941-43), American Academy of Psychiatry and Law, American Society of Criminology, American Justice Institute (member of advisory committee), American Civil Liberties Union (vice-chair of national committee), American Medical Association (fellow), American College of Physicians (life fellow), American College of Psychiatrists, American Medical Writers Association (life member; 2nd vice president, 1957-58; 1st vice president, 1958-59), American Association for the Advancement of Science, American Association for Child Psychoanalysis, National Commission for the Prevention of Child Abuse (co-chair of honorary board), American Association of Suicidology (honorary member), Medical Association for the Research of Nervous and Mental Diseases, Royal College of Psychiatrists (honorary fellow), Association of Clinical Pastoral Education, Association for Psychiatry Treatment Offenders, Sigmund Freud Archives, American Humanities Foundation, National Association for the Advancement of Colored Persons, National Congress of the American Indian, American Association of Botanical Gardens and Arboreta, American Horticultural Council, Friends of the Earth, Sierra Club, Save the Tallgrass Prairie Inc. (chair of national honorary board), Kansas Medical Society, Illinois Academy of Criminology, Illinois Committee on Family Law, Aspen Institute for Humanistic Studies (former trustee; currently honorary trustee), Chicago Psychoanalytic Association, American Indian Center (Chicago grand council), Chicago Orchestral Association (governor), Sigmund Freud Society (Vienna), University Presbyterian Club (Chicago), Country Lodge Presbyterian Club (Topeka, KS).

*AWARDS, HONORS:* Isaac Ray Award, 1962, First Distinguished Service Award, 1965, and First Founders Award, 1977, all from American Psychiatric Association; T. W. Salmon award, New York Academy of Medicine, 1967; Good Samaritan award, Eagles Lodge, 1968, 1969; Annual Service award, John Howard Association, 1969; Good Shepherd award, The Lambs (Chicago), 1969; American Academy of Psychiatry and Law award, 1974; Roscoe Pound award, National Council of Crime and Delinquency, 1975; Kansas Department of Corrections special award, 1976; Sheen award, American Medical Association, 1978; Presidential Medal of Freedom, 1981; D.Sc., Washburn University, 1949, University of Wisconsin, 1965, Oklahoma City University, 1966; L.H.D., Park College, 1955, St. Benedict College, 1963, Loyola University, 1972, DePaul University, 1974; LL.D., Jefferson Medical College of Philadelphia, 1956, Parsons College, 1960, Kansas State University, 1962, Baker University, 1965, Pepperdine University, 1974, John Jay College of Criminal Justice, 1978; numerous other awards.

*WRITINGS:*

*The Human Mind,* Knopf, 1930, 2nd edition, 1945.

*Man against Himself,* Harcourt, 1938.

(With wife, Jeanetta Menninger) *Love against Hate,* Harcourt, 1942.

(With G. Devereux) *A Guide to Psychiatric Books,* Grune & Stratton, 1950, 3rd revised edition, 1972.

*A Manual for Psychiatric Case Study,* Grune & Stratton, 1952, revised edition, 1962.

*Theory of Psychoanalytic Technique,* Basic Books, 1958, revised edition with Philip Holzman, Aronson, 1995.

*A Psychiatrists World* (selected papers), Viking, 1959.

*The Vital Balance: The Life Process in Mental Health and Illness,* Viking, 1963.

*The Crime of Punishment,* Viking, 1968.

*Sparks,* edited by Lucy Freeman, Crowell, 1973.

*A Celebration Issue Honoring Karl Menninger on His 80th Birthday: A Selection of His Previously Published Papers,* Menninger Foundation, 1973.

*Whatever Became of Sin?,* Hawthorn, 1973.

*The Human Mind Revisited,* International University Press, 1978.

(With Sarah R. Haavik) *Sexuality, Law, and the Developmentally Disabled Person: Legal and Clinical Aspects of Marriage, Parenthood, and Sterilization,* Paul Brookes, 1981.

*The Selected Correspondence of Karl A. Menninger, 1919-1945,* edited by Howard J. Faulkner and Virginia D. Pruitt, Yale University Press, 1989.

*The Selected Correspondence of Karl A. Menninger, 1946-1965,* edited by H. Faulkner and V. Pruitt, University of Missouri Press, 1995.

Also author, with others, of *Why Men Fail,* 1918, *The Healthy-Minded Child,* 1930, and *America Now,* 1938. Editor-in-chief, *Bulletin of the Menninger Clinic,* 1936-90; member of editorial board, *Archives of Criminal Psychodynamics, Psychoanalytic Quarterly, Excerpta Criminologica,* and *Academic Achievement.*

*SIDELIGHTS:* Psychiatrist Karl A. Menninger was internationally known for his treatment of the mentally ill. In addition to the practice of psychiatry, his work also extended to such related social issues as prison reform, child abuse, birth control, the plight of Native Americans, and the degradation of the environment. For his work on behalf of the betterment of society, Menninger was awarded the Presidential Medal of Freedom in 1981.

With his father Charles and brother William, Menninger founded the famous Menninger Clinic in 1919. The clinic, located in Topeka, Kansas, was the first psychoanalytic hospital established in the United States. A refuge for some of the nation's more well-to-do psychologically impaired, the clinic's mission was to replace the traditional confinement of the mentally ill with a more humane environment in which staff would engage in the psychoanalysis of patients, involving families in treatment and requiring the mentally impaired to perform everyday tasks that would help them maintain their connection to society-at-large. In 1941 the clinic became the

Menninger Foundation, today an internationally known center of psychiatric research and education. The importance of the clinic was noted in a citation given by the Albert Lasker Group Award in 1955: "The Menninger Foundation and Clinic, headed by Drs. Karl and William Menninger, has provided a sustained and highly productive attack against mental disease for many years. Inspired by their father, Dr. Charles Frederick Menninger, these brothers have developed an outstanding institution which has served as an example for other mental disease hospitals. . . . The influence of the Menninger Foundation and Clinic in increasing professional and public interest in the care of the mentally ill cannot be measured, but it is indelibly recorded as a great service to mankind."

During his sixty-plus years of affiliation with the clinic that bears his name, the charismatic Menninger became known as one of the staunchest advocates of psychoanalysis in the United States—Freud's daughter, Anna, joined the Menninger brothers to work with disturbed young people as early as 1915. He also wrote several books intended to provide both students of psychiatry and the general public with a fuller understanding of the nature of the human mind. His 1930 work, *The Human Mind,* was praised by critics as a valuable resource for social workers, prison administrators, clergymen, and lawyers, all of who would require an understanding of various psychological conditions during the course of dealing with the public. Referring to personality abnormalities as "jams in the mental machinery," Menninger provided well-documented examinations of numerous cases that both illustrated such mental abnormalities and provided suggestions for rehabilitation or other treatment. "Dr. Menninger has discarded the colossal humbug of the normal mind and has adopted the case method of presenting his subject," writes reviewer Smith Ely Jelliffe in *Nation.* "Every human mind is different and he tells us how and why. . . . Here is the simplest of skeletons filled in with a richness of detail that is informing and fascinating." In 1938's *Man against Himself* Menninger delved into the human impulse toward self-destruction, again using a case-by-case methodology. Covering a wide variety of mental aberrations—alcoholism, martyrdom, asceticism, and the drive to attempt suicide or other self-harm—Menninger credited what he termed the "death instinct" as being a major factor in such behavior, in contrast to some colleagues who maintained that man's tendency towards self-destruction was a misdirection of one's natural aggression. Throughout his life, Menninger worked for the early intervention in mental illness, believing that, if detected and treated early, many extreme deteriorations of the mental condition, such as suicide and schizophrenia, could be avoided.

Menninger's letters were collected and published in two volumes between 1989 and 1995. *The Selected Correspondence of Karl A. Menninger* proves Menninger to have been, in the words of *Washington Post Book World* reviewer Webster Schott, "one of our century's most prolific writers, as well as purposeful physicians." Dubbed as "psychiatry's great communicator" by Schott, Menninger was involved in a correspondence that extended to over 10,000 letters between the period between 1919 and 1965 that is covered in the collection. While praising the collection as "valuable and insightful" in terms of the psychiatrist's written correspondence, Gerald N. Grob notes in the *New York Times Book Review* that *The Selected Correspondence* is hampered by its introductory remarks, which draw on too slim a foundation in psychiatric knowledge. "One can only regret the missed opportunity to illuminate the history of psychiatry and psychoanalysis by presenting, insofar as is humanely possible, a more accurate and representative selection of letters to and from a man whose historical significance is unquestionable," Grob continues. However, T. P. Gariepy praises the work in *Choice,* maintaining that "Forensic psychiatrists and historians of medicine, psychiatry, and psychoanalysis . . . will find here a trove of interesting and useful documents."

Among Menninger's other books are *The Crime of Punishment, Whatever Became of Sin?, The Human Mind Revisited,* and *Sexuality, Law, and the Developmentally Disabled Person: Legal and Clinical Aspects of Marriage, Parenthood, and Sterilization,* the latter co-authored by Sarah R. Haavik. He was also the author of numerous magazine articles.

*BIOGRAPHICAL/CRITICAL SOURCES:*

*BOOKS*

Chandler, Caroline A., *Famous Modern Men of Medicine,* Dodd, 1965.

Davis, Elizabeth L., *Fathers of America,* Revell, 1958.

*PERIODICALS*

*Booklist,* April, 1930, p. 261.

*Chicago Tribune,* June 16, 1979.

*Choice,* March 1996, p. 1225.
*Christian Century,* August 22, 1990, p. 758.
*Look,* September 30, 1958.
*Los Angeles Times,* September 18, 1983.
*Nation,* April 16, 1930, pp. 458, 460; March 2, 1938, p. 198.
*New York Times,* November 6, 1955.
*New York Times Book Review,* February 23, 1930, p. 4; December 29, 1964, March 19, 1989.
*Reason,* December, 1993, p. 37.
*Saturday Evening Post,* April 7, 1962.
*Saturday Review,* January 25, 1964.

*OBITUARIES:*

*PERIODICALS*

*Chicago Tribune,* July 19, 1990.
*Los Angeles Times,* July 19, 1990.
*New York Times,* July 19, 1990.
*Time,* July 30, 1990, p. 65.
*Times* (London), July 20, 1990.
*U.S. News & World Report,* July 30, 1990, p. 10.*

* * *

**MERRILL, P. J.**
**See ROTH, Holly**

* * *

**MILLER, Judith 1948-**

*PERSONAL:* Born in 1948, in New York, NY. *Education:* Attended Ohio State University and Barnard College; received M.A. from Princeton University.

*ADDRESSES:* *Office—New York Times,* 229 West 43rd St., New York, NY 10036.

*CAREER:* *New York Times,* New York City, reporter, editor, and correspondent, 1977—, began as reporter on the Securities and Exchange Commission, became bureau chief in Cairo, Egypt, 1983, became correspondent in Paris, France, 1986, currently senior writer in New York. Freelance journalist, 1976.

*WRITINGS:*

*One, by One, by One: Facing the Holocaust,* Simon & Schuster (New York City), 1990.
(With Laurie Mylroie) *Saddam Hussein and the Crisis in the Gulf,* Random House (New York City), 1990.
*God Has Ninety-Nine Names: Reporting from a Militant Middle East,* Simon & Schuster, 1996.

Contributor to the *Progressive, New Republic, Foreign Affairs,* and many Middle Eastern journals. Also contributor to National Public Radio.

*SIDELIGHTS:* Since she joined the *New York Times* in 1977, Judith Miller has been a consistent contributor of reports and features on European and domestic politics and media. But she is best known for her work as a bureau chief in Cairo, Egypt, and as a special correspondent in the Middle East during the 1980s. She covered events such as the suicide attack on the Marine Corps barracks in Beirut, Lebanon, the hijacking of the cruise ship *Achille Lauro* and subsequent murder of Jewish passengers, the bombing of the U.S. embassy in Kuwait, and the Arab-Israeli peace process.

Miller's interview credits include most of the major players in Middle Eastern politics. She has provided *Times* readers with interviews of Jordan's King Hussein, former Israeli Prime Minister Shimon Peres, Egyptian President Hosni Mubarak, and Yasir Arafat of the Palestine Liberation Organization. Perhaps her biggest scoop came with the private interview that she secured with Libyan leader Muammar Qaddafi and her series of articles on the man and his country. "He has his own kind of bizarre ideology, a vision of an Islamic Utopia that he's creating in Libya. He's sincere about that," Miller told Joan Juliet Buck in a *Vogue* profile. Added Miller, "Qaddafi comes across in many ways as uneducated and so incredibly naive that it's hard to believe this guy is a killer, which he is."

Miller's experience in the Middle East has not only given her insights into the politics and personalities of that region, but also into the dilemma so closely associated with the Middle East in the minds of Westerners: terrorism. "I think . . . that part of the reason I feel so strongly about terrorism is that I've now covered enough of it to last me a lifetime," she explained in *Vogue.* "Terrorists are not all that clever. Some are well-organized, but I think that in lots of instances they've been as effective as they have because governments have acted stupidly." Miller offered the following advice: "The civilized world simply has to draw the line and say it's not true that one man's terrorist is another man's freedom fighter, because terrorism has a distinct and a specific meaning, and it is the wanton killing and deliberate murders of noncombatants, civilians, innocent people not involved in your conflict to inspire fear for political goals."

Miller has used her newspaper writing as a springboard for two books. Her first book grew out of a feature on the Holocaust—the slaughter of Jews by the Nazis during World War II—that she wrote while a correspondent in Paris in the mid-1980s. The resulting book, *One, by One, by One: Facing the Holocaust,* is, according to *New York Times Book Review* contributor Eli N. Evans, "a timely, provocative and in many respects deeply disturbing book about the ways in which five European countries and the United States are forgetting, distorting and politically manipulating the memory of the Holocaust." "She has discovered, to her dismay," wrote Eward Norden in *Commentary,* "that in Germany, Austria, Holland, France, and the USSR, the facts of the Holocaust are being cooked, that history is being mythologized for local consumption and political purposes."

Miller scrutinizes efforts in Germany at historical revisionism, especially in the wake of German reunification. She throws a spotlight on the election of former Nazi Kurt Waldheim as president of Austria to show that country's inability to come to terms with its collaboration. She contrasts the public celebration of the Dutch resistance and Holocaust victim and diarist Anne Frank with the disturbing fact that only twenty-five percent of Dutch Jews survived World War II. She finds France's uneasy memory of its role in Jewish deportations revived by the trial of Nazi war criminal Klaus Barbie. She discovers that the tragedy suffered by Russian Jews was overshadowed by the deaths of twenty million Russians. Finally, Miller looks at American remembrances of the Holocaust in events such as President Ronald Reagan's visit to the Bitburg Cemetery (where several Nazis were among those buried) and in the heated debate surrounding the U.S. Holocaust Memorial Museum in Washington, D.C.

"Judith Miller has had access that few freelance writers could equal," commented Evans. "She has taken her mission seriously and has written a troubling and thought-provoking exploration into a dark world of memory and redemption." Her mission, as Norden put it, is to call on all of these countries and others "to tell themselves and their children the whole truth, and to do this before the last collaborators with the Nazis and the last Jewish survivors are gone." "Unless we can keep it in mind that the Holocaust was comprised of the suffering of individuals, each with a face and name," added Norden, "ignorance and forgetfulness will prevail, depriving Jews and Gentiles of their 'surest defense' against the repetition of 'such gigantic cruelty.'"

Miller's second book, *Saddam Hussein and the Crisis in the Gulf,* was co-authored with Harvard scholar Laurie Mylroie as a quick response to the 1990 Iraqi invasion of Kuwait. "Written in three weeks and published in a fourth," wrote Stephen R. Shalom in the *Nation,* "[it] appeared a few months before the U.S. attack on Iraq." "While largely a synthesis of others' work, their book puts much essential background material on Iraq into one volume," commented Stanley Reed in *Business Week.* Miller and Mylroie profile the man that they call the Iraqi "Godfather," a man born into poverty in 1937 in a small village one hundred miles north of Baghdad. They outline his youth and then his emergence into the national scene in Iraq as a hit man for the Baath Party, which was struggling to control the country after the fall of King Faisal II in 1958.

When the Baathists finally seized power in 1963, Hussein took a position as interrogator and torturer. After a fall from grace and two years in prison, he reemerged to found a Baathist security force. On the inside with his own power base, Hussein continued his ruthless rise to the top. In 1979 he became president of Iraq and leader of the Baath Party and proceeded to execute hundreds of his opponents in the party. "The mechanics of Mr. Hussein's rise and his maintenance of power are skillfully described in *Saddam Hussein and the Crisis in the Gulf,* as is the history of Iraq's acquisition of weapons of mass destruction," wrote Marvin Zonis in the *New York Times Book Review.*

The book also covers the U.S. policy toward Iraq during Hussein's reign. It is this aspect of the book with which Shalom found fault. He especially found Mylroie's criticism of the United States for its pro-Baghdad stance prior to the invasion inconsistent. In her previous writings, noted Shalom, "Mylroie didn't just misjudge Iraq. She served as an apologist for and supporter of Saddam Hussein, a man whom after the invasion of Kuwait she presented as eternally evil. This transformation precisely parallels the official policy of the U.S. government." Zonis conceded that the authors miss some opportunities with this book, but in his assessment, "What they do deliver, however, is a frequently riveting account of how Saddam Hussein, ruthless visionary that he is, has driven his country and manipulated much of the world to satisfy his grandiose ambitions."

Miller's intimate knowledge of and years of experience reporting in the Middle East inform her ambitious book *God Has Ninety-Nine Names: Reporting from a Militant Middle East,* which is described by a *Kirkus Reviews* writer as "an intriguing, enlightening, often disheartening but occasionally hopeful tour" of the region. In the book, Miller gives historical and political profiles of ten countries spanning the area from Algeria to Iran, analyzing how each came to its present state of affairs. She also illuminates the great diversity within the world of Islam. Many reviewers were lavish in their praise of the author's work. *Business Week* critic Stanley Reed declared: "Readers will come away from this highly informative tour of the many faces of Islam with an almost tactile appreciation of the Gaza slums that produce suicide bombers and the grim, calculating mullahs who guide Hezbollah in southern Lebanon. . . . The author's wicked sense of humor leavens what could have become a depressing catalog of mayhem. She tells us that fundamentalists in Egypt have urged their followers not to eat squash and eggplants because of their supposed resemblance to sexual organs. The amorous antics of Libya's Muammar Quaddafi are a source of much fun."

Helen Winternitz noted in the *Los Angeles Times Book Review* that few people could have produced such a book: "[Miller's] writing is informed by her remarkable friendships with some of the most powerful figures in the Middle East, her tenancity at pursing interviews with some of the most potent of the militants, her large knowledge of the difficult territory and her attention to the forces of history. The book suffers only from her ambition to explain with microscopic intensity 10 disparate countries, an effort from which she emerges without trenchant conclusions. Her work does offer the patient reader a treasure trove of information, though." The *Kirkus Reviews* critic concluded that *God Has Ninety-Nine Names* is "a nuanced examination of Islamic militancy, crammed with information, that puts this growing movement and its most horrible terrorist manifestations into invaluable context."

*BIOGRAPHICAL/CRITICAL SOURCES:*

*BOOKS*

Miller, Judith, and Laurie Mylroie, *Saddam Hussein and the Crisis in the Gulf,* Random House, 1990.

*PERIODICALS*

*Atlanta Journal-Constitution,* June 9, 1996, p. L14.
*Business Week,* November 26, 1990, pp. 12, 14; May 20, 1996, p. 20.
*Christian Science Monitor,* July 10, 1996, p. 14.
*Commentary,* August, 1990, pp. 62-64; August, 1996, p. 102.
*Current History,* January, 1991.
*Economist,* October 6, 1990, p. 106; November 10, 1990, p. 107; July 20, 1996, p. S10.
*Foreign Affairs,* May-June, 1996, p. 122.
*Kirkus Reviews,* April 1, 1996, p. 512.
*Library Journal,* April 15, 1996, p. 106.
*Los Angeles Times Book Review,* July 7, 1996, p. 3.
*Nation,* February 25, 1991, pp. 241-243; August 12, 1996, p. 28.
*New Leader,* May 6, 1996, p. 19.
*New York Review of Books,* December 20, 1990, pp. 44-46; May 5, 1996, p. 9.
*New York Times,* May 20, 1996, p. C16.
*New York Times Book Review,* April 29, 1990, p. 7; November 11, 1990, p. 7; May 5, 1996, p. 9.
*Publishers Weekly,* March 16, 1990, p. 57.
*Time,* May 14, 1990, p. 89.
*U.S. Catholic,* October, 1990, pp. 48-51.
*Vogue,* August, 1986, pp. 323, 377-379.
*Wall Street Journal,* May 3, 1996, p. A10.
*Washington Post Book World,* June 23, 1996, p. 4.

* * *

**MOERI, Louise 1924-**

*PERSONAL:* Surname rhymes with "story"; born November 30, 1924, in Klamath Falls, OR; daughter of Clyde (a farmer) and Hazel (Simpson) Healy; married Edwin Albert Moeri (a civil servant), December 15, 1946; children: Neal Edwin, Rodger Scott, Patricia Jo Ann. *Education:* Stockton Junior College, A.A., 1944; University of California, Berkeley, B.A., 1946. *Religion:* Protestant.

*ADDRESSES: Home*—18262 South Austin Rd., Manteca, CA 95336.

*CAREER:* Manteca Branch Library, Manteca, CA, library assistant, 1961-78; writer.

*AWARDS, HONORS:* Literary Award, outstanding children's book by western writer, PEN Center U.S.A. West, 1990, for *The Forty-third War.*

*WRITINGS:*

*FOR CHILDREN*

*Star Mother's Youngest Child,* illustrated by Trina Schart Hyman, Houghton (Boston), 1975.
*A Horse for X. Y. Z.,* illustrated by Gail Owens, Dutton (New York City), 1977.
*How the Rabbit Stole the Moon,* illustrated by Marc Brown, Houghton, 1977.
*The Unicorn and the Plow,* illustrated by Diane Goode, Dutton, 1982.

*FOR YOUNG ADULTS*

*The Girl Who Lived on the Ferris Wheel,* Dutton, 1979.
*Save Queen of Sheba,* Dutton, 1981.
*First the Egg,* Dutton, 1982.
*Downwind,* Dutton, 1984.
*Journey to the Treasure,* Scholastic (New York City), 1986.
*The Forty-third War,* Houghton, 1989.

*SIDELIGHTS:* Adolescents confronted with adult-sized challenges are a special concern of fiction writer Louise Moeri. The author of several young adult novels that show how teens can come to terms with personal and family problems, Moeri tries to instill in her readers a sense of hope at life's possibilities. While Hollis Lowery-Moore writes in *Twentieth-Century Young Adult Writers* that "cynical readers may scoff at the happy endings achieved in Moeri's chronicles of adverse conditions and unthinkable hardships," the critic hastens to add that "the careful construction of credible characters and the tense plots ensure that most readers are cheering for these stalwart youngsters and will be dissatisfied with anything less than favorable resolutions."

The "adverse conditions" and "tense plots" that characterize Moeri's novels are all too familiar to the author, who clearly follows the cardinal rule of most fiction writers to "write what you know." Born in Klamath Falls, Oregon, in 1924, Moeri grew up during the Great Depression, and the lack of work and money forced her and her family to move several times during those difficult years. Like many working-class Americans, Moeri's parents were poor, and life for them and their children was difficult. "I was born into a troubled generation and into troubled times," the writer once explained to *CA.* "My childhood was lived against a background of fear and worry, the scars of which are still very evident in me today. It was many years before I realized that life without scars is not possible, and that the important thing is not what happens to you, but what you do with it."

Despite their impoverished circumstances, Moeri's parents managed to provide their daughter with a good education, "at the cost of such effort as I can only guess about now," the author noted. Young Moeri particularly enjoyed her hours spent at school. "Writing was at first just a curious and effortless adventure, and I was surprised to find that people thought I did it well," she recalled. Because she and her family frequently moved, Moeri often found herself in the role of outsider, the "new kid in class"—"the last one to find a friend, the last one to be chosen for any team," as she admitted. "And yet, in a family that utterly lacked stability and peace, I was taught some of the most valuable lessons. I learned that one's first commitment was to those human souls—parents, husband or wife, children, friends—with whom one had been entrusted. I learned that once I began something I must finish it. I learned to view myself, my actions, and the world around me through a framework of Christian principles. And I learned that any returns one might expect from life depended upon the amount of effort [one] put into it, taking also as my first obligation the need to locate whatever opportunities lay at hand and make the best possible use of them."

Eventually married and the mother of three children, Moeri continued to write for enjoyment—poetry and short stories were her favorites. Writing for children was "the direct outgrowth of my good fortune in getting a job in our local public library," she explained. "I shared these wonderful books with my own three children, and before long was caught up in the desire to write some of my own. Most of them failed to find a market, but *Jack and Jill* magazine finally purchased one, which they printed under the title 'A Shaggy Dog Story,' and I had the joy of seeing my work in print for the first time." Four picture books and several young adult novels would later follow Moeri's print debut.

Moeri's first published book was *Star Mother's Youngest Child,* an illustrated Christmas story about a lonesome elderly woman who finds an unkempt young child on her doorstep one Christmas Eve morning. Not realizing that the child is in fact an angel who has been allowed only one day to celebrate the Christmas season in human form, the old woman invites the rag-tag youngster in to help make both their holidays special. "Sensitive without being maudlin, the story is told in lilting prose," asserted *Horn Book* reviewer Mary M. Burns. Another favorable assessment of Moeri's debut came from Barbara Elleman of *Booklist,* who called *Star Mother's Youngest Child* "word- and picture-picture." Moeri followed this initial success with several more picture books for young children: *A Horse for X. Y. Z, How the Rabbit Stole the Moon,* and *The Unicorn and the Plow,* the latter published in 1982. Reviewing *A Horse for X. Y. Z.,* a *Kirkus Reviews* contributor commented: "A girls' story combining a fine horse, dangerous crooks, and rugged ordeals can hardly lose," adding that "Moeri brings more skill and conviction to the writing than the ingredients would lead you to expect." *How the Rabbit Stole the Moon,* a porquoi fable for primary graders about celestial luminaries, garnered praise from *Booklist* reviewer Elleman, who maintained that "fluidity of style and effortless handling of words highlight this original tale."

Moeri began writing fiction for older children with *The Girl Who Lived on the Ferris Wheel,* published four years after *Star Mother's Youngest Child.* In this novel eleven-year-old Til (Clothilde) fears the repeated abuse at the hands of her mentally disturbed mother, but feels helpless to save herself. Her main joy comes on Saturdays when she visits with her father, who has divorced her mother. The two ride on the ferris wheel, a favorite pastime of Til's dad, who is unaware that the ride secretly frightens the girl, symbolizing for her an endless, repetitive journey that she has no control over. Only gradually does Til realize that her mother's increasingly violent behavior is actually becoming life-threatening; her out-of-touch father is even slower to understand or accept the dangerous situation in which he has left his daughter. While noting that "Til's dilemma is convincing," reviewer Kate M. Flanagan contends in a *Horn Book* review of *The Girl Who Lived on the Ferris Wheel* that Moeri "creates the feeling of a movie thriller rather than an understanding of a prevalent social problem." A *Publishers Weekly* commentator, however, concluded that "Moeri's realistic characters and situations emphasize the need for urgent attention to a serious social problem."

Moeri's next novel, *Save Queen of Sheba,* was a well-received survival story set in the old American west. In this tale, twelve-year-old King David and his little sister, Queen of Sheba, survive an Indian attack but are left to fend for themselves while searching for the other survivors of the wagon train in the wilderness. Zena Sutherland of the *Bulletin of the Center for Children's Books* found *Save Queen of Sheba* "on the whole a deft sustaining of suspense and mood, impressive in a book that has so stark a setting and so sparse a cast." *Horn Book* reviewer Ann A. Flowers also commented favorably on the novel, asserting that "the children are intriguing characters" and the story "believable and human."

Survival of a more subtle nature is the order of the day in *First the Egg,* Moeri's 1982 novel about California high school senior Sarah Webster, cast in the role of "mother hen" during her Marriage and Family class. Paired with fellow student David Hanna and told by their teacher to "parent" a raw egg for an entire week as if it were their own infant, Sarah finds herself gaining a more mature outlook about both her family and her self through the course of the project. She also finds herself falling for David, a handsome but angry young man who acts out his distaste for the assignment by leaving the bulk of the work to Sarah. Zena Sutherland of the *Bulletin of the Center for Children's Books* called *First the Egg* "a remarkably discerning story," praising Moeri's "substantial characterization and dialogue." *Voice of Youth Advocates* contributor Carole A. Barham similarly maintained that "Moeri presents, within a bare-bones skeleton, an engaging, intriguing story about growing up."

Moeri focuses once again on themes of courage and survival amid crisis in her novels *Downwind* and *The Forty-third War.* Featuring a contemporary setting, *Downwind* relates the plight of a boy who must look after his two younger siblings as their family joins in a mass, frenzied exodus from their hometown after an accident threatens a meltdown at a local nuclear power plant. "This is a graphic look at a response to an emergency situation by the ill-prepared," noted *School Library Journal* contributor Wanna M. Ernst, who added that Moeri's characters are the focus of the story, so that "the emergency precipitating the evacuation could be any type of disaster." Moeri's award-winning adventure tale *The Forty-third War* takes place in an unnamed yet all-too-familiar area of Latin America. The novel finds twelve-year-old Uno Ramirez caught up in the throes of his politically unstable country's revolution after he and several other young boys from his village are captured by a party of raiding soldiers and forced to join the guerilla forces of the charismatic Captain Mendoza. After a weeks' training Uno joins a rebel patrol in the jungle, where he is wounded but rescued by his compadres. Uno's loyalty to the rebels deepens after the pro-government soldiers rape his sister, kill his father, and terrorize a nearby village. Praising Moeri for her well-researched and vivid portrayal of life among the rebel forces of such countries as El Salvador and Nicaragua, Ethel R. Twichell notes in *Horn Book* that "The unending wars in Central America are described with devastating accuracy in the microcosm of twelve-year-old Uno Ramirez's experiences." Betsy Hearne of the *Bulletin of the Center for Children's Books* similarly commented that in *The Forty-third War* "the scenes of conflict are taut and the protagonists' fears vividly projected."

In the years since she began her writing career, Moeri has watched her children, grandchildren, and now great-grandchildren grow up—"the most terrifying and joyous experience I could imagine," she admits to *CA*. "The family now ranges from a toddler barely plus one year old to a tall teenager facing adulthood. I have taken part in school visits, trips to the dentist, frantic late-night phone calls for help with homework ('Grandma, quick! What was the Edict of Nantes?'), and moments when 'nobody understands me.' I've loved every minute of it."

Outside of her immediate family, Moeri continues to be concerned with the lot of young people everywhere. "I am appalled at the way the world treats its children," she stated. "Fragile human lives are swept aside by armies on the march to some sought-for victory which, having lost the children along the way, can be no kind of victory. Even in the relatively stable societies, we have much to answer for in the way of ignorance, cruelty, and one of the greatest sins of all—indifference. I hope to carry on my small part of this struggle with books that shine some light on the lives of children."

*BIOGRAPHICAL/CRITICAL SOURCES:*

*BOOKS*

*Something about the Author Autobiography Series,* Volume 10, Gale (Detroit), 1990, pp. 165-181.

*Twentieth-Century Young Adult Writers,* St. James Press (Detroit), 1994, pp. 463-464.

*PERIODICALS*

*Booklist,* October 15, 1975, pp. 304-305; October 15, 1977, p. 378.

*Bulletin of the Center for Children's Books,* March, 1976, p. 115; December, 1977, p. 63; April, 1980, p. 158; September, 1981, p. 13; September, 1982, p. 16; January, 1983, p. 93; April, 1984, p. 152; November, 1989, pp. 66-67.

*Horn Book,* December, 1975, pp. 582-583; October, 1977, p. 533; January-February, 1980, pp. 69-70; October, 1981, pp. 536-537; October, 1982, p. 521.

*Kirkus Reviews,* June 15, 1977, p. 626; April 1, 1982, p. 419; September 1, 1989, pp. 1130-1131.

*Publishers Weekly,* December 24, 1979, p. 58; February 5, 1982, p. 387; November 19, 1982, p. 77; February 17, 1984, p. 90.

*School Library Journal,* September, 1984, pp. 120-121.

*Voice of Youth Advocates,* April, 1983, p. 38.

* * *

## MOORE, Marianne 1887-1972

*PERSONAL:* Born November 15, 1887, in Kirkwood, MO; died February 5, 1972; daughter of John Milton and Mary (Warner) Moore. *Education:* Bryn Mawr College, A.B., 1909; Carlisle Commercial College, graduate, 1910. *Religion:* Presbyterian. *Avocational interests:* Baseball.

*CAREER:* Author and poet. United States Indian School, Carlisle, PA, teacher, 1911-15; New York Public Library, New York City, assistant, 1921-25.

*MEMBER:* National Institute of Arts and Letters, American Academy of Arts and Letters, Bryn Mawr Club.

*AWARDS, HONORS:* Dial Award, 1924; Helen Haire Levinson Prize, 1932; Ernest Hartsock Memorial Prize, 1935; Shelley Memorial Award, 1941; Contemporary Poetry's Patrons Prize, 1944; Harriet Monroe Poetry Award, 1944; Guggenheim Memorial fellowship, 1945; National Institute of Arts and Letters, grant in literature, 1946, gold medal, 1953; National Book Award for poetry and Pulitzer Prize in poetry, 1952, for *Collected Poems;* Bollingen Prize in poetry, Yale University, 1953, for *Collected Po-*

*ems;* M. Carey Thomas Award, 1953; Poetry Society of America gold medal award, 1960, 1967; Brandeis Award for Poetry, 1963; Academy of American Poets fellowship, 1965, for distinguished poetic achievement over a period of more than four decades; MacDowell medal, 1967; named chevalier of the Legion of Honor, Order of Arts and Letters; named woman of achievement, American Association of University Women, 1968. Honorary degrees: Litt.D. from Wilson College, 1949, Mount Holyoke College, 1950, University of Rochester, 1951, Dickinson College, 1952, Long Island University, 1953, New York University, 1967, St. John's University, 1968, and Princeton University, 1968; L.H.D. from Rutgers University, 1955, Smith College, 1955, and Pratt Institute, 1958.

*WRITINGS:*

*POETRY*

*Poems,* Egoist Press, 1921, published with additions as *Observations,* Dial, 1924.
*Selected Poems,* introduction by T. S. Eliot, Macmillan, 1935.
*Pangolin, and Other Verse: Five Poems,* Brendin, 1936.
*What Are Years and Other Poems,* Macmillan, 1941.
*Nevertheless,* Macmillan, 1944.
*Collected Poems,* Macmillan, 1951.
*Like a Bulwark,* Viking, 1956.
*O to Be a Dragon,* Viking, 1959.
*A Marianne Moore Reader,* Viking, 1961.
*The Arctic Ox,* Faber, 1964.
*A Talisman,* Adams House, 1965.
*Tell Me, Tell Me: Granite, Steel, and Other Topics* (poetry and prose), Viking, 1966.
*The Complete Poems of Marianne Moore,* Macmillan, 1967, Penguin, 1987.
*Selected Poems,* Faber, 1969.
*Unfinished Poems,* P. H. and A.S.W. Rosenbach Foundation, 1972.

*POETRY; PUBLISHED IN LIMITED EDITIONS*

*Eight Poems,* illustrations by Robert Andrew Parker, New York Museum of Modern Art, 1962.
*Occasionem cognosce,* Stinehour Press, 1963.
*Dress and Kindred Subjects,* Ibex Press, 1965.
*Le mariage. . . ,* Ibex Press, 1965.
*Poetry and Criticism,* privately printed, 1965.
*Silence,* L. H. Scott, 1965.
*Tippoo's Tiger,* Phoenix Book Shop, 1967.

*OTHER*

(Co-translator) A. Stifter, *Rock Crystal,* Pantheon, 1945.
(Translator) *Selected Fables of La Fontaine,* Faber, 1955, revised edition, Viking, 1964.
*Predilections* (essays and reviews), Viking, 1955.
*Letters from and to the Ford Motor Company,* Pierpont Morgan Library, 1958 (first appeared in *New Yorker,* April 13, 1957).
(Compiler with others) *Riverside Poetry Three: An Anthology of Student Poetry,* Twayne, 1958.
*Idiosyncrasy and Technique: Two Lectures,* University of California Press, 1958.
*The Absentee: A Comedy in Four Acts* (play based on Maria Edgeworth's novel of the same name), House of Books, 1962.
(Contributor) *Poetry in Crystal,* Spiral Press, 1963.
*Puss in Boots, The Sleeping Beauty, and Cinderella* (retelling of three fairy tales based on the French tales of Charles Perrault), illustrated by Eugene Karlin, Macmillan, 1963.
(Contributor) A. K. Weatherhead, *The Edge of the Image,* University of Washington Press, 1968.
*The Accented Syllable,* Albondocani Press, 1969 (first appeared in *Egoist,* October, 1916).
(Contributor) *Homage to Henry James,* Appel, 1971.
*The Complete Prose of Marianne Moore,* edited by Patricia C. Willis, Penguin, 1986.

Contributor of articles, essays, and verse to numerous magazines. *Dial,* acting editor, 1925-29, editor, 1929.

*SIDELIGHTS:* Marianne Moore garnered significant critical acclaim and public recognition for her poetry during her six-decade career, including the rare triumph of winning poetry's "triple crown" of major awards-the National Book Award, the Pulitzer Prize, and the Bollingen Prize-for her 1951 work *Collected Poems.* Born and raised in Pennsylvania, Moore attended Bryn Mawr College, from which she graduated in 1909. During the next decade, Moore began writing poetry in earnest, finally emerging on the national literary scene in 1915, when several major literary magazines first published her poems. In 1918 Moore and her mother moved to New York City, where Moore was to live the remainder of her life. During the early 1920s, Moore worked for the New York Public Library while continuing to write poetry. In 1925 Moore became editor of the prestigious literary magazine *Dial,* a post she held until the magazine ceased publication in 1929. From that point onward, Moore made her living writing poetry and reviews.

Moore once told an interviewer for the *New York Times:* "Poetry. I, too, dislike it: There are things that are important beyond all this fiddle. [But,] if you demand on the one hand / the raw material of poetry in / all its rawness and / that which is on the other hand / genuine, then you are interested in poetry."

Moore continued: "I don't call anything I have ever written poetry. In fact, the only reason I know for calling my work poetry at all is that there is no other category in which to put it. I'm a happy hack as a writer. . . . I never knew anyone with a passion for words who had as much difficulty in saying things as I do. I seldom say them in a manner I like. Each poem I think will be the last. But something always comes up and catches my fancy."

In spite of Moore's rather humble thoughts, many critics believe in the significance of her poetry. For example, John Ashbery glowed: "I am tempted simply to call her our greatest modern poet. This despite the obvious grandeur of her chief competitors, including Wallace Stevens and William Carlos Williams. It seems we can never remind ourselves too often that universality and depth are not the same thing. Marianne Moore has no 'Arma virumque cano' prefacing her work: She even avoids formal beginnings altogether by running the first line in as a continuation of the title. But her work will, I think, continue to be read as poetry when much of the major poetry of our time has become part of the history of literature."

Ashbery isn't alone in his praise of Moore's poetry. James Dickey wrote: "Each of her poems employs items that Ms. Moore similarly encountered and to which she gave a new, Mooreian existence in a new cosmos of consequential relationships. What seems to me to be the most valuable point about Ms. Moore is that such receptivity as hers . . . is not Ms. Moore's exclusive property. Every poem of hers lifts us toward our own discovery-prone lives. It does not state, in effect, that I am more intelligent than you, more creative because I found this item and used it and you didn't. It seems to say, rather, I found this, and what did you find? Or, a better, what can you find?"

*Nation* critic Sandra Hochman agreed: "The art of Marianne Moore is not just the valuable art of observation. She is magical. Her poems do have riddles. They can irk us. But they finally carry us forward by the strength of language and, in her own words, the poet's 'burning desire to be explicit.' Nothing is wasted. All is transformed."

It is this desire that underlies Moore's poetry. James Dickey explained that "Ms. Moore tells us that facts make her feel 'profoundly grateful.' This is because knowledge, for her, is not power but love, and in loving it is important to know what you love, as widely and as deeply and as well as possible. In paying so very much attention to the things of this earth that she encounters, or that encounter her, Ms. Moore urges us to do the same, and thus gives us back, in strict syllables, the selves that we had contrived to lose. She persuades us that the human mind is nothing more than an organ for loving things in both complicated and blindingly simple ways, and is organized so as to be able to love in an unlimited number of fashions and for an unlimited number of reasons. This seems to me to constitute the correct poetic attitude, which is essentially a life-attitude, for it stands forever against the notion that the earth is an apathetic limbo lost in space." As Ms. Moore herself explained to Howard Nemerov: "I am . . . much aware of the world's dilemma. People's effect on other people results, it seems to me, in an enforced sense of responsibility—a compulsory obligation to participate in others' problems."

Marianne Moore is almost as famous for her practice of rewriting her previously published poems as for her poetry itself. This practice has often disturbed many of her followers. Jean Garrigrie explained: "Poets who revise their poems are apt to incur surprise or weak query (a guise of protest) from those who have long ago fallen in love with that 'one and only,' the original. The poet, patient about perfection, has a right to be impatient with such resistance. But there it is. And a good deal is involved. A line taken out of a poem sparingly built in the first place, that line's removal subtly alters the whole in tone. An 'excess' excised—a qualifying extension or elaboration—complicated one's responses, for one is busy dismissing and it takes time to adjust to the revision. What is being felt is the absence, almost as much as the new presence."

And Anthony Hecht once wrote that as "an admiring reader I feel that I have some rights in [this] matter. Her poems are partly mine, now, and I delight in them because they exhibit a mind of great fastidiousness, a delicate and cunning moral sensibility, a tact, a decorum, a rectitude, and finally and most movingly, a capacity for pure praise that has absolutely biblical awe in it. She (and Mr. Auden, too, as it will appear) however much I may wish to take exception to the changes they have made, have provided a field day for Ph.D. candidates for years to come, who can collate versions and come up with theories about why the changes were made."

In addition to her poetry, Moore wrote a significant number of prose pieces, including reviews and essays. Many of these were collected and published as *The Complete Prose of Marianne Moore.* The pieces in this work cover a broad range of subjects: painting, sculpture, literature, music, fashion, herbal medicine, and sports (Moore was an avid baseball follower). Calling the collection "a civilized delight," Chicago *Tribune Books* contributor Larry Kart remarked that "characteristic shafts of light refract from every corner of [Moore's] universe."

*BIOGRAPHICAL/CRITICAL SOURCES:*

*BOOKS*

Auden, W. H., *The Dyer's Hand and Other Essays,* Random House, 1962.

Birkerts, Sven, *The Electric Life: Essays on Modern Poetry,* Morrow, 1989.

*Contemporary Literary Criticism,* Gale, Volume 1, 1973, Volume 2, 1974, Volume 4, 1975, Volume 8, 1977, Volume 10, 1979, Volume 13, 1980, Volume 19, 1981, Volume 47, 1988.

Costello, Bonnie, *Marianne Moore: Imaginary Possessions,* Harvard University Press, 1981.

*Dictionary of Literary Biography,* Volume 45: *American Poets, 1880-1945, First Series,* Gale, 1986.

Engel, Bernard F., *Marianne Moore,* Twayne, 1964.

Gregory, Elizabeth, *Quotation and Modern American Poetry: Imaginary Gardens with Real Toads,* Rice University Press, 1995.

Hadas, P. W., *Marianne Moore: Poet of Affection,* Syracuse University Press, 1977.

Hall, Donald, *Marianne Moore: The Cage and the Animal,* Pegasus, 1970.

Jarrell, Randall, *Poetry and the Age,* Knopf, 1953.

Juhasz, Suzanne, *Naked and Fiery Forms: Modern American Poetry by Women, A New Tradition,* Harper, 1976.

Kreymborg, Alfred, *Our Singing Strength,* Coward-McCann, 1929.

Lakritz, Andrew M., *Modernism and the Other in Stevens, Frost, and Moore,* University Press of Florida, 1996.

Leavell, Linda, *Marianne Moore and the Visual Arts: Prismatic Color,* Louisiana State University Press, 1995.

Miller, Cristanne, *Marianne Moore: Questions of Authority,* Harvard University Press, 1995.

Molesworth, Charles, *Marianne Moore: A Literary Life,* Atheneum, 1990.

Nemerov, Howard, *Poets on Poetry,* Basic Books, 1966.

Rosenthal, M. L., *The Modern Poets,* Oxford University Press, 1965.

Schulman, Grace, *Marianne Moore: The Poetry of Engagement,* University of Illinois Press, 1986.

Schulze, Robin G., *The Web of Friendship: Marianne Moore and Wallace Stevens,* University of Michigan Press, 1995.

Sorrentino, Gilbert, *Something Said,* North Point Press, 1984.

Stapleton, L., *Marianne Moore,* Princeton University Press, 1978.

Tomlinson, Charles, editor, *Marianne Moore: A Collection of Critical Essays,* Prentice-Hall, 1970.

Vendler, Helen, *Part of Nature, Part of Us: Modern American Poets,* Harvard University Press, 1980.

*PERIODICALS*

*American Poetry Review,* Volume 17, number 4, July-August, 1988.

*Atlantic,* February, 1962.

*Chicago Review,* Volume 11, number 1, spring, 1957.

*College English,* Volume 14, number 5, February, 1953.

*Contemporary Literature,* Volume 27, number 4, winter, 1986; Volume 30, number 1, spring, 1989.

*Critical Inquiry,* Volume 13, number 3, spring, 1987.

*Detroit News,* February 6, 1972.

*Dial,* Volume 78, May, 1925.

*Esquire,* July, 1962.

*Freeman,* Volume 6, number 152, February 7, 1923.

*Harper's,* May, 1977.

*Hudson Review,* spring, 1968.

*Life,* January 13, 1967.

*McCall's,* December, 1965.

*Nation,* May 8, 1967.

*New Leader,* December 4, 1967.

*New Republic,* January 4, 1960; February 24, 1968.

*Newsweek,* January 2, 1967.

*New Yorker,* February 16, 1957; April 13, 1957; November 28, 1959; January 29, 1966; October 16, 1978.
*New York Times,* June 3, 1965; July 13, 1965; February 6, 1972; February 21, 1981; February 8, 1987; October 14, 1987.
*New York Times Book Review,* May 16, 1954; October 4, 1959; December 3, 1961; December 25, 1966; March 14, 1967; November 26, 1967.
*Parnassus: Poetry in Review,* Volumes 12 & 13, numbers 2 & 1, 1985.
*Poetry,* April, 1925; May, 1960; September, 1967.
*Publishers Weekly,* February 14, 1972.
*Quarterly Review of Literature,* Volume 4, number 2, 1948.
*Sagetrieb: Marianne Moore Special Issue,* Volume 6, number 3, winter, 1987.
*Sewanee Review,* Volume 60, number 3, July-September, 1952.
*Spectator,* Volume 187, number 6439, November 23, 1951.
*Times* (London), February 5, 1987.
*Tribune Books* (Chicago), March 8, 1987, p. 6.
*Twentieth Century Literature,* Volume 30, numbers 2 & 3, summer-fall, 1984.
*Virginia Quarterly Review,* Volume 58, number 4, autumn, 1982.
*Washington Post,* March 16, 1968; February 7, 1972; January 19, 1988.
*Washington Post Book World,* November 23, 1986, p. 1.*

* * *

**MORICE, Anne**
**See SHAW, Felicity**

* * *

**MORICE, Dave 1946-**
**(Dr. Alphabet, Joyce Holland)**

*PERSONAL:* Born September 10, 1946, in St. Louis, MO; son of Gilbert J. (a real estate agent) and Lillian G. (a librarian and secretary; maiden name, Murray) Morice; married Milagros Quijada, May 24, 1986 (divorced November 30, 1992); children: Danny. *Education:* St. Louis University, B.A., 1969; University of Iowa, M.F.A., 1972, M.A., 1988, Ph.D., 1996. *Politics:* Democrat.

*ADDRESSES: Home*—P.O. Box 3382, Iowa City, IA 52244.

*CAREER:* Writer, illustrator, educator. Presenter of poetry performances, as Dr. Alphabet, 1973—. Iowa Book and Supply, member of sales staff, 1977-80; *Poetry Comics,* publisher, 1979-82; University of Iowa, computer typesetter, 1980-83, visiting lecturer, 1989-96. Iowa Arts Council, writers-in-schools program, 1975-80; teacher of poetry writing to senior citizens.

*MEMBER:* Coordinating Council of Literary Magazines, Poets and Writers.

*AWARDS, HONORS:* Award from St. Louis University Poetry Contest, 1967, for "Skeletal"; TAMS Literary Award, Token and Medal Society, 1990, for the article "The Missouri Mule Gold Piece and Other Little Mysteries."

*WRITINGS:*

*Poems,* Al Buck Press (Iowa City), 1971.
*Tilt* (self-illustrated poems), Toothpaste Press, 1971.
(Illustrator) John Batki, *The Mad Shoemaker* (poems), Toothpaste Press, 1973.
*Paper Comet* (self-illustrated poems), Happy Press, 1974.
*Snapshots From Europe: Poems,* Toothpaste Press, 1974.
(Illustrator) Cinda Kornblum, *Bandwagon* (poems), Toothpaste Press, 1976.
(Illustrator) Allan Kornblum, *Threshold* (poems), Toothpaste Press, 1976.
*Poetry City, U.S.A.* (self-illustrated poem), Happy Press, 1977.
*Jnd-Song of the Golden Gradrti* (self-illustrated poems), Happy Press, 1977.
*Children Learn What They Live* (self-illustrated poems), Happy Press, 1979.
*The Cutist Anthology* (self-illustrated poems), Happy Press, 1979.
*Quicksand Through the Hourglass: Poems and Drawings* (self-illustrated), Toothpaste Press, 1979.
(Illustrator) Bobbie Louise Hawkins, *A Sense of Humor* (poems), Coffee House Press (Iowa City), 1983.
(Illustrator) Batki, *Why People Lack Confidence in Chairs* (poems), Coffee House Press, 1984.
(Author and illustrator, with Steve LaVoie) *Birth of a Brain/La Creacion de un Cerebro,* Happy Press, 1985.

(Illustrator) Lederer, *Nothing Risque, Nothing Gained: Ribald Riddles, Lascivious Limericks, Carnal Corn, and Other Good, Clean Dirty Fun,* Chicago Review Press, 1995.
(Illustrator) David Lehman, *The Questions of Postmodernism,* Holocene Press (Spartanburg, SC), 1995.
(Illustrator) Lederer, *Fractured English,* Pocket Books (New York City), 1996.
*Alphabet Avenue: Wordplay in the Fast Lane* (self-illustrated), Chicago Review Press, 1997.

*CHILDREN'S BOOKS*

*Dot Town,* Happy Press (Iowa City, IA), 1978.
*A Visit From St. Alphabet,* Toothpaste Press (West Branch, IA), 1980, 2nd edition, A Cappella/Chicago Review Press (Chicago, IL), 1993.
(Illustrator) *Poetry Comics: A Cartooniverse of Poems,* Simon & Schuster (New York City), 1980.
*The Happy Birthday Handbook,* Toothpaste Press, 1982.
*How to Make Poetry Comics,* Teachers and Writers (New York City), 1984.
(Illustrator) Edwin Finckel, *Now We'll Make the Rafters Ring: Classic and Contemporary Rounds for Everyone,* A Cappella/Chicago Review Press, 1993.
(Author of English-language text) Ursel Scheffler, *Sun Jack and Rain Jack,* illustrated by Jutta Timm, Gareth Stevens (Milwaukee, WI), 1993.
(Illustrator) *More Poetry Comics,* A Cappella/Chicago Review Press, 1994.
(Illustrator) Richard Lederer, *Pun and Games: Jokes, Riddles, Rhymes, Daffynitions, Tairy Fales, and More Wordplay for Kids,* Chicago Review Press, 1996.

*PLAYS*

*The Umbrella That Predicted the Future* (three-act), first produced in Iowa City, IA, at Wesley House Auditorium, 1974.
*A Light Draw* (one-act puppet play), first produced in Iowa City, at The Mill, 1975.
*Stargazers* (one-act), first produced in Iowa City, at The Wheel Room, 1977.
*The Naked Stage* (one-act), first produced in Iowa City, at The Mill, 1982.

*TEACHING MANUALS*

*A Tourist's Guide to Computers,* Simon & Schuster, 1982.
*The Adventures of Dr. Alphabet: 104 Unusual Ways to Write Poetry in the Classroom and the Community,* Teachers and Writers, 1995.

*OTHER*

Creator of classroom materials for elementary and junior high schools, and for senior citizen classes. Editor and illustrator of comic books, including *Dada Comix,* 1978, *Poetry Comics,* 1979-82, and *Phooey,* 1983-84. Editor, *Gum,* 1970-73; co-editor, *The No. II Son,* 1969, and *Candy,* 1973. Editor, *Matchbook* (magazine of one-word poetry), 1970-75; guest editor, *Out of Sight,* 1972. Author of "Kickshaws," a column in *Word Ways: A Journal of Recreational Linguistics,* 1986—.

*UNDER PSEUDONYM DR. ALPHABET*

*Poetry City, U.S.A.,* Happy Press, 1977.

*UNDER PSEUDONYM JOYCE HOLLAND*

*The Tenth J,* Toothpaste Press, 1972.
*Alphabet Anthology,* X Press (Iowa City), 1973.
*The Final E,* Happy Press, 1979.

*SIDELIGHTS:* Dave Morice told *CA:* "My work revolves around words and pictures. I like to find new forms that combine the two and that involve other forms of expression, such as sculpture and theater, as well. I also like to write and draw in traditional forms.

"When I was six years old, I wrote and illustrated rhyming 'porquois' poems, such as 'Why the Giraffe Has Spots,' and gave them to my mother. She gave me much encouragement to keep doing it, and I did. In high school, I almost wrote a novel titled *Frankenstein Versus the New York Yankees.*

"I minored in creative writing at St. Louis University. A few years after I graduated, one creative writing teacher told me he thought I'd be the only student who would not become a writer. While I was in the Iowa Writers Workshop, I took 'Life Drawing 2.' At the end of the semester, the teacher told me I should have taken 'Life Drawing 1.' My advice to beginning writers and illustrators is simple: don't take criticism too seriously.

"I view life as a series of moments. There are a few big moments, which we live to do—for instance, experiencing the birth of one's child. The big moments are separated by many little moments, which we do to live—the daily routines of eating, sleeping, reading, and feeding the cat. The big moments are transcendental.

"I mark the years of my life according to ongoing projects that evolve over a long period of time, take many little moments to accomplish, and generate a few big moments as a result. One of these projects was the Joyce Holland Literary Hoax. From 1972 to 1975 I wrote concrete poems and published them in literary magazines under the name Joyce Holland, without revealing my 'secret identity.' My girlfriend Pat Casteel played the physical role of Joyce Holland and gave readings in a number of places. She gave Joyce a personality.

"Another project was the Poetry Marathons. In 1973 I wrote the first one, a thousand poems in twelve hours at Epstein's Bookstore in Iowa City. Since then, I've written about sixty different marathons for various art festivals and school visits, including a Poem Wrapping a City Block, a Poem Off the Top of a Ten-Story Building, a Poem Across the Delaware River, and several Poems Wrapping Schools.

"In 1973 I also helped to found the Actualist Movement, a group of poets on the other side of the tracks from the Iowa Writers Workshop. We held three art festivals, called Actualist Conventions, organized several poetry reading series, and published many literary magazines and books. Actualism attempted to bring poetry to the people and to make it fun.

"In 1974 I made up an alter-ego, Dr. Alphabet, for appearances at art festivals, children's fairs, and school visits in general. I usually wear an 'alphabet hat,' which is a white tophat painted in different colors of letters of the alphabet. Sometimes I dress up in alphabet-spangled shirt, pants, and shoes, too, and write with an alphabet cane tipped with a felt marker.

"The Wooden Nickel Art Project began in 1985. I gave out artist's wooden nickels to friends, relatives, and strangers, asking them to write or draw anything they wanted on the blank side, and to sign and date the other side. I also sent the nickels to about two-thousand well-known people, from world leaders to children's writer and illustrators. Four hundred of them, including Bob Hope, Corazon Aquino, and Dr. Seuss, sent their nickels back with writing or drawing on them.

"For the past eight years, I've taught children's literature at the University of Iowa. This has given me a great opportunity to learn about children's books and to discuss them with students who are adults. For most of the students, it's a welcome reunion with characters that they met in childhood. They rediscover the magic that they once knew on a daily basis.

"Aside from the many benefits that children's books provide to children, they also offer a wider range of creative choices for those who write and draw children's picture books. Mainstream criticism rarely deals with children's authors and illustrators. Consequently, they don't have to conform to current trends; they have the freedom to use old or new forms in their book art.

"My favorite project is raising my son Danny. I've read children's books to him ever since he was born, and now he reads Shel Silverstein's poems to me. From my experiences with Danny, I've learned more about children, language, art, word play, teaching, cooking, and life than words can express. It's a never-ending, ever-changing process of learning."

* * *

**MORRIS, James (Humphrey)**
**See MORRIS, Jan**

* * *

**MORRIS, Jan 1926-**

*PERSONAL:* Formerly James Humphrey Morris; name changed to Jan Morris after sex change, 1972; born October 2, 1926, in Clevedon, Somerset, England; child of Walter and Enid (Payne) Morris; wife's name, Elizabeth (divorced); five children. *Education:* Christ Church, Oxford, B.A. (second class honors), 1951, M.A., 1961.

*ADDRESSES: Home*—Trefan Morys, Llanystumdwy, Gwynedd, Wales.

*CAREER:* *Western Daily Press,* Bristol, England, member of editorial staff, 1944; Arab News Agency, Cairo, Egypt, member of editorial staff, 1947-48; *Times,* London, member of editorial staff, 1951-56, and special correspondent in Egypt, Scandinavia, the Netherlands, India, and the United States; *Guardian,* Manchester, England, member of editorial staff, 1956-61; freelance writer, 1961—. *Military service:* British Army, Ninth Lancers, 1943-47; became lieutenant.

*MEMBER:* Royal Society of Literature (fellow).

*AWARDS, HONORS:* Commonwealth Fund fellow, 1953; Cafe Royal Prize, 1957, for *Coast to Coast;* George Polk Memorial Award, 1960; Heinemann Award, Royal Society of Literature, 1961, for *Venice;* D. Litt., University of Wales,

*WRITINGS:*

UNDER NAME JAMES MORRIS

*As I Saw the U.S.A.,* Pantheon, 1956 (published in England as *Coast to Coast,* Faber, 1956, second edition, 1962).

*Islam Inflamed: A Middle East Picture,* Pantheon, 1957 (published in England as *The Market of Seleukia,* Faber, 1957).

*Sultan in Oman: Venture into the Middle East,* Pantheon, 1957.

*Coronation Everest,* Dutton, 1958.

*South African Winter,* Pantheon, 1958.

*The Hashemite Kings,* Pantheon, 1959.

*The World of Venice,* Pantheon, 1960, revised edition, 1974 (published in England as *Venice,* Faber, 1960, revised edition, 1974, revised, Harcourt Brace, 1995).

*The Upstairs Donkey, and Other Stolen Stories* (juvenile), Pantheon, 1961.

*South America,* Manchester Guardian and Evening News Ltd., 1961.

*The Road to Huddersfield: A Journey to Five Continents* (Book-of-the-Month Club selection), Pantheon, 1963 (published in England as *The World Bank: A Prospect,* Faber, 1963).

*Cities,* Faber, 1963, Harcourt, 1964.

*The Outriders: A Liberal View of Britain,* Faber, 1963.

*The Presence of Spain,* Harcourt, 1964, published as *Spain,* Faber, 1970, reprinted, Prentice Hall, 1988.

*Oxford,* Harcourt, 1965, third edition, Oxford University Press, 1988, reprinted, 1993.

*Pax Britannica: The Climax of an Empire* (first book of trilogy), Harcourt, 1968.

*The Great Port: A Passage through New York,* Harcourt, 1969, reprinted, Oxford University Press, 1985.

(Author of introduction) Roger Wood, *Persia,* Thames & Hudson, 1969, Universe Books, 1970.

*Places,* Faber, 1972, Harcourt, 1973.

*Heaven's Command: An Imperial Progress* (second book of trilogy), Harcourt, 1973.

*Farewell the Trumpets: An Imperial Retreat* (third book of trilogy), Harcourt, 1978.

UNDER NAME JAN MORRIS

*Conundrum* (autobiography), Harcourt, 1974.

*Travels,* Harcourt, 1976.

(Editor) *The Oxford Book of Oxford,* Oxford University Press, 1978.

*Destinations: Essays from "Rolling Stone,"* Oxford University Press, 1980.

(Editor) *My Favorite Stories of Wales,* Lutterworth, 1980.

*The Venetian Empire: A Sea Voyage,* Harcourt, 1980.

*The Spectacle of Empire,* Doubleday, 1982.

*A Venetian Bestiary,* Thames & Hudson, 1982.

(Compiler) *Wales,* Oxford University Press, 1982.

*Stones of Empire: The Buildings of the Raj,* Oxford University Press, 1984.

*Among the Cities,* Oxford University Press, 1985.

*Journeys,* Oxford University Press, 1985.

*Last Letters from Hav: Notes from a Lost City* (novel), Random House, 1985.

*The Matter of Wales: Epic Views of a Small Country,* Oxford University Press, 1985.

*Scotland: The Place of Journeys,* Crown, 1986.

(With others) *Architecture of the British Empire,* Vendome, 1986.

*Manhattan, '45,* Oxford University Press, 1987.

*Hong Kong,* Random House, 1988 (published in England as *Hong Kong: Xianggang,* Viking, 1988).

(Author of introduction) John Ruskin, *The Stones of Venice,* Moyer Bell Limited, 1989.

*Pleasures of a Tangled Life* (autobiography), Random House, 1989.

*Ireland: Your Only Place,* Potter, 1990.

*City to City,* Macfarlane, Walter, & Ross, 1990, reprinted as *O Canada: Travels in an Unknown Country,* HarperCollins (New York City), 1992.

(Author of introduction) Fergus Bordewich, *Cathay: A Journey in Search of Old China,* Prentice Hall, 1991.

*Sydney,* Random House, 1992.

(Author of introduction) John Ryder, *Intimate Leaves from a Designer's Notebook,* Gwasg, 1993.

*Locations,* Oxford University Press, 1993.

*A Machynlleth Triad,* Viking, 1994.

*Fisher's Face, or, Getting to Know the Admiral,* Random House, 1995.

*The Princeship of Wales,* Gomer, 1995.

*The World of Venice,* Harcourt, 1995.

Also author of *Scotland: Place of Visions, Over Europe,* and *The Last Old Space.*

*SIDELIGHTS:* A critically acclaimed British journalist and travel essayist, Jan Morris has written numerous books on travels and adventures around the world. Known to readers under the name James Morris until changing genders in a sex-change operation, Morris is "a traveler whose journeys have been both physical and philosophical, a writer who has written of the clash of armies and the history of empires, a former soldier and foreign correspondent," writes Lynn Darling in the *Washington Post.* As a reporter for the London *Times* in the 1950s, Morris gained fame for covering the Mt. Everest climbing expedition of Sir Edmund Hillary. From 22,000 feet up the mountain and through an ingeniously organized communications system, Morris "scooped the world with the news of Hillary's . . . triumph," reports John Richardson. Morris later recounted the landmark event in the 1958 book *Coronation Everest.* Following her career as a journalist, Morris traveled around the world, reporting on wars and rebellions, while writing numerous history and travel books.

Among Morris's most acclaimed works are her travel accounts, which are praised for their original and readable look at different places and cultures around the world. "Her travel books are oddly reassuring, showing us that there are more ways of experiencing cultures than most of us supposed," writes Anatole Broyard in the *New York Times.* "In her wanderlust, she is like a lover looking for consummation—and she finds it in the most unlikely places." From *O Canada: Travels in an Unknown Country* to *Sydney,* she combines history, topography, and the social landscape in a unique manner: through her "attention to details," her "unpredictable but not capricious reactions," and "her willingness to show the sleight of hand behind travel-writing and destroy the illusion of all-knowingness," according to Stevenson Swanson in Chicago *Tribune Books.* In the essay collections *Locations* and *Journeys,* Morris combines impressions of trips taken during several decades, layering them to form a collage of the urban landscape but with an eye towards removing the outer shell of hyperbole. As Gary Krist explains in his review of *Journeys* for the *New York Times Book Review,* Morris "displays an uncanny ability to unearth the essential character of a place, a character that often lies hidden beneath tons of chamber-of-commerce cant." Equally insightful is her vast experience and deeply rooted love of history. "Among Morris' gifts is the ability to have a present trip call up an earlier expedition," writes Joan Tapper in the *Washington Post Book World,* "and one era—today's or even tomorrow's—suggest a distant, almost forgotten past."

The past in the form of the rise and fall of the British Empire is a topic that frequently falls to Morris's pen. Her trilogy that includes *Heaven's Command: An Imperial Progress, Pax Britannica: The Climax of an Empire,* and *Farewell the Trumpets: An Imperial Retreat* has been highly praised for its portrayal of the spectrum of British history, from Queen Victoria's claim of the throne in 1837 to the funeral of Winston Churchill in 1965. *The Spectacle of Empire,* which Morris published in 1982, expands the study by including a collection of photographs that, framed by Morris's prose, reveal what Sam Hall Kaplan refers to as "a heady, contradictory imperialistic mix of noblesse oblige, arrogance, racism, ostentation, plus sense of purpose and fair play" in his review in the *Los Angeles Times.* Morris provides a fitting end to her examination of the Empire with *Hong Kong: Epilogue to an Empire,* a book based on four decades of observations by the author.

The history of Venice has also captivated Morris for many years, and she has shared her interest with readers through several books. *The Venetian Empire: A Sea Voyage,* published in 1980, blends Morris's unique brand of travel writing with social and political history, beginning in 1203 with the destruction of the Byzantine city of Constantinople during the Fourth Crusade. A sequel of sorts to her popular 1960 travelogue *Venice, The Venetian Empire* involves Morris taking her readers on a trip through the Mediterranean, "disembarking wherever there is a sight to be seen or a story to be told," notes *Spectator* contributor J. G. Links, "in those eloquent and elegant words which fall so lightly from her pen."

1982's *A Venetian Bestiary,* which Links calls an epilogue to the author's previous writing on Venice, describes the creatures that have been immortalized in the city's art, literature, and legend. Well illustrated, the volume includes descriptions of the various animals—lions, bears, cats, dogs, exotic birds, and even crocodiles—that fell under the care of famous, and not so famous, Venetians over the centuries.

In 1995 Morris published *Fisher's Face: or, Getting to Know the Admiral,* a biography of a famed British Naval commander who died in 1920. Fascinated with the life of this man for decades, Morris based her book on a great deal of travel and research into Fisher's past. Born in Ceylon, Fisher joined the British Navy at age thirteen, dedicating the remainder of his life to His Majesty's service. Attaining the rank of First Sea Lord, Fisher is credited with transforming the British Navy into a modern institution, welcoming advanced technologies that replaced sailing ships with such modernities as oil-fired furnaces and iron hulls. However, *Fisher's Face* is less a book about British Naval history than it is about the character of the Admiral himself, and Morris, who "hero-worshipped Fisher for decades, and visited almost every building where he spent a night," has written what Nigel Nicolson calls "a book about his remarkable character," in a review for the *New York Times Book Review.* Nicolson adds that Morris uses so human-centered a viewpoint that she "can elaborate actual events by inventing the detail, and at one point imagines herself bending over the admiral, wounded in an imaginary battle." However, her respect for the man has not blinded the author to his faults; Fisher's bravado, cruelty, and philandering are amply documented. While agreeing that *Fisher's Face* is entertaining to read, Ken Ringle contends that Morris's volume falls short of the rigid criteria that would make it a useful biography. "Morris dances us past that hole in the scenery where real life lurks and the costumes fall away and power is more than a pose," the reviewer notes in the *Washington Post Book World.* "But we can't quite forget it's there. . . . And the reader is left with the gnawing certainty that Morris has dazzled herself with her own literary tricks and loved her subject not wisely but too well."

In addition to tours across nations, through historical epochs, and into the minds of men, modern cities receive their due scrutiny from Morris. In *Among the Cities,* which she published in 1985, Morris collects essays published after a trek she took to every major city on Earth: from Alexandria, Egypt, to Hamburg, Germany, and Los Angeles, California. "Serendipity, with a dash of contrivance, is Miss Morris's special skill," Nicholas Wollaston opines in his review of the book in the *Observer.* And remarking on the author's ruminations on the urban landscape that comprise Morris's *Destinations: Essays from Rolling Stone* in the *New York Times,* Anatole Broyard calls the collection "a book about great cities, their moods, their manners and their response to time. Jan Morris is a connoisseur of cities, someone who approaches them, as almost none of their inhabitants do, as places simply to *be.* She submits herself to cities and then tells us what they do to her, say to her."

Supplementing her travel books, Morris has written about her personal history. In the autobiographical *Conundrum,* she relates, "I was 3 or perhaps 4 years old when I realized that I had been born into the wrong body, and should really be a girl." In 1964, Morris began the transformation into the female Jan Morris by taking hormone pills; in 1972, the process was completed through surgery. A *Newsweek* writer calls *Conundrum* "certainly the best first-hand account ever written by a traveler across the boundaries of sex. That journey is perhaps the ultimate adventure for a human being, but although it has been the subject of myth and speculation since ancient times, it is an authentically modern experience." Regarding being a transsexual, Morris told Lorraine Kisly: "No one has ever been able to convince a real transsexual that his convictions about his true nature were wrong. No doctor or scientist can say where the conviction comes from, and for me it is a spiritual question, a matter of my soul, much deeper and broader than sexual preference or mode." The *Newsweek* writer comments that "Morris can offer no real answer to the central mystery; neither she nor the scientists of this era can explain with any certainty why a transsexual's mind and body are at odds with each other. What Jan Morris does offer, through her life and her work, is a window on the wondrous possibilities of humankind." Morris followed *Conundrum* with a second autobiographical book, *Pleasures of a Tangled Life,* which, as William French remarks in the Toronto *Globe and Mail,* "emphasiz[es] the happy side of her life and the sources of her pleasures."

*BIOGRAPHICAL/CRITICAL SOURCES:*

*BOOKS*

Morris, Jan, *Conundrum,* Harcourt, 1974.

Morris, Jan, *Pleasures of a Tangled Life,* Random House, 1989.

*PERIODICALS*

*Book World,* January 12, 1969.
*Chicago Tribune,* December 16, 1988; January 22, 1989.
*Christian Science Monitor,* October 13, 1959.
*Commentary,* March, 1989, p. 67.
*Economist,* March 18, 1995, p. 85.
*Globe and Mail* (Toronto), October 20, 1984; November 25, 1989.
*Harper's,* August, 1974.
*Los Angeles Times,* July 18, 1984; June 17, 1985.
*Los Angeles Times Book Review,* November 28, 1982, p. 2; January 15, 1989; July 9, 1995, pp. 1, 11.
*Maclean's,* December 21, 1992, p. 32.
*Manchester Guardian,* August 19, 1960.
*New Statesman,* December 5, 1959; October 25, 1968.
*New Statesman & Society,* March 10, 1995, p. 40.
*Newsweek,* August 5, 1963; April 8, 1974.
*New Yorker,* December 20, 1982.
*New York Review of Books,* May 2, 1974.
*New York Times,* May 17, 1980; May 31, 1984; March 1, 1985; March 19, 1987; May 22, 1987; January 3, 1989.
*New York Times Book Review,* April 14, 1974; November 19, 1978; December 5, 1982, p. 65; June 3, 1984, pp. 11-12; January 29, 1989, p. 35; November 12, 1989, p. 16; May 31, 1992, p. 32; December 6, 1992, p. 9; June 11, 1995, p. 36.
*New York Times Magazine,* March 17, 1974.
*Observer,* June 9, 1985; February 26, 1995, p. 15.
*Playboy,* January, 1991, p. 29.
*Saturday Evening Post,* July 3, 1965.
*Spectator,* October 25, 1980, p. 21; October 16, 1982, pp. 26-27; January 21, 1984, pp. 25-26; May 16, 1992, p. 31.
*Time,* April 3, 1987; January 16, 1989, p. 72.
*Times* (London), August 14, 1980; November 17, 1983; November 29, 1984; October 10, 1985; October 22, 1988.
*Times Literary Supplement,* October 7-13, 1988; December 8-14, 1989.
*Tribune Books* (Chicago), October 29, 1989; June 7, 1992, p. 5.
*Washington Post,* July 3, 1980; January 4, 1987; March 25, 1987.
*Washington Post Book World,* June 17, 1984, p. 11; October 15, 1989; June 11, 1995, p. 1.*

# N-O

**NARAYAN, R(asipuram) K(rishnaswami) 1906-**

*PERSONAL:* Born October 10, 1906, in Madras, India. *Education:* Maharaja's College (now University of Mysore), received degree, 1930.

*ADDRESSES:* *Home*—15 Vivekananda Rd., Yadavagiri 2, Mysore, India. *Agent*—Anthony Sheil Associates, 2-3 Maxwell St., London WC1B 3AR, England.

*CAREER:* Writer. Owner of Indian Thought Publications, Mysore, India.

*MEMBER:* American Academy and Institute of Arts and Letters (honorary member).

*AWARDS, HONORS:* National Prize of the Indian Literary Academy, 1958; Padma Bhushan, India, 1964; National Association of Independent Schools award, 1965; D.Litt., University of Leeds, 1967; English-Speaking Union Book Award, 1975, for *My Days: A Memoir;* American Academy and Institute of Arts and Letters citation, 1982.

*WRITINGS:*

*NOVELS*

*Swami and Friends: A Novel of Malgudi,* Hamish Hamilton (London), 1935, Fawcett (New York City), 1970, published with *The Bachelor of Arts,* Michigan State College Press (East Lansing), 1957.

*The Bachelor of Arts,* Nelson (London), 1937, published with *Swami and Friends,* Michigan State College Press, 1957.

*The Dark Room,* Macmillan (London), 1938.

*The English Teacher,* Eyre & Spottiswoode (London), 1945, published as *Grateful to Life and Death,* Michigan State College Press, 1953.

*Mr. Sampath,* Eyre & Spottiswoode, 1949, published as *The Printer of Malgudi,* Michigan State College Press, 1957.

*The Financial Expert,* Methuen (London), 1952, Michigan State College Press, 1953.

*Waiting for the Mahatma,* Michigan State College Press, 1955.

*The Guide,* Viking (New York City), 1958.

*The Man-Eater of Malgudi,* Viking, 1961.

*The Vendor of Sweets,* Viking, 1967, published as *The Sweet-Vendor,* Bodley Head (London), 1967.

*The Painter of Signs,* Viking, 1976.

*A Tiger for Malgudi,* Viking, 1983.

*Talkative Man,* Heinemann (London), 1986, Viking, 1987.

*The World of Nagaraj,* Viking, 1990.

*SHORT STORIES*

*Malgudi Days,* Indian Thought (Mysore, India), 1943.

*Dodu and Other Stories,* Indian Thought, 1943.

*Cyclone and Other Stories,* Indian Thought, 1944.

*An Astrologer's Day and Other Stories,* Eyre & Spottiswoode, 1947.

*Lawley Road,* Indian Thought, 1956.

*Gods, Demons and Others,* Viking, 1964, illustrated by R. K. Laxman, University of Chicago Press (Chicago), 1993.

*A Horse and Two Goats and Other Stories,* Viking, 1970.

*Old and New,* Indian Thought, 1981.

*Malgudi Days* (new collection), Viking, 1982.

*Under the Banyan Tree and Other Stories,* Viking, 1985.

*Malgudi Days II,* Viking, 1986.

*The Grandmother's Tale,* illustrated by Laxman, Indian Thought, 1992, published as *The Grandmother's Tale, and Selected Stories,* Viking, 1994.

*Salt & Sawdust: Stories and Table Talk,* Penguin (New Delhi), 1993.

Contributor of short stories to periodicals, including *New Yorker.*

*OTHER*

*Mysore,* Government Branch Press (Mysore), 1939.

*Next Sunday: Sketches and Essays,* Indian Thought, 1956, Pearl Publications, 1960.

*My Dateless Diary: A Journal of a Trip to the United States in October 1956,* Indian Thought, 1960, Penguin (New York City), 1965.

(Translator) *The Ramayana: A Shortened Modern Prose Version of the Indian Epic,* Viking, 1972.

*My Days: A Memoir,* Viking, 1974.

*Reluctant Guru,* Hind Pocket Books (New Delhi), 1974.

*The Emerald Route* (included play *The Watchman of the Lake*), Government of Karnataka (Bangalore), 1977, Ind-US Inc. (Glastonbury, CT), 1980.

(Translator) *The Mahabharata: A Shortened Prose Version of the Indian Epic,* Viking, 1978.

*A Writer's Nightmare: Selected Essays, 1958-1988,* Penguin, 1988, Penguin (New York City), 1989.

*A Story-Teller's World: Stories, Essays, Sketches,* Penguin, 1989, Viking, 1990.

(Editor) *Indian Thought: A Miscellany,* Penguin, 1997.

*ADAPTATIONS:* Narayan's *The Guide* was adapted for the stage by Harvey Breit and Patricia Rinehart and produced Off-Broadway at the Hudson Theatre, 1968.

*SIDELIGHTS:* R. K. Narayan is perhaps the best-known Indian writing in English today. His long and prolific career has been marked by well-received novels, novellas, and short stories, almost all of which are set in the fictional backwater town of Malgudi and its environs. Noting that Narayan has produced "India's most distinguished literary career of recent times," *New York Times Book Review* correspondent Shashi Tharoor went on to declare: "In the West, Mr. Narayan is widely considered the quintessential Indian writer, whose fiction evokes a sensibility and a rhythm older and less familiar to Westerners than that of any other writer in the English language."

According to Phil Hogan in the *Observer,* "Narayan . . . said he was 'a storyteller, nothing more, nothing less.' R. K. Narayan is no more just a storyteller than the Taj Mahal is a large building with a swimming pool. . . . Malgudi may be in the middle of nowhere but all life is here."

In a British Broadcasting Corporation radio interview, Narayan spoke to William Walsh of his use of the English language in his work: "English has been with us [in India] for over a century and a half. I am particularly fond of the language. I was never aware that I was using a different, a foreign, language when I wrote in English, because it came to me very easily. I can't explain how. English is a very adaptable language. And it's so transparent it can take on the tint of any country." Walsh added in his study *R. K. Narayan* that Narayan's English "is limpid, simple, calm and unaffected, natural in its run and tone, and beautifully measured" in a unique fashion that takes on an Indian flavor by avoiding "the American purr of the combustion engine . . . [and] the thick marmalade quality of British English."

Other critics have noted the rhythms of Narayan's style and the richness of his narrative. Melvin J. Friedman suggested in a comparison with Isaac Bashevis Singer that "both seem part of an oral tradition in which the 'spoken' triumphs over the 'written,'" and theorized that the similarities between Narayan's fiction and the Indian epics echo Singer's prose style and its "rhythm of the Old Testament." Eve Auchincloss noted that the translation-like quality of the language "adds curious, pleasing flavor."

Narayan's fictional setting is Malgudi, a village very similar to his childhood home, Mysore. In Malgudi every sort of human condition indigenous not only to India but to life everywhere is represented. Malgudi has perhaps inevitably drawn comparisons to William Faulkner's Yoknapatawpha County, both because Narayan returns to its setting again and again, and because he uses its eccentric citizens to meditate upon the human condition in a global context. "Narayan might . . . be called Faulknerian," wrote Warren French, "because against the background of a squalid community he creates characters with a rare quality that can only be called 'compassionate disenchantment.'" French also noted that both Narayan and Faulkner write frequently of "an unending conflict between individuality and the demands of tradition," typifying their respective geographical settings in such a way as to become universal by extension. Charles R. Larson demonstrated similar parallels but reflected that "while Faulkner's vision remains essentially grotesque, Narayan's has been predominantly comic, reflecting with humor the struggle of the individual consciousness to find peace within the framework of public life." In the *Times Literary Supplement,* Walsh stressed the universal quality of Malgudi: "Whatever happens in India happens in Malgudi, and whatever happens in Malgudi happens everywhere."

The characters in Narayan's novels and short stories often experience some kind of growth or change, or gain knowledge through the experiences they undergo. As Walsh observed, Narayan most often focuses on the middle class and its representative occupations, many of which provide the author with titles for his books: *The Bachelor of Arts, The English Teacher, The Financial Expert, The Guide, The Sweet-Vendor.* Walsh explained Narayan's typical structural pattern in terms of concentric circles, whereby the village represents the outer circle, the family is the inner circle, and the hero, the focus of each novel, stands at the hub. "His hero is usually modest, sensitive, ardent, wry about himself," wrote Walsh, "and sufficiently conscious to have an active inner life and to grope towards some existence independent of the family." Walsh further observed that the typical progress of a Narayan hero involves "the rebirth of self and the progress of its pregnancy or education," thereby suggesting the Indian concept of reincarnation. "Again and again Narayan gives us the account of an evolving consciousness," wrote Larson, "beginning in isolation and confusion and ending in wholeness (peace within the traditional Hindu faith)" while maintaining a unique freshness of presentation.

Closely related to Narayan's gift for characterization is his ability to present his material with sympathy and comic vision. *Los Angeles Times Book Review* contributor Judith Freeman wrote: "[Narayan] takes a Western reader into the very heart of an Indian village and the family compounds where the little dramas of marriage and money and kinship inevitably result in a tangle of human ties. The foreignness of the setting, rituals and traditions may seem to us exotic, but the underlying humanity of Narayan's dramas can't fail to strike a familiar chord." The critic added: "What is so lovely about Narayan's work, and what makes it so valuable in a world torn by racial misunderstanding, is the gentleness of his vision, the way he makes each of us a member of his wondrous universe." Walsh wrote of Narayan's "forgiving kindness" and labeled his novels "comedies of sadness . . . lighted with the glint of mockery of both self and others."

Narayan has been hailed as the last working writer in a generation that included W. H. Auden, Graham Greene, and Evelyn Waugh. Greene, for one, has found much to praise in Narayan's work, once citing his Indian contemporary as "the novelist I most admire in the English language." Few if any detractors have arisen as Narayan has entered his seventh decade of publishing with a well-received novel entitled *The World of Nagaraj* and a story collection, *The Grandmother's Tale.* "As his new collection of stories makes clear," Freeman observed, "age has not diminished his talent but simply added an extra dimension of wisdom to his remarkable and enduring vision."

In an *Observer* review of *The World of Nagaraj,* Hanif Kureishi wrote: "Narayan is a master, in control of all his subtle effects. He is very funny: his use of irony is superb, and there is much going on in the tiny world he describes." The critic concluded: "Next time you labour through a long, tediously clever new novel, think of the wisdom and humour Narayan gently slips into his small but luminous masterpieces." *The World of Nagaraj* offers a gentle tale of an easy-going townsman whose life is bedeviled by the dual trials of caring for his wayward nephew and trying to write a book about an obscure Indian saint. *New York Times Book Review* essayist Julian Moynahan declared that with *The World of Nagaraj* Narayan offers "the latest building block in a shining edifice . . . [a] subtly variegated and self-authenticating world of fiction in light of certain universal truths."

*The Grandmother's Tale and Selected Stories* is the closest publishers have come to printing an omnibus of Narayan's best short fiction. The title story was first published in India in 1992; other stories in the collection span the author's long career. In her *New York Review of Books* essay on the work, Hilary Mantel observed that Narayan makes his world familiar to non-Indian readers. "He can do this because he has such a sharp eye," Mantel explained, adding that "Life surprises him. . . . Any day, any street, any room in an accustomed house, any face known since childhood, can suddenly be fresh and strange and new; one reality peels away, and shows another underneath."

Mantel further maintained that through his body of work, Narayan has proven himself to be "a writer of towering achievement who has cultivated and preserved the lightest of touches." The critic concluded: "Celebrant of both the outer and inner life, he makes us feel the vulnerability of human beings and of their social bonds. Here is the town with its daylight bustle; . . . outside, and within, are the deep forests, where tigers roar in the night."

*BIOGRAPHICAL/CRITICAL SOURCES:*

*BOOKS*

Beatina, Mary, *Narayan: A Study in Transcendence,* P. Lang (New York City), 1993.

*Contemporary Literary Criticism,* Gale (Detroit), Volume 7, 1977; Volume 28, 1984; Volume 47, 1988, pp. 300-09.

*Contemporary Novelists,* St. James Press (Detroit), 1996, pp. 752-55.

Goyal, Bhagwat S., editor, *R. K. Narayan's India: Myth and Reality,* Sarup & Sons (New Delhi), 1993.

Hariprasanna, A., *The World of Malgudi: A Study of R. K. Narayan's Novels,* Prestige Books (New Delhi), 1994.

Kain, Geoffrey, editor, *R. K. Narayan: Contemporary Critical Perspectives,* Michigan State University Press (East Lansing), 1993.

Krishnan, S., editor, *Malgudi Landscapes: The Best of R. K. Narayan,* Penguin (New York City), 1992.

Pousse, Michel, *R. K. Narayan: A Painter of Modern India,* P. Lang, 1995.

*Season of Promise: Spring Fiction,* University of Missouri (Columbia), 1967.

Sharan, Nagendra Nath, *A Critical Study of the Novels of R. K. Narayan,* Classical Publishing (New Delhi), 1993.

Varma, R. M., *Major Themes in the Novels of R. K. Narayan,* Jainsons Publications (New Delhi), 1993.

Walsh, William, *R. K. Narayan,* Longman (New York City), 1971.

*PERIODICALS*

*Ariel,* January, 1984.

*Banasthali Patrika,* January 12, 1969; July 13, 1969.

*Books Abroad,* summer, 1965; spring, 1971; spring, 1976.

*Book World,* July 11, 1976; December 5, 1976.

*Christian Science Monitor,* February 19, 1970.

*Daedalus,* fall, 1989, p. 232.

*Encounter,* October, 1964.

*Harper's,* April, 1965.

*Journal of Commonwealth Literature,* December, 1966.

*Listener,* March 1, 1962.

*Literary Criterion,* winter, 1968.

*Literature East and West,* winter, 1965.

*London Magazine,* September, 1970.

*London Review of Books,* December 4, 1986, pp. 23-24.

*Los Angeles Times Book Review,* October 23, 1994, p. 12; December 11, 1994, p. 9; January 29, 1995, p. 8.

*Modern Fiction Studies,* spring, 1993, pp. 113-30.

*Nation,* June 28, 1975.

*New Republic,* May 13, 1967.

*New Statesman,* June 2, 1967.

*Newsweek,* July 4, 1976.

*New Yorker,* September 15, 1962; October 14, 1967; March 16, 1968; July 5, 1976, p. 82; August 2, 1982, p. 84.

*New York Review of Books,* June 29, 1967; October 8, 1987, p. 45; February 16, 1995, pp. 9-11.

*New York Times,* March 23, 1958, p. 5; August 1, 1965; June 20, 1976; August 8, 1983; March 14, 1987, p. 14.

*New York Times Book Review,* May 14, 1967; June 20, 1976; September 4, 1983, p. 4; July 8, 1990, p. 8; July 15, 1990, p. 8; September 11, 1994, p. 40.

*Observer* (London), March 25, 1990, p. 66; July 18, 1993, p. 57.

*Osmania Journal of English Studies,* Volume VII, number 1, 1970.

*Sewanee Review,* winter, 1975.

*Times Literary Supplement,* May 18, 1967; October 18, 1985, p. 1168; October 3, 1986, p. 1113; March 23-29, 1990, p. 328; July 23, 1993, p. 20.

*Village Voice,* November 5, 1985, p. 55.

*Wall Street Journal,* August 22, 1983, p. 14.

*Washington Post,* April 14, 1970.

*Washington Post Book World,* September 4, 1983, pp. 3, 9; July 28, 1985, pp. 7, 13; April 5, 1987, p. 7.

*World Literature Today,* spring, 1984, p. 325.*

* * *

## NASH, (Frediric) Ogden 1902-1971

*PERSONAL:* Born August 19, 1902, in Rye, NY; died of heart failure, May 19, 1971, in Baltimore, MD; buried in Little River Cemetery, North Hampton, NH; son of Edmund Strudwick and Mattie (Chenault) Nash; married Frances Rider Leonard, June 6, 1931; children: Linell Chenault, Isabel Jackson. *Education:* Attended Harvard University, 1920-21.

*CAREER:* Poet, author; began writing light verse about 1925. Taught one year at St. George's School, Providence, RI; was a bond salesman on Wall Street, briefly in the mid-1920s; worked in the copy department of Barron Collier, writing streetcar ads; worked in the editorial and publicity departments of Doubleday, Doran & Co., 1925; member of *New Yorker* editorial staff, 1932; became full-time writer. Gave frequent lectures and readings; appeared on radio shows, including "Information, Please!," and the Bing Crosby and Rudy Vallee hours, and on television panel shows, including "Masquerade Party."

*MEMBER:* American Academy of Arts and Sciences, National Institute of Arts and Letters.

*AWARDS, HONORS:* Sarah Josepha Hale Award, 1964.

*WRITINGS:*

(With Joseph Alger) *Cricket of Carador,* Doubleday, 1925.

(With Christopher Morley, Cleon Throckmorton, and others) *Born in a Beer Garden; or, She Troupes to Conquer,* Rudge, 1930.

*Free Wheeling* (also see below), Simon & Schuster, 1931.

*Hard Lines,* Simon & Schuster, 1931, enlarged edition with selections from *Free Wheeling* published as *Hard Lines, and Others,* Duckworth, 1932.

(Editor) P. G. Wodehouse, *Nothing but Wodehouse,* Doubleday, 1932.

*Happy Days,* Simon & Schuster, 1933.

*Four Prominent So and So's* (music by Robert Armbruster), Simon & Schuster, 1934.

*The Primrose Path,* Simon & Schuster, 1935.

*The Bad Parents' Garden of Verse,* Simon & Schuster, 1936.

*The Firefly* (screenplay; adapted from Otto A. Harbach's play), Metro-Goldwyn-Mayer (MGM), 1937.

(With Jane Murfin) *The Shining Hair* (screenplay), MGM, 1938.

*I'm a Stranger Here Myself,* Little, Brown, 1938.

*The Face Is Familiar: The Selected Verse of Ogden Nash,* Little, Brown, 1940, revised edition, Dent, 1954.

(With George Oppenheimer and Edmund L. Hartmann) *The Feminine Touch* (screenplay), MGM, 1941.

*Good Intentions,* Little, Brown, 1942, revised edition, Dent, 1956.

(Author of book with S. J. Perelman, and of lyrics) *One Touch of Venus* (musical; music by Kurt Weill; first produced on Broadway, 1943), Little, Brown, 1944.

*The Ogden Nash Pocket Book,* Blakiston, 1944.

*Many Long Years Ago,* Little, Brown, 1945.

*The Selected Verse of Ogden Nash,* Modern Library, 1946.

*Ogden Nash's Musical Zoo* (music by Vernon Duke), Little, Brown, 1947.

*Versus,* Little, Brown, 1949.

*Family Reunion,* Little, Brown, 1950.

*Parents Keep Out: Elderly Poems for Youngerly Readers,* Little, Brown, 1951, enlarged edition, Dent, 1962.

*The Private Dining Room, and Other New Verses,* Little, Brown, 1953.

(Editor) *The Moon Is Shining Bright as Day: An Anthology of Good-Humored Verse,* Lippincott, 1953.

*The Pocket Book of Ogden Nash,* Pocket Books, 1954.

*You Can't Get There from Here,* Little, Brown, 1957.

*The Boy Who Laughed at Santa Claus* (keepsake edition), Cooper & Beatty Ltd. (London), 1957.

*The Christmas That Almost Wasn't,* Little, Brown, 1957.

(Editor) *I Couldn't Help Laughing: Stories Selected and Introduced by Ogden Nash,* Lippincott, 1957.

*Verses from 1929 On,* Little, Brown, 1959 (published in England as *Collected Verse from 1929 On,* Dent, 1961).

*Custard the Dragon,* Little, Brown, 1959, reprinted with illustrations by Lynn Munsinger, 1995.

*Beastly Poetry,* Hallmark Editions, 1960.

*A Boy Is a Boy: The Fun of Being a Boy,* Watts, 1960.

*Scrooge Rides Again,* Hart, 1960.

(Editor) *Everybody Ought to Know: Verses Selected and Introduced by Ogden Nash,* Lippincott, 1961.

*Custard the Dragon and the Wicked Knight,* Little, Brown, 1961.

*The New Nutcracker Suite, and Other Innocent Verses,* Little, Brown, 1962.

*Girls Are Silly,* Watts, 1962.

*Everyone but Thee and Me,* Little, Brown, 1962.

*A Boy and His Room,* Watts, 1963.

*The Adventures of Isabel,* Little, Brown, 1963.

*The Untold Adventures of Santa Claus,* Little, Brown, 1964.

*An Ogden Nash Bonanza* (five-volume omnibus), Little, Brown, 1964.

*Marriage Lines: Notes of a Student Husband,* Little, Brown, 1964 (published in England as *Notes of a Student Husband,* Dent, 1964).

*The Animal Garden,* Evans, 1965.

*The Mysterious Ouphe,* Spadea Press, 1965.
*Santa Go Home: A Case History for Parents,* Little, Brown, 1967.
*The Cruise of the Aardvark,* M. Evans, 1967.
*There's Always Another Windmill,* Little, Brown, 1968.
*Funniest Verses of Ogden Nash: Light Lyrics by One of America's Favorite Humorists,* selected by Dorothy Price, Hallmark Editions, 1968.
(With Edward Lear) *The Scroobious Pip,* Harper, 1968.
(With others) *New Comic Limericks: Laughable Poems,* compiled by Ivanette Dennis, Roger Schlesinger, 1969.
*Bed Riddance: A Posy for the Indisposed,* Little, Brown, 1970.
*The Old Dog Barks Backwards,* Little, Brown, 1972.
*I Wouldn't Have Missed It: Selected Poems of Ogden Nash,* selected by Linnel Smith and Isabel Eberstadt, Little, Brown, 1972.
*Custard and Company,* Little, Brown, 1980.
*A Penny Saved Is Impossible,* Little, Brown, 1981.
*Ogden Nash's Zoo,* edited by Roy Finamore, Stewart, Tabori, 1986.
*Ogden Nash's Food,* Stewart, Tabori, 1989.
*Loving Letters from Ogden Nash: A Family Album,* Little, Brown, 1990.
*Candy Is Dandy: The Best of Ogden Nash,* selected by Smith and Eberstadt, Deutsch, 1994.
*Selected Poetry of Ogden Nash: 650 Rhymes, Verses, Lyrics, and Poems,* Black Dog & Leventhal, 1995.

Also author of lyrics for Off-Broadway production *The Littlest Revue* and for television show *Art Carney Meets Peter and the Wolf.* Wrote new verses to Saint-Saens's "Carnival of the Animals," narrated by Noel Coward, for Columbia; author of verses set to Prokofiev's "Peter and the Wolf" and Dukas's "Sorcerer's Apprentice." Contributor of verse to periodicals, including *New Yorker, Life, Saturday Evening Post, Holiday, Saturday Review, Harper's, Atlantic, Vogue, McCall's,* and *New Republic.*

*ADAPTATIONS:* Weston Woods adapted *Custard the Dragon* as a filmstrip with cassette in 1962 and as a film in 1964.

*SIDELIGHTS:* Ogden Nash was among America's most popular and most frequently quoted contemporary poets, drawing large and receptive audiences to his lectures and readings. Known for such lines as "Candy / Is dandy, / But liquor / Is quicker" and "If called by a panther / Don't anther," Nash was "secure in his possession of all the best and worst rhymes outside of the rhyming dictionaries," according to P. M. Jack. He called himself a "worsifier," and his "worses" bear the mark of a unique style—whimsical, offbeat, yet sophisticated—which he called "my individual method for concealing my illiteracy." He freely admitted to having "intentionally maltreated and man-handled every known rule of grammar, prosody, and spelling," yet the result, suggests Albin Krebs in a *New York Times* obituary, on closer examination reveals "a carefully thought-out metrical scheme and a kind of relentless logic." "I like the style because it gives me a mask," Nash told an interviewer for *Holiday,* a "front behind which I can hide. I can't go straight to the point about anything emotionally valid; that's one of my faults, I get ponderous. By backing off I can make the point without belaboring it."

Nash rose to prominence in 1931 with *Hard Lines,* his first book of poetry. In a contemporary *New York Herald Tribune Books* review, Lisle Bell marvels at Nash's inventive and imaginative verse: "Here the English language is not only flexible; it is double-jointed, ambidextrous, telescopic, kaleidoscopic, and slightly demented." Four years later, Nash again won acclaim with *The Primrose Path. New York Times Book Review* contributor C. G. Poore writes, "[Nash] is still fundamentally and magnificently unsound." The publication of *I'm a Stranger Here Myself* prompted *New York Herald Tribune Books* critic Thomas Sugrue to characterize Nash as "a modern counterpart of the eighteenth century essayist," a shrewd and devastatingly accurate satirist of his fellow citizens, particularly the pretentious and suburban variety. For his sharp wit, Nash is also compared to Dorothy Parker, P. G. Wodehouse, G. K. Chesterton, and Mark Twain. Peter Munro Jack writes in the *New York Times Book Review,* "Mr. Nash has as many rhymes as we have follies, as many aspects of meter as we have absurdities of demeanor."

*Good Intentions,* published in 1942, received mixed assessment and marks a transition in Nash's poetry. Noting the poet's more mature, detached philosophical voice in this volume, Sugrue writes in *New York Herald Tribune Books* that *Good Intentions* "shows no advance or mutation in technique, but it reflects a more mellow personality, a less subjective approach to life, and a deadlier, deeper wit." His next volume, *Versus,* is a reiteration of his characteristic style with similar results. David McCord writes in the *New York Herald Tribune Weekly Review,* "Even in the poorest of his verses—and they are not too many. . .—the surprising idea, the enchanting line, the unbelievable rhyme may still reward the hunter. Which only goes to prove again that Mr. Nash is well outside all the categories."

Nash was a frequent contributor to the *New Yorker,* a magazine largely devoted to the publication of serious literature and for which he also served as an editor. Yet Nash's light verse never received serious critical attention, though his adroit manipulation of language and verse schemes is highly regarded and often imitated. Reviewing 1950's *Family Reunion,* Irwin Edman writes in the *New York Herald Tribune Book Review,* "There may be deeper American poets—though this book is very wise—but surely there cannot be more completely beguiling ones." While commending Nash's unpredictable and amusing poetic turns, Richard L. Schoenwald criticizes the poet's persistent topicality and undemanding audience. In a *Commonweal* review of *You Can't Get There from Hear,* Schoenwald remarks, "Nash accepts America; America reciprocates. . . . They never see more than the surface because there is nothing to see. Nash never cuts into the depths." However, Reed Whitmore credits Nash with deflating the "lofty" pretensions of modern American poetry and sustaining public interest in the form. Whitmore writes in *New Republic,* "What [Nash] did he did well, and in so doing he. . . kept American verse more open and various in its aims and interests than it otherwise would have been." *New York Times Book Review* contributor Robert Kelly quotes Nash as remarking, "I'd rather be a great bad poet than a bad good poet." Kelly adds, "In that honesty, he worked to demystify poetry."

Nash also produced verse for children, some of which has been republished along with illustrations. *The Tale of Custard the Dragon* and *Custard the Dragon and the Wicked Knight* feature Custard, a shy dragon accused of cowardice by a young girl named Belinda and her circle of animal friends. In both stories Nash employs his usual nonsensical verse to describe how Custard unexpectedly rises to the occasion to vanquish a feared antagonist—first a pirate, then an evil knight. Illustrated versions of these classic stories appeared in the 1990s and were well received.

*Loving Letters from Ogden Nash,* edited by the poet's eldest daughter and published in 1990, contains Nash's affectionate letters to his wife and family between 1928 and his death in 1971. Though offering little insight into his artistic life, according to *Washington Post Book World* contributor Jonathan Yardley, Nash's private letters "give us an uncommonly kind and decent man, hard-working and loyal and conscientious, touched by but scarcely vain about such fame as he enjoyed during an era when millions of Americans still read and enjoyed light verse." Upon of the publication of Nash's correspondence, Richard Kostelanetz summarizes his achievement in *American Book Review:* "The major poets are those who realize significance in language, whose vision of the possibilities of poetry is distinctive, whose use of language has sufficient character or signature to make every poem they write recognizable as theirs. By these criteria, it seems to me, Ogden Nash ranks among the top dozen major American poets of the twentieth century; it is no small measure of his success that he wrote lines that will be remembered for as long as English is heard."

Looking back on his writing career, Nash once remarked: "The only lines I've ever written which I think have any chance of surviving me were lines written in my unregenerate youth." Contrary to his modest estimate, Nash is widely recognized as having had few peers, especially when it came to exposing human frailties and absurdities. As St. George Tucker Arnold, Jr., claims in his *Dictionary of Literary Biography* essay, "During his lifetime, Ogden Nash was the most widely known, appreciated, and imitated American creator of light verse. . . . [And his] reputation has grown still further in the years since his death." The poet was, in Eliot Fremont-Smith's words, "a master of a kind of civility in exposing silliness that has not been much nurtured in recent decades," retaining the possibility of "a wit expressed through a friendly wink or poke." Although some of his verse was quite serious, Nash characterized the body of his work as "fortunately slightly goofy and cheerfully sour." One critic describes him as a "philosopher, albeit a laughing one," expressing "the vicissitudes and eccentricitudes of domestic life as they affected an apparently gentle, somewhat bewildered man." Nash's death in 1971 inspired numerous tributes patterned after his own work, such as one by poet Morris Bishop, quoted in *Time:* "Free from flashiness, free from trashiness / Is the essence of ogdenashiness. / Rich, original, rash and rational / Stands the monument ogdenational."

*BIOGRAPHICAL/CRITICAL SOURCES:*

*BOOKS*

Axford, L. B., *An Index to the Poems of Ogden Nash,* Scarecrow, 1972.

Benet, Laura, *Famous American Humorists,* Dodd, 1959.
*Contemporary Literary Criticism,* Volume 23, Gale, 1983.
*Dictionary of Literary Biography,* Volume 11: *American Humorists, 1800-1950,* Gale, 1982.
Newquist, Roy, *Conversations,* Rand McNally, 1967.

*PERIODICALS*

*American Book Review,* June-July, 1991, p. 25.
*Booklist,* March 1, 1995, p. 1245; April 1, 1996, p. 1369.
*Commonweal,* August 23, 1957, p. 525.
*Holiday,* August, 1967.
*Horn Book Magazine,* November-December, 1991; July-August, 1995, p. 485.
*Life,* December 13, 1968.
*Los Angeles Times,* May 20, 1971.
*New Republic,* October 21, 1972, p. 31.
*New York,* April 15, 1996, p. 134.
*New York Herald Tribune Book Review,* February 17, 1935, p. 4; July 14, 1957; December 10, 1950, p. 4.
*New York Herald Tribune Books,* January 18, 1931, p. 7; June 5, 1938, p. 2; December 6, 1942, p. 2.
*New York Herald Weekly Book Review,* March 20, 1949, p. 4.
*New York Times Book Review,* June 19, 1938, p. 2; February 11, 1990, p. 7.
*Publishers Weekly,* December 22, 1989; August 2, 1991; May 8, 1995, p. 295; April 25, 1996, p. 74.
*School Library Journal,* July, 1995, p. 73; April, 1996, p. 127.
*Seventeen,* January, 1963.
*Spectator,* September 24, 1994, p. 36.
*Tribune Books* (Chicago), March 4, 1990, p. 5.
*Washington Post Book World,* February 11, 1990, p. 3.

*OBITUARIES:*

*PERIODICALS*

*New York Times,* May 20, 1971.
*Publishers Weekly,* May 31, 1971.
*Time,* May 31, 1971.
*Washington Post,* May 21, 1971.*

* * *

**NAUGHTON, Bill**
**See NAUGHTON, William John (Francis)**

**NAUGHTON, William John (Francis) 1910-1992 (Bill Naughton)**

*PERSONAL:* Born June 12, 1910, in Ballyhaunis, County Mayo, Ireland; died, 1992; son of Thomas (a coal miner) and Maria (Fleming) Naughton; married Ernestine Pirolt. *Education:* Educated in England.

*CAREER:* Writer and playwright. Worked as a laborer, lorry driver, weaver, coalbagger, and bleacher. *Wartime service:* Civil Defense driver in London, England, during World War II.

*AWARDS, HONORS:* Screenwriters Guild Awards, 1967 and 1968; Prix Italia, 1974, for *The Mystery;* Other Award, Children's Rights Workshop, 1978, for *The Goalkeeper's Revenge.*

*WRITINGS:*

*UNDER NAME BILL NAUGHTON*

*A Roof over Your Head* (autobiography), Pilot Press, 1945, revised edition edited by Vincent Whitcombe, Blackie & Son, 1967.
*Pony Boy* (juvenile novel), Pilot Press, 1946, revised edition, Hattap, 1966.
*Rafe Granite* (novel), Pilot Press, 1947.
*One Small Boy* (novel), MacKibbon & Kee, 1957, revised edition edited by David Grant, Hattap, 1970.
*Late Night on Watling Street, and Other Stories* (also see below), MacKibbon & Kee, 1959, Ballantine, 1967, revised edition, Longmans, Green, 1969.
*The Goalkeeper's Revenge and Other Stories* (also see below), Harrap, 1961.
*Alfie* (novel; also see below), Ballantine, 1966.
*Alfie Darling* (novel), Simon & Schuster, 1970.
*The Goalkeeper's Revenge* [and] *Spit Nolan* (*Spit Nolan* published separately, Creative Education, Inc., 1987), Macmillan, 1974.
*The Bees Have Stopped Working, and Other Stories,* Wheaton & Co., 1976.
*A Dog Called Nelson* (juvenile), Dent, 1976.
*My Pal Spadger* (juvenile), Dent, 1977.
*On the Pig's Back: An Autobiographical Excursion,* Oxford University Press, 1987.
*Saintly Billy: A Catholic Boyhood* (autobiography), Oxford University Press, 1988.
*Neither Use Nor Ornament* (autobiography), Bloodaxe, 1995.

*PLAYS*

*My Flesh, My Blood* (two-act comedy; first broadcast in 1957; revised version first produced as *Spring and Port Wine* in Birmingham, England, 1964, and at the West End, 1965; also produced as *Keep It in the Family* on Broadway at Plymouth Theatre, September 27, 1967), Samuel French, 1959, published as *Spring and Port Wine,* 1967.

*June Evening* (first broadcast in 1958; produced in Birmingham, England, 1966), Samuel French, 1973.

*Alfie* (three-act; first broadcast as *Alfie Elkins and His Little Life,* 1962; produced as *Alfie* in London, 1963), Samuel French, 1963.

*All in Good Time* (comedy; first produced in London, 1963; produced in New York City, 1965; televised as *Honeymoon Postponed,* 1961), Samuel French, 1964.

*He Was Gone When We Got There,* music by Leonard Salzedo, first produced in London, 1966.

*Annie and Fanny,* first produced in Bolton, Lancashire, England, at Octagon Theatre, 1967.

*Lighthearted Intercourse,* first produced in Liverpool, England, at Liverpool Playhouse, December 1, 1971.

(With others) *A Special Occasion: Three Plays* (includes *A Special Occasion;* also see below), Longman, 1988.

*OTHER*

Contributor to *Worth a Hearing: A Collection of Radio Plays* (contains *She'll Make Trouble,* first broadcast, 1958), edited by Alfred Bradley, Blackie & Son, 1967. Author of other radio plays, including *Timothy,* 1956; *Late Night on Watling Street,* 1959; *The Long Carry,* 1959; *Seeing a Beauty Queen Home,* 1960; *On the Run,* 1960; *Wigan to Rome,* 1960; *'30-'60,* 1960; *Jackie Crowe,* 1962; *November Day,* 1963; *The Mystery,* 1973; and *A Special Occasion,* 1982. Author of television plays, including *Nathaniel Titlark* series, 1957; *Jam Butty,* 1957; *Starr and Company* series, 1958; (with Alan Prior) *Yorky* series, 1960; (with Michael Caine) *Somewhere for the Night,* 1962; *Looking for Frankie,* 1963; and *It's Your Move,* 1967.

*ADAPTATIONS: Alfie,* a comedy-drama starring Shelley Winters and Michael Caine, was produced in 1966 by Paramount; *All in Good Time* was released as *The Family Way* by Warner Bros. in 1967; *Spring and Port Wine* was released by Warner-Pathe in 1970.

*SIDELIGHTS:* A prolific writer of books and plays for the stage, radio, and television, Bill Naughton grew up in the coal-mining county of Lancashire, England. His first book, *A Roof over Your Head,* is a semi-autobiographical volume that describes the typical life of poverty and hardship in Lancashire during the twenties. Lancashire is also the setting for many of Naughton's subsequent books and plays, including two of his most successful scripts, *Spring and Port Wine* and *All in Good Time.*

As in a number of Naughton's writings, family life is the subject of *Spring and Port Wine.* In this critically acclaimed play, Naughton relates a series of episodes that take place in a household during a spring weekend, with special attention paid to a young daughter who overindulges in port wine. *All in Good Time* deals with newlywed couples of Lancashire as they nervously face their wedding nights. One of Naughton's most popular radio plays, however, involves the adventures of a bachelor. *Alfie Elkins and His Little Life,* which was later revised as a stage play and novel entitled *Alfie,* concerns the love life of a cockney Don Juan. While often humorous, the play has also been praised for the author's ability to reveal his character's inner loneliness.

Beginning in the mid-1970s, Naughton retreated to a seaside bungalow on the Isle of Man because of what he felt was a "need to escape the 'idle life' of writing plays and get back to his real writing," according to a London *Times* writer. His work focused on condensing his journals and producing several autobiographical volumes about his childhood years in the working-class town of Bolton, England. The first of these, *On the Pig's Back,* briefly covers Naughton's World War II experience as a conscientious objector but focuses mainly on his early childhood in Bolton. The second volume, *Saintly Billy: A Catholic Boyhood,* covers Naughton's youth from ages ten to thirteen, focusing on the author's attraction to Catholicism and the poor but colorful mining community in Bolton. Volume three in Naughton's string of boyhood memoirs, *Neither Use Nor Ornament,* was published after the author's death in 1992. It covers only one month in Naughton's childhood, June of 1924, when the author turned fourteen and began the transition from boy to man. Reviewing *Saintly Billy* in the *Times Literary Supplement,* Dervla Murphy remarked that "Bill Naughton neither sentimentalizes nor dramatizes his boyhood. . . . A whole world is recreated through an accumulation of tiny details."

*BIOGRAPHICAL/CRITICAL SOURCES:*

*BOOKS*

*Dictionary of Literary Biography,* Volume 13: *British Dramatists since World War II,* Gale, 1982.

*PERIODICALS*

*New Statesman & Society,* July 7, 1989, p. 42; July 21, 1995, p. 39.
*Newsweek,* January 4, 1965; March 1 1965; October 9, 1967.
*New Yorker,* January 2, 1965.
*Observer,* March 20, 1988, p. 42.
*Time,* December 25, 1964.
*Times* (London), July 15, 1985.
*Times Literary Supplement,* April 1, 1988, p. 351; September 25, 1995, p. 32.

*OBITUARIES:*

*PERIODICALS*

*Chicago Tribune,* January 10, 1992, sec. 1, p. 10.
*Los Angeles Times,* January 11, 1992, p. A22.
*New York Times,* January 11, 1992, p. 26.
*Times* (London), January 10, 1992, p. 16.
*Washington Post,* January 13, 1992, p. B4.*

* * *

**NEWMAN, G(ordon) F. 1942-**

*PERSONAL:* Born in 1942 in Westminster, England; married Angela Harding (divorced); married Janet Orga (divorced); children: one son, one daughter. *Avocational interests:* Flying, fencing, chess.

*ADDRESSES: Home*—Wessington Court, Woolhope, Hereford HR1 4QN, England. *Agent*—Duncan Heath, 76 Oxford St., London W1N 0AX, England.

*CAREER:* Film producer, screenwriter, playwright, and author.

*MEMBER:* Writers Guild of Great Britain.

*AWARDS, HONORS:* Edgar Allan Poe Award from the Mystery Writers of America for *Sir, You Bastard;* Bafta Writer's Award, 1992, 1995.

*WRITINGS:*

*NOVELS*

*Sir, You Bastard,* W. H. Allen (London), 1970, Simon & Schuster (New York City), 1970, published as *Rogue Cop,* Lancer (New York City), 1973.
*You Nice Bastard,* New English Library (London), 1972.
*The Abduction,* New English Library, 1972.
*The Player and the Guest,* New English Library, 1972.
*Billy: A Family Tragedy,* New English Library, 1972.
*The Split,* New English Library, 1973.
*Three Professional Ladies,* New English Library, 1973.
*The Price,* New English Library, 1974, published as *You Flash Bastard,* Sphere Books (London), 1978.
*The Streetfighter,* Star Books (London), 1975.
*A Prisoner's Tale,* Sphere Books, 1977.
*The Guvnor,* Hart-Davis (London), 1977, published as *Trade-Off,* Dell (New York City), 1979.
*The Detective's Tale,* Sphere Books, 1977.
*A Villain's Tale,* Sphere Books, 1978.
*The List,* Secker & Warburg (London), 1980.
*The Obsession,* Granada (London), 1980.
*Charlie and Joanna,* Granada, 1981.
*The Men with the Guns,* Secker & Warburg, 1982.
*Law and Order,* Granada, 1983.
*Set a Thief,* M. Joseph (London), 1986.
*The Testing Ground,* M. Joseph, 1987.
*Trading the Future,* Macdonalds (London), 1992.
*Circle of Poison,* Simon & Schuster (New York City), 1995.

*PLAYS*

*Operation Bad Apple* (produced in London, 1982), Metheun (London), 1982.
*An Honourable Trade,* produced in London, 1986.
*The Testing Ground* (based on his novel of same title), produced in London, 1989.

Author of screenplay *Number One,* 1984. Author of television plays *Law and Order* (series), 1978, *Billy,* 1979, *The Nation's Health,* 1983, *Here Is the News,* 1989, *Black and Blue,* 1992, and *The Healer,* 1994.

*SIDELIGHTS:* G. F. Newman is best known for the "Terry Sneed" detective series, books featuring a crooked British police officer who nonetheless is an able detective and a foe of criminal forces. As Donald

C. Wall writes in the *St. James Guide to Crime and Mystery Writers,* "Despite his corruptness (and sometimes because of it), the power-hungry Sneed is an excellent detective. He manages, for example, to put away an important crook who had been hitherto untouchable and destroy the man's entire organization." Newgate Callendar in the *New York Times Book Review* calls Sneed "a smart, ruthless, ambitious and venal cop."

The first of the Sneed books, *Sir, You Bastard,* introduces the corrupt detective and traces the course of his first seven years on the force. "His education in the corrupt use of police techniques and powers," writes Wall, "enables him to fatten hidden bank accounts, convict crooks whether guilty or not, and advance in rank by blackmailing superiors or getting colleagues fired to create openings." As D. F. Lawler maintains in *Best Sellers,* "Sneed is certainly addressed correctly as 'Sir, You Bastard.'"

Further Sneed books chronicle what Wall describes as "the pervasive moral decay of society" as Sneed slowly comes to realize that many of the legal and political figures he encounters are as corrupt as the criminals they are set against. This same theme is also found in Newman's novel *The Guvnor,* in which Detective Chief Inspector John Fordham struggles to achieve justice in a society where corruption runs rampant. Unlike Sneed, however, Fordham "uses corrupt means only to effect justice, not to consolidate or add to his own power."

Besides his novels exploring the theme of social corruption, Newman has also written a wide range of other works dealing with such issues as child abuse, the John Kennedy assassination, and the lives of prostitutes. Wall concludes that Newman, because of the variety of his books, "is one of the most versatile and unpredictable of crime writers. . . . Newman's canvas is a broad one. He seems to have taken all society to be his subject, particularly its fringes, nor does he ever shy away from the sordid truths he encounters. His talent coupled with his uncompromising honesty mark him as a serious novelist who deserves to be widely read."

*BIOGRAPHICAL/CRITICAL SOURCES:*

*BOOKS*

*St. James Guide to Crime and Mystery Writers,* fourth edition, St. James Press (Detroit), 1996.

*PERIODICALS*

*Best Sellers,* June 1, 1971, p. 31.
*Library Journal,* July, 1971, p. 96.
*New York Times Book Review,* August 1, 1971, p. 16.
*Times Literary Supplement,* November 27, 1970, p. 1399.

* * *

**NEWMAN, Kim (James) 1959-**
**(Addison DeWitt)**

*PERSONAL:* Born July 31, 1959, in London, England; son of Bryan Michael (a potter) and Julia (a potter; maiden name, Christen) Newman. *Education:* Attended Bridgwater College, 1975-77; University of Sussex, B.A. (honors), 1980. *Politics:* Left. *Religion:* Agnostic.

*ADDRESSES: Home*—92 Fortis Green Rd., Muswell Hill, London N10 3HN, England. *Office*—City Limits, 313 Upper St., London N1 2QX, England. *Agent*—Antony Harwood, Gillon Aitken Ltd., 29 Fernshaw Rd., London SW10 0TG, England.

*CAREER:* Writer, 1981—. Performer in Club Whoopee band, 1981-84; broadcaster for *Kaleidoscope,* British Broadcasting Corp. (BBC) Radio, 1985—; director of Peace and Love Corp., 1985—. Member of City Limits Collective and Sheep Worrying Enterprises; affiliated with British Film Institute. Recordings with Band Club Whoopee include *Sheep Worrying* and *At the Club Whoopee,* both 1982.

*MEMBER:* British Fantasy Society, Performing Rights Society, Critics' Circle.

*WRITINGS:*

*NOVELS*

*The Night Mayor,* Carroll & Graf (New York City), 1990.
*Bad Dreams,* Carroll & Graf, 1991.
*Jago,* Carrol & Graf, 1993.
*Anno-Dracula,* Carroll & Graf, 1993.
*The Quorum,* Carroll & Graf, 1994.
*The Bloody Red Baron,* Carrol & Graf, 1995.

*PLAYS*

*Another England* (two-act), produced in Somerset, England, 1980.

*My One Little Murder Can't Do Any Harm* (one-act), produced in Somerset, 1981.

(With Brian Smedley) *The Gold Diggers of 1981* (three-act musical; book by Newman, music by Smedley), produced in Somerset, 1981, revised as *The Gold Diggers of 1986.*

(With others) *Your Television Knows Best* (musical revue), produced in Somerset, 1982.

(With Smedley) *The Roaring Eighties* (three-act musical; book by Newman, music by Smedley), produced in Somerset, 1982.

(With others) *In Search of Legends,* produced in Somerset, 1984.

Also author of one-act play *Deep South,* produced 1982. Lyricist and contributor to other theatrical works.

*OTHER*

*Nightmare Movies* (film criticism), Proteus Press, 1985, 2nd edition published as *Nightmare Movies: A Critical Guide to Contemporary Horror Films,* Harmony Books (New York City), 1988, 2nd edition published in England as *Nightmare Movies: A Critical History of the Horror Film, 1968-1988,* Bloomsbury (London), 1988.

(With Neil Gaiman) *Ghastly Beyond Belief* (humor), Arrow, 1985.

(Editor, with Stephen Jones) *Horror: The One Hundred Best Books,* Carroll & Graf, 1988.

*Wild West Movies; or, How the West Was Found, Won, Lost, Lied About, Filmed and Forgotten,* Bloomsbury, 1990.

(Editor, with Paul J. McAuley) *In Dreams,* Gollancz (London), 1992.

Also author of *Seminal Movies, The Atomic Cinema* and *The Movie Diary;* author of film books under the pseudonym Addison DeWitt.

Work represented in *Interzone: The First Anthology,* Dent, 1985. Contributor to *The Encyclopedia of Horror and the Supernatural,* Penguin, 1986. Contributor to periodicals, including *New Statesman & Society, Sheep Worrying, Monthly Film Bulletin, British Fantasy Newsletter, Halls of Horror, Knave, Brian, Fantasy Tales, Sight and Sound, Stills, Shock Xpress, City Limits, Venue, Club International, Penthouse, Interzone,* and the *New Musical Express.* Columnist for *Sheep Worrying,* 1981-85, *TNT,* 1984—, and *City Limits,* 1985—.

*SIDELIGHTS:* As a film critic, Kim Newman is best known for his books *Ghastly Beyond Belief,* a celebration of the most ridiculous moments from science fiction books and films co-authored with Neil Gaiman, and *Nightmare Movies,* a critical history of the horror film genre. But it is Newman's novels, combining horror and social satire, that have established him as "one of the best and brightest of horror fiction's new breed, knowledgeable of the genre's rich tradition but unwilling to be shackled by them," Douglas E. Winter explains in the *Washington Post Book World.*

In his critique of *Nightmare Movies, Foundation* reviewer Peter Nicholls remarks: "The horror film is not a field that can be profitably explored by the nice-minded. . . . Newman knows that much of the real action is in the sewers, the derelict hotels, the rotting slums of the genre. . . . He makes entirely accurate critical judgements while standing knee deep in the swamp, and is not too blinded by revulsion to see that some (a very few) of these movies are in their way works of art, and not to be wholly repudiated. There are very few critics around who can pull off this sort of conjuring trick."

In the late 1980s Newman began to expand his role as film critic into a career as a novelist. "My novel *The Night Mayor* is a fiction piece, but it contains elements of film criticism," he once explained to *CA;* "my critical work *Nightmare Movies,* and the half of *Ghastly Beyond Belief* that I am responsible for (the film half), are both structured in a semi-narrative way. As a freelance writer I have to think of commerce rather than art, but I don't think this precludes doing the best I can on each commission. I am at a point in my career where I am expanding my field of activity outside criticism. In other words, I think I want to be a novelist when I grow up."

Newman's horror novels range from studies of dangerous characters with supernatural powers, as in *Jago* and *The Quorum,* to alternate histories, as in *Anno-Dracula* and *The Bloody Red Baron.* In *Jago* Newman tells the story of cult leader Anthony William Jago, a defrocked priest whose psychic powers can unleash the most fearful emotions in his victims. Jago's plans for unleashing the apocalypse in a small British town lead to a psychic battle for control of the townspeople. A *Publishers Weekly* critic calls *Jago* "a distinguished literary effort rooted in the emotional interiors of three-dimensional characters," while finding that "Newman's prose is sophisticated and his narrative drive irresistible." Winter concludes that "Newman writes with great wit and unabashed enthusiasm. At his best moments, his prose is positively delirious, a white-knuckle carnival ride that cuddles the reader with comfort, then nosedives into breathtaking scenes of hallucination and horror."

In *Anno-Dracula* Newman writes an historical fantasy in which Count Dracula has married England's Queen Victoria, leading to a reign of vampire-monarchs preying upon a human populace. Writing in the *New York Times Book Review,* Nina Auerbach notes that "instead of invading civilization, [Newman's] vampires embody it. Their incessant intrigue, power games and casual oppression of the weak make *Anno-Dracula* no more (and no less) frightening than the Victorian society in which it is set." Throughout the book, Newman mixes real-life figures with fictional characters of the period, including Jack the Ripper, Bram Stoker, Dr. Jekyll, Inspector Lestrade (of the Sherlock Holmes' stories), and Dr. Moreau. "Newman's meticulous attention to historical detail occasionally seems superfluous in a work of such unabashed fantasy," notes a *Publishers Weekly* critic of *Anno-Dracula,* "but his prose is sure-handed and vivid." "The fin-de-siecle corruption," writes Marylaine Block in *Library Journal,* "is vividly portrayed. . . . This is literate, powerful, and ugly." Auerbach believes that "Newman's revision of Bram Stoker is brilliant."

Newman updates another horror genre staple in *The Quorum,* in which he recasts the familiar deal-with-the-devil story for 1990s England. In Newman's version of the tale, wealthy businessman Derek Leech offers three young friends a deal: they will enjoy success but only at the cost of another friend's misfortune. "Newman's tale," writes Stefan Dziemianowicz in the *Washington Post Book World,* "is an ambitious parable for our times. . . . *The Quorum* leaves you wondering uneasily how many of our most prominent public figures may be motivated by the prod of a pitchfork." A critic for *Publishers Weekly* admits that Newman "brings a new twist or two" to the deal-with-the-devil story, making *The Quorum* a "fine and funny romp."

*The Bloody Red Baron* picks up where *Anno-Dracula* ended, following the imaginary turn-of-the-century English vampire society ruled over by Dracula into the First World War. By the time the war begins, much of the world population has been turned into vampires, primarily because being a vampire is a necessary step to acquiring wealth and position in a society ruled by Dracula. When war breaks out, rival vampire air aces fight in the skies over Europe and such characters as Edgar Allan Poe, Hans Heinz Ewers, and Dr. Mabuse play major roles. "In the image of the immortal vampire," a *Publishers Weekly* reviewer writes, "Newman has found the perfect metaphor for history's larger-than-life personalities and the impact their appetites have upon civilization."

"I am a writer in much the same sense as I am right-handed, white, male, anglophone, heterosexual, hazel-eyed, and alive," Newman once told *CA.* "Nobody asked me to make a choice about any of these things, and I can take neither credit nor blame for them."

*BIOGRAPHICAL/CRITICAL SOURCES:*

*PERIODICALS*

*Booklist,* December 15, 1992, p. 715; September 1, 1993, p. 35; October 1, 1994, p. 240; November 1, 1995, p. 454.

*Fantasy Review,* September, 1985, p. 28.

*Foundation,* autumn, 1985.

*Library Journal,* November 15, 1991, p. 111; February 1, 1993, p. 113; August 1, 1993, p. 154; October 1, 1994, p. 115.

*Locus,* August, 1990, p. 29; December, 1990, p. 29; June, 1993, p. 19; February, 1994, pp. 36, 75; May, 1994, p. 25.

*Los Angeles Times Book Review,* January 20, 1991, p. 6.

*Necrofile,* winter, 1993, p. 17; summer, 1994, p. 1; winter, 1995, p. 4.

*New Statesman & Society,* August 14, 1992, p. 41; May 6, 1994, p. 37.

*New York Times Book Review,* October 21, 1990, pp. 7, 35; October 31, 1991, p. 16.

*Publishers Weekly,* July 27, 1990, p. 226; September 27, 1991, p. 43; November 16, 1992, p. 46; August 30, 1993, p. 78; October 11, 1993, p. 84; September 5, 1994, p. 89; October 2, 1995, p. 55.

*Science Fiction Chronicle,* December, 1990, p. 33; April, 1992, p. 29; March, 1993, p. 30.

*Times* (London), April 13, 1985.

*Variety,* September 10, 1990, p. 72.

*Voice of Youth Advocates,* February 1991, p. 365.

*Washington Post Book World,* March 26, 1989, p. 8; November 24, 1991, p. 8; April 4, 1993, p. 5; November 27, 1994, p. 8; December 31, 1995, p. 9.

*Wilson Library Bulletin,* April, 1990, p. 101; October, 1993, p. 102.*

* * *

**NIELSEN, Helen Berniece 1918-**
**(Kris Giles)**

*PERSONAL:* Born 1918, in Roseville, IL; daughter of Niels C. and May (Christensen) Nielsen. *Education:* Took extension course in journalism, attended Chicago Art Institute, and took U.S. defense course in aeronautical drafting. *Avocational interests:* Politics, Norwegian elkhounds.

*ADDRESSES: Home*—2622 Victoria Dr., Laguna Beach, CA 92651. *Agent*—Ann Elmo Agency, 60 E. 42nd St., New York, NY 10017.

*CAREER:* Old Globe Theatre Productions, Chicago, IL, costumer, 1934-35; freelance newspaper and commercial artist, 1937-41; Air Associates, Inglewood, CA, draftsman, 1942-43; Interstate Aircraft, Los Angeles, CA, draftsman, 1943-44; Van Tuyl Engineering, Los Angeles, loftsman, 1945; apartment house owner and manager, 1942-78. Member of California Democratic Council, 1956-66.

*MEMBER:* Authors Guild, Hollywood Highlands Democratic Club, Adlai Stevenson Democratic Club (secretary, 1954-55; president, 1956-57).

*WRITINGS:*

*The Kind Man,* Washburn (New York City), 1951.
*Gold Coast Nocturne,* Washburn, 1952, published as *Murder by Proxy,* Gollancz (London), 1952, published as *Dead on the Level,* Dell (New York City), 1954.
*Obit Delayed,* Washburn, 1953.
*Detour,* Washburn, 1953, published as *Detour to Death,* Dell, 1955.
*The Woman on the Roof,* Washburn, 1954.
*Stranger in the Dark,* Washburn, 1955.
*The Crime Is Murder,* Morrow (New York City), 1956.
*Borrow the Night,* Morrow, 1957, published as *Seven Days before Dying,* Dell, 1958.
*False Witness,* Ballantine (New York City), 1959.
*The Fifth Caller,* Morrow, 1959.
*Sing Me a Murder,* Morrow, 1960.
*Woman Missing and Other Stories,* Ace Books (New York City), 1961.
*Verdict Suspended,* Morrow, 1964.
*After Midnight,* Morrow, 1965.
*A Killer in the Street,* Morrow, 1967.
*Darkest Hour,* Morrow, 1969.
*Shot on Location,* Morrow, 1971.
*The Severed Key,* Morrow, 1973.
*The Brink of Murder,* Morrow, 1976.

Also author of scripts for television series, including *Alfred Hitchcock Presents, Perry Mason, Markham, Alcoa Theatre, 87th Precinct, Four STar Theatre* and *Checkmate.* Work appears in anthologies, including *Best Detective Stories,* 1955, 1959, *Alfred Hitchcock's Hangman's Dozen,* 1962, *Ellery Queen's Double Dozen,* 1964, and *Best Legal Stories,* 1970. Nielsen's manuscripts are collected at the Mugar Memorial Library, Boston University.

*ADAPTATIONS: Gold Coast Nocturne* was filmed under the title *Blackout; The Fifth Caller* and several short stories have been adapted for television.

*SIDELIGHTS:* Helen Nielsen writes mystery stories in which she carefully plays fair with the reader, providing enough information for the mystery to be solved. Nielsen mixes her detective puzzles with realistic character studies and often sets her stories in southern California, where she has lived since her childhood. Her California, however, is often the "the chilling rains or the thick, yellow, and dripping fogs" of winter, according to Mary Groff in the *St. James Guide to Crime and Mystery Writers.*

In *Woman on the Roof,* Nielsen tells the story of a paranoid woman investigating a murder at her brother's apartment complex in Los Angeles. L. G. Offord in the *San Francisco Chronicle* claims that "the oddness of the protagonist gives this novel a new flavor," while Anthony Boucher in the *New York Times* maintains that Nielsen's "portrait of a paranoid, not as a case history but as an understandable person, lifts [the novel] out of the common run." James Sandoe in the *New York Herald Tribune Book Review* offers the novel "worthy praise for its unpretentious artfulness."

*The Crime Is Murder* concerns a music festival at a small California resort town desperate for tourist revenue. Boucher notes that the novel is written "in a vein of quietly observant realism, underlined by sustained emotional horror." Offord finds the novel to be "done with Nielsen taste."

Although she usually sets her stories in California, Nielsen has on occasion moved to foreign locales. In *Stranger in the Dark,* the story takes place in Denmark. "The charm of the Danish background," notes Boucher, "and the adroitness of the twists and surprises make this one of the best recent cloak-and-dagger tales." *Shot on Location* is set in Greece, where an American general just back from Vietnam investigates the disappearance of a shady filmmaker. In this novel "Nielsen has successfully combined," according to J. L. Breen in *Library Journal,* "the chase-adventure-espionage tale with a formal, fairly clued detective puzzle, a rarer feat than one might imagine." Newgate Callendar in the *New York Times Book Review* writes that, although "there is no confusing the good and the bad guys," the novel is "a smooth piece of work . . . urbane and agreeable."

*BIOGRAPHICAL/CRITICAL SOURCES:*

*St. James Guide to Crime and Mystery Writers,* fourth edition, St. James Press (Detroit), 1996.

*PERIODICALS*

*Library Journal,* October 1, 1971, p. 96.
*Manchester Guardian,* July 31, 1959, p. 5.
*New York Herald Tribune Book Review,* September 5, 1954, p. 8; November 6, 1955, p. 16.
*New York Times,* October 21, 1951, p. 44; June 14, 1953, p. 19; September 5, 1954, p. 10; November 6, 1955, p. 54; January 8, 1956, p. 29; November 4, 1956, p. 39; February 22, 1959, p. 31.
*New York Times Book Review,* September 12, 1971, p. 42.
*Observer,* December 14, 1969.
*San Francisco Chronicle,* October 7, 1951, p. 22; September 12, 1954, p. 14; December 9, 1956, p. 31; March 15, 1959, p. 19.
*Saturday Review,* October 30, 1954, p. 37; December 3, 1955, p. 38; October 25, 1969; September 25, 1971, p. 54.
*Spectator,* August 18, 1973.

* * *

**NIXON, Richard M(ilhous) 1913-1994**

*PERSONAL:* Born January 9, 1913, in Yorba Linda, CA; died of complications following a stroke, April 22, 1994, in New York City; son of Francis Anthony (a store owner) and Hannah (Milhous) Nixon; married Patricia Ryan (deceased), June 21, 1940; children: Patricia (Mrs. Edward Finch Cox), Julie (Mrs. Dwight David Eisenhower II). *Education:* Whittier College, A.B. (with honors), 1934; Duke University, LL.B. (with honors), 1937. *Religion:* Society of Friends (Quaker).

*CAREER:* Thirty-seventh president of the United States. Bewley, Knoop & Nixon, Whittier, CA, general practice of law, 1937-42; Office of Emergency Management, Washington, DC, attorney in tire rationing division, 1942; U.S. Representative from 12th District of California, serving on Education and Labor Committee, Select Committee on Foreign Aid, and Committee on Un-American Activities, 1947-50; appointed to vacant seat in U.S. Senate, 1950; U.S. Senator from California, serving on Labor and Public Welfare Committee and Expenditures in Executive Departments Committee, 1951-53; vice president of the United States, serving as chair of President Eisenhower's Committee on Government Contracts, chair of the Cabinet Committee on Price Stability for Economic Growth, and as the personal representative of the president on goodwill trips to fifty-four countries, 1953-61; Republican candidate for the presidency, with Henry Cabot Lodge as running mate, 1960; Adams, Duque & Hazeltine, Los Angeles, CA, counsel, 1961-62; Republican candidate for governor of California, 1962; Mudge, Stern, Baldwin & Todd, New York City, member of firm, 1962-63; Nixon, Mudge, Rose, Guthrie & Alexander (later Nixon, Mudge, Rose, Guthrie, Alexander & Mitchell), New York City, partner, 1964-68; elected president of United States, with Spiro T. Agnew as vice president, 1968, reelected to office with landslide majority vote of electoral college, 1972, resigned, 1974. Trustee, Whittier College, 1939-68; honorary chair of Boys' Clubs of America; honorary chair of Fund for Democracy and Development, 1992. *Military service:* U.S. Naval Reserve, 1942-46; served in Pacific theatre of operations; became lieutenant commander.

*MEMBER:* French Fine Arts Academy (foreign associate member), Order of Coif.

*WRITINGS:*

*The Challenges We Face* (excerpts compiled from speeches and papers), McGraw, 1960.
*Six Crises* (autobiographical), Doubleday, 1962.
*The Inaugural Address of Richard Milhous Nixon,* Achille J. St. Onge, 1969.

*Setting the Course, The First Year* (policy statements), Funk, 1970.
*U.S. Foreign Policy for the 1970s: Report to Congress,* Harper, 1971.
*A New Road for America* (policy statements), Doubleday, 1972.
*Four Great Americans* (tributes to Dwight Eisenhower, Everett Dirksen, Whitney M. Young, and J. Edgar Hoover), Doubleday, 1973.
*The Nixon Presidential Press Conferences,* Earl M. Coleman, 1978.
*RN: The Memoirs of Richard Nixon,* Grosset, 1978.
*The Real War,* Warner Books, 1980.
*Leaders,* Warner Books, 1982.
*Real Peace: A Strategy for the West,* Little, Brown, 1983.
*No More Vietnams,* Arbor House, 1985.
*1999: The Global Challenges We Face in the Next Decade,* Simon & Schuster, 1988, published as *1999: Victory without War,* 1988.
*In the Arena: A Memoir of Victory, Defeat and Renewal,* Simon & Schuster, 1990.
*Seize the Moment: America's Challenge in a One-Superpower World,* Simon & Schuster, 1992.
*Beyond Peace,* Random House, 1994.

Also author of annual collections of State of the Union messages, news conference texts, messages to Congress, and major statements, published by Congressional Quarterly, five volumes, 1970-74; author of reports, speeches, addresses, official papers, and transcript collections published by U.S. Government Printing Office and other publishers.

*SIDELIGHTS:* When Richard M. Nixon first ran for public office in the late 1940s, it was the start of a distinguished and highly visible political career that would include terms as congressman, senator, vice president, and eventually president of the United States. Nixon was frequently embroiled in controversy throughout his career, whether as a member of Congress investigating communism for the House Un-American Activities Committee in the late 1940s or as a president criticized by liberals for continued U.S. involvement in Vietnam and by conservatives for establishing ties with Communist China. Nixon's position within the U.S. political record will most likely be usurped, however, by the scandal that drove him out of office in 1974: the infamous Watergate break-in and cover up, which involved several members of his administration and compelled Nixon to resign from the Presidency under threat of Congressional action. "Clare Boothe Luce once said that each person in history can be summed up in one sentence, . . ." Nixon related in a *Time* interview after his historic trip to China. "She said, 'You will be summed up, He went to China.' Historians are more likely to lead with 'He resigned the office.'"

Although Watergate ended his political career, Nixon remained in the public eye until his death in 1994 through the publication of several books focusing on Cold War issues and his own experiences. After recovering from a near-fatal bout of phlebitis in late 1974, as part of his "spiritual recovery" Nixon decided to write a personal account of his political career. *RN: The Memoirs of Richard Nixon* was published in 1978 to reviews that, while they differed in their assessment of the president himself, found the book interesting as a revelation of Nixon's character. *New York Times* critic Christopher Lehmann-Haupt, for example, observed that despite biases and flaws, *RN* "remains a fascinating performance. Whether one dislikes it or admires it, the voice of the prose reflects its author more distinctly than does that of any other American political memoir I can think of offhand, and, for reasons both negative and positive, that voice continues to hypnotize throughout the book's 1,100 pages." "This is a tremendous book, rich in concrete detail, a major political event, and as close as we are ever likely to get to that *sui generis* political creature, Richard Nixon," Jeffrey Hart of the *National Review* similarly claimed.

Many critics noted, in the words of *New York Times Book Review* contributor James MacGregor Burns, that "most of this huge volume [Nixon] devotes to a long statement for the defense." As a result, the critic continued, "the fact that [Nixon's] accounts are highly selective, that he seeks to score points in a continuing debate with the news media and his other adversaries, that his judgments range from the contentious to the tendentious, should not surprise us." "But even [these] flaws of the book help to tell the story," Elizabeth Drew suggested in the *Washington Post Book World,* "the story of an individual whose mind worked in a certain way." Clive James likewise commented that *RN,* despite its subjective slant, "is not a mean book. Nixon's faults are all on view, but so is the fact that they are faults in something substantial," James wrote in the *New Statesman.* "His claims to a place in history are shown to be not all that absurd," and his memoirs "constitute a readable book of no small literary merit and considerable human dignity." "For all of this book's predictable flaws," Drew concluded, "it is an interesting, sometimes even absorbing account that cannot be dismissed. Nixon is a major figure in our history, and here he gives us his own version of the years in which he dominated our national life."

Although his resignation removed Nixon from directly participating in political life, he noted in *Time* that "for whatever time I have left, . . . what is most important is to be able to affect the course of events." To that end, he wrote several books on foreign policy. The first, 1980's *The Real War,* outlines the history and possible future of the Cold War, and "is a straightforward call for the United States to mobilize *all* its power—military, economic, political, Presidential, clandestine, intellectual, informational and especially will power—to combat the Soviet Union on a global scale," according to Flora Lewis in the *New York Times Book Review.* Critics faulted the book, however, both for what Lewis termed "a highly selective approach" to historical examples and for Nixon's combative tone. As *New York Review of Books* critic Ronald Steel stated: "In this book instead of addressing himself seriously to the issues, [Nixon] panders to the public's anxieties. Instead of being constructive, he is once again being demolishing." But, said David E. Kaiser in a *New Republic* article, "one need not share Nixon's assumptions or value his role in American history in order to find this book provocative. Much of its argument draws effectively on history, it says publicly what many foreign policy specialists probably believe but dare not reveal, and its world view has an inner consistency that forces every reader to examine his own basic assumptions."

1983's *Real Peace: A Strategy for the West* addresses some of the same issues as Nixon's previous work, but with a view towards detente rather than confrontation during the then-ongoing Cold War with the U.S.S.R. "On balance," maintained Alvin Shuster in the *Los Angeles Times Book Review,* "[Nixon] has done well in taking critical issues before the country, in condensing and discussing them with a fair amount of clarity and force. There is no great writing here but he does manage to describe complex problems in understandable terms." Robert W. Tucker, however, felt that while Nixon's political assessments of the chances for "real peace" were interesting, the author omitted a concrete plan for attaining this peace. As the critic wrote in the *New York Times Book Review:* "The need for Mr. Nixon's real peace can scarcely be denied. How to move toward it remains the great question." But critics such as Joseph Sobran found *Real Peace* more specific in its approach than *The Real War,* especially in the realm of Third World relations. As Sobran commented in the *National Review,* Nixon's new book "is an incisive, often profound manifesto for 'hard-headed detente,' written with aphoristic punch. . . . *Real Peace* contains the antidote to its own single mistake, and much wisdom and practical shrewdness besides. It is a book we need."

In *No More Vietnams* Nixon traced the history of foreign involvement in Vietnam and proposed policies that would prevent another setback against communist encroachment. "Besides aggressive self-justification," Toronto *Globe and Mail* writer William Thorsell noted, "this book aims to inspire renewed U.S. commitment to military intervention around the world to stop a voracious communism." "'No More Vietnams' is two books," historian James Chace suggested in the *New York Times Book Review.* "The first is a highly selective history of the Vietnam War—a war, as he tells it, that we won. We then, however, 'lost the peace.' The second and more interesting book," the critic continued, is the chapter that outlines Nixon's program "to win the hearts and minds—and stomachs—of the third world." Echoing previous criticisms of Nixon's work, some reviewers faulted the former president's interpretation of past events, citing a lack of specific attributions. As *Chicago Tribune* writer Raymond Coffey observed, despite some strong arguments, "the big problem with the book is that its version of Vietnam history . . . is so blatantly, so outrageously self-serving that much of the weight and force of the Nixon prescription for the future . . . tend to be diminished."

Nevertheless, Steel admitted, "Nixon is an intelligent man and many things in his book are thoughtful and challenging. He is always interesting to listen to, particularly on foreign policy, a field in which he has concentrated so much of his energies." Hart went further in his praise, writing that *No More Vietnams* "is extraordinarily concise, providing, along with its strongly argued thesis . . . a history and an assessment of our Vietnam policy beginning with the Truman Administration in the immediate post-World War II period. Mr. Nixon's perspective here is presidential, his grasp of the history firm, and his judgments persuasive."

Nixon's 1988 work, titled *1999: Victory without War,* is "important because it is a serious, cogently argued attempt to get American politicians . . . to look forward and to evolve a set of policies that will bring the United States, and the rest of the world, safely into the 21st century," according to Paul Kennedy in the *Washington Post Book World.* "Although written by a politician whose right-wing and anti-communist convictions are frequently in evidence, it nonetheless offers perspectives that ought to interest Democrats as much as Republicans." *1999,* according to Thorsell, "restates Nixon's fundamental thesis—that the Soviet drive for world domination remains the central fact of global politics, and that the United States is the Soviet Union's only real opponent." To that end, Nixon outlines potential U.S. strategies for dealing with not only the Soviet Union, but Europe, Asia, and Third World nations. "He argues that one of the significant trends in the 21st century will be the rise of Western Europe, Japan and China to increasing importance in world politics, and he has a splendid chapter, both sympathetic and instructive, on the problems of the Third World," *New York Times Book Review* contributor Marshall D. Shulman summarized. This "effort to mark out a centrist position," the critic added, "may contribute to the emergence of a more coherent consensus for American foreign policy."

Some reviewers, however, criticize the author for overlooking the effects of then-Soviet president Mikhail Gorbachev's *glasnost* reforms as well as the economic costs of pursuing a "victory without war" against the Soviets. The book, wrote Stanley Hoffman in the *New Republic,* contains "an almost indiscriminate paranoia about the Soviet Union—and the absence of a political and financial price tag." "Nixon should stop trying so hard to sound like a statesman," James Fallows averred in the *New York Review of Books,* in favor of what the critic calls the former president's "canny, lawyerlike, poker-playing instinct for sizing up a situation and understanding the possibilities it allows." In contrast, Lehmann-Haupt, who found Nixon's work full of "clarity, simplicity, and anecdotal appeal," believed that "what needs to be stressed is that in the main '1999' reflects what [Nixon's] admirers have always insisted is the better side of him. In short, if there is a residue of the political opportunist in these pages, it is by and large overwhelmed by the student of statecraft that he has aspired with such doggedness and energy to become." "If he is a prideful prisoner of traumatic experience, and moved too much by the desire for vindication, Nixon is also the most rigorous thinker who has inhabited the White House since John F. Kennedy," Thorsell similarly concluded. "His categorical view of the world need not be shared, but his voice should be heard."

*National Review* contributor Herbert S. Parmet likewise praised the former president as "the most prominent, gifted, and contentious leader of post-World War II America," and termed 1990's *In the Arena: A Memoir of Victory, Defeat, and Renewal* "a useful introduction to [Nixon's] mind and personality." Consisting of a series of short chapters on various political and personal subjects, *In the Arena* "reveals Nixon the Elder, a long way from the Whittier lawyer, with a voice more mature but strikingly recognizable," in Parmet's view. The volume's more personal tone Lehmann-Haupt attributed to the author's use of dictation in writing the book; "it is a more relaxed book," the critic observed, and the chapters "read as if the author had unbuttoned his mind and set it free to gather wool." While this method allows the reader to glimpse and empathize with "a figure in many emotional guises," the critic added, it also "prompts [Nixon] to refer to episodes in his career that have not only been dealt with at length in his previous books, but that are also covered repeatedly in the present volume." As a result, Roger Morris suggested in the *New York Times Book Review,* "what may distinguish the book most . . . are the aphorisms that flow from the resonant and authentic Nixon voice."

Nevertheless, some critics thought that *In the Arena* devoted too much space to defending its author's political record and ideas. *Los Angeles Times Book Review* contributor John B. Judis, for instance, while noting that "sensible and interesting sections" existed, asserted that the volume's "attempts at self-justification and its neo-Cold War policy prescriptions reflect a man who is still bedeviled by his past." However, *Washington Post Book World* writer Bob Woodward maintained that despite "the limitations of this book, and there are many, Nixon once again provides convincing evidence that he is a masterful student of world politics. He repeatedly digs for and finds examples of successful leadership, deftly isolating the powerful personality traits of Eisenhower, De Gaulle, Chou En-Lai and other giants. . . . Nixon is best writing about his intensely personal struggles (few better understand the importance of raw emotion in political life) and about the larger international scene he continues to study avidly." "This is, in most ways, a wistful book, suggesting what has been lost all around rather than beating to death the what-could-have-beens," concluded Parmet. "The spirit may be forced, but the closing tone is nevertheless upbeat and reflective. Nixon lives on; some will say he has returned, as if he ever disappeared."

With the passing of the Cold War Era in the early 1990s, Nixon turned his attention to the topic of the

Free World and the spread of democracy. In 1992's *Seize the Moment: America's Challenge in a One-Superpower World* he published what Congressman Jack Kemp noted in the *American Spectator* as "what may be his most important book." Written before Gorbachev's fall from power in favor of Boris Yeltzin, the book is divided into discussions on the end of Cold War policies and their effects on various sections of the world, from Western Europe to the Islamic world, all framed by a discussion of the future foreign policy of the United States. "Of the Soviets, Nixon displays great clarity of vision," noted Elliott Abrams in *Commentary,* adding that the former president "unmistakably saw both [the fight between Gorbachev and Yeltsin and the collapse of the U.S.S.R.] coming, and, more to the point, welcomed them both as conducive to American interests." Rather than supporting a failing communist regime to further narrow U.S. financial interests, Nixon favored only one thing: the rise of democratic rule over communism. Praising the author for supporting a foreign policy that eschewed party affiliations in favor of this ultimate goal, Kemp called *Seize the Day* "a textbook for 'winning the peace,' and for realizing the dream of all people everywhere for rule of law, private property, and human rights."

Nixon's final published work was *Beyond Peace,* which was published posthumously in 1994. While continuing to maintain the conservative—and much criticized—approach to domestic policy characteristic of his entire political career, Nixon now saw a host of new responsibilities befalling Americans in the wake of the demise of the former U.S.S.R. In Nixon's view, political leaders should be judged according to their efforts in advancing freedoms in the new Eastern Europe, rather than how they manipulated political and economic institutions to conform with U.S. political interests. Some critics found a contradiction between the Nixon of political record and the authorial Nixon; as J. Anthony Lukas maintained in the *New York Times Book Review, Beyond Peace,* like many of Nixon's books, was "conceived as an artifact in a stunningly successful public relations campaign, designed to turn a deposed and disgraced President into a sagacious elder statesman. . . . [Hence] the yawning gap between the grandiloquent locutions of Nixonian rhetoric and the shabby realities of Nixonian politics." However, other critics disagreed, commenting on the earnestness of the work. Calling Nixon's last book "a succinct . . . analysis of how America must approach the dilemmas of the coming century at home and abroad," *Los Angeles Times Book Review* critic Robert Dallek added that *Beyond Peace* "will be seen as Nixon's last will and testament, a summing up of ideas that Nixon saw as his legacy to the country he loved, served and mis-served in his long career." Despite his involvement in one of the worst scandals to rock the U.S. Presidency, Nixon, through his writing, "carved out a sizable niche for himself in the public arena with his reputation for realism and sagacity in public affairs," Richard Bernstein concluded in the *New York Times.* "There are few retired Washington giants," Paul Johnson similarly remarked of the years following Nixon's retirement in *Commentary,* that "keep themselves so well briefed on the state of the world, or who have more worthwhile observations to make about it." The critic added that "there can be few men whose judgment of the American political scene is so shrewd and penetrating, as well as surprisingly objective. . . . He probably exercises more political influence than any other Western statesman not actually in office. Considering the depths of degradation from which he has climbed, this is a remarkable achievement." Rebounding from adversity was characteristic of Nixon, however, as he himself once acknowledged in *In the Arena:* "As I look back on the dark days after my resignation, my most vivid memory is of a conversation I had with Ambassador Walter Annenberg shortly after I returned to San Clemente in 1974. He said, 'Whether you have been knocked down or are on the ropes, always remember that life is ninety-nine rounds.' Today, the battle I started to wage forty-three years ago when I first ran for Congress is not over. I still have a few rounds to go."

*BIOGRAPHICAL/CRITICAL SOURCES:*

*BOOKS*

Ambrose, Stephen E., *Nixon,* Simon & Schuster, Volume 1: *The Education of a Politician 1913-1962,* 1987, Volume 2: *The Triumph of a Politician 1962-72,* 1989.

Bernstein, Carl, and Bob Woodward, *All the President's Men,* Simon & Schuster, 1974.

Bernstein, Carl, and Bod Woodward, *The Final Days,* Simon & Schuster, 1976.

Brodie, Fawn M., *Richard Nixon: The Shaping of His Character,* Harvard University Press, 1983.

Casper, D. E., *Richard M. Nixon,* Garland Publishing, 1988.

Crowley, Monica, *Nixon in Winter: The Last Campaign,* Random House, 1996.

Dudley, Mark E., *United States v. Nixon (1974): Presidential Powers,* Macmillian, 1994.

Ehrlichman, John, *Witness to Power: The Nixon Years,* Simon & Schuster, 1982.

Emery, Fred, *Watergate: The Corruption of American Politics and the Fall of Richard Nixon,* Time Books, 1994.

Frost, David, *"I Gave Them a Sword": Behind the Scenes of the Nixon Interviews,* Morrow, 1978.

Herda, D. J., *United States v. Nixon: Watergate and the President,* Enslow, 1996.

Hoff, Joan, *Nixon Reconsidered,* Basic Books, 1994.

Lindop, Edmund, *Richard M. Nixon, Jimmy Carter, Ronald Reagan,* Twenty-First Century Books, 1996.

Lukas, James Anthony, *Nightmare: The Underside of the Nixon Years,* Bantam, 1977.

Matthews, Christopher, *Kennedy & Nixon: The Rivalry that Shaped Postwar America,* Simon & Schuster, 1996.

Morris, Roger, *Richard Milhous Nixon: The Rise of an American Politician,* Holt, 1989.

Nixon, Richard M., *Six Crises,* Doubleday, 1962.

Nixon, Richard M., *RN: The Memoirs of Richard Nixon,* Grosset, 1978.

Nixon, Richard M., *In the Arena: A Memoir of Victory, Defeat and Renewal,* Simon & Schuster, 1990.

Safire, William, *Before the Fall,* Doubleday, 1975.

Sulzberger, C. L., *The World and Richard Nixon,* Prentice Hall, 1987.

White, Theodore, *Making of the President 1972,* Atheneum, 1973.

White, Theodore, *Breach of Faith,* Atheneum, 1975.

Wicker, Tom, *One of Us: Richard Nixon and the American Dream,* Random House, 1995.

Wills, Gary, *Nixon Agonistes,* Houghton, 1970, revised and enlarged edition, New American Library, 1979.

*The Young Nixon,* California State University Fullerton, Oral History Program, 1978.

Zeifman, Jerry, *Without Honor: Crimes of Camelot and the Impeachment of President Nixon,* Thunder's Mouth Press, 1996.

*PERIODICALS*

*American Spectator,* June, 1992, pp. 60-61.

*Chicago Tribune,* March 31, 1985.

*Commentary,* August, 1979; August, 1980; October, 1988; March 1992, pp. 62-64.

*Globe and Mail* (Toronto), May 4, 1985; June 11, 1988.

*Insight on the News,* April 16, 1990, p. 64; July 18, 1994, p. 29.

*Los Angeles Times Book Review,* October 31, 1982; January 15, 1984; April 28, 1985; May 8, 1988; April 29, 1990; May 8, 1994, pp. 2, 10.

*Nation,* July 8, 1978.

*National Review,* August 18, 1978; July 25, 1980; February 24, 1984; May 3, 1985; May 28, 1990.

*New Leader,* June 6, 1994, p. 4.

*New Republic,* June 14, 1980; June 10, 1985; May 23, 1988.

*New Statesman,* June 8, 1978.

*Newsweek,* May 8, 1978; May 19, 1986; May 2, 1994, p. 20.

*New York Review of Books,* June 29, 1978; June 26, 1980; May 30, 1985; July 21, 1988; July 14, 1994, p. 26.

*New York Times,* June 8, 1978; March 15, 1985; March 28, 1985; April 11, 1988; April 9, 1990.

*New York Times Book Review,* June 11, 1978; May 25, 1980; October 31, 1982; January 29, 1984; April 7, 1985; April 17, 1988; April 29, 1990; July 3, 1994, p. 8.

*Saturday Review,* June, 1980.

*Spectator,* July 15, 1978.

*Time,* June 9, 1980; April 2, 1990; May 2, 1994, p. 42.

*Times* (London), April 17, 1986.

*Times Literary Supplement,* July 7, 1978; September 19, 1986; January 27, 1989.

*Tribune Books* (Chicago), April 15, 1990; May 22, 1994, p. 3.

*U. S. News & World Report,* May 2, 1994, pp. 24, 37.

*Washington Post,* March 21, 1988.

*Washington Post Book World,* May 28, 1978; June 1, 1980; November 21, 1982; March 31, 1985; April 17, 1988; May 22, 1994, p. 2.

*OBITUARIES:*

*PERIODICALS*

*Chicago Tribune,* April 23, 1994, p. A1; April 24, 1994, pp. A1, A4.

*Los Angeles Times,* April 23, 1994, pp. A1, A13, A20, A22-24; April 24, 1994, pp. A1, A12, A14; April 26, 1994, pp. A1, A8.

*New York Times,* April 24, 1994, pp. A1, A28, A29-33; April 26, 1994, pp. B9, B11; April 27, 1994, p. A14; April 28, 1994, pp. A20-A21.

*Times* (London), April 25, 1994, pp. A1, A11, A16, A19.

*Washington Post,* April 24, 1994, pp. A1, A10; April 26, 1994, p. A1; April 27, 1994, p. B1; April 28, 1994, pp. A1, A12.*

**O'FAOLAIN, Julia 1932-**
**(Julia Martines)**

*PERSONAL:* Surname is pronounced O'Fay-lawn; born June 6, 1932, in London, England; daughter of Sean (a writer) and Eileen (Gould) O'Faolain; married Lauro Martines (a professor and historian); children: Lucien Christopher. *Education:* University College, Dublin, received B.A. and M.A.; graduate study at Universita di Roma and Sorbonne, University of Paris.

*ADDRESSES:* *Agent*—Rogers, Coleridge & White, 20 Powis Mews, London W11 1JN, England; and International Creative Management, 40 West 52ndSt., New York, NY 10019.

*CAREER:* Writer, translator, and language teacher.

*AWARDS, HONORS:* Arts Council of Great Britain grant, 1981; *No Country for Young Men* was named to the Booker Prize short list.

*WRITINGS:*

(Translator, under name Julia Martines) Gene Brucker, editor, *Two Memoirs of Renaissance Florence: The Diaries of Buonaccorso Pitti and Gregorio Dati,* Harper, 1967.
(Translator, under name Julia Martines) Piero Chiara, *A Man of Parts,* Little, Brown, 1968.
*We Might See Sights! and Other Stories,* Faber, 1968.
*Godded and Codded,* Faber, 1970, published as *Three Lovers,* Coward, 1971.
(Editor with husband, Lauro Martines) *Not in God's Image: Women in History from the Greeks to the Victorians* (nonfiction), Harper, 1973.
*Man in the Cellar* (short stories), Faber, 1974.
*Women in the Wall* (novel), Viking, 1975.
*Melancholy Baby, and Other Stories,* Poolbeg Press, 1978.
*No Country for Young Men* (novel), Allen Lane, 1980, Carroll & Graf, 1986.
*Daughters of Passion* (short stories), Allen Lane, 1982.
*The Obedient Wife* (novel), Allen Lane, 1982, Carroll & Graf, 1985.
*The Irish Signorina* (novel), Allen Lane, 1984.
*The Judas Cloth,* Sinclair-Stevenson, 1992, Minerva, 1993.

Contributor to anthologies, including *The Bodley Head Book of Irish Short Stories,* edited by David Marcus, Bodley Head, 1980, *The Penguin Book of Irish Short Stories,* edited by Benedict Kiely, Penguin, 1981, and *Fathers: Reflections by Daughters,* edited by Ursula Owen, Virago, 1983, *Telling Stories 3,* edited by Duncan Minshull, Sceptre, 1994, *Alternative Loves,* edited by David Marcus, Martello, 1994, *New Writing 3* British Council/Minerva, 1994, *New Writing 4* British Council/Minerva, 1995, and *New Writing 5* British Council/Minerva, 1996. Contributor of short stories and reviews to the London *Times, New Yorker, Kenyon Review, Saturday Evening Post, Scripsi, Vogue, Critic, Cosmopolitan, Irish Press, New York Times, Washington Post, Observer,* and other periodicals. Also contributor to "Kaleidoscope," a British Broadcasting Corporation radio program.

*WORK IN PROGRESS:* A novel, *Ulysses and Night Watchman,* set in a prison in Paris in 1939.

*SIDELIGHTS:* Irish writer Julia O'Faolain has garnered significant acclaim and attention for her novels, short story collections, and works of nonfiction. Drawing on her extensive foreign travels, O'Faolain has used Italy, France, Ireland, and the United States as settings for her stories.

Born in London in 1932, O'Faolain is the daughter of a wellknown writer, Sean O'Faolain. When Julia O'Faolain's first novel-*Three Lovers*—appeared, it was inevitable that comparisons between her novel and the work of her father would be made. But *Book World* critic J. R. Franks dismisses the issue by saying: "Yes, Julia O'Faolain is Sean's daughter. No, she does not write like her father. And maybe, if [*Three Lovers*] is a fair harbinger, she'll become the family-member whose name is used for identification." Franks's opinion is echoed by Sally Beauman, who notes in the *New York Times Book Review* that the author "writes firmly, with a voice all her own." Praising O'Faolain's "well planned, intelligent, concise" style, Beauman finds the author's writing "more pointed than that of [her father] with a cold female eye for the egocentricities of masculine behavior."

Two of O'Faolain's notable works focus on women in history. *Not in God's Image: Women in History from the Greeks to the Victorians,* edited by O'Faolain and her husband, Lauro Martines, is described by a *Christian Century* writer as a collection of readings from primary sources that "documents the subjection of women in Western civilization." An *Economist* critic states that "as a source-book on the history of women, [*Not in God's Image*] stands in a class quite of its own. . . . The authors deal skillfully with the constant larding of hypocrisy, ranging from recipes for damaged maidenhoods to advice on concealing intellect." Mary Ellmann also admires the work, writing in the *New York Review of Books* that O'Faolain's effort is "distinguished by genuine scholarship. Its feminist sympathy is apparent . . . but it pursues the point by hard work, not by swishy emotion. And what a picture unfolds!"

*Women in the Wall,* a novel based on the life of Queen Radegund, who in the sixth century founded the monastery of the Holy Cross, is another example of O'Faolain's interest in women's place in history. But according to *Times Literary Supplement* critic Lalage Pulvertaft, by adapting such characters as Queen Radegund and St. Agnes, the author tampered with history to "try and answer fundamental questions about women's role in society." Pulvertaft faults O'Faolain's motives in writing *Women in the Wall:* "In her fashionable wish to explain visions as sexuality, vocations as perverted power mania, [the author] misses the nub of the matter; that God, through Christ, had challenged women as well as men to be individuals, even if this meant attacking the institutions of society."

Doris Grumbach, on the other hand, reviewing the book for *New Republic,* calls O'Faolain "a novelist of great talent whose interest has . . . come close to a Poe-ian obsession with immurement. . . . The force of language, the subtle and entirely successful recreation by means of it of the spirit as well as the events of Gallic life 13 centuries ago, at the end of the Roman era and the beginning of the Christian, make *Women in the Wall* a remarkably modern historical novel, poignant and powerful. It absorbs the reader into a time when women were chattels, when 'inherited land followed the spear not the spindle,'—into a time when the greatest conqueror was not of the flesh but of the spirit, when the full force of early Christianity made fanatics and saints of its believers."

O'Faolain further indulges her interest in religious history with *The Judas Cloth,* a novel set in Italy that deals with the authoritarian rule of Pope Pius IX. Francis King describes the novel, which dramatizes the methods by which Pius had the Vatican Council declare him infallible, as a work possessing a "grandeur of theme [that] is matched by [its] boldness of execution to thrilling effect." London *Sunday Times* contributor Peter Kemp comments that *The Judas Cloth* is a "novel rich in bizarre theatre" and "unrolls with enormous bravura the twists and turns that transformed him [Pope Pius IX] from the 'Angel Pope', white hope of liberals and progressives, to a sclerotic reactionary so execrated that, for years, it was deemed unsafe to transport his mortal remains across a hostile city to his place of rest."

With *No Country for Young Men,* O'Faolain "tackles the legacy of Republicanism in Southern Ireland through the story of one family," according to Hermoine Lee in the *Observer.* This story follows the efforts of an American sympathizer in Ireland who, while conducting research for a pro-Republican film, is drawn into the lives of a family whose members have involved themselves in the Irish cause for years. Writing a novel that spans three generations is "an ambitious undertaking," says Patricia Craig in the *Times Literary Supplement;* however, the critic finds the book somewhat "unsure of its own purpose. *No Country for Young Men* is not a political thriller, not a stark tragedy, not a documentary of social behaviour, not a story of personal relations, not a family saga, not a piece of historical fiction; but it contains . . . elements of all these."

Other critics, though, found more to praise in the novel. Lee, while acknowledging that "at times the novel edges toward lecture-topics," concludes nonetheless that the book's "strong grasp of the relation between a family and a national history transcends its occasional imaginative sagginess." The work "reflects a concern for the nation that emerged from the Troubles, and a worry about the new Troubles," states William Trevor in *Hibernia.* Trevor continues: "As a novel, it is old-fashioned in the very best sense, tidily knitting together its disparate strands, athletically leaping about in time and place, telling several stories at once." And *Guardian* reviewer Robert Nye, while noting that there "have been many novels about twentieth century Ireland and its problems," says that *No Country for Young Men* is "one of the very best books of its kind that it has ever been my pain and my pleasure to read." In recognition of O'Faolain's achievement, the novel was named a finalist for Britain's prestigious Booker Prize.

Irish issues also surface in *The Obedient Wife,* but in a different setting. The tale of a Catholic housewife's infatuation with an Irish Catholic priest in Los Angeles, *The Obedient Wife* is "a novel about failures of instinct, as well as . . . social and conjugal failures," according to Patricia Craig in another *Times Literary Supplement* review. Craig adds: "There is plenty of scope for comedy in Julia O'Faolain's novel, but she has chosen not to present her material in a comic mode. . . . Instead she coolly assesses the circumstances and traits that have got her characters into their present predicament, and still more coolly allows their defects and misapprehensions to become apparent in the course of the narrative." *The Obedient Wife,* comments Craig, "is an exceptionally polished work; if its ending disappoints feminists, who require gestures of social rebelliousness from their fiction, just as Catholic readers used to require wholesomeness in theirs, it is none the less appropriate, in that it represents an assertion of the values its heroine has lived by."

O'Faolain's short story collection *Daughters of Passion* gathers pieces that had been previously published in magazines and anthologies. The protagonists of these stories are complex individuals; some are women whose identities are shaped by the men in their lives, and others are characters who adopt political views only to satisfy their most immediate needs. King described these stories as being "remarkable for their intellectual and emotional toughness."

Returning to an Italian setting for the novel *The Irish Signorina,* O'Faolain presents an intellectual Gothic romance. The book concerns a young Irish woman who visits a friend of her deceased mother and becomes involved with both the friend's grandson and her middle-aged son. O'Faolain develops a comparison between romanticism and rationalism and explores differing philosophies of life and love. The novel was not as well received as some of O'Faolain's other works, with most critics finding it didactic, overfilled with quotations and esoteric references, and, ultimately, contrived. Julia Whedon, for instance, writing in the *New York Times Book Review,* declares that the lengthy descriptions "together with a surfeit of quotations and mythological references" detract from the book's impact. Still, Whedon avers that O'Faolain "is clearly a gifted and devout observer."

O'Faolain is one of "the very few Irish writers who [is] truly international in range," declares Roger Garfitt in his contribution to the book *Two Decades of Irish Writing: A Critical Survey.* "Where she differs most sharply . . . from other Irish writers is in choosing to work from within the contemporary flux of modes and passions. Her characters generally have comparative economic freedom. . . . They do not escape, though, essentially the same challenges: only in their case the pressure comes from within, generally as a conflict between the direction of their own vitality and the assumptions of the way they have been brought up." Concludes Garfitt: "There is a power of mind behind her work, as well as an irreverently perceptive eye, that catches the intensity of human drives, the essential seriousness of the effort to live, without swallowing any of the trends in self-deception. She is an acute observer, who is involved at a level of concern deeper than the substance of her observations."

*BIOGRAPHICAL/CRITICAL SOURCES:*

*BOOKS*

*Contemporary Authors Autobiography Series,* Volume 2, Gale, 1985.

*Contemporary Literary Criticism,* Gale, Volume 6, 1976, Volume 19, 1981, Volume 47, 1988.

*Dictionary of Literary Biography,* Volume 14: *British Novelists since 1960,* Gale, 1983.

Dunn, Douglas, editor, *Two Decades of Irish Writing: A Critical Survey,* Dufor, 1975.

O'Faolain, Julia, *Women in the Wall,* Viking, 1975.

Owens Weeks, Ann, *Irish Women Writers,* University Press of Kentucky, 1990.

Rafroidi, Patrick, and Maurice Harmon, editors, *The Irish Novel in Our Times,* Volume 3, Publications de l'Universite de Lille, 1975- 1976.

*PERIODICALS*

*Best Sellers,* May 1, 1971.

*Book World,* June 13, 1971.

*Choice,* December, 1973; October, 1975.

*Colby Quarterly,* March, 1991.

*Economist,* February 17, 1973.

*Guardian,* June 5, 1980.

*Hibernia,* June 5, 1980.

*Irish Times,* September 26, 1992.

*Listener,* June 20, 1968; September 26, 1974; June 3, 1982.

*London Magazine,* September, 1968; November, 1970; October/November, 1974.

*London Review of Books,* June 23, 1994.

*New Republic,* May 10, 1975.

*New Statesman,* June 6, 1980; November 12, 1982.

*New York Review of Books,* November 1, 1973.

*New York Times Book Review,* May 9, 1971; December 1, 1985; July 20, 1986; February 1, 1987.

*Observer,* June 1, 1980.

*Saturday Review,* July 3, 1971.

*Spectator,* January 1, 1983, p. 22.

*Sunday Times* (London), November 15, 1992.

*Sunday Tribune* (Dublin), September 29, 1992.

*Times Literary Supplement,* April 4, 1975; June 13, 1980; July 23, 1982; October 26, 1984; September 25, 1992, p. 24.

**OLSON, Charles (John) 1910-1970**

*PERSONAL:* Born December 27, 1910, in Worcester, MA; died after a short illness, January 10, 1970, in New York, NY; son of Karl Joseph and Mary (Hines) Olson. *Education:* Wesleyan University, B.A., 1932, M.A., 1933; also studied at Yale University and Harvard University.

*CAREER:* Taught at Clark University, Worcester, MA, at Harvard University, Cambridge, MA, 1936-39, and at Black Mountain College, Black Mountain, NC, serving as rector at Black Mountain, 1951-56; taught at State University of New York, Buffalo, 1963-65, and University of Connecticut, 1969.

*AWARDS, HONORS:* Received two Guggenheim fellowships; grant from Wenner-Gren Foundation, 1952, to study Mayan hieroglyphic writing in Yucatan; Oscar Blumenthal-Charles Leviton Prize, 1965; *Los Angeles Times* Book Award, 1984, for *The Maximus Poems;* American Book Award, Before Columbus Foundation, 1988, for *The Collected Poems of Charles Olson.*

*WRITINGS:*

*Call Me Ishmael,* Reynal & Hitchcock, 1947, Grove, 1958.
*To Corrado Cagli* (poetry), Knoedler Gallery (New York), 1947.
*YM & X* (poetry), Black Sun Press, 1948.
*Letter for Melville* (poetry), Melville Society, Williams College, 1951.
*This* (poem; design by Nicola Cernovich), Black Mountain College, 1952.
*The Maximus Poems 1-10,* Jargon, 1953, *11-22,* Jargon, 1956, Jargon/Corinth, 1960.
*Mayan Letters,* edited by Robert Creeley, Divers Press, 1953.
*In Cold Hell, In Thicket,* [Dorchester, MA], 1953, Four Seasons Foundation, 1967.
*Anecdotes of the Late War* (antiwar document), Jargon, c. 1957.
*O'Ryan 2.4.6.8.10.,* White Rabbit Press, 1958.
*Projective Verse* (essay), Totem Press, 1959.
*The Distances* (poems), Grove, 1961.
*Maximus, From Dogtown I,* foreword by Michael McClure, Auerhahn, 1961.
*A Bibliography on America for Ed Dorn,* Four Seasons Foundation, 1964.
*Human Universe, and Other Essays,* edited by Donald Allen, Auerhahn, 1965.
*Proprioception,* Four Seasons Foundation, 1965.
*O'Ryan 1, 2, 3, 4, 5, 6, 7, 8, 9, 10,* White Rabbit Press, 1965.
*Selected Writings,* edited by Robert Creeley, New Directions, 1966.
*Stocking Cap* (story), Four Seasons Foundation, 1966.
*Charles Olson Reading at Berkeley,* Coyote, 1966.
*West,* Goliard Press, 1966.
*The Maximus Poems IV, V, VI,* Cape Goliard, in association with Grossman, 1968.
*Pleistocene Man,* Institute of Further Studies (Buffalo, NY), 1968.
*Causal Mythology,* Four Seasons Foundation, 1969.
*Letters for Origin, 1950-1956,* edited by Albert Glover, Cape Goliard, 1969, Grossman, 1970.
*Archaeologist of Morning* (collected poems), Cape Goliard, 1970, Grossman, 1971, new edition, Grossman, 1973.
*The Special View of History,* edited by Ann Charters, Oyez, 1970.
*Poetry and Truth: Beloit Letters and Poems,* edited by George F. Butterick, Four Seasons Foundation, 1971.
*Additional Prose,* edited by Butterick, Four Seasons Foundation, 1974.
*The Maximus Poems, Volume III,* Grossman, 1974.
*In Adullam's Lair,* To the Lighthouse Press, 1975.
*The Post Office,* Grey Fox, 1975.
*The Fiery Hunt and Other Plays,* edited by Butterick, Four Seasons Foundation, 1977.
(With James Den Boer) *Olson-Den Boer: A Letter,* Christophers Books, 1977.
*Muthologos: The Collected Lectures and Interviews,* edited by Butterick, Four Seasons Foundation, 1978.
(With Robert Creeley) *Charles Olson and Robert Creeley: The Complete Correspondence,* eight volumes, edited by Butterick, Black Sparrow, 1980-87.
*The Maximus Poems,* edited by Butterick, University of California Press, 1983.
*The Collected Poems of Charles Olson,* edited by Butterick, University of California Press, 1987.
*A Nation of Nothing but Poetry: Supplementary Poems,* with an introduction by Butterick, Black Sparrow, 1989.
*Charles Olson and Ezra Pound: An Encounter at St. Elizabeth's,* edited by Catherine Seelye, Paragon House, 1990.
*In Love, In Sorrow: The Complete Correspondence of Charles Olson and Edward Dahlberg,* edited and with an introduction by Paul Christensen, Paragon House, 1990.

*Maximus to Gloucester: The Letters and Poems of Charles Olson to The Gloucester Times, 1962-1969,* edited by Peter Anastas, Ten Pound Island Press, 1993.

*Selected Poems by Charles Olson,* edited by Creeley, University of California Press, 1993.

Author of dance-play "Apollonius of Tyana," 1951. Work is represented in anthologies, including *The New American Poetry: 1945-1969,* edited by Donald M. Allen, Grove, 1960, and *The Norton Anthology of Modern Poetry,* edited by Richard Ellmann and Robert O'Clair, Norton, 1973. Contributor to *Twice-A-Year, Black Mountain Review, Big Table, Yugen, Evergreen Review, Origin, Poetry New York,* and other periodicals.

*SIDELIGHTS:* Charles Olson was an innovative, award-winning poet and essayist whose work influenced numerous other writers during the 1950s and 1960s. In his influential essay on projective (or open) verse, Olson asserts that "a poem is energy transferred from where the poet got it (he will have some several causations), by way of the poem itself to, all the way over to, the reader. Okay. Then the poem itself must, at all points, be a high energy-construct and, at all points, an energy-discharge." Form is only an extension of content and "right form, in any given poem, is the only and exclusively possible extension of content under hand. . . . I take it that PROJECTIVE VERSE teaches, is, this lesson, that that verse will only do in which a poet manages to register both the acquisitions of his ear *and* the pressures of his breath." Olson goes by ear, and his lines are breath-conditioned. The two halves, he says, are: "the HEAD, by way of the EAR, to the SYLLABLE/the HEART, by way of the BREATH, to the LINE." He believes "it is from the union of the mind and the ear that the syllable is born. But the syllable is only the first child of the incest of verse. . . . The other child is the LINE. . . . And the line comes (I swear it) from the breath. . . ." Robert Creeley explains thus: "What he is trying to say is that the heart is a basic instance not only of rhythm, but it is the base of the measure of rhythms for all men in the way heartbeat is like the metronome in their whole system. So that when he says the heart by way of the breath to the line, he is trying to say that it is in the line that the basic rhythmic scoring takes place. . . . Now, the head, the intelligence by way of the ear to the syllable—which he calls also 'the king and pin'—is the unit upon which all builds. The heart, then, stands, as the primary feeling term. The head, in contrast, is discriminating. It is discriminating by way of what it hears." Olson believes that "in any given poem always, always one perception must must must MOVE, INSTANTER, ON ANOTHER!" So, all the conventions that "logic has forced on syntax must be broken open as quietly as must the too set feet of the old line."

Olson thus rejected "academic" verse, with its closed forms and alleged artifice. The *Times Literary Supplement* notes that "culture, civilization, history (except history as personal exploration as in Herodotus) and, above all, sociology, are dirty words for him." Olson said: "It comes to this: the use of a man, by himself and thus by others, lies in how he conceives his relation to nature. . . . If he is contained within his nature as he is participant in the larger force, he will be able to listen, and his hearing through himself will give him secrets objects share. And by an inverse law his shapes will make their own way. . . . This is not easy. Nature works from reverence, even in her destructions (species go down with a crash). But breath is man's special qualification as animal. Sound is a dimension he has extended. Language is one of his proudest acts. . . . I keep thinking, it comes to this: culture displacing the state." M. L. Rosenthal comments: "The problem is to get back to sources of meaning anterior to those of our own state-ridden civilization and so to recover the sense of personality and of place that has been all but throttled."

Robert Duncan, in his essay "Regarding Olson's *'Maximus,'*" writes: "Olson insists upon the active. Homo maximus wrests his life from the underworld as the Gloucester fisherman wrests his from the sea." Olson's striding poetic syllables, says Duncan, are "no more difficult than walking." Duncan traces Olson's aesthetics to nineteenth-century American sources: "I point to Emerson or to Dewey," writes Duncan, "to show that in American philosophy there are foreshadowings or forelightings of 'Maximus.' In this aesthetic, conception cannot be abstracted from doing; beauty is related to the beauty of a archer hitting the mark." A *Times Literary Supplement* reviewer observes that Olson's style is at times a "bouncy, get-in-with-it manner," often involving the "juxtaposition of a very abstract statement with a practical, jocular illustration of what the statement might imply." Wrote Olson: "It's as though you were hearing for the first time—who knows what a poem ought to sound like? until it's thar? And how do you get it thar ezcept as you do—*you,* and nobody else (who's a poet?. . .)"

Anyone familiar with contemporary poetry would agree with Robert Creeley when he calls Olson "central to any description of literary 'climate' dated 1958." Olson's influence extends directly to Creeley, Duncan, Denise Levertov, and Paul Blackburn, and, as Stephen Stepanchev notes, Olson's projective verse "has either influenced or coincided with other stirrings toward newness in American poetry." He himself owed a great deal to Ezra Pound, William Carlos Williams, and Edward Dahlberg. The scope of Olson's work is "as broad as Pound's," writes Kenneth Rexroth. It is not simple poetry, much of it being fragmentary and experimental. But it has, says Rosenthal, "the power of hammering conviction—something like Lawrence's but with more brutal insistence behind it. It is a dogmatic, irritable, passionate voice, of the sort that the modern world, to its sorrow very often, is forever seeking out; it is not a clear voice, but one troubled by its own confusions which it carries into the attack."

The magnitude of Olson's work can be viewed in the 1993 volume *Selected Poems,* which was edited by Creeley, "Olson's running mate' and poetic heir," according to Albert Mobilio in the *Village Voice Literary Supplement.* While Mobilio finds that the selections "tilt towards the *Maximus Poems,*" he remarks that "the appearance of a sleek , intelligently honed selection of Olson's unwieldy oeuvre is reason to cheer." In another review, a *Village Voice Literary Supplement* contributor cites Olson as "the most American of this century's poets" and praises the volume: "At last we have the quintessential American format—the portable—from which we can savor his rare and agile brilliance."

Olson's correspondence has been published in a number of volumes. It includes letters to other writers, such as Edward Dahlberg, published in *In Love, In Sorrow* as well as to the entire town of Gloucester via *The Gloucester Times* (*Maximus to Gloucester.*) The letters in *In Love, In Sorrow* illustrate the younger Olson's early relationship to Dahlberg as that of an apprentice. Over the twenty years of correspondence, that relationship changed to one of peers, then disintegrated as Olson's poetry matured. Albert Glover in *American Book Review* comments, "What distinguishes this correspondence . . . is the character of the figure to whom Olson writes and the nature of the issue that clearly hangs in the balance: identity. . . . these letters are addressed to a man who embodies authority, an older writer with experience and personal contacts useful to a beginner." Referring to Dahlberg's identity as a "confessional" writer, Glover notes, "I find in [the correspondence] more evidence of Olson's need to define an acceptable relation of personal life to creative work." Charles L. DeFanti in *Washington Post Book World* pursues a similar thread: "By itself, the psychopathology in the Dahlberg/Olson friendship is enough to maintain the reader's fascination, but Christensen wisely de-emphasizes clinical aspects in order to evaluate the literary issues surrounding these two bizarre American writers." Unfortunately, DeFanti continues, "Though this is a fascinating story, the wisdom of presenting it in this form is questionable." In particular, DeFanti cites the editing as "uneven," the texts incomplete, and ineffective or nonexistent notes: "Gaps in information are wide, references are obscure, and even fans of the two writers will need a Webster's Unabridged close at hand."

*Maximus to Gloucester,* Olson's correspondence to his hometown newspaper *The Gloucester Times,* fares better. Olson's original aim in writing these letters and poetry was to preserve Gloucester as a "living entity," according to Karl Young in *American Book Review.* Olson backed up the correspondence with activities such as the preservation of historic buildings in the city and saving wetlands. Ten Pound Island Press's motivation in publishing the texts in 1993 was to accomplish similar aims, as well as to "reintroduce Olson to Gloucester, this time as poet," notes Young. While the collection's primary audience may be assumed to be New England, Young declares that "it has a profound and emphatic significance [beyond New England]: it firmly and irrefutably throws the emphasis of Olson's work back on the local-on the detailed, immediate, and particular life of a *polis* that Olson thought essential to a proper vision of the world and existence in it."

Olson did not consider himself "a poet" or "a writer" by profession, but rather that nebulous and rare "archeologist of morning," reminiscent of Thoreau. He wrote on a typewriter. "It is the advantage of the typewriter that, due to its rigidity and its space precisions, it can, for a poet, indicate exactly the breath, the pause, the suspensions even of syllables, the juxtapositions even of parts of phrases, which he intends. For the first time the poet has the stave and the bar a musician has had. For the first time he can, without the convention of rime and meter, record the listening he has done to his own speech and by that one act indicate how he would want any reader, silently or otherwise, to voice his work."

*BIOGRAPHICAL/CRITICAL SOURCES:*

*BOOKS*

Allen, Donald M., editor, *The New American Poetry: 1945-1960,* Grove, 1960.

*Contemporary Authors Bibliographical Series,* Volume 2, Gale, 1986.

*Contemporary Literary Criticism,* Gale, Volume 1, 1973, Volume 2, 1974, Volume 5, 1976, Volume 6, 1976, Volume 9, 1978, Volume 11, 1979, Volume 29, 1984.

Foster, Edward Halsey, *Understanding the Black Mountain Poets,* University of South Carolina Press, 1995.

Maud, Ralph, *Charles Olson's Reading: A Biography,* Southern Illinois University Press, 1996.

*Olson: The Journal of the Charles Olson Archives,* University of Connecticut Library, 1974—.

Rexroth, Kenneth, *Assays,* New Directions, 1961.

Riddel, Joseph N., and Mark Bauerlein, editor, *The Turning Word: American Literary Modernism and Continental Theory,* University of Pennsylvania Press, 1996.

Rosenthal, M. L., *The Modern Poets,* Oxford University Press, 1965.

Stepanchev, Stephen, *American Poetry Since 1945,* Harper, 1965.

*PERIODICALS*

*American Book Review,* October, 1991, p. 24; August, 1993, p. 17.

*Antiquarian Bookman,* March 2-9, 1970.

*Black Mountain Review,* Number 6, 1956.

*Evergreen Review,* summer, 1958.

*Library Journal,* December, 1990, p. 169.

*London Review of Books,* March 10, 1994, p. 20.

*Los Angeles Times Book Review,* September 4, 1983.

*New Yorker,* May 23, 1994, p. 101.

*New York Times,* January 11, 1970.

*Publishers Weekly,* January 26, 1970.

*Review,* January, 1964.

*Times Literary Supplement,* November 25, 1965; September 30, 1988.

*Village Voice Literary Supplement,* November, 1993, p. 90; December, 1993.

*Washington Post Book World,* November 13, 1983; October 6, 1985; July 15, 1990, p. 4.

*West Coast Review,* spring, 1967.*

# P

**PALINURUS**
**See CONNOLLY, Cyril (Vernon)**

* * *

**PASTAN, Linda (Olenik) 1932-**

*PERSONAL:* Born May 27, 1932, in New York, New York United States; daughter of Jacob L. (a physician) and Bess (Schwartz) Olenik; married Ira Pastan (a molecular biologist), June 14, 1953; children: Stephen, Peter, Rachel. *Education:* Radcliffe College, B.A., 1954; Simmons College, M.L.S., 1955; Brandeis University, M.A., 1957. *Religion:* Jewish.

*ADDRESSES: Home*—11710 Beall Mountain Rd., Potomac, MD 20854. *Agent*—Jean V. Naggar Literary Agency, 336 East 73rd Street, New York, NY 10021.

*CAREER:* Writer. Lecturer at Breadloaf Writers Conference, Ripton, VT.

*AWARDS, HONORS:* Dylan Thomas Poetry Award, 1958, *Mademoiselle;* Swallow Press New Poetry Series award, 1972; National Endowment for the Arts fellow, 1972; Bread Loaf Writers Conference, John Atherton fellowship, 1974; Maryland Arts Council grant, 1978; De Castagnola Award, 1978, for *The Five Stages of Grief;* American Book Award poetry nomination, 1983, for *PM/AM: New and Selected Poems;* Bess Hokin Prize, *Poetry,* 1985; Maurice English Award, 1986; Virginia Faulkner Award, *Prairie Schooner,* 1992; poet laureate of Maryland, 1991-95, *The Imperfect Paradise* was nominated for the *Los Angeles Times* book award .

*WRITINGS:*

*POETRY*

*A Perfect Circle of Sun,* Swallow Press, 1971.
*Aspects of Eve,* Liveright, 1975.
*On the Way to the Zoo,* Dryad, 1975.
*The Five Stages of Grief,* Norton, 1978.
*Setting the Table,* Dryad, 1980.
*Waiting for My Life,* Norton, 1981.
*PM/AM: New and Selected Poems,* Norton, 1983.
*A Fraction of Darkness: Poems,* Norton, 1985.
*The Imperfect Paradise: Poems,* Norton, 1988.
*Heroes in Disguise,* Norton, 1991.
*An Early Afterlife,* Norton, 1995.
*Carnival Evening: New and Selected Poems 1968-1998,* Norton, 1998.

*SIDELIGHTS:* One of the prevailing themes of Linda Pastan's poetry is the complexity of domestic life. In what she terms "the war between desire and dailiness," Pastan "dissects the tension that divides womanly rituals of motherhood and housekeeping from the solitary rites of the poet," writes Phoebe Pettingell in the *New Leader.* Pastan relies on imagery and metaphor to infuse ordinary domestic matters with mystery and magic in a style reminiscent of Emily Dickinson, who, according to Dave Smith in the *American Poetry Review,* "took her dailiness to the heights of metaphysical vision. . . . It may be, Dickinson is Pastan's ghost, though less perhaps in sound than in what to look at and how to show it." Pastan's style is simple and understated; her poetry, therefore, is "never baroque, never sentimental, never suffused with a militant feminism," observes Samuel Hazo in the *Hudson Review.* Commenting on the economy of her language, *Chicago Tribune Book World* contributor L. M. Rosenberg writes that Pastan "knows the force of what's left unsaid, the importance of the white space around the written word. This makes her a poet of elegant spareness."

Pastan's "material chose her," according to Pettingell, "when she interrupted her writing career to [marry and] raise a family." The interruption immediately followed Pastan's graduation from Radcliffe, where, in her senior year, she won the *Mademoiselle* poetry contest. The runner-up was Sylvia Plath. Unlike Plath, however, Pastan relinquished her writing. "I was into the whole '50s thing, kids and the clean floor bit," she told *Washington Post* writer Michael Kernan. "I was unhappy because I knew what I should be doing." Pastan explained that her husband, tired "of hearing what a great writer I would have been if I hadn't got married," urged her to take her work seriously and write while the children were in school. Since that time, Pastan has dedicated herself to her poetry; her efforts were rewarded in 1983 when *PM/AM: New and Selected Poems* was nominated for an American Book Award.

In *Waiting for My Life,* a title that alludes to Pastan's interrupted writing career, "she broods on the rewards as well as the risks of domesticity," comments Sandra M. Gilbert in *Parnassus.* One of those risks, according to Pastan, is that those who are unfamiliar with domesticity will equate it with mundaneness. Gilbert, for example, wonders, "Is it because she is quite self-consciously a *woman* poet that Pastan so austerely ordains the necessity of acquiescence in the ordinary?" In *"Who Is It Accuses Us?"* Pastan defends both her lifestyle and her poetry by suggesting that domesticity is hazardous and requires physical and emotional fortitude. Another poem, *"The War between Desire and Dailiness,"* explores the conflict "between longing and order, body and soul, the woman and the poet," according to J. D. McClatchy in *Poetry.* At the end of the poem Pastan declares, "Let dailiness win," and though "it sounds as if she has chosen safety, . . . the line ends [the] poem with anything but conviction," observes Smith.

*Waiting for My Life* also depicts "parents musing on the lives of grown children, on their own altered flesh, the weather or, the slackened but not dead fevers of desire, those moments spent at windows in kitchens or gardens where we are astonished at the speed and movement that is all the not-us," Smith explains. In *"Meditation by the Stove,"* for instance, Pastan describes a housewife who contemplates neglecting her duties. Pettingell remarks that while there is "menace implicit" in the concluding lines "And I have banked the fires of my body / into a small domestic flame for others / to warm their hands on for a while," Pastan "knows what price men and women pay for domesticity, while realizing that not even poets want to live entirely alone, without responsibilities."

Both her subject matter and unaffected writing style make Pastan an accessible poet. Several critics note, however, that Pastan sometimes sacrifices subtly for accessibility. Mary Jo Salter, for example, comments in the *Washington Post Book World* that *Waiting for My Life* "is sometimes simple to a fault," citing the simile "the white curtains blow / like ghosts of themselves." Similarly, *Chicago Tribune Book World* contributor L. M. Rosenberg describes Pastan's poetry as "occasionally too easy" but later concedes that her "work is its own argument against charges of insufficiency." Peter Stitt, on the other hand, maintains in the *Georgia Review* that Pastan "does not cause brain strain, like the early Mark Strand, and she does not leave us breathless, sweating, far from civilization, like Galway Kinnell—but she is a wonderful writer nevertheless and works in a rich, human vein." *Waiting for My Life* "is full of surprises that make it far from daily," concludes Smith. "It keeps a low heat, but it is radiant heat nonetheless."

One way that Pastan elevates her subject matter is through metaphor. As Stephen Dobyns observes in the *Washington Post Book World:* "It is metaphor that drives all her poems, that lifts them from the mundane and gives them their degree of magic. . . . The poems are strongest when the commentary combines with the mysterious through metaphor to give us a new sense of the world, to make us see what has become commonplace as if for the first time." In *The Five Stages of Grief,* arranged according to the stages outlined in Elisabeth Kuebler-Ross's *On Death and Dying,* Pastan writes not only about death, but about death as a metaphor for "loss through divorce, adultery, argument, aging, children leaving home, identity crisis, silence, and innocence/wisdom," writes Karla Hammond in the *Prairie Schooner.* Several of the poems describe a discontented married woman who, after experiencing denial, anger, bargaining, and depression, finally reaches acceptance when she realizes that "even though their relationship has been strained to the point that it is no longer satisfactory to [her], she can find comfort only with her husband, with the familiar, with the imperfect," observes Benjamin Franklin V in the *Dictionary of Literary Biography.*

This metaphor "of the breaking marriage . . . is not a literal truth referring to the poet's life (other poems make this unmistakably clear) but a metaphor standing for the issue of loss and abandonment generally, as our children disappear from us into their own lives, as our parents disappear into their deaths, and so on," notes Stitt. "If there is an ultimate truth" in *The Five Stages of Grief,* "it is that grief (embodied in loss, separation, and death) like history, is a 'circular staircase' from which there is no human escape," comments Hammond, who later concludes that "this is a moving work in its subtlety, intensity and matter-of-factness. . . . It touches the lives of each of us on our journey from denial to acceptance."

In *PM/AM: New and Selected Poems* Pastan again "stresses the mystery of the ordinary, the strangeness to which we wake each 'AM' and out of which we lapse each 'PM,'" writes Gilbert. The early morning hours are especially important to Pastan, for she begins to write as soon as she wakes, hoping to "surprise her mind before the visions melt, while it is still running loose in that landscape of wishes, still detached from the engines of reason," according to Michael Kernan in the *Washington Post.* These fragments of dreams play a significant role in Pastan's writing, although, as she explained to Kernan, "it's not a matter of transcribing actual dreams, . . . but of using the unconscious state and its strange associations and the insights you get from them." Pastan's interest in the dream state manifests itself in several of the poems in *PM/AM: New and Selected Poems.* *"Waking,"* for example, describes the process of awakening as "watching our dreams move / helplessly away like fading / lantern fish." And in *"Dreams,"* originally published in *Waiting for My Life,* Pastan observes that dreams transport us to "the place where the children / we were / rock in the arms of the children / we have become." It is poems like these that "reveal a complex, original imagination finding magic in the commonplace and making dreams universally intelligible," writes *Detroit News* contributor Edward Morin.

The publication of *PM/AM: New and Selected Poems* has prompted several critics to review Pastan's progress as a writer. Kernan comments that in this book, "the sense of self-observation seems to have grown more acute, both in the quality of the observations and in the merciless cutting of lines and words . . . to clutch at some essence." *New York Times Book Review* contributor Hugh Seidman remarks: "One cannot deny that [Pastan's] vision has gained in depth over the years. [*PM/AM*] has a stateliness and solidity of tone not reached in earlier [books], and there is evidence of more emotional opening out in some of her newest pieces." Even those earlier poems "that seemed minor and fragmentary [the] first time around," writes a *Publishers Weekly* critic, "are transformed by the unity of their context" in *PM/AM.* Her poems, concludes *Voyages* critic Roderick Jellema, continue to "quietly unmake the set of the mind as they cut apart, deepen, and then reunify the ingredients of simple experience. And that's where discoveries about our lives and our world are made."

*The Imperfect Paradise* is a collection of poems in which Pastan writes of love and grief. Mortality, death, loss of a loved one, happiness, spiritual and physical love, and marital crisis are among the topics she explores, revealing her deepest thoughts, beliefs, and fears. Grace Bauer in the *Library Journal* calls Pastan's poems "direct and passionate, yet controlled." Bruce Bennett, writing in the *New York Times Book Review,* comments that "Ms. Pastan's unfailing mastery of her medium holds the darkness firmly in check," continuing on to conclude: "Enmeshed in the 'imperfect paradise' that constitutes our common life, Ms. Pastan sounds these depths ['whose measure we only guess'] in subtle and delicate ways."

*Heroes in Disguise* gathers poems on seasonal change, the resurfacing into adulthood of childhood experiences, and mortality. "Pastan like a seer delivers these poems," writes *Washington Post Book World* contributor Kathy S. Cohen, noting, "The clarity of middle age is here attached to the concept of generations." Most critics praise Pastan's serene tone of voice and insights into, as Lee Upton puts it in a *Belles Lettres* review, "matters of creation and judgment." Upton concludes that, while "the collection might have been culled of a few slighter poems in the later section, the book as a whole reflects Pastan's inviting spirit." And Sandra M. Gilbert notes in *Poetry* that "despite her restraints and constraints, Pastan . . . seems to me to have—or, anyway, to seek—affinities with that American muse who descends from a strange meeting between our two greatest poets [Walt Whitman and Emily Dickinson]." "Always interesting, balanced, seldom profound," writes Dick Allen in *The Hudson Review,* "this is a poetry we return to more for content than form, a poetry of the whole poem rather than the individual line."

*BIOGRAPHICAL/CRITICAL SOURCES:*

*BOOKS*

*Contemporary Literary Criticism,* Gale, Volume 27, 1984.

*PERIODICALS*

*American Poetry Review,* January, 1982.
*Belles Lettres,* fall, 1992, p. 30.
*Chelsea 60,* summer, 1996.
*Chicago Tribune Book World,* September 13, 1981; June 12, 1983.
*Detroit News,* September 27, 1981.
*Georgia Review,* winter, 1979, pp. 928-30; spring, 1983.
*The Hudson Review,* autumn, 1978; summer, 1992, p. 319.
*Library Journal,* May 15, 1988, p. 85.
*New England Review,* 1978, pp. 104-08.
*New Leader,* December 27, 1982.
*New York Times,* August 18, 1972.
*New York Times Book Review,* February 20, 1983; September 18, 1988, pp. 42, 44.
*Parnassus,* fall/winter, 1972, pp. 130-32; spring, 1983.
*Poetry,* September, 1982; June 12, 1983; August, 1992.
*Prairie Schooner,* fall, 1979.
*Publishers Weekly,* September 10, 1982; November 28, 1994, p. 53.
*Shenandoah,* summer, 1973, pp. 92-3.
*The Southern Review,* winter, 1992.
*Voyages,* spring, 1969, pp. 73-4.
*Washington Post,* December 17, 1983.
*Washington Post Book World,* May 21, 1978; July 5, 1981; November 7, 1982; February 2, 1986; December 22, 1991.

* * *

## PAULEY, Barbara Anne 1925-

*PERSONAL:* Born January 12, 1925, in Nashville, TN; daughter of William M. (a publisher) and Lucile (Dies) Cotton; married Robert Reinhold Pauley (an investment banker), June 22, 1946; children: Lucinda, Nicholas Andrew, Robert Reinhold, Jr., John. *Education:* Attended Wellesley College, 1942. *Politics:* Republican. *Religion:* Congregationalist.

*ADDRESSES: Office*—c/o Doubleday, 666 Fifth Ave., New York, NY 10103. *Agent*—Blassingame McCauley & Wood, 432 Park Ave. South, Suite 1205, New York, NY 10016.

*CAREER:* Freelance writer. Former editorial assistant, Ideal Publishing Corp.

*MEMBER:* Mystery Writers of America.

*WRITINGS:*

*Blood Kin,* Doubleday (New York City), 1972.
*Voices Long Hushed,* Doubleday, 1976.

Contributor of stories to romance magazines.

*SIDELIGHTS:* Barbara Anne Pauley focuses on "the passions, conflicts, and terrors of the Civil War," as Gina Macdonald explains in *Twentieth Century Romance and Historical Writers.* Her novels *Blood Kin* and *Voices Long Hushed* tell of women in the old South who find themselves entangled in family intrigues. The conflicts found in both novels, Macdonald writes, are "like those of the war itself, . . . family conflicts in which distant relatives conspire against the central characters—to acquire land or wealth or love, to hide sins, to work out personal hatreds."

In *Blood Kin,* Leslie Day Hallam tries to rebuild her impoverished life, and recapture some of the happiness of her childhood, at her family's plantation Sycamore Knob. Amid such troubling circumstances as a child with gruesome nightmares, a house fire, conflicting loyalties during the Civil War, and the machinations of jealous relatives, "romance blossoms, first in the sudden, physical passion that draws together an experienced man-of-the-world and an innocent girl, and then a gentler, self-giving love that grows with time and proximity," Macdonald relates. The *Booklist* reviewer notes that *Blood Kin* "contains familiar ingredients" but that "the soap-opera plot, reinforced with some perception of Southern temperament and thoroughbred horseflesh, just manages to hold to the end of the novel."

*Voices Long Hushed* follows the plight of Stacie, an orphan who discovers she has a mother accused of madness and murder. To prove her mother both sane and innocent, Stacie must "untangle the web of deceit spun by an odd assortment of distant, conniving relatives," Macdonald explains. The critic for *Booklist* notes that the novel's "traditional gothic elements are fortified by unusual twists that hold reader interest, and head-strong Stacie is an appealing character." The reviewer for *Library Journal* calls *Voices Long Hushed* "a very fancy amalgam of Gothic, historic, and suspense, hypnotic with money and menace, and written to a fare-thee-well."

*BIOGRAPHICAL/CRITICAL SOURCES:*

*BOOKS*

*Twentieth Century Romance and Historical Writers,* third edition, St. James Press (Detroit), 1994.

*PERIODICALS*

*Bestsellers,* May 1, 1973, p. 71.
*Booklist,* July 1, 1972, p. 930; May 1, 1976, p. 1243.
*Kirkus Reviews,* February 15, 1972, p. 221; January 1, 1976, p. 29.
*Library Journal,* July, 1972, p. 2440; May 16, 1976, p. 743.
*New York Times Book Review,* May 16, 1976, p. 34.
*Publishers Weekly,* February 2, 1976, p. 90.

* * *

**PERRY, Ritchie (John Allen) 1942-**
**(John Allen)**

*PERSONAL:* Born January 7, 1942, in King's Lynn, Norfolk, England; son of Hubert John (a teacher) and Ella (Allen) Perry; married Lynn Mary Charlotte Barton, November 23, 1976; children: Tina Elizabeth, Sara Charlotte. *Education:* St. John's College, Oxford, B.A. (honors), 1964.

*ADDRESSES:* *Agent*—Peters, Fraser & Dunlop, 5th Floor, The Chambers, Chelsea Harbour, Lots Rd., London SW10 0XF, England.

*CAREER:* Bank of London & South America Ltd., Brazil, managerial trainee, 1964-66; assistant teacher in Norfolk, England, 1966-74, and in Luton, England, 1975—.

*WRITINGS:*

*MYSTERY NOVELS*

*The Fall Guy,* Houghton (Boston), 1972.
*A Hard Man to Kill,* Houghton, 1973 (published in England as *Nowhere Man,* Collins [London], 1973).
*Ticket to Ride,* Collins, 1973, Houghton, 1974.
*Holiday with a Vengeance,* Collins, 1974, Houghton, 1975.
*Your Money and Your Wife,* Collins, 1975, Houghton, 1976.
*One Good Death Deserves Another,* Collins, 1976, Houghton, 1977.
*Dead End,* Collins, 1977.
*Dutch Courage,* Collins, 1978.
*Bishop's Pawn,* Pantheon (New York City), 1979.
*Grand Slam,* Pantheon, 1980.
*Fool's Mate,* Pantheon, 1981.
*Foul Up,* Doubleday (New York City), 1982.
*MacAllister,* Doubleday, 1984.
*Kolwezi,* Doubleday, 1985.
*Presumed Dead,* Doubleday, 1987.
*Comeback,* Doubleday, 1991.

*UNDER PSEUDONYM JOHN ALLEN*

*Copacabana Stud,* R. Hale (London), 1978.
*Up Tight,* R. Hale, 1979.

*JUVENILE*

*Brazil: The Land and Its People,* Macdonald Educational (London), 1977, Silver Burdett (Morristown, NJ), 1978.
*George H. Ghastly,* Hutchinson (London), 1981.
*George H. Ghastly to the Rescue,* Hutchinson, 1983.
*George H. Ghastly and the Little Horror,* Hutchinson, 1985.
*Fenella Fang,* Hutchinson, 1986.
*Fenella Fang and the Wicked Witch,* Hutchinson, 1989.
*The Creepy Tale,* Hutchinson, 1989.
*Fenella Fang and the Time Machine,* Hutchinson, 1991.
*The Runton Werewolf,* Hutchinson, 1994.
*Haunted House,* Ginn (Aylesbury), 1995.

*SIDELIGHTS:* In many of his thriller novels, Ritchie Perry has written of Philis, a British Intelligence operative based in Brazil whose cases take him throughout the world and involve him with terrorists, rival intelligence agencies and criminal organizations. "Perry's best work is his Philis series," writes George Kelley in the *St. James Guide to Crime and Mystery Writers.*

The Philis series begins with *The Fall Guy* in which Philis, a small-time smuggler in Brazil, is blackmailed by British Intelligence into working for them. By *Nowhere Man,* Philis is a regular agent but still "remains a cynical, selfish character with little loyalty to Britain," as Kelley explains. O. L. Bailey in *Saturday Review* calls Philis "a sufficiently maverick operative." Newgate Callendar in the *New York Times Book Review* describes Philis as "the independent, capable operative who can kill, who can flout authority, who is the hero of every man's dreams."

"*Bishop's Pawn,*" writes Kelley, "is the cleverest of Philis's adventures. . . . Philis [must] smuggle a defecting Polish Roman Catholic bishop out of East Germany. But the mission is complicated by the fact that the bishop turns out to have secretly been a mass murderer and war criminal in World War II. With that plotline and the hidden treasure looted from Italy during the German occupation, Philis has his hands full with this mission." Jean Strouse in *Newsweek* finds *Bishop's Pawn* "full of action and intrigue," while finding "Philis's smart-tough-funny mock-macho swagger often endearing." Robin Winks of the *New Republic* explains: "Everything unrolls with the comfortable sense that new double-crosses may be counted on every page and that in the end Philis will triumph."

Perry once told *CA:* "I'm a lazy slob. This is an opinion everybody shares, even my dog when I can't be bothered to take her for a walk. It was ingrained laziness which helped to start me writing—while I was sitting at a typewriter, nobody asked me to help with the household chores. Eventually the cynics around me (i.e., those doing all the chores) demanded some proof of my writing abilities and pride forced me to deliver. Hence my first book, back in 1972. As I like being able to tell impressionable young women that I am an author, I have continued writing ever since. However, the dilettante in me remains and I seldom work at my writing for more than ten hours a week. Indeed, I find it very difficult to take my books seriously as I have never, ever considered myself a creative person. A lot of my readers would probably agree with me."

*BIOGRAPHICAL/CRITICAL SOURCES:*

*BOOKS*

*St. James Guide to Crime and Mystery Writers,* fourth edition, St. James Press (Detroit), 1996.

*PERIODICALS*

*New Republic,* February 16, 1980, p. 37.
*Newsweek,* August 6, 1979, p. 73.
*New York Times Book Review,* September 9, 1979, p. 20.
*Saturday Review,* September 30, 1972, p. 79.

* * *

**PFAFF, Richard W(illiam) 1936-**

*PERSONAL:* Born August 6, 1936, in Oklahoma City, OK; son of Frederick Erwin (a businessman) and Flora Kathryn (Soergel) Pfaff; married Margaret Campbell, December 27, 1962; children: David Anthony. *Education:* Harvard University, A.B. (magna cum laude), 1957; Oxford University, B.A., 1959, M.A., 1963, D.Phil., 1965; attended General Theological Seminary, 1965-66. *Politics:* Democrat.

*ADDRESSES: Home*—334 Wesley Dr., Chapel Hill, NC 27516. *Office*—Department of History, CB 3195, University of North Carolina at Chapel Hill, Chapel Hill, NC 27599; fax: 919-962-1403.

*CAREER:* Ordained Episcopal priest, 1966; English teacher at private school in Kansas City, MO, 1959-60; Swarthmore College, Swarthmore, PA, assistant to the president, 1960-62; curate of Episcopal church in Suffern, NY, 1966-67; University of North Carolina at Chapel Hill, assistant professor, 1967-70, associate professor, 1970-75, professor of history, 1975—. Priest associate of Chapel of the Cross, Chapel Hill. Visiting fellow, Magdalen College, Oxford, 1989-90, and at Magdalene College, Cambridge, 1997.

*MEMBER:* American Society of Church History, Medieval Academy of America, Ecclesiastical Historical Society, Henry Bradshaw Society (honorary vice-president), Royal Historical Society (fellow), Society of Antiquaries of London (fellow), Phi Beta Kappa.

*AWARDS, HONORS:* Rhodes scholar, 1957-59 and 1962-63; fellow of National Endowment for the Humanities, 1972-73; National Humanities Center fellow, 1996-97.

*WRITINGS:*

*New Liturgical Feasts in Later Medieval England,* Oxford University Press (New York City), 1970.
*Montague Rhodes James,* Scolar Press, 1980.

*Medieval Latin Liturgy: A Select Bibliography,* University of Toronto Press (Toronto), 1982.

(Editor and author, with others) *The Eadwine Psalter,* Modern Humanities Research Association/Penn State University Press, 1992.

(Editor) *The Liturgical Books of Anglo-Saxon England,* Medieval Institute Publications, 1995.

Contributor to historical and medieval journals.

*WORK IN PROGRESS:* A history of the liturgy in medieval England.

* * *

**PIKE, Robert L.**
**See FISH, Robert L(loyd)**

* * *

**PIZZEY, Erin 1939-**

*PERSONAL:* Born February 19, 1939, in Tsingtao, China; separated; children: Ueo, Amos. *Education:* Educated in convent schools. *Politics:* "Apolitical."

*ADDRESSES: Home*—Cayman Islands. *Agent*—c/o Christopher Little, 49 Queen Victoria Street, London, EC4N 4SA, England.

*CAREER:* Founder and chairwoman of Chiswick Women's Aid, London, England; established several other shelters for abused women and children in Europe and North America. Writer.

*AWARDS, HONORS:* Italian Peace Prize, 1978; Nancy Astor Award for journalism, 1983, 1985; made honorary citizen of St. Giovanni D'Asso, Italy, 1992.

*WRITINGS:*

*NOVELS*

*The Watershed,* Hamish Hamilton (London), 1983.

*In the Shadow of the Castle,* Hamish Hamilton, 1984.

*First Lady,* Collins (London and New York City), 1986.

*The Consul General's Daughter,* Collins, 1987.

*The Snow Leopard of Shanghai,* Collins (London), 1989.

*Other Lovers,* HarperCollins (London and New York City), 1989.

*Swimming with Dolphins,* HarperCollins, 1990.

*Morningstar,* HarperCollins, 1992.

*For the Love of a Stranger,* HarperCollins, 1993.

*Kisses,* HarperCollins, 1995.

*The Wicked World of Women,* HarperCollins, 1996.

*OTHER*

*Scream Quietly or the Neighbours Will Hear,* Penguin, 1974.

*Infernal Child: A Memoir,* Gollancz (London), 1978.

*The Slut's Cook Book,* illustrated by Anny White, Macdonald (London), 1981.

(With Jeff Shapiro) *Prone to Violence,* Hamlyn (London), 1982.

*Erin Pizzey Collects,* Hamlyn, 1983.

Also author of screenplays *Requiem,* 1990, and *Shadows,* 1993; and television plays *Scream Quietly or the Neighbours Will Hear,* 1974; *That Awful Woman,* 1989; *Sanctuary,* 1989. Contributor to magazines.

*SIDELIGHTS:* Erin Pizzey is a feminist and activist who writes both nonfiction works about women's social problems, especially domestic violence, and romance novels that defy the conventions of their genre. "You might find it strange that a leading feminist . . . should also be known as a successful writer of romantic/blockbuster novels," noted P. Campbell in *Twentieth-Century Romance and Historical Writers.* "However, Erin Pizzey's books are not formula romances." Her characters are average, believable people who deal with tragedies and often emerge stronger than before.

"I write to tell the truth, however unpalatable, of women's lives," Pizzey commented in *Romance and Historical Writers.* Pizzey has recounted the real-life stories of abused women and children, and her work on their behalf, in *Scream Quietly or the Neighbours Will Hear, Infernal Child: A Memoir,* and *Prone to Violence.* Pizzey was a founder of Chiswick Women's Aid in London in 1971; it was the world's first shelter for battered women. *Scream Quietly or the Neighbours Will Hear* covers the beginnings of this organization. A *Publishers Weekly* reviewer pronounced the book "direct and lucid," as well as a "badly needed expose" on domestic violence. *America* commentator G. M. Anderson found the work "a pioneering book, and in terms of its impact one of the most important." Anderson lauded Pizzey's writing style as "informed with a determined individuality that [is] balanced by clarity and conciseness, and even by humor." *Infernal Child* provides both an update on Chiswick Women's Aid and insight into the experiences that shaped Pizzey's world view. Her father abused her mother, not physically, but emotionally; Pizzey believes that her commitment to helping victimized women had its roots in her observation of her father's behavior and in her eventual forgiveness of him. *Books and Bookmen* contributor Frank Longford deemed *Infernal Child* "a remarkable piece of autobiography," although he thought Pizzey's compassion for her father a bit excessive. Longford lauded Pizzey's generous spirit, but drew the line at "thanking God (which is what it comes to) for her father's maltreatment of his family as described." The account of Pizzey's cause-related work continues in *Prone to Violence,* written with fellow activist Jeff Shapiro. "The book should be read for its journalistic reporting of actual incidents; the psychologising of the authors is not of very much interest," remarked H. J. Eysenck in *Books and Bookmen.* Eysenck praised Pizzey's hands-on approach to treating social ills, though, finding it preferable to government solutions—which the reviewer characterized as bureaucratic and wasteful.

An abusive relationship is the subject of one of Pizzey's novels, *In the Shadow of the Castle.* The book's heroine, Bonnie, marries an older, wealthy man, Angus McPherson, who brutalizes her both emotionally and physically. Like many of the men in Pizzey's novels, he masks his true nature, concealing his cruelty with a charming demeanor. Bonnie endures his abuse for several years, but finally decides to leave him; unfortunately, he pursues her. "Bonnie's life as a battered wife is realistically and frighteningly portrayed," observed Campbell. Pizzey's other novels display a feminist bent as well. These include *First Lady,* a multigenerational family saga featuring several strong women characters, and *The Snow Leopard of Shanghai,* which chronicles a remarkable woman's life in mid-twentieth-century China.

Campbell described Pizzey as "an important voice in contemporary fiction" and praised her for exploring difficult topics with honesty and wit. "Everything from child abuse to homosexuality is treated seriously in Pizzey's novels, and her ability to create interesting characters in fascinating settings makes her a popular author," Campbell concluded. Pizzey commented to *CA:* "I am concerned about the need to understand human relationships. I work mostly with violent relationships and the needs of the women, children, and men which have to be met. All my writing reflects this search and helps me think ahead to how we can see the family in the future."

*BIOGRAPHICAL/CRITICAL SOURCES:*

*BOOKS*

*Twentieth-Century Romance and Historical Writers,* St. James Press (Detroit), 1994.

Pizzey, Erin, *Infernal Child: A Memoir,* Gollancz (London), 1978.

*PERIODICALS*

*America,* February 18, 1978, p. 126.

*Books and Bookmen,* January, 1979, pp. 31-32; December, 1982, p. 38.

*Publishers Weekly,* October 3, 1977, p. 87.

*Times Literary Supplement,* November 15, 1974, p. 1290.*

—*Sketch by Trudy Ring*

* * *

## POPPER, Karl R(aimund) 1902-1994

*PERSONAL:* Born July 28, 1902, in Vienna, Austria; died of pneumonia, cancer, and kidney failure, September 17, 1994, in Croydon, England; son of Simon Siegmund Carl (a barrister) and Jenny (Schiff) Popper; married Josefine Anna Henninger, April 11, 1930 (died November 17, 1985). *Education:* University of Vienna, Ph.D., 1928; University of New Zealand, M.A., 1938; University of London, D.Lit., 1948.

*CAREER:* University of Canterbury, Christchurch, New Zealand, senior lecturer in philosophy, 1937-45; University of London, London School of Economics and Political Science, London, reader, 1945-49, professor of logic and scientific method, 1949-69, professor emeritus, 1969-94. William James Lecturer in Philosophy, Harvard University, 1950; visiting professor, Institute for Advanced Studies, Vienna, 1956, University of California, Berkeley, 1962, University of Minnesota, 1962, Indiana University, 1963, New York University, 1963, Massachusetts Institute of Technology, 1963, and University of Denver, 1966; annual philosophical lecturer, British Academy, 1960; Herbert Spencer Lecturer, Oxford University, 1961 and 1973; Sherman Lecturer, University College,

University of London, 1961; Farnum Lecturer, Princeton University, 1963; Arthur Holly Compton Memorial Lecturer, Washington University, St. Louis, 1965; Kenan University Professor, Emory University, 1969; Ziskind Professor, Brandeis University, 1969; Romanes Lecturer, Oxford University, 1972; Henry D. Broadhead Memorial Lecturer, University of Canterbury, 1973; Darwin Lecturer, Cambridge University, 1977; Tanner Lecturer, University of Michigan, 1978; Doubleday Lecturer, Smithsonian Institution, 1979; distinguished lecturer at other institutions in England, Australia, and New Zealand.

*MEMBER:* International Academy for Philosophy of Science (fellow), Academic Internationale d'Histoire des Sciences, Academie Europeenne des Sciences, des Arts, et des Lettres (member of British delegation), Institut de France, Academie Royale Belgique, American Academy of Arts and Sciences (honorary foreign member), British Academy (fellow), British Society for the History of Science (chair of philosophy of science group, 1951-53), Aristotelian Society (president, 1958-59), British Society for the Philosophy of Science (president, 1959-61), Association for Symbolic Logic (member of council, 1951-54), Royal Institute of Philosophy (member of board, 1956-94), Royal Society of New Zealand (honorary member), Royal Society of London (fellow), Phi Beta Kappa (Harvard chapter; honorary member).

*AWARDS, HONORS:* Center for Advanced Study in the Behavioral Sciences fellow, 1956-57; LL.D., University of Chicago, 1962, and University of Denver, 1966; knighted by Queen Elizabeth, 1965; Prize of the City of Vienna, 1965, for contributions to the moral and mental sciences; Salk Institute for Biological Studies visiting fellow, 1966-67; Lit.D., University of Warwick, 1971, University of Canterbury, 1973, and Cambridge University, 1980; University of Copenhagen Sonning Prize, 1973; Grand Decoration of Honour in Gold, Austria, 1976; American Political Science Association Lippincott Award, 1976, for *The Open Society and its Enemies;* D.Litt., University of Salford, 1976, City University, London, 1976, and University of Guelph, 1978; Karl Renner Prize, 1978; Dr. rer. nat. h.c., University of Vienna, 1978; Dr. phil. h.c., University of Manheim, 1978, and University of Salzburg, 1979; American Museum of Natural History Gold Medal, 1979, for distinguished service to science; Ehrenzeichen fuer Wissenschaft und Kunst, Austria, 1980; Dr. rer. pol. h.c., University of Frankfurt am Main; Order of Merit of the Federal Republic of Germany, member, 1980, Grand Cross second class, 1983; Prix Alexis de Tocqueville, 1984; International prize, Catalonian Institute of Mediterranean Studies, 1989; honorary PhD., University of Eichstatt, 1991; honorary PhD., University of Madrid, 1991; Kyoto prize, Inamori Foundation, 1992; honorary PhD., University of Athens, 1992.

*WRITINGS:*

*Logik der Forschung: Zur Erkenntnistheorie der modernen Naturwissenschaft,* Springer Verlag, 1935, 8th revised and enlarged edition, J. C. B. Mohr, 1984, translation by author of original edition published as *The Logic of Scientific Discovery,* Basic Books, 1959, 11th revised edition, Hutchinson, 1983.

*The Open Society and Its Enemies,* Volume I: *The Spell of Plato,* Volume II: *The High Tide of Prophecy: Hegel, Marx, and the Aftermath,* Routledge & Sons, 1945, 14th revised edition, Princeton University Press, 1984.

*The Poverty of Historicism,* Beacon Press, 1957, 3rd edition, Routledge & Kegan Paul, 1961.

*Conjectures and Refutations: The Growth of Scientific Knowledge,* Basic Books, 1962, 5th edition, Routledge & Kegan Paul, 1974.

*Objective Knowledge: An Evolutionary Approach,* Clarendon Press, 1972, 7th revised edition, Oxford University Press (New York), 1983.

*The Philosophy of Karl Popper,* two volumes, edited by Paul A. Schilpp, Open Court, 1974, revised autobiographical section published separately as *Unended Quest: An Intellectual Autobiography,* Fontana, 1976.

(With John C. Eccles) *The Self and Its Brain,* Springer International, 1977, 4th edition, 1985.

*Die beiden Grundprobleme der Erkenntnistheorie,* Volume I, J. C. B. Mohr, 1980.

*Postscript to the Logic of Scientific Discovery,* Volume I: *Realism and the Aim of Science,* Volume II: *The Open Universe: An Argument for Indeterminism,* Volume III: *Quantum Theory and the Schism in Physics,* Hutchinson, 1982-83.

*A Pocket Popper,* Fontana, 1983.

*Auf der Suche nach einer besseren Welt,* R. Piper Verlag, 1984, translation by author published as *In Search of a Better World: Lectures and Essays from Thirty Years,* Routledge, 1992.

*The Myth of the Framework: In Defence of Science and Rationality,* Routledge, 1994.

*Knowledge and the Body-Mind Problem: In Defence of Interaction,* edited by Mark Amadeus Notturno, Routledge, 1994.

*Alles Leben ist Problemleosen,* Piper, 1995.

*The Lesson of this Century: With Two Talks on Freedom and the Democratic State,* Routledge, 1996.

*CONTRIBUTOR*

*Gesetz und Wirklichkeit,* [Innsbruck], 1949.
*Readings in Philosophy of Science,* Scribner, 1953.
*The State versus Socrates,* Beacon Press, 1954.
*Contemporary British Philosophy,* Allen & Unwin, 1956.
*British Philosophy in the Mid-Century,* Allen & Unwin, 1957.
*Observation and Interpretation,* Butterworth & Co., 1957, Dover, 1962.
*The Philosophy of History in Our Time,* Anchor Books, 1959, revised edition, 1961.
*Philosophy for a Time of Crisis: An Interpretation, with Key Writings by Fifteen Great Modern Thinkers,* Dutton, 1959.
*Theories of History,* Free Press of Glencoe, 1959.
*Society, Law, and Morality,* Prentice-Hall, 1961.
*Der Sinn der Geschichte,* C. H. Beck, 1961.
*Geist und Gesicht der Gegenwart,* Europa Verlag, 1962.
*Philosophy for a Time of Crisis, by Albert Einstein, E. M. Forster, Karl R. Popper, and Bertrand Russell,* Kinseido, 1962.
*Club Voltaire,* Szczesny Verlag, 1963.
*Plato: Totalitarian or Democrat?,* Prentice-Hall, 1963.
*The Philosophy of Rudolf Carnap,* Open Court, 1964.
*Theorie und Realitaet,* J. C. B. Mohr, 1964.
*Form and Strategy in Science,* D. Reidel, 1964.
*The Socratic Enigma,* Bobbs-Merrill, 1964.
*Human Understanding: Studies in the Philosophy of David Hume,* Wadsworth, 1965.
*Versaeumte Lektionen,* Sigbert Mohn Verlag, 1965.
*Philosophical Problems of the Social Sciences,* Macmillan, 1965.
*Mind, Matter, and Method: Essays in Honor of Herbert Feigl,* University of Minnesota Press, 1966.
*Quantum Theory and Reality,* Springer Verlag, 1967.

Also contributor to *Logik der Sozialwissenschaften,* 1965. Contributor of more than 100 articles to philosophy and science journals. Member of editorial board, *British Journal for the Philosophy of Science, Ratio, Monist, Dialectica,* and *Erfahrung und Denken.*

*SIDELIGHTS:* Regarded as a lucid, eloquent philosopher and one of the most distinguished of contemporary thinkers, Karl R. Popper is the author of "one of the most celebrated and controversial views of science to have been put forward in this century," writes Jonathan Lieberson in the *New York Review of Books.* Lieberson describes Popper as a logician of science "who has denied that science employs induction, and who has claimed that what demarcates science from nonscience, in particular metaphysics, is that scientists seek the truth by vigorously trying to falsify their theories." "For Popper," explains Anthony Quinton in the *Times Literary Supplement,* "scientific rationality is not a routine of fact-collecting but an alternation of adventurous guessing followed by rigorous testing. Its capacity for being tested, being possibly shown to be false by experience, is what makes a theory scientific, rather than pseudoscientific like alchemy and psycho-analysis or proto-scientific like the speculative atomism of the ancient Greeks."

Popper first articulated his view of "falsifiability" as the determining criterion of scientific knowledge in *Logik der Forschung,* his first book. Highly influential even in English-speaking countries, the 1935 work appeared in a series sponsored by the Vienna Circle of logical positivists, a group of philosophers at the University of Vienna who attempted to "purify" philosophy by discarding its metaphysical elements and making logic its organon. Though associated with the circle, Popper was not a member, as he disagreed with some of their principal doctrines. While Popper shared their belief that physical science is the most acceptable part of what is considered human knowledge, he rejected their traditional, Baconian view that scientific knowledge is acquired through induction. Popper maintained in *Logik der Forschung* that what makes a theory *scientific* is not its degree of probability based on the mechanical observation of numerous instances, but rather its ability to withstand determined efforts to refute, or falsify, it. He also believed the positivists were mistaken in dismissing metaphysics as nonsense, for although he too considered it nonscience, he claimed that metaphysics could anticipate science by suggesting falsifiable—hence, scientific—hypotheses.

Two years before his death in 1994, Popper published *In Search of a Better World,* an English translation of a 1984 collection of his occasional lectures and writings dating back to the 1950s. Though adding little to the substance of his major writings, as John Ziman notes in *Nature,* the volume represents a wide-ranging "retrospective" of Popper's work. According to *Choice* reviewer S. Fuller, "Here Popper makes his clearest claim to the title of 'public philosopher.'" While offering multidisciplinary speculation on themes as diverse as Beethoven and Athenian book publishing, the writings are unified by Popper's "three worlds" hypothesis, which posits that in addition to the material and subjective world there exists a third realm of objective structures such as art, science, and ideas that embody subjective creativity in irreducible forms. "This concept is not discussed much by philosophers or social scientists," Ziman observes, "and yet it could turn out to be the missing link between them. In effect, it provides a bridge between the subjectivity of the individual and the apparent objectivity of social institutions." However, Ziman continues, "Here again, Popper's instinctive recognition of an important idea is sound, but he holds back from the hard work of defining and refining it so that it can be used analytically as well as rhetorically."

Popper remains best known for his trenchant and controversial *Logik der Forschung,* translated and published as *The Logic of Scientific Discovery,* and *The Open Society and Its Enemies,* an anti-Marxist refutation of political historicism. According to Stephen Munhall in the *London Review of Books,* "Popper's conception of science has strongly influenced his view of the best approach to matters lying outside the domain of the natural sciences: his famous defence of the procedures and institutions of Western liberal democracy in *The Open Society* essentially depends on the claim that any other political arrangements will fail to acknowledge what his analysis of scientific method demonstrates—the provisional, fallible nature of human cognitive processes." *The Logic of Scientific Discovery* represents Popper's greatest expression of the skeptical critique and has become a classic text on the scientific method. As *Nation* contributor N. R. Hanson proclaims, "without any doubt this is one of the most important books in philosophy of science ever written."

*BIOGRAPHICAL/CRITICAL SOURCES:*

*BOOKS*

Ackerman, Robert, *The Philosophy of Karl Popper,* University of Massachusetts Press, 1976.

Bunge, Mario, editor, *The Critical Approach to Science and Philosophy: Essays in Honor of Karl R. Popper,* Free Press of Glencoe, 1964.

Clark, Peter, *Karl Popper: Philosophy and Problems,* Cambridge University, 1995.

Corvi, Roberta, *Introduction to the Thought of Karl Popper,* translation by Patrick Camiller, Routledge, 1996.

Feyerabend, Paul K., *Against Method,* Schoken, 1978.

Harper, David A., *Entrepreneurship and the Market Process: An Enquiry into the Growth of Knowledge,* Routledge, 1996.

Lakatos, Imre and Alan Musgrave, editors, *Criticism and the Growth of Knowledge,* Cambridge University Press, 1970.

Levinson, Paul, editor, *In Pursuit of Truth: Essays on the Philosophy of Karl Popper on the Occasion of His Eightieth Birthday,* Humanities, 1982.

Magee, Bryan, *Karl Popper,* Viking, 1973 (published in England as *Popper,* Fontana, 1973).

Miller, David, *Critical Rationalism: A Restatement and Defence,* Open Court, 1994.

O'Hear, Anthony, *Karl Popper,* Routledge & Kegan Paul, 1980.

Popper, Karl R., *Unended Quest: An Intellectual Autobiography,* Fontana, 1976.

Schilpp, Paul A., editor, *The Philosophy of Karl R. Popper,* two volumes, Open Court, 1974.

Shearmur, Jeremy, *The Political Thought of Karl Popper,* Routledge, 1996.

*PERIODICALS*

*Archiv fuer Rechts und Sozialphilosophie,* Volume XLVI, number 3, 1960.

*Choice,* May, 1993, p. 1481.

*London Review of Books,* June 10, 1993, p. 26.

*Manchester Guardian,* January 16, 1959.

*Nation,* June 27, 1959.

*National Review,* December 25, 1995, p. 46.

*Nature,* December 3, 1992, p. 425.

*New Scientist,* Volume V, number 124, 1959.

*New Society,* September 12, 1963.

*New York Review of Books,* November 18, 1982; December 2, 1982.

*New York Times,* January 1, 1995, p. 24.

*Times* (London), July 29, 1982.

*Times Literary Supplement,* December 3, 1982.

*OBITUARIES:*

*PERIODICALS*

*Economist,* September 24, 1994, p. 92.

*Time,* September 26, 1994, p. 17.

*Washington Post,* September 19, 1994, p. B4.*

**POTTER, Dennis (Christopher George) 1935-1994**

*PERSONAL:* Born May 17, 1935, in Joyford Hill, Gloucestershire, England; died of cancer, June 7, 1994, near Ross-on-Wye, England; son of Walter and Margaret Constance (Wales) Potter; married Margaret Morgan (a journalist), 1959; children: one son, two daughters. *Education:* New College, Oxford, B.A. (with honors), 1959. *Politics:* Labour.

*CAREER:* British Broadcasting Corp. (BBC-TV), London, England, member of current affairs staff, 1959-61; London Daily Herald, London, 1961-64, began as feature writer, became television critic; London Sun, London, editorial writer, 1964; freelance playwright, author, and journalist, 1964; television critic, Sunday Times, 1976-78. Labour candidate for Parliament from East Hertfordshire, 1964.

*AWARDS, HONORS:* Writer of the Year Awards from Writers Guild of Great Britain, 1966 and 1969; award from Society of Film and Television Arts, 1966; BAFTA Award, 1978, for "Pennies from Heaven," and 1980, for "Blue Remembered Hills;" Prix Italia, 1982, for "Blade on the Feather, Rain on the Roof, Cream in My Coffee;" honorary fellow, New College, Oxford, 1987.

*WRITINGS:*

*PLAYS*

*Vote Vote Vote for Nigel Barton,* 1965, revised version incorporating *Vote Vote Vote for Nigel Barton* and *Stand Up, Nigel Barton* (also see below), produced in Bristol at Theatre Royal, November 27, 1968, published in *The Nigel Barton Plays: Two Television Plays,* Penguin, 1967.

*Stand Up, Nigel Barton,* first televised, 1965, published in *The Nigel Barton Plays,* 1967.

*Son of Man* (first televised on British Broadcasting Corp. (BBC-TV), 1969, first produced in Leicester, 1969, produced in London at Round House Theatre, 1969), Deutsch, 1970.

*Lay Down Your Arms,* first televised on Independent Television (ITV), May 23, 1970.

*Traitor,* first televised on BBC-TV, October 14, 1971.

*Follow the Yellow Brick Road,* 1972, published in *The Television Dramatist,* edited by Robert Muller, Elek, 1973.

*Only Make Believe,* first televised, 1973, first produced in Harlow, 1974.

*Joe's Ark,* 1974, published in *The Television Play,* edited by Robin Wade, BBC Publications, 1976.

*Brimstone and Treacle* (first produced in Sheffield at the Crucible Theatre, October, 1977; also see below), Eyre Methuen, 1978.

*Pennies From Heaven* (screenplay; adapted from the television series by Potter), Metro-Goldwyn-Mayer, 1981.

*Brimstone and Treacle* (screenplay; adaptation of Potter's stage play), 1982.

*Sufficient Carbohydrate,* Faber & Faber, 1983.

*Gorky Park* (screenplay; adapted from the novel by Martin Cruz Smith), Orion, 1983.

*Waiting for the Boat* (three plays), Faber & Faber, 1984.

*Dreamchild* (screenplay), Curzon/Universal, 1985.

*Track 29* (screenplay; based on Potter's television play *Schmoedipus*), Island Pictures, 1988.

*The Singing Detective* (sextet; produced on BBC-Television, November 9, 1986), Random House, 1988, Vintage, 1988.

*Lipstick on Your Collar,* [London], 1993.

Also author of "The Confidence Course," 1965; "Alice," 1965; "Where the Buffalo Roam," 1966; "Emergency Ward Nine," 1966; "Message for Posterity," 1967; "A Beast With Two Backs," 1968; "The Bonegrinder," 1968; "Shaggy Dog," 1968; "Moonlight on the Highway," 1969; "Angels Are So Few," 1970; "Paper Roses," 1971; "Casanova" (six-play series), 1971; "A Tragedy of Two Ambitions" (adapted from story by Thomas Hardy), 1973; "Schmoedipus" (adapted from novel by Angus Wilson), 1974; "Late Call" (serial; adapted from novel by Wilson), 1975; "Double Dare," 1976; "Where Adam Stood" (adapted from *Father and Son* by Edmund Gosse), 1976; "Pennies From Heaven" (sextet), 1978; "The Mayor of Casterbridge" (adapted from novel by Hardy), 1978; "Blue Remembered Hills," 1979; "Blade on the Feather, Rain on the Roof, Cream in My Coffee," 1980; "Tender Is the Night" (sextet adapted from novel by F. Scott Fitzgerald), 1985; "Visitors," 1987; "Christabel" (quartet adapted from *The Past Is Myself* by Christabel Bielenberg), 1988; "Blackeyes," 1989; author and director of "Secret Friends" (adapted from Potter's novel *Ticket to Ride*), 1992.

*OTHER*

*The Glittering Coffin* (nonfiction), Gollancz, 1960.

*The Changing Forest: Life in the Forest of Dean Today* (nonfiction), Secker & Warburg, 1962.

*Hide and Seek* (novel), Deutsch, 1973.

*Ticket to Ride* (novel), Faber & Faber, 1986, Vintage Books, 1989.

*Blackeyes* (novel), Faber & Faber, 1987, Random House, 1988.

*Potter on Potter,* edited by Graham Fuller, Faber, 1993.

*Seeing the Blossom: Two Interviews and a Lecture,* Faber & Faber, 1994.

Also author of *Pennies from Heaven* (novel), 1982.

*SIDELIGHTS:* Dennis Potter's numerous television plays earned him a reputation as "one of the major dramatists writing for the medium." His first effort, "Vote Vote Vote for Nigel Barton," is a tragicomedy about a young Labour candidate's campaign for public office. This work and its companion play, "Stand Up, Nigel Barton," were together adapted for the stage under the title "Vote Vote Vote for Nigel Barton." Jeremy Kingston praised Potter's skill in combining elements of the two plays, noting that "the mingling of Nigel's past with his present and the tension between public and private face work as strongly on the stage as I am told they did on [television]." *New Statesman* critic Benedict Nightingale disagreed, claiming that Potter "shuffled" the plays together "like two decks of cards." He commented further that the play's attack upon "stupid and irrelevant reactionaries" causes it to fail as a political commentary.

Many of Potter's works generated controversy. His play "Son of Man" created a furor when it was first broadcast on BBC-TV and later when it was broadcast on KYW-TV in Philadelphia. Picketers protested that in the play Christ is portrayed as a "hippie." Potter's television play "Brimstone and Treacle" was also involved in conflict when BBC-TV decided against broadcasting it in response to protests by viewers of the BBC who considered the play too shocking for television. Those who feared censorship of the media, in turn, condemned the action of the BBC. The play was later produced for the stage and also published with a twenty-five-hundred-word introduction that presented the author's view of the quarrel. John Coleby, who reviewed the published version of the play, referred to it as "moving," "compelling," and "strong" but observed that "in the end the ingredients don't quite blend, the flavor is nondescript."

Potter also wrote the screenplay for "Pennies From Heaven," a film that impressed some critics and confused others with its combination of 1930s-musicals whimsy and Ingmar Bergman-like despair during the Depression. The *Chicago Tribune*'s Gene Siskel wrote, "One of the things we can make of [certain scenes] is that there was a huge gap between the grim realities of the Depression and the songs that were created in part to lift the nation's spirit." The *New York Times*'s Vincent Canby was less convinced of the film's merits. He conceded that some of the musical transitions—featuring actors lip-syncing songs by performers such as Bing Crosby—were "spectacularly effective," but added that Potter and director Herbert Ross created a work that is "chilly without being provocative in any intellectual way." Canby cited one scene in which the male protagonist lip-syncs a woman's voice as "briefly funny," then added that "the merciless eye of the camera and the film's deliberate pacing drain all real wit and spontaneity from the sequence."

Another Potter screenplay, "Dreamchild," takes place in the 1930s, when an elderly Alice Liddell Hargreaves (the "Alice" of Lewis Carroll's *Alice in Wonderland* and *Alice through the Looking-Glass*) travels to New York to receive an honorary degree. The unaccustomed pressures of American city life exhaust her and set her to dreaming about her childhood. Stephen Holden, writing in the *New York Times,* said that "Dreamchild" "paints the early 1930s in glowing storybook colors that complement the subtlety of the performances," and concluded that it is "a lovely, wistful little fairytale for adults." Gene Siskel, in the *Chicago Tribune,* stated that the film "goes its own special with precision and consummate skill," and declared, "See this fascinating and troubling and beautifully acted movie and your reading of 'Alice' never will be the same."

Potter followed with the television drama *The Singing Detective* and the film *Secret Friends,* which represents his directorial debut. *The Singing Detective* is a semi-autobiographic story involving a bedridden former detective with severe psoriasis. As Gerald Lubenow noted in *Newsweek,* "The New York Times's movie critic hailed [*The Singing Detective*] as one of the best films of the year—even though it was a six-part TV series." *Secret Friends* concerns a wildflower illustrator who experiences sudden anxiety over uncertainty as to whether or not he has murdered his wife. Though he criticized the film for its confusing temporal juxtapositions and unsurprising plot, *Commonweal* reviewer Richard Alleva commended Potter's cinematic technique, "the choice of camera angles, the duration of each shot, the alternation of fixed shots with long smooth pans, are all excellent." A *Rolling Stone* reviewer offered tempered criticism of *Secret Friends,* describing it as "a darkly seductive and witty thriller that will leave you elated or dozing" in response to Potter's "demanding conundrums."

Potter also produced several novels, including *Ticket to Ride* and *Blackeyes. Ticket to Ride,* upon which the film *Secret Friends* is based, involves an art director who loses his job and his memory, then lapses into mental illness as he suspects that he has committed a terrible crime. Patrick McGrath wrote in the *New York Times Book Review,* "in terms of narrative technique [the novel] is both unorthodox and frighteningly effective." A *British Book News* review similarly described the novel as "a terrifying psychological thriller." McGrath concluded, "the real accomplishment of 'Ticket to Ride' is not merely to depict these complicated psychic processes, but to demonstrate, with chilling plausibility, what they might look like in the mind of a mad murderer."

*Blackeyes* is the story of a writer who assembles the real-life experiences of his beautiful niece into a best-selling novel about a dim-witted model whose rapid ascent ends in her tragic suicide. The successful book humiliates his niece, however, as the story is filled with details of exaggerated promiscuity that she invented for her uncle in a deliberate attempt to embarrass him and to sabotage his writing career. "'Blackeyes' is clever, intricate and cold as a coroner's chisel," according to Peter S. Prescott in *Newsweek.* Shifting between multiple narrative perspectives, including that of the uncle, niece, and Potter himself, "the result," Prescott remarked, "is the sort of book that prompts a phrase like 'the first postmodernist/feminist/deconstructionist novel' to spring from a review's teeth."

Shortly before his death, Potter commented on his writing and career in an interview with John Wyver in *New Statesman & Society:* "I'm not a novelist and, although this is a difficult thing to say, I don't believe that the novel can occupy the territory that it used to occupy. Therefore there is something diminished about even the act of doing it." Potter continued, "One thing I knew in my head, but I didn't know as a reality until I made *Blackeyes,* was how extraordinarily emotional it is to make films, and those emotions were mapped into what *Blackeyes* was about. Whatever faults or vices I may have as a writer or indeed now as a director, what by some miracle I haven't lost touch with is a flood of feeling."

*BIOGRAPHICAL/CRITICAL SOURCES:*

*BOOKS*

Cook, John R., *Dennis Potter: A Life on the Screen,* Manchester University Press, 1995.

*PERIODICALS*

*British Book News,* December, 1986, p. 712.
*Chicago Tribune,* December 22, 1981; January 10, 1986.
*Christian Science Monitor,* November 26, 1969.
*Commonweal,* March 27, 1992, p. 24.
*Drama,* autumn, 1978.
*Encounter,* February, 1974.
*Library Journal,* May 1, 1993, p. 87.
*Listener,* November 15, 1973.
*Los Angeles Magazine,* July, 1989, p. 159.
*Los Angeles Times,* November 18, 1982; September 15, 1985; October 18, 1985.
*Los Angeles Times Book Review,* October 19, 1988.
*New Statesman & Society,* December 6, 1968; November 2, 1973; November 24, 1989, p. 16; December 15, 1989; February 19, 1993; April 22, 1994; June 17, 1994, p. 40; May 3, 1996, p. 20.
*Newsweek,* November 14, 1988, p. 80.
*New York,* February 24, 1992, p. 118.
*New York Times,* December 11, 1981; October 4, 1985.
*New York Times Book Review,* October 15, 1989, p. 37.
*Punch,* December 4, 1968; November 19, 1969.
*Rolling Stone,* February 20, 1992, p. 50.
*Stage,* October 21, 1971.
*Times* (London), December 9, 1983; February 14, 1984; September 9, 1986; October 1, 1987.
*Times Literary Supplement,* October 17, 1986, p. 169; March 26, 1996, p. 17.
*Variety,* March 18, 1970; July 25, 1990; April 11, 1994, p. 54.
*Washington Post,* January 17, 1986.

*OBITUARIES:*

*PERIODICALS*

*Chicago Tribune,* June 8, 1994, p. 10.
*Los Angeles Times,* June 8, 1994, p. A10.
*New York Times,* June 8, 1994, p. B11; June 12, 1994, p. H30.
*Times* (London), June 8, 1994, p. 19.
*Washington Post,* June 8, 1994, p. D6.*

**POWERS, J(ames) F(arl) 1917-**

*PERSONAL:* Born July 8, 1917, in Jacksonville, IL; son of James Ansbury (a dairy-and-poultry manager) and Zella (Routzong) Powers; married Elizabeth Alice Wahl (a writer), April 22, 1946; children: Katherine, Mary, James, Hugh, Jane. *Education:* Attended Northwestern University, 1938-40. *Religion:* Roman Catholic.

*CAREER:* Novelist and educator. Worked as a book store clerk, chauffeur, and insurance salesperson. Editor, Illinois Historical Records Survey, 1938; creative writing teacher at St. John's University, Collegeville, MN, 1947, Marquette University, Milwaukee, WI, 1949-50, University of Michigan, Ann Arbor, 1956-57, Smith College, Northhampton, MA, 1965-66, and St. John's University, 1976-93.

*MEMBER:* National Institute of Arts and Letters.

*AWARDS, HONORS:* O. Henry Award, 1947, for "The Valiant Woman"; National Institute of Arts and Letters grant, 1948; Guggenheim fellowship in creative writing, 1948; Rockefeller fellowship, 1954, 1957, 1967; National Book Award, 1963, for *Morte d'Urban;* nominated for National Book Award and National Book Critics Circle Award, both 1988, both for *Wheat that Springeth Green.*

*WRITINGS:*

*Prince of Darkness and Other Stories* (story collection; includes "Lions, Harts, Leaping Does" and "The Valiant Woman"), Doubleday (New York City), 1947.
*The Presence of Grace* (short stories), Doubleday, 1956.
*Morte d'Urban* (novel), Doubleday, 1962.
*Look How the Fish Live* (short stories), Knopf (New York City), 1975.
*Wheat that Springeth Green,* Knopf, 1988.

Work represented in anthologies. Contributor to the *New Yorker, Nation, Partisan Review, Reporter, Collier's, Kenyon Review,* and other periodicals.

*SIDELIGHTS:* In both novels and short fiction, J. F. Powers examines the relationship between the religious and secular worlds. Noted for his satirical portrayal of the plight of institutional Catholicism within the modern world, he is especially concerned, critic F. W. Dupee writes, with "the contradictions that beset Catholicism, in practice if not in theory, because of its claim to an earthly as well as a divine mission and authority." Leo J. Hertzel characterizes Powers's primary theme in such critically acclaimed novels as *Morte d'Urban* and the long-awaited *Wheat that Springeth Green* as "the problem of how to put the Christian's traditional smiling contempt of the world into action in the grim, restricted society of organized modern America."

Raised in a Catholic family in the predominately Protestant Midwest, Powers moved to Chicago after high school, where he undertook a series of odd jobs that sustained him during the lean years of the Depression. He also managed to take several evening classes at Northwestern University. The tense social and political environment surrounding the onset of World War II caused the author to rethink his spirituality; his choice to become a conscientious objector to U.S. participation in the battle underway in Europe resulted in more than a year of imprisonment. This experience, gained as a consequence of deeply held moral and political beliefs, would serve as the inspiration for Powers's first book, 1947's *Prince of Darkness and Other Stories.*

Powers often examines situations where the differences between the religious and secular worlds are most pronounced. Stated otherwise, in the words of Terry Teachout in *New Criterion:* "How is it that ordinary people, with all their commonplace failings, can do the work of God?" In the title story from *Prince of Darkness,* for instance, protagonist Father Ernest "Boomer" Burner must wrestle between his love of golf and his calling. Father Burner's indulgence in various earthly temptations eventually renders him almost demonic. The circumstances of his transformation are petty and ordinary to be sure; as Dupee states, Powers favors "the simple spectacle of priests going about the ordinary business of their professions." Clerical society proves an effective backdrop to the seduction of the individual, critic George Scouffas maintains, because "the Church offers a ready-made, highly developed, . . . organized [and] historically weathered pattern of order. . . . Opposed to the Church is the 'world,' or disorder. . . . This setting-up of opposing forces represents a formalization of a basic paradox in reality and experience."

Powers's short fictions, collected as *Prince of Darkness, The Presence of Grace,* and *Look How the Fish Live,* have been praised not only for their subject matter but also for the quality of their author's prose. "Powers' early stories were admired by readers who looked to discover . . . the metaphoric, 'poetic' qualities of lyric verse, . . ." notes William Pritchard in *New Republic.* "Powers had a genius for capturing some of the ways people talked; much of the pleasure in reading him had to do with the pure satisfactions of American speech accurately rendered."

The testing of one's faith as a movement towards spiritual rebirth is a motif that is repeated throughout both of Powers's novels, 1962's *Morte d'Urban* and *Wheat that Springeth Green,* published in 1988. In *Morte d'Urban,* winner of the National Book Award, Powers positions his ambitious middle-aged protagonist in such a situation: he must undergo a symbolic "death" of the spirit in order to gain a more steadfast spiritual outlook. Transferred to a remote monastery in Minnesota because of his inflated ego, Father Urban Roche, whose mantra is "Be a Winner," industriously sets about creating a luxurious retreat, a Club Med of the spirit, until his excesses lead to the ultimate spiritual collapse.

Power's second novel in more than two decades, *Wheat that Springeth Green,* is the story of Father Joe Hackett, a young, enthusiastic priest who gradually becomes disheartened over the inability of the Church's social outreach programs to make a positive difference in his community. Assigned to his own parish in a quiet, stable middle-class community, Hackett still seeks the spark that will ignite his spiritual resolve. Several decades pass; the priest reaches middle age; his disillusionment grows. Finally, the example of younger, more radical Father Bill inspires Powers's protagonist to leave the security of his suburban parish and help tackle the problems of the inner city.

The integrity of Powers's work comes from his deep understanding of his priestly protagonists, according to Harry Mark Petrakis in his review of *Wheat that Springeth Green* in *Tribune Books.* "Powers movingly describes the ordeal of a parish priest whose demeanor must never reveal doubt or weariness," Petrakis explains, "who must smile and console while sorely needing companionship and consolation himself, who is expected to be Godlike when he is only mortal." Such vivid characterization underlies both of Powers's novels, as each relates a similar tale. "[T]hose who were offended by [his] first novel . . . doubtless will be offended by this one as well," quips Jonathan Yardley in the *Washington Post Book World.* Commending the author for his daring in portraying the clergy as real people, the critic adds that "he shows us how deep their faith must be in order for them to maintain it against all odds. . . . *Wheat that Springeth Green* may be funny and irreverent, but in the last analysis it is as much an act of faith as anything done by the priests whose struggles it so lovingly depicts."

In much of his fiction, Powers employs a highly satiric style; as John V. Hagopian notes in his *J. F. Powers,* the writer is "known among his peers as a brilliant satirist." "The priesthood," reviewer Naomi Lebowitz writes, "offers a particularly good stage for Powers's form of comedy, for it serves as a microcosm of sin and virtue magnified in conflict by conscience." *New York Times Book Review* critic Hayden Carruth states that Powers "has revived the satire of the Golden Age . . . within a modern context of style and attitude." However, not all critics have found the writer's wit to be appropriate. Thomas Rowan, for example, calls it "mean-spirited" and suggests that Powers "has been peering too long at a few soiled pores on the face of the Catholic priesthood."

Although Powers's fiction is humorous, it also confronts and examines serious issues. A reviewer for *Time* comments that Powers is "the only man besides John Updike who can write about salvation and damnation in a world rapidly becoming trivialized by loneliness and loss of ardor." John P. Sisk admires Powers for his "ability to portray virtue in its complex relations with evil, an ability that includes, though it may go considerably beyond, the ability to confront ambivalence."

Summing up Powers's place in contemporary literature, Hagopian believes that the writer's "taut, understated ironies are out of step with current literary fashions, [and] as a consequence, Powers remains on the periphery of the literary stage, even though he is, as Frank O'Connor says, 'among the greatest of living story-tellers.'" Hagopian concludes that Powers works with "such immense skill and tough-minded compassion that his writing will surely endure."

*BIOGRAPHICAL/CRITICAL SOURCES:*

*BOOKS*

*Contemporary Literary Criticism,* Gale, Volume 1, 1973, Volume 4, 1975, Volume 8, 1978.

*Dictionary of Literary Biography,* Volume 130: *American Short Story Writers since World War II,* Gale, 1993.

Evans, Fallon, editor, *J. F. Powers,* B. Herder, 1968.

Hagopian, John V., *J. F. Powers,* Twayne, 1968.

Hyman, Stanley Edgar, *Standards: A Chronicle of Books for Our Time,* Horizon Press, 1966.
Kazin, Alfred, *Contemporaries,* Atlantic, 1962.
Kellogg, Gene, *The Vital Tradition: The Catholic Novel in a Period of Convergence,* Loyola University Press, 1970.
*The Picaresque Saint: Representative Figures in Contemporary Fiction,* Lippincott, 1959.
*The Short Story in America, 1900-1950,* Regnery, 1952.
Whitbread, Thomas B., editor, *Seven Contemporary Authors,* University of Texas Press, 1966.

*PERIODICALS*

*American Benedictine Review,* March, 1964.
*Atlantic,* November, 1962; November, 1975, p. 124.
*Catholic World,* September, 1952; November-December, 1989, p. 279.
*Commonweal,* October 12, 1962; November 4, 1988, p. 592; December 1, 1989, p. 680.
*Contemporary Literature,* spring, 1968.
*Critique,* fall, 1958.
*Encounter,* November, 1963.
*English Journal,* September, 1989, p. 89.
*Esquire,* December, 1975.
*Homiletic and Pastoral Review,* January, 1963.
*Hudson Review,* summer, 1976.
*Kenyon Review,* summer, 1958.
*Los Angeles Times,* September 15, 1988.
*Minnesota Review,* Volume 9, number 1, 1969.
*Nation,* September 29, 1962.
*National Review,* March 18, 1977, p. 347; March 10, 1989, p. 51.
*New Criterion,* January, 1989, pp. 69-74.
*New Leader,* October 13, 1975.
*New Republic,* April, 1956; September 24, 1962; November 29, 1975, p. 33; September 26, 1988, p. 36.
*Newsweek,* October 13, 1975.
*New York Review of Books,* November 13, 1975.
*New York Times,* September 25, 1975, p. 41.
*New York Times Book Review,* October 30, 1988, p. 47; February 4, 1990, p. 32.
*Observer,* April 7, 1985, p. 20; December 11, 1988, p. 47.
*Our Sunday Visitor,* September 2, 1963.
*Partisan Review,* spring, 1963; spring, 1973.
*Progressive,* October, 1962; December, 1975.
*Renascence,* summer, 1965.
*Sewanee Review,* January, 1977.
*Time,* November 3, 1975, p. 94; August 29, 1988, p. 69.
*Times Literary Supplement,* October 28, 1988, p. 1211.
*Tribune Books,* August 14, 1988, p. 5.
*Twentieth Century Literature,* July, 1968.
*Virginia Quarterly Review,* winter, 1976.
*Washington Post Book World,* August 14, 1988.
*Worship,* November, 1962.
*Yale Review,* December, 1962.*

* * *

**PREVERT, Jacques (Henri Marie) 1900-1977**

*PERSONAL:* Born February 4, 1900, in Neuilly-sur-Seine, France; died April 11, 1977, in Omonville-La-Petite, France; son of Andre (a clerk) and Suzann (Catusse) Prevert; married Simone Dienne, April 30, 1925 (marriage ended); married Janine Tricotet, March 4, 1947. *Education:* Educated in Paris, France.

*CAREER:* Poet, screenwriter, and dramatist. Exhibitions of his collages held in Paris, 1957 and 1982, and in Antibes, 1963. Appeared as an actor in several of his films.

*AWARDS, HONORS:* Grand Prix from Societe des Auteurs et Compositeurs Dramatiques, 1973; Grand Prix National from *Cinema,* 1975.

*WRITINGS:*

*IN ENGLISH TRANSLATION*

*Paroles* (poetry), Editions du Point du Jour, 1945, revised and augmented edition, Gallimard, 1966, translation by Lawrence Ferlinghetti published as *Selections from 'Paroles,'* City Lights, 1958.
(With Albert Lamorisse) *Bim, le petit ane* (juvenile), Guilde du Livre, 1951, translation by Bette Swados and Harvey Swados published as *Bim, the Little Donkey,* Doubleday, 1973.
(Author of introduction) *Couleur de Paris,* illustrated with photographs by Peter Cornelius, La Bibliotheque des Arts, 1961, translation by Jonathan Griffin and Margaret Shenfield published as *Paris in Colour,* Thames & Hudson, 1962, Bramhall House, 1963.
(Author of preface) *Les Halles: L'Album du coer de Paris,* illustrations by Romain Urhausen, Editions des Deux-Mondes, 1963, translation published as *Les Halles: The Stomach of Paris,* Atlantis

Books, 1964, published as *Les Halles de Paris* (French, German, and English text), Moos, 1980.

*Prevert II* (anthology), translation by Teo Savory, Unicorn Press, 1967.

*Les Enfants du paradis* (screenplay), Lorrimer Publishing, 1968, translation by Dinah Brooke published as *Children of Paradise,* Simon & Schuster, 1968.

*Le Jour se leve* (screenplay), translation by Brooke and Nicola Hayden, Simon & Schuster, 1970.

*To Paint the Portrait of a Bird—Pour faire le portrait d'un oiseau* (juvenile; bilingual French/English text), translation by Ferlinghetti, Doubleday, 1971.

*Words for All Seasons: Selected Poems,* translation by Teo Savory, 1979.

*Blood and Feathers: Selected Poems of Jacques Prevert,* translation by Harriet Zinnes, Schoken, 1987, reprinted Moyer Bell (New York), 1993.

*POETRY*

(With Andre Verdet) *Histoires* (title means "Stories"), Editions du Pre Aux Clercs, 1946, reprinted, Gallimard, 1974.

*Grand Bal du printemps* (title means "Grand Ball of Spring;" also see below), illustrated with photographs by Izis Bidermanas, Guilde du Livre, 1951.

*Charmes de Londres* (title means "The Charms of London" also see below), illustrated with photographs by Bidermanas, Guilde du Livre, 1952.

*Lumieres d'homme* (title means "Lights of Man"), Gu Levis Mano, 1955.

*La Pluie et le beau temps* (title means "Rain and Fine Weather;" also see below), Gallimard, 1955.

(With Joseph L. Artigas) *Miro,* Maeght, 1956.

(Contributor) Henry Decanaud, *La Pierre dans le souffle* (title means "The Stone in the Wind"), Seghers, 1959.

*Poemes,* edited by J. H. Douglas and D. J. Girard, Harrap, 1961.

*Histoires et d'autres histoires* (title means "Stories and Other Stories"), Gallimard, 1963.

*Varengeville,* illustrations by Georges Braque, Maeght, 1968.

*Poesies* (includes *Spectacle* [also see below] and *La Pluie et le beau temps*), Newton Compton, 1971.

*Choses et autres* (title means "Things and Others"), Gallimard, 1972.

*Grand Bal du printemps suivi de Charmes de Londres,* Gallimard, 1976

*Anthologie Prevert* (anthology with French text), edited and with English introduction and notes by Christiane Mortelier, Methuen Educational, 1981.

*Oeuvres Completes,* edited by Daniele Gasiglia-Laster and Arnaud Laster, Gallimard, 1992.

*SCREENPLAYS*

(With Paul Grimault) *La Bergere et le remoneur* (title means "The Shepherdess and the Chimney-sweep"), Les Gemeaux, 1947.

*Les Amants de Verone,* Nouvelle Edition, 1949.

Guy Jacob, Andre Heinrich, and Bernard Chardere, editors, *Jacques Prevert* (anthology), Imprimerie du Bugey, 1960.

*Les Visiteurs du soir,* published in *Deux films francais: Les Visiteurs du soir* [and] *Le Feu follet,* edited by Robert M. Hammond and Marguerite Hammond, Harcourt, 1965.

*Drole le drame* (also see below), Balland, 1974.

*Jenny; Le quai des brumes: Scenarios,* preface by Marcel Carne, Gallimard, 1988.

*La fleur de l'age; Drole de drame: scenarios,* Gallimard, 1988.

Also author of other screenplays, including "L'Affaire est dans le sac," 1932, "Ciboulettte," 1933, "L'Hotel du u Libre-Echange," 1934, "Un Oiseau rare," 1935, "Le Crime de Monsieest le Revelle," 1938, "Le Soleil a toujours raison," 1941, "Les Visiteurs du soir," 1942, "Lumiere d'ete," 1943, "Sortileges," 1945, "Les Portes de la nuit," 1946, "Notre Dame de Paris," r 1953, and "Les Amours celebres," 1961.

*OTHER*

*Contes pour les enfants pas sages* (title means "Stories for Naughty Children;" juvenile), Editions du Pre aux Clercs, 1947, reprinted, Gallimard, 1984.

(With Camilla Koffler) *Le Petit Lion* (title means "The Little Lion"), illustrated with photographs by Ylla, Arts et Metiers Graphiques 1947.

(Contributor) Joseph Kosman, *Le Rendezvous: Ballet en trois tableaux* (piano scores), Enoch, 1948.

(With Verdet) *C'est a Saint Paul de Vence,* Nouvelle Edition, 1949.

*Spectacle* (poems, plays, and prose), Gallimard, 1949, reprinted, 1972.

*Des Betes* (title means "The Animals"), illustrated wit photographs by Ylla, Gallimard, 1950.

*Guignol* (title means "Puppet Show"), illustrations by Elsa Henriquez, Guilde du Livre, 1952.

*Lettres des Iles Baladar* (title means "Letter from the Baladar r Islands"), Gallimard, 1952.

*L'Opera de la lune* (title means "Moon Opera"), lyrics by Christiane Verger, Guilde du Livre, 1953, reprinted, Editions G.P., 1974.

(With Georges Ribemont-Dessaignes) *Joan Miro,* Maeght, 1956.

(With Ribemont-Dessaignes) *Arbres* (title means "Trees"), Gallimard, 1956, 2nd edition, 1976.

*Images* (title means "Pictures"), Maeght, 1957.

*Dix-sept Chansons de Jacques Prevert* (title means "Seventeen Songs by Jacques Prevert"), music by Joseph Kosma, Folkuniversitetets Foerlag, 1958.

*Portraits de Picasso* (title means "Portraits of Picasso"), illustrated with photography by Andre Villers, Muggiani, 1959, reprinted, Ramsay, 1981.

(Contributor) Ylipe, *Magloire de Paris,* Losfeld, 1961.

(With Max Ernst) *Les Chiens ont soif* (title means "The Dogs Are r Thirsty"), Pont des Arts, 1964.

*Jacques Prevert presente "Le Circle d'Izis"* (title means "Jacques Prevert Presents 'The Circle of Izis'"), illustrated with photographs by Bidermanas, A. Sauret, 1965.

(With Helmut Grieshaber) *Carl Orff: Carmina burana,* Manus Presse, 1965.

*Georges,* illustrations by Ribemont-Dessaignes, Cagnes, 1965.

(Contributor) Alexander Calder, *Calder,* Maeght, 1966.

*Fatras,* illustrations by the author, Livre de Poche, 1966.

*Prevert vous parle* (title means "Prevert Speaks to You"), Prentice-Hall, 1968.

(Contributor) Cesare Vivaldi, *Mayo,* Instituto Editoriale Italiano, 1968.

*Imaginaires* (title means "Make-Believe"), A. Skira, 1970.

(With Andre Pozner) *Hebdomadaires* (title means "Weeklies;" interview), G. Authier, 1972.

(With Rene Bartele) *Images de Jacques Prevert* (title means "Pictures by Jacques Prevert"), Filipacchi, 1974.

*Le Jour des temps,* illustrations by Max Papart, Galerie Bosquet and Jacques Goutal Darly, 1975.

*A travers Prevert* (title means "Through Prevert"), Gallimard, 1975.

*Soleil de nuit,* Gallimard, 1980.

*Pages d'ecriture* (juvenile), Gallimard, 1980.

*Couleurs de Braque, Calder, Miro,* Maeght, 1981.

(Illustrator) Andre Pozner, *Jacques Prevert: Collages,* Gallimard, 1982.

*La cinquieme saison,* Gallimard, 1984.

*Chanson des cireurs de souliers,* illustrations by Marie Gard, Gallimard, 1985.

*Chanson pour chanter a tue-tete et a cloche-pied,* illustrations by Gard, Gallimard, 1985.

Also author of *Le Cheval de Troie,* 1946, *L'Ange garde-chiourme,* 1946, and *Vignette pour les vignerons,* 1951. Also author r of farces, pantomimes, ballets, and skits, including "Baptiste" (mime play) and "La Famille tuyau de poele" (title means "Top-hat Family"), 1935, and of lyrics for numerous popular songs, including "Les Feuilles mortes" (title means "Autumn Leaves"), set to music by Joseph Kosma. Work represented in numerous anthologies, including *Let's Get a Divorce,* edited by E. R. Bentley y Hill & Wang, 1958 and *Selections from French Poetry,* edited by K. F. Canfield, Harvey House, 1965. Contributor to *Coronet, Kenyon Review, Poetry,* and other periodicals.

*SIDELIGHTS:* On Jacques Prevert's death, Marcel Carne, the producer with whom Prevert collaborated on several major films, told the *New York Times:* "Jacques Prevert [was] the one and only poet of the French cinema. He created a style, original and personal, reflecting the soul of the people. His humor and poetry succeeded in raising the banal to the summit of art." Between 1937 and 1950 Prevert collaborated with Carne on eight major films and became one of France's most important screenwriters.

Prevert was a poet as well as a screenwriter, so the comparison Carne made between Prevert's cinematic work and poetry was not surprising. Prevert's general appeal as a poet was such that *New Republic* contributor Eve Merriman called the Frenchman "France's most popular poet of the 20th century." He began writing poetry in the early thirties but did not see his first volume of poetry, *Paroles,* published until 1946. The book was a best-seller, selling hundreds of thousands of copies. In *Jacques Prevert* William E. Baker noted that the titles of several of Prevert's early books of poetry—including *Paroles*—"in a very general way" described the poet's stylistic tendencies: "*Paroles* because the poet has a genius for making all sorts of ordinary idiom highly expressive, *Spectacle* because his verbal tricks often correspond to the antics of a clown or a magician, and *La Pluie et le beau temps* because the emotional tones of his symbols can have the classic simplicity of the summer-and-winter, sunshine-and-rain cycle of life and love."

Prevert was quite prolific, as evidenced by the more than 1500 pages of poetry and notes gathered for the volume *Oeuvres Completes.* According to Stephen Romer in the *Times Literary Supplement,* Prevert was also "famously careless about what happened to his poems," so the editors' ability to track down these works is impressive indeed. Regarding the poetry itself, Romer commented, "While [Prevert's] handling of linguistic device is usually deft and brilliant, his meaning could not be plainer; and we don't need to scruple about that word in Prevert."

*BIOGRAPHICAL/CRITICAL SOURCES:*

*BOOKS*

Andry, Marc, *Jacques Prevert,* Editions de Fallois, 1994.
Baker, William E., *Jacques Prevert,* Twayne, 1967.
Blakeway, Claire, *Jacques Prevert: Popular French Theatre and Cinema,* Associated University Presses (London), 1990.
*Contemporary Literary Criticism,* Volume 15, Gale, 1980.

*PERIODICALS*

*Booklist,* March 1, 1994, p. 1272.
*Library Journal,* December, 1987, p. 116.
*Modern Language Journal,* October, 1949.
*Times Literary Supplement,* January 19, 1973; September 25, 1992, p. 16.
*Wisconsin Studies in Contemporary Literature,* summer, 1966.
*World Literature Today,* autumn, 1985, p. 569.*

* * *

**PRICE, Anthony 1928-**

*PERSONAL:* Born August 16, 1928, in Hertfordshire, England; son of Walter Longsdon (an engineer) and Kathleen (an artist; maiden name, Lawrence) Price; married Ann Stone (a registered nurse), June 20, 1953; children: James, Simon, Katherine. *Education:* Merton College, Oxford, M.A. (with honors), 1952.

*ADDRESSES: Home*—Wayside Cottage, Horton-cum-Studley, Oxford OX33 1AW, England. *Agent*—A. P. Watt Ltd., 20 John St., London WC1N 2DR, England.

*CAREER:* Writer. Journalist with the Westminster Press, 1952-88; *Oxford Times,* Oxfordshire, England, editor, 1972-88. *Military service:* British Army, 1947-49; became captain.

*MEMBER:* Guild of British Newspaper Editors, Crime Writers Association (England), Detection Club.

*AWARDS, HONORS:* Silver Dagger from Crime Writers Association, 1971, for *The Labyrinth Makers;* Golden Dagger from Crime Writers Association, 1975, for *Other Paths to Glory;* Swedish Academy of Crime Fiction Award for best foreign crime book translated, 1979, for *Other Paths to Glory.*

*WRITINGS:*

*MYSTERY NOVELS*

*The Labyrinth Makers,* Gollancz (London), 1970, Doubleday (New York City), 1971.
*The Alamut Ambush,* Gollancz, 1971, Doubleday, 1972.
*Colonel Butler's Wolf,* Gollancz, 1972, Doubleday, 1973.
*October Men,* Gollancz, 1973, Doubleday, 1974.
*Other Paths to Glory,* Gollancz, 1974, Doubleday, 1975.
*Our Man in Camelot,* Gollancz, 1975, Doubleday, 1976.
*War Game,* Gollancz, 1976, Doubleday, 1977.
*The '44 Vintage,* Doubleday, 1978.
*Tomorrow's Ghost,* Doubleday, 1979.
*The Hour of the Donkey,* Gollancz, 1980.
*Soldier No More,* Gollancz, 1981, Doubleday, 1982.
*The Old Vengeful,* Gollancz, 1982, Doubleday, 1983.
*Gunner Kelly,* Gollancz, 1983, Doubleday, 1984.
*Sion Crossing,* Mysterious Press (New York City), 1985.
*Here Be Monsters,* Mysterious Press, 1985.
*For the Good of the State,* Gollancz, 1986, Mysterious Press, 1987.
*A New Kind of War,* Gollancz, 1987, Mysterious Press, 1988.
*A Prospect of Vengeance,* Gollancz, 1988.
*The Memory Trap,* Gollancz, 1989.

*OTHER*

*The Eyes of the Fleet: A History of Frigate Warfare, 1793-1815,* Hutchinson (London), 1990, Norton (New York City), 1996.

*SIDELIGHTS:* "Anthony Price," according to Karl G. Frederiksson in the *St. James Guide to Crime and Mystery Writers,* "has brought the concept of history into his spy novels in quite a unique manner. Suspense fiction which takes place in historical time, often including real historical persons, is nothing new. The same goes for the concept of the "detective as historian," uncovering things in the past. But Price has brought the *real* meaning of history into his novels, as something that happened perhaps a long time ago, but still has significance for us today. In almost all of his novels the plot is based on a historical episode, and the knowledge of the historical truth is necessary for the solution of the mystery."

*Times Literary Supplement* reviewer T. J. Binyon notes that Price's first novel, *The Labyrinth Makers,* "introduced the character who has since become his chief spy-catcher—Dr. David Audley of British Intelligence." In this novel, Audley is assigned to discover just why the Russians are so interested in a newly-located British plane that crashed in a lake in 1945. The *Best Sellers* critic finds the novel to be "as engrossing as a chess game," while Newgate Callendar in the *New York Times Book Review* calls it "an especially promising piece of work." The reviewer for the *Times Literary Supplement* judges *The Labyrinth Makers* "excellent, of a deft and polished kind and immensely enjoyable. . . . The hero, Dr. Audley, is exceptionally pleasant and acceptable."

In *Colonel Butler's Wolf,* Price draws on the real-life experiences of British traitor Kim Philby in an adventure in which Audley must uncover the reasons a Russian agent has infiltrated Oxford University. Utilizing Colonel Jack Butler as his operative, Audley succeeds in foiling a threat to British security. H. C. Velt in *Library Journal* calls the novel "unusually interesting and readable." The reviewer for the *Times Literary Supplement* credits Butler's "decency, training and good sense [with overcoming] an ingeniously subtle adversary."

Speaking of Price's work on the Audley series, Callendar claims that "Price, with his unsentimental view of the world, knows how to juggle the most convoluted intrigue and end up making sense." Fredriksson finds that Price "has succeeded in blending the intricacies of the spy novel with the plotting of the classical whodunnit. Apart from the moral riddles which always creep into the more serious British spy novels of the 'after-[Kim] Philby type' there is always a mystery to be solved, often with a historical dimension. This is not only achieved on a structural level, but is intricately blended into his literary style. Price stands out as a unique contributor to a genre in which British authors have always excelled."

Price once told *CA* that he tries "to combine the elements of the mystery story with those of the spy thriller, using my particular interests—history, particularly military history—as a background. My heroes and heroines are generally not secret agents so much as secret policemen (and women). My themes (I like to think) are nevertheless loyalty, duty, honor and patriotism, which I regard as the virtues of a free man in a free country. And if that's old fashioned, then so be it, by God!"

*BIOGRAPHICAL/CRITICAL SOURCES:*

*BOOKS*

*St. James Guide to Crime and Mystery Writers,* fourth edition, St. James Press (Detroit), 1996

*PERIODICALS*

*Best Sellers,* October 1, 1971, p. 307.
*Globe and Mail* (Toronto), August 13, 1988.
*Library Journal,* June 1, 1973, p. 1846.
*Los Angeles Times Book Review,* July 26, 1986.
*New York Times,* May 23, 1986.
*New York Times Book Review,* October 31, 1971, p. 30; July 30, 1972, p. 22; June 17, 1973, p. 32; June 17, 1984; September 15, 1985; August 16, 1987; July 19, 1988.
*Times* (London), January 22, 1987; December 24, 1987, November 12, 1988.
*Times Literary Supplement,* August 14, 1970, p. 906; July 7, 1972, p. 783; February 24, 1978; January 8, 1982; April 25, 1986; April 10, 1987.

# R

**RAND, Paul 1914-1996**

*PERSONAL:* Born August 15, 1914, in Brooklyn, NY; died of cancer, November 26, 1996, in Norwalk, CT; married second wife, Marion Swannie, 1975; children: (first marriage) Catherine. *Education:* Pratt Institute, graduate, 1932; studied at Parsons School of Design, 1932, and Art Students League of New York, 1934. *Religion:* Orthodox Jewish.

*CAREER:* Designer, typographer, painter, and teacher. Studio of George Switzer, New York City, apprentice, 1932-35; *Esquire* and *Apparel Arts* magazines, New York City, art director, 1936-41; William H. Weintraub Advertising Agency, New York, creative director, 1941-54; freelance designer, New York, beginning in 1955; design consultant to IBM, Cummins Engine Company, Westinghouse Electric Corporation, beginning in 1956; Cooper Union, Laboratory School of Design, New York City, instructor in graphic design, 1938-42, Pratt Institute, Brooklyn, NY, instructor in postgraduate course, 1946, Yale University, School of Art and Architecture, New Haven, CT, professor of graphic design, 1956-96, Yale Summer Program, Brissago, Switzerland, instructor, beginning in 1977, guest professor at Cooper Union, 1993, and other schools around the United States. Fulbright scholarship jury, former member; visitor at Museum School, Boston Museum of Fine Arts; member of art education advisory board, New York University. President's Fellow at Rhode Island School of Design. Numerous exhibitions of his work have been held in the United States, Europe, Japan, and Russia, and at museums that also hold some of his collections, including the Smithsonian in Washington, DC, Museum of Modern Art, New York, and Kunstgewerbemuseum, Zurich, Switzerland.

*MEMBER:* Royal Society of Arts (London; Benjamin Franklin fellow); Alliance Graphique International (Paris); Industrial Designers Society of America.

*AWARDS, HONORS:* Honorary Professor, Tama University, Tokyo, Japan, 1958; citation from Philadelphia College of Art, 1962; American Institute of Graphic Arts Gold Medal, 1966; named to New York Art Director's Club Hall of Fame, 1972; named Royal Designer for Industry, Royal Society of Arts, London, 1973; Florence Prize for Visual Communication, 1987; honorary master of arts, Yale University; honorary D.F.A. degrees from Philadelphia College of Art, Parsons School of Design, University of Hartford, and Kutztown University; other awards from *Financial World* for best design and typography of annual reports; Museum of Modern Art for fabrics design; *New York Times* jury for children's book illustrations; and Society of Typographic Arts for trademarks, and numerous other awards for design in advertising, brochures, reports, books, trademarks, packaging, fabric, interior architecture, and illustration for children's books.

*WRITINGS:*

*Thoughts on Design,* Wittenborn (New York City), 1946.

*The Trademarks of Paul Rand,* Wittenborn, 1960.

(Contributor) *Education of Vision,* Braziller (New York City), 1965.

(Contributor) *Homage to the Book,* West Virginia Pulp and Paper Co. (New York City), 1968.

*A Paul Rand Miscellany,* Walker Art Center, 1984.

*A Designer's Art,* Yale University Press (New Haven, CT), 1985.
*Design, Form, and Chaos,* Yale University Press, 1993.
(Contributor) *Looking Closer: Critical Writings on Graphic Design,* Allworth Press (New York City), 1994.
*From Lascaux to Brooklyn,* Yale University Press, 1996.

Contributor of numerous articles on design, advertising, and typography to such periodicals as *American Printer, Art and Industry, Graphic Forms, Type Talks, Penrose Annual, Journal of the American Institute of Graphic Arts, Typographica, Print, Daedalus,* and *Graphis.*

*ILLUSTRATOR*

*I Know a Lot of Things,* Harcourt (New York City), 1956.
*Sparkle and Spin,* Harcourt, 1957; reprinted, Abrams (New York City), 1991.
*Little I,* Harcourt, 1962; reprinted, Abrams, 1991.
*Listen, Listen!,* Harcourt, 1970.

Designer of hundreds of book covers and jackets for many publishers, including Knopf and Pantheon.

*SIDELIGHTS:* Paul Rand, celebrated American graphic designer of logos for International Business Machines (IBM), United Parcel Service (UPS), American Broadcasting Company (ABC), and Westinghouse, could be called the father of modern American graphic design. He was known in the graphic design and visual communications communities as a designer, typographer, painter, and teacher. His contributions in all these areas are vast, internationally renowned, and well-recognized by those who know of him and by those who receive only his messages, unaware of the artist who created them.

When Rand died on November 26, 1996, he left behind an artistic legacy that reached as far back as age three, when he was living in Brooklyn with his Orthodox Jewish parents. Rand was born on August 15, 1914, and by 1917 he was secretly drawing pictures of his neighborhood, though such practices were forbidden by his religion. When Rand was a teenager, the entrance fee for night classes at the Pratt Institute in Brooklyn cost $25.00, yet Rand was able to convince his father to pay the fee so Rand was able to attend the school while completing his high school education at Harren High School in Manhattan. From there Rand went on to study at the Parsons School of Design (New York) and the Art Students League (New York), studying with Georg Grosz. Ironically, Rand's true style emerged when he began studying foreign design magazines such as *German Gebrauchsgraphik* and *British Commercial Art* and the work of such design masters as A. M. Cassandre and Laszlo Moholoy-Nagy. While in design school, Rand brought to classes with him all the books and magazines from Europe containing the paintings, artists, and ideas then influencing him. Rand, talking in 1985 with Joseph Giovannini, contributor to the *New York Times Book Review,* explained, "my teachers never heard of them. They'd say I just didn't know how to draw. I'm sort of self-taught."

Rand found American illustrations in visual communication behind the times. Rand told Giovannini that there was "nothing called graphic design in this country" in the 1920s. In fact, realistic, detailed, narrative illustration with linear text predominated through the work of such artists as Maxfield Parrish and Norman Rockwell. As Rand was strongly being influenced by yet more European artists such as George Klee, Pablo Picasso, Henri Matisse, and Wassily Kandinsky, and even the design aesthetics of the German design school known as The Bauhaus, he sought to "explode" the tight, narrative illustrations of the turn-of-the-century advertising graphics still being used in the United States in the 1920s and replace them with simplicity of design. Following his formal education, Rand persisted in his work and went on to change the traditional face of American graphics forever.

Seeking opportunity to express his own interpretations of this European influence, Rand landed his first job as a designer for the George Switzer Agency in Manhattan. He designed packaging and lettering for many well-known clients. By age 23, Rand was working for Esquire-Coronet and developing his graphic skills as a page designer for such merchandise as fashions and gifts for *Apparel Arts* and *Esquire* magazines. He also designed avante-garde covers for the arts and culture magazine *Direction.* In 1941 Rand joined the newly established William Weintraub advertising agency as the art director, there developing designs for Dubonnet and Lee Hats, among others. In 1956, Rand joined with Eliot Noyes, the product and building design consultant at International Business Machines (IBM), and developed the familiar IBM logo with the characteristic block letters broken into horizontal lines. Rand went on to design the Westinghouse distinctive "W," UPS's package tied with string, and ABC's circle-encasing lower-case letters, all of which are in use today. As Rand designed the ABC trademark, he hinted at the simplicity of the alphabet as an effective design tool to convey a potentially complex aesthetic. Writing for *Contemporary Graphic Artists,* Dennis Wepman defined Rand as "noted for the economy of his design," since "he conveys a maximum of meaning with the fewest possible elements."

Rand's work has been presented on jacket, book, and magazine covers, on posters, typographies, and book pages (text design and margin arrangement), and in product advertisements and corporate trademarks. *Publishers Weekly* reviewer Jerome P. Frank named Rand as "the one who helped elevate commercial art that catered to the lowest common denominator to the portals of fine art." He was also a celebrated teacher on the university level, illustrator of four children's books, author of seven books, and contributor of a myriad of articles published in numerous trade journals of the day. Three of his most popular books include *Paul Rand: A Designer's Art* (1985), *Design, Form, and Chaos* (1993), and *From Lascaux to Brooklyn* (1996).

Alan Fern, reviewer for the *New York Times Book Review,* stated: "the curse of the designer is that he remains anonymous to those who use (and may even admire) his work." Rand's 1985 book *Paul Rand: A Designer's Art* shares his thoughts and ideas as well as samples of his work. As Rand asserted, "It is in a world of symbols that man lives." In *A Designer's Art* the design student finds the style and thoughts with which Rand used to change American visual communication. And Fern suggested, "Mr. Rand's writing is often poetic or allusive." Jerome Frank, reviewing for *Publishers Weekly,* believed Rand's essay espouses the "excellence in design . . . in a society that is today drifting almost casually toward the banal, the pretentious and the predictable." *A Designer's Art* discusses the roles color, symbol, humor, text, spacing, margins, and even politics play in the balancing the relationship between the message and the viewer.

Rand's 1993 book *Design, Form, and Chaos* is directed more at the general reader than the design student. Rand compared his own designs against current practices through critical analysis. Victor Margolin, reviewer for the *New York Times Book Review,* was critical in his assessment of Rand's tome. Seeing Rand's criticisms based on his comparisons, Margolin at once praised Rand for his work and ground-breaking achievements in American design and denounced Rand's unwillingness "to grapple with potentially valuable contributions of new ideas and new technology."

In Rand's 1996 *From Lascaux to Brooklyn,* Russell Clement, contributor to *Library Journal,* found, by way of history and practicality, an explanation of graphic design/visual communication, commending Rand's introductory first half as accessible to young and old alike and hailing the second half as a convincing analysis of aspects of design. Yet, Paul Shepheard, reviewer for the *New York Times Book Review,* found Rand's writing "immensely confusing." Shepheard felt that there are too many contradictions and ramblings in the book, and that it "seem[ed] to have been put together to support an ailing modernist program for graphic art, in which Paul Rand is a key figure." Still, Clement lauded Rand's "commonsense approach to the pursuit of quality in design theory and process," adding that *From Lascaux to Brooklyn* is "highly recommended for all academic libraries."

Rand's life's work is clear evidence of his understanding of the power of symbol, essential comprehension of subject, and skillful use of the less-is-more delivery, making him the forger of, as Philip Meggs asserted in *Contemporary Designers,* a "modernist approach into a graphic design style that was highly personal and uniquely American." Rand uncluttered the narrative illustration with simple effective color, symbol, and placement to present the idea to the viewer. He was a pioneer and master who explained, "When I designed the IBM logo, I just did it."

*BIOGRAPHICAL/CRITICAL SOURCES:*

*BOOKS*

Allner, Walter, *Posters: 50 Artists and Designers,* Reinhold (New York City), 1952.

*Champion Papers Book 35: A Special Issue on Paul Rand,* Champion, (Scottsdale, AZ), 1975.

*Contemporary Designers,* St. James Press, (Chicago), 1990.

*Contemporary Graphic Artists,* Gale, Volume 3, 1988.

Kamekura, Yusaku, *Paul Rand: His Work from 1946-58,* Knopf (New York City), 1959.

Klemin, Diana, *The Art of Art for Children's Books,* Clarkson Potter, 1966.

*PERIODICALS*

*American Artist,* June, 1942; October, 1953; October, 1970.
*American Book Collector,* April, 1987, p. 38.
*Architectural Review,* June, 1993, p. 97.
*Art Direction,* November, 1985, p. 126; May, 1993, p. 77.
*Bloomsbury Review,* November, 1988, p. 23.
*Christian Science Monitor,* December 23, 1985.
*Choice,* February, 1986, p. 859; July, 1993, p. 1763.
*Communications Arts,* January/February, 1979.
*Design,* June, 1993, p. 47.
*Design Quarterly,* winter, 1984, p. 1.
*Esquire,* August, 1953.
*Graphis,* September/October, 1993, p. 10.
*Idea,* November, 1976.
*Journal of Communication,* spring, 1994, p. 154+.
*Library Journal,* February 15, 1986, p. 175; April 15, 1996, p. 85.
*Newsweek,* June 23, 1986, p. 53.
*New York Times,* November 28, 1996, p. D19.
*New York Times Book Review,* November 3, 1985, p. 1; May 2, 1993, p. 31; June 6, 1993, p. 34; December 5, 1993, p. 42; March 24, 1996, p. 25.
*Print,* January/February, 1959; July/August, 1993, p. 273.
*Publishers Weekly,* October 4, 1985, p. 55; September 13, 1991, p. 81.
*School Arts,* March, 1981, p. 46.
*Time,* October 18, 1982, p. 84; December 9, 1996.
*Times Literary Supplement,* May 16, 1986, p. 528; July 23, 1993, p. 17.
*Upper and Lower Case,* March, 1977.

*OBITUARIES:*

*PERIODICALS*

*New York Times,* November 28, 1996, p. D19.
*Time,* December 9, 1996, p. 25.*

*—Sketch by Mari Artzner Wolf*

* * *

**RAYMOND, Rene (Brabazon) 1906-1985**
**(James Hadley Chase, James L. Docherty, Ambrose Grant, Raymond Marshall)**

*PERSONAL:* Born December 24, 1906, in London, England; died February 6 (one source says February 5), 1985, in Corseaux-sur-Vevey, Switzerland; married Sylvia Ray; children: one son. *Education:* Attended schools in Rochester, Kent, England.

*CAREER:* Writer. Door-to-door encyclopedia salesman in Hastings, England, in the mid-1920s; associated with Simkin Marshall (wholesale bookselling firm), London, England, in the late 1920s; editor of *RAF Journal. Military service:* Royal Air Force; became squadron leader.

*WRITINGS:*

(Under pseudonym James L. Docherty) *He Won't Need It Now,* Rich and Cowan (London), 1939, (under pseudonym James Hadley Chase) Panther (London), 1975.
(Editor with David Langdon) *Slipstream: A Royal Air Force Anthology,* Eyre & Spottiswoode (London), 1946.
*I'll Get You for This* (novel), Jarrolds (London), 1946, Avon (New York City), 1951, (under Chase pseudonym) Jarrolds, 1947, Avon, 1951.
(Under pseudonym Ambrose Grant) *More Deadly Than the Male,* Eyre & Spottiswoode, 1946, (under Chase pseudonym) Hamilton, 1960.

*NOVELS; UNDER PSEUDONYM JAMES HADLEY CHASE*

*No Orchids for Miss Blandish,* Jarrolds, 1939, Howell, Soskin (New York City), 1942, revised edition, Hamilton, 1961; published as *The Villain and the Virgin,* Avon (New York City), 1948, revised edition, 1961.
*The Dead Stay Dumb,* Jarrolds, 1939, Panther, 1971; published as *Kiss My Fist,* Eton (New York City), 1952.
*Twelve Chinks and a Woman,* Jarrolds, 1940, Howell, Soskin, 1941, revised edition published as *Twelve Chinamen and a Woman,* Novel Library (London), 1950, published as *The Doll's Bad News,* Panther, 1970.
*Miss Callaghan Comes to Grief,* Jarrolds, 1941.
*Miss Shumway Waves a Wand,* Jarrolds, 1944, Corgi, 1977.
*Eve,* Jarrolds, 1945, Corgi, 1975.
*I'll Get You for This,* Jarrolds, 1947, Avon, 1951 (see also above).
*The Flesh of the Orchid,* Jarrolds, 1948, Pocket Books (New York City), 1972.
*You Never Know With Women,* Jarrolds, 1949, Pocket Books, 1972.

*You're Lonely When You're Dead,* R. Hale (London), 1949, Duell, Sloan & Pearce (New York City), 1950.
*Figure It Out for Yourself,* R. Hale, 1950, Duell, Sloan & Pearce, 1951; published as *The Marijuana Mob,* Eton (New York City), 1952.
*Lay Her Among the Lilies,* R. Hale, 1950, Corgi, 1974; published as *Too Dangerous to Be Free,* Duell, Sloan & Pearce, 1951.
*Strictly for Cash,* R. Hale, 1951, Pocket Books, 1973.
*The Fast Buck,* R. Hale, 1952.
*The Double Shuffle,* R. Hale, 1952, Dutton (New York City), 1953.
*This Way for a Shroud,* R. Hale, 1953.
*I'll Bury My Dead,* R. Hale, 1953, Dutton, 1954.
*Tiger by the Tail,* R. Hale, 1954.
*Safer Dead,* R. Hale, 1954, published as *Dead Ringer,* Ace Books, 1955.
*You've Got It Coming,* R. Hale, 1955, Pocket Books, 1973, revised edition, R. Hale, 1975.
*There's Always a Price Tag,* R. Hale, 1956, Pocket Books, 1973.
*The Guilty Are Afraid,* R. Hale, 1957, New American Library (New York City), 1959.
*The Case of the Strangled Starlet,* New American Library, 1958 (published in England as *Not Safe to Be Free,* R. Hale, 1958, reprinted, 1979).
*Shock Treatment,* New American Library, 1959.
*The World in My Pocket,* R. Hale, 1959, Popular Library (New York City), 1962.
*More Deadly Than the Male,* Hamilton, 1960 (see also above).
*What's Better Than Money?,* R. Hale, 1960, Pocket Books, 1972.
*Come Easy—Go Easy,* R. Hale, 1960, Pocket Books, 1974.
*A Lotus for Miss Quon,* R. Hale, 1961.
*Just Another Sucker,* R. Hale, 1961, Pocket Books, 1974.
*I Would Rather Stay Poor,* R. Hale, 1962, Pocket Books, 1974.
*A Coffin from Hong Kong,* R. Hale, 1962.
*Tell It to the Birds,* R. Hale, 1963, Pocket Books, 1974.
*One Bright Summer Morning,* Hale, 1963, Pocket Books, 1974.
*The Soft Centre,* R. Hale, 1964.
*This Is for Real,* R. Hale, 1965, Walker & Co. (New York City), 1967.
*The Way the Cookie Crumbles,* R. Hale, 1965, Pocket Books, 1974.
*You Have Yourself a Deal,* R. Hale, 1966, Walker & Co., 1968.
*Cade,* R. Hale, 1966.
*Well Now, My Pretty—,* R. Hale, 1967.
*Have This One on Me,* R. Hale, 1967.
*An Ear to the Ground,* R. Hale, 1968.
*Believed Violent,* R. Hale, 1968.
*The Vulture Is a Patient Bird,* R. Hale, 1969.
*The Whiff of Money,* R. Hale, 1969.
*There's a Hippie on the Highway,* R. Hale, 1970.
*Like a Hole in the Head,* R. Hale, 1970.
*Want to Stay Alive?,* R. Hale, 1971.
*An Ace up My Sleeve* (also see below), R. Hale, 1971.
*Just a Matter of Time,* R. Hale, 1972.
*You're Dead without Money,* R. Hale, 1972.
*Knock! Knock! Who's There?,* R. Hale, 1973.
*Have a Change of Scene,* R. Hale, 1973.
*Three of Spades,* R. Hale, 1974.
*Goldfish Have No Hiding Place,* R. Hale, 1974.
*So What Happens to Me?,* R. Hale, 1974.
*Believe This, You'll Believe Anything,* R. Hale, 1975.
*He Won't Need It Now,* Panther, 1975 (see also above).
*The Joker in the Pack* (also see below), R. Hale, 1976.
*Do Me a Favour—Drop Dead,* R. Hale, 1976.
*I Hold the Four Aces* (also see below), R. Hale, 1977.
*Meet Mark Girland,* R. Hale, 1977.
*My Laugh Comes Last,* R. Hale, 1977.
*Consider Yourself Dead,* R. Hale, 1978.
*You Must Be Kidding,* R. Hale, 1979.
*Can of Worms,* R. Hale, 1979.
*You Can Say That Again,* R. Hale, 1980.
*Try This One for Size,* R. Hale, 1980.
*Hand Me a Fig Leaf,* R. Hale, 1981.
*Have a Nice Night,* R. Hale, 1982.
*We'll Share a Double Funeral,* R. Hale, 1982.
*Not My Thing,* R. Hale, 1983.
*Hit Them Where It Hurts,* R. Hale, 1984.
*Meet Helga Rolfe* (includes *An Ace Up My Sleeve, The Joker in the Pack, I Hold Four Aces*), R. Hale, 1984.
*Get a Load of This,* Hale, 1984.

*NOVELS; UNDER PSEUDONYM RAYMOND MARSHALL*

*Blondes' Requiem,* Jarrolds, 1945, Crown, 1946.
*No Business of Mine,* Jarrolds, 1947, R. Hale, 1976.
*The Pickup,* Harlequin (Toronto), 1955.
*Ruthless,* Harlequin, 1955.
*Never Trust a Woman,* Harlequin, 1957.

*NOVELS; ORIGINALLY UNDER PSEUDONYM RAYMOND MARSHALL, SUBSEQUENTLY UNDER PSEUDONYM JAMES HADLEY CHASE*

*Lady—Here's Your Wreath,* Jarrolds, 1940, (under Chase pseudonym) Hamilton, 1961.

*Just the Way It Is,* Jarrolds, 1944, (under Chase pseudonym) Panther, 1976.

*Make the Corpse Walk,* Jarrolds, 1946, (under Chase pseudonym) Hamilton, 1964.

*Trusted Like the Fox,* Jarrolds, 1948, (under Chase pseudonym) Hamilton, 1964.

*The Paw in the Bottle,* Jarrolds, 1949, (under Chase pseudonym) Hamilton, 1961.

*Mallory,* Jarrolds, 1950, (under Chase pseudonym) Hamilton, 1964.

*But a Short Time to Live,* Jarrolds, 1951, (under Chase pseudonym) Hamilton, 1960.

*In a Vain Shadow,* Jarrolds, 1951, (under Chase pseudonym) Hale, 1977.

*Why Pick on Me?,* Jarrolds, 1951, (under Chase pseudonym) Hamilton, 1961.

*The Wary Transgressor,* Jarrolds, 1952, (under Chase pseudonym) Hamilton, 1963.

*The Things Men Do,* Jarrolds, 1953, (under Chase pseudonym) Hamilton, 1962.

*Mission to Venice,* R. Hale, 1954, (under Chase pseudonym) Panther, 1973.

*The Sucker Punch,* Jarrolds, 1954, (under Chase pseudonym) Hamilton, 1963.

*Mission to Siena,* R. Hale, 1955, (under Chase pseudonym) Panther, 1966.

*You Find Him—I'll Fix Him,* R. Hale, 1956, (under Chase pseudonym) Panther, 1966.

*Hit and Run,* R. Hale, 1958, (under Chase pseudonym) R. Hale, 1978.

*PLAYS; UNDER PSEUDONYM JAMES HADLEY CHASE*

(With Arthur Macrea) *Get a Load of This,* produced in London, 1941.

(With Robert Nesbitt) *No Orchids for Miss Blandish* (adapted from Chase's novel of the same name), produced in London, 1942.

*Last Page* (produced in London, 1946), S. French (London), 1947.

*OTHER*

(Editor, with David Langdon) *Slipstream: A Royal Air Force Anthology,* Eyre and Spottiswoode, 1946.

*ADAPTATIONS:* Raymond was especially popular in France and Italy, where more than twenty of his novels were made into films. On the American film scene, Robert Aldrich produced *The Grissom Gang* in 1971, a Cinerama film release of writer Leon Griffith's screenplay, which was based on Raymond's *No Orchids for Miss Blandish.* Raymond wrote his own adaptation of the novel for the stage in 1942, which was filmed in 1948.

*SIDELIGHTS:* Rene Raymond shocked readers in the 1920s and 1930s with his hard-boiled crime novels, which were years ahead of their time in the graphic sex and violence they portrayed. During the course of his career, Raymond published more than one hundred books, some under the pseudonyms James Hadley Chase, James L. Docherty, Ambrose Grant, and Raymond Marshall. His first commercially successful book is probably the one for which he is best remembered. It was *No Orchids for Miss Blandish,* a thriller that details the kidnaping of an heiress by gangsters. It sold more than a million copies during its first year in print. Like most of his later work, *No Orchids* combines a fast pace, flashy characters, and a complex plot with elements of sex and violence.

Almost all of Raymond's books feature American settings and American protagonists—usually mobsters and private investigators. Raymond himself, however, was described by a London *Times* reporter as "a typical quiet Englishman," who gathered most of his background material from American slang dictionaries, police reports, and maps of U.S. cities. He had actually been in the United States only a few times, and even he never even visited the areas in which he usually set his stories.

According to Mary Ann Grochowski in *St. James Guide to Crime and Mystery Writers,* Raymond "propels the reader through complex, intricate plots with gaudy, explosive characters and a fast-moving, hard-boiled style." Some of his recurring characters are Brick-Top Corrigan, an unscrupulous private investigator; Don Micklem, a millionaire playboy; and Mark Girland, an ex-CIA agent who has gone freelance in order to support his expensive tastes in women. Girland is the main character in *You Have Yourself a Deal,* which is typical of Raymond's work. It includes a beautiful amnesiac with a mysterious tattoo on her left buttock, evil Russian and Chinese agents, and brutal interrogation sessions.

Contemporary reviewers sometimes gave Raymond his due as a storyteller, even if they disparaged the lurid elements that helped to make the author's work popular. Discussing *Figure It Out for Yourself,* a London *Times* reviewer allowed that "in spite of the garish properties of the story, the solution is carefully planned and the final revelation . . . is satisfactorily surprising." "If you like to read about violence, murder and insanity, they are all present here," wrote a *New York Times* contributor about the same book. The *New York Herald Tribune Book Review* reported that "Mr. Chase is well on his way to becoming the goriest writer in the detective story field, and his new novel virtually drips with blood." Grochowski concluded that Raymond's flaws "can all be overlooked when the reader has been captured by the fast-paced action and thrill-a-minute dialogue of [his] style."

Raymond himself was quoted in *St. James Guide to Crime and Mystery Writers* as saying: "My job is to write a book for a wide variety of readers. I do this job conscientiously. An introduction to my work would certainly not be of use to my general readers. They couldn't care less. All they are asking for is a good read: that is what I try to give them."

*BIOGRAPHICAL/CRITICAL SOURCES:*

*BOOKS*

*St. James Guide to Crime and Mystery Writers,* fourth edition, St. James Press (Detroit), 1996.
*Twentieth-Century Writing: A Reader's Guide to Contemporary Literature,* Transatlantic (Albuquerque, NM), 1969.

*PERIODICALS*

*Kirkus Reviews,* September 1, 1950; February 1, 1951.
*New Yorker,* September 6, 1941.
*New York Herald Tribune Book Review,* October 8, 1950, p. 34; May 20, 1951, p. 16; October 14, 1951, p. 22; January 19, 1953, p. 12; February 7, 1954, p. 10.
*New York Times,* August 24, 1941, p. 17; May 19, 1946, p. 30; October 15, 1950, p. 40; June 3, 1951, p. 19; October 14, 1951, p. 32; January 11, 1953, p. 28; January 10, 1954, p. 26.
*San Francisco Chronicle,* October 8, 1950, p. 14; April 8, 1951, p. 17; October 14, 1951, p. 20; January 18, 1953, p. 22; January 24, 1954, p. 19.
*Saturday Review of Literature,* May 18, 1946; April 28, 1951; October 20, 1951; February 7, 1953.
*Times* (London), August 31, 1940, p. 425; February 2, 1951, p. 65.

*OBITUARIES:*

*PERIODICALS*

*Los Angeles Times,* February 7, 1985.
*Time,* February 18, 1985.
*Times* (London), February 7, 1985.
*Washington Post,* February 11, 1985.*

* * *

**RITSOS, Giannes**
**See RITSOS, Yannis**

* * *

**RITSOS, Yannis 1909-1990**
**(Giannes Ritsos)**

*PERSONAL:* Name also transliterated as Giannes Ritsos; born May 1, 1909, in Monemvasia, Greece; died November 11, 1990, in Athens, Greece; son of Eleftherios (a land-owner) and Eleftheria (Vouzounara) Ritsos; married Fallitasa Georgiades (a medical doctor), 1954; children: Erie. *Education:* Educated in Greece. *Politics:* Communist. *Religion:* Greek Orthodox.

*CAREER:* Poet. Angelopoulos (law firm), Athens, Greece, law clerk, 1925; Mitzopoulos-Oeconomopoulos (notaries for National Bank of Greece), Athens, clerk, 1925-26; Lawyer's Association, Athens, assistant librarian, 1926; confined to a sanatorium because of tuberculosis, 1927-31; employed by a music theater during the 1930s; joined Communist Party, 1934; National Theatre of Greece, Athens, member of Chorus of Ancient Tragedies, 1938-45; member of National Resistance Movement (Communist guerrilla movement), 1944-49; Govostis (publisher), Athens, editor and proofreader, 1945-48, 1952-56; full-time writer, 1956-90. Actor and dancer for Lyriki Skini (Athens Opera House).

*MEMBER:* European Community of Writers, Society of Greek Writers, Society of Greek Dramatists,

Comite des Gens des Lettres, Societe des ecrivains et compositeurs dramatiques francais, Academy of Meinz, Academy Mallarme.

*AWARDS, HONORS:* State Prize Award for Poetry (Greece), 1956; Grand Prix International de la Biennale de Poesie de Knokke (Belgium), 1972; International Prize "Georgi Dimitroff" (Bulgaria), 1974; honorary doctorate from Salonica University (Greece), 1975, and University of Birmingham, 1978; Grand Prix Francais de la Poesie "Alfred de Vigny," 1975; International Prize for Poetry "Etna-Taormina" (Italy), 1976; International Prize for Poetry "Seregno-Brianza" (Italy), 1976; Lenin Peace Prize, 1977; Mondello Prize (Italy), 1978.

*WRITINGS:*

*POETRY; IN ENGLISH TRANSLATION*

*Romiosyne,* Kedros, 1966, translation by O. Laos published as *Romiossyni,* Dustbooks, 1969.

*Poems of Yannis Ritsos,* translated by Alan Page, Oxonian Press, 1969.

*Romiossini and Other Poems,* translated by Dan Georgakas and Eleni Paidoussi, Quixote Press, 1969.

*Gestures and Other Poems, 1968-1970,* translated by Nikos Stangos, Cape Golliard, 1971.

*Contradictions,* translated by John Stathatos, Sceptre Press, 1973.

*Dekaochto lianotragouda tes pikres patridas,* Kedros, 1973, translation by Amy Mims published as *Eighteen Short Songs of the Bitter Motherland,* North Central Publishing, 1974.

*Diadromos kai skala,* Kedros, 1973, translation by Nicos Germanacos published as *Corridor and Stairs,* Goldsmith Press (Ireland), 1976.

*Yannis Ritsos: Selected Poems,* translated by Stangos, Penguin, 1974.

*The Fourth Dimension: Selected Poems of Yannis Ritsos,* translated and introduced by Rae Dalven, David R. Godine, 1977.

*Chronicle of Exile,* translated and introduced by Minas Savvas, Wire Press, 1977.

*Ritsos in Parenthesis,* translated by Kimon Friar, Princeton University Press, 1979.

*Grafe tyflou,* Kedros, 1979, translated by Friar and Kostas Myrsiades as *Scripture of the Blind,* Ohio State University Press, 1979.

*Subterranean Horses,* translated by Savvas, Ohio State University Press, 1980.

*Erotica: Small Suite in Red Major, Naked Body, Carnal Word,* translated by Friar, Sachem Press, 1982.

*Selected Poems,* translated by Edmund Keely, Ecco Press, 1983.

*Exile and Return,* translated by Keely, Ecco Press, 1985.

*Monovasia and the Women of Monemvasia,* translated by Friar and Myrsiades, Nostos Books, 1988.

*Repetitions, Testimonies, Parentheses* (anthology), translated by Edmund Keeley, Princeton University Press, 1991.

*The Fourth Dimension,* translated by Peter Green, Princeton University Press, 1993.

*Late into the Night: The Last Poems of Yannis Ritsos,* translated by Martin McKinsey, Oberlin College Press, 1995.

*POETRY; IN GREEK*

*Trakter* (title means "Tractors"), Govostis, 1934.

*Pyramides* (title means "Pyramids"), Govostis, 1935.

*Epitaphios,* Rizospastis, 1936.

*To tragoudi tes adelphes mou* (title means "The Song of My Sister"), Govostis, 1937.

*Earini Symphonia* (title means "Spring Symphony"), Govostis, 1938.

*To emvatirio tou okeanou* (title means "The March of the Ocean"), Govostis, 1940.

*Palia Mazurka se rythmo vrohis* (title means "An Old Mazurka in the Rhythm of the Rain"), Govostis, 1942.

*Dokimasia* (title means "Trial"), Govostis, 1943.

*O syntrofos mas* (title means "Our Comrade"), Govostis, 1945.

*O anthropos me to gary fallo* (title means "The Man with the Carnation"), Politikes Ke Logotechnikes Ekdoseis, 1952.

*Agrypnia* (title means "Vigil"), Pyxida, 1954.

*Proino astro* (title means "Morning Star"), [Athens], 1955.

*He sonata tou selenophotos* (title means "Moonlight Sonata"), Kedros, 1956.

*Croniko* (title means "Chronicle"), Kedros, 1957.

*Apochairetisnos* (title means "Farewell"), Kedros, 1957.

*Hydria* (title means "The Urn"), Kedros, 1957.

*Cheimerinediaugeia* (title means "Winter Limpidity"), Kedros, 1957.

*Petrinos Chronos* (title means "Stony Time"), P.L.E., 1957.

*He Geitonies tou Kosmou* (title means "The Neighborhood of the World"), P.L.E., 1957.

*Otan erchetai ho xenos* (title means "When the Stranger Comes"), Kedros, 1958.

*Any potachti Politeia* (title means "Unsubjugated City"), P.L.E., 1958.

*He architectoniki ton dentron* (title means "The Architecture of the Trees"), P.L.E., 1958.

*Hoi gerontisses k'he thalassa* (title means "The Old Woman and the Sea"), Kedros, 1959.

*To parathyro* (title means "The Window"), Kedros, 1960.

*He gephyra* (title means "The Bridge"), Kedros, 1960.

*Ho mavros Hagios* (title means "The Black Saint"), Kedros, 1961.

*Pieimata Tomos* (collected poems), three volumes, Kedros, 1961-64.

*To nekro spiti* (title means "The Dead House"), Kedros, 1962.

*Kato ap' ton iskio tou vounou* (title means "Beneath the Shadow of the Mountain"), Kedros, 1962.

*To dentro tis phylakis Kai he gynaikes* (title means "The Prison Tree and the Women"), Kedros, 1963.

*Martyries* (title means "Testimonies"), Kedros, 1963.

*Dodeka pieimata gia ton Kavaphe* (title means "12 Poems for Cavafy"), Kedros, 1963.

*Paichnidia t'ouranou kai tou nerou* (title means "Playful Games of the Sky and the Water"), Kedros, 1964.

*Philoktetes,* Kedros, 1964.

*Orestes,* Kedros, 1966.

*Martyries* (title means "Testimonies II"), Kedros, 1966.

*Ostrava,* Kedros, 1967.

*Petres, Epanalepseis, Kinklidoma* (title means "Stones, Repetitions, Railings"), Kedros, 1972.

*He epistrophe tes Iphigeneias* (title means "The Return of Iphigenia"), Kedros, 1972.

*He Helene* (title means "Helen"), Kedros, 1972.

*Cheironomies* (title means "Gestures"), Kedros, 1972.

*Tetarte distase* (title means "Fourth Dimension"), Kedros, 1972.

*Chrysothemis,* Kedros, 1972.

*Ismene,* Kedros, 1972.

*Graganda,* Kedros, 1973.

*Ho aphanismos tis Milos* (title means "The Annihilation of Milos"), Kedros, 1974.

*Hymnos kai threnos gia tin Kypro* (title means "Hymn and Lament for Cyprus"), Kedros, 1974.

*To Kapnismeno tsoukali* (title means "The Soot-Black Pot"), Kedros, 1974.

*To kodonostasio* (title means "Belfry"), Kedros, 1974.

*Ho tichos mesa ston Kathrephti* (title means "The Wall in the Mirror"), Kedros, 1974.

*Chartina* (title means "Papermade"), Kedros, 1974.

*He Kyra ton Ambelion* (title means "The Lady of the Vineyards"), Kedros, 1975.

*He teleftaia pro Anthropou ekatontaeteia* (title means "The Last Century before Humanity"), Kedros, 1975.

*Epikairika* (title means "Circumstantial Verse"), Kedros, 1975.

*Ho hysterographo tis doxas* (title means "The Postscript of Glory"), Kedros, 1975.

*Hemerologia exorias* (title means "Diaries in Exile"), Kedros, 1975.

*Mantatofores,* Kedros, 1975.

*Pieimata Tomos IV* (collected poems), Kedros, 1976.

*To makrino* (title means "Remote"), Kedros, 1977.

*Gignesthai* (title means "Becoming"), Kedros, 1977.

*Epitome,* Kedros, 1977.

*Loipon?,* Kedros, 1978.

*Volidoskopos,* Kedros, 1978.

*Toichokollettes,* Kedros, 1978.

*To soma kai to haima,* Kedros, 1978.

*Trochonomos,* Kedros, 1978.

*He pyle,* Kedros, 1978.

*Monemvassiotisses,* Kedros, 1978.

*To teratodes aristioorghima,* Kedros, 1978.

*Phaedra,* Kedros, 1978.

*To roptro,* Kedros, 1978.

*Mia pygolampida fotizei ti nychta,* Kedros, 1978.

*Oneiro kalokerinou messimeriou,* Kedros, 1980.

*Diafaneia,* Kedros, 1980.

*Parodos,* Kedros, 1980.

*Monochorda,* Kedros, 1980.

*Ta erotica,* Kedros, 1981.

*Syntrofica tragoudia,* Synchroni Epochi, 1981.

*Hypokofa,* Kedros, 1982.

*Italiko triptycho,* Kedros, 1982.

*Moyovassia,* Kedros, 1982.

*To choriko ton sfougarhadon,* Kedros, 1983.

*Teiresias,* Kedros, 1983.

*OTHER*

*Pera ap'ton iskio ton Kyparission* (title means "Beyond the Shadow of the Cypress Trees"; three-act play; produced in Bucharest at the National Theatre, 1959), P.L.E., 1958.

*Mia gynaika plai sti thalassa* (title means "A Woman by the Sea"; three-act play; produced in Bucharest, 1959), P.L.E., 1959.

*Meletimata* (title means "Essays"), Kedros, 1974.

*Ariostos ho prosechtikos afhighite stigmes tou viou tou ke tou hypnou tou,* Kedros, 1982.
*Ti paraxena pragmata,* Kedros, 1983.

Ritsos' books have been translated into twenty-one languages.

*SIDELIGHTS:* "Yannis Ritsos," wrote Peter Levi in the *Times Literary Supplement* of the late Greek poet, "is the old-fashioned kind of great poet. His output has been enormous, his life heroic and eventful, his voice is an embodiment of national courage, his mind is tirelessly active." At their best, Ritsos' poems, "in their directness and with their sense of anguish, are moving, and testify to the courage of at least one human soul in conditions which few of us have faced or would have triumphed over had we faced them," as Philip Sherrard noted in the *Washington Post Book World.* Twice nominated for the Nobel Prize, Ritsos won the Lenin Peace Prize, the former Soviet Union's highest literary honor, as well as numerous literary prizes from across Eastern Europe prior to his death in 1990.

The hardship and misfortune of Ritsos' early life played a large role in all of his later writings. His wealthy family suffered financial ruin during his childhood, and soon afterward his father and sister went insane. Tuberculosis claimed his mother and an older brother and later confined Ritsos himself to a sanatorium in Athens for several years. Poetry and the Greek communist movement became the sustaining forces in his life.

Because his writing was frequently political in nature, Ritsos endured periods of persecution from his political foes. One of his most celebrated works, the "Epitaphios," a lament inspired by the assassination of a worker in a large general strike in Salonica, was burned by the Metaxas dictatorship, along with other books, in a ceremony enacted in front of the Temple of Zeus in 1936. After World War II and the annihilation of Greece's National Resistance Movement—a Communist guerrilla organization that attempted to take over the country in a five-year civil war—Ritsos was exiled for four years to the islands of Lemnos, Makronisos, and Ayios Efstratios. His books were banned until 1954. In 1967, when army colonels staged a coup and took over Greece, Ritsos was again deported, then held under house arrest until 1970. His works were again banned.

Ritsos' poetry ranges from the overtly political to the deeply personal, and it often utilizes characters from ancient Greek myths. One of his longer works and the subject of several translations, *The Fourth Dimension,* is comprised of seventeen monologues that most frequently involve the ancient King Agamemnon and the tragic House of Atreus. Narrated by such classical figures as Persephone, Orestes, Ajax, Phaedra, and Helen of Troy, *The Fourth Dimension* is a "beautifully written book . . . describing what happens when love and hate and sibling rivalry run amok," commented *Stand* reviewer Mary Fujimaki, who also praised the work's "colour, the excitement, the shifting back and forth from past to present that naturally makes the stories seem more familiar to modern readers." Shorter in length are the verses from 1991's *Repetitions, Testimonies, Parentheses,* a collection of eighty relatively brief poems that incorporate Greek myths and history. "Here . . . is the Ritsos of 'simple things,'" commented Minas Savvas in a review for *World Literature Today.* "The desire to draw out a moment or an object and magically expand it for its mystifying, arcane significance is wonderfully evident in these laconic, almost epigrammatic poems."

Many critics rank Ritsos' less political poems as his best work. George Economou, writing in the *New York Times Book Review,* stated that "in the short poems, most of which are not overtly political, Ritsos is full of surprises. He records, at times celebrates, the enigmatic, the irrational, the mysterious and invisible qualities of experience." Vernon Young in *Hudson Review* cited Ritsos' "remarkable gift . . . for suggesting the sound and color of silence, the impending instant, the transfixed hush." Similarly, John Simon pointed to the surreality of Ritsos' work. In a review of *Ritsos in Parenthesis* for *Poetry,* Simon wrote: "What I find remarkable about Ritsos' poetry is its ability to make extraordinary constructs out of the most unforcedly ordinary ingredients—surreality out of reality. And seem not even to make it, just find it." Simon also found a loneliness in Ritsos' poems. He explained: "Ritsos . . . is also a great bard of loneliness, but of loneliness ennobled and overcome. Poem after poem, image upon image, suffuses aloneness with a gallows humor that begins to mitigate its ravages and makes the person in the poem a Pyrrhic winner." Ritsos' final volume of verse, *Argha, poli argha mesa sti nihta,* was completed just prior to his death and published in its original Greek in 1991. "The imagistic dynamism, lyric intensity, and astonishing quasi-surrealistic expressions" that characterized the poet's work for his seventy-year career are, in the opinion of *World Literature Today* reviewer M. Byron Raizis, "manifest again, as refreshing and effective as any time during . . . his creative activity."

*BIOGRAPHICAL/CRITICAL SOURCES:*

*BOOKS*

*Contemporary Literary Criticism,* Gale, Volume 6, 1976, Volume 13, 1980, Volume 31, 1985.
Friar, Kimon, editor, *Modern Greek Poetry,* Simon & Schuster, 1973.
Papandreou, Chrysa, *Ritsos: Etude, choix de texte, et bibliographie,* Seghers (Paris), 1968.

*PERIODICALS*

*American Poetry Review,* September-October, 1973.
*Choice,* May, 1983; February, 1992, p. 903.
*Hudson Review,* winter, 1979-80.
*Nation,* March 19, 1977.
*New York Times Book Review,* July 10, 1977.
*Parnassus: Poetry in Review,* spring-summer, 1981.
*Poetry,* January, 1981.
*Publishers Weekly,* July 12, 1993, p. 75.
*Stand,* autumn, 1994, p. 88.
*Times Literary Supplement,* July 18, 1975; August 7, 1992, p. 9; June 12, 1994, p. 28.
*Washington Post Book World,* May 8, 1977.
*World Literature Today,* summer, 1977; summer, 1992, p. 557; winter, 1992, p. 179; winter, 1994, p. 180.

*OBITUARIES:*

*PERIODICALS*

*Chicago Tribune,* November 18, 1990.
*Los Angeles Times,* November 13, 1990.
*New York Times,* November 14, 1990.
*Times* (London), November 13, 1990.*

* * *

**ROBERTS, Lawrence**
**See FISH, Robert L(loyd)**

* * *

**ROTH, Holly 1916-1964**
**(K. G. Ballard, P. J. Merrill)**

*PERSONAL:* Born 1916, in Chicago, IL; died, 1964, after falling off a small sailing vessel while fishing in the Mediterranean; daughter of B. R. and Ethel (Ballard) Roth; married Josef Franta. *Avocational interests:* Yachting.

*CAREER:* Held various editorial positions with *Cosmopolitan,* Dell Books, *Seventeen, American Journal of Surgery,* and *New York Post.*

*MEMBER:* Mystery Writers of America (former secretary).

*WRITINGS:*

*The Content Assignment,* Simon & Schuster (New York City), 1954, published as *The Shocking Secret,* Dell (New York City), 1955.
*The Mask of Glass,* Vanguard (New York City), 1954.
*The Sleeper,* Simon & Schuster (New York City), 1955.
*The Crimson in the Purple,* Simon & Schuster, 1956.
*Shadow of a Lady,* Simon & Schuster, 1957.
(Under pseudonym K. G. Ballard) *The Coast of Fear,* Doubleday (New York City), 1957.
*The Van Dreisen Affair,* Random House (New York City), 1960.
(Under pseudonym K. G. Ballard) *Trial by Desire,* T. V. Boardman (London), 1959.
(Under pseudonym P. J. Merrill) *The Slender Thread,* Harcourt (New York City), 1959.
(Under pseudonym K. G. Ballard) *Bar Sinister,* Doubleday, 1960.
*Operation Doctors,* Hamish Hamilton (London), 1962, published as *Too Many Doctors,* Random House, 1963.
(Under pseudonym K. G. Ballard) *Gauge of Deception,* Doubleday, 1963.
*Button, Button,* Harcourt, 1966.

Contributor to *Saturday Evening Post, Redbook, Collier's,* and other magazines.

*SIDELIGHTS:* In a writing career lasting only twelve years, Holly Roth wrote several singular works in the mystery and espionage genres. "Everything that Miss Roth writes," Francis Iles once said in the *Guardian,* "really does deserve that hackneyed adjective 'distinguished.'"

Her first novel, *The Content Assignment,* "was also one of her most popular," according to Mary Ann Grochowski in the *St. James Guide to Crime and*

*Mystery Writers*. Telling a tale of romance and espionage set in the Berlin of the late 1940s, *The Content Assignment* moved Grochowski to praise its "witty, entertaining, descriptive style . . . , even though the hinges of the plot sometimes creak." As L. G. Offord explained in the *San Francisco Chronicle,* "if the story seems contrived, it's excellent contrivance."

In *The Crimson in the Purple,* Roth served up a Gothic mystery including "a creepy mansion setting, hints of ghostly menace, and a playwright who is also a licensed private detective," Grochowski wrote. James Sandoe in the *New York Herald Tribune Book Review* described the novel as "a forced hothouse bloom but once you get used to the temperature, a fruitily sinister specimen." Anthony Boucher in the *New York Times Book Review* explained that in *The Crimson in the Purple,* Roth "writes vividly of the theatre, blends deduction with character analysis, presents an attractively fallible hero, and frequently manages to convey . . . an almost Jacobean grue." Grochowski concluded that the novel was "a haunting tale of blackmail and fraud combined with murder."

Several critics remarked on Roth's ability to hold the reader's attention despite a minimum of plot in many of her novels. "Roth," wrote Sandoe, "works extravagence ingeniously. She makes do with remarkably little plot, yet sustains excitement straight through." Grochowski credited Roth's "good dialogue, fast-moving, action-packed scenes, vivid description, and effective use of the flashback" for the author's ability to consistently entertain her readers.

*BIOGRAPHICAL/CRITICAL SOURCES:*

*BOOKS*

*St. James Guide to Crime and Mystery Writers,* fourth edition, St. James Press (Detroit), 1996.

*PERIODICALS*

*Chicago Sunday Tribune,* March 13, 1960, p. 7.

*Guardian,* August 26, 1960, p. 5.

*New York Herald Tribune Book Review,* June 6, 1954, p. 12; January 16, 1955, p. 8; June 17, 1956, p. 9; March 31, 1957, p. 9; February 28, 1960, p. 15.

*New York Times,* January 16, 1955, p. 22; June 17, 1956, p. 16.

*New York Times Book Review,* March 13, 1960, p. 26; October 23, 1966, p. 59.

*San Francisco Chronicle,* February 7, 1954, p. 14.*

* * *

**ROY, Gabrielle 1909-1983**

*PERSONAL:* Born March 22, 1909, in St. Boniface, Manitoba, Canada; died of cardiac arrest, July 13, 1983, in Quebec City, Quebec, Canada; daughter of Leon (a colonization agent) and Melina (Landry) Roy; married Marcel Carbotte (a physician), August 30, 1947. *Education:* Educated in Canada; attended Winnipeg Normal School, 1927-29. *Religion:* Roman Catholic.

*CAREER:* Writer. Teacher in a Canadian prairie village school, 1928-29, and in St. Boniface, Manitoba, 1929-37; worked as freelance journalist for *Le Bulletin des agriculteurs, Le Jour,* and *Le Canada.*

*MEMBER:* Royal Society of Canada (fellow).

*AWARDS, HONORS:* Medaille of l'Academie Francaise, 1947; Prixfemina (France), 1947, for *Bonheur d'occasion;* received Canadian Governor General's Award for the following: *Bonheur d'occasion, Rue Deschambault,* and *Ces Enfants de ma vie,* Duvernay Prix, 1955; Companion of the Order of Canada, 1967; Canadian Council of the Arts Award, 1968; Prix David, 1971; Knight of the Order of Mark Twain.

*WRITINGS:*

*NOVELS*

*Bonheur d'occasion,* Societe des Editions Pascal (Montreal), 1945, translation by Hannah Josephson published as *The Tin Flute* (Literary Guild selection), Reynal, 1947.

*La Petite Poule d'eau,* Beauchemin (Montreal), 1950, translation by Harry L. Binsse published as *Where Nests the Water Hen: A Novel,* Harcourt, 1951, revised French language edition, Beauchemin, 1970.

*Alexandre Chenevert, Caissier,* Beauchemin, 1954, translation by Binsse published as *The Cashier,* Harcourt, 1955.

*Rue Deschambault,* Beauchemin, 1955, translation by Binsse published as *Street of Riches,* Harcourt, 1957, reprinted, University of Nebraska Press, 1993.

*La Montagne secrete,* Beauchemin, 1961, translation by Binsse published as *The Hidden Mountain,* Harcourt, 1962.

*La Route d'Altamont,* Editions HMH (Montreal), 1966, translation by Joyce Marshall published as *The Road Past Altamont,* Harcourt, 1966.

(With others) *Canada . . .* (includes *La Petite Poule d'eau*), Editions du Burin (St. Cloud, France), 1967.

*La Riviere sans repos,* Beauchemin, 1970, translation by Marshall published as *Windflower,* McClelland & Stewart, 1970.

*Cet ete qui chantait,* Editions Francaises, 1972, translation by Marshall published as *Enchanted Summer,* McClelland & Stewart, 1976.

*Un Jardin au bout du monde,* Beauchemin, 1975, translation by Alan Brown published as *Garden in the Wind,* McClelland & Stewart, 1977.

*Ces Enfants de ma vie,* Stanke, 1977, translation by Brown published as *Children of My Heart,* McClelland & Stewart, 1979.

*Fragiles Lumieres de la terre: Ecrits divers 1942-1970,* Quinze, 1978.

*My Cow Bossie,* McClelland & Stewart, 1988.

Contributor to anthologies, including *Great Short Stories of the World,* Reader's Digest, 1972, and *The Penguin Book of Canadian Short Stories,* Penguin, 1980.

*ADAPTATIONS: Bonheur d'Occasion* was made into a feature film, 1983.

*SIDELIGHTS:* Gabrielle Roy, who grew up in rural Manitoba, used Montreal, St. Boniface, and the wilds of northern Canada as settings for her novels. *Saturday Night* critic George Woodcock believed that the complex mixture of cultures in rural Manitoba explains why Roy is "a Canadian writer of truly multi-cultural background and experience." Hugo McPherson, writing in *Canadian Literature,* commented: "Roy's experience has taught her that life offers an endless series of storms and mischances."

After her father's death in 1927, Roy attended the Winnipeg Normal Institute rather than a university for financial reasons. Following graduation, she taught at the Institute Collegial Provencher in St. Boniface until 1937, when she taught briefly in Manitoba. In that same year, she sailed to London, where she studied acting for six months at the Guildhall School of Music and Drama. She decided, however, that she preferred to write, and she began submitting articles on Europe and Canada to newspapers in Saint-Boniface and Paris while continuing to travel throughout Europe. After returning to Canada in 1939, she settled in Montreal.

Roy filled her novels with people who are underprivileged, people of many nationalities and ethnicities, and minority people who have difficulty coping in a predominantly white society. "She records their plight with a tolerance and compassion that rests not on patriotism, humanism or religiosity, but on a deep love of mankind," McPherson stated. "Gabrielle Roy *feels* rather than analyzes, and a sense of wonder and of mystery is always with her." Jeannette Urbas, writing in *Journal of Canadian Fiction,* presented a similar view: "Roy immerses us directly in the suffering of her characters: we feel, we think, we live with them. The appeal is directly to the heart."

Roy, who was frequently compared to Willa Cather, provided insight into her own life with the publication of *The Road Past Altamont* and *Street of Riches.* These short story collections tell the story of Christine, a writer from Manitoba, who has wanderlust in her heart. The stories in *The Road Past Altamont,* in particular, reveal the profound influence of Roy's surroundings on her writing and life. As Penelope Power described it in *Kliatt,* "Landscape, travel and character are the three forces at work in Roy's family memories."

In addition to writing novels for adults, Roy also wrote children's books, including *My Cow Bossie.* A popular children's tale in its original French, *My Cow Bossie* was translated into English in 1988. It tells the tale of a young girl who receives a cow as a gift. Like many of Roy's books for adults, the work is set in Manitoba in the early 1900s and is reminiscent of the writings of Laura Ingalls Wilder. Anne Louise Mahoney, writing for *Canadian Children's Literature* commented that Roy "successfully weaves this appealing story with believable characters, unaffected dialogue, and honest emotions."

*Canadian Forum* critic Paul Socken stated that the link between all of Roy's writings is "people's lifelong struggle to understand the integrity of their own lives, to see their lives as a whole, and their need to create bridges of concern and understanding between themselves and others. . . . It is this very tension, and the success that she has demonstrated in dramatizing it, that makes Gabrielle Roy unique among Canadian writers."

*BIOGRAPHICAL/CRITICAL SOURCES:*

*BOOKS*

Amelinckx, Frans C. and Joyce N. Megay, editors, *Travel, Quest, and Pilgrimage as a Literary Theme: Studies in Honor of Reino Virtanen,* Society of Spanish and Spanish-American Studies, 1978, pp. 251-60.

Baby, Ellen R., *The Play of Language and Spectacle: A Structural Reading of Selected Texts by Gabrielle Roy,* ECW Press, 1985.

Chadbourne, Richard, and Hallvard Dahlie, editors, *The New Land: Studies in a Literary Theme,* Wilfrid Laurier University Press, 1978, pp. 92-120.

*Contemporary Literary Criticism,* Gale, Volume 10, 1979, Volume 14, 1980.

*Dictionary of Literary Biography, Volume 68: Canadian Writers, 1920-1959, First Series,* Gale, 1988.

*Dossiers de Documentation de la litterature canadienne-francaise,* Fides, 1967.

Gagne, Marc, *Visages de Gabrielle Roy,* Beauchemin, 1973.

Geniust, Monique, *La Creation romanesque chez Gabrielle Roy,* Cercle du Livre de France, 1966.

Grosskurth, Phyllis, *Gabrielle Roy,* Forum House, 1972.

Hesse, Marta Gudrun, *Gabrielle Roy,* Twayne, 1984.

Hesse, Marta Gudrun, *Gabrielle Roy par elle-meme,* Stanke, 1985.

Hind-Smith, Joan, *The Lives of Margaret Laurence, Gabrielle Roy, Frederick Philip Grove,* Clarke, Irwin, 1975, pp. 62-126.

Hughes, Terrance, *Gabrielle Roy et Margaret Laurence: Deux chemins, une recherche,* Editions du Ble, 1983.

Lecker, Robert, and Jack David, editors, *The Annotated Bibliography of Canada's Major Authors,* volume 1, ECW Press, 1979, pp. 213-63.

Lewis, Paula Gilbert, *The Literary Vision of Gabrielle Roy: An Analysis of Her Works,* Summa Publications, 1984.

Mitcham, Allison, *The Literary Achievement of Gabrielle Roy,* York Press, 1983.

Reisman Babby, Ellen, *The Play of Language and Spectacle: A Structural Reading of Selected Texts by Gabrielle Roy,* ECW Press, 1985.

Ricard, Francois, *Gabrielle Roy,* Fides, 1975.

Shek, Ben-Zion, *Social Realism in the French-Canadian Novel,* Harvest House, 1977, pp. 65-111 and 173-203.

Squier, Susan Merrill, editor, *Women Writers and the City: Essays in Feminist Literary Criticism,* University of Tennessee Press, 1984, pp. 193-209.

Urbas, Jeanette, *From "Thirty Acres" to Modern Times: the Story of French-Canadian Literature,* McGraw-Hill Ryerson, 1976, pp. 45-63.

Warwick, Jack, *The Long Journey: Literary Themes of French Canada,* University of Toronto Press, 1968, pp. 86-100, 140-44.

*PERIODICALS*

*American Review of Canadian Studies,* autumn, 1981, pp. 46-66.

*Antigonish Review,* winter, 1979, pp. 95-9; winter, 1982, pp. 49-55; autumn, 1983, pp. 35-46.

*Belles Lettres,* spring, 1994, p. 11.

*Canadian Children's Literature,* Nos. 35-36, 1984, pp. 27-37; No. 62, 1994, p. 60.

*Canadian Forum,* February, 1978.

*Canadian Literature,* summer, 1959, pp. 46-57; autumn, 1969, pp. 6-13; spring, 1981, pp. 161-71; summer, 1984, pp. 183-84.

*Canadian Modern Language Review,* October, 1964, pp. 20-6; No. 3, 1968, pp. 58-63; No. 2, 1974, pp. 96-100; October, 1983, pp. 105-10.

*Canadian Review of Comparative Literature,* June, 1984, pp. 205-15.

*Essays in French Literature,* November, 1981, pp. 86-99.

*Essays on Canadian Writing,* summer, 1978, pp. 66-71; spring, 1980, pp. 113-26.

*Etudes Francaises,* June, 1965, pp. 39-65.

*Etudes litteraires,* winter, 1984, pp. 441-55, 457-79, 481-97, 499-529.

*French Review,* December, 1981, pp. 207-15.

*Humanities Association Bulletin,* winter, 1973, pp. 25-31.

*Journal of Canadian Fiction,* spring, 1972, pp. 69-73; fall, 1972, pp. 51-54.

*Journal of Canadian Studies,* No. 3, 1968, pp. 3-10.

*Journal of Women's Studies in Literature,* No. 1, 1979, pp. 133-41 and 243-57.

*Kliatt,* May, 1994, p. 28.

*Los Angeles Times Book Review,* February 6, 1994, p. 12.

*Maclean's,* March 12, 1979.

*Malahat Review,* October, 1979, pp. 77-85.

*Modern Fiction Studies,* autumn, 1976, pp. 457-66.

*Modern Language Studies,* fall, 1981, pp. 44-50; spring, 1982, pp. 22-30.
*New York Times Book Review,* January 30, 1994, p. 28.
*North Dakota Quarterly,* No. 4, 1979, pp. 4-10.
*Quebec Studies,* spring, 1983, pp. 234-45; No. 2, 1984, pp. 105-17.
*Queen's Quarterly,* summer, 1962, pp. 177-97; summer, 1965, pp. 334-46.
*Revue de L'Universite d'Ottawa,* January-March, 1974, pp. 70-77; July-September, 1975, pp. 344-55; July-September, 1976, pp. 309-23; January-March, 1980, pp. 55-61.
*Saturday Night,* November, 1977.
*Studies in Canadian Literature,* No. 1, 1982, pp. 90-108.
*Tamarack Review,* autumn, 1956, pp. 61-70.
*Viewpoints,* winter, 1969, pp. 29-35.
*Voix et Images,* No. 3, 1977, pp. 96-115.

*OBITUARIES:*

*PERIODICALS*

*Chicago Tribune,* July 16, 1983.
*London Times,* July 18, 1983.
*New York Times,* July 15, 1983.
*Washington Post,* July 15, 1983.*

* * *

**RUCKMAN, Ivy 1931-**

*PERSONAL:* Born May 25, 1931, in Hastings, NE; daughter of Joy Uberto (a teacher and tree surgeon) and Lena Chloe (Osgood) Myers; married Edgar Baldwin Heylmun, December 17, 1955 (divorced, 1963); married Stuart Allan Ruckman (a dentist), June 6, 1965 (died, 1983); children: Kimberly Sue, William Bret, Stuart Andrew. *Education:* Hastings College, B.A., 1953; graduate study at University of Utah, 1963.

*ADDRESSES:* *Home*—3698 Golden Hills Ave., Salt Lake City, UT 84121.

*CAREER:* Writer, teacher, lecturer. High school English teacher in Casper, WY, 1953-57; Skyline High School, Salt Lake City, UT, English teacher, 1962-65, creative writing instructor, 1970-72.

*MEMBER:* Society of Children's Book Writers and Illustrators, Utah Children's Literature Association, Friends of the Salt Lake County Library System, Willa Cather Memorial Foundation.

*AWARDS, HONORS:* First place in Utah Fine Arts Contest, 1982, for *What's an Average Kid Like Me Doing Way Up Here?;* Outstanding Alumni Award, Hastings College, 1984; Mountain Plains Library Association Literary Contribution Award, 1985, for body of work; Notable Children's Trade Book in the Field of Social Studies, National Council on the Social Studies/Children's Book Council (NCSS/CBC), 1987, and Utah Children's Book Award nomination, 1988, for *This Is Your Captain Speaking;* Junior Literary Guild selection, Outstanding Science Trade Book for Children, National Science Teachers Association and the Children's Book Council (NSTA/CBC), 1984, Children's Choice selection, International Reading Association and Children's Book Council (IRA/CBC), 1984, Golden Sower (grades 4-6), Nebraska Library Association, 1986, Sequoyah Children's Book Award, Oklahoma Library Association, 1987, South Dakota Prairie Pasque Award, South Dakota Library Association, 1987, Maud Hart Lovelace Book Award, Friends of the Minnesota Valley Regional Library, 1988, and Iowa Children's Choice Award, Iowa Educational Media Association, 1989, all for *Night of the Twisters.*

*WRITINGS:*

*FOR YOUNG PEOPLE*

*Who Needs Rainbows?,* Messner (New York City), 1969.
*Encounter,* Doubleday (New York City), 1978.
*Melba the Brain,* illustrated by Ruth Van Sciver, Westminster, 1979.
*What's an Average Kid Like Me Doing Way Up Here?,* Delacorte (New York City), 1983, revised edition, Dell (New York City), 1988.
*In a Class By Herself,* Harcourt (New York City), 1983.
*The Hunger Scream,* Walker (New York City), 1983.
*Night of the Twisters,* Harper (New York City), 1984.
*This Is Your Captain Speaking,* Walker, 1987.
*No Way Out,* Harper, 1988.
*Who Invited the Undertaker?,* Harper, 1989.
*Melba the Mummy,* Dell, 1991.
*Pronounce It Dead,* Bantam (New York City), 1994.
*Spell It M-U-R-D-E-R,* Bantam, 1994.

Also editor of class-written television play for ABC-TV series *Room 222;* author of screenplay *Hell and High Water,* an adaptation of *No Way Out;* contributor of short stories to periodicals *Jack and Jill, Cricket,* and *Ranger Rick.*

*SIDELIGHTS:* Ivy Ruckman is the author of several award-winning novels for young adults. Very popular with students, Ruckman's novels have been cited for their well-paced plots, realistic dialogue, and plausible solutions to the kinds of problems teenagers face. One of her most popular works, *Night of the Twisters,* is unusual in her body of work for being based on an actual event, in this case a night during which a small town in Nebraska was hit by a series of tornadoes. *Night of the Twisters* is not unique among Ruckman's books in its reliance on action to propel the plot, however, inspiring some reviewers to recommend her books for reluctant readers. Other works deal with problems that are less dramatic, such as finding a boyfriend for a widowed mother, cross-generational relationships, or dealing with bullies at summer camp. Whatever her theme, Ruckman has been lauded throughout her career for her storytelling abilities, including swift pacing and strong character development, qualities that make her novels especially attractive to young adult readers.

The youngest of seven children born to a Nebraska family during the Great Depression, Ruckman maintains that her materially poor childhood enriched her immeasurably by forcing her to develop her imagination to the fullest. Throughout her childhood Ruckman was closest to her brother William, with whom she shared innumerable adventures, as she once told *CA:* "On a typical afternoon an upended stool became a ship's parapet, a rag mop displayed the colors. The longest stirring spoon in the kitchen stood by for an oar. The Captain and his First Mate, thus grandly appointed, rolled out to sea with solemn purpose—the capture of pirates. Together William and I built igloos in the Arctic tundra, stalked big game in steaming jungles while black panthers stalked us; we performed daring feats on a slender bar and did acrobatics on the broad-backed workhorses who always looked astonished to find themselves the dappled darlings of the circus ring. Christmas opulence, our contemporaries will remember, consisted of one or two gifts and a sack of nuts and candy from church. One year the two of us exchanged Woolworth 'diamond' rings, then spent the entire holidays slinking about the house as jewel thieves."

Books contributed to the rich imaginative life of Ruckman and her brother. "If our shoes didn't always fit during those magic years, we nonetheless had books. Our mother read *Robinson Crusoe* to us before I was old enough to understand it. Our real bonanza, however, was to be found in the trash that our father hauled from people in town who owned and discarded books. . . . We also salvaged bookkeeping ledgers from the trash pile if they contained empty pages for drawing or writing." William grew up to become a cardiovascular surgeon, while Ruckman began her career as a schoolteacher, turning to writing fulltime in 1974. Balancing her career with the demands of her family life was sometimes difficult, inspiring the author to pick up her pen wherever she happened to be, especially if she was outdoors. "I have a desk and a home office," Ruckman once commented, "but I end up writing everywhere—in the car, at auto repair shops, cross-legged on the porch swing, while lunching out. I do my best thinking and planning in the bathtub or the swimming pool. My husband, Allan, built a platform for me alongside our stream because I enjoy writing outdoors so much and because the properties of water seem to free my mind for creative thinking."

"For me, the writing itself is very difficult," Ruckman continued. "If I can produce two to four pages of prose in a day, I feel I've done well (at top speed one day I wrote thirteen pages of a novel; another time, creeping like a snail, I produced one paragraph). Because the *sound* of one's writing is so important, I rely heavily on my 'ear' for realistic dialogue, for the flow of my prose, for the sentence balance I want to achieve. The hardest part of writing, as I see it, is getting a story to work in the first place; the revising, or 'fine tuning,' is the most enjoyable. First and foremost, however, I want my characters to live and I want the reader to care about what happens to them. I become very much involved in the lives of my fictional 'children.' I succeed as a writer, I feel, only to the extent readers share my involvement."

Ruckman's novels for young adults address a variety of problems that young people may face. In *The Hunger Scream,* Lily, a teenage girl, becomes anorexic when her love for the boy next door is not requited, and her affection for him is disapproved of by her affluent parents because of his race. Ruckman was praised for her realistic portrayal of Lily's perspective, and for her attention to the often slow and painful recovery process. *This Is Your Captain Speaking* is another of Ruckman's early works focusing on family relations and social issues—in this case, old age and death. In the story, Tom befriends Roger, a resident at the retirement home where his mother works, as a way to escape his awkwardness in junior high school and his inability to approach Carmela, the girl he has a crush on. The subject of euthanasia arises as well as grief when Roger dies, and critics praised Ruckman's adroit blending of this serious business with the story of Tom's growing up and romance with Carmela. While some commentators faulted the author for failing to develop Roger as a well-rounded character, *This Is Your Captain Speaking* was widely praised as a sensitive, well-written book. Zena Sutherland of the *Bulletin of the Center for Children's Books* commented: "The story, capably written, gives a positive view of intergenerational friendship and a perceptive picture of grief and the acceptance of loss." *Booklist*'s Linda Ward Callaghan also offered a favorable review of *This is Your Captain Speaking,* maintaining that "Ruckman focuses on the serious business of junior high with humor and compassion."

One of Ruckman's most popular works with both critics and readers is *Night of the Twisters,* which concerns the actions of two adolescent boys after a series of tornadoes. Dan and his best friend Arthur, both twelve, are baby-sitting Dan's baby brother when a tornado strikes the house and the surrounding town, bringing suspenseful chaos and confusion as the boys attempt to contact family members and friends and help in the rescue effort. "The story is exciting and fast paced," enthused Elizabeth Mellett in her *School Library Journal* review. Some critics charged that characterization takes a back seat to action in this novel, but Sutherland of the *Bulletin of the Center for Children's Books* noted that Ruckman "produces dialogue that sounds appropriate for a stress situation, and gives her characters some depth and differentiation." *Booklist* reviewer Carolyn Phelan similarly asserted that "characterization is a bit flat, as it often is in adventure stories, but never inconsistent or unbelievable." Phelan concluded *Night of the Twisters* "a creditable adventure story with several vivid scenes."

*No Way Out,* like *Night of the Twisters,* is a suspenseful adventure story based on actual events. When a young couple takes an eleven-year-old boy hiking during their vacation, a flash flood brings disaster and a nightmarish struggle to survive. *Voice of Youth Advocates* contributor Colleen Macklin praised Ruckman's well-developed characters and noted that her attention to details of weather and geography underscores the credibility of this story. "The actions of the members of the party are authentic and readers will quickly sense that this author 'knows what she's talking about,'" Macklin commented.

In contrast to *Night of the Twisters* and Ruckman's other adventure stories, *Who Invited the Undertaker?* was dubbed by *School Library Journal* contributor Susan F. Marcus "a warm and happy family story about people who care about each other." In this work, seventh-grader Dale decides to take action when he hears his mother crying one night two years after his father's death. His solution, to place an ad in the personals column for her, does not bring the expected results, but does usher in welcome changes in their lives in the form of his mother's gradually increasing self-confidence. In a review in *Booklist,* Barbara Elleman praised Ruckman's "smooth integration of humor and a thoughtful underlying theme of family dynamics," concluding *Who Invited the Undertaker?* "heartwarming and true to contemporary times."

Ruckman is also the author of two mysteries for middle-grade readers. *Pronounce It Dead* and *Spell It M-U-R-D-E-R* both feature best friends Katy and Andrea, small-town girls who get into trouble when, in the first book, they decide to help out some kids who come to town with the County Fair and Livestock Show and wind up becoming involved with possible drug traffickers. In *Spell it M-U-R-D-E-R,* as the pair make their escape in a rowboat from an unhappy situation at summer camp they overhear a body being dumped into the lake. The girls' attempts to notify the police only raise the suspicion that they have been kidnapped. Reviews of these efforts were mixed. A commentator for *Voice of Youth Advocates* complained: "While Katy and Andrea are sixth-graders, these stories are extremely innocent for today's middle-schoolers. There is no 'murder' or 'death' in either story." *School Library Journal* contributor Julie Halverstadt, however, called *Spell It M-U-R-D-E-R* "perfect light summer fare." Similarly, Chris Sherman of *Booklist* dubbed *Spell It M-U-R-D-E-R* "a completely plausible mystery with likable characters who behave (and sound) like real kids."

*BIOGRAPHICAL/CRITICAL SOURCES:*

*BOOKS*

*Sixth Book of Junior Author and Illustrators,* H. W. Wilson (New York City), 1989, pp. 251-253.

*PERIODICALS*

*Booklist,* October 15, 1978, p. 369; April 1, 1983, p. 1037; May 15, 1983, p. 1197; November 1, 1983, p. 404; December 1, 1984, p. 528; November 15, 1987, p. 572; June 1, 1988, p. 1668; October 1, 1989, p. 355; July, 1994, p. 1949; January 1, 1995, p. 831.

*Bulletin of the Center for Children's Books,* April, 1969, p. 133; December, 1978, p. 71; March, 1980, p. 140; April, 1983, p. 157; May, 1983, p. 177; December, 1983, p. 77; November, 1984, pp. 54-55; November, 1987, p. 56.

*Catholic Library World,* May, 1979, p. 588; October, 1984, p. 142.

*Childhood Education,* fall, 1989, p. 45.

*English Journal,* November, 1990, p. 83.

*Horn Book,* October, 1983, p. 586; July, 1989, p. 72.

*Kirkus Reviews,* February 1, 1969, p. 107; November 1, 1978, p. 1194; October 1, 1987, p. 1467.

*Publishers Weekly,* June 24, 1988, p. 114.

*Reading Teacher,* May, 1990, p. 672.

*School Library Journal,* November, 1978, p. 78; January, 1980, p. 75; April, 1983, p. 116; August, 1983, p. 79; January, 1984, p. 88; December, 1984, p. 86; October, 1987, p. 89; August, 1988, p. 107; September, 1989, p. 277; August, 1994, p. 158.

*Voice of Youth Advocates,* October, 1983, p. 208; December, 1983, p. 280; June, 1984, p. 97; December, 1987, p. 46; October, 1988, p. 184; December, 1994, p. 280.

*Wilson Library Bulletin,* September, 1989, p. 11; March, 1990, p. 16.

* * *

## RUSSELL, Martin 1934-
## (James Arney, Mark Lester)

*PERSONAL:* Born September 25, 1934, in Bromley, England; son of Stanley William (a bank official) and Helen Kathleen (Arney) Russell. *Education:* Educated in England.

*ADDRESSES:* *Home*—15 Breckonmead, Wanstead Rd., Bromley, Kent, England.

*CAREER:* Writer. *Kentish Times,* Bromley, England, reporter, 1951-58; *Croydon Advertiser,* Croydon, Surrey, England, reporter and sub-editor, 1958-73. *Military service:* Royal Air Force, 1955-57.

*MEMBER:* Crime Writers Association.

*WRITINGS:*

*No Through Road,* Collins (London), 1965, Coward (New York City), 1966.
*No Return Ticket,* Collins, 1966.
*Danger Money,* Collins, 1968.
*Hunt to a Kill,* Collins, 1969.
*Deadline,* Collins, 1971.
*Advisory Service,* Collins, 1971.
*Concrete Evidence,* Collins, 1972.
*Double Hit,* Collins, 1973.
*Crime Wave,* Collins, 1974.
*Phantom Holiday,* Collins, 1974.
*The Client,* Collins, 1975.
*Murder by the Mile,* Collins, 1975.
*Double Deal,* Collins, 1976.
(Under pseudonym Mark Lester) *Terror Trade,* R. Hale (London), 1976.
*The Man without a Name,* Coward, 1977, published as *Mr. T.,* Collins, 1977.
*Dial Death,* Collins, 1977.
*Daylight Robbery,* Collins, 1978.
*A Dangerous Place to Dwell,* Collins, 1978, published as *Unwelcome Audience,* Walker (New York City), 1986.
*Touchdown,* Collins, 1979.
*Death Fuse,* Collins, 1980, St. Martin's (New York City), 1981.
*Catspaw,* Collins, 1980.
*Backlash,* Collins, 1981, Walker, 1983.
*All Part of the Service,* Collins, 1982.
*Rainblast,* Collins, 1982.
*The Search for Sara,* Collins, 1983, Walker, 1984.
(Under pseudonym James Arney) *A View to Ransom,* R. Hale, 1983.
*A Domestic Affair,* Collins, 1984, Walker, 1985.
*Censor,* Collins, 1984.
*The Darker Side of Death,* Collins, 1985.
*Prime Targets,* Collins, 1985.
*Dead Heat,* Collins, 1986.
*The Second Time Is Easy,* Collins, 1987.
*House Arrest,* Collins, 1988.
*Dummy Run,* Collins, 1989.
*Mystery Lady,* Collins, 1992.
*Leisure Pursuit,* Collins, 1993.

Editor, Crime Writers Association *Red Herrings,* 1979-81.

*SIDELIGHTS:* Martin Russell draws upon his years as a newspaper reporter in writing his mystery novels. As Martin Edwards remarks in the *St. James*

*Guide to Crime and Mystery Writers,* Russell's "writing is simple and clear and descriptions of people, and places are always kept to a minimum: with Russell, as with all good newspaper reporters, the story is everything." Russell once told *CA:* "A desire to explore the workings of the human mind, and to show the bizarre situations these can lead to, motivated me in my choice of the crime or mystery novel as a vehicle. I am intrigued by the Jekyll and Hyde in people."

Russell's fascination with bizarre situations is starkly apparent in *The Man without a Name,* the story of John Tiverton, who returns home from work one day to discover that his wife does not recognize him. When he refuses to leave the house as she requests, she calls the police and explains to them that her husband died six months before. Further investigation reveals family members and friends verifying Tiverton's death in a car accident. Tiverton must unravel the mystery of his own identity. As P. L. Adams writes in the *Atlantic,* Russell "writes in a crisp, persuasive style and quickly ensnares the reader with a puzzle." Tim Shepard in *Best Sellers* finds that the novel offers "believable intrigue, excitement, and suspense." The reviewer for the *Christian Science Monitor* calls *The Man without a Name* an "intelligent, nonviolent teaser."

Edwards remarks that "Russell specialises not in straightforward detection but in outlining a bizarre sequence of events and building suspense as his protagonists find themselves trapped in webs which are often of their own making. Russell can match Cornell Woolrich for ingenuity and is much better at tying up all the loose ends of his plots. . . . The best Russell stories are those which offer the most intriguing puzzles."

*BIOGRAPHICAL/CRITICAL SOURCES:*

*BOOKS*

*St. James Guide to Crime and Mystery Writers,* fourth edition, St. James Press (Detroit), 1996.

*PERIODICALS*

*Atlantic,* September, 1977, p. 96.
*Best Sellers,* September, 1977, p. 170.
*Christian Science Monitor,* September 14, 1977.
*School Library Journal,* October, 1977, p. 129.

# S-W

**SALE, Richard (Bernard) 1911-1993**
**(John St. John)**

*PERSONAL:* Born December 17, 1911, in New York, NY; died of complications from two strokes, March 4, 1993; son of Richard Bernard and Frances (Topinka) Sale; married second wife, Mary Loos (an author), December 17, 1946 (divorced); married Irma Foster, 1971; children: Lindsey (Mrs. Keith Tucker), Richard Townsend, Edward Clifford. *Education:* Attended Washington and Lee University, 1930-33. *Politics:* Independent. *Religion:* Christian.

*CAREER:* Freelance writer for magazines, 1930-44; writer for Paramount Pictures, Hollywood, CA, 1944; writer-director for Republic Pictures, Studio City, CA, 1945-48, 20th Century-Fox, Beverly Hills, CA, 1948-52, British Lion, London, England, 1953-54, United Artists, New York, NY, and Europe, 1954, and Columbia Pictures, Hollywood, CA, 1956; television writer, director, producer for Columbia Broadcasting System, 1958-59. Composer of music for several motion pictures.

*MEMBER:* Authors League of America, Writers Guild of America, Directors Guild of America, Academy of Motion Picture Arts and Sciences, National Academy of Television Arts, Delta Upsilon, Sigma Delta Chi, Balboa Angling Club, Shark Island Yacht Club.

*WRITINGS:*

*Not Too Narrow, Not Too Deep,* Simon & Schuster (New York City), 1936.
*Is a Ship Burning?,* Cassell (London), 1937, Dodd (New York City), 1938.
*Cardinal Rock,* Cassell, 1940.
*Lazarus No. 7,* Simon & Schuster, 1942, published as *Lazarus Murder Seven,* Quinn (New York City), 1943 (published in England as *Death Looks In,* Cassell, 1943).
*Sailor, Take Warning,* Wells Gardner (London), 1942.
*Passing Strange: A Story of Birth and Burial,* Simon & Schuster, 1942, published as *Passing Strange: A Mystery of Birth and Burial,* Quinn, 1943.
*Destination Unknown,* World's Work (Kingswood, Surrey), 1943, published as *Death at Sea,* Popular Library (New York City), 1948.
*Benefit Performance,* Simon & Schuster, 1946.
*Home Is the Hangman,* Popular Library (New York City), 1949.
*Murder at Midnight* (novellas), Popular Library, 1950.
*The Oscar,* Simon & Schuster, 1963.
*For the President's Eyes Only,* Simon & Schuster, 1971, published as *The Man Who Raised Hell,* Cassell, 1971.
*Square-Shooters,* Simon & Schuster, 1972.
*The White Buffalo,* Simon & Schuster, 1975.

*SCREENPLAYS*

(With others) *Strange Cargo,* 1937.
(With Grace Neville and Fred Niblo, Jr.) *Find the Witness,* 1937.
(With wife, Mary Loos) *The Dude Goes West,* 1938.
(With Joseph Hoffman) *Shadows over Shanghai,* 1938.
(With Loos) *Rendezvous with Annie,* 1946.
(With Loos and Lee Loeb) *Calendar Girl,* 1947.
(With others) *Northwest Outpost,* 1947.
(With Loos) *Driftwood,* 1947.

(With others) *The Inside Story,* 1948.
(With Jerry Gruskin and Thomas R. St. George) *Campus Honeymoon,* 1948.
(With others) *The Tender Years,* 1948.
*Lady at Midnight,* 1948.
(With Loos and Raphael Blau) *Mother Is a Freshman,* 1949.
(With Loos and Mary C. McCall) *Mr. Belvedere Goes to College,* 1949.
(With others) *Father Was a Fullback,* 1949.
(With Loos and Sy Gomberg) *When Willie Comes Marching Home,* 1950.
(With Loos) *A Ticket to Tomahawk,* 1950.
(With others) *I'll Get By,* 1950.
(With Loos) *Meet Me after the Show,* 1951.
(With Loos) *Let's Do It Again,* 1953.
(With others) *The French Line,* 1954.
(With others) *Woman's World,* 1954.
*Suddenly,* 1954.
(With Loos) *Gentlemen Marry Brunettes,* 1955.
(With others) *Over-Exposed!,* 1956.
(With William Wister Haines) *Torpedo Run,* 1958.
*The White Buffalo,* 1977.

Also author of television scripts for *Yancy Derringer, Bewitched, Wackiest Ship in the Army, FBI, Custer,* and *High Chapparal* series; author of television script *Assassination,* 1987.

*OTHER*

Contributor of 350 short stories and serials to *New Yorker, Saturday Evening Post, Country Gentleman, Scribner's Liberty, Blue Book, Good Housekeeping, Esquire, Coronet, Argosy, Detective Fiction Weekly, Adventure, Super Detective, Black Book Detective, Secret Agent X, Maclean's,* and other magazines. Yachting editor and contributor of other articles to *Orange County Illustrated,* beginning 1963.

*ADAPTATIONS: The Oscar* was filmed by Avco Embassy in 1966.

*SIDELIGHTS:* Richard Sale was a prolific writer of screenplays, mystery novels, adventure stories and television scripts. He began his career in the 1930s as a writer for the pulp magazines. By the late 1930s he was also publishing novels, turning to screenplays in the 1940s. Sale's more popular books include *Not Too Narrow, Not Too Deep; Is a Ship Burning?;* and *For the President's Eyes Only.*

*Not Too Narrow, Not Too Deep* is a suspenseful adventure about a group of ten convicts who escape from Devil's Island. They are soon joined by a mysterious eleventh person, a mystical figure who exerts unearthly control over their behavior and succeeds in rehabilitating the hardened criminals. Bill Crider in *St. James Guide to Crime and Mystery Writers* called the novel a "tour de force." William Doerflinger in *Saturday Review of Literature* found that Sale "succeeded in blending mysticism and brute realism into a striking piece of fiction."

*Is a Ship Burning?* tells the story of a cruise ship which catches fire and is lost at sea. Told from the viewpoint of the radio operator who survives the disaster, the novel is a fast-moving tale of suspenseful adventure. David Tilden in *Books* claimed: "I chased through the pages eagerly and was satisfied with the two hours' entertainment it afforded." F. T. Marsh in the *New York Times* similarly explained: "It will hold any man to a sitting for it is short, and, besides its dramatic action and masculine sentiment, it has a forthright decency about it, a generous spirit and a good will."

*For the President's Eyes Only* is, according to Crider, "a spy thriller that appeared a few years after the real vogue in such things had passed, probably the only reason it failed to become a bestseller. It has more action, adventure, intrigue, and glamour than any two or three similar novels, and a fine, tough hero besides. Reading it makes one wish that Sale had devoted less of his time to writing for movies and television and more to writing books like this."

*BIOGRAPHICAL/CRITICAL SOURCES:*

*BOOKS*

*St. James Guide to Crime and Mystery Writers,* fourth edition, St. James Press (Detroit), 1996.

*PERIODICALS*

*Books,* January 16, 1938, p. 7.
*Boston Transcript,* February 29, 1936, p. 4.
*Manchester Guardian,* July 28, 1936, p. 7.
*New York Times,* February 23, 1936, p. 21; January 16, 1938, p. 7.
*Saturday Review of Literature,* February 22, 1936.
*Times Literary Supplement,* August 1, 1936, p. 631.

*OBITUARIES:*

*PERIODICALS*

*Los Angeles Times,* March 8, 1993, p. A16.*

**SANDERS, Noah**
See **BLOUNT, Roy (Alton), Jr.**

* * *

**SAYERS, Valerie 1952-**

*PERSONAL:* Born August 8, 1952, in Beaufort, SC; daughter of Paul (a psychologist) and Janet (a homemaker; maiden name, Hogan) Sayers; married Christian Jara (a video producer), June 29, 1974; children: Christian Jara, Raul Jara. *Education:* Fordham University, B.A. (cum laude), 1973; Columbia University, M.F.A., 1976. *Politics:* "Left." *Religion:* Roman Catholic.

*ADDRESSES: Home*—Brooklyn, NY. *Agent*—Esther Newberg, International Creative Management, 40 West 57th St., New York, NY 10019.

*CAREER:* Writer. Worked variously as a waitress, freelance consultant and scriptwriter, associate editor at an anarchist publishing house, and part-time instructor at Polytechnic Institute of New York and City University of New York.

*MEMBER:* Authors Guild, Modern Language Association.

*WRITINGS:*

*Due East* (novel), Doubleday (New York City), 1987.
*How I Got Him Back; or, Under the Cold Moon's Shine* (novel), Doubleday, 1989.
*Who Do You Love?* (novel), Doubleday, 1991.
*The Distance Between Us* (novel), Doubleday, 1994.
*Brain Fever* (novel), Doubleday, 1996.

Contributor to the *New York Times Book Review.*

*SIDELIGHTS:* "If there is a place called the 'New South' in literature," Linda Barrett Osborne observed in the *Washington Post Book World,* "then Due East, S.C., Valerie Sayers' fictional coastal town, sits right on the map." All of Sayers's five novels have won critical acclaim as fresh reflections of modern life in the time-honored Southern literary tradition. With affectionate but unrelenting satire, Sayers has revised old Southern themes—particularly evoking the strong Southern faith in family—to accord with her view of an uncertain modern world.

Sayers's first work, *Due East,* "is one of those beautifully realized novels that takes over the reader's life," *Chicago Tribune* contributor Catherine Petroski raved. *Due East* is the story of fifteen-year-old Mary Faith Rapple and her father, Jesse. Mary Faith is an exceptionally bright and desperately lonely young woman who assumed a self-sufficient posture when her mother died three years earlier. Jesse is a gentle, if somewhat simple and confused, gas station manager, withdrawn into grief and alcohol after the loss of his wife. "The heart of this book," *Village Voice* reviewer Bret Harvey wrote, "is the relationship between father and daughter, which is clogged with unspoken tenderness and disappointment." As the novel opens, a lapse in communication and trust threatens to dissolve the bonds between Mary Faith and Jesse. When Mary Faith intentionally gets pregnant, Jesse's renewed attention to their relationship draws him out of his desolate state. His initial attempt to confront the situation is characteristically bungled: he falls into a lascivious love affair with—and impregnates—the mother of the man he thinks is the baby's father, while Mary Faith holds to her story of a virgin conception. *New York Times Book Review* contributor Jack Butler contended that this blend of comedy and melodrama effectively reveals some painful realities. "In 'Due East' things convincingly go askew," Butler remarked. "The characters formulate plans and follow them into total confusion."

Communication barriers between Jesse and Mary Faith are demonstrated through Sayers's use of two narrative voices: Mary Faith's first-person narration, and a third-person narrator reporting Jesse's point of view. According to Carl Mitcham in his *Commonweal* review of *Due East,* "each reaches out for the other and reacts to what are perceived as failures of love. The disjunction in narrative voices mirrors a deeper failure to bridge the gap between them." Mary Faith's voice and Jesse's omniscient narrator are presented in separate, alternating chapters until the novel's conclusion, when they are brought together for the first time. Sayers does not provide a definitive ending, but through this mingling of perspectives and an abatement of confusion, a tentative recovery is revealed. Harvey applauded the vivid evocation of family love in this understated resolution, saying that when Jesse, Mary Faith, and her baby settle down to dinner as a newly formed family, "you can practically hear the gentle clink of fork against plate." Butler concluded that "Ms. Sayers has that rare knack of appearing simply to open up a reality as if it were so clear before her eyes that she doesn't have to create it so much as invite us in."

*How I Got Him Back* relates the efforts of three women in Due East (one of them Mary Faith), struggling to hang on to their men. Mary Faith, after a four-year affair with Stephen Dugan, wants to marry him. Stephen's wife, Marygail, however, intends to win back his love and fortify their marriage. And Becky Perdue, one of the primary narrators of this novel, wants to win back her husband, Jack, who has left her for another woman. Also featured in this second novel are Tim Rooney, in love with Mary Faith and recovering from a nervous breakdown, and Father Berkeley, an alcoholic priest. All of the characters strive for spiritual peace and sanity—without much success—in a mixed-up world.

In bringing the town of Due East to life again, Sayers, according to critics, exhibits many of the strengths that made her first novel a success. Alfred Corn, in the *New York Times Book Review,* praised her "gift for voice" and her "honest, gritty commentary about human behavior in stressful circumstances," as well as her humor and unique insight. Maude McDaniel, in her *Chicago Tribune* review, described this "excellent book" as "an eclectic meld of love, hate, religious wrestling, guilt, female bonding, parental agonies, mild perversion, sexual frustration, psychosis and existential rage" that "touches on almost every reigning theme of contemporary writing." However several critics, including McDaniel, complained that there is actually too much going on in this novel. Corn maintained that the many narrative methods, "first-and third-person narration, letters, interior reverie, even a suite of rankly amateur poems written by Marygail," become distracting. McDaniels found the complexity and bleak outlook of *How I Got Him Back* somewhat overwhelming, but acknowledged that the novel's profusion of narrators, sub-plots, modern problems, and madness reflects the frenzied struggle for sanity that comprises Sayers's poignant portrait of life in the "New South."

At the time *Who Do You Love?* was published, Jonathan Yardley wrote in the *Washington Post Book World* that the town of Due East "gradually is acquiring a mythology all its own." In the *New York Times Book Review,* Howard Frank Mosher called Sayers' third novel her best to date, finding in it "humor and irony, family history, an unusual and fascinating setting, affecting characters." At the heart of the novel is Dolores Rooney, a thirty-seven-year-old transplanted New Yorker pregnant with her fifth child, who contemplates an affair with a visiting reporter from the North. Dolores is still haunted by two sexual encounters from her past. Because of her guilt and her still-lingering discomfort with the South, Dolores is, as Yardley pointed out, "a difficult woman, at times, a downright unpleasant one, who spends much of her time making things difficult for others"; still, her love for her family is "rough but real." Sharon Dirlam of the *Los Angeles Times Book Review* called this novel "a heavy little slice of life, narrow and rich." Mosher further enthused that upon finishing the novel "you have the satisfied sense of having spent much longer than a mere 24 hours in Due East."

The historical setting of *Who Do You Love?* keeps the novel from being a simple story of one family's problems and relationships; the action commences on the evening of November 21, 1963, ending only after the assassination of John F. Kennedy. The nation's tragedy particularly resonates for a family who, like the president, is liberal Roman Catholic in a conservative Protestant country. For Yardley, "Sayers moves the novel toward this cataclysmic moment with immense skill and subtlety," but Pinckney Benedict, writing in the *Chicago Tribune,* found this ending to be "telegraphed on the first page." Benedict complained that "the book's final episode, in which the Rooney family and all of Due East react to the news that President Kennedy has been assassinated, doesn't really resolve the various storylines." Yet the story belongs to Dolores Rooney, not to the slain president, as she transcends her idiosyncrasies and own shadows of guilt. By the time the novel reaches its "wonderfully affirmative ending," said Mosher, "[Dolores] manages to achieve . . . a remarkably wise insight into herself and her relationship with her big, squabbling, funny, smart, problem-ridden and immensely likeable family."

In *The Distance Between Us,* wrote a *Publishers Weekly* reviewer, Sayers "ventures to new geographical . . . and emotional territories" before returning her characters to Due East. The heroine of this story is Franny, Kate Rooney's best childhood friend. Franny is a promiscuous Catholic girl who flees her small southern town for New York. Along the way, Franny captivates several men who represent different classes. "Investigating these social differences against the background of '60s is one of Sayers's aims here, and she acquits herself beautifully," noted the *Publishers Weekly* writer. Franny's metamorphosis from "bad" teenager to would-be artist with four children, however, is the main thrust of this novel, but a complaint was voiced by *Publishers Weekly* that it "happens too slowly." The novel has also raised certain questions about its similarities to Sayers' own life. Yardley declared that the novel is a "big, fat, shapeless lump of a thing, crammed to overflowing with what looks like ill-disguised autobiography."

Franny finds herself in a triangle as her wealthy ex-boyfriend and her husband collaborate on a play. This plot machination occasionally leads Sayers, according to *Publishers Weekly,* to "strain too hard to assemble her cast at key moments," resulting in scenes that are "sometimes unconvincing and trite." Also of concern to critics was a screenplay, written by Franny's husband and inserted in the middle of the novel. While *Publishers Weekly* found "these pages [to] have a riveting immediacy," for Kate Wilson of *Entertainment Weekly,* the "sinewy screenplay makes the novel look baggy by contrast." Despite these narrative lapses, the quality of Sayers' work is apparent to many readers. Jill McCorkle in the *New York Times Book Review* noted that "Ms. Sayers is a first-rate writer, her prose rich with memorable descriptions that bring her landscapes, particularly the Southern ones, into sharp focus." And if the characters live, as Liz Rosenberg writing in *Chicago Tribune,* put it, "in . . . messy glory," their "race to nowhere," said a contributor to *Kirkus Reviews,* is "full of memorable voices, color, and the tang of living."

In her fifth novel, *Brain Fever,* Sayers again moves away from her home territory as she re-introduces Tim Rooney, now in his fifties, and follows him from Due East to New York City and back again. The landscape is as varied as the emotional content; *New York Times Book Review* critic Elizabeth Benedict noted the book's "large ambition, compassion and psychological depth." A few days before his impending marriage to Mary Faith Rapple, the heroine of *Due East,* Tim neglects to take his antidepressants, stuffs $15,000 into his shoes and heads to New York to find his ex-wife. Tim narrates his descent into madness, which for Michael Parker, writing in the *Washington Post Book World,* was one the least successful parts of the story. "Tim's voice," he said, "only intermittently sounds like a man who hits bottom when standing in the middle of Union Square dressed in black pajamas." Parker also pointed out that "as the story forges northward, both protagonist and author trade familiar territory for the woolly risks of what seems another planet from Due East." Sybil S. Steinberg of *Publishers Weekly* also missed the familiar territory of Due East. She found "too much touristy scene-setting in the novel," concluding in her review that Sayers' "usual tart observations of Southern characters and landscapes, and of the Catholic Church, don't travel well."

Still, there is much to enjoy in this novel that Joanne Wilkinson of *Booklist* called a "painful and often moving portrait of a man who is having a nervous breakdown." Likening it to a sucker punch, she declared, "when you finally see the emotional wallop coming, it's too late to duck." Particularly successful is the character of Mary Faith Rapple. Though the novel is told primarily from Tim's point of view, Sayers does give voice to Mary Faith, who undertakes a journey to New York City, along with a priest, to save Tim. One of the chapters Mary Faith narrates is "the most moving in the novel," said Benedict. "It is Ms. Sayers at her very best."

The forceful writing and Southern wit of the Due East novels, in the opinion of several critics, place Sayers in the ranks of such revered Southern writers as Eudora Welty and Flannery O'Connor. The fictional town of Due East is, according to Liz Rosenberg writing in the *Chicago Tribune,* "as clearly delineated as Faulkner's famous Yoknapatawpha County." In writing about *Brain Fever,* a critic for *Kirkus Reviews* called Sayers "a writer for whom life is not an abstract notion but a quirkily real, always exactly rendered place where ordinary people can be touched by unexpected grace as they struggle to survive."

Sayers told *CA:* "My novel in progress and my published novels all take place in the fictional town of Due East, South Carolina. I was raised in a little coastal town—Beaufort, South Carolina—suspiciously like Due East. I moved to New York at seventeen, but evidently have a compunction to return to that particular southern landscape."

*BIOGRAPHICAL/CRITICAL SOURCES:*

*BOOKS*

*Contemporary Literary Criticism,* Volume 50, Gale (Detroit), 1987.

*PERIODICALS*

*Booklist,* February 1, 1996, p. 918.
*Chicago Tribune Books,* March 8, 1987; February 19, 1989; March 10, 1991, p. 6; March 20, 1994, p. 6.
*Commonweal,* May 22, 1987.
*Entertainment Weekly,* March 4, 1994, p. 61.
*Kirkus Reviews,* November 15, 1993, p. 1418; December 1, 1995, p.1664.
*Library Journal,* December, 1995.
*Los Angeles Times Book Review,* January 27, 1989; March 10, 1991, p. 6.
*New York Times Book Review,* March 8, 1987; January 29, 1989; April 7, 1991, p. 3; February 20, 1994, p. 23; March 17, 1996, p. 8.
*Publishers Weekly,* December 6, 1993, p. 56; February 7, 1994, p. 66; December 18, 1995, p. 40.
*Times Literary Supplement,* March 11, 1988.
*Village Voice,* May 19, 1987.
*Washington Post Book World,* May 12, 1987; February 24, 1991, p. 3; January 23, 1994, p. 3; February 25, 1996, p. 7.*

* * *

**SHAW, Felicity 1918-1989**
**(Anne Morice)**

*PERSONAL:* Born in 1918 in Kent, England; died in 1989; daughter of Harry (a general practitioner) and M. R. (Morice) Wolthington; married Alexander Shaw (a film director), 1939; children: three. *Education:* Attended secondary school in London, England. *Politics:* "Varies." *Religion:* Church of England.

*CAREER:* Writer.

*WRITINGS:*

*The Happy Exiles,* Harper (New York City), 1956.
*Sun Trap,* Anthony Blond (London), 1958.
*Dummy Run* (two-act play), first produced in Henley-on-Thames, England, at Kenton Theatre, 1977.

*MYSTERY NOVELS UNDER PSEUDONYM ANNE MORICE*

*Death in the Grand Manor,* Macmillan (London), 1970.
*Murder in Married Life,* Macmillan, 1971.
*Death of a Gay Dog,* Macmillan, 1971.
*Murder on French Leave,* Macmillan, 1972.
*Death and the Dutiful Daughter,* Macmillan, 1973, St. Martin's (New York City), 1974.
*Death of a Heavenly Twin,* St. Martin's, 1974.
*Killing with Kindness,* Macmillan, 1974, St. Martin's, 1975.
*Nursery Tea and Poison,* St. Martin's, 1975.
*Death of a Wedding Guest,* St. Martin's, 1976.
*Murder in Mimicry,* St. Martin's, 1977.
*Scared to Death,* Macmillan, 1977, St. Martin's, 1978.
*Murder by Proxy,* St. Martin's, 1978.
*Murder in Outline,* St. Martin's, 1979.
*Death in the Round,* St. Martin's, 1980.
*The Men in Her Death,* Macmillan, 1981.
*Hollow Vengeance,* St. Martin's, 1982.
*Sleep of Death,* Macmillan, 1982, St. Martin's, 1983.
*Murder Post-Dated,* St. Martin's, 1984, published as *Getting Away with Murder?,* Macmillan, 1984, G. K. Hall (Boston), 1985.
*Dead on Cue,* Macmillan, 1985.
*Publish and Be Killed,* Macmillan, 1986, St. Martin's, 1987.
*Treble Exposure,* Macmillan, 1987, St. Martin's, 1988.
*Design for Dying,* St. Martin's, 1988.
*Planning for Murder,* Macmillan, 1990.

*OTHER*

A collection of Shaw's manuscripts is housed at the Mugar Memorial Library, Boston University.

*SIDELIGHTS:* Under the pseudonym Anne Morice, Felicity Shaw wrote mystery novels featuring the character Tessa Crichton Price, an actress who, in the classic mystery tradition of Agatha Christie or Ngaio Marsh, solves crimes which are presented with enough clues so that the reader has a fair chance to solve them too. As Carol Cleveland wrote in the *St. James Guide to Crime and Mystery Writers,* in the typical Price adventure "a cast of characters is introduced and placed in a situation that simmers with incipient violence. The exposition is sometimes so leisurely that murder is not committed until halfway through the book, but the characters are so lively and Tessa's commentary so entertaining that the pace is not noticeably slowed. In the classic detective tradition, all the necessary clues are faithfully laid out, attention is masterfully misdirected from them, and Tessa explains all in a final conversation." Before writing mysteries, Shaw wrote two mainstream novels examining British social relationships.

The Morice mysteries are marked by a biting view of society. As Cleveland described it, "although the form is classic, the flavor of the social world that Morice explores is much sharper than Christie's or Marsh's. Ordinary society as Tessa describes it consists of a thin film of civility floating on a thick stew of folly, passion, vice, and warped development. Both in Tessa's life and in Morice's philosophy, all the world's a stage, on which professional and amateur actors intermingle, often playing out private dramas with murderous plots." Cleveland concluded that Shaw's work under the Morice pseudonym "provides a high quality of entertainment for adults: a realistic imitation of the social world and vigorous exercise for any reader's wits."

The sharp observation of social reality found in Shaw's mysteries was first evident in her 1956 novel, *Happy Exiles,* the story of a young British woman living in an Asian colonial settlement. The book was praised for its accurate, biting depiction of British colonial life. Anne Ross in the *New York Herald Tribune Book Review* praised the "charm, irony and some extremely witty dialogue" to be found in the novel, while the critic for the *Times Literary Supplement* noted Shaw's "sharp eye for the tell-tale signs of social inferiority" and "admirably poised satiric comedy." Anne Richards in the *New York Times* found that "the conversations—rambling, boring or tautly acid as the occasion offers—ring with on-the-spot authenticity." "Anyone," wrote Faubion Bowers in *Saturday Review,* "who has a taste for Ivy Compton Burnett, Nancy Mitford, Angela Thirkell, or Margery Sharp will find Felicity Shaw a very welcome extension of those ranks."

Shaw once told *CA:* "I have never engaged in any research, beyond making a telephone call to one of numerous friends connected with the theater, films, and television. Perhaps the single slightly unusual thing about my life has been the number and variety of foreign countries I have lived in (Egypt, Kenya, Cyprus, Sudan, Tunisia, Uganda, India, France, Taiwan, and the United States), and from this the vast collection of friends I have been lucky enough to acquire in different parts of the world."

*BIOGRAPHICAL/CRITICAL SOURCES:*

*BOOKS*

*St. James Guide to Crime and Mystery Writers,* fourth edition, St. James Press (Detroit), 1996.

*PERIODICALS*

*Booklist,* May 15, 1956, p. 374.
*Bookmark,* June, 1956, p. 213.
*Christian Science Monitor,* July 19, 1956, p. 7.
*Kirkus,* March 15, 1956, p. 223.
*Murderess Ink,* October, 1979.
*Murder Ink,* September, 1977.
*New York Herald Tribune Book Review,* June 3, 1956, p. 2.
*New York Times,* June 3, 1956, p. 22.
*San Francisco Chronicle,* July 15, 1956, p. 26.
*Saturday Review,* June 2, 1956, p. 11.
*Spectator,* July 27, 1956, p. 154.
*Springfield Republican,* July 29, 1956, p. 5C.
*Times Literary Supplement,* August 3, 1956, p. 461.*

* * *

**SHERWOOD, John (Herman Mulso) 1913-**

*PERSONAL:* Born May 14, 1913, in Cheltenham, England; son of Charles Edward and N. Claire (Flecker) Sherwood; married Joan Mary Yorke, 1953; children: Mary Claire. *Education:* Attended Marlborough College; Oriel College, Oxford, Lit.Hum., 1935. *Religion:* Anglican Church.

*ADDRESSES: Home*—North End Cottage, 36 High St., Charing Ashford, Kent TN27 OHX, England. *Agent*—A. P. Watt & Son, 20 John St., London WC1N 2DR, England.

*CAREER:* Freelance writer. Curcher's College, Petersfield and Blackpool Grammar School, teacher of Classics, 1935-39; worked in the control commission for Germany, 1945-46; British Broadcasting Corporation (BBC), London, England, held variety of jobs in external services, 1946-63, head of French Language services, 1963-73. *Military service:* British Army, Intelligence Corps, 1940-45; became major.

*MEMBER:* Crime Writers Association, Association of Broadcasting Staff, Royal Automobile Club, Bushmen.

*AWARDS, HONORS:* Radio documentary prize, Italia Prize Competition, 1961.

*WRITINGS:*

*Dr. Bruderstein Vanishes,* Doubleday (New York City), 1949 (published in England as *The Disappearance of Dr. Bruderstein,* Hodder & Stoughton [London], 1949).
*Mr. Blessington's Imperialist Plot,* Doubleday, 1951.
*Ambush for Anatol,* Doubleday, 1952.
*Two Died in Singapore,* Hodder & Stoughton, 1954.
*Vote against Poison,* Hodder & Stoughton, 1956.
*Undiplomatic Exit,* Doubleday, 1958.
*The Sleuth and the Liar,* Doubleday, 1961 (published in England as *The Half Hunter,* Gollancz [London], 1961).
*No Golden Journey: A Biography of James Elroy Flecker,* Heinemann (London), 1973.
*Honesty Will Get You Nowhere,* Gollancz, 1977.
*The Limericks of Lachasse,* Macmillan (London), 1978.
*The Hour of the Hyenas,* Macmillan, 1979.
*A Shot in the Arm,* Gollancz, 1982, published as *Death at the BBC,* Scribner (New York City), 1983.
*Green Trigger Fingers,* Scribner, 1984.
*A Botanist at Bay,* Scribner, 1985.
*The Mantrap Garden,* Scribner, 1986.
*Flowers of Evil,* Scribner, 1987.
*Menacing Groves,* Gollancz, 1988, Scribner, 1989.
*A Bouquet of Thorns,* Scribner, 1989.
*The Sunflower Plot,* Scribner, 1990.
*The Hanging Garden,* Scribner, 1992.
*Creeping Jenny,* Scribner, 1993.
*Bones Gather No Moss,* Scribner, 1994.

Also author of scripts for British Broadcasting Corp.

*SIDELIGHTS:* John Sherwood has written two series of mystery novels since the late 1940s. In his first series, Charles Blessington, a British civil servant, figures in whimsically humorous adventures. The second series focuses on the elderly widow Celia Grant, who works as a professional horticulturalist and amateur sleuth. Judith Rhodes in the *St. James Guide to Crime and Mystery Writers* states that all of Sherwood's books exhibit "action, humour, and sheer improbability."

The Blessington series of novels involve a mild-mannered treasury department bureaucrat in a number of outlandish international incidents. In *Mr. Blessington's Imperialist Plot,* for example, Blessington is kidnapped in the Balkans by Soviet agents. The critic for the *New York Herald Tribune Book Review* calls the book "good adventure [with] lots of impressive-sounding background." L. G. Offord in the *San Francisco Chronicle* finds the book has a "generally light-hearted atmosphere" and "some happy kidding of Communist cliches." In *Ambush for Anatol,* Blessington chases a currency exchange racketeer and blackmailer. Anthony Boucher in the *New York Times* calls the novel "a delightfully persuasive and amusing melodrama." While Drexel Drake in the *Chicago Sunday Tribune* describes *Ambush for Anatol* as "thrilling entertainment," James Sandoe in the *New York Herald Tribune Book Review* praises the "very sprightly foolishness" and "all sorts of incidental, humorous perceptions."

Sherwood's other series concerns the widow Celia Grant, who owns a small nursery in a Sussex village and solves crimes on the side. "It is in the Celia Grant mysteries," Rhodes believes, "that Sherwood demonstrates how skilfully he can characterize and plot." Similar to Agatha Christie's character Miss Marple, Celia finds herself unexpectedly involved in murder mysteries and criminal conspiracies while plying her unassuming trade in the English countryside. Celia's gardening skills take her to such settings as Monk's Mead, an historical garden, in *The Mantrap Garden,* and earn her a commission to recreate an Elizabethan garden in *The Sunflower Plot.* As Rhodes explains, "in choosing the relatively narrow setting of horticulture for this series, Sherwood in no way prohibits himself or his sleuth from participating in far wider spheres of activity. Indeed, it provides a convenient entree into the traditional country-house-and-garden murder setting."

Sherwood told *CA:* "I started writing mysteries as a sideline after serving in Army Intelligence in Germany in the chaotic period which followed the defeat of Hitler, having found that my experiences there could best be written up in fictional form. I have gone on writing mysteries ever since. The form suits me as a vehicle for social comment, and since my retirement, writing them fills my need for something to occupy my mind when I am not thinking about anything else. I work out my plots while lying on the beach during my summer holiday (much more restful than trying to read) and write them up in winter. Exhorted four years ago by Gollancz to adopt a recurring detective, I invented a female horticultural expert who also detects, because no other crime writer seemed to have a gardener-detective, and because gardening is my other hobby."

*BIOGRAPHICAL/CRITICAL SOURCES:*

*BOOKS*

*St. James Guide to Crime and Mystery Writers,* fourth edition, St. James Press (Detroit), 1996.

*PERIODICALS*

*Chicago Sunday Tribune,* November 23, 1952, p. 10.
*Manchester Guardian,* November 14, 1958, p. 6.
*New York Herald Tribune Book Review,* March 11, 1951, p. 18; November 23, 1952, p. 26; November 9, 1958, p. 12.
*New York Times,* July 31, 1949, p. 15; November 30, 1952, p. 44; November 9, 1958, p. 36.
*San Francisco Chronicle,* February 18, 1951, p. 23; December 21, 1952, p. 10; December 21, 1958, p. 21.
*Saturday Review,* December 13, 1958, p. 32.
*Spectator,* November 21, 1958, p. 728.

* * *

**SIMIC, Charles 1938-**

*PERSONAL:* Born May 9, 1938, in Belgrade, Yugoslavia; immigrated to U.S., 1954, naturalized citizen 1971; son of George (an engineer) and Helen (Matijevic) Simic; married Helene Dubin (a designer), October 25, 1965; children: Anna, Philip. *Education:* New York University, B.A., 1967. *Religion:* Eastern Orthodox.

*ADDRESSES: Home*—P.O. Box 192, Strafford, NH 03884-0192. *Office*—Department of English, University of New Hampshire, Durham, NH 03824.

*CAREER:* Poet and educator. *Aperture* (photography magazine), New York City, editorial assistant, 1966-69; University of New Hampshire, Durham, associate professor of English, 1974—. Visiting assistant professor of English, State University of California, Hayward, 1970-73, Boston University, 1975, and Columbia University, 1979. *Military service:* U.S. Army, 1961-63.

*AWARDS, HONORS:* PEN International Award for translation, 1970; Guggenheim fellowship, 1972-73; National Endowment for the Arts fellowship, 1974-75, and 1979-80; Edgar Allan Poe Award from American Academy of Poets, 1975; National Institute of Arts and Letters and American Academy of Arts and Letters Award, 1976; National Book Award nomination, 1978, for *Charon's Cosmology;* Harriet Monroe Poetry Award from University of Chicago, Di Castignola Award from Poetry Society of America, 1980, and PEN translation award, all 1980; Fulbright travelling fellowship, 1982; Ingram Merrill fellowship, 1983-84; MacArthur Foundation fellowship, 1984-89; Pulitzer Prize nominations, 1986 and 1987; Pulitzer Prize, 1990, for *The World Doesn't End;* National Book Award finalist in poetry, 1996, for *Walking the Black Cat.*

*WRITINGS:*

*POETRY*

*What the Grass Says,* Kayak, 1967.
*Somewhere among Us a Stone Is Taking Notes,* Kayak, 1969.
*Dismantling the Silence,* Braziller, 1971.
*White,* New Rivers Press, 1972, revised edition, Logbridge Rhodes, 1980.
*Return to a Place Lit by a Glass of Milk,* Braziller, 1974.
*Biography and a Lament,* Bartholemew's Cobble (Hartford, CT), 1976.
*Charon's Cosmology,* Braziller, 1977.
*Brooms: Selected Poems,* Edge Press, 1978.
*School for Dark Thoughts,* Banyan Press, 1978, sound recording of same title published by Watershed Tapes (Washington, DC), 1978.
*Classic Ballroom Dances,* Braziller, 1980.
*Austerities,* Braziller, 1982.
*Weather Forecast for Utopia and Vicinity,* Station Hill Press, 1983.
*Selected Poems 1963-1983,* Braziller, 1985.
*Unending Blues,* Harcourt, 1986.
*Nine Poems,* Exact Change, 1989.
*The World Doesn't End,* Harcourt, 1989.
*The Book of Gods and Devils,* Harcourt, 1990.
*Hotel Insomnia,* Harcourt Brace, 1992.
*A Wedding in Hell: Poems,* Harcourt, 1994.
*Walking the Black Cat: Poems,* Harcourt Brace (New York City), 1996.

*TRANSLATOR*

Ivan V. Lalic, *Fire Gardens,* New Rivers Press, 1970.
Vasko Popa, *The Little Box: Poems,* Charioteer Press, 1970.

*Four Modern Yugoslav Poets: Ivan V. Lalic, Branko Miljkovic, Milorad Pavic, Ljubomir Simovic,* Lillabulero (Ithaca, NY), 1970.

(And editor with Mark Strand) *Another Republic: Seventeen European and South American Writers,* Viking, 1976.

*Key to Dream, According to Djordje,* Elpenor, 1978.

V. Popa, *Homage to the Lame Wolf Selected Poems,* Field (Oberlin, OH), 1979.

(With Peter Kastmiler) Slavko Mihalic, *Atlantis,* Greenfield Review Press, 1983.

(With others) Henri Michaux, *Translations: Experiments in Reading,* OARS, 1983.

Tomaz Salamun, *Selected Poems,* Viking, 1987.

Lalic, *Roll Call of Mirrors,* Wesleyan University Press, 1987.

Ristovic, Aleksandar, *Some Other Wine or Light,* Charioteer Press, 1989.

Tadic, Nicola, *Night Mail: Selected Poems,* Oberlin College Press, 1992.

*Horse Has Six Legs: Contemporary Serbian Poetry,* Graywolf Press, 1992.

*OTHER*

*The Uncertain Certainty: Interviews, Essays, and Notes on Poetry,* University of Michigan Press (Ann Arbor), 1985.

*Wonderful Words, Silent Truth,* University of Michigan Press, 1990.

*Dime-Store Alchemy: The Art of Joseph Cornell,* Ecco, 1992.

*The Unemployed Fortune-Teller: Essays and Memoirs,* University of Michigan Press, 1994.

*Orphan Factory: Essays and Memoirs,* University of Michigan, 1997.

Contributor to anthologies, including *Young American Poets,* Follett, 1968; *Contemporary American Poets,* World Publishing, 1969; *Major Young American Poets,* World Publishing, 1971; *America a Prophesy,* Random House, 1973; *Shake the Kaleidoscope: A New Anthology of Modern Poetry,* Pocket Books, 1973; *The New Naked Poetry,* Bobbs-Merrill, 1976; *The American Poetry Anthology,* Avon, 1976; *A Geography of Poets,* Bantam, 1979; *Contemporary American Poetry, 1950-1980,* Longman, 1983; *The Norton Anthology of Poetry,* Norton, 1983; *Harvard Book of American Poetry,* Harvard University Press, 1985; and *The Harper American Literature,* Volume 2, Harper, 1987. Author of introductions, *Homage to a Cat: As It Were: Logscapes of the Lost Ages,* by Vernon Newton, Northern Lights, 1991, and *Prisoners of Freedom: Contemporary Slovenian Poetry,* edited by Ales Debeljak, Pedernal, 1992.

Contributor of poetry to more than one hundred magazines, including *New Yorker, Poetry, Nation, Kayak, Atlantic, Esquire, Chicago Review, New Republic, American Poetry Review, Paris Review,* and *Harvard Magazine.*

*SIDELIGHTS:* Charles Simic, a native of Yugoslavia who immigrated to the United States during his teens, has been hailed as one of his adopted homeland's finest poets. Simic's work, which includes *Unending Blues, Walking the Black Cat,* and *Hotel Insomnia,* has won numerous prestigious awards, among them the 1990 Pulitzer Prize and the coveted MacArthur Foundation "genius grant." Although he writes in English, Simic draws upon his own experiences of war-torn Belgrade to compose poems about the physical and spiritual poverty of modern life. *Hudson Review* contributor Liam Rector notes that the author's work "has about it a purity, an originality unmatched by many of his contemporaries."

The receipt of a Pulitzer Prize for *The World Doesn't End* may have widened Simic's audience, but the poet has never lacked admirers in the community of creative writers. In the *Chicago Review,* Victor Contoski characterizes Simic's work as "some of the most strikingly original poetry of our time, a poetry shockingly stark in its concepts, imagery, and language." *Georgia Review* correspondent Peter Stitt writes: "The fact that [Simic] spent his first eleven years surviving World War II as a resident of Eastern Europe makes him a going-away-from-home writer in an especially profound way. . . . He is one of the wisest poets of his generation, and one of the best." In a piece for the *New Boston Review,* Robert Shaw concludes that Simic "is remarkably successful at drawing the reader into his own creative moment."

Simic spent his formative years in Belgrade. His early childhood coincided with World War II; several times his family evacuated their home to escape indiscriminate bombing. The atmosphere of violence and desperation continued after the war as well. Simic's father left the country for work in Italy, and his mother tried several times to follow, only to be turned back by authorities. In the meantime, young Simic was growing up in Belgrade, where he was considered a below-average student and a minor troublemaker.

When Simic was fifteen his mother finally arranged for the family to travel to Paris. After a year spent studying English in night school and attending French public schools during the day, Simic sailed for America and a reunion with his father. He entered the United States at New York City and then moved with his family to Chicago, where he enrolled in high school. In that environment—a suburban school with caring teachers and motivated students—Simic began to take new interest in his courses, especially literature. After graduation he managed to attend college at night while holding a full-time job as an office boy with the *Chicago Sun Times.*

Simic's first poems were published in 1959, when he was twenty-one. Between that year and 1961, when he entered the service, he churned out a number of poems, most of which he has since destroyed. Simic finally earned his bachelor's degree in 1966. His first full-length collection of poems, *What the Grass Says,* was published the following year. In a very short time, Simic's work—original poetry in English and translations of important Yugoslavian poets—began to attract critical attention. In *The American Moment: American Poetry in the Mid-Century,* Geoffrey Thurley notes that the substance of Simic's earliest versa—its material referents—"are European and rural rather than American and urban. . . . The world his poetry creates—or rather with its brilliant semantic evacuation decreates—is that of central Europe—woods, ponds, peasant furniture." *Voice Literary Supplement* reviewer Matthew Flamm also contends that Simic was writing "about bewilderment, about being part of history's comedy act, in which he grew up half-abandoned in Belgrade and then became, with his Slavic accent, an American poet."

Simic's work defies easy categorization. Some poems reflect a surreal, metaphysical bent and others offer grimly realistic portraits of violence and despair. *Hudson Review* contributor Vernon Young maintains that memory—a taproot deep into European folklore—is the common source of all of Simic's poetry. "Simic, a graduate of NYU, married and a father in pragmatic America, turns, when he composes poems, to his unconscious and to earlier pools of memory," the critic writes. "Within microcosmic verses which may be impish, sardonic, quasi-realistic or utterly outrageous, he succinctly implies an historical montage." Young elaborates: "His Yugoslavia is a peninsula of the mind. . . . He speaks by the fable; his method is to transpose historical actuality into a surreal key. . . . [Simic] feels the European yesterday on his pulses."

Some of Simic's best known works challenge the dividing line between the ordinary and extraordinary. He gives substance and even life to inanimate objects, discerning the strangeness in household items as ordinary as a knife or a spoon. Shaw writes in the *New Republic* that the most striking perception of the author's early poems was that "inanimate objects pursue a life of their own and present, at times, a dark parody of human existence." *Chicago Review* contributor Victor Contoski concludes: "Simic's efforts to interpret the relationship between the animate and inanimate have led to some of the most strikingly original poetry of our time, a poetry shockingly stark in its concepts, imagery, and language." As Anthony Libby puts it in the *New York Times Book Review,* Simic "takes us to his mysterious target, the other world concealed in this one."

Childhood experiences of war, poverty, and hunger lie behind a number of Simic's poems. *Georgia Review* correspondent Peter Stitt claims that the poet's most persistent concern "is with the effect of cruel political structures upon ordinary human life. . . . The world of Simic's poems is frightening, mysterious, hostile, dangerous." Thurley also declares that Simic "creates a world of silence, waiting for the unspeakable to happen, or subsisting in the limbo left afterwards. . . . The dimension of menace in Simic becomes metaphysics in itself." Simic tempers this perception of horror with gallows humor and an ironic self-awareness. Stitt claims: "Even the most somber poems . . . exhibit a liveliness of style and imagination that seems to re-create, before our eyes, the possibility of light upon the earth. Perhaps a better way of expressing this would be to say that Simic counters the darkness of political structures with the sanctifying light of art."

Critics find Simic's style particularly accessible, a substantial achievement for an author for whom English is a second language. According to Shaw, the "exile's consciousness still colors [Simic's] language as well as his view of existence. Having mastered a second language, Simic is especially aware of the power of words, and of the limits which words grope to overcome. His diction is resolutely plain: as with the everyday objects he writes about, he uncovers unexpected depth in apparently commonplace language." In the *New Letters Review of Books,* Michael Milburn writes: "Charles Simic is a poet of original vision. . . . Simic practically taunts the reader with a familiarity bordering on cliche. He seems to challenge himself to write as plainly as possible, while still producing works of freshness and originality.

[His works] literally beckon us off the street and into a world that at first looks indistinguishable from our own. . . . But a brilliant method lies behind Simic's plainness. . . . Casual, unobtrusive language expresses the most fantastic images." Milburn concludes that the poet "mines ingredients of language and experience that readers may take for granted, and fuses them in a singular music."

For more than fifteen years Simic has taught English, creative writing, and criticism at the University of New Hampshire. Because of Simic's numerous literary awards, his writing has earned a wide audience in both the United States and abroad. Diane Wakoski notes in *Poetry* that Simic's work is "cryptic and fascinating. . . . This is the kind of poem you can turn inside out, make symbolic, make metaphoric, make religious, make aesthetic, and still have a beautiful cryptic little piece, written as if it were a folk poem or perhaps a child's verse that wasn't intended to be complex at all." According to David Ignatow in the *New York Times Book Review,* Simic's poems show "that it is possible to write intensely personal poetry without openly placing oneself at the center. . . . His poems echo and re-echo in the mind, as of memories of lives, impulses and cataclysms long since buried within us." Likewise, *New York Times Book Review* contributor Stephen Dobyns contends that when one reads a Simic piece, "one has a sense of the world made bigger and taken out of the hands of the bandits and the captains. A poem may create only a very small scene, but that scene continues to expand and ramify within the imagination." Milburn notes that reading Simic's poems "is less a matter of self-discipline than of giving in to the temptation of beauty." The critic concludes: "Simic's poems are the kind one thinks of when asked to define poetry."

In addition to poetry and prose poems, Simic has also written several works of prose nonfiction, including 1992's *Dime-Store Alchemy: The Art of Joseph Cornell.* A literary paean to one of the most innovative visual artists of the twentieth century, Simic's book highlights Cornell's life work, which included minimalist sculptures using found objects to create intriguing surrealist collages, by creating verbal collages that are themselves composed of still smaller units of prose. "As in his poems, Simic's style in *Dime-Store Alchemy* is deceptively offhand and playful," notes Edward Hirsch in the *New Yorker,* "moving fluently between the frontal statement and the indirect suggestion, the ordinary and the metaphysical."

Simic once commented: "The tradition that I find myself philosophically and temperamentally in tune with is that of Emily Dickinson, Robert Frost and Wallace Stevens. I have been called a 'surrealist,' a 'magic realist' and a 'plain old realist,' and I accept all three."

*BIOGRAPHICAL/CRITICAL SOURCES:*

*BOOKS*

*Contemporary Authors Autobiography Series,* Volume 4, Gale (Detroit), 1986.

*Contemporary Literary Criticism,* Gale, Volume 6, 1976; Volume 9, 1978; Volume 22, 1982; Volume 49, 1988; Volume 68, 1991.

Thurley, Geoffrey, *The American Moment: American Poetry in the Mid-Century,* St. Martin's, 1978.

Weigl, Bruce, editor, *Charles Simic: Essays on the Poetry,* University of Michigan Press, 1996.

*PERIODICALS*

*America,* January 13, 1996, p. 18.

*Antioch Review,* spring, 1977.

*Boston Review,* March/April, 1981; April, 1986.

*Chicago Review,* Volume 48, number 4, 1977.

*Chicago Tribune Book World,* June 12, 1983.

*Choice,* March, 1975.

*Gargoyle,* number 22/23, 1983.

*Georgia Review,* winter, 1976; summer, 1986.

*Hudson Review,* spring, 1981; autumn, 1986.

*Los Angeles Times Book Review,* March 16, 1986; December 7, 1986; December 27, 1992, pp. 1, 8.

*New Boston Review,* March/April, 1981.

*New Letters Review of Books,* spring, 1987.

*New Republic,* January 24, 1976; March 1, 1993, p. 28.

*New Yorker,* December 21, 1992, pp. 130-35; June 28, 1993, p. 74.

*New York Times,* May 28, 1990.

*New York Times Book Review,* March 5, 1978; October 12, 1980; May 1, 1983; January 12, 1986; October 18, 1987; March 21, 1993, pp. 14, 16.

*Ploughshares,* Volume 7, number 1, 1981.

*Poet and Critic,* Volume 9, number 1, 1975.

*Poetry,* December, 1968; September, 1971; March, 1972; February, 1975; November, 1978; July, 1981; October, 1983; July, 1987; April, 1996, p. 33.

*Poetry Review,* June, 1983.

*Publishers Weekly,* November 2, 1990; September 21, 1992, p. 78.

*Stand,* summer, 1984.
*Village Voice,* April 4, 1974; February 28, 1984.
*Virginia Quarterly Review,* spring, 1975.
*Voice Literary Supplement,* December, 1986.
*Washington Post,* April 13, 1990.
*Washington Post Book World,* November 2, 1980; April 13, 1986; May 7, 1989; January 3, 1993, pp. 9-10.

* * *

**SIMON, Kate (Grobsmith) 1912-1990**

*PERSONAL:* Born Kaila Grobsmith, December 5, 1912, in Warsaw, Poland; immigrated to United States, 1917, naturalized citizen; daughter of Jacob (in the shoe design business) and Lina (a corsetiere; maiden name, Babicz) Grobsmith; married Robert Simon, 1947 (divorced, 1960); married a second time; children: a daughter. *Education:* Hunter College of the City University of New York, B.A., 1935.

*CAREER:* Writer. Worked for Book-of-the-Month Club, for a printing firm, and for *Publishers Weekly;* book reviewer for *New Republic* and *Nation;* freelance writer for Alfred A. Knopf, Inc., 1952-55.

*MEMBER:* PEN, Authors League.

*AWARDS, HONORS:* Awards of honor from Hunter College and English-Speaking Union; National Book Critics Circle named *Bronx Primitive: Portraits in a Childhood* among the most distinguished books published in 1982.

*WRITINGS:*

*New York Places and Pleasures: An Uncommon Guidebook,* illustrations by Bob Gill, Meridian Books, 1959, 4th revised edition, Harper, 1971.
*New York,* photographs by Andrea Feininger, Viking, 1964.
*Mexico: Places and Pleasures,* Doubleday, 1965, 3rd edition, Crowell, 1979.
*Paris Places and Pleasures: An Uncommon Guidebook,* Putnam, 1967.
*London Places and Pleasures: An Uncommon Guidebook,* Putnam, 1968.
*Italy: The Places in Between,* Harper, 1970, revised and expanded edition, Harper, 1984.
*Rome: Places and Pleasures,* Knopf, 1972.
*England's Green and Pleasant Land,* Knopf, 1974.
*Fifth Avenue: A Very Social Story,* Harcourt, 1978.
*Bronx Primitive: Portraits in a Childhood* (autobiography), Viking, 1982.
*A Wider World: Portraits in an Adolescence* (autobiography), Harper, 1986.
*A Renaissance Tapestry: The Gonzaga of Mantua* (nonfiction), Harper, 1988.
*Etchings in an Hourglass,* Harper (New York City), 1990.

Contributor of articles to periodicals, including the *New York Times, Vogue, Harper's, National Geographic, Harper's Bazaar, Saturday Review, Holiday,* and *Travel and Leisure.*

*SIDELIGHTS:* According to *Time* magazine reviewer R. Z. Sheppard, Kate Simon was "one of those rare writers who is preternaturally incapable of composing a dull sentence." Widely praised for her colorful, richly detailed prose, Simon first established her literary reputation as an author of travel guides, which Sybil S. Steinberg described in a *Publishers Weekly* article as being "in a class by themselves, distinctly personal guides of rare good taste and discernment, expressed in an urbane and witty style." Simon captivated her readers—globetrotters and armchair travelers alike—after the 1959 publication of her first book, *New York Places and Pleasures.* "There is no more wonderful guidebook than this," J. H. Plumb announced in the *New York Times Book Review,* proclaiming the eventual best-seller a work "written with a real love for a city and sparkling with gaiety, wit, and recondite knowledge."

Simon went on to write similar guides for such cities and countries as Mexico, Paris, London, and Italy, eliciting accolades for "her saunterings in areas which only the most enterprising tourists would find for themselves," as a *Times Literary Supplement* reviewer commented; for giving "the distinct impression [she] did all this research on her own two feet and not in a library," according to *Washington Post Book World*'s John Crosby; and for writing "for travelers who want to possess [a place], not for vacationers seeking a brief flirtation," as Stanley Carr stated in the *New York Times Book Review.* Plumb remarked that Simon "has made of the guidebook, one of the dullest forms of literature, a brilliant work of art. And to do that requires genius."

Simon also demonstrated her descriptive powers in *Fifth Avenue: A Very Social Story,* a 1978 book that delved into the glamorous past of New York City's

Fifth Avenue and the mansions that once lined it. The work also explores the lives of the great homes' occupants, including such famous and wealthy families as the Vanderbilts, the Astors, the Stuyvesants, the Guggenheims, and the Rockefellers. "Ambling up Fifth Avenue in a leisurely, neo-Proustian fashion," remarked *Saturday Review* critic Robert F. Moss, Simon "mixes elaborate architectural commentary with an unauthorized biography of nineteenth-century American nobility." Bruce Bliven Jr., writing for the *New York Times Book Review,* judged *Fifth Avenue* "a generous book—large and handsome—filled with a multitude of treasures and pleasures," adding that "we owe a debt to the author for capturing as much of [the mansions] as she has in words, which is preservation of a kind."

Until publication of the first segment of her three-part autobiography, titled *Bronx Primitive: Portraits in a Childhood,* few of Simon's readers could have guessed that she began life in a Warsaw, Poland, ghetto. She was not, as *Los Angeles Times* writer Elaine Kendall pointed out, "wheeled through the Borghese Gardens in her pram; shepherded through the city museums on rainy afternoons; [and] rewarded for good behavior with petits fours at Rumplemeyer's." Rather, at age four Simon immigrated to the United States, a steerage passenger aboard the *Susquehanna* accompanied by her mother and younger brother (her father having made the journey three years earlier). Simon would spend the remainder of her childhood in a poor immigrant neighborhood in the northernmost borough of New York City, where "her Borghese garden was Crotona Park, her cultural mecca the neighborhood library, [and] her Museum of Natural History the tenement hallways," noted Kendall.

In *Bronx Primitive* Simon recounts this childhood, casting her father as an overbearing and selfish shoemaker who decided that young Kate would become a famous concert pianist and make him rich, a husband and father who was more concerned for his newly arrived immigrant cousins than for his own wife and children. Simon reserves higher regard for her mother, a proud woman who later confessed to her daughter that she had had thirteen abortions—which, as *Time*'s Sheppard related, "was not a neighborhood record." Simon's younger sister was born only after Dr. James—brother of novelist Henry James and compassionate gynecologist to the poor—refused to give Simon's mother her fourteenth abortion. With the arrival of the new baby, eldest Kate, who had been expected to also care for her younger brother, took charge of another sibling, while her brother was allowed to amuse himself as he pleased. "While he," Simon reflected, "the grasshopper, sang and danced, I, the ant, sat demurely rocking the carriage. He was in the full sun, I in the shade; he was young, I was old."

Within this familial framework, however, life for the author was not undiluted dissatisfaction, squalor, and pain; Simon invokes fond memories in *Bronx Primitive* as well. She tells, for instance, of the two weeks her family spent at a small rented beach house on Coney Island, and describes an outing with her mother and brother: "When my mother walked into the street in her new brown suit and beaver hat on the first day of Passover, she was so beautiful that I couldn't see her; her radiance blinded me. My brother, in spite of our steady urge to mayhem, appeared all gold and dazzling as he played stickball in the street." In this scene Simon herself felt "complete and smooth as a fresh pea pod."

Critics greeted *Bronx Primitive* enthusiastically, praising Simon's aptitude for description and applauding the lucid, unidealized tone of the work. "She approaches [her experiences] with a clear eye in two senses," observed *Washington Post* critic Linda Barrett Osborne. "She is both strongly visual and vivid in re-creating scenes and people, and uncompromisingly straightforward in assessing them. She makes the era attractive because her style is lively, humorous, tough, and not sentimental or nostalgic." Echoing Osborne, Helen Yglesias wrote in the *New York Times Book Review* that "the reader is in safe hands, delivered from the dangers of shallow nostalgia or a generalizing sentimentality." As Kendall concluded, Simon "recalls the 1920s with piercing clarity, and while the ingredients are familiar, the results are often unexpected. There are unfiltered memories of the immigrant experience, with the grounds still settling and a slight sharp aftertaste."

Simon followed *Bronx Primitive* with a second volume of memoirs titled *A Wider World: Portraits in an Adolescence.* In this book the author has become a rebellious, quick-witted, and artistically gifted Depression-era teenager who embraces literature-induced fantasies of worldliness, fame, and romantic passion, seeing herself as "the girl who was to be immortal, the bright fantasist and loony wanderer." Informed by her father upon graduation from primary school that she could only attend high school for one year of secretarial training, Simon responds with what Sheppard termed "pluck and clarity of intent [that] are completely captivating." Her determination lands her in the academically challenging James Monroe High School, where she shines as a sharp English student and essayist. At fifteen she breaks free of her father's tyrannical grip and leaves home to become a live-in babysitter for the eccentric and politically radical Bergson family, who introduce Simon to a potent world of culture. She adopts an avant-garde bohemian lifestyle, the trappings of which include a long, gray raincoat, gold borsalino hat, gypsy earrings, beads, and black stockings. To further prove her independence she also shares a flat for a time with the shy and sensitive Davy, earning a reputation among her high school classmates as an "utterly uninhibited sexpot and total free spirit"—despite the fact that the couple's awkwardness prevents them from consummating their relationship for several years.

Simon's treatment of sexuality in *A Wider World* is forthright and even humorous at times, as when she describes an arrangement wherein Jones, a free-love friend-of-a-friend, eagerly agrees to initiate the virginal young Kate. His lesson is unsuccessful, however; during his preamble on the wonders of nature's fecundity, she falls asleep. But the author acknowledges the darker side of sexuality, too, when recounting her two abortions, the first of which was "the result of drinking deeply of synthetic gin and romping with an anonymous beauty over house roofs and down some stairs or other, to roll on the grass in a nearby park." Simon's frank but gruesome recollection of the actual abortion procedure prompted *Washington Post Book World* contributor Robert Lekachman to comment that "right-to-lifers could read with profit what it was like to get a cheap abortion without anesthesia."

Such straightforward, vivid writing earned Simon critical applause similar to that which greeted *Bronx Primitive.* Comparing *A Wider World* with such celebrated American works as Willa Cather's *My Antonia,* F. Scott Fitzgerald's *The Great Gatsby,* and Mario Puzo's *The Godfather, New York Times Book Review* writer Robert Pinsky decided that Simon's "modest, distinctive and feminist account may be all the more essentially American precisely because the transitional climb is a matter not of heroic determination or overwhelming genius, but of shining intelligence, good luck, and a tough, likable vitality." The critic also deemed Simon "unsentimental, judgmental, passionate in dislike and in loyalty, [and] coolly meticulous of eye," and praised "her clean and unpretentious prose style, her aristocratic disdain for cant, her frank worldliness and the unforced breadth of reference." *New York Times* critic Michiko Kakutani echoed Pinsky, finding in *A Wider World* "memories [that] move us not with the faded, antique charm of dog-eared photos in an album, but with the hard, bright passions of life." Sheppard concluded that "together, *Bronx Primitive* and *A Wider World* qualify as a minor American classic."

Simon turned to the concerns of another country in another era for her next book, 1988's *A Renaissance Tapestry: The Gonzaga of Mantua.* In the *New Yorker* Naomi Bliven likened the work to Simon's earlier travel series, calling *A Renaissance Tapestry* "an all-inclusive tour of four extraordinary centuries conducted at an easy tempo by an unpretentious, friendly, knowledgeable guide." The Gonzaga family ruled Mantua, a province of the Lombardy region of northern Italy, from the early fourteenth century until the early eighteenth century. Focusing primarily on the lives of Francesco Gonzaga, Marquis of Mantua, and his wife, Isabella d'Este, from the late fifteenth century to the early sixteenth century, Simon presents a history of politics, war, and culture in which the lords of Mantua served as soldiers of fortune for wealthier rulers of other Italian city-states, prospered from sound farming practices in the region's fertile land, founded Italy's first tapestry industry, and became known as excellent horse breeders. The author also describes the Gonzaga penchant for ostentation ("their clothes were gaudy, their jewels flashy, their dwarfs the smallest they could find," noted Bliven) and fratricide, while portraying them as earnest patrons of the arts whose payroll included artists Leonardo da Vinci, Titian, Andrea Mantegna, and Peter Paul Rubens, as well as composer Claudio Monteverdi and architect Filippo Brunelleschi. Remarking on *A Renaissance Tapestry* in the *New York Times Book Review,* Mark Phillips wrote that "a colorful, troubled, egotistical age is alive in Miss Simon's readable narrative." Bliven commended Simon on her characteristically forthright, unaffected style: "Her narrative poise . . . eschews the 'gee whizz' wonderment that often addles writers about the Renaissance. Her book is simply accurate, and its unargumentative precision demonstrates—at this moment in history, anyhow—the Italian Renaissance has lost some of its appeal."

The last work to be published by Simon prior to her death in February of 1990 was *Etchings in an Hour-*

*glass,* the third part of her autobiography. Following in the tradition of *Bronx Primitive* and *A Wider World, Etchings* explores facets of the author's adult life: her first husband's illness, a difficult second marriage, friends and lovers, parenting, the death of her daughter at age twenty-two, and her own battle with the cancer that would ultimately prove victorious. A *Publishers Weekly* critic praised the book, noting that Simon brought to bear "the same omnivorous interest, realism and passion, tempered by humor" that characterized her two previous memoirs. Reviewing Simon's collected autobiographical writings in the *New York Times Book Review,* Doris Grumbach noted that "The three volumes together may well become a classic of autobiography. Few people in our time have so keenly remembered, and so frankly recounted in print, the vagaries, defeats, successes and losses of a gallant and independent life."

*BIOGRAPHICAL/CRITICAL SOURCES:*

*BOOKS*

Simon, Kate, *Bronx Primitive: Portraits in a Childhood,* Viking, 1982.
Simon, Kate, *A Wider World: Portraits in an Adolescence,* Harper, 1986.

*PERIODICALS*

*Los Angeles Times,* May 4, 1982.
*Ms.,* June, 1982; July, 1986.
*Newsweek,* May 12, 1986.
*New Yorker,* July 28, 1962; May 10, 1982; April 11, 1988.
*New York Times,* March 24, 1970; March 3, 1978; May 24, 1982; February 15, 1986; April 5, 1988.
*New York Times Book Review,* June 16, 1968; September 8, 1968; June 7, 1970; April 16, 1978; May 23, 1982; February 23, 1986; April 10, 1988; August 19, 1990, p. 3.
*Observer* (London), February 14, 1971.
*Publishers Weekly,* May 14, 1982; June 15, 1990, p. 60.
*Saturday Review,* June 26, 1965; April 29, 1978.
*Sewanee Review,* spring, 1991, pp. 41-42.
*Time,* July 14, 1967; April 19, 1982; February 24, 1986.
*Times Literary Supplement,* August 1, 1968; February 19, 1970.
*Washington Post,* May 11, 1982.
*Washington Post Book World,* September 1, 1968; April 10, 1988.

*OBITUARIES:*

*PERIODICALS*

*New York Times,* February 5, 1990.
*Time,* February 19, 1990, p. 91.*

* * *

## SIMPSON, George Gaylord 1902-1984

*PERSONAL:* Born June 16, 1902, in Chicago, IL; died of pneumonia, October 6, 1984, in Tucson, AZ; son of Joseph Alexander (a lawyer) and Helen Julia (Kinney) Simpson; married Lydia Pedroja, February 2, 1923 (divorced April, 1938); married Anne Roe (a psychologist and writer), May 27, 1938; children: (first marriage) Helen (Mrs. Wolf Vishniac), Gaylord (Mrs. Frank Bush; deceased), Joan (Mrs. James Bums), Elizabeth (Mrs. John Wuri). *Education:* University of Colorado, student, 1918-19, 1920-22; Yale University, Ph.B., 1923, Ph.D., 1926. *Politics:* Democrat. *Religion:* "Nondogmatic." *Avocational interests:* Travel.

*CAREER:* American Museum of Natural History, New York City, field assistant, 1924, assistant curator, 1927, associate curator of vertebrate paleontology, 1928-42, curator of fossil mammals, 1942-59; chairman of department of geology and paleontology, 1944-58; Columbia University, New York City, professor of vertebrate paleontology, 1945-59; Harvard University, Museum of Comparative Zoology, Cambridge, MA, Alexander Agassiz Professor of Vertebrate Paleontology, 1959-70; University of Arizona, Tucson, professor of geoscience, 1967-82; Simroe Foundation, Tucson, president and trustee, 1968-84. National Research Council fellow in biological science, British Museum of Natural History, 1926-27. Special lectureships at Princeton University, Harvard University, Yale University, University of California, Columbia University, and other universities, 1946-83. Member of American Museum of Natural History expeditions to western United States, 1924, 1929, 1932, 1935, 1936, 1946-50, and 1952-54, southeastern United States, 1929-30, Patagonia region of Argentina and Chile, 1930-31, 1933-34, Venezuela, 1938-39, Brazil, 1954-55, 1956, Spain,

1960, East Africa, 1961, and others. *Military service:* U.S. Army, 1942-44; became major.

*MEMBER:* Paleontological Society, American Society of Mammalogists, American Society of Zoologists (president, 1964), Geological Society of America (fellow), Society for the Study of Evolution (president, 1946), Society of Systematic Zoology (president, 1962-63), Society of Vertebrate Paleontology (president, 1942-43), American Academy of Arts and Sciences (fellow; councillor, 1960-63), American Philosophical Society (fellow; councillor, 1946-49), National Academy of Sciences, Academia de Ciencias (Venezuela, Brazil, Argentina), Sociedad Cientifica Argentina (corresponding member), Sociedad Argentina de Estudios Geographia Gaea (honorary correspondent), Asociacion Paleontologica Argentina (honorary member), Deutsche Gesellschaft fur Saugetier Kunde, Senkenbergische Naturforschende Gesellschaft, Accademia Nazionale dei Lincei (Italy), Academia Nazionale dei XL (Italy), Phi Beta Kappa, Sigma Xi; foreign member of Royal Society, Linnean Society, and Zoological Society (all London); also member of numerous other societies throughout the world.

*AWARDS, HONORS:* Lewis Prize, American Philosophical Society, 1942; National Academy of Sciences, Thompson Medal, 1943, and Elliott Medal, 1944, 1961; Gaudry Medal, Societe Geologique de France, 1947; Hayden Medal, Philadelphia Academy of Sciences, 1950; Penrose Medal, Geological Society of America, 1952; Andre H. Dumont Medal, Geological Society of Belgium, 1953; Darwin-Wallace Medal, Linnean Society of London, 1958; Darwin Plakette, Deutsche Akademie Naturforscher Leopoldina, 1959; Darwin Medal, Royal Society of London, 1962; Linnean Gold Medal, 1962; National Medal of Science, 1965; Verrill Medal, Yale University, 1966; distinguished achievement medal, American Museum of Natural History, 1969; Wilbur Cross Medal, Yale Graduate Association, 1969; Paleontological Society Medal, 1973; International Award for distinguished contributions to natural history, Smithsonian Institution, 1976; distinguished service award, American Institute of Biological Science, 1978. Honorary degrees from Yale University, 1946, Princeton University, 1947, University of Durham, 1951, Oxford University, 1951, University of Glasgow, 1951, University of New Mexico, 1954, University of Chicago, 1959, Cambridge University, 1965, University of Paris, 1965, York University, 1966, Kenyon College, 1968, University of Colorado, 1968, Universidad de La Plata, 1978.

*WRITINGS:*

*A Catalogue of the Mesozoic Mammalia in the Geological Department of the British Museum,* British Museum, 1928, reprinted, Ayer Co., 1980.

*American Mesozoic Mammalia,* Elliot's Books, 1929.

(Contributor) *Memoirs of the Peabody Museum of Yale University,* Volume III, Yale University Press, 1929, reprinted, Ayer Co., 1980.

*Attending Marvels: A Patagonian Journal,* Macmillan, 1934, reprinted, University of Chicago Press, 1982.

*The Fort Union of the Crazy Mountain Field, Montana, and Its Mammalian Faunas,* U.S. National Museum, 1937, reprinted with *Paleocene Primates of the Fort Union, with Discussion of Relationships of Eocene Primates* by James W. Gidley, AMS Press, 1978.

(With wife, Anne Roe) *Quantitative Zoology,* McGraw, 1939, revised edition (with Anne Roe and Richard Lewontin), Harcourt, 1960.

*Los Indios Kamarakotos,* Revista de Fomento (Caracas), 1940.

*Tempo and Mode in Evolution,* Columbia University Press, 1944, reprinted, 1984.

*The Principles of Classification and a Classification of Mammals,* American Museum of Natural History, 1945.

*The Beginning of the Age of Mammals in South America,* American Museum of Natural History, Part I, 1948, Part II, 1967.

*The Meaning of Evolution: A Study of the History of Life and Its Significance for Man,* Yale University Press, 1949, revised and abridged edition, New American Library, 1951, revised edition, Yale University Press, 1967.

*Horses: The Story of the Horse Family in the Modern World and Through Sixty Million Years of History,* Oxford University Press, 1951, published with new preface, Anchor Books, 1961.

*Life of the Past* (an introduction to paleontology), Yale University Press, 1953.

*The Major Features of Evolution,* Columbia University Press, 1953.

*Evolution and Geography* (Condon Lectures), Oregon State System of Higher Education, 1953.

(With Carlos de Paula Cauto) *The Mastodonts of Brazil,* American Museum of Natural History, 1957.

(With C. S. Pittendrigh and L. H. Tiffany) *Life: An Introduction to Biology,* Harcourt, 1957, revised edition (with William S. Beck) with instructor's manual, 1965, abridged edition, with student guide, 1970, 3rd edition (with William S. Beck and Karel F. Liem), Harper (New York City), 1991.

(Editor with Anne Roe) *Behavior and Evolution,* Yale University Press, 1958.
*Principles of Animal Taxonomy,* Columbia University Press, 1961.
*This View of Life: The World of an Evolutionist,* Harcourt, 1964.
*The Geography of Evolution* (collected essays), Chilton, 1965.
*Mammals Around the Pacific,* University of Washington Press, 1966.
*Biology and Man,* Harcourt, 1969.
*Penguins: Past and Present, Here and There,* Yale University Press, 1976.
*Concession to the Improbable: An Unconventional Autobiography,* Yale University Press, 1979.
*Splendid Isolation: The Curious History of South American Mammals,* Yale University Press, 1980.
*Why and How: Some Problems and Methods in Historical Biology,* Pergamon, 1980.
(Author of introduction) Charles Darwin, *Book of Darwin,* WSP, 1983.
*Fossils and the History of Life,* W. H. Freeman, 1984.
*Discoverers of the Lost World: An Account of Some of Those Who Brought Back to Life South American Mammals Long Buried in the Abyss of Time,* Yale University Press, 1984.
*Simple Curiosity: Letters from George Gaylord Simpson to His Family, 1921-1970,* edited by Leo F. Laporte, University of California Press, 1987.
*The Dechronization of Sam Magruder: A Novel,* edited and with a memoir by Joan Simpson Burns, introduction by Arthur C. Clarke, afterword by Stephen Jay Gould, St. Martin's Press (New York City), 1996.

Contributor of numerous articles, reports, essays, and reviews, to journals.

*WORK IN PROGRESS:* Essays and reviews for journals.

*SIDELIGHTS:* George Gaylord Simpson was renowned as an empirical paleontologist and as a principal founder of modern evolutionary theory. Simpson told *CA:* "I am primarily an earth scientist but have written not only technical studies but also textbooks and popular books covering broad fields in a number of different sciences. Outside of the sciences I read detective stories and study languages and linguistics from ancient Egyptian to modern Arabic, Hawaiian, and other languages." F.N. Egerton noted in *Choice* that Simpson's books were "highly regarded [for] popularizing his science and exploring the relation between evolution and religion and philosophy."

Simpson's book *Splendid Isolation: The Curious History of South American Mammals* presented its topic "successfully and readably, though the subject matter is highly specialized and somewhat technical," wrote David Snow in the *Time Literary Supplement.* Excavating South America's past, Simpson pieced together evidence which shows the relationship between its geologic history and the evolution of its mammals. Mammals distinctly South American, he found, developed where the continent was separated from North America during the late Cretaceous and the Tertiary periods. When continental drift united the two land masses, South America's peculiar mammals began their struggle to survive the invasion by North America's more advanced species. "This book shows Simpson's characteristic thoroughness, carefully measured thought, and admirable clear prose style," commented a *Washington Post Book World* reviewer. "Although aimed at anyone with a general interest in natural history," Snow added, *Splendid Isolation* "will . . . be referred to as much by working biologists as by the general reader and will be enjoyed by both."

*Simple Curiosity: Letters from George Gaylord Simpson to His Family, 1921-1970* is an epistolary account of Simpson's life. The letters trace his personal affairs, including his service in military intelligence during World War II, his divorce and remarriage, and his scientific expeditions. The letters reveal that vanity, laziness, and raw curiosity were among the reasons he was drawn to science and that he could be sociable with friends but insolent toward colleagues. The letters also reveal his perspicacity. Yet, Stephen Jay Gould maintained in the *New York Times Book Review:* "These letters do not show us the real man. They simply remind us once again that people have the damnedest ability to compartmentalize their lives; one can be a fine statesman and a cad at home, a financial genius and an insensitive lout, a lover of dogs and a murderer of people."

After his death, Simpson's sister discovered a short science fiction manuscript in his desk. *The Dechronization of Sam Magruder* is a scientific autobiography of sorts grounded in the twenty-second century. In 2162 Magruder, a scientist working on the theory of time, accidentally sends himself back 80 million years with no way to return to the present.

He soon realizes he is the only human alive among the dinosaurs—and that he has the unparalleled opportunity to resolve mysteries about the dinosaurs. He records his scientific observations on stone slabs that are found by a geologist 80 million years later. Writing in the *New York Times Book Review,* Alan Lightman commended Simpson's "didactic but excellent physical descriptions of dinosaurs and their various adaptations."

*BIOGRAPHICAL/CRITICAL SOURCES:*

*BOOKS*

Simpson, George, *Concession to the Improbable: An Unconventional Autobiography,* Yale University Press, 1979.

*PERIODICALS*

*Bloomsbury Review,* May/June, 1996, p. 14.
*Booklist,* December 1, 1995, p. 610.
*Choice,* April, 1988, p. 1268.
*Los Angeles Times Book Review,* March 10, 1996, p. 10.
*Natural History,* May, 1994, p. 62.
*Nature,* April 26, 1984.
*New York Times Book Review,* March 23, 1980; February 14, 1988, p. 14; January 28, 1996, p. 13.
*Publishers Weekly,* November 27, 1995, p. 52.
*Science,* May 16, 1980; November 16, 1984.
*Science Books & Films,* September, 1980, p. 24.
*Times Literary Supplement,* August 1, 1980; November 2, 1984.
*Washington Post Book World,* September 4, 1983.

*OBITUARIES:*

*PERIODICALS*

*Chicago Tribune,* October 9, 1984.
*Los Angeles Times,* October 10, 1984.
*New York Times,* October 8, 1984.
*Washington Post,* October 13, 1984.*

* * *

**SIMPSON, Louis (Aston Marantz) 1923-**

*PERSONAL:* Born March 27, 1923, in Kingston, Jamaica, British West Indies; United States citizen; son of Aston and Rosalind (Marantz) Simpson; married Jeanne Rogers, 1949 (divorced, 1954); married Dorothy Roochvarg, 1955 (divorced, 1979); married Miriam Butensky Bachner, 1985; children: (first marriage) Matthew; (second marriage) Anne, Anthony. *Education:* Columbia University, B.S., 1948, A.M., 1950, Ph.D., 1959.

*ADDRESSES: Home*—186 Old Field Rd., Setauket, New York, NY 11733-1636.

*CAREER:* Bobbs-Merrill Publishing Co., New York City, editor, 1950-55; Columbia University, New York City, instructor in English, 1953-59; New School for Social Research, instructor in English, 1955-59; University of California, Berkeley, 1959-67, began as assistant professor, became professor of English; State University of New York at Stony Brook, professor of English and comparative literature, 1967-91, distinguished professor 1991-93, professor emeritus, 1993—. Has given poetry readings at colleges and poetry centers throughout the United States and Europe and on television and radio programs in New York, San Francisco, and London. *Military service:* U.S. Army, 1943-46; became sergeant; awarded Bronze Star with oak leaf cluster, Purple Heart (twice), Presidential Unit Citation.

*MEMBER:* American Academy in Rome.

*AWARDS, HONORS:* Fellowship in literature (Prix de Rome) at American Academy in Rome, 1957; *Hudson Review* fellowship, 1957; Columbia University, distinguished alumni award, 1960, Medal for Excellence, 1965; Edna St. Vincent Millay Award, 1960; Guggenheim fellowship, 1962, 1970; American Council of Learned Societies grant, 1963; Pulitzer Prize for poetry, 1964, for *At the End of the Open Road;* Medal for Excellence, Columbia University, 1965; Commonwealth Club of California poetry award, 1965; American Academy of Arts and Letters award in literature, 1976; D.H.L., Eastern Michigan University, 1977; Institute of Jamaica, Centenary Medal, 1980; Jewish Book Council, Award for Poetry, 1981; Elmer Holmes Bobst Award, 1987; Hampden Sydney College, D.Litt., 1990.

*WRITINGS:*

*The Arrivistes: Poems, 1940-49,* Fine Editions, 1949.
*Good News of Death and Other Poems,* Scribner, 1955.

(Editor with Donald Hall and Robert Pack) *The New Poets of England and America,* Meridian, 1957.

*A Dream of Governors* (poems), Wesleyan University Press, 1959.

*Riverside Drive* (novel), Atheneum, 1962.

*James Hogg: A Critical Study,* St. Martin's, 1962.

*At the End of the Open Road* (poems), Wesleyan University Press, 1963.

(Contributor) Thom Gunn and Ted Hughes, editors, *Five American Poets,* Faber, 1963.

*Selected Poems,* Harcourt, 1965.

(Editor) *An Introduction to Poetry,* St. Martin's, 1967, 2nd edition, 1972.

*Adventures of the Letter I* (poems), Harper, 1971.

*North of Jamaica* (autobiography), Harper, 1972, published as *Air with Armed Men,* London Magazine Editions, 1972.

*Three on the Tower: The Lives and Works of Ezra Pound, T. S. Eliot and William Carlos Williams* (literary criticism), Morrow, 1975.

*Searching for the Ox* (poems), Morrow, 1976.

*A Revolution in Taste: Studies of Dylan Thomas, Allen Ginsberg, Sylvia Plath and Robert Lowell* (literary criticism), Macmillan, 1978, published in England as *Studies of Dylan Thomas, Allen Ginsberg, Sylvia Plath and Robert Lowell,* Macmillan, 1979.

*Armidale* (poems), BOA Editions, 1979.

*Out of Season* (poems), Deerfield Press, 1979.

*Caviare at the Funeral* (poems), Franklin Watts, 1980.

*A Company of Poets* (literary criticism), University of Michigan, 1981.

*The Best Hour of the Night* (poems), Ticknor and Fields, 1983.

*People Live Here: Selected Poems 1949-1983,* BOA Editions, 1983.

*The Character of the Poet* (literary criticism), University of Michigan, 1986.

*Collected Poems,* Paragon House, 1988.

*Selected Prose,* Paragon House, 1988.

*Wei Wei and Other Friends* (poems), Typographeum, 1990.

*In the Room We Share* (poems), Paragon House, 1990.

*Ships Going into the Blue: Essays and Notes on Poetry,* University of Michigan Press (Ann Arbor), 1994.

*The King My Father's Wreck* (memoir), Story Line Press, 1995.

*There You Are: Poems,* Story Line (Brownsville, OR), 1995.

*Modern Poets of France: A Bilingual Anthology* (poems), Story Line Press, 1997.

Contributor of poems, plays, and articles to literary periodicals, including *American Poetry Review, Listener, Hudson Review, Paris Review,* and *Critical Quarterly.*

*SIDELIGHTS:* Jamaican-born poet and educator Louis Simpson, author of poetry collections that include the Pulitzer Prize-winning *At the End of the Open Road, Searching for the Ox,* and *There You Are,* is noted for simple, controlled verses that reveal hidden layers of meaning. Critic Yohma Gray writes in praise of the poet's ability to make his readers heed that which usually passes undiscerned. "Even in the most mundane experience there is a vast area of unperceived reality," the critic notes, "and it is Louis Simpson's kind of poetry which brings it to our notice. It enables us to see things which are ordinarily all about us but which we do not ordinarily see; it adds a new dimension to our sensational perception, making us hear with our eyes and see with our ears." Gray maintains that poetry seeks the same goal as religious belief: "to formulate a coherent and significant meaning for life. The poetry of Louis Simpson offers us that meaning."

In a discussion of Simpson's early poetry, Gray comments that the author "never departs from traditional form and structure and yet he never departs from contemporary themes and concerns." Gray describes one poem, for example, in which Simpson "handles a modern psychological situation in the delicate cadence of seventeenth-century verse." Ronald Moran makes a similar comment in regard to *The Arrivistes,* Simpson's first book. Moran finds that Simpson often sounds "like an Elizabethan song-maker or like a Cavalier poet." Gray argues that this juxtaposition of traditional form (ordered meter and rhyme) and modern subjects emphasizes, particularly in the poems about the world wars, the chaotic quality and the tensions of contemporary life. Gray finds that Simpson neither complains nor moralizes about modern problems; rather he clarifies difficulties and presents rational insights.

After 1959, the publication date of *A Dream of Governors,* there was a perceived change in Simpson's work; reviewer Stephen Stepanchev contends that it changed for the better. Notes Stepanchev: "The prosaism of his early work—which required metrics and rhyme in order to give it character as verse—now gave way to rich, fresh, haunting imagery. His philosophical and political speculations achieved a distinction and brilliance that they had lacked before." A *Chicago Review* critic had more cautious praise for the shift in Simpson's poetry, writing that, "*A Dream of Governors* has wit, sophistication, perceptiveness, intelligence, variety, and knowingness, but it comes perilously close to being a poetry of chic." The reviewer goes on to say that this early work lacks a depth of feeling.

However, he continues, "*At the End of the Open Road* (1963) . . . is a different story entirely. Simpson has found the secret of releasing the meaning and power of his themes. . . . It is not that his stanzas . . . are becoming more flexible and experimental: this in itself does not mean very much. . . . What is more fundamental, it seems to me, is that greater stylistic flexibility should be the sign of growth in the character and thought of the speaker. Simpson is becoming more able to be a part of what he writes about, and to make what he writes about more a part of him." *New York Time Book Reviews* Edward Hirsch agrees that the Pulitzer Prize-winning *At the End of the Open Road* indicates a growth and finesse in Simpson's poetry, opining "It is not only a major breakthrough in his own work; it is also one of the tours de force of American poetry in the 60's." Hirsch describes *At the End of the Open Road* as "a sustained meditation on the American character" noting, "the moral genius of this book is that it traverses the open road of American mythology and brings us back to ourselves; it sees us not we wish to be but as we are."

Not all critics appreciated the change in Simpson's verse. In a review of 1965's *Selected Poems,* which contains twelve new poems in addition to selections of earlier work, Harry Morris states that "Simpson's first three volumes are better" than his new poetry. Morris believes that Simpson's "new freedoms" have not helped him convey his themes more effectively. T. O'Hara, in a critique of *Adventures of the Letter I,* also questions Simpson's new manner: "What has happened to Louis Simpson's energy?. . . It almost appears that success has mellowed the tough poetic instinct that once propelled him, for this present collection barely flexes a muscle." Yet Marie Borroff, speaking of the same book, avows that "when the remaining decades of the twentieth century have passed ignominiously into history along with the 1960's, these stanzas and other gifts will remain to us." And Christopher Hope deems *Adventures* "a work of pure, brilliant invention."

A mix of criticism continued in reviews of *Searching for the Ox.* Derwent May finds the quiet, reflective mood of the poems attractive. Nikki Stiller, on the other hand, feels that "Louis Simpson's work now suggests too much comfort: emotional, physical, intellectual. He has stopped struggling, it seems, for words, for rhythms, for his own deepest self." Yet in contrast to this, Peter Stitt remarks that *Searching for the Ox* "is a tremendously refreshing book. . . . The style in which [the poems] are written presents us with no barriers—it is plain, direct and relaxed. Moreover, the poems tell a story, or stories, in which we can take a real interest."

Simpson's ability to have his poems relate stories of interest is evident as well in *Collected Poems.* Selections from his poetry created from 1940 through the 1980's, *Collected Poems* focuses on the lives of everday citizens. "For the last two decades [Simpson's] appetite has increasingly been for recreating quintessentially American stories of ordinary people . . . living out lives of quiet desperation," finds Hirsch, noting "he has turned his ardor and ingenuity to uncovering the secret and public lives of people stripped of their expectations and bewildered by their fates." "Simpson takes part in the existence of other people, and pecks or picks about the shopping mall with them, or the redwoods and the Golden Gate, or Paris, or the battlefields of the Second World War which so nearly unmade him," observes *Times Literary Supplement*'s William Scammell, adding, "And he manages to do this without relinquishing his own firm sense of identity, or slumping into a reverent pantheistic incoherence." Scammell concludes with praise for *Collected Poems* as "a masterclass for reader and writer alike, alive on every page." "But mastery is not the right metaphor to end on," he surmizes, "for Simpson is someone who stands outside aestheticism, outside schools and movements."

In *There You Are: Poems,* the poet again "send[s] us into the lives of people and their stories" comments Mark Jarman in the *Hudson Review.* A *Publishers Weekly* contributor states that in *There You Are* while "combining straightforward diction with oblique insights, Simpson limns people and stories with an irony tempered by compassion." Jarman hails Simpson as "a poet of the American character and vernacular." Praising Simpson's storytelling skill and style, Jarman claims "that no one writing today has a better understanding of narrative as a figure of speech. Each of his stories is like a piece standing for life as a whole, existing in a kind of chaste simplicity and yet, to paraphrase Simpson himself, giving off vibrations."

Simpson occasionally ventures from verse into other genres: novel, autobiography, and literary criticism. Robert Massie writes of the poet's 1962 novel *Riverside Drive* in the *New York Times Book Review:* "Into fragments of dialogue, [Simpson] packs more meaning and drama than many novelists can bring off in a chapter. . . . As novels go, *Riverside Drive* is not a tragedy to shake the Gods—but it should stir most of its readers. From the first chapter to the last, it has the ring of truth." Concerning Simpson's literary critical study *A Revolution in Taste,* Paul Zweig comments that the author "has provided a series of engaging portraits of poets whom he presents less as cultural exemplars than as individuals struggling, as Baudelaire wrote, to absolve the pain of their lives with the grace of an enduring poem. It is the life narrowing intensely and heatedly into the act of writing that interests Simpson, the life pared to the poem. And this has enabled him to write a series of compact literary biographies that have the pithiness of a 17th-century 'character' and a literary good sense that reminds me of [Samuel] Johnson's 'Lives of the Poets.'"

Simpson has also written several volumes of autobiography, including 1972's *North of Jamaica* and *The King My Father's Wreck,* published in 1994. The latter work recounts the poet's early years in Jamaica and his transition to adulthood and literary maturity through a selection of essays. Focusing on specific images from his past—his mother's disappearance from home when he was a young boy, his excitement at the prospect of becoming a U.S. citizen, a dissatisfying job working as an editor for a publishing house, the experiences he encountered in the armed forces during World War II that led to later protestations over the conflict in Vietnam, returning a book to his Jamaican school sixty years after borrowing it—*The King My Father's Wreck* is written in the same spare style that is characteristic of Simpson's verse. The poet's "insistent voice" imbues his reminiscences with "more dramatic emotional topography than most," comments a *Publishers Weekly* reviewer, thereby "rewarding adventurous readers."

*BIOGRAPHICAL/CRITICAL SOURCES:*

*BOOKS*

*Contemporary Literary Criticism,* Gale (Detroit), Volume 4, 1975, Volume 7, 1977, Volume 9, 1978, Volume 32, 1985.

Hungerford, Edward, ed., *Poets in Progress: Critical Prefaces to Thirteen Modern American Poets,* Northwestern University Press, 1967.

Lazer, Hank, editor, *On Louis Simpson: Depths beyond Happiness,* University of Michigan, 1988.

Lensing, George S., and Ronald Moran, *Four Poets and the Emotive Imagination,* Louisiana State University Press (Baton Rouge), 1976.

Moran, Ronald, *Louis Simpson,* Twayne, 1972.

Roberson, William H., *Louis Simpson: A Reference Guide,* G. K. Hall, 1980.

Stepanchev, Stephen, *American Poetry since 1945,* Harper, 1965.

Stitt, Peter, *The World's Hieroglyphic Beauty: Five American Poets* University of Georgia, 1985.

*PERIODICALS*

*American Poetry Review,* January-February, 1979.

*Best Sellers,* June 15, 1972.

*Chicago Review,* Volume XIX, number 1, 1966.

*Harper's,* October, 1965.

*Hudson Review*, Autumn, 1996.

*Listener,* November 25, 1976.

*London Magazine,* February-March, 1977.

*Los Angeles Times Book Review,* April 30, 1995, p. 13.

*Midstream,* December, 1976.

*New Statesman,* January 31, 1964.

*New York Herald Tribune Book Review,* November 15, 1959; May 13, 1962.

*New York Times Book Review,* September 27, 1959; May 13, 1962; May 9, 1976; December 17, 1978; January 29, 1984; November 13, 1988.

*New York Times Magazine,* May 2, 1965.

*Parnassus*, Volume 21, pp. 138-145.

*Poetry,* April, 1960.

*Publishers Weekly,* October 24, 1994, p. 58; July 31, 1995.

*Saturday Review,* May 21, 1960.

*Saturday Review/World,* April 3, 1976.

*Sewanee Review,* spring, 1969.

*Time,* May 18, 1962.

*Times Literary Supplement,* June 9, 1966; January 4, 1980; July 4, 1986; May 5, 1989.

*Washington Post Book World,* March 5, 1995, p. 12.

*Yale Review,* March, 1964; October, 1972.

* * *

**SLESAR, Henry 1927-**
**(O. H. Leslie, Jay Street)**

*PERSONAL:* Born June 12, 1927, in Brooklyn, NY; son of Benjamin and Sophie (Motlin) Slesar; married

Oenone Scott, August 3, 1952 (divorced, 1969); married Jan Maakestad, December 12, 1970 (divorced, 1974); married Manuela Jone, June 1, 1975; children: Leslie Ann. *Education:* Attended School of Industrial Art, New York, NY. *Avocational interests:* Music, both jazz and classical.

*ADDRESSES: Home*—125 E. 72nd St., New York, NY 10021. *Agent*—Jerome S. Siegel, 8733 Sunset Blvd., Hollywood, CA 90069.

*CAREER:* Young & Rubicam (advertising agency), New York City, copywriter, 1945-49; Robert W. Orr & Associates (advertising agency), New York City, creative director, 1949-57; Fuller & Smith & Ross (advertising agency), New York City, creative director, 1957-60; Donahue & Coe (advertising agency), New York City, creative director, 1960-64; Slesar & Kanzer, New York City, president, 1964-69; Slesar & Manuela, New York City, president, 1974—; headwriter of daytime serials *The Edge of Night,* 1968-79, and *Somerset,* 1971-73. *Military service:* U. S. Army, 1946-47.

*MEMBER:* Mystery Writers of America, Science Fiction Writers of America, National Academy of Television Arts and Sciences, Authors League.

*AWARDS, HONORS:* Edgar Award, Mystery Writers of America, 1959, for *The Gray Flannel Shroud.*

*WRITINGS:*

*The Gray Flannel Shroud,* Random House (New York City), 1959.

*Enter Murderers,* Random House, 1960.

*Clean Crimes and Neat Murders,* introduction by Alfred Hitchcock, Avon (New York City), 1961.

*A Crime for Mothers and Others,* Avon, 1962.

*The Bridge of Lions,* Macmillan (New York City), 1963.

*The Right Kind of House* (one-act play), Dramatic Publishing, 1963.

*The Seventh Mask,* Ace Books (New York City), 1969.

*The Thing at the Door,* Random House, 1974.

*Death on Television: The Best of Henry Slesar's Alfred Hitchcock Stories,* edited by Francis Nevins and Martin Greenberg, Southern Illinois University Press (Urbana), 1989.

*SCREENPLAYS*

(With John Kneubuhl) *Two on a Guillotine,* Warner Bros., 1968.

(With Christopher Wicking) *Murders in the Rue Morgue,* American International, 1970.

Also author, with Louis Vittes, of screenplay *The Eyes of Annie Jones,* 1963. Also author of over 100 television scripts for *Alfred Hitchcock Presents, Twilight Zone,* and other series; also author of thirty-nine radio scripts for *CBS Radio Mystery Theatre.* Work is represented in over eighty-five anthologies. Contributor of over 500 short stories and novelettes to various magazines, including *Ellery Queen's Mystery Magazine* and *Alfred Hitchcock's Mystery Magazine.*

*SIDELIGHTS:* A prolific television writer whose work for the *Alfred Hitchcock Presents* series includes some of that program's classic episodes, Henry Slesar has also written a number of mystery novels and over 500 short stories. "Slesar's ability to delight his readers is exemplified throughout his work," according to Frances D. McConachie in the *St. James Guide to Crime and Mystery Writers.*

In his Edgar Award-winning novel *The Gray Flannel Shroud,* Slesar "combines the detective and the crime story with romance," McConachie explains. "The novel presents legitimate clues, colorless yet sympathetic suspects, and a puzzle—who killed Bob Bernstein, the friendly photographer, Anne Gander, the 'voluptuous' model and Willie Shenk, the 'pretty boy' thug." Advertising executive Dave Robbins, while tending the needs of his important Burke Baby Foods account, turns amateur sleuth to solve the murders. James Sandoe in the *New York Herald Tribune Book Review* finds the novel exhibits "a quick and happily lasting appeal" as well as a "sardonic persuasion." Anthony Boucher believes the novel could have used "much second-thought revision," but finds it to have "some very amusing and presumably authentic stuff about advertising campaigns." Drexel Drake in the *Chicago Sunday Tribune* calls *The Gray Flannel Shroud* a "richly satirical portrayal of advertising 'genius' at work."

*The Thing at the Door* is a thriller concerning a young heiress being terrorized by mysterious noises during the night. Private eye Steve Tyner investigates the situation to determine whether the noises are delusions or attempts upon the rich woman's life. In this book, according to McConachie, "Slesar skillfully unravels a psychological drama of suspense." Julian Barnes in the *New Statesman* notes that the book reminds readers that "the fears we had as children never really lose their grip." H. C. Veit in

*Library Journal* calls *The Thing at the Door* "a good slick thriller."

*BIOGRAPHICAL/CRITICAL SOURCES:*

*BOOKS*

*St. James Guide to Crime and Mystery Writers,* fourth edition, St. James Press (Detroit), 1996.

*PERIODICALS*

*Chicago Sunday Tribune,* March 8, 1959, p. 6.
*Guardian,* May 12, 1961, p. 9.
*Kirkus,* November 1, 1958, p. 834; June 15, 1960, p. 470.
*Library Journal,* September 1, 1974, p. 2093.
*New Statesman,* August 29, 1975, p. 258.
*New York Herald Tribune Book Review,* February 1, 1959, p. 9; August 28, 1960, p. 12.
*New York Times,* February 1, 1959, p. 18; August 28, 1960, p. 12.
*New York Times Book Review,* December 15, 1974, p. 10.
*San Francisco Chronicle,* February 15, 1959, p. 28; October 9, 1960, p. 30.
*Saturday Review,* March 7, 1959, p. 38; September 24, 1960, p. 34.
*Times Literary Supplement,* June 23, 1961, p. xi; December 26, 1975, p. 1544.

* * *

## SOWELL, Thomas 1930-

*PERSONAL:* Born June 30, 1930, in Gastonia, NC; married Alma Jean Parr; children: two. *Education:* Harvard University, A.B. (magna cum laude), 1958; Columbia University, A.M., 1959; University of Chicago, Ph.D., 1968.

*ADDRESSES: Office*—Hoover Institution, Stanford, CA 94305.

*CAREER:* U.S. Department of Labor, Washington, DC, economist, 1961-62; Rutgers University, Douglass College, New Brunswick, NJ, instructor in economics, 1962-63; Howard University, Washington, DC, lecturer in economics, 1963-64; American Telephone & Telegraph Co., New York City, economic analyst, 1964-65; Cornell University, Ithaca, NY, assistant professor of economics, 1965-69, director of Summer Intensive Training Program in Economic Theory, 1968; Brandeis University, Waltham, MA, associate professor of economics, 1969-70; University of California, Los Angeles, associate professor, 1970-74, professor of economics, 1974-80; Urban Institute, Washington, DC, project director, 1972-74; Center for Advanced Study in the Behavioral Sciences, Stanford, CA, fellow, 1976-77; Hoover Institution, Stanford, senior fellow, 1977, 1980—. Visiting professor, Amherst College, 1977. *Military Service:* U.S. Marine Corps, 1951-53.

*WRITINGS:*

*Economics: Analysis and Issues,* Scott, Foresman (Glenview, IL), 1971.
*Black Education: Myths and Tragedies,* McKay (New York City), 1972.
*Say's Law: An Historical Analysis,* Princeton University Press (Princeton, NJ), 1972.
*Classical Economics Reconsidered,* Princeton University Press, 1974.
*Affirmative Action: Was It Necessary in Academia?,* American Enterprise Institute for Public Policy Research (Washington, DC), 1975.
*Race and Economics,* McKay, 1975.
*Patterns of Black Excellence,* Ethics and Public Policy Center, Georgetown University (Washington, DC), 1977.
(Editor) *American Ethnic Groups,* Urban Institute (Washington, DC), 1978.
(Editor) *Essays and Data on American Ethnic Groups,* Urban Institute, 1978.
*Markets and Minorities,* Basic Books (New York City), 1981.
(Editor with others) *The Fairmont Papers: Black Alternatives Conference, December, 1980,* ICS Press (San Francisco), 1981.
*Pink and Brown People, and Other Controversial Essays,* Hoover Institution (Stanford, CA), 1981.
*Knowledge and Decision,* Basic Books, 1983.
*Ethnic America: A History,* Basic Books, 1983.
*The Economics and Politics of Race: An International Perspective,* Morrow (New York City), 1983.
*Compassion Versus Guilt, and Other Essays,* Quill (New York City), 1984.
*Marxism: Philosophy and Economics,* Morrow, 1985.
*Civil Rights: Rhetoric or Reality?,* Morrow, 1985.
*Assumptions versus History,* Hoover Institution, 1986.
*A Conflict of Visions: Ideological Origins of Political Struggles,* Morrow, 1987.

*Judicial Activism Reconsidered* (essays), Hoover Institution, 1989.

*Choosing a College: A Guide for Parents and Students,* Perennial Library (New York City), 1989.

*Preferential Policies: An International Perspective,* Morrow, 1990.

*Inside American Education: The Decline, the Deception, the Dogmas,* Free Press (New York City), 1992.

*Race and Culture: A World View,* Pennsylvania State University Press (University Park, PA), 1992.

*The Vision of the Anointed: Self-Congratulation as a Basis for Social Policy,* Basic Books, 1995.

*Migrations and Cultures: A World View,* Basic Books, 1996.

Work represented in anthologies, including *Readings in the History of Economic Thought,* edited by I. H. Rima, Holt, 1970; and *Discrimination, Affirmative Action and Equal Opportunity: An Economic and Social Perspective,* edited by W. E. Block and M. A. Walker, Fraser Institute, 1982. Author of column for *Forbes* magazine, 1991—. Contributor to numerous periodicals, including *New York Times Magazine, Ethics, American Economic Review, Social Research, Education Digest, Western Review, University of Chicago Magazine, Oxford Economic Papers,* and *Economica.*

*SIDELIGHTS:* Called "a free-market economist and perhaps the leading black scholar among conservatives" by Fred Barnes of the *New York Times Book Review,* Thomas Sowell has written numerous controversial books about economics, race, and ethnic groups. His support for a laissez-faire economic system with few government constraints and his vocal opposition to most of the social programs and judicial actions favored by most other black spokespeople have made him a target for much criticism. Yet, Steven E. Plaut of *Commentary* calls Sowell "one of America's most trenchant and perceptive commentators on the subject of race relations and ethnicity." Davis Holmstrom, writing in the *Los Angeles Times,* maintains that "in the writing of economist Thomas Sowell, scholarship, clarity and genuine information come together as nicely and perfectly as a timeless quote." Because of his "insights on some of the most pressing social-science concerns of our times," according to the *Wall Street Journal*'s Joel Kotkin, Sowell is "in a very real sense, a modern successor to the kind of acute, culture-based social science epitomized by Max Weber."

Sowell has done extensive research into the economic performance of racial and ethnic groups throughout the world, trying to determine the factors which make some groups more successful than others. He has presented his research findings and the conclusions he has drawn from them in such books as *Race and Economics, American Ethnic Groups, Markets and Minorities, Ethnic America: A History, The Economics and Politics of Race: An International Perspective, Civil Rights: Rhetoric or Reality?, Migrations and Cultures,* and *Race and Culture: A World View.* These books have attempted to disprove a number of popularly held beliefs while bringing new and potentially valuable information to light. As George M. Fredrickson notes in the *New York Times Book Review,* "Sowell is engaged in a continuing polemic against the basic assumptions of liberals, radicals and civil rights leaders. But the quality of his evidence and reasoning requires that he be taken seriously. His ideological opponents will have to meet his arguments squarely and incisively to justify the kind of policies currently identified with the pursuit of racial equality and social justice."

Sowell's own life story seems to illustrate many of the values he now expounds. Born in North Carolina, Sowell attended a segregated high school where he was at the top of his class. "We never wondered why there weren't any white kids there," he tells Joseph Sobran in the *National Review.* "We never thought we'd be learning more if there *had* been white kids there. In fact, we never *thought* about white kids." A graduate of Harvard University, Columbia University, and the University of Chicago, Sowell went on to hold a number of positions in government and academia before joining the Hoover Institution in 1980. Through it all, Sobran remarks, Sowell has been "matter-of-fact about his race and its bearing on his intellectual life."

At least one critic, however, sees more personal notes in some of Sowell's writing. Scott McConnell of the *Wall Street Journal* finds *The Vision of the Anointed: Self-Congratulation as a Basis for Social Policy* to be an "uncompromising and often angry book." He posits his explanation of this display of emotion: "Mr. Sowell—a black intellectual whose prose seldom sends out even the faintest glint of ethnic references—draws from a well of both sorrow and anger when he reflects on some remarkable facts"; these facts point out that blacks either were bettering their own lives without the help of twentieth-century social policy or have actually suffered more under the auspices of social changes designed to help people, such as the prodefendant *Miranda* decision.

One of Sowell's most controversial contentions is that a racial or ethnic group's economic success is not seriously hindered by discrimination from society at large. Sowell believes that migrants bring to their new homelands their own habits and beliefs—what he calls cultural capital—and this is the determining factor in their future economic success or failure. "This is a theory," writes Thurston Clarke in the *New York Times Book Review,* "that deflates any windbag oratory about the United States being a unique land of opportunity, where migrants succeed by discarding their former culture and leaping naked into the great melting pot." Sowell cites, for instance, the case of the Italian immigrants in the United States: "'Too proud to take charity, they were not too proud do the hardest and dirtiest work spurned by others.'"

In *The Economics and Politics of Race* Sowell gives several examples of minority groups around the world who have fared well despite prejudice against them, and of other groups with little discrimination to overcome who have done poorly. The Chinese minorities in Southeast Asian countries, despite intense resistance from the native populations, have done very well economically. They often dominate their local economies. European Jews have also faced opposition from majority population groups. Yet they too have performed outstandingly well and enjoy a high level of economic success. On the other hand, Plaut gives an example of underachievement from Sowell's *The Economics and Politics of Race:* "In Brazil and other parts of South America blacks face less racism than do American blacks. . . . Yet for all this tolerance, Brazil shows a larger gap in black-white earnings, social position, and education than does the United States."

The key factor in an ethnic group's economic success, Sowell argues is "something economists refer to as human capital—values, attitudes and skills embodied in a culture," as Stanley O. Williford explains it in the *Los Angeles Times Book Review.* An ethnic or racial group which emphasizes hard work, saving money, and acquiring an education will generally do well whatever the political or social climate. *Newsweek*'s David Gelman notes that Sowell "has a conservative message to impart. Essentially, it is that diligence, discipline and entrepreneurial drive can overthrow the most formidable barriers of poverty and bigotry." Thurston Clarke in the *New York Times Book Review* points out that Sowell's assertions "will unsettle multiculturalists who believe that all cultures make equivalent contributions to human progress." Yet, according to Jacob Cohen writing in the *National Review,* in *Race and Culture* Sowell "has produced a book that will compel every careful reader, and not just those on the Left, to rethink their most confident views on matters of race and culture"; *Race and Culture* challenges both sides to rethink the effect of individual effort on economic performance.

Because of this belief in human capital, Sowell argues against continued efforts by the federal government to end racial discrimination, a problem he believes was largely eliminated during the civil rights struggle, and calls instead for a greater emphasis on free-market economics. A healthy, growing economy, Sowell believes, does the most good for minority groups who suffer from poverty. As Aaron Wildavsky writes in the *National Review,* "When labor is scarce and the markets for it are competitive, wages go up regardless of the prejudices of employers." Sowell points out in *Civil Rights: Rhetoric or Reality?* that "the economic rise of minorities preceded by many years passage of the Civil Rights Act . . . [and] that this trend was not accelerated either by that legislation or by the quotas introduced during the seventies," as Tony Eastland reports in the *American Spectator.* Sowell believes that minority groups, Chris Wall writes in the *Los Angeles Times Book Review,* are "crying racism at every turn to divert attention from the fact that their cultures or subcultures may be economically unproductive."

Sowell dismisses much of what black civil rights leaders believe necessary for the betterment of American blacks. He questions, for example, the value for black students of integrated public schools, called for by the Warren court in the case *Brown* vs. *Board of Education.* Sobran reports that Sowell finds the court's contention "that segregated schools produced inferior black education . . . expresses and justifies a destructively paternalistic attitude, according to which a black child can't learn anything except in close proximity to a white one. With forced busing, [Sowell] reflects ironically, the white man's burden has become 'the white *child's* burden—to go forth and civilize the heathen.'"

Sowell, in fact, finds grave fault with the U.S. educational system in terms of what it offers to many children other than black children, for, according to the *New Republic*'s Alan Wolfe, "American students, like their textbooks, have been 'dumbed down.'" In *Inside American Education,* Sowell makes the claim that, "'It is not merely that Johnny can't read, or even that Johnny can't think. Johnny doesn't even know what thinking is.'" As explained by Wolfe, Sowell further rails against the "therapeutic" ideology in education today—"All should be taught to appreciate themselves, even if they don't know a thing." Sowell claims that, to protect their jobs, educators simply advance "unprepared children" through the system.

Many students who diverge from the academic norm are particularly at risk. In *Inside American Education,* Sowell enumerates two such groups: bilingual students and athletes. Bilingual students cause an inflow of federal money for special education classes which, says Michael Schwartz in the *Wall Street Journal,* "creates an incentive for keeping as many students as possible in such programs for as long as possible." Thus students may be held back in these classes even when it is not in their best interest. The demands of the game may be what keeps the athlete from learning. Combined with his or her already "'sub-standard academic background,'" the athlete, writes Sowell, "'usually finds himself out on the street with no skills, no degrees, and perhaps no character.'"

Other government programs, including affirmative action racial quotas and public welfare, are also attacked by Sowell, particularly in *Inside American Education.* He maintains that black students, who would do well at second-tier educational institutions such as many state universities, may instead find themselves near the bottom of the class at Harvard or even as college dropouts. In analyzing this problem, Schwartz contends that "the administrators of these institutions [i.e., Harvard] can cheerfully pat themselves on the back for having proved numerically that they provided educational 'opportunity' to minority students." Sowell also quotes a Harvard dean as saying, "if we're driven exclusively by academic qualities, we would have a much less interesting student body." As Schwartz explains it, "It is a case of ideology over education."

Some critics of Sowell's books on education protest that his rhetoric is overinflated. John Brademas, a reviewer for the *New York Times Book Review,* maintains that in *Inside American Education* Sowell's "generalizations are so extravagant and his tone so self-righteous and bombastic that he undermines his case. He is his own worst enemy." Brademas goes on to further contend that, with regard to the challenges facing American education, Sowell "offers little constructive counsel on how to deal with them." Peter Schrag, writing in *The Nation,* calls this same book "a near-perfect inventory of what the far right is saying about our schools and colleges, some of it true enough but much of it exaggerated."

Many others, however, find this same work coherent and exact. Michael Schwartz in the *Wall Street Journal* found that *Inside American Education* "demonstrates an impressive range of knowledge and acuity of observation." Chester E. Finn, Jr., in the *National Review,* simply calls it a "splendid new book." Some of these contradictions in interpretation of the book's effectiveness come from an inherent difference between conservatives and liberals on what the role of public education should, in fact, be. Conservatives such as Sowell believe, according to the *New Republic*'s Alan Wolfe, that "the education of children is a secondary goal: serving some larger political purpose comes first." Wolfe continues, "When the schools take on so many functions other than the transmission of knowledge they inevitably become battlegrounds in ideological wars, and all who fight in these wars have a panacea, not a well-thought-out solution to the educational crisis in America."

In another work, *Preferential Policies: An International Perspective,* Sowell argues against equal opportunity hiring and admissions policies, which mandate that employers and school officials judge minority applicants by different, more relaxed, criteria than they judge other applicants. Sowell believes that these policies result in less-qualified candidates gaining preferential treatment over better-qualified candidates and eventually lower the standards by which all individuals are measured. Citing examples from such countries as Sri Lanka, Nigeria, and India, as well as the United States, Sowell contends that preferential policies can be found around the globe.

Adolph L. Reed, Jr., reviewing *Preferential Policies* in the *Washington Post Book World,* found Sowell's thesis unconvincing, stating that "the relation between his examples and his underlying argument—that preferential policies undermine their own objectives and cause more problems then they resolve—is tortured and unconvincing." Andrew Hacker, however, in the *New York Times Book Review,* found that Sowell does make an important point about the effect of these policies, namely that "those who lose out [to preferential policies] are generally lower-middle-class candidates, who adhered to the rules and find themselves displaced by others deemed entitled to exemptions." He added, "Whether in fire departments or on campuses, groups at the end of the queue are being played off against one another—hardly the best way to promote racial amity."

In fact, Sowell is convinced, Nathan Glazer writes in the *New Republic,* "that hardly anything government will do can help blacks and other minorities with high levels of poverty and low levels of educational and economic achievement, and that almost anything government will do will only make matters worse." In a *Choice* review of *Civil Rights,* R. J. Steamer admits that "Sowell's revolutionary view—that government programs such as affirmative action, forced busing, and food stamps will not bring the disadvantaged black minority into the economic and social mainstream and might better be abandoned—will anger many." One such angered critic is Gelman, who claims that Sowell "seems to fault blacks for resting on their grievances instead of climbing aboard the success wagon." But Sowell sees government programs and those who call for them as part of a self-destructive mind-set. The black civil rights establishment, Sowell believes, "represents a thin layer of privileged blacks who have risen socially by echoing liberal ideology, with its view of blacks in general as helpless victims who depend on political favors for whatever gains they can make," Sobran explains.

The consistent differences between Sowell's views and those of other black commentators, and the differences between those of the political left and right, moved Sowell to examine the underlying assumptions that create this dichotomy. In *A Conflict of Visions: Ideological Origins of Political Struggle,* he describes "two divergent views of man and society that he convincingly contends underlie many of the political, economic and social clashes of the last two centuries and remain very much with us today," as Walter Goodman of the *New York Times* explains. Sowell posits the unconstrained and the constrained views of man. "The unconstrained see human beings as perfectible," Otto Friedrich of *Time* writes, "the constrained as forever flawed." Sowell writes in the book that "the constrained vision is a tragic vision of the human condition. The unconstrained vision is a moral vision of human intentions."

These two visions are, Daniel Seligman writes in *Fortune,* "the mind-sets that originally made [intellectuals] gravitate to some ideas instead of others." Those with an unconstrained view of man, for example, tend to believe that social problems can be ultimately solved, and that man will usually act rationally. Such beliefs can lead to social engineering efforts to correct perceived societal ills. Those with a constrained view of man see him as imperfect and human nature as unchanging. They often call for a limited government, a strong defense, and strict criminal penalties.

Sowell admits that not all people hold to one or the other vision consistently. And such ideologies as Marxism and fascism are compounds of both the constrained and unconstrained visions. Yet, critics see much of value in Sowell's plan. "Right or wrong in his main thesis," Sobran states, "he is full of stunning insights." "The split between the constrained and the unconstrained," Barnes notes, "works as a framework for understanding social theories and politics." Goodman finds that *A Conflict of Visions* "does lay out styles of thinking that we can readily recognize today in the divisions between left and right." And Michael Harrington, who explains in his *Washington Post Book World* review that "I reject the basic assumptions and the very intellectual framework" of the book, nonetheless concludes that "its insights and *apercus* reveal a serious mind honestly and fairly . . . trying to grapple with those visionary premises on which our supposedly objective data are so often based and ordered."

Sowell further expands upon the idea of the liberal vision in *The Vision of the Anointed.* The "anointed," Sowell argues in this book, are the people who view the world as a place where "criminals can be 'rehabilitated,' irresponsible mothers taught 'parenting skills,' and where all sorts of other social problems can be 'solved.'" Sowell contrasts the vision of these liberals with the realization of the conservatives "that liberal schemes to eradicate these evils a) never work, and b) inevitably impose huge social costs of their own," writes Robert P. George in the *National Review.* Sowell maintains that the anointed have, in fact, caused damage to the social policy of America, particularly because their "*prevailing* vision" is taken as true even without empirical evidence to prove this to be so.

Richard Epstein, writing in the *New York Times Book Review,* points out that *The Vision of the Anointed* stops before political shifts that seem to have taken power away from the liberals. "Sowell . . . surely has given voice to many of [the new American political majority's] longstanding frustration," writes Epstein. "It is too bad that he has overstated his case and failed to suppress his obvious enmity toward his intellectual and political targets. Mr. Sowell has written an important and incisive book, even with its flaws. But with a bit more moderation at the margin, he could have written a better one still."

During his career as a leading black economist, Sowell "has spoken out often, with considerable force and eloquence, against many of the assumptions about black life in the United States that are widely held by the black leadership and its white allies," Jonathan Yardley reports in the *Washington Post Book World.* His arguments are beginning to attract converts the black community. As Glazer notes, "One has the impression that increasingly he is heeded, that this unbending analyst is having a greater influence on the discussion of matters of race and ethnicity than any other writer of the past ten years." Harrington, a socialist who admits that he is "utterly at odds" with Sowell's political beliefs, still calls him "one of the few conservative thinkers in America today who is interesting as a theorist."

*BIOGRAPHICAL/CRITICAL SOURCES:*

*BOOKS*

Sowell, Thomas, *Civil Rights: Rhetoric or Reality?,* Morrow, 1985.
Sowell, *A Conflict of Visions: Ideological Origins of Political Struggles,* Morrow, 1987.

*PERIODICALS*

*American Political Science Review,* June, 1991.
*American Spectator,* July 1984; November, 1990; October, 1995, p. 75.
*Book World.* April 7, 1996.
*Change,* January, 1990.
*Choice,* September, 1984; November, 1990.
*Commentary,* December, 1983; September, 1996, p. 78.
*Commonweal,* January 13, 1995, p. 22.
*Foreign Affairs,* Volume 70, number 3, 1991.
*Fortune,* March 16, 1987; February 13, 1989.
*Library Journal,* March 1, 1996, p. 91.
*Los Angeles Times,* March 22, 1985.
*Los Angeles Times Book Review,* September 6, 1981; January 8, 1984.
*Nation,* May 10, 1993, p. 638.
*National Review,* October 16, 1981; February 13, 1987; June 25, 1990; February 15, 1993, p. 49; November 7, 1994, p. 69; October 23, 1995, p. 52; November 25, 1996, p. 65.
*New Republic,* November 21, 1983; June 11, 1984; February 8, 1993, p. 25.
*Newsweek,* August 24, 1981.
*New York Review of Books,* October 12, 1989; January 12, 1995, p. 29.
*New York Times,* January 24, 1987.
*New York Times Book Review,* October 16, 1983; January 25, 1987; July 1, 1990; March 28, 1993, p. 11; November 27, 1994, p. 28; July 30, 1995, p. 6; June 2, 1996, p. 9.
*Publishers Weekly,* April 27, 1990; February 19, 1996, p. 195.
*Time,* March 16, 1987.
*Times Literary Supplement,* September 22, 1995, p. 10.
*Wall Street Journal,* September 25, 1989; February 12, 1993; July 22, 1994; July 28, 1995, p. A9.
*Washington Monthly,* June, 1990.
*Washington Post Book World,* April 29, 1984; January 4, 1987; September 9, 1990; April 7, 1996, p. 4.
*Wilson Quarterly,* Volume 14, number 3, 1990.*

* * *

**SPICER, Bart 1918-**
**(Jay Barbette, a joint pseudonym)**

*PERSONAL:* Born in 1918 in Richmond, VA; married Betty Coe (a writer).

*CAREER:* Freelance writer. Worked as journalist and radio writer; in public relations for Universal Military Training. Formerly associated with Scripps-Howard Syndicate and World Affairs Council. *Military service:* U.S. Army; served in the South Pacific; became captain.

*WRITINGS:*

*NOVELS*

*The Dark Light,* Dodd (New York City), 1949.
*Blues for the Prince,* Dodd, 1950.
*Black Sheep, Run,* Dodd, 1951.
*The Golden Door,* Dodd, 1951.
*The Long Green,* Dodd, 1952, published as *Shadow of Fear,* Collins (London), 1953.
*The Wild Ohio,* Dodd, 1953.
*The Taming of Carney Wilde,* Dodd, 1954.
*The Day of the Dead,* Dodd, 1955.
*The Tall Captains,* Dodd, 1957.

*Brother to the Enemy,* Dodd, 1958.
*Exit, Running,* Dodd, 1959.
*The Day before Thunder,* Dodd, 1960.
*Act of Anger,* Atheneum (New York City), 1962.
*The Burned Man,* Atheneum, 1966.
*Kellogg Junction,* Atheneum, 1969.
*Festival,* Atheneum, 1970.
*The Adversary,* Putnam (New York City), 1974.

*WITH WIFE, BETTY COE SPICER, UNDER JOINT PSEUDONYM JAY BARBETTE*

*Final Copy,* Dodd (London), 1950.
*Dear Dead Days,* Dodd, 1953, published as *Death's Long Shadow,* Bantam (New York City), 1955.
*The Deadly Doll,* Dodd, 1958.
*Look Behind You,* Dodd, 1960.

*OTHER*

Translations of Spicer's books have been published in France, Germany, Spain, Sweden, Denmark, Norway, the Netherlands, Japan, Italy, Yugoslavia, and the Soviet Union.

*ADAPTATIONS:* Spicer's novels have been adapted for television.

*SIDELIGHTS:* Bart Spicer began his writing career in the late 1940s as a writer of hardboiled mystery novels in the tradition of Raymond Chandler and Dashiell Hammett. In the 1960s he turned to writing suspense novels aimed, as Art Scott notes in the *St. James Guide to Crime and Mystery Writers,* "at the bestseller market rather than the specialized mystery readership." In both genres, Spicer has earned a considerable reputation for his work.

Spicer's hardboiled mysteries feature the character Carney Wilde, a Philadelphia private detective whose cases take him throughout the United States and often involve neglected sections of society. In the novel *Blues for the Prince,* for example, Wilde investigates a murder among the jazz crowd. The critic for the *New York Herald Tribune Book Review* claims that Spicer does an "excellent job . . . showing the relationship between whites and Negroes both in the unbiased world of jazz and the more deeply biased outside world." The reviewer for *Saturday Review of Literature* finds that "devotees of jazz and blues should find it extra interesting."

Scott notes that "the Wilde books are beautifully crafted. Spicer's plotting is coherent, with credible twists and surprises; his style strikes a satisfying balance between the telegraphic and the over-ripe; he writes convincing dialogue and makes imaginative use of the 'hard-boiled simile.' Wilde himself is an admirable, believable hero, not the formularized caricature that can be found in too many tough-guy series of the period. Wilde's first-person narration flows smoothly, steering clear of both excessive wisecrackery and windy philosophizing. The secondary characters, continuing and otherwise, are varied and interesting (Spicer's treatment of the cops, and Wilde's relations with them, is particularly good), and the settings are fresh."

In the 1960s Spicer began to explore other types of fiction, including courtroom drama. In *Act of Anger,* Spicer follows the murder trial of a young Mexican-American accused of killing a wealthy gay in the desert of New Mexico. V. P. Hass in the *Chicago Sunday Tribune,* although finding the book to contain some unnecessarily strong scenes, calls it "compelling courtroom fiction." Martin Levin in the *New York Times Book Review* judges Spicer to be "a capable narrator with an interesting view of this particular murder, which he translates into an exciting denouement." William Hogan in the *San Francisco Chronicle* ranks *Act of Anger* above *Anatomy of a Murder,* another popular courtroom drama of the time. "*Act of Anger,*" writes Hogan, "is by a professional. . . . It is in every sense above-average entertainment."

Scott concludes that all of Spicer's writing has displayed a "fine prose style, sharp eye for detail and characterization, and overall high marks as fictional entertainment."

*BIOGRAPHICAL/CRITICAL SOURCES:*

*BOOKS*

*St. James Guide to Crime and Mystery Writers,* fourth edition, St. James Press (Detroit), 1996.

*PERIODICALS*

*Chicago Sunday Tribune,* August 12, 1962, p. 3.
*New York Herald Tribune Book Review,* June 4, 1950, p. 15.
*New York Times,* November 18, 1951, p. 50; March 30, 1952, p. 34; March 21, 1954, p. 23; March 6, 1955, p. 23; November 23, 1958, p. 50.
*New York Times Book Review,* October 11, 1959, p. 30; September 9, 1962, p. 42.

*San Francisco Chronicle,* August 7, 1962, p. 31.
*Saturday Review of Literature,* May 20, 1950, p. 36.
*Springfield Republican,* January 18, 1959, p. 4D.

* * *

**STEIN, Joseph 1912-**

*PERSONAL:* Born May 30, 1912, in New York, NY; son of Charles and Emma (Rosenblum) Stein; married Sadie Singer (died, 1974); married Elisa Loti (a psychotherapist, former actress), 1976; children: Daniel, Harry, Joshua; step-children: John, Jenny Lyn. *Education:* City College (now City College of the City University of New York), B.S.S., 1935; Columbia University, M.S.W., 1937.

*ADDRESSES: Office*—1130 Park Avenue, New York, NY 10128; fax 212-410-3458. *Agent*—Paramuse Artists, 1414 Avenue of the Americas, New York, NY 10019.

*CAREER:* Playwright. Psychiatric social worker, 1939-45; writer for radio, television, and stage, beginning 1946, including work for radio's "Henry Morgan Show" and "Kraft Music Hall," and television's "Your Show of Shows," "Sid Caesar Show," and others.

*MEMBER:* Dramatists Guild of the Authors League of America; Executive Council of Dramatists Guild.

*AWARDS, HONORS:* Antoinette Perry (Tony) Award of American Theater Wing for best musical, New York Drama Critics Award, and Newspaper Guild Award, all 1965, all for *Fiddler on the Roof;* Tony Award nomination for best musical, 1969, for *Zorba,* and 1987, for *Rags;* Lawerence Oliver award nomination, 1989, for *The Baker's Wife.*

*WRITINGS:*

*PLAYS*

(With Will Glickman) *Lend an Ear,* produced in New York City at National Theatre, 1948.

(With Glickman) *Mrs. Gibbons' Boys* (produced on Broadway at Music Box Theatre, 1949), Samuel French (New York City), 1958.

(With Glickman) *Alive and Kicking,* produced on Broadway at Winter Garden Theatre, 1950.

(With Glickman) *Inside U.S.A.,* produced in New York City at Century Theatre, 1951.

(With Glickman) *Plain and Fancy* (produced on Broadway at Mark Hellinger Theatre, 1955), Random House (New York City), 1955.

(With Glickman) *Mr. Wonderful* (produced on Broadway at Broadway Theatre, 1956), Hart Stenographic Bureau, 1956.

(With Glickman) *The Body Beautiful* (produced on Broadway at Broadway Theatre, 1958), Samuel French (New York City), 1958.

*Juno* (based on Sean O'Casey's play *Juno and the Paycock;* produced on Broadway at Winter Garden Theatre, 1959), Hart Stenographic Bureau, 1959.

(With Robert Russell) *Take Me Along,* produced on Broadway at Shubert Theatre, 1959.

*Enter Laughing* (based on the autobiography by Carl Reiner; produced on Broadway at Henry Miller's Theatre, 1963), Samuel French (New York City), 1963, reprinted, 1984; film version produced by Columbia, 1967.

*Fiddler on the Roof* (based on short stories by Sholom Aleichem; produced on Broadway at Imperial Theatre, 1964; film version produced by United Artists, 1971), Crown (New York City), 1965.

*Zorba* (based on Nikos Kazantzakis' book *Zorba the Greek;* produced on Broadway at Imperial Theatre, 1968), Random House (New York City), 1969.

(With Hugh Wheeler and others) *Irene,* produced on Broadway at Minskoff Theatre, 1973.

*King of Hearts* (based on the film of the same name), produced on Broadway at Minskoff Theatre, 1978.

(With Alan Jay Lerner) *Carmelina* (based on the film *Buona Sera, Mrs. Campbell*), produced on Broadway at St. James Theatre, April, 1979.

*The Baker's Wife* (based on a 1937 French film), produced in New York at York Theatre Company, 1985; produced in London at Phoenix Theatre, 1989.

*Before the Dawn* (adaptation of the play *A Ladies' Tailor* by Aleksandr Borshchagovsky), produced in New York at American Place Theatre, 1985.

*Rags,* produced on Broadway at Mark Hellinger Theatre, 1986.

*SIDELIGHTS:* Playwright Joseph Stein told *CA:* "I, in a career that spans four decades, have been connected with some of Broadway's biggest hits (*Fiddler on the Roof, Zorba, Enter Laughing, Take Me Along,* etc.) as well as some major disappointments, notably the musical *Rags.*

"My work deals largely with the relationships and emotional drives of basic, unsophisticated 'simple' people . . . (the Jews of the Russian 'shtetl' in *Fiddler on the Roof;* the Greek peasants of *Zorba;* the Amish of *Plain and Fancy;* the poor Dubliners of *Juno;* the immigrants of *Rags;* the French country folk of *The Baker's Wife,* etc.) their conflicts, their struggles, their romances. My tone is generally warm-hearted, affectionate and laced with humor.

"Ironically, both my major success, *Fiddler on the Roof,* which continues to play all over the world, and perhaps my major disappointment, *Rags,* dealt with the Jewish experience, and in a sense, followed each other chronologically. As *Fiddler on the Roof* ended with the central characters leaving for America, *Rags* opens with the central characters arriving on these shores.

"Although *Fiddler on the Roof* had some difficulty getting produced (there was much concern that it would only appeal to a narrow ethnic audience) it subsequent history was most successful. *Rags,* on the other hand, was felled at the outset by a negative review by New York's principal critic. The cast, including its leading player, the opera star Teresa Stratas, were so enthusiastic about the show that they all offered to defer their salaries to keep it open, and after the closing curtain, they paraded down Broadway, together with the audience, chanting 'Keep *Rags* open!'. But it was not to be; the producers had run out of funds.

"However, *Rags* was subsequently revived Off-Broadway to a very favorable reaction, and it continues to play in regional theaters with considerable success.

*BIOGRAPHICAL/CRITICAL SOURCES:*

*BOOKS*

Guernsey, Otis L., Jr., editor, *Broadway Song and Story: Playwrights/Lyricists/Composers Discuss Their Hits,* Dodd, Mead, 1986.

*PERIODICALS*

*New York Times,* April 10, 1979; April 22, 1979; March 25, 1985; August 17, 1986; August 22, 1986; September 21, 1986.

*Washington Post,* March 4, 1979; April 22, 1979.

## STEINER, Wendy 1949-

*PERSONAL:* Born March 20, 1949, in Winnipeg, Manitoba, Canada; came to the United States in 1970; daughter of William Harrison (an educational psychologist) and Ida (Abramson) Lucow; married Peter Steiner (a professor of Slavic language and literature), February 2, 1973. *Education:* McGill University, B.A., 1970; Yale University, M.Phil., 1972, Ph.D., 1974.

*ADDRESSES: Office*—Department of English, University of Pennsylvania, Philadelphia, PA 19104.

*CAREER:* Yale University, New Haven, CT, assistant professor of English, 1974-76; University of Michigan, Ann Arbor, assistant professor of English, 1976-79; University of Pennsylvania, Philadelphia, assistant professor, 1979-82, professor of English, 1982—. Member of several committees; lecturer.

*MEMBER:* Academy of Literary Studies, Modern Language Association of America, Semiotic Society of America (member of executive board, 1978-80).

*AWARDS, HONORS:* Woodrow Wilson fellowship, 1970-71; doctoral fellowships, Yale University, 1970-74, and Canada Council, 1971-74; Rackham research fellowship, University of Michigan, 1977; Josephine Nevins Keale fellowship, University of Michigan, 1978-79; National Endowment for the Humanities research stipend, 1980; research fellowship, University of Pennsylvania, 1981.

*WRITINGS:*

(Translator from the French) Jan Mukarovsky, *Structure, Sign and Function,* Yale University Press (New Haven, CT), 1977.

*Exact Resemblance to Exact Resemblance: The Literary Portraiture of Gertrude Stein,* Yale University Press, 1978.

(Translator from the Czech with husband, Peter Steiner) *Selected Writings of Roman Jakobson,* Volume V, Mouton (Hawthorne, NY), 1979.

(Editor) *The Sign in Music and Literature,* University of Texas Press (Austin), 1981.

(Editor) *Image and Code,* Michigan Studies in the Humanities, 1981.

(Translator from the French) Sergej Karcevskii, *The Prague School: Selected Writings, 1929-1946,* University of Texas Press, 1982.

*The Colors of Rhetoric: Problems in the Relation between Modern Literature and Painting,* University of Chicago Press (Chicago), 1982.

(Author of introduction) Gertrude Stein, *Lectures in America,* Beacon Press (Boston), 1985.

*Pictures of Romance: Form against Context in Painting and Literature,* University of Chicago Press, 1988.

*The Scandal of Pleasure: Art in an Age of Fundamentalism,* University of Chicago Press, 1995.

*CONTRIBUTOR*

(With P. Steiner) Jan Mukarovsky, *On Poetic Language,* [Lisse, Netherlands], 1976.

R. W. Baily and others, editors, *The Sign: Semiotics around the World,* Michigan Studies in the Humanities, 1978.

Andre Helbo, editor, *Le Champ semiologique,* Le Creuset (Brussels, Belgium), 1979.

John Odmark, editor, *Linguistic and Literary Studies in Eastern Europe,* Walter Benjamins, 1979.

Karl Menges and Daniel Rancour-Laferriere, editors, *Axia,* Akademischer Verlag Stuttgart, 1981.

Miroslav Cervenka and others, editors, *The Structure of the Literary Process,* John Benjamins (Philadelphia), 1982.

*Andres Serrano, Works 1983-1993,* Institute of Contemporary Art, University of Pennsylvania (Philadelphia), 1994.

Contributor to journals, including *New Literary History, Critical Inquiry, Semiotica, Poetics-Today,* and *Yale University Library Gazette.*

*WORK IN PROGRESS: Storied Pictures: Narrativity in Literature and Painting;* contributing to Volume V of *The Cambridge History of American Literature;* contributing to *Columbia Literary History of the United States.*

*SIDELIGHTS:* Into the center of the often rancorous debate about art in the public sphere comes Wendy Steiner, a professor of English at the University of Pennsylvania and semiotician, and her book *The Scandal of Pleasure: Art in an Age of Fundamentalism.* Steiner sees art under attack from a host of quarters, on the right and on the left, in the halls of Congress and the halls of academe. She finds examples of these attacks in "a deconstructionist critic 'steeled against the pleasures of art' or Islamic fundamentalists who could not stand Salman Rushdie's 'wicked fun,'" observes Andrew Delbanco in the *New York Times Book Review.* And, as Pat C. Hoy points out in the *Sewanee Review,* "She is as critical of the liberal left (Catherine MacKinnon and Andrea Dworkin) as she is of the conservative right (Jesse Helms and Alfonse D'Amato), and she shows us how at various times their 'literalism' becomes indistinguishable." Ultimately "what disturbs Ms. Steiner . . . are [these] unimaginative responses to works of the imagination," explains Delbanco.

In this context, *The Scandal of Pleasure* stands as "a stimulating book," in the view of Delbanco, one which combines "moderation with passion." The reviewer adds that the book represents "a splendid rebuttal of those on the left and right who think that the pleasures induced by art are trivial or dangerous. Indeed, Ms. Steiner has written one of the most powerful defenses of the potentiality of art that I have read in a long time." In taking on the extremes, Steiner also offers those in the middle—a public confused into not knowing what to think about art or into fearing it—a way to put art in perspective. She shows, according to Alan Wolfe in *Commonweal,* that "culture liberates us from literalism. Art gives pleasure, and if each person's pleasure is different from others, so be it, for there is no expertise where aesthetic appreciation is concerned." He adds that in Steiner's view, "Art stretches the mind, not for a particular purpose, but because human beings come with minds that crave being stretched."

With this appreciation of the purpose of art in mind, Steiner also argues that there is no reason for the public to fear the negative effects of art. "Ms. Steiner believes that art provokes but does not coerce," observes Delbanco, "that its pleasure is sensuous but mediated by the viewer's judgment: this is why 'we will not be led into fascism or rape or child abuse or racial oppression through esthetic experience.'" Wolfe concludes, "Not only does [*The Scandal of Pleasure*] represent the reality of our culture wars with uncommon good sense, but is also an aesthetic pleasure in its own right. When she sticks to art, Steiner reminds us of the treasures the culture war is taking away from us."

*BIOGRAPHICAL/CRITICAL SOURCES:*

*PERIODICALS*

*American Spectator,* March, 1996, p. 66.

*Art in America,* April, 1996, p. 37.

*Commonweal,* April 5, 1996, p. 28.

*Insight on the News,* February 19, 1996, p. 31.

*Journal of Aesthetics and Art Criticism,* winter, 1989, p. 91

*Los Angeles Times Book Review,* December 14, 1995, p. 8.
*New Statesman and Society,* February 2, 1996, p. 37.
*New York Times,* December 26, 1995, p. C19.
*New York Times Book Review,* December 31, 1995, p. 6.
*Quarterly Journal of Speech,* November 1989, p. 475.
*Sewanee Review,* April, 1996, p. 330.*

* * *

**STREET, Jay**
**See SLESAR, Henry**

* * *

**STUART, Ian**
**See MacLEAN, Alistair (Stuart)**

* * *

**SWENSON, May 1919-1989**

*PERSONAL:* Born May 28, 1919, in Logan, UT; died December 4, 1989, in Ocean View, DE, (some sources say Bethany Beach, DE or Salisbury, MD); daughter of Dan Arthur (a teacher) and Anna M. (Helberg) Swenson. *Education:* Utah State University, B.A., 1939.

*CAREER:* Poet, 1949-89. Formerly worked as an editor for New Directions, New York City; writer in residence at Purdue University, West Lafayette, IN, 1966-67, University of North Carolina, 1968-69 and 1974, Lothbridge University, Alberta, Canada, 1970, and University of California, Riverside, 1976. Lectured and gave readings at more than fifty American universities and colleges, as well as at the New York YM-YWHA Poetry Center, and San Francisco Poetry Center. Conductor of workshops at University of Indiana Writers Conference and Bread Loaf Writers Conference, Vermont. Participant at the Yaddo and MacDowell colonies for writers.

*MEMBER:* Academy of American Poets (Chancellor, 1980), American Academy and Institute of Arts and Letters.

*AWARDS, HONORS:* Poetry Introductions Prize, 1955; Robert Frost Poetry Fellowship for Bread Loaf Writers' Conference, 1957; Guggenheim fellowship, 1959; William Rose Benet Prize of the Poetry Society of America, 1959; Longview Foundation award, 1959; National Institute of Arts and Letters award, 1960; Amy Lowell Travelling Scholarship, 1960; Ford Foundation grant, 1964; Brandeis University Creative Arts Award, 1967; Rockefeller Writing fellowship, 1967; Distinguished Service Medal of Utah State University, 1967; Lucy Martin Donnelly Award of Bryn Mawr College, 1968; Shelley Poetry Award, 1968; National Endowment for the Arts Grant, 1977; National Book Award nomination, 1978, for *New and Selected Things Taking Place;* Academy of American Poets fellowship, 1979; Bollingen Poetry Award, 1981; MacArthur Award, 1987; National Book Critics Circle award nomination (poetry), 1987, for *In Other Words.* Honorary degrees from Utah State University, 1987.

*WRITINGS:*

*POETRY*

*Another Animal,* Scribner, 1954.
*A Cage of Spines,* Rinehart, 1958.
*To Mix With Time: New and Selected Poems,* Scribner, 1963.
*Poems to Solve* (for children "14-up"), Scribner, 1966.
*Half Sun Half Sleep* (new poems and her translations of six Swedish poets), Scribner, 1967.
*Iconographs* (includes "Feel Me"), Scribner, 1970.
*More Poems to Solve,* Scribner, 1971.
(Translator with Leif Sjoberg) *Windows and Stones, Selected Poems of Tomas Transtromer* (translated from Swedish), University of Pittsburgh Press, 1972.
*New and Selected Things Taking Place* (includes "Ending"), Little, Brown, 1978.
*In Other Words,* Knopf, 1988.
*The Centaur,* illustrated by Barry Moser, Macmillan (New York), 1994.
*Nature: Poems Old And New,* Houghton Mifflin (Boston), 1994.
*May Out West,* Utah State University Press (Logan), 1996.

*PLAYS*

*The Floor* (one-act), first produced under the program title *Doubles and Opposites* in New York at American Place Theater, May 11, 1966, on a triple bill with "23 Pat O'Brien Movies," by Bruce Jay Friedman, and "Miss Pete," by Andrew Glaze.

*CONTRIBUTOR*

*A Treasury of Great Poems,* edited by Louis Untermeyer, Simon & Schuster, 1955.
*New Poets 2,* Ballantine, 1957.
*New Poets of England & America,* edited by Donald Hall, Robert Pack, and Louis Simpson, Meridian, 1957.
*A Country in the Mind,* edited by Ray B. West, Angel Island Publications, 1962.
*Twentieth-Century American Poetry,* edited by Conrad Aiken, Modern Library, 1963.
*100 American Poems of the Twentieth Century,* Harcourt, 1963.
*The Modern Poets,* edited by John Malcolm Brinnin and Bill Read, McGraw, 1963.
*The New Modern Poetry,* edited by M. L. Rosenthal, Macmillan, 1967.

*OTHER*

Works represented in other anthologies. Poems also included in translation in anthologies published in Italy and Germany. Contributor of poetry, stories, and criticism to *Poetry, Nation, Saturday Review, Atlantic, Harper's, New Yorker, Southern Review, Hudson Review,* and other periodicals. Swenson's work is included in the sound recording *Today's Poets: Their Poems, Their Voices,* Volume 2, Scholastic Records, 1968, and recordings for the Library of Congress, Spoken Arts Records, Folkways Records, and others. Her poems have been set to music by Otto Leuning, Howard Swanson, Emerson Meyers, Joyce McKeel, Claudio Spies, Lester Trimble, and Warren Benson.

*SIDELIGHTS:* During her prolific career, May Swenson received numerous literary-award prizes and nominations for her poetry. Often experimental in both form and appearance, her poems earned her widespread critical acclaim. As Priscilla Long comments in *The Women's Review of Books,* "Swenson was a visionary poet, a prodigious observer of the fragile and miraculous natural world."

Swenson's poetry has been praised for its imagery, which is alternately precise and beguiling, and for the quality of her personal and imaginative observations. In addition, her poetry "exhibits . . . her continuing alertness to the liveliness of nature. Correspondences among all life forms pour from her work, confirming that nothing is meaningless. The universe's basic beauty and balance is the stuff and soul of her poems," Eloise Klein Healy observes in the *Los Angeles Times.*

Richard Howard emphasizes in a *Tri-Quarterly* review that Swenson's enterprise is "to get out of herself and into those larger, warmer energies of earth, and to do so by liturgical means." Howard writes: "When May Swenson, speaking in her thaumaturgical fashion of poetry, says that 'attention to the silence in between is the amulet that makes it work,' we are reminded, while on other occasions in her work we are reassured, that there is a kind of poetry, as there used to be a kind of love, which dares not speak its name." Thus Swenson's "orphic cadences," her "siren-songs, with their obsessive reliance on the devices of incantation," are the means by which she seeks to "discover runes, the conjurations by which she can not only apostrophize the hand, the cat and the cloud in their innominate otherness, but by which she can, in some essential and relieving way, become them, leave her own impinging selfhood in the paralyzed region where names are assigned, and assume instead the energies of natural process."

In *Book Week,* Chad Walsh notes: "In most of Miss Swenson's poems the sheer thingness of things is joyfully celebrated." Walsh calls her "the poet par excellence of sights and colors." Stephen Stepanchev, author of *American Poetry since 1945,* agrees that Swenson's "distinction is that she is able to make . . . her reader see clearly what he has merely looked at before." Stepanchev, however, is one of the few critics to find her poems less than completely effective. "Miss Swenson," he writes, "works in a free verse that is supple but rather prosaic, despite her picturemaking efforts."

Howard, writing of Swenson's development as a poet, states that "from the first . . . Swenson has practiced, in riddles, chants, hex-signs and a whole panoply of invented sortilege unwonted in Western poetry since the Witch of Endor brought up Samuel, the ways not only of summoning Being into her grasp, but of getting herself out of that grasp and into alien shapes, into those emblems of power most often identified with the sexual." Of the more recent poems, Howard writes: "They are the witty, resigned poems of a woman . . . eager still to manipulate the phenomenal world by magic, but so possessed, now, of the means of her identity that the ritual, spellbinding, litaneutical elements of her art, have grown consistent with her temporal, conditioned, suffering experience and seem—to pay her the highest compliment she could care to receive—no more than natural."

Reviewing *Half Sun Half Sleep, New York Times Book Review* contributor Karl Shapiro writes: "[Swenson's] concentration on the verbal equivalent of experience is so true, so often brilliant, that one watches her with hope and pleasure, praying for victory all the way." In a *Poetry* review of *Half Sun Half Sleep,* William Stafford says of this collection: "No one today is more deft and lucky in discovering a poem than May Swenson. Her work often appears to be proceeding calmly, just descriptive and accurate; but then suddenly it opens into something that looms beyond the material, something that impends and implies. . . . So graceful is the progression in her poems that they launch confidently into any form, carrying through it to easy, apt variations. Often her way is to define things, but the definitions have a stealthy trend; what she chooses and the way she progresses heap upon the reader a consistent, incremental effect." And Shapiro offers this analysis of Swenson's achievement in this book: "The whole volume is an album of experiments . . . that pay off. It is strange to see the once-radical *carmen figuratum,* the calligraphic poem, spatial forms, imagist and surreal forms—all the heritage of the early years of the century—being used with such ease and unselfconsciousness."

Swenson herself wrote that the experience of poetry is "based in a craving to get through the curtains of things as they *appear,* to things as they are, and then into the larger, wilder space of things as they *are becoming.* This ambition involves a paradox: an instinctive belief in the senses as exquisite tools for this investigation and, at the same time, a suspicion about their crudeness." Swenson also noted: "The poet, tracing the edge of a great shadow whose outline shifts and varies, proving there is an invisible moving source of light behind, hopes (naively, in view of his ephemerality) to reach and touch the foot of that solid whatever-it-is that casts the shadow. If sometimes it seems he does touch it, it is only to be faced with a more distant, even less accessible mystery. Because all is movement—all is breathing change."

Among the "strategies and devices, the shamanism and sorcery this poet deploys," as Howard admiringly describes them, is Swenson's use of the riddle in *Poems to Solve.* The book may be enjoyed by both children and adults; the poems here are another serious attempt to accommodate "the mystery that only when a thing is apprehended as something else can it be known as itself." Swenson wrote of these poems: "It is essential, of course, with a device such as this to make not a riddle-pretending-to-be-a-poem but a poem that is also, and as if incidentally, a riddle—a solvable one. The aim is not to mystify or mislead but to clarify and make recognizable through the reader's own uncontaminated perceptions."

*Nature: Poems Old and New,* published four years after Swenson's death, emphasizes Swenson's sympathy for and identification with the outdoors. "Swenson was an unrelentingly lyrical poet," writes Priscilla Long in the *Women's Review of Books,* "a master of the poetic line in which similar sounds accumulate and resonate so that the poem exists, beyond its meanings, as a rattle or a music box, or, in moments of greatness, a symphony." Her collection *Nature* is "so inward, independent, and intense, so intimate and impersonal at once," declares critic Langdon Hammer in the *Yale Review,* that "it has been difficult to place in the field of contemporary poetry." Several other critics, however, identify the work as an appreciation of Swenson's profound talent, collecting the best of her work between two covers. "The poetry thinks, feels, examines," asserts a *Publishers Weekly* contributor; "it's patiently, meticulously sensuous, and adventurously varied in form, much as nature is." "These poems, harvested from her life's work and arranged in this delightful format," states Rochelle Natt in the *American Book Review,* "promote a lasting vision of Swenson's valuable contribution to American poetry."

*BIOGRAPHICAL/CRITICAL SOURCES:*

*BOOKS*

Brinnin, John Malcolm, and Bill Read, editors, *The Modern Poets,* McGraw, 1963.

*Contemporary Literary Criticism,* Gale, Volume 4, 1975; Volume 14, 1980, Volume 61, 1990.

*Contemporary Poets,* St. Martin's Press, 1980.

Deutsch, Babette, editor, *Poetry in Our Time,* 2nd edition, Doubleday, 1963.

*Dictionary of Literary Biography,* Volume 5: *American Poets since World War II,* Gale, 1980.

Hoffman, Daniel, editor, *The Harvard Guide to American Writing,* Belknap Press, 1977.
Nemerov, Howard, editor, *Poets on Poetry,* Basic Books, 1966.
*Poems for Young Readers: Selections from Their Own Writing by Poets Attending the Houston Festival of Contemporary Poetry,* National Council of Teachers of English, 1966.
Stepanchev, Stephen, *American Poetry Since 1945,* Harper, 1965.
Untermeyer, Louis, editor, *A Treasury of Great Poems, English and American,* Simon & Schuster, 1955.

*PERIODICALS*

*American Book Review,* September, 1995, p. 14.
*Atlantic,* February, 1968.
*Booklist,* June 1, 1993.
*Book Week,* June 4, 1967, Volume 4, number 30.
*Christian Science Monitor,* February 12, 1979.
*Los Angeles Times,* March 22, 1979.
*New York Times,* March 19, 1979; June 16, 1987.
*New York Times Book Review,* September 1, 1963; May 7, 1967; February 11, 1979; June 12, 1988; January 19, 1992.
*Poetry,* December, 1967; February, 1979; February, 1993.
*Prairie Schooner,* spring, 1968.
*Publishers Weekly,* May 30, 1994, pp. 46-47.
*Tri-Quarterly,* fall, 1966.
*Women's Review of Books,* January, 1995, pp. 8-9.
*Yale Review,* January, 1995, pp. 121-41.

*OBITUARIES:*

*PERIODICALS*

*Chicago Tribune,* December 10, 1989.
*Los Angeles Times,* December 14, 1989.
*New York Times,* December 5, 1989.
*Washington Post,* December 8, 1989.*

* * *

**SZIRTES, George 1948-**

*PERSONAL:* Born November 29, 1948, in Budapest, Hungary; son of Laszlo (an engineer) and Magdalena (a photographer; maiden name, Nussbacher) Szirtes; married Clarissa Upchurch (an artist), July 11, 1970; children: Thomas Andrew, Helen Magdalena. *Education:* Harrow School of Art, 1968-69; Leeds College of Art, B.A., 1972; University of London, A.T.C., 1973.

*ADDRESSES:* *Home*—16 Damgate Street, Wymondham, Norfolk, NR18 OBQ, England.

*CAREER:* Writer. Instructor in writing at schools and colleges in England, 1975-81; St. Christopher School, Letchworth, England, director of art, 1981-87; Senior lecturer in poetry, Norfolk Institute of Art and Design, beginning in 1991. Freelance writer and translator, 1987—. Etchings exhibited at Victoria and Albert Museum. Member of literature panel of Eastern Arts Association, 1981—.

*MEMBER:* International PEN, Royal Society of Literature (fellow).

*AWARDS, HONORS:* Co-recipient of Geoffrey Faber Memorial Prize from Faber & Faber Ltd. Arts Council, 1980, for *The Slant Door;* Arts Council fellowship, 1984; Poetry Book Society choices and recommendations, 1984, 1986, and 1988; British Council fellowship, 1985; Cholmondely Prize for Poetry from the Marchioness of Cholmondely, 1987; Dery prize for translation, 1991; Gold Star of the Hungarian Republic for translation, 1991.

*WRITINGS:*

*POETRY*

*Poems,* Perkin (Leeds), 1972.
*The Iron Clouds,* Dodman Press (Hitchin, Hertfordshire), 1975.
*Visitors,* Dodman Press, 1976.
(With Neil Powell and Peter Scupham) *A Mandeville Troika,* Mandeville Press (Hitchin, Hertfordshire), 1977.
*An Illustrated Alphabet,* Mandeville Press, 1978.
(With Alistair Elliott, Craig Raine, Alan Hollinghurst, Cal Clothier, and Anne Cluysenaar) *Poetry Introduction 4,* Faber (London), 1978.
*At the Sink,* Dodman Press, 1978.
*Silver Age,* Dodman Press, 1978.
*The Slant Door,* Secker & Warburg (London), 1979.
*Sermon on a Ship,* Dodman Press, 1980.
*Homage to Cheval,* Priapus Press (Berkhampstead, Hertfordshire), 1981.
*November and May,* Secker & Warburg, 1981.
*The Kissing Place,* Starwheel Press (Hitchin, Hertfordshire), 1982.

*Short Wave,* Secker & Warburg, 1984.
*The Photographer in Winter,* Secker & Warburg, 1986.
*Metro,* Oxford University Press (Oxford), 1988.
*Bridge Passages,* Oxford University Press, 1991.
*Blind Field,* Oxford University Press, 1994.
*Selected Poems, 1976-1996,* Oxford University Press, 1996.

*TRANSLATOR OR EDITOR*

(Editor) *A Starwheel Portfolio, The Transparent Room, Strict Seasons, Spring Offensive, Cloud Station, States of Undress* (verse and etching portfolios), Starwheel Press, 6 volumes, 1978-84.
(Translator) Imre Madach, *The Tragedy of Man,* Corvina (London and Budapest), 1988; Puski (New York City), 1988.
(Translator) Istvan Vas, *Through the Smoke: Selected Poems,* Corvina, 1989.
(Translator) Dezso Kosztolanyi, *Anna Edes,* Quartet (London), 1991; New Directions (New York City), 1993.
(Editor) Otto Orban, *The Blood of the Walsungs: Selected Poems,* Bloodaxe (Newcastle upon Tyne), 1993.
(Editor and translator) Zsuzsa Rakovszky, *New Life,* Oxford University Press, 1994.

*CONTRIBUTOR*

*Writers of East Anglia,* edited by Angus Wilson, Secker & Warburg, 1977.
*New Poems, 1977/78,* edited by Gavin Ewart, Hutchinson (London), 1978.
*Poems for Shakespeare,* edited by Patricia Beer, Shakespeare Trust (England), 1979.
*Poetry Book Society Anthology,* edited by Peter Porter, Poetry Book Society (England), 1980.
*The Music of What Happens,* edited by Derwent May, BBC Publications (London), 1981.
*Between Comets,* edited by William Scammell, Taxus (England), 1984.
*British Poetry since 1945,* edited by Edward Lucie-Smith, Penguin (New York City), 1985.
*Slipping Glimpses,* edited by Carol Rumens, Poetry Book Society, 1985.
*The Words Book, 1985-86,* edited by Philip Vine, Words Publications (England), 1986.
*With a Poet's Eye,* edited by Pat Adams, Tate Gallery (London), 1986.

Also contributor to *New Poetry,* Volumes 1-5, Arts Council/Hutchinson. Contributor to periodicals, including *Times Literary Supplement, New Statesman, Listener, Encounter,* and *Quarto.*

*SIDELIGHTS:* From his early surrealistic and painterly style of poetry to his growing interest in themes dealing with his native Hungary, George Szirtes has gained critical recognition as an important poet in the literary world. "People find Szirtes's poetry attractive because they recognise in it a basic understanding of human feeling and a proverbial sense of language," comments London *Observer* contributor Peter Porter. This appeal may in part be due to the influence of Szirtes's background and experience upon his poetry. "I arrived in England as a refugee in 1956," he tells *CA.* "My early education was science based, but I began writing and painting at school. I studied fine art and travelled in Europe on a scholarship, the longest stay being in Italy. I was exhibiting pictures at this time, but probably the most important influence on my writing was the poet Martin Bell, who was one of my tutors. After marriage to the artist Clarissa Upchurch, and a brief but intense religious period during which I was baptised, I taught full- and part-time in various institutions." Armed with these diverse credentials, Szirtes has slowly made a place for himself among English poets.

The poet's work first appeared in magazines in 1973, the influence of his training as a painter making his writing saliently visual. "Szirtes chooses words like pigments," Peter Porter writes in *Contemproary Poets,* "as though they could be modified in their mixing." However, some critics like Alan Brownjohn of *Encounter* feel that Szirtes's work is at its best when he gets away "from some habits of using the painter's eye for intriguing detail to get poems off the ground and employing a rather garish, surrealistic fantasy." *The Slant Door* contains much of this surrealism, but it also marks the point where the poet "moves very steadily towards a greater confidence, clarity, and originality of outlook," Brownjohn further remarks.

Szirtes told Porter in a *Contemporary Poets* interview that *The Slant Door* is structurally about the conflict between "the possibility of happiness" and the "apprehension of disaster," the two states of mind which he believes "define the territory" in which he best moves. Overall, the critical reaction to *The Slant Door* has been positive. William Palmer of *Poetry Review* sums up the author's effort as being "one of the best first books of poetry in the past few years, that is if we judge by successful poems and not by promise or critically adduced intentions."

*November and May* was, for Szirtes, a transitional book, one in which, as he told Porter, he concentrated "less on the finished object" and "more on the process of the poem," so that, as he told *CA:* "If I had to summarize my aims at the time, I would [say] that I felt my task was to preserve as fresh whatever was delightful and miraculous." A number of critics have found the poems in the book grimmer and more morose than his earlier work. "Szirtes is more interested in evoking the sadness involved in attempting to explain than in offering explanations," says *Times Literary Supplement* contributor Tim Dooley. His focus turns from the clearer, starker style for which *The Slant Door* was lauded to the "'mundane apparition,' the unattended moment of mystery or menace; to look out, too, for the words and rhythms that will evoke this malady of the quotidian with oblique forcefullness, deadened, remote decorum of manner," as Alan Jenkins of *Encounter* describes it. This predilection for expressing disturbing ideas while maintaining a somber tone has been compared to that of Irish poet Louis MacNeice, while Szirtes's love for the tangible has caused him to be compared to Geoffrey Grigson, the British poet. By such a contrast of the philosophical with the visually real, *November and May* and *The Slant Door* complement each other well.

With Szirtes's two visits to his native Hungary in 1984 and 1985, the poet rediscovered a personal subject to write about. *Short Wave,* a book which contains more than Szirtes's usual number of love poems, was his first to begin to "explore the idea and feel of Europe," explains the poet to *CA*. Porter writes about this work: "*Short Wave* is a book of considerable accomplishment. Szirtes's voice is now completely his own." Though some critics like Andrew Motion of *Poetry Review* feel that this book creates a "sense of blandness when . . . considered as a whole," others like John Lucas of *New Statesman* believe that "*Short Wave* is a truly original volume of poems. It is witty but in no superficial sense." However, where *Short Wave* is the first poetry collection in which the author expresses an original voice by exploring his homeland, his next two books do this in even greater depth.

*The Photographer in Winter* (1986) deals largely with the Hungary of the 1940s and 1950s. It "offers a powerful epigraph and model of ancestral allusion," explains *Books and Bookmen* contributor Barbara Hardy. This collection covers almost everything that Szirtes associates with the Hungary of the past, from the title poem, which is about the poet's mother, to descriptions of Hungarian architecture and satires on politics and propaganda. Simon Rae comments in *London Magazine:* "Szirtes tends to see the past frozen into stone, petrified into a photographic image that cannot develop or be changed, but only assimilated—by art—into some sort of pattern." The central element of *The Photographer in Winter* deals with investigating, as Szirtes tells *CA,* "the life of my mother before I was born (the time she spent in the Budapest ghetto and in the concentration camp) and relates this to the unhappy devotion she bore for her brother who failed to respond to her affection." Such themes, though personal, are written from a standpoint "unsettlingly poised between commitment and detachment," observes Lachlan Mackinnon of *Times Literary Supplement* about *The Photographer in Winter.* Perhaps this is due to Szirtes's largely English viewpoint which prevents him from being in complete contact with his Hungarian past. Mackinnon continues by saying that *The Photographer in Winter* "contains an implicit criticism of much English poetry for its inwardness, its political isolation." But other critics such as Barbara Hardy do not see anything negative about Szirtes's dual identity. "He belongs with [his compatriots]," says Hardy, "but he lends a strong voice to English poetry."

When Szirtes writes about Hungary, he does it from the point of view of someone looking back in time, and he does so again in *Metro,* a book in which the poet uses the metaphor of the underground train as a vehicle for the narrative. The same woman photographer from *The Photographer in Winter* is revealed to be the poet's mother, and she becomes, as Mark Wormald points out in the *Times Literary Supplement,* "a guide on a journey through an unreal city of the imagination." She is also the medium through which Szirtes reconstructs "both the terrors of the Holocaust in 1945 Budapest and the cloudy details of his family's past." Mark Ford, in the *London Review of Books,* notes how the poem's narrative cuts between the poet's "own childhood memories of Hungary and the fates of various branches of the Szirtes family" as well as "his mother's love for a disdainful older brother, lost during the war, her courtship, and the circumstances surrounding her arrest." The 780-line title poem presents the Budapest of 1944-45 constructed out of "relics, photographs, family gossip and chance memories," according to Ford, making the city a setting for "a generalized European urban chaos." Such a technique, which employs both the television reporter's use of the quick-cut, as well as the visual artist's use of collage, is viewed as creating an engaging panorama, one which barrages the reader with image and sound. Overall, critics like Ford find *Metro* "a rather somber book, with the tragedies of East European history felt in some degree in nearly all its contents."

*Bridge Passages,* which Szirtes calls his "third 'Hungarian' book" in an interview with *Contemporary Poets,* includes poems that are "the closest I have got to reportage in that they respond on a daily level to the rapid political change of 1989." Though a "Hungarian" book, *Bridge Passages* also includes poems wherein the poet explores how his immigration to England has affected him. This is shown in the poem "English Words," in which he describes learning that "somehow it was possible to know / the otherness of people and not be afraid," and that naturalization is language-based, so that the immigrant works to "say a word until it loses meaning / and taste the foreignness of languages, / your own included." Stan Smith, writing in *London Review of Books,* suggests that the title *Bridge Passages* "indicates a fine balance between connection and disconnection, a ubiquitous history and the trivia of everyday life," and that "in these bridge-passages of history, the fracturing of ideologies offers a brief chance of 'understanding what remains the same.'"

*Blind Field* finds Szirtes returning to the theme of photography, a subject that "consolidates his very individual position in contemporary poetry," according to Tim Dooley in the *Times Literary Supplement.* The book is written in three sections, the first of which, Dooley explains, "postulates a hidden community, or 'blind field,' existing outside the frozen moment of the photographic images." The central section, "Transylvania," a long, two-part poem written in terza rima, details the poet's visit to his mother's home town in Cluj-Napoca, Romania. Szirtes told Porter that "at its center is an ice-skating scene" which is designed to "hold it together." According to Dooley, "Transylvania" is "a bitter parody of pastoral and a sense of the tragic dislocation of a generation." The final section, "Blind Fold," shifts to a more personal and varied content, poems about the poet's wife, and poems about what Szirtes told Porter included "immediate family histories." *Blind Field,* in Dooley's opinion, is "an interesting and worthwhile addition to Szirtes's work."

*Selected Poems, 1976-1996* brought together poems that show the full range of Szirtes's work over two decades. Dooley calls Szirtes "An insider's outsider" who has "cleared a particular territory for himself in ostensibly decorous poems which can startle with unanticipated perceptions." Szirtes is considered to offer in his poetry a unique blend of the visual artist's sensibility as well as explorations of personal connection to Eastern European history and experience. He is also esteemed as a practitioner in the English poetic tradition. Readers of Szirtes's contemporary poetry will discover a poet who works in traditional forms, stanzas, and regular meter, and who produces both serious long poems as well as short parodies and satires. Porter finds that although "it is difficult to place Szirtes in the league of today's poets, serious readers . . . may have reason to believe that Szirtes' talent is one of the strongest of all."

In addition to his work as a poet, Szirtes has established himself as an editor and award-winning translator of Hungarian poetry into English, offering readers "fine English versions," according to George Gomori in the *Times Literary Supplement,* of the poems of Imre Madach, Istvan Vas, Dezso Kosztolanyi, Otto Orban, and Zsuzsa Rakovsky.

*BIOGRAPHICAL/CRITICAL SOURCES:*

*BOOKS*

*Contemporary Literary Criticism,* Volume 25, Gale (Detroit), 1988.
*Contemporary Poets,* fourth edition, St. James Press (Detroit), 1996.

*PERIODICALS*

*Books,* July, 1991, p. 5.
*Books and Bookmen,* April, 1986, pp. 21-22.
*British Book News,* April, 1982, pp. 253-254; June, 1986, p. 364.
*Economist,* March, 1989, p. 44.
*Encounter,* November, 1979, pp. 70-77; August, 1982, pp. 55-61.
*Edinburgh Review,* spring, 1982.
*Hungarian Quarterly* (Budapest), winter, 1994, pp. 20-22.
*Listener,* December 1, 1988, p. 40.
*Literary Review,* January, 1984.
*London Magazine,* March, 1980; August-September, 1986, pp. 132-135.
*London Review of Books,* January 19, 1989, pp. 14-15; January 9, 1992, pp. 22-23.

*New Hungarian Quarterly* (Budapest), spring, 1989, pp. 149-159; spring, 1990, pp. 26-29.
*New Statesman,* (London), January 1, 1982, pp. 18-19; January 13, 1984, pp. 24-25; August 26, 1988.
*New Statesman and Society,* August 26, 1988, p. 38.
*Observer* (London), August 19, 1979, p. 37; January 22, 1984, p. 53; June 1, 1986, p. 22; November 30, 1986, p. 21; August 7, 1988, p. 41.
*Poetry Review,* December, 1980, pp. 68-70; December, 1981; April, 1984, p. 64; summer, 1990, pp. 24-27.
*Quarto,* February, 1982.
*Stand,* 1983, pp. 75-76; 1985, pp. 64-65; spring, 1991, p. 49; spring, 1992, p. 64.
*Sunday Times,* September 14, 1986.
*Times Literary Supplement,* July 2, 1982, p. 720; June 1, 1984, p. 610; January 13, 1984; November 28, 1986, p. 1355; September 2, 1988, p. 957; August 16, 1991, p. 24; February 2, 1996, p. 28.*

*—Sketch by Robert Miltner*

* * *

**THALER, Michael C. 1936-**
**(Mike Thaler)**

*PERSONAL:* Born in 1936, in Los Angeles, CA; son of Ben (in sales; a poet and sculptor) and Jean (Rosensweig) Thaler; married Laurel Lee (a professor and writer), March 3, 1995. *Education:* Attended the University of California, Los Angeles. *Avocational interests:* Collecting art, netsuke, model and toy race cars, t-shirts, and laughter.

*ADDRESSES: Home and office*—1305 Heater Ct., West Linn, OR 97068-2736. *Agent*—(literary) Andrea Brown, P.O. Box 429, El Granada, CA 94018-0429; (multimedia) Creative Artists Agency, 9830 Wilshire Blvd., Beverly Hills, CA 90212; (school visits) Riddle King Tours—Kay Meekins, 1318 Pisgah Church Rd., Greensboro, NC 27455.

*CAREER:* Author and illustrator, 1961—. Songwriter, sculptor, game designer, teacher, and lecturer. Public Broadcasting Service (PBS), creator of "Letterman" for the children's television series *The Electric Company.* Teacher of workshops on making riddles, making creative books, stories, and creative dramatics. Co-designer of software and computer games, including *The Riddle King's Riddle Magic* (software), and board games, including *Scrambled Legs* and *The Riddle King's Riddle Race.*

*MEMBER:* PEN International, American Society of Composers, Authors, and Publishers (ASCAP).

*AWARDS, HONORS:* Children's Choice, International Reading Association and Children's Book Council, 1982, for *Moonkey.*

*WRITINGS:*

*UNDER NAME MIKE THALER*

*The Magic Boy,* Harper (New York City), 1961.
*The Clown's Smile,* Harper, 1962, new edition, illustrated by Tracey Cameron, 1986.
*The King's Flower,* Orion Press, 1963.
*Penny Pencil: The Story of a Pencil,* Harper, 1963.
*Moonboy,* Harper, 1964.
*The Prince and the Seven Moons,* illustrated by Ursula Arndt, Macmillan (New York City), 1966.
(Editor with William Cole) *The Classic Cartoons: A Definitive Gallery of the Cartoon as Art and as Humor,* World Publishing (New York City), 1966.
*The Rainbow,* illustrated by Donald Leake, H. Quist, 1967.
*The Smiling Book,* illustrated by Arnie Levin, Lothrop (Philadelphia), 1971.
*My Little Friend,* illustrated by Levin, Lothrop, 1971.
*The Staff,* illustrated by Joseph Schindelman, Random House (New York City), 1971.
*How Far Will a Rubberband Stretch?,* illustrated by Jerry Joyner, Parents Magazine Press (New York City), 1974.
*Magic Letter Riddles,* Scholastic (New York City), 1974.
*What Can a Hippopotamus Be?,* illustrated by Robert Grossman, Parents Magazine Press, 1975.
*Wuzzles,* Scholastic, 1976.
*Soup With Quackers! Funny Cartoon Riddles,* F. Watts (Danbury, CT), 1976.
*Riddle Riot,* Scholastic, 1976.
(With Cole) *Knock Knocks: The Most Ever,* F. Watts, 1976.
*Funny Bones: Cartoon Monster Riddles,* F. Watts, 1976.
*Silly Puzzles,* Xerox Publications, 1976.
*Dazzles,* Grosset, 1977.
(With Cole) *Knock Knocks You've Never Heard Before,* F. Watts, 1977.

(With Cole) *The Square Bear and Other Riddle Rhymes,* Scholastic, 1977.

*Never Tickle a Turtle: Cartoons, Riddles, and Funny Stories,* F. Watts, 1977.

*There's a Hippopotamus Under My Bed,* illustrated by Ray Cruz, F. Watts, 1977.

*What's Up, Duck? Cartoons, Riddles, and Jokes,* F. Watts, 1978.

*The Chocolate Marshmelephant Sundae,* F. Watts, 1978.

*The Yellow Brick Toad: Funny Frog Cartoons, Riddles, and Silly Stories,* Doubleday, 1978.

(With Cole) *Give Up? Cartoon Riddle Rhymes,* F. Watts, 1978.

*Madge's Magic Show,* illustrated by Carol Nicklaus, F. Watts, 1978.

(With Cole) *Backwords,* Random House, 1979.

*Picture Riddles,* Random House, 1979.

*Unicorns on the Cob,* Grosset, 1979.

*Screamers,* Grosset, 1979.

*Steer Wars,* Grosset, 1979.

*The Nose Knows,* Grosset, 1979.

*Grin and Bear It,* Grosset, 1979.

*Toucans on Two Cans,* Grosset, 1979.

*The Complete Cootie Book,* Avon (New York City), 1980.

*My Puppy,* illustrated by Madeleine Fishman, Harper, 1980.

*Moonkey,* illustrated by Giulio Maestro, Harper, 1981.

*The Moose Is Loose,* illustrated by Tony Gaffr, Scholastic, 1981.

*A Hippopotamus Ate the Teacher,* illustrated by Jared Lee, Avon, 1981.

*Oinkers Away: Pig Riddles, Cartoons, and Jokes,* Archway, 1981.

*Scared Silly: A Monster Riddle and Joke Scare-a-Thon Featuring Bugs Mummy and Count Quackula,* Avon, 1982.

*Story Puzzles,* Scholastic, 1982.

*The Pac-Man Riddle and Joke Book,* Archway, 1982.

*Paws: Cat Riddles, Cat Jokes, and Catoons,* Archway, 1982.

(With Cole) *Monster Knock Knocks,* Archway, 1982.

*Owly,* illustrated by David Wiesner, Harper, 1982.

*The Moon and the Balloon,* illustrated by Madeleine Fishman, Hastings House, 1982.

*Stuffed Feet,* Avon, 1983.

*It's Me, Hippo!,* illustrated by Maxie Chambliss, Harper, 1983.

*Riddle Rainbow,* Hastings House, 1984.

*Montgomery Moose's Favorite Riddles,* illustrated by Neal McPheeters, Scholastic, 1985.

*Cream of Creature From the School Cafeteria,* illustrated by Jared Lee, Avon, 1985.

*Funny Side Up! How to Create Your Own Riddles,* Scholastic, 1985.

*Upside Down Day,* illustrated by Jared Lee, Avon, 1986.

*King Kong's Underwear,* Avon, 1986.

*Hippo Lemonade,* illustrated by Maxie Chambliss, Harper, 1986.

*Mr. Bananahead at Home,* Scholastic, 1987.

*Hink Pink Monsters,* illustrated by Fred Winkowski, Scholastic, 1987.

*In the Middle of the Puddle,* illustrated by Bruce Degen, Harper, 1988.

*Pack 109,* illustrated by Normand Chartier, Dutton (New York City), 1988.

*Come and Play, Hippo,* illustrated by Maxie Chambliss, Harper, 1989.

*Godzilla's Pantyhose,* Avon, 1989.

*Frankenstein's Pantyhose,* Avon, 1989.

*The Riddle King's Camp Riddles,* illustrated by Paul Harvey, Random House, 1989.

*The Riddle King's Food Riddles,* illustrated by Harvey, Random House, 1989.

*The Riddle King's Pet Riddles,* illustrated by Harvey, Random House, 1989.

*The Riddle King's School Riddles,* illustrated by Harvey, Random House, 1989.

*Catzilla,* Simon & Schuster (New York City), 1991.

*Seven Little Hippos,* illustrated by Jerry Smath, Simon & Schuster, 1991.

*Cannon the Librarian,* illustrated by Lee, Avon, 1993.

*Colossal Fossil,* illustrated by Rick Brown, W. H. Freeman, 1994.

*Miss Yonkers Goes Bonkers,* illustrated by Lee, Avon, 1994.

*Earth Mirth: The Ecology Riddle Book,* illustrated by Rick Brown, Scientific American Books for Young Readers, 1994.

*Bad Day at Monster Elementary,* Avon, 1995.

*"LAGOON ELEMENTARY" SERIES; ILLUSTRATED BY JARED LEE*

*The Teacher From the Black Lagoon,* Scholastic, 1989.

*The Principal from the Black Lagoon,* Scholastic, 1993.

*The Gym Teacher from the Black Lagoon,* Scholastic, 1994.

*The School Nurse from the Black Lagoon,* Scholastic, 1995.

*The Librarian from the Black Lagoon,* Scholastic, 1997.

*"BULLY BROTHERS" SERIES; ILLUSTRATED BY JARED LEE*

*The Bully Brothers Trick the Tooth Fairy,* Grosset, 1993.
*The Bully Brothers: Gobblin' Halloween,* Grosset, 1993.
*The Bully Brothers: Making the Grade,* Scholastic, 1995.
*The Bully Brothers at the Beach,* Scholastic, 1996.

*"FUNNY FIRSTS" SERIES; ILLUSTRATED BY JARED LEE*

*Camp Rotten Time,* Troll Communications, 1994.
*Fang the Dentist,* Troll Communications, 1994.
*My Cat Is Going to the Dogs,* Troll Communications, 1994.
*The Schmo Must Go On,* Troll Communications, 1995.
*I'm Dracula, Who Are You?,* Troll Communications, 1996.
*Love Stinks,* Troll Communications, 1996.
*Moving to Mars,* Troll Communications, 1996.

*"LAFFALONG" SERIES; ILLUSTRATED BY JERRY SMATH*

*Never Mail an Elephant,* Troll Communications, 1993.
*Uses for Mooses and Other Popular Pets,* Troll Communications, 1993.
*Never Give a Fish an Umbrella,* Troll Communications, 1996.

*"HAPPILY EVER AFTER" SERIES; ILLUSTRATED BY JARED LEE*

*Cinderella Bigfoot,* Scholastic, 1997.
*Hanzel and Pretzel,* Scholastic, 1997.
*Schmoe White and the Seven Dorfs,* Scholastic, 1997.
*The Princess and the Pea-ano,* Scholastic, 1997.

*ACTIVITY BOOKS; WITH JANET PULLEN*

*The Riddle King's Giant Book of Jokes, Riddles, and Activities,* Modern, 1987.
*The Riddle King's Jumbo Book of Jokes, Riddles, and Activities,* Modern, 1987.
*The Riddle King's Super Book of Jokes, Riddles, and Activities,* Modern, 1987.
*The Riddle King's Book of Jokes, Riddles, and Activities,* Modern, 1988.

*RECORDINGS*

*The Riddle King Tells His Favorite Riddles, Jokes, Stories, and Songs with Steve Charney,* Caedmon, 1985.
*The Riddle King's Riddle Song: Scholastic Songs with Steve Charney,* Scholastic, 1987.

Other cassette recordings include *These Are the Questions, My Blanket Is the Sky,* and *Sing Me a Rainbow.*

*OTHER*

Contributor of cartoons to magazines, including *Harper's Bazaar, Horizon, Humpty Dumpty,* and *Saturday Evening Post.* Thaler's books have been published in England, Canada, France, and Japan.

*ADAPTATIONS:* The "Bully Brothers" series has been optioned by ABC-TV and CBS-TV for a television series.

*SIDELIGHTS:* An author and illustrator of numerous picture books, beginning readers, and original joke and riddle books for children, Thaler has teamed with illustrator Jared Lee to produce scores of entertaining and well-received works for children. In a review of their most recent effort, which comprises *Hanzel and Pretzel, Schmoe White and the Seven Dorfs,* and other books in their "Happily Ever After" series, *Cincinnati Enquirer* commentator Sara Pearce dubbed Thaler and Lee "the court jesters of children's literature." Through each of his books for children, Thaler shares his lighthearted vision of life and encourages young people to indulge in their natural sense of wonder.

Born in Los Angeles, California, in 1936, Thaler attended classes at the University of California, Los Angeles before breaking away to follow his dreams. "What I really hoped to earn a living at was doing cartoons for adults," Thaler once told *CA.* "Actually, they weren't even funny cartoons, they were the 'save-the-world' kind. Then one day Ursula Nordstrom, an editor at Harper & Row, saw a picture story I had done for *Harper's Bazaar* . . . and asked if I had ever thought of doing children's books." Thaler completed his first book for children, *The Magic Boy,* in 1961. The story of a young boy who could juggle rainbows that never dropped, *The Magic Boy* was the first in a long line of books for children by this prolific writer/illustrator.

"Writing a story is like painting a picture," Thaler once explained to *CA.* "You put down one color, and then you put down a second color next to it, and it changes the first color. You put down words next to words and they change, too. So when you put two or three words together, there's an interaction." During the writing process, Thaler tries to tap the feelings of his inner child—"I sort of feel like I am more of a receiver than an originator, that I am merely the radio the music plays through. It's like the stories are already there. I am simply putting them down on paper."

Among the many picture books Thaler has written, and often illustrated, are *What Can a Hippopotamus Be?, Madge's Magic Show,* the award-winning *Moonkey,* and 1982's *Owly,* the story of a young owl full of curiosity about the world around him. Owly has a never-ending list of questions for his busy mother, who, instead of answering them herself, sends the young owlet out into the world to discover the answers for himself in a book that *Bulletin of the Center for Children's Books* reviewer Zena Sutherland noted "has a loving relationship and an interesting concept as appeals." The beginning reader *It's Me, Hippo!* contains four stories that feature the portly title character involved in a range of activities alongside a group of his African animal friends in what a *Publishers Weekly* reviewer called a "buoyant collection." Animals are also featured in *Hippo Lemonade, Moonkey,* and *In the Middle of the Puddle.* In this latter work, Fred the frog and Ted the turtle find their comfortably sized puddle stretched into a sea after a long rainstorm. "Paced by the phrase repetition that small children relish . . . this charmer will delight youngsters on rainy and sunny days," asserted Beth Ames Herbert in her review of the picture book for *Booklist.*

"When you do children's [picture] books, there can be no waste, no fat," Thaler explained. "It has to be all muscle and bone. There has to be character development, plot and depth, all in thirty-two pages. And it has to be beauty and energy." According to the author, the words under the illustration are what fuel the story. "Words give an emotional feeling. They give you energy." While Thaler once believed children's books should also contain a message, he has since changed his mind. "Just the laughter of children is the message. Laughter is a message in itself."

Thaler claims to have a poor reputation for understanding other people's jokes, so in his books he finds it simpler just to make up his own. He tries to extend that originality to every part of each of his riddle books—from jokes and riddles to the stories and drawings that he includes alongside them. While many riddle books contain just lists of riddles, Thaler's books are unusual in that he uses his ability as an artist to play up the visual humor through comic illustrations. In 1977's *Never Tickle a Turtle: Cartoons, Riddles, and Funny Stories,* which is illustrated with black and white cartoons, Thaler appeals to a variety of ages by featuring visual puns along with his jokes and riddles. *The Yellow Brick Toad* contains an entire collection of jokes, riddles, stories, and cartoons featuring the high-hopping amphibians. Similarly, *Oinkers Away!* is full of swine humor, complete with illustrations by Thaler that add to the fun.

In addition to working on new books, Thaler travels to schools across the country, reading from his books and encouraging the children he meets to develop their own creativity. "I find riddles to be a valuable educational tool," he noted. "They get kids into all sorts of things—synonyms, rhythm, spelling syntax, syllables and, more importantly, into the dictionary, a marvelous source of riddles." During his visits to schools Thaler encourages students to make up their own stories, draw their own cartoons, and write their own "books" in order to help them build on their personal creativity and developing sense of humor. "There is pure creativity when you are around kids," he exclaimed. "The energy of children is the most amazing, important source of energy in this whole country. It should be protected and helped to develop. Teachers to me are the most important people in the world because they are shaping the future. The possibilities of kids are the possibilities of the future."

"There was a time in my life when everything had to be serious," Thaler admitted to *CA.* "Now I have learned that laughter is important, and I feel it is important for children to have a good body of humor, an intelligent body of humor." Thaler weaves his belief in the power of humor into each of his many books, joining it with another principle. "Love and creativity are the two basic elements of life to me," he explained. "If you put love and creativity into everything you do, you've got it made. This is the philosophy I live by, and the philosophy I teach."

*BIOGRAPHICAL/CRITICAL SOURCES:*

*PERIODICALS*

*Booklist,* March 15, 1977, p. 1008; June 1, 1988, pp. 1679-1680; September 15, 1990, p. 173; April 1, 1991, p. 1578.
*Bulletin of the Center for Children's Books,* January, 1979, p. 90; July-August, 1982, p. 216.
*Cincinnati Enquirer,* March 18, 1997, p. C5.
*Junior Bookshelf,* February, 1978, p. 15.
*Kirkus Reviews,* February 1, 1979, p. 131.
*Publishers Weekly,* January 27, 1975, p. 285; December 2, 1983, p. 86; March 8, 1993, p. 77; September 20, 1993, p. 30.
*School Library Journal,* December, 1975, p. 49; April, 1977, p. 72; May, 1978, p. 82; March, 1979, p. 122; November, 1981, p. 83; September, 1982, p. 112; December, 1983, p. 80; December, 1988, p. 94; August, 1991, p. 156; November, 1991, p. 107.

* * *

**THALER, Mike**
**See THALER, Michael C.**

* * *

**TRIMBLE, Marshall I(ra) 1939-**

*PERSONAL:* Born January 16, 1939, in Mesa, Arizona; son of Ira (a stockman/railroader) and Juanita (a waitress) Trimble; married Gena Powell (an executive on the Salt River Project), August 8, 1974; children: Roger. *Education:* Arizona State University, B.A., 1961, M.A., 1963.

*ADDRESSES: Home*—6401 E. Hummingbird Lane, Paradise Valley, AZ 85253. *Office*—9000 E. Chaparral Rd., Scottsdale, AZ 85250.

*CAREER:* Historian, writer, teacher, folksinger. Scottsdale Community College, Scottsdale, AZ, teacher of Arizona history, 1972—.

*AWARDS, HONORS:* Finalist, Ben Franklin Award for humor, for *It Always Rains after a Dry Spell;* named Arizona's official State Historian, 1997.

*WRITINGS:*

*Arizona: A Panoramic History of a Frontier State,* foreword by Barry M. Goldwater, Doubleday (New York City), 1977.
*Discover Arizona Heritage,* Arizona Highways, 1979.
*Arizona Adventure: Action-Packed True Tales of Early Arizona,* Golden West, 1982.
*CO Bar: Bill Owen Depicts the Historic Babbitt Ranch,* foreword by John G. Babbitt, Northland, 1982.
*In Old Arizona: True Tales of the Wild Frontier,* Golden West, 1985.
(With Bob Hirsch) *Outdoors in Arizona: A Guide to Camping,* illustrated by Joe Beeler, Arizona Department of Transportation, 1986.
*Roadside History of Arizona,* illustrated by Joe Beeler, Mountain Press, 1986.
*Diamond in the Rough: An Illustrated History of Arizona,* Donning (Norfolk, VA), 1988.
(With James E. Cook and Sam Negri) *Travel Arizona: The Back Roads: Twenty Back Road Tours for the Whole Family,* Arizona Department of Transportation, 1989.
*Arizona: A Cavalcade of History,* Treasure Chest (Tucson, AZ), 1989.
*It Always Rains after a Dry Spell,* illustrated by Jack Graham, Treasure Chest, 1992.
*Marshall Trimble's Original Arizona Trivia,* Golden West, 1996.

Consultant to *America the Beautiful: Arizona,* by Ann Heinrichs, Childrens Press, 1991; contributor to *Arizona Highways Album: The Road to Statehood,* by Dean Smith, Arizona Highways, 1987. Editor of Arizona Trivia boardgame; author of scripts for the *Portrait of America* television series on *Arizona;* stories have appeared in *Arizona Highways* and *Western Horseman,* among others; *Legends in Levis,* a cassette recording of Trimble singing old cowboy songs.

*SIDELIGHTS:* Marshall Trimble told *CA:* "I graduated from college in 1961 and became a teacher. During the evenings/summer I worked as a folk singer. I cut four records in 1964.

"In 1972, I began teaching Arizona history at Scottsdale Community College. I'm still there. My first book, published by Doubleday & Co. in 1977 was *Arizona: A Panoramic History of a Frontier State*. The book was a big seller and I went on the speaking circuit. That work led to convention shows, television and radio work. That makes up a major part of my career today.

"I visit a lot of schools, especially 4th grade, to promote Arizona history to youngsters. I sing old cowboy songs and tell stories and tall tales."

*BIOGRAPHICAL/CRITICAL SOURCES:*

*PERIODICALS*

*Arizona Highways,* April, 1976.
*Arizona Republic,* June 6, 1976; May 13, 1977; July 3, 1977; July 10, 1977.
*Phoenix,* November, 1976.
*Phoenix Gazette,* January 12, 1974.
*Scottsdale Progress,* June 24, 1976; August 3, 1977.

* * *

**UCHIDA, Yoshiko 1921-1992**

*PERSONAL:* Surname is pronounced "Oo-*chee*-dah"; born November 24, 1921, in Alameda, CA; died after a stroke, June 21, 1992, in Berkeley, CA; daughter of Dwight Takashi (a businessman) and Iku (Umegaki) Uchida. *Education:* University of California, Berkeley, A.B. (cum laude), 1942; Smith College, M.Ed., 1944. *Politics:* Democrat. *Religion:* Protestant. *Avocational interests:* Fine arts, folk crafts.

*CAREER:* Elementary school teacher in Japanese relocation center in Utah, 1942-43; Frankford Friends' School, Philadelphia, PA, teacher, 1944-45; membership secretary, Institute of Pacific Relations, 1946-47; secretary, United Student Christian Council, 1947-52; full-time writer, 1952-57; University of California, Berkeley, secretary, 1957-62; full-time writer, 1962-92.

*AWARDS, HONORS:* Ford Foundation research fellow in Japan, 1952; Children's Spring Book Festival honor award, *New York Herald Tribune,* 1955, for *The Magic Listening Cap;* Notable Book citation, American Library Association, 1972, for *Journey to Topaz;* medal for best juvenile book by a California author, Commonwealth Club of California, 1972, for *Samurai of Gold Hill;* Award of Merit, California Association of Teachers of English, 1973; citation, Contra Costa chapter of Japanese American Citizens League, 1976, for outstanding contribution to the cultural development of society; Morris S. Rosenblatt Award, Utah State Historical Society, 1981, for article, "Topaz, City of Dust"; Distinguished Service Award, University of Oregon, 1981; Commonwealth Club of California medal, 1982, for *A Jar of Dreams;* award from Berkeley Chapter of Japanese American Citizens League, 1983; *School Library Journal,* Best Book of the Year citation, 1983, for *The Best Bad Thing;* New York Public Library, Best Book of the Year citation, 1983, for *The Best Bad Thing;* Best Book of 1985 citation, Bay Area Book Reviewers, 1985, for *The Happiest Ending;* Child Study Association of America, Children's Book of the Year citation, 1985, for *The Happiest Ending;* San Mateo and San Francisco Reading Associations, Young Authors' Hall of Fame award, 1985, for *The Happiest Ending;* Friends of Children and Literature award, 1987, for *A Jar of Dreams;* Japanese American of the Biennium award, Japanese American Citizens Leagues, 1988, for outstanding achievement.

*WRITINGS:*

*JUVENILES*

*The Dancing Kettle and Other Japanese Folk Tales,* illustrations by Richard C. Jones, Harcourt, 1949, reprinted, Creative Arts Book Co., 1986.
*New Friends for Susan,* illustrations by Henry Sugimoto, Scribner, 1951.
(Self-illustrated) *The Magic Listening Cap—More Folk Tales from Japan,* Harcourt, 1955, reprinted, Creative Arts Book Co., 1987.
(Self-illustrated) *The Full Circle* (junior high school study book), Friendship, 1957.
*Takao and Grandfather's Sword,* illustrations by William M. Hutchinson, Harcourt, 1958.
*The Promised Year,* illustrations by Hutchinson, Harcourt, 1959.
*Mik and the Prowler,* illustrations by Hutchinson, Harcourt, 1960.
*Rokubei and the Thousand Rice Bowls,* illustrations by Kazue Mizumura, Scribner, 1962.
*The Forever Christmas Tree,* illustrations by Mizumura, Scribner, 1963.
*Sumi's Prize,* illustrations by Mizumura, Scribner, 1964.
*The Sea of Gold, and Other Tales from Japan,* illustrations by Marianne Yamaguchi, Scribner, 1965.

*Sumi's Special Happening,* illustrations by Mizumura, Scribner, 1966.

*In-Between Miya,* illustrations by Susan Bennett, Scribner, 1967.

*Hisako's Mysteries,* illustrations by Bennett, Scribner, 1969.

*Sumi and the Goat and the Tokyo Express,* illustrations by Mizumura, Scribner, 1969.

*Makoto, the Smallest Boy: A Story of Japan,* illustrations by Akihito Shirawaka, Crowell, 1970.

*Journey to Topaz: A Story of the Japanese-American Evacuation,* illustrations by Donald Carrick, Scribner, 1971.

*Samurai of Gold Hill,* illustrations by Ati Forberg, Scribner, 1972.

*The Old Man with the Bump* (cassette based on story from *The Dancing Kettle*), Houghton, 1973.

*The Birthday Visitor,* illustrations by Charles Robinson, Scribner, 1975.

*The Rooster Who Understood Japanese,* illustrations by Robinson, Scribner, 1976.

*The Two Foolish Cats* (filmstrip with cassette based on a story from *The Sea of Gold*), Encyclopaedia Britannica Educational, 1977.

*Journey Home* (sequel to *Journey to Topaz*), illustrations by Robinson, McElderry Books, 1978.

*The Fox and the Bear* (cassette based on a story from *The Magic Listening Cap*), Science Research Associates, 1979.

*A Jar of Dreams,* McElderry Books, 1981.

*The Best Bad Thing* (sequel to *A Jar of Dreams*), McElderry Books, 1983.

*Tabi: Journey through Time, Stories of the Japanese in America,* United Methodist Publishing House, 1984.

*The Happiest Ending* (sequel to *The Best Bad Thing*), McElderry Books, 1985.

*The Two Foolish Cats,* illustrations by Margot Zemach, McElderry Books, 1987.

*The Terrible Leak,* Creative Education, 1990.

*The Magic Purse,* illustrations by Keiko Narahashi, McElderry Books, 1993.

*The Bracelet,* illustrations by Joanna Yardley, Philomel, 1993.

*The Wise Old Woman,* illustrations by Martin Springett, McElderry Books, 1994.

*FOR ADULTS*

*We Do Not Work Alone: The Thoughts of Kanjiro Kawai,* Folk Art Society (Japan), 1953.

(Translator of English portions) Soetsu Yanagi, editor, *Shoji Hamada,* Asahi Shimbun Publishing, 1961.

*The History of Sycamore Church,* Sycamore Congregational Church, 1974.

*Desert Exile: The Uprooting of a Japanese-American Family,* University of Washington Press, 1982.

*Picture Bride* (novel), Northland Press, 1987.

*The Invisible Thread* (an autobiography for young adults), J. Messner, 1991, reprinted, Beech Tree, 1995.

*OTHER*

Contributor to many books, including *Flight Near and Far,* Holt, 1970; *Scribner Anthology for Young People,* Scribner, 1976; *Literature and Life,* Scott, Foresman, 1979; *Fairy Tales of the Sea,* Harper, 1981; *Anthology of Children's Literature,* Scott, Foresman, 1984; and *Explorations,* Houghton, 1986. Author of regular column, "Letter from San Francisco," in *Craft Horizons,* 1958-61. Contributor to exhibit catalogue of Oakland Museum, 1976. Contributor of adult stories and articles to newspapers and periodicals, including *Woman's Day, Gourmet, Utah Historical Quarterly, Far East,* and *California Monthly.* The Kerlan Collection holds Uchida's manuscripts for *In-Between Miya* and *Mik and the Prowler.* Other manuscript collections are at the University of Oregon Library, Eugene, and the Bancroft Library, University of California, Berkeley.

*SIDELIGHTS:* Yoshiko Uchida's appreciation for her Japanese heritage inspired her to become the author of many books on Japanese culture for readers of all ages. "In fiction, the graceful and lively books of Yoshiko Uchida have drawn upon the author's own childhood to document the Japanese-American experience for middle-grade readers," Patty Campbell commented in the *New York Times Book Review.* Among her nonfiction works for adults are studies of Japanese folk artists such as *We Do Not Work Alone: The Thoughts of Kanjiro Kawai,* as well as a memoir of wartime imprisonment, *Desert Exile: The Uprooting of a Japanese-American Family.*

After the bombing of Pearl Harbor, Americans of Japanese descent were incarcerated by order of the U.S. government. Uchida was a senior at the University of California, Berkeley, when her family was sent to Tanforan Racetracks, where thousands of Japanese-Americans lived in stables and barracks. After five months at Tanforan, they were moved to Topaz, a guarded camp in the Utah desert. Uchida taught in the elementary schools there until the spring of 1943, when she was released to accept a fellowship for graduate study at Smith College. Her parents were also released that year.

Uchida earned a Master's Degree in education, but because teaching limited her time for writing, she found a secretarial job that allowed her to write in the evenings. As she explained in her contribution to *Something about the Author Autobiography Series,* "I was writing short stories at the time, sending them to the *New Yorker, Atlantic Monthly* and *Harper's*—and routinely receiving printed rejection slips. After a time, however, the slips contained encouraging penciled notes and a *New Yorker* editor even met with me to suggest that I write about my concentration camp experiences. . . . And many of the short stories I wrote during those days were published eventually in literature anthologies for young people."

By the time *Woman's Day* accepted one of her stories, Uchida found that writing for children promised more success. Her first book, *The Dancing Kettle and Other Japanese Folk Tales,* was well received, and when a Ford Foundation grant enabled Uchida to visit Japan, she collected more traditional tales. In addition, she became fascinated with Japanese arts and crafts, and learned more about them from Soetsu Yanagi, the philosopher, and other founders of the Folk Art Movement in Japan. But her most important gain from the visit, she wrote, was the awareness "of a new dimension of myself as a Japanese-American and [a] deepened . . . respect and admiration for the culture that had made my parents what they were."

The final children's books Uchida wrote before her death in 1992 reflect her interests not only in Japan but also in her Japanese-American heritage. *The Magic Purse,* for instance, offers a tale with many mythical Japanese elements. In the book, a poor farmer journeying through a swamp encounters a beautiful maiden held captive by the lord of the swamp. She persuades him to carry a letter for her to her parents in another swamp, giving him a magic purse as a reward for his efforts. The purse contains gold coins that forever multiply, and the coins make the farmer a rich man, even as he returns year after year to the swamp to make peace with the swamp lord and to remember the maiden. *The Bracelet,* meanwhile, is set in California during World War II and features a seven-year-old Japanese-American girl, Emi, who is being shipped off to an internment camp with her mother and sister; her father has already been taken to another camp. Once at the camp (Tanforan Racetracks, the same camp that the author lived in as a girl), Emi realizes that she has lost the gold bracelet that her best friend Laurie gave to her as a parting gift. Despite being despondent over the loss of the bracelet, Emi comes to understand that her memory of Laurie is something more precious than the bracelet, because the memory will stay with her forever. In *The Wise Old Woman,* Uchida's final children's book, the author tells the story of a small village in medieval Japan in which the cruel young village lord has decreed that any person reaching seventy years of age must be taken into the mountains and left to die. A young farmer, unable to bear the thought of taking his mother away and letting her die, instead builds a secret room where she can hide. Later, a neighboring ruler comes to the village and declares that the village will be destroyed unless its citizens can carry out three seemingly impossible tasks. When the farmer's mother proves to be the only one capable of figuring out how to complete the tasks, the cruel young lord realizes the error of his age decree and revokes it, leaving the old woman—and others like her—free to remain with their families.

The death of the author's mother in 1966 prompted Uchida to write a book for her parents "and the other first-generation Japanese (the Issei), who had endured so much." The result was the book *Journey to Topaz: A Story of the Japanese-American Evacuation.* Based on her own experiences in the camps during the war, it marked a shift in emphasis from Japanese culture to the Japanese-American experience in the United States. Every book Uchida wrote after *Journey to Topaz* responded to the growing need for identity among third generation Japanese-Americans. Uchida once explained to *CA:* "Through my books I hope to give young Asian-Americans a sense of their past and to reinforce their self-esteem and self-knowledge. At the same time, I want to dispel the stereotypic image still held by many non-Asians about the Japanese and write about them as real people. I hope to convey the strength of spirit and the sense of hope and purpose I have observed in many first-generation Japanese. Beyond that, I write to celebrate our common humanity, for the basic elements of humanity are present in all our strivings."

*BIOGRAPHICAL/CRITICAL SOURCES:*

*BOOKS*

*Children's Literature Review,* Volume 6, Gale, 1984.
*Something about the Author Autobiography Series,* Volume 1, Gale, 1986.

*Twentieth-Century Children's Writers,* 3rd edition, St. James Press, 1989.

*PERIODICALS*

*Children's Book World,* November 5, 1967.
*Five Owls,* January/February, 1994.
*New York Times Book Review,* February 9, 1986; November 14, 1993, p. 21.
*Publishers Weekly,* October 24, 1994, p. 61.
*School Library Journal,* November, 1993, p. 103; December, 1993, p. 95; July, 1995, p. 75.
*Young Readers' Review,* January, 1967.

*OBITUARIES:*

*PERIODICALS*

*Chicago Tribune,* June 28, 1992, section 2, p. 6.
*Los Angeles Times,* June 27, 1992, p. A26.
*New York Times,* June 24, 1992, p. A18.
*School Library Journal,* August, 1992, p. 23.*

* * *

**WAYS, C. R.**
**See BLOUNT, Roy (Alton), Jr.**

* * *

**WINSTON, Daoma 1922-**

*PERSONAL:* Born November 3, 1922, in Washington, DC; daughter of Joel (a businessman) and Ray (Freedman) Winston; married Murray Strasberg (a physicist), August 26, 1944. *Education:* George Washington University, A.B. (with distinction), 1946.

*ADDRESSES: Home*—Washington, DC. *Agent*—Jay Garon-Brooke Associates, 101 W. 55th St., New York, NY 10019-5348.

*CAREER:* Novelist.

*MEMBER:* Authors League of America, Mystery Writers of America, Phi Beta Kappa.

*WRITINGS:*

*NOVELS*

*Tormented Lovers,* Monarch (Derby, CT), 1962.
*Love Her, She's Yours,* Monarch, 1963.
*The Secrets of Cromwell Crossing,* Lancer Books (New York City), 1965.
*Sinister Stone,* Paperback Library (New York City), 1966.
*The Wakefield Witches,* Award (New York City), 1966.
*The Mansion of Smiling Masks,* New American Library (New York City), 1967.
*Shadow of an Unknown Woman,* Lancer Books, 1967.
*Castle of Closing Doors* (bound with *Night of Evil,* by Genevieve St. John), Belmont-Tower (New York City), 1967.
*The Carnaby Curse* (bound with *House of Hell,* by Virginia Coffmann), Belmont-Tower, 1967.
*Shadow on Mercer Mountain,* Lancer Books, 1967.
*Pity My Love,* Belmont-Tower, 1967.
*The Traficante Treasure,* Lancer Books, 1968.
*The Moderns,* Pyramid Publications (New York City), 1968.
*The Long and Living Shadow,* Belmont-Tower, 1968.
*Bracken's World No. 1,* Paperback Library, 1969.
*Mrs. Berrigan's Dirty Book,* Lancer Books, 1970.
*Beach Generation,* Lancer Books, 1970.
*Bracken's World No. 2: Wild Country,* Paperback Library, 1970.
*Dennison Hill,* Paperback Library, 1970.
*House of Mirror Images,* Lancer Books, 1970.
*Bracken's World No. 3: Sound Stage,* Paperback Library, 1970.
*The Love of Lucifer,* Lancer Books, 1970.
*The Vampire Curse,* Paperback Library, 1971.
*Flight of a Fallen Angel,* Lancer Books, 1971.
*The Devil's Daughter,* Lancer Books, 1971.
*The Devil's Princess,* Lancer Books, 1971.
*Seminar in Evil,* Lancer Books, 1972.
*The Victim,* Popular Library (New York City), 1972.
*The Return,* Avon (New York City), 1972.
*The Inheritance,* Avon, 1972.
*Kingdom's Castle,* Berkley Publishing (New York City), 1972.
*Skeleton Key,* Avon, 1972, published as *The Mayeroni Myth,* Lancer Books, 1972.
*Moorhaven,* Avon, 1973.
*The Trap,* Popular Library, 1973.
*The Unforgotten,* Berkley Publishing, 1973.
*Emerald Station,* Avon, 1974.

*The Haversham Legacy,* Simon & Schuster (New York City), 1974.
*Mills of the Gods,* Avon, 1974.
*Return to Elysium,* Avon, 1975.
*A Visit after Dark,* Ace Books (New York City), 1975.
*Death Watch,* Ace Books, 1975.
*The Golden Valley,* Simon & Schuster, 1975.
*Walk around the Square,* Ace Books, 1975.
*The Dream Killers,* Ace Books, 1976.
*Gallows Way,* Simon & Schuster, 1976.
*The Adventuress,* Simon & Schuster, 1978.
*The Lotteries* (Literary Guild alternate selection), Morrow (New York City), 1980.
*A Sweet Familiarity,* Arbor House (New York City), 1981.
*Mira,* Arbor House, 1981.
*The Hands of Death,* Piatkus (Essex, England), 1982.
*Family of Strangers,* Piatkus, 1982.
*The Fall River Line,* St. Martin's (New York City), 1983.
*Maybe This Time,* Century (London), 1988.
*A Double Life,* Severn House (London), 1991.
*Hannah's Gate,* Piatkus, 1992.
*Curse of Hannah's Gate,* Piatkus, 1993.

*OTHER*

*Doubtful Mercy* (poems), Decker Press, 1950.

Contributor to *Mirror, Mirror, Fatal Mirror,* 1973. Also contributor to *Writer.*

*SIDELIGHTS:* Daoma Winston has produced a substantial number of novels, mostly in the gothic and romance genres, often with historical backgrounds. "Background" may be an appropriate way of describing her use of history; as Marion Hanscom noted in *Twentieth-Century Romance and Historical Writers,* Winston "neither delves nor probes into the political and philosophical events that took place during the periods of her stories, but rather uses those times as "set decoration' against which to place her characters." This set dressing sometimes includes references, though, to real historical characters and happenings; American presidents, industrialists, and temperance crusader Carry Nation are passengers on the ships of *The Fall River Line,* and President Andrew Johnson's impeachment trial comes up in *The Haversham Legacy.* While Winston's novels are light on historical analysis, they are heavy on descriptions of period clothing, customs, and dwellings, Hanscom pointed out, crediting the author with "a special talent" for such delineations.

Many of Winston's novels have a strong woman as the central character. These heroines frequently suffer through troubled love affairs and other melodramatic crises; insanity, intrigue, adultery, and murder crop up in Winston's plots. Miranda Jervis, the protagonist of *The Haversham Legacy,* joins the Haversham branch of her family in Washington, DC, just after the Civil War, and soon finds that these relatives are mostly gamblers, scoundrels, or addicts of one sort or another. In *Gallows Way,* Marietta Garvey, a plantation mistress in the antebellum South, contends with a conniving younger sister and an irresponsible stepbrother, then marries a man who is involved in helping slaves escape to freedom. Nineteenth-century shipping heiress Augusta Kincaid, heroine of *The Fall River Line,* endures her husband's affair with her sister.

The Winston novels set in modern times portray long-suffering women (and sometimes men) as well. The eponymous protagonist of *Mira* has a son who is a member of a racist gang, a husband who is an arms dealer, and a lover who is a survivor of child abuse. *A Sweet Familiarity* focuses on a young man who has recovered from mental illness brought on by his girlfriend's accidental death and his father's suicide, only to meet a woman whom he believes to be the girlfriend's reincarnation.

Winston's work has not gained much attention from reviewers. The few critiques it has received are mixed. A *Publishers Weekly* commentator called *Gallows Way* a "smoothly written plantation Gothic . . . a satisfying and exciting read"; reviews in the same publication described *A Sweet Familiarity* as "much ado . . . without much substance" and *The Fall River Line* as "lacking in drama." *Library Journal* contributor Andrea Lee Shuey, though, had a more positive summation of *The Fall River Line,* saying "the times depicted were eventful, and so is the novel." Another *Library Journal* critic, Terrill Brooks, dubbed *Mira* "chilling reading" and recommended it. Hanscom observed that Winston's novels generally provide "a quick, easy read" and characterized the author as "a speedy, prolific, unpretentious writer."

Winston once told *CA:* "I didn't begin a career in writing. I always wrote, and always knew that that would be my major interest in life. I wanted to tell stories about people; their needs hopes and dreams;

about their weaknesses and their strengths. When on a book, I work about six hours a day, seven days a week, with small bites of time taken from each day to attend to those chores everyone must deal with."

Winston continued: "I tell aspiring writers who ask me, first of all to read, read, read. Then to write only what they themselves most enjoy reading. And thirdly to make a habit of writing every single day, even if it's only a few words. But I am always uneasy about giving advice to hopefuls. Survival as a professional writer is difficult, demanding emotionally and physically. And publishing today makes it more and more risky for the beginner."

*BIOGRAPHICAL/CRITICAL SOURCES:*

*BOOKS*

*Twentieth-Century Romance and Historical Writers,* St. James Press (Detroit), 1994.

*PERIODICALS*

*Library Journal,* March 1, 1981, p. 578; October 1, 1981, p. 1946; April 15, 1984, p. 825.

*Publishers Weekly,* November 1, 1976, p. 66; March 13, 1981, p. 75; August 14, 1981, p. 51; March 23, 1984, pp. 66-67.*